A Comprehensive
Guide to Intellectual
and Developmental Disabilities

Second Edition

edited by

Michael L. Wehmeyer, Ph.D.
University of Kansas

Ivan Brown, Ph.D.
Brock University

Maire Percy, Ph.D.
University of Toronto
Surrey Place Centre

Karrie A. Shogren, Ph.D.
University of Kansas

and

Wai Lun Alan Fung, M.D., Sc.D.
University of Toronto

·P·A·U·L·H·
BROOKES
PUBLISHING CO ®

Baltimore • London • Sydney

Paul H. Brookes Publishing Co.
Post Office Box 10624
Baltimore, Maryland 21285-0624
USA

www.brookespublishing.com

Typeset by Progressive Publishing Services, Emigsville, Pennsylvania.
Manufactured in the United States of America by
Sheridan Books, Inc., Chelsea, Michigan.

Cover image ©istockphoto/mymrin.

Chapter 1 definition reprinted from *International Statistical Classification of Diseases and Related Health Problems 10th Revision (ICD-10)-2015-WHO Version,* Mental Retardation (F70–F79), Copyright (2015). Chapter 3 definition from the American Association on Intellectual and Developmental Disabilities (AAIDD). (2013). *Definition of intellectual disability.* Retrieved from http://aaidd.org/intellectual-disability/definition, p.1; reprinted by permission. Chapter 47 excerpt from Bradley, E., Sinclair, L., & Greenbaum, R. (2012). Trauma and adolescents with intellectual disabilities: interprofessional clinical and service perspectives. *Journal of Child & Adolescent Trauma,* 5(1) (33–46), reprinted by permission of Taylor & Francis Ltd, http://www.tandfonline.com.

The publisher and the authors have made every effort to ensure that all of the information and instruction given in this book are accurate and safe, but they cannot accept liability for any resulting injury, damage, or loss to either person or property, whether direct or consequential and however it occurs. Medical advice should only be provided under the direction of a qualified health care professional.

Most of the vignettes presented in this book are composite accounts that do not represent the lives or experiences of specific individuals, and no implications should be inferred. In a few cases, actual people's stories have been used with permission.

Library of Congress Cataloging-in-Publication Data
The Library of Congress has cataloged the print edition as follows:

Names: Wehmeyer, Michael L., editor.
Title: A comprehensive guide to intellectual and developmental disabilities / edited by Michael L. Wehmeyer,
    Ph.D., University of Kansas, Ivan Brown, Ph.D., Brock University, Maire Percy, Ph.D., University of
    Toronto, Surrey Place Centre, Toronto, Karrie A. Shogren, Ph.D., University of Kansas, and Wai Lun Alan
    Fung, M.D., Sc.D., University of Toronto.
Description: Second edition. | Baltimore: Paul H. Brookes Publishing, Co., [2017] | Includes bibliographical
    references and index.
Identifiers: LCCN 2016028967 (print) | LCCN 2016035428 (ebook) | ISBN 9781598576023 (hardcover) | ISBN
    9781598579062 (pdf) | ISBN 9781598575644 (epub)
Subjects: LCSH: Developmentally disabled. | People with mental disabilities. | Developmental
    disabilities. | Mental retardation. | Developmentally disabled—Services for. | People with mental
    disabilities—Services for.
Classification: LCC HV1570 .C66 2017 (print) | LCC HV1570 (ebook) | DDC 362.1968—dc23
LC record available at https://lccn.loc.gov/2016028967

British Library Cataloguing in Publication data are available from the British Library.

2021   2020   2019   2018   2017

10   9   8   7   6   5   4   3   2   1

Contents

I Intellectual and Developmental Disabilities in Today's Context

II Human Development

III Etiology and Conditions

About the Editors

Michael L. Wehmeyer, Ph.D., Ross and Marianna Beach Distinguished Professor of Special Education; Director and Senior Scientist, Beach Center on Disability; Co-Director, Kansas University Center on Developmental Disabilities, University of Kansas, 1200 Sunnyside Avenue, Room 3136, Lawrence, KS 66045.

Michael L. Wehmeyer is Ross and Marianna Beach Distinguished Professor of Special Education; Director and Senior Scientist, Beach Center on Disability; and Co-Director, Kansas University Center on Developmental Disabilities, all at the University of Kansas. Dr. Wehmeyer is the author or coauthor of more than 350 peer-reviewed journal articles or book chapters and has been an author or editor for 35 books on disability- and education-related issues, including issues pertaining to self-determination, conceptualizing intellectual disability and supports, applied cognitive technologies, and the education and inclusion of learners with extensive and pervasive support needs. Dr. Wehmeyer is Past President and a Fellow of the American Association on Intellectual and Developmental Disabilities (AAIDD); Past President of the Council for Exceptional Children's Division on Career Development and Transition; a Fellow of the American Psychological Association, Intellectual and Developmental Disabilities Division (Division 33); and a Fellow and former Vice President for the Americas of the International Association for the Scientific Study of Intellectual and Developmental Disabilities. He is former Editor of the journal *Remedial and Special Education* and is a founding Co-editor of the AAIDD journal *Inclusion.* He is a coauthor of the AAIDD *Supports Intensity Scale* (2004) and the 2010 AAIDD *Intellectual Disability: Definition, Classification, and Systems of Supports* manual. He has been recognized for his research and service with awards from numerous associations and organizations, including the American Psychological Association Distinguished Contributions to the Advancement of Disability Issues in Psychology Award, the AAIDD Research Award, the Distinguished Researcher Award for lifetime contributions to research in intellectual disability by The Arc of the United States, the Burton

Blatt Humanitarian Award from the Council for Exceptional Children (CEC) Division on Autism and Developmental Disabilities, and the CEC Special Education Research Award for 2016. Dr. Wehmeyer holds undergraduate and master's degrees in special education from the University of Tulsa and a master's degree in experimental psychology from the University of Sussex in Brighton, England, where he was a Rotary International Fellow from 1987 to 1988. He earned his Ph.D. in human development and communication sciences from the University of Texas at Dallas, where he received a 2014 Distinguished Alumni Award.

Ivan Brown, Ph.D., Adjunct Professor, Centre for Applied Disability Studies, Brock University, St. Catharines, ON, Canada; Director, Academy on Education, Teaching and Research, International Association for the Scientific Study of Intellectual & Developmental Disabilities; Founding editor of *Journal on Developmental Disabilities*

Ivan Brown is an internationally recognized expert in intellectual and developmental disabilities. He has a strong history of community involvement in disability, serving on numerous government, legal, and community agency committees, task forces, and boards and acting in leadership roles with several professional organizations. In particular, he was a longtime member of the Board of Directors of the Ontario Association on Developmental Disabilities and served a term as its Chair. For almost 2 decades, he has held positions in the International Association for the Scientific Study of Intellectual and Developmental Disabilities, is a Fellow of that organization, sits on the governing Council, and is currently Co-chair of the Quality of Life Special Interest Research Group and Director of its Academy for Education, Teaching, and Research. Dr. Brown has published widely in the academic literature and has written or edited 14 scholarly books and many journal articles and book chapters, and he has authored numerous reports and measurement scales. With co-editor Professor Maire Percy, he has edited three editions of the highly success-ful text *Developmental Disabilities in Ontario*. In addi-tion, he has been a member of the editorial boards of several journals in the field of intellectual and developmental disabilities over the years and has contributed hundreds of peer reviews. During his career at the University of Toronto, he initiated several major quality of life studies and managed two national research centers with a special focus on disability issues as they relate to health promo-tion, child welfare, and indigenous populations. As a retiree, Dr. Brown remains an active contributor to the field of intellectual and developmental disabili-ties through ongoing lecturing; leading workshops; writing and editing; consulting; volunteering with disability organizations; serving as Director of the International Association for the Scientific Study of Intellectual and Developmental Disabilities' Acad-emy on Education, Teaching and Research; and teaching as an adjunct professor of Applied Dis-ability Studies at Brock University in Canada.

Maire Percy, Ph.D., Professor Emeritus, Depart-ments of Physiology and Obstetrics and Gynaeco-logy, Faculty of Medicine, University of Toronto; Former Director of the Neurogenetics Laboratory, Surrey Place Centre; Vice-Chair, Research Ethics Board, Surrey Place Centre, 2 Surrey Place, Toronto, ON M5S 2C2, Canada

Maire Percy is an internationally recognized Cana-dian neurogeneticist, a full emeritus professor of the University of Toronto (Physiology and Obstetrics and Gynaecology), and Vice Chair of the Research Ethics Board at Surrey Place Centre (an organiza-tion dedicated to improving the quality of life for people with developmental disabilities and their families). From 1989 to 2012, she was Director of the Surrey Place Centre Neurogenetics Laboratory. She obtained degrees from the University of Toronto (B.Sc., physiology and biochemistry; M.A., medical biophysics; Ph.D., biochemistry; and A.R.C.T. from the Royal Conservatory of Music of Toronto, piano). As a Medical Research Council postdoctoral fellow, she trained in immunology and genetics at the Agri-cultural Research Council of Animal Physiology (Babraham, United Kingdom) and the Hospital for Sick Children (Toronto, Canada). Supported initially by a National Health Research Scholar Award, she established award-winning research and student

training/mentoring programs to identify genetic, metabolic, and environmental risk factors caus-ing or contributing to serious human diseases and disorders, including dementia among older people with Down syndrome. Material from an innovative and interactive graduate course that she developed (called The Neuroscience of Developmental Dis-abilities) motivated the conception of two textbooks co-edited with her colleague, Ivan Brown: *Develop-mental Disabilities in Ontario* (now in its third edi-tion) and the first edition of *A Comprehensive Guide to Intellectual and Developmental Disabilities*. Although formally retired, she continues to publish research articles and book chapters, review articles and grant applications, organize community courses for later-life learners, and serve on the editorial boards of two journals (*Journal on Developmental Disabilities* and *International Journal of Developmental Disabilities*). Honors include the Ontario Association on Develop-mental Disabilities Award of Excellence and the June Callwood Award for important contributions to the field of developmental disabilities. Asteroid 32207 is named after her.

Karrie A. Shogren, Ph.D., Professor, Department of Special Education; Co-Director and Senior Sci-entist, Kansas University Center on Developmental Disabilities; Associate Director, Beach Center on Disability, University of Kansas, 1200 Sunnyside Avenue, Room 3136, Lawrence, KS 66045

Karrie A. Shogren is Professor of Special Education; Co-Director and Senior Scientist, Kansas University Center on Developmental Disabilities; and Associate Director, Beach Center on Disability, all at the Uni-versity of Kansas. Dr. Shogren's research focuses on self-determination and systems of support for peo-ple with disabilities as well as applications of posi-tive psychology and strengths-based approaches to people with intellectual and developmental disabil-ities; she has a specific interest in contextual factors that affect student outcomes. Her work focuses on developing and researching the efficacy and effec-tiveness of assessment and intervention approaches for students with and without disabilities to pro-mote self-determination, with a particular focus on the role of these approaches in the transition to adult life and engagement in meaningful adult roles and responsibilities. Dr. Shogren has published more than 100 articles in peer-reviewed journals, is the author or coauthor of 10 books, and is a coauthor of *Intellectual Disability: Definition, Classification, and Systems of Support,* the 11th edition of the American Association on Intellectual and Developmental Disabilities' (AAIDD's) seminal definition of *intellectual disability* (formerly *mental retardation*). In addition, she is a coauthor of AAIDD's *Supports Intensity Scale—Children's Version* and *Supports Intensity Scale—Adult Version.* Dr. Shogren has received grant funding from several sources, including the Institute of Education Sciences and National Institute on Disability, Independent Living, and Rehabilitation Research. Dr. Shogren is Co-editor of *Inclusion* and *Remedial and Special Education* and Associate Editor of *Research and Practice for Persons with Severe Disabilities.* She has received the Council for Exceptional Children's Division for Research Distinguished Early Career Research Award and the American Association on Intellectual and Developmental Disabilities Early Career Award. Dr. Shogren completed bachelor and master's degrees in psychology at Ohio State University and the University of Dayton, respectively, and her doctoral degree at the University of Kansas.

Wai Lun Alan Fung, M.D., Sc.D., Assistant Professor, University of Toronto Faculty of Medicine; Chair of Research Ethics Board and Medical Director of Research, Department of Psychiatry, North York General Hospital, 4001 Leslie Street, Toronto, ON M2K 1E1, Canada

Wai Lun Alan Fung is a medical specialist in psychiatry who is also board certified in the subspecialties of Behavioral Neurology & Neuropsychiatry (United Council for Neurologic Subspecialties, United States) and Sleep Medicine (American Board of Psychiatry and Neurology). He serves as Medical Director of Research of the Department of Psychiatry, as well as Chair of the Research Ethics Board, at North York General Hospital—an affiliated teaching hospital of the University of Toronto Faculty of Medicine in Toronto, Ontario, Canada. He is also Assistant Professor of Psychiatry at the University of Toronto as well as Affiliate Scientist of the Toronto General Research Institute. As a neuropsychiatrist focusing on genetic disorders, he has particular clinical and academic interests in 22q11.2

deletion syndrome (22q11.2DS) and Huntington disease in adults and in adolescents making the transition to adulthood. His interests in intellectual and developmental disabilities were first ignited through a medical school research project as part of Ivan Brown's pioneering Family Quality of Life in Intellectual Disabilities study. Dr. Fung has subsequently continued his professional involvement with intellectual and developmental disabilities through his work in 22q11.2DS. He was the lead coauthor of the first set of guidelines for managing adult patients with 22q11.2DS, endorsed by the 22q11.2 Society (the international professional organization dedicated to the study of chromosome 22q11.2 and related disorders). He has also served as Founding Knowledge Officer of The 22q11.2 Society. During 2012–2015, he served as Founding Co-Director of the Dalglish Family 22q Clinic at Toronto General Hospital in Canada—the first comprehensive, multidisciplinary clinic of its kind worldwide fully dedicated to the care of adults with 22q11.2DS and their families. He is a member of the International Consortium on Brain and Behavior in 22q11.2DS as well as an investigator member of the Huntington Study Group. He has also served in leadership roles in such professional organizations as the American Psychiatric Association and the American Neuropsychiatric Association. His other professional interests include neuropsychiatric genetics and pharmacogenetics; the cultural and spiritual dimensions of mental health care; medical quality improvement through knowledge mobilization, utilization of information technology, intra- and interprofessional collaboration, and education; and patient- and family-centered collaborative care. He has published in leading journals such as *Journal of the American Medical Association, JAMA Psychiatry, Lancet Psychiatry, American Journal of Psychiatry, British Journal of Psychiatry, World Psychiatry, Neurology, Genetics in Medicine,* and *Social Science and Medicine.* Dr. Fung completed his undergraduate and medical degrees, as well as his residency training in psychiatry, at the University of Toronto. He also completed a master's degree in epidemiology at the University of Cambridge, United Kingdom, and a research doctorate and research fellowship in neuropsychiatric genetic epidemiology at Harvard University. He is a Fellow of both the Royal College of Physicians of Canada and the American Psychiatric Association.

Contributors

Kruti Acharya, M.D.
Assistant Professor
Departments of Disability and Human
  Development and Pediatrics
University of Illinois at Chicago
1640 West Roosevelt Road (MC 626)
Chicago, IL 60608

Heather M. Aldersey, Ph.D.
Assistant Professor
Queen's National Scholar
School of Rehabilitation Therapy
Queen's University
31 George Street
Kingston, ON K7L3N6
Canada

F. Daniel Armstrong, Ph.D.
Professor and Executive Vice Chair
Department of Pediatrics
Director
Mailman Center for Child Development
Senior Associate Dean of Faculty Affairs (Interim)
University of Miami Miller School of Medicine
Post Office Box 016820 (D-820)
Miami, FL 33101

Marjorie Aunos, Ph.D.
Psychologist
Centre Intégré Universitaire de Santé et Services
  Sociaux de l'Ouest de l'Ile de Montréal (CIUSSS
  ODIM)
8000 Notre-Dame
Lachine, QC H8R 1H2
Canada

Michael Bach, Ph.D.
Executive Vice President
Canadian Association for Community Living
4700 Keele Street, Kinsmen Building
York University
Toronto, ON M3J 1P3
Canada

Daniel Baker, Ph.D.
Internal Reviewer
Minnesota Department of Human Resources
Post Office Box 64251
St. Paul, MN 55164-0251

Deborah Barbouth, M.D.
Assistant Professor
Division of Clinical and Translational
  Genetics
Dr. John T. Macdonald Foundation Department of
  Human Genetics
University of Miami, Miller School of Medicine
1501 NW 10th Avenue, BRB, Room 373
Miami, FL 33136

Anne S. Bassett, M.D.
Professor
University of Toronto
The Dalglish Family 22q Clinic
Toronto General Hospital
200 Elizabeth Street, 8NU-802
Toronto, ON M5G 2C4
Canada

Joseph M. Berg, MB.BCh., M.Sc.
(deceased)
Professor Emeritus, Faculty of Medicine
University of Toronto
Canada

Cathy Binger, Ph.D.
Associate Professor
University of New Mexico
1700 Lomas Boulevard NE
MSC01 1195
1 University of New Mexico
Albuquerque, NM 87131

Anne Black, C.Y.W., B.A., M.Ed.
Contract Lecturer
School of Child and Youth Care
Ryerson University
350 Victoria Street
Toronto, ON M5B 2K3
Canada

Peter Blanck, Ph.D., J.D.
University Professor and Chairman
Burton Blatt Institute
Syracuse University
900 South Crouse Avenue
Crouse-Hinds Hall, Suite 300
Syracuse, NY 13244

Matthew Bogenschutz, Ph.D.
Assistant Professor
School of Social Work
Virginia Commonwealth University
Post Office Box 842027
Richmond, VA 23284

Erik Boot, M.D., Ph.D.
Physician for people with intellectual disability
The Dalglish Family 22q Clinic, Toronto General
    Hospital, University Health Network
Norman Urquhart, 8-802
585 University Avenue
Toronto, ON, M5G 2N2
Canada

Kenneth Boss, M.D., M.ADS
Psychiatrist
Developmental Disabilities Service
North Bay Regional Health Centre
50 College Drive
North Bay, ON P1B 0A4
Canada

Elspeth Bradley, Ph.D., MB.BS.
Associate Professor, Department of Psychiatry,
    University of Toronto
On staff, The Centre for Addiction and Mental
    Health and St. Michael's Hospital, Toronto
Consultant, Cota Developmental and Dual
    Diagnosis Services, Toronto and The Meta Centre
401 Champagne Drive
Toronto, ON M3J 2C6
Canada

Nancy Brady, Ph.D.
Associate Professor
Speech-Language-Hearing: Sciences & Disorders
University of Kansas
1000 Sunnyside Avenue
Lawrence, KS 66045

W. McIntyre Burnham, Ph.D.
Professor Emeritus
University of Toronto
Department of Pharmacology and Toxicology, MSB
1 King's College Circle
Toronto, ON M5S 1A8
Canada

Nancy J. Butcher, Ph.D.
Research Scientist
The Children's Hospital of Philadelphia Research
    Institute
Leonard Madlyn Abramson Research Center,
    Room 916-H
3615 Civic Center Boulevard
Philadelphia, PA 19104

Ella Callow, J.D.
Legal Director
The National Center on Parents with Disabilities
    and their Families
3075 Adeline Street, Suite 120
Berkeley, CA 94703

Tina Campanella, M.A.
Chief Executive Officer
Quality Trust for Individuals
    with Disabilities
4301 Connecticut Avenue NW, Suite 310
Washington, DC 20008

Tom Cheetham, M.D.
Deputy Commissioner of Health Services
Tennessee Department of Intellectual and
    Developmental Disabilities
400 Deaderick Street
10th Floor, Citizen's Plaza
Nashville, TN 37243

Joan Christopher, J.D.
Research Instructor
Coordinator for Advocacy and
    Self-Determination
Georgetown University Center for Excellence in
    Developmental Disabilities
3300 Whitehaven Street NW, Third Floor
Washington, DC 20007

Trudy Clifford, R.N., CERT PHN
Nurse Service Coordinator and Clinic
    Coordinator (Retired)
FASD Diagnostic Clinic for Adults
Surrey Place Centre
2 Surrey Place
Toronto, ON M5S 2C2
Canada

Rosemary A. Condillac, Ph.D., BCBA-D
Associate Professor
Centre for Applied Disability Studies
Brock University
500 Glenridge
St. Catharines, ON L2S 3A1
Canada

Glen Dunlap, Ph.D.
Professor
Nevada Center for Excellence
    in Disabilities
University of Nevada, Reno
MS 0285
Reno, NV 89557

Amy Dwyre D'Agati, M.S.
Senior Associate
TransCen, Inc.
401 North Washington Street, Suite 450
Rockville, MD 20850

Anna J. Esbensen, Ph.D.
Assistant Professor of Pediatrics
Research Director, Jane and Richard Thomas
    Center for Down Syndrome
Cincinnati Children's Hospital Medical
    Center
3430 Burnet Ave
MLC 4002
Cincinnati, OH 45229

Darcy Fehlings, M.D.
Head
Division of Developmental Paediatrics
Department of Paediatrics
University of Toronto
Holland Bloorview Kids Rehabilitation
    Hospital
150 Kilgour Rd.
Toronto, ON M4G 1R8
Canada

Maurice Feldman, Ph.D.
Professor
Centre for Applied Disability
    Studies
Brock University
1812 Sir Isaac Brock Way
St. Catharines, ON L2S3A1
Canada

Robert Fletcher, D.S.W., ACSW, LCSW
Founder and Chief Executive Officer
NADD
132 Fair Street
Kingston NY 12401

Cynthia J. Forster-Gibson, Ph.D., M.D.
Physician Lead
Genetics Program
Trillium Health Partners
2200 Eglinton Avenue West
Mississauga, ON L5M 2N1
Canada

Elaine B. Frankel, Ed.D.
Professor
School of Early Childhood Studies
Ryerson University
350 Victoria Street
Toronto, ON M5B 2K3
Canada

Ann Fudge Schormans, Ph.D.
Associate Professor
School of Social Work
McMaster University
309A Kenneth Taylor Hall
1280 Main Street West
Hamilton, ON L8S 4M4
Canada

Diane Galambos, Ed.D.
Professor and Academic Program Coordinator
    (Retired)
Sheridan College
1430 Trafalgar Road
Oakville, ON L6H 2L1
Canada

Peggy Goldstein, Ed.D.
Associate Professor
Florida Atlantic University
College of Education, ES 223
3200 South College Avenue
Fort Lauderdale, FL 33314

Tawara D. Goode, M.A.
Assistant Professor and Director
National Center for Cultural Competence
Associate Director
Georgetown University Center of Excellence in
    Developmental Disabilities
Georgetown University Center for Child and
    Human Development
3300 Whitehaven Street NW, Suite 3300
Washington, DC 20007

Dorothy Griffiths, CM, OOnt, Ph.D.
Professor
Brock University
St. Catharines, ON L2S 3A1
Canada

Laura Hahn, Ph.D.
Assistant Professor
Department of Speech and Hearing Sciences
University of Illinois at Urbana-Champaign
901 South Sixth Street, MC 482
Champaign, IL 61820

**Angela Hassiotis, Ptychion (Higher Education
    Degree) Medical School, University
    of Athens; Ph.D.**
Professor of Psychiatry of Intellectual Disability
Division of Psychiatry
University College London
6th Floor, Maple House
149 Tottenham Court Road
London W1T 7NF
United Kingdom

Tamar Heller, Ph.D.
Distinguished Professor and Head
Department of Disability and Human Development
University of Illinois at Chicago
1640 West Roosevelt Road
Room 435, MC 626
Chicago, IL 60608

Jessica A. Hellings, MB.BCh., M.Med. Psych. (S.A.), FAPA
Director
Regional Center Psychiatry Program
Kansas City Regional Office
821 Admiral Boulevard
Kansas City, MO 64106

John Heng, M.A.
Doctoral Candidate
Assistant Professor
King's University College
Western University
266 Epworth Avenue
London, ON N6A 2M3
Canada

Amy S. Hewitt, Ph.D.
Director
Research and Training Center on Community Living
Institute on Community Integration
University of Minnesota
150 Pillsbury Drive SE
214 Pattee Hall
Minneapolis, MN 55455

Jordan Hoath, B.A., B.Ed.
Behaviour Consultant
Centre for Behaviour Health Sciences
570 Bryne Drive , Unit H
Barrie, ON L4N 9P6
Canada

Jeanette Jeltje Anne Holden, Ph.D., FCCMG
(deceased)
Professor, Departments of Psychiatry and Physiology, Queen's University
Director, Autism Research Program and DNA Research Laboratory, Ongwanada
Kingston, ON
Canada

Carolyn Hunt, M.D.
Developmental Pediatrician
Grandview Children's Centre
Associate Professor
University of Toronto
600 Townline Road South
Oshawa, ON L1H 7K6
Canada

Stephanie Ioannou, M.A., BCBA
Behaviour Therapist
Vita Community Living Services
4301 Weston Road
Toronto, ON M9L 2Y3
Canada

Barry J. Isaacs, Ph.D.
Director
Research, Evaluation and Education
Surrey Place Centre
2 Surrey Place
Toronto, ON M5S 2C2
Canada

Matthew P. Janicki, Ph.D.
Co-Chair
National Task Group on Intellectual Disabilities and Dementia Practices
Associate Research Professor
Department of Disability and Human Development
College of Applied Health Sciences
University of Illinois at Chicago
Suite 436 DHSP
1640 West Roosevelt Road (MC 626)
Chicago, IL 60608

Chet D. Johnson, M.D.
Professor of Pediatrics
University of Kansas School of Medicine
3901 Rainbow Boulevard
Kansas City, KS 66160

Nancy Jokinen, Ph.D.
Associate Professor
School of Social Work
University of Northern British Columbia
3333 University Way
Prince George, BC V2N 4Z9
Canada

Wendy Alegra Jones, M.Ed., M.S.W.
Senior Policy Associate
National Center for Cultural Competence
Georgetown University Center of Excellence in Developmental Disabilities
Georgetown University Center for Child and Human Development
3300 Whitehaven Street NW, Suite 3300
Washington, DC 20007

Emoke Jozsvai, Ph.D.
Psychologist
Surrey Place Centre
2 Surrey Place
Toronto, ON M5S 2C6
Canada

Jennifer Kent-Walsh, Ph.D., CCC-SLP, S-LP(C)
Professor and FAAST Center Director
Department of Communication Sciences and
    Disorders
University of Central Florida
Post Office Box 162215
Orlando, FL 32816

E. Louise Kodituwakku, Ph.D.
Assistant Professor in Pediatrics
Senior Clinical Psychologist
Center for Development and Disability
University of New Mexico School of
    Medicine
2300 Menaul NE
Albuquerque, NM 87107

Piyadasa W. Kodituwakku, Ph.D.
Associate Professor of Pediatrics and
    Neurosciences
Center for Development and Disability
University of New Mexico School of Medicine
2300 Menaul NE
Albuquerque NM 87101

Julie Koudys, Ph.D.
Assistant Professor
Centre for Disability Studies
Brock University
500 Glenridge Avenue
St. Catharines, ON L2S 3A1
Canada

Traci LaLiberte, Ph.D.
Executive Director
Center for Advanced Studies in
    Child Welfare
University of Minnesota
1404 Gortner Avenue
205 Peters Hall
Saint Paul, MN 55108

Jason P. Lerch, Ph.D.
Senior Scientist
The Hospital for Sick Children
25 Orde Street
Toronto, ON M5T 3H7
Canada

Sheldon Z. Lewkis, Ph.D.
Private Practice Psychologist
1128 Alberni Street, Suite 2807
Vancouver, BC V6E 4R6
Canada

Elizabeth Lightfoot, Ph.D.
Professor
Doctoral Program Director
School of Social Work
University of Minnesota
105 Peters Hall
St. Paul, MN 55108

Bengt Lindqvist, M.D.HC, Ph.D.HC
Co-Director
Disability Rights Promotion
    International
York University
4700 Keele Street
Room 5021, TEL Building
Toronto, ON M3J 1P3
Canada

Joanne C.Y. Loo, Ph.D.
Research Analyst II
The Dalglish Family 22q Clinic
Toronto General Hospital
200 Elizabeth Street, 8NU-802
Toronto, ON M5G 2C4
Canada

John S. Lovering, M.D.
(deceased)
Developmental Pediatrician and Assistant
    Professor, Department of Pediatrics
University of Toronto
Canada

Richard G. Luecking, Ed.D.
President Emeritus
TransCen, Inc.
401 North Washington Street, Suite 450
Rockville, MD 20850

Karolina Machalek, M.P.H.
Policy Analyst
Public Health Agency of Canada
130 Colonnade Road
Ottawa, ON K1A 0K9
Canada

William MacKay, Ph.D.
Professor
Department of Physiology
University of Toronto
Medical Sciences Building
1 King's College Circle
Toronto, ON M5S 1A8
Canada

William E. MacLean, Jr., Ph.D.
Senior Scientist
Waisman Center
University of Wisconsin–Madison
1500 Highland Avenue, Room S 101A
Madison, WI 53705

Diana R. Mager, M.Sc., Ph.D., R.D.
Associate Professor, Clinical Nutrition
Department of Agricultural, Food & Nutritional
    Science
Department of Pediatrics
University of Alberta
2-021D Clinical Research Unit
Alberta Diabetes Institute
University of Alberta
8602-112 Street
Edmonton, AB T6G 2E1
Canada

Jonathan G. Martinis, J.D.
Legal Director
Quality Trust for Individuals with Disabilities
4301 Connecticut Avenue NW, Suite 310
Washington, DC 20008

Philip McCallion, Ph.D.
Distinguished Professor
Director
Center for Excellence in Aging and Community
    Wellness
School of Social Welfare
University at Albany
135 Western Avenue
Albany NY 12222

Catherine McClain, M.D.
Professor Emeritus
Center for Development and Disability
Medical Director
Center for Development and Disability
University of New Mexico
2300 Menaul NE
Albuquerque, NM 87107

Donna McDonald-McGinn, M.S., LCGC
Clinical Professor of Pediatrics, The Perelman
    School of Medicine of the University of
    Pennsylvania
Chief, Section of Genetic Counseling
Director, 22q and You Center
Associate Director, Clinical Genetics Center
The Children's Hospital of Philadelphia
34th Street and Civic Center Boulevard
Philadelphia, PA 19104

Shirley McMillan, B.Sc.N., M.N.
Advanced Practice Nurse
Surrey Place Centre
2 Surrey Place Centre
Toronto, ON M5S 2C2
Canada

Patricia Minnes, Ph.D.
Professor Emerita
Department of Psychology
Queen's University
62 Arch Street
Kingston, ON K7L 3N6
Canada

J. Dale Munro, M.S.W., RSW
Individual, Couple, and Family
    Therapist
Clinical Affiliate
Redpath Centre
341 Talbot Street, Suite 212
London, ON N6A 2R5
Canada

**Trevor R. Parmenter, A.M., B.A., Ph.D., FACE,
    FAAIDD, FIASSIDD, FASSID**
Professor Emeritus
Sydney Medical School
University of Sydney
Australia

Paula E. Pasquali, Ph.D.
Health and Wellness Consultant (private
    practice)
Whitehorse, Yukon
Canada

Adrienne Perry, Ph.D., BCBA-D
Professor
Department of Psychology
York University
4700 Keele Street
Toronto, ON M3J 1P3
Canada

Paula Campos Pinto, Ph.D.
Assistant Professor
School of Social and Political
    Sciences
University of Lisbon
ISCSP
Rua Almerindo Lessa
1300-663 Lisboa
Portugal

Vee P. Prasher, MB.ChB., M.MedSc., M.D., Ph.D., MRCPsych
Consultant and Visiting Professor
Birmingham Community NHS Trust
Birmingham Learning Disability Service
The Greenfields
30 Brookfield Road
Birmingham B30 3QY
United Kingdom

John P. Radford, Ph.D.
Professor Emeritus
Department of Geography
York University
4700 Keele Street
Toronto ON M3J 1P3
Canada

Ambreen Rashid, MB.BS., MRCPsych
ST Psychiatrist in Intellectual Disabilities
The Royal College of Psychiatrists
21 Prescot Street
London E1 8BB
United Kingdom

Marcia H. Rioux, Ph.D.
Distinguished Research Professor
York University
4th HNES Building
4700 Keele Street
Toronto, ON M3J 1P3
Canada

Pat Rogan, Ph.D.
Professor of Special Education
Indiana University School of Education, Indianapolis
902 West New York Street
Indianapolis, IN 46202

Abigail Schindler, M.S.
Research Specialist
Institute on Disability and Human Development
University of Illinois at Chicago
1640 West Roosevelt Road, MC 626
Chicago, IL 60608

Jan Scholz, D.Phil.
Postdoctoral Research Fellow
Mouse Imaging Centre
Hospital for Sick Children
25 Orde Street
Toronto ON, M5T 3H7
Canada

Janice Seabrooks-Blackmore, Ph.D.
Associate Professor of Exceptional Student Education
University of North Florida
College of Education and Human Services
Building 57, Suite 3500
1 UNF Drive
Jacksonville, FL 32224

Dick Sobsey, Ed.D.
Professor Emeritus
Department of Educational Psychology
University of Alberta
6-102 Education North
Edmonton, AB T6G 2G5
Canada

Denise Poston Stahl, Ph.D.
Research Associate (retired)
Beach Center on Disability
University of Kansas

William F. Sullivan, M.D., C.C.F.P., Ph.D.
Associate Professor
Department of Family and Community Medicine
University of Toronto
St. Michael's Family Medicine Associates
St. Michael's Hospital and Medical Services
Surrey Place Centre
2 Surrey Place
Toronto, ON, M5S 2C2
Canada

Jane Summers, Ph.D.
Director
Interprofessional Practice, Underserved Populations Program
Centre for Addiction and Mental Health
Professional Practice Office
80 Workman Way
Toronto, ON M6J 1H4
Canada

Leeping Tao, M.N.–ACNP
RN(EC), Nurse Practitioner—Adult
University Health Network
Princess Margaret Hospital
610 University Avenue
Toronto, ON M5G 2M9
Canada

Valerie K. Temple, Ph.D.
Clinical Psychologist
Surrey Place Centre
2 Surrey Place
Toronto, ON M5S 2C2
Canada

James R. Thompson, Ph.D.
Professor and Senior Scientist
Department of Special Education
Beach Center on Disability
University of Kansas
1200 Sunnyside Avenue
3124 Haworth Hall
Lawrence, KS 66045

Miles D. Thompson, Ph.D.
Research Associate
University of Toronto
Department of Pharmacology and Toxicology
  Medical Sciences Building, Room 4207
1 King's College Circle
Toronto, ON M5S 1A8
Canada

Ann P. Turnbull, Ed.D.
Ross and Marianna Beach Distinguished Professor
  Emerita
Cofounder, Beach Center on Disability
University of Kansas
1200 Sunnyside Avenue
3111 Haworth Hall
Lawrence, Kansas 66045

Kathryn Underwood, Ph.D.
Associate Professor
Faculty of Community Services
School of Early Childhood Studies
Ryerson University
350 Victoria Street
Toronto, ON M5B 2K3
Canada

Kristine Wiest Webb, Ph.D.
Professor
Department of Exceptional, Deaf, and Interpreter
  Education
University of North Florida
Building 57, Room 3514
1 UNF Drive
Jacksonville, FL 32224

Introduction

We are very pleased to bring you the second edition of *A Comprehensive Guide to Intellectual and Developmental Disabilities*. This text is intended to appeal to people whose careers or personal lives include disability. The information presented is purposely designed to be useful to a broad audience yet reflect current trends, policies, and practices that are common across many areas of the world.

Students of disability in colleges and universities will find this text a valuable guide to their learning. We consider this to be particularly important because these students are the future professionals and community leaders in the field of intellectual and developmental disabilities. This book is also intended for use by direct support staff, educators, health care workers, social workers, academics, policy makers, government leaders, those concerned with legal and ethical issues, and many others. Perhaps most important, the book provides one way for people with disabilities themselves and their family members to learn about a broad range of issues in the field of intellectual and developmental disabilities. At a time when many families want to have a stronger voice in determining support for their family members with disabilities, such information is needed. Finally, it is our hope that the material contained between these covers will help the general public to better understand intellectual and developmental disabilities and to include people with disabilities of all ages in the communities where they live.

As was the case with the first edition, in this new edition we have attempted to capture cutting-edge core and practical information in the intellectual and developmental disabilities field and to present it in a format for learning and for day-to-day use. The main goal of the book is to promote the sharing of information, experience, solutions, and insights in order to support people with intellectual and developmental disabilities and their families to improve the quality of their lives.

We have assembled this book for three additional reasons. First, interest in a book of this nature arose from our collective experiences as researchers and teachers, as well as from networking throughout our activities with a number of intellectual and developmental disability professional groups. We realized that support providers of all disciplines, students, educators, researchers, policy makers, and others would benefit from a book about intellectual and developmental disabilities that presents core and practical information from a multidisciplinary perspective. Because the field is changing so quickly and because most people do not have a broad understanding of all the issues in the field, much valuable information is not readily accessible to the people who need it at the very times they need it most. Second, this text brings together formal knowledge and informal knowledge—based on the extensive experiences of clinicians, educators, and researchers—in ways that have not been done before. Finally, a good response to the new philosophical, policy directions, and support approaches that have emerged requires solid knowledge of the field.

One of the primary intents of this book is to capture as much as possible of the environment that influences the lives of people with intellectual and developmental disabilities. In doing so, our aim is to encourage readers to place the lives of people with intellectual and developmental disabilities—and the field itself—within this environment and to explore, as much as possible, the interrelationship among people, the field, and the environment. We have tried to capture a great deal of the complexity in the broad field of intellectual and developmental disabilities in the 50 chapters of this book. In doing so, we have not been able to include every aspect of life of people with intellectual and developmental disabilities, nor have we been able to raise every issue that is of importance to them. Nonetheless, we have brought readers a comprehensive set of chapters under one cover about intellectual and developmental disabilities.

It is our hope and intent that the second edition of *A Comprehensive Guide to Intellectual and Developmental Disabilities* will be informative and helpful in your understanding of intellectual and developmental disabilities. We hope that this book will encourage you to network with others in the field and to learn about intellectual and developmental disabilities in many different ways. Above all, we trust that your learning from the materials contained within these covers will help you to enhance your own lives and the lives of the people with intellectual and developmental disabilities whom you know.

Acknowledgments

Three dear friends and colleagues who authored chapters for the first edition of the text and have since passed away are honored and remembered: Jeanette Jeltje Anne Holden, geneticist (Chapter 15); Joseph M. Berg, psychiatrist and geneticist (Chapter 49); and John S. Lovering, developmental pediatrician (Chapter 49). We are indebted to Tom Dearie—communications architect at Threesixty Creative and design instructor at Toronto Image Works Institute, Toronto, Canada—for provision of high-resolution diagrams; to Robyn Alvarez; and to the editorial staff at Brookes Publishing (especially Rebecca Lazo, Nicole Schmidl, Kim Beauchamp, and Stephen Krauss) for their expert assistance and continued faith in this endeavor.

Credit must be given to Jeff Orchard of Front Porch Publishing, producer of the first edition of *Developmental Disabilities in Ontario* in 1999—the prototype for this book—and the Ontario Association on Developmental Disabilities, which published the second edition of *Developmental Disabilities in Ontario* in 2003 and the third edition in 2011. Brookes Publishing and the Ontario Association on Developmental Disabilities have mutually agreed to share content in a collaborative effort to reach a broader readership in both the United States and Canada. As such, portions of this second edition of *A Comprehensive Guide to Intellectual and Developmental Disabilities* have been updated, expanded, and adapted from the first, second, and third editions of *Developmental Disabilities in Ontario*. This spirit of cooperation between the two publishers has helped to make this book one of the most comprehensive textbooks on intellectual and developmental disabilities available today.

I

Intellectual and Developmental Disabilities in Today's Context

What Is Meant by the Terms *Intellectual Disability* and *Developmental Disabilities?*

Ivan Brown, Michael L. Wehmeyer, and Karrie A. Shogren

WHAT YOU WILL LEARN

- Differing meanings of disability terms according to who is using them and the purposes for which they are used
- Disability terms as social constructs, the meanings of which emerge from several sources
- Personal, public, critical, and definitional meanings of *intellectual disability* and *developmental disabilities*
- Advantages and disadvantages of using disability terms
- Current usage of the terms *intellectual disability* and *developmental disability*

In this text, the terms *intellectual disability* and *developmental disabilities* are used to identify the characteristics of two somewhat different, but overlapping, groups of people. These people, part of the wide variety of people that make up the human population, have existed in all cultures of the world across human history (Wehmeyer, 2013b). In fact, they are not distinct groups of people at all; rather, they are a collection of individuals who each add one piece to the mosaic that illustrates the rich, interesting diversity that is characteristic of the human condition.

It has only been since about the mid-1800s that people have begun to use terms to describe and classify in detail the individuals now thought of as having disabilities. This has been done primarily to identify people who need learning and lifestyle supports to function more successfully in typical contexts, although use of terms for these and other purposes has been controversial and misuse has occurred. Table 1.1 lists terms that are currently used and some of the historical terms, most of which have taken on pejorative meanings. Still, the terms *intellectual disability* and *developmental disabilities* are widely used at the time of this book's publication, and for this reason they are used throughout the text.

This chapter explores what is meant by the terms *intellectual disability* and *developmental disabilities.* Readers will come to understand that the meanings differ somewhat, depending on who is using the terms and their purposes for using them. They will also come to understand that there is no one simple meaning for these terms but, rather, that a broader approach to conceptualizing terms is most helpful to understanding them and to the way people use these terms in their lives and work. For students and disability professionals in particular, it is important to understand and apply the multiple meanings of these terms.

MEANINGS OF *INTELLECTUAL DISABILITY* AND *DEVELOPMENTAL DISABILITIES*

In this section, meanings of *intellectual disability* and *developmental disabilities* that are particularly important to professionals and support providers

Table 1.1. Some other terms used to describe intellectual disability and developmental disabilities

Terms currently in use
Intellectual disability
Developmental disabilities

Terms sometimes used, but not preferred
Mental disability
Mental handicap
Developmental handicap
Challenged

Terms used in some countries
Learning disabilities (United Kingdom)
Mental retardation

Historical terms
Mental retardation
Mental deficiency
Feeble-minded
Moron
Imbecile
Idiot
Natural fool

are described from four different perspectives: personal meaning, public meaning, critical meaning, and definitional meaning. They are described here as separate meanings for purposes of clarity, but in reality most people in the field of disability supports understand *intellectual disability* and *developmental disabilities* as some blend of the four meanings. As noted in other chapters of this book, definitional meanings very often are taken as the only meaning, especially when children or adults are being considered for diagnosis or eligibility for services. However, as shown in this chapter, *intellectual disability* and *developmental disabilities* mean much more than meeting the criteria set out in a definition. The contention of this chapter is that it is necessary to understand the terms *intellectual disability* and *developmental disabilities* as a fluid blending of all four meanings for the promotion of disability in the culture and for effective work in the field today.

The rationale for such a contention is that terms such as *intellectual disability* and *developmental disabilities* are always socially constructed from several sources. By this we mean that such terms do not have fixed meanings but, rather, take on meanings that are shaped and colored in response to an amalgam of such things as personal experiences, knowledge, salient philosophies, organizational structures, and social and cultural conditions and

values. Because these influences vary across time and place, the terms *intellectual disability* and *developmental disabilities* can take on subtle, or even more distinct, differences in meaning from one period of time to another or from one region to another within the same time period. They may also differ somewhat in meaning among groups of people who view disabilities from their unique perspectives.

Personal Meaning

Disability of any kind has, first and foremost, a personal meaning for a person because it is a part of his or her whole life over the entire life span. At the personal level, there is no disability—intellectual, developmental, or otherwise. There is not something that can be described as a condition or a limitation or a challenge. Nor is there something that can be defined as abnormal or unfortunate. It is not anything other than an aspect of a person's life; it is just part of who the person is. Each person uses what abilities and resources are available to live in a way that is personal and that serves his or her individual needs and preferences. The personal meaning of *disability* may be the most important perspective because it describes the very core of disability within human life, and an understanding of this meaning probably needs to shape all other responses to it.

This is not what has occurred in the past. *Intellectual disability* and *developmental disabilities* are terms devised by professionals to describe people who function and behave in ways that seem different from the majority of people. There are personal consequences to the fact that people are labeled as having a disability or, less formally, as being in some way different from the general population. This very labeling or being considered different can create within the labeled people a sense that "something is wrong with me" and "I am different," and it can create in other people a sense that they can view and treat people with disabilities as different. Knowledge that people regard themselves, and other people regard them, as "disabled" can result in a personal meaning attached to *intellectual disability* or *developmental disabilities* that can affect self-perception and self-confidence, often in negative ways (Wehmeyer, 2008).

It may seem surprising that many people have not developed a deeper understanding of the personal experience of people with intellectual disability or developmental disabilities, but there

Pubic is shaped by literal + sociocultural meaning.

are beginning to be many excellent first-person accounts available that help professionals, family members, and members of the general community to understand them better. Advocacy organizations such as People First (People First, 2016) promote ways for people with disabilities to help inform others. The Internet contains numerous personal stories about what it is like to lead the life of a person with a disability (e.g., Regional Oral History Office, n.d.) from the perspective of the people themselves or from the perspective of a family member. The National Leadership Consortium (n.d.) provided an excellent list of children's books about disability, and Kaplan (2009) listed books that depict characters with disabilities in a positive light. In addition, the Council for Exceptional Children's Division on Autism and Developmental Disabilities (n.d.) makes annual awards to authors of children's books who depict people with intellectual and developmental disabilities in a positive manner. There are also lists of movies that depict intellectual and developmental disabilities (e.g., MUBI, 2013).

The best understanding about the personal meaning of *intellectual disability* and *developmental disabilities*, though, probably comes from direct conversation and interaction with individuals and with members of their families. Listening to and learning about the full scope of their everyday lives can result in a clearer understanding of what disability means to them personally.

Public Meaning

The meaning of the terms *intellectual disability* and *developmental disabilities*, as understood and used by members of the general public who are not in daily contact with people with a disability, is typically somewhat different from that which is understood and used by people with disabilities and their families and by professionals who work in the field of disability supports. Yet, these meanings guide the depiction of disability among people in the general public when they talk or think about disability in the public media (e.g., newspapers, television); in popular culture (e.g., books, movies, games); in workplaces; in social, cultural, and religious institutions; and even in law-related circles (e.g., police, courts, legislative bodies). The public meaning develops not from personal or professional experience but, rather, from the public depiction of *disability*. However, because this public depiction shapes so many outcomes for people with disabilities, it is important to consider.

The public meaning of *intellectual disability* and *developmental disabilities* emerges as a consequence, and as a confluence, of two main factors: the public's understanding of the literal meaning of the terms used to describe them and the sociocultural meanings associated with those terms. Each of these two factors is described next.

Literal Meanings of the Terms The literal meaning of a term refers to its semantics, or the general (not scientific) understanding of the words that make up a term. It represents the simplest and broadest understanding of a term because it goes no further than an understanding of what the term's words mean. This literal meaning is the basic foundation for how a term is conceptualized and, for this reason, it is a good place to begin to understand what members of the general public mean by it. Literal meanings vary slightly from one source to another. However, *ability* generally refers to a capacity or capability, and *dis-*, as a prefix, has a negative or reversing effect on the meaning of the word. The prefix *dis-* is used with *ability* in this way to mean *not able,* except that there is an implication that one is not able due to a specific reason or cause. Thus, *disability* means more than simply not able; it means not able because of something that deprives a person of performing or accomplishing something. The adjective *intellectual*, as paraphrased from the *Oxford Advanced Learner's Dictionary of Current English, Sixth Edition* (Oxford University Press, 2000), refers to a person being able to think logically or understand something. When the word *intellectual* is used as an adjective to qualify the noun *disability*, the separate meanings of the two words become enmeshed to form just one meaning in the mind of the public. Thus, at the literal (word meaning) level, *intellectual disability* refers to a person's lack of ability to think in a logical way or understand things and that this lack of ability deprives him or her of performing or accomplishing specific things.

Similarly, the word *developmental,* as an adjective on its own, refers to a condition or state of development (Oxford University Press, 2000). When *developmental* is put together with *disability* and the two words are used as one term, *developmental disability* refers to something in the way a person develops over time that deprives him or her of being able to perform or accomplish specific things.

The public meanings of *intellectual disability* and *developmental disabilities* are very much based on what the words in the terms literally mean. Often, they go no further than this.

Sociocultural Meanings Associated with the Terms

The literal meanings of *intellectual disability* and *developmental disability* contribute to how these terms are understood and used in the public sphere, but they are also shaped by broader social and cultural perceptions (Foreman, 2005). Within the public domain, perceptions of what abilities people should have, and thus the things that they should be able to perform and accomplish, differ considerably from one group of people to another and from one time period to another. Tolerance of people who have too few or too many abilities also differs among cultures and over time periods. Many interweaving factors are part of the emergence of such perceptions and levels of tolerance—social and political structures, economic conditions, cultural values and attitudes, and environmental demands—but somehow, in all social orders, a general understanding emerges about what constitutes typical development and what things almost all people should be able to do. This general understanding forms the basis of what a person is expected to be able to do in his or her social and cultural environment. Thus, the word *ability*, in addition to its literal meaning, takes on a particular meaning that is derived from social expectations.

People who do not have the ability to do the things that are expected of most people in their living environments are considered, from the public perspective, to have disabilities or other limiting conditions. When there is some evidence of limitation—even very cursory evidence such as physical appearance—in intellectual or other functioning, the terms *intellectual disability* or *developmental disabilities* are frequently used by members of the public to qualify and understand the lack of ability to do the things that are expected of most people in their environments.

There are many reasons why people do not have the capacity to meet socially derived expectations in their particular environments, many of which are detailed in this text. These include the following, among other things: genetic inheritance, chance occurrences both before and after conception, injury, lack of learning opportunities, languages understood and used, poor family and social support, physical barriers (e.g., steps rather than ramps), systems that are too complex (e.g., electronic banking, complicated application procedures for services, use of written words rather than icons on signs), practices that are inappropriately difficult (e.g., sending letters to people who have visual impairments or who cannot read), and unavailability of resources (e.g., money, housing, support personnel) in the immediate and broader environments. Furthermore, very often there is a combination of several reasons.

Critical Meaning

Since about 1990, there has emerged worldwide a strong voice from within the wider disability community declaring itself to be a valid and necessary part of the human social order (Oliver, 1990). This movement, reflecting the critical (value-based and goal-oriented) disability perspective, has a decades-long history, but its strong emergence reflects the influence of other established identity theories—such as those related to race, feminism, gender identity, and oppression (Asch, 2001). The critical disability perspective, building on views advanced by these other theories, regards disability terminology and many of the enormous number of systems and social conventions that have emerged from such terminology as the wrongly focused, somewhat unnecessary, and sometimes illegitimate constructed ideas of *other* people. It views the discourse of disability (i.e., the formal ideas, discussions, and writings about disability) as the domain mainly of people with disabilities themselves and considers that it is primarily people with disabilities who can move the field forward in ways that are truly helpful and valid. It examines power in its various forms—intellectual, political, economic, moral—and considers recognition of all difference as a social necessity (Davis, 2010).

The critical disability movement is also strongly influenced by the philosophy of equal human rights for people with disabilities, a sister movement that has championed disability rights worldwide. Human rights emphasizes that all people, regardless of their abilities or limitations, are members of the human family and as such are equally entitled to the same rights. Gaining such equality involves putting laws in place that clearly specify rights, but it also is a matter of people with disabilities claiming equal rights

Growing Expectations of Ability

Many of the expectations associated with carrying out the practical and social activities of everyday life are becoming increasingly complex. This complexity broadens the public meaning of disability to some extent because many people need assistance to cope with it.

A large majority of the world's population now lives in urban areas, where it is typically necessary to use complicated transportation systems; shop in a large choice of venues; take specific action to maintain personal relationships; and deal with ever-changing technology (e.g., banking, elevators, computers, social networking), crowds, and many other challenges. Although many accommodations have been made in most cities to make daily life activities easier for people with disabilities, the very nature of urban life increases the expectation that people should be able to perform numerous everyday activities that are rather complex.

Whether or not people live in urban areas, daily life is becoming more complex. Technology used in the home—involving such things as telephones, televisions, equipment to play music and movies, and many adaptive devices—has been extremely helpful to many people with disabilities. At the same time, it changes at a rather rapid pace—a pace that is often bewildering even to those who eagerly embrace it. Literacy is a required skill in today's urban world. Computer literacy (i.e., the ability to use computer equipment to communicate with others and gather information) is very helpful to some people with disabilities and is quickly becoming a required skill; *the e-divide* is a term to describe those who are and are not computer literate. It is still too early to describe how much of an asset computer literacy will be to people with various types of disabilities (Davies, Stock, & Wehmeyer, 2004), but it is quite possible that it will be another way that they are separated from others in their environments (i.e., they are on the "wrong" side of the e-divide).

Growing Acceptance of Disability

Paradoxically, the 21st century has seen a trend toward altering the social view of intellectual and developmental disabilities so that members of the general public are more tolerant of them. It is increasingly recognized that people have a broad range of skills and lifestyles, and there is growing acceptance of people of varying skill levels and lifestyle choices. This view holds not only that all people should be free to live their lives in general accordance with the rules of society but also that they must be supported in doing so if help is required.

Considerable effort has been made, especially since approximately 1980, to remove some of the social and environmental barriers to inclusion so that all people—regardless of ability level, age, cultural background, and so forth—can live more ably in the general society. As a result, the public meaning of *intellectual and developmental disabilities* has narrowed somewhat. Increasing numbers of people with these disabilities are included in society and are carrying out many socially expected life functions quite ably and independently.

and being seen by others as being fully entitled to them. A closely related philosophical underpinning is social responsibility, which emerges out of the social model (Shakespeare, 2010), where disability is considered to exist not because of impairment (which is a part of all social orders in any case) but because of a society's inability to accept its responsibility to provide the necessary means to include and accommodate all of its members. The critical disability movement also includes what is referred to as political necessity, or the need to speak out about past oppression, to make the experience of disability explicitly known to both those who have disabilities and those who do not, to advocate, and to act in a political way to bring about needed change. As such, its main thrusts are empowerment, equality, self-determination, and emancipation (Pothier & Devlin, 2006).

For people with intellectual disability and developmental disabilities, involvement in the critical disability movement has been limited. One organization that has perhaps come closest to this type of involvement is People First, an international organization with chapters in many countries that advocates for the voice of people with intellectual and developmental disabilities to be heard and for their human rights to be respected. There has also developed a strong professional, family, and self-advocate interest in self-determination and community inclusion. In addition, there are in every community active people with disabilities and family members who may well never have heard of the critical disability movement but understand from their own experiences the need to express similar views.

The broader critical disability movement has had a considerable impact on the meaning of *disability*, including intellectual disability and developmental disabilities. There has emerged since 1990 a strong body of critical writing from scholars with disabilities and their allies, and—perhaps as a consequence—Disability Studies as a program of learning that promotes the critical perspective has emerged in institutions of higher learning around the world.

The critical meaning of *disability* adds to other held meanings of *intellectual disability* and *developmental disabilities*. It is leading to an understanding that the ways people with disabilities have been conceptualized and treated in the past—the meanings ascribed to *disability*—may have been well intended but must be deconstructed and reconceptualized because they have also resulted in limitations and caused harm that needs to be redressed. This movement is also leading our field to understand that there is a need to have people with disabilities define the experience and discourse of disability themselves in the future. In short, the critical meaning of *intellectual disability* and *developmental disabilities* is oppression of individuals by others in positions of power and the need for equality, self-expression, self-determination, and, eventually, emancipation.

Definitional Meaning

Disability professionals are individuals whose work, and often whose full careers, involve supporting people who have disabilities in a wide variety of ways (e.g., lifestyle, residential, educational, vocational, medical). At the present time and into the foreseeable future, there remains a perceived need for disability professionals to define the terms *intellectual disability* and *developmental disabilities* more specifically (and more narrowly) than can be done using the personal, public, and critical meanings.

This need arises from specific purposes for using these terms, such as establishing entitlement to educational, medical, or social services. Responding to this need, many professional organizations, government bodies, and other groups have set out their own formal definitions of *intellectual disability* or *developmental disabilities* in which they specify the essential criteria for identifying them.

From this view, *intellectual disability* and *developmental disabilities* are terms that are defined by characteristics that are specific and unique to the condition or state of functioning or by the impact of the condition or state of functioning on life outcomes. Formal definitions of *intellectual disability* and *developmental disabilities* emphasize the results of sound scientific assessment as the best way to show adherence to their definitions' criteria. These definitions may (or may not) consider the personal, public, and critical disability meanings discussed in this chapter, but just as each of these meanings has a particular intent or, perhaps, bias, so too do definitional meanings.

One of the criticisms of definitional meanings is that although they are specific and usually rely on scientific methodology for evidence, their "specifics" can differ among particular groups or organizations that create and use them for varying purposes. The meaning of something then becomes what it has been defined to be at a particular point in time (and almost all definitions change over time). Thus, definitions of the same thing can differ somewhat, and each can represent the focus or intent of whoever created it and put it into practice. This is especially problematic if a definitional meaning for something is the only meaning used, as is often the case with government and service organizations.

***Definitions of* Intellectual Disability**   Even given the previous discussion, many jurisdictions and systems around the world have relied quite heavily on the definitional meaning of *intellectual disability* and *developmental disabilities* from one or more of the following entities: the American Association on Intellectual and Developmental Disabilities (AAIDD), the American Psychiatric Association (APA), or the World Health Organization (WHO). For this reason, it is essential to understand such definitions, especially how and why they are used. We begin with the WHO's definitions of disability, as both the AAIDD and APA definitions are aligned with the WHO conceptualization of *disability*.

World Health Organization Definitions One role of the WHO has been to create taxonomies (lists, or organization structures) for diseases and disorders to provide a consistent means to track and monitor health- and illness-related issues throughout the world. The primary vehicle by which this is accomplished is the *International Statistical Classification of Diseases and Related Health Problems,* more commonly referred to as the International Classification of Diseases, or ICD, and now in its 10th revision. Within ICD-10, the term *mental retardation* is defined as follows:

> A condition of arrested or incomplete development of the mind, which is especially characterized by impairment of skills manifested during the developmental period, which contribute to the overall level of intelligence, i.e. cognitive, language, motor, and social abilities (see Centers for Disease Control and Prevention [CDC], n.d., p. 553).

This definition, first introduced in 1990, considers mental retardation to be a disorder and a "condition of arrested or incomplete development of the mind" (CDC, n.d.). It also contains the three elements found in most of the widely used definitions up to that point: 1) intellectual impairment (cognitive, language, motor); 2) social (e.g., adaptive behavior) deficits; and 3) onset during the developmental period (prior to the age of 18). The ICD system remains the dominant classification system in the world, and we will return to this system shortly in a discussion of how the 11th revision of ICD may change the terms used.

In essence, the ICD views intellectual disability within a pathology or deficits framework. Although the ICD-10 continued this emphasis, the WHO became increasingly aware of the dissatisfaction from disability advocates and others who consider disability from personal or critical perspectives and are unwilling to accept pathology-based definitions of the construct. As early as 1980, the WHO began to release alternative ways to think about disability that were outside of typical pathology-based models. The *International Classification of Impairments, Disabilities, and Handicaps (ICIDH;* WHO, 1980) was the WHO's first attempt to separate disability from disease conceptualizations. The ICIDH recognized that disability certainly results from an impairment to body functions or structures (e.g., in the case of intellectual disability, from impairments to the central nervous system) but that personal and environmental/contextual factors affect the manifestation of disability as a function of that impairment. The ICIDH introduced the notion that one must consider activity restrictions that result from interactions between the person's impairments and the demands of the context or environment when defining disability.

In 2001, the WHO took these ideas a step further, introducing the *International Classification of Functioning, Disability and Health (ICF)* to replace the ICIDH. Unlike previous classification systems, the ICF significantly defined *disability* within, and not apart from, a context of typical human functioning. Within ICF, *functioning* is an umbrella term for all life activities of an individual and encompasses the three dimensions of body structures (anatomical parts of the body) and functions (physiological and psychological functions of body systems), personal activities (the execution of tasks or actions), and participation (involvement in a life situation). Problems or limitations in functioning are labeled a disability. Disability can result from any problem in one or more of the three dimensions of human functioning: problems in body structures and functions are referred to as *impairments*, problems in personal activities are referred to as *activity limitations*, and problems in participation are referred to as *participation restrictions*. The ICF situates these impairments, activity limitations, and participation restrictions within the interactions between health conditions, environmental factors, and personal factors.

The key issue as it pertains to understanding disability within the context of the ICF is that disability exists only as a function of the relationship between a person's capacities and the demands of the typical environment or context. Disability exists when there is a gap between personal capacity and environmental demands that affects the person's ability to engage in activities and participate in typical activities in that context. Furthermore, the degree of disability diminishes to the degree that this gap can be reduced or eliminated. Disability is, within ICF, a state of functioning, not a characteristic of or problem with the person.

The ICF is not perfect. Many disability critics believe that the ICF has too strong a medical model focus because it conceptualizes disability as an impairment that is influenced by personal and environmental factors but does not encompass disability arising out of social factors such as marginalization, discrimination, and oppression. Nevertheless, for many professionals, the ICF introduced the first comprehensive conceptualization of disability that allowed a strengths-based focus. Within ICF, intellectual disability is, first and foremost, a disability as understood by the ICF framework. It is a disability that results from body or structure limitations that affect cognition or intellectual capacity.

American Association on Intellectual and Developmental Disabilities Definition In 1992, the then-named American Association on Mental Retardation (AAMR) issued the 9th edition of its widely used manual on mental retardation terminology, classification, and systems of support (Luckasson et al., 1992). Though the term *mental retardation* was retained in this edition (and in the 10th edition, published in 2002), the AAMR 9th edition framed its definition within the WHO ICIDH model of disability, and subsequent editions also aligned with the WHO ICF framework. Now named AAIDD, the association's manual on intellectual disability is in its 11th edition (Schalock et al., 2010) and, in addition to continuing to more closely align the definition and classification process with the ICF, this edition replaced the term *mental retardation* with *intellectual disability* to be more in keeping with international usage. Within the AAIDD 2010 manual, *intellectual disability* is defined as follows: "Intellectual disability is characterized by significant limitations both in intellectual functioning and in adaptive behavior as expressed in conceptual, social, and practical adaptive skills. This disability originates before age 18" (p. 8).

Schalock and colleagues (2010) referred to this as the "operational" definition of the construct, referring to the definition that should be used for diagnostic purposes. Note that this retains the three traditional prongs of definitions of *intellectual disability:* limitations in intellectual functioning and adaptive behavior occurring in the developmental period. This is "operationalized" in standard diagnostic processes by taking measures of intelligence and adaptive behavior.

The AAIDD definition embraces the spirit and intent of the ICF, however, by adding to the definition a series of five assumptions in the application of the operational definition. These assumptions are as follows (Schalock et al., 2010, p. 1):

1. Limitations in present functioning must be considered within the context of community environments typical of the individual's age peers and culture.

2. Valid assessment considers cultural and linguistic diversity as well as differences in communication, sensory, motor, and behavioral factors.

3. Within an individual, limitations often coexist with strengths.

4. An important purpose of describing limitations is to develop a profile of needed supports.

5. With appropriate personalized supports over a sustained period, the life functioning of the person with intellectual disability generally will improve.

The AAIDD framework involves a strengths-based approach that emphasizes the development of individualized supports to reduce or close the gap between a person's capacities and the demands of the environment. In essence, it provides a method for designing supports that enable a person to function within his or her context by working toward increasing personal capacity; making modifications to the activity, task, context, or environment; and putting in place additional supports as necessary (Schalock et al., 2010).

According to Thompson and colleagues (2009), supports are "resources and strategies that aim to promote the development, education, interests, and personal well-being of a person and that enhance individual functioning" (p. 135). Luckasson and Spitalnik (1994) suggested that "supports refer to an array, not a continuum, of services, individuals, and settings that match the person's needs" (p. 88). First, supports have the unambiguous intent to enhance community integration and inclusion by enabling people to gain access to a wide array of resources, information, and relationships. Second, supports are individually designed and determined with the active involvement of key stakeholders in the process, particularly the person benefiting from that support. Third, a supports model requires an active and ongoing evaluation of the ecological aspects of the disability (because the disability can only be defined within the context of the functional limitation and the social context), and efforts to design supports focus heavily on changing aspects of the environment or social context or providing individuals with additional skills or strategies to overcome barriers in those environments.

American Psychiatric Association Definition The APA released the latest version of its *Diagnostic and Statistical Manual of Mental Disorders,*

Fifth Edition (DSM-5), in May of 2013, following a decade-long planning process. Like the change in terminology from the 10th to the 11th editions of the AAIDD terminology and classification manual, the *DSM-5* updates the term *mental retardation* used in the prior version to *intellectual disability (intellectual developmental disorder).* The parenthetical "intellectual developmental disorder" included after the term *intellectual disability* in the *DSM-5* is an example of the ongoing evolution of terms and language to describe conditions and states of functioning, such as the types of conditions and functioning that are now called *intellectual disability.* In part, the APA states that the parenthetical intellectual developmental disorder is intended to reflect the fact that when *DSM-5* was being developed, the WHO was also initiating a revision of the ICD (intended to become ICD-11). As described previously, since ICD-10 had been released in 1990, the WHO had released the ICF and, fundamentally, removed the term *disability* from the taxonomy of disorders and diseases. The ICD is a classification of diseases and disorders and, in fact, has a rule that the term *disability* cannot be used within ICD (because, as noted, disability within the WHO family of classifications is handled within ICF and is not a disorder or a disease). Yet, because most of the world and particularly developing countries use the ICD to allocate scarce resources for people with intellectual disability, leaving it out of the ICD-11 simply was not an option. The switch from the term *mental retardation,* as used in ICD-10, was a given. The conundrum was what term to use instead. A WHO task force recommended the use of the term *intellectual developmental disorders* to replace *mental retardation* (Carulla et al., 2011), and the timing of the publication of *DSM-5* was such that the committee opted to include that term in parentheses following the term *intellectual disability.* The problem is that advocates in the field of intellectual and developmental disabilities, many of whom hold personal and critical views of disability, object to the use of the term *disorder,* arguing that this was a step back toward a pathology-based understanding of the construct (Wehmeyer, 2013a). As noted, however, there is a naming convention within ICD that prohibits the use of the term *disability.* The less-than-satisfying compromise, especially for advocates, seems to be *disorders of intellectual development* (ICD-11 is in beta testing at the time of this chapter's writing, so we cannot absolutely confirm the final terminology). This term avoids a primary problem with *intellectual developmental disorders* as

recommended by the original task force in that its acronym is not IDD, which many advocates thought could be conflated with the acronym for *intellectual and developmental disabilities* (obviously, also IDD). According to the beta-version of ICD-11, *disorders of intellectual development* refers to "a group of etiologically diverse conditions originating during the developmental period characterized by significantly below average intellectual functioning and adaptive behavior that is approximately two or more standard deviations below the mean" and occurring during the developmental period (Tassé, Luckasson, & Nygren, 2013, p. 128).

Returning, then, to the APA *DSM-5* definition, the *DSM-5* manual defines *intellectual disability (intellectual developmental disorder)* as involving the following (2014, p. 1, sec. 2):

> Impairments of general mental abilities that impact adaptive functioning in three domains, or areas. These domains determine how well an individual copes with everyday tasks:
>
> - The conceptual domain includes skills in language, reading, writing, math, reasoning, knowledge, and memory.
> - The social domain refers to empathy, social judgment, interpersonal communication skills, the ability to make and retain friendships, and similar capacities.
> - The practical domain centers on self-management in areas such as personal care, job responsibilities, money management, recreation, and organizing school and work tasks.
>
> While intellectual disability does not have a specific age requirement, an individual's symptoms must begin during the developmental period and are diagnosed based on the severity of deficits in adaptive functioning. The disorder is considered chronic and often co-occurs with other mental conditions like depression, attention-deficit/hyperactivity disorder, and autism spectrum disorder.

Intelligence test scores are purposely not included in this definition, so that they are "not overemphasized as the defining factor" (APA, 2014, pp. 1–2, section 3). APA does note, however, in the text that accompanies its definition that

> IQ or similar standardized test scores should still be included in an individual's assessment. In *DSM-5,* intellectual disability is considered to be approximately two standard deviations or more below the population, which equals an IQ score of about 70 or below. (2014, p. 2, section 2)

Defining **Developmental Disabilities** The
previous three sections describe the definitional
meanings of *intellectual disability* from the perspective
of three professional or governmental organizations.
In many parts of the world, the term *developmental
disabilities* is used to mean the same thing as *intellectual disabilities*. In parts of Canada, for example,
developmental disabilities is the term used in legislation, in government and organizations' documents,
and in the disability support environment, but for
purposes of diagnosis or determining eligibility for
services, definitional criteria for *intellectual disabilities*
that are similar to those described in the previous
section are used. The term *developmental disabilities* is
also used in various countries around the world to
refer to a somewhat broader group of conditions and
states of functioning than can be described by the
definitional criteria for *intellectual disability*. The reason for this is that in every country, there are people
who do not meet the definitional criteria for *intellectual disabilities* or another commonly used term
(i.e., those used in mental health, physical health,
and other areas), yet they function such that they
require support.

In the United States, there is a specific, technical, and definitional meaning of *developmental
disabilities* as well that differs from that of *intellectual disability*. In fact, in many ways, the term *developmental disabilities* exists mainly in the sphere of
definitional meanings, because the term was put
in place by the 91st United States Congress with
passage of the Developmental Disabilities Services
and Facilities Construction Amendments of 1970
(PL 91-517), reflected in its most recent version as
the Developmental Disabilities Assistance and Bill
of Rights Act Amendments of 2000, PL 106-402;
DD Act). Thompson and Wehmeyer (2008) conducted a search for the term *developmental disabilities* (or *developmental disability*) and determined that
before 1971, there were only three documents that
included this term.

The DD Act was the direct result of the deinstitutionalization movement and of the need to
create comprehensive community-based service
systems for people with both intellectual disability
and closely related physical disabilities. Lakin and
Bruininks (1985) noted that the DD Act defined disabilities as developmental when such a disability "(a)
originated in childhood (the developmental period
from birth to 18), (b) constituted a significant handicap, and (c) were expected to continue indefinitely"
(p. 4). A *developmental disability* was defined as "a

disability attributable to mental retardation, cerebral palsy, epilepsy, or other neurologically handi-
capping conditions found to be related to mental
retardation or requiring treatment similar to that
for mentally retarded individuals" (Developmental Disabilities Services and Facilities Construction
Amendments of 1970, U.S.C. § 135).

Over the years, the definition of *developmental
disabilities* has been modified and changed to reflect
changes in the field. The current version of the definition from the 2000 reauthorization of the DD Act
is as follows (Developmental Disabilities Assistance
and Bill of Rights Act Amendments of 2000, PL 106-
402, 45 CFR 1385.3—Definitions):

> Developmental disabilities (DD) are severe, life-
> long disabilities attributable to mental and/or
> physical impairments, manifested before age 22.
> Developmental disabilities result in substantial
> limitations in three or more areas of major life
> activities:
>
> * capacity for independent living
> * economic self-sufficiency
> * learning
> * mobility
> * receptive and expressive language
> * self-care
> * self-direction
>
> Without appropriate services and supports, the
> choices open to people with developmental disabil-
> ities, including where they live, work, and play, are
> minimal. They are isolated rather than fully inte-
> grated and included in the mainstream of society.
> Persons with developmental disabilities require
> individually planned and coordinated services
> and supports (e.g., housing, employment, educa-
> tion, civil and human rights protection, health care)
> from many providers in order to live in the com-
> munity.

In the United States, then, some but not all
people who are considered to have an intellectual
disability are also considered to have a developmental disability, as it is defined in the 2000 DD
Act. Similarly, some but not all people who meet
the definition for *developmental disability* as it is set
out in the DD Act are considered to have an intellectual disability. These are not completely overlapping groups. The term *developmental disabilities*
also includes people with physical disabilities
(e.g., cerebral palsy, spina bifida) that emerge during the developmental period. Increasingly, some
manifestations of autism spectrum disorder are

included as developmental disabilities (though, again, not all).

Another umbrella term that is not as widely used, *cognitive disabilities,* overlaps to some degree with both intellectual disability and developmental disabilities. It typically refers to any disability that affects cognitive functioning, including intellectual disability, traumatic brain injury, Alzheimer's disease or senile dementia, and, in some cases, learning disabilities.

SHOULD DISABILITY TERMS BE USED?

The use of terms, and the meanings ascribed to them, has been controversial for several decades. There are a number of reasons that general and specialized terms are useful, but misuse has no doubt also occurred (Foreman, 2005). Moreover, people who might be described as having disabilities themselves often eschew the use of any term that sets them apart, marginalizing them. For this reason, practitioners, students, and teachers must use terms with caution, and always be aware—even in writing and reading this book—that the terms *intellectual disability* and *developmental disability* and their many related terms are considered by some to be demeaning and inappropriate. Why, then, are such terms used at all?

Use of Disability Terms as Scientific Thinking

Despite the view that disabilities are a natural and acceptable part of the human condition, people with and without disabilities have been categorized in response to the strong trend in recent centuries to conceive the world in "scientific" ways. The word *normal* emerged to describe some people and the word *abnormal* then described those people who were not considered to be normal (Davis, 2010). Within the field that is now known as intellectual and developmental disabilities, subcategories have been described and refined over the past 150 years. For example, John Langdon Down, best known for first describing what is called Down syndrome today, wrote about what he called his "ethnic classification of idiots" in 1866 (Ward, 2002). Since the early 1900s, people with disabilities have been described and classified in increasingly complex ways (see Chapters 2 and 3). The rationale for doing this was to identify those people who need special learning and lifestyle support and to capture the

ever-expanding knowledge of disability. There were other, more sinister, reasons as well, such as controlling propagation of "feeble-minded" people through sterilization, isolation, and other means so that society could be "improved" over time (Smith & Wehmeyer, 2012). Over the past few decades, numerous new categories have emerged to describe people with disabilities that reflect new knowledge of environmental, genetic, and other biological causes of disability (see especially Chapters 9, 10, 11, and 12). The use of categorization within more general terms such as *intellectual disability* is at an historic high.

The question of who should create and use terms and categories—if they should be used at all— is also controversial. Historically, people have been ascribed terms and are placed into categories based on physical or behavioral characteristics that can be described by "other" people, usually disability or medical professionals, and not by people with disabilities themselves. This is a matter of considerable concern among those who advocate for self-determination and those who promote a critical disability perspective.

Dangers of Using Disability Terms

Terms that are related to intellectual and developmental disability have been misused, both directly and indirectly, in numerous well-documented ways. These include isolating people from their families, friends, and communities; segregating people in schools, residences, and workplaces; denying personal freedoms and human rights; and preventing procreation (Roeher Institute, 1997; Wehmeyer, 2013b; Zola, 1993). These misuses have had a significant negative impact on individuals' lives, and many of them continue in some form today. For reasons such as these, the cautions about misuse of terms that are found throughout the disability literature need to be clearly understood and assiduously applied.

Another danger more closely related to the meaning of terms is that terms used to describe people on the margins of society have a habit of taking on negative connotations. This occurs with disability terms because disability is devalued, and negative stereotyping emerges as a consequence (Blaska, 1993). Terms used in the past as roughly equivalent to the current *intellectual disability* and *developmental disabilities* have all fallen out of favor and been replaced by other more "appropriate" terms. It is almost impossible in the 21st century to believe that people with limited intellectual functioning were once referred to as idiots, morons, imbeciles, feeble-minded, and mentally deficient by well-meaning and caring people.

Throughout the last half of the 20th century, the term *mentally retarded* was quite respectable around the world, whereas most people now feel thoroughly insulted if they are referred to by that term. Some groups of people, such as people who have low hearing or vision, sometimes avoid the term *disability* altogether, not wanting to be associated with it, and instead describe their lifestyle as a subculture (e.g., Freebody & Power, 2001; Kaplan, 2005). As the complex meanings of the terms as described above changed over time, there was little choice but to change the terms to something less stigmatizing.

Why is there such a turnover of terms? Because of the lack of value placed on disability, using terms to refer to people whose lower abilities leads others to believe they are on the margins of society results in a cycle of devaluation and degradation. The terms classify people, either formally or informally, as different. Classifying others as different carries with it perceptions that they are "not worthy" and "outsiders." Such perceptions lead others to treat people classified as different as if they really are different. Finally, treating people differently leads them to act differently. The irony is that because they act differently, those who classified them in the first place feel assured that their classification has been correct all along and was therefore justified. Thus, the cycle may continue. This situation suggests that terms such as *intellectual disabilities* and *developmental disabilities* are harmful and are perhaps best abandoned wherever possible.

Reasons for Using Disability Terms

The terms *intellectual disability* and *developmental disability* and related terms are useful for several purposes. Six of the most important are highlighted in this section.

1. The principal argument that is used to support the use of terms such as *intellectual disability* and *developmental disability* is that they help to identify, and thus to assist, people who have extraordinary support needs. Within the present context, it is often useful to classify people as having such

disabilities so that they may receive the supports they need to function successfully across multiple domains. This support may occur at any age and in many places, such as in family homes, in health services, in schools, in workplaces, or in the homes of adults with disabilities. Governments that fund such supports and agencies that provide them often want to be assured that their efforts are going to the intended recipients. Thus, classifying people as having intellectual disability or developmental disabilities can often lead to much-needed supports and life improvements. In practice, either formal or informal definitions may be used for such purposes, although there is often considerably more flexibility to respond to the needs of individuals when informal definitions are used.

2. People who are somewhat marginalized in society, such as people with intellectual disability and developmental disabilities, often need specific civic and legal protection to express themselves personally and to participate fully in their communities. Terms that are identified with such groups can be used in legislation and legal documents to set out such protections. At the same time, including terms in such documents demonstrates a commitment by the broader society to include identified marginalized groups.

3. Professionals who work in the intellectual and developmental disabilities field, parents, and others sometimes need to use these terms to clarify to others what might be expected of a person with a disability. At times, people find it helpful to use other terms that have similar meanings to help others understand the nature of a disability. For example, a professional who is explaining, for the first time, the nature of delayed development in a young child to parents who have had no experience with disabilities might say something such as

> Your child appears to have a developmental delay. Some people call this a handicap, or challenged, or intellectual disability, but these all basically mean the same thing—that your child will be able to do many of the things that other children her age can typically do, but it will take her more time and effort to learn to do them. Some of those things she may not learn to do at all. However, she will learn other things that are important to her. (A. Perry, personal communication, September 17, 2002)

4. The terms *intellectual disability* and *developmental disability*, and their numerous subterms, are useful to classify various categories of disabilities.

By allowing for precision, such classification helps to broaden knowledge of specific disabilities through research and practice and to understand better what services and treatments are required for people to live in the best possible ways.

5. Individual self-advocates and groups of self-advocates, such as People First and numerous others, take advantage of terms such as *intellectual disability* and *developmental disabilities* to make their cause known to others in ways that can be clearly understood. Parent and family groups, some of which play a strong advocacy role in various jurisdictions, often find it very helpful to draw attention to what it means to have a child or family member with an intellectual or developmental disability and to show that this experience is different from that of having a child or family member without a disability.

6. Leaders in the field of intellectual and developmental disabilities—such as academics, researchers, policy makers, and heads of organizations—need a term that describes their area of interest and that focuses attention on a specific set of issues. Having a field that is identified by the name of the disability adds legitimacy to this area of interest and its set of issues and sets it apart as something that is worthwhile. In the same line of thinking, national and international organizations find it helpful to use these terms to describe their focus of interest. Some examples include the International Association for the Scientific Study of Intellectual and Developmental Disabilities, AAIDD, and the Australasian Society for Intellectual Disability.

So Should Disability Terms Be Used?

Use and nonuse of the terms *intellectual disability* and *developmental disabilities* might follow the wisdom of the much-used illustration of the use of terms in general in academia. According to this illustration, a botanist, to work efficiently, may well need to know the classification system that describes all the plants that grow in a garden and might need to use the scientific names that have been given to them. People strolling through the same garden enjoying the sights and the fragrances of the plants in bloom do not need to know this information or use the terms at all. What this illustration teaches is that disability terms may be used when it is helpful and not used when there is no need to do so.

CURRENT HELPFUL USES OF DISABILITY-RELATED TERMS

For young children, the term *developmental delay* is commonly used instead of *intellectual disability* or *developmental disabilities*. The reasoning is that all aspects of development are still in progress. It is possible that the delay is caused by a condition that will not persist over time and that there will not be an ongoing disability.

Currently, it is quite acceptable to talk about intellectual disability or developmental disabilities as subsets of larger groupings of disability categories, about the field of intellectual and developmental disabilities, or about people with intellectual and developmental disabilities as a whole population. When referring to a specific individual, however, the practice is to simply use the person's name.

Sometimes, for purposes of clarification, a term such as *intellectual disability* or *developmental disabilities* is added in people-first format, as in the following example: "Sarah, a woman with intellectual disability." Alternatively, professionals who work in services for people with disabilities very often use the verb *support* when clarification is needed. Thus, they would say, "Sarah, a woman we support." This is thought to be more respectful of the person and to promote current thinking that the principal purpose of services is to support individuals in ways that will maximize their potential and their enjoyment of life.

People First, a large international organization that represents people with intellectual and developmental disabilities, suggests that people-first language should always be used. It is interesting to note that people with disabilities seldom refer to themselves by terminology at all in the course of carrying out their daily lives (Finlay & Lyons, 2005). The principal reason for this has been documented in many personal stories: it is that people with intellectual or developmental disabilities see themselves simply as human beings, living in a world with other human beings. Like most people, though, they recognize that they have more things in common with some people than others, and thus they often associate naturally with other people who have similar abilities and interests (see Table 1.2).

SUMMARY

The terms *intellectual disability* and *developmental disabilities* are widely used throughout the world. Four

Table 1.2.   Acceptable use of *intellectual disability, developmental disabilities,* and related terms[a]

Term (applicable group)	Generally acceptable use	Example
Intellectual disability (adults or children)	The term in general	"The meaning of *intellectual disability*"
	Adjective for an individual	"Sarina, a woman with an intellectual disability"
Developmental disabilities (adults or children)	A group of disabilities	"The disabilities related to the development of abilities"
	A field of study or service	"Supports for developmental disabilities"
	Adjective for a group of people	"Individuals with developmental disabilities"
Developmental disability (adults or children)	The term in general	"A definition of *developmental disability*"
	Adjective for an individual	"Jose, a man with a developmental disability"
Developmental delay (children only)	The field of study or service	"Study in developmental delay"
	Adjective for a group of children	"Education for children with developmental delay"
	Adjective for an individual child	"Kareem, a boy with a developmental delay"

[a]As of this writing in 2016

meanings of the terms *intellectual disability* or *developmental disabilities* that are particularly important today—personal, public, critical, and definitional meanings—illustrate four perspectives on understanding what the terms mean. It is useful for practitioners to understand disability terms as a blend of all four meanings. The personal meaning emerges from the life experiences of people with disabilities and their families. The public meaning is the way disability is conceptualized in the broader culture. The critical meaning, which emerges from the main ideas of the critical disability movement, recognizes that treatment of people with disabilities in the past has not always been helpful and that past wrongs need to be redressed; equality and self-determination are basic principles that support the view that people with disabilities are a legitimate part of the human condition that needs to be respected. Definitions of *intellectual disability* and *developmental disability* are widely used, especially for determining eligibility for services and supports. There is danger, however, in overrelying on the definitional meanings alone. The question of whether disability terms should be used, and for what purposes, has been controversial for several decades, as there are both advantages and disadvantages to doing so. People-first language is typically used today to describe people with disabilities; when it is not necessary to identify disability for clarification, use of the person's name is most acceptable.

FOR FURTHER THOUGHT AND DISCUSSION

1. Examine your own personal ideas and values around the term *intellectual disability,*

and describe the meaning you attach to the term.

2. To what degree should there be internationally understood meanings of the terms *intellectual disability* and *developmental disability?* What are the advantages and disadvantages to having such internationally understood meanings?

3. Do the terms *intellectual disability* and *developmental disability* encompass and reflect the values you hold for your field?

4. Examine the literal meaning of the term *intellectual disability* and the common definitional meanings for this term used in your country. What are some of the factors in your country that contribute to the public meaning of *intellectual disability?* How do these factors alter how people in your country think of the term's meaning?

5. The term *developmental delay* is often used for children because they are still in their developmental years. Should different terms be used for children and adults? What are the advantages and disadvantages of using different terms for children and adults? When shaping your response, consider adolescents. If different terms are used for children and adults, at what age or stage of life is it best to change from using one term to using the other?

REFERENCES

American Psychiatric Association. (2013). *Diagnostic and statistical manual of mental disorders* (5th ed.). Washington, DC: Author.

American Psychiatric Association. (2014). *DSM-5 implementation and support.* Retrieved from http://www.dsm5.org/Pages/Default.aspx

Asch, A. (2001). Critical race theory, feminism, and disability: Reflections on social justice and personal identity. *Ohio State Law Journal, 62,* 1–17.

Blaska, J. (1993). The power of language: Speak and write using "person first." In M. Nager (Ed.), *Perspectives on disability* (2nd ed., pp. 25–32). Palo Alto, CA: Health Markets Research.

Carulla, L.S., Reed, G.M., Vaez-Azizi, L.M., Cooper, S.A., Leal, R.M., Bertelli, M.,...Saxena, S. (2011). Intellectual developmental disorders: Towards a new name, definition, and framework for "mental retardation /intellectual disability" in ICD-11. *World Psychiatry, 10*(3), 175–180.

Centers for Disease Control and Prevention. (n.d.). *ICD-10-Volume-1 (2013).* Retrieved from http://www.cdc.gov /nchs/data/dvs/2e_volume1_2013.pdf

Council for Exceptional Children, Division on Autism and Developmental Disabilities. (n.d.). *The Dolly Gray Children's Literature Award.* Retrieved from http:// daddcec.org/Awards/DollyGrayAwards.aspx

Davies, D.K., Stock, S.E., & Wehmeyer, M.L. (2004). Computer-mediated, self-directed computer training and skill assessment for individuals with mental retardation. *Journal of Developmental and Physical Disabilities, 16,* 95–105.

Davis, L.J. (2010). *The disability studies reader* (3rd ed.). New York, NY: Routledge.

Developmental Disabilities Assistance and Bill of Rights Act Amendments of 2000, PL 106-402, 42 U.S.C. §§ 6000 *et seq.*

Developmental Disabilities Services and Facilities Construction Amendments of 1970, PL 91-517, 42 U.S.C. §§ 6000 *et seq.*

Dictionary.com unabridged. (n.d.) *ability.* Retrieved from http://dictionary.reference.com/browse/ability

Finlay, W.M.L., & Lyons, E. (2005). Rejecting the label: A social constructionist analysis. *Mental Retardation, 43,* 120–134.

Foreman, P. (2005). Language and disability. *Journal of Intellectual and Developmental Disability, 30,* 57–59.

Freebody, P., & Power, D. (2001). Interviewing deaf adults in postsecondary educational settings: Stories, cultures, and life histories. *Journal of Deaf Studies and Deaf Education, 6,* 130–142.

Kaplan, D. (2005). *The definition of disability.* Retrieved from http://www.accessiblesociety.org/topics/demographics-identity/dkaplanpaper.htm

Kaplan, M. (2009). *List of books where people with disabilities are shown in a positive light.* Retrieved from http://www .articlesbase.com/book-reviews-articles/list-of-books-where-people-with-disabilities-are-shown-in-a-positive-light-1530258.html

Lakin, K.C., & Bruininks, R.H. (1985). Contemporary services to handicapped children and youth. In R.H. Bruininks & K.C. Lakin (Eds.), *Living and learning in the least restrictive environment* (pp. 3-22). Baltimore, MD: Paul H. Brookes Publishing Co.

Luckasson, R., Coulter, D.L., Polloway, E.A., Reiss, S., Schalock, R.L., Snell, M.E.,...Stark, J.A. (1992). *Mental retardation: Definition, classification, and systems of supports* (9th ed.). Washington, DC: American Association on Mental Retardation.

Luckasson, R., & Spitalnick, D.M. (1994). Political and programmatic shifts of the 1992 AAMR definition of intellectual disability. In V.J. Bradley, J.W. Ashbaugh, & B.C. Blaney (Eds.), *Creating individual supports for people with developmental disabilities: A mandate for change at many levels* (pp. 81–95). Baltimore, MD: Paul H. Brookes Publishing Co.

MUBI. (2013). *Disability in film.* Retrieved from https:// mubi.com/lists/disability-in-film

National Leadership Consortium. (n.d.). *Recommended books about the disability experience.* Retrieved from http://www .nlcdd.org/resources-books-movies-disability.html

Oliver, M.J. (1990). *The politics of disablement: Critical texts in social work and the welfare state.* Basingstoke, United Kingdom: Macmillan.

Oxford University Press. (2000). *Oxford advanced learner's dictionary of current English* (6th ed.). Oxford, United Kingdom: Author.

People First. (2016). *People First.* Retrieved from http:// www.peoplefirst.org/

Pothier, D., & Devlin, R. (2006). *Critical disability theory: Essays in philosophy, politics, policy, and law.* Vancouver, Canada: UBC Press.

Regional Oral History Office. (n.d.). *ROHO news.* Retrieved from http://bancroft.berkeley.edu/ROHO /projects/rosie/

Roeher Institute. (1997). *Disability, community and society: Exploring the links.* Toronto, Canada: Author.

Schalock, R., Borthwick-Duffy, S., Bradley, V., Buntinx, W., Coulter, D., Craig, E.,...Wehmeyer, M. (2010). *Intellectual disability: Definition, classification, and systems of supports* (11th ed.). Washington, DC: American Association on Intellectual and Developmental Disabilities.

Shakespeare, T. (2010). The social model of disability. In L.J. Davis (Ed.), *The disability studies reader* (3rd ed., pp. 266–273). New York, NY: Routledge.

Smith, J.D., & Wehmeyer, M.L. (2012). *Good blood, bad blood: Science, nature and the myth of the Kallikaks.* Washington, DC: American Association on Intellectual and Developmental Disabilities.

Tassé, M.J., Luckasson, R., & Nygren, M. (2013). AAIDD proposed recommendations for ICD–11 and the condition previously known as mental retardation. *Intellectual and Developmental Disabilities, 51*(2), 127–131.

Thompson, J.E., & Wehmeyer, M.L. (2008). Historical and legal issues in developmental disabilities. In H.P. Parette & G.R. Peterson-Karlan (Eds.), *Research based practices in developmental disabilities* (2nd ed., pp. 13–42). Austin, TX: PRO-ED.

Thompson, J.R., Buntinx, W., Schalock, R.L., Shogren, K.A., Snell, M.E., Wehmeyer, M.L.,...Yeager, M.H. (2009). Conceptualizing supports and the support needs of people with intellectual disability. *Intellectual and Developmental Disabilities, 47,* 135–146.

Ward, C. (2002). *History of Down's syndrome.* Retrieved from http://www.intellectualdisability.info/changing-values/history-of-downs-syndrome

Wehmeyer, M.L. (2008). The impact of disability on adolescent identity. In M. Sadowski (Ed.), *Adolescents at school: Perspectives on youth, identity, and education* (2nd ed., pp. 167–184). Cambridge, MA: Harvard Education Press.

Wehmeyer, M.L. (2013a). Disability, disorder, and identity. *Intellectual and Developmental Disabilities, 51*(2), 122–126.

Wehmeyer, M.L. (Ed.). (2013b). *The story of intellectual disability: An evolution of meaning, understanding, and public perception.* Baltimore, MD: Paul H. Brookes Publishing Co.

World Health Organization. (n.d.). *Mental retardation (F70-F79).* Retrieved March 9, 2015 from http://apps.who.int/classifications/icd10/browse/2015/en#/F70-F79

World Health Organization. (1980). *International classification of impairments, disabilities, and handicaps.* Retrieved from http://apps.who.int/iris/bitstream/10665/41003/1/9241541261_eng.pdf

World Health Organization. (2001). *International Classification of Functioning, Disability and Health (ICF).* Geneva, Switzerland: Author.

World Health Organization. (2015). Mental retardation (F70-F79). In *International Statistical Classification of Diseases and Related Health Problems, 10th revision (ICD-10) -2015-WHO version for 2015.* Retrieved from http://apps.who.int/classifications/icd10/browse/2015/en#/F70-F79

Zola, I.K. (1993). Self, identity and the naming question: Reflections on the language of disability. In M. Nager (Ed.), *Perspectives on disability* (2nd ed., pp. 15–23). Palo Alto, CA: Health Markets Research.

2

Historical Overview of Intellectual and Developmental Disabilities

Ivan Brown, John P. Radford, and Michael L. Wehmeyer

WHAT YOU WILL LEARN

- The presence of disabilities throughout human history
- How disabilities have been conceptualized and treated in various ways throughout human history
- How people with disabilities have been treated kindly and maltreated, sometimes simultaneously
- How the institutional era loomed large in the history of intellectual and developmental disabilities
- Approaches to understanding the early 21st century's emphasis on equality, community living, and social inclusion in the context of the history of disabilities

Other chapters in this book primarily address recent and current issues in intellectual and developmental disabilities, although many ground their material in historical aspects that have influenced their specific topics. This chapter provides an historical overview of intellectual and developmental disabilities. Understanding how intellectual and developmental disabilities were perceived and treated in various ages gives some perspective on the way modern societies view disability.

Perception and treatment of disability has differed considerably over time and across regions of the world, and it is not possible in this chapter to capture all of the known details. Rather, major trends that may influence current thinking are provided with accompanying examples. Of necessity, particular emphasis is given to the trends in geographic areas that have become more affluent nations, where historical information is more readily and widely available to the authors.

Although disability has always been present, it has been perceived differently over time. Even since the early 1900s, thinking about disability has changed markedly. For this reason, it is essential to remember that when intellectual disability is spoken of, particularly in a historical context, people in earlier times did not think of disability as it is thought of today (Berkson, 2006; Stainton, 2001; Wehmeyer, 2013). Also, people who lived in one historical era did not necessarily think of disability in the same way as people who lived in other eras or even in other parts of the world during the same era. Indeed, the word *disability* is very much a social concept (or social construct), because its meaning is not stable across time and place; rather, its very meaning and the connotations that accompany that meaning emerge from a variety of social and other environmental factors that are present in particular places and times (see also Chapter 1 for more information on the social meaning of terms). Thus, the terms *disability* and *intellectual disability* are used in this chapter purely for the sake of convenience, and it must be understood that many different descriptive terms have been used across time. Some such terms that are familiar are *fools, idiots, feeble-minded,* and *morons,* but there were many others. At the time of their use, such terms described groups of people or their development in ways that were largely value neutral. At other times (especially when terms had been in use for a while), they became derogatory or were used to categorize people in an unfair way—in the sense that today's "labels" are often considered overly restrictive, even if they are descriptive. The following sections further explore these ideas.

DISABILITY IN ANTIQUITY

Detailed and relevant recorded documentation of disability in early history is a rare commodity. Consequently, investigation of disability in ancient times has necessarily spilled over into such disciplines as archaeology, anthropology, and genealogy. Although evidence is scarce, from a logical perspective, there is no reason to think that intellectual disability did not exist from the dawn of time

Evidence of disability in ancient cultures is sometimes categorized into two broad classes: natural (evidence from the remains of humans—e.g., bones, teeth) and cultural (evidence from cultural artifacts and recorded histories). Valuable clues to the existence of intellectual disability and treatment of people with disabilities, in general, may be drawn from each of these two sources. Natural evidence is almost invariably supplemented by cultural evidence—that is, written and graphic documentation, domestic relics, tools, art, architecture, and even spoken chronicles passed down through generations.

Archeological evidence shows that disability has existed since the dawn of humankind, and studies of Neanderthal specimens show that disability perhaps even predates that (Berkson, 2004). In spite of restrictions to historical knowledge, interesting evidence has been collected over the years from which some general conclusions can be drawn. Such evidence comes from a variety of times and places, but it was considerably mitigated by the emergence of artistic expression about 50,000 years ago, by people in what is now Europe and Western Asia changing from nomadic hunters and gatherers to settled agrarians approximately 10,000 years ago and by the beginning of recorded history about 5,000 years ago.

The earliest evidence of disability, and, potentially, of concern for people with disabilities, dates to 50,000 years ago with the discovery of the remains of Neanderthal people near a village called Shanidar in what is now northern Iraq (Craig, 2013). Among the remains discovered in the mid-20th century at this site was a Neanderthal man, called Shanidar I,

who had experienced significant head and/or brain trauma that appeared to result in impairments to his limbs and, possibly, to his vision. Yet this man lived to an old age (for Neanderthals), an outcome not possible, anthropologists have suggested, without the aid and support of his fellow proto-humans (Trinkaus & Zimmerman, 1982).

The passing millennia contain evidence for the presence of people with disabilities across ancient societies, although not specifically evidence pertaining to intellectual disability. Berkson (2004) concluded that it is clear from the available evidence that prehuman hominids, early Homo sapiens, and early civilizations lived with the following conditions:

- A variety of physical malformations

- Anemia

- Blindness

- Broken limbs

- Down syndrome (and probably other syndromes)

- Head injuries

- Hydrocephaly (enlargement of the head caused by an abnormal accumulation of cerebrospinal fluid in the cranium)

- Microcephaly (smaller than normal circumference of the head because the brain had not developed properly or had stopped growing) and anencephaly (a congenital neural tube birth disorder that causes the absence of a major portion of the brain, skull, and scalp and is incompatible with life)

- Mobility impairments

- Osteoarthritis

- Paralysis

Somewhat paradoxically, advances in the human condition—notably a settled lifestyle that allowed agriculture, technology, and the arts to flourish—also contributed to the development of diseases and conditions that encouraged an increase in disabilities (e.g., overcrowding; diseases from cultivated plants and animals; polluted water; unclean environments; increase in rodents; increase in insects). For example, disabilities resulted from such things as malaria, smallpox, the plague, and measles—which spread rapidly throughout concentrated settlements—and from a variety of birth malformations (Centers for

Disease Control and Prevention, 2004; Pangas, 2000; Warkany, 1959).

How Disability Was Viewed in Antiquity

Only scattered bits of archeological and written historical information are available about how people with disabilities were treated in very early human social groups (Berkson, 2004). Because there is evidence from a few parts of the world that some adults with these conditions lived into their adult years and were buried after death, it seems reasonable to assume that they must have been treated by their families or wider social groups with a degree of care and, possibly, compassion.

There is somewhat more evidence from early civilizations that left pictorial and written records of their lives. Beliefs and superstitions regarding the origins and meanings associated with disabilities varied widely but probably had a strong impact on the social responses to disabilities; explanations for disabilities included (Edgerton, 1968; Warkany, 1959)

- Demon possession

- Sexual congress with animals or demons

- Sins or other misdeeds of parents or other ancestors

- Influence of the stars and the moon

- Omens and warnings provided by the gods

- Predictions of the future

- Signs of displeasure of the gods

From written or pictorial evidence, it appears that people with disabilities were sometimes protected, even esteemed at times. For example, people who were achondroplastic dwarfs (having the most common type of dwarfism, which is characterized by average-size trunk, short arms and legs, and a slightly enlarged head and prominent forehead) were held in high esteem in dynastic Egypt (e.g., Jeffreys & Tait, 2000). Humanitarian, equitable, and/or charitable treatment was also recorded in several ancient societies. The tendency to act with a degree of kindness and helpfulness toward those members of one's own social order who are in some distress may be not only a developed social value but also an adaptive aspect of genetic heritage that is shared with other animals. Certainly, this trait can be widely observed in many higher order species

of the animal kingdom. However, Kanner's (1964) observation that there is no real evidence that the needs of early humans with the equivalent of intellectual or developmental disabilities were attended to in any systematic way appears to be still valid.

Moreover, at the same time that people with disabilities were being helped in some ways in cultures that had recorded history, they were frequently maltreated or devalued in other ways. This duality has persisted in the treatment of people with intellectual and developmental disabilities, in a variety of ways, to modern times (Wehmeyer, 2013; Woodill & Velche, 1995). Some examples from early civilizations include the following:

- Caring for people with disabilities was set out as a moral obligation in the Torah, the Bible, and the Quran (Brown & Brown, 2003). For example, Kanner (1964) noted that Mohammed advised, as recorded in the fourth verse of the fourth sura, "to feed and house those without reason and to give them kindly words" (p. 3). Similarly, both the Old Testament and the New Testament of the Bible contain explicit instructions to treat disability with compassion (Berkson, 2006). Berkson also noted that in early Christianity, the notion emerged, especially in the writings of St. Augustine, of disability as a natural phenomenon rather than a punishment. At the same time, though, a man who was "blemished" was considered unfit to "offer the bread of his God" (Leviticus 22:17, as cited in Brown & Brown, 2003).

- In classical Greek culture, pensions were provided to people with disabilities, especially for people with physical disabilities that resulted from military service. Hippocrates demonstrated great concern for children with disabilities and attributed certain disabilities to "natural causes" rather than to possession by demons or wrath of the gods (Craig, 2013). Nonetheless, he lived in a civilization that generally believed that the birth of a child with a disability or other deformity was a show of anger by the gods, that held negative attitudes toward them, and that routinely ignored or rejected people with disabilities (Garland, 1995).

- Philip II of Macedon, father of Alexander the Great, raised a son named Arridaios who probably had an intellectual disability. It seems that Alexander treated this brother with kindness, having him accompany his great armies through Persia and India and ensuring that he lived in comfort throughout his life. After Alexander's death, Arridaios became Philip III for a brief period before he was murdered as a pawn in the political machinations of those vying for power. However, it seems from historical accounts that it was widely accepted at the time that Philip II would have been fully justified in having his son suffocated or otherwise disposed of at birth or in his early childhood (e.g., see Green, 1991).

- In Roman civilization, certain advanced medical procedures were intended to prevent or cure some disabilities (Berkson, 2006). At the same time, it was common practice to use people with various physical and mental disabilities as a source of amusement and entertainment (Brown & Brown, 2003). Moreover, Roman civilization, like classical Greek civilization, regarded individuals with disabilities as a scourge and ostracized or otherwise denigrated them accordingly (Berkson, 2004, 2006). In the first century A.D., Roman society considered infants with physical disabilities to be a sign of a "god's power or a god at play, showing humor. Pliny was quoted as saying, 'Nature creates monsters [newborns with malformations] for the purpose of astonishing us and amusing herself'" (as cited in Northampton General Hospital, 2016). The Law of the Twelve Tables that emerged during the 5th century B.C.E. was highly influential throughout the Roman Empire and reflected both positive and negative perspectives of disabilities. For example, infanticide was reinforced, but ongoing care of people with disabilities was ensured by making males in the family legally responsible for them (Berkson, 2006).

It cannot be denied that, in ancient times, people with disabilities were subjected to various forms of discrimination, segregation, persecution, and attempted eradication (including infanticide, especially through the practice of exposure, whereby newborns were left outside to die; see Berkson, 2006, for a description). At the same time, though, certain stories and recorded actions appear to offer some evidence of interest in treating or curing disability. This interest might be interpreted in at least two ways: 1) as an attempt to eradicate disability and therefore an indication of the ongoing negative attitudes toward disability or 2) as an effort

to demonstrate compassion and therefore an indication of a desire to help better the lives of people with disabilities. Whatever the intended meaning, some examples of treatments include the following (Berkson, 2004):

- Calls for divine intervention

- Herbal remedies

- Prosthetic devices (e.g., crutches; artificial limbs, eyes, and teeth)

- Surgery (e.g., amputating limbs, removing cataracts, drilling holes in the skull)

Overall, although disability existed and was recognized in antiquity, it is not known precisely how it was conceptualized. From the information that is available, it seems likely that disability was viewed more negatively than positively. Still, the beginnings of compassion toward people with disabilities, and the beginnings of positive action to care for and improve the lives of those people with disabilities, appears to have developed over this very long era. Furthermore, as Craig (2013) noted, there is a sequence of life circumstances established in antiquity with regard to people with disability, and that would include people with intellectual disability, repeated throughout history. That is, in prehistory and into the earliest times in antiquity, people with intellectual disability were likely unnoticed if their level of impairment required minimal support. In early hunter-gatherer and agrarian societies, people with intellectual disability probably functioned as the rest of society. Clearly the presence of any physical impairment stigmatized people, although there is evidence of humane treatment of people with physical disabilities, at least in early agrarian societies.

DISABILITY IN THE MEDIEVAL ERA (MIDDLE AGES)

Historians from a distinctly European perspective refer to the medieval era, also sometimes called the Middle Ages, as the long period approximately spanning the years 300 to around 1500 CE. As Wickham (2013) noted, it is important to keep in mind that during this period there was, in essence, no formal conception of "intelligence" and, again, due to conditions during this period, concerns about intellectual disability were fairly minimal. That said, as Wickham suggested, the study of intellectual disability, and disability in general, is a study of poverty and the lives of people who were the poorest in these societies, and the evidence pertaining to the lives of people with disabilities in this span is, in part, provided by the growing civic responses to such people.

References to something similar to an intellectual disability are scarce during this long period, and most historians only refer to evidence from the 11th century onward. From this evidence, two terms appear to have been in popular usage: *natural fool* and *idiot*. Although many people with intellectual impairment may have been thought of in this way, the terms referred more generally to people who did not accept the typical responsibilities of adult life for a variety of undefined reasons. Stainton (2001) wrote that these terms were unspecific and ambiguous, and that, although understood in a general way, they lacked any objective conceptual criteria.

Of importance for the development of systematic approaches to supporting people with intellectual and developmental disabilities, in the 1100s there began to emerge a distinction between people with mental illness (the insane) and people with intellectual disability. Kranzler (1993) quoted Spanish rabbi Moses Maimonides as among the earliest people to make such distinctions:

> The insane person [*shoteh*] is unacceptable as a witness by biblical law, because he is not subject to the commandments. By *shoteh* is to be understood not only one who walks around naked, breaks things and throws stones, but anyone whose mind has become disturbed so that his thinking is consistently confused in some domain although with respect to other matters he speaks to the point and asks pertinent questions, his evidence is nevertheless inadmissible and he is included among the insane.
>
> The intellectually deficient who cannot recognize contradictions and are unable to comprehend things as ordinary people do and those who are extremely agitated and frantic are classed with the insane. Discretionary power is vested in the judge in this matter, as it is impossible to lay down detailed rules on this subject. (Kranzler, 1993, p. 50–51)

Furthermore, legal rulings and laws beginning in the 1300s began to differentiate between people with mental illness and people who were deemed idiots, where an idiot was someone whose mental impairment was considered as occurring at birth and continuing lifelong (Wickham, 2013). Wickham documented multiple examples of English law through the 1300s and 1400s as it pertained to Prerogativa Regis (the prerogative of the king) and

the disposition of property. She also documented instances of guardianship over people deemed to be idiots as early as the late 1200s.

Influences on the Way Disabilities Were Addressed

Four other interrelated characteristics of this era distinguish how conditions that might now be considered disabilities were addressed. These characteristics are discussed in the following sections.

Moral Perspective   Disability was primarily viewed from a moral perspective. That is, people with disabilities were thought to illustrate that God made humankind as a species of imperfect beings; at the same time, they represented gifts from God toward which charity should be demonstrated by others. Small charitable institutions, supported by monasteries, were common by the 11th century. In England, for example, there were four main types of such institutions: almshouses, hospices for poor wayfarers and pilgrims, leper houses, and hospitals for the sick and infirm poor (Carlin, 1989). Of these, almshouses—places that cared for poor children and sometimes their parents, orphans, juvenile delinquents, and sometimes indigent adults who were elderly or mentally ill—were the most common. Although it seems that some people with intellectual impairments were cared for in these institutions, it was poverty rather than intellectual impairment that was the main criterion for care. In fact, some such institutions excluded those who were deemed incurable, including people deemed to be idiots (Stainton, 2001).

Probably of greater importance was the more general acceptance that charity toward those less fortunate was a religious and moral obligation. This trend became widely accepted because it was actively promoted by medieval religious institutions. This trend no doubt worked in favor of the well-being of people with intellectual impairment, yet it set them apart as well.

Lack of Distinction Between the Body and the Mind   During the medieval era, there was no generally understood distinction between the body and the mind. This is exemplified by the many historical accounts from the Middle Ages of the activities of "fools"—people whose appearance, characteristics, speech, and actions were somewhat outside the accepted norm. Although fools were usually appreciated for their wit and for their representation of the full range of human characteristics, they typically had some physical and cognitive differences that were not particularly distinguished from one another.

Lack of Expectations for Large Segments of the Population   Economic activity during the Middle Ages was primarily organized around agriculture. Because this required a great deal of manual labor, there typically were few specific expectations for learning or intellectual capacity among large segments of the population. This was especially the case for those with lower socioeconomic status. Many of the people that today would be considered to have disability were probably not particularly disadvantaged, and thus might well not have been singled out, because there was no need to do so and because they were capable of functioning quite well alongside others of comparable socioeconomic status (Wickham, 2013).

Understanding Among People with Disabilities   People with intellectual and other conditions thought of today as disabilities sometimes shared a mutual understanding and communal bond. Although it is not clear how common this was, these individuals appeared at times to share resources and assist one another (Brown & Brown, 2003). For example, Woodill and Velche explained that

> Those who were intellectually or physically different were often found living…as poor beggars. Being a disabled beggar at that time was an advantage, in that it was easier to receive alms from the rich if disability were present. Organized guilds of disabled beggars existed, sometimes sharing their "take" and helping each other. (1995, p. 2)

Woodill and Velche also cited the associations of blind people at Barcelona and Valencia, which had bylaws that were written in 1329 and "provided for the mutual loan of guides, visits to each other in case of sickness, and a fair division of alms received" (p. 9). These and other characteristics contributed to tolerance and resulted in many people with intellectual impairment being able to live relatively well in their home communities.

This was by no means the case for all people, however, and it would be hasty to conclude that the "fools and idiots" were treated well or were well off. Many lived in their family homes, with varying degrees of care, while others lived in houses of refuge, were accommodated privately by charity,

were homeless, or ended up in prison or institutions. There was poor access to medical help, and infant mortality was high and life expectancy short. In some places, tolerance and charity were the exception rather than the rule, and many individuals held fearful or derogatory attitudes toward people with intellectual and physical differences. Kanner (1964) quoted the French psychiatrist Jean Étienne Esquirol (1772–1840), who referred to the ongoing nature of this perspective: "[T]he idiot has always been in misfortune and misery. The state of…the idiot is always the same" (p. 102).

Summary of Influences   On the whole, then, the Middle Ages was a time when intellectual disability, or disability at all for that matter, was not conceptualized in any clear or separate way. Rather, it appears to be part of the broader and loosely defined terms *natural fool* and *idiot*. Perhaps for this reason, very little systematic policy or service provision was available for people with disabilities (Wickham, 2013). One important feature of this era was the rise of charity as a social and moral obligation. This resulted in the establishment of medieval charitable institutions supported by religious institutions and sometimes by the state, although less formal charity was also actively promoted. The people chosen as recipients of charity did not necessarily have intellectual impairments; however, values related to caring for people on the margins of society were established that developed in a more formal, although uneven, way over the next centuries.

THE EXPANSION OF DISABILITY AS DIFFERENCE

The Industrial Revolution brought about huge social and personal changes, especially in the ways people earned their living (increasingly through industry rather than agriculture), in demographics (large numbers of people moving to towns and cities), and in the rapid growth of scientific thought as the basis for perceiving how all things function. These changes set the context for the growth of the view of disability as "difference" and the view that disability could be categorized separately from other human conditions. Several key knowledge trends that developed toward the end of the medieval period and throughout the rise of science and industrialization of the 18th and 19th centuries supported the growth of these views (*General sources:*

Brown & Brown, 2003; Stainton, 1994, 2001; Trent, 1994; Wehmeyer, 2013; Wolfensberger, 1972, 1976; Wright, 2001; Wright & Digby, 1996):

- *Descriptions of conditions:* Slowly over time, description of concepts related to what later was understood to be disability evolved and were recorded in printed documents. One often-cited example is the 1534 description by Anthony Fitzherbert, an English judge and expert on English law: "He who shall be found to be a sot and idiot from birth, is such a person who cannot accompt or number twenty pence, nor can tell who his Father, or Mother, nor how old he is etc" (as cited in Whitaker, 2013, p. 20).

- *Phenomenology:* This view held that a person has individual characteristics throughout the lifespan. This opened thinking to describe intellectual "deficit" as a characteristic that is placed within the individual person and persists throughout the person's lifespan.

- *Separation of the mind and body:* The view arose that the mind and body were two separate entities and functioned somewhat independently. This allowed for the mind and the intellect to be scientifically studied in isolation from the body.

- *Redefinition of nature:* Nature was understood to be governed by fixed, logical laws. This contrasted with earlier views that nature was precisely what one saw in the world, including the physical environment, culture, and social and political structures.

- *Theological debates:* Differences of opinion concerning the responsibility of humans for their own salvation resulted in the emergence of the view that individuals have to seek and work for the privilege of salvation. Yet, there were evidently some of God's own creation who did not appear to have the intellectual capacity to do this, so they needed to be thought of and treated separately.

- *Right of individuals to think and decide:* John Locke and others brought forth the view that individuals have not only the right, but also the moral obligation, to use their own intellectual capacity to reason and reach conclusions about virtually all aspects of human life and society. This included even how societies were governed (a perspective that was especially influential in the United States and France, but later throughout the developed world). Once this view was accepted, the group of people who did not appear to have the intellectual skills to think at a conceptual level and to make decisions for themselves became an obvious exception.

- *The Industrial Revolution:* The Industrial Revolution opened up an infinite number of possibilities for inventions and new ideas. It also resulted in the sudden rise of towns and cities, as well as the movement of large numbers of people from rural areas and their stable, agricultural way of life. The rise of towns and cities, and the industrial economy that supported them, brought numerous social problems with which the new industrial order was ill equipped to cope. Poverty, homelessness, and crime were considerably more important criteria for determining need than intellectual disability. Still, it seems reasonable to assume that those with intellectual disability might have found the complexities of living in the chaos of the newly formed industrial towns and cities difficult to manage and thus were more likely to be identified as being "different."

- *Legislation that addressed social problems:* Laws and other responses to social problems arose throughout the English-speaking world and in most European countries. The United States developed its own complex series of laws to address social problems; these are well-documented in a number of books, articles, and postings on the Internet (see also Scheerenberger, 1987; Trattner, 1999; Trent, 1994).

Legislation in Britain, spanning a number of centuries, was particularly influential. The Elizabethan Poor Law of 1601 amalgamated a number of previous English laws and established a compulsory "poor rate" to be levied on every parish; the creation of "overseers" of relief; the "setting the poor on work"; and the collection of a poor relief from property owners (Bloy, 2002a). The Poor Law Amendment Act of 1834, however, is often seen as one of the most important pieces of legislation for setting the scene for the development of institutions for people of "difference." This act established workhouses throughout England and Wales and later in Ireland (1838) and Scotland (1845). Once implemented, this act established workhouses in every parish, or groups of parishes, that were overseen by Boards of Guardians; stopped outdoor relief (relief outside the workhouse); set in place the principle of "less eligibility" or making workhouse conditions sufficiently harsh that people would be discouraged from wanting to receive help; and established the principle of segregation of the workers (Bloy, 2002b). This law was later amended many times. Numerous other laws followed that addressed the construction and governance of the many types of asylums and institutions that grew up over the ensuing decades, their reasons for being, and the "inmates" who were to live in them (e.g., see Bloy, 2002b, for documentation).

Rise of Asylums

The previously described trends provide a great deal of the context that served as the catalyst in the 1800s for the emergence, in the more developed countries, of a mindset of social reform that was in keeping with the fast-developing reliance on scientific knowledge. Many jurisdictions began to move toward what was then thought of as a logical and progressive solution to the social problems that had arisen: establishing specialized institutions that were designed specifically to accommodate people who could not meet the daily living demands of their environments. In fact, this solution was so highly thought of that people—often described as dangerous and harmful to society—were moved into institutions for a variety of reasons, some of which seem counterproductive or even horrifying to us in the beginning of the 21st century: receiving training or education (schools or industrial centers), being a fool or an idiot, not having parents (orphanages), being old, being poor (poorhouses), being in debt (debtor's prisons), having mental health problems (lunatic asylums), and others. People with intellectual, physical, and other disabilities or with mental health problems were especially moved to these institutions.

The institution was conceived as an instrument of reform by its early founders and supporters, whose intentions were for the most part honorable. It was an innovative way to deal with the many social problems that proliferated as industrialization progressed and was in keeping with scientific thinking of the time (i.e., society worked like a giant machine made up of many parts, each of which contributed to the overall functioning). It also responded to a dominant philosophy of the time,

humanitarianism, that looked at all people with a sense of compassion and, especially for those who were less fortunate, considered that people deserved to have opportunities to learn, advance their skills, and contribute positively to their society. In some instances, this appeared to have worked very well, as there was some success with rehabilitation and retuning people to productive lives outside the institutions (Woodill & Velche, 1995).

At the same time, there was pressure from prisons and overcrowded asylums. Managers of asylums considered people with intellectual impairment to be unresponsive to their treatment programs, largely "incurable," and a waste of the energies of their staffs. People who were considered "mentally defective" were often placed in separate annexes or wings of the asylums, where they typically received nothing more than very basic custodial care. Specialized institutions for such people seemed to be the answer.

Thus, advocates for the early institutions saw a need for specialized training facilities that would prepare people with disabilities for a life in the world outside or, if this was not considered possible, would provide for their safety and comfort (Brown & Brown, 2003). This modern approach to addressing the specific needs of people with disabilities was characterized by considerable thought that was supported by medical, educational, religious, and other leaders in many countries. Schools for children with learning difficulties, hearing and visual impairments, and other disabilities were developed. Special health care facilities emerged to address such issues as hygiene, new and experimental physical therapies, and the treatment of conditions specific to the residents of institutions (e.g., epilepsy, vision and hearing problems). Buildings that functioned as places of care and training—both life skills and vocational—were set up in cities for children and adults with disabilities. Sites were established in the countryside that provided a clean fresh-air environment—a welcome relief from the polluted air and dirty streets of the cities—and a full range of life activities. Many of these, including several throughout the United Kingdom and North America in the late 1800s, functioned as model farms, with residents working not only to provide for their own needs but also to produce quality products for sale to others. Typically, these institutions were designed and built to comprise a number of large buildings set on ample, well-groomed grounds that were designed to give a sense of tranquility (Wolfensberger, 1972).

Early Focus on Education and Learning

The initial focus in the growth of institutions was on children with disabilities who were amenable to training, especially children with deafness, blindness, physical impairments, or mild cognitive impairments. In the middle of the 19th century, educational thinkers began to claim that these children could be intensively trained and educated within a controlled environment and prepared for a return to their home communities, where they would be able to adapt and contribute to community life (Woodill & Velche, 1995).

In Germany, an approach toward disability was adopted that was fairly progressive for its time, and German disability educators were leading pioneers in developing special schools for children deemed idiots in the early 19th century (Woodill & Velche, 1995). A document published in 1820 by educator Johann Traugott Weiss is thought to be the first concrete plan designed to provide instruction to children with disabilities (Kanner, 1964). A growing optimism toward the possibilities of education and training led to the belief that "idiots" could develop skills that would allow them to function in the outside world, given proper conditioning and an environment conducive to drawing out their latent abilities. The expectation was to implement a vigorous and efficient program that would return the children to the general classroom as quickly as possible so as not to alienate them any longer than necessary. France, England, the United States, and other countries were quick to follow suit and soon established their own institutions for learning (Wehmeyer, 2013). At the same time, an inclination toward investigating the physiological basis of idiocy was taking the scientific community by storm, and an understanding of disability that became the basis of the medical model came to the forefront of science. Consequently, the approach toward what would later come to be known as intellectual and developmental disabilities moved away from a custodial nature and embraced methods of learning and causes of disability (Woodill & Velche).

The Supportive and Nonsupportive Role of Science

The early "idiot asylums" of the mid-19th century represented the application of Enlightenment ideas to the "problem" of disability. As a result, the asylums were originally designed to provide healthy environments to prepare people (mainly children) for life in the outside world. Science, widely considered to be the way to progress, was mobilized to support these views. New methods of training and learning sprang up to support the work in the schools and training centers, and these and other positive interventions were supported by a growing knowledge of the neurological and environmental roots of disability.

At the same time, however, the quickly expanding scientific knowledge of the 19th century also acted against the success of the asylums. Social Darwinism, a philosophy that viewed human social evolution as favoring those humans most "fit" to match the conditions and demands of their environments (Hawkins, 1997), suggested that people with disabilities were among the "unfit." A growing knowledge of genetics was used to reinforce this view and, furthermore, to support the growth of eugenics, a movement that held that society could be improved by encouraging propagation among the more desirable portions of the general population and discouraging propagation among the less desirable portions. Intelligence testing was developed around the beginning of the 20th century, primarily to distinguish between those able and unable to learn in the school systems, but it was also used as an instrument to weed out those deemed incapable of learning, fit only for "training" at best. These applications of scientific knowledge justified the perpetuation of custodial asylums as warehouses for as many "hopeless cases" and "problem populations" as could be squeezed in (Smith & Wehmeyer, 2012).

Impact of Institutions

It is difficult for present-day readers to imagine the scale of the institution movement. In the first 4 decades of the 20th century, the number and size of institutions for people with intellectual disability dramatically increased (Wehmeyer, 2013). On top of this, there were lunatic asylums, workhouses, and many other types of institutions. An enormous social and economic investment—which was supported by political, scientific, religious, medical, and other leaders of the time—had gone into establishing these settings as an integral part of society. This had a tremendous impact on the way people thought of the "unfortunates." They were seen as people unable, unworthy, or unfit to contribute to society and who were therefore best housed apart from society.

Early Attempts to Understand and Classify

Establishing institutions changed attitudes toward disability, mostly by setting people apart and dictating to them a lifestyle that differed from that of most people of the times. One way this is illustrated is by the shifts in terms used to describe people for whom the institutions were designed. The most durable term to describe those people who would now be thought of as having intellectual disability was *idiot*, a word that was well-established in medieval England as a descriptive term. Over the course of the asylum era, idiocy came to be understood as a "condition," called *feeble-mindedness*, with a single etiology. Kanner (1964) paraphrased Gertrude Stein in a somewhat tongue-in-cheek description of the prevailing attitude of the time as "the feebleminded were the feebleminded were the feebleminded" (p. 102), signifying that this general group of people were seen as having ongoing undesirable characteristics.

To the extent that any differentiation was attempted for idiots or the feeble-minded, medical and educational professionals, who were for the most part proponents of trying to understand disability in a scientific way, focused on quantifying degrees of idiocy. A general, but not particularly clear, distinction was made between imbeciles, who had cognitive deficiencies but could communicate verbally, and three classes of idiots: 1) those who could use a few words and short sentences, 2) those who could utter monosyllables and grunts, and 3) those who had no language at all (Kanner, 1964). John Langdon Down (later known as John Langdon Haydon Down)—who was a physician to the Asylum for Idiots at Earlswood in London and is now known for his identification of Down syndrome—put forward three categories of idiocy: 1) congenital idiocy (never had mental power), 2) developmental idiocy (deterioration after a satisfactory start), and 3) accidental idiocy (caused by illness or injury). Yet, it was Down's 1866 "clinical lecture and report" describing a condition that came to be known as *mongolism* (now known as *Down syndrome*)—and other loosely described conditions named for major racial groups around the world that apparently reminded Down of the physical characteristics of certain inmates in his asylum—that precipitated a real interest in etiology and hence a move from thinking of feeble-mindedness in a homogeneous way toward thinking of it in terms of more comprehensive etiological classification systems (Kanner).

In the early years of the 20th century, a preoccupation among the middle class with mental deficiency and feeble-mindedness led educators and other professionals to identify the *moron* as a hidden group with "subnormal" intelligence apparently lurking within society's "problem populations." At the same time, advances in the testing and measurement of intelligence, particularly the work of the French psychologist Alfred Binet, allowed for what was believed to be a scientific method of describing categories of deficiency. This gave rise to the broad use of such terms as *moron, imbecile,* and *idiot.*

These terms were not originally intended to have negative connotations, but because they were brought forward to describe separate groups of people who were not socially valued, they quickly became pejorative. Similarly, later in the 20th century, subclassifications and a growing understanding of the causes and contributing conditions of intellectual and developmental disabilities contributed to a view that people with disabilities are "different." This resulted in *mental retardation, mental handicap, developmental handicap,* and other terms that are considered to be derogatory in many countries (see Chapter 1).

It has become apparent that the institutional era was marked as much by attitudes as by buildings. Only a small proportion of people considered idiots, feeble-minded, or mentally deficient were actually institutionalized. This was not due to a belief that community living was superior; rather, it was mainly due to lack of space and resistance to the level of public spending that would have been required. It was widely believed that in a perfect society, all such people would be "put away" and it was often said that those who remained in the community "belonged in an institution." Opposition to such views existed but was a minority opinion and not well documented (Woodill & Velche, 1995). The institutions created a sanctuary for mental deficiency within the social order, and it was widely believed that these places were both proper and beneficial, not only for society but also for those who spent their lives in them.

Decline of Institutions

If the institutions began as positive steps forward in the care and treatment of people with disabilities, why did they not succeed? As Brown and Brown (2003) put it, it is now well known that even though "many institutions started out as the benign well-oiled machines they were envisioned to be, they rusted out in time" (p. 61).

The optimism of the pioneers of institutionalization was, in fact, rather short-lived, and the institutions began to decline even as more and more were built and expanded. Several interrelated factors contributed to this decline, and public attitudes gradually began to change. The most important factors associated with the decline of institutions included the following:

- *Lack of progress:* The reformers were unable to demonstrate noteworthy progress. The need to justify their existence as therapeutic facilities led, in some cases, to setting up demonstration projects in which education programs were applied only to children with the mildest forms of disability. Gradually, the ideal of improved skills and health and successful return to community life faded, and the managers resigned themselves to a custodial, rather than an educational, role. The institutions became places in which people grew old, and this was a powerful social symbol that idiocy or mental deficiency was both permanent and incurable.

- *Lack of knowledge:* The institutions were not only places of care and training for those who were housed in them. They were also places of experimentation and places of learning for those who ran them. Authorities and professionals of the time simply had little knowledge about how to handle the many types of disabilities and conditions they faced; although they experienced many successes, they also experienced a great many failures.

- *Stereotypes:* Formerly held stereotypes of idiocy as an ongoing, permanent condition were not forgotten and proved durable, especially when the institutions lacked evidence of success. This led to a view that the residents of institutions were not capable of improving and that they "belonged" in places that were away from society.

- *Overcrowding:* The capacity of institutions to function effectively was soon curtailed by overcrowding. The very view that institutions could help people with "social" problems resulted in an overreliance on institutions to solve many more problems than they were capable of addressing. More and more people were moved into

institutions as it became increasingly accepted that social problems were best dealt with there. In addition, not as many people as anticipated developed sufficient independent living skills to move out of institutions. The growing number of residents increased demands on the institutions' available funds and staff, and many of the more capable people with disabilities were retained because of their value as workers, further contributing to the problem of overcrowding (Trent, 1994). Allocating time and other resources to individuals became increasingly more difficult, and attention was gradually shifted away from growth and development toward providing basic care. In these overcrowded institutions, the original purposes of providing training, opportunities, and rehabilitation faded in importance. Living conditions deteriorated markedly in a great many institutions, such that family and service groups eventually began to advocate for change and closures. In some cases, such changes and closures were precipitated by disclosure of treatment and conditions that now seem quite shocking. One well-documented example was Pennhurst, an institution for people with intellectual and developmental disabilities that was located in Pennsylvania (United States) and operated from the early 1900s to the 1980s. An investigation of Pennhurst, prompted particularly by a series of unexplained deaths of residents, revealed the deteriorating level of treatment that residents received (El Peecho Productions, 2004). In addition, the investigation uncovered many cases of abuse and inhumane treatment that resulted in lawsuits, one of which resulted in a judgment by the U.S. Supreme Court. (For information on the court's judgment, see Legal Information Institute, 2005; for information on photographic documentation submitted in 1977 court proceedings, see El Peecho Productions, 2004.) The institutions became overcrowded and living conditions deteriorated, and the original purposes of providing training, opportunities, and rehabilitation faded in importance.

- *Use of drugs:* Medical advances, especially in the 20th century, increased the possibility that pharmacological treatment could alleviate immediate behavior issues and other problems. This made the institutions more manageable for overworked staff but shifted the emphasis away from developing health and independent living skills toward controlling behavior and maintaining care. This shift contributed to further overcrowding and lack of progress.

- *Reduced public interest and funding:* Moving people with disabilities to institutions segregated them from society at large, removing them from the public's attention. Somewhat ironically, the very institutions that were intended to function efficiently as the part of society that addressed the needs of people with disabilities lost the ability to function efficiently, in part because they were out of society's view. Reduced visibility led to reduced—and insufficient—funding for the large number of people who lived in institutions.

- *Improving community conditions:* With technological and social advances, living conditions, especially in cities, gradually improved. Cleaner water and air, broader sources of food, better working conditions, viable public transportation, and many other improvements made communities more attractive and viable places for people with disabilities to live. Thus, the need for people with disabilities to be housed in institutions was reduced.

- *Growth of interest in equality and human rights:* The growing trends toward acceptance of equality among people and valuing human rights (see Chapters 3 and 5) worked against isolating people—often without their consent—in institutions. These trends also strengthened the views that people with disabilities were equally entitled to all that society had to offer, which was not possible living within institutions, and, eventually, that fair treatment of people with disabilities is a social responsibility that requires inclusion.

- *Dramatic failure of eugenics:* Eugenics, the science of purposely influencing the genetic makeup of a society, had critics but was widely practiced in many developed countries. Eugenics sought to improve society by isolating and reducing reproduction among "the feeble-minded" or otherwise "unfit" (Smith & Wehmeyer, 2012). These trends have been documented for several countries, including the United Kingdom (Kevles, 1985), the United States (Smith & Wehmeyer), and Canada (McLaren, 1990). The application of eugenics escalated dramatically in Nazi Germany during the period 1933–1945, when a series of public policies were instituted to create a pure and able Aryan

race. At first, this took the form of favoring some types of people while blatantly persecuting and removing the personal rights of others. Later, during the Second World War, great numbers of "undesirable" people were killed, including millions of Jews; approximately 5,000 children with disabilities; and thousands of other people with mental illness, other disabilities, and various differences (e.g., ethnic minorities, Romani or "gypsies," then-called homosexuals). The discovery of these atrocities at the end of the war, coupled with other changing social attitudes and values, led to a quick decline of eugenics as a credible social philosophy.

INCLUSION IN COMMUNITIES

No single event marked the end of the institutional era. Instead, the transition has extended over many decades, and institutions still operate worldwide. The pressure for change came from outside the institution system and largely from outside the professions that had delivered services both within the institutions and in the wider community. Indeed, the professionals who believed they were providing a specialized and necessary set of services, along with some groups of parents who believed their sons and daughters to be safe and well cared for within the institutions, were often resistant to change. The impetus to end the institutional era was supported and sometimes led by academics, governments, staff, and other professionals but mainly came from the voluntary sector, especially from parent and other advocacy groups that strongly criticized living conditions in the institutions. Sometimes the groups called for increased funding and improved institution programs. Increasingly, though, they argued for resources to provide care and support in community settings as an alternative to large institutions.

Conceptual Basis for Community Living

An emerging body of theory, developed in close association with advocacy groups, shifted the trend away from institutions that were physically and psychologically separated from mainstream society. A movement that was primarily identified by its own interpretation of the term *normalization* set forth principles that endeavored to demolish the restricting constructs of disability by altering the environment of people with disabilities. Bengt

Nirje, the movement's pioneer, offered a conceptualization of disability with three interconnected components that raised the importance of environment. First, there is the primary medical or physical condition that is usually the most visible but is increasingly open to medical and other scientific advances. Second, there is the broader environment—the living conditions, daily routines, economic status, and prevailing social attitudes. The third component is the identity, or self-image, of the person with a disability. Such self-image is influenced by the physical condition, but this is not all-important. Rather, self-image develops as a reflection of the attitudes and values of those in the broader environment (Nirje, 1969).

In Nirje's view, the key to reform was to intervene in this complex interrelationship by altering the environment. However, what kind of environment is most suitable? The answer, quite simply, was the same rich variety of social niches within which other people create their lifeworlds—in other words, a set of "normal" environments.

People with intellectual and developmental disabilities, Nirje argued, should be afforded normal daily, weekly, and yearly routines; ordinary housing; ordinary economic circumstances; and the usual life opportunities. Similar ideas were advanced by others, notably Wolf Wolfensberger, whose 1972 book *The Principle of Normalization in Human Services* is the classic and most comprehensive statement of the concept and its application. Normalization, it was claimed, was all about abandoning the stereotypes and ideologies of difference and substituting the principle of inclusion.

The implications were significant. Numerous books and articles were published that described the reasons for deinstitutionalization and its implications for policy and practice. Policy had to be changed, funding mechanisms had to be altered from maintaining and expanding institutions to providing for community living, service delivery systems had to be reinvented to support more independent community living, and a whole new emphasis on professional training had to be developed (Casey, McGee, Stark, Menolascino, 1985; Paul, Stedman, & Neufeld, 1977). For people with intellectual and developmental disabilities, the closing of institutions changed the opportunities that were available for participating in daily community life as individuals were introduced (not always willingly) to the new concept of normalized living.

As Wolfensberger forecasted, the effects of a movement that required the total inclusion of people with disabilities into the community were felt in every aspect of human services.

Reasons for Controversy over Deinstitutionalization

For people with an early 21st-century perspective, it is perhaps difficult to appreciate why these proposals were so controversial. In the society of the early 1970s, though, people were still attuned to the difference of disability, and normalization was widely misunderstood or at least misrepresented. Some charged that to portray the person with an intellectual or developmental disability as normal was to deny reality. Here, it seemed to the critics, was another instance of unfounded optimism.

Some of the opposition stemmed from a sense of protectiveness. "Normal" environments can be hazardous, and it was considered by many that some people had needs that could only be met in the safety of the institution. Family members who had placed their relatives in closed institutions were often worried by the prospect of having to provide unaccustomed care in their homes. Many others were concerned—with some justification, as it turned out in many jurisdictions—that the money saved from institutional closure would not be fully reinvested in community services. The advocates of normalization responded to this by claiming that all individuals benefit from a degree of uncertainty. They grow through problem solving and should be allowed to experience the "dignity of risk," a term that became widespread to describe the view that protection and care need to be balanced with respecting and supporting the wishes and choices of people with disabilities, even if those wishes and choices involve some possible risk (see especially Wolfensberger, 1972).

Community Living

Despite these reservations, the principles of normalization, consolidated first in Scandinavia, began to be adopted in almost every jurisdiction in Western Europe, North America, Australia, New Zealand, and other countries during the 1970s and 1980s. Over a relatively short period of time, the principles were incorporated into official policy in many other countries as well, although the effects were felt more gradually in practice.

Closing institutions and moving residents to communities was applied in uneven ways, both across and within countries. The main reasons for this were differences in political will, availability of financial resources to close institutions and support moves, local values and attitudes, traditional ways of housing people with disabilities, the presence or absence of local advocacy and conceptual leadership, the response by professionals and families, and the philosophies of funders of institutions (mostly governments). Among the many issues faced by those charged with closing institutions and establishing community living services were staffing problems; funding limitations; resistance by some professional groups and labor unions, who feared lower standards of care as well as loss of jobs; resistance by some parent groups, who feared loss of security and poorer care in the community; and municipal zoning bylaws that excluded group homes from residential neighborhoods. All of this resulted in the institutions proving to be more durable, and community homes much harder to find, than expected. Some countries (e.g., Norway) closed all of their institutions rather quickly, whereas most other countries have taken a more gradual approach that avoids many of the short-term challenges but delays community inclusion. In many countries (e.g., Italy, the Netherlands), there are still many institutions, although most of these have been modernized considerably so that they are more homelike. In still other countries, deinstitutionalization is an ideal that is only beginning to be realized, often because there is low funding or it is not a sociopolitical priority.

The concepts associated with community living are widely accepted throughout the world, turning idealism into reality for a great many people. Due to human rights awareness and closely linked legislation (see Chapter 5), it is gradually becoming more acceptable for people with disabilities to live in a broad array of neighborhoods and carry out all of their daily life activities in their home communities. Now the principles of normalization are questioned by those who believe they do not go far enough.

The increasingly important concepts of inclusion, quality of life, and self-determination in the field of intellectual and developmental disabilities have begun to illustrate exactly how to "go farther" to achieve the vision established by the normalization principle (Brown & Brown, 2003). Since the early 1990s, ideas associated with these concepts have become paramount in more affluent countries and increasingly so in less affluent countries as well. The focus is on trying to ensure that people who live in the community are able to have complete, fulfilling lives and that they can contribute to society in ways that are satisfying to themselves and others. The most hopeful indication of moving ahead into the future is that overt hostility toward people with disabilities is becoming the exception rather than the rule.

SUMMARY

It is essential to understand that disability was not always understood as it is today. Still, it is possible to learn valuable lessons from evidence of how people with various disabilities were treated in former times. Disability existed since prehistoric times, and early civilizations often promoted compassion for conditions resulting in disability, although there was overt discrimination as well. The medieval era in Europe featured the growth of charity as a moral obligation and a broad public recognition of natural fools and idiots; however, the conditions attached to these terms were not clearly conceptualized as disability and superstitious beliefs were widespread. The rise of science and the influence of new thinking that came with industrialization encouraged more detailed descriptions of disability. Industrialization also brought on serious social problems that were eventually dealt with by building many large institutions for people who did not fit into the mainstream. These were not always built just for people with disabilities but often included them. Institutions were conceived of and built as progressive, positive solutions to social problems, but they eventually failed for a number of reasons. The decline and closure of institutions was precipitated by the growth of the philosophical view of normalization through community living. Although deinstitutionalization is still not the dominant policy of some countries, community living is now the norm in most. In many places, the current emphasis is on inclusion, individual ability, personal fulfillment, and enjoyment of life.

FOR FURTHER THOUGHT AND DISCUSSION

1. In early societies, there was evidence of compassion toward people with disabilities, but there was also discrimination. Think of the life of one person you know who has an intellectual or developmental disability. By describing a broad range of life activities for this person, show how compassion and discrimination are still being demonstrated.

2. In medieval times, natural fools and idiots were some of the people to whom the rich were morally obliged to provide charity. Was this a good idea? Are there people today who "deserve" charity?

3. Place yourself in the early 1900s and ask, "Why were asylums espoused as a solution? What were the problems that needed solutions? Were asylums a good solution?"

4. Setting people with intellectual and developmental disabilities apart as "different" helped in understanding them, but it was also detrimental. Weigh the benefits against the detriments as you argue for what should have been done.

5. Despite deinstitutionalization and a community living approach, to what degree does society still think in terms of an "institutional" model of care?

6. What are the three most important lessons you have learned from the past? Write two or three paragraphs about each to describe your reasons.

REFERENCES

Berkson, G. (2004). Intellectual and physical disabilities in prehistory and early civilization. *Mental Retardation, 42,* 195–208.

Berkson, G. (2006). Mental disabilities in Western civilization from Ancient Rome to the Prerogativa Regis. *Mental Retardation, 44,* 28–40.

Bloy, M. (2002a). *The 1601 Elizabethan Poor Law.* Retrieved from http://www.victorianweb.org/history/poorlaw/elizpl.html

Bloy, M. (2002b). *The Poor Law: Introduction.* Retrieved from http://www.victorianweb.org/history/poorlaw/plintro.html

Brown, I., & Brown, R.I. (2003). *Quality of life and disability: An approach for community practitioners.* London, United Kingdom: Jessica Kingsley.

Carlin, M. (1989). Medieval English hospitals. In L. Granshaw & R. Porter (Eds.), *The hospital in history* (pp. 21–40). London, United Kingdom: Routledge.

Casey, K., McGee, J., Stark, J., & Menolascino, F.J. (1985). *A community-based system for the mentally retarded: The ENCOR experience.* Lincoln, NE: University of Nebraska Press.

Centers for Disease Control and Prevention. (2004). *The history of malaria: An ancient disease.* Retrieved from http://www.cdc.gov/malaria/history/index.htm#ancienthistory

Craig, E.M. (2013). At the dawn of civilization: Intellectual disability in prehistory and ancient times (9000 BCE–500 CE). In M. Wehmeyer (Ed.), *The story of intellectual disability: An evolution of meaning, understanding, and public perception* (pp. 19–45). Baltimore, MD: Paul H. Brookes Publishing Co.

Edgerton, R.B. (1968). Mental retardation in non-Western societies: Toward a cross-cultural perspective on incompetence. In H.C. Haywood (Ed.), *Social-cultural aspects of mental retardation* (pp. 523–560). New York, NY: Appleton-Century-Crofts.

El Peecho Productions. (2004). *Pennhurst information.* Retrieved from http://www.elpeecho.com/pennhurst/pennhurst.htm

Fitzherbert, A. (1534/1793). *Natura Brevium.* Dublin, Ireland: H. Watts.

Garland, R. (1995). *The eye of the beholder: Deformity and disability in the Graeco-Roman world.* Ithaca, NY: Cornell University Press.

Green, P. (1991). *Alexander of Macedon, 356–323 B.C.: A historical biography.* Berkeley: University of California Press.

Hawkins, M. (1997). *Social Darwinism in European and American thought 1860–1945: Nature as model and nature as truth.* Cambridge, United Kingdom: Cambridge University Press.

Jeffreys, D., & Tait, J. (2000). Disability, madness, and social exclusion in dynastic Egypt. In J. Humphrey (Ed.), *Madness, disability and social exclusion: The archaeology and anthropology of "difference"* (pp. 87–95). London, United Kingdom: Routledge.

Kanner, L. (1964). *A history of the care and study of the mentally retarded.* Springfield, IL: Charles C. Thomas.

Kevles, D.J. (1985). *In the name of eugenics: Genetics and the uses of human heredity.* Cambridge, MA: Harvard University Press.

Kranzler, H.N. (1993). Maimonides' concept of mental illness and mental health. In R. Rosner & S.S. Kotek (Eds.), *Moses Maimonides: Physician, scientist, and philosopher* (pp. 49–57). Northvale, NJ: J. Aronson.

Legal Information Institute. (2005). *Supreme Court collection: Pennhurst State School and Hospital v. Halderman.* Retrieved from http://supct.law.cornell.edu/supct/html/historics/USSC_CR_0451_0001_ZO.html

McLaren, A. (1990). *Our own master race.* Toronto, Canada: McLelland and Stewart.

Nirje, B. (1969). The normalization principle and its human management implications. In R. Kugel & W. Wolfensberger (Eds.), *Changing patterns in residential services for the mentally retarded* (pp. 179–195). Washington, DC: President's Committee on Mental Retardation.

Northampton General Hospital. (2016). *Dr Gosset paper on congenital abnormalities 1956.* Retrieved from http://www .northamptongeneral.nhs.uk/AboutUs/Ourhistory/ Dr-Gosset/Downloads/Dr-Gosset-paper-on-congenital-abnormalities-1956.pdf

Pangas, J.C. (2000). Birth malformations in Babylon and Assyria. *American Journal of Medical Genetics, 91,* 318–321.

Paul, J.L., Stedman, D.J., & Neufeld, G.R. (Eds.). (1977). *Deinstitutionalization: Program and policy development.* Syracuse, NY: Syracuse University Press.

Scheerenberger, R.C. (1987). *A history of mental retardation: A quarter century of promise.* Baltimore, MD: Paul H. Brookes Publishing Co.

Smith, J.D., & Wehmeyer, M.L. (2012). *Good blood, bad blood: Science, nature and the myth of the Kallikaks.* Washington, DC: American Association on Intellectual and Developmental Disabilities.

Stainton, T. (1994). *Autonomy and social policy: Rights, mental handicap and social care.* London, United Kingdom: Avebury.

Stainton, T. (2001). Medieval charitable institutions and intellectual impairment c.1066–1600. *Journal on Developmental Disabilities, 8*(2), 19–29.

Trattner, W.I. (1999). *From poor law to welfare state: A history of social welfare in America* (6th ed.). New York, NY: The Free Press.

Trent, J.W. (1994). *Inventing the feeble mind: A history of mental retardation in the United States.* Berkeley: University of California Press.

Trinkaus, E., & Zimmerman, M.R. (1982). Trauma among the Shanidar Neanderthals. *American Journal of Physical Anthropology, 57*(1), 61–76.

Warkany, J. (1959). Congenital malformations in the past. *Journal of Chronic Diseases, 10,* 84–96.

Wehmeyer, M.L. (Ed.). (2013). *The story of intellectual disability: An evolution of meaning, understanding, and public perception.* Baltimore, MD: Paul H. Brookes Publishing Co.

Whitaker, S. (2013). *Intellectual disability: An inability to cope with an intellectually demanding world.* London, United Kingdom: Palgrave Macmillan.

Wickham, P. (2013). Poverty and the emergence of charity: Intellectual disability in the Middle Ages (500 CE to 1500 CE). In M.L. Wehmeyer (Ed.), *The story of intellectual disability: An evolution of meaning, understanding, and public perception* (pp. 63–77). Baltimore, MD: Paul H. Brookes Publishing Co.

Wolfensberger, W. (1972). *The principle of normalization in human services.* Toronto, Canada: National Institute on Mental Retardation.

Wolfensberger, W. (1976). The origins and nature of our institutional models. In R. Kugel & A. Shearer (Eds.), *Changing patterns in residential services for the mentally retarded.* Washington, DC: President's Committee on Mental Retardation.

Woodill, G., & Velche, D. (1995). From charity and exclusion to emerging independence: An introduction to the history of disabilities. *Journal on Developmental Disabilities, 4*(1), 1–11.

Wright, D. (2001). *Mental disability in Victorian England: The Earlswood Asylum 1847–1901.* Oxford, United Kingdom: Oxford University Press.

Wright, D., & Digby, A. (Eds.). (1996). *From idiocy to mental deficiency.* London, United Kingdom: Routledge.

3

Changing Perspectives on Intellectual and Developmental Disabilities

Michael Bach

This chapter looks at three different perspectives on intellectual and developmental disabilities and at how these have influenced supports to people with disabilities. Perspectives have shifted over time as the limitations of certain concepts of disability became apparent and alternatives were put forth. Underlying the shifting perspectives are different responses to the following questions: What is disability? How should society identify and come to know the needs of people labeled this way? What are family, community, and state obligations to this group?

UNDERSTANDING DISABILITIES

Intellectual and developmental disabilities are often understood to be one of a cluster of categories

Author's note: The author is grateful to Maureen Connolly and Ivan Brown for their helpful suggestions and additions to the chapter.

used to refer to people whose intellectual capacities, communication skills, and/or behavior are determined to be developing, or to have developed, at a slower rate or to a lesser extent than what is deemed to be typical. In defining *intellectual and developmental disabilities* this way, the focus is on what scientific, legal, and service communities have determined to be "normal" paths of human development. These terms suggest that there is a normal path to human development and to human intellectual activity and that people who are deemed to have disabilities in these areas are somehow different because they do not fit within the normal path. The notion that normalcy can be reliably defined in these areas—as well as the advisability of even doing so—have increasingly come into question since the mid-1990s (Amundson, 2000; Davis, 2010; Withers, 2012).

Today, what is considered to be normal or abnormal, competent or incompetent, or abled or disabled is a matter of perspective—the vantage point from which one views the world and others. This view, referred to as *postmodernism,* claims that, for everything, there can be several or multiple "truths" and that these "truths" about the same thing sometimes compete with one another. The word *truth* is placed in quotation marks on purpose, because truth is recognized to be a social construction—that is, an idea or an understanding constructed at a particular time by particular people. Certain constructions come to be normalized as a common-sense way of seeing the world. For example, McIntosh (2002) and Peters (2000) showed how others actively socially construct people with disabilities as being passive and in need of control and management. Also, as Fawcett (2000) suggested, those humans with the power to generate and control the use of knowledge and language often pathologize other humans because of their particular intellectual, physical, and genetic characteristics.

However, even deeply rooted and accepted truths can be challenged. New social constructions are born as those who have been objectified by dominant ways of seeing and knowing speak back and challenge so-called truths that do not actually reflect their own ways of seeing themselves—often experienced as violations to their dignity and equal respect. This is certainly the case as women, ethno-racial, and sexual minorities challenge dominant gendered, sexist, racialized, and heteronormative labels and categories. Similarly, people with intellectual and developmental disabilities, and their advocates, increasingly challenge the idea that intellectual and developmental disabilities are by definition "deficits" or "impairments," and instead some are beginning to call for recognition of "cognitive diversity." Around the world, people with intellectual and developmental disabilities and their families are calling for an end to poverty and exclusion, for a right to live in communities outside of institutional care, for full inclusion in quality education, and for the right to have their legal capacity and decisions over their own lives respected, including the right to vote, to marry, and to control their own bodies and their own property (Inclusion International, 2006, 2009, 2012, 2014).

In this respect, legitimate knowledge about disabilities emerges from the diverse voices of people with disabilities themselves rather than from others talking about them. These and other views may seem to compete with one another, and indeed many do, but each represents its own "truth" about how disabilities are understood. Together, these views aid understanding that intellectual or developmental disability is not a fixed and absolute fact or feature of a person. It is a human-made lens shaped through culture, law, and political struggles throughout history (Carlson, 2010). The starting point is to recognize, as critical theorists in this area have done since the latter part of the 20th century, that intellectual or developmental disability—or one of its predecessor categories such as mental retardation, mental deficiency, or feeble-mindedness—are unstable and heterogeneous

categories. As Carlson noted, they are constructed through various disciplines and power relations that often end up leaving people with intellectual disabilities objectified as different from the norm:

> What is fascinating about mental retardation as a classification is its persistence. Perhaps it is precisely because of, not in spite of, its heterogeneity, instability, ability to generate prototype effects, and its place within various constellations of power that it survived for so long. As long as there are experts in different disciplines to define them, institutions to house them, schools to teach them, scientists to study them, psychologists to test them, educators to classify them, people to judge them, and theorists to debate the validity of the label itself, persons with intellectual disabilities will continue to be objects of knowledge. (2010, p. 101)

Three of the most important lenses for viewing intellectual and developmental disability—legal, biomedical, and social and human rights perspectives—are discussed in this chapter, and an emerging "radical disability" lens is touched upon as well.

DEVELOPMENTAL DISABILITY AS A LEGAL STATUS

There are many legal and social histories to the terms *intellectual disability* and *developmental disability* (and similar terms that predate them). They evolved in tandem with the institution of legal personhood, which expresses what defines individuals to whom rights and responsibilities apply in any particular legal context. Early Roman law established the legal category of *personne*, and thus provided a legal norm from which those now thought of as having intellectual or developmental disabilities began to be marked as different. Carrithers, Collins, and Lukes (1985) reviewed the development of notions of personhood in different cultures over the centuries preceding and succeeding this early Roman innovation and showed how the category of person, just like the category of intellectual disability, is subject to shifting perspectives and conflicts over what counts as personhood.

In this section, I pick up the threads of the legal history of personhood in English law in the 14th century, where the roots of the terms *intellectual disability* and *developmental disability* can be found in legal distinctions that still influence public policy and services today. The 14th century English statute under Edward II, titled *De Prerogativa Regis*, or the royal prerogative, now referred to as the *parens patriae* jurisdiction, imposed an obligation on the state to provide for those deemed incompetent to manage their personal or financial affairs. Chapter IX of the law states, "The King shall have the Custody of the Lands of natural Fools, taking the Profits of them without Waste or Destruction, and shall find them their necessaries" (Shelford, 1833, p. 10).

Determinations of incompetency to manage one's estate or person were made by jury trials at inquisitions called for the purpose. These determinations were the purview of the courts and juries exclusively, but they acted on the royal prerogative—the *parens patriae* power (Neugebauer, 1996). As Foucault (1965) argued, it was from the 14th century on that reason and rationality became the defining feature of what it meant to be a person, and culture, science, and public policy since that time rests largely on this assumption. Development of statutory law during this period suggests that what *reason* comes to mean is constructed in tandem with the legal articulation of lunacy and idiocy.

State obligations to people with a disability were consolidated in England with the passage of the Poor Law in 1601 (Hirst & Michael, 2003; King, 2000; Rushton, 1988). This statute established a distinction between the "worthy" and the "unworthy" poor and was later adopted in many of England's colonies. Adults with disabilities considered unable to work were, by this law, deemed worthy and entitled to state provision. The law contributed to a marginalized economic and social status for people with disabilities that still continues. By linking disability and inability to work, the law and its ensuing amendments institutionalized the idea that people with disabilities did not fit into the labor market, an assumption that still drives much employment-related policy. In addition, by considering people with disabilities as "worthy poor," the state promised slightly better provision than for the "unworthy" poor—those who were deemed able-minded and able-bodied but unwilling to work. However, the cost of obtaining richer provision was the adoption of disability as a legally sanctioned charity status, one that people with disabilities are still trying to shake in favor of recognition as full citizens.

As contracts between people increasingly came to define both economic and social relationships, especially with industrialization beginning in the 18th century, a figure of "market man," a freely contracting agent, began to emerge. To protect the sanctity of contracts, parties had to be seen to fully understand their nature and consequences. Thus, industrialization and the infrastructure of contract law that supported it established requirements for what it meant to be a person at law and to be recognized as such in social and economic relationships (Cossman, 1990; Poole, 1985, 1991). People with intellectual or developmental disabilities thus came to be seen as a threat to the upholding of contract law—they were not seen as having the necessary reason and rationality to exercise responsibility in entering into and fulfilling contracts. So a means other than providing them a right to enter contracts had to be found to ensure their basic needs were met.

The 1890 English Lunacy Act was a successor to *De Prerogativa Regis* and consolidated legal provisions related to lunacy and the *parens patriae* jurisdiction of the courts. The legislation was made effective under colonial law in many other countries under British colonial rule. By conferring a differential legal status on people with a developmental disability, the *parens patriae* power helped to institutionalize the idea that what made a human being a person was the ability to meet certain tests of reason. Institutional care for people labeled as "idiots," "fools," or "lunatics" grew in succeeding years for those who were not considered to have the requisite "reason" to be recognized as a person, and thus to enter contracts or take on other rights and responsibilities. Consequently, such people were shut more and more away from the mainstream of society.

The traces of these legal boundaries of intellectual and developmental disability are still embedded in law. The statutory equation in guardianship law, for example, between legal capacity and mental capacity demonstrates the deeply entrenched assumption that in order to have legal power over one's life respected and protected, one must meet certain standards of intellectual functioning. Despite international human rights treaties to challenge this equation between the right to legal capacity and having certain levels of mental capacity, and the obligation to provide support in decision making rather than to rely on substituted decision making, domestic law in many countries is still shedding this centuries-old assumption (Bach & Kerzner, 2010).

THE BIOMEDICAL VIEW

By the 18th century, a legal perspective on disability was beginning to be supplanted by a biomedical one. With the rise of institutional care, the need grew for regulation, licensing, and due process in committal to institutions. The growing medical profession was called upon to play this regulatory role and, over the 18th and 19th centuries, the powers to determine competence shifted from juries of inquisition under the courts to physicians. By the end of the 18th century, the Royal College of Physicians in England was responsible for the licensing of "madhouses." By mid-19th century, resident physicians were required in madhouses of more than 100 people. In the same period, the Association of Medical Officers of Hospitals for the Insane was established, and the organization published a diagnostic manual that included such categories as "mania," "melancholy," "monomania," "dementia," "moral insanity," "idiocy," "imbecility," "general paralysis," and "epilepsy" (Weistubb, 1990). The manual is one of the precursors of the *Diagnostic and Statistical Manual of Mental Disorders, Fifth Edition* (American Psychiatric Association, 2013), widely used to "diagnose" intellectual, developmental, and other disabilities.

The idea that disability was not a status that was conferred, but was in fact an individual deficit, gained strength in the early 20th century when Binet and Simon developed the first intelligence test to identify children in France who were not progressing in school. The test was adapted and, increasingly over the 20th century, became the most common instrument for diagnosing "feeble-mindedness," "mental deficiency," and "mental retardation." Standardized intelligence tests were developed for different age ranges and normal deviations were constructed as a means of identifying as subnormal those who fell below the range considered to be normal. Developmental tests were later designed to measure how closely individuals met "developmental" targets at each age. The discrepancy in measures on language, motor, and behavioral development assisted in defining various categories of what is now called *intellectual and developmental disability*.

These various strands in the evolution of the law and science of disability converged with research and public policy in disability generally. Many definitions were generated over the 20th century and, in 1980, the World Health Organization (WHO) suggested three elements of a definition within what came to be known as the *International Classification of Impairments, Disability and Handicaps*:

- *Impairment.* In the context of health experience, an impairment is any loss or abnormality of psychological, physiological, or anatomical structure or function.

- *Disability.* In the context of health experience, a disability is any restriction or lack (resulting from an impairment) of ability to perform an activity in the manner or within the range considered normal for a human being.

- *Handicap.* In the context of health experience, a handicap is a disadvantage for a given individual, resulting from an impairment or disability, that limits or prevents the fulfilment of a role that is normal (depending on age, sex, social and cultural factors) for that individual. (Wood, 1980, pp. 27–29)

This definition, with its focus on abnormality and lack of ability in relation to a norm and on placing pathology within the individual's body (Siebers, 2008; Straus, 2010), is consistent with the language of intellectual and developmental disability since its inception in law more than 600 years ago. It is also consistent with the many other definitions where developmental or intellectual disability is related to "deficits" or "impairments" in conceptual, practical, and social intelligence (Greenspan & Driscoll, 1997) or lower than "normal" functioning in intellectual abilities (e.g., reasoning, acculturation knowledge, short and long-term memory, visual and auditory processing, processing speed, quantitative knowledge; Horn & Noll, 1997).

The main limitation of the biomedical view is that it categorizes individuals as abnormal in relation to norms of intelligence, even though these vary through history. Thus, as Goodey (2011) suggested, a person identified in the 21st century as "intellectually disabled" would not have the same qualities as a person seen to be lacking the needed capabilities to meet norms of intelligence in the classical Greek era. Intellectual disability is always defined (by others) in relation to norms of intelligence and intellectual capacity, which are themselves bound by social, cultural, and economic contexts. For example, the most recent definition of intellectual disability adopted by the American Association on Intellectual and Developmental Disabilities (AAIDD) uses these norms (AAIDD, 2013; Schalock et al., 2010). To AAIDD, *intellectual disability* is a disability that becomes apparent before the age of 18 and that is characterized by significant limitations in intellectual functioning (general mental capacity; e.g., learning, reasoning, problem solving) and in adaptive behavior (everyday social and practical skills), both measured against normative standards set by professionals.

Measurement of population characteristics can be conducted in ways to statistically define certain "norms" of development, but these norms remain just that—statistical constructions. Deviations from the norms do not signify "abnormal" development; they merely represent statistical deviations from a presumed norm. In this view, if children, youth, or adults do not proceed developmentally through a set of common functions, developmental stages, or critical developmental periods, then they are to be considered abnormal or to have deviations in physical, emotional, or skill development. This assumption, which has served to frame much of the practice in education, developmental psychology, and social science research, is increasingly being called into question (Amundson, 2000; Skrtic, 1991). It has been suggested that rather than being scientific and objective, the concept of functional normality reflects the beliefs, preferences, and cultural expectations of a majority of the members of society. As Amundson suggested, if what it means to be normal is indeed a product of the culture, then the yardsticks for measuring normalcy lack universal and scientific validity, and "disadvantages experienced by people assessed as abnormal derive not from biology, but from implicit social judgments about the acceptability of certain kinds of biological variation" (p. 33). The definition of *normal* becomes arbitrary, relative, and specific to the historical context in which it occurs (Goodey, 2011).

A critique of normalcy does not suggest that particular individuals do not have real limitations and difficulties or face barriers as a result or that they do not require early intervention to help remediate limitations or address diseases and ill health. It simply means that each person must be considered as a unique person. A person's developmental progress will proceed like no other person's, even though at a population level, trends in development can be found across children and subgroups of children.

Mackelprang and Salsgiver (1999) pointed to some of the intellectual foundations of a broader view of developmental theory that begin to address the cultural biases of predominant approaches based on normalcy. This work stresses that the focus in developmental theory must be shifted from measuring the gap between age and expected developmental achievements and measuring the standard deviations of that gap to focusing on the conditions that enable children and adults with disabilities to carry out "developmental tasks" that are culturally shared and defined. To be able to communicate with others, for instance, is a developmental task whose

achievement need not be measured by verbal language skills in the dominant language. Moving into adulthood need not be defined by the capacity for independence, which would exclude from successful adult achievement those who require ongoing personal supports. It can also be defined by the control one is given over one's supports; development of mutually supportive, interdependent relationships; and the opportunity to develop and pursue a wider range of goals.

The WHO definition, its antecedents, and its contemporaries all placed *disability* firmly within the individual while recognizing that it often brings needs for support from others and social stigma for not measuring up to the norm. This is also the case with the AAIDD definition, which recognizes that

> In defining and assessing intellectual disability… additional factors must be taken into account, such as the community environment typical of the individual's peers and culture. Professionals should also consider linguistic diversity and cultural differences in the way people communicate, move, and behave. (2013, p. 1)

A biomedical view of disability is not inherently harming to people with intellectual or developmental disabilities. It can provide an understanding of a person's genetic differences and possible consequences. It can provide information (e.g., through a diagnosis) at an early stage of a person's life about the particular challenges to be faced in communication, motor, and behavioral development, and thus it can encourage access to early intervention programs and other developmental supports. Such information is vital to a child and to his or her family seeking to nurture as many life chances as possible.

The "harm" in a biomedical perspective comes from using it as the only way of viewing a person. This often leads to the assumption that all the challenges to be faced arise from genetic or other differences. In order to address the challenges that arise from a devalued legal and social status, a broader perspective for viewing a person is needed—one that sheds light on how the legal system and economic, social, educational, and other environments in which a person lives can determine his or her life chances. A social and human rights perspective on developmental disability can help to shed this light.

THE SOCIAL MODEL OF DISABILITY

An alternative social and human rights model of disability—often referred to simply as the *social model*—has been advanced by those who find in the WHO and other definitions a "reductionist" tendency—reducing the disability to individual characteristics (Barnes, 1991; Oliver, 1996; Pothier & Devlin, 2006; Rioux, 1996; Rioux, Basser, & Jones, 2011). In a social model, disability arises from the discrimination and disadvantage individuals experience in relation to others because of their particular differences and characteristics. This shift in thinking finds a primary source in feminist and other identity theories of "difference" wherein the challenge is to recognize such differences as gender, race, sexual identity, and disability without assigning social or economic value on the basis of these differences (Carlson, 2010; Garland-Thomas, 2010; Minow, 1990).

A parallel and closely related body of theory in disability, critical disability theory, contends that past and current conceptualizations of disability and their accompanying policies and practices have been both discriminatory and oppressive, and that redress is necessary through overt action that seeks to situate disability in a full and value-neutral way within the human condition. Critical disability theory's value-based approach, which identifies and brings into focus past and current harm from social, cultural, and political relationships, and emphasizes the need to redress this harm, lends a call to action to the social model that is helpful to society assuming its responsibility for providing in an equitable way for all of its citizens, including those with all disabilities (see, e.g., Davis, 2010; Hosking, 2008; Meekosha & Shuttleworth, 2009; Pothier & Devlin, 2006).

The social model, in today's context, embraces human rights as a key method for society to assume its responsibility to ensure equal treatment and opportunities for all of its citizens (Rioux, Pinto, & Parekh, 2015). This reintroduces the notion of people with disabilities as legal entities described at the beginning of this chapter but stresses equality and citizenship rights in a way that brings into question the status that was first carved out for them under statutes such as *De Prerogativa Regis* and also questions the forms of institutional and community care that have taken away their basic rights to self-determination, citizenship, and freedom from discrimination in employment. Instead, the social model suggests a reconstruction of the legal, social, and economic status of people with disabilities, starting with recognition that, first and foremost, people are full, rights-bearing citizens. The purpose of this reconstruction is not to restrict opportunities, but to ensure that opportunities to a full life are protected and enhanced and that these will be appropriate to capabilities of people with all disabilities (Brown, Hatton, & Emerson, 2013).

In a social model of disability, the "pathology," to use Rioux's (1996) terminology, is not individual, but rather social in nature. The unit of analysis shifts from the individual to the legal, social, economic, and political structures that calculate value and status on the basis of difference. Informed by principles of human rights and an equality of outcomes that takes account of differences, the social model does not reject biomedical knowledge of impairments and research on individual rehabilitation. Rather, it celebrates impairment as part of the human condition and looks at achieving equity for people with impairments in terms of the social, cultural, and political contexts (Goodley, 2011).

There remains some question about the place of "impairment" within the social and human rights model of disability. In the response of Disabled Peoples' International (DPI) to the WHO definition, the term *handicap* was dropped, but "impairment" and "functional limitation" were kept as the foundation of the definition (DPI, 1982). Oliver (1996) suggested that this emphasis reinforces normalizing tendencies within the definition that need to be questioned. In keeping with Oliver's view, Shakespeare (1996) suggested that only by turning to the stories and experience of people with disabilities themselves can a legitimate place be given to their lived realities of impairment as the meaning they give to their physical and intellectual differences. He also called for recognition that with impairments can come "intrinsic limitations" (Shakespeare, 2006, p. 41), a reality that must be figured into understanding the disadvantage people with disabilities face. Thomas (2004) continued this thread in her outline of a "social relational model" of disability, which recognizes that physical or cognitive impairments can have real effects and limitations in a person's life. These approaches acknowledge the reality of impairment while challenging the assumption that one person is given the status to define another as "impaired" from some "objective" criteria of "normal" functioning. It is argued that by their very nature, such assessments reinforce a norm at the same time as they define someone as deficient in relation to the norm. Rather, impairment is a lived and subjective reality, given meaning within the individual and in collective narratives expressed by people with disabilities themselves and those who are in personal relationships with them. Frazee (1997) has stressed the importance of creating a "culture" of disability wherein people's differences, or impairments if they define them as such, can be named, given meaning, celebrated, and thereby transformed into a cultural and personal resource, even while people may experience limitations and needs for support.

The notions of a "social model of disability," "personal experience of impairment," and a "culture of disability" may not at first glance provide much hope of liberation to people with more profound intellectual and developmental disabilities, and indeed there has not been nearly as much attention in critical disability studies to the lived realities of this group. Many who are labeled with an intellectual or developmental disability have very challenging needs, are unable to communicate in ways that most others understand, sometimes act in ways that bring alarm to others, and sometimes demand attention from family and support workers. Those who advocate a social rather than biomedical perspective for understanding disability argue that it is most important to bring this perspective to individuals who are in such a situation. It is they whose voices about their own lives and life conditions are least likely to be heard but need to be for an understanding of disability (see Charlton, 1998, 2010; Couser, 1997, 2010). It is they who are most at risk of being devalued in society for their differences, who are defined as furthest from the norm, and who are perceived to be lacking a personal story or narrative that others value. As Eva Kittay—a philosopher who has a daughter with a profound intellectual disability—argued, the differences people with intellectual and developmental disabilities have in relation to others cannot be defined away as "social constructions." These differences are real. It is the defining of them as "problems" that must be addressed:

> The cognitive impairments of the severely and profoundly retarded are not merely contingently disabling. Unlike many disabilities, Sesha's [her daughter's] are not simply social constructions. Someone such as my daughter could not survive, much less thrive, without constant vigilant attention....We might say, however, that in the case of developmental disabilities, especially severe ones, though the disability itself is not socially constructed, the view that mental retardation is a "problem" rather than a possible outcome of human physiology is. (Kittay, 2002, p. 265)

CHALLENGES IN MOVING A SOCIAL MODEL INTO REALITY

How can a social and human rights model best be moved into law, policy, and practice in a way that makes a practical difference in addressing the inequalities and disadvantages experienced by people with intellectual and developmental disabilities? How can that be done in a way that also recognizes that the term *intellectual disability* does not signify a homogenous group and is but one of the identities (although often the dominant one) that people live with at the intersection with their gender, ethno-racial-cultural identity, sexual orientation, and other identities—the intersections that the "radical" model calls upon everyone to recognize (Withers, 2012)? Through the 1980s and 1990s, much was accomplished in codifying in law human rights protections for people with disabilities and prohibitions against discrimination on this basis. In 2006, the United Nations' *Convention on the Rights of Persons with Disabilities* (United Nations, 2006) established a comprehensive human rights standard to guide states (countries) in developing their own human rights and to provide a basis for global monitoring of human rights and disability. The dilemma now is how to put those commitments into reality.

Although human rights laws have advanced, not as much has changed in the lives of people with disabilities in terms of poverty rates, unemployment, exclusion from regular education, exclusion from community activities, exclusion from housing, and rates of abuse (especially neglect; see Chapter 35). Moreover, the inequities affecting people with disabilities within countries and between countries grow. The WHO, for example, estimates a far lower participation rate of children with disabilities than children without disabilities in primary and secondary education (WHO, 2011). In the more affluent countries of the world, where children with disabilities are required to go to school, it is still challenging to move from a segregated to an inclusive approach, as the social model would require.

So, if legal change that significantly addresses the centuries of differential legal status imposed on people with disabilities has been accomplished, what are the next steps? In sectors across society—education, recreation, employment, public sector services, health care, and others—there is a growing commitment to, and belief in, the equality of people with disabilities. However, the leadership, relationships, and knowledge required in these sectors to make full inclusion a reality is often missing. Closing the gap between exclusion and inclusion will require new roles and partnerships, including actors who for many years advocated for legal change working alongside service providers and people with disabilities themselves. For example, more individualized and person-centered planning, funding, and support services are essential if people with intellectual and developmental disabilities are going to be supported to maximize achievement, contribution, success, and belonging, each person along his or her unique developmental path. However, funding arrangements and service delivery systems in education, residential, employment, and community supports still largely foreclose this possibility because of their emphasis on congregate and often segregated approaches. Systems are beginning to change as individualized and person-directed approaches are tested and increasingly adopted (Kendrick, 2011). Nonetheless, the limits of reform will depend on the extent to which a fuller transformation can be made from the predominant biomedical view of disability to a social or human rights approach and even more radical views.

In addition, recognition will be required that people with intellectual and developmental disabilities are not a homogenous group. They are located simultaneously in gendered, racialized, and culturally defined roles and relationships that also structure the limits and possibilities of reform at any point in time and place. For a social and human rights model of disability to take full account of the realities of people with intellectual and developmental disabilities, it must also attend to this more radical perspective on the multiple, sometimes conflictual, and always evolving nature of social identities. This perspective helps people to better understand the double and triple disadvantage some individuals face and also to identify opportunities to build common understanding and solidarity with groups who share forms of social and economic exclusion. These alliances can help to further unsettle the hold that negative and devaluing constructions of intellectual disability have held over people's lives and developmental possibilities.

IMPORTANCE OF A HUMAN RIGHTS APPROACH

This brief overview of the terms *intellectual disability* and *developmental disability,* public policy, and their

historical roots makes clear that there are different ways of making sense of the terms *intellectual disabilities* and *developmental disabilities.* Since the late 20th century, a broad perspective has begun to take shape that goes significantly beyond delineating norms to guide the assessment of disability (e.g., intelligence, adaptive behaviors, social competencies, genetic structure), focusing instead on what needs to be done so that people, whatever their personal challenges and social and economic disadvantage, can exercise their human rights and full citizenship.

The discourse of human rights has not yet influenced thinking in the area of intellectual and developmental disability as much as it has in other areas, such as gender, race, sexual identity, or physical disability (Carlson, 2010). Nonetheless, with the recognition that the label has brought with it a devalued legal, social, and economic status, a human rights framework now has an irrevocable impact on understanding intellectual and developmental disability. Since 1948, when the *Universal Declaration of Human Rights* was adopted, and more recently with the United Nations *Convention on the Rights of Persons with Disabilities,* human rights provisions have been successively passed by national and state or provincial governments. The implications of these changes are being witnessed in the reform of federal and regional statutes—for the right to vote, the right to participate on juries, the right to have access to health care, the right to education, and other rights.

The adoption of a human rights perspective for understanding state obligations to its citizens is arguably the most profound conceptual advance for understanding intellectual and developmental disability since the terminology was first born in law hundreds of years ago. Human rights provisions have become indispensable foundations for a social model of disability and indeed have helped make a social model perspective on disability possible in law, policy, and practice. They are a crucial instrument in challenging the discrimination and inequality that arises from assigning people with intellectual and developmental disabilities differential and devalued legal, social, and economic status on the basis of assessed, or assumed, intellectual differences.

By stressing the value of human rights in understanding intellectual and developmental disability, a social model needs not reject biomedical information. There is much to be learned and valued from an understanding of people's particular differences and the biomedical consequences and challenges they bring. A social model recognizes a biomedical view as one source of information for understanding disability. However, it changes the vision and purpose of intervention from "fixing," "impairments," and "abnormalities" to supporting people to exercise their human rights and thereby become full and valued members of society.

Although the implications of human rights obligations are still to be fully worked out, the vantage point they allow helps to reveal the inequalities in status between people with disabilities and the rest of the population and among people with disabilities themselves. They provide a legitimate ground on which to restructure the institutions and policies that have brought inequality in the past and to consider what entitlements people require in order to fully exercise their citizenship and equality rights. They also demand a restructuring of outmoded approaches to service delivery that still congregate and segregate people on the basis of intellectual and developmental disabilities. As understandings of these inequalities in status inch further and further into public consciousness, it can be hoped that genetic, behavioral, communicational, and intellectual differences will be seen for what they are—signs of diversity, horizons of human possibility, and a place to nurture support, belonging, and reciprocity.

SUMMARY

Intellectual and developmental disability is usually thought of as an intellectual deficit or developmental delay arising from a genetic "deficiency" or other condition, which becomes visible in the early years of life. Stepping back from this assumed definition, it can be seen that *disability* is, first and foremost, a term applied by some people to others. The term is rooted in legal distinctions that go back hundreds of years to a time when the state first became concerned with distinguishing those considered to have the requisite "reason" to manage property and financial affairs.

The biomedical view, in which intellectual and developmental disability tends to be seen primarily as a delay in normal human development, arose as the medical profession was increasingly called upon to determine to whom the category would be applied. A social and human rights model of disability has more recently emerged to question the exclusive focus in a biomedical perspective on "deficits"

and "delays." It aims to shed light on the social, economic, and political barriers to full citizenship that come when a person is labeled as intellectually "delayed" or "disabled."

The legal, biomedical, and social perspectives on disability all underlie public policies for people with intellectual and developmental disabilities. There has been a gradual shift in public policy from "care" for people with disabilities to policies that enable greater social and economic inclusion of such people. However, concerns are growing that there is a "re-medicalization" of disability underway that will be used to distinguish between those who are deemed worthy of public support and those who are not. With human rights commitments now in place, the next step is to develop the knowledge needed for all sectors of society to build inclusive policies and practices that enable people with intellectual and developmental disabilities to take their rightful place.

FOR FURTHER THOUGHT AND DISCUSSION

1. Why do you think it is that a person with a disability has a right to health care and medical interventions in many countries (even if this right is not always fulfilled) but can only obtain disability-related supports as a matter of charity?

2. What arguments would you use to encourage a potential employer who would like to hire a person with a disability but who is concerned about the functional and behavioral assessments provided by a vocational counselor?

3. You are supporting a young person with a developmental disability and her parents. The mother is 3 months pregnant and finds out that her second child will have Down syndrome. The mother turns to you for advice on whether she should abort her fetus. How do you counsel her?

4. Children have a right to education. However, some are excluded from attending their neighborhood school because they do not have the communication capacities or the needed augmentative communication systems are considered too expensive or cumbersome in the classroom. Should education be a matter of right or of capacity? Can functional and other biomedical assessments be used to help a child and a school to more fully exercise the right to education? In what ways might they undermine the possibility of full inclusion?

5. What is the difference between a physician's knowledge about the human rights of a person with a disability, knowledge about how to provide medical care to a person with an intellectual disability, and knowledge about how to ensure that a person with an intellectual disability can have access to the physician's office and be supported to make health care decisions?

REFERENCES

American Association on Intellectual and Developmental Disabilities. (2013). *Definition of intellectual disability.* Retrieved from http://aaidd.org/intellectual-disability/definition

American Psychiatric Association. (2013). *Diagnostic and statistical manual of mental disorders* (5th ed.). Washington, DC: Author.

Amundson, R. (2000). Against normal function. *Studies in History and Philosophy of Biomedical Science, 31,* 33–53.

Bach, M., & Kerzner, L. (2010) *A new paradigm for protecting autonomy and the right to legal capacity.* Toronto, Canada: Law Commission of Ontario.

Barnes, C. (1991). *Disabled people in Britain and discrimination.* London, England: Hurst.

Brown, I., Hatton, C., & Emerson, E. (2013). Quality of life indicators for individuals with intellectual disabilities: Extending current practice. *Intellectual and Developmental Disabilities, 51*(5), 316–332.

Carlson, L. (2010). *The faces of intellectual disability: Philosophical reflections.* Bloomington: Indiana University Press.

Carrithers, M., Collins, S., & Lukes, S. (1985). *The category of the person.* Cambridge, England: Cambridge University Press.

Charlton, J. (1998). *Nothing about us without us: Disability, oppression and empowerment.* Berkeley: University of California Press.

Charlton, J. (2010). The dimensions of disability oppression. In L.J. Davis (Ed.), *The disability studies reader* (3rd ed., pp. 52–62). New York, NY: Routledge.

Cossman, B. (1990). A matter of difference: Domestic contracts and gender equality. *Osgoode Hall Law Journal, 28*(2), 303–377.

Couser, G.T. (1997). *Recovering bodies: Illness, disability and life writing.* Madison: University of Wisconsin Press.

Couser, G.T. (2010). Disability, life narrative and representation. In L.J. Davis (Ed.), *The disability studies reader* (3rd ed., pp. 531–534). New York, NY: Routledge.

Davis, L.J. (Ed.). (2010). *The disability studies reader* (3rd ed.). New York, NY: Routledge.

Disabled Peoples' International. (1982). *Proceedings of the First World Congress.* Singapore: Author.

Fawcett, B. (2000). *Feminist perspectives on disability.* London, England: Prentice-Hall.

Foucault, M. (1965). *Madness and civilization* (R. Howard, Trans.). New York, NY: Random House.

Frazee, C. (1997). Prideful culture. *Entourage, 10,* 87–94.

Garland-Thomas, R. (2010). Integrating disability, transforming feminist theory. In L.J. Davis (Ed.), *The disability studies reader* (3rd ed., pp. 353–373). New York, NY: Routledge.

Goodey, C.F. (2011). *A history of intelligence and 'intellectual disability': The shaping of psychology in early modern Europe.* Farnham, United Kingdom: Ashgate.

Goodley, D. (2011). *Disability studies: An interdisciplinary introduction.* Thousand Oaks, CA: Sage.

Greenspan, S., & Driscoll, J. (1997). The role of intelligence in a broad model of personal competence. In D. Flanagan, J. Genshaft, & P. Harrison (Eds.), *Contemporary intellectual assessment: Theories, tests, and issues* (pp. 131–150). New York, NY: Guilford Press.

Hirst, D., & Michael, P. (2003). Family, community and the "idiot" in mid-nineteenth century North Wales. *Disability and Society, 18,* 145–163.

Horn, J., & Noll, J. (1997). Human cognitive capabilities: Gf-Gc theory. In D. Flanagan, J. Genshaft, & P. Harrison (Eds.), *Contemporary intellectual assessment: Theories, tests, and issues* (pp. 53–91). New York, NY: Guilford Press.

Hosking, D.L. (2008). *Critical disability theory.* Paper presented at the 4th Biennial Disability Studies Conference, Lancaster, United Kingdom. Retrieved from http://www.lancaster.ac.uk/fass/events/disabilityconference_archive/2008/papers/hosking2008.pdf

Inclusion International. (2006). *Hear our voices: People with an intellectual disability and their families speak out on poverty and inclusion.* Toronto, Canada: Author.

Inclusion International. (2009). *Better education for all: When we're included too.* Salamanca, Spain: Instituto Universitario de Integración en la Comunidad (INICO).

Inclusion International. (2012). *Inclusive communities = stronger communities.* London, England: Author.

Inclusion International. (2014). *Independent but not alone: Global report on the right to legal capacity.* London, England: Author.

Kendrick, M. (2011). Empowerment and self-direction relative to the design and governance of personalized service arrangements. *Journal of Human Development, Disability, and Social Change, 19*(2), 57–68.

King, S. (2000). *Poverty and welfare in England, 1700–1850.* Manchester, England: Manchester University Press.

Kittay, E.F. (2002). When caring is just and justice is caring. In E.F. Kittay & E.K. Feder (Eds.), *The subject of care: Feminist perspectives on dependency* (pp. 257–276). Lanham, MD: Rowman and Littlefield.

Mackelprang, R., & Salsgiver, R. (1999). *Disability: A diversity model approach in human services practice.* Pacific Grove, CA: Brooks/Cole.

McIntosh, P. (2002). An archi-texture of learning disability services: The use of Michel Foucault. *Disability and Society, 17,* 65–79.

Meekosha, H., & Shuttleworth, R. (2009) What's so "critical" about critical disability studies? *Australian Journal of Human Rights, 15*(1), 47–75.

Minow, M. (1990). *Making all the difference: Inclusion, exclusion, and American law.* Ithaca, NY: Cornell University Press.

Neugebauer, R. (1996). Mental handicap in medieval and early modern England: Criteria, measurement and care. In D. Wright & A. Digby (Eds.), *From idiocy to mental deficiency: Historical perspectives on people with learning disabilities* (pp. 22–43). London, England: Routledge.

Oliver, M. (1996). Defining impairment and disability: Issues at stake. In C. Barnes & G. Mercer (Eds.), *Exploring the divide: Illness and disability* (pp. 39–54). Leeds, England: University of Leeds, Disability Press.

Peters, S. (2000). Is there a disability culture? A syncretisation of three possible world views. *Disability and Society, 15*(4), 583–601.

Poole, R. (1985). Morality, masculinity and the market. *Radical Philosophy, 39,* 16–23.

Poole, R. (1991). *Morality and modernity.* London, England: Routledge.

Pothier, D., & Devlin, R. (2006). *Critical disability theory: Essays in philosophy, politics, policy, and law.* Vancouver, Canada: UBC Press.

Rioux, M.H. (1996). Ethical and socio-political considerations on the development and use of classification. *Canadian Journal of Rehabilitation, 9*(2), 61–67.

Rioux, M., Basser, L.A., & Jones, M. (Eds.). (2011). *Critical perspectives on human rights and disability law.* Leiden, The Netherlands: Martinus Nijhoff.

Rioux, M.H., Pinto, P.C., & Parekh, G. (2015). *Disability rights monitoring, and social change: Building power out of evidence.* Toronto: Canadian Scholars' Press.

Rushton, P. (1988). Lunatics and idiots: Mental disability, the community and poor law in north east England, 1600–1800. *Medical History, 32,* 34–50.

Schalock, R.L., Borthwick-Duffy, S.A., Bradley, V.J., Buntinx, W.H.E., Coulter, D.L., Craig, E.M....Yeager, M.H. (2010). *Intellectual disability: Definition, classification, and systems of supports* (11th ed.). Washington, DC: American Association on Intellectual and Developmental Disabilities.

Shakespeare, T. (1996). Disability, identity, difference. In C. Barnes & G. Mercer (Eds.), *Exploring the divide: Illness and disability* (pp. 94–113). United Kingdom: University of Leeds, Disability Press.

Shakespeare, T. (2006). *Disability rights and wrongs.* London, England: Routledge.

Shelford, L. (1833). *A practical treatise on the law concerning lunatics, idiots and persons of unsound mind. with an appendix of the statutes of England, Ireland, and Scotland, relating to such persons; and precedents and bills of costs.* London, England: S. Sweet, Chancerry Lance, and Stevens & Sons, Bell Yard.

Siebers, T. (2008). *Disability theory.* Ann Arbor: University of Michigan Press

Skrtic, T.M. (1991). *Behind special education: A critical analysis of professional culture and school organization.* Denver, CO: Love.

Straus, J.N. (2010). Autism as culture. In L.J. Davis (Ed.), *The disability studies reader* (3rd ed., pp. 535–559). New York, NY: Routledge.

Thomas, C. (2004). Developing the social relational in the social model of disability: A theoretical agenda. In C. Barnes & G. Mercer (Eds.), *Implementing the social model of disability: Theory and research.* Leeds, United Kingdom: Disability Press.

United Nations. (2006). *Convention on the rights of persons with disabilities.* Retrieved from http://www.un.org/disabilities/convention/conventionfull.shtml

Weistubb, D. (1990). *Enquiry on mental competency: Final report.* Toronto, Canada: Osgoode Hall Law School.

Withers, A.J. (2012). *Disability politics and theory.* Halifax, Canada: Fernwood.

Wood, P. (1980). *International classification of impairments, disabilities, and handicaps.* Geneva, Switzerland: World Health Organization.

World Health Organization. (2011). *World report on disability.* Geneva, Switzerland: WHO Press.

4

Trends and Issues in Intellectual and Developmental Disabilities

Trevor R. Parmenter and James R. Thompson

WHAT YOU WILL LEARN

- International sociopolitical trends in intellectual and developmental disabilities
- International trends in disability pertaining to inclusive practices
- Types and ranges of services provided internationally
- Challenges for the field in the future

The field of intellectual and developmental disabilities, like all others, has a set of core issues that do not change substantially over time. Such issues include identifying and implementing the best approaches to supporting people and their families, ensuring that services are available and accessible, and promoting the dignity of people with disabilities as fully participating members of society.

Yet, this field has by no means remained static, either. The time since the 1960s has yielded tremendous change and growth, particularly in more economically developed countries. On the whole, these changes have resulted in vast improvements in the lives of people with intellectual and developmental disabilities and their families, and they have drawn attention to many other changes that could lead to further improvements in the future.

Such changes have not occurred in isolation, however. The intellectual and developmental disabilities field has broadened and diversified or constricted and narrowed in response to numerous social, economic, political, and environmental factors that are both national and international in origin. Like other fields, interests and priorities have emerged and declined over time. Issues that were considered to be of utmost importance in one decade seemed less important the following decade and were replaced by others that were seen as more timely and urgent.

In this chapter, some of the most important international trends and issues that are currently important to the field of intellectual and developmental disabilities are highlighted to provide a context for understanding people with disabilities, as well as the service systems that have been established to support them, in a more complete way. Such trends and issues are likely to become more important or less important over time. For the present and the near future, however, they are important for two reasons: 1) they guide thinking about the field and how to approach support for people with disabilities and 2) they provide the "top layer" of an ever-changing groundwork out of which future trends and issues will emerge.

INTERNATIONAL SOCIOPOLITICAL TRENDS

The 1960s and 1970s were decades in which dramatic changes occurred in public policies and professional practices affecting people with intellectual and developmental disabilities. During these 2 decades, the sociopolitical concept of normalization and the corresponding deinstitutionalization and mainstreaming movements led to efforts to establish local, community-based services across the globe. This new, community-based service system sharply contrasted with traditional services provided in disability centers and residential institutions. These 2 decades of dramatic change paved the way for the United Nations (UN) to declare 1981 the International Year of Disabled Persons, and advances in protecting the civil rights of people with disabilities were evident in specific countries (e.g., the Americans with Disabilities Act [ADA] of 1990 [PL 101-336] in the United States).

Although there has been progress on many fronts in the field of intellectual and developmental disabilities since the early 1980s, such advances for people with intellectual and developmental disabilities across the world are best characterized as incremental rather than landmark. The advances have been incremental, to a large extent, because of broader societal contexts that have curtailed bold advances. Beginning in the 1980s, considerable shifts in thinking within most developed nations affected many aspects of the social order in an ongoing way, including, to some degree, how people with disabilities were perceived and treated. Key interrelated aspects of these shifts are explained in the following subsections.

Toward a Global Economy

During the last decades of the 20th century, an increasingly global economy created pressure on countries, especially those that were strongest economically, to relax government regulations and restrictions on the ways the economy functioned nationally and internationally. The core element was a growing view that economic policies must allow businesses the freedom to choose which resources they could use and how such resources could be used. For example, this concept proposed that businesses should have considerable freedom to use raw materials, labor, and services from whatever countries of the world could provide them in the most cost-effective way. It was reasoned that products produced by businesses in such a climate would be less expensive to consumers, therefore increasing consumer purchasing power and, ultimately, resulting in a higher standard of living for all. Critics of this view contended that allowing businesses to

"shop around the world" for cost-effective resources would result (and has resulted) in strong countries exploiting weaker countries, especially in terms of worker wages.

At any rate, these views resulted in changes to the political discourse, and later to the public discourse, that were highly influential in many of the more developed countries by the early 1990s. Such changes were strongly influenced by the economic policies initiated by governments in the United Kingdom and the United States in the 1980s, and later by those of other developed countries such as Australia, where "economic rationalization" became a widely used description of a new set of policies and ways of thinking. These governments' policies supported the overall view that a strong economy would create a better environment within which all could prosper, including people who had traditionally been living at the margins of society. A strong economy, it was thought, could be created by reducing the tax burden on citizens and by reducing government restrictions on businesses. A strong economy also made maximum use of available resources, and there was considerable emphasis on what was referred to as "making do with less," "trimming the fat," or "utility maximization." The resulting booming economy, it was believed, would create wealth that would "trickle down" to those who were not able to benefit directly from the policies (e.g., many people with disabilities).

The overall benefits of these policies are a matter of debate, and people with different economic and political viewpoints arrive at vastly different conclusions. Analyzing global economic indicators is well beyond the scope of this chapter, but it is clear that significant economic benefits for people with disabilities and other disadvantaged people did not occur on a widespread scale. For example, a first step was typically a strong emphasis on reducing or eliminating budget deficits. This was accomplished through budget cuts that resulted in a reduction or loss of numerous formerly funded social and other programs, including those for people with disabilities, and the stagnation of many others. Such moves did not help people with disabilities and in many cases actually acted as a barrier to maintaining the services that did exist and to expanding new ways of thinking. Thus, the degree to which these policies were beneficial for those with fewer advantages now seems to be in doubt (e.g., see Sommeiller & Price, 2014), although this will be more fully assessed and evaluated with the passage of time. Still, there is no doubt that the previously described overall changes in thinking in regard to a government's obligations to its more vulnerable citizens represented a change that was highly influential internationally and continues to be influential.

Perceived Need to Contain Public Spending

At about the same time, there developed a concern that the degree to which governments had been funding social and many other programs was not sustainable in the long term and that government overspending in these areas was depleting resources that were needed to restock the economy and to provide for people in the future. This trend appears to have arisen from some discontent in two areas. First, political parties that then formed governments considered the public to be unrealistically overreliant on them to resolve all social and economic problems. Second, the public came to believe that it was increasingly being asked to pay for more programs that were not necessarily useful or fully justified. As a consequence, government leaders and other policy makers in the most developed countries began to change the way their funds were generated (primarily through taxes) and redistributed by cutting or freezing taxes or reducing tax increases, as well as reducing the number and scope of many of the programs and initiatives formerly funded (including some programs for people with intellectual and developmental disabilities).

The overall result of such moves was a stronger emphasis on economic investment and prosperity and on decreased government responsibility, with a corresponding increased individual, community, and corporate responsibility. In shifting responsibility this way, the state began to play more of a supportive rather than a leadership role in addressing the needs of vulnerable populations. Within disability services, the thinking was that rather than commit to providing comprehensive care from cradle to grave, as was formerly (but imperfectly) the case, it was more economically viable to offer a "safety net" approach, by which public money to fund supports would only be offered to certain individuals whose needs were sufficiently substantial to merit such assistance.

Many governments also adopted the theme of mutual obligation that requires people receiving financial or other support to contribute to their country's economy, especially by obtaining a job or attending training. Although this policy may have had some effect in removing people without disabilities from welfare support, data on the numbers of people with disabilities without employment provide evidence of structural barriers that prevent this population from obtaining meaningful work (e.g., see Siperstein, Parker, & Drascher, 2013).

Public policies since the 1980s have tended to emphasize economic strength, and there has been a reduced emphasis on social equity. There has been a concomitant move to downsize government bureaucracies and to change the relationships between government institutions and the public into economic partnerships, as evidenced by a shift toward requiring individuals, families, and local communities to assume greater responsibility for arranging services and supports and to make greater use of existing community and family resources. DiRita, Parmenter, and Stancliffe (2008) observed that public policies affecting people with intellectual and developmental disabilities since the 1970s can be characterized by "entrenched moral grounding in utilitarianism," and noted that "this suggests a conception of the person with ID [intellectual disability] reflective of conditional tolerance rather than acceptance of moral equality, and places them in a precarious situation, i.e., contingent on economic health" (p. 624).

Growth of Individualism

An emphasis on the needs and wishes as well as the responsibilities of individuals has accompanied the previously described changes and constitutes what is referred to as *individualism*. The growth of individualism in society more generally influenced a similar emphasis within the field of intellectual and developmental disabilities. The concepts of freedom of individual choice, respect for the individual perspective, more control by individuals over their own lives, release from government regulation (e.g., direct funding to people with disabilities or their families), self-determination, and individual and family empowerment have all taken on increasing importance since the early 1990s. Person-centered approaches have been adopted by many service provider organizations in response to a perceived need to emphasize the individual (see this chapter's Person-Centered Approaches section for a fuller discussion). These are important trends for people with disabilities that have helped develop an understanding that people with disabilities have unique needs, wishes, life goals, and capabilities that need to be respected when providing support.

At the same time, however, the emphasis on individualism presents certain threats to vulnerable groups of people such as those with intellectual and developmental disabilities. First, although individualism works to encourage as much personal independence as possible, people in this population, by definition, require supports that others in the general population do not need. The thrust within individualism compromises the integrity of individuals with disabilities by expecting them to act on their own behalf in "normative" ways, which may not be characteristic of or realistic for them. It also contributes further to their being ascribed lower social status and being less valued than other human beings, precisely because they are not always able to act on their own behalf to improve their own lives. The individualistic view of the self militates against people with disabilities as dependents and therefore contributes to "dependence" being viewed negatively. The challenge is for society to create environments where the interdependence of individuals is a central feature and where individuals perceive their identity and the conceptualization of self in the context of a mutually dependent society.

A second problem with individualism is that it seems to act contrary to those elements that build social cohesion and a sense of mutual obligation toward one's fellow citizens, especially people who are marginalized and relatively powerless. It is ironic that the focus on individualism does not sit comfortably with the call by many developed economies for a greater emphasis on the development of social capital and community capacity building. This call is a direct corollary to the policies of downloading responsibilities for providing supports from governments to communities, families, and individuals.

Finally, the growth of individualism also seems to have contributed rather significantly to the growing gap between the rich and the poor in both developed and developing countries. This gap constitutes a further impediment for social justice policies for disadvantaged groups in societies and is particularly relevant to people with disabilities, who are highly associated with poverty (Emerson, 2004; Leake, 2012).

Environmental Degradation and Primary Prevention

The assault on the world's ecosystems continues to have profound negative effects on the health of the world's population. The rapid growth of the production of new chemicals has increased the risk for birth defects. It is estimated that there are approximately five million chemicals to which the population has significant exposure. Occupational and environmental exposures to toxic solutions continue to contribute to birth defects worldwide (Rauch & Lanphear, 2012). Lead exposure and nutritional deficiencies also continue to be significant causes of birth defects in both developed and developing countries (Attina & Trasande, 2013). Iodine deficiency is still a major cause of intellectual disability, and mild to moderate deficiencies have been identified in 32 countries, more than half of which are in the industrialized world (Shaw & Friedman, 2011). Lack of immunization programs (e.g., against rubella), and in some cases lack of commitment to them, continues to be a major problem in primary prevention of disability. The rampant spread of the human immunodeficiency virus (HIV), especially in Africa, is among the most common infectious causes of intellectual and developmental disability. Effective nuclear waste disposal and the minimization of the risks of nuclear accidents, which could also lead to disabilities, continue to be challenges.

These are just a few examples of environmental degradation and the enormous problems that the human race faces in dealing with them. There are many others. Unfortunately, such problems are usually associated either directly or indirectly with disability and have strong impacts on both the breadth and nature of the work of the intellectual and developmental disability field.

INTERNATIONAL TRENDS IN DISABILITY

A number of important international trends have developed specifically in the field of intellectual and developmental disabilities that are influenced by the broader trends described in the previous section but also reflect the changing values, concepts, and knowledge that have emerged within the field. The following subsections highlight trends that have greatly influenced current thinking about disability and the provision of supports to people with disabilities.

Pause in Funding Increases and Philosophical Approach

The previously described trends and policies since 1980 have, in general, been accompanied by and resulted in a pause in both funding increases and philosophical approach. Funds of services for people with disabilities have been frozen, reduced, or increased only slightly in most countries. There have been exceptions to the funding pause, especially where funds are provided strategically (i.e., for specific programs—e.g., employment training— or for specific subpopulations—e.g., children with autism). On the whole, though, there have been no substantial increases in funding for people with disabilities in most countries for many years.

In keeping with this, the prevailing approach in disability philosophy since the 1980s has been to reflect on and scrutinize what services are for, how they are obtained, and what needs they are meeting. The time of philosophical pause has been a time of rethinking and reevaluating the efficiency and cost-effectiveness of services rather than a time for generating new philosophical approaches. Although this philosophical pause has been countered to some degree by the expansion of new ideas associated with broad concepts such as inclusion, social-ecological understandings of disabilities, self-determination, and quality of life (see the following subsection for a more complete description), overall, there has been less emphasis on providing support that is based on principles and ideology and more emphasis on encouraging support that is responsive to such ideas as using alternative resources, financial accountability, and community and family involvement.

Emphasis on Inclusion, Supports, Quality of Life, and Human Rights

Despite the pause described in the preceding section—and, to some extent, in reaction to it—people with disabilities are probably more accepted in society now than ever before. A number of interrelated clusters of concepts have contributed to this. The principles of normalization and community living have been strongly embraced and solidified within the field and to some degree within the general population (see Chapter 2). These principles, along with important developments in rights (see the discussion that follows), have helped to stress equality between people with and without disabilities.

Inclusion has become the overall term for a strong international movement that seeks to improve the life circumstances of people with intellectual and other disabilities in the context of their communities. As the name implies, inclusion strives to ensure that people with disabilities should not only live in communities but also be valued, accepted, respected, involved, and have the same life opportunities as people without disabilities (Amado, Stancliffe, McCarron, & McCallion, 2013).

Understanding intellectual disability and related developmental disabilities contextually, as an interaction between the person and the environment instead of as a defect within the person, is the essence of a social-ecological understanding of disability. As was discussed in Chapter 1, the World Health Organization also described a social-ecological conceptualization of disability in its 1980 publication *International Classification of Impairments, Disabilities, and Handicaps (ICIDH)* and its 2001 publication *International Classification of Functioning, Disability and Health (ICF)*. Viewing disability as a mismatch between the person's capacities and the context in which the person functions logically leads to a focus on providing individualized supports. Supports bridge the gap between personal competency and environmental demands, and therefore bridge the gap between people's current life experiences and conditions and the life they aspire to have. Several new assessment tools to measure the support needs of people with intellectual and developmental disabilities were developed during the first decade of the 21st century in response to a social-ecological understanding of disability. These include the Supports Intensity Scale (Thompson et al., 2004) and the I-CAN (Riches, Parmenter, Llewellyn, Hindmarsh, & Chan, 2009).

The concept *quality of life* emerged and expanded during the 1990s. It is an ideal emphasizing the quality within individuals' lives and ways to bring maximum enjoyment of life for each individual. *Inclusion* and *quality of life* are companion terms because both pursue similar general goals. Having accepted that people with disabilities can and must live in neighborhoods and communities alongside people without disabilities, these concepts seek to enhance the overall quality of people's living circumstances and life experiences. Since the 1990s, there has been considerable emphasis in many countries on promoting both inclusion and quality of life for children and adults with intellectual and developmental disabilities (Verdugo, Navas, Gomez, & Schalock, 2012).

Underlying recent accomplishments in inclusion and quality of life is a belief in the equality of people with and without disabilities. This belief is being realized primarily through important developments in the rights of people with disabilities (see Chapters 5 and 6 for fuller details). In 2006, the UN *Convention on the Rights of Persons with Disabilities* (CRPD) was adopted. The CRPD is an international treaty that requires parties to the convention (i.e., countries that sign it) to protect the human rights and ensure the basic freedoms of people with disabilities. The articles included in the CRPD address a wide array of issues including environmental accessibility, protection from inhumane treatment (e.g., torture in the name of behavioral intervention), choice making, community living, and access to education. Countries signing the treaty agree to adopt legislation that will ensure its implementation (UN, 2014). As of July 28, 2014, 143 countries ratified the treaty (United Nations Treaty Collection, 2014).

There is no denying the fact that legislation enacted in most Western countries has underpinned the provision of a wide range of supports, which has enabled the fuller participation of people with a disability into regular community life. However, rights legislation may be seen as a necessary, but not sufficient, condition for people with disabilities to enjoy the acceptance of the community. Similarly, it is suggested that the moral language of rights may be necessary, but not sufficient, to ground moral responsibility for people with a disability.

As a universal approach, the rights movement may need to be adapted or reconceptualized. This may be especially true in cultures that do not have a social system with a strong commitment to social welfare or social justice or in cultures that emphasize the notion of a person's obligations to the community or tribe more strongly than is the case in many Western cultures (see also Chapters 5 and 6). Notwithstanding, the emphasis on human rights and disability has led to some very positive steps forward in perceiving and treating people with intellectual and developmental disabilities as both valued and equal, and it has provided a strong philosophical foundation for other complementary concepts such as inclusion and quality of life.

Community Living and Community Supports

Changing approaches to conceptualizing intellectual and developmental disabilities led to an international trend to close institutions (see discussion in Chapter 2). In turn, closing institutions and moving people to community settings has had a tremendous impact on how society views intellectual and developmental disabilities. The philosophical significance of the shift from institutional to community living is that all people should be valued in society and that all people have a place within society, but at a very practical level, it has meant that people with intellectual and developmental disabilities now live in neighborhoods everywhere with a much higher degree of acceptance than was the case a generation ago.

Some people still live in large government- and non–government-run facilities. The number of people in such settings is gradually being reduced in response to a firm commitment by governments in most countries to close them as soon as is feasible. In a number of countries, moving thousands of people from institutional living to community living has involved considerably more logistical problems than were anticipated when the initiative was first given consideration in the 1970s (see Chapter 2). As a result, there are still thousands of people living in congregate care facilities in most countries across the world. In less developed countries, institutional care or living with family often remain the major ways to accommodate people with intellectual and developmental disabilities. In the growing economies of Asia, the move to more normalized environments has been slow; however, population density is a key factor in many of these countries, and Western-style residential models may not be applicable. Moreover, contemporary Western philosophies have not always had a major impact on these countries, as many do not have similar social welfare and social justice histories.

The large majority of the developed economies have made a commitment to close their large facilities. For instance, the United Kingdom, New Zealand, and Norway have closed all of their congregate care facilities (e.g., see Braddock, Emerson, Felce, & Stancliffe, 2001). In countries where this has not occurred, there has been considerable progress. For example, in the United States, the population of people living in state-operated institutions decreased from 194,650 in 1967 to 29,574 in 2011, and 168 institutions have closed (or are in the process of closing) since 1969 (Braddock et al., 2013). In some countries, a lack of community alternatives has been one of the major reasons for maintaining institutions, especially for people with very high support needs. The problem is often a lack of options; there is simply no place in the community that is adequately funded to provide needed supports to which these individuals can move.

Perhaps the biggest challenge in assisting people to move from congregate to community living is doing so in ways that respect the dignity of people (e.g., provide people with personal choices and opportunities for self-expression; provide people with personalized supports that result in happier, more fulfilled lives). There is ample evidence that people who have moved from congregate facilities to community-based living are very likely to experience an improved quality of life across a wide array of indicators (Lemay, 2009). However, there is also strong evidence that quality of life is still less than desirable for many people (Mansell & Beadle-Brown, 2010). A move into a community setting does not guarantee people will become part of a community. There has possibly been too much emphasis on the physical environment to the detriment of deciding how people can be best supported to optimize their quality of life in community settings. This issue continues to be a challenge for policy planners and support providers.

Types and Range of Services and Supports Available

A comprehensive set of community services and supports is available to most people with intellectual and developmental disabilities and their families, as described throughout this book. Although not available everywhere, these supports and services are accessible in a great many countries and regions of countries by people who have demonstrated need. Yet, life in community settings—including adaptation to ongoing changes that occur, such as changes in transportation, communication, technology, and types of services—has produced new challenges for the types and range of supports that need to be made available. Despite the promise of specialized assistive technologies designed specifically for use by people with disabilities, as well as everyday technologies such as smartphones (emerging from the technology boom since the 1980s), very few people with intellectual

and developmental disabilities use technological supports in their daily lives (Palmer, Wehmeyer, Davies, & Stock, 2012). In addition, there are ongoing issues in obtaining and using the services and supports that are available, including unequal access to services and sources of funding, gaps in services (e.g., between school and adult community living), lack of continuity within and among services, services that do not respond to the specific needs of individuals, and difficulties in gaining access to needed services.

Loss of Advocates and Specialists

Somewhat ironically, the move away from institutional care and toward community support has contributed to a sense in many jurisdictions that there is a loss of passionate spokespeople for intellectual and developmental disabilities (Dumeresq & Lawton, 2003). Perhaps the main factor that affects this sense is that there has been an increasing emphasis on using generic, rather than specialized, professionals and services (e.g., health care professionals, psychologists).

A major difficulty that has been a problem for community support is the high turnover of front-line staff (Hewitt & Larson, 2007; see Chapter 26). This results in a paucity of experienced support workers and also effective advocates at the level of the individual with disabilities. Ways to address shortages of trained personnel in the field of intellectual and developmental disabilities, and ways to encourage such personnel to have ongoing careers in the human services field, are concerns in many countries. Paradoxically, the loss of professionals as advocates may make this challenge all the more difficult.

Professional groups have not yet taken all of the necessary steps to ensure that there will be enough professionals with specialized training in intellectual and developmental disabilities. For some professions, although this differs among countries and regions of countries, there are experienced and trained professionals readily available to respond to the needs of people with disabilities. For many other professions, however, there is a scarcity of such professionals. For example, in many areas it is difficult to identify lawyers, psychiatrists, family physicians, therapists, nurses, home care staff, counselors, addictions workers, and many other professionals to address the needs of people with disabilities.

Increasing Knowledge about Disabilities

Another important trend is the continually increasing knowledge base about factors that cause or contribute to the occurrence of intellectual and developmental disabilities. Especially since 1990, there has been a dramatic increase in understanding of the roles of environmental hazards such as alcohol abuse, brain injury from accidents involving impaired driving and child abuse, low socioeconomic status, genetics, and many other factors (see Chapters 9 and 10 for complete details). Such advances are positive in that they have added considerably to knowledge of the factors that cause or contribute to disabilities and, in some cases, to effective interventions. In a number of cases, they are also beginning to have important implications for preventing and treating intellectual and developmental disabilities.

Implications of New Genetic and Clinical Knowledge   Until the mid-20th century, infectious diseases and malnutrition were major causes of sickness and death in the world. Because of advances in treatment of such problems, genetic disorders are now major health problems in industrialized countries. In the United States, for example, 3%–5% of infants are born with a birth defect of chromosomal, gene, or multifactorial origin, and the important role of genetics in pediatric illnesses is being increasingly recognized (Parker et al., 2010). Because genetic diseases are chronic, they require lifelong attention, as well as expensive support, therapy, and specialized care. Thus, genetic knowledge has also created some new problems for the intellectual and developmental disabilities field. For example, for some time it has been possible for parents to know during pregnancy if their child will have Down syndrome (see Chapters 10 and 14) or for parents to know before birth that there is a possibility their child will have fragile X syndrome (see Chapter 15) and to choose not to continue the pregnancy. Such choices are not for everyone, however, and such knowledge can pose terrible ethical dilemmas. It is clear that the prevalence of Down syndrome has decreased as the result of being able to diagnose it by serum analysis of the mother or by ultrasound (see Chapters 10 and 14), but it is not known if the ability to diagnose fragile X and other disorders by DNA analysis actually is resulting in decreased prevalence of such disorders. Upon examining data from 13 European countries,

Loane et al. (2013) concluded that the availability of prenatal screening and cultural attitudes toward abortion led to a wide variation among populations in regard to the prevalence of live births of infants with disabilities.

Genetic advances have raised broader ethical concerns in the field of intellectual and developmental disabilities that go beyond simple prevention. The possibility of genetic intervention as the key to preventing disabilities raises new and troubling questions about when and how to make decisions about whether to intervene genetically or medically. It also raises important questions especially for those who advocate the value placed on the lives of individuals with disabilities and about the value placed on disability as part of any social order (Kaposy, 2013). Disability advocates often argue that disability adds to the richness of the human condition and therefore has a legitimate and important place in any social order. With the possibility of genetic intervention, however, it is not clear that advocates—especially those who do not themselves have disabilities— would present the same views. These types of concerns stress a need for professionals and self-advocates in the field of disabilities to continuously assess their core values and to assume leadership in helping to shape and expand positive values for people with disabilities. They also stress a need to expand the role of ethical considerations in testing and carrying out interventions that will almost certainly result from a rapidly growing knowledge of genetic disabilities.

The need for disability professionals and self-advocates to take on this responsibility is especially important because new genetic knowledge gained through the Human Genome Project is increasing exponentially. It is anticipated that such new knowledge will have a particularly profound impact on the profession of nursing and that nurses will become more and more involved in referring people for genetic testing and for managing the genetic health aspects of individuals (Gharaibeh, Oweis, & Hamad, 2010). Health care systems will have to provide resources for meeting such training needs, for educating the public as well as professionals about genetic disorders, for meeting the demands for diagnosing new disorders, and for supporting individuals and families with newly diagnosed genetic disorders. Disability professionals and self-advocates will need to provide guidance and ethical leadership if these challenges are to be met adequately.

Self-Advocacy by People with Disabilities

The worldwide growth of self-advocacy groups is a potentially vital force for people with intellectual and developmental disabilities achieving equal citizenship with citizens from the general population. There has been considerable growth in self-advocacy groups since the 1970s when they first emerged. For example, the People First movement has spread to several countries, including some in the Middle East. A number of international self-advocacy conferences have been held in Canada, the United Kingdom, and the United States. At other conferences, self-advocacy has been one important aspect of the overall programs. For example, at the American Association on Intellectual and Developmental Disabilities 2014 annual meeting, self-advocate Jenny Hatch presented a plenary address regarding her struggles (both interpersonal as well as legal) to use supported decision making to direct her life.

There has been increasing recognition of the rights of people with intellectual and developmental disabilities to have a voice in how they would like to live their lives. As such, people with disabilities are asserting their need to be consulted on a variety of policy and service issues, including involvement in setting the research agenda. The growth in the empowerment of people with disabilities to make their own decisions and choices has been one of the major forces of the early 21st century. Testimony to this development is the increasing number of people with an intellectual or developmental disability who are marrying or forming long-term relationships, having children, going to college, working in full-time jobs, and directing their own supports as they live lifestyles of their own choosing in their home communities.

Person-Centered Approaches

Another important international trend, related to the growth of individualism, is the growing emphasis on person-centered approaches (see especially Chapter 24 for a more detailed discussion). This is resulting in community disability service agencies redefining their overall roles and the roles of their employees. Person-centered approaches refer to methods of providing support to people with intellectual and developmental disabilities and their families that place their wants and needs at the center of the supports they receive. Person-centered approaches imply that service organizations should neither predetermine what services are important to people with disabilities nor make the key decisions about the best ways to implement those services; rather, they should respond in individual ways to the needs and wishes of the people they support. For these approaches to be realized, service organizations need to be flexible in their organizational structure and have the capacity to respond to a wide variety of needs and wishes in ways that are sometimes new and that require creative solutions.

Proponents of person-centered planning (PCP) approaches have expressed skepticism about formalizing these processes through specifying explicit procedures and outcomes. They argued that flexible guidelines for conducting planning meetings, roles for people that are not clearly defined, and a lack of formal requirements (e.g., forms requiring certain sections to be completed and signatures) liberates people to creatively problem solve. They contrast PCP to the constraints many people experience when engaged in more formalized planning processes such as developing an annual plan that is required by governmental regulations (see O'Brien, O'Brien, & Mount, 1997). Others disagree, arguing that it is impossible to scientifically study approaches that are so nebulously defined. For instance, Osborne (2005) charged that PCP processes have fuzzy goals and outcomes, and he characterized them as a *faux fixe* in the field.

A trend that is influencing services to people with intellectual and developmental disabilities and one that is related to person-centered approaches in many countries is the growth of direct funding—public money being dispersed by governments or government agents directly to individuals with disabilities or their families. Direct funding, or consumer-controlled funding in some countries, is based on the principle that services can be delivered in a more cost-efficient and effective way because many individuals and families are in the best position to know what supports they need and are capable of using the money responsibly and effectively. One direct funding model makes an amount of money, typically up to a maximum, available to any individuals with intellectual and developmental disabilities or their families who apply for it. Another model assigns funding levels to individuals or families following an individual assessment. In some cases, money moves directly from government or other funding agents to individuals and families; in other cases, money is provided to community organizations that take responsibility for identifying, approving, and monitoring individuals or families who need funding and who use the method effectively.

The slogan "fund people not programs" concisely sums up the rationale for individual budgets. It is assumed that if people with disabilities and their closest allies (e.g., family members, friends) are in control of funds, then service provider organizations will be highly motivated to be responsive to the needs of the person with the disability. A funding structure that puts people with disabilities in control of their own allocations enables them to direct their own services and supports.

Direct funding can offer families a degree of financial support and independence, but it is often only a portion of what they need. Furthermore, it places on them the ultimate responsibility for care of family members with disabilities, which some people with disabilities and families want but others do not. For adults with intellectual or developmental disabilities who wish to spend more years with their families, direct funding is highly desirable, but it also has the potential to restrict a family member with a disability from moving out of the family home. That is, if a family needs the income associated with the member with a disability, there may be pressure from family members to keep the member with the disability residing in the family home. The implications of providing funding directly to individuals and families have not yet been critically examined in any depth but will undoubtedly be an area of great interest in the coming years.

CHALLENGES FOR THE FIELD

The field of intellectual and developmental disabilities has faced challenges for many decades and will continue to do so in the future. Nine important questions that emerge from the broader trends described in this chapter are presented here as examples (adapted from Brown & Percy, 2003).

1. What Is Meant by *Intellectual and Developmental Disabilities?*

The terms used, and the meanings attached to those terms, change over time (see Chapter 1 for full details). For the allocation of special services and for access to generic community services and supports such as education, health care, and employment, it is helpful to know specifically what the

terms *intellectual disability* and *developmental disabilities* mean. It is especially important to know this if resources are scarce or if priorities are shifting. Two interesting questions are the degree to which those in the field need to understand the operational meanings of terms such as *intellectual disability* and *developmental disabilities* for the purposes of supporting people with disabilities effectively and in cost-efficient ways, and whether this need differs according to the purpose for which the terms are being used.

2. How Can Useful Information and Tracking Systems Be Developed?

Most countries have not implemented a systematic mechanism to track questions such as the following:

- How many people within a given population meet diagnostic criteria for intellectual or developmental disabilities? Of this group, how many meet criteria but currently do not have a diagnosis?

- How many people can services systems identify as having needs?

- What kinds of services do these people need and use?

- Where do they live?

- What are their age ranges?

- What are their levels of need?

- What are their sources of financial support?

- What is the degree to which they have family and other social support?

- What are their living conditions?

In addition, in most Western countries there are few mechanisms to track two groups of people who are important to disability services. First, people who will probably require support in the future are not being clearly identified for purposes of future planning. For example, school systems vary considerably in regard to the extent to which they plan for ways to address the needs of students once they leave school. There is also great diversity in the extent to which adult community service provider organizations plan in advance for those who are preparing to leave school and need community support as adults (see Chapter 37). Second, many people have been assisted by the service system in the past but no longer require support because they have learned independent living skills or are supported by family or others. For the most part, these people simply become lost to the service system. It would be helpful to track these people because valuable indicators of the success of the service system include successful independent living and the degree to which family and community support can be put in place.

Following these types of information over time and analyzing trends would help 1) plan services and resources needed for what people will require in the future, 2) identify those who need but are not receiving any support because they are not known to the service system, 3) develop a better understanding of how people with intellectual and developmental disabilities can be supported by other sectors outside the education and service systems, and 4) provide a better measure of evaluation and accountability for public funds used in disability services.

3. What Are the Service Implications of People Living Longer?

There is a growing trend for people with intellectual and developmental disabilities to live much longer, due to improved living conditions and better medical treatment. Medical and technological advances also make it increasingly possible for older adults or those who are medically fragile to participate in community life much more than was possible even in the late 1980s. Sometimes, this requires special equipment or additional personnel. A challenge is to find ways to provide support to people who are living longer and to identify ways to balance the need for this support with the needs of others with disabilities.

4. What Are the Implications of New Genetic Knowledge?

Genetic knowledge has been increasing at a dramatic rate since the mid-1990s. Such knowledge has helped society to understand a number of causes that result in disability and to shape medical and social support interventions, but it has opened up the need for new interventions and supports and has suggested numerous ethical challenges. It appears that there is a strong need for increased expertise within the field of intellectual and developmental disabilities especially to guide how new disability-related genetic knowledge should be generated; understand the utility of information generated for the field; help disseminate new genetic knowledge in ways that are understandable to people with disabilities, their families, and disability practitioners; and provide leadership in developing practical applications of new genetic knowledge.

5. How Effective Can Individualized Funding Be?

Although most countries have no comprehensive programs for individualized funding, a number of important shifts have tied funding closer to individual needs. The shift toward individualized funding may continue in the future, but major challenges will need to be faced if it is to be equitable (to respond fairly to the needs of individuals with intellectual and developmental disabilities and their families) and accountable (to ensure that the public's money is well spent). As a starting point, a method will have to be developed to assess needs and services in a standard way. This will involve determining what services should cost, who should receive them, and the extent to which public money should be used to fund them.

6. Are Services an Entitlement?

There is a growing sense, especially among parents, that services for their children with disabilities and services for families that support children with such disabilities should be an entitlement. Parents are often surprised to discover that in most countries, they are not entitled by law or policy to most services but rather that they may gain access to those that are provided and available, assuming that they meet the qualifying criteria. The difficulty is that the services that are available are not always those that are needed, there are long waitlists for services in some areas, and people with intellectual or developmental disabilities do not always meet the qualifying criteria (e.g., the ability to travel independently is sometimes a criterion for access to vocational support programs). A discussion of entitlement to services is particularly timely in view of the shift toward shared responsibility among government, communities, and families. In practice, this has meant that families assume the primary responsibility for their children while they are still in school, with support services provided by various community agencies and government funding sources. Increasingly, families are continuing to assume the primary responsibility for young adults and even, in many cases, older adults with intellectual and developmental disabilities as well—usually without entitlement to services—and the degree to which families are willing or able to do this needs to be carefully monitored.

7. To What Extent Does the Public Have a Right to Know How Service Funds Are Used?

A challenge that is related to individualized funding and increased responsibility for families is accountability for the specific ways public funds are used. It is reasonable for funding sources to want to know how effective their funds are in helping individuals and families to reach identified goals. On the other hand, interesting ethical questions arise, such as whether individuals with disabilities who receive disability financial support, individuals or families who receive tax deductions, or families who receive funding under a government-funded program should choose how the money is used or if it should be used in ways specified by the funder. For example, Josef receives a government-sponsored disability pension, to which he is entitled by legislation, but he lives with his family and his family members support his daily living needs financially (i.e., they buy his food and clothing and do not charge him rent). He spends most of his money on his own entertainment and traveling with groups around the country. Should Josef be free to spend public money in this way, or should he only receive it if he needs it to pay for basic needs?

8. Can Life-Span Planning Be Initiated?

It appears at the present time that it would be very helpful to develop a system of life-span (long-range) planning for people with intellectual and developmental disabilities. The current emphasis is more on providing services than on identifying children with disabilities and planning for their needs over their life span. Making the shift to life-span planning will require considerable restructuring of services and current ways of thinking.

A shift toward life-span planning should spark considerable creativity in both policy and practice. For example, it should encourage creative and individualized solutions to planning for future financial needs (e.g., savings accounts, trust funds, property) and other personal support needs (e.g., designating family members who will assume responsibility at various stages of life, connecting individuals with needed community supports). Policy will need to set the environment for such activities, and the practical work will need to be done by community service organizations, self-advocacy, family advocacy, and other groups, as well as by individuals with disabilities and their family members.

9. What Are the Best Models of Support?

At one time, it was assumed that a good model of support was for people with disabilities to live in large state-run institutions. As noted previously, this view has been in decline for many years. As of this chapter's writing in 2016, only a small minority of people advocate for maintaining institutions as part of a jurisdiction's service delivery system. The vast majority contend that adults with intellectual and developmental disabilities must have opportunities to live in community homes or supported independent living, or that public funds should be used to support families with members with disabilities living in the family home. However, "place of residence" will not, by itself, ensure opportunities for a meaningful, fulfilling life. As Thompson (2013) pointed out, people with intellectual and developmental disabilities

> Have the same basic wants and desires as everyone else. They certainly want to be safe and happy, but they also want their rights acknowledged and respected. They want a home to live in; and, a home is not simply a physical structure that provides shelter from the elements. They want meaningful work and other opportunities to make contributions to the world. They want all kinds of relationships with people with and without disabilities, because people without relationships are lonely. They want family relationships, close friends, romantic friends, casual friends, etc. They want meaningful ways to spend their time, and that includes hobbies in which to immerse themselves as well as opportunities for life-long learning. They want choices so that their lives are unique, and they do not want a series of "canned programs" targeted only to people with disabilities. (p. 516)

Therefore, residential options must be considered in the context of a person's entire life. Just because a person lives in a community home or in his or her family's home does not mean he or she has access to meaningful work, a full range of relationships, learning opportunities, and other aspects associated with a high quality of life. It remains an ongoing challenge for the field to put into practice models that best enhance the lives of those it supports. In the meantime, it is important to assess current models in an ongoing way. For example, although some people may want to live with their families or live alone in their own home, other people might be lonely in such situations and have a more fulfilling life if they lived with several housemates. Although a return to large, congregate institutional settings should most certainly be rejected, there is a need to better understand how to identify an ideal size of home for different individuals and not simply assume that "smaller is always better."

In doing this, a challenge that must be addressed is how to take into account the views of people with intellectual and developmental disabilities themselves. An additional challenge for service providers and families in particular is how to react if the views of people with disabilities differ from the principles of current best models of care and support or if they contradict the wishes and values of supporting family members. Alternative models of support need to extend beyond those traditionally provided by disability-specific programs. These, too, will pose some interesting questions and challenges for the field. Some examples include the following:

- People with disabilities have numerous health problems and needs associated with growing older (see Chapters 44 and 49). To what degree should these needs be addressed by general health services rather than services funded by disability-specific resources? For example, should older people with intellectual and developmental disabilities who need ongoing care live in group homes, nursing homes, or other facilities?

- Some types of disabilities do not typically meet criteria for access to the long-term care system. Should disability services deal with dementia and other mental health problems rather than incorporating dementia into generic services?

- In most developed countries at the beginning of the 21st century, it is not always clearly specified which services are funded by disability ministries or departments and which are funded by other ministries or departments, such as the department of health or the department of education. The general approach appears to be that if a problem that involves intellectual and developmental disability is not picked up by another ministry or department, then the disability service may address it.

- Various government entities and various nongovernment bodies, both private and public, provide infrastructures for similar types of supports. The question of how to maximize the efficient use of financial and human resources is an ongoing challenge.

- Disability service organizations could evolve to work in partnership with government, other community services and resources, and families in a variety of ways.

- Although advocacy by people with disabilities and their families should be encouraged, it is important to ensure that the strength of one's advocacy skills or power of one's advocacy network does not lead to extreme inequalities in the distribution of public funds or quality of service. There will always be finite resources, and if those who can advocate most effectively are able to secure far more resources and far better services than those who either by nature are less assertive or simply come from "low power" families that do not have the skills or the confidence to battle with a jurisdiction's service system, the result will be a grossly unfair service system benefiting people who are assertive and well-connected at the expense of those who are not.

SUMMARY

The field of intellectual and developmental disabilities has a set of issues that have been relatively stable over time, but others have been influenced by current sociopolitical trends and trends within the disability field. Within developed countries, there has been an emphasis since the 1980s on economic prosperity and economic accountability at the cost of stressing social justice, although some progress has been made. There have been policy shifts toward supporting individuals, families, and communities; providing for those most in need; and sharing responsibility with communities and families. The international field of intellectual and developmental disabilities itself has been experiencing a philosophical and funding pause but, at the same time, has generated important new knowledge and ideas, especially those related to conceptualizing disability in a more functional manner, community living, self-advocacy, and PCP approaches. Overall, the field of intellectual and developmental disabilities has made steady progress since the 1980s, although not as dramatic as progress made during the 1960s and 1970s. Opportunities for people with disabilities are far better today than they were in the past. Still, there are a number of long-standing challenges and multiple new challenges that have arisen due to recent trends.

FOR FURTHER THOUGHT AND DISCUSSION

1. To what degree should trends within the field of intellectual and developmental disabilities change in response to broader national and international trends?

2. How important is it for services for people with intellectual and developmental disabilities to be based on strong philosophical principles?

3. Debate the pros and cons of taking a person-centered approach. Illustrate your points by referring to people with intellectual and developmental disabilities or their families.

4. How feasible is it to implement a broad program of direct funding to families of people with intellectual and developmental disabilities? Illustrate by describing families you know.

5. Putting current models of service and support aside, create a fictional system of service and support that addresses the problems and challenges identified in this chapter. In doing so, be sure to develop ideas that are practical and that work in the best interests of people with intellectual and developmental disabilities.

REFERENCES

Amado, A.N., Stancliffe, R.J., McCarron, M., & McCallion, P. (2013). Social inclusion and community participation of individuals with intellectual/developmental disabilities. *Intellectual and Developmental Disabilities, 51,* 360–375.

Americans with Disabilities Act (ADA) of 1990, PL 101-336, 42 U.S.C. §§ 12101 *et seq.*

Attina, T.M., & Trasande, L. (2013). Economic costs of childhood lead exposure in low- and middle-income countries. *Environmental Health Perspectives, 121,* 1097–1102.

Braddock, D., Emerson, E., Felce, D.,& Stancliffe, R.J. (2001). Living circumstances of children and adults with mental retardation or developmental disabilities in the United States, Canada, England and Wales, and Australia. *Mental Retardation and Developmental Disabilities Research Reviews, 7,* 115–121.

Braddock, D., Hemp, R., Rizzolo, M.C., Tanis, E.S., Haffer, L., Lulinski, A., & Wu, J. (2013). *State of the states in developmental disabilities 2013.* Washington, DC: American Association on Intellectual and Developmental Disabilities.

Brown, I., & Percy, M. (2003). Current trends and issues in developmental disabilities in Ontario. In I. Brown & M. Percy (Eds.), *Developmental disabilities in Ontario* (2nd ed., pp. 43–55). Toronto, Canada: Ontario Association on Developmental Disabilities.

DiRita, P.A., Parmenter, T.R., & Stancliffe, R.J. (2008). Utility, economic rationalism and the circumscription of agency. *Journal of Intellectual Disability Research, 52,* 618–625.

Dumeresq, M., & Lawton, S. (2003). The role of the professional supporting people with developmental disabilities. In I. Brown & M. Percy (Eds.), *Developmental disabilities in Ontario* (2nd ed., pp. 493–507). Toronto, Canada: Ontario Association on Developmental Disabilities.

Emerson, E. (2004). Poverty and children with intellectual disabilities in the world's richer countries. *Journal of Intellectual and Developmental Disability, 29,* 319–338.

Gharaibeh, H., Oweis, A., & Hamad, K.H. (2010). Nurses' and midwives' knowledge and perceptions of their role in genetic teaching. *International Nursing Review, 57,* 435–442. doi: 10.1111/j.1466-7657.2010.00814.x

Hewitt, A., & Larson, S. (2007). The direct support workforce in community supports to individuals with developmental disabilities: Issues, implications, and promising practices. *Mental Retardation and Developmental Disabilities Research Reviews, 13,* 178–187. doi: 10.1002/mrdd.20151

Kaposy, C. (2013). A disability critique of the new prenatal test for down syndrome. *Kennedy Institute of Ethics Journal, 23*(4), 299–324.

Leake, D.W. (2012). Self-determination requires social capital, not just skills and knowledge. *Review of Disability Studies, 8,* 34–43.

Lemay, R.A. (2009). Deinstitutionalization of people with developmental disabilities: A review of the literature. *Canadian Journal of Community Mental Health, 28,* 181–194.

Loane, M., Morris, J.K., Addor, M.-C., Arriola, L., Budd, J., Foray, B.,...Dolk, H. (2013). Twenty-year trends in the prevalence of Down syndrome and other trisomies in Europe: Impact of maternal age and prenatal screening. *European Journal of Human Genetics, 21,* 27–33.

Mansell, J., & Beadle-Brown, J. (2010). Deinstitutionalisation and community living: Position statement of the Comparative Policy and Practice Special Interest Research Group of the International Association for the Scientific Study of Intellectual Disabilities. *Journal of Intellectual Disability Research, 54,* 104–112.

O'Brien, C.L., O'Brien, J., & Mount, B. (1997). Person-centered planning has arrived...or has it? *Mental Retardation, 35,* 480–484.

Osborne, J.G. (2005). Person-centered planning: A *faux fixe* in the service of humanism? In J.W. Jacobson, R.M. Foxx, & J.A. Mulick (Eds.), *Controversial therapies for developmental disabilities: Fad, fashion, and science in professional practice* (pp. 313–329). Mahwah, NJ: Lawrence Erlbaum.

Palmer, S.B., Wehmeyer, M.L., Davies, D.K., & Stock, S.E., (2012). Family members' reports of the technology use of family members with intellectual and developmental disabilities. *Journal of Intellectual Disability Research, 56,* 402–414.

Parker, S.E., Mai, C.T., Canfield, M.A., Wang, R.R., Meyer, R.E., Anderson, P.,...Correa, A. (2010). Updated national birth prevalence estimates for selected birth defects in the United States, 2004–2006. *Birth Defects Research Part A Clinical and Molecular Teratology, 88,* 1008–1016.

Rauch, S.A., & Lanphear, B.P. (2012). Prevention of disability in children: Elevating the role of the environment. *The Future of Children, 22,* 193–217.

Riches, V.C., Parmenter, T.R., Llewellyn, G., Hindmarsh, G. & Chan, J. (2009). I-CAN: A new instrument to classify support needs for people with disability: Part I. *Journal of Applied Research in Intellectual Disabilities, 22,* 326-339.

Shaw, J.G., & Friedman, J.R. (2011). Iron deficiency anemia: Focus on infectious diseases in lesser developed countries. *Anemia, 2011,* 1–10. doi:10.1155/2011/260380

Siperstein, G.N., Parker, R.C., & Drascher, M. (2013). National snapshot of adults with intellectual disabilities in the labor force. *Journal of Vocational Rehabilitation, 39,* 157–166.

Sommeiller, E., & Price, M. (2014). *The increasing unequal states of America: Income inequality by state, 1917–2011.* Washington, DC: Economic Analysis and Research Network.

Thompson, J.R. (2013). Presidential address—race to catch the future. *Intellectual and Developmental Disabilities, 51,* 512–521.

Thompson, J.R., Bryant, B.R., Campbell, E.M., Craig, E.M., Hughes, C.M., Rotholz, D.A.,…Wehmeyer, M.L. (2004). *Supports Intensity Scale Users Manual.* Washington, DC: American Association on Mental Retardation.

United Nations. (2014). *Convention on the rights of people with disabilities.* Retrieved from http://www.un.org /disabilities/convention/conventionfull.shtml

United Nations Treaty Collection. (2014). *Status as at: 28-06-14 05:00:54 EDT. 15. Convention on the rights of persons with disabilities.* Retrieved from https://treaties.un.org /Pages/ViewDetails.aspx?src=TREATY&mtdsg_no=IV -15&chapter=4&lang=en

Verdugo, M.A., Navas, P., Gomez, L.E., & Schalock, R.L. (2012). The concept of quality of life and its role in enhancing human rights in the field of intellectual disability. *Journal of Intellectual Disability Research, 56,* 1036–1045.

World Health Organization. (1980). *International Classification of Impairments, Disabilities, and Handicaps (ICIDH).* Geneva, Switzerland: Author.

World Health Organization. (2001). *International Classification of Functioning, Disability and Health (ICF).* Geneva, Switzerland: Author.

5

International Human Rights and Intellectual Disability

Paula Campos Pinto, Marcia H. Rioux, and Bengt Lindqvist

WHAT YOU WILL LEARN

- Comprehensive nature of the United Nations international human rights system
- Implementation obligations of countries that sign international documents (States Parties) and difficulties monitoring progress
- The rights of people with disabilities as set out by the *Convention on the Rights of Persons with Disabilities* (2006)
- How the *Convention on the Rights of Persons with Disabilities* can be applied effectively to people with intellectual disabilities

Human rights are principles for ensuring that people are able to live with dignity, free from fear, harassment, or discrimination. They allow people to have choices and opportunities to participate fully in society as individuals and members of communities. All people have human rights just because they are human. Values held and advanced throughout recorded human history and centuries of sociopolitical development show that human rights cover all areas of life. Among the most important of these are the right to life; the right not to be subject to torture; legal rights, such as equal protection of the law;

political rights, such as freedom of expression and the right to take part in government; and the rights to form a family, to own property, to work, to receive education and health care, and to participate in the cultural life of communities.

This chapter explains human rights, particularly in terms of disability. The discussion begins with an outline of the various international human rights treaties—including the *Convention on the Rights of Persons with Disabilities* (CRPD), the first human rights treaty of the 21st century and the most relevant to the field of disability. It then examines areas of rights that are particularly relevant to people with intellectual disabilities. The chapter concludes by emphasizing the importance of monitoring to promote and advance human rights.

THE INTERNATIONAL HUMAN RIGHTS SYSTEM

Human rights are set out in writing in legal documents that obligate governments to respect, protect, and fulfill their basic standards. The legal human rights documents at the international level are international human rights treaties.

Although the philosophical principles behind it are much older, the first treaty in the modern system of international human rights began when the member States of the United Nations proclaimed the *Universal Declaration of Human Rights* on December 10, 1948. This declaration emerged primarily as the international response to the discovery of the horrors of the concentration camps in Eastern Europe at the end

---

This chapter uses the term *persons with disabilities* (vs. *people with disabilities*) in keeping with the terminology used in the *Convention on the Rights of Persons with Disabilities* (2006).

The authors are grateful to Anne Carbert, who contributed as a coauthor to the content of this chapter in the first edition.

of World War II. The Universal Declaration remains a powerful statement of the basic rights of all human beings. It is an enunciation of the rights and freedoms essential for life with dignity and well-being.

In the decades following the adoption of the Universal Declaration, the UN created more detailed human rights obligations by adopting successive international treaties. There are now nine treaties central to the UN human rights system, the most recent of which is focused on disability:

1. *International Covenant on Economic, Social and Cultural Rights* (1966)

2. *International Covenant on Civil and Political Rights* (1966)

3. *International Convention on the Elimination of All Forms of Racial Discrimination* (1965)

4. *Convention on the Elimination of All Forms of Discrimination Against Women (CEDAW)* (1979)

5. *Convention Against Torture and Other Cruel, Inhuman or Degrading Treatment or Punishment* (1984)

6. *Convention on the Rights of the Child (CRC)* (1989)

7. *International Convention on the Protection of the Rights of All Migrant Workers and Members of Their Families* (1990)

8. *International Convention for the Protection of All Persons from Enforced Disappearance* (2006)

9. *Convention on the Rights of Persons with Disabilities* (2006)

See the web site of the Office of the UN High Commissioner for Human Rights (n.d.a) for additional information on these treaties.

With the exception of the *International Convention on the Protection of the Rights of All Migrant Workers and Members of Their Families* and the *International Convention for the Protection of All Persons from Enforced Disappearance,* all these treaties have supplementary optional agreements, called *Optional Protocols,* which suggest preferred obligations further to the central text of the treaties for governments that subscribe to them.

Country Obligations to International Treaties

By becoming parties to international human rights treaties, governments of countries (referred to as *states* in international law) around the world have assumed legal obligations to uphold the human rights that are laid out in the Conventions and to ensure that all of their citizens enjoy these rights without discrimination. These obligations are threefold: to respect, to protect, and to fulfill the human rights of their citizens. *To respect* means that the government must not violate a right. This may be accomplished by refraining from intervention whenever government's actions are likely to give way to a violation of a particular human right. *To protect* requires that the government takes action in order to prevent violations of rights by state and nonstate actors. In the classical approach, the protection of human rights strictly involved dealing with individual claims against the state; current conceptions, however, extend this protection against all potential violators, with the state still holding the duty of assuring that all rights are available to all citizens. For instance, some persons with disabilities have been victims of abuse and discrimination by their family members and personal caregivers, and protection against these private forms of violence requires a broad understanding of the meaning of the state's obligations to protect human rights. Finally, the obligation *to fulfill* entails states' duties to take positive action in the form of legislative, administrative, judicial, and other measures to ensure that the right in question is implemented to the greatest extent possible. Although this obligation is equally valid to all governments signatory of any international human rights treaty, authors usually agree that standards are higher for states with more resources than for those with fewer resources (Alston & Quinn, 1987; Eide, 2001; Nowak, 2003). Indeed, a very important concept in international human rights is the idea of "progressive realization." It recognizes that even though a country has ratified a Convention, it may not be able to implement every article as soon as it ratifies. The expectation is that the country will act in good faith and will work toward full ratification over a number of years or even decades. In other words, a country commits itself to moving in the direction of full compliance.

Numerous international documents and declarations, some of which are referred to throughout this chapter, reinforce the implementation of these major international human rights treaties by emphasizing state responsibilities to guarantee human rights. In many instances, these agreements highlight particular issues of concern such as the rights of women (CEDAW), children (CRC), and people with disabilities (CRPD). The importance of a convention such as the one on disability is that although it does not create any new rights, it carefully articulates what rights mean for the group of people worldwide who are marginalized and disadvantaged by their disability. It provides a great deal of information about how the rights apply specifically to individuals with disabilities.

Monitoring Implementation of Human Rights by States Parties

Human rights treaties are supported by mechanisms to monitor the implementation of the human rights they set out to guarantee. These mechanisms include committees that review states' own progress reports on their implementation of treaty rights. For example, the Committee on the Rights of Persons with Disabilities is a body of independent experts that monitors the implementation of the 2006 CRPD by the States Parties (countries that have signed international treaties). All States Parties have agreed to a requirement to submit regular reports to this Committee on how the rights are being implemented within their countries. States Parties are required to report initially within 2 years of signing the Convention and thereafter every 4 years. The Committee examines each report submitted and makes suggestions and general recommendations that it considers appropriate. The Committee on the Rights of Persons with Disabilities, like some of the other committees, also receives reports from disability rights organizations that provide their perspectives about the ways in which their rights are being respected or not respected. These "shadow" or "alternative" reports are important to the Committee reviewing a country's compliance with the CRPD, as they give the view of the people who are most affected. The Committee takes these reports very seriously, recognizing that the implementation of any Convention will look different to governments and to people who live in their communities (Rioux, Pinto, & Parek, 2015). Finally, individuals and groups from countries that have subscribed to the Optional Protocol to the CRPD can submit to the Committee complaints alleging that their rights have been violated.

The UN Commission on Human Rights also performs a monitoring role. Comprised of 53 of the countries that are members of the UN, the commission meets every year to consider global human rights issues. It has the power to create mechanisms and special procedures to promote the implementation of human rights, and it appoints independent experts to investigate important human rights themes such as health, food, education, adequate housing, torture, violence against women, and disability. The mandates of the current Special Rapporteur on the Rights of Persons with Disabilities, for instance, include, among others, developing regular dialogue with states and other relevant stakeholders for the exchange and promotion of good practices related to the realization of the rights of persons with disabilities; receiving and exchanging information and communications on violations of the rights of persons with disabilities; making recommendations and providing technical assistance on how to better promote and protect the rights of persons with disabilities; raising awareness of the rights of persons with disabilities; and reporting annually to the Human Rights Council and the UN General Assembly.

Despite the existence of all these mechanisms, monitoring and enforcing international laws and agreements remains a challenge for a number of reasons (Chambers, 2007). First, disability rights legislation often lacks enforcement mechanisms at the state (country) level. Second, monitoring bodies can make recommendations, but they lack the power to impose actual sanctions. Third, access to international courts is only possible after exhausting all options within the domestic judicial system, which makes international courts not readily accessible to individuals with disabilities.

HUMAN RIGHTS SPECIFIC TO COUNTRIES

In addition to human rights set out in international treaties, most countries of the world have numerous laws, documents, and policies that specify the human rights of the citizens of their countries. The main purpose of country-specific systems of human rights is to establish systems within the legal contexts of each country for implementing the obligations of international treaties and, at the same time, to implement the specifications of the country's own human rights. In many cases, a country's own human rights are the same as, or are complementary to, the human rights described in international documents, but in other cases, they may extend beyond them (e.g., the adoption by some countries of legal same-sex marriage). Country-specific systems of human rights may also create mechanisms for citizens to seek remedies if they consider their rights to be violated.

Within countries, formal legal statements about human rights are found in constitutions, bills of rights, and human rights legislation. For example, in Canada there is a Charter of Rights and Freedoms, part of the Canadian Constitution, which says that all people have the right to equality before and under the law (i.e., in process and outcome) even if they have a physical or mental disability. The importance of this legal inclusion in the highest law of the country is that legal action can be undertaken to challenge laws in Canada that do not make sure that equality is being applied.

In the United States, as well, a number of laws exist to protect the rights of individuals with disabilities. The Americans with Disabilities Act (ADA) of 1990 (PL 101-336) prohibits discrimination on the basis of disability in employment, state and local government, public accommodations, commercial facilities, transportation, and telecommunications. In addition, the U.S. government has enacted specific legislation to ensure the full participation of persons with disabilities in all spheres of life. These include, among others, the Telecommunications Act of 1996 (PL 104-104), which provides for accessibility to all telecommunications equipment and services; the Individuals with Disabilities Education Improvement Act of 2004 (PL 108-446; updated from the original Education for All Handicapped Children Act of 1975, PL 94-142), which makes available to all eligible children with disabilities a free appropriate public education to meet their individual needs; and the Architectural Barriers Act of 1968 (PL 90-480), which imposes federal standards for physical accessibility to all buildings and facilities designed, constructed, or altered with federal funds or leased by a federal agency (Chambers, 2007).

In many countries, disability rights protections may also emerge from rulings within the legal system. For example, in the United States in 1999, the Supreme Court issued the *Olmstead v. L.C.* decision. In *Olmstead*, the Court ruled that Title II of the Americans with Disabilities Act (ADA) prohibits the unnecessary institutionalization of people with disabilities. Justice Ruth Bader Ginsburg, delivering the opinion of the Court, wrote that

> States are required to place persons with mental disabilities in community settings rather than in institutions when the State's treatment professionals have determined that community placement is appropriate, the transfer from institutional care to a less restrictive setting is not opposed by the affected individual, and the placement can be reasonably accommodated, taking into account the resources available to the State and the needs of others with mental disabilities. (p. 22)

The Supreme Court ruled that services to people with disabilities must be provided "in the most integrated setting possible" and that Ms. Curtis and Ms. Wilson were entitled to community options that would allow them to live outside nursing homes. *Olmstead* is a historic decision that opens the door for individuals with disabilities and their families to request and expect a full range of community services as alternatives to services provided in institutionalized settings.

HUMAN RIGHTS AND DISABILITY

A central principle of international human rights treaties—one that is formalized in the CRPD (2006)—is that human rights for people with disabilities, sometimes referred to as *disability rights*, are not separate from the rights specified for all people (Rioux, Basser, & Jones, 2011). Individuals with disabilities are people with the same rights as all others. In addition to general human rights, both the Convention and specific laws within countries set out more specific interpretations of rights, policies, and programs for persons with disabilities for the purposes of providing more specific protection against discrimination and ensuring better quality of life.

Persons with disabilities have not always enjoyed equal rights and still do not enjoy full equal rights at the beginning of the 21st century. In an important case related to sterilization of a young woman with an intellectual disability in Canada, the court held the following:

> There are other reasons for approaching an application for sterilization of a mentally incompetent person with utmost caution. To begin with, the decision involves values in an area where our social history clouds our vision and encourages many to perceive the mentally handicapped as somewhat less than human. This attitude has been aided and abetted by now discredited eugenic theories whose influence was felt in this country as well as the United States. (Rioux et al., 2011, pp. 251–252)

In other words, the Canadian Supreme Court recognized that contemporary actions must be put in the context of historical attitudes that sheltered discrimination.

Times do change, as do attitudes and recognition of the underlying worth of all people. One encouraging discussion is the exploration of the legal concept of *incapacity*, which raises many questions in terms of individual rights. There is now a welcome move to rethink that concept and think instead about *supported decision making*. These issues raise new challenges in law and policy. There are still full-service institutions in both more affluent and less affluent countries of the world in which people are housed or, as some would say, warehoused. The Disability Rights International (DRI) web site (http://www.driadvocacy.org/about), for example, discusses how there are still many lingering ideas from the past when it was assumed that people with disabilities should receive treatment, be marginalized in private residences, or be maltreated in other ways, all without rights. For example, there are children with autism and other developmental disabilities who still receive electric shock treatment as a form of behavior therapy in some places, some children are housed in private residences or institutions with little or no official oversight and there are even suggestions that some children with disabilities have been "trafficked" into forced labor or sex slavery (DRI, 2014).

The shift toward the implementation of equal human rights within disability—persons with disabilities fully enjoying their human rights, recognizing that disability rights are human rights that are specified for all people—has been strongly influenced by voices from the critical disability movement. This movement recognizes that there have been barriers to equal rights in the past: legal barriers, such as laws that discriminate; conceptual barriers, such as values, attitudes, and perceptions of disability that support marginalization; and neglect barriers, which include a wide number of measures that are not taken that otherwise would act to help include all citizens, especially those who are currently marginalized. The critical disability movement seeks, among other things, to remove such barriers. It also seeks to shift past conceptualizations of disability, and the unhelpful social responses to those conceptualizations, to positive conceptualizations of disability that reflect the lived experience and social contributions of persons with disabilities and the active role of societies in ensuring that all citizens enjoy all human rights equally.

It has become increasingly common in recent years to recognize persons with disabilities as full citizens entitled to equal rights. Viewing persons with disabilities in this way, as the CRPD affirms, is a radical conceptual change for many people, organizations, and governments (Rioux et al., 2011). However, the exclusion so often experienced by persons with disabilities is now increasingly being seen as the result of social and environmental failures to acknowledge and respond constructively to difference. People are realizing that the barriers faced by persons with disabilities violate their human rights, perpetuate social isolation and exclusion, and place persons with disabilities at greater risk of discrimination, abuse, and poverty (e.g., see Oliver, 1990). From this perspective, it is no longer the responsibility of an individual with disability to either adapt or face exclusion. The trend is for societies and governments to embrace everyone and create policies, laws, programs, and services that acknowledge difference and respect each person's dignity. As a UN's study on human rights and disability stated,

> Seeing persons with disabilities as subjects rather than objects entails giving them access to the full benefits of basic freedoms that most people take for granted and doing so in a way that is respectful and accommodating of their difference. (Quinn & Degener, 2002, p. 13)

Governments are responsible for implementing the human rights of all citizens. This means the onus is on the governments to find ways to end widespread discrimination and to promote the full participation of persons with disabilities. It is now clear that many government practices and policies violate the human rights of persons with disabilities by explicitly preventing them from exercising their rights or by failing to address their needs. In the context of increased human rights awareness, and particularly since the adoption of the CRPD, governments can no longer justify denying children with disabilities education, preventing persons with disabilities from forming families, prohibiting ownership of property or access to health care, and denying other rights and freedoms the rest of humanity takes for granted.

A human rights approach presents the promise and challenge of creating a society that respects the dignity and equality of each person, regardless of differences among individuals. Internationally accepted human rights standards, as articulated in the CRPD and other international treaties and declarations, have become critical tools for disability advocacy and for responding to injustice.

The Emergence of a Human Rights Approach to Disability

The movement that culminated in 2006 with the adoption by the UN General Assembly of the CRPD developed gradually over the previous several decades. In 1969, organizations of people with disabilities in both sides of the Atlantic began to articulate how the design and structure of societies, as well as the general attitudes toward persons with disabilities, severely limited their opportunities. As this new perspective gathered support, the UN designated 1981 as the International Year of Disabled Persons. The International Year focused global attention on the situation of the estimated 600 million persons with disabilities around the world and led to the adoption of the *World Programme of Action Concerning Disabled Persons* (UN General Assembly, 1982). The World Programme was a strategy to promote the equalization of opportunities to achieve the full participation of persons with disabilities in social life and national development.

The World Programme created momentum for many significant developments in the 1990s. First, more specific international commitments were adopted to promote and protect the rights of persons with disabilities, chief among them the *Standard Rules on the Equalization of Opportunities for Persons with Disabilities,* adopted by the UN General Assembly in 1993. These international documents drew attention to the rights and abuses experienced by persons with disabilities and the policies and actions needed to protect and promote their rights. The Standard Rules clearly stipulated that governments are responsible for taking steps to remove obstacles preventing the full participation of persons with disabilities and must act to empower them and to create an accessible society. A Special Rapporteur was appointed to monitor the implementation of the Standard Rules and to report regularly to the UN.

In 1994, the UN Committee on Economic, Social and Cultural Rights—the body of experts responsible for monitoring the implementation of the *International Covenant on Economic, Social and Cultural Rights*—issued a detailed analysis of how the Covenant applies in the context of disability. The Committee's analysis, titled the *General Comment 5: Persons with Disabilities,* explicitly stated that the Covenant applies fully to all members of society, including persons with disabilities, and that discrimination on the basis of disability is prohibited. Furthermore, the Committee required States Parties to take appropriate measures to enable persons with disabilities to overcome any disadvantages resulting from their disabilities that inhibit the enjoyment of Covenant rights. It recognized that this may involve the provision of supports, services, and aids to enable social and economic inclusion, self-determination, and the realization of all rights in the treaty. The Committee's analysis was a historic recognition that persons with disabilities are entitled to equal effective enjoyment of treaty rights without discrimination and that governments have legal responsibilities to ensure the enjoyment of human rights for persons with disabilities.

Another significant development in the emergence of the human rights approach to disability was the first legally binding international treaty specifically devoted to the rights of Persons with disabilities: the *Inter-American Convention on the Elimination of All Forms of Discrimination Against Persons with Disabilities* (2001). This treaty was adopted in 1999 by the Organization of American States and officially came into force in 2001. Under the terms of this treaty, governments agreed to adopt legislation and social, educational, or labor-related measures to fully include persons with disabilities in society. The treaty calls for rehabilitation, education, job training, and other measures to promote the independence and quality of life of persons with disabilities.

At the turn of this century, the UN Commission on Human Rights (1998, 2000) also passed two important resolutions specifically confirming the rights of persons with disabilities. The Commission recognized that inequality or discrimination based on disability violates human rights (Resolution 1998/31). The Commission further called on the High Commissioner for Human Rights to strengthen the protection and monitoring of human rights of persons with disabilities (Resolution 2000/51).

In 2001, the Office of the High Commissioner for Human Rights published a study on human rights and disability (Quinn & Degener, 2002). This study reviewed the obligations of States Parties under international human rights treaties and explained how the relevant enforcement mechanisms were working in the context of disability. More important, it argued for the adoption of a thematic convention on the rights of persons with disabilities. In December 2001, building on the support for a human rights approach to disability, the UN General Assembly accepted the Mexican government's proposal and established an Ad Hoc Committee tasked with the development of a comprehensive international convention to promote and protect the rights of persons with disabilities. The Ad Hoc Committee met eight times between 2002 and 2006, and on December 13, 2006, the UN General Assembly adopted by consensus the CRPD and its Optional Protocol. (The Optional Protocol establishes procedures for strengthening and monitoring the implementation of the Convention, notably an individual communications procedure allowing individuals or groups of individuals to make claims as victims of violations of rights and an inquiry procedure giving the Committee on the Rights of Persons with Disabilities—a new body established by the Convention—authority to conduct inquiries on disability rights violations.) This first Convention of the new millennium and its Optional Protocol opened up for signature at the UN Headquarters in New York on March 30, 2007, collecting a historic 82 signatures on the opening day. The treaty and protocol entered into force on May 3, 2008, after receiving the 20th ratification by signing countries of the Convention and the 10th ratification of the Optional Protocol.

The *Convention on the Rights of Persons with Disabilities*

The CRPD is a human rights document that reaffirms clearly that all persons with all types of

disabilities must enjoy all human rights and freedoms on an equal basis with others. The Convention does not create new rights. Rather, it clarifies and qualifies how all categories of rights apply to persons with disabilities and identifies areas where protections have to be reinforced or adaptations made for persons with disabilities to effectively exercise their rights.

A cornerstone of the Convention is its conceptualization of disability. Acknowledging in the Preamble that disability is "an evolving concept," the Convention does not offer a definition of disability, instead describing disability in its Article 1 as follows: "Persons with disabilities include those who have long-term physical, mental, intellectual and sensory impairments which in interaction with various barriers may hinder their full and effective participation in society on an equal basis with others" (CRPD, 2006, p. 4). The Convention also reaffirms the indivisibility, interdependence, and interrelatedness of all human rights and fundamental freedoms, and the need for persons with disabilities to be guaranteed their full enjoyment. Figure 5.1 provides an overview of the CRPD's provisions.

The Convention promotes and protects the human rights and freedoms of persons with disabilities in all spheres of life. It enunciates areas where States Parties need to intervene so that persons with disabilities can fully enjoy their rights. These, among

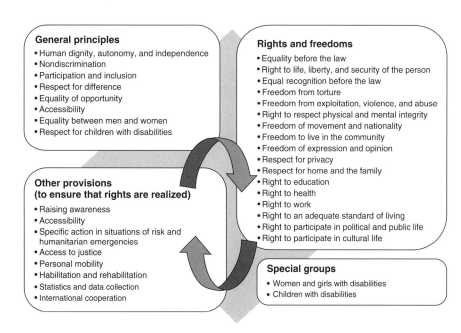

Figure 5.1. Provisions of the *Convention on the Rights of Persons with Disabilities* (2006) at a glance.

others, include raising awareness about disability and disability discrimination; promoting accessibility to the built environment, transportation, and information; ensuring access to justice for persons with disabilities; and undertaking the systematic collection of data on disability issues as a basis for the formulation of policy to implement the treaty. Furthermore, to guide states and other actors in the implementation of these obligations, the Convention spells out eight general principles for a human rights approach to disability. These principles, which can be found in the majority of human rights treaties, are human dignity, autonomy and independence, nondiscrimination, participation and inclusion, equality of opportunities, accessibility, equality between women and men, and respect for the evolving capacities of children. Finally, recognizing that some groups are more exposed than others to multiple and intersecting forms of discrimination based on age, sex, or other grounds, the treaty calls special attention to the situation of women and girls, as well as of children with disabilities.

The full inclusion of disability in the international human rights system represents a milestone in the process of achieving rights for persons with disabilities. For the first time, the rights and fundamental freedoms of persons with disabilities are set out in a single, comprehensive document that precludes discrimination on the basis of disability in all spheres of life: social, economic, civil, political, and cultural. The adoption and entry into force of the Convention means that even States that have not become parties to the Convention, as well as those that have signed it but have not yet concluded the ratification process, now have an internationally agreed-upon outline for the protection and promotion of disability rights. Moreover, the debates generated by the negotiation of the Convention and its final adoption have raised awareness of the multiple forms of discrimination and social injustices experienced by persons with disabilities around the world today and have firmly inscribed disability in the international agenda as a human rights issue.

There is still a long way to go to translate rights-based rhetoric into real improvements that positively affect the lives of persons with disabilities. However, the political and symbolic power of the Convention should not be underestimated. In the hands of individuals with disabilities and disability organizations, the Convention has become a valuable tool to advocate for positive change all around the world. The treaty represents the international acknowledgment that persons with disabilities have been discriminated against, that this discrimination must end, and that such persons must be entitled to the same rights, opportunities, and freedoms as all other citizens.

HUMAN RIGHTS FOR PEOPLE WITH INTELLECTUAL DISABILITIES

To illustrate how human rights relate to the situation of persons with intellectual disabilities, this section looks at four key rights: the right to education, the right to live independently and be included in the community, the right to equality before the law, and rights that are particularly relevant to women and girls with intellectual disabilities. For each topic, common experiences of persons with disabilities—collected through Disability Rights Promotion International (DRPI; 2014), an international initiative dedicated to monitoring the rights of persons with disabilities—are connected to specific rights in the CRPD and other international human rights treaties.

Education

First proclaimed in the *Universal Declaration of Human Rights,* the right to education is now found in several UN human rights treaties, including the following:

- *International Covenant on Economic, Social and Cultural Rights,* Article 13

- *Convention on the Rights of the Child,* Articles 28 and 29

- *Convention on the Elimination of All Forms of Discrimination Against Women,* Article 10

- *International Convention on the Elimination of All Forms of Racial Discrimination,* Article 5 (e) (v)

- *Convention on the Rights of Persons with Disabilities,* Article 24

These treaties address access to education as well as the aims and content of education. Human rights principles support accessible public education that includes children with disabilities in general education programs. In the specific context of disability rights, Article 24 of the CRPD affirms the right to education and stresses the need for governments to ensure equal access to an "inclusive education system at all levels" and provide reasonable accommodation and individual support services to

---

Mission of Disability Rights Promotion International

Disability Rights Promotion International (DRPI) is a collaborative project that established a comprehensive, sustainable international system to monitor human rights of people with disabilities. Monitoring involves collecting and verifying information about human rights abuses. Working in partnership with disability organizations, human rights experts, academics, and others advocating for equal rights, DRPI has developed monitoring tools and has trained people with disabilities on five continents to become monitors of disability rights.

To capture the depth and scope of the discrimination faced by people with disabilities, DRPI's activities emphasize the following:

An individual violations focus

- Fact finding with respect to alleged individual violations of the human rights of persons with disabilities

A systems focus

- Studying legislative frameworks to document the way in which laws violate or protect disability rights and to assess how relevant laws are implemented and enforced in order to inform struggles for legislative reform

- Tracking case law before the courts and statutory human rights bodies

- Analyzing general government policies and programs to provide evidence and awareness for change

A media focus

- Tracking media imagery and coverage of disability to document myths and stereotypes perpetuated by media portrayals of people with disabilities and highlight effective reporting of disability issues

- Thorough and accurate data expose the extent of discrimination faced by people with disabilities on a daily basis around the world; such data are useful for advocacy activities— that is, for preparing parallel or shadow reports to United Nations monitoring bodies and for providing documentation for governments to develop policy and plans that include people with disabilities in their societies

For more information and reports on DRPI studies, visit the project web site at http://drpi.research.yorku.ca/.

---

persons with disabilities to facilitate their education. This involves access to the learning of braille, sign language, and other alternative forms of communication. To ensure the realization of education rights, the treaty further calls on States Parties to take appropriate measures to employ teachers with disabilities and other teachers who are qualified in sign language and/or braille, and to train professionals and staff who work at all levels of education (CRPD, 2006).

General Comment 9 of 2007, elaborated by the Committee on the Rights of the Child, reinforces this interpretation by reaffirming that children with disabilities "have the same right to education as all other children and should enjoy this right without any discrimination" and recognizing "the need for modification to school practices and for training of regular teachers to prepare them to teach children with diverse abilities and ensure that they achieve positive educational outcomes" (2007, *General Comment 9*, para. 62). In its analysis, the Committee clearly stated that "inclusive education should be the goal of educating children with disabilities" but the "manner and form of inclusion must be dictated by the individual educational needs of the child" (para. 66). Encouraging team work and mutual support among parents, teachers, and other specialized professionals as the best way to respond to the individual needs of each child with disabilities (para. 63), the Committee recalled that "the education of a child with disability includes the strengthening of positive self-awareness," thus highlighting the role of education in the empowerment of children with disabilities (para. 64).

The right to education is very closely interconnected with the exercise of many other human rights. For example, education enhances enjoyment of the right to work, of rights to political participation, and of the right to take part freely in cultural activities. Education also supports fuller participation in civil society. Thus, barriers faced in gaining access to education have a wide and harmful impact on the lives of persons with disabilities. Yet, this is an area where many persons with disabilities, and particularly persons with intellectual disabilities, face increased challenges.

Data from the World Health Survey shows that respondents with disabilities experience significantly lower rates of primary school completion and fewer mean years of education than respondents without disabilities (WHO, 2011). DRPI monitoring studies have also found that in many countries, children with disabilities do not attend school and receive little or no education at all (to view full reports, see DRPI, 2014). Many of those who do go to school, both in high- and low-income countries, attend separate schools for children with disabilities, are placed in segregated classes in general education schools, or encounter teaching methods and curricula that do not respond to their needs.

The *World Report on Disability* (WHO, 2011) identifies two broad types of barriers to education: systemwide problems and school-based problems. Divided ministerial responsibilities (often with a limited role for the Ministry of Education) and lack of appropriate legislation, policy, and funding hamper the ability of governments to provide education to students with disabilities of the same quality that is offered to all other learners. Rigid approaches to education and assessment, inadequate training of teachers and school staff, physical barriers to school buildings, lack of accessible transportation, negative attitudes toward persons with disabilities, stigmatization, violence, bullying, and abuse are further problems encountered

in schools by many children with disabilities. These barriers may lead some families with students who have disabilities to believe that special schools are the best places for their children's education (WHO, 2011).

Persons with disabilities are entitled to the full enjoyment of their human rights, including the right to education. For persons with intellectual disabilities to enjoy this right, they must have access to education in an inclusive setting, with adequate support, and with teaching methods and content that responds to their particular learning needs and promotes their fullest potential.

Living Arrangements and Inclusion in the Community

Persons with intellectual disabilities typically have little opportunity to freely choose where and with whom they live. As few options exist for affordable, supportive, and independent living, they are often dependent on family members for housing or on other options, including full-service institutions (see Brown, 2014 for a description of commonly available housing options). This compounds their isolation and exclusion from the communities to which they should belong.

Adequate housing is a human right recognized in several treaties as part of the right to an adequate standard of living (food, clothing and housing). For example, this right is found in the following agreements:

- *International Covenant on Economic, Social and Cultural Rights,* Article 11(1)

- *Convention on the Elimination of All Forms of Discrimination Against Women,* Article 14

- *Convention on the Rights of the Child,* Article 27

Having a secure place to live is a central part of human dignity. Indeed, an adequate housing environment is essential to quality of life and well-being (Brown, 2014). The Committee on Economic, Social and Cultural Rights elaborated on the content of the right to adequate housing, stating that "adequate shelter means…adequate privacy, adequate space, adequate security, adequate lighting and ventilation, adequate basic infrastructure, and adequate location with regard to work and basic facilities—all at reasonable cost" (1991; *General Comment 4,* para. 7). The Committee also emphasized that the right to

---

Persons with Intellectual Disability Speak Out

"There is a tremendous amount of discrimination that goes on....When you're in the workplace, you're supposed to be competing against people who don't have mental illness, and you're supposed to be as good as them, and that's difficult, right?" (Canada, 2010; Male, 41 years old)

   "I feel bad because I'm very useless at home, sitting around all day, watching television, listening to music, and I do get bored. And I'd like to get a job, to get my own money, to not depend on anybody." (Montenegro, 2013; Female, 23 years old)

   "My partner, my wife whom I trusted, decided while I was in the hospital, to request my interdiction and seize the goods we had acquired together." (Colombia, 2013; Male, 47 years old)

   "I filed my case of property rights in consultation with disabled people's organizations. I had no one to support [me] in the judiciary process, I couldn't hire solicitors; eventually the court decision couldn't favor me." (Nepal, 2013; Female, 31 years old)

---

housing "cannot be viewed in isolation from other human rights"; the full enjoyment of freedom of expression, freedom of association, freedom of residence, and the right to participate in public decision making are indispensable to the realization of the right to housing (para. 9).

The interrelatedness of the right to housing to other rights is particularly important for persons with disabilities and is explicitly recognized in the CRPD, which states in article 19:

> States Parties to this Convention recognize the equal right of all persons with disabilities to live in the community, with choices equal to others, and shall take effective and appropriate measures to facilitate full enjoyment by persons with disabilities of this right and their full inclusion and participation in the community. (p. 13)

To ensure that persons with disabilities have the opportunity to freely choose their housing and be included in the community, the Convention calls on States Parties to provide "a range of in-home, residential and other community support services" and to guarantee that "community services and facilities for the general population are available on an equal basis to persons with disabilities and are responsive to their needs" (CRPD, 2006, Article 19 [a] and [b]). In other words, the CRPD recognizes that to be able to fully exercise choice in relation to where and with whom to live, persons with disabilities need to secure adequate assistance and an enabling environment. Persons with intellectual disability, for instance, may need an advocate supporting them to handle money or make choices and will only be able to participate if information is provided in easy-to-read and understandable formats. The CRPD Committee asserted

that "accessibility is a precondition for persons with disabilities to live independently and participate fully and equally in society" (2014, *General Comment 2,* para. 1).

DRPI monitoring projects have documented the barriers faced by persons with intellectual disabilities to have control over their lives, live independently, and be included in the community. The lack of appropriate supports, inadequate and unresponsive services, laws and policies contradictory to a rights-based approach, and the pervasive stigmatization of persons with intellectual disabilities are the challenges most often reported, resulting in exclusion, isolation, and the continuing segregation of persons with intellectual disabilities in institutions. Although many countries have undertaken the transition from institutionalized to community care, too often, lack of careful planning and inadequate allocation of human resources and funding result in significant unmet needs for assistance and support services and in ongoing exclusion. The Convention states that governments are expected to abolish such legislation and practices, to set standards for rights-based services, to enforce them, and to monitor compliance so as to promote inclusive communities where all citizens, including persons with intellectual disabilities, enjoy life with dignity and rights.

Right to Equality Before the Law

The right to equality before the law is an inherent civil and political right accorded to all people, with roots in the *Universal Declaration of Human Rights.* A number of subsequent international human rights instruments specifically guarantee this right, including the *International Covenant on Civil and Political Rights,* Article 4, and the *Convention on the Elimination of All Forms of Discrimination Against Women,* Article 15, which recognizes women's legal capacity on an equal basis with men, including in relation to concluding contracts, administering property, and exercising their rights in the justice system.

Recognizing that many persons with disabilities, and particularly those with intellectual and psychosocial disabilities, have historically been denied their full legal capacity, Article 12 of the CRPD reaffirms that persons with disabilities "have the right to recognition everywhere to be equal before the law" (2006, p. 10). Thus, States Parties are required to examine their legislation to ensure that their laws and policies do not restrict in any way the right to legal capacity, notably under substitute-decision-making protocols, or mental health laws that permit enforced treatment. The Convention also requires governments to take all appropriate measures to provide the following:

> Access by persons with disabilities to the support they may require in exercising their legal capacity,...effective safeguards to prevent abuse in accordance with international human rights law...[and] to ensure the equal right of persons with disabilities to own or inherit property, to control their own financial affairs and to have equal access to bank loans, mortgages and other forms of financial credit (CRPD, 2006, Article 12 [2] [3] and [4]).

The initial reports reviewed by the Committee on the Rights of Persons with Disabilities have demonstrated that many challenges exist in the implementation of Article 12, in both high- and low-income countries. In virtually all Concluding Observations issued to 2014, the CRPD Committee expressed concerns about the contradictions and gaps in States Parties legislation and policies regarding the scope of the right to equality before the law (see United Nations, Office of the High Commissioner for Human Rights [n.d.c] for a searchable treaty body database where full documents can be found). The body tasked with monitoring the implementation of the Convention has therefore delivered a General Comment providing guidance on the interpretation of this right (Committee on the Rights of Persons with Disabilities, 2014, *General Comment 1*). In its analysis, the Committee recalls that the adoption of a rights-based model of disability fundamentally "implies a shift from the substitute decision-making paradigm

to one that is based on supported decision-making" (2014, *General Comment 1*, para. 3). It goes on to explain that enjoying legal capacity entails being recognized "both as a holder of rights and an actor under the law," or, in other words, as a person entitled to full protection of his or her rights by the legal system and an agent "with power to engage in transactions and create, modify or end legal relationships" (2014, *General Comment 1*, para. 12). This latter is considered by the Committee to be the dimension of the right most frequently denied or restricted to persons with intellectual disabilities. Article 12 requires, instead, that persons with disabilities are provided with adequate supports to exercise their legal capacity. Such supports "must respect the rights, will and preferences of persons with disabilities and should never amount to substitute decision-making" (2014, *General Comment 1*, para. 17). The Comment clarifies that the concept of "protection of best interest," which has served in the past to legitimize substitute decision making, must be abandoned in the context of the CRPD and replaced by the notion of "will and preferences" of the person, to ensure that he or she will exercise legal capacity. Supports to be provided can thus encompass both informal and formal arrangements, of varying degrees and intensity:

> For example persons with disability may choose one or more trusted support persons to assist them in exercising their legal capacity for certain types of decisions, or may call on other forms of support, such as peer support, advocacy (including self-advocacy support), or assistance with communication. Support to persons with disabilities in the exercise of their legal capacity might include measures relating to universal design and accessibility—for example, requiring private and public actors, such as banks and other financial institutions, to provide information in an understandable format or to provide professional sign language interpretation in order to enable persons with disabilities to perform the legal acts required to open an account, conclude contracts, or conduct other social transactions. Support can also constitute the development and recognition of diverse, non-conventional methods of communication, especially for those who use non-verbal forms of communication to express their will and preferences. (2014, *General Comment 1*, para. 17)

Such supports must be available "at nominal or no cost to persons with disability, and lack of financial resources should not be a barrier to accessing support in the exercise of legal capacity" (2014, *General Comment 1*, para. 34 [e]).

Recognition of legal capacity for persons with disabilities is linked to the enjoyment of many other rights. The Committee highlights, in particular, interrelationships with the right to access to justice (Article 13), the right to be free from involuntary detention in a mental facility and not to be forced to undergo mental health treatment (Article 14), the right to respect for one's physical and mental integrity (Article 17), the right to liberty of movement and nationality (Article 18), the right to choose where and with whom to live (Article 19), the right to freedom of expression (Article 21), the right to marry and found a family (Article 23), the right to consent to medical treatment (Article 25), and the right to vote and stand for election (Article 29) (*General Comment 1*, para. 31). The consultation with and active involvement of persons with disabilities and their organizations in the development and implementation of legislation to ensure the exercise of legal capacity is recommended as a strategy to achieve change (para. 50).

In short, rather than using perceived or actual deficits in mental capacity as a justification for denying legal capacity, the challenge brought about by the CRPD emphasizes the need to change and reshape the broader social context to create a nondiscriminatory society, one that accepts diversity, facilitates autonomy, and ensures that all citizens, regardless of their different abilities, are treated equal to one another, under and before the law.

Rights of Women and Girls with Intellectual Disability

The CRPD explicitly recognizes that women and girls with disabilities may be subject to multiple and intersecting forms of discrimination based on gender and disability (Article 6). Data from DRPI studies shows that multiple discrimination affects many aspects of women's lives by limiting educational and employment opportunities and increasing their risk of poverty, neglect, social isolation, abuse, and dependence on others (for full reports, see Disability Rights Promotion International, 2014). Many women with intellectual disabilities are still subject to forced sterilization and are denied control of their reproductive health and decision (Pinto, 2015). Invisibility and isolation leave women with disabilities vulnerable to human rights abuse, including sexual violence (International Network of Women with Disabilities, 2011).

A study conducted in Sweden involving 1,063 women with intellectual disabilities found that 33% had experienced threats, violence, or sexual abuse by men. Half of those women had, on at least one occasion, been physically injured by the men as a result of violence and/or sexual assault (Swedish Research Institute for Disability Policy, 2007). Other research, undertaken by the U.S. Department of Justice (2009) based on the National Crime Victimization Survey, showed that the age-adjusted rate of nonfatal violent crime against persons with disabilities was 1.5 times higher than the rate for persons without disabilities and that females with a disability had a higher victimization rate than males with a disability (see also Chapter 35 on maltreatment and disability).

Given the high incidence of violence experienced by women with intellectual disabilities, there is a clear need for governments to take action to protect women with disabilities by encouraging them to report abuse and by instituting policies aimed at preventing and detecting abuse. These policies should include measures aimed at the "development, advancement and empowerment of women and girls with disabilities" as stated in the CRPD (Article 6 [2]).

Furthermore, there is a strong need for governments to actively ensure the enjoyment of all human rights to improve the quality of life of women with disabilities and reduce the risk factors for abuse. As early as 1991, the Committee on the Elimination of Discrimination Against Women that monitors the *Convention on the Elimination of All Forms of Discrimination Against Women* recognized that women with disabilities "suffer from double discrimination" and are a "vulnerable group." The Committee recommended that States Parties "provide information on women with disabilities in their periodic reports, and on measures taken to deal with their particular situation" (Committee on the Elimination of Discrimination Against Women, 1991, *General Recommendation 18*).

The CRPD Committee is drafting at the time of writing (2016) a new *General Comment* on Article 6 (Women and Girls with Disabilities; see United Nations, Office of the High Commissioner for Human Rights, n.d.b). According to the outline, the *General Comment* will specify the normative content of Article 6 with a particular emphasis on the concept of "intersectional discrimination" and will clarify States Parties' obligations differentiating between nondiscrimination duties and empowerment duties.

It will also stress the interrelation between the provisions addressing women and girls with disabilities and their link to other CRPD provisions, and will call upon States Parties to gather gender-disaggregate data and statistics and to include the gender perspective in CRPD national monitoring mechanisms.

Monitoring the Implementation of the Rights of Persons with Intellectual Disabilities

Article 33 of the CRPD establishes specific obligations to States Parties regarding implementation and monitoring of the rights of persons with intellectual disabilities and requires the involvement of civil society, in particular, persons with disabilities and their representative organizations, in those processes:

1. States Parties shall, in accordance with their legal and administrative systems, maintain, strengthen, designate or establish within the State Party, a framework, including one or more independent mechanisms, as appropriate, to promote, protect and monitor implementation of the present Convention.

2. Civil society, in particular persons with disabilities and their representative organizations, shall be involved and participate fully in the monitoring process. States Parties are obliged to submit periodic reports on measures taken to give effect to its obligations under the Convention and on the progress made in that regard (Article 35). Under the Optional Protocol, individuals or groups who claim to be victims of a violation by a State Party can also file complaints with the CRPD Committee, once efforts to resolve those issues at national level have been made and all possibilities for appeal have been exhausted (Articles 1 and 2).

Disability organizations are increasingly making use of these opportunities to have their voices heard at the international level. Participatory emancipatory monitoring is essential to fully understand what is being done in countries (Rioux et al., 2015). Many persons with disabilities contribute to state reporting processes while also providing their own accounts of the realization of human rights through national disability coalitions that elaborate in parallel or shadow reports and submit them to the CRPD Committee. More important, there are now a number of country monitoring projects that include the voices of persons with disabilities in new and broader ways. These not only cover an accounting of laws, policies, and programs but also, significantly, monitor the lived experiences of people with disabilities—their stories—enabling a way to measure the gap between the policy, law, and legislation and the implementation of those in the communities in which people live. A growing number of intellectual disability organizations are participating in monitoring processes regarding other human rights treaties, by offering comments that raise awareness of human rights violations against persons with disabilities (e.g., the work done by DRPI, Disability Rights International, the International Disability Alliance, and the Zero Project conducted by the ESSL Foundation in Austria). This twin-track approach to disability rights monitoring needs to be strengthened to ensure that the mainstreaming of disability in the international human rights system results in social, legal, and political changes that make a difference in the quality of life of persons with disabilities around the world.

SUMMARY

The human rights approach to disability that emerged in the early 1980s led to the 2006 adoption of the CRPD by the UN General Assembly. Under international law, persons with disabilities are now recognized as full citizens, entitled to equal rights and support to ensure those rights. There is also a growing understanding that the rights of the core international human rights treaties in the UN's human rights system apply equally to persons with disabilities. Thus, governments of countries that have signed the Convention (States Parties) can no longer justify denying persons with disabilities rights such as education, adequate and freely chosen housing and inclusion in the community, employment, equality before the law, and freedom from violence. The CRPD clarified the obligations and legal duties of States Parties to respect and ensure the equal enjoyment of all human rights by all persons with disabilities, and it contributed to a better understanding of their experiences. It identified areas where adaptations are necessary so that persons with disabilities can exercise their rights and areas where protections must be reinforced because those rights have historically been violated. Monitoring the implementation of human rights has become an important tool in the hands of governments, and more particularly of disability rights advocates, to promote change at national and local levels. Ensuring the equal effective enjoyment of human rights for persons with disabilities will improve the lives of persons with disabilities and create societies that respect the dignity and equality of each human being.

FOR FURTHER THOUGHT AND DISCUSSION

1. It appears to take decades for the equal rights of marginalized groups to be recognized. Women, indigenous peoples, persons with disabilities, and others continue to strive for equality. What are some of the barriers preventing the equal enjoyment of human rights by all?

2. How would you explain why persons with intellectual disabilities are so often the last in line to have their rights recognized?

3. Many people argue that persons with intellectual disabilities can be excluded from schools and general education classrooms because they learn differently, even though basic education is accepted as a right for other children. How would you frame a rights argument to counter that exclusion?

4. How can teachers, rehabilitation counselors, and other specialized professionals help promote and monitor the human rights of persons with intellectual disabilities?

REFERENCES

Alston, P., & Quinn, G. (1987). The nature and scope of States Parties obligations under the *International Covenant on Economic, Social and Cultural Rights. Human Rights Quarterly, 9,*156–229.

Americans with Disabilities Act (ADA) of 1990, PL 101-336, 42 U.S.C. §§ 12101 *et seq.*

Architectural Barriers Act of 1968, PL 90-480, 42 U.S.C. §§ 4151 *et seq.*

Brown, I. (2014). Care, residential. In A.C. Michalos (Ed.), *Encyclopedia of quality of life research* (pp. 553–564). Dordrecht, Netherlands: Springer.

Chambers, D. (2007). Role of advocacy in ensuring disability rights and entitlements. In I. Brown & M. Percy (Eds.), *A comprehensive guide to intellectual and developmental disabilities* (pp. 69–84). Baltimore, MD: Paul H. Brookes Publishing Co.

Committee on Economic, Social and Cultural Rights. (1991, December 13). *General Comment 4: Right to adequate housing.* E/1992/23.

Committee on Economic, Social and Cultural Rights. (1994, December 9). *General Comment 5: Persons with disabilities.* E/1995/22.

Committee on the Elimination of Discrimination Against Women. (1991, January 4). *General Recommendation 18: Disabled women.* A/46/38.

Committee on the Rights of Persons with Disabilities. (2014, May 19). *General Comment 1: Article 12: Equal recognition before the law.* CRPD/C/GC/1.

Committee on the Rights of Persons with Disabilities. (2014, May 22). *General Comment 2: Article 9: Accessibility.* CRPD/C/GC/2.

Committee on the Rights of the Child. (2007, February 27). *General Comment 9: The rights of children with disabilities.* CRC/C/GC/9.

Convention Against Torture and Other Cruel, Inhuman or Degrading Treatment or Punishment. (1984). General Assembly, Res. 39/46, 39 UN GAOR Supp. (No.51) at 197, entered into force June 26, 1987.

Convention on the Elimination of All Forms of Discrimination Against Women. (1979). General Assembly Res. 34/180, 34 UN GAOR Supp.(No. 46) at 193, entered into force Sept. 3, 1981.

Convention on the Rights of Persons with Disabilities. (2006). General Assembly Res. A/RES/ 61/106, entered into force May 3, 2008.

Convention on the Rights of the Child. (1989). General Assembly Res. 44/25, Annex, 44 UN GAOR Supp.(No. 49) at 167, entered into force Sept. 2, 1990.

Disability Rights International. (2014). *Disability Rights International: About us.* Retrieved from http://www.driadvocacy.org/about/

Disability Rights Promotion International. (2014). *Disability Rights Promotion International.* Retrieved from http://drpi.research.yorku.ca/

Education for All Handicapped Children Act of 1975, PL 94-142, 20 U.S.C. §§ 1400 *et seq.*

Eide, A. (2001). Economic, social and cultural rights as human rights. In A. Eide, C. Krause, & A. Rosas (Eds.), *Economic, social and cultural rights: A textbook* (2nd rev. ed., pp. 3–8). The Hague, The Netherlands: Kluwer Law International.

Individuals with Disabilities Education Improvement Act (IDEA) of 2004, PL 108-446, 20 U.S.C. §§ 1400 *et seq.*

Inter-American Convention on the Elimination of All Forms of Discrimination Against Persons with Disabilities. Organization of American States, General Assembly AG/RES. 1608, entered into force Sept. 14, 2001.

International Convention for the Protection of All Persons from Enforced Disappearance. (2006). General Assembly Res. A/RES/ 61/177, entered into force Dec. 23, 2010.

International Convention on the Elimination of All Forms of Racial Discrimination. (1965). General Assembly Res. 2106A (XX) 660 U.N.T.S.195, entered into force Jan. 4, 1969.

International Convention on the Protection of the Rights of All Migrant Workers and Members of Their Families. (1990). General Assembly Res. 45/186 annex, 45 U.N. GAOR Supp. (No. 49A) at 262, entered into force Jul. 1, 2003.

International Covenant on Civil and Political Rights. (1966). General Assembly Res. 2200A (XXI), 999 U.N.T.S. 171, entered into force Mar. 23, 1976.

International Covenant on Economic, Social and Cultural Rights. (1966). General Assembly Res. 2200A (XXI), U.N.T.S. 3, entered into force Jan. 3, 1976.

International Network of Women with Disabilities. (2011). *Violence against women with disabilities.* Retrieved from http://www.centerwomenpolicy.org/programs/waxman fiduccia/2011OnlineSeriesBarbaraWaxmanFiduccia.asp

Nowak, M. (2003). *Introduction to the international human rights regime.* Leiden, The Netherlands: Brill Academic.

Oliver, M. (1990). *Politics of disablement.* New York, NY: Macmillan.

Olmstead v. L.C., 527 U.S. 581 (1999).

Pinto, P.C. (2015). Women, disability and the right to health. In P. Armstrong & J. Deadman (Eds.), *Women's health: Intersections of policy, research and practice* (2nd ed.). Toronto, Canada: Women's Press.

Quinn, G., & Degener, T. (2002). *Human rights and disability: The current use and future potential of United Nations human rights instruments in the context of disability.* Retrieved from http://www.ohchr.org/Documents /Publications/HRDisabilityen.pdf

Rioux, M., Basser, L.A., & Jones, M. (Eds.). (2011). *Critical perspectives on human rights and disability law.* Leiden, The Netherlands: Brill, Nijhoff.

Rioux, M., Pinto, P.C., & Parek, G. (Eds.). (2015). *Disability, rights monitoring, and social change: Building power out of evidence.* Toronto, Canada: Canadian Scholar's Press.

Swedish Research Institute for Disability Policy. (2007). *Men's violence against women with disabilities.* Retrieved from http://www.wwda.org.au/swedishstudy1.doc

Telecommunications Act of 1996, Pub. LA. No. 104-104, 110 Stat. 56 (1996).

United Nations Commission on Human Rights. (1998, April 17). *Human rights of persons with disabilities.* C.H.R. res. 1998/31, ESCOR Supp. (No. 3) at 117. Retrieved from http://www1.umn.edu/humanrts/UN/1998/Res031 .html

United Nations Commission on Human Rights. (2000, April 25). *Human rights of persons with disabilities.* C.H.R. res. 2000/51. Retrieved from http://ap.ohchr.org /documents/alldocs.aspx?doc_id=4740

United Nations General Assembly. (1948, December 10). *Universal Declaration of Human Rights.* General Assembly Res. 217A (III), UN Doc A/810 at 71.

United Nations General Assembly. (1982, December 3). *World Programme of Action Concerning Disabled Persons.* General Assembly Res. 37/52.

United Nations General Assembly. (1993, December 20). *Standard Rules on the Equalization of Opportunities for Persons with Disabilities.* General Assembly Res. 48/96, annex.

United Nations, Office of the High Commissioner for Human Rights. (n.d.a). *The core international human rights instruments and their monitoring bodies.* Retrieved from http://www.ohchr.org/EN/ProfessionalInterest/Pages /CoreInstruments.aspx

United Nations, Office of the High Commissioner for Human Rights. (n.d.b). *Outline document for the preparation of a General comment on UNCRPD article 6.* Retrieved from http://www.ohchr.org/Documents/HRBodies/CRPD /OutlinedraftgeneralcommentonArticle6.doc

United Nations, Office of the High Commissioner for Human Rights. (n.d.c). *Treaty body database.* Retrieved from http://tbinternet.ohchr.org/_layouts/treatybodyexternal /TBSearch.aspx?Lang=en&TreatyID=4&DocTypeID=5

U.S. Department of Justice, Office of Justice Programs. (2009). *First international study on crime against people with disabilities.* Retrieved from http://bjs.ojp.usdoj.gov /index.cfm?ty=pbdetail&iid=2022

World Health Organization. (2011). *World report on disability.* Geneva, Switzerland: Author.

6

Advocacy and Legal Considerations to Ensure Civil Rights

Peter Blanck, Tina Campanella, and Jonathan G. Martinis

WHAT YOU WILL LEARN

- What is meant by advocacy and its role in civil rights
- The work of disability rights advocates and their role in obtaining civil rights and protections
- How laws, internationally, bolster a focus on human rights and protections
- How guardianship status affects a person's civil rights
- What is meant by supported decision making and how it is supported in international law

Since the late 20th century—and in particular since the passage of the Americans with Disabilities Act (ADA) of 1990 (PL 101-336)—people with intellectual and developmental disabilities have won the opportunity to exercise many civil rights others take for granted. Advocacy in many countries and in its many forms played an important role in affirming this access to individual rights under law for children and adults with disabilities (Blanck, 2014a). In most places in the world, people with disabilities may no longer be warehoused in institutions and nursing homes, excluded from government programs and public places that everyone else can use, and denied equal employment for no reason other than the presence of a disability. However, interpreting, applying, and protecting these legal and basic human rights has raised new questions: for instance, questions focused not on whether discrimination is wrong but on what discrimination is and how it can be identified and remedied.

International law—laws from other countries and United Nations (UN) transnational treaties—have an important role in answering these emerging questions (Blanck, Waterstone, Myhill, & Siegal, 2014). Movements and organizations (often called nongovernmental organizations, or NGOs) that support the rights of people with disabilities increasingly involve global efforts, especially with advances in mobile Internet communications and technologies (e.g., the use of web-based social media platforms such as Facebook) (Blanck, 2014b).

In this chapter, we first consider the role that advocacy (by individuals, families and friends, groups, and organizations) has played in establishing and protecting the rights of people with intellectual and developmental disabilities, with a focus on developments in the United States. Next, we examine how international law is helping these entities understand, extend, and advocate for the rights of individuals with intellectual and developmental disabilities. Finally, we explore, using real-world scenarios, the ways that advocacy based on international law and movements is helping to protect and advance the civil rights of people with intellectual and developmental disabilities across the world.

ADVOCACY AND RIGHTS OF PEOPLE WITH INTELLECTUAL AND DEVELOPMENTAL DISABILITIES

The dictionary definition of *advocacy* is "active support, especially of a cause" (Collins English Dictionary, n.d.). Advocacy is speaking up, speaking out, "speaking truth to power" for or against something, with the goal of that thing being done or stopped. Advocacy takes many shapes and styles. It includes supporting the rights of a single person, championing and challenging laws and policies, speaking and acting publicly for or against conditions or proposals, and filing lawsuits seeking to change the status quo. Advocates may be people directly affected by what they are supporting or opposing as well as friends, family members, professionals, elected officials, and fellow citizens.

One example of disability civil rights advocacy that received wide attention in the United States involved a man named Don who had intellectual disability and did not speak verbally (Blanck, 2014b). Don was working in a sheltered (segregated) workplace, which typically employed people with intellectual and developmental disabilities and paid far less than minimum wage. Don communicated using an electronic communication device. The U.S. Equal Employment Opportunity Commission and local disability advocates represented Don in an ADA employment discrimination case. Don had been fired from his job at a restaurant chain, even though his job performance was excellent and his co-workers enjoyed working with him. A regional manager had visited the restaurant and, upon seeing Don, took the local supervisor aside and criticized her for hiring one of "those people." After returning to the restaurant, the regional manager fired Don.

Don's ADA legal case went to trial and the jury found against the company, awarding Don $70,000 in damages for his lost wages. In addition, to make its point that this sort of discrimination would not be tolerated, the jury awarded Don $13 million in punitive damages. Surprisingly, the company appealed the jury award on the grounds that Don's disability made it highly unlikely that he would experience distress because of his termination. However, the court imposed the maximum allowable damages, stating that "the breathtaking magnitude of an eight-figure punitive damages award demonstrates that the jury wanted to send a loud, clear message" (Blanck, 2014b, p. 15). That message was that disability discrimination was illegal and would not be accepted in that community.

Disability Rights Advocacy

Throughout history, effective and impassioned advocacy—like those advocates involved in Don's case—has helped establish legal rights and ensured that people were respected, protected, and implemented. The same is true for people with intellectual and developmental disabilities. The work and commitment of countless family members and *self-advocates*—the term many people with disabilities use to describe themselves—has created and advanced the disability rights movement. Progress toward equality has been born out of the lived stories of individuals with disabilities seeking their rights to participate fully in daily life (Blanck, 2014b). As never before, people with disabilities are pursuing their rights to join fully in their communities. Sometimes they are successful; often they are not. Some have sought to change the law and influence its interpretation and implementation.

The journey toward disability rights has not been easy: people with disabilities faced (and still face) societal, governmental, and legal systems that often view them as fundamentally different and in some cases, less than human—with one example being the infamous *Buck v. Bell* case, in which the U.S. Supreme Court held that states could sterilize people considered, at that time, mentally defective (Smith & Nelson, 1989).

In response, self-advocates, their families and friends, and organizations used individual and group advocacy to demand equal treatment, rejecting the stereotyped notion that people with disabilities were incapable and unworthy of equality. In the following subsections are only a few of their stories.

Models for Action

Ed Roberts, who had quadriplegia due to polio, was one of the first self-advocates in the United States. Roberts was accepted to the University of California at Berkeley, but he soon learned that there was no accessible housing on campus. With several other students with disabilities, he formed a campus program with the goal of integrating students with disabilities in university life (Scotch, 1989). Their efforts were successful, leading to more people with disabilities attending the university.

Roberts then focused his efforts on increasing people with disabilities' access to community activities and opportunities, creating the Berkeley Center for Independent Living in 1972 (Scotch, 1989). Roberts' model has flourished: there are now close to 500 Centers for Independent Living in the United States providing independent-living-skills education, training and resources, peer counseling, and advocacy to millions of people with disabilities nationwide (U.S. Administration for Community Living, 2014).

Grassroots Organizing At a time when there were no formal services for children with intellectual and developmental disabilities, groups of parents around the United States (and beyond) decided things needed to change. Driven by the belief that life could be better for their children, these families sought resources and worked together to provide educational, social, and other opportunities for their children. In the 1950s, what started as grassroots, local efforts became formally organized into a national association—the National Association for Retarded Children—known today as The Arc.

The number of parents and friends associated with The Arc grew steadily in the 1960s and early 1970s. As the numbers grew, so did the organization's influence on legislation and policy at the local and national levels. Many of the services and funding schemes that support people with disabilities today are the result of advocacy from parents and other members associated with The Arc. As a movement, The Arc shows the grassroots power of people coming together to achieve common goals. In more than 60 years of advocacy and activism, The Arc has played a significant role in increasing knowledge about intellectual and developmental disabilities, changing perceptions about the abilities and future promise of children and adults with disabilities, and demonstrating that with opportunity and support, people with intellectual and developmental disabilities can be contributing, active members of their communities.

Starting a National Movement In 1974, a group of people with intellectual and developmental disabilities attended a professional conference about the "mentally handicapped" (Schalock, Baker, & Croser, 2002). Angry that professionals and providers were making decisions about their lives without consulting them, they formed People First—named for their desire to be recognized and respected as people instead of "disabled." Active today in the United States and internationally, the goal of People First is to ensure that individuals with intellectual and developmental disabilities are the leaders on issues involving their lives and the supports and services they need and want (Schalock et al.).

The People First effort took root and continues to grow: by 1984, one team of researchers estimated that there were nearly 5,000 people in 152 self-advocacy groups nationwide (Rhoades, Browning, & Thorin, 1986). By 1994, those numbers had grown to 11,600 people in 500 organizations in 43 states. By 2010, there were more than 800 organizations in the United States (Caldwell, 2010). Self-advocacy organizations such as People First, the Autistic Self Advocacy Network (ASAN), and Self Advocates Becoming Empowered continue the "nothing about us without us" movement, driving America's national conversation and fighting to ensure that people with disabilities have an equal opportunity to take part in everyday life activities.

Ensuring Education As recently as the 1970s, almost 2 million American children with disabilities were denied the chance to go to public school. In 1971, a group of Pennsylvania self-advocates and parents challenged state laws authorizing schools to exclude children who had not attained a mental age of 5 years. The Pennsylvania Association for Retarded Children (PARC) sued the state, state officials, and school boards, arguing that these laws violated the children's rights (Blanck, 2014a). They said that all children, even those with the most severe disabilities, can benefit from education and that the state laws had been used to deny those benefits to children with disabilities (*PARC v. Commonwealth*, 1972).

The case eventually was settled by the parties. However, the laws allowing schools to refuse to educate children were declared unconstitutional and the state was required to "place each mentally retarded child in a free, public program of education and training appropriate to the child's capacity" (*PARC v. Commonwealth*, 1972).

After the PARC case, students and parents filed dozens of lawsuits aimed at protecting the rights of every child to receive an appropriate education. These actions led to passage in 1974 of the federal Education for All Handicapped Children Act of 1975

(PL 94-142). The law, now called the Individuals with Disabilities Education Improvement Act (IDEA) of 2004 (PL 108-446), requires every state to provide a free appropriate public education in the least restrictive environment to all children, regardless of their disabilities. Similar laws have been enacted across the world (see Chapter 36), leading to the education of tens of millions of children with disabilities who would have otherwise been denied this right.

Demanding Progress In the United States, the Rehabilitation Act of 1973 (PL 93-112) further expanded the civil rights protections of people with disabilities, prohibiting programs receiving federal funding from discrimination on the basis of disability (Schalock et al., 2002). Four years after it was passed, however, the Office for Civil Rights of the U.S. Department of Health, Education, and Welfare (HEW) had not implemented the regulations needed to make the law effective in practice (Freeman & Johnson, 1999).

Frustrated by the delay, the American Coalition of Citizens with Disabilities sent a letter to President Jimmy Carter demanding that HEW finalize the regulations by April 4, 1977 (Freeman & Johnson, 1999). On April 5, groups of individuals with disabilities, including individuals from Ed Roberts' Berkeley Center for Independent Living, launched protests that involved a sit-in at the HEW offices in San Francisco, California (Freeman & Johnson). The sit-in continued for 24 days until, on April 28, 1977, the regulations were finalized, creating the greatest expansion and protection of the rights of people with disabilities to that time.

USING INTERNATIONAL LAW TO DEFINE, UNDERSTAND, AND PROTECT THE RIGHTS OF AMERICANS WITH INTELLECTUAL AND DEVELOPMENTAL DISABILITIES

In the United States, as in many other countries, there now are many federal and state laws addressing the civil rights of people with intellectual and developmental disabilities. The next two sections focus on how international law may be used to help understand, define, and protect these rights by providing answers to questions and uncertainties left by those laws. To illustrate this, we focus on one major American law: the ADA of 1990 (PL 101-336), which was mentioned previously and used in Don's civil rights legal case.

Called the "most significant piece of disability rights legislation ever enacted" (Schalock, et al., 2002, p. 4), the ADA was signed by President George H.W. Bush with these words on July 26, 1990: "let the shameful wall of exclusion finally come tumbling down" (as cited in U.S. Equal Employment Opportunity Commission, n.d.). The ADA recognized that people with disabilities have the right to life, liberty, and happiness, and it states that "physical or mental disabilities in no way diminish a person's right to fully participate in all aspects of society" (ADA 1990, 42 U.S.C. §§ 12101, Findings and Purpose). The ADA acknowledged that people with disabilities have been denied these basic civil rights due to, as it states,

> Outright intentional exclusion, the discriminatory effects of architectural, transportation, and communication barriers, overprotective rules and policies, failure to make modifications to existing facilities and practices, exclusionary qualification standards and criteria, segregation, and relegation to lesser services, programs, activities, benefits, jobs, or other opportunities. (ADA, 42 U.S.C. §§ 12101[1] and [3]).

To remedy this history of neglect and segregation, the ADA broadly established that people with disabilities have the right under law to equal access in employment, government services, and public places and accommodations (Blanck, 2015; Schur et al., 2014). Even so, years of analysis, debate, and litigation have raised new questions about the reach of the ADA: When is someone "disabled" for purposes of the law, as opposed to lacking the general knowledge, skills, or abilities to do something? When is someone the victim of disability discrimination (as Don was), as opposed to being not qualified for a particular job, or to receive a particular benefit, or to take part in an activity offered to the public?

The text of the ADA does not directly answer many of these interpretive questions, although federal agencies such as the U.S. Department of Justice and the U.S. Equal Employment Opportunity Commission have provided guidance on such issues (Blanck et al., 2014). The ADA, and laws like it, often are limited by their text: that is, they forbid discrimination generally but do not always explain what specific actions are discriminatory, what public and private entities should do to avoid discriminating, and what should be done to fix discrimination. The interpretation of the law ultimately is left to the courts to decide. However, stereotyped and prejudiced beliefs about people with disabilities, and what they can and cannot do, are deeply embedded in societal practices so that changing patterns of action is not easy, even when a court orders it so. That is why these issues often are addressed by many courts and government agencies, relying on sources other than the actual law itself (e.g., using social science research studies). Therefore, important interpretive questions, such as those previously identified here, need to be answered through advocacy and evidence-based study.

In this interconnected world, American disability advocates also increasingly examine and build on international law (and other countries' domestic laws) to "fill in the gaps"—that is, to help analyze, understand, and define their rights as well as to identify cutting-edge ways to defend them. For instance, where the ADA's text and its interpretation by federal agencies may not directly provide helpful answers, disability advocates are looking to the underlying principles of the ADA and then reviewing international laws with the same intent to advocate that the ADA should be interpreted in accordance with them.

However, before exploring how international law may be used to protect rights, it must first be determined whether it may be used effectively at all. Why would advocates use another country's laws, which Americans had no part in writing, to analyze laws written by their representatives?

The U.S. Constitution recognized the importance of international law, giving the president the power to enter into transnational treaties with the advice and consent of Congress. Treaties are considered "the supreme law of the land," much the same as laws passed by Congress and signed by the president. Sometimes, the U.S. Congress and the president attach "Reservations, Understandings, and Declarations" (RUDs; Congressional Research Service, 2001) to treaties, to explain how they should be interpreted and to identify sections of the treaty intended to be "the supreme law of the land" and those sections that are not (Congressional Research Service, 2001).

As this chapter was being written, the U.S. Senate was debating whether to ratify the UN *Convention on the Rights of Persons with Disabilities* (CRPD). The CRPD is a comprehensive international treaty, setting forth specific rights of people with disabilities, and corresponding responsibilities of signatory governments, intended to "ensure the full and equal enjoyment of all human rights and fundamental freedoms by all persons with disabilities, and to promote respect for their inherent dignity" (UN, 2006).

Should the U.S. Senate eventually ratify the CRPD, the treaty will become "the supreme law of the land" except for those areas identified by RUDs as not having the same effect as a law passed by Congress and signed by the president. Where the ADA doesn't address a particular issue but the CRPD does (and that part of the CRPD is not covered by a RUD), the CRPD will act to modify the ADA by expressing people's rights in that situation.

However, even if the CRPD does not become "the supreme law of the land," it and other international laws and practices still help Americans with intellectual and developmental disabilities advocate for themselves and others. This is because although international law is not always mandatory, it may always be instructive—it can help disability advocates argue that an American law should be interpreted in a certain way because an international law on the same topic is interpreted that way.

In other words, even prior to the possible ratification of the CRPD, if the ADA does not say whether a particular action is discriminatory but the CRPD does, disability advocates may argue for Congress to amend the ADA, or to pass new regulations interpreting the law based on the CRPD, to make the ADA clearer and more effective. In litigation, attorneys may request that courts interpret the ADA in accord with the CRPD—to fill in the gaps of the ADA with language from a law accepted by the world community that has the same purpose. In both instances, advocates would contend that the intent of the ADA is to bar discrimination on the basis of disability and that amending or interpreting the law in accord with the CRPD, which has the same purpose, will accomplish that purpose.

CASE ILLUSTRATION: THE RIGHT TO DIRECT ONE'S OWN LIFE

With the previous background, we explore in this section a situation in which international law may be used to understand, analyze, and protect civil rights under the ADA.

Part 1: Justin, Guardianship, and Supported Decision Making

Say you are an advocate, helping people with disabilities protect their rights and seeking systemwide changes in law to benefit all people with disabilities. Justin and his friends come to your office and ask for your help. Justin has an intellectual disability.

Recently, Justin graduated high school and held his first job. Like most people, Justin is independent minded and wants to make his own decisions. He has friends who provide him with support when he needs it and he wants to live with them.

Justin's parents want to become his legal guardians—they want a court to appoint them to make all decisions for him and to have those decisions be final. Justin's parents believe that they have his best interests at heart and, even if he disagrees, that they should have the power to decide where he lives and what he does because that will keep him safe.

Justin does not want a legal guardian. He acknowledges that he has some limitations, but he believes he just needs "a little help" in making everyday decisions. Justin and his friends want to use an alternative to guardianship called supported decision making (SDM) (Blanck & Martinis, 2015). They believe that SDM will help Justin to live more independently, productively, and safely and—of particular importance—to maintain maximum control over his own life using all of his abilities.

After doing some research, you learn that in the United States, adult guardianship is a legal process governed by state law with different rules and systems in each state. In general, though, a person is placed in guardianship when a court decides that he or she cannot make some or all decisions, that he or she is in need of "protection," and that there are no less-restrictive options than guardianship.

The estimated number of adults under partial or total (plenary) guardianship in the United States has tripled since 1995 (Reynolds, 2002; Schmidt, 1995; Uekert & Van Duizend, 2011). The majority of guardianships are plenary or "full" (e.g., Teaster, Wood, Lawrence, & Schmidt, 2007). A plenary guardian, therefore, has broad court-endorsed powers to make all decisions, in all situations, for a person. That is the type of guardianship Justin's parents want.

From your research, you learn that guardianship is an important issue for people with intellectual and developmental disabilities. It is controversial because sometimes it takes away individuals' legal rights to make decisions about their own lives and treats people as not being capable of making their own decisions. One member of the U.S. Congress said,

> The typical ward has fewer rights than the typical convicted felon.... By appointing a guardian, the court entrusts to someone else the power

to choose where they will live, what medical treatment they will get and, in rare cases, when they will die. (Pepper, 1987, p. 21)

You learn more about SDM (from reading different state laws and sections of the CRPD), which Justin wants to use instead of being subjected to a plenary guardianship. SDM focuses on providing people the help and information they need and want to understand the situations they face and the choices they must make so they can make their own decisions to the best extent possible in any given circumstance (Blanck & Martinis, 2015; Dinerstein, 2012).

SDM increasingly is used by people with intellectual and developmental disabilities because it has the potential to help people be more independent and have better quality of life (Kohn, Blumenthal, & Campbell, 2013). To use SDM, people with intellectual and developmental disabilities identify trusted supporters—who may be friends, family members, and professionals—to help them in specific situations. The focus of SDM is to establish relationships that the person wants and organize them in the way the person, with input from his or her supporters, believes will work best. A person may have one supporter for financial issues and another for health care decisions or may use the same people to provide support across situations. SDM relationships may be formal, created by a written agreement outlining what type of support will be given and when (and may even be endorsed by a court), or informal, with people available to give advice when needed (Dinerstein, 2012).

You also learn that researchers have shown that people with intellectual and developmental disabilities who exercise more self-determination—who have more control over their lives—tend to have better jobs, have a higher quality of life, learn to be better problem-solvers, and are better able to resist and avoid abuse (Khemka, Hickson, & Reynolds, 2005; Schur, Kruse, & Blanck, 2013; Wehmeyer & Schwartz, 1998). On the other hand, people denied self-determination may, as Deci (1975) noted, "feel helpless, hopeless and self-critical, and will not behave because [they] can see no use in behaving" (p. 308). Losing the right to make decisions may cause people to have symptoms similar to clinical depression (Garber & Seligman, 1980), with a study by Winick (1995) finding that taking away the right to make decisions may "foster feelings of depression and worthlessness" (p. 6).

What are some of the questions you might have? Would you want to know which, if any, of Justin's civil rights may be affected if his parents become his plenary guardians? What is lost if Justin's parents become his guardians? What may Justin gain if he can use SDM? Without considering the ADA or international law, what ways could you advocate for Justin and people in the same situation?

Part 2: What Does the Americans with Disabilities Act Say?

The ADA does not mention the words *guardianship* and *supported decision making*. Instead, the ADA is written broadly to provide a clear and comprehensive mandate for the elimination of discrimination against individuals with disabilities. Congress found discrimination against people with disabilities includes not only "outright intentional exclusion," but also "the discriminatory policies of… overprotective rules and policies" (ADA 1990, 42 U.S.C. §§ 12101[a][5]).

The ADA's primary goal is to ensure "equality of opportunity, full participation, independent living and economic self-sufficiency" for people with disabilities (ADA 1990, 42 U.S.C. §§ 12101[a][7]). One of the ways the ADA accomplishes this is to forbid discrimination against people with disabilities by state and local governments.

Regulations written by federal agencies interpreting Title II of the ADA, the section of the law dealing with the actions of state and local government agencies, require governments to "administer services, programs, and activities in the most integrated setting appropriate to the needs of qualified individuals with disabilities" (28 C.F.R. § 35.130[d] [2008]). The "most integrated setting" is one "that enables individuals with disabilities to interact with non-disabled individuals to the fullest extent possible" (28 C.F.R. pt 35, app. A, subsec. B [2008]). The U.S. Supreme Court has recognized this important principle as part of the ADA's "integration mandate" (Blanck, 2014a).

The ADA requires state and local governments to make "reasonable modifications in policies, practices, or procedures when the modifications are necessary to avoid discrimination on the basis of disability" (28 C.F.R. § 35.130[b][7]). These modifications—also known as accommodations and adjustments—to state laws and practices enable people with disabilities covered by the law to participate fully in all the programs and services offered to the public (Blanck, Goldstein, & Myhill, 2013).

What questions does this information bring to mind? Do you wonder how an unjustified guardianship may violate the ADA if the law does not mention protections against unwarranted guardianship? What is Justin's argument to advocate that he has a legal right to use SDM instead of plenary guardianship? What types of advocacy might you use to help Justin achieve his goals? What types of advocacy would you use to advocate for systemwide changes in state laws and practices to help people in the same situation as Justin achieve their goals?

One important U.S. Supreme Court case found that people with disabilities should not be forced to live in segregated and large institutions operated by the state when they choose not to and when they have the ability to live in the community in integrated ways. The Supreme Court said that "unjustified isolation…is properly regarded as discrimination based on disability," because "confinement in an institution severely diminishes the everyday life activities of individuals, including family relations, social contacts, work options, economic independence, educational advancement, and cultural enrichment" (*Olmstead v. L.C.*, 1999, 600–601). Extending this idea, Salzman (2010) concluded that "unjustified" guardianship may result in the same type of discrimination as "unjustified" institutionalization.

Given this information, how would you advocate for Justin to use SDM instead of guardianship? How would you use this idea to advocate for systemwide changes in state laws to help people in the same situation as Justin?

Part 3: What Can Americans Learn from International Law?

The ADA and its regulations, although clear on the centrality of disability civil rights and equal opportunity for independence in daily life, do not address issues associated with legal guardianship and SDM. Many advocates, therefore, consider the principles in international laws to examine these issues and argue that the ADA should be interpreted in a consistent way.

As was true in the United States, other countries' laws historically have excluded people with disabilities from society and denied them basic civil rights that people were free to exercise

(Logue & Blanck, 2010). Governments often treated people with intellectual and developmental disabilities as outsiders from society, different and deviant, needing to be controlled for the benefit of society and protected from themselves (Flynn & Arstein-Kerslake, 2014).

With the advent of the ADA, CRPD, and other countries' domestic laws, there is a clear shift toward recognizing and respecting the human rights of people with disabilities. The *Universal Declaration on Human Rights* (UN, 1948) recognizes the rights of all people to be treated with dignity and receive equal treatment under the law. The *International Covenant on Economic, Social and Cultural Rights* (UN, 1976) declares that all people have the right to self-determination.

Passage and ratification of the CRPD by more than 100 nations from around the world represented a global high-water mark in disability human rights. The CRPD is intended to "protect and ensure the full and equal enjoyment of all human rights and fundamental freedoms by all persons...and to promote respect for their inherent dignity" (UN, 2006). Leading international disability rights legal scholar Gerard Quinn and his colleague commented that the CRPD creates unprecedented bridges of knowledge and rights among people with and without disabilities across the globe (Quinn & Flynn, 2012).

To help reach its goals, the CRPD enshrines two principles critical to SDM. First, CRPD Article 12 states that people with disabilities "enjoy legal capacity on an equal basis with others in all aspects of life" (UN, 2006). Second, the CRPD requires governments to "provide access by persons with disabilities to the support they may require in exercising their legal capacity" (UN, 2006).

Taken together, these principles mean that people with disabilities have a human right to take part in all decision making that affects their rights. The UN handbook for parliamentarians on the CRPD identifies SDM as a way to ensure these rights:

> With supported decision-making, the presumption is always in favour of the person with a disability who will be affected by the decision. The individual is the decision maker; the support person(s) explain(s) the issues, when necessary, and interpret(s) the signs and preferences of the individual. Even when an individual with a disability requires total support, the support person(s) should enable the individual to exercise his/her legal capacity to the greatest extent possible, according to the wishes of the individual. (UN, 2007).

Countries around the world have embraced SDM in varying degrees. For example, several Canadian provinces have given people with disabilities a legal right to use SDM. In Yukon, Alberta, and British Columbia, people with disabilities may enter into representation agreements with a support network made up of one or more trusted people. These agreements are a "sign to others, including doctors, financial institutions and service providers, that the individual has given the network the authority to assist him/her in making decisions and represent him/her in certain matters" (UN, 2007).

In the United Kingdom, when people with disabilities need help making decisions regarding important health and support issues and do not have people in their lives to provide it, they can access services from the Independent Mental Capacity Advocate (IMCA) program (United Kingdom Office of the Public Guardian, 2007). In general, IMCAs work with the person—collecting information about the decision to be made and the person's values and preferences by speaking with the person, reviewing documents, and interviewing providers. The IMCA then issues a report recommending a course of action (Crane, 2015).

In Sweden, people with disabilities may ask for and designate a personal ombudsman to help them make decisions. The ombudsman must work only with that person and follow his or her will and preferences. In addition, a court may appoint a mentor, called a "god-man," for the person, if the person agrees. The god-man acts as the person's agent and can make some decisions and enter into contracts on the person's behalf. However, the god-man is supposed to receive the person's consent for all nonroutine decisions. If the god-man makes a decision the person does not agree with, the person may cancel or invalidate it. Also, the person may end the relationship at any time (Salzman, 2010).

SUMMARY

This chapter examined how advocacy by individuals, families and friends, groups, and organizations is establishing and protecting the civil rights of people with intellectual and developmental disabilities in the United States and abroad. Developments in international law—transnationally as in the CRPD and in the domestic laws of other countries—is helping Americans understand and self-advocate for the full and equal rights of individuals with intellectual and developmental disabilities. Using fact-based scenarios, we illustrated ways that advocacy based on these developments are advancing the rights of people with intellectual and developmental disabilities in the United States and in other countries in regard to the emerging area of SDM.

FOR FURTHER THOUGHT AND DISCUSSION

1. Design an advocacy campaign using international law principles to advocate for Justin to use SDM instead of plenary guardianship. What methods would you use?

2. Design an advocacy campaign using international law principles to advocate for systemwide state law changes to support people like Justin who want to use SDM instead of plenary guardianship. What methods would you use?

3. Even if the CRPD is ratified by the U.S. Senate, Article 12, which is where the right to SDM is stated, it will not be the "supreme law of the land." How does this affect your advocacy campaign for Justin?

REFERENCES

Americans with Disabilities Act (ADA) of 1990, PL 101-336, 42 U.S.C. §§ 12101 et seq.

Blanck, P. (2014a). *eQuality: The struggle for web accessibility by persons with cognitive disabilities.* New York, NY: Cambridge University Press.

Blanck, P. (2014b). The struggle for web equality by persons with cognitive disabilities. *Behavioral Sciences and the Law, 32*(1), 4–32.

Blanck, P. (2015). ADA at 25 and people with cognitive disabilities: From voice to action. *Inclusion, 3*(2), 46–54.

Blanck, P., Goldstein, B., & Myhill, W. (2013). *Legal rights of persons with disabilities: An analysis of federal law* (2nd ed.). Palm Beach Gardens, FL: LRP.

Blanck, P., & Martinis, J. (2015). "The right to make choices": National Resource Center for Supported Decision-Making. *Inclusion, 3*(1), 24–33.

Blanck, P., Waterstone, M., Myhill, N., & Siegal, C. (2014). *Disability civil rights law and policy: Case and materials* (3rd ed.). Minneapolis, MN: West.

Caldwell, J. (2010). Leadership development of individuals with developmental disabilities in the self-advocacy movement. *Journal of Intellectual Disability Research, 54,* 1004–1014.

Collins English Dictionary. (n.d.). *Collins English dictionary: Complete and unabridged* (10th ed.). Retrieved from http://www.dictionary.com

Congressional Research Service, 106th Congress. (2001). *Study on treaties and other international agreements: The role of the United States Senate, S. Rep. No. 106-7* (Comm. Print 2001). Washington, DC: U.S. Library of Congress.

Crane, S.A. (2015). Is guardianship reform enough? Next steps in policy reforms to promote self-determination among people with disabilities. *Journal of International Aging Law & Policy, 8,* 177–210.

Deci, E. (1975). *Intrinsic motivation.* New York, NY: Plenum Press.

Dinerstein, R. (2012). Implementing legal capacity under article 12 of the UN convention on the rights of persons with disabilities: The difficult road from guardianship to supported decision making. *Human Rights Brief, 19,* 8–12.

Education for All Handicapped Children Act of 1975, PL 94-142, 20 U.S.C. §§ 1400 et seq.

Flynn, E., & Arstein-Kerslake, A. (2014). Legislating personhood: Realising the right to support in exercising legal capacity. *International Journal of Law in Context, 10*(1), 81–104.

Freeman, J., & Johnson, V. (1999). *Waves of protest: Social movements since the sixties.* Oxford, United Kingdom: Rowman & Littlefield.

Garber J., & Seligman, M. (Eds.). (1980). *Human helplessness: Theory and applications.* London, United Kingdom: Academic Press.

Individuals with Disabilities Education Improvement Act (IDEA) of 2004, PL 108-446, 20 U.S.C. §§ 1400 et seq.

International Covenant on Economic, Social and Cultural Rights, art. 1, Dec. 16, 1966, 993 U.N.T.S. 3, 7 (1976).

International Covenant on Economic, Social and Cultural Rights. General Assembly Res. 2200A (XXI), U.N.T.S. 3, entered into force Jan. 3, 1976.

Khemka, I., Hickson, L., & Reynolds, G. (2005). Evaluation of a decision-making curriculum designed to empower women with mental retardation to resist abuse. *American Journal on Mental Retardation, 110,* 193–204.

Kohn, N., Blumenthal, J., & Campbell, A. (2013). Supported decision-making: A viable alternative to guardianship. *Pennsylvania State Law Review, 117,* 1111–1157.

Logue, L., & Blanck, P. (2010). *Race, ethnicity, and the treatment of disability in post-Civil War America.* New York, NY: Cambridge University Press.

Longhurst, N.A. (1994). *The self-advocacy movement by people with developmental disabilities: A demographic study and directory of self-advocacy groups in the United States.* Washington, DC: American Association on Mental Retardation.

Olmstead v. L.C., 527 U.S. 581 (1999).

Pennsylvania Association for Retarded Children v. Commonwealth, 343 F. Supp. 279 (1972).

Pepper, C. (1987). Prepared statement, U.S. Subcommittee on Health and Long Term Care of the House Select Committee on Aging, 100th Cong. *Abuses in guardianship of the elderly and infirm: A national disgrace* (H.R. Rpt. 100-639, 21).

Quinn, G., & Flynn, E. (2012). Transatlantic borrowings: The past and future of EU nondiscrimination law and policy on the ground of disability. *American Journal of Comparative Law, 60*(1), 23–48.

Rehabilitation Act of 1973, PL 93-112, 29 U.S.C. §§ 701 et seq.

Reynolds, S.L. (2002). Guardianship primavera: A first look at factors associated with having a legal guardian using a nationally representative sample of community-dwelling adults. *Aging and Mental Health, 6,* 109–120.

Rhoades, C.M., Browning, P.L., & Thorin, E. (1986). A self-help advocacy movement: A promising peer support system for mentally handicapped people. *Rehabilitation Literature, 47*(1), 2–7.

Salzman, L. (2010). Rethinking guardianship (again): Substituted decision making as a violation of the integration mandate of Title II of the Americans with Disabilities Act. *University of Colorado Law Review, 81,* 157.

Schalock, R.L., Baker, P.C., & Croser, M.D. (2002). *Embarking on a new century: Mental retardation at the end of the 20th century.* Washington, DC: American Association on Mental Retardation.

Schmidt, W.C. (1995). *Guardianship: Court of last resort for the elderly and disabled.* Durham, NC: Carolina Academic Press.

Schur, L., Kruse, D., & Blanck, P. (2013). *People with disabilities: Sidelined or mainstreamed?* New York, NY: Cambridge University Press.

Schur, L., Nishii, L., Adya, M., Kruse, D., Bruyere, S., & Blanck, P. (2014). Accommodating employees with and without disabilities. *Human Resource Management, 53*(4), 593–621. doi:10.1002/hrm.21607

Scotch, R.K. (1989). Politics and policy in the history of the disability rights movement. *Milbank Quarterly, 67*(2), 380–400.

Smith, J.D., & Nelson, K.R. (1989). *The sterilization of Carrie Buck: Was she feebleminded or society's pawn?* New York, NY: New Horizon Press.

Teaster, P., Wood, E., Lawrence, S., & Schmidt, W. (2007) Wards of the state: A national study of public guardianship. *Stetson Law Review, 37,* 193.

Uekert, B.K., & Van Duizend, R. (2011). Adult guardianships: A "best guess" national estimate and the momentum for reform. In C.R. Flango, A.M. McDowell, C.F. Campbell, & N.B. Kauder (Eds.), *Future trends in state courts 2011* (pp. 107–112). Washington, DC: National Center for State Courts.

United Kingdom Office of the Public Guardian. (2007). *Making decisions: The independent mental capacity advocate.* Retrieved from https://www.gov.uk/government/uploads/system/uploads/attachment_data/file/365629/making-decisions-opg606-1207.pdf

United Nations. (2006). *Convention on the Rights of Persons with Disabilities,* G.A. Res. 61/106, U.N. GAOR, 61st Sess., U.N. Doc. A/Res/61/106 (Dec. 13, 2006).

United Nations. (2007). *From exclusion to equality: Realizing the rights of persons with disabilities.* Retrieved from http://www.un.org/disabilities/documents/toolaction/ipuhb.pdf

United Nations General Assembly. (1948, December 10). *Universal Declaration of Human Rights.* General Assembly Res. 217A (III), UN Doc A/810 at 71.

U.S. Administration for Community Living. (2014). *New Law Expands ACL's Capacity to Serve Americans with Disabilities.* Retrieved from http://www.acl.gov/NewsRoom/blog/2014/2014_07_22.aspx

U.S. Equal Employment Opportunity Commission. (n.d.). *Remarks of President George Bush at the signing of the Americans with Disabilities Act.* Retrieved from http://www.eeoc.gov/eeoc/history/35th/videos/ada_signing_text.html

Wehmeyer, M.L., & Schwartz, M. (1998). The relationship between self-determination and quality of life for adults with mental retardation. *Education and Training in Mental Retardation and Developmental Disabilities, 33*(1), 3–12.

Winick, B. (1995). The side effects of incompetency labeling and the implications for mental health law. *Psychology, Public Policy and Law, 1*(1), 6–42.

Self-Advocacy

Karrie A. Shogren

In the intellectual and developmental disability field, self-advocacy has had a significant and sustained impact since the 1960s. Self-advocacy can be viewed both as a social movement (Wehmeyer, Bersani, & Gagne, 2000) and as a set of skills needed to successfully participate in advocacy (Test, Fowler, Brewer, & Wood, 2005). As a social movement, self-advocacy brought together people with intellectual and developmental disabilities and those who support them to emphasize the inherent right of people with intellectual and developmental disabilities to be causal agents—the people who make things happen in their own lives—and to receive supports and services to enable this outcome. The self-advocacy movement changed perceptions of the role of people with intellectual and developmental disabilities, emphasized that self-advocates could serve as leaders and organizers, and pushed for the integration of these values in the structure and delivery of supports and services. As a set of skills, self-advocacy involves knowledge of one's strengths, interests, needs, and rights as well as the ability to communicate that knowledge and act as a leader. These skills enable a person to engage in advocacy and participate in social movements.

This chapter provides a brief overview of the development of self-advocacy in the intellectual disability field, explores how self-advocacy is a social movement and what it has been able to achieve as such, and suggests some strategies to promote skills associated with self-advocacy.

DEVELOPMENT OF THE SELF-ADVOCACY MOVEMENT

The self-advocacy movement emerged in the 1960s with "social clubs" in Sweden organized by Bengt Nirje, a leader in the normalization movement, that provided opportunities for people with intellectual and developmental disabilities to organize and to develop and express self-determination (Caldwell, 2011). As the self-advocacy movement matured, organizations were formed in the United States and internationally that were created and run by people with intellectual and developmental disabilities. The first groups in North America were established in early 1970s. The first national conference in the United States was held in 1990, and a national organization (Self-Advocates Becoming Empowered) was established in 1994. There are more than 800 active self-advocacy groups in the United States (Caldwell, 2010) and in 43 countries around the world (Caldwell, 2011). Self-advocacy groups provide learning opportunities, social support, and community for people with intellectual and developmental disabilities. These groups vary significantly based on local interests, preferences, and activities. Some more strongly emphasize advocacy, others more strongly emphasize social support, and still others focus on community engagement.

SELF-ADVOCACY AS A SOCIAL MOVEMENT

The self-advocacy movement can be understood as a social movement or a "collective, organized, sustained, and noninstitutional challenge to authorities, powerholders, or cultural beliefs or practices" (Goodwin & Jasper, 2003, p. 3). Social movements emerge as people form networks to advocate and develop a collective identity around a shared issue (Polletta & Jasper, 2001). The self-advocacy movement emerged after other social movements within the disability field, namely the parent movement (Turnbull, Shogren, & Turnbull, 2011), the independent living movement (Shapiro, 1993), and the normalization (Nirje, 1969) and deinsitutionalization (Bradley, 1994) movements. In each of these movements, different groups came together to develop a collective identity and challenge the status quo of disability services and supports, beginning with parents uniting around the lack of supports and resources available, particularly in the United States, for appropriately educating their children with disabilities. The normalization movement emphasized the inherent right of people with intellectual and developmental disabilities to participate in normative activities, and the deinstitutionalization movement emphasized the inherent right of people with disabilities to community-based, person-centered living, services, and supports. The independent living movement focused on changing the built environment to make it fully accessible for people with disabilities, with leaders from the physical disability community. The self-advocacy movement built on this lineage of advocacy in the disability field and was led by people with intellectual and developmental disabilities and others who supported them, with an emphasis on challenging existing segregation, discrimination, and stereotypes that created barriers

for the full participation of people with intellectual and developmental disabilities in society.

Social movements in the disability field were also influenced by other civil rights movements, including the women's rights movement and the African American rights movement in the United States. The unique feature of the self-advocacy movement was that people with intellectual and developmental disabilities were leaders and organizers, targeting issues of equitable treatment, community participation, and person-centered supports and services. Ultimately, self-advocates developed a collective identity advocating that they themselves should 1) be the people in charge of their lives, 2) be able to establish their own personal goals, and 3) be able to inform others how to organize and provide supports and services that supported those personal goals. A common rallying cry for the self-advocacy movement is "nothing about us without us." Up until this point, people with intellectual and developmental disabilities had been recipients of the benefits of other advocacy movements but had not yet emerged as leaders and organizers.

Self-Advocacy's Role in Changing Perceptions of Disability

The self-advocacy movement has played a key role in shaping and changing the supports and services provided for people with intellectual and developmental disabilities. More fundamentally, perhaps, it had to first change perceptions of the role of people with intellectual and developmental disabilities in shaping those supports and services. Prior to the emergence of the broader disability rights movement, disability was largely viewed through a medical or remediation lens. Disability was understood as an individual pathology, wherein the condition resided within a person and needed to be cured or remediated. The terminology used to refer to those with intellectual and developmental disabilities reflected this understanding. For example, terms such as *mental retardation,* which was the diagnostic term used prior to intellectual disability, reflected the idea that the problem was internal to a person. As Wehmeyer and colleagues (2008) wrote about the term *mental retardation,*

> The first such assumption was that the disability resided within the person. To have mental retardation was to be defective. The loci of that defect was the mind....The nature of the defect of the mind (mental deficiency) was inferior mental

performance (mental subnormality) characterized by mental slowness (mental retardation). (p. 312)

When disability is understood as a problem within a person, there can be many negative consequences. For example, in the late 19th century and well into the 20th century, institutions became the primary place for people with intellectual and developmental disabilities to receive services and supports. Such institutions removed people with intellectual and developmental disabilities from their communities and created segregation and a separate system. Although initially the focus of institutions was education and rehabilitation, over time the focus shifted to control and congregate care. Both children and adults with intellectual and developmental disabilities were removed from the community on the assumption that they were defective, a "menace" to society, and belonged in an institution (Trent, 1994). The changing focus on institutions reflected changes in society occurring during this time, including widespread immigration, a growing emphasis on intelligence testing, and an increasing recognition that many people with intellectual and developmental disabilities had support needs that would be present throughout the life span. When the dominant model of understanding disability was based on deficits and services were organized to control rather than empower individuals, it was challenging for the public (and people with disabilities themselves) to see people with intellectual and developmental disabilities as self-advocates and as causal agents over their lives.

However, beginning in the mid- to late-20th century, models of understanding disability began to change significantly—and the disability rights and self-advocacy movements exerted a significant influence. The social-ecological model of disability was adopted by the World Health Organization (1980, 2001, 2007), and the same model was incorporated into conceptualization of intellectual disability of the American Association on Intellectual and Developmental Disabilities (Schalock et al., 2010). The social-ecological model explicitly recognizes that disability is not a deficit that resides within the person but instead is the result of an interaction of personal capacities and environmental demands. Cultural models of disability have also emerged that focus on disability identity and challenge notions of disability as a deficit, instead focusing on how disability is a shared identity with unique cultural values and experiences that should be celebrated (Danforth & Gabel, 2006; Davis, 2013). The self-advocacy

movement changed perceptions of the role of people with intellectual and developmental disabilities, emphasizing that notions of disability identity and community extended to those with intellectual and developmental disabilities and that self-advocates could serve as leaders and organizers with those who support them in a social movement.

Self-Advocacy's Role in Changing Perceptions of Disability Support

The self-advocacy movement built on the foundation created by the normalization and deinstitutionalization movements to shift services and supports from a congregate, institutional model to a community-based model based on the needs and preferences of each person with an intellectual and developmental disability—not program or facility needs, preferences, or conveniences. Self-advocates participated in efforts to change terminology, particularly in the United States, moving from *mental retardation* to *intellectual disability*, a term that explicitly recognizes the social-ecological model by using the term *disability* to reflect the mismatch between cognitive functioning and environmental demands and to emphasize the responsibility of society for adequately including and providing for all of its citizens, including all those with disabilities. Overall, the shift to a social-ecological model of disability is highly consistent with the values of the self-advocacy movement. Furthermore, practicing self-advocacy is consistent with a social-ecological model, as it enables people with intellectual and developmental disabilities to 1) speak for themselves, 2) identify the community environments they enjoy, and 3) participate in identifying goals and needed supports. The impact has been described by one self-advocate: "I think I found my voice when I went to my first self-advocacy meeting and people were talking about dreams and hopes. I got to thinking about my dreams and hopes" (Shogren & Broussard, 2011, p. 91).

There still remains significant work to be done, however. As Powers et al. (2002) wrote, "People with disabilities are increasingly asserting their rights and responsibilities as citizens, services users and leaders…[; nonetheless,] major obstacles remain in services and systems that prevent people with disabilities from expressing their citizenship" (p. 132). Societal attitudes may not always reflect a social-ecological approach to disability. People with disabilities, particularly those with intellectual and developmental disabilities, continue to experience disparities in employment and community participation outcomes. Self-advocates and the self-advocacy movement continue to rally around these disparities and attempt to raise awareness and make changes to the service system and in the attitudes of the public. However, to act as self-advocates and to engage in the self-advocacy movement, it is critical to also have the skills associated with effective self-advocacy.

STRATEGIES TO PROMOTE ADVOCACY AND SELF-ADVOCACY

In the professional literature, numerous definitions of self-advocacy have been provided. A research team (Test, Fowler, Wood, Brewer, & Eddy, 2005) identified 20 definitions from a search of the literature and input from researchers, teachers, parents, and people with disabilities on how they defined self-advocacy. These authors identified four components that were fundamental to self-advocacy definitions:

1. Knowledge of self

2. Knowledge of rights

3. Communication of one's knowledge of self and rights

4. Leadership

Essentially, to advocate for oneself—either personally to ensure one's interests and preferences are respected or collectively through the self-advocacy movement—people with intellectual and developmental disabilities must understand themselves and their rights and be able to communicate effectively about these things using leadership skills. In the following subsections, each of these four components of self-advocacy is used as an organizing concept for suggesting strategies to help youth and adults with intellectual and developmental disabilities develop and express self-advocacy skills. Table 7.1 provides an overview of these strategies.

Knowledge of Self

Knowing oneself—including one's interests, preferences, strengths, and needs—is considered fundamental to engaging in self-advocacy. Ongoing opportunities to experience different environments,

Table 7.1.   Strategies to promote self-advocacy skills

Key self-advocacy skills	Strategies to promote self-advocacy skills
Knowledge of self	Having opportunities to experience different environments, activities, and interest areas
	Completing a preference assessment
	Developing PowerPoint presentations about one's strengths and support needs
	Participating in self-advocacy groups
	Participating in available programs/curricula:
	• *Choose and Take Action* curriculum (Martin et al., 2004)
	• *Self-Advocacy Strategy for Education and Transition Planning* (Van Reusen, Bos, Schumaker, & Deshler, 1994)
	Learning about one's disability and the history of the disability rights movement (Campbell-Whatley, 2008)
Knowledge of rights	Learning about one's rights as a citizen
	Participating in self-advocacy groups and conferences
	Participating in available programs/curricula:
	• *Partners in Policymaking* (http://partnersonlinecourses.com/)
	Learning about postsecondary education rights and responsibilities (Wood et al., 2010)
Communication of one's knowledge of self and rights	Receiving assertiveness training
	Experiencing opportunities to express rights and be mentored in this expression
	Expressing needed supports and accommodations
Leadership	Receiving opportunities for mentored leadership
	Leading self-advocacy meetings
	Engaging in political advocacy
	Participating in available programs/curricula:
	• Youth Leadership Forums (http://www.envisionexperience.com)

activities, and interest areas are necessary to enable people with disabilities to learn about themselves and to grow confidence in expressing knowledge about themselves.

It is important to note that people can communicate these interests, preferences, strengths, and needs in diverse ways. Some people may do this verbally and independently, whereas others may require more supports. For example, preference assessment (i.e., presenting options and seeing which item or activity an individual prefers) can be useful for garnering such information. Technology can allow people with intellectual and developmental disabilities and communication support needs to express their needs, such as pointing to or touching preferred items on a computer screen or using communication devices and programs.

Curriculum materials have been developed particularly for adolescents with disabilities to use to gain knowledge of themselves and their interests and preferences. For example, the *Choose and Take Action* curriculum (Martin et al., 2004) can be used with adolescents and adults with disabilities to support vocational assessment that enables people to learn about their interests, preferences, and goals for the future in the domain of employment. This curriculum includes 20-second video clips of a variety of entry-level jobs. Support providers (e.g., teachers, vocational rehabilitation professionals, parents) can set up a preference assessment with the videos for which the person with a disability watches between 8 and 32 clips that are randomly paired. After watching each pair of videos, the person picks the one he or she prefers. The videos are paired until a top choice emerges. The program then creates a plan that shows the top settings (e.g., hospital, office), activities (e.g., cleaning, taking care of animals), and characteristics (e.g., many people, outside, quiet). After watching or trying the preferred settings, activities, and characteristics in the actual community site, the person indicates if this is actually a preferred job. Through this systematic process, the people learn more about themselves, their interests, and their preferences, and ideas for vocational opportunities are generated. Researchers (Martin, Mithaug, Oliphint, Husch, & Frazier, 2002) found that young adults with intellectual and developmental disabilities had more positive job outcomes when using effective vocational preference assessment than when someone else selected a job for them.

A tool more specifically focused on education and transition planning that has primarily been used with adolescents with disabilities but that could also have relevance to postsecondary education planning is the *Self-Advocacy Strategy for Education and Transition Planning* (Van Reusen, Bos, Schumaker, & Deshler, 1994). The purpose of the Self-Advocacy Strategy is to enable students to learn strategies to enhance their participation at meetings and be better able to understand and express their strengths, interests, preferences, and goals.

Another highly relevant aspect of knowing oneself is understanding one's disability and the history of the disability rights movement. For example, Campbell-Whatley (2008) developed a 13-week curriculum to teach students about their disabilities, emphasizing individualized understandings of strengths and support needs, successful people with disabilities, and the characteristics of disability supports and services. After the curriculum was implemented, adolescents showed increased understandings of their strengths and support needs as well as improved self-concept (Campbell-Whatley). Other strategies include developing PowerPoint presentations to share information about one's strengths and weaknesses and develop goals for the future (Shogren, 2013) and participating in self-advocacy groups.

Knowledge of Rights

Understanding oneself and one's interests, preferences, goals, and support needs is one component of self-advocacy, but another key component is understanding one's rights and responsibilities as a citizen. People with intellectual and developmental disabilities need to understand rights to advocate at a personal level and need to appreciate the context of the self-advocacy movement. At the personal level, this might involve advocating for equality of opportunity or reasonable accommodations. Unfortunately, people with intellectual and developmental disabilities all too often face societal barriers to achieving their goals, particularly related to employment. As one self-advocate described the job search process, the prospective employers were "looking at my disability and not the person I am. If they really look at me as a person and not as a disability they would know me better and I can talk to them" (Shogren & Broussard, 2011, p. 91). This person was told—even though there was an active job posting—that the budget was not approved or that she was not right for the job. However, she kept going back to the job site and asking about the status of her application because she knew she had the right to have her application receive equal consideration.

There are a variety of ways for people with intellectual and developmental disabilities to learn about their rights. One way is through participation in self-advocacy meetings and in self-advocacy conferences. For example, Self-Advocates Becoming Empowered (http://www.sabeusa.org/), a national self-advocacy group in the United States, has a national conference each year, and many other self-advocacy groups organize not just local meetings but also meetings at the state or provincial level. The national and state- or province-level meetings often include sessions that provide education on rights and acting as an effective advocate. In addition to teaching about rights, Self-Advocates Becoming Empowered and other groups also focus on teaching and supporting the development of the expression of one's responsibilities as a citizen. For example, voting is an area in which people with intellectual and developmental disabilities often experience discrimination either through the denial of voting rights or because of cognitive inaccessibility of voting materials. Projects have emerged to document such discrimination and to create educational opportunities for people with disabilities to learn about the voting process and how to exercise their voting rights.

Other training opportunities have emerged that have trained self-advocates internationally about rights and advocacy. Partners in Policymaking, for example, was established in 1987 by the Minnesota Governor's Council on Developmental Disabilities. As of the 25th anniversary of the program in 2012, there were more than 21,000 Partners graduates in the United States and more than 2,000 graduates internationally. The Partners in Policymaking web site has a variety of tools that can be used to support the growth and development of advocacy skills (http://mn.gov/mnddc/pipm/).

Interventions have also been developed to teach youth and adults about their rights and responsibilities in the postsecondary education context. For example, Wood, Kelley, Test, and Fowler (2010) developed an intervention about rights and responsibilities in postsecondary settings under the Americans with Disabilities Act (ADA) of 1990 (PL 101-336). The researchers adapted a document from the U.S. Department of Education called *Students with Disabilities Preparing for Postsecondary Education: Know Your Rights and Responsibilities* (the original version is available at http://www2.ed.gov/about /offices/list/ocr/transition.html). They found that when students preparing for the transition to college had audio support for reading the text and explicit instruction on how to advocate, they were more able to understand the information and generalize it to new situations. For example, students took part in mock interviews with staff from disability services offices in postsecondary settings and were able to communicate about their required accommodations after explicit instruction.

Communication of One's Knowledge of Self and Rights

Knowing oneself and knowing about one's rights are important elements of self-advocacy. However, self-advocates also need to be able to communicate this knowledge effectively to others. Many self-advocates emphasize their responsibility to support the self-advocacy movement and the next generation of self-advocacy leaders. Self-advocate leaders have said that being a self-advocate involves "[getting] out there and [making] it better for someone else who can't yet speak up for themselves" and "being able to advocate for myself and others too if they need it" (Shogren & Broussard, 2011, p. 91).

In reviewing the literature on self-advocacy, Test, Fowler, Brewer, and Wood (2005) identified the importance of body language, listening skills, recruiting help, and assertiveness in effectively communicating with others to ensure that one's preferences, interests, and rights are acknowledged and respected. Assertiveness, particularly when advocating for oneself or for the broader group of individuals with intellectual and developmental disabilities as part of the self-advocacy movement, is key. Assertiveness involves knowing the result one wants (e.g., receiving reasonable accommodations, using a person-centered planning process), having confidence in one's ability to express what one wants, and being able to negotiate and engage respectfully with others (Weston & Went, 1999).

Having opportunities to learn about oneself and one's rights will help build confidence. Opportunities to communicate these interests, preferences, and rights to others also build confidence and assertiveness skills. Expressing goals and seeing how others react is important to learning how to communicate, negotiate, and be respectful and confident. Observing others engaging in these activities and having opportunities to role-play can provide support for youth and young adults having their first self-advocacy opportunities. This is the reason programs such as Partners in Policymaking and participation at self-advocacy meetings and conferences can be useful.

It is also important to learn how to identify and request needed supports and accommodations. Beginning this process in the school context, such as during the individualized education program (IEP) meeting, can be useful, but it is also necessary to consider how this generalizes and does not generalize to the postsecondary school environment and employment environment and supports planning in adulthood.

Although mentioned previously, it is worth noting again that people with intellectual and developmental disabilities vary significantly in how they communicate their interests, preferences, needs, and wants. Some people may do this independently. Others may engage members of their support team to translate certain behaviors as indicators of interests and preferences. For example, some people may verbally communicate preferences, whereas others may use pictures or technology and may need a circle of support to help contextualize their unique communication modes. However, even people who require intensive supports to identify and communicate their preferences can still be self-advocates. The importance of opportunities and structuring the environment to be respectful of and responsive to diverse communication modes, whether verbal or behavioral, is that it can lead to all people being able to express their interests, preferences, needs, and rights in unique and individual ways.

Leadership

Leadership is about learning the roles played by members of a group and assuming responsibilities related to a role within the group. For example, leadership opportunities have emerged for self-advocates within the self-advocate movement. Opportunities for leading group meetings, organizing social events, and engaging in political advocacy all create natural opportunities for learning roles, observing others performing the roles, and eventually taking on those roles. Many self-advocates emphasize the importance of having people support them in

growing into any of these roles. As it is for all people, mentorship is important for people with intellectual and developmental disabilities. Opportunities for leadership outside of self-advocacy groups may also be pursued, and these often build additional leadership skills. For example, people with intellectual and developmental disabilities are sometimes invited to serve as members on boards of parent and professional organizations in the disability field. It is important, however, in such situations that the roles reflect not tokenism but meaningful opportunities for people with intellectual and developmental disabilities to participate. Caldwell, Hauss, and Stark (2009) examined the participation of people with developmental disabilities and their family members on committees and advisory boards and found that several things were important to promoting meaningful participation, including individualized supports (e.g., accommodations including access to material in advance to process its meaning and materials written in jargon-free language) and financial supports for attendance at meetings. Also, providing clear communication channels, training and supports on how to act as leaders, and expectations for participation and action, as well as communicating the value of the person being on the committee, were all necessary to promoting meaningful leadership and participation.

Opportunities also exist for youth with intellectual and developmental disabilities. Youth Leadership Forums are intensive training programs for adolescents with disabilities that typically involve a residential experience, often in a university setting, during the summer, with education and networking sessions and ongoing mentoring and support during the year. Adolescents are matched with adult mentors with disabilities who provide education and mentoring on leadership skills, career exploration, civil rights, and ways to handle discrimination throughout the year (Wehmeyer, Gragoudas, & Shogren, 2006).

FUTURE DIRECTIONS

Some have suggested that a "second phase" of the disability rights movement has begun (Longmore, 2003) that focuses on disability identity and culture, building on the first generation of the movement that focused on advocacy and rights. Although advocacy and rights are still critical, given that those with disabilities remain a minority and marginalized group, this second generation adds the celebration of the unique culture and identity associated with having a disability. As described previously, social movements are sustained through shared experiences that bring people together to build a collective identity; in this second phase, the collective identity may focus on culture and identity as well as rights. This shift has been shaped by progress that has occurred in the field (e.g., the passage of the ADA, the movement toward community-based supports and services), although there remains significant work to be done.

Nonetheless, progress has not been equivalent for all disability groups. Distinctions persist between disability groups in the disability rights movement; some have discussed a "hierarchy of disability" in the disability community, with those with intellectual and developmental disabilities often being viewed differently and more negatively than those with other disabilities (Caldwell, 2011). This occurs not only in the disability rights movement but also in society in general. People still question the degree to which people with intellectual and developmental disabilities can be self-advocates. Some people ask how those with significant support needs related to intellectual functioning can understand their own rights, communicate their rights effectively, and be effective leaders. Yet, as self-advocates themselves have said, the attitudes and biases of others are often the biggest barrier. Yes, people with intellectual and developmental disabilities need ongoing support to navigate the complexities of legal rights and advocacy; however, self-advocates argue they also have a great deal to teach others, if people only open their minds:

> I get frustrated by some people...Like one [parent group] who tells the legislature that their son and daughter have the mind of a 6 year old child.... They look down on us and not value as a person and its demeaning instead of a positive.... We need to do education over and over and over again.... I feel like it has to be a two way street because they need to learn from us and we need to learn from them. (Shogren & Broussard, 2011, p. 94)

Ultimately, people with intellectual and developmental disabilities and those who act as their supporters and allies must work in partnership to learn together, advocate together, and change perceptions together (as has occurred in other civil rights movements). By challenging the notion that an intellectual or developmental disability is a problem and

shifting to models that recognize intellectual and developmental disabilities as a form of diversity associated with a unique identity and community, support providers can serve as allies in the movement while fostering the leadership of those with intellectual and developmental disabilities. Examples abound of self-advocates and their allies taking on leadership roles in advocacy and educating the public and their governing bodies about their experiences as minoritized people.

Ongoing efforts are needed to change societal perceptions of people with intellectual and developmental disabilities and to bring together disability groups to broaden the celebration of disability culture and increase the establishment of a cross-disability agenda for continued change and advocacy. This is particularly important given the growing movement in policy and practice toward generic services and supports that are not based on a specific disability label. For such services and supports to be effective, they need to be inclusive of all people, recognizing the diverse support needs that exist within the disability community.

Within the self-advocacy movement, many current leaders cite the importance of their personal experiences with oppression and discrimination in institutions and segregated settings in shaping their desire to advocate and make change. Some have questioned how the next generation of leaders, many of whom have not had direct experience with institutions, will view advocacy and their role in promoting change from within the communities where they live. There is still significant oppression and discrimination, but the nature of oppression may be changing. Efforts are needed to understand current and changing issues in self-advocacy and how the next generation of leaders in self-advocacy needs and wants to be supported (see Chapter 3).

Furthermore, although those with intellectual and developmental disabilities experience disparities in their access to technology, emerging technologies and the use of social media are increasingly changing communication, social relationships, and community organizing (see Chapter 1). Such changes will shape the ways in which people organize and develop collective identities, including leaders in the self-advocacy movement. These emerging technologies create new opportunities for those with severe disabilities and significant communication support needs to enhance their participation in the self-advocacy movement.

Ultimately, there remains significant work to be done to ensure that people with disabilities, particularly those with intellectual and developmental disabilities, experience equality of opportunity and have access to the opportunities and supports to live the lives that they want in their community. Ongoing advocacy within the disability community, of which the self-advocacy movement is part, is needed. Continued attention to the movement, as well as supporting the development of skills that enable self-advocacy, will be critical to the future of the self-advocacy, and the meaningful participation of people with intellectual and developmental disabilities in the decisions that affect their lives and their community. Shaping public perceptions of intellectual and developmental disabilities, including promoting the understanding that those with intellectual and developmental disabilities can serve as advocates and leaders with support from their allies, has the potential to lead to higher expectations, greater opportunities, and a celebration of the capacity of those with intellectual and developmental disabilities to act as leaders and change agents, living and learning and growing in inclusive communities.

SUMMARY

In the intellectual and developmental disability field, the self-advocacy movement has had a significant and sustained impact. Self-advocacy can be viewed both as a social movement and as a set of skills needed to successfully participate in advocacy. As a social movement, self-advocacy brought together people with intellectual and developmental disabilities and those who support them to emphasize the inherent right of people with intellectual and developmental disabilities to be causal agents—the people who make things happen in their own lives—and to receive supports and services to enable this outcome. The self-advocacy movement changed perceptions of the role of people with intellectual and developmental disabilities, emphasized that self-advocates could serve as leaders and organizers, and pushed for the integration of these values in the structure and delivery of supports and services. As a set of skills, self-advocacy involves knowledge of one's strengths, interests, needs, and rights as well as the ability to communicate that knowledge and act as a leader. These skills enable a person to engage in advocacy and participate in social movements.

FOR FURTHER THOUGHT AND DISCUSSION

1. What are some of the ways in which a person's self-advocacy could be supported in typical, day-to-day activities?

2. What might be some barriers to the progress of the self-advocacy movement through the next decade?

3. What are the benefits of a person with intellectual or developmental disabilities becoming part of a self-advocacy group?

4. Discuss the implications of ongoing segregated settings and practices on the development of self-determination skills.

5. How might young people become involved in self-advocacy?

REFERENCES

Americans with Disabilities Act (ADA) of 1990, PL 101-336, 42 U.S.C. §§ 12101 *et seq.*

Bradley, V.J. (1994). Evolution of a new service paradigm. In V.J. Bradley, J.W. Ashbaugh, & B.C. Blaney (Eds.), *Creating individual supports for people with developmental disabilities: A mandate for change at many levels* (pp. 11–32). Baltimore, MD: Paul H. Brookes Publishing Co.

Caldwell, J. (2010). Leadership development of individuals with developmental disabilities in the self-advocacy movement. *Journal of Intellectual Disability Research, 54*(11), 1004–1014.

Caldwell, J. (2011). Disability identity of leaders in the self-advocacy movement. *Intellectual and Developmental Disabilities, 49*(5), 315–326.

Caldwell, J., Hauss, S., & Stark, B. (2009). Participation of individuals with developmental disabilities and families on advisory boards and committees. *Journal of Disability Policy Studies, 20*(2), 101–109.

Campbell-Whatley, G.D. (2008). Teaching students about their disabilities: Increasing self-determination skills and self-concept. *International Journal of Special Education, 23*(2), 137–144.

Danforth, S., & Gabel, S.L. (2006). *Vital questions facing disability studies in education.* New York, NY: Peter Lang.

Davis, L.J. (Ed.). (2013). *The disability studies reader* (4th ed.). New York, NY: Routledge.

Goodwin, J., & Jasper, J.M. (Eds.). (2003). *The social movements reader: Cases and concepts.* Oxford, England: Blackwell.

Longmore, P. (2003). *Why I burned my book and other essays on disability.* Philadelphia, PA: Temple University Press.

Martin, J.E., Huber Marshall, L., Wray, D., Wells, L., O'Brien, J., Olvey, G. & Johnson, Z. (2004). *Choose and take action: Finding the right job for you.* Longmont, CO: Sopris West.

Martin, J.E., Mithaug, D.E., Oliphint, J.H., Husch, J.V., & Frazier, E.S. (2002). *Self-directed employment: A handbook for transition teachers and employment specialists.* Baltimore, MD: Paul H. Brookes Publishing Co.

Nirje, B. (1969). The normalization principle and its human management implications. In R.B. Kugel & W. Wolfensberger (Eds.), *Changing residential patterns for the mentally retarded* (pp. 179–195). Washington, DC: President's Committee on Mental Retardation.

Polletta, F., & Jasper, J.M. (2001). Collective identity and social movements. *Annual Review of Sociology, 27,* 283–305.

Powers, L.E., Ward, N., Ferris, L., Nelis, T., Ward, M., Wieck, C., & Heller, T. (2002). Leadership by people with disabilities in self-determination systems change. *Journal of Disability Policy Studies, 13*(2), 126–134.

Schalock, R.L., Borthwick-Duffy, S., Bradley, V., Buntix, W.H.E., Coulter, D.L., Craig, E.P.M., …Yeager, M.H. (2010). *Intellectual disability: Definition, classification, and systems of support* (11th ed.). Washington, DC: American Association on Intellectual and Developmental Disabilities.

Shapiro, J.P. (1993). *No pity: People with disabilities forging a new civil rights movement.* New York, NY: Three Rivers Press.

Shogren, K.A. (2013). *Self-determination and transition planning.* Baltimore, MD: Paul H. Brookes Publishing Co.

Shogren, K.A., & Broussard, R. (2011). Exploring the perceptions of self-determination of individuals with intellectual disability. *Intellectual and Developmental Disabilities, 49*(2), 86–102. doi: 10.1352/1934-9556-49.2.86

Test, D.W., Fowler, C.H., Brewer, D.M., & Wood, W.M. (2005). A content and methodological review of self-advocacy intervention studies. *Exceptional Children, 72,* 101–125.

Test, D.W., Fowler, C.H., Wood, W.M., Brewer, D.M., & Eddy, S. (2005). A conceptual framework of self-advocacy for students with disabilities. *Remedial and Special Education, 26,* 43–54.

Trent, J.W. (1994). *Inventing the feeble mind: A history of mental retardation in the United States.* Berkeley: University of California Press.

Turnbull, H.R., Shogren, K.A., & Turnbull, A.P. (2011). Evolution of the parent movement: Past, present, and future. In J.M. Kauffman & D.P. Hallahan (Eds.), *Handbook of special education* (pp. 639–653). New York, NY: Routledge.

Van Reusen, A.K., Bos, C.S., Schumaker, J.B., & Deshler, D.D. (1994). *The self-advocacy strategy for education and transition planning.* Lawrence, KS: Edge Enterprises.

Wehmeyer, M.L., Bersani, H., Jr., & Gagne, R. (2000). Riding the third wave: Self-determination and self-advocacy in the 21st century. *Focus on Autism and Other Developmental Disabilities, 15*(2), 106–115.

Wehmeyer, M.L., Buntix, W.H.E., Lachapelle, Y., Luckasson, R.A., Schalock, R.L., Verdugo, M.A.,…Yeager, M.H. (2008). The intellectual disability construct and its relation to human functioning. *Intellectual and Developmental Disabilities, 46,* 311–318. doi: 10.1352/1934-9556(2008)46

Wehmeyer, M.L., Gragoudas, S., & Shogren, K.A. (2006). Self-determination, student involvement, and leadership development. In P. Wehman, *Life beyond the classroom: Transition strategies for young people with disabilities* (4th ed., pp. 41–69). Baltimore, MD: Paul H Brookes Publishing Co.

Weston, C., & Went, F. (1999). Speaking up for yourself: Description and evaluation of an assertiveness training group for people with learning disabilities. *British Journal of Learning Disabilities, 27*(3), 110–115. doi: 10.1111/j.1468-3156.1999.tb00099.x

Wood, C.L., Kelley, K.R., Test, D.W., & Fowler, C.H. (2010). Comparing audio-supported text and explicit instruction on students' knowledge of accommodations, rights, and responsibilities. *Career Development for Exceptional Individuals, 33*(2), 115–124. doi: 10.1177/0885728810361618

World Health Organization. (1980). *International classification of impairments, disabilities, and handicaps.* Geneva, Switzerland: Author.

World Health Organization. (2001). *International classification of functioning, disability and health.* Geneva, Switzerland: Author.

World Health Organization. (2007). *International classification of functioning, disability and health: Children and youth version.* Geneva, Switzerland: Author.

8

Making Services More Effective Through Research and Evaluation

An Introductory Guide

Barry J. Isaacs

WHAT YOU WILL LEARN

- How the research literature informs the supports provided to people with intellectual and developmental disabilities
- Steps to plan a program evaluation
- Contextual factors that support the use of research and program evaluation in working with people with intellectual and developmental disabilities
- The need for building research and evaluation capacity in service organizations

Two excellent sources of information for improving services are the existing research literature and knowledge gained from evaluating existing interventions and programs. Yet the degree to which community-based agencies use these sources varies. Some agencies do not use them at all because they lack the capacity to do so. In other cases, lack of knowledge or negative attitudes toward terms such as *evidence-based practice* (EBP) and *program evaluation* may discourage their use. Often there is little or no incentive or time to take advantage of the research literature or to do program evaluation. This chapter highlights the need to do both. It also dispels the misconception that EBP does not allow for clinical judgment. In addition, concrete steps to plan program evaluations are described and issues of organizational capacity are briefly discussed.

USING THE RESEARCH LITERATURE

Research is one important source of information to guide decision making and service and/or support planning for people with intellectual and developmental disabilities. It can be applied at levels ranging from policy, legislation, and programs that are implemented across an entire service system in a country or region to the service options individual support workers discuss with the people they support. For example, a state or province might decide to develop a program for the delivery of individualized funding (a method of funding services that is tailored to a person's needs) to people with intellectual and developmental disabilities because research has shown positive effects of such approaches (e.g., Lord & Hutchison, 2008). Those developing the program can use other research that shows some of the challenges involved in individualized funding (e.g., Bigby & Fyffe, 2009; Lord, 2000; Lord & Hutchison; Stainton, 2002, 2009) to help them design an effective program that avoids some of the problems encountered in other places. At an organizational level, there are many prepackaged social skills interventions available, and an agency might decide to purchase and implement a particular one because it has been shown to be effective with the types of people with disabilities it generally supports. Research is also used by professionals at an individual level to decide what specifically might work with a particular person who has a specific set of needs.

Any of the applications of research to inform services or supports described previously might be referred to as forms of EBP. EBP is defined as the integration of three elements into intervention decisions for people with disabilities: the best available research evidence, clinical expertise, and client characteristics and preferences (see APA Presidential Task Force on Evidence-Based Practice, 2006). What is the process through which EBP is implemented? A common view is that of the single clinician making decisions for individuals. Service delivery is often, however, more complicated. For example, service may be delivered through clinical teams or in large programs mandated to provide specific kinds of interventions.

Mitchell (2011) outlined four different ways EBP can be implemented that account for these types of complexities: 1) empirically supported treatments (EST), 2) integrative approaches, 3) common elements of effective evidence-based interventions, and 4) common factors and characteristics of effective programs. The EST approach is perhaps the most common view of EBP. It is characterized by the use of discrete treatments delivered in a prescribed way that are shown to be effective for particular problems with particular types of individuals. There are various names for these kinds of interventions, such as empirically supported interventions (McBeath, Briggs, & Aisenberg, 2010) and empirically supported therapies (Chambless & Hollon, 1998). Rigorous evidence such as multiple, high-quality, randomized controlled trials are usually required for an intervention to qualify as an EST (e.g., Chambless & Hollon). The focus on studies with random assignment of participants to treatment and nontreatment groups requires high-level treatment fidelity (i.e., that interventions are delivered in a specific way) and has led to criticisms that ESTs are impractical and have limited relevance to the diverse and often complex people seen in many disability support settings (McBeath et al., 2010; Mitchell).

The integrative approach to EBP focuses on the adaptation of EST to fit individual needs and service contexts. Sometimes under this approach, contexts are also adapted to help accommodate interventions (Mitchell, 2011).

In a third approach to EBP, elements common to many ESTs focused on similar problems for similar populations can be identified and applied as needed based on evidence, experience, and underlying theories of change. For example, Garland, Hawley, Brookman-Frazee, and Hurlburt (2008) identified 21 elements common to at least half of a list of eight parent-mediated ESTs for disruptive behavior in children. These elements were divided into four categories: 1) therapeutic content, such as principles of positive reinforcement; 2) treatment techniques, such as modeling; 3) aspects of working alliance, such as consensual goal setting; and 4) treatment parameters, such as at least 12 sessions. In another example, Chorpita, Becker, and Daleiden (2007) listed the elements that are common to childhood depression interventions. These include psychoeducation, problem-solving activity scheduling, and social skills training. The identification of common elements does not necessarily replace the use of ESTs, but knowledge of common elements can, for example, guide the choice of a specific treatment manual (Chorpita et al.). Another application of this approach might train clinicians on a small number of practice elements common to the most efficacious treatments, thus providing the clinicians with additional options to offer clients (Chorpita et al.). Overall, this approach to practice is attractive for a number of reasons. Among these are that it allows for clinical judgment while maintaining an emphasis on evidence of effectiveness, it reduces the need to train staff in entire ESTs that may be complex and overlapping (Mitchell, 2011), and it acts as a basis for the evaluation of services by providing a list of elements it should be comprised of (Garland et al., 2008).

Finally, Mitchell (2011) identified an approach to EBP based on common factors and characteristics of effective programs. These factors and characteristics refer to the structure and context of service provision as opposed to specific procedures. Mitchell used the example of supports to children which, to be effective, should be client-centered, developmentally appropriate, address practical needs, foster good client–worker relationships, and address varied needs in a comprehensive way.

Whatever form of EBP is followed, the idea is to use the evidence that is gained from research when setting up a new intervention, amending an intervention, or evaluating an intervention with a view to making it as effective as possible. If there is no known linkage between an intervention and research knowledge (i.e., practitioners just do not know whether their practice is based on theoretical and research knowledge), the four approaches to EBP described previously are good ways to explore and establish such a linkage. If none exists, or if the analysis suggests improvements, appropriate amendments can be made. This chapter highlights an example of one instance where such a linkage was explored by a program operating in Ontario, Canada, and explains how the program was altered so that its practice was more evidence based.

Evidence-Based Practice Based on Quality of Life Research

Since about 1990, numerous studies on quality of life have been carried out in various parts of the world. A large study in Ontario, Canada (Brown, Raphael, & Renwick, 1997), found numerous factors that were associated with better quality of life for adults with intellectual and developmental disabilities, such as living in the community, living independently, exercising choice, and many others. Staff from one program in Ontario that teaches life skills to young adults with intellectual and developmental disabilities read these results with interest, conducted a library search to find that studies in other countries supported the findings, and decided to use this evidence to redesign their interventions based on quality of life concepts and principles. They changed their content to cover those aspects of life that were found to be most important to people's quality of life, and they altered their process to reflect the helpful actions of quality of life (e.g., exercising choice, focusing on skills and personal interests that are pleasing). Outcomes to evaluate the success of their program were also based on quality of life research evidence: improved self-confidence, statements of satisfaction and pleasure, and greater independence and self-determination. In short, this program moved toward EBP by using research evidence to amend and improve its own program.

Although there are many gaps in available knowledge from research, there is a large and varied array of research on interventions to support people with intellectual and developmental disabilities and to address many different types of needs. Developmental service agencies could adopt any one or more of the approaches to EBP described earlier to take advantage of this literature. To do so would require access to this literature, and skills to review it that may not be available in some organizations. In these cases, agencies could develop partnerships with universities or colleges where these resources are available. Literature reviews could be generated as part of student or faculty projects, serving the needs of both the agency and the university.

PROGRAM EVALUATION

Besides using the existing research literature, agencies should be evaluating the services they provide. Evaluation provides accountability to those who oversee programs. It also provides information that can be used in a feedback loop to improve services. The following subsections discuss program evaluation along with concrete steps for planning evaluations.

What Is Program Evaluation?

Program evaluation is a specific type of research. Here are two definitions:

> Evaluation is the systematic assessment of the operation and/or the outcomes of a program or policy, compared to a set of explicit standards, as a means of contributing to the improvement of the program or policy. (Weiss, 1998, p. 4)

> Program evaluation is the use of social science research procedures to systematically investigate the effectiveness of social intervention programs that is adapted to their political and organizational environments and designed to inform social action in ways that improve social conditions. (Rossi, Freeman, & Lipsey, 1999, p. 20)

Elaborating on some key elements of these definitions will help to develop a better understanding of program evaluation.

What Is Evaluated?

This chapter is concerned with evaluating programs targeting people with intellectual and developmental disabilities and those who care for them. Owen (2007) identified three levels at which programs operate and can be evaluated. At the mega level are the government offices or private boards that are ultimately responsible for the overall policies that govern programs and are concerned with their larger impacts. At the macro level there are the local or regional offices, agencies, divisions, and so on that are responsible for delivering the program in a specific geographic area or are a defined group within the larger program. At the micro level are the individual agencies within regions, the specific services within agencies, and the component parts of these services. Although evaluations of programs at the mega and macro levels are important, this chapter focuses on ways managers and staff can evaluate at the micro level. Examples of these are individual interventions or supports that exist within larger programs (e.g., service coordination, behavior management, psychotherapy) or specific components of these interventions (e.g., relaxation exercises in psychotherapy).

There are two aspects of programs that evaluations usually address. The first is program processes. When evaluating processes, the goal of an evaluation might be to determine if the program is being implemented as intended. Evaluation questions may include the following: Are certain key activities being carried out? How often are these key activities occurring? How many individuals are receiving services from the program? Sometimes, however, particularly with older programs that have not been evaluated, the goal of the evaluation may be to clarify what is going in the program. Who is the program serving? What are the key components of the program? What are the key activities and intended outcomes of the program?

The second aspect of programs that evaluations usually address is the achievement of outcomes. Outcomes should be distinguished from outputs. Outputs are the products or services that are delivered to program recipients (Rossi, Lipsey, & Freeman, 2004). Outcomes are the changes or benefits experienced by people with disabilities or their families as a result of the program. Outcomes can be short term, such as reductions in behavior problems or enhanced social skills. These more immediate benefits can also contribute to long-term outcomes, such as improved quality of life. Program evaluation that focuses on the outcomes of a specific intervention is often referred to as research.

How Is It Evaluated?

Evaluation is systematic. The approaches used in evaluation are the same as those used in social science research, such as psychology, sociology, or social work. These methods include complex experimental designs with control groups, surveys, reviews of clinical records, focus groups, and interviews. The data collected may be quantitative or qualitative. It is very important to remember that the methods used to evaluate a program must fit the program context. Some methods, such as studies with random assignment to groups, require many resources and strict adherence to program fidelity, making them impractical in many service contexts. Furthermore, these designs require some program participants to be randomly denied treatment, or at least have treatment delayed, and this can cause ethical concerns. A few simple designs that can be

implemented with relative ease in community agencies are included in the following sections of this chapter.

Why Conduct Program Evaluation?

Evaluation of services is undertaken for two main reasons. The first reason is accountability, meaning that evaluation provides evidence as to whether services are reaching the goals and objectives they were meant to achieve. This is important because services cost money. If some services are not reaching their intended goals and objectives, the money to fund them might be put to more effective use elsewhere. The second reason is that evaluation provides information that can be used to make services more effective and/or more efficient. In this chapter, the evaluation approaches described primarily address improving program effectiveness. Data from these types of evaluations, however, can also be used for accountability purposes.

What Are the Steps for Planning an Evaluation?

Good planning is a key to successful program evaluation. Owen (2007) and Bamberger, Rugh, and Mabry (2006) identified several issues to consider in an evaluation plan. These have been adapted in the following subsections to suit the specific needs of managers, clinical personnel, and frontline staff working in developmental service agencies.

Step 1: Clearly Articulate the Overall Purpose of the Evaluation Evaluations can have several purposes: to determine if the program is effective, if it is efficient, if it is being implemented as intended, or whether it should be continued or expanded. Evaluations are often undertaken to see how programs can be improved. Understanding the overall purpose of an evaluation is necessary for determining the specific evaluation questions.

Step 2: Determine Who Will Use the Information and How The question here, who will use the information and how, is tied directly into the purpose of the evaluation. Results from evaluations designed to improve a service, support, or intervention will likely be used by managers and staff. Results from evaluations designed to determine whether a program will continue are more likely to be used only by managers or funders. Clearly articulating at the beginning who will use the information, and how it will be used, increases the likelihood that the results actually will be used.

Step 3: Determine the Resources Available for the Evaluation

Lack of resources (e.g., staff, budget) for evaluation is a common problem in community-based agencies. Often, staff lack time to participate in program evaluation, individuals with appropriate evaluations skills may be lacking, and there may be no budget for things such as computers, software, or the required measures and tests. Overcoming these issues is challenging. Often the real solutions lie at the organizational level and involve building evaluation capacity and instilling a culture of evaluation, which will be discussed later in the chapter. Given these realities, each evaluation can only work within its current circumstances, and the evaluation plan must be achievable within the currently available resources. This means that the use of some types of methods, tools, or equipment may not be feasible and alternatives need to be explored. Bamberger et al. (2006) provided several recommendations for scaling back evaluation plans to meet tight budgets. It is important to remember that during the planning stage, suggestions for possible evaluation questions and data that could be collected to answer them mount quickly (Owen, 2007). As a general recommendation, particularly if resources are scarce, evaluation questions should be prioritized and the simplest design possible— collecting only the data needed to answer the most important questions—should be used (Bamberger et al., 2006).

Step 4: Determine How Much Time Is Available to Complete the Evaluation

Some evaluations may have strict time lines because the information is needed by a certain date. In other cases, time lines are predetermined. Time lines may be determined by the time period set out by funders or those needing to have evaluation results. Another example is that the evaluation of a group intervention must, more or less, begin around the same time as the intervention and end roughly when the intervention does. The terms "more or less" and "roughly" are used purposely here because some pretesting and follow-up may also occur. Bamberger et al. (2006) pointed out that the strategies used to meet the challenge of limited resources also address time challenges. Thus, where there is limited time to plan and carry out an evaluation, adjustments might

be needed to the overall evaluation design, methods, and the amount and nature of the data collected. For example, organizing comparison or control groups takes time, and designs that include such features may not be possible when time and resources are limited. In other cases, interventions may be underway already before the evaluation is planned, and thus only data collected during or after the program delivery can be considered.

Some types of evaluation activities are designed to be ongoing and, therefore, not time limited. In such cases, it is still wise to consider efficient methods to limit the time and resources that need to be expended.

Step 5: Identify the Other Stakeholders Involved in Jointly Planning and Carrying Out the Evaluation

The degree to which those carrying out the evaluation work with other program stakeholders varies. They may act completely independently (which is rare) or they may involve a very wide array of stakeholders in the planning and execution of an evaluation (Rossi et al., 2004; Weiss, 1998). Although there are many different types of stakeholders associated with programs (e.g., policy makers, funders, and even the general public), the most common are the management and staff who are involved in planning and carrying out evaluation (Weiss). Service recipients may also be included. A participatory action approach to evaluation involves working in partnership with a variety of stakeholders, with an emphasis on service recipients, to plan, carry out, and use the results of an evaluation. This type of approach would be extremely valuable in giving people with intellectual and developmental disabilities and their families a voice in program improvement (Sample, 1996).

There are many reasons for including a range of program stakeholders. When trying to improve a service, involvement of staff and managers in the planning and execution of the evaluation will increase the likelihood that the evaluation is successful. Resistance to evaluation may be encountered because program staff and managers might see it as extra work for which they have little time, may feel threatened by it, or may see it as irrelevant to their work. Including these stakeholders in the planning of the evaluation increases the likelihood that evaluation questions are relevant and important to them. This, in turn, may help to foster cooperation when the evaluation is carried out and the results are used (see Weiss, 1998, pp. 101–103).

The decision about which stakeholders to include in the planning of an evaluation depends on the overall purpose, the specific evaluation questions, the budget, and the time lines. Often smaller, internally initiated evaluations include only program staff and managers, because this group knows the program well, has definite ideas about the relevant questions for evaluation and program improvement, and is readily accessible. When planning an evaluation, it is wise to consider carefully what would be accomplished by including various stakeholder groups (Weiss, 1998).

Step 6: Clarifying the Underlying Program Theory or Logic

To carry out an evaluation, the elements of the program to be studied must be clearly defined. For example, if the purpose of the evaluation is to determine program effectiveness, then the intended outcomes of the program must be clearly articulated and agreed upon by interested stakeholders. If the program elements under study are not well defined, then some process to define them is needed. Need for this sort of clarification is common and is sometimes, in and of itself, the goal of an evaluation (Owen, 2007).

Logic models are practical and straightforward tools that help to specify underlying program theory (Isaacs, Clark, Correia, & Flannery, 2009; Rossi et al., 2004). A logic model is a pictorial representation of a program. In a logic model, program elements are identified and linked. A list of the program elements often included in logic models are as follows:

- *Components:* Groups of closely related activities that form the main functions of the program (e.g., assessment, mediator-based intervention)

- *Activities:* The things that are done within the program components to work toward the desired outcomes

- *Inputs:* Resources, such as staff, used to carry out the program activities

- *Outputs:* A direct measure of the program activities, including the number of assessment reports, training sessions delivered, or clients supported

- *Target groups:* The individuals or groups toward which the activities are directed (e.g., clients, caregivers, professionals)

- *Outcomes:* The intended benefits experienced by the program recipients. Often short- and long-term outcomes are specified in logic models. An example of a short-term outcome might be

reduction in problem behavior after behavioral intervention. Improved quality of life is an example of a long-term outcome for the same type of program. Outcomes must be distinguished from outputs. *Outcomes* refer to change experienced by program recipients. *Outputs* are more like products that are produced by the program. Just because a person with disability received a service (output) does not mean he or she experienced change (outcome).

There are many formats for logic models. An example of one logic model developed to evaluate improvement in program activities and outcomes of a behavior therapy intervention for people with intellectual and developmental disabilities is shown in Figure 8.1. This format was adapted from Porteous, Sheldrick, and Stewart (2002). Notice that this model does not include inputs and outputs. There are many papers on logic models with varying formats that include other elements (Cooksy, Gill, & Kelly, 2001; Dwyer & Makin, 1997; Hernandez, 2000; McLaughlin & Jordan, 1999; Millar, Simeone, & Carnevale, 2001; Rush & Ogborne, 1991; Schalock & Bonham, 2003).

The information to build a logic model can come from several sources (Owen, 2007). These sources might include 1) program documentation such as policies and procedures, 2) literature review on the program being evaluated, 3) experts in the field the program is associated with (e.g., if a behavior therapy intervention is being evaluated, experts in behavior therapy), and 4) program stakeholders.

Program stakeholders are a rich and important source of information on the program in that they know best how it works, its subtleties and nuances, what is working well and not so well, and more. In addition, including stakeholders in the logic model building process fosters their buy-in, which is important to the success of the evaluation. Before consulting with stakeholders, however, it is best to review the literature and program documentation and talk to others in the field. The information garnered from these other sources will inform the discussions with program stakeholders.

To build a logic model, meet with the program stakeholders identified in Step 5 to discuss and build consensus on the program (e.g., components, activities, inputs, outputs, target groups, outcomes) that will be included in the model. Then produce a draft model. Meet with the stakeholders again to discuss the model and agree on revisions. The model should then be revised and discussed again. This process

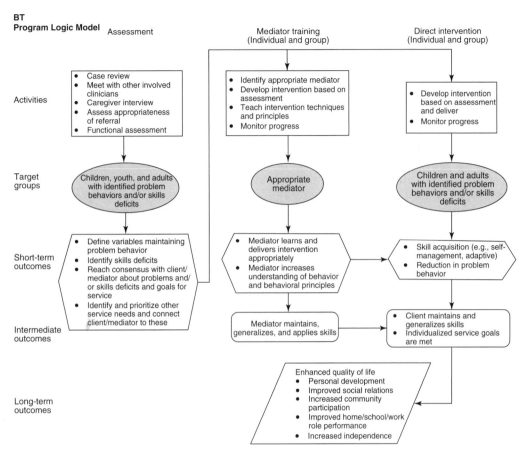

Figure 8.1. Logic model for a behavior therapy service. (From Isaacs, B.J. [n.d.]. Logic Model for a behavior therapy service. Barry Isaacs and the Behavior Therapy Discipline Group, Surrey Place Centre, Toronto, Canada; reprinted with permission; *Source:* Porteous, Sheldrick, & Stewart, 2002.)

continues until a final model is agreed upon (Isaacs et al., 2009). It is common for a program evaluation specialist to work with stakeholders during this process by facilitating the meetings, producing the first draft, and revising the model based on feedback.

Step 7: Specify the Evaluation Questions   The next step is to work with program stakeholders to specify the evaluation questions. The group or individuals who asked for the evaluation to be done should definitely have input into the questions. It is also important that those who will assist in carrying out the evaluation have input, as they will be more likely to answer evaluation questions they had a hand in formulating. For example, program staff are more likely to provide data or assist in the recruitment of program recipients if these data will be used to answer questions they think are the questions that should be asked. Not including the most appropriate stakeholders at this stage may also result in evaluation questions that are seen as irrelevant by those who should be using the information to improve the program (Weiss, 1998).

Program logic models are excellent tools for specifying evaluation questions. Working with stakeholders identified in Step 5, the evaluation team can go through the logic model and discuss particular aspects of it that would be important to evaluate. Then, specific questions should be developed around those aspects. Using the logic model in Figure 8.1, behavior therapists and their managers might identify specific short-term outcomes such as "mediator learns and delivers intervention appropriately" and "reduction in problem behavior/issue" as priorities for evaluation. The questions for evaluation are then 1) Do mediators learn and deliver intervention appropriately? and 2) Are significant reductions in problem behavior/issues in clients occurring? Another question that might arise is "What are the most common problems/issues with which clients are presenting?"

Step 8: Determine the Measures That Are Used and Develop Criteria for Success   The evaluation questions also specify the variables of interest. The next question is how to measure these variables. There are many types of measures that can be used. Tests, rating scales, or questionnaires (preferably with good reliability—i.e., consistent—and validity—i.e., measure what they are intended to measure), checklists, and frequency counts are just some examples. Any of these types of data may be based on reports from staff, parents, clients, or other observer reports. Data may also be found in clinical files or existing databases. Following along from the example in the preceding subsection, behavioral problems or issues could be assessed using any number of valid and reliable scales or through caregivers counting the frequency of occurrence of the behaviors targeted for reduction.

If outcomes are being measured, criteria for success should also be established beforehand. One easy criterion when using quantitative measures, such as scales, is statistical significance. In other words, client scores on measures are significantly better after therapy than before, as determined by a statistical procedure such as a *t* test. It is very important, however, to understand that statistical significance does not necessarily mean that a meaningful benefit was experienced by a client. Therefore, in some cases, criteria based on clinical significance might need to be established (Hayes, Barlow, & Nelson-Gray, 1999).

Step 9: Choose an Evaluation Design and Outline the Procedures   There are several different parameters along which evaluation designs can be categorized. Broadly, designs can be distinguished by the overall approach: quantitative, qualitative, or both (i.e., mixed methods). In some respects, the overall approach is determined by the measures used. Staying with the previous example, it is feasible to examine parents' experiences of change in behavior through interviews. This, however, does not mean that the overall approach will be strictly qualitative. A quantitative approach to sampling could be used, such as choosing a specific number of clients from different age groups so that the results might be representative of all clients in service. This would be in contrast to qualitative approaches that might use snowball sampling (asking participants to recommend other participants) and saturation (stopping recruitment when interviews are not revealing any new insights).

Qualitative data may be collected through a variety of methods. Interviews and focus groups are common methods used. More in-depth designs

also involve observation. Qualitative approaches are useful when evaluating program processes but also can be used to examine outcomes.

Quantitative designs may be categorized into group designs and single-case time series designs. These designs also vary in complexity. Group designs may include a comparison or control group (i.e., a group that is not exposed to the program being evaluated) that is compared to a group of individuals that get the program. Individuals might be assigned to these groups randomly or using some other method, such as date referral. Designs that do not use random assignment are referred to as quasi-experimental. These designs are considered weaker than designs that employ random assignment because there are other variables besides the program that could explain the results.

Including a comparison group often requires a great deal of planning and extra work. The simplest group designs do not include comparison groups. The AB, or pre-post design, in which measures are taken on program participants at the beginning and then again at the end of program, is common in applied service settings. These designs are easier to implement than comparison group designs because there are fewer participants to collect data from, and participants are likely more accessible because they are all in contact with the program being evaluated. AB designs, however, are considered a fairly weak design because program recipients may have experienced some positive change during the course of the program (assuming their scores were better at postmeasurement than at premeasurement), but it is always possible that the positive change occurred for reasons other than the program (e.g., maturation, changes in the environment).

Another possible approach to evaluating outcomes is to use single-case time series designs. These designs are often used to evaluate clinical interventions. The main feature of these designs is that data are collected repeatedly, at regular intervals before an intervention begins. This period of data collection is referred to as the baseline. This collection of data at the same intervals continues throughout the intervention and may continue after the intervention stops. The assumption is that when the data are graphed, the line showing the trend during baseline will be at a different level than that representing the intervention phase. See Figure 8.2 for an example using an AB time series design to evaluate an intervention to reduce aggression.

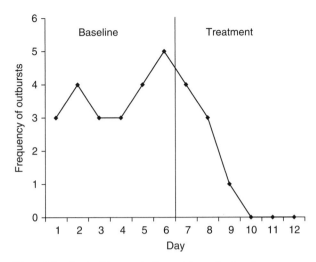

Figure 8.2. Graph of data evaluating an intervention to reduce aggressive outbursts using an AB time series design.

Time series designs vary in complexity and there are many different types. Like its group counterpart, the AB time series design is not considered strong because it lacks experimental control. Repeating, or replicating, the AB time series design across several individuals, however, does provide some evidence that an intervention is effective (Hayes et al., 1999). The reversal and multiple baseline are two examples of time-series designs with good experimental control. A detailed discussion of evaluation designs is beyond the scope of this chapter, but see Bamberger et al. (2006) and Rossi et al. (2004) for more discussions of group designs and qualitative approaches to evaluation, and see Hayes et al. (1999) for a discussion of single-case designs.

Once an overall design has been identified, the specific procedures for carrying out the evaluation and reporting the results should be developed. The following should be documented in detail:

1. What participants will be recruited and how (see next section for a discussion of participant consent)

2. A plan of what data will be collected, when in relation to the program (i.e., before, during, and/or after), and by whom

3. The planned procedures for analysis (e.g., if the evaluation is a quantitative group design, the statistical tests that will be conducted should be specified)

4. How the results will be reported, to what stakeholders, and for what purpose

Although the steps detailed in the previous subsections may seem like a lot of work, it is important to remember that evaluation does not have to be complex. Here are few recommendations that might help get sustainable evaluation started in agencies:

1. Be sure there is time dedicated for evaluation.

2. Begin with small projects with simple designs.

3. Consult with an expert in evaluation. In consulting with an expert, build in processes whereby the stakeholders such as program staff and managers learn about evaluation.

4. Be sure the results are reported and used.

How Does One Obtain Consent in Research Involving Participants with Intellectual and Developmental Disabilities?

Free and informed consent is a basic requirement in research involving human participants. *Free and informed consent* means that individuals are free to choose whether to take part in any research project; they cannot in any way be forced, influenced, or coerced into participating. It also means that a person who consents to participate understands fully what he or she is agreeing to. Just some of the information that must be communicated to each participant before he or she consents includes the following:

• The activities participants are expected to engage in

• That participation is voluntary and declining to participate holds no negative consequences

• The risks and benefits of participating

Participants with intellectual and developmental disabilities should always be included in the consent process, but determining if individuals have the capacity to consent is not always a simple process. Capacity to consent is not static; it changes over time. Furthermore, just because someone has diminished capacity does not mean he or she is unable to consent to participate in a particular research activity. Therefore, in all research, consent should be viewed as an ongoing process.

Special procedures should also be developed for aiding the consent process with individuals who have intellectual and developmental disabilities. These might include involving someone who knows the individual well and can help him or her to understand the research activities. Communication aids, such as pictures, may also be developed. In circumstances where individuals do not have the capacity to consent, a substitute decision maker may provide consent on behalf of the participant in accordance with policy and laws in the jurisdiction where the research is being carried out.

BUILDING EVALUATION CAPACITY

A previous section introduced the idea that the solutions to successfully engaging in evaluation lie at the organizational level. Many smaller agencies providing services to individuals with intellectual and developmental disabilities, and even some larger ones, do not engage in evaluation in a way that makes clear whether the people they are supporting are actually experiencing positive gains. There are several reasons for this. Agencies are often not provided funding to support program evaluation. Agency staff may lack the time, knowledge, and skills needed to engage in program evaluation. There may also be a view among agency staff that evaluation is not important or helpful. The concept of evaluation capacity building (ECB) is concerned with addressing these issues.

The objectives of ECB are to build evaluation knowledge, increase skills, enhance evaluation resources, and foster positive attitudes toward evaluation in organizations with the goal of enabling sustainable evaluation practice (Preskill & Boyle, 2008). Preskill and Boyle developed a model that describes how ECB initiatives should be designed and implemented to maximize success. The model takes into account many factors that need to be considered, including the following:

- The current evaluation capacity of the organization in question (i.e., evaluation knowledge, skills, and attitudes)

- Organizations' characteristics, such as learning capacity, leadership, culture, and structures

- The motivations, expectations, and assumptions associated with a given ECB initiative

- ECB teaching strategies, such as education and training for staff, involvement in evaluation, and technical assistance

- Elements of sustainable evaluation practice, such as resources dedicated to evaluation, evaluation policies and procedures, and a record of using results

Evaluation is difficult to carry out and sustain if there is little capacity in an organization for it. Thus, it is important that the leadership in any organization wanting to engage in evaluation also engages in ECB. The model provided by Preskill and Boyle (2008) provides an excellent guide as to how that may be done. An organization that engages successfully in ECB should end up with a strong evaluation culture in which staff are involved in evaluation, the results are used, mistakes are tolerated and learned from, and there is willingness to change (Mayne, 2009).

SUMMARY

Using existing research literature and engaging in program evaluation are two important sources of information to guide improvement of services and support for individuals with intellectual and developmental disabilities. There are various models of ECB that allow for the integration of research evidence, clinical experience, and client characteristics and preferences in approaches to service and supports. In addition to adopting one or more of these models, developmental service agencies should also be evaluating the services they provide. Program evaluation provides accountability and information for improving services. Evaluation should have a clear purpose and be carefully planned. Issues of organizational capacity to carry out sustained evaluation should also be addressed.

FOR FURTHER THOUGHT AND DISCUSSION

1. Think of a clinical setting you have visited or worked in.
   a. To what extent is the practice there evidence based?
   b. If it is not evidence based, why not? If it is, what factors support and encourage evidence-based practice?

c. What program evaluation activities are carried out there?

d. What are the barriers to program evaluation there?

2. Think of a service or support you are familiar with.

a. What are the core components of that service?

b. What are the short- and long-term outcomes?

c. What are some of the important evaluation questions for that service?

REFERENCES

APA Presidential Task Force on Evidence-Based Practice. (2006). Evidence-based practice in psychology. *American Psychologist, 61,* 271–285.

Bamberger, M., Rugh, J., & Mabry, L. (2006). *Real world evaluation: Working under budget, time, data and political constraints.* Thousand Oaks, CA: Sage.

Bigby, C., & Fyffe, C. (2009). An overview of issues in the implementation of individualised funding. In C. Bigby & C. Fyffe (Eds.), *Achieving their own lives: The implementation of individualised funding for people with intellectual disability. Proceedings of the Third Annual Roundtable on Intellectual Disability Policy* (pp. 3–12). Melbourne, Australia: School of Social Work and Social Policy, La Trobe University. Retrieved from http://espace.library.curtin.edu.au/cgi-bin/espace.pdf?file=/2009/07/03/file_1/119375

Brown, I., Raphael, D., & Renwick, R. (1997). *Quality of life—dream or reality? Life for people with developmental disabilities in Ontario.* Toronto, Canada: Centre for Health Promotion, University of Toronto.

Chambless, D.L., & Hollon, S.D. (1998). Defining empirically supported therapies. *Journal of Consulting and Clinical Psychology, 66*(1), 7–18.

Chorpita, B.F., Becker, K.D., & Daleiden, E.L. (2007). Understanding the common elements of evidence-based practice: Misconceptions and clinical examples. *Journal of the American Academy of Child and Adolescent Psychiatry, 46*(5), 647–652.

Cooksy, L.J., Gill, P., & Kelly, A. (2001). The program logic model as an integrative framework for a multimethod evaluation. *Evaluation and Program Planning, 24,* 119–128.

Dwyer, J.J.M., & Makin, S. (1997). Using a program logic model that focuses on performance measurement to develop a program. *Canadian Journal of Public Health, 88*(6), 421–425.

Garland, A.F., Hawley, K.M., Brookman-Frazee, L., & Hurlbut, M.S. (2008). Identifying common elements of evidence-based psychosocial treatments for children's disruptive behavior problems. *Journal of the American Academy of Child and Adolescent Psychiatry, 47*(5), 505–514.

Hayes, S.C., Barlow, D.H., & Nelson-Gray, R.O. (1999). *The scientist practitioner: Research and accountability in the age of managed care* (2nd ed.). Needham Heights, MA: Allyn and Bacon.

Hernandez, M. (2000). Using logic models and program theory to build outcome accountability. *Education and Treatment of Children, 23*(1), 24–40.

Isaacs, B., Clark, C., Correia, S., & Flannery, J. (2009). Utility of logic models to plan quality of life outcome evaluations. *Journal of Policy and Practice in Intellectual Disabilities, 6*(1), 52–61.

Lord, J. (2000). *More choice and control for people with disabilities: Review of individualized funding and support.* Toronto, Canada: Ontario Federation for Cerebral Palsy. Retrieved from http://www.johnlord.net/more-choice-and-control-for-people-with-disabilities/

Lord, J., & Hutchinson, P. (2008). Individualized funding in Ontario: Report of a provincial study. *Journal on Developmental Disabilities, 14*(2), 44–53.

Mayne, J. (2009). Building an evaluative culture: The key to effective evaluation and results management. *Canadian Journal of Program Evaluation, 24*(2), 1–30.

McBeath, B., Briggs, H.E., & Aisenberg, E. (2010). Examining the premises supporting the empirically supported intervention approach to social work practice. *Social Work, 55*(4), 347–357.

McLaughlin, J.A., & Jordan, G.B. (1999). Logic models: A tool for telling your program's performance story. *Evaluation and Program Planning, 22*(1), 65–72.

Millar, A., Simeone, R.S., & Carnevale, J.T. (2001). Logic models: A systems tool for performance management. *Evaluation and Program Planning, 24*(1), 73–81.

Mitchell, P.F. (2011). Evidence-based practice in real-world services for young people with complex needs: New opportunities suggested by recent implementation science. *Children and Youth Services Review, 33,* 207–216.

Owen, J.M. (2007). *Program evaluation: Forms and approaches.* New York, NY: Guilford Press.

Porteous, N.L., Sheldrick, B.J., & Stewart, P.J. (2002). Introducing program teams to logic models: Facilitating the learning process. *Canadian Journal of Program Evaluation, 17*(3), 113–141.

Preskill, H., & Boyle, S. (2008). A multidisciplinary model of evaluation capacity building. *American Journal of Evaluation, 29*(4), 443–459.

Rossi, P.H., Freeman, H.E., & Lipsey, M.W. (1999). *Evaluation: A systematic approach* (6th ed.). Thousand Oaks, CA: Sage.

Rossi, P.H., Lipsey, M.W., & Freeman, H.E. (2004). *Evaluation: A systematic approach* (7th ed.). Thousand Oaks, CA: Sage.

Rush, B., & Ogborne, A. (1991). Program logic models: Expanding their role and structure for program planning and evaluation. *Canadian Journal of Program Evaluation, 6*(2), 95–106.

Sample, P.L. (1996). Beginnings: Participatory action research and adults with developmental disabilities. *Disability and Society, 11*(3), 317–332.

Schalock, R.L., & Bonham, G.S. (2003). Measuring outcomes and managing results. *Evaluation and Program Planning, 26*(3), 229–235.

Stainton, T. (2002). Taking rights structurally: Disability rights and social worker responses to direct payments. *British Journal of Social Work, 32*, 751–763.

Stainton, T. (2009). Individualised funding: An international review of approaches, outcomes and challenges. In C. Bigby & C. Fyffe (Eds.), *Achieving their own lives: The implementation of individualised funding for people with intellectual disability. Proceedings of the Third Annual Roundtable on Intellectual Disability Policy* (pp. 14–21). Melbourne, Australia: School of Social Work and Social Policy, La Trobe University.

Weiss, C.H. (1998). *Evaluation* (2nd ed.). Upper Saddle River, NJ: Prentice-Hall.

II

Human Development

9

Introduction to Early Development

A Multidisciplinary Perspective

Maire Percy and Chet D. Johnson

WHAT YOU WILL LEARN

- Stages of development before birth
- Some important epigenetic processes in development: cellular differentiation, X-chromosome inactivation, genomic imprinting, metabolic programming, perinatal programming
- Disruption of development by teratogens
- Highlights of embryonic and fetal development and developmental milestones after birth
- Complications associated with pregnancy, labor, and birth
- Development after birth
- Approaches to prenatal detection of developmental disabilities
- Approaches to prevention, intervention, and cure of developmental disabilities, including stem cell research and ethical dilemmas

Scientists now recognize that human development is not exclusively regulated by the "blueprint" contained in DNA. Many different factors can affect how a child develops. Factors sometimes referred to as *environmental* include nutritional status and health care during pregnancy and afterward, socio-economic status, relationships during the first years, and quality of child care, especially during the first 3 years of life. Environmental factors affecting development also include exposures to toxic substances and other adverse events. The factors that influence development and how they work are becoming clearer. In biology, the term *nurture* refers to the effects that various environmental influences and factors have in total on an organism (in this chapter an *organism* is a developing human body). Indeed, the ways in which nurture can interact with nature to influence who each person is and who he or she may become are quite remarkable.

The purpose of this chapter is to provide an introduction to early development and the possibilities that exist, or that are being envisioned, for modifying this process. Such information should help individuals in the field to make informed choices relevant to prevention, intervention, or even cures. Readers are reminded that the term *developmental disabilities* includes intellectual disability and other disabilities that are apparent during childhood.

STAGES OF DEVELOPMENT BEFORE BIRTH

This section provides an introduction to conception and the embryonic and fetal processes. (Readers may also want to refer to the short video clip *Human Development* at http://www.youtube.com /watch?v=UgT5rUQ9EmQ.)

Conception

At birth, the ovaries of females contain precursors of all the ova they will ever produce. These immature ova are called oocytes. The testes of males from puberty onward produce new sperm continually. Sperm and ova are called germ cells.

Conception occurs when a sperm fertilizes an ovum and the number of chromosomes is doubled (see discussion in the next paragraph). The word *sperm* comes from the Greek word *sperma* meaning seed; it refers to the reproductive cells in males. The word *ovum* refers to the reproductive cells of females; in Latin, it means egg. Mature sperm and ova are called gametes.

Sperm and ova contain only 23 chromosomes, half the number found in other cells of the body (46 chromosomes, arranged in 23 pairs). Of the 23 chromosomes in sperm or ova, one is the sex chromosome. Half of the sperm have an X sex chromosome, whereas the other half have a Y sex chromosome. All ova have one X sex chromosome. If the sperm that fertilizes an ovum has an X sex chromosome, the fertilized egg will have two X sex chromosomes and will develop into a female. If the sperm has a Y sex chromosome, the fertilized egg will have one X and one Y sex chromosome and will develop into a male.

Zygotic Period (Germinal Period)

Once a female egg has become fertilized and the chromosome number increases from 23 to 46, it is known as a *zygote*. Zygotes undergo a 2-week period of rapid cell division before becoming embryos. In the process of cell division, each cell doubles and divides into two daughter cells, a process called mitosis (see Chapter 10). This 2-week stage is known as the zygotic or germinal period of development and covers the time of conception to implantation of the embryo into the uterus.

Embryonic and Fetal Periods

The embryonic period refers to development occurring between weeks 2 and 8. The term *fetus* refers to the unborn offspring from the end of the 8th week after conception (when major structures recognizable in adults have formed) until birth. Development in the embryonic period is remarkable in the sense that cells formed during the process of mitosis from one fertilized ovum move to different places in the zygote and begin to differentiate to form different tissues in the body. Understanding how the fertilized egg can develop into all of the different tissues in the body is one of the great challenges in human biology. Some mechanisms that regulate development of the fertilized egg are described in the next section.

SOME IMPORTANT PROCESSES IN PRENATAL DEVELOPMENT

The DNA—and genes that are sections of DNA—that make up the chromosomes inherited from both parents are very important in determining how humans develop. However, there is increasing recognition that development is also affected by mechanisms that regulate the activity of genes. These are called epigenetic mechanisms. Epigenetic mechanisms do not change the sequence of the building blocks in DNA, but they instruct cells to turn certain genes on or off. In the following subsections, we highlight developmental processes that occur during the embryonic and fetal stages and explain how epigenetic mechanisms are involved.

Cellular Differentiation

During the zygotic stage, cells have the potential to develop into any one of many different cell types and are referred to as *pluripotent cells* (Reik, 2007). As the result of epigenetic mechanisms, methyl groups on DNA are removed or inactivated during the zygotic stage. However, after more divisions, methylation is reintroduced and cells undergo differentiation. This means that as cell division proceeds, the daughter cells become more and more specialized. Different types of specialized cells make different sets of proteins. It is these different sets of proteins that cause cells in different tissues to have different shapes and membranes as well as different structures and functions (Kiefer, 2007; Leese, 2005).

Chromosome Inactivation

Development also includes an epigenetic process called X-chromosome inactivation (or lyonization; see Chapter 10 for additional information). At an early stage in development, most genes on one or other of the two X chromosomes in cells of females become inactivated so that they do not have twice as many X chromosome genes as the male. In the past, it was thought that genetic defects on the X chromosome would only affect males and that females would be protected because they inherit two X chromosomes: if one is defective, the other can compensate for it. However, this is not always the case. In some cases, females do have symptoms of X-linked conditions (e.g., Duchenne muscular dystrophy, fragile X syndrome). For more information about X-chromosome inactivation and its consequences, see Chapter 10 and the X chromosome guide on the Genetics Home Reference web site at http://ghr.nlm.nih.gov/chromosome=X.

Genomic Imprinting

Another epigenetic process called genomic imprinting is also important in development. Genes can occur in alternative forms that are known as *alleles*. For most genes, alleles inherited from the mother and from the father are both expressed. However, this is not the case for the relatively small groups of genes located on certain chromosomes that are subject to genomic imprinting. Genomic imprinting occurs during sperm and ova formation and persists throughout embryonic and fetal development. In genomic imprinting, methyl groups are added to certain regions of certain genes, causing them to be turned off. In these cases, genes on the maternal allele are expressed because the paternal allele is imprinted (and thus turned off), or genes on the paternal allele are expressed because the maternal allele is imprinted. Because genomic imprinting affects some genes, genetic information is needed from both a mother and a father for normal development of offspring. On the other hand, interference with genomic imprinting can result in developmental disorders such as Prader-Willi and Angelman syndromes (see Chapter 13). For an introduction to genomic imprinting, see the following web sites: National Human Genome Research Institute at http://www.genome.gov/27532724 and Learn.Genetics at http://learn.genetics.utah.edu.

Metabolic Programming

Development is affected by factors other than those discussed previously. There is evidence that a wide range of environmental factors acting during critical periods of early development can affect health in adults. For example, if a woman does not have adequate nutrition prior to conception, her child might develop high blood pressure, heart disease, or diabetes later in life. This hypothesis was originally proposed in the 1980s by the physician and epidemiologist Dr. David Barker. The idea evolved into the fetal origins theory, and it presently is called metabolic programming. Epigenetic processes also are involved in this physiological process, but understanding of this area is in its infancy. (See Fowden & Forhead, 2009, and Wong-Goodrich et al., 2008, for more information.)

Perinatal Programming

The concept of metabolic programming has since expanded into an idea called perinatal programming. Physicians and researchers are exploring the idea that environmental factors—including the ways in which mothers, fathers, and other people interact with an infant, bacterial and viral infections, and nutritional deficiencies after birth—can change the way an infant's brain genes express themselves and the way an infant develops and may even result in neurodevelopmental disorders, including memory disorders. For example, there is evidence of an association between a mother having the flu during pregnancy and an increased risk of schizophrenia or autism in offspring. Also, animal studies have shown how the impact of a mother's "love"—maternal licking and grooming—affects behavior in later generations. Rat pups that are frequently licked and groomed by their mothers (or a surrogate mother) appear to have lower stress, are more social, have greater cognitive skills, and are more responsive to reward motivations than those that are not. Furthermore, the rats that receive such attention pass on this trait to their own offspring (Champagne, 2008). It is believed that the hormone oxytocin is responsible for positive maternal behavior and that licking and grooming triggers the production of proteins called growth factors in the rat pups. These growth factors, in turn, prevent certain genes in the brains of the rat pups from becoming methylated. There is much interest in determining if similar mechanisms affect human health and behaviors (Galbally, Lewis, Ijzendoorn, & Permezel, 2011).

Highlights of Embryonic and Fetal Development

Table 9.1 lists some of the highlights of embryonic and fetal development. The Visible Embryo web site (http://www.visembryo.com) enables one to navigate through the 40 weeks of pregnancy and see the changes in each stage of human development shown in this table.

Table 9.1.   Highlights of embryonic and fetal development

Conception	Conception takes place in one of the fallopian tubes midway through the menstrual cycle.
3 weeks	The blastocyst implants in the uterus; the primitive placenta produces the pregnancy hormone human chorionic gonadotrophin. The blastocyst is a berry-like structure consisting of an outer cell mass (trophoblast), an inner cell mass, and the cavity.
4 weeks	The embryo consists of two layers—the epiblast and hypoblast—from which all body parts develop. The primitive placenta also is made of two layers. Present at this time are the amniotic sac, the amniotic fluid, and the yolk sac. The future brain and nervous system are visible after approximately 4 weeks of gestation.
5 weeks	The embryo is approximately 1 mm across. It is made of three layers—the ectoderm, mesoderm, and endoderm. The ectoderm gives rise to the neural tube (which gives rise to brain, spinal cord, nerves, and backbone), skin, hair, nails, mammary and sweat glands, and tooth enamel. The mesoderm gives rise to the heart and circulatory system, muscles, cartilage, bone, and subcutaneous tissue. The endoderm gives rise to the lungs, intestine, rudimentary urinary system, thyroid, liver, and pancreas. The primitive placenta and umbilical cord are already delivering oxygen and nourishment.
6 weeks	The embryo is 4–5 mm across. The head appears large; dark spots mark where the eyes and nostrils will be; shallow pits on the sides of the head mark developing ears; arms and legs appear as protruding buds; hands and feet look like paddles with webbing between the digits. Below the opening that will be the mouth are small folds from where the neck and lower jaw develop. The heart is already beating 100–130 beats per minute. Blood is beginning to circulate. The intestines are developing. Tiny breathing passages appear where the lungs will be. Muscle fibers are beginning to form.
7 weeks	The embryo is approximately 0.5 in. long.
2 months	The embryo is the size of a lima bean. It moves and shifts constantly. It has distinct, slightly webbed fingers. An embryo is called a fetus at the end of the first trimester (9 weeks).
3 months	The fetus is approximately 2 in. long. The skin is transparent; the face is becoming humanlike.
4 months	The fetus is approximately 4.5 in. long. The blood volume of a fetus is 10 to 12% of the body weight. In a 4-month fetus with a weight of 100g, this would be 10-12 mL (between 2 and 3 tsp) (Smith & Cameron, 2002). At 4 months of development, the fetal heart pumps this blood through the body approximately 2000 times every day. For details about the fetal circulation see the University of Rochester Medical Center Health Encyclopedia website (https://www.urmc.rochester.edu/encyclopedia/content.aspx?ContentTypeID=90&ContentID=P02362). The body is covered with downy hair.
5 months	The fetus is approximately 10 in. long from head to heel. A protective substance coats the skin.
6 months	The fetus is approximately 12 in. long and weighs approximately 1 lb. Blood vessels become visible through the skin, which is wrinkled. The lips, eyebrows, and eyelids are distinct.
7 months	The fetus is approximately 15 in. long and weighs approximately 2.25 lb. Body fat begins to form.
8 months	The fetus weighs approximately 4 lb. It may have "peach fuzz" on the head. It may have turned its head down in preparation for birth.
9 months	At birth, the baby is approximately 18 in. long and weighs approximately 6 lb., but weight at birth is variable.

Sources: Harding and Bocking (2006), University of Maryland Medical Center (2011), and The Visible Embryo (n.d.).
Key: mm, millimeter; in., inch; lb., pound; g, gram; mL, milliliter; tsp, teaspoon.)

DISRUPTION OF PRENATAL DEVELOPMENT BY TERATOGENS

Typical fetal development depends on the mother's good health and nutritional status. Because pregnancy is a period of rapid growth for both mother and fetus, both mother and fetus are vulnerable to disruptions in the supply of nutrients and micronutrients in the diet. Fetal growth and development can be adversely affected by many different factors, including teratogens. The word *teratogen* is derived from the Greek words *terato* (monster) and *gen* (to give rise to). Teratogens are factors that interfere with normal embryonic and fetal differentiation,

and teratology is the study of congenital anomalies (those present at birth) and their causes, whether they are genetic or environmental in origin (Arndt, Stodgell, & Rodier, 2005). It is suspected that many teratogens exert their effects via epigenetic mechanisms.

A large number of teratogenic agents have been identified. These include diethylstilbestrol (a drug used to prevent miscarriages and premature deliveries in the 1950s, 1960s, and early 1970s and also used in some countries as an emergency contraceptive or "morning after pill" to prevent implantation of a fertilized ovum in the womb), thalidomide (a drug used to treat morning sickness in the early

1960s), Agent Orange (a toxic agent used to defoliate trees, especially during the Vietnam war), valproic acid (an anticonvulsant), and misoprostol (a drug originally developed to prevent stomach ulcers in people who take certain arthritis or pain medications, including aspirin, but that also has been used in some countries to induce abortion). The rubella virus (which causes German measles) also is teratogenic. In addition, alcohol is a teratogen, and use of alcohol during pregnancy can result in fetal alcohol spectrum disorder (see Chapter 18). Isotretinoin (13-cis-retinoic acid, a vitamin A derivative), which may be used to treat severe acne, is a strong teratogen: a single dose taken by a pregnant woman may result in serious birth defects. Because of this effect, most countries have systems in place to ensure that isotretinoin is not given to pregnant women and that the patients are aware how important it is to prevent pregnancy during, and at least 1 month after, treatment. Whether isotretinoin also affects sperm is controversial; on the basis of adverse effects in studies with rats, birth control is advocated for males undergoing high-dose or prolonged treatment for acne (Gencoglan & Tosun, 2010). Excessive exposures to mercury

are problematic during prenatal development and throughout life. There also is evidence that excessive exposures to aluminum can be problematic. See the Health Canada web sites for information about toxicity of mercury (http://www.hc-sc .gc.ca/hl-vs/iyh-vsv/environ/merc-eng.php) and aluminum (http://www.hc-sc.gc.ca/fn-an/securit/addit /aluminum-eng.php). Table 9.2 provides an extensive list of known teratogens and other factors causing or contributing to developmental disabilities.

Examples of effects caused by teratogens include some cases of cleft lip and/or palate, anencephaly (a neural tube defect in which a large part of the brain and skull are missing), or ventricular septal defects (one or more holes in the wall of the heart located between the two ventricles), which are medically serious abnormalities present at birth. By interfering with the development of the brain and nervous system, teratogens also can result in developmental disability. It is important to note that at least five teratogens are associated with increased risk of autism; these include maternal rubella infection, ethanol, thalidomide, valproic acid, and misoprostol (Arndt et al., 2005). Fetal death, prematurity, growth retardation, and unexplained dysmorphology

Table 9.2. Some known teratogens and other factors causing developmental disabilities

Category	Examples
Drugs	Alcohol; vitamin A derivatives (13-cis-retinoic acid, isotretinoin [Accutane], etretinate); certain sedative and anxiety-reducing drugs (temazepam [Restoril; Normison], nitrazepam [Mogadon], nimetazepam [Erimin]); certain anticancer drugs (aminopterin, busulfan; cyclophosphamide); androgenic hormones (testosterone); blood pressure medications (captopril, enalapril); coumadin (blood thinner); diethylstilbestrol (synthetic estrogen); anticonvulsants (diphenylhydantoin [Phenytoin, Dilantin, Epanutin], trimethadione, valproic acid]; lithium; methimazole (antithyroid drug); penicillamine (copper-binding drug used to treat rheumatoid arthritis and Wilson disease); tetracyclines (antibiotic); thalidomide
Environmental chemicals	Chlorobiphenyls (PCBs, used as plasticizers, lubricants, and dielectrics); dioxin; ethidium bromide (chemical often used in molecular biology labs); hexachlorobenzene (fungicide); hexachlorophene (disinfectant); organic mercury; uranium; methoxyethyl ethers (type of organic solvent)
Ionizing radiation	Atomic weapons, radioactive iodine, radiation therapy
Infections	Cytomegalovirus (a type of herpes virus that causes enlargement of epithelial cells, especially the salivary glands); intrauterine herpes simplex virus (cold sore virus) infection; parvovirus B-19 (causes several different autoimmune diseases); rubella virus (German measles); syphilis (a sexually transmitted disease); toxoplasmosis (a parasitic disease passed from animals to humans, often not causing symptoms); Venezuelan equine encephalitis virus (mosquito borne). In 2016, Zika virus (mosquito-borne) was classified as a teratogen that causes microcephaly and other serious brain anomalies (Karwowski et al., 2016; Meaney-Delman et al., 2016).
Metabolic imbalances	Thyroid disorders (e.g., from iodine deficiency), diabetes, folic acid deficiency, elevated body temperature due to failed body regulation, unmanaged phenylketonuria (see Chapter 13), virilizing tumors (tumors that produce male hormones causing growth of facial hair). Lupus erythematosis (an autoimmune disease) is associated with increased risk of having a miscarriage or still birth or of having an infant born prematurely or with a low birth weight (Bermas, 2016).
Unhealthy lifestyle factors	Smoking tobacco, use of alcohol, use of street drugs, abuse of certain prescription medication, excessive consumption of caffeine (e.g., in beverages such as coffee and soft drinks)

Sources: Gilbert (2000), Shepard and Lemire (2007), The Hospital for Sick Children (2016), and University of Oxford (2010); see also Chapter 13.

(structural abnormalities) are all suggestive of teratogenic effects. The study of teratogens also is important because disorders resulting from them can be prevented by education of the community. Four factors that are important in teratogenicity are as follows:

1. Embryo/fetus age, or the gestational age of the fetus at the time of the exposure to the teratogen: Different organs of the body are forming at different times; therefore, the sensitivity to the teratogen and the organ affected by the teratogen will vary. Generally, the embryonic stage (i.e., the period of 14–56 days of gestation) is a time of greater vulnerability than the fetal period (i.e., the second and third trimesters). For a period of approximately 2 weeks from the time of conception until implantation, teratogenic insults to the embryo are likely to result either in miscarriage (or resorption) or in intact survival. Because the embryo is undifferentiated at this stage, repair and recovery can occur through multiplication of pluripotent cells. If the teratogen persists beyond this period, however, congenital malformations may result.

2. Dosage of the teratogen

3. Fetal genotype, which may make the fetus more or less resistant to the teratogen

4. Maternal genotype: Pregnant women differ in their ability to detoxify teratogens.

By considering the sequence of events involved in normal embryonic and fetal development, it is easy to see how teratogens may have different effects depending upon when they are encountered. Women who are planning to become pregnant or who are pregnant should get advice from their doctors or prenatal clinics about what potential teratogens to avoid and whether there are any potential problems associated with prescription medications or over-the-counter substances they may be taking or consider using. For additional information, see the Motherisk web site at http://www.motherisk.org/women/index.jsp.

COMPLICATIONS ASSOCIATED WITH PREGNANCY, LABOR, AND BIRTH

Many pregnancies are uneventful. However, sometimes complications occur during a pregnancy or during labor and the birth process itself that can affect an infant's health and development and/or result in physical or intellectual disability. These are discussed in the following subsections. In many instances, good health care can avert or lessen the effects of complications in mothers and infants.

Complications of Pregnancy

Complications of pregnancy are problems experienced by the mother, the fetus, or both. Some of the most common complications include ectopic pregnancy (a pregnancy that is not in the uterus), Rh negative disease (this occurs if the mother has Rh negative blood and the father has Rh positive blood), group B streptococcus infection (the bacteria causing this infection is often present in the gastrointestinal tract but sometimes can be passed on to an infant), preterm labor, and low gestational birth weight. For information about these conditions and interventions for them, see the American Pregnancy Association web site at http://www.americanpregnancy.org/pregnancycomplications/.

Complications of Labor and Delivery

Occasionally, women who have had normal pregnancies can experience complications during labor or delivery. Such complications can deprive the infant of oxygen or increase the risk of acquiring an infection and result in developmental delay, intellectual disability, and/or physical disabilities. Examples of labor or delivery complications include premature labor and premature delivery, a labor that lasts too long, abnormal presentation of the infant in the birth canal, premature rupture of the membranes around the infant, or umbilical prolapse (i.e., the umbilical cord precedes the infant into the birth canal). For more information about these conditions and interventions for them, refer to the American Pregnancy Association web site at http://www.americanpregnancy.org/pregnancycomplications/.

Complications Associated with Premature Birth

Infants born before the 37th week of gestation are considered to be premature. There are many complications associated with premature birth that can result in physical, developmental, or intellectual disability. These include immature lungs, increased risk of acquiring pneumonia, other infections, jaundice, intraventricular hemorrhage (hemorrhage into the ventricles of the brain; see Chapter 11), inability to maintain normal body temperature, and immature digestive tracts. For more information about these disorders and interventions for them, see the American Pregnancy Association web site at http://www.americanpregnancy.org/labornbirth/complicationspremature.htm.

DEVELOPMENT AFTER BIRTH

There are countless books and other resources readily available on the development and care of infants. Although these vary in quality, friends, relatives, and infant care specialists can help select those that are the most reliable and useful. The best materials are those that reflect current medical and developmental knowledge, are in keeping with current health care and child-rearing practices, describe health problems that infants might encounter, clearly explain the expected stages of development, and provide practical advice for caregivers.

Development During the First Year

During the first year of life, an infant grows and develops rapidly. The child's weight doubles by age 5–6 months and triples by his or her first birthday. Some of the major achievements in the development of an infant are called developmental milestones. Many organizations have published developmental checklists (e.g., the Centers for Disease Control and Prevention web site provides milestones typically observed from 2 months after birth to 5 years of age: http://www.cdc.gov/ncbddd/actearly/milestones/).

It must be emphasized that there is considerable variation among infants in their development rate; however, a substantial deviation from the norm, especially in walking or talking, sometimes may reflect a problem with brain development and the presence of intellectual disability. The time of onset of developmental disability depends on its nature. Symptoms may be evident at birth or manifest later in childhood. Children who have conditions such as encephalitis or meningitis (infections of the brain) may later show signs of cognitive impairment or cognitive difficulties. Early intervention programs are very important in supporting families and helping infants and young children to reach developmental milestones and their full potential (Shonkoff, 2009).

Development Throughout the Life Span

Until the early 20th century, the process of development from birth to adulthood was largely ignored, and children tended to be viewed as little adults. It is now recognized that from birth into early childhood, children go through cognitive, emotional, physical, social, and educational growth. Many different theories have been proposed to account for childhood development. Since the late 1990s, there has been an emphasis on identifying typical ages at which various milestones occur.

APPROACHES TO PRENATAL DETECTION OF DEVELOPMENTAL DISABILITIES

As discussed previously in this chapter and in Chapter 10, particularly, various genetic and environmental factors can affect development and result in physical and/or developmental disabilities. Certain disorders resulting in disability can be detected in a number of ways before an infant is born, including ultrasound scans and maternal serum screening as well as amniocentesis, chorionic villus sampling, and percutaneous umbilical cord sampling.

Ultrasound Scans and Maternal Serum Screening

In 2016, the American College of Obstetricians and Gynecologists issued new guidelines for prenatal screening and testing of pregnant women. It is recommended that all expectant mothers be offered screening testing ideally at their first prenatal visit (Prenatal Information Research Consortium, 2016). The most common form of prenatal screening is to look directly at the fetus with ultrasound (sound wave) scans. Ultrasound is usually done to determine an accurate gestational age, but the procedure also will pick up certain types of physical abnormalities such as a gross brain defect, a very large or very small head, certain structural heart defects, poor fetal growth, and certain abnormal features that suggest the presence of Down syndrome (see Chapter 14). It also will detect the presence of twins, triplets, or even more infants. Since the beginning of the 21st century, major improvement in ultrasound imaging resolution continues to take place. Although ultrasound scans conducted prior to 1992 were considered not to be harmful to fetuses, the safety of newer technologies simply is not known. Fetuses are now examined at early and vulnerable stages of development, and the acoustic energy applied is considerably greater than that used previously (Houston, Odibo, & Macones, 2009). Based on the majority of epidemiologic studies, diagnostic ultrasound during pregnancy is generally considered to be safe. Experts recommend careful adherence to established policies and further studies to determine risk and benefit.

Screening for Down syndrome and neural tube defects (e.g., spina bifida) can be done using a blood sample from a pregnant woman at 15–17 weeks of gestation for a process called maternal serum screening. Several substances can be measured in such blood samples in order to determine the risk that the woman may be carrying a fetus with these conditions. Some prenatal clinics offer pregnant women screening for Down syndrome using both ultrasound and maternal serum testing. Because such testing is associated with false positive and false negative rates, some pregnant women choose to have diagnostic testing for Down syndrome using an invasive test that analyzes cells from the fetus (see next subsection).

Amniocentesis, Chorionic Villus Sampling, and Percutaneous Umbilical Blood Sampling

Women at risk of having a child with a birth defect, and women older than the age of 35 (i.e., at increased risk of having a child with Down syndrome due to maternal age), may choose to have amniocentesis (analysis of the fluid and or fetal cells gathered from the womb's amniotic fluid), chorionic villus sampling (CVS; analysis of cells from the placenta), or percutaneous umbilical blood sampling (PUBS; analysis of blood from the umbilical cord); see illustrations of these procedures in Figure 9.1. Tests that can be done on such samples include analysis for the presence of particular proteins, as well as analysis of cells in the samples or that are cultured from the samples, under the microscope for the presence of extra or missing chromosomes or structurally altered chromosomes. Certain biochemical errors, such as a reduced level of a particular enzyme that results in a particular disorder, can be detected by measuring levels of certain

metabolites or measuring the activity of particular enzymes in cells. As explained in Chapter 10, to look for particular defects in DNA extracted from cells, long stretches of DNA along the chromosomes can now be copied billions of times in a procedure called the polymerase chain reaction (PCR). The PCR procedure is so sensitive that it can detect different types of genetic defects in single cells. Furthermore, as explained in Chapter 10, the application of microarray procedures has the potential for identifying defects in DNA or RNA in amniotic fluid, and samples can be obtained very quickly using CVS or PUBS procedures.

Amniocentesis, CVS, and PUBS have relative advantages and disadvantages. Amniocentesis is usually performed in the second trimester of pregnancy, between the 15th and 18th weeks, though it can be done during weeks 12–20. Amniocentesis before the 14th week is associated with a risk of miscarriage (0.25%–0.5%). By the second trimester, there is enough amniotic fluid surrounding the fetus to make it easier for the doctor to take an adequate sample without putting the fetus at risk. Because cells from the amniotic fluid are usually cultured to get a large sample of the fetus's cells, results from amniocentesis often take up to 2 weeks to obtain.

CVS can be performed between the 10th and 12th weeks of pregnancy. The risk of miscarriage associated with CVS (0.5%–1%) is slightly higher than in amniocentesis. CVS has been associated with the occurrence of limb defects in infants, but this happens rarely and mainly when the test is carried out before the 10th week of pregnancy.

PUBS is done at 18 weeks of pregnancy or later, when diagnostic information cannot be obtained through ultrasound, amniocentesis, or CVS, or results from these tests are not conclusive. In contrast to the other procedures, PUBS cannot detect neural tube defects, but it can detect chromosomal abnormalities, hemophilia and anemia, some metabolic disorders, infections such as toxoplasmosis and rubella, and causes of some structural problems such as intrauterine growth restriction. Results from PUBS usually are available within 72 hours. PUBS also can be used to give blood transfusions to the fetus and to administer medication directly. This procedure is considered to be safe, though invasive. The miscarriage rate associated with PUBS is 1%–2%.

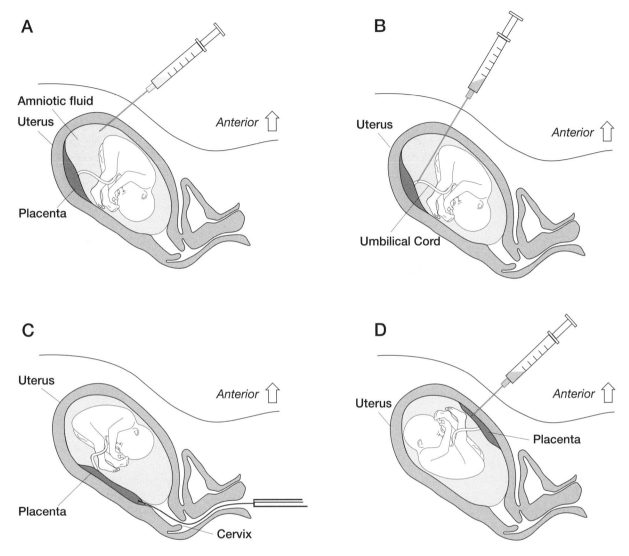

Figure 9.1. Amniocentesis (Panel A), percutaneous umbilical cord sampling (Panel B), and chorionic villus sampling (Panels C and D). (Copyright © Tom Dearie, Threesixty Creative/Infographix.)

APPROACHES TO PREVENTION, INTERVENTION, AND CURE

Future issues in the area of genetics and development include the prevention and cure of genetic disorders as well as the use of cloning and stem cells. Inherent in these topics are various ethical and social issues, including the ethical, legal, and social concerns arising from new genetics findings.

Prevention Via Genetic Counseling

The availability of technology that can detect genetic defects causing developmental disabilities is valuable to many parents. Knowing the exact cause of the problem helps parents to understand the likely outcome for their child and to choose the best option. Such information is absolutely essential for researchers to develop rational treatments or even cures. It also provides people with choices for family planning. For example, after undergoing genetic counseling, parents may choose not to have a family or to have a therapeutic abortion if a life-threatening problem is identified in the fetus.

Sex selection techniques based on in vitro fertilization can reduce a mother's risk of giving birth to an infant with X-linked disorders. If couples know that they carry genes for life-threatening illnesses that they do not want to pass on to their children, they can choose to have a procedure called preimplantation genetic diagnosis. This procedure begins with a process of in vitro fertilization, mixing sperm from the father with ova from the mother in a dish in the laboratory rather than having fertilization occur within the mother's body after intercourse. Single cells from the fertilized ova are then subjected to DNA analysis for a large number of disorders. Only those ova that do not show evidence of genetic defects are implanted. A few thousand of these procedures have already been performed for couples who have genetic defects causing life-threatening conditions. In Europe and in a few centers in the United States, in vitro fertilization with washed sperm is being used to reduce the chance of HIV infection in an infant whose father is HIV positive.

As discussed in other chapters, some people with a developmental disability receive a genetic diagnosis. Although there are many benefits that can result from genetic diagnosis, there also are ethical concerns. Some women would never consider having a therapeutic abortion. Others feel great relief at receiving a genetic diagnosis. However, they must think carefully about whether they should tell other biological members of their family about the disorder and how they should communicate the information. Professionals should be sensitive to the attitudes of individuals and support the choices that they make. Another concern is whether it is really ethical to test children for genetic disorders when there is no cure for them. In addition, assigning a genetic diagnosis can have unexpected consequences in the sense that once a diagnosis is made, the information is filed in the health records of the child and will probably be available for life to all future health professionals. This may be extremely helpful in many cases, but children and adults sometimes experience discrimination because of labels given to them by professionals. In Canada, it has been the case that despite universal health care, people with genetic disorders may have problems obtaining extra health insurance or assistance with paying for such things as corrective surgery or dental work arising from a disability.

Fetal Surgery

Some potentially life-threatening conditions diagnosed before birth are suitable for surgical intervention in utero. Surgical interventions have included intrauterine blood transfusion, operations on the placenta and umbilical cord, repair of congenital diaphragmatic hernia associated with occlusion of lung growth, and treatment of urinary obstruction. Even nonlethal conditions such as repair of myelomeningocele (protrusion of the spinal membranes and spinal cord through a hole in the vertebral column) are now considered potential indications. Although many fetal interventions are investigational, randomized clinical trials have established the safety and potential of some types of fetal therapy (Deprest et al., 2010).

Gene Therapy

In the past, only a few genetic disorders could be detected and treated early enough to prevent disease. However, as explained in Chapter 10, the Human Genome Project is significantly increasing the ability to discover more effective therapies and prevent inherited disease. It is anticipated that future advances in genetic technology known as gene therapy will actually be able to correct certain human genetic diseases, thereby improving the lives of children and their families. This technology is only beginning to develop and, although extremely promising, has not yet advanced to the point where interventions are developed and available.

There are two types of gene therapy: germ line gene therapy and somatic cell therapy. Germ line gene therapy refers to therapy in which germ cells (sperm or ova) are modified by the introduction of functional genes into their genomes. In this case, change due to therapy would be heritable and passed on to later generations. In somatic gene therapy, the therapeutic genes are transferred into the somatic cells (all body cells that are not germs cells) of a patient, and any effects will be restricted to the individual patient only and not transmitted to offspring.

Many jurisdictions presently do not allow germ line gene therapy, so discussion of gene therapy usually refers to correction of genetic disease by modification of the somatic genome. Somatic gene therapy approaches include the following:

- Replacement of the defective gene with normal DNA to reverse the genetic defect

- Transplantation of cells that have been genetically engineered to express molecules that are missing

- Transplantation of stem cells or of tissues produced from stem cells

As mentioned, the development of gene therapies is still in the infancy stage. It is believed that such therapies are likely to have most benefit for people who have single-gene disorders associated with a severe phenotype, including Lesch-Nyhan syndrome and phenylketonuria (PKU). Gene therapy is far less likely to provide treatment of mild intellectual disability, which accounts for approximately 85% of all cases of intellectual disability (King, Toth, Hodapp, & Dykens, 2009). Therapy that involves the transplantation of stem cells (or tissues derived from stem cells) is a particularly exciting area of research. (For more information about stem cells, see the subsection with this name later in the chapter.) Initially there was hype and hope that stem cell therapies would revolutionize medicine. Transplantation techniques are proving difficult to develop, but as of 2016 stem cells (i.e., induced pluripotent stem cells) have become an important tool for testing drugs as well as for modeling and investigating human diseases (Scudellari, 2016). See Daniels (2016) for information about how stem cell therapy has made some landmark advances in different types of vision impairments.

Cloning

A major achievement in the field of biology has been the ability to clone—or to produce genetically identical copies of cells or organisms. In 1952, a tadpole was cloned. For many years, scientists have been able to grow colonies or clones of cells in tissue culture or in animal hosts. The first report of cloning a mammal was in 1997. This involved the creation of the beloved Dolly the sheep by a process called reproductive cloning or nuclear transfer technology. Genetic material from the nucleus of a cell derived from the udder of an adult sheep was transferred into an egg in which the nucleus (containing its genetic material) had been removed. The reconstructed egg containing the DNA from the donor cell was then treated with chemicals in order to stimulate cell division. Once the cloned embryo had reached a suitable stage, it was transferred to the uterus of a female host, where it continued to develop until birth. Strictly speaking, Dolly was not 100% genetically identical to the sheep from which the udder cell DNA was derived because the egg from which the nucleus was removed still contained mitochondria (the energy-generating organelles of cells), which carry their own DNA segments (see Chapter 10). Since Dolly, researchers have used nuclear transfer technology to clone a number of different animals, including sheep, goats, cows, mice, pigs, cats, rabbits, and a gaur (Indian bison).

As explained in more detail in the next subsection, the discovery of stem cells has led to an activity called therapeutic cloning. This refers to the production of human embryos for use in research. The purpose of such cloning is to generate a supply of stem cells for the study of human development, the replacement of damaged tissues and organs, and the treatment of disease. Stem cells are important to biomedical researchers because they can be used to generate virtually any type of specialized cell in the human body. However, extraction of stem cells from a 5-day-old embryo results in its destruction, raising ethical concerns. Furthermore, using in vitro fertilization technology, it may become possible for parents to choose the traits they would like to see in their child. This process of human reproductive cloning (choosing only healthy embryos, or embryos of a particular gender, for implantation) should be distinguished from therapy. Reproductive cloning has not yet been carried out and is illegal in many countries.

Another human cloning concept that is, as yet, theoretical is *replacement cloning*, a combination of therapeutic and reproductive cloning. In this approach, an extensively damaged, failed, or failing body part or parts would be replaced (through cloned replacement), possibly followed by whole or partial brain transplant.

Stem Cells

Stem cells are primitive cells that have the capacity to self-renew as well as to differentiate into one or more mature cell types. As of the time of this writing in 2016, four different types of stem cells have been described.

Embryonic stem cells are taken from the inner cell mass of an embryo after 5 days of cell division. They are pluripotent (i.e., can differentiate into approximately 200 different cell types and into cells of the three germ cell layers). Because of their capacity of unlimited expansion and pluripotency, they are potentially useful in regenerative medicine. Because they have long telomeres (regions of DNA located at the ends of chromosomes), they are classified as "young" cells. Being derived from embryonic tissue, however, there are ethical objections associated with their investigation and applications because extraction of stem cells destroys the embryo.

Tissue or adult stem cells produce cells specific to the tissue in which they are found. They are relatively unspecialized and are predetermined to give rise to specific cell types when they differentiate. Their regenerative power is not strong in comparison to embryonic stem cells, and they are not young. However, their use is not subject to ethical objection.

Induced pluripotent stem cells (iPSCs) are created by genetically engineering normal adult cells to revert to embryonic stem cell status. They are young; however, again, because they are derived from adult cells, they are not subject to ethical objection. To create these cells, adenoviruses are injected into the cell. Adenoviruses do not change the DNA of their host. They go into the nucleus of the host and work directly on the proteins without altering the chromosomes (Stadtfeld, Nagaya, Utikal, Weir, & Hochedlinger, 2008). Shinya Yamanaka and Sir John Gurdon were awarded the 2012 Nobel prize in physiology of medicine for their discovery that mature cells can be reprogrammed to become pluripotent (Colman, 2013).

Parthenogenetic (or parthenogenic) stem cells are obtained from unfertilized oocytes, the cells that, if allowed to develop, would become ova. They are, by definition, young. These cells are not associated with ethical objections associated with the use of embryonic tissue.

A Canadian group discovered a way to differentiate adult skin cells into blood cells without the need to program them to a primordial state (Szabo et al., 2010). In this approach, patients could have small pieces of their own skin removed, cultured in vitro, and then differentiated into blood cells of their own genetic makeup. Potentially, these cells could then be used for blood transfusion without the concern of immune rejection. Once such blood cells can be produced in sufficient numbers, this protocol can be tested in humans. For information about stem cells and how the field is advancing, see the Learn.Genetics web site (http://learn.genetics.utah.edu/content/stemcells/) or the National Institutes of Health Stem Cell Information website (http://stemcells.nih.gov/info/Pages/Default.aspx).

Ethical and Moral Implications

For different reasons, many people find some or all of the preceding concepts to be ethically and morally problematic, unacceptable, or completely wrong. The process of inclusion (i.e., the philosophy and practice of including all people who belong to a society in the functioning of the society) and prevention (i.e., the philosophy and practice of applying current knowledge about the causes of developmental disabilities to preventing them) are conflicting trends in the field of developmental disabilities. Because radical decisions have been made by some governments in the past, including involuntary sterilization during the eugenics movement and the practice of allowing infants born with Down syndrome to die from lack of medical treatment, it is imperative that the scientific and medical communities and governments hear the views of consumers and families about ethical issues that involve new genetic findings. Fortunately, as part of the Human Genome Project, research is now being conducted on such topics as discrimination in insurance and employment, genetic testing, screening and counseling, and genetic therapies to cure conditions that lead to intellectual disability.

SUMMARY

Embryonic and fetal development depend upon many factors that can include nurture as well as nature. Good nutrition and maternal health, prenatally and perinatally, are key to the development of a healthy infant and to its good health later in life. Early intervention programs are very important in helping infants and young children to reach developmental milestones. This chapter also introduced readers to topical issues in the area of genetics and development, such as screening for genetic disorders, as well as future approaches for their prevention and cure, including potential applications of cloning and stem cells. These are issues about which some individuals have strong moral objection and which are topics of continued ethical and moral debate.

FOR FURTHER THOUGHT AND DISCUSSION

1. What are some risks and benefits associated with fetal screening using ultrasound?

2. Despite strong scientific evidence for prenatal care and early intervention for children and families, lack of support for pregnant women, young children, and families is a worldwide problem that has received limited attention. What steps might be taken, and by whom, to address this universal problem?

3. Check the Health Canada web sites given in the chapter for information about consequences of excessive exposures to mercury and aluminum.

Is there enough information on these sites for people to make decisions about how to reduce their own exposures and those of their infants to these metals? What actions might concerned citizens take to increase awareness of potential hazards that might result from excessive exposures to these metals?

4. The frequency of developmental disabilities is known to be higher in areas of poverty than in affluent areas. What factors might account for this finding?

REFERENCES

Arndt, T.L., Stodgell, C.J., & Rodier, P.M. (2005). The teratology of autism. *International Journal of Developmental Neuroscience, 23*(2–3), 189–199.

Bermas, B.L. (2016). *Patient information: Systemic lupus erythematosus and pregnancy (beyond the basics).* Retrieved from http://www.uptodate.com/contents/systemic-lupus-erythematosus-and-pregnancy-beyond-the-basics

Champagne, F.A. (2008). Epigenetic mechanisms and the transgenerational effects of maternal care. *Frontiers in Neuroendocrinology, 29*(3), 386–397.

Colman, A. (2013). Profile of John Gurdon and Shinya Yamanaka, 2012 Nobel laureates in medicine or physiology. *Proceedings of the National Academy of Sciences, U.S.A., 110*(15), 5740–5741.

Daniels, J.T. (2016). Biomedicine: Visionary stem-cell therapies. *Nature, 531*, 309–310.

Deprest, J.A., Flake, A.W., Gratacos, E., Ville, Y., Hecher, K., Nicolaides, K., … Harrison, M.R. (2010). The making of fetal surgery. *Prenatal Diagnosis, 30*(7), 653–667.

Fowden, A.L., & Forhead, A.J. (2009). Hormones as epigenetic signals in developmental programming. *Experimental Physiology, 94*(6), 607–625.

Galbally, M., Lewis, A.J., Ijzendoorn, M., & Permezel, M. (2011). The role of oxytocin in mother–infant relations: A systematic review of human studies. *Harvard Reviews in Psychiatry, 19*(1), 1–14.

Gencoglan, G., & Tosun, M. (2010). Effects of isotretinoin on spermatogenesis of rats. *Cutaneous and Ocular Toxicology, 30*(1), 55–60.

Gilbert, S.F. (2000). Environmental disruption of normal development. In S.F. Gilbert, *Developmental biology* (6th ed.). Sunderland, MA: Sinauer Associates. Retrieved from http://www.ncbi.nlm.nih.gov/books/NBK9998/

Harding, R., & Bocking, A.D. (Eds.). (2006). *Fetal growth and development.* Cambridge, United Kingdom: Cambridge University Press.

Houston, L.E., Odibo, A.O., & Macones, G.A. (2009). The safety of obstetrical ultrasound: A review. *Prenatal Diagnosis, 29*(13), 1204–1212.

Karwowski, M.P., Nelson, J.M., Staples, J.E., Fischer, M., Fleming-Dutra, K.E., Villanueva, J., Powers, … Rasmussen, S.A. (2016). Zika virus disease: A CDC update for pediatric health care providers. *Pediatrics, 137*(5). pii: e20160621. doi: 10.1542/peds.2016-0621

Kiefer, J.C. (2007). Epigenetics in development. *Developmental Dynamics, 236*(4), 1144–1156.

King, B.H., Toth, K.E., Hodapp, R.M., & Dykens, E. M. (2009). Intellectual disability. In B.J. Sadock, V.A. Sadock, & P. Ruiz (Eds.), *Comprehensive textbook of psychiatry* (9th ed., pp. 3444–3474). Philadelphia, PA: Lippincott Williams & Wilkins.

Leese, H.J. (2005). Rewards and risks of human embryo creation: A personal view. *Reproduction, Fertility, and Development, 17*(3), 387–391.

Meaney-Delman, D., Rasmussen, S.A., Staples, J. E., Oduyebo, T., Ellington, S.R., Petersen, E.E., … Jamieson, D.J. (2016). Zika virus and pregnancy: What obstetric health care providers need to know. *Obstetrics & Gynecology, 127*(4), 642–648.

Prenatal Information Research Consortium. (2016, April 29). ACOG issues new prenatal testing guidelines. *Practice Bulletin, 153.* Retrieved from https://prenatalinformation.org/2016/04/29/acog-issues-new-prenatal-testing-guidelines/

Reik, W. (2007). Review article. Stability and flexibility of epigenetic gene regulation in mammalian development. *Nature, 447*(7143), 425–432.

Scudellari, M. (2016). How iPS cells changed the world. *Nature, 534*(7607), 3101–3102.

Shepard, T.H., & Lemire, R.J. (2007). *Catalog of teratogenic agents* (12th ed.). Baltimore, MD: Johns Hopkins University Press.

Shonkoff, J.P. (2009, Fall). The road to a new energy system: Mobilizing science to revitalize early childhood policy. *Issues in Science and Technology, XXVI*(1). Retrieved from http://issues.org/26-1/shonkoff/

Smith, G.C., & Cameron, A.D. (2002). Estimating human fetal blood volume on the basis of gestational age and fetal abdominal circumference. *British Journal of Obstetrics & Gynaecology, 109*(6), 721–722.

Stadtfeld, M., Nagaya, M., Utikal, J., Weir, G., & Hochedlinger, K. (2008). *Induced pluripotent stem cells generated without viral integration.* doi:10.1126/science.1162494

Szabo, E., Rampalli, S., Risueño, R.M., Schnerch, A., Mitchell, R., Fiebig-Comyn, A., … Bhatia, M. (2010). Conversion of human fibroblasts to multilineage blood progenitors. *Nature, 468*, 521–526.

The Hospital for Sick Children. (2016). *Things to avoid during pregnancy: Teratogens.* Retrieved from http://www.aboutkidshealth.ca/en/resourcecentres/pregnancybabies/pregnancy/healthcareinpregnancy/pages/things-to-avoid-during-pregnancy-teratogens.aspx

University of Maryland Medical Center. (2011). *Fetal development.* Retrieved from http://www.umm.edu/ency/article/002398.htm

University of Oxford. (2010). *List of known and suspected teratogens.* Retrieved January 15, 2010, from http://msds.chem.ox.ac.uk/teratogens.html

Visible Embryo. (n.d.). *The visible embryo.* Retrieved from http://www.visembryo.com

Wong-Goodrich, S.J., Glenn, M.J., Mellott, T.J., Blusztajn, J.K., Meck, W.H., & Williams, C.L. (2008). Spatial memory and hippocampal plasticity are differentially sensitive to the availability of choline in adulthood as a function of choline supply in utero. *Brain Research, 1237,* 153–166.

10

Introduction to Genetics, Genomics, Epigenetics, and Intellectual and Developmental Disabilities

Maire Percy, Sheldon Z. Lewkis, Miles D. Thompson, Ivan Brown, Deborah Barbouth, and F. Daniel Armstrong

WHAT YOU WILL LEARN

- The concepts of genetics, genomics, and epigenetics, as well as their importance and a brief history
- Fundamentals of human genetics, including DNA, RNA, how proteins are made from DNA, and processes involved in cell division
- Introduction to genetic disorders, including causes and inheritance patterns, unusual features of genetics, the genetic basis of certain intellectual or developmental disabilities, and testing for genetic disorders
- Epigenetic processes and how diet, lifestyle, and environment can influence health
- Advances and initiatives in the field, including "next generation" sequencing, the Precision Medicine Initiative Cohort Program, direct-to-consumer genetic testing, the PhenX Toolkit, and the Roadmap Epigenetics Mapping Consortium
- Challenges and future applications to disability and disease

This chapter provides an introduction to some important concepts in human genetics. It is divided into eight main sections that cover key issues. Within these sections are mentioned some notable advances and initiatives in the field.

Genetics is the branch of biology that studies heredity—the passing of inherited traits (features that distinguish one person from another) from parents to offspring. Genetics is the study of how and why traits are transmitted from parents to children and what causes normal and abnormal variations of inherited traits. It provides information that will aid understanding of human genetic inheritance as well as the genetic causes of certain developmental disabilities (e.g., Down syndrome, fragile X syndrome [FXS]).

In a technical sense, genetics is concerned with patterns and means of inheritance of traits as well as elucidation of the functioning of single genes and DNA and related molecules, including the influences of environmental factors, in health and disease. Genomics is a discipline of genetics that encompasses the study of all genes, their interrelationships, and their combined influence on the growth and development of an organism, as well as related techniques. The term *genome* refers to the entirety of an organism's genetic information. Epigenetics is a branch of genetics that studies how gene expression can be altered without involving changes to the underlying DNA sequence.

Having an introductory knowledge of genetics (including the related disciplines of genomics and epigenetics) is important for several reasons:

1. Genetics explains much of why humans are the way they are. On average, each person carries genes for at least seven serious genetic disorders (Milunsky, 1977). However, effects of genes are now known to be influenced by epigenetic processes triggered by environmental factors that include exposures to toxins in the environment, infection, diet and nutrition, and behavioral factors.

2. Genetics can aid understanding of the mechanisms and extent to which diet, lifestyle, and environment influence health.

3. New knowledge about genetic causes of disabilities is leading to improved methods for their diagnosis. Being able to diagnose a disorder leads to better forms of intervention and treatment. This also is encouraging searches for better treatments, prevention, and even cures.

4. Genetics technology is advancing quickly, and the application of genetic and genomic technology is rapidly becoming a defining component of efforts to move to precision medicine for a variety of disorders and diseases beginning in the neonatal period (Petrikin, Willig, Smith, & Kingsmore, 2015) and extending throughout the life span (Mohler, Najafi, Fain, & Ramos, 2015). (Precision medicine is a personalized approach to health care that takes into account an individual's genetics as well as environmental and lifestyle factors for disease prevention and treatment.) For this reason, genetics, genomics, and epigenetics need to be core components of a curriculum for interdisciplinary training at every level, in the classroom and at the bedside.

5. A fundamental understanding of genetics, genomics, and epigenetics can be of benefit to everyone, particularly to those whose lives are affected by disabilities.

A BRIEF HISTORY OF GENETICS

The field of genetics is evolving rapidly, and advances have resulted in several Nobel Prizes being awarded for some of the discoveries described herein. More specific information on this is included throughout the chapter, but readers are also encouraged to review the Nobel Prize web site (Nobelprize.org, 2016).

The beginning of genetics as a science goes back to some observations and experiments conducted by Gregor Mendel. Mendel, born in 1822, was an Augustinian monk and also taught natural science to high school students. He crossed peas of different varieties and observed that certain traits were inherited in certain proportions. His findings were first presented in 1865.

The use of the word *genetics* as a noun was introduced by William Bateson in 1905 in a presentation that popularized Mendel's forgotten works. It is derived from the Greek word *genetikos,* meaning "genitive," which is related to the word *genesis,* or origin. Prior to Mendel's discoveries, a French naturalist and biologist—Jean Baptiste Lamarck—proposed in 1829 that characteristics developed during a lifetime are transmitted as inheritable traits to offspring. This hypothesis was later discounted but has been revived as the result of the discovery of some cellular mechanisms that are described as being epigenetic. The word *epigenetic* is derived from the Greek word *epi,* meaning "above," and literally means "above genetics." So, Lamarck's idea was actually far from incorrect.

The rediscovery of Mendel's work in the early 20th century was the first among a series of more than 90 key milestones in the development of genetics as a discipline. Historically, discovery of the double helix structure of DNA in the early 1950s was arguably one of the most important scientific advances of the 20th century. For a detailed outline of historic milestones in the field of genetics, see the web site of the National Human Genome Research Institute (NHGRI) at http://www.genome.gov/25019887/.

Interest in genetics in the 21st century has been greatly stimulated by the Human Genome Project (HGP), completed in 2003. This 13-year, international research project was huge in terms of its cost and technological challenges, and in these respects has been said to rival putting humans on the moon. The HGP determined the sequence of all of human DNA and identified the approximately 25,000 genes that human DNA contains. DNA (i.e., deoxyribonucleic acid) is the substance in nuclei of cells that contains the "blueprint" for the basic instructions of structure and physiology. The genes are found in the 23 sets of organelles called chromosomes in the nucleus of most of human cells. Red blood cells are an exception, because they do not contain a nucleus. For an introduction to the HGP, see the NHGRI web site at http://www.genome.gov/10001772.

The mapping of the human genome was a first step in better understanding variations in sequences of genetic material and how these affect the occurrence or nonoccurrence of different characteristics or diseases, as well as how those conditions might be modified in specific ways for individuals. Combined with access to large amounts of data contained in electronic health records and the capability of rapidly emerging bioinformatics technology, the understanding of the human genome has opened the doors to the possibility of precision medicine, an approach that potentially affects diagnosis and treatment for every condition, disorder, or disease. In January 2015, U.S. President Barack Obama launched a major initiative to create a large research cohort (Precision Medicine Initiative Cohort Program) to accelerate progress in the application of genomic knowledge to human diseases and conditions (see National Institutes of Health, n.d.a).

What researchers are still grasping to understand is how a single fertilized ovum "knows" how to develop into a complex organism containing many different types of cells. Another question is why apparently identical twins can sometimes be physically and/or psychologically different from one another (Higgins, 2008). It is now known that these phenomena and others occur, in part, because of epigenetic biological processes that turn selective genes on or off in cells in response to day-to-day experiences and interactions with the environment. Some of the instructions for turning genes on or off are inherited, and some result from interactions with the environment.

BASICS OF HUMAN GENETICS

This section explains the relationship between DNA, chromosomes, and genes in cells and provides an overview of how DNA functions as genetic material. Also explained is how cells make protein using information in DNA and differences between DNA and RNA.

Fundamental Components of a Cell

As shown in Figure 10.1, every cell has an outer membrane. The membrane helps the cell hold its contents and shape. The membrane also regulates what gets into and out of the cell, and it contains the cytoplasm. Cytoplasm is a gelatinous substance in which all of cellular metabolism, including protein production, takes place. Proteins are molecules that carry out much of the work in cells. (Hemoglobin is one very important and well-known protein; it

is located in red blood cells and is involved in the transport of oxygen and carbon dioxide).

Within each cell is a structure called the nucleus, which contains 23 pairs of chromosomes (23 from the mother and 23 from the father). Each chromosome is made up of pairs of linear strands of DNA that are tightly coiled. The tight coiling of DNA results because the DNA strands wrap themselves around proteins called histones. Because DNA molecules are composed of two closely linked linear chains of DNA, they are said to be double stranded. The DNA molecules contain short stretches of DNA called genes. Each gene contains information for the production of a specific protein. What people look like and how they function depend upon what proteins are made using information contained in the genes in DNA.

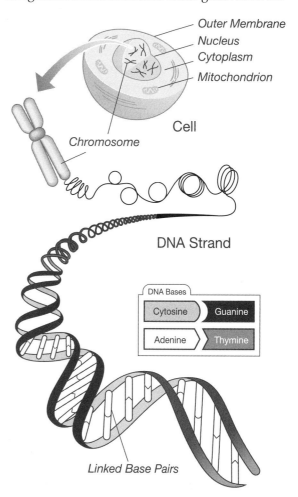

Figure 10.1. Fundamental components of a cell. This diagram shows the relationship between double-stranded DNA in a cell nucleus (genomic DNA) and chromosomes. The inset shows the four different bases in DNA and how interactions between individual bases opposite each other on the two DNA strands form rungs in the DNA "ladder." See Figure 10.2 for more information. (*Source:* Percy, Lewkis, & Brown, 2003. *Illustration:* Copyright © Tom Dearie, Threesixty Creative/Infographix.)

The Structure of DNA

The basic structure of DNA is shown in Figure 10.2. James Watson and Francis Crick shared a Nobel Prize in Physiology or Medicine in 1962, along with their collaborator Maurice Wilkins, for their work on the structure of DNA (Maddox, 2003).

The building block of DNA molecules are nucleotides. Each nucleotide molecule is composed of components—called a base, a sugar, and a phosphate—that are bonded together. These components are sometimes called groups. Different nucleotides contain different bases but identical sugar and phosphate groups. There are four different bases in DNA. They are adenine (A), thymine (T), guanine (G), and cytosine (C). T and C groups are large, whereas A and G groups are small. The nucleotides are held together in single linear DNA strands by the phosphate groups in adjacent nucleotides. The two strands of a DNA molecule are held together by interactions between the base component of a nucleotide in one DNA strand and the base of one directly opposite in the second DNA strand. An A on one side of the ladder is always paired with a T on the other side, and a G with a C (Figure 10.2).

This base pairing makes a DNA molecule take a shape like a twisted ladder. The interconnected phosphate groups in each DNA strand form the sides of the ladders, and the interacting pairs of bases form the rungs. The linear order of nucleotides in a DNA molecule constitutes the "information coding." The order in which the four different varieties of nucleotides are strung together make the linear sequence of every gene unique. The four bases can create a code for something as complex as the development of a human through the specific ordering of pairs in the sequence.

Nuclear DNA consists of almost 6 billion (6×10^9) nucleotide (base) pairs. Every million base pairs take up a linear space of 0.34 millimeters (mm) or 0.34×10^{-2} centimeters (cm). So the length of DNA in each cell is 204 cm or approximately 2 meters. Because there are approximately 50 trillion (50×10^{12}) cells in the adult human body, the length of stretched out DNA in the human body is $2 \times 50 \times 10^{12}$ (100×10^{12}) meters. The extended DNA in a human body would stretch from earth to the sun and back 350 times.

The DNA present in the nucleus of cells is called genomic DNA. Most of the text in this chapter deals with this type of DNA. DNA is also present in the cell structures called mitochondria. Each mitochondrion

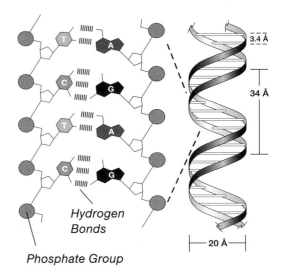

Hydrogen Bonds

Phosphate Group

Figure 10.2. The structure of DNA. Left: A two-dimensional representation of the two complementary strands of DNA, showing AT and GC base pairs (A/T and G/C are complementary base pairs). Right: The double helix model of DNA proposed by Watson and Crick (1953). The horizontal "rungs" represent the paired bases. (*Source*: Percy, Lewkis, & Brown, 2003. *Illustration*: Copyright © Tom Dearie, Threesixty Creative/Infographix.)

contains a circle of double-stranded DNA consisting of 16,569 nucleotide pairs. Each mitochondrion encodes several proteins, and each cell has thousands of mitochondria. Mitochondrial DNA (mtDNA) accounts for about 0.3% of total cellular DNA. Mitochondria are the "powerhouses" of the body. Proteins made from mtDNA are all subunits that take part in the important energy-generating pathway of mitochondria, known as oxidative phosphorylation. Mitochondria replicate themselves in a cell independently of the processes that are necessary for cell division. Mitochondria present in sperm cells get eliminated during early cell divisions after an embryo is formed. This means that the DNA in the mitochondria of most cells in the body is derived from the mother.

How Information in Genes of DNA Results in Proteins

This section provides an overview of how information in genes of DNA results in the production of specific protein molecules. What a cell does depends upon what proteins it makes. What proteins a cell makes depends upon what genes in the cell are active (turned on) or not active (turned off) and what forms of mature RNA are made from the active genes.

The first event in the production of a protein is the copying of the gene for that protein from the strand of a DNA molecule where it is located. The gene is copied onto a molecule of RNA (i.e., ribonucleic acid). This process is called transcription. Transcription takes place only from genes that are active. The second event involves a number of biochemical steps in which the cell uses information in RNA to assemble protein molecules from basic building blocks called amino acids. The process of using different RNA molecules to direct the production of different protein molecules is called translation.

There are only about 25,000 genes in the human genome but more than 120,000 different types of proteins. Thus, a single gene contains information used to make several proteins. Moreover, sometimes genes are active and result in protein production and sometimes they are inactive with no protein being produced. There is also an increasing awareness that interactions with the environment can trigger mechanisms in cells that turn genes on or off. These factors all contribute to phenotype (i.e., an individual's observable or measureable traits, including the physical and biochemical characteristics).

We next explain how regions of DNA corresponding to genes get copied into "working" molecules of RNA and how these RNA molecules are used by cellular machinery called ribosomes to make specific proteins, linear chains of building blocks called amino acids (Figure 10.3). Also explained is how RNA differs from DNA.

As mentioned, the first step in the production of a specific protein is the copying of the gene for this protein into RNA. This RNA is called messenger RNA (mRNA). mRNA strands are working copies of genes located in the cell that are distinct from the genes in the DNA. Not all genes in DNA get copied into mRNA at the same time—only those that are needed by the cell. mRNA molecules then move from the cell nucleus to structures in the cell cytoplasm called ribosomes, which contain all the necessary machinery for making proteins. In order to be "read" by the ribosomal machinery, pieces of RNA that are not needed are removed. The pieces of RNA that are removed are called introns, and those that are kept are called exons. RNA processed in this way is called mature RNA.

Within ribosomes, the mature mRNA molecule is "read" by a process called translation (Figure 10.3). Key to this process are molecules called transfer RNAs (tRNAs), which are essential for the ribosomal machinery to read mRNA. Translation involves the formation of complexes between the mRNA molecule and tRNAs. There are as many

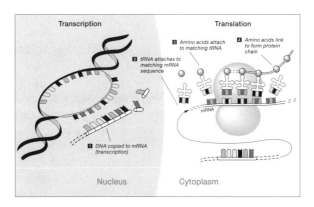

Figure 10.3. How protein is formed from DNA. DNA in a gene is copied in a process called transcription into a molecule called messenger RNA (mRNA; Step 1). This mRNA moves from the nucleus (left-hand panel) into the cytoplasm (right-hand panel) where it undergoes translation. Translation involves complexing of mRNA (long strand, right-hand panel) with ribosomes (round structures, right-hand panel). It also involves complexing of small RNA molecules called transfer RNA (tRNA) to different regions of the mRNA (Step 2). The tRNA molecules are key to translation because one end binds to a trinucleotide sequence in the mRNA molecule and the other binds to only one amino acid (Step 3). Ribosomal machinery then links amino acids attached to tRNA molecules into a linear protein chain (Step 4). The amino acids, of course, are not identical. (*Source*: Percy, Lewkis, & Brown, 2003. *Illustration*: Copyright © Tom Dearie, Threesixty Creative/Infographix.)

different tRNA molecules as there are amino acids. Each tRNA molecule is unique and does two important things: One end contains a unique set of three nucleotides (called a base triplet) that bind to a complementary nucleotide set in the mRNA molecule. The other end contains a region that binds uniquely to only one of 20 different amino acids, which are the basic building blocks of proteins. Because one tRNA can bind only to one trinucleotide sequence in mRNA and only to one amino acid, the order in which different tRNAs bind to different base triplets in mRNA (which corresponds to the order of unique base triplets in DNA) determines the order of amino acids in protein chains. As depicted in Figure 10.3, the ribosomal machinery joins amino acids attached to the tops of their respective tRNA molecules into a linear protein chain. The unique sets of base triplets in mRNA molecules (and the corresponding sets in DNA) are called codons. The complementary sets of base triplets in tRNA molecules are sometimes called anticodons. For example, the codon ACG in DNA specifies the complementary codon CGU in mRNA, which in turn specifies incorporation of the amino acid arginine at that position. In 1968, the Nobel Prize for Physiology or Medicine was awarded jointly to Robert Holley, Har Gobind Khorana, and Marshall Nirenberg for deciphering the genetic code and discovering its function in the synthesis of proteins (Raju, 1999a).

Although many genes produce only one mature species of mRNA molecule and one protein, some precursor mRNA molecules are processed in different ways to yield different functional species of mature mRNAs, which are translated into proteins. DNA sequence variation can influence every step along this pathway, often in association with disorders such as autism spectrum disorder (ASD: Guigó & Valcárcel, 2015; Xiong et al., 2015). After protein chains are made, two or more polypeptide chains may combine to form a single protein molecule. Proteins also may be cleaved or modified chemically (e.g., by adding carbohydrate, phosphate, or certain other groups at particular sites).

Differences Between DNA and RNA

As mentioned, mRNA molecules are working copies of DNA ultimately created for the purpose of protein construction. Like DNA, RNA molecules are composed of nucleotides. However, in RNA nucleotides, the sugar group is ribose rather than deoxyribose, and thymine (T) bases are replaced by uracil (U) bases. In contrast to DNA molecules, which are double-stranded, mRNA molecules are single-stranded, though these single strands fold up in complex ways. Different types of mRNA molecules and different types of proteins are produced from the same DNA sequence via a process called alternative RNA splicing. In this process, pieces of RNA that are not needed by a cell are removed prior to the act of translation. The process of alternative RNA splicing explains, in part, why there are many more proteins in the body than genes in the human body. Much of DNA does not code for genes; instead, it gets translated into RNA molecules that have regulatory functions. Such RNA molecules include microRNAs (miRNAs) and long non-coding mRNAs (see later sections about these forms of RNA).

Processes Involved in Cell Division

An introduction to genetics should involve an introduction to the processes involved in cell division and in the production of sperm and ova. This section describes two different forms of cell division: mitosis and meiosis. Also explained are the concepts of genetic recombination and chromosomal nondisjunction. Fundamental to cell division is the double-stranded nature of DNA. The sequence of bases on one strand is specified by the sequence on the other and vice versa. All cells in the body, except for the sperm and ova (eggs) are referred to as somatic cells. The number of chromosomes in somatic cells (46, or 23 pairs) is constant. The set of 46 chromosomes is referred to as the diploid number and is indicated by $2n$, where n is the haploid number (i.e., 23). Because ova and sperm (also called gametes) have only half of the diploid number of chromosomes (23), they are said to be haploid.

In order to maintain the same number of chromosomes in cells, two types of cell division occur. Mitosis occurs in cells in somatic tissues during growth and repair. It ensures constancy of chromosome number in cells and constancy of genetic material. Meiosis is a specialized form of cell division that results in the formation of four daughter cells, each with a haploid number of chromosomes. Meiosis occurs only in germ cells of genital tissue and results in formation of the gametes. In males, each spermatocyte forms four functional spermatids, which develop into sperm. The formation of sperm takes place on a continual basis from the time of sexual maturity. In females, each oocyte results in the formation of only one ovum; the other three daughter cells become nonfunctional polar bodies. The formation of ova is largely complete at birth. Each gamete's chromosomes produced in meiosis have a unique combination of genes derived from both parents. During meiosis, each chromosome pair in a germ cell mixes the paternal and maternal genetic material in that cell by the process of genetic recombination (Figure 10.4). Thus, each unpaired chromosome in a sperm or ovum has genetic material derived from both of the chromosomes that form a pair in the germ cell. Meiosis is fundamental to sexual reproduction and ensures genetic variability of species.

Of the 23 chromosome pairs (autosomes), 22 are labeled 1–22 in decreasing order of their length (although chromosome 22 is larger than chromosome 21). One of the 23 pairs is termed the sex pair. In females, the sex pair is comprised of two X chromosomes. Conversely, males have a sex pair comprised of an X and a Y chromosome. (The X and Y chromosomes are not actually X or Y shaped.)

Figure 10.5 shows the process of meiosis. Sometimes, the process of meiosis is abnormal and not all the chromosomes come apart. The consequence is that one cell gets both sister chromatids that each

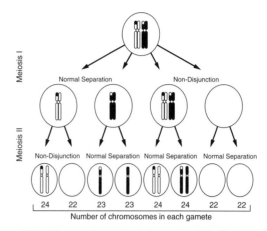

Figure 10.5. Diagram of normal and abnormal meiosis. Normal meiosis delivers one sister chromatid to each gamete. However, nondisjunction of sister chromatids can result in gametes receiving both or neither of a chromatid pair. The resulting gametes have too few or too many chromosomes. (*Source*: Percy, Lewkis, & Brown, 2003. *Illustration*: Copyright © Tom Dearie, Threesixty Creative/Infographix.)

become a chromosome, whereas the other cell gets none. This abnormal process of meiosis is called nondisjunction. Nondisjunction can occur during particular stages of meiosis called meiosis I or meiosis II (see Figure 10.5). This results in an ovum or sperm having two copies of one particular chromosome or missing a copy of that chromosome.

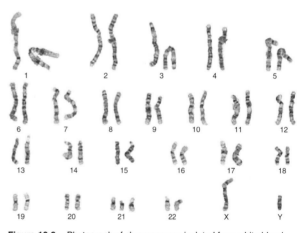

Figure 10.6. Photograph of chromosomes isolated from white blood cells of a male child with Down syndrome. Chromosomes are tightly bound strands of DNA bound to proteins found in the cell nucleus. In this photograph, the chromosomes have been stained with Giemsa (G banding) in a standard fashion. They are numbered from 1 to 22 in order of decreasing length (except that chromosome 21 is smaller than chromosome 22), with the X and Y chromosomes shown separately. This standard arrangement of an individual's chromosomes is known as a karyotype. Healthy, typically developing individuals have 22 pairs of chromosomes plus two sex chromosomes. The presence of three chromosome 21s in this photo indicates Down syndrome. (Karyotype courtesy of Dr. Kathy Chun and Mr. Shawn Brennan, TML—Cancer Cytogenetics Laboratory, Banting Institute, Toronto.)

Figure 10.4. Crossing over and recombination during meiosis. During the early stages of cell division in meiosis, two chromosomes of a homologous pair may exchange segments in the manner shown, producing genetic variation in germ cells. This process ensures that each ovum and sperm produced will have a unique collection of alleles. This process is beneficial for survival. (*Source*: Percy, Lewkis, & Brown, 2003. *Illustration*: Copyright © Tom Dearie, Threesixty Creative/Infographix.)

During meiosis, translocation sometimes occurs; that is, chromosomes sometimes get attached to one another, and these do not separate properly. Figure 10.6 provides a photograph of chromosomes isolated from cultured white blood cells from a male child with Down syndrome, a common disorder resulting from nondisjunction of chromosome 21 (see Chapter 14).

As explained more fully in the second part of the next section, the cells of an individual do not always have the same genetic makeup. This is a phenomenon called mosaicism. Mosaicism can result from errors in cell division. However, a unique and normal type of mosaicism occurs in all females because one of the two X chromosomes in each of

their cells becomes inactivated at a very early stage of development (see Figure 10.7).

INTRODUCTION TO GENETIC DISORDERS

This section looks at alternative forms of genes and other abnormalities that can cause genetic disorders.

Some Causes of Genetic Disorders

Normally, a person has two copies of every gene, one from the mother, the other from the father. These copies sometimes are identical, but sometimes they are not. Alternative forms of a gene are called alleles. Different alleles code for variations in inherited characteristics such as eye color. In some cases, allelic variation can be so abnormal that genetic disorders can result. Procedures called genetic linkage analysis and association studies have been traditional means for identifying regions of the genome with large genetic effects and particular genes that contribute to a disease (Cui, Li, Li, & Wu, 2010). Genetic linkage analysis continues to be important in the age of whole-genome sequencing (Ott, Wang, & Leal, 2015).

Mutations

Mutations are permanent errors in DNA sequence that affect protein expression or function or RNA expression or function. Those that cause genetic disorders often result from the production of abnormal proteins as the result of errors in DNA sequences. However, in addition to malfunctioning protein, changes or errors in DNA also can result in the underexpression, overexpression, or complete absence of proteins. Furthermore, RNA abnormalities that have no effect on protein sequence can still be problematic. Mutations can occur in mtDNA as well as in genomic DNA. DNA mutations occur as the result of the following:

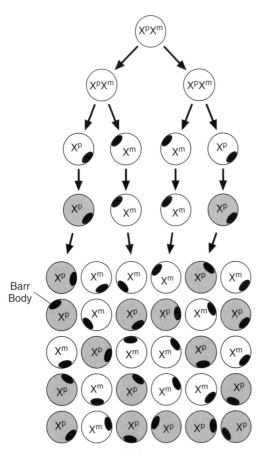

Figure 10.7. The process of lyonization, or random X chromosome inactivation, in female somatic cells. The ovals within the circles represent the Barr bodies that are formed from the inactivated paternal or maternal X chromosome. In any somatic cell in a female, either the paternally inherited X chromosome (X^p) or the maternally inherited X chromosome (X^m) may be active; which chromosome is active is usually a matter of chance. Once one X chromosome has become inactivated in a cell, this X chromosome remains inactivated in all of the descendants of that cell. (*Source*: Percy, Lewkis, & Brown, 2003. *Illustration*: Copyright © Tom Dearie, Threesixty Creative/Infographix.)

- Small changes in nucleotide sequences

- Deletions (i.e., loss or absence of crucial regions of DNA)

- Duplications (i.e., the production of one or more copies of any piece of DNA)

- Amplifications (e.g., of regions of DNA called trinucleotide repeat regions—sequences of three nucleotides that get repeated over and over again)

- Translocations (i.e., transfer of a chromosomal segment to a new region)

- Inversions (i.e., a type of mutation in which an entire section of DNA is reversed)

Other DNA Changes

There also are other changes in DNA that may affect its function. These include the following:

- *Single nucleotide polymorphisms (SNPs).* SNPs (pronounced "snips") are DNA sequence variations resulting in a difference in a single nucleotide. SNPs are found every 100–300 nucleotides throughout the genome. They can occur in both coding regions (i.e., genes) and noncoding regions of the genome. Many SNPs have no effect on cell function, but others may affect the function of a protein and predispose people to disease or influence their response to a drug.

- *Copy number variations (CNVs).* These are the most common type of genetic variation in humans. A CNV is a segment of DNA for which differences in copy number (i.e., number of copies of a particular region or portions of it) are found when two or more genomes are compared. The segment involved in a CNV may range from one kilobase to several megabases in size. CNVs can be inherited, or they may arise de novo (Morrow, 2010). Identical twins sometimes have different CNVs.

If a protein does not function properly, and if this protein is particularly important in brain cells, then brain structuring and/or physiology will be affected. Because cellular DNA is faithfully reproduced when a cell divides to produce daughter cells, mistakes that are present in a DNA molecule usually also are produced. This is the basis of inheritance of genetic forms of developmental disabilities. Generally, one gene produces one protein. However, some genes can produce more than one type of protein because different species of RNA can be produced from the same gene. Developmental disabilities that result from dysfunction or absence of only one protein are the ones for which the prospects of a cure are the most likely in the foreseeable future. One example is FXS, in which there is deficiency of FMR1 protein (see Chapter 15).

As already mentioned and as discussed in more detail later, epigenetic mechanisms also can affect gene function. Epigenetic modifications can be inherited, and they also can arise during development and throughout the life span in response to interaction with the environment.

Mosaicism and Lyonization

It is not always the case that all somatic cells have identical chromosomes. Sometimes cells may gain or lose one or more chromosomes during the process of division. Individuals who carry somatic cells with the normal diploid number and cells that have one or more chromosomes missing or one or more extra chromosomes are said to carry more than one cell line. When individuals carry two or more different cell lines, they are said to have mosaicism. The development of mosaicism can occur in any dividing tissue before or after birth and throughout one's life. Mosaicism that normalizes the DNA content of a tissue or organ is beneficial. For example, as explained in Chapter 14, individuals who are mosaic for trisomy 21 (i.e., who have some normal cells in their tissues along with trisomy 21 cells) may have fewer features of Down syndrome than individuals with complete trisomy 21. Errors sometimes occur in chromosomal segregation during mitosis after zygote formation (see Chapter 9) in a process also resulting in mosaicism. (The term *zygote* refers to the fertilized egg, the result of fusion between an ovum and a sperm.)

Another type of mosaicism occurs in all females. In females, one of the two X chromosomes in each somatic cell is inactivated, becoming the "Barr body." This process has been called lyonization after Mary Lyon, the scientist who discovered it. Which X chromosome is inactivated (i.e., the one that originally came from the sperm or the one from the ovum) is thought to be determined randomly. Inactivation of one X chromosome in each cell of the developing embryo starts to occur about 3 days after fertilization, when the embryo is comprised of approximately 32 cells. Should one of the X chromosomes be defective, the process of lyonization ensures that some cells in the female always will have a normal X chromosome that is active.

This process tends to spare females from the effects of defective genes on the X chromosome. In contrast, if a gene on the X chromosome in a male is defective, there is no normal copy of that gene to compensate, as males have only one X chromosome. Lyonization explains why female carriers of an X-linked disorder are often spared from full effects of the disorder, whereas male carriers are strongly affected. Fragile X syndrome (see Chapter 15), Duchenne muscular dystrophy, and Lesch-Nyhan syndrome (see Chapter 21) are examples of serious X-linked developmental disabilities. Figure 10.7 illustrates the process of lyonization in somatic cells of females.

CLASSIFICATION OF GENETIC DISORDERS AND INHERITANCE PATTERNS

We have already discussed ways in which mistakes in cells can arise. Sometimes these result in genetic disorders associated with developmental and/or intellectual disability. In this section, we discuss the three common classifications of genetic disorders: chromosomal, single gene, and non-Mendelian. Disorders caused by single genes are less frequent than disorders resulting from multiple genes acting on their own or in conjunction with environmental factors.

Chromosomal Disorders

Chromosomal disorders or syndromes are caused by a person having too many or two few chromosomes or by a change in the structure of a chromosome that disrupts its function. About 60% of all first-trimester miscarriages (spontaneous abortions) occur as a result of a chromosomal abnormality. The term *syndrome* refers to a set of clinically recognizable symptoms occurring together. Most chromosomal disorders are not actually inherited, even though they are considered to be genetic. Rather, they occur sporadically (i.e., irregularly, without any pattern or order in time, with no evidence of being inherited). Examples of chromosomal disorders resulting from an abnormal number of chromosomes are Down syndrome (trisomy 21; see Chapter 14), Patau syndrome (trisomy 13), Edwards syndrome (trisomy 18), Turner syndrome (monosomy X; see Chapter 21), and Klinefelter syndrome (XXY; see Chapter 21). Examples of chromosomal disorders in which there are a normal number of chromosomes but a segment of DNA is deleted include cri du chat syndrome (missing part of the short arm of chromosome 5; see Chapter 21), many cases of Prader-Willi and Angelman syndromes (both of which stem from a missing part of the long arm of chromosome 15; see Chapter 21), and Williams syndrome (missing part of the long

arm of chromosome 7; see Chapter 21). As explained in the Other Disorders section below, Prader-Willi and Angelman syndromes are also classified as "congenital imprinting disorders."

Single-Gene Disorders

Genetic disorders caused by a sequence change or chromosome abnormality affecting only one gene are called single-gene disorders. Single-gene disorders are sometimes called Mendelian disorders because their inheritance pattern is predictable according to Mendel's principles. Inborn errors of metabolism are a subtype of single-gene disorder, which occur when cells cannot produce proteins or enzymes needed to convert certain chemicals into others, or when cells cannot transport substances from one place to another. About one in 1,500 children is born with a defective enzyme that results in an inborn error of metabolism. More than 350 inborn errors of metabolism have been identified, many of which impair the function of the brain. One example of an inborn error of metabolism is phenylketonuria (PKU), which most frequently results from mutations in the phenylalanine hydroxylase gene. Intellectual and developmental disabilities associated with PKU can sometimes be mitigated by early diagnosis and treatment. See Chapter 21 for more information about PKU as well as other examples of single-gene disorders.

Single-gene disorders are the easiest to diagnose because they are caused by a change in a single gene. Disorders that result from changes in single genes are inherited in one of three ways: dominant inheritance, recessive inheritance, and X-linked inheritance.

Dominant Inheritance   In dominant inheritance, one affected parent of either sex has a defective gene that dominates over its normal gene counterpart. Every child has a 50% chance of inheriting from the affected parent either the defective gene (and the disease) or the normal gene. Myotonic dystrophy, neurofibromatosis (see Chapter 21) and tuberous sclerosis (see Chapter 21) are examples of autosomal dominant developmental disabilities.

Recessive Inheritance   In recessive inheritance, both parents are usually unaffected, but each carries a defective gene that, by itself, does not cause problems. Parents of children with autosomal recessive traits are called carriers because each parent carries one copy of the abnormal trait but does not actually show it. The disorder or disease occurs when a person receives two copies of the recessive gene (i.e., one from each parent). There is a 25% chance that a person will inherit two copies of the defective gene and show the abnormality, a 50% chance a person will be a carrier, and a 25% chance that a person will neither be a carrier nor be affected. The highest incidence of autosomal recessive disorder in the United States is sickle cell anemia, with Smith-Lemli-Opitz syndrome (Chapter 21) and PKU (Chapter 21) serving as examples of disorders commonly associated with intellectual and developmental disabilities. It is recognized that recessive genes causing certain serious genetic disorders can have beneficial functions in certain situations. For example, having one copy of the autosomal recessive hemoglobin S gene for sickle cell anemia protects against malaria infection (Eiguero et al., 2015). Certain other disorders of hemoglobin structure or function (e.g., α-thalassemia) may also protect against malaria (Taylor, Cerami, & Fairhurst, 2013). Genes associated with cystic fibrosis may protect against vitamin D deficiency effects, tuberculosis, and hypertension (high blood pressure) (Lubinsky, 2012).

X-Linked Inheritance In X-linked disorders (sometimes called sex-linked disorders), the defective gene is carried on the X chromosome of the mother, who usually shows few or no symptoms of the disorder. The disorder is expressed when a male receives the defective gene. Each male child has a 50% chance of being affected, and 50% of female children will carry the defective gene but will usually not be highly affected because of lyonization. Examples of X-linked single-gene disorders are Duchenne muscular dystrophy, Lesch-Nyhan syndrome, and FXS.

Fragile X is caused by an unusually large CGG repeat region in the FMR1 gene on the X chromosome, called a mutation. Such mutations contain more than 200 copies of the trinucleotide CGG and result in silencing of the FMR1 gene via methylation (the addition of methyl groups to FMR1 DNA; see Chapter 15). It is well known that CGG repeat regions of FMR1 that are larger than normal but contain 55–200 copies of CGG, called premutations, are associated with neurodevelopmental disorders other than fragile X. These include ASD, seizures, and attention-deficit/hyperactivity disorder (ADHD) as well as fragile X-associated tremor/ataxia

syndrome (FXTAS) in males (see Chapter 15). With FXTAS and the other previously mentioned disorders, the molecular mechanism is not related to the silencing (methylation) of the FMR1 gene but to toxicity resulting from an increase in FMR1 mRNA (Hagerman & Hagerman, 2013; Lozano, Rosero, & Hagerman, 2014). (See the section of this chapter on epigenetics for a discussion about methylation and gene silencing.)

Non-Mendelian Genetic Disorders

Non-Mendelian is a general term that refers to any pattern of inheritance in which traits do not segregate in accordance with Mendel's simple laws of inheritance. In clinical genetics, traits that are maternally inherited (e.g., mitochondrial disorders) or multifactorial in nature tend to be referred to as non-Mendelian.

Other Disorders

Polygenic disorders result from a deleterious combination of two or more genes in the absence of environmental factors. Many mental health conditions are suspected to be polygenic. Examples currently thought to be polygenic by some scientists include ADHD (Martin, Hamshere, Stergiakouli, O'Donovan, & Thapar, 2014) and schizophrenia (Agerbo et al., 2015). (See Chapters 23 and 30 for more information about ADHD and schizophrenia.)

Multifactorial disorders are caused by a combination of genetic mutations and environmental exposures. One example of a multifactorial disability is spina bifida, a neural tube defect. Spina bifida results from failure of fusion of the caudal neural tube during early embryonic development. It is one of the most common malformations of human structure and is thought to result from a combination of genetic and environmental factors. Certain chromosomal abnormalities, mutations in single genes, and exposures to teratogens are associated with spina bifida (see Chapters 9, 13, and 33). In addition, deficiency of folic acid plays an important role. Up to 70% of spina bifida cases can be prevented by maternal periconceptional folic acid supplementation. (The term *periconceptional* refers to the period from before conception to early pregnancy.) The mechanisms underlying this protective effect are unknown, but they may involve genes that regulate folate transport and metabolism. Vitamin B_{12} sufficiency also may be important in prevention of spina bifida (see Chapter 13). Other common examples of disorders considered to be multifactorial are Alzheimer's disease (see Chapter 49), cancer, hypertension, ischemic heart disease (the word *ischemic* refers to any form of blockage in a blood vessel), and type 2 diabetes (van Heyningen & Yeyati, 2004).

Congenital imprinting disorders are a group of rare congenital diseases affecting growth, development, and metabolism (Eggermann et al., 2015). For most genes, two active copies of each gene are inherited: one from the mother and one from the father. For some others, one active copy is inherited as well as one that has been silenced through the addition of methyl groups to DNA during egg or sperm formation. Genes inactivated in this way usually remain silenced throughout life. However, during egg and sperm formation they become reset. Regardless of the parent of origin, certain genes are always silenced in the egg and others are always silenced in the sperm (University of Utah, n.d.). Incorrect imprinting of a particular gene can result in an individual having two active or two inactive copies instead of one active copy. This can lead to severe developmental abnormalities, cancer, and other problems. Prader-Willi syndrome and Angelman syndrome are two very different chromosomal disorders resulting from different imprinting problems that occur in the same region of chromosome 15 (see Chapter 21). In Prader-Willi syndrome, individuals are missing gene activity that normally comes from the father. In Angelman syndrome, individuals are missing gene activity that normally comes from the mother (University of Utah, n.d.; see also Chapter 21).

UNUSUAL FEATURES OF GENETICS

In the previous sections, the focus was on genes in cell nuclei and two types of RNA: mRNA and tRNA. Only 10%–15% of the bases in DNA make up the genes. DNA also is present in cellular mitochondria. This section provides information on mtDNA, some types of DNA once labeled as "junk," and prion disorders that are transmitted by protein and not by microorganisms containing nucleic acid. The section concludes with a brief introduction to noncoding RNAs and their functions.

Mitochondrial DNA Variation

In contrast to genomic DNA, which is inherited from both parents in equal proportions, mtDNA is inherited only from the mother. This is because sperm cells do not contribute mitochondria to the embryo (as they are degraded upon fusion of sperm and egg). Mutations in mtDNA are transmitted to all of a woman's offspring but none of a man's offspring. Examples of developmental disabilities resulting from mtDNA mutations (i.e., mitochondrial inheritance) are certain mitochondrial myopathies, such as mitochondrial encephalopathy, lactic acidosis, and stroke-like episodes (MELAS). Another mitochondrial disorder is Leber hereditary optic neuropathy.

DNA Satellite Sequences

A large percentage of DNA (85%–90%) has no identified function and is sometimes said to be "silent." Some of the remaining base sequences perform crucial functions such as helping to turn genes on and off and holding chromosomes together. DNA that does not have a specific, identified function has historically been referred to as "junk DNA."

Part of this junk DNA includes unusual regions called DNA satellite sequences. These are repetitive sequences made up of one or more of the four DNA bases (i.e., A, C, G, T) repeated over and over again. The repetitive nature of these satellite sequences makes them unstable. Satellite sequences are very prone to changing in length as they are transmitted from one generation to another. The term *microsatellite* is applied to very short repetitive sequences. Variations of microsatellite sequences called trinucleotide repeat regions are now known to play an important role in quite a number of disorders that affect the central nervous system. Trinucleotide repeat regions consist of a three-nucleotide sequence repeated over and over again (e.g., CGG-CGG-CGG-CGG-CGG).

It is suspected that microsatellites are involved in regulating the amount of protein produced by particular genes and that such regulation may be important in adaptation to environmental changes. Certain trinucleotide repeat regions are known to grow in length as they are transmitted, if they are or become unstable. Examples of developmental disabilities that are caused by expansions of trinucleotide repeat regions are FXS, myotonic dystrophy (type 1), and Huntington disease (see Ellegren, 2004; Nussbaum, McInnes, & Willard, 2016; Orr & Zoghbi, 2007). Expansion of trinucleotide repeat regions may cause particular disorders to become expressed at an earlier and earlier age and/or more severely as they are transmitted through several generations in a family (e.g., FXS, myotonic dystrophy), a phenomenon called genetic anticipation.

Perhaps the most important type of satellite sequence is a region of repetitive DNA located at the ends of chromosomes, called telomeric DNA. When DNA replicates, there is difficulty copying the DNA at the chromosome ends. The impact of this problem is avoided, however, because at the ends of every chromosome is a region of satellite DNA called a telomere. With cell division, the telomeric DNA at the chromosome ends becomes shorter and shorter. If telomeres become excessively short, DNA replication is negatively affected, and this may lead to onset of serious illness or death. Through a simple blood test, it is now possible to test for telomere length in white blood cells. If the length is found to be unduly short, then lifestyle changes are recommended. Healthy eating and exercise are known to be associated with an increase in the activity of the enzyme telomerase, which is involved in telomere synthesis (these findings relate to epigenetics). The Nobel Prize in Physiology or Medicine in 2009 was awarded jointly to Elizabeth Blackburn, Carol Greider, and Jack Szostak for their work on telomeres and telomerase (Corey, 2009).

Transposons

Transposons are sequences of DNA that can move or transpose themselves to different regions of the genome. In the past, transposons have been considered to be a form of junk DNA. They also have been called "jumping genes" and "selfish DNA" because their main function seems to be to replicate themselves. One type of transposon gets copied and the copy gets inserted at a new position in the genome. Another type gets cut out and moved to a new position. Transposons were first discovered by Dr. Barbara McClintock, who received the Nobel Prize in Physiology or Medicine in 1983 for her discovery of genetic elements that were mobile and could move from one place to another within the genome of a cell (Raju, 1999b).

The HGP determined that a large portion of the human genome (44%) consists of transposons, though only about 0.05% are known to be active as of 2016. There is great interest in the active transposons, as they continue to generate genetic diversity as well as cause genetic disease (Mills, Bennett, Iskow, & Devine, 2007).

The most common form of transposon in humans is Alu. The Alu sequence is about 300 bases long. There are between 300,000 and 1 million copies of Alu in the human genome. Alu insertions that have altered normal gene function have been linked with various cancers (e.g., breast cancer) and other disorders including type 2 diabetes and neurofibromatosis (see Chapter 21).

Neurodegenerative Prion Disorders

A discussion of genetics would not be complete without mentioning the prion disorders. Prions are short proteins (peptides) that have infectious properties like bacteria or viruses, even though they contain no RNA or DNA. The Nobel Prize in Physiology or Medicine 1997 was awarded to Stanley B. Prusiner for his work on prions and their role in fatal forms of dementia called prion disorders (Bonn & Ault, 1997; Raju, 2000). Prion disorders are all associated with a spongy, "Swiss-cheese" appearance of the brain and a proliferation of nonneuronal brain cells called astroglia (Prusiner, 2001). Well-known prion disorders in animals include scrapie (a progressive disease that occurs in sheep and mice and frequently causes itching so intense that the animals seek relief by scraping off their wool or fur) and bovine spongiform encephalopathy (BSE; otherwise known as "mad cow disease").

Human prion diseases include kuru, Creutzfeldt-Jakob disease (CJD), Gerstmann-Sträussler disease, and fatal familial insomnia. Kuru is a disease that was first recognized in New Guinea in the early 1900s in a group taking part in a cannibalistic ritual: eating flesh and brain tissue from dead people who were important in the community. The reason for current interest in prion disorders is that a new variant of CJD (vCJD), discovered in 1990 and apparently related to BSE, has been reported in the United Kingdom and possibly in other countries as well. It is thought that eating beef infected with BSE resulted in transmission of vCJD. BSE was nicknamed mad cow disease because it caused nervous, aggressive behavior in normally peaceful animals. It is believed that cattle became infected because they were fed improperly sterilized food derived from scrapie-infected sheep. As of 2014, 1 in 2,000 people in the United Kingdom were found to carry proteins related to mad cow disease, though only 177 died from consumption of meat products contaminated with BSE in the late 1980s and early 1990s (Diack et al., 2014).

People have been cautioned not to handle scrapie-infected meat and bone meal with bare hands or to inhale it. Unfortunately, prions are very resistant to heat and cannot be destroyed by autoclaving (a process of sterilization involving treatment at high temperature and pressure that is often used to decontaminate biohazardous waste as well as surgical and dental instruments). One might ask what other animal products might be contaminated with prions (e.g., gelatin; collagen; tallow; leather; laboratory reagents such as calf serum, bovine serum albumin, and other bovine proteins).

In parts of Europe, livestock other than cattle, such as pigs, poultry, goats, and sheep, have become infected by BSE (by the same means as cattle). However, as of 2016, BSE is not a major problem in the United States or Canada. To date, only a very small number of isolated cases of BSE have been found in cattle in these countries.

Although it is not understood exactly how, prion proteins become folded in an abnormal way that causes neighboring prion molecules to take on the same abnormal structure. It is this abnormal folding that results in disease. (For more information about prions and prion diseases, see the Genetics Home Reference web site at http://ghr.nlm.nih.gov /condition/prion-disease/ and Rhodes, 1998).

Noncoding RNAs

Most RNA that is transcribed from DNA does not code for proteins and is classified as noncoding RNA (ncRNA). This RNA has been demonstrated to be essential for brain development and higher cognitive abilities and has been implicated in the development and pathophysiology of psychiatric disorders as well as many other diseases (Barry, 2014). ncRNAs may be potential targets for therapeutic intervention. Two classes of ncRNA whose functions are under investigation are the miRNAs and long ncRNAs (lncRNAs).

miRNAs are very small RNA molecules that regulate gene activity. They act by binding to complementary sequences in regulatory regions at the ends of mRNA molecules—regions called three prime untranslated regions. Such binding usually represses the translation of mRNA into protein or promotes mRNA degradation. miRNAs can change the way basic processes—including cell death, cell proliferation, tissue development, and the immune response—take place. More than 1,000 different miRNA molecules are encoded in the human

genome, and each one may affect the expression of hundreds of mRNAs. Researchers have found that the amounts of certain miRNAs produced in cells may be significantly altered in certain diseases (e.g., FXS, Alzheimer's disease [see Chapter 49], prion diseases; Provost, 2010).

lncRNAs are defined as those that are larger than 200 nucleotides. Only a few of these have been characterized, but there may be many thousands of them. Many lncRNAs have been found to be associated with development, neurodevelopmental disorders, and various diseases, but the mechanisms by which the lncRNAs control cellular processes are still under investigation (van de Vondervoort et al., 2013). See the section on epigenetics for more information.

TESTING FOR GENETIC DISORDERS

Testing for genetic disorders involves the application of laboratory procedures to detect alterations in DNA or chromosomes. The results of such tests can be used to diagnose genetic disorders and to identify individuals who carry altered DNA but may not be severely affected by a disorder. Testing also can be used to determine if an individual might pass a copy of an abnormal gene to his or her child. Genetic testing can be done on cells, blood, and amniotic fluid. This section discusses different ways in which genetic abnormalities can be detected.

One approach looks for changes in chromosome number or structure under the microscope (a procedure called cytogenetics). As already mentioned, another approach involves whole-exon or whole-genome sequencing. A third approach involves the application of molecular probes designed to attach to particular regions of DNA that are suspected of being altered and then using a special procedure to visualize the molecular probes that have bound. Some genetic alterations can be detected using functional or biochemical tests that demonstrate the presence of an altered gene through the presence of abnormal proteins or no proteins at all.

Alterations in DNA gene copy number (i.e., in gene dosage) are associated with normal human variation, but some are responsible for genetic syndromes. A technique called chromosomal microarray analysis (CMA) is able to screen the entire genome in a single test (South et al., 2013). On its own, CMA provided evidence for genetic involvement in 15%–20% of cases of unexplained intellectual or developmental disability, ASD, or multiple congenital abnormalities excluding Down syndrome and other recognizable chromosomal syndromes (Miller et al., 2010). In the case of ASD alone, the diagnostic yield of CMA was reported to be 9.3% (Tammimies et al., 2015).

CMA may not detect low-level mosaicism for unbalanced rearrangements and balanced translocations, so karyotyping is still recommended as a second tier. (The term *karyotype* refers to making a photograph of a set of chromosomes arranged in standard fashion.) CMA is also being used to screen for genetic abnormalities in embryos created by in vitro fertilization as early as 3 days of age because as many as 70% of embryos fertilized in vitro may have chromosomal abnormalities (Novik et al., 2014). The Nobel Prize in Physiology or Medicine 2010 was awarded to Robert Edwards for his breakthrough work regarding in vitro fertilization, a technique that has enriched the lives of infertile couples worldwide (Kirby, 2010).

Next-generation sequencing refers to the technologies that allow a very rapid sequencing of a large number of DNA segments (whole-exome sequencing) up to the entire genome (whole-genome sequencing). The use of whole-exome sequencing and whole-genome sequencing for diagnosis and research is growing, including the potential use in detecting life-threatening conditions in the newborn period as part of the newborn screening programs (American College of Medical Genetics and Genomics Board of Directors, 2012). However, it has also created a growing market for direct-to-consumer genetic testing. This form of testing is also known as "at-home genetic testing"; individuals obtain their own samples, often by swabbing the inside of the cheek, and mail these to a testing laboratory. In this approach, a doctor or insurance company is not necessarily involved.

For more information about at-home testing, see the Genetics Home Reference web site (U.S. National Library of Medicine, 2016a). For more information about genetic testing in general, see the Genetics Home Reference web (U.S. National Library of Medicine, 2016b). For a "proof of principle" application of whole-exome sequencing that found "needle in the haystack" mutations in the PIGV gene, causing a rare developmental disability called Mabry syndrome, see Krawitz et al. (2010) and Thompson et al. (2010).

EPIGENETICS AND EPIGENETIC PROCESSES

It is now understood that DNA is not a static blueprint but, rather, offers a dynamic span of possibilities in terms of gene expression. In their role in producing proteins, genes can be activated (upregulated) or suppressed (downregulated). Changes of this type can occur quickly and depend on the influence of factors outside of the cell—specifically, the immediate physiological and metabolic environment around the cell (Lipton, 2005, 2013; Turner, 2009). The extracellular environment that has this controlling influence on gene expression is determined by a range of factors (e.g., nutrition, physical exercise, quality of sleep, psychological experience, environmental toxins). Research is revealing at more and more subtle levels the range and quality of human experience that results in extracellular change, which in turn transmits a signal into the cell nucleus, triggering changes in the regulation of gene expression. It appears that there is a close interface between human experience and gene expression. Depending on the influence of the extracellular environment, the action of a cell within a given tissue is determined by which combination of genes at which moment is being upregulated or downregulated.

The concept of epigenetics was introduced briefly near the beginning of this chapter. However, different investigators have different explanations for the term (Deans & Maggert, 2015). Originally, *epigenetics* referred to processes by which a fertilized zygote developed into a mature, complex organism. However, the field is now focusing on changes in gene expression in a cell that are produced by modifications to chromatin within the cell nucleus that do not involve changes to the DNA sequence itself and where these modifications are triggered by changes in the immediate environment around the cell that depend on the organism's experience. This is the process by which human experience is transduced via rapid and flexible gene response into change in physiology and anatomy, thereby affecting development and, with repeated experience, the baseline state of health. (Chromatin is a complex of DNA, RNA, histone proteins, and nonhistone proteins, including enzymes called transcription factors. The basic repeating unit of chromatin is referred to as a nucleosome, which is conceptualized as being composed of eight core histone proteins [octamer] around which DNA of a length of 147 base pairs is wrapped. Extending out from each histone of the octamer is a flexible strand of histone protein; known as "tails," these extensions generally vary between 15 and 40 amino acids in length.)

Genes may be downregulated or upregulated on a moment-to-moment basis, depending on the matrix of mental and outer influences in play. This can result in an immediate appreciable effect on the body or change in the longer term, when accumulated alterations in the function of genes reach a critical mass. Studies involving monozygotic twins (Chiarella, Tremblay, Szyf, Provençal, & Booij, 2015) who share more or less the same genetic sequence provide striking examples of the role of environment in determining phenotype, including behavior. Epigenetic molecular analysis has elucidated the origin of these differences to be at the level of alterations in the chromatin leading to shift in gene expression, and not to involve change in the DNA sequence per se. Other epigenetic studies have revealed equally striking and flexible gene responses associated with the state of "well-being," a far more subtle circumstance pointing to the important link between state of mind (i.e., thoughts, beliefs, choices) and somatic health. For example, seeking happiness by engaging in hedonic pursuits (i.e., gratification via pleasurable sensations) and striving to find deeper meaning in one's life or by connecting with something larger than the self both result in feelings of emotional well-being. However, they transduce very differently at the molecular level regarding expression of genes involved in inflammation and immune response and may, over the long term, have strikingly different effects on baseline health (Fredrickson et al., 2013). (These latter findings are still considered controversial, however.)

The present epigenetic literature relating to how genes are up- or downregulated—for example, in response to stress—is dominated by description of three epigenetic processes (or "mechanisms") taking place within the chromatin and each with a number of variations. The two most established classes of epigenetic processes (Turgeon, Aravin, Sukumar, & Marsden, 2014) refer either to modification to the DNA of nucleosomes or, alternatively, to histone tails (Figures 10.8 and 10.9).

The molecular pathway—from detection of extracellular physiologic or metabolic changes relevant to gene expression, to transmission of this information to the chromatin, and the selection and triggering of these processes or others—is an

area of rapidly evolving research. One of these processes is DNA methylation/hydroxymethylation, and it involves changing gene expression by removing a hydrogen atom in DNA cytosine (at a specific position within the cytosine) and replacing it with either a chemical structure known as a methyl group ($-CH_3$) or a hydroxymethyl group ($-CH_3OH$). It is considered to be the case that DNA methylation generally inhibits gene expression. A second epigenetic gene regulation process, posttranslational histone modification, involves modification of the tails associated with the large histone proteins around which the DNA helix is wound. Various chemical structures have been identified

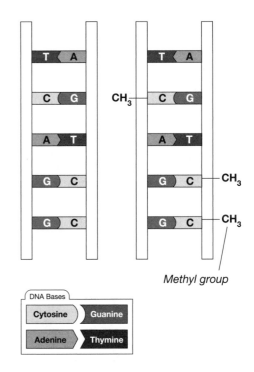

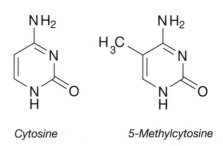

Cytosine   *5-Methylcytosine*

Figure 10.8. One epigenetic mechanism for activating or repressing gene activity is addition of methyl groups (CH_3) to the DNA base cytosine (C). In this figure, the vertical rods depict the linear backbone of the two strands of DNA. When CH_3 groups become attached to certain C residues, DNA in that region cannot be copied into mRNA. (*Source*: Percy, Lewkis, & Brown, 2003. *Illustration*: Copyright © Tom Dearie, Threesixty Creative/Infographix.)

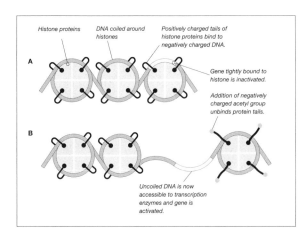

Figure 10.9. A second epigenetic mechanism for controlling gene activity is modification of histone proteins that help to keep DNA coiled. The top panel (A) shows DNA interacting with histone proteins that are not modified; the tails of the histone proteins wrap themselves around the DNA. When DNA is tightly coiled it cannot be copied into RNA. The bottom panel (B) shows what happens when acetyl groups are added to the histone tails; they can no longer bind the DNA. This allows the DNA to assume a more open configuration that allows a DNA strand to be copied into RNA. (*Source*: Percy, Lewkis, & Brown, 2003. *Illustration*: Copyright © Tom Dearie, Threesixty Creative/Infographix.)

that can bind to specific amino acids at specific locations in the histone tails, and in their patterning of doing so, affect gene expression. These chemical structures include methyl, acetyl (–COCH$_3$), and phosphoryl (–PO$_3^{2-}$) groups, among others. See Figures 10.8 and 10.9.

A third type of epigenetic gene regulation process is RNA based. It involves forms of RNA that unlike messenger RNA, do not code for protein. ncRNAs involved in epigenetics include microRNAs and lncRNAs that are longer than 200 nucleotides. How ncRNAs interact with other chromatin constituents to modulate gene expression seems to be less clear than the chemical binding described in the two processes described earlier in the subsection. However, known processes that affect functions of ncRNAs include alterations of DNA methylation on noncoding regions of DNA and alterations of methylation on the RNAs themselves (Lo & Zhou, 2014).

The previously described epigenetic chemical modifications of DNA or histones are referred to as marks. They achieve their effect of upregulating or downregulating gene expression by physically altering accessibility of DNA to DNA-binding proteins such as transcriptional regulators by altering the three-dimensional DNA conformation. In the case of posttranslational histone modifications, regulatory information is communicated by the specific combination of histone marks; this is known as the "histone code hypothesis."

Epigenetic marks on the DNA or histones may remain in place throughout the lifetime of cell divisions; they are also reversible (Cao, 2014). These modifications can occur throughout a lifetime and also occur prenatally in relation to the prenatal extracellular environment (i.e., the maternal blood supply). Many specific alterations of gene expressions originating in fetal development have been identified and linked to circumstances that affect the fetal extracellular environment, such as the level of stress experienced by the mother (Lo & Zhou, 2014; see also Chapter 33).

Epigenetic changes can also be ancestral; they can be induced in male or female germ cells and transmitted via mitosis to offspring (Turner, 2009). As demonstrated in an animal model, such transmission can involve demethylation of a gene in the germline (Szyf, 2014), though how environmental exposures induce changes to the germline is largely unknown.

The field of epigenetics also explores the real-time dynamic gene response of factors well established to influence health, such as diet. It invites consideration of the role of other factors that might affect gene expression and health as well as delineation of how these factors affect gene expression. On a philosophical note, research to date appears to support a number of beliefs that are well known in native traditions throughout the world: that a person's well-being is not independent of the well-being of the environment and the quality of his or her relationship to it, that mental experience can shape health in general, and that the impact of at least some experiences of one's ancestors can be passed on.

The National Institutes of Health Roadmap Epigenomics Mapping Consortium (National Institutes of Health, n.d.b) is working to determine the locations of methyl groups in human DNA as well as other stable changes in representative cells that constitute epigenomic marks. As explained by David Allis, whereas the HGP "provided the blueprint for life, the epigenome will tell us how the whole thing gets executed" (as cited in Bradbury, 2003, p. 1).

CHALLENGES AND FUTURE OPPORTUNITIES FOR DISABILITY AND DISEASE

Despite the major scientific advances in both genetic and genomic knowledge and the explosion of new technologies, application of genetic information to human disease and disorder remains limited because of shortages in trained health care providers (Uscher, 2013). Ultimately, it will be human health care professionals who will use genetic information to provide care, and there are unfortunately shortages of clinical geneticists and genetic counselors. Reimbursement for these clinical activities is often well below reimbursement for other types of health care, providing little incentive for young professionals to pursue clinical genetics careers. Unless these work force and reimbursement issues are addressed, the potential benefits of advances in genetic and genomic science and technology are likely to be unrealized in human health care.

Another limitation in the application of basic discoveries in genetics and genomics has been the ability to link these discoveries to the range of symptoms and symptom severity of many diseases and disorders due to inadequate or inconsistent phenotyping. Fortunately, this problem has been recognized, and a major National Institutes of Health initiative (see PhenX Toolkit, n.d.) is underway in the United States to create a library of standardized measures of common disease phenotypes in an effort to accelerate application of genetic and genomic knowledge in biomedical research. The Toolkit is also providing standardized measures of and environmental exposures for use in such studies.

When the complete mapping of the human genome was announced, a distinguished geneticist remarked that this was the equivalent of putting the needle at the beginning of the first groove in a long-playing 33 1/3 rpm record album. It represented the start. The application of genetic and genomic technology has advanced rapidly since the HGP announcement, and the cost of performing whole-genome and whole-exome sequencing has declined dramatically, making them viable and cost-effective clinical and research tools. At the same time, tremendous advances in bioinformatics technology are increasingly making it possible to analyze large and complex genetic and genomic datasets. Combined with the adoption of electronic health records, the genetic, genomic, and bioinformatics advances provide an infrastructure for "big data" analyses that have never previously been possible.

For many diseases, such as cancer, these new technologies offer hope for individualized, personal medicine that provides targeted, highly effective therapy while minimizing toxic, unnecessary side effects. For many of the primary genetic disorders, particularly those that result in moderate intellectual and developmental disabilities, the time to human benefit may be a bit more prolonged. There are certainly opportunities to improve the accuracy of newborn screening and provide site-of-service newborn screening that allows immediate access to genetic counseling and early intervention (when available). For conditions that are not immediately detectable at birth (e.g., FXS, some of the leukodystrophies), improved newborn screening technology offers opportunities for natural history studies that may lead to early intervention or treatment that is not possible as of this writing in 2016.

Most of the genetic and genomic efforts to date have focused on diagnosis. The future holds great promise for the use of genetic and genomic advances to develop new targeted drugs, repurpose old drugs, and provide biomarkers for gene and stem cell therapies (Schaaf, Zschocke, & Potocki, 2012). A potential consequence of these advances will be reduction in the cost of many expensive current treatments, making access to effective care available to many more individuals. One of the outcomes of effective, lower cost care will be an ultimate reduction in health disparities. These advances, if realized, offer new hope to those living with intellectual and developmental disabilities, and possibly prevention or reduction of severity for those affected in the future.

SUMMARY

The genetic phenomena described in this chapter are among the most profound biological discoveries since Gregor Mendel discovered the classical patterns of single-gene inheritance through his studies of plants. This chapter outlined the roles of mutated genomic and mitochondrial DNA, amplifications of trinucleotide repeat regions, common polymorphic variants, prions and high-throughput sequencing, and epigenetic processes in normal human development and in disorders. The chapter concluded with a discussion of challenges and future directions in this exciting field.

FOR FURTHER THOUGHT AND DISCUSSION

1. What steps need to be taken in the consent process for children with intellectual and developmental disabilities whose genetic/genomic

information may be linked to health challenges they will not face until later in life?

2. What policy changes will be necessary to provide uninsured or poorly insured individuals with intellectual and developmental disabilities with access to the advances in diagnosis and treatment that result from progress in genetics and genomic research?

3. The term *environment* includes such factors as stress, diet, toxins, and use of various forms of manufactured products. What are the implications of epigenetics in terms of people's relationships to such environmental factors?

4. Are there concerns that should be addressed if advances in low-cost sequencing expand the number of conditions that can be identified by newborn screening that currently have no treatment but that might benefit future individuals if natural history studies were initiated to better understand the developmental process and identify potential treatments?

REFERENCES

Agerbo, E., Sullivan, P.F., Vilhjálmsson, B.J., Pedersen, C.B., Mors, O., Borgium, A.D.,...Mortensen, P.B. (2015). Polygenic risk score, parental socioeconomic status, family history of psychiatric disorders, and the risk for schizophrenia: A Danish population-based study and meta-analysis. *JAMA Psychiatry, 72*(7), 635–641.

American College of Medical Genetics and Genomics Board of Directors. (2012). Points to consider in the clinical application of genomic sequencing. *Genetics in Medicine, 14,* 759–761.

Barry, G. (2014). Integrating the roles of long and small non-coding RNA in brain function and disease. *Molecular Psychiatry, 19,* 410–416.

Bonn, D., & Ault, A. (1997). Prusiner awarded the Nobel prize for work on prions. *Lancet, 350*(9084), 1079.

Bradbury, J. (2003). Human Epigenome Project—Up and running. *PLOS Biology, 1*(3), e82. Retrieved from http://journals.plos.org/plosbiology/article?id=10.1371/journal.pbio.0000082

Cao, J. (2014). The functional role of long non-coding RNAs and epigenetics. *Biological Procedures Online, 2014 Sep 15.* doi:10.1186/1480-9222-16-11

Chiarella, J., Tremblay, R.E., Szyf, M., Provençal, N., & Booij, L. (2015). Impact of early environment on children's mental health: Lessons from DNA methylation studies with monozygotic twins. *Twin Research and Human Genetics, 18*(6), 623–634.

Corey, D.R. (2009). Telomeres and telomerase: From discovery to clinical trials. *Chemistry and Biology, 16*(12), 1219–1223.

Cui, Y., Li, G., Li, S., & Wu, R. (2010). Designs for linkage analysis and association studies of complex diseases. *Methods in Molecular Biology, 620,* 219–242.

Deans, C., & Maggert, K.A. (2015). What do you mean, "epigenetic"? *Genetics, 199*(4), 887–896.

Diack, A.B., Head, M.W., McCutcheon, S., Boyle, A., Knight, R., Ironside, J.W., & Manson, J.C. (2014). Variant CJD. 18 years of research and surveillance. *Prion, 8*(4), 286–295.

Eggermann, T., Perez de Nanclares, G., Maher, E.R., Temple, I.K., Tümer, Z., Monk, D.,...Netchine, I. (2015). Imprinting disorders: A group of congenital disorders with overlapping patterns of molecular changes affecting imprinted loci. *Clinical Epigenetics, 14*(7),123. doi:10.1186/s13148-015-0143-8

Eiguero, E., Delicat-Loembet, L.M., Rougeron, V., Arnathau, C., Roche, B., Becquart, P.,...Prugnolle, F. (2015). Malaria continues to select for sickle cell trait in Central Africa. *Proceedings of the National Academies of Sciences USA, 112*(22), 7051–7054.

Ellegren, H. (2004). Microsatellites: Simple sequences with complex evolution. *Nature Reviews in Genetics, 5*(6), 435–445.

Fredrickson., B.L., Grewen, K.M., Coffey, K.A., Algoe, S.B., Firestine, A.M., Arevalo, J.M.,...Cole, S.W.A. (2013). Functional genomic perspective on human well-being. *Proceedings of the National Academy of Sciences USA, 110,* 13684–13689.

Guigó, R., & Valcárcel, J. (2015). RNA. Prescribing splicing. *Science, 347*(6218), 124–125.

Hagerman, R., & Hagerman, P. (2013). Advances in clinical and molecular understanding of FMR1 premutation and fragile X associated tremor/ataxia syndrome. *Lancet Neurology, 12*(8), 786–798.

Higgins, E.S. (2008). The new genetics of mental illness. *Scientific American Mind, 19,* 40–47. doi:10.1038/scientificamericanmind0608-40

Kirby, T. (2010). Robert Edwards: Nobel Prize for father of in-vitro fertilisation. *Lancet, 376*(9749), 1293.

Krawitz, P.M., Schweiger, M.R., Rödelsperger, C., Marcelis, C., Kölsch, U., Meisel, C.,...Robinson, P.N. (2010). Identity-by-descent filtering of exome sequence data identifies PIGV mutations in hyperphosphatasia mental retardation syndrome. *Nature Genetics, 42*(10), 827–829.

Lipton, B.H. (2005). *The biology of belief: Unleashing the power of consciousness, matter and miracles.* New York, NY: Hay House.

Lipton, B.H. (2013). *The honeymoon effect.* Carlsbad, CA: Hay House.

Lo, C.L., & Zhou, F.C. (2014). Environmental alterations of epigenetics prior to the birth. *International Review of Neurobiology, 115,* 1–49.

Lozano, R., Rosero, C.A., & Hagerman, R.J. (2014). Fragile X spectrum disorders. *Intractable Rare Diseases Research, 3*(4), 134–146. doi:10.5582/irdr.2014.01022

Lubinsky, M. (2012). Hypothesis: Cystic fibrosis carrier geography reflects interactions of tuberculosis and hypertension with vitamin D deficiency, altitude and temperature. Vitamin D deficiency effects and CF carrier advantage. *Journal of Cystic Fibrosis, 11*(1), 68–70.

Maddox, B. (2003). The double helix and the "wronged heroine." *Nature, 421*(6921), 407–408.

Martin, J., Hamshere, M.L., Stergiakouli, E., O'Donovan, M.C., & Thapar, A. (2014). Genetic risk for attention-deficit/hyperactivity disorder contributes to neurodevelopmental traits in the general population. *Biological Psychiatry, 76*(8), 664–671.

Miller, D.T., Adam, M.P., Aradhya, S., Biesecker, L.G., Brothman, A.R., Carter, N.P.,…Ledbetter, D.H. (2010). Consensus statement: Chromosomal microarray is a first-tier clinical diagnostic test for individuals with developmental disabilities or congenital anomalies. *American Journal of Human Genetics, 86*(5), 749–764.

Mills, R.E., Bennett, E.A., Iskow, R.C., & Devine, S. (2007). Which transposable elements are active in the human genome? *Trends in Genetics, 23*(4), 183–191.

Milunsky, A. (1977). *Know your genes.* Boston, MA: Houghton Mifflin.

Mohler, J., Najafi, B., Fain, M., & Ramos, K.S. (2015). Precision medicine: A wider definition. *Journal of the American Geriatric Society, 63*(9), 1971–1972.

Morrow, E.M. (2010). Genomic copy number variation in disorders of cognitive development. *Journal of the American Academy of Child and Adolescent Psychiatry, 49*(11), 1091–1104.

National Institutes of Health. (n.d.a). *Precision Medicine Initiative Cohort Program.* Retrieved from https://www.nih.gov/precision-medicine-initiative-cohort-program

National Institutes of Health. (n.d.b). *Roadmap Epigenomics Project.* Retrieved from http://www.roadmapepigenomics.org/

Nobelprize.org. (2016). *Nobel Prizes and laureates.* Retrieved from http://nobelprize.org/nobel_prizes

Novik, V., Moulton, E.B., Sisson, M.E., Shrestha, S.L., Tran, K.D., Stern, H.J.,…Stanley, W.S. (2014).The accuracy of chromosomal microarray testing for identification of embryonic mosaicism in human blastocysts. *Molecular Cytogenetics, 7*(1), 18. doi:10.1186/1755-8166-7-18

Nussbaum, R.L., McInnes, R.R., & Willard, H.F. (2016). Introduction to human genetics. *Thompson & Thompson genetics in medicine* (8th ed.). Philadelphia, PA: W.B. Saunders.

Orr, H.T., & Zoghbi, H.Y. (2007). Trinucleotide repeat disorders. *Annual Review of Neuroscience, 30,* 575–621.

Ott, J., Wang, J., & Leal, S.M. (2015). Genetic linkage analysis in the age of whole-genome sequencing. *Nature Reviews in Genetics, 16*(5), 275–284.

Percy, M., Carter, M., Lewkis, S.Z., Thompson, M., & Brown, I. (2011). Introduction to human genetics. In I. Brown & M. Percy (Eds.), *Developmental disabilities in Ontario* (3rd ed., pp. 145–168). Toronto, Canada: Ontario Association on Developmental Disabilities.

Percy, M., Lewkis, S., & Brown, I. (2003). An introduction to genetics and development. In I. Brown & M. Percy (Eds.), *Developmental disabilities in Ontario* (2nd ed., pp. 89–108). Toronto, Canada: Ontario Association on Developmental Disabilities.

Percy, M., Lewkis, S., & Brown, I. (2007). Introduction to genetics and development. In I. Brown & M. Percy (Eds.), *A comprehensive guide to intellectual and developmental disabilities* (pp. 87–108). Baltimore, MD: Paul H. Brookes Publishing Co.

Petrikin, J.E., Willig, L.K., Smith, L.D., & Kingsmore, S.F. (2015). Rapid whole genome sequencing and precision neonatology. *Seminars in Perinatology, 39*(8), 623–631.

PhenX Toolkit. (n.d.). *Welcome to the PhenX Toolkit.* Retrieved from https://www.phenxtoolkit.org

Provost, P. (2010). MicroRNAs as a molecular basis for mental retardation, Alzheimer's and prion diseases. *Brain Research, 1338,* 58–66.

Prusiner, S.B. (2001). Shattuck lecture: Neurodegenerative diseases and prions. *New England Journal of Medicine, 344,* 1516–1526.

Raju, T.N. (1999a). The Nobel chronicles. 1968: Har Khorana (b 1922); Robert Holley (1922–93); Marshall Nirenberg (b 1927). *Lancet, 354*(9179), 690.

Raju, T.N. (1999b). The Nobel chronicles. 1983: Barbara McClintock (1902–92). *Lancet, 354*(9194), 2007.

Raju, T.N. (2000). The Nobel chronicles. 1997: Stanley Ben Prusiner (b 1942). *Lancet, 356*(9225), 260.

Rhodes, R. (1998). *Deadly feasts: Tracking the secrets of a terrifying new plague.* New York, NY: Simon & Schuster.

Schaaf, C.P., Zschocke, J., & Potocki, L. (2012). *Human genetics: From molecules to medicine.* Philadelphia, PA: Lippincott Williams & Wilkins.

South, S.T., Lee, C., Lamb, A.N., Higgins, A.W., & Kearney, H.M; Working Group for the American College of Medical Genetics and Genomics Laboratory Quality Assurance Committee. (2013). ACMG Standards and Guidelines for constitutional cytogenomic microarray analysis, including postnatal and prenatal applications: Revision 2013. *Genetics in Medicine, 15*(11), 901–909.

Szyf, M. (2014). Lamarck revisited: Epigenetic inheritance of ancestral odor fear conditioning. *Nature Neuroscience, 17,* 2–4.

Tammimies, K., Marshall, C.R., Walker, S., Kaur, G., Thiruvahindrapuram, B., Lionel, A.C.,…Fernandez, B.A. (2015). Molecular diagnostic yield of chromosomal microarray analysis and whole-exome sequencing in children with autism spectrum disorder. *JAMA: The Journal of the American Medical Association, 314*(9), 895–903.

Taylor, S.M., Cerami, C., & Fairhurst, R.M. (2013). Hemoglobinopathies: Slicing the Gordian knot of *Plasmodium falciparum* malaria pathogenesis. *PLPS Pathogens, 9*(5), e1003327. doi:10.1371/journal.ppat.1003327

Thompson, M.D., Nezarati, M.M., Gillessen-Kaesbach, G., Meinecke, P., Mendoza-Londono, R., Mornet, E.,…Cole, D.E. (2010). Hyperphosphatasia with seizures, neurologic deficit, and characteristic facial features: Five new patients with Mabry syndrome. *American Journal of Medical Genetics A, 152A*(7), 1661–1669.

Turgeon, P.J., Aravin, N., Sukumar, A.N., & Marsden, P.A. (2014). Epigenetics of cardiovascular disease—A new "beat" in coronary artery disease. *Medical Epigenetics, 2*(1), 37–52.

Turner, B.M. (2009). Epigenetic responses to environmental change and their evolutionary implications. *Philosophical Transactions of the Royal Society B: Biological Sciences, 364*(1534), 3403–3418.

University of Utah, Learn.Genetics. (n.d.). *Genomic imprinting.* Retrieved from http://learn.genetics.utah.edu/content/epigenetics/imprinting/

U.S. National Library of Medicine. (2016a). *What is direct-to-consumer genetic testing?* Retrieved from https://ghr.nlm.nih.gov/handbook/testing/directtoconsumer

U.S. National Library of Medicine. (2016b). *What is genetic testing?* Retrieved from https://ghr.nlm.nih.gov/handbook/testing/directtoconsumer

Uscher, J. (2013). Increasing the ranks of medical geneticists. *AAMC Reporter.* Retrieved from the Medical Education site of the Portfolio of Jen Uscher at http://jenuscher.com/static/media/portfolio/Increasing_the_Ranks.pdf

van de Vondervoort, I.I.G.M., Gordebeke, P.M., Khoshab, N., Tiesinga, P.H.E., Buitelaar, J.K.T., Aschrafi, A., & Glennon, J.C. (2013). Long non-coding RNAs in neurodevelopmental disorders. *Frontiers in Molecular Neuroscience, 6,* 53. doi:10.3389/fnmol.2013.00053

van Heyningen, V., & Yeyati, P.L. (2004). Mechanisms of non-Mendelian inheritance in genetic disease. *Human Molecular Genetics, 13*(Suppl. 2), R225–R233.

Watson, J.D., & Crick, F.H.C. (1953). A structure for deoxyribose nucleic acid. *Nature, 171,* 737–738.

Xiong, H.Y., Alipanahi, B., Lee, L.J., Bretschneider, H., Merico, D., Yuen, R.K.,…Frey, B.J. (2015). The human splicing code reveals new insights into the genetic determinants of disease. *Science, 347*(6218), 1254806. doi:10.1126/science.1254806

11

Introduction to the Nervous Systems

William MacKay and Maire Percy

WHAT YOU WILL LEARN

- The importance of having an overview of the nervous systems
- The features of the central and peripheral nervous systems, including the gut microbiome
- Brain structure and function
- Some factors affecting brain structure and function
- Importance of the blood–brain barrier and the hypothalamic–pituitary–adrenal axis
- New directions in brain and neuroscience research

Knowledge of the neurobiological basis of different intellectual and developmental disabilities and of environmental or life experience influences on brain development and function should lead to better interventions and treatments for these disorders as well as to better educational strategies. This chapter provides an introduction to the nervous systems and cutting-edge research to encourage clinicians to determine which parts of the nervous systems are affected, and how, in every case of intellectual or developmental disability.

THE NERVOUS SYSTEMS

Abnormalities in, or insults to, the developing or mature brain or the sensory organs can result in deficits of communication, learning, behavior, and/or motor ability. Such problems may involve the central nervous system (CNS), the peripheral nervous system (PNS), or both.

Central Nervous System

The CNS is divided grossly into two parts: the brain and the spinal cord. The skull protects the brain and the vertebrae of the spinal column protect the spinal cord. In addition, a set of membranes (the meninges) covering the surface of the brain and spinal cord protects and nourishes the CNS. Fluid in the brain and spinal cord called cerebrospinal fluid (CSF) supports and cushions these tissues from trauma. CSF is made by the choroid plexus, a ribbon of tissue that is highly vascularized (i.e., contains a lot of blood vessels) and lines the CSF-filled ventricles of the brain (see Figure 11.1 for an illustration of the ventricles). The volume of CSF is normally constant at about 215 milliliters (mL), although it is continually secreted at a rate of approximately 550 mL per day. To prevent buildup of intracranial pressure (pressure inside the skull), the CSF flows out of the fourth ventricle into the subarachnoid space (the area under the arachnoid mater, which is the middle membrane of the brain meninges) to eventually drain into either the venous or lymphatic system. (The lymphatic system is a network of tissues and organs consisting mainly of lymph vessels, lymph nodes, and lymph that includes the tonsils, adenoids, spleen, and thymus.) CSF is made from the blood by filtration, diffusion, and active transport of blood constituents. It washes away waste products of metabolism, drugs, and other substances that may gain access to the brain from the blood. CSF is clear and colorless, and it contains only a few lymphocytes (white blood cells); small amounts of protein, glucose, potassium;

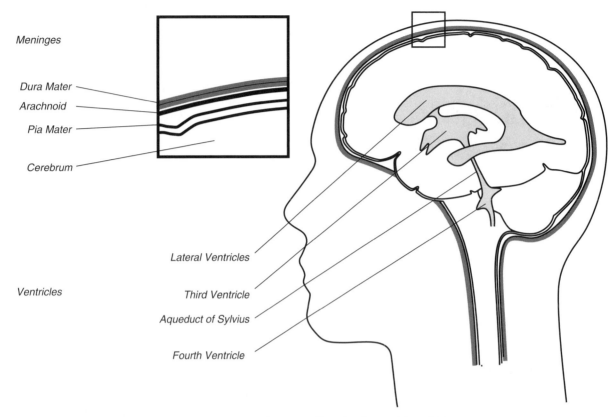

Figure 11.1. Meninges and ventricles of the brain. (Copyright © Tom Dearie, Threesixty Creative/Infographix.)

and relatively large amounts of sodium chloride (salt). When the intracranial pressure is increased (e.g., as a result of brain injury, hydrocephalus—excessive accumulation of fluid in the brain—or a brain tumor), this can cause agitation, confusion, changes in behavior, decreased response, and coma.

Analysis of the CSF can give clues in cases of CNS disease. Total protein is increased in infections and viral diseases, and CSF cell counts increase in cases of meningitis (inflammation of the meninges) or encephalitis (infections of the brain).

The various parts of the brain work together to enable perception and thinking as well as coordination of appropriate behaviors and body maintenance. The brain's survival depends on receiving (via the circulation of blood) an adequate supply of fuel (mainly glucose), other nutrients, and oxygen. The front part of the brain is supplied with blood by the internal carotid arteries, which branch and become the anterior and middle cerebral arteries, and the back part by the vertebral arteries, which merge to become the basilar artery. These arteries are joined together by smaller connections to form

the Circle of Willis (see Figure 11.2; for an animation of blood flow through the Circle of Willis see the North Harris College Biology Department web site at http://www.apchute.com/cardio/circle.htm). Reduced blood flow in the cerebral arteries radiating out from the Circle of Willis is a common cause of stroke (death of brain cells in a focal zone) due to either a blockage in the blood supply (an infarction) or to bleeding into the tissue from a ruptured blood vessel (a hemorrhage). Drainage of blood from the brain occurs via deep veins and sinuses that finally drain into the internal jugular veins. In a healthy brain, a homeostatic mechanism known as autoregulation allows blood flow to stay constant even when physiologic conditions change radically. However, if the blood supply to the brain is seriously decreased as the result of heart failure or other factors, then this may contribute to the development of dementia, including Alzheimer's disease (see Chapter 49 for greater detail).

The average adult human brain weighs 1.3–1.4 kilograms (kg) (approximately 3 pounds). It contains about 87 billion nerve cells (neurons) and five to

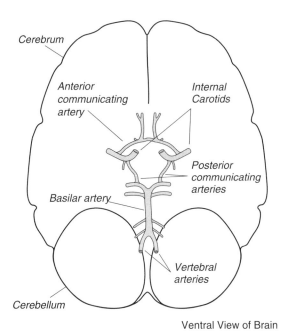

Ventral View of Brain

Figure 11.2. In the brain, anterior and posterior as well as right and left arteries join to create an interconnected blood supply in a structure called the Circle of Willis. (Copyright © Tom Dearie, Threesixty Creative/Infographix.)

10 times that number of three different types of non-neural support cells called glia:

1. Microglia are the macrophages (phagocytic cells) of the brain. Phagocytes engulf and absorb waste material, harmful microorganisms, or other foreign substances in the blood vessels and tissues.

2. Astrocytes provide nutritional support to neurons, especially lactate and glutamine molecules. They communicate with neurons and modulate signaling between neurons.

3. Oligodendrocytes encircle the axons of many neurons to form myelin sheaths in the white matter. (Myelin is an insulating material that usually is around only the axon of a neuron.)

Gray matter refers to brain tissue that is composed of the bodies of nerve cells (i.e., the neurons) and the initial parts of the processes (axons and dendrites) that emerge from the neurons. Information processing takes place in the gray matter. The nerve impulses for information transmission throughout the nervous systems are initiated here and then are sent away to specific targets via axons that make up the white matter. White matter is by this means responsible for information transmission. The form of the brain is reminiscent of a mushroom: the giant

cerebrum (analogous to the cap) is supported by the brainstem (the stalk), which is continuous with the spinal cord. The spinal cord is the main information pathway connecting the brain and PNS. It is comprised largely of white matter arranged in tracts of longitudinal fibers around a central core of gray matter; this central core of gray matter surrounds a small, longitudinal canal continuous with the ventricles of the brain and filled with CSF. The spinal cord is approximately 43 centimeters (cm) long in adult women and 45 cm long in adult men and weighs approximately 35–40 grams (g) (Gray, 1918). (*General sources:* Bear, Connors, & Paradiso, 2007; MacKay & Percy, 2007, 2011.)

Peripheral Nervous System

The PNS is divided into three parts: the somatic nervous system, the autonomic nervous system, and the enteric nervous system of the gut. The somatic nervous system is comprised of the afferent nerve network, which includes most sensory nerves leading to the spinal cord and brain, and the efferent nerve network, which includes all motor nerves leading from the brain and spinal cord to the muscles. (*Afferent* means carrying impulses toward the CNS; *efferent* means leading away.) In general, the somatic system mediates sensation and all body movement. The brain typically processes the information from the afferent network and responds through the efferent nerve network to elicit a response in the muscles. Sometimes, however, the brain does not fully process the information before a reflex arc within the spinal cord triggers a movement. Reflex arcs coordinate stereotyped reactions that are either protective in dangerous situations or regulatory. The term *regulatory* refers to the maintenance of a specific motoric function, be it postural balance, finger grip, or eye position. Certain stimuli, such as touching a hot surface, stimulate activity in a protective reflex arc. Nerve impulses travel up the afferent nerve, through several interneurons in the spinal cord, to eventually activate selected motor (efferent) neurons. (Interneurons are connector neurons that process signals from one or more sensory neurons and relay signals to motor neurons.) Finally, the reflex signal travels down the appropriate efferent nerves to jerk the hand away from the hot surface. This automatic response system results in reactions that are much quicker than is possible with consciously willed responses and better scaled to the magnitude of the stimulus.

The autonomic nervous system controls smooth muscles, both in viscera (internal organs) and in blood vessels, and it controls secretion from glands. It is involved in functions such as blood pressure, heart rate, breathing, digestion, excretion, body temperature, and copulation. The effector channels of the autonomic system are classified as either sympathetic or parasympathetic. The sympathetic system prepares the body for arousal and sudden stresses. The parasympathetic system supports maintenance and restorative functions including digestion. Efferents of the sympathetic nervous system originate in the thoracic segments of the spinal cord and are distributed to various parts of the body via the sympathetic chain of ganglia on either side of the vertebral column. (The term *ganglia* refers to PNS structures containing a collection of nerve cell bodies.) Sympathetic nerves also contain sensory afferents conveying metabolic information from internal organs to the CNS. Efferents of the parasympathetic nervous system originate in the brainstem and in the lowest segments of the spinal cord. Neurological functions located here include those necessary for survival (e.g., breathing, digestion, heart rate, blood pressure). Again, sensory afferents mingle with efferents in parasympathetic nerves. For example, the large vagus nerve conveys information about blood pressure, levels of carbon dioxide in the blood, and the amount of food in the stomach. The sympathetic nervous system prepares the body for activities associated with fight or flight; it prepares for stressful events ranging from facing a violent confrontation to running from danger. In the fight-or-flight reaction, adrenaline and noradrenaline (hormones released by the medulla of the two adrenal glands) cause various parts of the body to respond in much the same way as the sympathetic nervous system. Because adrenaline and noradrenaline are released into the blood stream, they continue to exert effects after a stressful event has stopped. In the fight-or-flight reaction, blood sugar is increased, extra red blood cells are released from the spleen, peripheral blood vessels constrict, the pulse quickens, blood pressure elevates, and digestion stops. Parasympathetic function is largely nutritive, restorative, and restful; it organizes recovery from any emergency state that the sympathetic nervous system creates.

As noted previously, the sympathetic and parasympathetic systems are structurally distinct entities. Some functions of these two systems oppose one another—as in a push–pull balancing act—but other functions are complementary in nature (see Table 11.1).

Reflexes also operate within the autonomic nervous system, generally to regulate homeostatic functions such as blood pressure or body temperature. Moreover, many afferents within autonomic nerves transmit pain information. In the CNS, information about organ pain often converges with pain signals from surface areas of the body. As a result, the source of the information sometimes gets confused. This is called referred pain. One example is the referred pain that some people feel in the shoulders and arms when they are having a heart attack.

The autonomic nervous system influences all aspects of digestion, including gut motility, ion transport associated with secretion and absorption, and gastrointestinal blood flow. Much of the control of the gastrointestinal system results from the feedback of digestive system hormones acting both on vagal afferents and directly on the CNS. However, the gastrointestinal tract also has its own local nervous system referred to as the enteric nervous system (Grundy & Schemann, 2005).

The enteric nervous system contains as many neurons as the spinal cord. It is primarily composed of two networks of neurons extending from the esophagus to the anus, both of which are imbedded

Table 11.1. Some contrasting and complementary effects of sympathetic and parasympathetic arousal

Sympathetic nervous system	Parasympathetic nervous system
Pupil dilation and opening of the eyelids	Pupil constriction
Stimulation of the sweat glands	Activation of the salivary glands
Constriction of blood vessels in the skin and gut	Promotion of urination
Increase of the heart rate	Decrease of the heart rate
Dilation of the bronchial tubes	Constriction of the bronchial tubes
Inhibition of the secretions in the digestive system	Stimulation of intestinal movement and secretions of the stomach
Ejaculation of semen	Penile erection

Influence of the Microbiome on the Brain and Nervous System

The microbiome (spectrum of bacteria in the intestines) influences brain function including development of the nervous system. The gut microbiome is probably dysfunctional in autism. For example, some children with autism have a higher-than-normal concentration of *Clostridium* bacteria in the gut. These bacteria can produce neurotoxins plus the metabolite propionic acid. Propionic acid crosses the blood–brain barrier (BBB); injection of it directly into the brain ventricles of rats causes symptoms associated with autism, such as repetitive and antisocial behaviors and cognitive impairments (MacFabe, 2013; Midtvedt, 2012). There is evidence that "good" bacteria can reverse symptoms of autism in a mouse model (Hsiao et al., 2013).

---

in the wall of the digestive tract and innervate the gastrointestinal muscles, pancreas, and gall bladder (i.e., the viscera). Disorders of the gastrointestinal system, such as celiac disease (intolerance to gluten) or the intestinal inflammation that is common in people with autism, involve the enteric nervous system. In addition, the gut microbiome, via metabolites and secreted signaling molecules, significantly influences both vagal afferents and the brain. (The term *microbiome* refers to particular microorganisms present in particular regions of the body.) Indeed, in the very young, the microbiome appears to influence brain development. The gut–brain interaction is bidirectional: feeling sick to the stomach or "having butterflies" when nervous is an effect of a psychological disturbance to the enteric nervous system. (*General sources:* Bear et al., 2007; MacKay & Percy, 2007, 2011.)

BRAIN STRUCTURE AND FUNCTION

There are various elements of brain structure and function. These are explored in the following sections.

Cells of the Brain and Synapses

The functional units of all nervous systems are nerve cells or neurons that transmit and process information via electrochemical signaling, and the neuroglia that perform "housekeeping" functions such as insulation, infection fighting, maintenance of ion balance, and transfer of nutrients between brain capillaries and neurons. The anatomical and biochemical connections between neurons are called synapses. There are two types of synapses: chemical and electrical. At chemical synapses, communication between two cells is mediated by specialized molecules, or neurotransmitters (see the Neurotransmitters section later in this chapter). At electrical synapses, structures called gap junctions

join cells and signals are transmitted via ion currents without involvement of neurotransmitters. Specialized membranes of nerve cell axons enable them to conduct electrical impulses over long distances. The conduction of electrical impulses depends on the ability of axonal membranes to undergo rapid changes in permeability to small, positively charged ions. Conduction of impulses along axonal membranes consumes relatively little energy when compared with synaptic signal transmission. The needed energy is largely derived from the aerobic metabolism of lactate and glutamine, supplied to neurons by astroglia. In turn, the astroglia are ultimately dependent on glucose from the bloodstream. Consequently, the brain is very sensitive to disruption of a regular supply of glucose and of oxygen. In an infant, the developing brain is continually forming and reforming synapses. A synaptic connection is preferentially made between neurons that are simultaneously active. When frequently stimulated, synapses become stronger (a process called long-term potentiation). Signaling chemicals are sent out that make the connections stronger and more permanent. A diagram of a neuron and a chemical synapse is given in Figure 11.3. Neurons are specialized cells in the brain. If a single neuron is magnified approximately 1,000 times, it looks like an uprooted tree. The "branches" at one end of the neuron are dendrites, and the long "trunk" is the axon. Dendrites and axons connect with neighboring cells. Dendrites receive signals from other cells. Axons pass signals on to other cells. The transfer of signals from axons to dendrites occurs at specialized junctions, or synapses. The narrow gap between an axon terminal and a dendrite is called the synaptic cleft. A neuron signals information by transmitting electrical impulses along its axon. When impulses reach the end of the axon, they

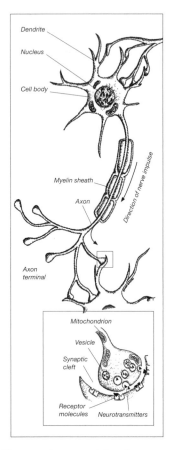

Figure 11.3. Diagrammatic representation of a neuron and a chemical synapse. (*Source*: Percy, Lewkis, & Brown, 2003. Diagram kindly provided by Rivka Birkan and Simon Wong.)

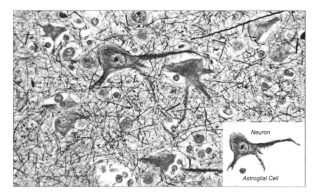

Figure 11.4. Cross-section of the cortex (outer region) of the human brain showing interconnections between neurons (the neuronal network). (*Source*: Percy, Lewkis, & Brown, 2003. Photograph kindly provided by Dr. Catherine Bergeron, University of Toronto.)

trigger the release of neurotransmitters that are stored in pouches called vesicles. The neurotransmitters released from vesicles rapidly diffuse across the synaptic cleft and bind to receptor molecules in the postsynaptic membrane of the dendrite. A cross-section of the human brain showing interconnections between neurons (i.e., interneurons) is shown in Figure 11.4. In this photograph, a small section of a normal human brain cortex has been fixed and stained with Bielschowsky silver stain. The large triangular cells with an oval nucleus are the neurons. The neurons are connected to one another by an intricate network of long processes (dendrites and axons; see Figure 11.3). Small nonneuronal cells are either astrocytes or microglia.

Neurotransmitters

Neurotransmitters are classified into two broad categories depending on the effects that they

trigger when they bind to specific receptors on the postsynaptic cell: ionotropic and metabotropic. First, at ionotropic synapses, transmitter–receptor binding causes the opening of diffusion channels through the postsynaptic membrane of a target neuron. Ion diffusion through the open channels then generates a postsynaptic potential, which may be either excitatory or inhibitory depending on the properties of the channel. An electrical impulse is generated in the postsynaptic neuron if there is sufficient summation of the excitatory synaptic potentials. Ionotropic transmitters are glutamate, gamma aminobutyric acid (GABA), glycine, acetylcholine, and serotonin. Glutamate is the main excitatory transmitter; GABA is the main inhibitory transmitter. Second, these same transmitters and many others—including catecholamines, peptides, and fatty acid amides—can bind to metabotropic receptors. In this case, transmitter–receptor binding initiates a cascade of enzyme activations or deactivations in the postsynaptic neuron that results in changes of the levels of "second messenger" molecules and subsequently other signaling agents. The influence of the metabolic cascade lasts many minutes or longer. In general, this process has a modulatory effect, suppressing or enhancing adjacent ionotropic transmission. Some metabotropic transmitters are gases, such as nitric oxide, that cannot be stored in vesicles. Instead, they are synthesized when an electrical impulse arrives at the end of the axon, and then they promptly diffuse everywhere in the vicinity. (*General sources:* Bear et al., 2007; MacKay & Percy, 2007, 2011.)

Parts of the Brain

The brain has both external and internal parts. These are described next.

External Structure   The brainstem provides the connection between the brain and the spinal cord. It controls many vital and involuntary body functions such as blood pressure, breathing, and pulse; coordinates posture and locomotion; and regulates the level of consciousness. The cerebellum is a structure that greatly improves the fine temporal control of all body movements, from postural balance to speech and manual skills.

Figure 11.5 illustrates the lobes of the cerebrum. These include the frontal lobes, parietal lobes, temporal lobes, occipital lobes, and the olfactory bulbs. The frontal lobes control personality, expression of emotion, motivation, and planning, plus initiation of motor actions. They also inhibit inappropriate or impulsive action. Moreover, they store information and affect a person's ability to concentrate, plan strategically, and think in abstract terms. The parietal lobes control a person's awareness of his or her body parts and his or her position in space. In addition, they mediate physical sensations such as touch, kinesthesia (sense of body posture and movement), temperature, and pain. The temporal lobes embody memory, intellectual abilities, and impulse control. They also process visual and auditory input, making these lobes essential for object and color recognition, language comprehension, and music appreciation.

The occipital lobes are the site of entry-level processing of visual information. This information is transmitted to the inferior temporal lobes for object recognition (ventral visual pathway) and to the parietal lobes for recognition of spatial relationships and direction (dorsal visual pathway). The olfactory bulbs (not shown in Figure 11.5) are narrow extensions from the undersurface of the frontal lobes, one on each side of the midline. The olfactory bulbs transmit smell information from the nose to the brain and are necessary for having the sense of smell. Neurogenesis (creation of new neurons from stem cells or progenitor cells) in the adult brain takes place continually in the olfactory bulbs and also in the dentate gyrus region of the hippocampus. (*General source:* Bear et al., 2007.)

Inner Structure   Figure 11.6 shows the brain's inner structure. The amygdala is an almond-shaped neural structure in the anterior part of the temporal lobe of the cerebrum. It is intimately connected with the hypothalamus, the hippocampus, and the cingulate gyrus. As part of the limbic system, the amygdala plays an important role in motivation and emotional behavior. The limbic system is a complex set of structures located on both sides of the thalamus, just under the cerebrum. It includes the hypothalamus, the hippocampus, the amygdala, and several other areas located nearby. It is primarily responsible for emotions and also plays an important role in the formation of memories. An interesting feature of the hypothalamus is its production of

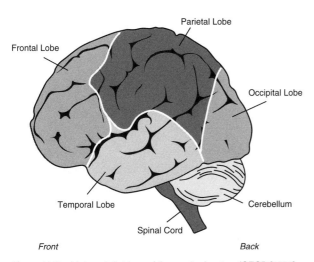

Figure 11.5.   Major subdivisions of the cerebral cortex. (OECD [2002], *Understanding the Brain: Towards a New Learning Science*, OECD Publishing. [p. 45], http://dx.doi.org/10.1787/9789264174986-en; reprinted by permission.)

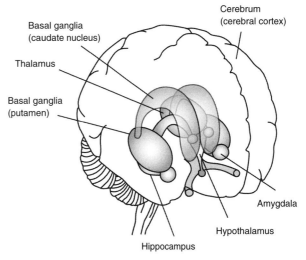

Figure 11.6.   Inner structure of the human brain, including the limbic system. (OECD [2002], *Understanding the Brain: Towards a New Learning Science*, OECD Publishing. [p. 57], http://dx.doi.org/10.1787/9789264174986-en; modified by William MacKay and redrawn by Tom Dearie with permission.)

a hormone called oxytocin. This is best known for its role in inducing labor. However, it has been nicknamed the "cuddle hormone," because in animal models it plays a role in the expression of maternal, sexual, social, stress, and feeding behaviors as well as in learning and memory (Ross & Young, 2009). The basal ganglia are large structures toward the center of the brain that surround the thalamus. The basal ganglia have both limbic and motor functions. They participate in making decisions, integrating feelings, and habit formation. They are involved with setting the body's idle or anxiety level. In addition, the basal ganglia help to modulate motivation and are likely involved with feelings of pleasure and ecstasy. Closely associated with the basal ganglia is a small region in the upper brainstem known as the substantia nigra ("black substance"). It contains neurons that produce and release dopamine, a neurotransmitter that acts within the basal ganglia to facilitate both movement-related and reward-related signals.

The cerebral cortex is the highest brain part in terms of abstraction and aspects unique to humans. Phylogenetically, it is the most recent addition to the brain, and in human development it is the last brain area to fully mature. It governs thoughts, senses, and skilled body motion. It consists of two (left and right) highly folded sheets of gray matter, called hemispheres. Each hemisphere has a temporal, frontal, parietal, and occipital lobe, plus an olfactory bulb. Sensory processing is highly localized, such that visual input is processed in the occipital and inferior temporal lobes, auditory in the upper temporal lobe, and somatosensory in the anterior parietal lobe.

The hippocampus forms the medial edge of the temporal lobe in both hemispheres and is essential for memory and learning. As already mentioned, the hippocampus is a component of the limbic system as well. The hippocampus contains the dentate gyrus, one of two brain regions in which neurogenesis is known to take place in adults.

The thalamus and hypothalamus serve as the interface between the brainstem and cerebrum; they are located just above the brainstem. The hypothalamus oversees the endocrine system to regulate thirst, hunger, body temperature, sleep, moods, sex drive, and the release of hormones from various glands. It also controls the hypothalamic–pituitary–adrenal (HPA) axis (for more details, see the Hypothalamic–Pituitary–Adrenal Axis and Stress section of this chapter). In general, the hypothalamus communicates with the body via the autonomic nervous system and the pituitary gland (or "master gland"),

which produces hormones that are important in regulating growth and metabolism. The hypothalamus is also part of the limbic system, the network mediating emotional experience and autonomic behaviors.

The thalamus is located in the center of the brain, beneath the cerebral hemispheres and next to the third ventricle. It is formed of gray matter and can be thought of as a processing station for nerve impulses being sent to the cerebral cortex or basal ganglia. (*General source:* Bear et al., 2007; MacKay & Percy, 2007, 2011.)

SOME FACTORS AFFECTING BRAIN STRUCTURE AND FUNCTION

Stage of development, side of the brain, and gender affect brain structure and function. These factors are addressed in the following subsections.

Stage of Development

Before Birth to the Second Year of Life Compared with other organs, the human brain develops over a long period of time. Development begins in the first weeks after conception, with most of the basic brain structure completed before birth. The brain is very vulnerable to environmental changes in early pregnancy and during the brain growth spurt that begins in the last trimester of pregnancy and extends to the end of the second year in life. Factors such as lack of oxygen, traumatic physical injury, lack of essential fatty acids or folic acid and other vital nutrients, infections, drugs, toxins (including maternal use of alcohol), stress, and lack of stimulation can particularly affect normal development of the brain. Developing fetuses and infants are much more vulnerable to toxins than adults for the following reasons:

- Their brains are developing rapidly.

- Chemical exposures have a bigger effect on fetuses and infants than on adults simply because of body size difference.

- Their BBBs are not mature and allow substances to enter the CNS that adult brains would exclude.

- Their systems for detoxifying and excreting chemicals are not fully developed.

- They have more years than adults during which a problem caused by an exposure can develop.

(*General sources:* Environmental Working Group, 2005; MacKay & Percy, 2007, 2011; Restak, 2001.)

Using Neuroplasticity to Address Neurological Weaknesses

Neuroplasticity can be used to advantage in order to correct brain deficiencies. This is the fundamental premise of the Arrowsmith Program in Toronto, Canada. For example, dysfunction of the region at the junction of the parietal, temporal, and occipital lobes results in an inability to combine separate details into a single whole, making reading an analog clock to tell the time a challenge. In the Arrowsmith Program, this deficit in understanding symbol relations is overcome by a progressive series of exercises in clock reading. Rigorous training with the exercises not only results in clock reading proficiency but also in a generalized and permanent improvement in symbol comprehension. Speech is understood in real time, text and mathematics comprehended, and even ironic jokes appreciated for the first time (Arrowsmith-Young, 2012).

A child's brain is characterized by plasticity. *Plasticity* means that connections between neurons can form, strengthen, weaken, or disappear according to the rate of information flow. Between 10 and 18 months, an infant's emotions begin to develop. Emotion involves the entire nervous system, but two parts of the nervous system are particularly important for emotion: the limbic system (see Figure 11.6) and the autonomic nervous system (see the preceding Peripheral Nervous System section). The limbic system not only plays an important role in emotional life and how people respond to stress, but it also is important in the formation of memories. Emotion and sensory perception (smelling, hearing, seeing, feeling, and tasting) are vital for survival, growth, development, and the experience of bodily pleasure. Learning between the ages of 3 and 10 years plays a key role in establishing connections in the child's brain. Life experiences significantly affect brain development. Unfortunately, severe stress, particularly that which lasts a long time, can adversely affect a child's brain development and functioning when he or she becomes an adult. (*General sources:* Bear et al., 2007; Doidge, 2007; Restak, 2001; Shore, 1997.)

Adolescence Puberty is said to be as critical a time for typical brain development as are the growth spurts in the fetal or infant brain. Puberty is marked by striking changes in neuroendocrine function. In particular, levels of steroidal gonadal hormones (sex hormones) increase markedly. These steroidal hormones have profound effects on the structure and function of the maturing nervous system, and they influence the development of various steroid-dependent behaviors characteristic of adulthood (e.g., sexuality). They also affect stress reactivity. Changes in neuronal circuitry in adolescence involve steroid-hormone-induced sculpt-

ing of certain synapses and the pruning of others. Because the areas of the brain involved in emotion mature earlier than those involved in judgment and reasoning, adolescents tend to make decisions more impulsively than adults, who balance emotion with reason and use both abilities to reach decisions. (*General sources:* MacKay & Percy, 2007, 2011; Restak, 1999.)

Aging The brain in older individuals is characterized by challenges with memory, and more time is needed to learn new information. Yet, intelligence, abstract thinking, and verbal expression tend to remain the same with age. Life experiences provide older people with wisdom, making them more rational and flexible. Lifestyle is thought to be very important in the preservation of memory with aging. Mental and physical exercise promote increased blood circulation to the brain and stimulate the production of neurotrophic factors that maintain and enhance important synaptic connections. Good nutrition also is extremely important, especially a rich and varied supply of antioxidants. (*General sources:* Bengmark, 2006; Hess, 2005; Restak, 2001.)

The Right Brain and the Left Brain

The two hemispheres of the cerebral cortex are linked by the corpus callosum, the band of white matter through which the hemispheres communicate and coordinate. Generally, the right hemisphere controls the left side of the body and the left hemisphere controls the right side. When the left brain has been damaged, some of the lost functions can be taken over by the right brain. Nevertheless, the two hemispheres have some separate specializations. The left hemisphere predominates in reasoning ability (i.e., the detailed sequential thinking common in science and mathematics) and written and spoken language. In contrast, the right hemisphere predominates in spatial or integrative tasks, insight, imagination, and appreciation of art and music. Generally speaking, the left brain excels at information processing based on fine distinctions in temporal order and the right brain tends to ignore precise timing in favor of details regarding how information is grouped together (*General sources:* Doidge, 2007; Haier, Jung, Yeo, Head, & Alkire, 2005; Restak, 2001.)

The Male Brain and the Female Brain

There has been much controversy as to whether there are structural and functional differences between the brain in males and females. A few hypothalamic centers concerned with sex hormones are clearly different. Although there are no significant differences in general intelligence between males and females, there is evidence that women have more white matter and men more gray matter correlated to intellectual skill. Although there may be other explanations, it has been suggested that such differences may help to explain why men tend to be better in tasks requiring local processing and enhanced systemizing (e.g., mathematics), whereas women tend to excel at integrating and assimilating information as required for empathy and language proficiency. In a study by Haier and colleagues, 84% of gray matter correlated to intelligence was found in the frontal region in women, as compared to 45% in men. Moreover, 86% of white matter correlated to intelligence was found in the frontal region in women, as compared to 0% in men (Haier et al., 2005). The more frontally focused basis of intelligence processing in women may explain why brain injuries affecting the frontal lobes tend to be more detrimental to cognitive performance in women than in men. (*General sources:* Haier et al., 2005; Legato, 2005.)

IMPORTANCE OF THE BLOOD–BRAIN BARRIER AND HYPOTHALAMIC–PITUITARY–ADRENAL AXIS

The BBB, as well as the HPA axis and stress, affect brain development and function. Each topic is explored next.

Blood–Brain Barrier

Typical brain function depends on the integrity of the BBB (Francis, van Beek, Canova, Neal, & Gasque, 2003; see Figure 11.7). The BBB is made of the closely knit sheets of endothelial cells that form the walls of blood vessels in the brain. The BBB separates the brain and surrounding tissues that contain neurons, astrocytes, and microglia from circulating blood; tightly regulates the transport of nutrients and signaling molecules into the brain; and maintains proper biochemical conditions for normal brain function. It normally blocks circulating bacteria and viruses (pathogens) from entering the brain and thus acts as a sentry to defend against infection. If a pathogen gains entry to the endothelial cells, genes are activated that produce protein factors that recruit white blood cells to the brain to fight the infection. Group B *streptococcus* (Doran, Liu, & Nizet, 2003) and HIV (Manji, Jäger, & Winston, 2013) are two pathogens that manage to gain access to the BBB. The former results in meningitis, which can result in intellectual disability; the latter can lead to dementia and different types of neuropathy. The BBB of fetuses and infants is not fully formed, perhaps explaining in part why their brains are so vulnerable to the effects of infection and toxic substances.

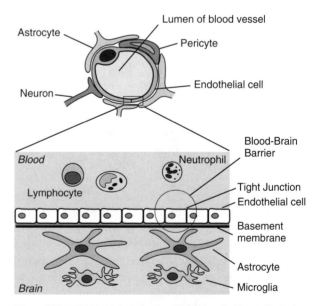

Figure 11.7. The blood–brain barrier. (From Francis, K., van Beek, J., Canova, C., Neal, J.W., & Gasque, P. [2003]. Innate immunity and brain inflammation: The key role of complement. *Expert Reviews in Molecular Medicine*, 5[15], 1–19. Reproduced with permission.)

Hypothalamic–Pituitary–Adrenal Axis and Stress

The HPA axis (see Figure 11.8) is a communication system between the hypothalamus and pituitary gland, which are in the brain, and the adrenal glands, which are located just above the kidneys. Various types of stress (psychological, emotional, and physical—including the tissue injury associated with infection, hypoglycemia, cold exposure, and pain) activate the HPA axis in the CNS and the sympathetic nervous system in the PNS. As explained at the end of this section, there is increasing evidence that abnormal functioning of the HPA axis, resulting from experiencing severe stress prenatally or postnatally, is involved in different types of intellectual and developmental disabilities, in challenging behavior, and in mental illnesses (which generally are more prevalent in people with intellectual disability), as well as in certain physical illnesses such as cardiovascular disease. Conversely, there also is evidence that in an appropriate environment, the HPA axis can be normalized (see also the Psychoneuroimmunology section of this chapter).

Proper functioning of the HPA axis plays an important role in development, health, and

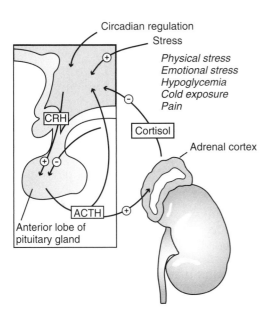

Figure 11.8. The hypothalamic–pituitary–adrenal axis. (From Kirk, L.F., Jr., Hash, R.B., Kanner, H.P., & Jones, T. [2000]. Cushing's disease: Clinical manifestations and diagnostic evaluation. *American Family Physician*, 52[5], 1121. Original artwork © 2000 D. Klemm. Reprinted by permission.) (*Key:* ACTH: acrenocorticotrophic hormone; CRH: corticotropin releasing hormone.)

resistance to stress (see Figure 11.8). Activation of the HPA axis ultimately results in the release of the hormone cortisol from the cortex of the two adrenal glands. Cortisol increases the level of blood sugar and increases the vascular tone, resulting in increased blood pressure. Blood sugar is increased because cortisol promotes the conversion of protein from muscle, glycogen from the liver, and fatty acids from fat tissue into intermediates that get converted into glucose. Cortisol also alters the balance of cells in the blood. It results in lowered numbers of lymphocytes (including T cells), eosinophils, basophils, monocytes, and macrophages, but in increased numbers of neutrophils and red blood cells. It also increases the blood hemoglobin level. The paraventricular nucleus of the hypothalamus releases corticotropin-releasing hormone (CRH). In turn, CRH acts on the pituitary gland, which releases adrenocorticotrophic hormone (ACTH). ACTH then causes the adrenal cortex to release cortisol. It is this combined system of CRH–ACTH–cortisol release that is referred to as the HPA axis. Positive and negative feedback occurs at various sites in the brain to ensure that cortisol production stays within certain limits, depending on the body's requirements. Excessive cortisol production has a negative effect on the immune system, suppressing the production of cytokines (immunoregulatory proteins) such as IL-1, IL-2, IL-6, and TNF-alpha, which are produced by cells of the immune system (lymphocytes, macrophages, monocytes, neutrophils, and—within the CNS—microglia). In major depression, cortisol sensitivity is reduced and cytokine levels are high.

Appropriate responsiveness of the stress system to stressors is necessary for a sense of well-being, adequate performance of tasks, and positive social interactions. In contrast, inappropriate responsiveness of the stress system may impair growth and development and may account for a number of endocrine, metabolic, autoimmune, and psychiatric disorders that affect intellect, development, or both. Studies in rodents and nonhuman primates have shown that maternal stress during pregnancy can influence the developing fetus and can result in a delay of motor and cognitive development, impaired adaptation to stressful situations, small birth size, and an increased risk of cardiovascular disease in later life. It is thought that excessive cortisol production in the mother affects the way in which the HPA axis functions in the fetus. There also is evidence that stress after birth can alter functioning of the HPA axis. For example, individuals with posttraumatic stress disorder as the result of sexual abuse have enhanced sensitization of the HPA axis. Furthermore, chronic excess cortisol secretion is believed to damage the hypothalamus and affect the normal sleep–wake cycle (MacKay & Percy, 2011; O'Connor, O'Halloran, & Shanahan, 2000; Reynolds, Labad, Buss, Ghaemmaghami, & Räikkönen, 2013).

FUTURE DIRECTIONS IN BRAIN AND NEUROSCIENCE RESEARCH

The next sections highlight developments in several areas that hold promise for providing new insights into typical brain function and the neurodevelopmental or neurological basis of intellectual and developmental disabilities and other brain disorders.

Measuring Brain Activity and Structure

Three different approaches provide quantitative information about functions of the brain and which areas are involved in different intellectual, developmental, and related disabilities. One very important approach involves the analysis of brain tissue donated to organizations called "brain banks" (Kretzschmar, 2009; National Geographic, 2014). Many different histochemical, biochemical, molecular biological, and biophysical techniques can be applied to brain tissues collected at autopsy. Computer-assisted analysis of brain images taken with powerful microscopes (image analysis) enables the results to be expressed quantitatively. The second approach involves the application of different neuroimaging techniques and electrophysiological techniques to study the brain in living people. (See University of Saint Andrews [2014] and Chapter 12 for an overview of different types of brain imaging techniques.) The third approach to providing quantitative information involves quantitative neuropsychological assessments. These assessments include a variety of tests of cognitive/intellectual, language, visual-perceptual, scholastic, motor, sensory, and emotional/behavioral abilities and functions (Malik & Kishner, 2015; National Academy of Neuropsychology Policy and Planning Committee, 2008).

The coordinated application of all three approaches is proving to be key to identifying physiological, neurocognitive, and neurobehavioral consequences of single-gene mutations associated with intellectual disability (e.g., fragile X syndrome [FXS]; Rett syndrome, an X-linked disorder that mainly affects females—males fetuses with the syndrome generally do not survive to term), identifying syndromes resulting from exposures to toxic substances (e.g., fetal alcohol spectrum disorder), and providing new insights into approaches for intervention. (For more information on the cited syndromes and disorders, see this book's chapters about those topics.)

Psychoneuroimmunology

Psychoneuroimmunology is a relatively recent field of science that studies the ways in which a person's mental state influences development or expression of a disorder, disease, or injury; susceptibility to co-occurring physical and mental illnesses; and the healing process. Specifically, it studies the relationship between psychological processes and the nervous and immune systems of the body. (The immune system includes all the processes that protect an organism from infection, other invaders, and disease.) Communication between the brain, the stress response, and the immune system is maintained by molecules called cytokines and neurohormones. These molecules carry messages from cells in the brain to the immune system and to other tissues in the body and from the immune system and other tissues back to the brain. Some important research questions with implications for prevention and intervention in the intellectual and developmental disabilities field are the following:

- How does maternal stress result in an increased risk of preterm births?

- How do stresses encountered in the neonatal intensive care unit affect premature infants and infants of low birth weight who are at high risk of developing an intellectual or developmental disability or both?

- What are the psychoneuroimmunological consequences of deprivation or abuse in early childhood?

Neurogenesis in the Adult Brain

One of the most intriguing questions facing neuroscientists is the function of neurogenesis (formation of new neurons) that takes place in the adult brain (i.e., in the hippocampus and olfactory lobes). On one hand, it has been thought that the insertion of new neurons into circuits established during fetal and early neonatal development might be important in learning and memory and that impairment of adult neurogenesis might contribute to certain conditions such as depression, epilepsy, ischemia, or neurodegenerative diseases (Cleva, Kelly, Wischerath, & Foster Olive, 2011; Ming & Song, 2011). On the other hand, it now is recognized that although boosting neural proliferation through several weeks of exercising before learning can enhance memory formation in adult mice, neuron growth that occurs after information is learned can degrade these memories. As of 2015, it is suspected that adult neurogenesis may play an important role in erasing old memories and making way for new ones (Akers et al., 2014). Studies have identified defective adult neurogenesis in mouse models of certain intellectual disabilities (e.g., FXS, Down syndrome, Rett syndrome), potentially paving the way for new treatment approaches to alleviate cognitive deficits and unusual behaviors associated with these and other intellectual and developmental disabilities (Contestabile et al., 2013; Luo et al., 2010; Zhang et al., 2014).

Rewiring the Brain

The belief at one time was that brains were hardwired for life and that mental abilities that were not working appropriately or that were altered or lost because of damage or disease could not be improved or healed. It is now known that synapses in the brain and neural pathways can be changed in response to changes in behavior, environment, neural processes, thinking, emotions; changed by other noninvasive procedures that include light, sound, vibration, movement, and exercise; and also changed by invasive procedures such as deep brain stimulation (Doidge, 2015). For more information about biomedical processes involved in neuroplasticity and exciting new developments in the field, readers are directed to Chapter 12.

SUMMARY

For any intellectual or developmental disability, it is important to determine which part(s) of the nervous system is/are affected and why. With such knowledge, more effective interventions can be designed. The nervous system includes the central and peripheral systems. The central system includes the brain and spinal cord; the peripheral system includes the somatic, autonomic, and enteric (gut) nervous systems. Bacteria that live in the gut are referred to as the *gut microbiome;* understanding the role of the gut microbiome in behavior and brain function is a new biomedical frontier. The sympathetic arm of the autonomic system prepares the body for fight or flight, whereas the parasympathetic arm is largely restorative. The functional units of all nervous systems are the neurons and "housekeeping" neuroglia (astrocytes, microglia, and oligodendrocytes). Important components of the neuron are axons (fibers that conduct electrical impulses away from the cell body) and dendrites (fibers that conduct impulses from adjacent cells toward the cell body). Connections between neurons are called synapses. Neurotransmitters relay information from some neurons to others via synaptic connections. Brain function and health is dependent upon an adequate supply of blood and glucose, as well as cerebrospinal fluid. The various sections of the brain carry out and coordinate specific tasks. External, visible parts of the brain include the cerebrum, the cerebellum, the hind portion of the brain stem, and the spinal cord. Internal structures include the hippocampus, basal ganglia, thalamus, hypothalamus, and amygdala. Brain structure and function change throughout development, adolescence, and aging; the fetal and infant brain are particularly vulnerable to toxins and other insults. The two hemispheres of the cerebrum have specialized functions that may differ in males and females. Typical brain function requires an intact BBB. Proper functioning of the HPA axis plays an important role in development, health, and resistance to stress. New directions in brain research are shedding new light on intellectual and developmental disabilities as well as other disorders and diseases of the brain. Such research includes coordinated studies of brain tissue deposited in brain banks, application of imaging techniques to living individuals, and psychological assessment; psychoneuroimmunological studies, particularly of the role of stress in physical and mental ill health and healing; and studies of neurogenesis and brain plasticity that aim to facilitate brain rewiring and improve brain function.

FOR FURTHER THOUGHT AND DISCUSSION

1. What actions can concerned citizens take to ensure that neurotoxic substances are not a threat to daily living?

2. Why do environmental hazards place infants' brains more at risk than adults' brains?

3. How can the average citizen help researchers to better understand brain function and development?

REFERENCES

Akers, K.G., Martinez-Canabal, A., Restivo, L., Yiu, A.P., De Cristofaro, A., Hsiang, H.L.,…Frankland, P.W. (2014). Hippocampal neurogenesis regulates forgetting during adulthood and infancy. *Science, 344*(6184), 598–602.

Arrowsmith-Young, B. (2012). *The woman who changed her brain.* Toronto, Canada: Simon & Schuster.

Bear, M.F., Connors, B.W., & Paradiso, M.A. (2007). *Neuroscience: Exploring the brain* (3rd ed.). Philadelphia, PA: Lippincott Williams & Wilkins.

Bengmark, S. (2006). Impact of nutrition on ageing and disease. *Current Opinion in Clinical Nutrition and Metabolic Care, 9*(1), 2–7.

Cleva, R.M. , Kelly, C., Wischerath, K.C., & Foster Olive, M. (2011). Extinction learning and adult neurogenesis. *Neuropsychopharmacology, 36,* 360–361.

Contestabile, A., Greco, B., Ghezzi, D., Tucci, V., Benfenati, F., & Gasparini, L. (2013). Lithium rescues synaptic plasticity and memory in Down syndrome mice. *Journal of Clinical Investigation, 123*(1), 348–361.

Dantzer, R., & Kelley, K.W. (2012). Psychoneuroimmunology. In M. Gelder, N. Andreasen, J. Lopez-Ibor, & J. Geddes (Eds.), *New Oxford textbook of psychiatry* (2nd ed.). Oxford, United Kingdom: Oxford University Press.

Doidge, N. (2007). *The brain that changes itself.* Toronto, Canada: Penguin.

Doidge, N. (2015). *The brain's way of healing.* New York, NY: Viking Press.

Doran, K.S., Liu, G.Y., & Nizet, V. (2003). Group B streptococcal beta-hemolysin/cytolysin activates neutrophil signaling pathways in brain endothelium and contributes to development of meningitis. *Journal of Clinical Investigation, 112,* 736–744.

Ebstein, R.P., Israel, S., Chew, S.H., Zhong, S., & Knafo, A. (2010). Genetics of human social behavior. *Neuron, 65*(6), 831–844.

Environmental Working Group. (2005, July 14). *Body burden: The pollution in newborns.* Retrieved from http://www.ewg.org/research/body-burden-pollution-newborns

Francis, K., van Beek, J., Canova, C., Neal, J.W., & Gasque, P. (2003, May 23). Innate immunity and brain inflammation: The key role of complement. *Expert Reviews in Molecular Medicine,* 1–19.

Gray, H. (1918). The spinal cord or medulla spinalis. In *Anatomy of the human body.* Retrieved from http://www.bartleby.com/107/185.html

Grundy, D., & Schemann, M. (2005). Enteric nervous system. *Current Opinion in Gastroenterology, 21,* 176–182.

Haier, R.J., Jung, R.E., Yeo, R.A., Head, K., & Alkire, M.T. (2005). The neuroanatomy of general intelligence: Sex matters. *Neuroimage, 25*(1), 320–327.

Hess, T.M. (2005). Memory and aging in context. *Psychology Bulletin, 131*(3), 383–406.

Hsiao, E.Y., McBride, S.W., Hsien, S., Sharon, G., Hyde, E.R., McCue, T.,…Mazmanian, S.K. (2013). Microbiota modulate behavioral and physiological abnormalities associated with neurodevelopmental disorders. *Cell, 155*(7), 1451–1463.

Kelley, K.W., & McCusker, R.H. (2014). Getting nervous about immunity. *Seminars in Immunology, 26*(5), 389–393. doi:10.1016/j.smim.2014.01.011

Kirk, L.F., Jr., Hash, R.B., Katner, H.P., & Jones, T. (2000). Cushing's disease: Clinical manifestations and diagnostic evaluation. *American Family Physician, 62*(5), 1119–1127, 1133–1134.

Kretzschmar, H. (2009). Brain banking: Opportunities, challenges and meaning for the future. *Nature Reviews Neuroscience, 10,* 70–78.

Legato, M.J. (2005). Men, women, and brains: What's hardwired, what's learned, and what's controversial. *Gender Medicine, 2*(2), 59–61.

Luo, Y., Shan, G., Guo, W., Smrt, R.D., Johnson, E.B., Li, X., … Zhao, X. (2010). Fragile X mental retardation protein regulates proliferation and differentiation of adult neural stem/progenitor cells. *PLOS Genetics, 6*(4), e1000898.

MacFabe, D. (2013). Autism: Metabolism, mitochondria, and the microbiome. *Global Advances in Health and Medicine, 2*(6), 52–66.

MacKay, W., & Percy, M. (2007). Introduction to the nervous systems. In I. Brown & M. Percy (Eds.), *A comprehensive guide to intellectual and developmental disabilities* (pp. 109–124). Baltimore, MD: Paul H. Brookes Publishing Co.

MacKay, W., & Percy, M. (2011). Introduction to the nervous systems. In I. Brown & M. Percy (Eds.), *Developmental disabilities in Ontario* (3rd ed., pp. 185–206). Toronto, Canada: Ontario Association on Developmental Disabilities.

Malik, A.B., & Kishner, S. (2015, March 11). *Neuropsychological evaluation.* Retrieved from http://emedicine.medscape.com/article/317596-overview

Manji, H., Jäger, H.R, & Winston, A. (2013). HIV, dementia and antiretroviral drugs: 30 years of an epidemic. *Journal of Neurology, Neurosurgery and Psychiatry, 84*(10), 1126–1137.

Midtvedt, T. (2012). The gut: A triggering place for autism—possibilities and challenges. *Microbial Ecology in Health and Disease, 2012, 23,* 18982. Retrieved from http://dx.doi.org/10.3402/mehd.v23i0.18982

Ming G.-I., & Song, H. (2011). Adult neurogenesis in the mammalian brain: Significant answers and significant questions. *Neuron, 70*(4), 687–702.

National Academy of Neuropsychology Policy and Planning Committee. (2008). Learning disabilities: The need for neuropsychological evaluation. *Archives of Clinical Neuropsychology, 23*(2), 217–219.

National Geographic. (2014). *Brain bank.* Retrieved from http://video.nationalgeographic.com/video/brain-bank-sci

O'Connor, T.M., O'Halloran, D.J., & Shanahan, F. (2000). The stress response and the hypothalamic–pituitary–adrenal axis: From molecule to melancholia. *QJM, 93*(6): 323–333. Retrieved from http://qjmed.oxfordjournals.org/content/93/6/323.full

OECD Publishing. (2002). *Understanding the brain: Towards a new learning science*. Retrieved from http://dx.doi.org/10.1787/9789264174986-en

Organisation for Economic Co-operation and Development. (n.d.). *Major subdivisions of the cerebral cortex*. Retrieved from http://www.oecd.org/dataoecd/50/25/15355617.gif

Percy, M., Lewkis, S., & Brown, I. (2003). An introduction to genetics and development. In I. Brown & M. Percy (Eds.), *Developmental disabilities in Ontario* (2nd ed., pp. 89–116). Toronto, Canada: Ontario Association on Developmental Disabilities.

Restak, R.M. (1999). *The secret life of the brain*. New York, NY: Canada Press.

Restak, R.M. (2001). *The secret life of the brain*. Washington, DC: Joseph Henry Press. Retrieved from http://www.pbs.org/wnet/brain/3d/index.html

Reynolds, R.M., Labad, J., Buss, C., Ghaemmaghami, P., & Räikkönen, K. (2013). Transmitting biological effects of stress in utero: Implications for mother and offspring. *Psychoneuroendocrinology, 38*(9), 1843–1859.

Ross, H.E., & Young, L.J. (2009). Oxytocin and the neural mechanisms regulating social cognition and affiliative behavior. *Frontiers in Neuroendocrinology, 30*(4), 534–547.

Shore, R. (1997). *Rethinking the brain: New insights into early development*. New York, NY: Families and Work Institute.

University of Saint Andrews, School of Psychology and Neuroscience. (2014). *Brain imaging techniques. Introduction to brain imaging and other methods*. Retrieved from https://www.st-andrews.ac.uk/psychology/research/brainimaging/

Zhang, Y., Mao, R.R., Chen, Z.F., Tian, M., Tong, D.L, Gao, Z.R.,...Qiu, Z. (2014). Deep-brain magnetic stimulation promotes adult hippocampal neurogenesis and alleviates stress-related behaviors in mouse models for neuropsychiatric disorders. *Molecular Brain, 7*, 11. doi:10.1186/1756-6606-7-11

Brain Plasticity

Jan Scholz and Jason P. Lerch

Brain plasticity refers to the brain's capability to change during development, aging, and disease and in response to environment and experience. Neurons, which are the brain's fundamental processing units, exchange information with each other at the synapses (where two neurons make physical contact). The brain can adapt temporarily by modifying these connections, or it can also change permanently by growing and removing new connections or neurons—a process referred to as *structural plasticity*. This chapter focuses on the mechanisms underlying structural plasticity and the circumstances that lead to it.

LEARNING, MEMORY, AND THE BRAIN

The brain consists of large numbers of neurons that communicate with each other through electrical

Authors' note: The authors wish to thank the following people for their comments and discussions over the years about brain plasticity: Mark Henkelman, John Sled, Brian Nieman, Dulcie Vousden, and Rylan Allemang-Grand from the Mouse Imaging Centre; Heidi Johansen-Berg and Cassandra Sampaio-Baptista from Oxford University; Sheena Josselyn and Paul Frankland from the Hospital for Sick Children; and Alan Evans from McGill University.

and chemical signaling. It is through this signaling that sights and sounds from the outside world are encoded, movements are planned, and commands are communicated to muscles and glands. To learn is thus to modify the signaling between neurons, by either creating new connections or changing the strength with which signaling occurs. To study how the connections in the brain alter with learning and experience is to study brain plasticity.

The Importance of the Sea Slug

There is a rich and centuries-old scientific tradition of studying learning and memory in human subjects, embodied especially in the writings of Ebbinghaus and William James. Although tremendously enriching to the psychology of learning, the complexity of human thought combined with the difficulty of conducting experimental investigations meant that deciphering the biological bases of learning awaited experimentation on simpler animals.

The key breakthrough studies on the cellular bases of learning and memory came from Eric Kandel and colleagues and their work with the Californian sea slug, *Aplysia Californica*, for which Kandel was awarded the Nobel Prize in Medicine in 2000 (see Sweatt, 2009, for an in-depth treatment of this topic). The researchers studied two simple but important types of learning: habituation and sensitization. The sea slug has a gill and siphon complex; if the gill is touched or given a light electric shock, the animal will withdraw the gill and siphon into the mantle cavity. Repeated light touch of the gill, however, allows the slug to habituate to such touches; eventually, it will not react to these repeated touches, because it learns that these touches do not represent a threat after all. Similarly, increasing the strength of the electric shock sensitizes the animal; afterward, even a very light touch will cause it to withdraw the gill. In short, there is a threshold of gill stimulation that causes the sea slug to withdraw the gill; this threshold can be either decreased or increased over time. These simple forms of learning, combined with the sea slug having very large neurons for its body size, opened the door to understanding the molecular and cellular bases of learning.

The first key conclusion was that the cellular bases of learning and memory differ for short-term memories and long-term memories. In the short term, stimulation of the siphon causes the sensory neuron to stimulate its motor neuron, causing an influx of calcium (Ca^{2+}), changing the electrical excitability of the neurons. This in turn signals to the muscles to contract the siphon. In addition, the sensory neuron stimulates an interneuron; this interneuron releases a neurotransmitter (serotonin), which leads to the activation of a series of second messengers in the motor neuron. Second messengers are long-lasting molecules that relay signals to targets within the cell. These second messengers, acting through multiple cellular processes, cause subsequent stimulation of the motor neuron to produce increased release of neurotransmitters, thus having a greater effect on the muscles controlling the siphon. In other words, the first time one touches the siphon of the sea slug, a slight withdrawal of the siphon is produced, but at the same time the motor neuron has been sensitized so that further touching of the siphon produces a greater effect.

The effects described above are, however, transient. A second set of mechanisms is required to make long-term memories. Repeated activation of the second messengers triggered by the interneuron starts a cascade, ultimately altering gene expression; that is, the extent to which genes produce their final product, usually proteins, is changed. This causes whole new synapses to be made; in other words, long-term memory formation requires changes in the physical structure of the brain. Stimulation of the sensory neuron thus has a greater effect on the motor neuron

controlling gill withdrawal, because there are now more synaptic connections affected by the initial input.

IMAGING BRAIN PLASTICITY IN HIGHER ANIMALS

Until the 1960s, a central assumption in the field of neuroscience was that once matured, the adult brain remains stable except for processes related to aging or disease. As described in the previous section, simple animal models, such as the sea slug, allowed great insight into what happens in neurons when humans learn.

With the development of new imaging techniques, researchers are now able to detect even subtle structural changes at much larger spatial scales in the brain in humans. Imaging techniques for visualizing brain structures include magnetic resonance imaging (MRI) and two-photon imaging. MRI in humans can capture the entire brain at a resolution of about 1 cubic millimeter. MRIs allow for a whole range of measures of brain structure. As an example, an MRI could be used to visualize the delineation of the gray-white matter boundary of the temporal lobe. This boundary can then be compared with that of other individuals to detect deviations possibly related to factors such as aging or disease. Underlying these macroscopic morphological changes are microscopic alterations of neuronal cells, including synapses. However, these structures are too small to be resolved with MRI and require invasive techniques, such as two-photon imaging. To learn more about the latest brain imaging techniques and view examples of brain structures visualized with MRI and two-photon imaging, visit The McConnell Brain Imaging Center at McGill University (https://www.mcgill.ca/bic). This site describes the most cutting-edge research in brain imaging and is also home to BrainWeb, a Simulated Brain Database (SBD) that contains a set of realistic MRI data volumes produced by an MRI simulator.

Because of the imaging techniques available today, it is now understood that the brain changes in response to a variety of experiences and environmental perturbations. In this section, we briefly describe how modern neuroscience observes and quantifies structural changes in the brain.

The term *structural plasticity* usually refers to modifications of neurons, such as the growths of synapses and spines and changes in dendritic complexity. Structural changes have also been observed in the fibers that connect the neurons, the axons. The axons are wrapped in myelin, which promotes faster transmission of nerve signals. It has been suggested myelination increases to facilitate communication between different brain areas and that under certain conditions even new axons might sprout (Hihara et al., 2006). Although we do not discuss this here in greater detail, it is important to note that these changes might be accompanied by changes in other cell populations of the brain, such as glial cells, the housekeeping cells of the brain. Changes in vasculature, the blood supply of the brain, have also been observed (Anderson et al., 1994).

Observing processes related to structural plasticity has always been a trade-off between spatial resolution, temporal sampling rate, and coverage. Put differently, imaging finer details is usually only possible by imaging for a longer time and/or by imaging a smaller part of the brain. Although two-photon imaging and histology can resolve fine details down to individual spines protruding from dendrites in a specific area of the brain, MRI can only define gross anatomical structures but across the whole brain.

Due to their invasiveness, two-photon imaging and histology are used only in animal models of structural plasticity. Thus, many more specifics are known about processes related to plasticity in the animal brain than in the human. However, the hope is that by conducting more MRI experiments in animals followed by histology-grade techniques, the cellular processes observed in animals may be linked to the changes observed by MRI in humans.

BRAIN PLASTICITY DURING DEVELOPMENT AND AGING

In this section, we briefly discuss the gross changes observed in the brain during development and aging. The mammalian brain develops rapidly from a homogeneous neural tube into a complex brain structure with numerous anatomical subdivisions. During development, neurons differentiate, proliferate, and eventually migrate to their final position in the brain, where they form connections to other neurons. The total number of neurons does not change markedly after birth (Larsen et al., 2006). However,

there is a significant turnover during the whole life span; old neurons will get replaced by new ones such that the total number of neurons stays relatively constant (Spalding et al., 2013).

The visual cortex is an intensely studied brain region during development and has served as a valuable model of the effect of experience on cortical plasticity. Monocular deprivation experiments were one of the first attempts to show nervous-system plasticity during development (Wiesel & Hubel, 1963). The experiment requires that one eye is kept shut permanently. If the deprivation happens during a critical developmental period, the visual cortex develops differently, such that the visual cortex is permanently less responsive to inputs from the deprived eye, even if normal binocular vision is restored. However, if vision is restored to the deprived eye during the critical period, the visual cortex can recover to its nondeprived state.

These and other studies indicate that brain plasticity is elevated during certain developmental stages, the critical periods. Changes in sensory experience during critical periods might have long-lasting effects and might not be reversible during later stages of life. This suggests that brain injury and childhood experiences related to maternal care and social or environmental factors might have long-lasting effects on the brain and thus behavior.

Conversely, aging has been associated with decremental structural brain changes such as cortical thinning and white matter degeneration. These changes are often paralleled by cognitive decline and diminished sensorimotor performance. In particular learning, memory, and executive function mediated by the medial temporal and prefrontal cortex show considerable age-related decline in humans (reviewed in Burke and Barnes, 2006). This raises the question whether the senescent brain still possesses enough plasticity to counter or slow these changes and recover after injury or disease.

Of interest, it seems that the neuronal morphology is remarkably stable across age, indicating that it is not the gross shape of the neurons that deteriorates. So far, evidence favors the hypothesis that decreased synapse number and Ca^{2+} dysregulation are related to age-related decline in plasticity (Burke & Barnes, 2006). As mentioned in the first section, influx of Ca^{2+} ions into the neuron is essential for modulation of electrical activity, transmitter release, and ultimately structural reorganization. Thus, both decreased synapse number and Ca^{2+} dysregulation (wherein calcium is not properly controlled and therefore becomes toxic) might limit the aging brain's plasticity and decrease its tolerance for insult and disease.

In summary, both development and aging have specific implications for brain plasticity. Although the young brain is quick to adapt to new experiences, its plasticity is also most pronounced during specific critical periods and in specific functional brain regions. Any experience or lack of experience might have long-lasting effects on brain structure and behavior. The neural matter in the healthy brain stays remarkably structurally stable during aging. Contrary to common folk wisdom, there is no conclusive evidence that neural matter necessarily deteriorates by itself. Rather, neurological disease and aging vasculature cause neuronal degeneration, suggesting that a healthy brain can stay plastic and able to learn for a long time.

EXPERIENCE-RELATED BRAIN PLASTICITY

The ability to learn and adapt to the environment is prevalent in mammals, particularly in rodents and primates, which often possess this capability well into their adulthood and often throughout their entire life span. This fact has allowed these mammals to develop more complex forms of behavior, such as manipulation of objects and intricate social interactions. As discussed previously, the brain can adapt quickly and temporarily but also changes its structure permanently to allow memory and retention of skills.

In this section, we discuss evidence for systems-level structural changes in response to experience and learning new skills. These studies will illustrate how complex experiences can have long-lasting effects on the brain, visible with in vivo imaging methods. Of importance, these structural changes are larger in extent and might encompass several brain regions in contrast to the single-neuron changes found in the sea slug and the cell-specific developmental changes in the mouse visual cortex.

The first studies using MRI in humans to investigate experience-related brain plasticity were cross-sectional in their design. That means they contrasted the brain anatomy of individuals who had been trained on a specific task with the brain anatomy of individuals who remained naive, the so-called controls. Cross-sectional studies cannot unambiguously determine the cause of structural differences, as the relationship might be either pre-existing (e.g., genetic) or a result of the intervention (i.e., experience-related).

For example, a famous study compared taxi drivers to controls and found that the hippocampus, a navigation- and memory-related brain structure, was enlarged in taxi drivers (Maguire et al., 2000). It is possible that people who had a larger hippocampus chose to become taxi drivers because they were better navigators. An alternative explanation is that taxi drivers' hippocampi grew as they became better at navigating around the city. Longitudinal studies that image the same subject before and after the intervention are generally considered to provide better evidence that a certain experience is the cause of the structural brain changes.

Expert populations, such as taxi drivers, have been of particular interest, because it is conceivable that the long and intensive exposure to a specific environmental stimulus might be associated with especially large structural differences between experts and non-experts. Professional musicians have increased gray matter density, a measure derived from T1-weighted MRI, compared to amateurs or controls (Bermudez, Lerch, Evans, & Zatorre, 2009; Gaser & Schlaug, 2003; Sluming et al., 2002). In both taxi drivers and musicians, practice seems to correlate with the extent of the changes, suggesting that more frequent or more intense practice might be associated with more pronounced brain changes.

Studies have also shown experience-related changes in the brain's white matter, where the tracts that connect different brain areas are located. In professional concert pianists, fractional anisotropy, a measure related to myelination and fiber organization, correlates with piano practicing time (Bengtsson et al., 2005). This suggests that piano training can induce white matter plasticity, especially during a time when the involved fiber tracts have not yet fully matured.

Finally, it might not be necessary to practice tens of thousands of hours spread over years for these structural changes to occur. Volumetric increases in motor-related brain areas have been found in children undergoing only 15 months of musical training (Hyde et al., 2009).

The first striking longitudinal evidence for learning-related plasticity in the adult human brain was found in healthy volunteers who learned to juggle (Draganski et al., 2004). Gray matter density increased in mid-temporal area (hMT/V5) after 3 months of juggling training. The mid-temporal area is involved in the retention of visual-motion information (Sereno, Pitzalis, & Martinez, 2001), and its structural reorganization might therefore contribute to the improved visuomotor skill in the jugglers. Following studies also have shown gray matter density changes in elderly adults (Boyke, Driemeyer, Gaser, Büchel, & May, 2008), and that the white matter underlying these gray matter changes also adapted (Scholz, Klein, Behrens, & Johansen-Berg, 2009).

Training effects on brain structure are not limited to motor tasks. Medical students who were scanned before and after an intense 3-month study period showed gray matter increase in the hippocampus and in posterior and lateral parietal cortex bilaterally (Draganski et al., 2006).

Combined, these studies suggest that the young brain and adult brain are structurally malleable in response to learning and training. Both gray and white matter structure seem to carry behavioral significance and seem to reorganize in response to experience. Visuomotor as well as cognitive tasks seem to trigger processes of structural reorganization. This capacity seems to persist even in elderly individuals. The cellular underpinnings, however, remain elusive. This gap in knowledge is being bridged using animal models that allow MRI followed by histology to test for molecular and cell-specific changes. The hope is to translate these findings to the human case via the acquired MRI. One of the earliest examples of this type of translational research was one of our studies, wherein learning-related brain plasticity was observed on MRIs of mice being trained on the Morris water maze task (Lerch et al., 2011). Histology then showed that the MRI-detectable brain plasticity was related not to more neurons or astrocytes but instead to changes in axons and dendrites, likely implicating increased branching and numbers of synapses (Lerch et al.).

BRAIN PLASTICITY IN THE CONTEXT OF DISEASE AND INSULT

The evidence for the structural malleability of the brain even in the adult individual suggests that it might be possible to ameliorate age-related cognitive decline and treat neurological disease and insults by boosting the brain's innate plasticity. In this section, we briefly discuss how neurological disease affects plasticity and brain structure.

Neurodevelopmental disorders are often associated with deficits in neuronal plasticity. One example of such a disorder is fragile X syndrome (FXS), which is linked to the disruption of a single gene. Development and maintenance of neuronal networks are impaired in individuals with FXS (Huber, Gallagher, Warren, & Bear, 2002). Specifically, spines, which form the basis for synapses, remain immature and fail to form fully functioning synapses. As described previously, learning and memory depend crucially on synaptic plasticity. Individuals with FXS often present with a developmental delay and other symptoms that are likely due to the decreased efficiency of established neural networks during early brain development.

The same way that neurodevelopment can be impaired by reduced plasticity, cognitive decline during aging can be worsened by decreasing plasticity. In Alzheimer's disease, amyloid-β protein causes rapid disruption of synaptic plasticity and thus memory impairment. Individuals with Alzheimer's disease thus often suffer from profound episodic memory loss (i.e., inability to remember past events) even before substantial cognitive decline.

Finally, next to disorders and disease that affect individuals during various periods of their lives, there are neurological insults and injuries that test the brain's ability to adapt and reorganize to the limit. Traumatic brain injuries (TBI) are caused by external forces large enough to affect the structure and functioning of the brain. Both primary brain injuries directly caused by the impact and progressive secondary brain injuries, such as raised intracranial pressure, edema, and ischemia, can affect the brain's functioning severely. Less well known is that secondary injuries can, in some cases, affect the brain's functioning for months or even years. These secondary injuries stem from a number of processes such as inflammation (i.e., the release of chemical compounds and immune cells within the brain). The resulting maladaptive plasticity has been suggested as one of the potential neuronal mechanisms accounting for the chronic physical, mental, and emotional impairments experienced by young TBI survivors (Li et al., 2014).

BOOSTING PLASTICITY AS TREATMENT

Mounting evidence in favor of adult brain plasticity has stirred the desire to harvest the brain's innate malleability to overcome or at least attenuate the impact of neurological disease, injury, and natural aging. However, although structural changes have now been found in response to a range of tasks and training regimes, it is less clear how this can benefit patients and the elderly.

It has been shown that during certain critical periods of development the brain undergoes important and pronounced structural changes. This finding suggests that earlier intervention might have a higher probability of success in altering the brain's developmental path. The hypothesis that young brains are more plastic has been exploited in treatment of children (8–10 years) with poor reading skills. After children underwent 100 hours of intensive reading training, researchers found increases in fractional anisotropy, a measure of white matter integrity, in the left anterior centrum semiovale, correlated with improvement in phonological decoding ability (Keller & Just, 2009). This suggests that in the young brain, targeted behavioral intervention can bring about changes in task-specific cortico-cortical white matter tracts that are associated with improved behavioral performance. Similarly, cognitive-behavioral therapy (CBT) has been shown to be particularly effective in pediatric obsessive-compulsive disorder, improving both patient outcome and increasing gray matter volume in the frontal cortex (Huyser et al., 2012). CBT interventions clearly target the brain's ability to rewire itself and thus represent brain plasticity in therapeutic action.

In middle-age and elderly healthy volunteers, 8 weeks of training on a mnemonic technique improved memory performance and showed increases in cortical thickness in the right fusiform cortex (Engvig et al., 2010). This suggests it might be possible that systematic mental exercise may have the power to slow age-related cognitive decline by counteracting structural brain deterioration. In a more simple form, targeted training tasks have become popular as "brain training" games or applications during recent years. Although practicing improves performance on these specific tasks, it has been questioned how well the acquired skills generalize. A comprehensive study followed more than 10,000 participants as they practiced a range of cognitive tasks designed to improve reasoning, memory, planning, visuospatial skills, and attention over a period of 6 weeks (Owen et al., 2010). No evidence was found for transfer effects to untrained tasks, even when those tasks were similar to the one practiced. Unfortunately, the study did not take any measurements of brain structure. Thus, it is still an open question how the presence or absence of structural brain changes relates to changes in performance of practiced tasks and comparable tasks that were not practiced. In summary, specialized cognitive training regimes might be effective to reconstitute certain faculties by modulating the underlying neural substrate. However, specialized training might fail to counteract a broader age-related cognitive decline, which encompasses a whole range of cognitive faculties.

Improving fitness has been proposed as a possible measure to increase overall brain health. Animal studies have demonstrated that exercise benefits brain health by decreasing inflammation and a number of pathological processes. In addition, exercise decreases the age-related decrease in hippocampal neurogenesis and facilitates release of neurotrophic factors that promote proliferation of neurons and synapses (Voss, Vivar, Kramer, & van Praag, 2013). As seen in previous sections of this chapter, these are important processes that support brain plasticity. In humans, aerobic exercise and cardiorespiratory fitness have been found to contribute to healthy brain aging (Hayes, Hayes, Cadden, & Verfaellie, 2013). Increased fitness is associated with attenuated age-related decreases in frontoparietal white and gray matter regions (Colcombe et al., 2003). The beneficial effects of exercise on brain structure are also behaviorally and clinically relevant. Exercise has been shown to improve performance on motor and memory tasks (Hayes et al., 2013) and reduce the risk of cognitive impairment (Erickson et al., 2010).

In concert, these studies suggest that behavioral performance can be improved by specific training interventions. These interventions seem to work, at least in part, by altering the underlying neural substrate. The possibility of altering brain structure suggests a mechanism to target age- or disease-related deterioration in these areas. However, the specificity of these interventions might limit their effectiveness in improving general brain health and behavioral performance across a range of skills. Exercise has the potential to improve brain plasticity across a larger number of brain areas and slow age-related decline across a range of faculties. Ultimately, behavioral interventions such as CBT should be considered for any disorder, in particular pediatric disorders, in which targeting the plastic brain can bring about at least some amelioration of the condition.

SUMMARY

The brain is remarkable for its ability to modify itself in response to changing environments. The scientific community is beginning to understand the physiological and molecular mechanisms that make this adaptability possible. Novel ways of measuring brain plasticity in humans are being developed, yet in many ways the field is still in its infancy. Ultimately, understanding how the brain changes itself will lead to more targeted therapies to improve outcomes in many mental health disorders that affect the brain's capacity to adapt.

FOR FURTHER THOUGHT AND DISCUSSION

1. How many different forms of memory can you think of? Try to distinguish them in terms of what gets remembered (e.g., personal events versus facts, visual versus auditory) and how long they last (e.g., seconds, minutes, years).

2. Building on the first question, which types of memory do you think require more permanent structural changes in the brain and which might work through temporary synaptic changes?

3. Discuss the pros and cons of using animal models versus human individuals when investigating structural brain plasticity.

REFERENCES

Anderson, B.J., Li, X., Alcantara, A.A., Isaacs, K.R., Black, J.E., & Greenough, W.T. (1994). Glial hypertrophy is associated with synaptogenesis following motor-skill learning, but not with angiogenesis following exercise. *Glia, 11*(1), 73–80.

Bengtsson, S.L., Nagy, Z., Skare, S., Forsman, L., Forssberg, H., & Ullén, F. (2005). Extensive piano practicing has regionally specific effects on white matter development. *Nature Neuroscience, 8*(9), 1148–1150.

Bermudez, P., Lerch, J.P., Evans, A.C., & Zatorre, R.J. (2009). Neuroanatomical correlates of musicianship as revealed by cortical thickness and voxel-based morphometry. *Cerebral Cortex, 19*(7), 1583–1596.

Boyke, J., Driemeyer, J., Gaser, C., Büchel, C., & May, A. (2008). Training-induced brain structure changes in the elderly. *Journal of Neuroscience, 28*(28), 7031–7035.

Burke, S.N., & Barnes, C.A. (2006). Neural plasticity in the ageing brain. *Nature Reviews Neuroscience, 7*(1), 30–40.

Colcombe, S.J., Erickson, K.I., Raz, N., Webb, A.G., Cohen, N.J., McAuley, E., & Kramer, A.F. (2003). Aerobic fitness reduces brain tissue loss in aging humans. *Journals of Gerontology Series A: Biological Sciences and Medical Sciences, 58*(2), M176–M180.

Draganski, B., Gaser, C., Busch, V., Schuierer, G., Bogdahn, U., & May, A. (2004). Neuroplasticity: Changes in grey matter induced by training. *Nature, 427*(6972), 311–312.

Draganski, B., Gaser, C., Kempermann, G., Kuhn, H.G., Winkler, J., Büchel, C., & May, A. (2006). Temporal and spatial dynamics of brain structure changes during extensive learning. *Journal of Neuroscience, 26*(23), 6314–6317.

Engvig, A., Fjell, A.M., Westlye, L.T., Moberget, T., Sundseth, Ø., Larsen, V.A., & Walhovd, K.B. (2010). Effects of memory training on cortical thickness in the elderly. *NeuroImage, 52*(4), 1667–1676.

Erickson, K.I., Raji, C.A., Lopez, O.L., Becker, J.T., Rosano, C., Newman, A.B.,...Kuller, L.H. (2010). Physical activity predicts gray matter volume in late adulthood: The cardiovascular health study. *Neurology, 75*(16), 1415–1422.

Gaser, C., & Schlaug, G. (2003). Brain structures differ between musicians and non-musicians. *Journal of Neuroscience, 23*(27), 9240–9245.

Hayes, S.M., Hayes, J.P., Cadden, M., & Verfaellie, M. (2013, July). A review of cardiorespiratory fitness-related neuroplasticity in the aging brain. *Frontiers in Aging Neuroscience, 5*, 31.

Hihara, S., Notoya, T., Tanaka, M., Ichinose, S., Ojima, H., Obayashi, S.,...Iriki, A. (2006). Extension of corticocortical afferents into the anterior bank of the intraparietal sulcus by tool-use training in adult monkeys. *Neuropsychologia, 44*(13), 2636–2646.

Huber, K.M., Gallagher, S.M., Warren, S.T., & Bear, M.F. (2002). Altered synaptic plasticity in a mouse model of fragile X mental retardation. *Proceedings of the National Academy of Sciences of the United States of America, 99*(11), 7746–7750.

Huyser, C., van den Heuvel, O.A., Wolters, L.H., de Haan, E., Boer, F., & Veltman, D.J. (2012). Increased orbital frontal gray matter volume after cognitive behavioural therapy in paediatric obsessive compulsive disorder. *World Journal of Biological Psychiatry, 14*(4), 319–331.

Hyde, K.L., Lerch, J., Norton, A., Forgeard, M., Winner, E., Evans, A.C., & Schlaug, G. (2009). The effects of musical training on structural brain development: A longitudinal study. *Annals of the New York Academy of Sciences, 1169*, 182–186.

Keller, T.A., & Just, M.A. (2009). Altering cortical connectivity: Remediation-induced changes in the white matter of poor readers. *Neuron, 64*(5), 624–631.

Larsen, C.C., Bonde Larsen, K., Bogdanovic, N., Laursen, H., Graem, N., Samuelsen, G.B., & Pakkenberg, B. (2006). Total number of cells in the human newborn telencephalic wall. *Neuroscience, 139*(3), 999–1003.

Lerch, J.P., Yiu, A.P., Martinez-Canabal, A., Pekar, T., Bohbot, V.D., Frankland, P.W.,...Sled, J.G. (2011). Maze training in mice induces MRI-detectable brain shape changes specific to the type of learning. *NeuroImage, 54*(3), 2086–2095.

Li, N., Yang, Y., Glover, D.P., Zhang, J., Saraswati, M., Robertson, C., & Pelled, G. (2014). Evidence for impaired plasticity after traumatic brain injury in the developing brain. *Journal of Neurotrauma, 31*(4), 395–403.

Maguire, E.A., Gadian, D.G., Johnsrude, I.S., Good, C.D., Ashburner, J., Frackowiak, R.S., & Frith, C.D. (2000). Navigation-related structural change in the hippocampi of taxi drivers. *Proceedings of the National Academy of Sciences of the United States of America, 97*(8), 4398–4403.

Owen, A.M., Hampshire, A., Grahn, J.A, Stenton, R., Dajani, S., Burns, A.S.,...Ballard, C.G. (2010). Putting brain training to the test. *Nature, 465*(7299), 775–778.

Scholz, J., Klein, M.C., Behrens, T.E.J., & Johansen-Berg, H. (2009). Training induces changes in white-matter architecture. *Nature Neuroscience, 12*(11), 1370–1371.

Sereno, M.I., Pitzalis, S., & Martinez, A. (2001). Mapping of contralateral space in retinotopic coordinates by a parietal cortical area in humans. *Science, 294*(5545), 1350–1354.

Sluming, V., Barrick, T., Howard, M., Cezayirli, E., Mayes, A., & Roberts, N. (2002). Voxel-based morphometry reveals increased gray matter density in Broca's area in male symphony orchestra musicians. *Neuroimage, 17*(3), 1613–1622.

Spalding, K.L., Bergmann, O., Alkass, K., Bernard, S., Salehpour, M., Huttner, H.B.,...Frisén, J. (2013). Dynamics of hippocampal neurogenesis in adult humans. *Cell, 153*(6), 1219–1227.

Sweatt, J.D. (2009). *Mechanisms of memory* (2nd ed.). London, United Kingdom: Academic Press.

Voss, M.W., Vivar, C., Kramer, A.F., & van Praag, H. (2013). Bridging animal and human models of exercise-induced brain plasticity. *Trends in Cognitive Sciences, 17*(10), 525–544.

Wiesel, T.N., & Hubel, D.H. (1963). Single-cell responses in striate cortex of kittens deprived of vision in one eye. *Journal of Neurophysiology, 26,* 1003–1017.

III

Etiology and Conditions

13

Factors Causing or Contributing to Intellectual and Developmental Disabilities

Maire Percy, Ivan Brown, and Wai Lun Alan Fung

WHAT YOU WILL LEARN

- Importance of education about factors that cause or contribute to intellectual and developmental disabilities (i.e., risk factors)
- Overview of causal or contributing factors
- Biomedical, social, behavioral, and educational risk factors
- Prevention of intellectual and developmental disabilities
- Comorbid sensory impairments and mental health disorders
- Future directions in the field

The purpose of this chapter is to draw awareness to different factors that can cause or contribute to intellectual and/or developmental disabilities. There are several reasons why this chapter is important. First, obtaining an explanation for why a person has been diagnosed with intellectual disability as early as possible (i.e., an early diagnosis) provides relief to families and others who care for the child. Second, an early diagnosis facilitates access to supports and services earlier than in the absence of a diagnosis; in some cases, these may prevent actual or further impairment from developing. Third, an early diagnosis may help to prevent recurrences of certain types of intellectual and developmental disabilities within an affected individual's family. Fourth, having information about the causes of intellectual and

developmental disabilities helps administrators and policy makers allocate funding for supports and services, because these often are geared to specific types of disabilities. Finally, before an explanation is sought for what may have caused intellectual or developmental impairments, professionals and families should consider any negative consequences that might arise from a child becoming "labeled." Sometimes, complex ethical, legal, and social issues can arise that might interfere with obtaining medical or life insurance or with employment, or labels might upset family members. Should such concerns arise, it is important that appropriate guidelines, laws, policies, or strategies be developed and implemented to guard against them (Percy, 2007; Percy & Brown, 2011).

OVERVIEW

Using criteria in the fourth edition of the *Diagnostic and Statistical Manual of Mental Disorders, Fourth Edition, Text Revision (DSM-IV-TR)*, intellectual disability has been estimated to affect approximately 2%–3% of the general population worldwide, the prevalence being lower in developed than developing countries (American Psychiatric Association [APA], 2000). On the basis of *DSM-5* criteria, the prevalence is approximately 1% (APA, 2013). However, in a study of 1997–2008 data representative of U.S. households, as many as 1 in 6 children in the United States is affected by some type of developmental disorder, including attention-deficit/hyperactivity disorder (ADHD), intellectual disability, cerebral palsy, autism spectrum disorder (ASD), seizures, stuttering or stammering, moderate to profound hearing loss, blindness, learning disorders, and/or other developmental delays (Boyle et al., 2011). Most cases of intellectual disability are mild, with less than 0.5% being severe (Rauch et al., 2012).

Intellectual disability is sometimes classified as syndromic (in which intellectual impairments associated with other medical and behavioral signs and symptoms are present) and nonsyndromic (in which intellectual impairments appear without other medical and behavioral signs and symptoms). Syndromic intellectual impairments account for 30%–50% of cases (Kaufman, Ayub, & Vincent, 2010; Rauch et al., 2012; Srour & Shevell, 2014.)

Many different factors that cause or contribute to intellectual and developmental disabilities have been identified. One quarter to one half of intellectual or developmental disability diagnoses are associated with genetic factors (Srour & Shevell, 2014). Although some publications report that the cause of intellectual disability is unknown in up to half of cases, a population study in a middle-income country identified causal factors in approximately 90% of a birth cohort (Karam et al., 2015). Studies of children indicate that 1.5 times as many males are affected with intellectual disability as females, but the male-to-female proportion decreases with increasing severity of intellectual impairment (McLaren & Bryson, 1987). In autism spectrum disorder (ASD), the most widely reported male-to-female ratio is 4-5:1 (Lai, Lombardo, Auyeung, Chakrabarti, & Baron-Cohen, 2015).

The American Association on Intellectual and Developmental Disabilities (AAIDD) focuses on four different types of factors that cause or contribute to intellectual disability (biomedical, social, behavioral, and educational) and on the timing of exposure to these factors (prenatal, perinatal, and postnatal) (AAIDD, 2010). Biomedical factors include genetic disorders and various factors adversely affecting health. Social factors include adverse family social interactions, lack of access to health care, and parental neglect. Behavioral factors include any behavior that adversely affects functioning, such as maternal alcohol or substance abuse. Educational factors include lack of accessibility to educational experiences that support adaptive skills, such as family support and/or special education, especially

early in life. Sometimes the term *environmental* is used to denote health-related, social, behavioral, and educational factors. *Prenatal* means occurring before birth; *perinatal* relates to the period shortly before and after birth (traditionally, from the 20th week of gestation to the 28th day of newborn life). *Postnatal* means after birth (traditionally, the first 6 weeks after birth). Nongenetic factors are sometimes referred to as environmental factors.

Factors involved in intellectual and developmental disabilities are often referred to as risk factors. Many forms of intellectual and developmental impairment are thought to result from more than one factor (McLaren & Bryson, 1987). Risk factors can be causal or contributing. The term *causal* implies that the factor (or factors acting in combination) actually causes the intellectual impairment or developmental delay (i.e., that the probability of causing the intellectual impairment or developmental delay is 100% or close to this). *Contributing* implies that the factor(s) in question is/are not sufficient on its/their own to cause the intellectual impairment or developmental delay. Conversely, some factors can help to prevent intellectual impairment or developmental delay or reduce its severity. The study of factors involved in intellectual and developmental disabilities is complex and challenging. For example, having an extra chromosome 21 is known to cause Down syndrome, and Down syndrome is associated with intellectual disability. However, the degree of intellectual disability in people with Down syndrome is highly variable, and the nature of this variability is not yet understood. This may involve multiple biomedical and/or psychosocial factors. Susser (2002) noted that ideas of what are causal factors in human disease have "changed over the years as societies, understanding of disease, and technical resources have changed." Furthermore, this field of study continues to evolve (Xiang et al., 2015).

An introduction to risk factors for intellectual and developmental disabilities should include a brief review of genetics, the "nature versus nurture" debate, the subspecialty of genetics called epigenetics, and brain plasticity.

A Brief Review of Genetics

Every cell in the human body contains 46 chromosomes: 23 from the mother and 23 from the father. Chromosomes are structures in the nucleus of the cells made up of tightly coiled strands of DNA.

Along these strands are sections referred to as genes. Genes contain information that both enables the body to grow and work and determines how the body grows and works. Genes are passed from parents to children. Twenty-two of the 23 chromosome pairs are called autosomes; these are not involved in sex determination. The chromosomes that determine sex (the sex chromosomes) are the X in females and the Y in males. Females have two X chromosomes; males have one X and one Y. DNA is also present in mitochondria, the energy-producing organelles of cells. Mitochondrial DNA is inherited from the mother. When the first cell is formed from the mother and father, mitochondria from the father are destroyed. In this first cell, very occasionally a chromosome (or more) is structurally not normal, or there can be too many or too few of them, or they can be changed in very minor ways. Sometimes genetic abnormalities are inherited from one parent or from both parents, but sometimes they are not and occur de novo (i.e., spontaneously; Nussbaum, McInnes, & Willard, 2015). Inheritance of a genetic disorder can be dominant (a mutation in just one of two copies of a gene is sufficient to cause a problem) or recessive (mutations are needed in both copies of a gene to have an effect). There is no controversy that eye and hair color are specified by variants of specific genes encoded in each human cell.

A Brief Review of Nature versus Nurture

The nature theory supports the idea that even more abstract traits such as intelligence, personality, aggression, and sexual orientation are encoded in a person's DNA. The nurture theory, on the other hand, proposes that behavioral aspects of humans originate only from the environmental factors of upbringing. There was considerable debate over several decades about whether nature or nurture predominates in matters of child development. It is now generally agreed that both play important roles, that they interact in sometimes complex ways, and that the relative importance of nature or nurture varies considerably from one person to another.

A Brief Review of Epigenetics

Epigenetics is the study of changes in gene activity that are caused by things other than the makeup of the genes themselves. From conception to the end of life, genes are coded to function in specific ways that determine growth and changes over the lifespan, but genes are not always active. Through biochemical processes collectively known as genetic imprinting, genes can be turned "on" or "off"—something like a light switch–or they can be "dimmed"—something like a light-switch dimmer. One imprinting process involves the addition of methyl groups to particular cytosine residues in DNA, a process called methylation. This is often a good thing. For example, during the early adolescent years, genetic imprinting permanently turns off certain growth genes so that the body stops growing taller; otherwise, a person would continue to grow taller and taller throughout life. A second example of imprinting involves silencing of many genes on one of the two X chromosomes in females at an early stage in development. This is so that females have approximately the same number of active genes on their two X chromosomes as males do on their one X. An interesting aspect of epigenetic research that has emerged in recent years is showing that life's events, positive or negative, can also influence genes being turned on or off. For example, prenatal exposure to alcohol has been found to result in unique DNA methylation changes in offspring, both in mice and humans (Laufer et al., 2015). Thus, although understanding of epigenetics is in its infancy, epigenetic research is helping to resolve the nature versus nurture debate. Environmental factors and experiences can indeed shape who people are and have profound consequences about how they live (Percy & Brown, 2011).

A Brief Review of Brain Plasticity

The term *brain plasticity* (or *neuroplasticity*) refers to changes in neural connections that occur in the brain when people learn new things or memorize new information (see Chapter 12). Using the brain in new and different ways causes it to create new "pathways" that did not previously exist. These changes can occur throughout life, which makes clear the importance of mental exercise at all life stages. Studies point to the involvement of epigenetic processes in these brain changes. For example, whereas DNA methylation (addition of methyl groups to DNA) is necessary to inhibit genes involved in memory suppression, DNA demethylation (removal of methyl groups from DNA) is important in activating genes whose expression is positively correlated with memory formation (Miller & Sweatt, 2007).

The next four main sections highlight different risk factors that cause or contribute to intellectual and developmental disabilities. The first three main sections deal with factors that are biomedical in nature, and the fourth deals with social, behavioral and educational risk factors.

BIOMEDICAL RISK FACTORS FOR INTELLECTUAL AND DEVELOPMENTAL DISABILITIES: INTRODUCTION

This risk factors introductory section explains why the developing fetus is particularly susceptible to damage by certain risk factors and provides an overview of biomedical risk factors.

Fetal Vulnerability

The developing fetus is particularly susceptible to damage at certain developmental stages (Table 13.1). Substances and agents that induce the production of physical deformities in the fetus, including the central nervous system, are called teratogens. See also Chapter 9.

Biomedical Risk Factors

Biomedical risk factors for intellectual and developmental disabilities, based on the AAIDD system for classifying risk factors, are presented in Table 13.2. Involvement of factors other than biomedical ones is difficult to substantiate. Hence, it is not surprising that factors identified from research studies are primarily biomedical in nature.

BIOMEDICAL RISK FACTORS FOR INTELLECTUAL AND DEVELOPMENTAL DISABILITIES: GENETIC CAUSES

This main section, which is divided into several subsections, provides details about the genetic basis of intellectual and developmental disabilities.

Table 13.1.   Fetal vulnerability at different stages of development

Developmental stage[a]	Developmental features	Potential issues
Fertilization	Restoration of diploid number, establishment of sex, triggering of first cleavage division	
First week	Embryo is transported from site of fertilization to site of implantation in the uterus; formation of blastula	50%–70% of pregnancies end in spontaneous abortions within the first 2 weeks due to • Chromosomal abnormalities, which result in 60% of miscarriages • Failure of zygote to implant • Maternal immune response • Physical teratogens such as heat and ionizing radiation (e.g., x rays, gamma rays)
Second week	Embryo implants into lining of uterus; amniotic cavity and primitive yolk sac are formed	
Third through eighth weeks	Organogenesis—beginning of the development of body form	Chemical teratogens (e.g., alcohol) and maternal metabolic upsets (e.g., obesity, diabetes, thyroid malfunction) may produce major malformations.
Second trimester	Multiplication of neurons	
Third trimester to 18–24 months after birth	Brain growth spurt: glial cell multiplication, dendritic arborization, synaptogenesis, and myelination	The brain is very vulnerable to malnutrition, endogenous and environmental poisons, and hormonal imbalances; in utero effects of teratogens may include minor malformations and neurobehavioral and neurocognitive effects.

Sources: Brent (2004), Dobbing (1981), Guze (2005), D. Laslo personal communication (April 25, 1999), and Rice and Barone (2000).

[a]Pregnancy is measured from the start of a woman's last menstrual period. It usually lasts 40 weeks or about 9 calendar months. The first trimester lasts from 0 to 13 weeks, the second from 14 to 27 weeks, and the third from 28 to 40 weeks.

Table 13.2. Biomedical risk factors for intellectual and developmental disabilities

	Associated developmental period(s)		
Risk factor	Prenatal	Perinatal	Postnatal
Genetic	Chromosomal disorders (changes in number or structure)		
	Transmitted single gene defects (autosomal, X- or Y-linked)		
	De novo mutations (including known syndromes and nonsyndromic intellectual and developmental disabilities)		
	Copy number variants		
	Complex or multifactorial disorders		
	Mitochondrial disorders (defects in mitochondrial DNA)		
Health related	Maternal infections (e.g., cytomegalovirus, rubella, Zika virus)	Infections acquired from the mother during birth or shortly afterward (e.g., cytomegalovirus, herpesvirus types 1 and 2, HIV, streptococcus B)	Infections acquired after birth (e.g., whooping cough, measles, meningitis, HIV, influenza Haemophilus b)
	Maternal malnutrition from poor diet, including iodine deficiency	Malnutrition (e.g., resulting from poor quality or insufficient quantity of breast milk or infant formula)	Malnutrition (e.g., resulting from poor or inadequate diet)
	Maternal metabolic disorders (e.g., obesity, diabetes, thyroid dysfunction, phenylketonuria [PKU])		
	Traumatic brain injury (e.g., from physical assault, motor vehicle accidents, falls)	Traumatic brain injury (e.g., from birth complications, child battering, motor vehicle accidents, falls)	Traumatic brain injury (e.g., from child battering, motor vehicle accidents, accidents, falls)
	Maternal exposures to teratogens (e.g., alcohol, drugs)	Conditions resulting in lack of oxygen (asphyxia)	Stroke (mainly from sickle cell anemia)
			Brain tumors
			Conditions resulting in lack of oxygen
	Maternal exposures to toxins and toxic metals (e.g., lead, mercury, aluminum)	Exposures to toxins and toxic metals	Exposures to toxins and toxic metals
	Rh disease of the fetus	Prematurity for any reason	Seizure disorders
	Maternal stress	Caregiver stress	Caregiver stress
	Lack of prenatal screening for potentially treatable conditions (e.g., diabetes, thyroid disorders, Rh disease, maternal PKU)	Lack of neonatal screening for potentially treatable conditions (e.g., congenital hypothyroidism, PKU)	Lack of neonatal screening for potentially treatable conditions (e.g., congenital hypothyroidism, PKU)
	Parental age effects (refers to the statistical relationship between the age of a parent and effects on the child; see the chapter text for examples)		
	Abnormal maternal microbiome effects[a]	Abnormal maternal and/or infant microbiome effects[a]	Abnormal infant microbiome effects[a]

(continued)

Table 13.2. *(continued)*

Risk factor	Associated developmental period(s)		
	Prenatal	Perinatal	Postnatal
Congenital brain anomalies	Anencephaly, encephalocele, spina bifida (bifida occulta, meningocele, and myelomeningocele), lissencephaly, hydranencephaly		
Other	Consanguinity (having offspring from union to a second cousin or closer)		

Sources: American Association on Intellectual and Developmental Disabilities (2010), Percy (2007), and Percy and Brown (2011).

ᵃThe term *microbiome* refers to the collection of microorganisms that inhabit various places in or on one's body, primarily in the gut. The microbiome carries out various functions which are thought to be vital for human development, health, and survival. See text of this chapter as well as Chapters 9 and 11.

Overview

Genetic causes of intellectual and developmental disabilities are often subdivided into a number of different categories, as shown in Table 13.2. In 2004, approximately 7,500 different genetic disorders were known. As of 2015, more than 18,000 single-gene disorders had been identified. Of these, more than 6,000 are known to be heritable (i.e., passed down through generations; R. R. McInnes, personal communication, January 18, 2015). As of 2014, 450 genes were implicated in intellectual impairments and developmental disorders, with 400 attributed to syndromic intellectual impairments and developmental disorders and 50 to nonsyndromic intellectual impairments and developmental disorders (Srour & Shevell, 2014).

Variability of Expression of Genetic Disorders

Genetic disorders associated with intellectual and developmental disabilities are variable in their expression. For example, although some people with a given genetic disorder have intellectual impairments or developmental disorders, others do not. Noonan syndrome is an example of a common genetic disorder in which only approximately one third of affected children have mild intellectual disability (see Chapter 21). The reason a disorder can vary so much in the way it is expressed is thought to be the result of the nature and severity of the mutation causing the condition, effects of background genes (i.e., genes not carrying the abnormality that causes the genetic disorder but that modify the effects of the mutant gene), and other biomedical factors and differing life experiences (see Table 13.2).

The Most Common Genetic Disorders

Worldwide, the most common intellectual and developmental disabilities with a genetic basis are Down syndrome, 22q11.2 deletion syndrome (which includes previously identified syndromes such as DiGeorge syndrome and velocardiofacial syndrome; see Chapter 17), and fragile X syndrome (FXS). The estimated birth incidence of Down syndrome is between 1 in 1,000 and 1 in 100. The birth incidence of 22q11.2 deletion syndrome is approximately 1 in 2,000. One in 3,600 to 1 in 4,000 males and 1 in 4,000 to 1 in 6,000 females have FXS. Down syndrome is the most common etiology for intellectual disability resulting from an aberration of chromosome number. It is usually caused by the presence of an additional chromosome 21 and is referred to as trisomy 21 (i.e., having three copies of chromosome 21 instead of the usual two copies). Most cases of Down syndrome are not inherited and occur spontaneously without a family history. The birth incidence of Down syndrome increases markedly after a maternal age of 35 years (see Chapter 14). 22q11.2 deletion syndrome is a chromosomal disorder resulting from a missing piece of chromosome 22. Expression of this disorder is very variable and may include delayed growth and speech development and learning disabilities. Affected children are at risk of also having ADHD or ASD. Later in life, people with this syndrome are at increased risk of developing other mental health problems (see Chapter 17). FXS is the most common inherited etiology resulting in intellectual or developmental disability. FXS is an X-linked single gene disorder caused by unstable mutations in the FMR1 gene. Though both men and women can carry X chromosomes with FMR1 mutations, mutated FMR1 is transmitted only by females, and the mutations tend to get larger as they are passed on from one generation to the next. Males are affected more severely by FXS than females because they have only one X chromosome; females with FXS tend to be spared because they carry one normal X as well as the X with a mutation (see Chapter 15).

Inborn Errors of Metabolism

As of 2014, 89 potentially treatable genetic disorders called inborn errors of metabolism (i.e., genetic disorders in which the body cannot properly turn food into energy) had been identified (van Karnebeek, 2014). These disorders include phenylketonuria (PKU), galactosemia, Hunter syndrome, and Lesch-Nyhan syndrome (see Chapter 21). Effects of PKU can be prevented if this disorder is identified by genetic screening at birth and a special diet lacking in phenylalanine is adopted. Mothers who carry a PKU gene should adhere to a strict diet during pregnancy. Effects of galactosemia can be attenuated by adherence to a diet lacking in galactose. The U.S. Food and Drug Administration approved a treatment for Hunter syndrome that involves intravenous administration of the enzyme that is deficient in this disorder (da Silva, Strufaldi, Andriolo, & Silva, 2016). Quite a number of different disorders, including Hunter syndrome and Lesch-Nyhan syndrome, are being treated on an experimental basis with cord blood stem cell transplants.

Sex Chromosome Disorders and Imprinting Disorders

Turner syndrome and Klinefelter syndrome are disorders involving abnormalities in the number of sex chromosomes. These syndromes are sometimes, but not always, associated with mild intellectual impairment and physical anomalies (see Chapter 21).

Two very different but related genetic conditions resulting in intellectual impairment or developmental disorder are Prader-Willi syndrome and Angelman syndrome. These are both caused by small deletions in exactly the same region of chromosome 15 or by duplication of one chromosome 15 and loss of the other. Prader-Willi syndrome is often caused by deletions in the paternal chromosome 15 or by duplication of the maternal chromosome 15. Angelman syndrome is often caused by deletions in the maternal chromosome 15 or by duplication of the paternal chromosome 15 (see Chapter 21).

(This parent of origin phenomenon arises because genes on chromosome 15 are expressed only if they have not been marked by the imprinting process; maternal and paternal chromosome 15s have different imprinting patterns.)

Other Disorders

Congenital hypothyroidism is a disorder resulting from thyroid hormone deficiency that is easily treated. This affects approximately 1 in 4,000 newborns in North America. Congenital hypothyroidism can result from genetic mutations or from iodine deficiency (see Chapter 21).

De novo single nucleotide mutations and loss of function mutations (i.e., small genetic changes not transmitted by parents that can occur in individuals with intellectual and developmental disabilities) have emerged as possible risk factors for moderate and severe levels of intellectual impairment (Hamdan et al., 2014) and ASD (Gamsiz et al., 2015). Copy number variants (CNVs) also are associated with intellectual disability and ASD (Kaminsky et al., 2011). CNVs are specific types of alteration in genomic DNA that result in the cell having an abnormal number of copies of a DNA segment equal to or greater in size than 1,000 base pairs. A CNV can refer to the addition or deletion of such a segment. These may be transmitted by parents or arise de novo. Because de novo mutations and CNVs are common in the general population, establishing that they are pathologically involved in intellectual disability or ASD, and how, remains challenging.

ASD has a prevalence that is an order of magnitude larger than Down syndrome. ASD is multifactorial, meaning that it is thought to result from a variety of factors. Suspected risk factors include complex genetic interactions, nutritional deficiencies (e.g., vitamin D deficiency) or overloads, pre- and postnatal exposure to chemicals or viruses, errors during the embryonic neural tube closure process, dysfunctional immune systems, a dysfunctional gut microbiome, maternal diabetes in the first 26 weeks of pregnancy, and even allergies (see Chapter 16). Furthermore, a number of different genetic disorders associated with features similar to those seen in ASD sometimes are incorrectly diagnosed as ASD. These include PKU, FXS, tuberous sclerosis, Williams syndrome, Prader-Willi and Angelman syndromes, Rett syndrome, and 22q11.2 deletion syndrome (see Chapter 21). In a recent analysis of U.S. medical records, counties with higher rates of genital deformities in newborn males had higher rates of ASD and intellectual disability. This highlights the possibility of congenital exposure to harmful environmental factors such as pesticides in both disorders (Rzhetsky et al., 2014).

Mitochondrial disorders resulting from mutations in mitochondrial DNA are not common. Overall, they affect approximately 1 in 5,000 individuals across all ages. Mutations can be maternally inherited (see previous discussion) or occur sporadically. Mutations in mitochondrial DNA often affect multiple organ systems that require a lot of energy (e.g., heart, brain, muscles). Two examples of mitochondrial disorders that affect brain function are myoclonic epilepsy with ragged-red fibers—a disorder affecting many parts of the body—and mitochondrial myopathy, encephalopathy, lactic acidosis, and stroke syndrome—a progressive neurodegenerative disorder (Nussbaum et al., 2015).

Other Factors that Affect Genetic Causes of Disabilities

Two other factors that affect genetic causes of intellectual and developmental disabilities are ethnic origin and survival advantage. Ethnic origin may influence the chances of a child being affected by, or being a carrier of, a genetic disability. Disorders that have a high prevalence in certain ethnic groups, regardless of where individuals from those groups live now, result from probable common ancestry. This explains why there are many more people in these groups who carry a gene for the disorder than in the general population. This phenomenon is sometimes referred to as a founder effect. For example, there is a high frequency of Tay-Sachs disease (a fatal genetic disorder in which harmful quantities of a fatty substance called a ganglioside accumulate in the nerve cells of the brain) among Ashkenazic (central, northern, or eastern European) Jews but not among Sephardic (Spanish, Portuguese, or Middle Eastern) Jews. In contrast, PKU is mostly found in Caucasians and is rare in people of (or descended from) African or Asian ethnic groups. FXS is reported to be particularly common in Finland and in Quebec (Percy, 2007; Percy & Brown, 2011). Consanguineous parentage (i.e., union of closely related kin) increases the risk for conditions with autosomal recessive inheritance.

Survival advantage is a phenomenon associated with some recessive mutant genes. In such cases, mutant genes that are harmful when present in two copies have some survival advantage when only one copy has been inherited. Sickle-cell anemia (a condition in which red blood cells are sickle-shaped rather than round) and beta thalassemia (a disorder in which the body cannot make the beta chains of hemoglobin, the red cell protein that carries oxygen and carbon dioxide in the blood) are two recessive genetic disorders that are sometimes associated with intellectual and developmental disabilities and in which being the carrier of one mutant gene has an advantage. The trait for sickle-cell anemia, found in many people of African origin, is connected with a resistance to malaria; two sickle-cell genes result in the expression of anemia and resistance to malaria, whereas a carrier possessing a single sickle-cell gene is resistant to malaria and lacks the anemia. The trait of beta thalassemia, found in people of Mediterranean origin, similarly is connected with a resistance to malaria (Mount Sinai Hospital, 2013). Treatment for the anemia in both disorders requires blood transfusions, which leads to iron overload and organ failure if the body iron load is not normalized by treatment with drugs that remove iron from the body.

BIOMEDICAL RISK FACTORS FOR INTELLECTUAL AND DEVELOPMENTAL DISABILITIES: HEALTH-RELATED FACTORS

Numerous health-related factors are risk factors for intellectual and developmental disabilities (see Table 13.2). The following sections elaborate on some of these factors. Some of these factors are largely preventable.

Malnutrition

Malnutrition is suspected of being a cause of or contributing factor to intellectual impairment in a large proportion of affected individuals. Maternal malnutrition prior to conception may be the largest culprit. Although adults are remarkably resistant to the effects of malnutrition, the developing fetal brain is very susceptible. Protein-energy undernutrition and deficiencies of certain vitamins (e.g., folic acid, vitamin B_{12}, vitamin A) and minerals (e.g., iodide, iron, zinc) are problems not only in underdeveloped countries but in developed countries, including the United States and Canada (Bailey, West, & Black, 2015). As of 2010, one quarter of the world's population younger than 5 years of age was found to be underweight (UNICEF, 2010). About one in 12 newborns in the United States is underweight (March of Dimes Foundation, 2016). In North America, *underweight* is defined as having a birth weight of less than 2,500 grams (or 5.5 pounds). For couples planning pregnancy, there are many regional programs to address the challenge of how to prevent low birth weight infants (CDC, 2015; March of Dimes Foundation). The following subsections discuss several specific factors that contribute to malnutrition.

Protein-Energy Undernutrition Protein-energy undernutrition refers to a reduced protein intake over an extended period of time (Scheinfeld, 2015). This reduced intake eventually leads to depletion of the tissue protein reserve and lowering of blood protein levels, compromising proper function of nerve, muscle, and intellectual function. The latter may be irreversible if protein deprivation occurs during periods of brain development. Economic, social, and cultural factors (e.g., poor feeding habits, superstitions, belief in incorrect information about health and nutrition) all contribute to protein malnutrition in many countries. Infants and young children are very vulnerable. There are two disorders of protein-calorie malnutrition: marasmus and kwashiorkor (Scheinfeld, 2015). Which form develops depends upon the relative availability of nonprotein and protein sources of energy. In marasmus, there is severe deficiency of calories in the diet, including calories from protein. This results in severe growth failure and emaciation. Kwashiorkor results from premature abandonment from breast feeding, usually when a second child is born and replaces the first born at the mother's breast. Children with kwashiorkor have an odd reddish-orange color of the hair as well as a characteristic red skin rash. In kwashiorkor, the total calorie intake may be adequate but there is a deficiency of protein in the diet. Kwashiorkor often is associated with a maize-based diet. Protein-calorie malnutrition results in more severe infections than would occur in a state of adequate nutrition.

Folic Acid and Vitamin B$_{12}$ Deficiencies
Folate (or folacin) is a water-soluble B vitamin that all people need in order for their bodies to make new cells. A folic acid deficiency may result from low dietary intake of folic acid (eating the wrong foods) and/or as the result of one's genetic makeup. Folic acid deficiency is a risk factor for neural tube defects such as spina bifida (a birth defect in the bony encasement of the spinal cord) and anencephaly

(a birth defect characterized by missing or a very reduced amount of brain tissue). Pregnant women (especially women who have diabetes, epilepsy, or a family history of neural tube defects) should take a daily folic acid supplement before and during pregnancy to reduce the risk of having an infant with a neural tube defect. The United States, Canada, and some other countries fortify grain products, such as bread and pasta, with folic acid. As of this writing in 2016, there is concern that excessive synthetic folic acid intake may be associated with certain adverse health effects. Folic acid supplementation masks and exacerbates effects of vitamin B$_{12}$ deficiency. Prenatal folic acid supplement may be associated with an increased risk of unilateral neuroblastoma in a subset of the population homozygous for a particular variant of the dihydrofolate reductase gene. Finally, high maternal red cell folate in pregnancy has been associated with insulin resistance in offspring (Selhub & Rosenberg, 2016).

Vitamin B$_{12}$ is a water-soluble vitamin found in animal products, including fish, meat, poultry, eggs, milk, and milk products. Vitamin B$_{12}$ deficiency during pregnancy also is a risk factor for neural tube defects (Thompson, Cole, & Ray, 2009). Though confirmation is needed, it is prudent for women considering pregnancy to be B$_{12}$ replete and have a serum value not below 300 nanograms per liter at the time of conception.

Vitamin A Deficiency and Excess Vitamin A (retinol) is a fat-soluble vitamin that is found mainly in fish liver oils, liver, egg yolks, butter, and cream. Vitamin A precursors (e.g., carotene) are found in green leafy and yellow vegetables. Vitamin A is crucial for normal nervous system development and is important for proper function of the immune system. Vitamin A deficiency (VAD) is the leading cause of preventable blindness in children and raises the risk of disease and death from severe infections accompanied by diarrhea and measles. In pregnant women, VAD causes night blindness and may increase the risk of maternal mortality. For pregnant women in high-risk areas, VAD can occur during the last trimester, when demand by both the unborn child and the mother is highest. VAD may also be associated with elevated mother-to-child transmission of human immunodeficiency virus (HIV). Secondary VAD results when vitamin A precursors cannot be converted into vitamin A; from problems with absorption, storage, or transport of vitamin A (as in celiac disease, a disorder resulting from intolerance to a protein called gluten that is found in wheat and many other grains); or from intestinal infections. VAD is a public health problem in 118 countries, especially in Africa and Southern and Eastern Asia. It is common in protein-energy malnutrition.

More of vitamin A is not necessarily better. Too much is toxic and can result in death. Women of child-bearing age need to be very careful. Women who are pregnant should carefully check the amount of vitamin A in their multivitamins and consult with their doctor to make sure the dose is safe.

Vitamin D Deficiency Vitamin D is a fat-soluble substance that is called a vitamin, although it is actually a prohormone. It is known as the "sunshine vitamin" because it is produced in the body as the result of mild sun exposure. It also is consumed in certain foods (e.g., fatty fish, fish oil) and supplements. Vitamin D sufficiency is essential for preventing rickets in children and for good bone health (National Institutes of Health, n.d.). Vitamin D deficiency is unusually common in people with intellectual and developmental disabilities, partly because of insufficient exposure to sunlight (Frighi et al., 2014). In addition to involvement in bone health, vitamin D deficiency is suspected of contributing to abnormal fetal development (Hart et al., 2015), to ASD (Fernell et al., 2015), and to a wide range of neurological and neuropsychiatric disorders (Dursun, 2010; Groves, McGrath, & Burne, 2014). Furthermore, there is evidence that the vitamin D system is regulated by epigenetic mechanisms and is important in maintenance of the epigenome (Fetahu, Höbaus, & Kállay, 2014). These issues must be addressed in prospective research studies, and the importance of maintaining vitamin D sufficiency must be communicated to professionals and the public.

Iodine Deficiency Iodine is a trace mineral used by the thyroid gland to produce the important thyroid hormone called thyroxine. Thyroid dysfunction resulting from iodine deficiency disorder is the single most common cause of preventable developmental disability and brain damage in the world; more than 54 countries are still iodine deficient (World Health Organization [WHO], 2015). In North America, salt is usually iodized. Nevertheless, in the United States, mild iodine deficiency may still be problematic (Stagnaro-Green, Dogo-Isonagie, Pearce, Spencer, & Gaba, 2015). Iodine deficiency is also still problematic in some other developed countries, such as Switzerland and Germany. Iodine deficiency in children can cause stunted growth; apathy; difficulty with movement, speech, and hearing; and intellectual impairment. Iodine deficiency in pregnant women causes miscarriages and stillbirths; if the fetus survives, severe maternal iodine deficiency retards fetal growth and brain development. Infants with iodine deficiency are usually given L-thyroxine for a week plus iodide to quickly restore a normal thyroid state. Iodide supplementation is then continued.

More iodine is not necessarily better. Chronic iodine toxicity results when iodine intake is 20 times greater than the daily requirement. Paradoxically, too much iodine can lead to hypothyroidism, as can too little (Vitti, 2014).

Iron Deficiency Iron, a trace metal that is essential for life, is absorbed in the intestines. It comes in two forms: heme iron (found in meats), which is well absorbed, and nonheme iron (found in leafy vegetables–e.g., spinach), which is not as well absorbed. Most of the consumed iron goes to form hemoglobin, the substance that helps red blood cells transport oxygen from the lungs to the rest of the body. The rest of the iron is stored for future needs and mobilized when dietary intake is inadequate. Because iron also plays a key role in helping to prepare the immune system to do its job, a deficiency may lead to colds. Low iron levels can also cause fatigue, pallor, and listlessness—hallmarks of anemia.

Iron deficiency affects more than 2 billion people in the world; 30% of the population is anemic. In developing countries, approximately 50% of pregnant women and 40% of children are iron deficient (WHO, 2015). Iron deficiency anemia during the third trimester of fetal development affects one third of the pregnancies in the United States and has been associated with adverse postnatal behavioral outcomes. Complications of iron deficiency anemia in infants and children include developmental delays; behavior disturbances such as decreased motor activity, social interaction, and attention to tasks; compulsive eating of nonfood items (pica) and ice; and irreversible impairment of learning ability. In adults, iron deficiency anemia can result in a low capacity to perform physically demanding labor. Iron deficiency anemia also contributes to lead poisoning in children by increasing the gastrointestinal tract's ability to absorb heavy metals, including lead. (A common source of lead overload is exposure to dust from lead-based paint in old houses.) Iron deficiency anemia is associated with conditions that may independently affect infant and child development. Iron deficiency during pregnancy contributes to maternal mortality and fetus/infant mortality in the perinatal period. During the first two trimesters of pregnancy, it is associated with increased risk for preterm delivery and for delivering a low birth weight infant.

Iron deficiency can result from poor diet (e.g., a poor vegetarian diet), parasitic diseases (e.g., from worm and malaria infections), and abnormal uterine bleeding. Iron therapy in anemic children can often, but not always, improve behavior and cognitive performance, lead to normal growth, and hinder infections. Researchers at Guelph University in Canada created replicas of a small river fish—associated with luck in village folklore—to be put into iron cooking pots. When put into cooking pots in a village in Cambodia, these fish supplied up to 75% of the daily iron requirement and resulted in an enormous decrease in anemia, dizziness, and headaches in village women (Dalal, 2014). Of note, however, is that excessive iron can be damaging. Too much supplemental iron in a malnourished child or in people from certain ethnic backgrounds promotes fatal infections, because the excess iron is available for pathogen use. Also, excessive body iron resulting from excessive iron therapy, repeated blood transfusions, or iron overload resulting from a genetic condition called hemochromatosis is problematic (Moalem, Weinberg, & Percy, 2004).

Toxic Threats

Toxic threats to a child's environment during prenatal, neonatal, or postnatal development can have adverse outcomes ranging from severe intellectual impairment or developmental delay to more subtle changes, such as problems with attention, memory, learning, social behavior, and intellectual ability, depending on timing and dose of the toxic threat. Furthermore, infants and children have unique patterns of exposure and special vulnerabilities to pesticides (Landrigan, Kimmel, Correa, & Eskenazi, 2004). Toxic threats include exposures to methylmercury, polychlorinated biphenyls (PCBs), ethanol, lead, arsenic, toluene, manganese, fluoride, chlorpyrifos (a pesticide), tetrachloroethylene (PERC), polybrominated diphenyl ethers (PBDEs), and dichlorodiphenyltrichloroethane (DDT/DDE) (Grandjean & Landrigan, 2014). Additional toxic threats include exposures to aluminum, dioxins, ionizing radiation (i.e., x rays, gamma rays), and environmental tobacco

smoke, as well as maternal use of alcohol, tobacco, marijuana, and cocaine. Other exposures suspected of being a threat include maternal consumption of antidepressants and antianxiety drugs and maternal exposure to dental x rays (Percy & Brown, 2011). By learning about different types of toxic threats and their sources, by taking efforts to avoid them, and by promoting hand washing and good dietary habits, parents and caregivers can play an important role in reducing exposures to toxicants present in consumer products. Many places are undertaking initiatives to reduce sources of toxic threats in the environment. (For more information, see Hamblin [2014], Mercola [2008, 2010], and Winneke [2011].)

Maternal Metabolic Effects

Certain metabolic abnormalities in the mother may have harmful effects on the developing fetus. Such effects are called gestational programming (Ross & Desai, 2005). Examples are described in the following subsections.

Maternal Obesity and Diabetes   Being overweight during pregnancy is associated with a greatly increased risk of neural tube defects such as spina bifida and anencephaly (Stothard, Tennant, Bell, & Rankin, 2009). Obesity is becoming a worldwide epidemic. Associated with obesity is the occurrence of type 2 diabetes, a disorder in which the level of blood sugar is excessively high. Some women have diabetes before they become pregnant. Others develop it during pregnancy, a form called gestational diabetes. About 3% of pregnant women have problems with their blood sugar. Presently, it is not clear whether it is obesity or high blood sugar that results in the neural tube defects. Infants born to mothers with diabetes tend to be very large. This poses risks to their health and to the mothers, who may require delivery by caesarean section. Furthermore, infants born to diabetic mothers may have cognitive dysfunction and also develop diabetes themselves. Maternal diabetes diagnosed at 26 weeks of gestation or earlier was recently established as a significant risk factor for ASD (Xiang et al., 2015). It is very important that pregnant women control their blood sugar levels.

Abnormal Thyroid Function   Abnormal thyroid function in a pregnant mother, in the fetus, or in the newborn all have repercussions on neuropsychological development. There are three sets of clinical thyroid disorders that affect fetal development:

those that affect the infant only, those that affect only the maternal thyroid gland, and iodine deficiency that affects maternal and fetal thyroid function. Hypothyroidism (a condition in which the thyroid does not make enough thyroid hormone) in pregnant women is associated with an increased risk of miscarriage, preeclampsia (i.e., high blood pressure sometimes with fluid retention and loss of protein in the urine), abruptio placentae (premature separation of the placenta from the uterus), low birth weight infants, still births, and fetal distress in labor. Children born to mothers with untreated hypothyroidism during pregnancy score lower on IQ tests than children of healthy mothers. Thus, it is important for pregnant mothers with hypothyroidism to be adequately treated during their pregnancies. Congenital hypothyroidism of the fetus affects approximately 1 in 4,000 newborn infants, resulting in permanent developmental delay and growth defects (see Chapter 21). In the United States, Canada, and other developed countries, newborns are screened for hypothyroidism and are given early thyroid replacement therapy, when necessary, to prevent severe intellectual and developmental disabilities. Causes of this congenital hypothyroidism can be genetic or environmental (e.g., caused by iodine deficiency). (For more information, see Gruters & Krude, 2012, & LaFranchi, 2016.)

Maternal Stress

Prospective studies have revealed that a mother's depression, anxiety, or emotional stress while pregnant increases the risk for her child having adverse outcomes that include emotional problems, symptoms of ADHD, ASD, or impaired cognitive development. Based upon information from animal models, the mechanisms underlying these changes are being explored (Glover, 2015).

Infections

Infections with various microorganisms and viruses are known to be causal or contributing factors for intellectual and developmental disabilities. This subsection provides some detail about such risk factors, including human immunodeficiency virus (HIV) and Zika virus.

Intrauterine and Perinatal Infections   The acronym TORCH stands for toxoplasmosis, other (syphilis, varicella-zoster, parvovirus B19), rubella, cytomegalovirus, and herpesvirus infections. These infections used to cause a large percentage of intellectual impairments and developmental disorders in children (Stegman & Carey, 2002). However, with the availability of improved vaccines, prevention methods, and early identification, these infections in many instances can now be prevented or treated early enough to prevent damage to the central nervous system of the fetus. The application of antibiotics to cut umbilical cords prevents much newborn infection. However, there has been an unfortunate resurgence of some vaccine–preventable diseases in North America because some families deliberately refuse vaccination. New challenges also include pediatric HIV, and perinatal bacterial infections with Group B *streptococcus* and *Listeria monocytogenes*. There is also concern that unidentified multiple organisms causing bacterial vaginal infections may be causing intellectual and developmental disabilities in some children (Smith, 2014).

Human Immunodeficiency Virus Infection
Infection with HIV occurs by the transfer of blood, semen, vaginal fluid, pre-ejaculate fluid, or breast milk. It is spread mostly through unprotected sexual contact. Mother-to-child transmission of HIV occurs when an HIV-positive mother passes the virus to her child during pregnancy, labor, delivery, or breastfeeding. New HIV infections among children have declined by 50% worldwide since 2010 (UNAIDS, 2016). This has resulted because of effective voluntary testing and counseling services, access to antiretroviral therapy, safer delivery practices, and the widespread availability and safer use of breast milk substitutes, especially in the developed world. However, there are unique challenges in the developing world—HIV infection is rampant, especially among teenagers, and many people are not aware that they are infected. Also, there are many barriers that need to be overcome with respect to HIV prevention and treatment. One is the very high cost of antiretroviral drugs; a second is lack of health infrastructure to effectively provide essential public health services (Maartens, Celum, & Lewin, 2014).

Zika Virus   In April, 2016, the CDC declared prenatal infection with Zika virus, carried by a particular type of mosquito, to be a teratogen causing microcephaly as well as other serious neurological diseases (Rasmussen, Jamieson, Honein, & Petersen, 2016; see also Chapter 9). First identified in Brazil early in 2015, the virus has spread rapidly throughout the Americas. Efforts are being mounted to find ways of preventing adverse outcomes especially from virus infection during pregnancy.

Rh Disease in the Newborn

Rh factor is an inherited protein found on the surface of red blood cells. Most people have this protein (i.e., they are Rh positive), but some do not (i.e., they are Rh negative). Rh-negative pregnant women who carry an Rh-positive infant sometimes become sensitized to Rh protein and make antibodies to the Rh protein that destroy fetal red blood cells. Rh disease was once a leading cause of fetal and newborn death as well as of intellectual disability. Fortunately, Rh disease can be prevented by giving mothers a purified blood product called Rh immune globulin (RhIG) to prevent sensitization. These shots are given to the mother at 28 weeks of pregnancy and again within 72 hours of giving birth if a blood test shows that her infant is Rh positive (March of Dimes Foundation, 2016).

Preterm Delivery and Low Birth Weight

Preterm delivery (birth occurring before 36 weeks of gestation) is associated with increased risk for intellectual impairment or developmental delay. The more premature or underweight the newborn, the greater the risks of illness (e.g., infection, respiratory distress), impairments such as cerebral palsy and learning problems, hearing and vision problems, and death. Factors that predispose to prematurity are multiple births, regardless of the cause, placental failure, and excess amniotic fluid. Preterm delivery is known to place the immature brain at risk of hemorrhage, which can result in tissue damage. Low birth weight is also associated with increased risk for intellectual impairment or developmental delay, even if an infant is full term. The frequency of preterm and low birth weight infants is increasing in North America. This increased frequency may, in part, be related to the use of in vitro fertilization and/or to women having children at a later age than in previous decades (Jarjour, 2015).

Premature Cutting of the Umbilical Cord

For more than 200 years, there has been an awareness that the umbilical cord should be cut after the infant has drawn its first breath and after the cord stops pulsating. However, since 1980, cords are often clamped as soon as possible after birth or following delivery of the fetal head in order to obtain cord blood samples for diagnosis of asphyxia. There is increasing support for delayed cord clamping because it increases the baby's hemoglobin levels and iron stores, thereby countering anemia, which can result in altered behavioral and neural development. Such consequences are considered beneficial as long as an infant does not have severe, untreated jaundice. Severe, untreated jaundice can result in permanent brain damage called kernicterus. Jaundice in newborns is treated by phototherapy (i.e., exposure to ultraviolet light) (McDonald, Middleton, Dowswell, & Morris, 2013).

Advanced Parental Age

Studies of parental age are providing new information about factors that cause or contribute to intellectual and developmental disabilities and to ASD. Trisomy 21, 13, and 18 are three syndromes associated with intellectual and developmental disabilities that increase in frequency with increasing maternal age as the result of mistakes in cell division that occur during the time of conception. General cognitive impairment also is associated with advanced maternal age (Cohen, 2014). Evidence from multiple sources supports the hypothesis that paternal and maternal advancing age are risk factors for ASD but that different mechanisms are involved. Higher rates of de novo mutations in older fathers may account for the paternal effect, but the mechanism underlying the maternal effect is different (Lee & McGrath, 2015). However, it should be noted that ASD is considered to be a multifactorial and heterogeneous disorder and that factors as esoteric as the gut microbiome may be involved in affected individuals.

Brain Injury

As detailed in Table 13.2, brain injury can result from various factors. Brain injury resulting from head injury is a common cause of intellectual disability and cerebral palsy. Many circumstances can lead to head injury, including falls; child battering; bicycle, scooter, and sports accidents; accidents with guns, and car accidents. Surveillance and intervention activities could prevent many cases of brain injury.

SOCIAL, BEHAVIORAL, AND EDUCATIONAL RISK FACTORS FOR INTELLECTUAL AND DEVELOPMENTAL DISABILITIES

Biomedical factors are important in the etiology of intellectual and developmental disabilities; however, they do not always act alone. Various other factors can interact with such factors or independently of them over the lifetime of individuals and even act across generations (AAIDD, 2010; Emerson, 2010). By understanding intergenerational causes, appropriate supports can be used to prevent and reverse the effects of risk factors. Some examples of social, behavioral, and educational risk factors contributing to intellectual and developmental disabilities are given in Table 13.3.

Table 13.3.   Examples of social, behavioral, and educational risk factors for intellectual and developmental disabilities

Etiological classification	Associated developmental period(s)		
	Prenatal	Perinatal	Postnatal
Social	Adverse family social interactions • Negative or stressful interactions with spouse/partner, children, other family, friends, or caregivers • Social isolation • Low socioeconomic status	Adverse family social interactions (same as for prenatal)	Adverse family social interactions (same as for perinatal)
	Lack of access to health care • No insurance • Lack of a regular health care provider • Travel to health care services is difficult	Lack of access to health care (same as for prenatal)	Lack of access to health care (same as for perinatal)
	Parental neglect • Family poverty	Parental neglect • Family poverty • Leaving a baby unattended	Parental neglect • Family poverty • Leaving a baby unattended • Inadequate stimulation • Institutionalization
Behavioral	Behaviors that adversely affect functioning • Parental alcohol and drug abuse • Parental smoking • Parental immaturity	Behaviors that adversely affect functioning • Parental rejection of caregiving • Parental abandonment of child • Child abuse and neglect • Domestic violence • Inadequate safety measures • Social deprivation • Difficult child behaviors • Institutionalization	Behaviors that adversely affect functioning (same as for perinatal)
Educational	Lack of access to educational experiences • No or poor information about good prenatal care	Lack of access to educational experiences • No or poor information about good neonatal care and parenting • No information about family support services	Lack of access to educational experiences • No information about good postnatal care and parenting • No information about family support services • No information about educational supports • No knowledge of developmental milestones

Sources: American Association on Intellectual and Developmental Disabilities (2010) and Kaderavek (2014).

The following examples illustrate how socio-logical, behavioral, and educational factors are involved in intellectual and developmental disabilities. We have discussed how certain prenatal and genetic risk factors can result in the emergence of intellectual and developmental disabilities. Of importance, research has shown that the developmental trajectories of children with an early diagnosis of intellectual and developmental disabilities can be altered by a favorable early environment (e.g., positive interactions with their mothers) and that such interactions can promote resilience (i.e., ability to cope with stress and adversity) (Fenning & Baker, 2012).

It is known that parents do much more than ensure that their offspring are adequately nourished and sheltered. Deprivation and neglect from living in an orphanage can result in odd behaviors, delayed language, and various other challenges, including intellectual and developmental disabilities. However, children who are placed into foster care or adopted by about age 2 are more likely to grow up with "typical brains" than those who are not (Marshall, 2015; Powell, 2010; Sheridan, Drury, McLaughlin, & Almas, 2010).

ASD is a neurodevelopmental disorder characterized by impaired social interaction, impaired verbal and nonverbal communication, and restricted and repetitive behavior that may or may not be associated with intellectual disability. There is evidence that early intensive behavior intervention is beneficial for some young children with ASD and has positive effects on the clinical manifestations compared to other interventions available in the community (Reichow, Bartin, Boyd, & Hume, 2014).

Advanced maternal age and chromosomal nondisjunction are known risk factors for having a child with Down syndrome. Meiosis I is responsible for approximately 77% and meiosis II for 23% of maternal nondisjunction, but why this happens is not clear. Hunter et al. (2013) found that low socioeconomic status is significantly associated with chromosome 21 nondisjunction occurring during meiosis II in mothers of children with Down syndrome, independently of their age. Further studies are needed to explore which aspects of low maternal socioeconomic status, such as environmental exposures or poor nutrition, may account for these results.

CO-OCCURRENCE OF SENSORY IMPAIRMENTS, CHALLENGING BEHAVIORS, AND MENTAL HEALTH DISORDERS IN PEOPLE WITH INTELLECTUAL AND DEVELOPMENTAL DISABILITIES

Sensory impairments (impairments in vision or hearing), challenging behaviors, and mental health disorders are unusually common in people with intellectual and developmental disabilities. Because sensory impairments are underrecognized among people with intellectual and developmental disabilities, changes in behavior or challenging behaviors are often attributed to the intellectual impairment or to mental health disorders rather than to sensory impairment and resulting communication difficulties. Sensory impairments and challenging behaviors exacerbate one another. Because sensory impairments limit sensory stimulation, learning opportunities, and social interaction, they can result in underdevelopment of learning and brain activity. In turn, this can lead to more challenging behavior. To provide the best quality of life, it is imperative that hearing and vision be evaluated at as early an age as possible and at regular intervals throughout life and that appropriate supports are provided.

Co-occurring Sensory Impairments and Intellectual and Developmental Disabilities

The prevalence of sensory impairments (visual and hearing) is much greater in adults with intellectual and developmental disabilities than in the general population. The prevalence of hearing loss is approximately 1 in 1,000 in the general population and is about 40 times higher in people with intellectual and developmental disabilities. The prevalence of visual impairment is approximately 0.5%–2% in the general population and at least 8.5 times higher in people with intellectual and developmental disabilities. Comorbidity (i.e., the presence of both) of hearing and vision impairment also is more common in people with intellectual and developmental disabilities. The frequency of sensory impairments increases with severity of intellectual impairment and increasing age (Kiani & Miller, 2010).

Vision loss in people with intellectual and developmental disabilities may be congenital, arise

Table 13.4. Factors resulting in vision loss in people with intellectual and developmental disabilities

Time of onset	Factor
Congenital (genetic in nature)	Down syndrome (predisposes to early age cataracts and later onset vision problems)
	Inborn errors of metabolism (e.g., mucopolysaccharidoses)
	Other specific syndromes (e.g., Leber congenital amaurosis, Batten disease, Bardet-Biedel syndrome)
Pregnancy or at birth (acquired)	Intrauterine infection (e.g., rubella, cytomegalovirus, syphilis, toxoplasmosis, herpes)
	Fetal alcohol spectrum disorder (associated with anatomical abnormalities of the eye and various vision problems)
	Asphyxia
	Prematurity (e.g., resulting in cerebral hemorrhage, resulting in the need for artificial respiration)
Later onset ophthalmological problems (acquired)	Self-injurious behavior, directed at or near the eyes
	Advanced age
Later onset cerebral conditions (acquired)	Meningitis
	Significant head trauma
	Brain tumor
	Asphyxia by near drowning or near sudden infant death

From the Rehabilitation Research and Training Center on Developmental Disabilities and Health (RRTCDD). (2015b). *Visual Impairment.* Retrieved from http://www.rrtcadd.org/resources/Resources/Topics-of-Interest/Health-Promotion/visual-imp.PDF, p. V7; adapted by permission. For additional resources, please visit the Rehabilitation Research and Training Center on Developmental Disabilities and Health (www.RRTCDD.org).

during pregnancy or birth, or stem from later onset ophthalmological problems or cerebral conditions (Table 13.4). Similarly, hearing loss may be congenital, arise during pregnancy or birth, or be of later onset (Rehabilitation Research and Training Center on Developmental Disabilities and Health, 2015a).

At least 50% of cases of congenital hearing loss are caused by genetic disorders, which are primarily a result of inheriting recessive genes (Kiani & Miller, 2010). Congenital hearing loss is associated with procreation within a close family network, poverty, and inadequate access to health care and immunization in the general population. Cytomegalovirus infection plays a major role in acquired hearing loss (Deltenre & Van Maldergem, 2013). In Down syndrome, structural anomalies of sensory organs are common (e.g., narrow ear canals, keratoconus—a degenerative disorder of the eye in which structural changes within the cornea cause it to thin and change to a more conical shape than the more normal gradual curve), and sensory impairments may occur several decades earlier than in the general population (Kiani & Miller, 2010; see also Chapters 14 and 49). Certain syndromes or conditions are associated with intellectual and developmental disabilities and combined hearing and vision loss. These include prematurity, congenital rubella syndrome, meningoencephalitis, and Usher syndrome, among others. (For information about Usher syndrome, see Mathur & Yang, 2015.) Many individuals with congenital deafblindness have some degree of intellectual impairment.

Co-occurring Challenging Behaviors, Mental Health Disorders, and Intellectual and Developmental Disabilities

The prevalence of challenging behaviors, including mental health disorders, is three to four times more common in people with intellectual and developmental disabilities than in the general population. People with ASD, severe disabilities, and sensory impairments and communication disorders are more likely to demonstrate these behaviors. Moreover, as mentioned earlier, quite a number of genetic disorders are associated with behaviors resembling those seen in individuals with ASD. People with intellectual and developmental disabilities also are at increased risk of having comorbid mental health disorders, including ADHD, schizophrenia, depression, and bipolar disorder. As already noted, sensory impairments can exacerbate challenging behaviors and mental health disorders. Because challenging behaviors often serve as a form of communication, efforts should be made to identify the cause of these and implement supports to subdue them (see Chapter 23). Ideally, a sensory impairment team, care pathway, and clinical network should be developed within every disability support service to work across the professional and organizational boundaries and in close collaboration with audiology and ophthalmology services (Kiani & Miller, 2010).

INTELLECTUAL AND DEVELOPMENTAL DISABILITIES AND PREVENTION

Since the mid-1980s, advances in research and public education endeavors have reduced the incidence of intellectual and developmental disabilities (The Arc, n.d.). In particular, newborn screening programs have prevented the development of intellectual impairment and developmental disorder from PKU, congenital hypothyroidism, and other causes by early and appropriate therapy. Rh disease resulting in severe jaundice in the newborn has been prevented by the use of anti-RhIG in the mother. Immunization programs can reduce intellectual impairment or developmental delay resulting from infectious causes. For example, vaccination programs in young children have prevented many cases of *Haemophilus influenzae* type b, measles, encephalitis, and rubella (German measles). Other interventions also reduce occurrences of intellectual impairment or developmental disorders (Percy & Brown, 2011); examples follow.

- Having access to early comprehensive prenatal care and preventive measures prior to and during pregnancy increases a woman's chances of not having a child with intellectual impairment or developmental disorders.

- Counseling women with PKU to use a restricted phenylalanine diet for 3 months prior to pregnancy and during pregnancy prevents intellectual impairment or developmental disorders in their infants.

- Removal of lead from the environment reduces the chances of brain damage in children.

- Safe storage of toxins prevents accidental exposures.

- Use of child safety seats, bicycle helmets, and sports helmets reduces occurrences of head trauma in children.

- Installation of pool fencing prevents asphyxia from near drowning.

- Measures to avoid drunk driving help prevent accidents that result in brain injury and intellectual impairment.

- Enrolling high-risk infants and toddlers into early intervention programs has positive effects on intellectual functioning.

- Identifying children's special educational needs and providing appropriate supports and services helps enable them to develop to their full potential.

For more information, see chapters for specific disorders (e.g., Chapters 14–20) as well as ones with broader perspectives (e.g., Chapters 21, 33, and 34).

SUMMARY

Since 2000, tremendous technical advances have been made with respect to the ability and feasibility of detecting abnormalities in DNA of individuals. In particular, complete sequencing of genomic DNA is becoming economically as well as practically feasible. This latter technique is leading to new information about the involvement of genetic mutations in intellectual and developmental disabilities and ASD and to new strategies for obtaining a genetic diagnosis (Ellison, Rosenfeld, & Shaffer, 2013). New approaches are being developed to determine whether new mutations are pathologically associated with particular disorders (Xiong et al., 2015). The recognition that life experiences and different bacteria in the gut (i.e., the microbiome), via epigenetic mechanisms, can modify brain function as well as infant development in positive and negative ways has created awareness of the probable complexity of the mechanisms that cause variation in intellectual and developmental disability phenotypes (see Chapters 11 and 23). The potential involvement of vitamin D deficiency in intellectual and developmental disabilities and associated mental disorders warrants particular attention. Also, insights about what aspects of cognitive function and behavior are genetic and what are not also are coming from comparison studies of "identical" twins (who were once thought to be exact genetic photocopies of one another but are not) and of fraternal twins (whose genes are different but upbringings are very similar). Because epigenetic processes are potentially reversible and theoretically amenable to manipulation, there is optimism that changes in lifestyle and environment (including physical exercise, social activity, and exercises to develop brain function), and also new forms of pharmacological intervention directed at modification of epigenetic processes, may be fruitful avenues for intervention in intellectual and developmental disorders and certain disorders of mental health. Finally, much can be learned about risk factors for intellectual and developmental disabilities from detailed longitudinal studies of individuals in families including the prenatal, neonatal, and postnatal stages of development as well as the transition to adulthood and aging.

FOR FURTHER THOUGHT AND DISCUSSION

1. What can be done to target and educate prospective mothers about the dangers of folic acid and vitamin B_{12} deficiencies, drinking, smoking, preterm birth, low birth weight infants, as well as other preventable causes of developmental disabilities?

2. What actions might be taken to curb brain injury due to drunk driving, accidental falls, and child battering?

3. What actions might policy makers take to ensure that health professionals are appropriately paid for providing services to people with intellectual and developmental disabilities?

4. What strategies should be undertaken to create awareness of toxic threats to the health of infants and children?

REFERENCES

American Association on Intellectual and Developmental Disabilities. (2010). *Intellectual disability: Definition, classification, and systems of supports* (11th ed.). Washington, DC: Author.

American Psychiatric Association. (2000). *Diagnostic and statistical manual of mental disorders* (4th ed., text rev.). Washington, DC: Author.

American Psychiatric Association. (2013). *Diagnostic and statistical manual of mental disorders* (5th ed.). Washington, DC: Author.

The Arc. (n.d.). *Causes and prevention of intellectual disabilities*. Retrieved from http://www.thearc.org/page.aspx?pid=2453

Bailey, R.L., West, K.P., Jr., & Black, R.E. (2015). The epidemiology of global micronutrient deficiencies. *Annals of Nutrition and Metabolism, 66*(Suppl. 2), 22–33.

Boyle, C.A., Boulet, S., Schieve, L.A., Cohen, R.A., Blumberg, S.J., Yeargin-Allsopp, M.,...Kogan, M.D. (2011). Trends in the prevalence of developmental disabilities in US children, 1997–2008. *Pediatrics, 127*(6), 1034–1042.

Brent, R.L. (2004). Environmental causes of human congenital malformations: The pediatrician's role in dealing with these complex clinical problems caused by a multiplicity of environmental and genetic factors. *Pediatrics, 113*(Suppl. 4), 957–968.

Centers for Disease Control and Prevention (CDC). (2015). *Preterm birth*. Retrieved from http://www.cdc.gov/reproductivehealth/maternalinfanthealth/pretermbirth.htm

Cohen, P.N. (2014, April 4). Parental age and cognitive disability among children in the United States. *Sociological Science*. Retrieved from https://www.sociologicalscience.com/parental-age-cognitive-disability/

da Silva, E.M., Strufaldi, M.W., Andriolo, R.B., & Silva, L.A. (2016). Enzyme replacement therapy with idursulfase for mucopolysaccharidosis type II (Hunter syndrome). *Cochrane Database of Systematic Reviews, Feb 5*(2), CD008185. doi:10.1002/14651858.CD008185.pub4

Dalal, M. (2014, May 29). *Lucky iron fish in cooking pots tackle anemia*. Retrieved from http://www.cbc.ca/news/health/lucky-iron-fish-in-cooking-pots-tackle-anemia-1.2658632

Deltenre, P., & Van Maldergem, L. (2013). Hearing loss and deafness in the pediatric population: Causes, diagnosis, and rehabilitation. *Handbook of Clinical Neurology, 113*, 1527–1538.

Dobbing, J. (1981). The later development of the brain and its vulnerability. *Journal of Inherited Metabolic Disease, 5*(2), 88.

Dursun, S. (2010). Vitamin D for mental health and cognition. *Canadian Medical Association Journal, 182*(17), 1886. doi: 10.1503/cmaj.110-2125

Ellison, J.W., Rosenfeld, J.A., & Shaffer, L.G. (2013). Genetic basis of intellectual disability. *Annual Review of Medicine, 64*, 441–450.

Emerson, E. (2010). Socio-economic position. In J.H. Stone & M. Blouin (Eds.), *International encyclopedia of rehabilitation*. Retrieved from http://cirrie.buffalo.edu/encyclopedia/en/article/313/

Fenning, R.M., & Baker, J.K. (2012). Mother–child interaction and resilience in children with early developmental risk. *Journal of Family Psychology, 26*(3), 411–420.

Fernell, E., Bejerot, S., Westerlund, J., Miniscalco, C., Simila, H., Eyles, D.,...Humble, M.B. (2015). Autism spectrum disorder and low vitamin D at birth: A sibling control study. *Molecular Autism, 6*, 3. Retrieved from http://www.ncbi.nlm.nih.gov/pmc/articles/PMC4396835

Fetahu, I.S., Höbaus, J., & Kállay, E. (2014).Vitamin D and the epigenome. *Frontiers in Physiology, 29*(5), 164.

Frighi, V., Morovat, A., Stephenson, M.T., White, S.J., Hammond, C.V., & Goodwin, G.M. (2014). Vitamin D deficiency in patients with intellectual disabilities: Prevalence, risk factors and management strategies. *British Journal of Psychiatry, 205*(6), 458–464.

Gamsiz, E.D., Sciarra, L.N., Maguire, A.M., Pescosolido, M.F., van Dyck, L.I., & Morrow, E.M. (2015). Discovery of rare mutations in autism: Elucidating neurodevelopmental mechanisms. *Neurotherapeutics, 12*(3), 553–571.

Glover, V. (2015). Prenatal stress and its effects on the fetus and the child: Possible underlying biological mechanisms. *Advances in Neurobiology, 10*, 269–283.

Grandjean, P., & Landrigan, P.J. (2014). Neurobehavioural effects of developmental toxicity. *Lancet Neurology, 13*(3), 330–338.

Groves, N.J., McGrath, J.J., & Burne, T.H. (2014). Vitamin D as a neurosteroid affecting the developing and adult brain. *Annual Review of Nutrition, 34*, 117–141.

Gruters, A., & Krude, H. (2012, February). Detection and treatment of congenital hypothyroidism. *Nature Reviews Endocrinology, 8*(2), 104–113.

Guze, C. (2005). *Teratogens*. Retrieved July 15, 2005, from http://www.carolguze.com/text/442-13-teratogens.shtml

Hamblin, J. (2014, March 18). The toxins that threaten our brains. *The Atlantic*. Retrieved from http://www.theatlantic.com/features/archive/2014/03/the-toxins-that-threaten-our-brains/284466/

Hamdan, F.F., Srour, M., Capo-Chichi, J.M., Daoud, H., Nassif, C., Patry. L.,…Michaud, J.L. (2014). De novo mutations in moderate or severe intellectual disability. *PLOS Genetics, 10*(10), e1004772. doi:10.1371/journal.pgen.1004772

Hart, P.H., Lucas, R.M., Walsh, J.P., Zosky, G.R., Whitehouse, A.J., Zhu, K.,…Mountain, J.A. (2015). Vitamin D in fetal development: Findings from a birth cohort study. *Pediatrics, 135*(1), e167–173. doi:10.1542/peds.2014-1860

Hunter, J.E., Allen, E.G., Shin, M., Bean, L.J., Correa, A., Druschel, C.,…Sherman, S.L. (2013). The association of low socioeconomic status and the risk of having a child with Down syndrome: A report from the National Down Syndrome Project. *Genetics in Medicine, 15*(9), 698–705.

Jarjour, I.T. (2015). Neurodevelopmental outcome after extreme prematurity: A review of the literature. *Pediatric Neurology, 52*(2), 143–152.

Kaderavek, J.N. (2014). Children with intellectual disability. In J.N. Kaderavek, *Language disorders in children* (2nd ed., pp. 82–92). New York, NY: Pearson Education.

Kaminsky, E.B., Kaul, V., Paschall, J., Church, D.M., Bunke, B., Kunig, D.,…Martin, C.L. (2011). An evidence-based approach to establish the functional and clinical significance of copy number variants in intellectual and developmental disabilities. *Genetics in Medicine, 13*(9), 777–784.

Karam, S.M., Riegel, M., Segal, S.L., Félix, T.M., Barros, A.J., Santos, I.S.,…Black, M. (2015). Genetic causes of intellectual disability in a birth cohort: A population-based study. *American Journal of Medical Genetics Series A, 167*(6), 1204–1214.

Kaufman, L., Ayub, M., & Vincent, J.B. (2010). The genetic basis of non-syndromic intellectual disability: A review. *Journal of Neurodevelopmental Disorders, 2*(4), 182–209.

Kiani, R., & Miller, H. (2010). *Sensory impairment and intellectual disability. Advances in Psychiatric Treatment, 16*(3), 228–235.

LaFranchi, S. (2016). *Clinical features and detection of congenital hypothyroidism*. Retrieved from http://www.uptodate.com/contents/clinical-features-and-detection-of-congenital-hypothyroidism

Lai, M. C., Lombardo, M.V., Auyeung, B., Chakrabarti, B., & Baron-Cohen, S. (2015). Sex/gender differences and autism: Setting the scene for future research. *Journal of the American Academy of Child and Adolescent Psychiatry, 54*(1), 11–24.

Landrigan, P.J., Kimmel, C.A., Correa, A., & Eskenazi, B. (2004). Children's health and the environment: Public health issues and challenges for risk assessment. *Environmental Health Perspectives, 112*, 257–265.

Laslo, D. (1999, April 23). *Embryonic neurodevelopment, neural tube defects, and folic acid*. Presentation in Neuroscience of Developmental Disabilities: PSL1062S [Seminar], Department of Physiology, University of Toronto, Canada.

Laufer, B.I., Kapalanga, J., Castellani, C.A., Diehl, E.J., Yan, L., & Singh, S.M. (2015). Associative DNA methylation changes in children with prenatal alcohol exposure. *Epigenomics, 7*(8), 1259–1274.

Lee, B.K., & McGrath, J.J. (2015). Advancing parental age and autism: Multifactorial pathways. *Trends in Molecular Medicine, 21*(2), 118–125.

Maartens, G., Celum, C., & Lewin, S.R. (2014). HIV infection: Epidemiology, pathogenesis, treatment, and prevention. *Lancet, 384*(9939), 258–271.

March of Dimes Foundation. (2016). *Rh disease*. Retrieved from http://www.marchofdimes.org/complications/rh-disease.aspx

Marshall, E. (2015, January 26). *Childhood neglect erodes the brain*. Retrieved from http://news.sciencemag.org/brain-behavior/2015/01/childhood-neglect-erodes-brain

Mathur, P., & Yang, J. (2015). Usher syndrome: Hearing loss, retinal degeneration and associated abnormalities. *Biochimica et Biophysica Acta, 1852*(3), 406–420.

McDonald, S.J., Middleton, P., Dowswell, T., & Morris, P.S. (2013, July 11). Effect of timing of umbilical cord clamping of term infants on mother and baby outcomes. *Cochrane Database System Review, 7*, CD0040747. Retrieved from http://www.cochrane.org/CD004074/PREG_effect-of-timing-of-umbilical-cord-clamping-of-term-infants-on-mother-and-baby-outcomes

McLaren, J., & Bryson, S.E. (1987). Review of recent epidemiological studies of mental retardation: Prevalence, associated disorders, and etiology. *American Journal of Mental Retardation, 92*(3), 243–254.

Mercola, J. (2008, December 23). *How to avoid the top ten most common toxins*. Retrieved from http://articles.mercola.com/sites/articles/archive/2005/02/19/common-toxins.aspx

Mercola, J. (2010, April 13). *BPA toxins puts newborns, mothers at risk*. Retrieved from http://www.huffingtonpost.com/dr-mercola/bpa-toxins-puts-newborns_b_457590.html

Miller, C., & Sweatt, J.D. (2007). Covalent modification of DNA regulates memory formation. *Neuron, 53*(6), 857–869.

Moalem, S., Weinberg, E.D., & Percy, M.E, (2004). Hemochromatosis and the enigma of misplaced iron: Implications for infectious disease and survival. *Biometals, 17*(2), 135–139.

Mount Sinai Hospital. (2013). *Ethnicity-based conditions*. Retrieved from http://www.mountsinai.on.ca/care/pdmg/genetics/ethnicity-based-conditions

National Institutes of Health, Office of Dietary Supplements. (n.d.). *Nutrient recommendations: Dietary reference intakes (DRI)*. Retrieved from https://ods.od.nih.gov /Health_Information/Dietary_Reference_Intakes.aspx

Nussbaum, R.L., McInnes, R.R., & Willard, H.F. (2015). *Thompson & Thompson genetics in medicine* (8th ed.). Philadelphia, PA: Elsevier.

Percy, M. (2007). Factors that cause or contribute to developmental disabilities. In I. Brown & M. Percy (Eds.), *A comprehensive guide to intellectual and developmental disabilities* (pp. 125–148). Baltimore, MD: Paul H. Brookes Publishing Co.

Percy, M., & Brown, I. (2011). Factors that cause or contribute to intellectual and developmental disabilities. In I. Brown & M. Percy (Eds.), *Developmental disabilities in Ontario* (3rd ed., pp. 207–226). Toronto, Canada: Ontario Association on Developmental Disabilities.

Powell, A. (2010, October 10). Breathtakingly awful. *Harvard Gazette*. Retrieved from http://news.harvard .edu/gazette/story/2010/10/breathtakingly-awful/

Rasmussen, S.A., Jamieson, D.J., Honein, M.A., & Petersen, L.R. (2016). Zika virus and birth defects: Reviewing the evidence for causality. *The New England Journal of Medicine, 374*, 1981–1987. doi: 10.1056/NEJMsr1604338

Rauch, A., Wieczorek, D., Graf, E., Wieland, T., Endele, S., Schwarzmayr, T.,...Strom, T. M. (2012). Range of genetic mutations associated with severe non-syndromic sporadic intellectual disability: An exome sequencing study. *Lancet, 380*(9854), 1674–1682.

Rehabilitation Research and Training Center on Developmental Disabilities and Health. (2015a). *Guidelines on hearing impairment in ID*. Retrieved from http://www .rrtcadd.org/resources/Resources/Topics-of-Interest /Health-Promotion/hearing-imp.PDF

Rehabilitation Research and Training Center on Developmental Disabilities and Health. (2015b). *Guidelines on vision impairment in ID*. Retrieved from http://www .rrtcadd.org/resources/Resources/Topics-of-Interest /Health-Promotion/visual-imp.PDF

Reichow, B., Bartin, E.E., Boyd, B.A., & Hume, K. (2014, November 3). Early intensive behavioral intervention (EIBI) for young children with autism spectrum disorders (ASD): A systematic review [Monograph]. *Campbell Systematic Reviews, Issue 9*. Retrieved from http://www.campbellcollaboration.org /lib/?go=monograph&year=2014

Rice, D., & Barone, S., Jr. (2000). Critical periods of vulnerability for the developing nervous system: Evidence from humans and animal models. *Environmental Health Perspectives, 108*(Suppl. 3), 511–533.

Ross, M.G., & Desai, M. (2005). Gestational programming: Population survival effects of drought and famine during pregnancy. *American Journal of Physiology. Regulatory, Integrative and Comparative Physiology, 288*, R25–R33.

Rzhetsky, A., Bagley, S.C., Wang, K., Lyttle, C.S., Cook, E.H., Jr., Altman, R.B., & Gibbons, R.D. (2014). Environmental and state-level regulatory factors affect the incidence of autism and intellectual disability. *PLOS Computational Biology, 10*(3), e1003518. doi:10.1371/journal.pcbi.1003518

Scheinfeld, N.S. (2015). *Protein-energy malnutrition*. Retrieved from http://emedicine.medscape.com/article /1104623-overview

Selhub, J., & Rosenberg, I.H. (2016). Excessive folic acid intake and relation to adverse health outcome. *Biochimie, 126*, 71–78.

Sheridan, M., Drury, S., McLaughlin, K., & Almas, A. (2010). Early institutionalization: Neurobiological consequences and genetic modifiers. *Neuropsychology Review, 20*(4), 414–429.

Smith, D.C. (2014). *Bacterial infections and pregnancy*. Retrieved from http://emedicine.medscape.com/article /235054-overview#a3

Srour, M., & Shevell, M. (2014). Genetics and the investigation of developmental delay/intellectual disability. *Archives of Disease in Childhood, 99*(4), 386–389.

Stagnaro-Green, A., Dogo-Isonagie, E., Pearce, E.N., Spencer, C.A., & Gaba, N. (2015). Marginal iodine status and high rate of subclinical hypothyroidism in Washington DC in women planning conception. *Thyroid, 25*(10), 1151–1154.

Stegman, B.J., & Carey, J.C. (2002). TORCH Infections. Toxoplasmosis, other (syphilis, varicella-zoster, parvovirus B19), rubella, cytomegalovirus (CMV), and herpes infections. *Current Women's Health Reports, 2*, 253–258.

Stothard, K.J., Tennant, P.W., Bell, R., & Rankin, J. (2009). Maternal overweight and obesity and the risk of congenital anomalies: A systematic review and meta-analysis. *JAMA: The Journal of the American Medical Association, 301*(6), 636–650.

Susser, M.W. (2002). *Causality, causes, and causal inference*. Retrieved from http://www.encyclopedia.com

Thompson, M.D., Cole, D.E., & Ray, J.G. (2009). Vitamin B-12 and neural tube defects: The Canadian experience. *American Journal of Clinical Nutrition, 89*(2), 697S–701S.

UNAIDS. (2016). *Fact sheet 2016*. Retrieved from http:// www.unaids.org/en/resources/fact-sheet

UNICEF. (2010). *Nutrition*. Retrieved from http://www .unicef.org/nutrition/

van Karnebeek, C.D. (2014). [Inborn errors of metabolism are not hopeless; early identification of treatable conditions in children with intellectual disability]. *Nederlands Tijdschrift voor Geneeskunde, 158*, A8042.

Vitti, P. (2014). *Iodine deficiency disorders*. Retrieved from http://www.uptodate.com/contents/iodine-deficiency -disorders

Winneke, G. (2011). Developmental aspects of environmental neurotoxicology: Lessons from lead and polychlorinated biphenyls. *Journal of the Neurological Sciences, 308*(1–2), 9–15.

World Health Organization. (2015). *Micronutrient deficiencies*. Retrieved from http://www.who.int/nutrition /topics/ida/en/

Xiang, A.H., Wang, X., Martinez, M.P., Walthall, J.C., Curry, E.S., Page, K.,...Getahunm, D. (2015). Association of maternal diabetes with autism in offspring. *JAMA: The Journal of the American Medical Association, 313*(14), 1425–1434.

Xiong, H.Y., Alipanahi, B., Lee, L.J., Bretschneider, H., Merico, D., Yuen, R.K.,...Frey, B.J. (2015). RNA splicing. The human splicing code reveals new insights into the genetic determinants of disease. *Science, 347*(6218), 1254806. doi:10.1126/science.1254806.

14

Down Syndrome

Anna J. Esbensen and William E. MacLean, Jr.

WHAT YOU WILL LEARN

- Initial identification of Down syndrome
- Causes of Down syndrome
- How Down syndrome affects brain function, cognition, temperament, motor skills, and language
- Common health and mental health concerns
- Implications for educational practices
- Experiences of families

The aim of this chapter is to provide an introduction to Down syndrome, the most common developmental disability with a chromosomal basis.

HISTORY

Down syndrome was originally termed "mongolism" by John Langdon Down in 1866. While serving as the medical superintendent of the first "idiot" asylum in England, Down observed a group of residents with facial features that were so similar that they seemed to be from the same family (Wright, 2011). The facial features that most intrigued Down were the oblique angle of these individuals' eyes, epicanthic skin folds on the inner corner of their eyes, flat mid-face, and the fact that their tongue appeared larger than typical. This cluster of features was instantly recognizable—even at birth. Subsequent accounts of mongolism added small stature, an incurved fifth finger, single palmar crease, and Brushfield spots as associated physical characteristics (Wright, 2011). Behaviorally, the primary defining characteristic of mongolism was "mental deficiency"—the predominant term in the 19th century for the condition now known as intellectual disability. Although John

Langdon Down is generally credited with providing the first systematic account of the condition that now shares his name, pioneering French psychiatrist Jean-Étienne Esquirol and his student Edouard Sequin actually described children with the same physical features as having "mongolism" in the mid-1800s (Roubertoux & Kerdelhué, 2006).

At the time that John Langdon Down made his historic observations, there was considerable interest in classification of people by racial or ethnic groups. For example, according to one classification system, people were described as Aztecs, Caucasians, Ethiopians, Malayans, and Mongolians. Down was familiar with this classification system and attempted to apply it to all of the residents in his care at Earlswood Asylum. Although erroneous in his assumption that people with Down syndrome had features characteristic of the Mongolian race, the term remained in public and professional use for over a century (Rodríquez-Hernández & Montoya, 2011).

Growing dissatisfaction with the term *mongolism* during the early 1960s led to consideration of several alternatives, including trisomy 21 anomaly, Down's syndrome or anomaly, Langdon-Down anomaly, and congenital acromicria (referring to the small hands and feet of those affected). *Down's syndrome* became the preferred term, recognizing Down's seminal description and perhaps the influence of his grandson Norman Langdon-Down. In the United States and some other countries, the possessive was later dropped and the term became *Down syndrome*. Norman Langdon-Down was a medical superintendent of Normansfield, an asylum that catered to the upper class, which was opened by John Langdon Down in 1868. Norman was part of a legacy at Normansfield that passed from father to sons to grandson over a period of 102 years (Ward, 1999). In an almost unbelievable coincidence, John Langdon Down's other grandson, Jonathan, was born with Down syndrome after his grandfather's death in 1896.

Soon after John Langdon Down's seminal description, numerous case reports of mongolism were published in the medical literature. In the decades that followed, there was considerable speculation about the cause of mongolism. In the context of the eugenics movement in England, speculation included well-known infirmities of that era such as alcohol use by parents, syphilis, and tuberculosis, among others. Hypotheses also emerged in relation to inherited thyroid dysfunction, a common medical condition among people with Down syndrome, and "uterine exhaustion" among mothers of advanced age who gave birth to children with Down syndrome. However, there was speculation that the cause was genetic, given the observed similarity among children affected.

With the discovery in the late 1950s that humans had 23 pairs of chromosomes and with the refinement in visualizing chromosome pairs with karyotyping methods, scientists could examine the number, arrangement, and characteristics of chromosomes. With this technology, it was only a matter of time before the etiology of Down syndrome would be discovered. In 1959, a team of investigators led by Jerome LeJeune, a French geneticist, established the genetic basis of Down syndrome: a third copy of the 21st chromosome (Lejeune, Gautier, & Turpin, 1959). Before karyotyping, diagnoses relied on clinical descriptions largely from Down's observations; karyotyping provided a reliable method for diagnosis and for prenatal diagnosis when amniocentesis became widely available.

ETIOLOGY

Although Lejeune and his colleagues are generally credited with the discovery that a third copy of the 21st chromosome is present in people with Down syndrome, there were other teams of researchers simultaneously pursuing cytogenetic studies to determine a genetic basis for Down syndrome. One group, led by Patricia Jacobs of Edinburgh, Scotland, may have been the first to discover that trisomy 21 was responsible, but the Lejeune et al. (1959) paper was actually published about 2 weeks earlier than the paper authored by Jacobs and her colleagues (Jacobs, Baikie, Court Brown, & Strong, 1959). In a fascinating account of this time period, Gautier and Harper (2009) suggested that it was Lejeune, after hearing of Jacobs' work at a conference at McGill University, who rushed the French findings to publication in a journal with an extremely short publication lag. In some professional circles, the determination of the etiology of Down syndrome is actually regarded as a codiscovery by the two research groups. Furthermore, in recognition of the 50th anniversary of the codiscovery, Gautier asserted that she alone was responsible for producing the scientific evidence of trisomy 21 for the French team but that Lejeune assumed first authorship of the paper to advance his career (Gautier & Harper).

Subsequent research established that chromosomal trisomies occur quite frequently in humans, involving nearly every autosomal chromosome pair. Whereas most trisomy conditions are incompatible with life and are believed to result in spontaneous abortions during pregnancy, others are not. In the case of trisomy 21, or Down syndrome, nondisjunction (i.e., the failure of chromosome pairs to separate during meiosis prior to ovulation) is not a lethal condition. In fact, it is the only autosomal trisomy that allows survival into adulthood. Nondisjunction can be of maternal or paternal origin but among people with Down syndrome the origin is overwhelmingly maternal—more than 90% (Hultén et al., 2010).

Although the majority of people with Down syndrome have trisomy 21, approximately 4% have a condition called translocation in which a portion of an extra chromosome 21 is attached to chromosome 14, 21, or 22. There is no evidence that the translocation subtype differs from trisomy 21 in cognitive or medical dimensions. Finally, for 1%–2% of people with Down syndrome, the nondisjunction occurs after the egg is fertilized and results in trisomy in some, but not all, of the cells. This condition is referred to as mosaic, and those affected typically have less obvious physical features than children with trisomy 21 and typically score 15 points higher on IQ tests than children with trisomy 21 or translocation subtypes.

Down syndrome is the most common chromosomal disorder associated with intellectual disability. With an incidence of 1 in 700 births, there are more than 400,000 people with Down syndrome living in the United States. Advanced maternal age has been associated with an increased likelihood of a child with Down syndrome. Risk increases rapidly from maternal age 30 (1 in 1,000) to age 45 (1 in 50). Although multiple factors may account for nondisjunction, it is commonly believed that aging of the maternal ovum is responsible. Despite assumptions that advances in the ability to make prenatal diagnoses might lead to fewer children with Down syndrome being born, studies show that the prevalence of Down syndrome among children and adolescents in the United States is actually increasing (Shin et al., 2009). Speculation is that the increase is related to a trend toward increased rates of childbearing in older women, who are at greater risk of having children with chromosomal disorders, particularly Down syndrome, and toward more aggressive medical treatment of conditions associated with Down syndrome in early childhood.

NEUROLOGY

The neuroanatomy of the brain of individuals with Down syndrome at birth is very similar to that of the general population. During infancy, neuropathological differences emerge in some individuals. Myelination can be delayed (Wisniewski, 1990), the growth of the frontal lobes slows, the superior temporal gyrus can narrow, the size of the cerebellum and brain stem can be smaller, and fewer cortical granular neurons can be present (as reviewed in Fidler & Nadel, 2007). In both MRI scans of individuals with Down syndrome and in mouse models, consistent anatomical features are present, including reductions in the prefrontal cortex, cerebellum, temporal lobe, and hippocampal formation.

These anatomical differences can have functional implications for the cognition of individuals with Down syndrome. Prefrontal cortex differences can affect episodic and working memory abilities, temporal lobe differences can affect auditory processing, and several studies have demonstrated difficulties in verbal working memory (Fidler, Most, & Philofsky, 2008; Klein & Mervis, 1999). Hippocampal differences can also affect episodic memory (generally verbal).

HEALTH CONCERNS

Down syndrome is characterized by a variety of health conditions that warrant special attention throughout the lifespan. Although these conditions are not unique to Down syndrome, they do occur with considerable frequency among people with Down syndrome as compared with the general population, suggesting heightened risk. For example, among children with Down syndrome, the risk for childhood acute lymphoblastic leukemia is 20 times higher than in the general population. Similarly, children with Down syndrome have a higher risk of congenital heart disease (40%–60%) than the general population (3%). In general, congenital heart disease includes a number of specific conditions that affect the structure or function of the heart and related circulatory system that are present at birth. The most frequent forms of congenital heart disease among people with Down syndrome involve the incomplete development of the upper and lower chambers of the heart, or the valves connecting them, thus compromising circulation and allowing oxygen-rich and oxygen-poor blood to mix. Surgical correction is often necessary to correct these defects and to sustain life.

Children with Down syndrome may also be affected by a variety of gastrointestinal conditions, some of which may be life-threatening. Again, these conditions are not unique to Down syndrome but occur with considerable frequency (12%–25%) in comparison with the general population. The most prevalent conditions are gastrointestinal malformations (affecting 6.7% of children with Down syndrome) that can occur at any point along the gastrointestinal tract but are more frequent in the small intestine, in the lower bowel, and at the junction of the trachea and esophagus (Freeman et al., 2009). In addition to congenital malformations affecting gastrointestinal functioning, people with Down syndrome are susceptible to gastroesophageal reflux disease and food sensitivities, as well as the gluten intolerance associated with celiac disease.

A characteristic looseness of ligaments, tissue that connects bones or cartilage in a joint, is thought to be responsible for a host of orthopedic problems associated with Down syndrome. The most clinically significant of these conditions is atlantoaxial instability—a partial displacement or subluxation of the vertebrae closest to the skull. Occurring in 15% of children with Down syndrome, this condition can result in spinal nerve entrapment that, if not diagnosed and treated, could lead to spinal cord compression and paralysis (Cohen, 2006).

Visual and hearing impairments are common among children and adolescents with Down syndrome and continue into adulthood. Children with

Down syndrome are more likely than are other children to need corrective lenses due to nearsightedness, farsightedness, or astigmatism. A misalignment of the eyes, or strabismus, is also common among people with Down syndrome. There is also an increased risk of cataracts through the lifespan, beginning at birth (congenital) and associated with early aging among adults. Congenital malformations affecting the middle ear and eustachian tubes, common among people with Down syndrome, increase susceptibility to middle ear infections that increase risk for conductive hearing loss. Hearing impairments generally occur earlier among adults with Down syndrome than in the general population. For example, high-frequency sensorineural hearing impairments occur 30–40 years earlier among adults with Down syndrome than when onset is observed in the general population (Buchanan, 1990). Hearing impairments can have a profound impact on the aging adult with Down syndrome, especially in light of the fact that, as found in one study, only 41% of adults with hearing loss were using hearing devices and 80% of care providers were unaware of the hearing loss (Van Buggenhout et al., 1999).

There is a rise in the rate of seizures as individuals with Down syndrome age from adolescence to adulthood (Puri, Ho, & Singh, 2001). The elevated rate of seizures among adults with Down syndrome may be related to their increased risk of dementia and also to a genetic marker for myoclonus epilepsy being located on chromosome 21 (Hattori et al., 2000). However, the rise also parallels the increased risk among typically developing adults.

Individuals with Down syndrome have an elevated rate of thyroid dysfunction and hypothyroidism, and this rate increases with age (Coleman, 1994; Prasher, 1994). Obesity is a concern with 45%–79% of males and 56%–96% of females with Down syndrome reported to be overweight (as reviewed in Esbensen, 2010). Several medical conditions contribute to the increased risk for obesity, including hypothyroidism, metabolic rates, and behavioral patterns (eating and exercise). Obesity and hypothyroidism also put adults with Down syndrome at greater risk of sleep apnea, a condition they are already predisposed to given their facial and physical features. Approximately 30%–55% of children with Down syndrome have obstructive sleep apnea, and the risk is reported to increase into adulthood (as reviewed in Esbensen, 2010).

In the early 20th century, the average life expectancy for an individual with Down syndrome was 9 years of age. As of the beginning of the 21st century, adults with Down syndrome are experiencing an average life expectancy of 60 years of age. Advances in medical technology, services, advocacy, and early detection of associated medical conditions have likely contributed to the lengthening of the lifespan of individuals with Down syndrome (Bittles & Glasson, 2004; Yang, Rasmussen, & Friedman, 2002). With this new population of aging adults with Down syndrome, health professionals have identified several age-related changes in the health of adults with Down syndrome.

Findings in the 1960s suggested that individuals with Down syndrome were at increased risk of Type 1 diabetes, with earlier ages of onset. However, more recent studies report age of onset comparable to the general population and a lower risk for mortality due to Type 1 diabetes than in the general population or among adults with intellectual disability due to other causes (as reviewed in Esbensen, 2010). Rates of Type 2 diabetes are reported to be lower than in the general population (Silverman, 2010).

Although stability in cognitive and functional ability is generally present prior to age 50, the risk of dementia increases dramatically at this age (Hawkins, Eklund, James, Foose, & Krauss, 2003). The prevalence of dementia among adults with Down syndrome younger than 40 is 8.9% and increases to 17.5% among 50- to 54-year-olds and to 32.1% among 55- to 59-year-olds (Coppus et al., 2006). After the age of 60, approximately 50%–60% of adults with Down syndrome exhibit symptoms of dementia (Holland, Hon, Huppert, & Stevens, 2000; Zigman, Schupf, Sersen, & Silverman, 1996). Although most adults with Down syndrome have the physical signs in their brain (plaques and tangles) associated with dementia, not all individuals exhibit the clinical features. Current research is focused on understanding the associated risk factors that lead to the expression of clinical symptoms. This topic is covered more extensively in Chapter 49.

Women with Down syndrome have a 4–6 year earlier onset of menopause than women in the general population. This elevated rate has implications for health risks in heart disease, osteoporosis, breast cancer, and depression (as reviewed in Esbensen, 2010).

Several skin and hair changes are experienced by adults with Down syndrome that give the appearance of accelerated aging, such as premature graying of hair, hair loss, and decreased elasticity of skin. Other skin conditions include atopic and seborrhoeic dermatitis, xerosis, and fungal infections. Hair loss is present in 6%–18% of adults with Down syndrome (Prasher, 1994) and likely related to an immunological deficiency. Some hypotheses are posited to explain this premature aging, such as that enzymes located on chromosome 21 affect the function of tissue and its altered structure or that low levels of DNA repair enzymes found in adults with Down syndrome contribute to an accumulation of unrepaired DNA damage (Madan, Williams, & Lear, 2006; Sinha, 2005).

In contrast, adults with Down syndrome experience lower rates of solid tumors, cardiovascular and cerebrovascular disease, emphysema, fractures, hypercholesterolemia, and coronary heart disease compared with the general population (as reviewed in Esbensen, 2010). Several hypotheses have been put forward to explain these reduced risks, which tend to represent suppressor genes located on chromosome 21, lower blood pressure, and lower resting heart rates (Kerins, Petrovic, Bruder, & Gruman, 2008; Prasher, 1994; Satge et al., 1998).

BEHAVIORAL PHENOTYPE

The behavioral phenotype of individuals with Down syndrome generally describes their cognitive and language development, personality or socioemotional functioning, psychopathology, and motor skills. Individuals with Down syndrome generally fall within the range of intellectual disability and, as a group, demonstrate a pattern of cognitive strengths and limitations. Development is often relatively typical in the first year and gradually slows during the toddler years. During the school-age years, relative cognitive strengths are commonly found in the visual domain and include visual processing (Hodapp et al., 1992), visuospatial short-term memory (Gathercole & Alloway, 2006), visuoconstructive abilities (Klein & Mervis, 1999), processing of visual stimuli (Zoia, Pelamatti, & Rumiati, 2004), and imitation abilities (Kanno & Ikeda, 2002; Zoia et al.). Relative cognitive limitations are commonly found in the verbal domain and include verbal processing tasks (Hodapp & Dykens, 2004). Within the verbal domain, comprehension and vocabulary are generally strengths relative to syntactic abilities (Hodapp & Dykens). Relative to their peers with similar cognitive abilities, individuals with Down syndrome also commonly have difficulties with working memory, short-term verbal memory, and long-term memory (as reviewed in Fidler et al., 2008).

Descriptions of personality traits of people with Down syndrome often include being affectionate, social, and having an easy temperament (as reviewed in Esbensen, Seltzer, & Abbeduto, 2008). Relative strengths in social skills have been supported in the literature in studies of eye gaze, facial displays, and social interactions (as reviewed in Fidler & Nadel, 2007), and less significant externalizing behavior problems are reported than those exhibited by their peers with other intellectual and developmental disabilities (Greenspan & Delaney, 1983; Hodapp & Dykens, 1994). Individuals with Down syndrome are also reported to have higher functional abilities in comparison to their peers with other intellectual and developmental disabilities (as reviewed in Esbensen et al.). Individuals with Down syndrome are also more likely to apply their social strengths by using social interactions in attempts to avoid difficult tasks (Kasari & Freeman, 2001).

Motor and speech development is often affected by the low muscle tone exhibited by people with Down syndrome. The wide gait common in children with Down syndrome affects balance and coordination of gross motor development. Additional difficulties in gross and fine motor skills are also affected by difficulties with motor planning, balance, strength, and hand strength. Despite these motor difficulties, the sequence of motor development is generally the same as among typically developing children but with milestones being met at a significantly delayed rate and the rate becoming more delayed for more advanced motor skills (Bruni, 2006; Frank & Esbensen, 2015; Winders, 2013).

LANGUAGE

The language development of children with Down syndrome has been studied extensively by investigators from a variety of communication-related fields. As a result, there is an extremely rich literature regarding the linguistic profile of Down syndrome that includes receptive and expressive language, vocabulary, grammar, pronunciation and articulation, and the pragmatic use of language in social situations (Abbeduto, Warren, & Conners, 2007).

Given the strong association between cognitive and language development, it follows that a delay in cognitive development would be associated with similar delays in language development. Studies that compare children with Down syndrome of a particular age with typically developing children who are chronologically younger but of comparable cognitive developmental level, as determined by mental age scores, generally show that the two groups are similar in their levels of receptive language, vocabulary, and pragmatic use of language. However, children with Down syndrome demonstrate significantly greater delays in expressive language than would be expected for their level of cognitive development. Although there is evidence that this delay exists during the prelinguistic period, it is clearly apparent when considering the developmental milestone associated with a child speaking his or her first word. In comparison with typically developing children, who usually speak their first word before 12 months of age, the average age for children with Down syndrome is 21 months. Delays in expressive vocabulary remain throughout childhood and may become even more significant in adolescence (McDuffie & Abbeduto, 2009). Grammar, the rules that define language use, is another area characterized by extremely delayed development for people with Down syndrome. Specific examples of delayed grammar development relate to the placement of adjectives and nouns in phrases, the appropriate use of tense, and the complexity of sentence structure. Martin, Klusek, Estigarribia, and Roberts (2009) concluded that syntax deficits in young people with Down syndrome cannot be explained by cognitive level alone.

Finally, differences in pronunciation and articulation are also evident in the expressive language of people with Down syndrome. Various physiological issues involving the structure and function of the oral cavity, palate, vocal cords, and facial muscles, and abnormalities of the tongue, undoubtedly play a role in articulation impairments. As a result, the intelligibility of spoken communication is often compromised. In extreme cases, in perhaps as many as 15% of children with Down syndrome, the difficulty in saying sounds, syllables, and words reaches the threshold for a diagnosis of verbal apraxia.

In contrast to the difficulties described with regard to expressive language, grammar, and speech production, children with Down syndrome have a relative strength in nonverbal communication skills such as the use of gestures and imitation that contribute to their effectiveness in social situations. This strength, in combination with difficulties with verbal expression and articulation, led to consideration of augmentative and alternative methods of communication for children with Down syndrome.

In these instances, sign language instruction or pictorial representations may strengthen communication effectiveness until spoken language is acquired.

Knowledge of language development in Down syndrome has been enhanced by comparing the abilities of people with Down syndrome with those of people with other genetic syndromes such as Williams syndrome or fragile X syndrome, as well as with groups of people with intellectual disability with mixed diagnoses. For example, people with Down syndrome and Williams syndrome have very similar intellectual level but demonstrate remarkable differences in expressive language. People with Williams syndrome exhibit language use far above their level of cognitive development and in stark contrast to people with Down syndrome in terms of syntax, semantics, storytelling abilities, and narrative enhancement. In many respects, the abilities of people with Williams syndrome are comparable to their typically developing peers. These comparative studies assist in determining the syndrome-specific features of Down syndrome, which could inform efforts to develop etiology-specific language interventions.

EDUCATION

Contrary to earlier beliefs that children with intellectual disability would not benefit from participation in public education, decades of research has demonstrated otherwise. Sweeping legislative mandates (discussed in detail in Chapter 36) set the stage for children with Down syndrome and other disabilities to receive early intervention services until 3 years of age and special education services from 3 to 21 years of age. These mandates guaranteed access to a free appropriate public education in the least restrictive environment for all students with disabilities. Young adults leaving the educational system in the early 21st century have had a far different educational experience than any previous cohort. The opportunity for children with disabilities to participate in general education settings with typically developing peers was a major shift in the history of education worldwide. With this opportunity, what are the educational issues that affect people with Down syndrome?

Although it is not uncommon for ideology to shift practice, often without consideration of available data, it is reassuring that there are studies regarding the relative value of particular educational placements. For example, a study from England suggested that for teenagers with Down syndrome, there are advantages to general educational settings in comparison with segregated classrooms (Buckley, Bird, Sacks, & Archer, 2006). In this study, teenagers in general education classrooms showed higher levels of communication—particularly, expressive language and literacy skills—and fewer behavioral difficulties than teenagers in segregated classrooms.

Despite evidence suggesting that children with disabilities benefit from instruction in inclusive settings, not all children with Down syndrome have that experience. Efforts are underway to understand this issue from the standpoint of the educator and the parent—both of whom are critical stakeholders in discussions regarding where services are provided.

Given the current emphasis on establishing etiology-specific characteristics, the question emerges whether that information should inform educational practices. In other words, are there aspects of the behavioral phenotype associated with Down syndrome that may be relevant for educators? Research has identified functioning areas in which children with Down syndrome, as a group, appear to differ from children with other etiologies or for whom etiologies have not yet been determined. Although not every child with Down syndrome has the same pattern of performance, there is an emerging pattern of educationally relevant strengths and weaknesses that may inform education practices. For example, a significant aspect of the Down syndrome behavioral phenotype is intellectual disability. Of relevance to educational performance, studies indicate that intellectual level is a very strong predictor of academic performance (Sloper, Cunningham, Turner, & Knussen, 1990). That is, children functioning in the mild range of intellectual disability obtain higher levels of academic achievement than children in the moderate or severe ranges. Subsequent research has identified other aspects of the Down syndrome behavioral phenotype that may be relevant to educational performance. A review of these studies by Daunhauer and Fidler (2011) indicates that relative strengths include receptive language and language comprehension, visual-perceptual processing, social engagement, social orientation, and social competency regarding friendships. Relative weaknesses include expressive language, executive functioning, motor development, and challenges performing goal-directed

behavior. The time is ripe for the development of innovative practices related to the Down syndrome behavioral phenotype.

Daunhauer, Fidler, and Will (2014) focused on school function in relation to students with Down syndrome. *School function* refers to nonacademic aspects of a school program and is defined as "a student's ability to perform important functional activities that support or enable participation in the academic and related social aspects of an educational program" (Coster, Deeney, Haltiwanger, & Haley, 1998, p. 2). Examples include manipulating books and tools for writing, responding to questions about the curriculum material, the ability to manage self-care and personal needs, interacting with peers during learning tasks, and requesting assistance when needed. Daunhauer et al. assessed 29 students with Down syndrome in kindergarten through sixth grade with the School Function Assessment (SFA) measure. The resulting school function profile revealed areas of relative strength and challenge among the various domains and functioning areas. For example, relatively high scores were obtained for travel, maintaining and changing position, setup and cleanup, eating and drinking, and going up and down stairs. Areas of greatest challenge included computer and equipment use, compliance with adult directives and school rules, and completion of tasks requiring behavior regulation and written work, among others. The assumption is that enhanced performance on nonacademic tasks, such as those measured on the SFA, may enhance performance in academic content areas.

Students with intellectual disability and their parents are increasingly seeking postsecondary education opportunities (Grigal & Hart, 2010). The marketplace has responded with 220 programs, with locations in nearly every U.S. state. The programs vary in a number of ways, but the essence of postsecondary education includes person-centered planning, participation in campus life, participation in regularly scheduled academic courses, and an emphasis on life skill development, social integration, and employment. The National Down Syndrome Society has been instrumental in promoting postsecondary experiences for young adults with Down syndrome. Participation in postsecondary education has been associated with substantially higher rates of competitive employment among people with intellectual disability.

FAMILY

A diagnosis of Down syndrome can have an impact on the larger family system, and the impact may vary across the lifespan. At birth, the diagnosis can have an impact on parents and their understanding and accepting of the diagnosis. As the child ages, the behavioral phenotype of the individual with Down syndrome will continue to affect the well-being of family members.

Despite advances in prenatal screening (Bianchi et al., 2014), most diagnoses of Down syndrome continue to be made postnatally (Skotko, 2005a). How the diagnosis is first presented to the family has a significant impact on parental well-being and acceptance of the genetic diagnosis and may help to shape early parenting beliefs (Skotko & Bedia, 2005). In previous decades, parents often reported feeling dissatisfied with how the diagnosis was communicated from a medical professional and anxious about their child's future (Skotko; Skotko & Bedia, 2005). Recent work in the field of genetic counseling has informed clinicians on how best to communicate a diagnosis to families. Children with Down syndrome born after 2000 have increasingly had their diagnoses communicated to families in a manner that included the positive aspects of raising a child with Down syndrome (Skotko). The impact on the family when the diagnosis is made prenatally is comparable to postnatal diagnoses. However, parents receiving prenatal diagnoses often report feeling the added pressure to make a decision regarding terminating or continuing with the pregnancy (Skotko, 2005b).

Many studies have examined the impact of raising a child with Down syndrome on parental well-being through childhood, adolescence, and adulthood. Although the impact of raising a child with an intellectual disability is generally associated with negative outcomes in comparison to raising a typically developing child, the impact (e.g., pessimism, stress, depressed mood, positive well-being, marital satisfaction) is generally comparable to or better than raising a child with idiopathic intellectual disability, autism spectrum disorder (ASD), or another genetic syndrome (Fidler, Hodapp, & Dykens, 2000; Hauser-Cram, Warfield, Shonkoff, & Krauss, 2001; Ly & Hodapp, 2002; Skotko, Levine, & Goldstein, 2011). Difficulties in parenting or marital relationships are often associated with behavioral problems exhibited by the child with Down syndrome (Cahill & Glidden, 1996).

The pattern of comparable or better outcomes experienced by parents of children with Down syndrome in comparison to parents of children with other developmental disabilities continues into adolescence and adulthood (Abbeduto et al., 2004; Esbensen & Seltzer, 2011). Despite adolescents with Down syndrome experiencing increased risk for

---

When Alice was born with Down syndrome, her parents were told to institutionalize her because she would never have the quality of life of a typically developing person. Her parents ignored that advice and decided to raise her at home with their other three children. At home, Alice's parents had the same expectations for her as they did for her older siblings. They encouraged Alice's language and social development and insisted that she be included in activities for children her same age. With the support of an early intervention program, they augmented Alice's verbal language development, which was very slow to develop, with sign language, and learned ways to promote her cognitive development in the context of everyday activities. At 5 years of age, Alice entered kindergarten with her neighborhood peers. She remained in public schools, spending the majority of her day in the regular classroom with the support of special education teachers. At age 21, Alice earned a certificate of attendance and participated in graduation exercises with her peers. With her parents' support, Alice attended a local college, where she took classes based on her interests, had a job on campus, and learned how to live independently.

As a part of her college program, Alice participated in an employment planning program that emphasized self-determination and client-centered planning. The team helped Alice identify employment options that fit her interests and abilities. With their support, Alice obtained training in food preparation and was a paid apprentice in a local bakery. With this experience, she and several friends, who also had developmental disabilities, began a food preparation microenterprise with the support of their parents.

medical concerns in adolescence (e.g., the onset of celiac disease, worsening of sleep apnea), parents continue to experience positive well-being in comparison to parents of children with other developmental disabilities (Abbeduto et al.). The improved outcomes are again often related to contextual factors, such as associated behavioral concerns, a finding also replicated among parents of adults with Down syndrome (Corrice & Glidden, 2009). With the longer lifespans experienced by adults with Down syndrome, their parents are also adjusting to their own aging and the need for continued care of their child. Again, despite the high rates of health problems experienced by adults with Down syndrome, mothers continue to demonstrate a life-course pattern of positive profiles and adaptation.

Findings are mixed regarding the impact of having a sibling with Down syndrome. Several studies indicate positive outcomes, particularly in relation to peers with siblings with other developmental disabilities (Bolton et al., 1994; Seltzer, Krauss, Orsmond, & Vestal, 2000). However, others have identified higher rates of behavior problems (Cuskelly & Dadds, 1992; Cuskelly & Gunn, 1993). Parenting practices, family resources, self-appraisals, and the behavioral profile of the child with Down syndrome likely all influence outcomes of siblings.

MENTAL WELLNESS

During childhood and adulthood, individuals with Down syndrome are commonly found to exhibit lower rates of psychopathology in comparison to their peers with other intellectual and developmental disabilities (Dykens, Hodapp, & Finucane, 2000; Mantry et al., 2008). However, common behavioral concerns include inattention, hyperactivity, impulsivity, noncompliance, and aggression. Rates of attention-deficit/hyperactivity disorder are three to five times higher among children with Down syndrome in comparison to the general population, and two to three times higher in comparison to children with other intellectual and developmental disabilities (Dekker & Koot, 2003; Ekstein, Glick, Weill, Kay, & Berger, 2011; Froehlich et al., 2007).

Similarly, individuals with Down syndrome present with other clinical diagnoses or psychopathology that warrant treatment, including oppositional behaviors, depression, and anxiety disorders. Externalizing problem behaviors are often less prevalent among individuals with Down syndrome in comparison to their peers with other intellectual and developmental disabilities. Rather, individuals with Down syndrome often exhibit noncompliance in the form of avoidance behaviors. These behaviors are commonly described as "stubborn" and may include wandering (McGuire & Chicoine, 2006; Pueschel, Bernier, & Puzzullo, 1991).

Depression is a frequently reported clinical diagnosis in individuals with Down syndrome (Collacott, Cooper, & McGrother, 1992; Myers & Pueschel, 1991). However, the prevalence and incidence of depression is not higher than that observed among adults with other intellectual and developmental disabilities (Mantry et al., 2008). Furthermore, there are several medical comorbidities that may present as depression and need to be taken into account during diagnosis. For example, hypothyroidism may present with lethargy and decreased interest in activities. Sleep apnea may also present with fatigue, irritability, and lack of interest in activities. Celiac disease, B_{12} deficiency, and sensory loss—all common in individuals with Down syndrome—also present with a behavioral profile that mirrors depression.

Anxiety disorders are less common among individuals with Down syndrome than their peers with intellectual and developmental disabilities; however, obsessive or compulsive behaviors are commonly reported (Capone, Goyal, Ares, & Lannigan, 2006; Mantry et al., 2008). These behaviors may stem from a need for sameness or a repetitive quality in behaviors (Evans & Gray, 2000). Individuals with Down syndrome often benefit from this need of sameness or routines. These features can be adaptive or beneficial when they contribute to increased organization, care with appearance, increased independence, and accurate work performance. However, these same features can also contribute to challenging behaviors, such as difficulties with transitions or difficulties being flexible with changes to routine.

Self-talk and having imaginary friends is common among individuals with Down syndrome. It is also very common among typically developing children, who learn to self-monitor or internalize these thoughts as they grow older. In contrast, self-talk and imaginary friends may not internalize among adults with Down syndrome. Instead of representing psychoses or hallucinations, self-talk among individuals with Down syndrome is viewed as normative behavior for recalling daily events. However, self-talk can become more pronounced, both in volume and intensity, during times of stress or loneliness (McGuire & Chicoine, 2006).

Researchers are interested in the rate of ASD among children with Down syndrome. Rates of ASD are somewhat higher than those observed in the general population but substantially lower than in other genetic etiologies such as fragile X. Children with Down syndrome who receive diagnoses of ASD display increased impairment in terms of cognition, language abilities, and adaptive behavior and exhibit more problem behaviors than children with Down syndrome without ASD (Hepburn & MacLean, 2009; Molloy et al., 2009). A biological mechanism is conjectured to be responsible for the co-occurrence of ASD and Down syndrome in some children—potentially involving chromosome 21.

CURRENT AND FUTURE DIRECTIONS

The decades since the 1990s have brought unparalleled changes to the lives of people with Down syndrome. Advances in medicine and greater health care access have been associated with substantial gains in longevity. Delineation of the Down syndrome behavioral phenotype has provided a better understanding of the characteristics that appear to define Down syndrome and those that occur with the same frequency in people with intellectual disabilities without a diagnosis of Down syndrome or in the general population. Careful study of aging in people with Down syndrome has enhanced understanding of Alzheimer's disease for individuals with Down syndrome and for the general population. Awareness of the co-occurrence of mental health issues and intellectual disability in the field more generally has led to greater understanding of such issues in people with Down syndrome. Increased rates of ASD and externalizing behavior disorders in children, as well as depression in adults, has informed the delivery of mental health services in this population. Together, these advances have culminated in a wealth of resources and organizations that are targeted toward individuals with Down syndrome and their families.

Children with Down syndrome have been afforded participation in early intervention programs, have benefited from inclusive education practices, and have access to postsecondary educational opportunities. Compared with earlier generations, people with Down syndrome entering adulthood are better prepared for participation in the community in a variety of adult roles. Access to technology provides supports for many people with Down syndrome to live independently in the community.

Translational research, where basic science is applied in a clinical setting, is advancing, and

---

Autism and Down Syndrome

Laurie and Harold Roberts were first-time parents expecting that Laurie's pregnancy would result in a typically developing child without congenital disorder. Routine prenatal screening revealed otherwise. At 9 weeks of gestation, chorionic villus sampling indicated that their son—whom they later named Liam—had Down syndrome. Although unexpected, the diagnosis was taken in stride. Harold's cousin Ben has Down syndrome. Ben is an engaging young adult who is outgoing, friendly, and socially skilled. He had some medical challenges, but they did not hold him back from full-time employment at a local business. Like many people with Down syndrome, Ben has a full life with friends and family—living an inclusive life in his local community.

Six months later, Liam was born and referred for early intervention services at a local developmental preschool. Expecting that Liam would develop like Ben, the Roberts were surprised when the early intervention teachers expressed concerns about Liam's development in the toddler classroom. The teachers noticed that Liam was socially isolated, made infrequent eye contact, engaged in a variety of repetitive motor behaviors such as hand flapping, and did not respond when his name was called. Although the Roberts had observed some of these characteristics at home, they attributed them to Liam's global developmental delay, which was significant.

After discussing the concerns with Liam's pediatrician, the Roberts turned to an autism program at a local university for an evaluation. The results of the evaluation indicated that Liam met the diagnostic criteria for ASD. Approximately one in 20 children with Down syndrome share Liam's diagnosis of ASD.

knowledge gained from clinical trials will potentially affect learning and cognition among individuals with Down syndrome (Bartesaghi et al., 2015). However, with these many advances comes greater responsibility. Continued care for an aging population, implementation of effective interventions and programs, and continued randomized clinical trials are all warranted to continue to support individuals with Down syndrome and their families.

SUMMARY

Down syndrome is the most prevalent chromosomal disorder and the most common genetic cause of intellectual disability. Individuals with Down syndrome most frequently have an extra 21st chromosome, which often causes cognitive, language, and motor delays in addition to a variety of dysmorphic features. With improvements in medical care and services, individuals with Down syndrome are experiencing healthier, more active, and longer lives. However, there is an ongoing need to identify new treatment targets and approaches that are likely to further reduce impairments in daily functioning, improve quality of life, improve education practices, and reduce family burden.

FOR FURTHER THOUGHT AND DISCUSSION

1. Advances in prenatal testing permit earlier detection of Down syndrome during pregnancy. What implications do you think this has for termination versus continuing the pregnancy? What information do you think should be given to families, when do you think it should be given, and how do you think this information should be shared with prospective parents?

2. If a pill could "cure" Down syndrome, do you think parents should give it to their child? If so, what do you think is "ill" about Down syndrome? If not, what alternative therapies would you provide to families?

3. Speech therapy is generally sought in childhood to improve language and articulation. Given the chronic language impairment, what are your thoughts about ongoing need for speech therapy for adults?

4. With the longer lives experienced by adults with Down syndrome, what implications do you think this has for disability services, families, health care, and social opportunities?

REFERENCES

Abbeduto, L., Seltzer, M.M., Shattuck, P., Krauss, M.W., Orsmond, G., & Murphy, M.M. (2004). Psychological well-being and coping in mothers of youths with autism, Down syndrome, or fragile X syndrome. *American Journal on Mental Retardation, 109,* 237–254.

Abbeduto, L., Warren, S.F., & Conners, F.A. (2007). Language development in Down syndrome: From the prelinguistic period to the acquisition of literacy. *Mental Retardation and Developmental Disabilities Research Reviews, 13,* 247–261.

Bartesaghi, R., Haydar, T.F., Delabar, J.M., Dierssen, M., Martínez-Cué, C., & Bianchi, D.W. (2015). New perspectives for the rescue of cognitive disability in Down syndrome. *The Journal of Neuroscience, 35*(41), 13843–13852.

Bianchi, D.W., Parker, R.L., Wentworth, J., Madankumar, R., Saffer, C., Das, A.F.,...Sehnert, A.J. (2014). DNA sequencing versus standard prenatal aneuploidy screening. *New England Journal of Medicine, 370,* 799–808.

Bittles, A., & Glasson, E. (2004). Clinical, social, and ethical implications of changing life expectancy in Down syndrome. *Developmental Medicine and Child Neurology, 46,* 282–286.

Bolton, P., Macdonald, H., Pickles, A., Rios, P., Goode, S., Crowson, M.,...Rutter, M. (1994). A case-control family history study of autism. *Journal of Child Psychology and Psychiatry, 35,* 877–900.

Bruni, M. (2006). *Fine motor skills for children with Down syndrome: A guide for parents and professionals.* Bethesda, MD: Woodbine House.

Buchanan, L.H. (1990). Early onset of presbyacusis in Down syndrome. *Scandinavian Audiology, 19,* 103–110.

Buckley, S., Bird, G., Sacks, B., & Archer, T. (2006). A comparison of mainstream and special education for teenagers with Down syndrome: Implications for parents and teachers. *Down Syndrome Research and Practice, 9,* 54–67.

Cahill, B.M., & Glidden, L.M. (1996). Influence of child diagnosis on family and parental functioning: Down syndrome versus other disabilities. *American Journal of Mental Retardation, 101,* 149–160.

Capone, G., Goyal, P., Ares, W., & Lannigan, E. (2006). Neurobehavioral disorders in children, adolescents, and young adults with Down syndrome. *American Journal of Medical Genetics, Part C, 142C,* 158–172.

Cohen, W.I. (2006). Current dilemmas in Down syndrome clinical care: Celiac disease, thyroid disorders, and atlanto-axial instability. *American Journal of Medical Genetics Part C, 142C,* 141–148.

Coleman, M. (1994). Thyroid dysfunction in Down syndrome: A review. *Down Syndrome Research and Practice, 2,* 112–115.

Collacott, R.A., Cooper, S.A., & McGrother, C. (1992). Differential rates of psychiatric disorders in adults with Down's syndrome compared with other mentally handicapped adults. *British Journal of Psychiatry, 161,* 671–674.

Coppus, A., Evenhuis, H., Verberne, G.J., Visser, F., Van Gool, P., Eikelenboom, P., & Van Duijin, C. (2006). Dementia and mortality in persons with Down's syndrome. *Journal of Intellectual Disability Research, 50,* 768–777.

Corrice, A.M., & Glidden, L.M. (2009). The Down syndrome advantage: Fact or fiction? *American Journal of Intellectual and Developmental Disabilities, 114,* 254–268.

Coster, W., Deeney, T., Haltiwanger, J., & Haley, S. (1998). *School Function Assessment (SFA).* San Antonio, TX: Psychological Corporation.

Cuskelly, M., & Dadds, M. (1992). Behavioural problems in children with Down's syndrome and their siblings. *Journal of Child Psychology and Psychiatry, 33,* 749–761.

Cuskelly, M., & Gunn, P. (1993). Maternal reports of behavior of siblings of children with Down syndrome. *American Journal on Mental Retardation, 97,* 521–529.

Daunhauer, L.A., & Fidler, D.J. (2011). The Down syndrome behavioral phenotype: Implications for practice and research in occupational therapy. *Occupational Therapy in Health Care, 25*(1), 7–25.

Daunhauer, L.A., Fidler, D.J., & Will, E. (2014). School function in students with Down syndrome. *American Journal of Occupational Therapy, 68,* 167–176.

Dekker, M.C., & Koot, H.M. (2003) DSM-IV disorders in children with borderline to moderate intellectual disability. II: Child and family predictors. *Journal of the Amerian Academy of Child and Adolescent Psychiatry, 42,* 923–931.

Dykens, E.M., Hodapp, R.M., & Finucane, B.M. (2000). *Genetics and mental retardation syndromes: A new look at behavior and interventions.* Baltimore, MD: Paul H. Brookes Publishing Co.

Ekstein, S., Glick, B., Weill, M., Kay, B., & Berger, I. (2011). Down syndrome and attention-deficit/hyperactivity disorder. *Journal of Child Neurology, 26,* 1290–1295.

Esbensen, A.J. (2010). Health conditions associated with aging and end of life of adults with Down syndrome. *International Review of Research in Mental Retardation, 39,* 107–126.

Esbensen, A.J., & Seltzer, M.M. (2011). Accounting for the "Down syndrome advantage." *American Journal of Intellectual and Developmental Disabilities, 116,* 3–15.

Esbensen, A.J., Seltzer, M.M., & Abbeduto, L. (2008). Family well-being in Down syndrome and fragile X syndrome. In J.E. Roberts, R.S. Chapman, & S.F. Warren (Eds.), *Speech and language development and intervention in Down syndrome and fragile X syndrome* (pp. 275–295). Baltimore, MD: Paul H. Brookes Publishing Co.

Evans, D., & Gray, F. (2000). Compulsive-like behavior in individuals with Down syndrome: Its relation to mental age level, adaptive and maladaptive behavior. *Child Development, 71,* 288–300.

Fidler, D.J., Hodapp, R.M., & Dykens, E.M. (2000). Stress in families of young children with Down syndrome, Williams syndrome, and Smith-Magenis syndrome. *Early Education and Development, 11,* 395–406.

Fidler, D., Most, D., & Philofsky, A. (2008). The Down syndrome behavioural phenotype: Taking a developmental approach. *Down Syndrome Research and Practice, 12*(3), 37–44.

Fidler, D.J., & Nadel, L. (2007). Education and children with Down syndrome: Neuroscience, development, and intervention. *Mental Retardation and Developmental Disabilities Research Reviews, 13,* 262–271.

Frank, K., & Esbensen, A.J. (2015). Development of fine motor and self-care milestones for individuals with Down syndrome using retrospective chart review. *Journal of Intellectual Disability Research, 59,* 719–729.

Freeman, S.B., Torfs, C.P., Romitti, P.A., Royle, M.H., Druschel, C., Hobbs, C.A., & Sherman, S.L. (2009). Congenital gastrointestinal defects in Down syndrome: A report from the Atlanta and National Down Syndrome Projects. *Clinical Genetics, 75,* 180–186.

Froehlich, T., Lanphear, B., Epstein, J., Barbaresi, W., Katusic, S., & Kahn, R. (2007). Prevalence and treatment of attention-deficit/hyperactivity disorder in a national sample of U.S. children. *Archives of Pediatric and Adolescent Medicine, 161,* 857–864.

Gathercole, S.E., & Alloway, T.P. (2006). Practitioner review: Short-term and working memory impairments in neurodevelopmental disorders: Diagnosis and remedial support. *Journal of Child Psychology and Psychiatry, 47,* 4–15.

Gautier, M., & Harper, P.S. (2009). Fiftieth anniversary of trisomy 21: Returning to a discovery. *Human Genetics, 126,* 317–324.

Greenspan, S., & Delaney, K. (1983). Personal competence of institutionalized adult males with or without Down syndrome. *American Journal of Mental Deficiency, 88,* 218–220.

Grigal, M., & Hart, D. (2010). *Think college! Postsecondary education options for students with intellectual disabilities.* Baltimore, MD: Paul H. Brookes Publishing Co.

Hattori, M., Fujiyama, A., Taylor, T.D., Watanabe, H., Yada, T., Park, H.-S.,…Yaspo, M.-L. (2000). The DNA sequence of human chromosome 21. *Nature, 405,* 311–319.

Hauser-Cram, P., Warfield, M.E., Shonkoff, J.P., & Krauss, M.W. (2001). Children with disabilities: A longitudinal study of child development and parent well-being. *Monographs of the Society for Research in Child Development, 66,* Serial No. 266.

Hawkins, B.A., Eklund, S.J., James, D.R., Foose, A.K., & Krauss, M.W. (2003). Adaptive behavior and cognitive function of adults with Down syndrome: Modeling change with age. *Mental Retardation, 41,* 7–28.

Hepburn, S.L., & MacLean, W.E. (2009). Maladaptive and repetitive behaviors in children with Down syndrome and autism spectrum disorders: Impications for screening. *Journal of Mental Health Research in Intellectual Disabilities, 2,* 67–88.

Hodapp, R.M., & Dykens, E.M. (1994). Mental retardation's two cultures of behavioral research. *American Journal on Mental Retardation, 98,* 675–687.

Hodapp, R., & Dykens, E. (2004). Genetic and behavioural aspects: Application to maladaptive behavior and cognition. In J. Rondal, R. Hodapp, S. Soresi, E. Dykens, & L. Nota (Eds.), *Intellectual disabilities: Genetics, behaviour and inclusion* (pp. 13–48). London, United Kingdom: Whurr.

Hodapp, R.M., Leckman, J.F., Dykens, E.M., Sparrow, S.S., Zelinsky, D., & Ort, S. (1992). K-ABC profiles in children with fragile X syndrome, Down syndrome, and nonspecific mental retardation. *American Journal on Mental Retardation, 97,* 39–46.

Holland, A., Hon, J., Huppert, F., & Stevens, F. (2000). Incidence and course of dementia in people with Down's syndrome: Findings from a population-based study. *Journal of Intellectual Disability Research, 44,* 138–146.

Hultén, M.A., Patel, S.D., Westgren, M., Papadogianna-kis, N., Jonsson, A.M., Jonsson, J., & Iwarsson, E. (2010). On the paternal origin of trisomy 21 Down syndrome. *Molecular Cytogenetics, 3,* 4.

Jacobs, P.A., Baikie, A.G., Court Brown, W.M., & Strong, J.A. (1959). The somatic chromosomes in mongolism. *Lancet, 1*(7075), 710.

Kanno, K., & Ikeda, Y. (2002). Word-length effect in verbal short-term memory in individuals with Down's syndrome. *Journal of Intellectual Disability Research, 46,* 613–618.

Kasari, C., & Freeman, S.F. (2001). Task-related social behavior in children with Down syndrome. *American Journal on Mental Retardation, 106,* 253–264.

Kerins, G., Petrovic, K., Bruder, M., & Gruman, C. (2008). Medical conditions and medication use in adults with Down syndrome: A descriptive analysis. *Down Syndrome Research and Practice, 12,* 141–147.

Klein, B.P., & Mervis, C.B. (1999). Contrasting patterns of cognitive abilities of 9- and 10-year-olds with Williams syndrome or Down syndrome. *Developmental Neuropsychology, 16*(2), 177–196.

Lejeune, J., Gautier, M., & Turpin, R. (1959). Etude des chromosomes somatiques de neuf enfants mongoliens. [Study of somatic chromosomes of nine children with mongolism.] *C. R. Academy Science (Paris), 248,* 1721–1722.

Ly, T.M., & Hodapp, R.M. (2002). Maternal attribution of child noncompliance in children with mental retardation: Down syndrome versus other causes. *Journal of Developmental and Behavioral Pediatrics, 23,* 322–329.

Madan, V., Williams, J., & Lear, J. (2006). Dermatological manifestations of Down's syndrome. *Clinical and Experimental Dermatology, 31,* 623–629.

Mantry, D., Cooper, S.-A., Smiley, E., Morrison, J., Allan, L., Williamson, A.,…Jackson, A. (2008). The prevalence and incidence of mental ill-health in adults with Down syndrome. *Journal of Intellectual Disability Research, 52,* 141–155.

Martin, G.E., Klusek, J., Estigarribia, B., & Roberts, J.E. (2009). Language characteristics of individuals with Down syndrome. *Topics in Language Disorders, 29,* 112–132.

McDuffie, A., & Abbeduto, L. (2009). Developmental delay and genetic syndromes: Down syndrome, fragile X syndrome, and Williams syndrome. In R. Schwartz (Ed.), *Handbook of child language disorders* (pp. 44–66). New York, NY: Psychology Press.

McGuire, D., & Chicoine, B. (2006). *Mental wellness in adults with Down syndrome: A guide to emotional and behavioral strengths and challenges.* Bethesda, MD: Woodbine House.

Molloy, C.A., Murray, D.S., Kinsman, A., Castillo, H., Mitchell, T., Hickey, F.J., & Patterson, B. (2009). Differences in the clinical presentation of trisomy 21 with and without autism. *Journal of Intellectual Disability Research, 53,* 143–151.

Myers, B., & Pueschel, S.M. (1991). Psychiatric disorders in persons with Down syndrome. *Journal of Nervous and Mental Disease, 179,* 609–613.

Prasher, V. (1994). Screening of medical problems in adults with Down syndrome. *Down Syndrome Research and Practice, 2,* 59–66.

Pueschel, S.M., Bernier, J.C., & Pezzullo, J.C. (1991). Behavioural observations in children with Down's syndrome. *Journal of Mental Deficiency Research, 35,* 502–511.

Puri, B., Ho, K., & Singh, I. (2001). Age of seizure onset in adults with Down's syndrome. *International Journal of Clinical Practice, 55,* 442–444.

Rodríquez-Hernández, M.L., & Montoya, E. (2011). Fifty years of evolution of the term Down's syndrome. *The Lancet, 378,* 402.

Roubertoux, P.L., & Kerdelhué, B. (2006). Trisomy 21: From chromosomes to mental retardation. *Behavior Genetics, 36,* 346–354.

Satge, D., Sommelet, D., Geneix, A., Nishi, M., Malet, P., & Vekemans, M. (1998). A tumor profile in Down syndrome. *American Journal of Medical Genetics, 78,* 207–216.

Seltzer, M.M., Krauss, M.W., Orsmond, G.I., & Vestal, C. (2000). Families of adolescents and adults with autism: Uncharted territory. *International Review of Research in Mental Retardation, 23,* 267–294.

Shin, M., Besser, L.M., Kucik, J.E., Lu, C., Siffel, C., & Correa, A. (2009). Prevalence of Down syndrome among children and adolescents in 10 regions of the United States. *Pediatrics, 124,* 1565–1571.

Silverman, W. (2010, January 20). *Dementia among adults with Down syndrome: Individual differences in risk and progression* [Webinar in the Aging and End of Life Series]. Retrieved from https://aaidd.org/education /webinars/aging-and-end-of-life-series/2010/01/20 /default-calendar/dementia-among-adults-with-down-syndrome-individual-differences-in-risk-and-progression

Sinha, S. (2005). Anti-oxidant gene expression imbalance, aging and Down syndrome. *Life Sciences, 76,* 1407–1426.

Skotko, B. (2005a). Mothers of children with Down syndrome reflect on their postnatal support. *Pediatrics, 115,* 64–77.

Skotko, B.G. (2005b). Prenatally diagnosed Down syndrome: Mothers who continued their pregnancies evaluate their health care providers. *American Journal of Obstetrics and Gynecology, 192,* 670–677.

Skotko, B., & Bedia, R.C. (2005). Postnatal support for mothers of children with Down syndrome. *Mental Retardation, 43,* 196–212.

Skotko, B.G., Levine, S.P., & Goldstein, R. (2011). Having a son or daughter with Down syndrome: Perspectives from mothers and fathers. *American Journal of Medical Genetics Part A, 155,* 2335–2347.

Sloper, P., Cunningham, P., Turner, S., & Knussen, C. (1990). Factors related to the academic attainment of children with Down's syndrome. *British Journal of Educational Psychology, 60,* 284–298.

Van Buggenhout, G., Trommelen, J., Schoenmaker, A., De Bal, C., Verbeek, J., Smeets, D., Fryns, J.-P. (1999). Down syndrome in a population of elderly mentally retarded patients: Genetic-diagnostic survey and implications for medical care. *American Journal of Medical Genetics, 85,* 376–384.

Ward, O. (1999). John Langdon Down: The man and the message. *Down Syndrome Research and Practice, 6*(1), 19–24.

Winders, P.C. (2013). *Gross motor skills for children with Down syndrome: A guide for parents and professionals.* Bethesda, MD: Woodbine House.

Wisniewski, K. (1990). Down syndrome children often have brain with maturation delay, retardation of growth, and cortical dysgenesis. *American Journal of Medical Genetics, 37,* 274–281.

Wright, D. (2011). *Downs: The history of a disability.* New York, NY: Oxford University Press.

Yang, Q., Rasmussen, S.A., & Friedman, J. (2002). Mortality associated with Down's syndrome in the USA from 1983 to 1997: A population-based study. *The Lancet, 359,* 1019–1025.

Zigman, W.B., Schupf, N., Sersen, E., & Silverman, W. (1996). Prevalence of dementia in adults with and without Down syndrome. *American Journal on Mental Retardation, 100,* 403–412.

Zoia, S., Pelamatti, G., & Rumiati, R.I. (2004). Praxic skills in Down and mentally retarded adults: Evidence for multiple action routes. *Brain and Cognition, 54,* 7–17.

15

Fragile X Syndrome

Cynthia J. Forster-Gibson and Jeanette Jeltje Anne Holden

WHAT YOU WILL LEARN

- The nature of fragile X syndrome and how it affects individuals
- The genetics of fragile X, the pattern of heredity, and genetic testing
- How fragile X syndrome affects families
- Needs of and services for people with fragile X syndrome
- Some interesting areas of fragile X syndrome research

Fragile X syndrome (FXS) is the most common known inherited form of intellectual disability worldwide. Some effects of this syndrome include intellectual and developmental disabilities, characteristic physical features and atypical behaviors, and other health effects as discussed later in this chapter.

THE NATURE OF FRAGILE X SYNDROME

The number of people reported to have FXS is reported to be approximately 1 in 4,000 males and 1 in 8,000 females in the general population (Peprah, 2012). The prevalence of unaffected carriers of an abnormal fragile X gene is approximately 1 in 290 in males and 1 in 148 in females (Maenner et al., 2013).

The gene for FXS is located on the X chromosome. This gene is called fragile X mental retardation 1 (FMR1). Mutations of the FMR1 gene usually result from an increase in size of a specific region of the gene (described in the Size of the FMR1 Gene section). Small increases in size may have little to no effect, whereas larger increases may cause severe cognitive disability and physical changes (i.e., FXS). Males with FXS typically need specialized help at school, supported employment, and assistance with community living. Females with FXS usually have milder cognitive impairment and fewer clinical features.

Public awareness about FXS is limited. Even health care professionals, educators, and other service providers may have little information about this syndrome. The effects of FXS on a family are not limited to the individual with the syndrome but can also influence family planning and affect education, health care, financial planning, and life planning for siblings, other family members, and future descendants.

As of this writing in 2016, there is no cure for FXS. Researchers from around the world are actively carrying out research aimed at finding a cure or improving treatment for this syndrome.

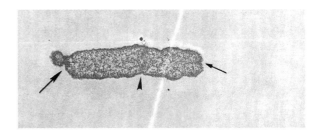

Figure 15.1. First transmission electron micrograph of a fragile X chromosome. The FMR1 gene is located in the region near the bottom end of the chromosome, denoted by the largest arrow. (This scanning EM image was kindly provided by Dr. G.Y. Wen and Dr. E.C. Jenkins of the New York State Institute for Basic Research in Developmental Disabilities [Wen et al., 1997]).

Authors' note: The authors wish to thank the following people for their comments and contributions to this chapter: P. Frost, J. Henderson, A. Holmes, B.A. Lee, R. Lokkesmoe, P. Minnes, J. Naschen, S. Stone, R. Wiens, and M. Wing.

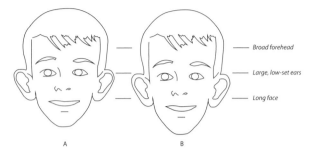

Figure 15.2. Male affected by fragile X syndrome (FXS) at younger (A) and older (B) ages. Notable features may be present in males with FXS. (*Sources:* Laschiewitcz, Dawson, & Spiridigliozzli, 2000; National Human Genome Research Institute, 2016). The sketch in Panel A is a composite of representative images of boys ages 5–8 diagnosed with FXS. The sketch in Panel B shows increased prominence of the jaw and facial lengthening that may become more evident in older males with FXS. Features of FXS are less pronounced in females. (Copyright © 2016 Tom Dearie, Threesixty Creative/ Infographix.)

Why Is It Called Fragile X Syndrome?

The term *fragile X syndrome* comes from the observation of a fragile site (a small break) on the tip of the X chromosome of males and some females who have this disorder (see Figure 15.1).

How Fragile X Syndrome Affects Individuals

The effects of the fragile X gene mutation (summarized in Table 15.1) vary from one person to another. (See Bagni, Tassone, Neri, and Hagerman, 2012 for a review.) Most males with FXS have some degree of cognitive impairment, and many have behavioral problems, including aggression, anxiety, and autistic behaviors. About one in three meet criteria for a diagnosis of autism. Physical features often include a long face with prominent jaw and ears, high arched palate, flat feet, and loose joints. These features may become more evident with age (see Figure 15.2). Most females who have FXS have milder impairments—including learning difficulties, anxiety, and shyness—and some physical features similar to males. These characteristics are part of the phenotype of FXS.

Individuals who have FXS can be very shy and display stereotypies such as hand flapping, resembling the behaviors seen in children with autism (see Chapter 16 for more information about autism). Approximately 30% of boys with FXS meet full criteria for a diagnosis of autism, and many more have some of the features of autism (Gabis, Baruch, Jokel, & Raz, 2011).

Fragile X Subphenotypes

The term *phenotype* refers to the characteristics that are common to a particular genetic disorder. Some people with FXS belong to a subgroup of FXS with a phenotype that resembles another genetic disorder. These subgroups include the following:

- *Obesity phenotype:* Truncal obesity; short, broad hands and feet; hyperpigmentation; and small genitals; occasionally referred to as Prader-Willi-like phenotype because some of these characteristics resemble another genetic disorder called Prader-Willi syndrome

- *Overgrowth phenotype:* Above-average birthweight, increased head circumference, includes extreme overall body overgrowth and increased height in childhood and adulthood, resembles Sotos syndrome and has been referred to as Sotos-like

THE GENETICS OF FRAGILE X

The FMR1 gene was identified in 1991. Everyone has a copy of the FMR1 gene on his or her X chromosomes. However, people with FXS have an abnormal (or mutant) FMR1 gene. Kremer et al. found in 1991 that people with FXS actually have a larger FMR1 gene than those in the general population.

The following genetic information is included for two reasons: 1) to provide a more in-depth understanding of the nature of the fragile X gene mutation and 2) to provide an appreciation for the complexity of information that families encounter when they receive a diagnosis of FXS in a family member.

Genetic Effects of Fragile X Syndrome

The effects of FXS and the pattern of heredity are influenced by 1) the size of the FMR1 gene, 2) the gender of the parent, and 3) the gender of the child.

Size of the FMR1 Gene DNA is made up of four different bases (molecules) called adenine, thymine, cytosine, and guanine (A, T, C, G). Each gene has a specific number of bases in a specific sequence. When the FMR1 gene has a mutation, it has too many bases. The extra bases come in sets of three, CGG CGG CGG and so on, called triplet repeats.

Table 15.1. Characteristics of individuals with fragile X syndrome (full mutation)[a]

Characteristic	As manifested in childhood and adolescence	As manifested in adulthood
Physical	Large protruding ears, flat feet, loose joints, strabismus, scoliosis, development of macroorchidism (large testicles) in males during puberty	As in childhood; potential for distinguishing features to become more evident and include long, narrow face and prominent jaw
Behavioral	Hyperactivity, features like those seen in individuals with autism, poor eye contact, shyness, social anxiety, sensitivity to touch/sound, hand biting/flapping, aggressive outbursts	Potential decrease in functional behavioral concerns; potential increase in anxiety (Gabis, Baruch, Jokel, & Raz, 2011)
Learning	Cognitive delay, attention difficulty with or without hyperactivity	Mild to severe developmental disability
Health	Otitis media, sinusitis, orthopedic problems, club foot deformity, minor heart anomalies, kidney dysfunction, orthodontic problems, strabismus, obstructive sleep apnea, gastroesophageal reflux, possible precocious puberty	Mitral valve prolapse, hypertension, obstructive sleep apnea
Neurological	Hypotonia, seizures	Seizures

[a]These characteristics are not always present. Features tend to be milder in females.

The number of triplet repeats can be classified into one of four categories: normal, full mutation, premutation, and intermediate or gray zone (Figure 15.3).

Normal FMR1 Repeats (Approximately 6–54 Copies of the CGG Repeat)
When the number of CGG repeats within the FMR1 gene is between approximately 6 and 54, individuals are said to have a normal FMR1 gene.

Full Mutation
When the number of copies of the CGG repeat exceeds 200, the mutation is described as being a full mutation. The full mutation prevents the gene from producing the protein that it codes for. This causes the clinical phenotype associated with FXS. Almost all males with a full mutation are affected with FXS. Approximately half of all females with a full mutation are affected.

Whether a female is affected depends to some extent on whether the X chromosome with the mutant FMR1 gene is active or inactive. Remember that although females have two X chromosomes, only one in each cell is active. Which one is active and which one is not is determined at an early stage of cell division in the embryo. If, in a female, the active X chromosome in the majority of cells has the mutant FMR1 gene, this would result in the girl being affected.

Females who have the full mutation will either pass their mutated gene or their normal gene to sons or daughters. The mutation size in the sperm of males

with a full mutation contracts to a premutation size. Any daughter they have will be a premutation carrier.

Premutation (Approximately 55–200 Copies of the CGG Repeat)
Individuals with FMR1 genes having approximately 55–200 repeats are said to have a premutation. Males and females with the premutation do not have FXS. They may be called premutation carriers. Whether premutation carriers have cognitive or behavioral differences is an area of controversy (Hunter, Abramowitz, Rusin, & Sherman, 2009). Some female carriers develop

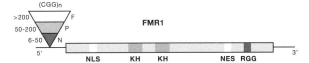

Figure 15.3. Schematic representation of the FMR1 gene. The coding region of the FMR1 gene that specifies FMR1 RNA is depicted by the horizontal rectangular bar. Noncoding regions of the gene, called untranslated regions (UTRs), are depicted by the horizontal lines on either side of the bar. The region called the 5'UTR is denoted by 5' and that called the 3'UTR is denoted by 3'. The CGG repeat region that is expanded in fragile X syndrome is located in the 5'UTR. The relative sizes of the CGG repeat region are shown for healthy individuals who do not have fragile X (approximately 6–54 repeats), for people who have a premutation (approximately 55–200 repeats), and for people who have a full mutation (>200 repeats). The terms *NLS, KH, NES,* and *RGG* refer to regions of FMR1 DNA that affect important functions of FMR1 protein. The KH and RGG regions of FMR1 protein are involved in RNA binding. The NES region helps the protein to move from the cell nucleus to the cytoplasm. The NLS region helps the protein to move from the cytoplasm to the cell nucleus. (From Oostra, B.A., Hoogeveen, A.T., & Willemsen, R. [n.d.]. *Fragile X syndrome and FMR1.* Retrieved August 12, 2010, from http://www2.eur.nl/fgg/kgen/research/fmr1.html, reprinted by permission.)

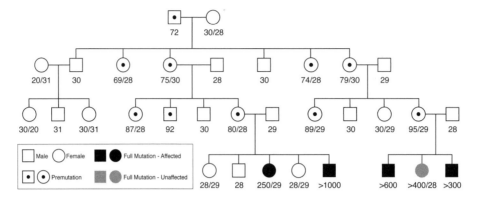

Figure 15.4. Pedigree of family with the fragile X syndrome, showing inheritance of the FMR1 gene. The numbers under the pedigree symbols indicate the number of CGG repeats in the FMR1 gene on each chromosome. Females have two X chromosomes and hence have two FMR1 genes; males have a single X chromosome and hence a single FMR1 gene. Sons inherit the X chromosome (and FMR1 gene) from their mothers and Y chromosome from their fathers. Daughters receive X chromosomes from both their mothers and fathers. (From Lee, B. A., MacKenzie, J.J., & Holden, J.J.A. [2003]. Fragile X syndrome. In I. Brown & M. Percy [Eds.], *Developmental disabilities in Ontario* [2nd ed., p. 237]. Toronto, Canada: Ontario Association on Developmental Disabilities; reprinted by permission.)

premature ovarian failure (early menopause and changes in their menstrual cycle) and older male and female carriers sometimes develop the fragile X-associated tremor/ataxia syndrome (FXTAS), a condition in which the person has tremors and balance problems.

Depending on the size of the repeat, if a female carrier of a premutation passes this gene to her child, it may expand to a full mutation or remain within the premutation size (see Figure 15.4). Premutations in the 55–65 repeat range rarely expand to full mutations, but those that are greater than about 80 repeats do. Thus, the risk for a carrier mother to have a child who is affected with FXS depends to a large extent on the size of the repeat within her mutated FMR1 gene. Males with the premutation pass the premutation on to all of their daughters. The chance of the mutation expanding to a full mutation is extremely small.

Intermediate or Gray Zone (Approximately 45–54 Copies of the CGG Repeat) People with an intermediate-size repeat (approximately 45–54 repeats) do not have FXS; however, the repeat size may be increased in their children to a premutation size (Nolin et al., 2011).

The Gender of the Parent Thousands of families with FXS have been studied to determine the likelihood that premutation and full mutation carriers will have affected offspring. The findings indicate that when the FMR1 premutation is passed from fathers to daughters, it has a very low

probability of expanding to a full mutation. However, when the same-size premutation is carried in mothers and is passed to either sons or daughters, it often expands to a full mutation (see Figure 15.4).

The Gender of the Child Males with a full mutation are almost always affected with FXS. Not all females with a full mutation are affected, and those who are affected are generally less affected than males.

GENETIC TESTING FOR FRAGILE X SYNDROME

The first genetic test for FXS was done by looking at the X chromosome. Testing is now done by directly examining the CGG repeat size of the FMR1 gene. (Figure 15.5 depicts the relationship between DNA and chromosomes.)

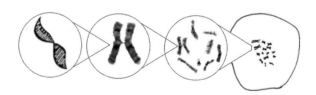

Figure 15.5. The relationship between DNA and chromosomes. DNA (extreme left) is tightly coiled and bound with proteins to form chromosomes (remaining figures). The chromosomes are located within the nucleus of the cell. (From Lee, B. A., MacKenzie, J.J., & Holden, J.J.A. [2003]. Fragile X syndrome. In I. Brown & M. Percy [Eds.], *Developmental disabilities in Ontario* [2nd ed., p. 240]. Toronto, Canada: Ontario Association on Developmental Disabilities; reprinted by permission.)

Chromosome Test

Until 1991, genetic testing for FXS relied on the examination of chromosomes to search for the little break or fragile site at the end of the X chromosome. Although this test was an important step in distinguishing fragile X from other causes of developmental disability, the test was not always reliable and sometimes resulted in misdiagnoses.

Gene Test

Since the discovery of the FMR1 gene in 1991, two tests have been developed: polymerase chain reaction (PCR) and Southern blotting. Both gene tests examine the number of repeats in the FMR1 genes from individuals, using a small sample of blood or even a swab of cells from the inside of the cheek. The PCR test is more accurate for determining the number of repeats, especially when the number is less than about 200. It is difficult to determine accurately the number of repeats when the size is much larger than that. However, because males with 200 repeats are as affected as those with 450 repeats, having accurate numbers for full mutations is not necessary. A simple method of doing PCR to determine the number of repeats in the FMR1 gene using only a small spot of blood was developed, making the test very inexpensive (Holden, Chalifoux, Wing, DiTullio, & Julien-Inalsingh, 1996) and enabling the study of large populations.

Who Is Eligible for Testing?

Anyone with a family history of FXS, or anyone who has a developmental disability or autism spectrum disorder of unknown cause, is eligible for testing. The family history shown in Figure 15.4 illustrates no instances of developmental disability prior to the youngest generation. However, genetic testing of other family members revealed the FMR1 premutation in several family members and that the expansion had increased in size from generation to generation until it reached the full mutation in five members of the last generation. Four of the five are affected with FXS, with one daughter being unaffected. Because all individuals with FXS inherit an abnormal FMR1 gene from a parent, relatives of an affected individual are eligible for testing.

FXS can appear in a family unexpectedly. This is because small premutations, which have been present in the family for several generations, expand

in size, finally reaching a size that is clinically significant (i.e., produces symptoms in the person having the mutation).

The Accuracy of Fragile X Testing

Testing for the standard FMR1 mutation (i.e., expansion of the number of CGG repeats) using the gene test is extremely precise and approaches 100% accuracy.

When to Provide Testing

Genetic testing can be performed for individuals at any age as well as for the developing fetus. The decision to have genetic testing for oneself, for a child, or for a relative is a personal choice and can evoke a variety of emotions. Professional assistance can be helpful when dealing with such challenging issues. The testing of children who are not old enough to provide their own consent is a controversial issue. Genetic testing should only be done with appropriate counseling.

IMPACT ON FAMILIES

Families in which at least one member has FXS face unique challenges. In dealing with these challenges, family members experience a range of emotions, including joy, pride, and love, but often also a sense of loss, fear, guilt, and other difficult emotions. Studies involving several families affected by fragile X revealed various experiences of stress (Minnes & Steiner, 2009; Nachshen & Minnes, 2005). These included difficulty getting a diagnosis, lack of knowledge about FXS in professionals, difficulty explaining FXS to others, difficulty finding appropriate community living, problems with family relationships, difficulties with the education system, issues regarding sexuality, challenges in finding recreation, and complications in long-term planning. These areas of stress reflect the need for public awareness about FXS and more information for professionals in the health care and education systems.

SUPPORTS AND SERVICES FOR PEOPLE WITH FRAGILE X SYNDROME

Supports and services to address various needs in people affected by FXS are described in the following subsections.

Health Care Needs

Although some people with FXS do not have medical complications, it is important to recognize that both children and adults with FXS are at higher risk for some problems than unaffected individuals of the same age. Table 15.2 summarizes some of the problems that might arise in children, as well as how the problems might be manifested and what assessments or management tools should be implemented. For example, recurrent otitis media is common in FXS, and tubes to drain fluid from the middle ear may be indicated.

It is important to remember that adults with FXS may have health problems that have been overlooked. A tool to help primary care providers looking after people of all ages with FXS has been developed, giving information about health problems in FXS and suggesting appropriate approaches to management. The tool is called a Health Watch Table and is available at http://www.surreyplace.on.ca/resources-publications/primary-care/tools-for-primary-care-providers.

Educational Needs

Students with developmental disabilities may be eligible for inclusion in general education classrooms but may require special assistance. Students with FXS sometimes benefit from short periods away from regular classroom activity. Teachers can benefit from information on educational strategies designed specifically for children with FXS (for more information, see National Fragile X Foundation, 2016).

Other Services and Supports for Individuals with Fragile X Syndrome

Primary care may be provided by pediatricians to children (or family physicians to children and adults) who make referrals to specialized services as required. Interventions may include behavioral or medical therapies to modify sleep disturbances, hyperactivity, and short attention span and may address other concerns. Specialized services include the following:

- Assessment of fine motor or gross motor functioning

- Assessment of speech and language development

- Assessment of learning abilities

- Behavioral assessment

- Occupational therapy (to improve participation in activities of daily living independently) or physiotherapy (to maintain health and ability by physical sense—e.g., special exercises)

Table 15.2.   Checklist of possible health care needs of children with fragile X syndrome[a]

Problem area	Clinical expression	Assessment/management
Feeding difficulties	Poor weight gain	Feeding team
Visual	Squint/refractive errors	Early consult with pediatric ophthalmologist if eyes are not straight or if there is a suggestion of poor vision
Auditory/ears	Chronic otitis media (ear infection or earache), conductive hearing loss	Early vigorous treatment, hearing assessment, otolaryngology consult regarding ventilation tubes
Dental	Caries, malocclusion	Initial dental examination by age 2 (may require sedation)
Musculoskeletal	Low muscle tone, flat feet, scoliosis, loose joints	Physiotherapist, orthopedic or occupational therapist
Cardiovascular	Cardiac murmurs/clicks, high blood pressure	Echocardiogram, cardiologist, prophylactic antibiotics are rarely needed
Genitourinary	Bed-wetting, late toilet training, urinary tract infections, hernia	Behavioral interventions, medication, renal ultrasound
	Large testes	Not a problem, but concerned parents benefit from reassurance on this matter
Endocrine	Early puberty	Endocrinologist, medications
Central nervous system	Seizure disorder, cognitive delay, low muscle tone, behavior disorders, psychiatric disorders	Pediatric neurologist, electroencephalogram, anticonvulsant medication, early developmental assessment, psychology assessment

[a]All health care should be coordinated by one primary physician.

Health professionals involved in such service provision include the following:

- Pediatricians (especially developmental pediatricians)
- Psychologists or psychiatrists
- Speech-language pathologists
- Behavioral consultants
- Occupational therapists
- Physiotherapists
- Psychometrists

Specialized Intervention Strategies for People with Fragile X Syndrome

Several intervention strategies have been developed to help reduce difficult behaviors in special circumstances and improve the quality of life for individuals with FXS. Changes in routine may result in behavioral outbursts, much like the response of children with autism to change. Loud noises and bright lights can be distracting and cause problems in a learning environment. Table 15.3 lists some causes of behavioral disturbances and how to address them.

Programs and Services Beneficial to Children with Fragile X Syndrome

Five types of beneficial programs and services exist:

1. *Infant development/stimulation programs:* From birth to 2 years of age, such programs provide in-home support with suggestions for parents on how to provide intervention for a child with a developmental disability.

2. *Hanen Centre:* The Hanen Centre provides programs that may help parents, educators and professionals assist children in developing communications skills. Information can be found at http://www.hanen.org. Speech language pathologists (speech therapists) can be very helpful if there are concerns regarding language development.

3. *Child care placements:* Child care placements can help by providing a stimulating environment with peers.

4. *Preschool development services:* These services may be provided in the home or child care environment with activities to stimulate development and plan the transition to school.

5. *Special education services.* In the United States, the Individuals with Disabilities Education Improvement Act (IDEA) of 2004 (PL 108-446) mandates special education services from birth to 21 years of age. Programs vary depending on the individual's needs (see https://www.fragilex.org/treatment-intervention/education/).

Community Programs to Facilitate Child Development

Services for children with developmental disabilities vary among communities. Child development centers

Table 15.3. Examples of what may cause behavioral disturbances and how to address them

Causes	Strategies to try
Changes in routine	
Has the routine suddenly changed? Is there a new teacher? Have seating arrangements been changed?	Keep the routine as predictable as possible. Introduce changes regularly. Give appropriate notice of changes. (*Note:* An excessive amount of notice may cause anxiety.)
Loud noises	
Are there loud or unpredictable noises? Did the alarm go off? Did someone's cell phone ring?	Keep unpredictable sounds (e.g., alarms, cell phones) to a minimum as possible. Avoid loud or abrupt noises. Use soothing, uninterrupted sounds, such as quiet, steady hums, classical music, and nature sound recordings.
Lights	
Is the lighting too bright? Are there flashing lights?	Make use of daylight/natural lighting (vs. fluorescent lighting) whenever possible. Reduce brightness—use pink or other soft-tone lightbulbs.
Crowds	
Are there too many people around? Are they too close together?	Maintain a sense of spaciousness; avoid crowds. Choose aisle seats or back sections for more space and an easy exit.

may be part of hospital services, health units, or specialized child care centers, depending on the size of the community. These resources include government financial assistance, respite care, and behavior management. Readers should contact the following organizations for information about such services: the National Fragile X Foundation (http://www.fragilex.org) and the FRAXA Foundation (http://www.fraxa.org) in the United States and the Fragile X Research Foundation of Canada (http://www.fragilexcanada.ca) in Canada.

FRAGILE X RESEARCH

Every 2 years, researchers from around the world come together to discuss their research findings at the International Fragile X Conference. Some areas of ongoing research are described in the following subsections.

The FMR1 Protein

The FMR1 gene codes for the FMR1 protein, which is lacking in people with FXS. It is particularly abundant in neurons in the brain and may play a role in modulating the signaling that occurs between neurons. Researchers are learning the precise role of FMR1 protein in different cells. For a review, see Pfeiffer and Huber (2009).

Strategies Designed to Maximize Functioning of Individuals with Fragile X Syndrome

A wide range of treatments for improving function in people with FXS is available, including psychopharmacology (reviewed by Bagni et al., 2012). The identification of appropriate medical therapies has been influenced by research into the effect of FMR1 mutations in FXS. The identification of the fragile X gene, FMR1, and its product, FMR1 protein, have allowed researchers to begin to understand how the lack of FMR1 protein leads to certain aspects of FXS. Much of this research has been done using animal models, which allow for research that cannot be attempted on human subjects. Mice with the fragile X gene mutation have been developed and are being used to explore treatments for fragile X. For example, Bilousova and colleagues (2009) showed potential benefit in using an antibiotic (minocycline) to reduce anxiety in a mouse model of fragile X. Other work by Wang et al. (2008)

suggested an important role for dopamine regulation in FXS, also using a mouse model. Clinical trials of some of these agents are ongoing.

Premature Ovarian Failure/ Primary Ovarian Insufficiency

Women with premutations can have irregular menses and decreased fertility and may go into menopause at an early age, leading to concerns about family planning and health. It is important for women with premutations who are experiencing very irregular or no menses to consult their physician and be tested to determine whether they should be considering any therapy, such as hormone replacement. Research in mice is beginning to show how this happens and perhaps how treatment might be developed (Lu et al., 2012).

Fragile X-Associated Tremor/Ataxia Syndrome

Older adults who have the premutation may develop FXTAS, a neurological condition that is sometimes described as being like Parkinson's disease. It is more common in males but also can occur in females. It does not occur in full mutation carriers. This area of research was reviewed by Brouwer, Willemsen, and Oostra (2009).

Distributions of FMR1 Alleles and Prevalence of Mutant Alleles in Different Populations

Many studies have looked at the prevalence of the fragile X full mutation, premutation, and gray zone alleles in different populations. Peprah (2012) reviewed the results of population studies and how this information aids understanding of the mechanism of trinucleotide repeat expansion in FXS.

Educational Strategies

In the United States, various educational strategies are being researched. Dr. Marcia Braden (Colorado) is studying learning and behavior management strategies for students with FXS and has developed the Logo Reading System (http://www.marciabraden.com/Products). Dr. Michelle Mazzocco (Maryland) is examining math skills in girls with fragile X in order to adapt math programs to optimize learning in these girls (Murphy & Mazzocco, 2008). Increasing understanding of learning difficulties for fragile X students is important in devising effective learning strategies.

Health Care Concerns

Dr. Patricia Minnes, at the Department of Psychology of Queen's University in Ontario, Canada, has been working with families affected by fragile X and studies parents' concerns about, and views on, enhancing health care of their children with FXS (Minnes & Steiner, 2009).

SUMMARY

FXS is one cause of developmental disability in males and females. This syndrome is hereditary, with females usually being less affected than males. Affected individuals generally have good health but can require specialized services or medication. Health care services are provided through family physicians and pediatricians. Affected individuals often require special education assistance.

Families of individuals affected with FXS frequently experience challenges associated with raising a child with a developmental disability, including finding information, services, and support. Family members generally encounter a lack of awareness of FXS in the community and among professionals. Unaffected family members can also carry the fragile X mutation, and this often affects their family planning decisions. Research, public awareness, and support for people with FXS are growing around the world.

FOR FURTHER THOUGHT AND DISCUSSION

1. Parents of students with fragile X do not always inform teachers and other students about the fragile X diagnosis. Discuss possible advantages and disadvantages of sharing or not sharing this information.

2. If fragile X carrier women were identified, they could be offered the option of prenatal diagnosis and pregnancy termination. Should screening be carried out? To whom should screening be available (e.g., newborn females, teenagers, pregnant women)? Should the cost of screening be paid by health insurers or national health services?

3. Prenatal screening can identify the size of the mutation in a female fetus but cannot predict whether she will be affected. Should a pregnancy termination be offered for a female fetus with the fragile X full mutation?

4. When a person receives a diagnosis of fragile X, other family members also have a high probability of carrying the mutation. Genetic counselors recommend that family members tell their relatives about fragile X so that they too can get genetic counseling and testing for the mutation. Geneticists and genetic counselors often encounter family members who, for a variety of reasons, have chosen not to tell other relatives about fragile X. Should this task be left to the family member who received the diagnosis? If the genetics department knows the names of the extended family members, does it have an obligation to tell them about the fragile X diagnosis? Would this be a violation of confidentiality?

5. Several research initiatives are looking at the possibility of gene therapy for FXS. This involves the delivery of a working copy of the fragile X gene into the cells of the brain in the hope that the gene would make the needed protein and reverse the cognitive disabilities associated with this syndrome. Discuss arguments for and/or against such therapy.

REFERENCES

Bagni, C., Tassone, R., Neri, G., & Hagerman, R. (2012). Fragile X syndrome: Causes, diagnosis, mechanisms, and therapeutics. *Journal of Clinical Investigation, 122*(12), 4314–4322.

Bilousova, T.V., Dansie, L., Ngo, M., Aye, J., Charles, J.R., Ethell, D.W., & Ethell, I.M. (2009). Minocycline promotes dendritic skhourypine maturation and improves behavioral performance in the fragile X mouse model. *Journal of Medical Genetics, 46*(2), 94–102.

Brouwer, J.R., Willemsen, R., & Oostra, B.A. (2009). The FMR1 gene and fragile X-associated tremor/ataxia syndrome. *American Journal of Medical Genetics, 150B*(6), 782–798.

Gabis, L.V., Baruch, Y.K., Jokel, A., & Raz, R. (2011). Psychiatric and autistic comorbidity in fragile X syndrome across ages. *Journal of Child Neurology, 26*(8), 940–948.

Holden, J.J.A., Chalifoux, M., Wing, M., DiTullio, K., & Julien-Inalsingh, C. (1996). The fragile-X syndrome: Current understanding and testing procedures. *Journal on Developmental Disabilities, 2*(1), 82–90.

Hunter, J.E., Abramowitz, A., Rusin, M., & Sherman, S. (2009). Is there evidence for neuropsychological and neurobehavioral phenotypes among adults without

FXTAS who carry the FMR1 premutation? A review of current literature. *Genetics in Medicine, 11*(2), 79–89.

Individuals with Disabilities Education Improvement Act (IDEA) of 2004, PL 108-446, 20 U.S.C. §§ 1400 *et seq.*

Kremer, E.J., Pritchard, M., Lynch, M., Yu, S., Holman, K., Baker, E.,...Richards, R.I. (1991). Mapping of DNA instability at the fragile X to a trinucleotide repeat sequence p(CCG)n. *Science, 252*(5013), 1711–1714.

Laschiewitcz, A.M., Dawson, D.V., & Spiridigliozzli, G.A. (2000). Physical characteristics of young boys with fragile X syndrome: Reasons for difficulties in making a diagnosis in young males. *American Journal of Medical Genetics, 92,* 229–236.

Lee, B. A., MacKenzie, J.J., & Holden, J.J.A. (2003). Fragile X syndrome. In I. Brown & M. Percy [Eds.], *Developmental disabilities in Ontario* (2nd ed.). Toronto, Canada: Ontario Association on Developmental Disabilities.

Lu, C., Lin, L., Tan, H., Wu, H., Sherman, S.L., Gao, F.,... Chen, D. (2012). Fragile X premutation RNA is sufficient to cause primary ovarian insufficiency in mice. *Human Molecular Genetics, 21*(23), 5039–5047.

Maenner, M.J., Baker, M.W., Broman, K.W., Tian, J., Barnes, J.K., Atkins, A.,...Mailick, M.R. (2013). FMR1 CGG expansions: Prevalence and sex ratios. *American Journal of Medical Genetics, 162B*(5), 466–473.

Minnes, P., & Steiner, K. (2009). Parent views on enhancing the quality of health care for their children with fragile X syndrome, autism or Down syndrome. *Child: Care, Health and Development, 35*(2), 250–256.

Murphy, M.M., & Mazzocco, M.M. (2008). Rote numeric skills may mask underlying mathematical disabilities in girls with fragile X syndrome. *Developmental Neuropsychology, 33,* 345–364.

Nachshen, J.S., & Minnes, P. (2005). Empowerment in parents of school-aged children with and without developmental disabilities. *Journal of Intellectual Disability Research, 49,* 889–904.

National Fragile X Foundation. (2016). *Education.* Retrieved from https://fragilex.org/treatment-intervention/education/

National Human Genome Research Institute. (2016). *Learning about fragile X syndrome.* Retrieved from https://www.genome.gov/19518828/learning-about-fragile-x-syndrome/

Nolin, S.L., Glicksman, A., Ding, X., Ersalesi, N., Brown, W.T., Sherman, S.L., & Dobkin, C. (2011). Fragile X analysis of 1112 prenatal samples from 1991 to 2010. *Prenatal Diagnosis, 31,* 925–931.

Oostra, B.A., Hoogeveen, A.T., & Willemsen, R. (n.d.). *Fragile X syndrome and FMR1.* Retrieved August 12, 2010, from http://ww2.eur.nl/fgg/kgen/research/fmr1.html

Peprah, E. (2012). Fragile X syndrome: The FMR1 CGG repeat distribution among world populations. *Annals of Human Genetics, 76*(2), 178–191.

Pfeiffer, B.E., & Huber, K.M. (2009). The state of synapses in fragile X syndrome. *Neuroscientist, 15,* 549–567.

Wang, H., Wu, L.-J., Kim, S.S., Lee, F.J.S., Gong, B., Toyoda, H.,...Zhuo, M. (2008). FMRP acts as a key messenger for dopamine modulation in the forebrain. *Neuron, 59*(4), 634–637.

Wen, G.Y., Jenkins, E.C., Yao, X.-L., Yoon, D., Brown, W.T., & Wisniewski, H.M. (1997). Transmission electron microscopy of chromosomes by longitudinal section preparation: Application to fragile X chromosome analysis. *American Journal of Medical Genetics, 68,* 445–449.

16

Autism Spectrum Disorder

Adrienne Perry, Julie Koudys, Glen Dunlap, and Anne Black

WHAT YOU WILL LEARN

- The history of autism spectrum disorder diagnoses and terminology
- The definition and prevalence of autism spectrum disorder
- Early intervention, education, and services to support people with autism spectrum disorder
- The importance of family involvement in supporting people with autism spectrum disorder

It is often said that no two people with autism spectrum disorder (ASD) are alike. The three profiles highlighted in this chapter demonstrate a number of important things about ASD. First, ASD may seem very different from one person to another, depending on the person's age, level of cognitive functioning, personality, and particular pattern of symptoms and behavior. Also, people with ASD may have other disorders or difficulties as well as ASD, and they will have particular strengths and talents as well. Like all people, children and adults with ASD live, learn, work, and play in a variety of community environments.

CHARACTERISTICS OF AUTISM SPECTRUM DISORDER

This section begins with a brief historical perspective on ASD, which is followed by a more detailed description of the current definition of ASD. The diagnostic process is then described, together with other disorders that may be confused with or may overlap with ASD. Trends in ASD prevalence and research into the causes of ASD are then summarized.

History of Autism Spectrum Disorder Diagnosis and Terminology

The disorder now called ASD was first described by Leo Kanner in 1943. Since that time, understanding of ASD has grown and the definition of autism has changed several times. Another major change in terminology is in progress. Until 2013, most professionals in North America used the terminology defined in the *Diagnostic and Statistical Manual of Mental Disorders, Fourth Edition, Text Revision* (*DSM-IV-TR*; American Psychiatric Association [APA], 2000), and in this transition period this terminology is still often used, so it is good to be familiar with it. The *DSM-IV-TR* included a general category of pervasive developmental disorders (or PDDs), which involve difficulties with social interaction, verbal and nonverbal communication, and repetitive behavior. Five specific disorders were defined: Autistic Disorder, Asperger's Disorder, Pervasive Developmental Disorder-Not Otherwise Specified (PDD-NOS), Rett's Disorder, and Childhood Disintegrative Disorder.

In 2013, however, the fifth edition of the *DSM* (*DSM-5*; APA, 2013) replaced the general category of PDDs with one broad diagnostic term: Autism Spectrum Disorder (ASD). This change reflects research showing that the specific definitions of the subtypes were not always reliable and also the belief that there is a spectrum, or continuum of symptom severity, as well as a range of developmental levels, rather than five distinct disorders. In addition, in *DSM-5*, the criteria were reduced in number and fall into only two broad areas of difficulty: 1) persistent deficits in social communication and interaction, and 2) restricted, repetitive patterns of behavior, interests, or activities. The broad diagnostic label *Autism*

219

BEN

Ben is 2½ and he loves trains. He is content to play alone with them for hours. He does not pretend to make them go on the track or have crashes, imagine what the cars are carrying, or talk as he plays. He just lines up the trains in the same way every time and gets very upset if anyone rearranges his trains. Sometimes Ben carries a train around with him and rubs it against his chin or waves it in front of his eyes. He never brings a train to show his parents and never points to the trains to show his sister. Ben does not talk at all, rarely looks at other people, and rarely smiles.

CAROLYN

Carolyn is 12 and is great at doing puzzles quickly, even if they are upside down. She struggles with her schoolwork, especially language arts and social studies, but is quite good at spelling and math and has an excellent memory. Carolyn was in special education classes when she was younger but is now in a general education class. She seems very friendly and talkative. She asks questions of everyone she comes in contact with, even if people are not interested in talking to her, and does not know how to relate to her peers any other way. Other teens do not like being with her and some bully her. Lately, she is showing signs of depression. She is enrolled in a social skills group at a local mental health agency.

JEFF

Jeff is 23 and has lived, for the past 2 years, in a group home with four other young men who have developmental disabilities, but Jeff doesn't really interact with the other residents—only with staff. Jeff just got a job in a warehouse. Although he has the skills needed to do the actual work, Jeff still requires a lot of support, and his employer insists that a staff person is with him at all times. One reason is that Jeff sometimes has seizures at work. Also, Jeff has a hard time when asked to do new things or when tasks are changed slightly from what he is used to; he will bang his head and scream when he gets frustrated in such situations. At the group home, three staff members work with Jeff and his housemates to teach them how to cook, clean their rooms, and do their laundry.

Spectrum Disorder now replaces other specific terms previously known as Autistic Disorder, Asperger's Disorder, PDD-NOS, and Childhood Disintegrative Disorder. *Autism Spectrum Disorder* is a much broader term, referring to a wide spectrum, compared with the term *autism,* which was used to mean just Autistic Disorder and was seen as the disorder at the severe end of the spectrum.

There has been some controversy about the new definition. Some individuals formerly diagnosed with Asperger syndrome, or what the *DSM-IV-TR* called Asperger's Disorder, are concerned about losing their specific identity and simply being included in the much broader category of ASD along with individuals who are very different from them. In addition, some people are concerned that research into causes and treatments will be more complicated now that there is just one disorder that includes people who may be very different from one another. Some studies have suggested that people with milder symptoms or higher IQs may not actually meet criteria for ASD,

but other researchers do not find this. It will take years before the full impact of this major change is known.

Definition and Description of Autism Spectrum Disorder

Per the *DSM-5* definition, *ASD* involves, first and foremost, pervasive difficulties in reciprocal social communication and interaction. All three of the criteria in Section A must be met. This includes deficits in *social-emotional reciprocity.* People with ASD may prefer isolation and ignore other people (e.g., Ben, who is described in the profiles) and may be unresponsive or aloof when others try to interact with them. Other people may respond to social initiation as best they can but seldom, if ever, initiate social contact. Children with ASD tend not to show others something they have made or point out things of interest, such as Ben, who did not show his trains to his parents. Even "high-functioning" people with ASD can have great difficulty thinking about the

Figure 16.1. Repetitive or stereotyped behaviors in autism might include repetitive play or object use, such as lining up trains or toy cars. (Image © istockphoto/Linda Epstein.)

feelings and thoughts of other people. Some people with ASD may appear not to notice if another person is hurt or upset, do not understand when people are joking or being sarcastic, and may not seem to have empathy for others. They often have difficulty engaging in back-and-forth conversations, even if they can speak well, but they may like to talk about topics of interest to them, not realizing others are not interested (e.g., Carolyn).

People with ASD also have deficits in *nonverbal communicative behaviors*. These include such things as eye contact that may be very brief, odd, or almost nonexistent (e.g., Ben); infrequent smiling or other facial expression; and great difficulty with the use of gestures and behaviors to engage the attention of another person in a social interaction. They often do not point to show something, for example, as in the case of Ben. Sometimes a person with ASD will speak or use a gesture but not combine it with eye contact and smiling as would be expected (e.g., he or she may point at something but not look to see if the other person is looking at what he or she is pointing at).

Deficits in *developing and maintaining relationships* are also characteristic of ASD. This social deficit does not necessarily involve withdrawing from social contact, but there is difficulty developing and sustaining relationships with other people. It is very

difficult for children with ASD to make friends even if they want to (e.g., Carolyn), and individuals such as Jeff often have no friends at all. Children with ASD often have difficulty with imitation and with pretend play. For example, a child such as Ben may repeatedly open and close the window of a playhouse, whereas another child might ask someone else to play and pretend to sell him or her an ice cream cone in the playhouse.

The other part of the diagnosis involves two (or more) of the four symptoms listed under Section B in the *DSM-5*. Repetitive or stereotyped behaviors (often assumed to be self-stimulatory) may include rocking, hand flapping, and other unusual body movements. The behaviors may also involve manipulation of objects, such as repeatedly jiggling, spinning, tapping, rubbing, or lining up certain objects (e.g., Ben lining up his trains; see Figure 16.1 for another example). Some individuals with ASD may also use verbal or vocal behavior in an unusual manner. They may exhibit echolalia, or repeat the words or phrases of others, either right away (immediate echolalia) or sometime later (delayed echolalia). Some individuals engage in complex routines and rituals and get very upset if these cannot be completed. Sometimes, people with ASD are extremely rigid and react strongly to small changes. For example, an altered school bus route or a new picture on the wall may be upsetting enough to precipitate a tantrum in some children. There can be unusual preoccupations and interests (e.g., a fixation with traffic lights) or intense interests in unusual topics (e.g., the call letters of radio stations) and limited interest in other toys or activities. Finally, unusual reactions to sensory input are also common. For example, an individual with ASD may demonstrate a fascination with visual stimuli such as lights, mirrors, or spinning fans, or may have very negative reactions to seemingly minor sensory input, such as the sound of the vacuum cleaner or the feeling of a shirt label.

Part of the definition of ASD is that the symptoms begin in early childhood, although in certain cases, it may not be clear until the child is a little older (e.g., when the child goes to kindergarten) and the social demands are too much for the child.

Diagnosis of Autism Spectrum Disorder

Despite increased awareness of the need for early assessment and diagnosis, children with ASD are diagnosed, on average, at about 4 years of age

(Centers for Disease Control and Prevention [CDC], 2012), although parents often begin reporting concerns when their child is 2 or even younger. Many parents are told to "wait and see" or that their child "will likely grow out of it," but this is usually not good advice. Parents should be believed and respected. When ASD is suspected (warning signs are described below in the next paragraph), children should be referred as soon as possible for a comprehensive diagnostic assessment. If there is a long waiting list, it may be wise to begin early intervention even before a formal diagnosis is obtained.

There has been a lot of research looking at early signs of ASD from home videos (e.g., from the child's first birthday party); from parent surveys about early concerns; and from watching the development, from birth on, of the younger siblings of children with autism, some of whom also go on to show ASD. Early "red flags" to watch for in children at 18 months or 2 years (Anagnostou et al., 2014) include not responding to their names, not making eye contact, not pointing to show or share interest, not speaking, not using gestures, and not imitating. There may or may not be repetitive behavior (e.g., excessive rocking or flicking fingers) or loss of previously gained skills (e.g., the child had a few words and then lost them). However, it is more important to pay attention to the things the toddler should be doing and is not doing, such as pointing, smiling, and imitating.

Making the diagnosis of ASD is a complex task and should be done only by a qualified professional (usually a psychologist, developmental pediatrician, neurologist, or child psychiatrist) or multidisciplinary team, based on some combination of the following: direct observation of the child, a review of the child's history, diagnostic interviews with parents, completion of rating scales designed to measure ASD, and assessment of the child's cognitive and language level. It is important to consider 1) differential diagnosis—that is, whether the child's symptoms are best accounted for by ASD or by some other disorder such as intellectual disability or attention-deficit/hyperactivity disorder—and/or 2) comorbidity—that is, whether the child has more than one diagnosis, such as ASD and an intellectual disability (discussed further in the next section). Children should also have a full medical workup to rule out any genetic or other syndromes and should have their hearing tested. For more in-depth information about best practices

in the assessment and diagnosis of ASD, see Anagnostou et al. (2014) and Nachshen et al. (2008).

Overlap with Other Developmental Problems and Other Disabilities

It is very common for children and adults with ASD to also have another diagnosis or other difficulties. The one of greatest relevance for this book is intellectual disability, which often co-occurs with ASD. Under the former *DSM-IV-TR* system, about 70% of individuals with Autistic Disorder had comorbid intellectual disability. The number is, of course, lower (perhaps about one third; CDC, 2012) if the broader ASD spectrum is considered, as many people included on the spectrum have higher cognitive functioning. When providing support or intervention, it is important to understand that ASD can be more or less severe, as can be the degree of cognitive impairment. Thinking back to the profile of Jeff, some of his support needs emerge from his level of cognitive functioning more than his ASD.

Another type of comorbidity is in the area of mental health and behavioral disorders or symptoms. Attentional problems, emotion regulation difficulties, and issues with anxiety and depression are quite common. It is important to remember that just because someone has ASD, it does not mean he or she might not have other problems needing intervention, such as in the profile of Carolyn, who was having emotional problems related to being bullied, as any child might experience in that situation.

Prevalence of Autism Spectrum Disorder

The prevalence of ASD is about 1 in 100, or 1%, which means it is very common, but this includes the whole spectrum. Some studies have even reported 1 in 68 (CDC, 2014), but the methods they used may lead to higher numbers (Mandell & Lecavalier, 2014). The prevalence of those with *DSM-IV-TR* Autistic Disorder and an intellectual disability is a smaller number, perhaps in the region of 1 in 500. ASD occurs in all racial, ethnic, and socioeconomic groups. It is more common in boys than in girls (approximately 4:1). The frequency of ASD (the broad spectrum at least) seems to be increasing, and certainly the demand for services and educational resources is increasing significantly. However, it is not known whether this is a true increase in prevalence or whether it is due to the different definition being used (ASD versus just Autistic Disorder), earlier diagnosis, increased awareness of autism among community professionals and the public, increased resources (in some jurisdictions) for intervention, or the research methods used (file review only vs. actual assessments; small sample vs. whole state/province/country). A study by Baxter et al. (2014) reviewed worldwide prevalence studies and concluded there has been no real increase when these factors are considered.

Causes of Autism Spectrum Disorder

A great deal of research has been done and continues to be done to determine the cause(s) of ASD. Although many questions remain unanswered, the following is known: 1) ASD is not caused by poor parenting (this is an old idea that has been discredited) and 2) ASD is a biological disorder, but there is probably no single, straightforward cause. A variety of sources (Anagnostou et al., 2014; Volkmar et al., 2014) indicated that the causes of ASD are "multifactorial," meaning that there are many factors (genetic, epigenetic, and nongenetic factors) that occur in combination. Several lines of research support this idea.

Approximately 10%–15% of people with autism also have another neurological, chromosomal, or genetic diagnosis, such as Down syndrome, fragile X syndrome, or tuberous sclerosis. Family studies show that there is a genetic component to at least some cases of autism (this is an active research area). Studies suggest that a family that has one child with autism has a higher than average chance of having a second child who is also affected; yet, according to Volkmar et al. (2014), numbers vary considerably across studies, from 2% to 18%. Also, twin studies show that identical twins (who have identical genes) are much more likely to be concordant—that is, both have ASD—than are fraternal twins. This supports a genetic cause, although again the actual numbers vary across studies. The fact that this does not always happen, however, indicates that other, nongenetic factors are likely also involved.

Other research findings point to biological factors that may or may not be genetic. People with autism have a higher than average rate of seizures (seizures occur in approximately 20%–25% of individuals with ASD), indicating abnormal electrical activity in the brain. A small percentage of children who are born prematurely or with low birth weight are at greater risk for having ASD. Children born to older fathers and mothers are at a higher risk for having ASD (Volkmar et al., 2014). Researchers are trying to pinpoint which area(s) of the brain may contribute to ASD. This research is very complex and hard to interpret because of slightly different research methods, slightly different definitions of ASD, and so on. It is likely that whatever goes wrong in the developing brain happens quite early in fetal development and affects a number of different brain areas. The neurochemicals that the brain uses to pass messages along various pathways are also being investigated. Although much remains unknown, the neurotransmitter serotonin has been reported to be elevated in several studies (Volkmar et al., 2014).

Environmental factors have also been suggested as potential causes. The theory that vaccines cause ASD has been disproved (Volkmar et al., 2014). Other theories about environmental factors such as pollution or toxic waste causing ASD, or in utero exposure to substances such as different types of medications, are not supported by any firm evidence to date, but research is ongoing.

INTERVENTIONS FOR PEOPLE WITH AUTISM SPECTRUM DISORDER

ASD is generally considered a lifelong disorder. However, better diagnosis, intervention, and education programs are making a real difference, and the future for children with ASD in the early 21st century is much more optimistic than was the case in the past. Still, many individuals with ASD will need significant supports throughout their lives. The treatment and educational approaches selected should be individualized for each person but should be evidence based, meaning they have research evidence to show they work. Several practice guidelines have been published that provide recommendations for effective treatment (National Autism Center [NAC], 2009, 2011; Perry & Condillac, 2003; Wong et al., 2013).

Early Intervention

Early intensive behavioral intervention (EIBI) programs or comprehensive treatment models, some of which have been in operation since the 1960s, have been shown to result in significant improvements in children's cognitive level (or IQ), adaptive behavior, language, and ability to function in school (Eldevik et al., 2009; NAC, 2009; Reichow, 2012). There is significant variability in children's outcomes, however, which is the subject of ongoing research. It may be related to child factors (e.g., pretreatment age IQ), treatment factors (e.g., quantity, quality of treatment), and perhaps family factors (Perry et al., 2011; Reichow, 2012).

The most well-known of these EIBI programs was developed by Ivar Lovaas in California in the 1960s. The results were very surprising at that time. Almost half of the very young children (age 2 to 3 1/2) receiving 40 hours per week of treatment for about 2 years achieved "best outcome" (i.e., IQ in the average range and unassisted placement in a general education classroom; Lovaas, 1987). Since then, numerous other EIBI programs have been developed, many of which have carried out research to demonstrate their effectiveness (e.g., Howard, Sparkman, Cohen, Green, & Stanislaw, 2005), including some large-scale community applications (Perry et al., 2008).

Other comprehensive early intervention approaches that have been shown effective include Pivotal Response Treatment (PRT; Schreibman & Koegel, 2005), the Early Start Denver Model (ESDM; Dawson et al., 2010), and the Learning Experiences and Alternate Program (LEAP) for Preschoolers and their Parents model (Strain & Bovey, 2011). PRT has been used with preschoolers and their parents as well as with older children. PRT uses behavioral principles in a naturalistic way, encouraging child-directed learning and natural reinforcers, and it focuses on "pivotal" behaviors such as child motivation. It has been shown to be evidence-based (National Research Council, 2001; Wong et al., 2013). The ESDM approach combines behavioral, developmental, and relationship-based approaches and is delivered intensively by therapists and parents in the home. Dawson et al. (2010) showed that this approach can be very effective with toddlers ages 18 to 30 months. The LEAP model involves children with ASD receiving specialized behavioral intervention in naturalistic, inclusive preschool settings rather than using one-to-one teaching in home or segregated settings. Teachers are given special training and consultation, typical peers are trained in how to interact with the children with ASD, and parents receive training that helps them manage their child with ASD and reduce their own stress. The LEAP approach, and the naturalistic teaching that is part of it, has been shown to be effective based on a number of studies over 3 decades (National Research Council, 2001; Wong et al., 2013; see Strain & Bovey, 2011, for details).

These comprehensive early behavioral intervention programs differ somewhat in terms of where the intervention takes place (e.g., home, clinic, preschool), the specific teaching methods used, the type of children involved (e.g., age, developmental level), the theoretical background (more behavioral vs. more developmental), the extent of parent and peer involvement, the degree to which they are adult directed or child directed, and so forth, although there are many similarities across approaches (e.g., promoting active engagement of the child). Research has not been done to directly compare different specific methods or approaches, so it cannot be concluded whether one is better than the others. It may be possible that certain approaches are better matched to specific child and family characteristics, but this has not yet been demonstrated.

The early intervention programs with the strongest support generally rely on the use of applied behavior analysis (ABA) and behavioral teaching strategies (NAC, 2009). More specifically, some characteristics of successful early behavioral intervention include the following:

1. It begins very early. Considerable evidence suggests best outcomes are much more likely if children begin very young, ideally before age 4.

2. It is intensive (often 20–40 hours per week for 1–2 years), although the intensity and duration of treatment may vary based on the model of treatment (e.g., programs with increased parental involvement may provide fewer hours of staff-delivered treatment).

3. It uses structured behavioral teaching principles (e.g., reinforcement, shaping).

4. It is comprehensive. That is, it teaches skills in all areas of development, including language, play, social skills, academics, self-help skills, and others.

5. It is individualized based on the person's strengths, needs, and preferences.

6. It uses highly trained staff who are supervised frequently by highly trained behavior analysts.

7. It involves frequent data collection and uses data to make decisions about children's progress and to guide next steps of treatment.

8. It involves systematic, supported inclusion with typically developing peers. Some approaches emphasize this more than others and do it sooner than others.

9. It involves parents in programming, sometimes conducting extra hours of therapy or helping the child generalize skills to natural settings (Perry, 2002). This early intensive behavioral approach is the kind of program that would be appropriate for Ben. For more details about EIBI and its strong evidence base, please see Perry, Koudys, and Blacklock (2016).

Even with the best early intervention, however, the majority of children with ASD will need supports in school and in adult life. Older children and adults can still continue to benefit from a similar approach involving structured teaching and individualized goals in a comprehensive range of areas of functioning. Teaching vocational skills and life skills becomes more important as individuals with ASD get older. These skills need to be learned and applied in a variety of environments. The next subsection briefly examines effective strategies for school-age children and adolescents with ASD.

Educational Intervention

As with the other forms of intervention discussed in this chapter, educational programming should be evidence based and effective. Compared with the early intervention literature, there is not the same body of evidence to guide individuals working with school-age children with ASD. However, hundreds of small studies have looked at intervention approaches to teach specific skills to individuals or small groups of children and adolescents. Iovannone, Dunlap, and others (Dunlap, Iovannone, & Kincaid, 2008; Iovannone, Dunlap, Huber, & Kincaid, 2003) reviewed the literature regarding effective educational practices for children with ASD older than age 5 and formulated six core elements that are evidence based and should be included in comprehensive educational intervention programs: 1) use systematic instruction; 2) create individualized supports and services; 3) provide comprehensible and structured learning

environments; 4) have a specialized curriculum focus; 5) use a functional approach to problem behavior; and 6) involve families and typically developing peers.

Systematic reviews of more recent literature have been conducted. These reviews identified a variety of focused intervention practices that are considered evidence-based practice (NAC, 2009; Wong et al., 2013). Many of these strategies, such as discrete trial teaching, prompting, and reinforcement, are commonly used within EIBI. However, those strategies, among others, were also found to be effective for older children and adolescents. Many of the strategies fall broadly into the six core elements initially identified by Iovannone and colleagues.

Systematic Instruction Effective educational intervention is systematic—that is, carefully planned and structured, as well as constantly evaluated and modified based on data. Similar to the research on early intervention, most of the published literature for school-age children is based on principles derived from ABA, including such diverse approaches as self-management to promote independent academic work, naturalistic intervention to teach things such as grocery shopping skills, and discrete trial teaching to teach academic skills. Other evidence-based behavioral teaching strategies include modeling appropriate behavior (e.g., raising one's hand while in a group), prompting the performance of a skill (e.g., providing physical guidance to print letters), task analysis to divide larger activities into smaller steps (e.g., separating the tasks required to complete a worksheet and teaching one task at a time, such as "First, print the date"), and the use of a time delay to encourage a child to respond independently (e.g., pausing before prompting a child to respond to a greeting). All involve data collection and analysis. It may be difficult to collect certain kinds of data in school settings (e.g., the trial-by-trial data often used in EIBI programs), but it is important that there are adequate data on the child's skills to make data-based decisions about questions such as "When do we move on to the next set of reading words?" and "Has she mastered appropriate greetings?"

Individualized Supports and Services Given the individual differences among students with ASD in terms of symptoms, characteristics, behaviors, and functioning level, educational programs need to be tailored to suit each child. Individualization needs to take into account student likes and dislikes, strengths and preferences, and motivation. Active engagement in the learning environment is essential. As such, strategies that enhance engagement and motivation should be integrated into each child's education. In part, this means the use of instructional materials and tasks that are interesting to the student (e.g., for Carolyn, who loves puzzles, use a map puzzle to learn geography), and the use of effective motivational systems (i.e., reinforcement). Reinforcement does not just mean using candies to reward correct responses. It could include check marks for correct written work, high-fives for spontaneous social initiation, and effective use of naturally occurring activities or tangible reinforcers. Giving students choices in terms of activities or reinforcers also assists with motivation for task-related behavior and minimizes problem behavior. (For a comprehensive review of effective reinforcement practices, refer to Miltenberger, 2012.)

Comprehensible and Structured Learning Environments

Children with ASD benefit from a structured environment. That means the structure of the day (or task or lesson) is predictable and understandable. A number of supportive strategies may be helpful, such as environmental arrangements or visual cues to help complete a sequence of activities, visual boundaries or organization systems to increase on-task behavior and task completion, providing warnings or time lines before transitions, and so forth. Some (but not all) people with autism respond well to visual supports. These may be used to provide structure and predictability (e.g., having a picture activity schedule showing the order of daily activities) or to help break a task down into steps (e.g., following pictures of the sequence for making a sandwich might work with Jeff). Pictures, or words in some cases, can also help people be more independent if they can use the pictures or words to cue themselves rather than waiting for someone to tell them what to do next.

Specialized Curriculum Focus

Within the individualized approach, there should be a functional curriculum that addresses the specific characteristics of ASD. This means there should be explicit teaching of social-communicative skills that are meaningful for the child's life. Sometimes very

basic social skills (e.g., taking turns) and specific social skills (e.g., asking other children to join in a game) must be taught and practiced in real-life settings. The nature of the specific instructional targets may vary a great deal, depending on the person. PRT, which was mentioned previously in this chapter, is an example of a comprehensive treatment model used with toddlers and older children that teaches pivotal learning variables to teach communication, language, play, and social behaviors—behaviors often referred to as "core deficits" in ASD. Examples of other evidence-based practices to teach social, play, or communicative skills include the use of video modeling to teach play sequences, scripting to teach reciprocal conversation, social narratives to reduce interfering behavior, social skills training to increase prosocial behavior, and structured play groups to teach appropriate social interaction during a structured activity, such as building with blocks.

Improving communication skills is likely to be a goal for all people with ASD. For people with good verbal skills, such as Carolyn, this may mean enhancing reciprocal conversation skills. For individuals with few or no verbal abilities, such as Ben and Jeff, this may mean teaching another form of communication, such as an augmentative and alternative communication (AAC) system. Different communication systems have advantages and disadvantages for different people with ASD (in terms of portability, appeal, cost, effectiveness, understandability, and so forth). AAC approaches include nonsymbolic gestures (e.g., leading someone by the hand to obtain an object), learned cultural gestures (e.g., waving), and formal systems of symbolic gestures (i.e., sign language). Sign language can be helpful as long as the individual has the fine motor skills to produce accurate signs and people in the environment understand the signs, but often the individual learns only a few simple signs that are useful in daily life (e.g., MORE, BREAK, DRINK, TOILET). Also, there has been an increase in the use of speech-generating applications on tablets or notebook computers. Although the opportunity to enhance communication using a socially acceptable device is exciting, so far the research remains limited as to their actual effectiveness in improving functional communication.

Technology can be used for more than communication. The use of technology-aided instruction and intervention has been shown to be effective in improving daily living skills, increasing self-management and task completion, and enhancing social-communicative behavior, among others. However, more research is required to better understand whether these devices are associated with substantial improvements in communication, and if so, for whom. As with other facets of treatment for children with ASD, decisions about communication should be based on evidence. The Picture Exchange Communication System (PECS; Bondy & Frost, 1994) is an example of an AAC system that utilizes many behavioral teaching strategies (prompting, task analysis, reinforcement) and is considered evidence-based practice. It has been very effective with children with a range of support needs. PECS would likely be a good choice for Ben. Parents sometimes worry that learning one of these AAC systems will discourage their child's development of speech. In fact, the opposite is true—AAC systems not only help children communicate their needs at the time but also may help children to speak later as well (Mirenda & Fossett, 2011).

Functional Approach to Problem Behavior
Effective school-based intervention includes a functional approach to understanding a child's problem behavior. Some people with ASD may exhibit severe problem behaviors, such as tantrums, aggression, destruction, or self-injurious behavior. These behaviors are not part of the definition of ASD, but they may be related to the level of functioning or skill deficits, such as poor communication skills or difficulties adapting to change or understanding social situations. Helping students with these problems is a crucial part of their educational program.

Current approaches to managing challenging behavior emphasize comprehensive approaches that first seek to prevent the unwanted behavior(s) from occurring by making environmental changes, and then seek to teach skills that replace the unwanted behaviors, described later in this section. This approach is often referred to as positive behavior support (PBS; Koegel, Koegel, & Dunlap, 1996). First, it is important to rule out any medical issues, especially pain. For example, a child who is biting his hand may actually have a toothache. Maybe the child is hungry, thirsty, or tired. Also, the environment and type of schoolwork needs to be examined. Is the classroom too loud? Are the tasks too boring or too difficult? Sometimes, it is quite easy to prevent

the problem behavior by changing environmental factors that precede the behavior, a strategy referred to as antecedent-based intervention.

If the behavior persists, a behavior support plan may need to be developed based on the results of a functional behavioral assessment (FBA). Note that the term *functional* is used here in a slightly different way than it was previously used in the chapter to refer to a functional curriculum. In this case, it refers to the reason the behavior is happening. Challenging behaviors do not happen "out of the blue"; it is the responsibility of professionals and support providers to figure out the reason(s) why they occur. For example, is it the only way the person has of getting something that he or she wants? Is it an effective way for the person to avoid a hard task? Has the behavior been reinforced by other people's attention?

Once the function is determined, an intervention plan to reduce or change it can be designed based on that function. Many classroom-based strategies can be used, such as providing scheduled antecedent events and interrupting interfering behavior and redirecting to a more appropriate behavior (also known as response interruption/redirection). One of the most important principles is to teach the person alternative, more appropriate behaviors and skills that meet the same function. For example, a student can be taught the skill of requesting a break (whether verbally or using a break card) in order to receive a break from a difficult task instead of waiting until he or she is frustrated and throws books. Also, there are a variety of positive reinforcement-based approaches that involve differential reinforcement of the absence of the problem behavior (i.e., giving attention when a child is behaving appropriately), reinforcing the alternative behavior or replacement skill (e.g., "Oh, good, you raised your hand—I'll be right there"), or reinforcing other incompatible behaviors (e.g., putting hands in pockets instead of flapping hands). Often, these reinforcement strategies are combined with extinction, or the removal of reinforcement for the interfering behavior. For more information about FBAs and managing challenging behavior, refer to Miltenberger (2012).

Family and Peer Involvement
Parents should be actively involved in assessing and determining their child's learning goals, should have input into the methods and motivational strategies used, and should help determine progress (e.g., by reporting how well skills are generalized to the home setting).

There should be frequent communication between home and school. In some cases, parents can supplement programming by either practicing specific skills with their child or by doing informal generalization (e.g., helping the child use a skill in a different setting and with different people). Research increasingly suggests that parent-implemented intervention, in which parents are actively involved in delivering individualized intervention through structured parent training programs, is also effective. For more information about families and PBS, see Lucyshyn, Dunlap, and Albin (2002), a book written about and with parents.

Involvement with typically developing peers is also an important part of learning for most children with ASD. Systematically incorporating opportunities for peer-mediated instruction and intervention may help children with ASD learn new communication or social skills within the natural environment. However, simple exposure or integration with typical peers will likely not be sufficient. As was true with Carolyn, peers are not necessarily helpful. Rather, peers need to be systematically taught strategies to engage with children with ASD and rewarded for these efforts (e.g., Petursdottir, McComas, McMaster, & Horner, 2007). Also, children with ASD will likely require ongoing support, using evidence-based strategies such as those listed earlier in the chapter, in order to effectively develop new social behaviors. Children such as Carolyn may require instruction on basic social concepts (e.g., how to start a conversation), followed by opportunities to practice or role-play the desired skills (e.g., approach your friends, make a comment on what they are doing), feedback on their performance, and ongoing prompting and reinforcement of these behaviors in the natural environment (e.g., "Great job commenting on your friend's activity; now let's practice doing that and making eye contact at the same time").

Services for Adults with Autism Spectrum Disorder

In contrast to the growing body of evidence-based practice for preschool and school-age children and adolescents with ASD, far less is known about effective supports for adults. For a person such as Jeff, a number of the previously described evidence-based practices may be helpful, such as the use of antecedent interventions and functional assessment to address problem behavior, and the use of behavioral teaching strategies to enhance functional skills, but there are obviously important differences to consider when serving an adult population, such as sexuality, privacy, and so on. More research is needed in order to better understand how to adjust practices to accommodate for increasing chronological age, varying abilities, behavioral and mental health issues, and adult-specific issues related to living and working in the community. For some individuals with ASD who have relatively high verbal ability, there is emerging evidence to suggest that cognitive-behavioral therapy can be effectively adapted to address comorbid mental health issues—especially anxiety (e.g., Singh et al., 2011). However, the majority of the research to date has been conducted with children and adolescents. In many jurisdictions, services for adults with autism are particularly problematic. There is a serious shortage of appropriate supports needed for living and working in the community for an individual such as Jeff and for families whose adult son or daughter lives at home.

Medication

Medications are quite often used for individuals with ASD, but there are no medications that actually treat the ASD itself. However, in some cases, medication—usually together with behavioral approaches—may be helpful to treat 1) particular symptoms such as irritability or high activity level or 2) the comorbid disorders individuals may have such as depression or anxiety. See Volkmar et al. (2014) for more information on specific medications and what research has been done.

New and Controversial Approaches

In the ASD field, new treatment methods tend to spring up regularly—often methods that are not evidence based. Parents and others who care about children and adults with ASD naturally seek out treatments. As a result, they may be tempted to try new approaches and are vulnerable to being disappointed by those that are ineffective or even harmful. It is important to learn how to evaluate the next "miracle cure" that comes along. The following are points to keep in mind and questions to ask regarding new or controversial treatment techniques:

- Be open minded but skeptical.

- Ask what research has been done to demonstrate the approach's effectiveness.

- Beware if the approach is being promoted as a miracle, a "cure," or a breakthrough.

- Beware if the approach is claimed to work for everyone and/or is implemented the same way for everyone (rather than being based on an individualized assessment).

- Ask whether the approach is monitored and changed regularly based on some form of data.

- Ask who is qualified to provide the treatment and/or what training and supervision the person receives.

- Think about what harm the approach could cause in terms of potential side effects and risks.

Then consider the costs in money, time, and energy to the person with ASD, his or her family, and any professionals or paraprofessionals who work with the person. Do a risk–benefit analysis, taking all of these points into consideration. If a decision is made to try a new approach, do not discontinue other approaches known to be beneficial and try to evaluate the effectiveness of the new approach systematically to determine whether it really works.

There have been a number of expert panels and processes resulting in lists of treatment approaches that are considered evidence based (e.g., the ones discussed previously in this chapter) and some that are not (e.g., NAC, 2009; Perry & Condillac, 2003; Wong et al., 2013). It is important to realize that there are two different ways that a treatment could be considered as not evidence based: 1) there is just not much evidence either way (in which case, the questions and guidelines mentioned earlier in this subsection may be helpful) or 2) there may be multiple studies showing the approach does not work, in which case it should not be used. Some of the approaches that fall into this category that should not be used or recommended include facilitated communication, patterning, gentle teaching, auditory training, secretin injections, vitamin B_6/magnesium supplementation, chelation, and the gluten- and casein-free diet.

SUMMARY

ASD is a complex and highly variable disorder involving core difficulties with social communication and repetitive behavior. Individuals with ASD may also have intellectual disability, behavioral issues, and psychiatric disorders or difficulties. Evidence-based, individualized interventions and supports are crucial for individuals with ASD of all ages.

FOR FURTHER THOUGHT AND DISCUSSION

1. How might changes in the way ASD is defined in the *DSM-5* affect educational practice?

2. The reported prevalence of ASD has increased dramatically in the early 21st century. Why might that be?

3. What are the benefits and drawbacks of various early intervention programs focused on young children with ASD?

4. What roles can newly emerging electronic and information technologies play in the education of children with ASD?

5. Why do controversial treatments and approaches seem to proliferate within the area of ASD? How can one determine what is valid and what is not with regard to intervention and treatment?

6. What systemic changes need to occur to support adults with ASD to live, learn, work, and play in their communities? What barriers exist to achieving these outcomes?

REFERENCES

American Psychiatric Association. (2000). *Diagnostic and statistical manual of mental disorders* (4th ed., text rev.). Washington, DC: Author.

American Psychiatric Association. (2013). *Diagnostic and statistical manual of mental disorders* (5th ed.). Arlington, VA: Author.

Anagnostou, E., Zwaigenbaum, L., Szatmari, P., Fombonne, E., Fernandez, B.A., Woodbury-Smith, M.,... Scherer, S.W. (2014). Autism spectrum disorder: Advances in evidence-based practice. *Canadian Medical Association Journal, 186*(7), 509–519. doi:10.1503/cmaj.121756

Baxter, A.J., Brugha, T.S., Erskine, H.E., Scheuer, R.W., Vos, T., & Scott, J.G. (2014). The epidemiology and global burden of autism spectrum disorders. *Psychological Medicine, 45*(3), 601–613.

Bondy, A., & Frost, L. (1994). The Picture Exchange Communication System. *Focus on Autistic Behavior, 9,* 1–19.

Centers for Disease Control and Prevention. (2012). Prevalence of autism spectrum disorders—Autism and

Developmental Disabilities Monitoring Network, 14 sites, United States, 2008. *MMWR Surveillance Summaries, 61,* 1–19.

Dawson, G., Rogers, S., Munson, J., Smith, M., Winter, J., Greenson, J.,...Varley, J. (2010). Randomized, controlled trial of an intervention for toddlers with autism: The Early Start Denver Model. *Pediatrics, 125,* e17–e23.

Dunlap, G., Iovannone, R., & Kincaid, D. (2008). Essential components for effective educational programs. In J. Luiselli, D.C. Russo, W.P. Christian, & S.M. Wilczynski (Eds.), *Effective practices for children with autism: Educational and behavior support interventions that work* (pp. 111–136). New York, NY: Oxford University Press.

Eldevik, S., Hastings, R.P., Hughes, J.C., Jahr, E., Eikeseth, S., & Cross, S. (2009). Meta-analysis of Early Intensive Behavioral Intervention for children with autism. *Journal of Clinical Child and Adolescent Psychology, 38,* 439–450.

Howard, J.S., Sparkman, C.R., Cohen, H.G., Green, G., & Stanislaw, H. (2005). A comparison of intensive behavior analytic and eclectic treatments for young children with autism. *Research in Developmental Disabilities, 26,* 359–383.

Iovannone, R., Dunlap, G., Huber, H., & Kincaid, D. (2003). Effective educational practices for students with autism spectrum disorders. *Focus on Autism and Other Developmental Disabilities, 18,* 150–165.

Kanner, L. (1943). Autistic disturbance of affective contact. *Nervous Child, 2,* 217–250.

Koegel, L.K., Koegel, R.L., & Dunlap, G. (Eds.). (1996). *Positive behavioral support: Including people with difficult behavior in the community.* Baltimore, MD: Paul H. Brookes Publishing Co.

Lovaas, O.I. (1987). Behavioral treatment and normal educational and intellectual functioning in young autistic children. *Journal of Consulting and Clinical Psychology, 55,* 3–9.

Lucyshyn, J.M., Dunlap, G., & Albin, R.W. (Eds.). (2002). *Families and positive behavior support: Addressing problem behaviors in family contexts.* Baltimore, MD: Paul H. Brookes Publishing Co.

Mandell, D., & Lecavalier, L. (2014). Should we believe the Centers for Disease Control and Prevention's autism spectrum disorder prevalence estimates? *Autism, 18,* 482–484.

Miltenberger, R.G. (2012). *Behavior modification: Principles and procedures* (5th ed.). Belmont, CA: Wadsworth, Cengage Learning.

Mirenda, P., & Fossett, B. (2011). Augmentative communication. In A. Bondy & L. Frost (Eds.), *A picture's worth: PECS and other visual communication strategies in autism* (2nd ed., pp. 43–64). Bethesda, MD: Woodbine House.

Nachshen, J., Garcin, N., Moxness, K., Tremblay, Y., Hutchinson, P., Lachance, A.,...Ruttle, P.L. (2008). *Screening, assessment, and diagnosis of autism spectrum disorders in young children: Canadian best practice guidelines.* Montreal, Canada: Miriam Foundation.

National Autism Center. (2009). *The National Standards Project: Addressing the need for evidence-based practice guidelines for autism spectrum disorders.* Randolph, MA: Author.

National Autism Center. (2011). *Evidence-based practice and autism in the schools: A guide to providing appropriate*

interventions to students with autism spectrum disorders. Randolph, MA: Author.

National Research Council. (2001). *Educating children with autism.* Washington, DC: National Academies Press.

Perry, A. (2002). Intensive early intervention program for children with autism: Background and design of the Ontario preschool autism initiative. *Journal on Developmental Disabilities, 9*(2), 121–128.

Perry, A., & Condillac, R.A. (2003). *Evidence-based practices for children and adolescents with autism spectrum disorders: Review of the literature and practice guide.* Toronto, Canada: Children's Mental Health Ontario.

Perry, A., Cummings, A., Dunn Geier, J., Freeman, N.L., Hughes, S., LaRose, L.,...Williams, J. (2008). Effectiveness of intensive behavioral intervention in a large, community-based program. *Research in Autism Spectrum Disorders, 2,* 621–642.

Perry, A., Cummings, A., Dunn Geier, J., Freeman, N.L., Hughes, S., LaRose, L.,...Williams, J. (2011). Predictors of outcome for children receiving intensive behavioral intervention in a large, community-based program. *Research in Autism Spectrum Disorders, 5,* 592–603.

Perry, A., Koudys, J., & Blacklock, K. (2016). Early intensive behavioral intervention and training. In N.N. Singh (Ed.), *Clinical handbook of evidence-based practices for individuals with intellectual disabilities* (pp. 531–535). New York, NY: Springer.

Petursdottir, A.L., McComas, J., McMaster, K., & Horner, K. (2007). The effects of scripted peer tutoring and programming common stimuli on social interactions of a student with autism spectrum disorder. *Journal of Applied Behavior Analysis, 40*(2), 353–357.

Reichow, B. (2012). Overview of meta-analyses on early intensive behavioral intervention for young children with autism spectrum disorders. *Journal of Autism and Developmental Disorders, 42,* 512–520.

Schreibman, L., & Koegel, R.L. (2005). Training for parents of children with autism: Pivotal responses, generalization, and individualization of interventions. In E.D. Hibbs & P.S. Jensen (Eds.), *Psychosocial treatment for child and adolescent disorders: Empirically based strategies for clinical practice* (2nd ed., pp. 605–631). Washington, DC: American Psychological Association.

Singh, N.N., Lancioni, G.E., Manikam, R., Winton, A.S.W., Singh, A.N.A., Singh, J., & Singh, A.D.A. (2011). A mindfulness-based strategy for self-management of aggressive behavior in adolescents with autism. *Research in Autism Spectrum Disorders, 5,* 1153–1158.

Strain, P.S., & Bovey, E.H. (2011). Randomized, controlled trial of the LEAP model of early intervention for young children with autism spectrum disorders. *Topics in Early Childhood Special Education, 31,* 133–154.

Volkmar, F., Siegel, M., Woodbury-Smith, M., King, B., McCracken, J., & State, M. (2014). Practice parameter for the assessment and treatment of children and adolescents with autism spectrum disorder. *Journal of the American Academy of Child and Adolescent Psychiatry, 53*(2), 237–257.

Wong, C., Odom, S.L., Hume, K., Cox, A.W., Fettig, A., Kucharczyk, S.,...Schultz, T.R. (2013). *Evidence-based practices for children, youth, and young adults with autism spectrum disorder.* Chapel Hill: University of North Carolina.

17

22q11.2 Deletion Syndrome

Nancy J. Butcher, Erik Boot, Joanne C.Y. Loo,
Donna McDonald-McGinn, Anne S. Bassett, and Wai Lun Alan Fung

WHAT YOU WILL LEARN

- 22q11.2 deletion syndrome as a common multisystem disorder and cause of intellectual disability
- Common clinical features of individuals with a 22q11.2 deletion and their variable expressivity
- Cognitive and behavioral development in people with 22q11.2 deletion syndrome
- Changing issues across the life span
- Recommendations for anticipatory support, treatments, and genetic counseling

22q11.2 deletion syndrome (22q11.2DS) is a common multisystem disorder associated with intellectual and developmental disabilities. It displays considerable variations in the spectrum and severity of its expression across individuals, and the cardinal features may change with age. Prominent features in childhood can include heart problems at birth (congenital heart defects), abnormalities in the hard and soft palate (e.g. velopharyngeal insufficiency), low calcium levels (hypocalcemia), problems with the immune system, and the presence of autism spectrum disorder (ASD), attention deficit disorders, and anxiety disorders. In adolescence and adulthood, there is a high risk of neuropsychiatric disorders such as anxiety disorders and schizophrenia spectrum disorders.

As there is such a wide variation in the features of 22q11.2DS, different groups of signs and

symptoms (syndromes) were historically described as separate conditions (U.S. National Library of Medicine Genetics Home Reference, 2016; adapted from 22q11.2 Deletion Syndrome—Genetics Home Reference. Available from http://ghr.nlm.nih.gov/condition/22q112-deletion-syndrome):

- Autosomal dominant Opitz G/BBB syndrome
- CATCH 22 syndrome
- Cayler cardiofacial syndrome
- Conotruncal anomaly face syndrome (CTAF)
- Deletion 22q11.2 syndrome
- DiGeorge syndrome
- Sedlackova syndrome
- Shprintzen syndrome
- Velo-cardio-facial syndrome
- Velocardiofacial syndrome (VCFS)

In the early 1990s, it was found that these individuals shared the same genetic change: a deletion (missing piece of DNA) in the long arm (q11.2 region) of one of the pairs of chromosome 22. To avoid confusion, the preferred name of the condition is 22q11.2 deletion syndrome, based on its underlying genetic cause.

PREVALENCE

22q11.2DS is the most common microdeletion syndrome in humans, occurring in one in an estimated 2,000–4,000 live births. Both sexes and all racial

---

Authors' note: Nancy J. Butcher and Erik Boot contributed equally to the writing of this chapter.

and ethnic groups are affected (McDonald-McGinn et al., 2015). The 22q11.2 deletion is the second most common genetic cause of developmental delay after Down syndrome, accounting for more than 2% of individuals with developmental disabilities (Rauch et al., 2006). The actual prevalence of 22q11.2DS is likely to be even higher, as it remains an underdiagnosed condition because of its highly variable expressivity (Bassett et al., 2011; see Table 17.1). Due to improved pediatric survival rates, individuals with 22q11.2DS are an increasing population, as the majority now live into adulthood (Bassett et al.; Fung et al., 2015).

GENETICS

22q11.2DS is associated with a deletion of a small region of DNA on chromosome 22. About 90% of affected individuals have a large (approximately 3 million base pairs [Mb]) deletion that spans 90 genes including 46 that are protein-coding. The smaller proximal deletion (approximately 1.5 Mb) that encompasses 30 protein-coding genes occurs in about 10% of individuals. Other "atypical" deletions within the 3 Mb deletion region are also possible but are more rarely detected. There appears to be no relationship between the size of the deletion and the main clinical expressions of 22q11.2DS.

Approximately 90% of cases of 22q11.2DS result from a de novo (spontaneous) mutation, meaning that neither parent has the deletion. In the other 10% of individuals, the deletion is found to be inherited from one of the parents. An individual with 22q11.2DS has a 50% chance of passing along the deletion each time he or she has a child; boys and girls are equally likely to be affected.

Diagnosis of 22q11.2DS requires clinical genetic testing, which first became available in 1992 through fluorescence in situ hybridization (FISH) testing. FISH studies use a probe such as N25 or TUPLE1 that localizes to the proximal 22q11.2 deletion region to test for the deletion. Thus, in a subset of individuals, atypical deletions that occur outside of the FISH probe region may not be detected using this technique. Typical and atypical 22q11.2 deletions have become detectable through newer techniques such as Multiplex Ligation-dependent Probe Amplification (MLPA) and clinical genome-wide microarrays. These genome-wide options are now indicated for individuals of any age with unexplained developmental delay or intellectual disability, multiple congenital anomalies, or ASD (Miller et al., 2010), and should be considered in individuals with schizophrenia (Baker, Costain, Fung, & Bassett, 2014).

Table 17.1.   Common clinical manifestations in 22q11.2 deletion syndrome

Feature[a]	Management
Learning or intellectual disability and developmental delay (90%)	Developmental and cognitive assessment, special education, life skills assessment, vocational counseling and training
Heart defects (50%–75%)	Echocardiogram, electrocardiography
• Requiring surgery (30%–40%)	• Cardiac surgery, cardiac follow-up
Palatal abnormalities (roof of the mouth) and related (75%)	Palatal surgery
• Poor feeding	• Nasogastric tube feeding and/or gastrostomy tube placement
• Hypernasal speech (> 90%)	• Speech-language assessment, speech therapy, surgery
Abnormal facial features (> 90%)	N/A
• Variable, often mild	
Immune system–related diseases (75%)	Immunological evaluation, follow-up
• Lymphocytopenia	
• Recurrent infections (e.g., middle ear infections, 35%–40%)	
• Autoimmune diseases	
• Noninfectious respiratory disease (10%–20%)	
• Seborrhea or dermatitis (35%)	

Table 17.1

Feature[a]	Management
Endocrine (hormones) related diseases	
• Hypocalcemia and/or hypoparathyroidism (> 60%)	• Monitoring of ionized calcium and parathyroid hormone; supplementation of vitamin D (and calcium, if needed)
• Abnormal thyroid hormone levels (> 25%)	• Monitoring of thyroid-stimulating hormone levels; thyroid hormone supplementation
• Obesity (35%)	• Weight monitoring, diet, and regular exercise
• Hypomagnesemia	• Monitoring of magnesium, supplementation
Growth	Monitoring with 22q11.2DS growth charts (http://www.22q.org/resources-for-22q/growth-charts-2/)
• Faltering growth, short stature (20%)	• Growth hormone supplementation
Neuromuscular/musculoskeletal abnormalities	Radiography and/or orthopedic assessments, surgery, physiotherapy
• Scoliosis and kyphosis	
• Deformities of the cervical spine	
• Leg pains of unknown cause in childhood	
• Patellar dislocation	
Blood disorders/cancer	Surveillance, vigilance regarding cancer
• Thrombocytopenia (30%)	
• Malignancies	
Gastroenterological abnormalities	
• Dysmotility/dysphagia (35%)	• Tube feeding, food preparation changes
• Gastroesophageal reflux (10%)	• Lifestyle changes (e.g., low-fat diet), medication
• Gallstones in the gallbladder (20%)	• Diet, pain management, surgery
• Constipation	• High-fiber diet, laxatives, increase fluid intake
Genitourinary abnormalities (> 30%)	Ultrasound
• Improperly formed urinary tract	• Nephrologic, urologic, and/or gynecologic evaluation
• Dysfunctional voiding (10%)	• Urologic or gynecologic evaluation
Sensory abnormalities	
• Impaired sense of smell	• Vigilance with food expiration dates, toxic fumes, and smoke
• Eye problems (e.g., focusing errors, 60%–70%)	• Eye examination at young age, individualized follow-up
• Hearing loss (40%)	• Audiological examination, hearing aids, ear syringing for common wax buildup
Neuropsychiatric disorders	Monitoring for changes in behavior, emotional state, and thinking
• Childhood neuropsychiatric disorders (e.g., attention-deficit/and hyperactivity disorder, autism spectrum disorder)	Psychopharmacological treatments Psychological interventions (e.g., cognitive behavioral therapy)
• Anxiety and mood disorders	
• Schizophrenia and other psychotic disorders (30%–40%)	
Neurologic	
• Recurrent seizures (40%), epilepsy (5%)	• Neurological assessment, monitoring of calcium and magnesium levels, magnetic resonance imaging (MRI), electroencephalogram (EEG)
• Early-onset Parkinson's disease	• Neurological examination, functional neuroimaging
Dental	
• Enamel disturbances/chronic cavities	• Regular checkups, special care dentistry

Sources: Bassett et al. (2011) and Kapadia and Bassett (2008).
[a]Rates provided in parentheses are approximate estimates of lifetime prevalence.

CLINICAL MANIFESTATIONS AND MANAGEMENT

22q11.2DS is typically a multisystem disorder (see Table 17.1). Yet, the syndrome displays considerable variation in the spectrum and severity of its clinical manifestations (Bassett et al., 2011; Fung et al., 2015). This applies to individuals from different families as well as to individuals within the same family (Cirillo et al., 2014). Moreover, the manifestations may vary depending on the age of the individual (Bassett et al.). Management must be targeted to best suit the individual, his or her age and developmental stage, existing manifestations, severity, and need for treatment (Bassett et al.). Interventions include educational, behavioral, vocational, and medical and pharmacological strategies that integrate multiple professionals as well as the family and other support people (Table 17.1).

Congenital Cardiovascular Defects

Improperly formed parts of the heart or blood vessels (congenital cardiovascular defects) are a core feature of 22q11.2DS (McDonald-McGinn & Sullivan, 2011). An example is tetralogy of Fallot, a defect that involves four anatomical abnormalities of the heart and is present in about 10%–20% of individuals with 22q11.2DS. Another example is interrupted aortic arch type B (the aorta is the main blood vessel of the heart) (Bassett et al., 2011; McDonald-McGinn & Sullivan). Milder congenital heart defects (e.g., a hole in the wall of the bottom two heart chambers, known as ventricular septal defect) may escape medical attention. Therefore, all individuals with a 22q11.2 deletion should be evaluated for heart defects at diagnosis.

Palatal Abnormalities and Related Manifestations

The development and functioning of the palate (roof of the mouth) is affected in the majority of individuals with a 22q11.2 deletion. This often contributes to poor feeding in infants and, later, to speech difficulties such as hypernasal speech (McDonald-McGinn & Sullivan, 2011). Such palatal abnormalities typically include weakness of the closing of muscles that separate the nose and mouth (velopharyngeal insufficiency). More significant defects can include soft tissue and frank anatomical clefts. Cleft lip is relatively uncommon. Speech therapy may improve velopharyngeal function. The decision about whether surgery is required must be individualized

to the anatomy and the goals of each individual. Poor coordination of the involved muscles and shortness of breath due to cardiac defects can further contribute to feeding and swallowing problems in infancy (McDonald-McGinn, Kohut, & Zackai, 2010). The neuromuscular incoordination and its surgical treatment may also contribute to risk for sleep apnea.

Facial Features

The facial features of an individual with 22q11.2DS may include a long, narrow face, a prominent nasal root with a fullness superior to the nasal tip, widely spaced eyes (hypertelorism) with hooded eyelids and narrow space between upper and lower eyelids, a small mouth, and/or malformed ears (see Figure 17.1). Nevertheless, the facial features may be very subtle and may be missed even by specialists, especially in non-Caucasian individuals (Liu et al., 2014; Monteiro et al., 2013).

Immune System–Related Diseases

In many children with 22q11.2DS, the immune system's ability to fight infectious disease is compromised (immunodeficiency; McDonald-McGinn & Sullivan, 2011). Most people with 22q11.2DS do not develop life-threatening infections. Still, infections may be prolonged, and the frequency of upper respiratory tract infections is increased, especially in children. Immunological evaluation is recommended at diagnosis. Follow-up into adulthood is recommended for those who have a history of autoimmune conditions or recurrent infections (Bjork, Oskarsdottir, Andersson, & Friman, 2012). Diseases that may occur in 22q11.2DS when the immune system mistakenly attacks healthy body tissue (autoimmune diseases) include psoriasis, juvenile rheumatoid arthritis, and thyroid disease.

A   B

Figure 17.1. Mild dysmorphic facial features of a woman with 22q11.2 deletion syndrome (left, age 11 years; right, age 25 years). (Kapadia, R.K., and Bassett, A.S. Recognizing a common genetic syndrome: 22q11.2 deletion syndrome. *Canadian Medical Association Journal [CMAJ], 178*[4], doi:10.1503/cmaj.071300. © 2008 Canadian Medical Association or its licensor. This work is protected by copyright and the making of this copy was with the permission of Access Copyright. Any alteration of its content or further copying in any form whatsoever is strictly prohibited unless otherwise permitted by law.)

Endocrine-Related Diseases

Low serum levels of calcium (hypocalcemia) are common in 22q11.2DS and are generally the result of inadequate parathyroid hormone secretion (hypoparathyroidism) (Cheung et al., 2014). Clinical presentations vary widely, ranging from symptomless to life-threatening situations such as serious irregular heartbeats (cardiac arrhythmias) or severe seizures. Milder symptoms include fatigue, emotional irritability, and abnormal involuntary movements. Monitoring of calcium levels and parathyroid hormone is recommended for all individuals at diagnosis and with stress, such as at surgery, pregnancy, and acute illness (Bassett et al., 2011). In addition, regular testing of calcium levels is important, as hypocalcemia can emerge at any age. Thyroid diseases are also more common; too much thyroid hormone production (hyperthyroidism) is found in about 5% of individuals and too little thyroid hormone production (hypothyroidism) is found in about 30% of individuals (Bassett et al.; Cheung et al.).

Growth

Growth faltering (failure to thrive) is common in children with 22q11.2DS, particularly those younger than 5 years of age. Rarely this may be caused by growth hormone deficiency (Habel, McGinn, Zackai, Unanue, & McDonald-McGinn, 2012). Weight usually recovers but recovery in height is incomplete and short stature may be found in about one in five adults. 22q11.2DS-specific growth charts have been developed (Habel et al.): see http://www.22q.org/resources-for-22q/growth-charts-2/.

Neuromuscular and/or Musculoskeletal Abnormalities

Deformities of the neck vertebrae (cervical spine) and an abnormal curvature of the spine (e.g., scoliosis) are prevalent (>45%) in people with 22q11.2DS (Bassett et al., 2011; McDonald-McGinn, Kohut, & Zackai, 2010). Several other musculoskeletal abnormalities (e.g., supernumerary or absent ribs) are less common but occur at a rate higher than seen in the general population. Careful examination of the musculoskeletal system should be conducted at diagnosis. The clinical consequences of cervical spine abnormalities (e.g., instability, spinal cord compression) are variable but may require surgery in some cases (Boot et al., 2015).

Hematology and/or Cancer

Many individuals with 22q11.2DS have a low platelet count (thrombocytopenia). Other blood disorders, such as a low red cell blood count (anemia), also occur at a rate higher than in the general population (Bassett et al., 2011; McDonald-McGinn et al., 2010). The overall risk of developing a pediatric cancer (malignancy) appears to be slightly increased. A specific increase in rates of hepatoblastoma, a type of liver cancer, has been reported in 22q11.2DS (Bassett et al.).

Gastroenterological Abnormalities

Many children with 22q11.2DS have difficulties in swallowing (dysphagia) (McDonald-McGinn et al., 2010). Dysphagia may also be present in adulthood and present difficulties in swallowing food and medications. Additional gastroenterological symptoms may include stomach contents coming back up the esophagus (gastroesophageal reflux), gallstones in the gallbladder, constipation, and structural bowel anomalies that are present at birth and that require surgical correction.

Genitourinary Abnormalities

Malformations of the urinary tract (e.g., a missing kidney) have been identified in nearly a third of individuals with a 22q11.2 deletion (Bassett et al., 2011). In males, the absence of one or both testicles from the scrotum (cryptorchidism) and an abnormally placed opening of the urethra (hypospadias) have also been observed (Bassett et al.). Physical examinations (focusing on location of the opening of the urethra and presence of the testicles in the scrotum) and ultrasound (focusing on urinary tract malformations) should be performed at diagnosis.

Sensory-Related Abnormalities

Many children and adults with 22q11.2DS have hearing loss and/or narrow external ear canals (Bassett et al., 2011; Persson, Friman, Oskarsdottir, & Jonsson, 2012; Vieira et al., 2015). Recurrent ear infections often require surgical tube placements. An impaired sense of smell is an important but often overlooked feature of 22q11.2DS (e.g., Romanos et al., 2011). This may not only affect the flavor and the enjoyment of food, but may also be dangerous because it can hinder the detection of potentially toxic fumes, smoke, and spoiled food. Several features of 22q11.2DS relate to the eyes, although severe eye problems are uncommon (e.g., Casteels, Casaer, Gewillig, Swillen, & Devriendt, 2008). These include errors in the focusing of the eyes (refractive errors), problem with eye alignment (strabismus), and twisted blood vessels, known as vascular tortuosity, that are observable but with no clinical consequences.

Dental

Abnormal development of teeth, enamel disturbances, and chronic cavities are common in 22q11.2DS (e.g., Nordgarden et al., 2012).

Neurologic

Seizures and epilepsy occur at a higher than normal frequency in individuals with a 22q11.2 deletion. Recurrent seizures are common, and approximately 5%–7% of the affected individuals have epilepsy, compared with 0.5%–1.0% of the general population (Bassett et al., 2011). Seizures may be related in part to factors such as hypocalcemia, surgery, sleep deprivation, fever, and/or concomitant medication use (e.g., antipsychotic drugs). In 22q11.2DS, optimal seizure control is comprised of not only lifestyle recommendations (e.g., optimize sleep) and antiepileptic drug treatment, but also careful attention to and management of medical conditions that require specific treatment (e.g., hypocalcemia; Table 17.1).

Recent evidence suggests that adults with 22q11.2DS are at increased risk of developing early-onset (<50 years) Parkinson's disease (Butcher et al., 2013), a progressive disorder of the nervous system that is more commonly found in the general population of older adults. Hallmark symptoms include tremor, stiffness, slowness in moving, and balance problems. Periodic neurological assessment for parkinsonism (symptoms of Parkinson's disease) should be considered for adults with 22q11.2DS, especially for those presenting with changes in movements. Causes of parkinsonism and other movement problems may be multifaceted and warrant careful, systematic investigation; side effects from medications (e.g., antipsychotic-induced parkinsonism), musculoskeletal abnormalities, seizures, hypocalcemia, and/or abnormal levels of thyroid hormones may also play a role in presenting movement problems (Boot et al., 2015).

Neuropsychiatric Manifestations

Psychiatric conditions are much more commonly diagnosed in individuals with 22q11.2DS than in the general population and are of great concern to individuals with 22q11.2DS and their families (Fung et al., 2010; Schneider et al., 2014). Individuals may experience a wide range of treatable psychiatric disturbances across the life span. Attention-deficit/hyperactivity disorder (ADHD) is diagnosed in approximately 40% of children and may persist into adulthood. The majority of these individuals have the inattentive subtype, characterized by inattentive concentration or a deficit of sustained attention. Autism spectrum disorder may also be frequent. Unlike in the general population, where it is more common in males, ASD in 22q11.2DS is equally distributed between males and females. Treatable anxiety and mood disorders, often existing simultaneously, are common from childhood on in 22q11.2DS (Schneider et al., 2014).

A major concern for individuals with 22q11.2DS and family members is the markedly elevated risk for developing a schizophrenia spectrum disorder. Schizophrenia and other psychotic disorders are diagnosed in up to 30% of adults with 22q11.2DS. Schizophrenia presenting in an individual with 22q11.2DS is essentially indistinguishable from schizophrenia in the general population with respect to early symptoms, age at onset, clinical features, cognitive profile (except for lower mean IQ and physical features), and so forth. Recurrent psychiatric evaluations should be performed in all individuals with 22q11.2DS to facilitate appropriate diagnosis and timely treatment, in particular in adolescence and young adulthood. Family members and other support people can assist in this by keeping charts and diaries of symptoms and behaviors and by promptly seeking professional help. Individuals and families should be informed about the lifelong genetic vulnerability to major psychiatric illnesses and the many treatments available for those conditions.

The management of psychiatric disorders in 22q11.2DS follows the same biopsychosocial principles as those applied in the general population and in other conditions associated with an intellectual disability. Standard pharmacological treatments are currently recommended for treating individuals with 22q11.2DS who develop a neuropsychiatric condition (e.g., psychostimulants for ADHD, antidepressants and antianxiety medications for anxiety or depression, antipsychotic medications for psychoses; Bassett et al., 2011; Fung et al., 2015; Butcher et al., 2015). Attention to 22q11.2DS-related issues is important, such as the possibility of an increased risk of associated seizures. This seizure risk may be especially of concern during treatment with clozapine (an antipsychotic medication) (Butcher et al., 2015). Also, vigilance for the emergence of symptoms of Parkinson's disease during antipsychotic treatment is also recommended (Butcher et al., 2013). Standard evidence-based psychotherapeutic approaches (e.g., cognitive behavioral therapy) may also be helpful for conditions such as anxiety and depression.

There have been concerns regarding the safety and efficacy of psychostimulant medication, the mainstay of pharmacological interventions in ADHD, in those with 22q11.2DS. Although limited research suggests that the use of the psychostimulant methylphenidate is effective and safe in those with 22q11.2DS, a comprehensive cardiovascular evaluation before and during treatment is recommended, whether or not a congenital heart defect is present (Green et al., 2011). Vigilance regarding the positive emergence of other psychiatric symptoms is also advisable. Optimizing treatment of other associated conditions (e.g., thyroid disease, hypocalcemia, sleep apnea) and minimizing external factors (e.g., high caffeine intake) are particularly important in 22q11.2DS.

INTELLECTUAL AND ADAPTIVE FUNCTIONING ACROSS THE LIFE SPAN

Developmental delay and learning or intellectual disability affect the majority (>90%) of individuals with 22q11.2DS (Table 17.1). The IQ distribution curve in individuals with 22q11.2DS is shifted to the left (with mean IQ about 70) of the IQ distribution in the general population (where the mean IQ is 100; Moreno-de-Luca et al., 2013). There is significant variation between individuals in terms of intellectual functioning (i.e., reasoning, learning, problem solving) and adaptive functioning (e.g., daily living skills, socializing, occupational activities) (Butcher et al., 2012). Moreover, intellectual and adaptive functioning may change over time. Repeated formal assessments are recommended to inform individuals, families, and clinicians, especially at major transitions (e.g., to adulthood).

Infancy and Early Childhood

Delayed developmental milestones are common in young children with 22q11.2DS. These often include delays in achieving motor milestones such as crawling and walking and/or speech and language development (Roizen et al., 2007; Swillen et al., 1997). For example, the average age for beginning to talk (e.g., can put two words together) is between 24 and 36 months, compared with an average age of about 12 to 16 months in typically developing children. Notably, the presence of such developmental delays does not appear to be necessarily predictive of later cognitive functioning in children with 22q11.2DS (Roizen et al.).

Evaluation for delays in achievement of developmental milestones should be conducted regularly using standard screening tools so that early interventions can be implemented. For some children, a prolonged kindergarten before entering elementary school may be helpful. Additional supports that may be necessary when starting school should be considered in advance to facilitate a smooth transition, such as special education classes or pairing with a teacher's aide.

School-Age Children

School-age children with 22q11.2DS most commonly present within the borderline to mild range of impairment in intellectual functioning. Moderate to severe impairments in intellectual functioning appear to be relatively rare, but 22q11.2DS may be underrecognized in this population. Performance IQ scores are reported to be higher than verbal IQ scores in studies of children (Duijff et al., 2013; Swillen et al., 1997), though this may not be observable later on. Boys and girls have similar cognitive profiles.

Children with 22q11.2DS generally show an atypical profile across multiple neurocognitive domains that may affect their academic progress and day-to-day functioning. Areas of relative strength often include reading, spelling, and rote verbal learning and memory. Mathematics, visuospatial skills (e.g., the ability to analyze and understand space in two and three dimensions) and visuospatial memory, attention, working memory, and motor functioning are common areas of deficits (Moss et al., 1999; Sobin et al., 2005). Formal cognitive assessments that include evaluation of the strengths and weaknesses of the child are needed and should be repeated regularly. Studies that have assessed children at two or more points in time have found that the cognitive abilities of some children with 22q11.2DS decline over time (Duijff et al., 2012; Vorstman et al., 2015).

Special assistance in classes is often necessary for children with 22q11.2DS (Moss et al., 1999; Sobin et al., 2005). The decision about whether the child attends the general education classroom or is placed in a special education classroom should be informed by the child's needs and abilities. In any case, speech-language therapy as well as occupational and/or physical therapy is often indicated (Sobin et al.; see Table 17.1). Interventions should be tailored to the individual's strengths and weaknesses. Frequent communication between parents, the school, and teachers is important for proper management. Comorbid medical (e.g., hearing loss) and neuropsychiatric conditions (e.g., ADHD) that may affect functioning should be assessed and treated as needed (Table 17.1).

Adolescents

The global cognitive profile of adolescents with 22q11.2DS is overall similar in pattern to that observed in children; borderline to mild deficits in intellectual functioning are most common. A repeat cognitive assessment should also be considered during the adolescent years, as the cognitive profile, including strengths and weaknesses, may have changed from childhood. Notably, IQ decline is observable in a subset of individuals with 22q11.2DS (Duijff et al., 2013). Conversely, some children showed some cognitive and/or functional improvements over time. Severe cognitive deterioration in this age range appeared to be rare.

As individuals with 22q11.2DS enter adolescence, social, academic, and other functional support needs may become more apparent (e.g., "growing into deficit") as their peers and siblings make age-appropriate progress in these areas. This may be independent of or in addition to an absolute decline in cognitive capabilities (Duijff et al., 2013). Changes in cognition and behavior may be associated with the emergence of neuropsychiatric conditions commonly associated with 22q11.2DS (Table 17.1), such as schizophrenia, and should be monitored carefully to facilitate early interventions and treatment (Vorstman et al., 2015).

As adolescents approach the legal age of adulthood, the use of supported decision making may need to be considered as a result of impaired cognitive competency that may affect individuals' financial management, personal care, and decision-making abilities. Some individuals with 22q11.2DS may function independently with little assistance whereas others may require a high level of support. Internet safety (e.g., vulnerability to financial and/or sexual exploitation) is a growing concern for adolescents and adults (Buijs et al., 2016; Fung et al., 2015). Postsecondary education and vocational placement should be considered whenever possible.

Adulthood

22q11.2DS in adulthood is characterized by widespread cognitive and functional impairments that affect most major aspects of daily adult life (Fung et al., 2015). As in earlier stages of development, there is considerable variability between individuals. Schizophrenia is an important mediator of cognitive functioning in adults. In adults with 22q11.2DS, the average IQ is lower in individuals with schizophrenia than in those who do not have psychotic symptoms (Butcher et al., 2012; Chow, Watson, Young, & Bassett, 2006; Vorstman et al., 2015). Individuals with schizophrenia also tend to perform worse on tests of social cognition, verbal learning, and motor skills (Chow et al., 2016). In general, neurocognitive performance profiles are typically reported to be similar in pattern to the cognitive impairments reported in general forms of schizophrenia (Chow et al., 2016).

In adulthood, employability and activities of daily living are often relative strengths. It has been reported that more than two thirds of individuals with 22q11.2DS are employed in some capacity during adulthood (Butcher et al., 2012). The types of jobs are diverse, although most are entry-level positions such as work in fast-food restaurants and coffee shops or positions such as janitorial or cleaning staff. Some may hold jobs that require more advanced skills, such as trade positions (e.g., pipe fitter, hair dresser), working with the general public (e.g., receptionist, store clerk), or technical positions (e.g., computer store staff, web designer).

Although many adults with 22q11.2DS are employed in some capacity, few are financially independent, likely relating to difficulties maintaining employment due to medical or psychiatric issues, the types of jobs in which they are employed (e.g., lower-wage, part-time work), and/or poor money management skills. Financial assistance from family and government sources is common, as is living with parents or other relatives. Some people with

22q11.2DS marry and/or have children, more often for those with borderline to average intellect and no psychotic illness (Butcher et al., 2012).

The cognitive capacity of older adults with 22q11.2DS has been little studied, but recent evidence suggests that significant intellectual deterioration may affect some adults, in particular those with a history of psychosis (Evers et al., 2014). Cognitive and functional deterioration associated with the progression of Parkinson's disease has also been reported in adults with 22q11.2DS (Butcher et al., 2013). Additional studies are needed to better delineate the prevalence and severity of changes in cognitive abilities in older adults with 22q11.2DS as well as the underlying etiology.

GENETIC COUNSELING

The 22q11.2 deletion associated with 22q11.2DS has the same one in two chance of being transmitted from an affected individual at each pregnancy. In other words, affected individuals, males and females, have a 50% chance of having an affected child with each pregnancy. However, the range and symptoms vary greatly, and even those from within the same family may have different manifestations (Bassett et al., 2011).

Genetic counseling for individuals and families affected by 22q11.2DS is often provided by a trained genetic counselor or medical geneticist. Nevertheless, all clinicians involved in the care of individuals with a 22q11.2 deletion should be able to convey the general information provided in genetic counseling sessions, particularly as it pertains to their medical specialty (Chan et al., 2015).

Genetic counseling should include a discussion of 22q11.2 deletion causes, detection, variability of expression, interventions, anticipatory care, and preconception and prenatal options (Chan et al., 2015; Fung et al., 2015). Financial, social, and academic support that may be available should also be explored. Parents have expressed that they would like help with telling their affected children about the condition. Counselors may help by advising on the selection of a proper time and an appropriate set of words to use (Faux, Schoch, Eubanks, Hooper, & Shashi, 2012).

Follow-up counseling sessions, which allow counselors to reinforce concepts and convey updated information, are necessary as the individual moves into each new life stage. This is especially important for teenagers with 22q11.2DS, with whom reproductive risks and transition to adulthood should be discussed (Chan et al., 2015).

Genetic counseling sessions should be tailored to each person's developmental stage, intellectual capacity, communication skills, sensory functioning, and potential psychiatric conditions (Chan et al., 2015; Fung et al., 2015). The counselor may need to use simple sentences. Some individuals may benefit from special notes and visual aids (e.g., documents and pictures that they can take home) to understand and retain the information discussed in the counseling session. Those with shorter attention spans may require repetition of information. Some may prefer input from their family or support team members during counseling sessions (Chan et al., 2015).

A number of studies have shown that some genetic counselors do not discuss psychiatric problems at the initial meeting, especially if the person is younger than 13 years old (Martin et al., 2012; Morris, Inglis, Friedman, & Austin, 2013). The reasons for nondisclosure include stigma against psychiatric problems, lack of knowledge or awareness, and concerns about information overload (Martin et al., 2012). However, many parents of affected children would want to know about the symptoms before they occur in order to minimize the "surprise" factor (Faux et al., 2012). Following individuals for psychiatric problems from an early stage allows psychiatric illnesses to be diagnosed and treated early, which in turn leads to better outcomes (Martin et al., 2012).

Knowledge about 22q11.2DS is increasing. Genetic counselors and medical personnel should provide care for affected individuals based on the most up-to-date information available (see Table 17.2 for a list of related resources).

SUMMARY

22q11.2DS, named after its underlying cause of a missing piece of DNA on chromosome 22, is a relatively common disorder associated with intellectual and developmental disabilities. 22q11.2DS can affect almost any part of the body but displays significant variation in the spectrum and severity of the associated clinical features between individuals. Commonly associated major features may include learning or developmental disabilities, psychiatric disorders, congenital heart defects, and hypernasal speech. Standard best-practices treatment guidelines

Table 17.2.   Resources regarding 22q11.2 deletion syndrome (22q11.2DS)

The Dalglish Family 22q Clinic at Toronto General Hospital, Toronto, ON, Canada: http://22q.ca

22q Deletion Syndrome Clinic at the Hospital of Sick Children, Toronto, ON, Canada: http://www.sickkids.ca/CGenetics/What-we-do/22q-deletion-syndrome-clinic/index.html

22q and You Center at The Children's Hospital of Philadelphia, PA, United States: http://www.chop.edu/service/22q-and-you-center/home.html

22q Healthy Minds Clinic at the Cognitive Analysis and Brain Imaging Laboratory from the MIND Institute at the University of California, Davis, in Sacramento, CA, United States: http://www.ucdmc.ucdavis.edu/mindinstitute/research/cabil/healthymindsclinic.html

The 22q11.2 Society, London, United Kingdom: http://22qsociety.org/

22q11.2 Deletion Syndrome at GeneReviews: Bookshelf from the National Center for Biotechnology Information, U.S. National Library of Medicine, Bethesda, MD, United States: http://www.ncbi.nlm.nih.gov/books/NBK1523/

The International 22q11.2 Foundation in Matawan, NJ, United States: http://22q.org

are generally recommended for managing the associated conditions. Molecular diagnosis at any age has important implications for management but is often overlooked, especially in the growing adult population.

The cognitive and behavioral trajectories for individuals with 22q11.2DS are diverse. Intellect in the borderline to mild range of intellectual disability is most common. Intellectual and functional abilities may change over the lifetime. Neuropsychiatric disorders, including anxiety disorders and schizophrenia, develop in a substantial proportion of people with 22q11.2DS. Individual-centered anticipatory care—including the provision of comprehensive information, guidance and support, and screening for and coordinated management of associated medical conditions—is indicated for all those with 22q11.2DS. This requires a multidisciplinary approach involving family members, professionals, paraprofessionals, and other support people.

FOR FURTHER THOUGHT AND DISCUSSION

1. Do you know someone with 22q11.2DS? After reading this chapter, is there anything that you would have done or could do differently?

2. What services are available in your area to help support children and adults with 22q11.2DS and their families?

3. If you teach or provide medical care for an individual with 22q11.2DS whom you notice is increasingly irritable and anxious, what steps could you take?

4. If a child is diagnosed at a very young age, when and how should the parents disclose the diagnosis to the child?

5. Should an affected adolescent tell his or her friends and/or classmates about having a 22q11.2 deletion? If so, what should he or she say?

6. Should an affected adult tell his or her boss about having a 22q11.2 deletion? If so, when? What are the risks and advantages of doing so?

7. What knowledge on 22q11.2DS is still needed? What research studies could be performed?

8. True or false: The increased risk for developing a psychiatric illness in 22q11.2DS is similar to other genetic syndromes associated with an intellectual disability.

9. Should 22q11.2DS be added to newborn screening tests?

10. How many medication pills will someone with a 22q11.2 deletion have taken on average over his or her life?

11. An individual with 22q11.2DS begins to have difficulty with his or her movements such as balance problems and/or stiffness. What are the possible causes to consider, and why might (urgent) medical attention be required?

REFERENCES

Baker, K., Costain, G., Fung, W.L.A., & Bassett, A.S. (2014). Chromosomal microarray analysis—a routine clinical genetic test for patients with schizophrenia. *Lancet Psychiatry*, *1*(5), 329–331.

Bassett, A.S., McDonald-McGinn, D.M., Devriendt, K., Digilio, M.C., Goldenberg, P., Habel, A.,…International 22q11.2 Deletion Syndrome Consortium. (2011). Practical guidelines for managing patients with 22q11.2

deletion syndrome. *Journal of Pediatrics, 159*(2), 332–339. e331. doi:10.1016/j.jpeds.2011.02.039

Bjork, A.H., Oskarsdottir, S., Andersson, B.A., & Friman, V. (2012). Antibody deficiency in adults with 22q11.2 deletion syndrome. *American Journal of Medical Genetics, Part A, 158A*(8), 1934–1940. doi:10.1002/ajmg.a.35484

Boot, E., Butcher, N., van Amelsvoort, T., Lang, A.E., Marras, C., Pondal, M.,…Bassett, A.S. (2015). Movement abnormalities in adults with 22q11.2 deletion syndrome. *American Journal of Medical Genetics, Part A, 167A*(3), 639–645.

Buijs, P.C., Boot, E., Shugar, A., Fung, W.L.A., & Bassett, A.S. (2016). Internet safety issues for adolescents and adults with intellectual disabilities. *Journal of Applied Research in Intellectual Disabilities.* doi: 10.1111/jar.12250. [Epub ahead of print].

Butcher, N., Chow, E., Costain, G., Karas, D., Ho, A., & Bassett, A. (2012). Functional outcomes of adults with 22q11.2 deletion syndrome. *Genetics in Medicine, 14*(10), 836–843. doi:10.1038/gim.2012.66

Butcher, N.J., Fung, W.L.A., Fitzpatrick, L., Guna, A., Andrade, D.M., Lang, A.E.,…Bassett, A.S. (2015). Response to clozapine in a clinically identifiable subtype of schizophrenia: 22q11.2 deletions mediate side effect risk and dosage. *British Journal of Psychiatry, 206*(6), 484–491.

Butcher, N., Kiehl, T., Hazrati, L., Chow, E., Rogaeva, E., Lang, A., & Bassett, A. (2013). Association between early-onset Parkinson disease and 22q11.2 deletion syndrome: Identification of a novel genetic form of Parkinson disease and its clinical implications. *JAMA Neurology, 70*, 1359–1366.

Casteels, I., Casaer, P., Gewillig, M., Swillen, A., & Devriendt, K. (2008). Ocular findings in children with a microdeletion in chromosome 22q11.2. *European Journal of Pediatrics, 167*(7), 751–755. doi:10.1007/s00431-007-0582-0

Chan, C., Costain, G., Ogura, L., Silversides, C.K., Chow, E.W., & Bassett, A.S. (2015). Reproductive health issues for adults with a common genomic disorder: 22q11.2 deletion syndrome. *Journal of Genetic Counseling, 24*(5), 810–821.

Cheung, E.N., George, S.R., Costain, G.A., Andrade, D.M., Chow, E.W., Silversides, C.K., & Bassett, A.S. (2014). Prevalence of hypocalcemia and its associated features in 22q11.2 deletion syndrome. *Clinical Endocrinology, 81*(2), 190–196.

Chow, E.W., Watson, M., Young, D.A., & Bassett, A.S. (2006). Neurocognitive profile in 22q11 deletion syndrome and schizophrenia. *Schizophrenia Research, 87*(1–3), 270–278. doi:10.1016/j.schres.2006.04.007

Cirillo, E., Giardino, G., Gallo, V., Puliafito, P., Azzari, C., Bacchetta, R.,…Pignata, C. (2014). Intergenerational and intrafamilial phenotypic variability in 22q11.2 deletion syndrome subjects. *BMC Medical Genetics, 15*(1), 1. doi:10.1186/1471-2350-15-1

Duijff, S.N., Klaassen, P.W., de Veye, H.F., Beemer, F.A., Sinnema, G., & Vorstman, J.A. (2012). Cognitive development in children with 22q11.2 deletion syndrome. *British Journal of Psychiatry, 200*(6), 462–468. doi:10.1192/bjp.bp.111.097139

Duijff, S.N., Klaassen, P.W., Swanenburg de Veye, H.F., Beemer, F.A., Sinnema, G., & Vorstman, J.A. (2013). Cognitive and behavioral trajectories in 22q11DS from childhood into adolescence: A prospective 6-year follow-up study. *Research in Developmental Disabilities, 34*(9), 2937–2945. doi:10.1016/j.ridd.2013.06.001

Evers, L.J., van Amelsvoort, T.A., Candel, M.J., Boer, H., Engelen, J.J., & Curfs, L.M. (2014). Psychopathology in adults with 22q11 deletion syndrome and moderate and severe intellectual disability. *Journal of Intellectual Disability Research, 58*(10), 915–925. doi:10.1111/jir.12117

Faux, D., Schoch, K., Eubanks, S., Hooper, S.R., & Shashi, V. (2012). Assessment of parental disclosure of a 22q11.2 deletion syndrome diagnosis and implications for clinicians. *Journal of Genetic Counseling, 21*(6), 835–844. doi:10.1007/s10897-012-9535-5

Fung, W.L.A., Butcher, N.J., Costain, G., Andrade, D.M., Boot, E., Chow, E.W.C.,…Bassett, A.S. (2015). Practical guidelines for managing adults with 22q11.2 deletion syndrome. *Genetics in Medicine, 17*(8), 599–609. doi:10.1038/gim.2014.175

Fung, W.L.A., McEvilly, R., Fong, J., Chow, E.W.C., & Bassett, A.S. (2010). Elevated prevalence of generalized anxiety disorder in adults with 22q11.2 deletion syndrome. *American Journal of Psychiatry, 167*(8), 998.

Green, T., Weinberger, R., Diamond, A., Berant, M., Hirschfeld, L., Frisch, A.,…Gothelf, D. (2011). The effect of methylphenidate on prefrontal cognitive functioning, inattention, and hyperactivity in velocardiofacial syndrome. *Journal of Child and Adolescent Psychopharmacology, 21*(6), 589–595. doi:10.1089/cap.2011.0042

Habel, A., McGinn, M.-J., II, Zackai, E.H., Unanue, N., & McDonald-McGinn, D.M. (2012). Syndrome-specific growth charts for 22q11.2 deletion syndrome in Caucasian children. *American Journal of Medical Genetics, Part A, 158A*(11), 2665–2671. doi:10.1002/ajmg.a.35426

Kapadia, R.K., & Bassett, A.S. (2008). Recognizing a common genetic syndrome: 22q11.2 deletion syndrome. *CMAJ. 178*(4), 391–393. doi: 10.1503/cmaj.071300

Liu, A.P., Chow, P.C., Lee, P.P., Mok, G.T., Tang, W.F., Lau, E.T.,…Chung, B.H. (2014). Under-recognition of 22q11.2 deletion in adult Chinese patients with conotruncal anomalies: Implications in transitional care. *European Journal of Medical Genetics, 57*(6), 306–311. doi:10.1016/j.ejmg.2014.03.014

Martin, N., Mikhaelian, M., Cytrynbaum, C., Shuman, C., Chitayat, D.A., Weksberg, R., & Bassett, A.S. (2012). 22q11.2 deletion syndrome: Attitudes towards disclosing the risk of psychiatric illness. *Journal of Genetic Counseling, 21*(6), 825–834. doi:10.1007/s10897-012-9517-7

McDonald-McGinn, D., Kohut, T., & Zackai, E. (2010). Deletion 22q11.2 (velo-cardio-facial syndrome/DiGeorge syndrome). In S.B. Cassidy & J.E. Alanson (Eds.), *Management of genetic syndromes* (pp. 263–284). Hoboken, NJ: Wiley-Blackwell.

McDonald-McGinn, D., & Sullivan, K. (2011). Chromosome 22q11.2 deletion syndrome (DiGeorge syndrome/velocardiofacial syndrome). *Medicine, 90*(1), 1–18.

McDonald-McGinn, D.M., Sullivan, K.E., Marino, B., Philip, N., Swillen, A., Vorstman, J.A.,…Bassett, A.S.

(2015). 22q11.2 deletion syndrome. *Nature Reviews Disease Primers, 1*, 15071. doi: 10.1038/nrdp.2015.71

Miller, D.T., Adam, M.P., Aradhya, S., Biesecker, L.G., Brothman, A.R., Carter, N.P.,...Ledbetter, D.H. (2010). Consensus statement: Chromosomal microarray is a first-tier clinical diagnostic test for individuals with developmental disabilities or congenital anomalies. *American Journal of Human Genetics, 86*(5), 749–764.

Monteiro, F.P., Vieira, T.P., Sgardioli, I.C., Molck, M.C., Damiano, A.P., Souza, J.,...Gil-da-Silva-Lopes, V.L. (2013). Defining new guidelines for screening the 22q11.2 deletion based on a clinical and dysmorphologic evaluation of 194 individuals and review of the literature. *European Journal of Pediatrics, 172*(7), 927–945. doi:10.1007/s00431-013-1964-0

Moreno-De-Luca, A., Myers, S.M., Challman, T.D., Moreno-De-Luca, D., Evans, D.W., & Ledbetter, D.H. (2013). Developmental brain dysfunction: Revival and expansion of old concepts based on new genetic evidence. *Lancet Neurology, 12*(4), 406–414. doi: 10.1016/S1474-4422(13)70011-5

Morris, E., Inglis, A., Friedman, J., & Austin, J. (2013). Discussing the psychiatric manifestations of 22q11.2 deletion syndrome: An exploration of clinical practice among medical geneticists. *Genetics in Medicine, 15*(9), 713–720.

Moss, E.M., Batshaw, M.L., Solot, C.B., Gerdes, M., McDonald-McGinn, D.M., Driscoll, D.A.,...Wang, P.P. (1999). Psychoeducational profile of the 22q11.2 microdeletion: A complex pattern. *Journal of Pediatrics, 134*(2), 193–198.

Nordgarden, H., Lima, K., Skogedal, N., Folling, I., Storhaug, K., & Abrahamsen, T.G. (2012). Dental developmental disturbances in 50 individuals with the 22q11.2 deletion syndrome; relation to medical conditions? *Acta Odontologica Scandinavica, 70*(3), 194–201. doi:10.3109/00016357.2011.629624

Persson, C., Friman, V., Oskarsdottir, S., & Jonsson, R. (2012). Speech and hearing in adults with 22q11.2 deletion syndrome. *American Journal of Medical Genetics, Part A, 158A*(12), 3071–3079. doi:10.1002/ajmg.a.35589

Rauch, A., Hoyer, J., Guth, S., Zweier, C., Kraus, C., Becker, C., & Trautmann, U. (2006). Diagnostic yield of various genetic approaches in patients with unexplained developmental delay or mental retardation. *American Journal of Medical Genetics, Part A, 140*(19), 2063–2074.

Roizen, N.J., Antshel, K.M., Fremont, W., AbdulSabur, N., Higgins, A.M., Shprintzen, R.J., & Kates, W.R. (2007). 22q11.2DS deletion syndrome: Developmental milestones in infants and toddlers. *Journal of Developmental and Behavioral Pediatrics, 28*(2), 119–124.

Romanos, M., Schecklmann, M., Kraus, K., Fallgatter, A.J., Warnke, A., Lesch, K.P., & Gerlach, M. (2011). Olfactory deficits in deletion syndrome 22q11.2. *Schizophrenia Research, 129*(2–3), 220–221. doi:10.1016/j.schres.2010.12.015

Schneider, M., Debbané, M., Bassett, A.S., Chow, E.W.C., Fung, W.L.A., Van den Bree, M.B.M.,...Eliez, S. (2014). Psychiatric disorders from childhood to adulthood in 22q11.2 deletion syndrome: Results from the International Consortium on Brain and Behaviour in 22q11.2 Deletion Syndrome. *American Journal of Psychiatry, 171*(6), 627–639.

Sobin, C., Kiley-Brabeck, K., Daniels, S., Khuri, J., Taylor, L., Blundell, M.,...Karayiorgou, M. (2005). Neuropsychological characteristics of children with the 22q11 deletion syndrome: A descriptive analysis. *Child Neuropsychology, 11*, 39–53.

Swillen, A., Devriendt, K., Legius, E., Eyskens, B., Dumoulin, M., Gewillig, M., & Fryns, J.P. (1997). Intelligence and psychosocial adjustment in velocardiofacial syndrome: A study of 37 children and adolescents with VCFS. *Journal of Medical Genetics, 34*(6), 453–458.

U.S. National Library of Medicine Genetics Home Reference. (2016). *22q11.2 deletion syndrome.* Retrieved from http://ghr.nlm.nih.gov/condition/22q112-deletion-syndrome

Vieira, T.P., Monteiro, F.P., Sgardioli, I.C., Souza, J., Fett-Conte, A.C., Monlleo, I.L.,...Gil-da-Silva-Lopes, V.L. (2015). Clinical features in patients with 22q11.2 deletion syndrome ascertained by palatal abnormalities. *Cleft Palate-Craniofacial Journal, 52*(4), 411–416. doi:10.1597/13-233

Vorstman, J.A., Breetvelt, E., Duijff, S.N., Jalbrzikowsk, M., Vogels, A., Swillen, A.,...International 22q11.2 Brain Behavior Syndrome Consortium. (2015). Cognitive decline preceding the onset of psychosis in patients with 22q11.2 deletion syndrome. *JAMA Psychiatry, 72*(4), 377–385.

18

Fetal Alcohol Spectrum Disorder, Part I

Diagnosis, Neurobehavioral Functions, and Interventions in Children

Catherine McClain, E. Louise Kodituwakku, and Piyadasa W. Kodituwakku

WHAT YOU WILL LEARN ABOUT

- Introduction to fetal alcohol spectrum disorder
- Diagnostic criteria used to identify children with prenatal alcohol exposure
- Latest estimates of incidence in the general population and maternal drinking as a risk factor
- Key findings from the latest neuroimaging and neuropsychological studies
- Some behavioral and pharmacological interventions and other supports to help affected children and their families

In this chapter, we present a brief overview of fetal alcohol spectrum disorder (FASD). The chapter focuses on diagnostic guidelines and prevalence; neural, cognitive, and behavioral effects of prenatal alcohol exposure; and interventions and supports for children and their families.

DIAGNOSTIC GUIDELINES FOR FETAL ALCOHOL SPECTRUM DISORDER AND PREVALENCE ESTIMATES

In 1973, Jones, Smith, Ulleland, and Streissguth described a triad of features found in the offspring of 11 women who had a history of significant alcohol use during pregnancy. This triad consisted of 1) growth deficiency, 2) facial anomalies, and 3) central nervous system (CNS) dysfunction and subsequently became known as fetal alcohol syndrome (FAS; Jones et al.). Although there are numerous references in the early literature describing the harmful effect of alcohol on the unborn child, until this triad in association with maternal alcohol consumption during pregnancy was identified, the relationship between alcohol consumption during pregnancy and fetal harm was not an accepted truth. Since that link was first made, knowledge has grown significantly about prenatal alcohol exposure and its effects on the structure of the body and the brain as well as development, behavior, emotion, adaptive functioning, learning, and cognition. Prenatal alcohol exposure is the leading preventable cause of intellectual disability and birth defects and can result in a range of adverse outcomes—subtle to serious. Current emphasis is on finding markers for the early identification of mothers who are drinking and the identification of children who have been exposed to alcohol prenatally, as well as on defining intervention strategies that best support the development, learning, and behavior of children who had been exposed to alcohol prenatally.

Approaches to Diagnosis

Exposure to alcohol in utero results in a spectrum of disorders that have similar physical and/or

243

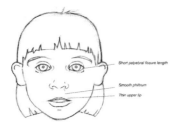

Short palpebral fissure length

Smooth philtrum

Thin upper lip

Figure 18.1. Facial anomalies in children with fetal alcohol syndrome. (Copyright © 2016 Tom Dearie, Threesixty Creative/Infographix.)

neurobehavioral characteristics and are referred to as FASD, an umbrella term that encompasses a number of diagnostic categories. In the United States, at least four sets of diagnostic guidelines are currently used: Institute of Medicine diagnostic criteria (Stratton, Howe, & Battaglia, 1996), University of Washington FASD 4-Digit Diagnostic Code (Astley & Clarren, 2000), Centers for Disease Control and Prevention (CDC) diagnostic guidelines (CDC, 2004), and Hoyme and colleagues' (2005) clarification of the Institute of Medicine diagnostic criteria. The different sets of diagnostic criteria generally agree on the major diagnostic categories but differ on specific criteria necessary to meet specific diagnoses. Prenatal diagnosis of FASD is not yet possible.

The Hoyme et al. (2005) description of FASD encompasses the following diagnoses:

1. *FAS with confirmed maternal alcohol exposure:* Confirmation of a history of excessive maternal alcohol use during pregnancy is a necessary component of making this diagnosis. These children show at least two components of the characteristic pattern of facial abnormalities that includes a flat philtrum (the area between the nose and the upper lip), a thin upper lip, and short palpebral fissures (the opening of the eye); either prenatal or postnatal growth deficiency (less than the 10th percentile in height or weight); and evidence of CNS abnormalities exhibited by either a small head circumference, a structural brain abnormality, and/or signs of cognitive and/or behavioral neurodevelopmental abnormalities. Characteristic facial abnormalities are illustrated in Figure 18.1.

2. *FAS without confirmation of maternal alcohol exposure:* For the child who shows all of the physical and neurodevelopmental characteristics of FAS as stated in the first category and where there is suspected prenatal exposure to alcohol but no clear confirmation that the mother drank while pregnant, this diagnosis may be used. However, it is important, whenever possible, to confirm the history of maternal alcohol exposure as the etiology of the child's disorder and to ensure that these findings are not due to another dysmorphic syndrome.

3. *Partial fetal alcohol syndrome (pFAS) with confirmation of maternal alcohol exposure:* In this group of children, excessive maternal alcohol use during pregnancy is confirmed and the child shows two or more of the characteristic facial abnormalities. The child exhibits either growth deficiency or CNS/neurodevelopmental abnormalities.

4. *Alcohol-related birth defects (ARBD):* This diagnosis is made when there is confirmed maternal alcohol use during pregnancy and the child has congenital abnormalities involving one or more organ systems as well as at least two of the characteristic facial abnormalities. These congenital anomalies are believed to occur as a result of alcohol disrupting the processes involved in the formation of organ systems.

5. *Alcohol-related neurodevelopmental disorder (ARND):* In ARND, there is confirmation of maternal alcohol exposure and evidence of CNS/neurodevelopmental abnormalities. These children have normal growth patterns and have typical facial features. Cognitive changes such as language delays, hyperactivity, attention deficits, or intellectual delays may be the only signs significant of prenatal alcohol exposure in most children (Kuehn et al., 2012). Developmental and behavioral differences follow a pattern explained later in this chapter; these are not explained by other genetic factors and are not secondary to another developmental disorder.

FASD can be identified at birth or during infancy when the child is severely affected. However, more frequently, the diagnosis is made during the preschool through school-age years once the child's cognition, speech and language, attention, fine and gross motor skills, and behavior can be more accurately evaluated using standardized neuropsychological assessments. Early diagnosis that leads to early intervention is strongly encouraged. A diagnosis of FASD is typically made by a multidisciplinary team that may consist of a physician, a neuropsychologist, and other health professionals.

As of this writing in 2016, there are no reliable means of diagnosing children with ARND because those with ARND may not show clinically discernable physical anomalies. A document by a joint committee of the National Institutes of Health and CDC (Interagency Coordinating Committee on Fetal Alcohol Spectrum Disorders, 2011) underscores the considerable challenge of recognizing ARND in primary health care of children. Furthermore, diagnosis of FASD in adolescents and adults presents a unique set of challenges because some of the morphological anomalies resulting from alcohol exposure have been found to diminish with maturation. With age, the nose tends to become longer and the chin bigger and, for some, height, weight, and/or head circumference may fall within normal parameters (Streissguth, 1994). Adolescents with FASD, particularly girls, tend to gain weight (Fuglestad et al., 2014; Werts, Van Calcar, Wargowski, & Smith, 2014), which makes it hard to recognize minor anomalies on the face.

Prevalence Estimates of Fetal Alcohol Spectrum Disorder

Prenatal alcohol exposure is thought to be the leading preventable cause of birth defects and intellectual disability resulting in a significant burden to society. The estimated lifetime additional cost of raising a child with FASD in the United States in 2002 was estimated to be $2 million, with a range of $0.5–$4 million (Lupton, Burd, & Harwood, 2004). This estimate included the cost of medical treatment, special education services, residential care, and loss of productivity. The true costs are most likely significantly higher given that the study did not include all medical expenses, behavioral health services, criminal justice services, or support for the family and loss of productivity of caregivers.

Prevalence estimates vary significantly depending on the population studied and methods used. Figures for the United States, using surveillance data, range from 0.5 (FAS only) to 9.1 cases of FASD per 1,000 live births, or almost 1% (CDC, 2014.) However, using active case ascertainment strategies in a school setting in a middle-class community in the United States, followed by comprehensive multidisciplinary evaluations, May et al. (2014) reported an FASD prevalence rate of 2.4%–4.8%. In certain at-risk populations, such as children at environmental risk (i.e., in an environment where alcohol is abused) or the offspring of those from communities where

high alcohol consumption is societally accepted, the prevalence rates may be significantly higher. A community in South Africa was found to have the highest prevalence in the world reported so far, at an overall rate of 13.6%–20.9% (May et al., 2013). An international study using active case ascertainment of children in child care systems (orphanages, foster care, boarding schools, adoption centers, and child welfare) found prevalence rates of 6% (60 per 1,000) for FAS and 16.9% (169 per 1,000) for FASD (Lange, Shield, Rehm, & Popova, 2013).

FASD often is not diagnosed, and the prevalence rates may be considerably higher than reported. In an attempt to facilitate greater recognition of the disorder by primary care providers and early referral for a comprehensive FASD assessment as well as ongoing intervention and support, the American Academy of Pediatrics published the Fetal Alcohol Spectrum Disorders Toolkit (2016).

Identification of women abusing alcohol while pregnant is the goal of prenatal screening, leading to intervention that will prevent the occurrence of FASD. Biomarkers identified in dried blood spots obtained during neonatal screening may help health professionals in the early identification of infants who have been prenatally exposed (Bakhireva et al., 2014). Measuring the length of the palpebral fissure and neurobehavioral screening may also assist in the early identification of those children who may have FASD so that further diagnostic testing can be completed to determine if FASD is the correct diagnosis (Koren et al., 2014).

Involvement of Maternal Drinking and Other Risk Factors

There is no known safe amount of alcohol during pregnancy, and when the mother drinks, so does her infant. Alcohol (i.e., ethanol) is quickly absorbed by the stomach; it enters the mother's blood stream and easily crosses the placenta to reach the fetus, reaching a concentration similar to the mother's. Once in the fetal blood stream, alcohol is excreted through fetal urine and fetal exhalations into the amniotic fluid, where it is absorbed again through fetal inspiration and, in very early pregnancy, transdermally, extending the duration the fetus is exposed (Burd, Blair, & Dropps, 2012). Alcohol is toxic to cells: it causes cell death and tissue damage and interferes with cell growth. In an adult, ethanol is metabolized by the liver through oxidation into acetaldehyde by alcohol dehydrogenase to acetate then oxidation of acetate by aldehyde dehydrogenase. The fetal liver, however, is not mature enough to adequately detoxify alcohol.

The degree and location of fetal organ damage is dependent on the timing, amount, and duration of alcohol exposure during the periods of critical development for the differing organ systems, and there is no safe time during pregnancy for alcohol exposure. Prenatal alcohol exposure can result in miscarriages, infant death, or a range of lifelong disabilities. Exposure during the first trimester may result in damage to developing organs such as the heart, eyes, ears, and kidneys as well as to the face and extremities. Second trimester exposure increases the risk of spontaneous abortion, and third trimester exposure has the greatest negative effect on height and weight. Because the brain develops throughout gestation, there is greater opportunity for prenatal alcohol exposure to affect its structure and function. Alcohol acts as a teratogen in the brain by decreasing cell populations, interfering with cell migration, increasing rates of cell loss, and causing both functional and structural abnormalities. Not all fetuses are affected equally, as some are genetically more sensitive to the teratogenic effect of alcohol than others.

Approximately 12% of pregnancies have some degree of prenatal alcohol exposure, and the CDC reports that approximately 2% of pregnant women report heavy drinking, although in most pregnancies the mother quits drinking once she finds out she is pregnant. (See National Institutes of Health [n.d.] for definitions of drinking levels.) Not all exposed pregnancies result in a child with FASD, and adverse outcomes are associated with the additional risks of maternal smoking, inadequate nutrition, limited or delayed prenatal care, and older maternal age. However, studies have shown that as many as 80% of the offspring of women drinking heavily during pregnancy have one or more abnormalities associated with prenatal alcohol exposure, with the highest percentage having some sort of cognitive impairment (Kuehn et al., 2012). The greatest risk for poor outcomes was in those children whose mothers binge drank (five or more drinks at a time) and those whose mothers had a high total weekly intake consisting of an average of 64.5 standard drinks or 903 grams of alcohol a week (Kuehn et al.). Research has shown that the risk of having a child with FAS is higher in older mothers and in those women who have had multiple pregnancies (Kvigne et al., 2003).

RELATION BETWEEN BRAIN CHANGES, COGNITION, AND BEHAVIOR IN CHILDREN WITH FETAL ALCOHOL SPECTRUM DISORDER

As mentioned previously, the identification of children with ARND has proved to be a challenging clinical problem because this group of children may not show any of the dysmorphic features seen in those with FAS or pFAS. Therefore, clinicians have to rely on cognitive-behavioral data and prenatal exposure history to make a diagnosis. The use of cognitive-behavioral data for diagnosing ARND will be feasible only if such data are uniquely different from those obtained from children with disorders that mimic FASD in some respects, particularly attention-deficit/hyperactivity disorder (ADHD) and conduct disorder. Therefore, the question of whether children with FASD show unique changes in their brain structure and/or function and a unique cognitive-behavioral profile has received considerable attention in the field. In this section, we summarize the literature on cognitive-behavioral functioning in children with FASD, with an emphasis on the latest findings. Because cognitive and behavioral difficulties in these children are known to result from alcohol-induced brain damage, we briefly review the findings from the most recent neuroimaging studies first, followed by an overview of cognitive-behavioral outcomes.

Neuroimaging Studies

The effects of prenatal alcohol exposure on the human brain have been investigated using a number of imaging methodologies: magnetic resonance imaging (MRI), functional MRI (fMRI), diffusion tensor imaging (DTI), electroencephalography (EEG), and magnetoencephalography (MEG) (for details, see Moore, Migliorini, Alejandra Infante, & Riley [2014]). MRI studies have revealed evidence of structural damage in the brain, particularly a reduction in brain volume and alterations of shape. Chen, Coles, Lynch, and Hu (2012) divided the brain into 88 regions to find out if some regions were more damaged by prenatal alcohol exposure than other regions. These investigators found widespread volume reductions in the alcohol-exposed brain, with a few regions showing greater reduction: particularly, the back part of the corpus callosum (the band of fiber that connects the two hemispheres), the caudate nucleus (a curved structure beneath the front part of the brain), and the cerebellum (small brain) were found to show significant volume reductions (Chen et al.). Rajaprakash, Chakravarty, Lerch, and Rovet (2014) found that even children with ARND showed volume reductions in multiple regions in the brain, including the frontal, parietal, and temporal lobes. Further analyses revealed that these volume reductions were in the cortical surface area rather than in thickness.

It is now known that when specific regions of the brain are activated, blood flow to those regions changes, and that such changes can be detected by MRI. It is also known that oxygen-rich blood and oxygen-poor blood have different magnetic properties, resulting in stronger MRI signals associated with oxygen-rich blood. Capitalizing on these findings, investigators have developed a technique called fMRI to detect which regions of the brain are activated by different tasks. Using this technique, a number of investigators have demonstrated that individuals with FASD show different patterns of activation compared with typically developing controls during performance of learning and memory tasks (see Moore et al. [2014] for details). This finding suggests that the brains of children with prenatal alcohol exposure function differently from those of typically developing children. An important discovery related to brain activation is that different regions of the brain interact even when an individual is not performing a particular task. Investigations into such "resting state networks" have proved useful in the assessment of functional connectivity in the brain. A number of investigators have found functional connectivity disruptions in children and adolescents with FASD (Kim, Wozniak, Mueller, & Pan, 2015; Wozniak et al., 2013). The MRI technique DTI has allowed investigators to evaluate the integrity of the brain's white matter (bundles of axon fibers that connect different regions of the brain). This technique capitalizes on the fact that magnetic resonance signals are sensitive to the random motions (diffusion) of water molecules in tissue. Diffusion tenor imaging studies have revealed reduced white matter, particularly in the corpus callosum, in children and adolescents with prenatal alcohol exposure.

MEG is an imaging method that measures magnetic fields produced by neuronal activity in the brain. This powerful technique has a very high temporal resolution, allowing investigators to measure neural activity with millisecond accuracy. Coffman et al. (2013) recorded MEG while children with FASD and neurotypical controls performed a simple visual task in which participants were asked to look from a central fixation point on screen toward a sudden-onset stimulus on periphery. Because something that suddenly appears on the periphery is looked at without even thinking, such eye movements are called reflexive eye movements. These investigators found that the FASD group showed slower MEG responses even in the very early stages of visual processing. The investigators also obtained evidence that children with FASD were slower than typically developing controls in the processing of auditory stimuli (Coffman et al., 2013).

Synopsis of Imaging Results In summary, MRI studies have revealed that children with FASD show a broad range of structural differences in the brain, including changes in brain size and shape. fMRI studies have shown that children with FASD show different activation patterns compared with controls during the performance of various tasks. There is also evidence that prenatal alcohol exposure is associated with anomalies in the white matter and disruptions in functional connectivity. MEG studies have provided evidence that children with FASD process both auditory and visual stimuli at a slower rate.

Cognitive-Behavioral Outcomes

Given that MRI data show that children with FASD exhibit widespread anomalies in the brain, a central question related to the neurobehavioral functioning of these children concerns whether they exhibit generalized cognitive impairments. Alternatively, because some regions of the brain have been found to show more pronounced alterations, one can ask whether the functions that are supported by such regions are more affected than those supported by other regions. Because we have reviewed the literature pertinent to these questions (Kodituwakku & Kodituwakku, 2014; Kodituwakku, Segall, & Beatty, 2011), here we provide only a summary of the findings. We have organized the section on cognitive-behavioral outcomes under three main headings: elementary functions, complex functions, and behavioral observations.

Elementary Functions The term *elementary functions* refers to very basic sensory and cognitive processes such as orienting responses (orienting attention to an unexpected noise or a visual stimulus) or eyeblink conditioning. Researchers find the study of elementary functions in children with neurodevelopmental disorders is of high clinical value because these functions are universal (shared by both animals and humans) and their neurobiological basis is well defined. Being universal, they can be investigated in a broad spectrum of subjects across different cultures and across the life span.

Orienting Responses   Several studies have examined eye movements (saccades) and responses to auditory stimuli (e.g., tones) in children with FASD. It is known that the vagus nerve responds quickly to metabolic changes in the brain by regulating the heart's "pacemaker." That is, when metabolic demand is low, vagal tone increases and signals the heart to lower its output; when metabolic demand increases (e.g., for processing new information), vagal tone decreases, signaling the heart to increase its output. Kable and Coles (2004) capitalized on this observation to investigate information processing in 6-month-old infants with prenatal alcohol exposure. These investigators found that infants with prenatal alcohol exposure were slower in the processing of visual and auditory stimuli but showed higher levels of arousal compared with nonexposed infants. This finding is consistent with eye movement studies of older children with FASD, in which investigators have found slower responses and more errors in children with prenatal alcohol exposure (Green et al., 2009).

Eyeblink Conditioning   An example of classical learning occurs when the eyeblink reflex is conditioned to a neutral stimulus (e.g., a tone) that predicts an unconditioned stimulus (e.g., a puff of air). Because it is naturally elicited by a puff of air, the eyeblink response is called an unconditioned response. In a typical eyeblink conditioning experiment, a tone (conditioned stimulus) is consistently presented immediately prior to the delivery of an air puff to the eye (unconditioned stimulus) so that an association between the two stimuli is formed. Once the association is established, the conditioned stimulus begins to elicit the eyeblink reflex. A number of investigators have reported that children with FASD are impaired on this learning task (Jacobson, Stanton, et al., 2011).

Complex Functions   Included under complex functions are those abilities that are typically evaluated in clinical assessments. These include intellectual, attention, executive function, language, and memory and learning. There also exist a few studies that have investigated visual perceptual and visual constructional abilities, number sense and numerical reasoning abilities, and social cognition in children with FASD. Next, we present the highlights of the latest findings in these areas.

Intellectual Ability   Because IQ tests are readily available, intellectual ability has been assessed in almost all published human studies of FASD. These studies have consistently shown that intellectual ability is diminished in children with FASD, particularly in those children exposed to substantial amounts of alcohol. Many studies have shown that children with substantial alcohol exposure score 1–2 standard deviations (average IQ scores from 70 to 85) below the population mean of IQs (Mattson et al., 2013). However, recent data from large-scale studies of FASD from Europe and Australia show that children exposed to mild to moderate amounts of alcohol prenatally who grow up in middle-class socioeconomic environments do not show exposure-related effects on IQ (Kesmodel et al., 2012). These findings suggest that the effect of prenatal alcohol exposure on cognitive development may be moderated by other variables such as genetic and socioeconomic variables.

Attention   The word *attention* refers to a number of things, including the ability to engage in one task while ignoring others and the ability to focus and maintain interest in a given task. Previous studies had shown that children with FASD had impairments in most areas of attention (see Kodituwakku and Kodituwakku [2011] for details). In 2010, Kooistra, Crawford, Gibbard, Ramage, and Kaplan compared the performance of three groups of children—namely, FASD, ADHD, and typically developing—on the Attention Network Test, which assesses three attentional networks: alerting, orienting, and executive. The executive network supports the ability to perform a task despite having interference in the background. Results showed that children with FASD and ADHD (i.e., combined type; those with hyperactivity and inattentiveness) had difficulty with executive attention (Kooistra et al.). It should be noted that performance of the executive component of the test is more demanding than that of other components. In a multicenter study of FASD, investigators (Mattson et al., 2013) found that relatively complex attentional tests (spatial working memory), but not relatively simpler ones (e.g., simple reaction time from the Cambridge Neuropsychological Test Automated Battery), discriminated children with FASD from comparison groups (ADHD, typically developing).

Executive Function   Consistent with this pattern are the findings from the studies of executive functions in children with FASD. *Executive function* is an umbrella term that refers to a broad range of higher order abilities involved in attaining goals in an efficient manner. These include planning, execution of planned actions in the face of interference, correction of errors using feedback, and flexible shifting of attention. Studies that have examined these abilities in children with FASD have shown that prenatal alcohol exposure is associated with impaired performance on more demanding rather than on less demanding items on executive function measures. For example, children with FASD have difficulty with complex planning problems but not with simple ones (see Kodituwakku & Kodituwakku [2011] for details).

Language   Studies of language skills in children with FASD have produced mixed results. Some early studies of children exposed to light to moderate amounts of alcohol prenatally failed to find an association between prenatal alcohol exposure and language skills (Greene, Ernhart, Martier, Sokol, & Ager, 1990). In contrast, the studies that examined language skills in children exposed to substantial amounts of alcohol have consistently reported a broad spectrum of impairments, including articulation problems (oral-motor abilities), difficulty in the grammatical arrangement of words in sentences (syntax), and limited understanding of word meanings (semantics). Some investigators have found an age effect on language, with younger children with prenatal alcohol exposure showing global impairments and older children displaying impairments only on complex language tasks such as social communication and verbal fluency.

As mentioned previously, a number of studies from Europe and Australia failed to find intellectual impairments in children exposed to light to moderate amounts of alcohol prenatally. Zuccolo and colleagues (2013) found that children exposed to moderate amounts of alcohol prenatally scored higher on a test of academic achievement (including a test of vocabulary) than those exposed to lighter drinking. The authors explained this counterintuitive finding in terms of socioeconomic background

difference: moderate drinkers came from higher socioeconomic backgrounds than did lighter drinkers. However, O'Leary, Zubrick, Taylor, Dixon, and Bower (2009) pointed out that the timing of exposure may be an important factor that determines language difficulties in children with FASD. Those investigators found that exposure to alcohol during the third trimester may pose a risk for language delay in children with FASD.

Memory and Learning   Clinical descriptions of children with prenatal alcohol exposure often include statements such as "what is learned one day is gone the next day." This statement captures a fundamental difficulty that children with prenatal alcohol exposure show: a difficulty in learning new information. Animal research has established that the hippocampus, the part of the brain critically involved in memory, is highly sensitive to the effects of alcohol exposure. Using broad neuropsychological batteries of memory and learning, investigators have demonstrated that children with FASD are impaired in both verbal and visual memory. It is also noteworthy that children with FASD also have difficulty in learning complex information that requires organization. Consistent with this finding is the observation that children with prenatal alcohol exposure are able to retrieve the newly learned information when they are provided with memory support. For example, a number of studies have reported that children with FASD perform better on recognition memory tasks (where memory support is given by showing the items to be recalled with distracters) than on free-recall tasks (where no memory support is provided). (See Kodituwakku et al. [2011] for details.)

Other Functions   There is a growing body of literature on visual-perceptual skills, social sense, and number sense in children with FASD (see Mattson et al. [2013] for a detailed review of the literature). Several studies have reported that children with FASD show relatively little impairment on relatively simple visual perceptual tasks such as facial recognition. In contrast, children with prenatal alcohol exposure tend to perform poorly on visual-motor integration tests (e.g., copying relatively complex shapes).

The observation that children with FASD have more difficulty with math than with other academic subjects has led investigators to probe deeply into the source of math difficulties in children affected by prenatal alcohol exposure. Jacobson, Dodge, et al.

(2011) found that a fundamental deficit in magnitude estimation was responsible for math difficulties in children with FASD (e.g., of 6 and 11, which number is closer to the solution of 2 × 4?). Using fMRI, these investigators also examined brain activation during the performance of this type of task by children with FASD. They found that the control group showed activation in the regions that are known to be associated with number processing (e.g., frontal-parietal). In contrast, the FASD group failed to engage these regions during number estimation, suggesting a neurobiological basis for their math difficulties.

Because children with FASD are known to have poor social skills, some investigators have examined the association between prenatal alcohol exposure and social sense. To answer the question whether children with FASD have a core deficit in social sense, Bishop, Gahagan, and Lord (2007) compared children with prenatal alcohol exposure to those with autism, which is a neurodevelopmental disorder characterized by social and communication difficulties. In this study, the investigators utilized the Autism Diagnostic Observation Schedule to compare the two groups. Results showed that both groups had impairments in social communication but that those impairments had different origins. Whereas the autism group had a fundamental deficit in social communication (core deficit), the children in the prenatal alcohol exposure group had social difficulties associated with their limited executive control skills (e.g., impulsivity). Greenbaum, Stevens, Nash, Koren, and Rovet (2009) found that these children's social difficulties were distinctly different from those found in children with ADHD.

Behavioral Observations The two studies cited in the section on social cognition raise an important question pertinent to identifying children with FASD: Do children with prenatal alcohol exposure have a unique (signature) behavioral profile? Researchers have attempted to answer this question by having parents and teachers complete questionnaires such as the Child Behavior Checklist and the Behavior Rating Inventory of Executive Function. Stevens and colleagues (2013) reported that children with FASD were rated by their caregivers as showing a broad range of behavioral problems, including those labeled internalizing problems (e.g., anxiety, depression) and those labeled externalizing problems (e.g., hyperactivity, aggression, conduct disorder). A recent study compared chil-

dren with FASD and those with ADHD on a questionnaire called Sluggish Cognitive Tempo (Graham et al., 2013). The results of this study revealed that several test items (e.g., forgets details, confused, and drowsy) separated the FASD group from those with ADHD. Previous studies had reported that children with FASD were rated as "acting young for their age" and showing inattentive behaviors.

Another important finding pertinent to the behavioral profile of FASD is increased psychiatric problems (O'Connor, 2014; Rangmar et al., 2015) and limited adaptive behaviors that persist through adulthood. The term *adaptive behaviors* refers to those skills required for independent living, such as taking care of daily needs and appropriately interacting with others. A number of investigators have reported that children and adolescents with FASD show marked impairments in adaptive behaviors, which eventually can lead to dependent living during adulthood (Thomas, Kelly, Mattson, & Riley, 1998; Whaley, O'Connor, & Gunderson, 2001). It has been documented that in addition to dependent living, adults with FASD display a broad range of secondary disabilities. Particularly, getting and keeping a job, finding "ordinary work" outside of a sheltered workshop setting, and living independently are difficult for the majority of adults with FASD; hence, they often rely on social welfare programs (Rangmar et al., 2015; Spohr, Willms, & Steinhausen, 2007). Persistent impairments in cognitive functioning (e.g., attentional deficits) and social skills are, in part, to blame for affected adults' inability to hold down a job or to care for themselves (Spohr et al., 2007; Streissguth, 1994). Many studies have indicated that adults with FASD had significantly higher rates of alcohol and illicit drug abuse as well as a greater likelihood of getting into trouble with the law than their age-matched peers (Rangmar et al., 2015; Streissguth et al., 2004). However, after accounting for the effects of exposure to adverse environmental conditions, the prevalence of substance abuse and criminality among adults with FASD was found to be less than or equivalent to that in the general population (Rangmar et al., 2015).

Synopsis of Cognitive-Behavioral Outcomes

Neurobehavioral studies of FASD show that children with prenatal alcohol exposure display difficulties across the board. On tests of intellectual ability, children with FASD have been found to score, on average, 15–30 points below the expected level. There is evidence that verbal and nonverbal intellectual abilities are impaired in children exposed to substantial amounts of alcohol. Investigation into other areas of cognitive functioning (e.g., memory and learning, language, visual perception, social sense, and number processing) has revealed that children with FASD have greater difficulty handling complex information. We have proposed that this difficulty in handling complex information may be associated with slow information processing. Recent MEG studies of sensory processing support the idea that children and adolescents with FASD process information at a slower rate compared with their typically developing age peers (Coffman et al., 2013). FASD is a lifelong disorder that can result in difficulties in attaining successful independence in adulthood and the need for ongoing supportive services.

INTERVENTIONS AND SUPPORTS TO FULFILL THE CHILD'S POTENTIAL

The majority of children with FASD are known to experience numerous adverse conditions such as exposure to violence, physical and sexual abuse, and neglect. Having limited cognitive and emotional resources, these children find it difficult to handle these adverse conditions effectively. Data from the Seattle prospective study underline the importance of minimizing these adverse conditions to achieve better life outcomes. Streissguth and colleagues (2004) identified a number of factors associated with better life outcomes in children with FASD: having a stable, nurturing home; lack of multiple placements; good quality parenting; being diagnosed before the age of 6; not experiencing physical, sexual, or emotional abuse; and being evaluated for and receiving early intervention services.

We proposed a framework for designing effective interventions for children with FASD (Kodituwakku & Kodituwakku, 2011) in which we identified two other key elements that may lead to better outcomes: providing evidence-based, guided experiences and managing comorbid conditions such as ADHD and depression. With regard to evidence-based, guided experiences, we emphasized the importance of improving self-regulatory skills during the preschool age, using concrete examples and hands-on experiences in teaching math and other

abstract concepts, repeating information, and creating strategies to improve active engagement in learning. However, children with FASD may fail to benefit from these experiences unless their comorbid conditions are managed well.

Therefore, the success of an intervention program designed for children with FASD will involve an optimal combination of three key elements: structured and loving environment, guided experiences, and management of comorbid conditions. Researchers have piloted a number of interventions for children with FASD, combining these elements to varying degrees. The following subsections present some of those interventions. See Paley and O'Connor (2011) and Bertrand (2009) for details.

Parent-Assisted Children's Friendship Training

O'Connor and colleagues (2006) at University of California, Los Angeles, used a 12-week program to teach children with FASD social skills through friendship training. Parents attended concurrent classes to learn how to support children learning new social skills such as conversational skills, making a good first impression, handling rejection and bullying, and being a good host when a child comes to the house. This program proved to be effective in improving social skills in children with FASD.

Safety Skills

Children with FASD are at increased risk for unintentional injuries mainly due to their impulsivity, poor judgment, and other cognitive difficulties. Therefore, Coles, Strickland, Padgett, and Bellmoff (2007) at Emory University, Atlanta, Georgia, designed a computer-based intervention program aimed at improving street and fire safety. Children with FASD practiced safety skills in a "virtual world" while receiving immediate feedback on their performance. Results showed that computer-based training was effective in that participants had achieved improved knowledge and behavior related to safety.

Language and Literacy Training

The main goal of a pilot project conducted by Adnams and colleagues (2007) of the University of Cape Town, South Africa, was to enhance phonological awareness in children prenatally exposed to alcohol and to promote their acquisition of preliteracy and early literacy skills. The treatment group received two half-hour sessions twice weekly over 9 months of literacy and language training. Results indicated that the group receiving treatment showed improvement in letter knowledge, syllable manipulation, word and nonword reading, and nonword spelling. However, these achievements did not translate into improvement in scholastic ability.

The Math Interactive Learning Experience

The Math Interactive Learning Experience is a psychoeducational program developed by Kable, Coles, and Taddeo (2007) of Emory University for teaching math skills. The program contains strategies to help compensate for core neurodevelopmental deficits in FASD such as poor working memory. In one reported study, children with FASD received intensive short-term memory training. Children also received training in regulatory skills such as focus, plan, and act. Kable et al. reported that the program is effective in improving math skills in children with FASD.

Working Memory Strategies

Strategies to improve the working memories of children with FASD were developed by Loomes, Rasmussen, Pei, Manji, and Andrew (2008) to promote the use of rehearsal strategies. Children who learned the strategies showed significant improvement in their ability to recall a series of numbers across three sessions.

Families Moving Forward

Families Moving Forward is an intervention program developed by Olson and colleagues at the University of Washington (Bertrand, 2009; Olson, Oti, Gelo, & Beck, 2009) to increase parental self-efficacy and subsequently reduce children's behavior problems. Intervention specialists worked with the parents and school for 9–11 months in biweekly sessions using a model of supportive behavioral consultation with the ability to work on individual problems within the group. More important, the program sought to modify the underlying negative parental responses to the child by explaining the underlying cause of the behaviors. Caregivers reported a decrease in negative behaviors upon completion of the program.

Self-Regulation

Because children with FASD show impairments in self-regulation, Chasnoff and colleagues piloted the utility of the Alert Program (reported by Bertrand, 2009; Wells, Chasnoff, Schmidt, Telford, & Schwartz, 2012) in teaching regulatory skills to children with FASD. This program uses the metaphor of a car engine to teach children to regulate their behavior. Children are told that they can make their "engine" run fast, slow, or just right. The parents of the children involved with this program reported significant improvement in measures of executive functioning, particularly self-regulation.

Medications and Novel Therapies

As mentioned previously, the majority of children with FASD show comorbid problems, with ADHD and depression being the most common disorders. A number of studies have assessed the effectiveness of stimulant medication in the treatment of ADHD in children with FASD. These studies seem to indicate that hyperactive and impulsive behaviors improve with medication but that inattentive behaviors do not. Inattentive behaviors include disorganization, difficulty in sustaining attention on a task, and daydreaming. It is possible that slow information processing in children with signs of FASD is associated with these inattentive behaviors. A study conducted at UCLA (Frankel, Paley, Marquardt, & O'Connor, 2006) found that children with FASD who received neuroleptic medications benefited more from social skills training than those who were not on medication. Some novel therapies are also being tested in children with FASD. For example, a pilot study is underway in Minnesota aimed at testing the efficacy of choline supplementation in the treatment of learning and memory problems in children (Wozniak et al., 2013).

SUMMARY

Although significant advances have taken place in the area of FASD in terms of understanding the neurobiology of alcohol's teratogenic effects and developing interventions, one simple fact remains true: FASD is 100% preventable. Therefore, continued efforts focused on the prevention of maternal drinking during pregnancy are of high social and clinical significance. Practitioners are often reluctant to even ask about alcohol use during pregnancy due to the fear that they may offend the mother. The effectiveness of strategies such as putting warning labels on bottles of alcohol is questionable because the prevalence of FASD remains unchanged or is increasing.

Therefore, the development of novel strategies aimed at addressing the risk factors associated with alcohol use during pregnancy is important. Equally important is the prevention of secondary disabilities in children with prenatal alcohol exposure. This will require the development of early intervention programs by optimally combining the elements of effective intervention programs listed in this chapter.

FOR FURTHER THOUGHT AND DISCUSSION

1. What are the main challenges of diagnosing FASD in children's primary care?

2. Considering that children with FASD experience numerous adverse life conditions in addition to alcohol-induced brain damage, how would you design an intervention program for a preschool-age child affected by prenatal alcohol exposure?

3. Given current knowledge of FASD, what type of policies do you advocate with regard to drinking during pregnancy?

REFERENCES

Adnams, C.M., Sorour, P., Kalberg, W.O., Kodituwakku, P., Perold, M.D., Kotze,A.,...May, P.A. (2007). Language and literacy outcomes from a pilot intervention study for children with fetal alcohol spectrum disorders in South Africa. *Alcohol, 41*(6), 403–414.

American Academy of Pediatrics. (2016). *Fetal alcohol spectrum disorders toolkit.* Retrieved from http://www.aap.org/fasd.

Astley, S.J., & Clarren, S.K. (2000). Diagnosing the full spectrum of fetal alcohol-exposed individuals: Introducing the 4-digit diagnostic code. *Alcohol and Alcoholism, 35*(4), 400–410.

Bakhireva, L.N., Leeman, L., Savich, R.D., Cano, S., Gutierrez, H., Savage, D.D., & Rayburn, W.F. (2014). The validity of phosphatidylethanol in dried blood spots of newborns for the identification of prenatal alcohol exposure. *Alcoholism: Clinical and Experimental Research, 38*(4), 1078–1085.

Bertrand, J. (2009). Interventions for children with fetal alcohol spectrum disorders (FASDs): Overview of findings for five innovative research projects. *Research in Developmental Disabilities, 30*(5), 986–1006.

Bishop, S., Gahagan, S., & Lord, C. (2007). Re-examining the core features of autism: A comparison of autism spectrum disorder and fetal alcohol spectrum disorder. *Journal of Child Psychology and Psychiatry, 48*(11), 1111–1121.

Burd, L., Blair, J., & Dropps, K. (2012). Prenatal alcohol exposure, blood alcohol concentrations and alcohol elimination rates for mother, fetus and newborn. *Journal of Perinatology, 32*(9), 652–659.

Centers for Disease Control and Prevention. (2004). *Fetal alcohol syndrome: Guidelines for referral and diagnosis.* Retrieved from http://www.cdc.gov/ncbddd/fasd/documents/fas_guidelines_accessible.pdf

Centers for Disease Control and Prevention. (2014). *Fetal alcohol spectrum disorders (FASDs): Data and statistics.* Retrieved from http://www.cdc.gov/ncbddd/fasd/data.html

Chen, X., Coles, C.D., Lynch, M.E., & Hu, X. (2012). Understanding specific effects of prenatal alcohol exposure on brain structure in young adults. *Human Brain Mapping, 33*(7), 1663–1676.

Coffman, B.A., Kodituwakku, P., Kodituwakku, E.L., Romero, L., Sharadamma, N.M., Stone, D., & Stephen, J.M. (2013). Primary visual response (M100) delays in adolescents with FASD as measured with MEG. *Human Brain Mapping, 34*(11), 2852–2862.

Coles, C.D., Strickland, D.C., Padgett, L., & Bellmoff, L. (2007). Games that "work": Using computer games to teach alcohol-affected children about fire and street safety. *Research in Developmental Disabilities, 28*(5), 518–530.

Frankel, F., Paley, B., Marquardt, R., & O'Connor, M. (2006). Stimulants, neuroleptics, and children's friendship training for children with fetal alcohol spectrum disorders. *Journal of Child and Adolescent Psychopharmacology, 16*(6), 777–789.

Fuglestad, A.J., Boys, C.J., Chang, P.N., Miller, B.S., Eckerle, J.K., Deling, L.,...Wozniak, J.R. (2014). Overweight and obesity among children and adolescents with fetal alcohol spectrum disorders. *Alcoholism: Clinical and Experimental Research, 38*(9), 2502–2508.

Graham, D.M., Crocker, N., Deweese, B.N., Roesch, S.N., Coles, C.D., Kable, J.A.....Mattson. S.N. (2013). Prental alcohol exposure, attention-deficit/hyperactive disorder, and sluggish cognitive tempo. *Alcoholism: Clinical and Experimental Research, 37*, E338–346.

Green, C.R., Mihic, A.M., Brien, D.C., Armstrong, I.T., Nikkel, S.M., Stade, B.C.,...Reynolds, J.N. (2009). Oculomotor control in children with fetal alcohol spectrum disorders assessed using a mobile eye-tracking laboratory. *European Journal of Neuroscience, 29*(6), 1302–1309.

Greenbaum, R.L., Stevens, S.A., Nash, K., Koren, G., & Rovet, J. (2009). Social cognitive and emotion processing abilities of children with fetal alcohol spectrum disorders: A comparison with attention deficit hyperactivity disorder. *Alcoholism: Clinical and Experimental Research, 33*(10), 1656–1670.

Greene, T., Ernhart, C.B., Martier, S., Sokol, R., & Ager, J. (1990). Prenatal alcohol exposure and language development. *Alcoholism: Clinical and Experimental Research, 14*(6), 937–945.

Hoyme, H.E., May, P.A., Kalberg, W.O., Kodituwakku, P., Gossage, J.P., Trujillo, P.M., & Robinson, L.K. (2005). A practical clinical approach to diagnosis of fetal alcohol spectrum disorders: Clarification of the 1996 institute of medicine criteria. *Pediatrics, 115*(1), 39–47.

Interagency Coordinating Committee on Fetal Alcohol Spectrum Disorders. (2011). *Consensus statement: Recognizing alcohol-related neurodevelopmental disorder (ARND) in primary health care of children.* Retrieved from http://www.niaaa.nih.gov/sites/default/files/ARND ConferenceConsensusStatementBooklet_Complete .pdf

Jacobson, J.L., Dodge, N.C., Burden, M.J., Klorman, R., & Jacobson, S.W. (2011). Number processing in adolescents with prenatal alcohol exposure and ADHD: Differences in the neurobehavioral phenotype. *Alcoholism: Clinical and Experimental Research, 35*(3), 431–442.

Jacobson, S.W., Stanton, M.E., Dodge, N.C., Pienaar, M., Fuller, D.S., Molteno, C.D.,…Jacobson, J.L. (2011). Impaired delay and trace eyeblink conditioning in school-age children with fetal alcohol syndrome. *Alcoholism: Clinical and Experimental Research, 35*(2), 250–264.

Jones, K.L., Smith, D.W., Ulleland, C.N., & Streissguth, P. (1973). Pattern of malformation in offspring of chronic alcoholic mothers. *Lancet, 1*(7815), 1267–1271.

Kable, J.A., & Coles, C.D. (2004). The impact of prenatal alcohol exposure on neurophysiological encoding of environmental events at six months. *Alcoholism: Clinical and Experimental Research, 28*(3), 489–496.

Kable, J.A., Coles, C.D., & Taddeo, E. (2007). Socio-cognitive habilitation using the math interactive learning experience program for alcohol-affected children. *Alcoholism: Clinical and Experimental Research, 31*(8), 1425–1434.

Kesmodel, U.S., Eriksen, H.L., Underbjerg, M., Kilburn, T.R., Stovring, H., Wimberley, T., & Mortensen, E.L. (2012). The effect of alcohol binge drinking in early pregnancy on general intelligence in children. *BJOG: An International Journal of Obstetrics and Gynaecology, 119*(10), 1222–1231.

Kim, J., Wozniak, J.R., Mueller, B.A., & Pan, W. (2015). Testing group differences in brain functional connectivity: Using correlations or partial correlations? *Brain Connectivity, 5*(4), 214–234. doi: 0.1089/brain.2014.0319

Kodituwakku, P.W., & Kodituwakku, E.L. (2011). From research to practice: An integrative framework for the development of interventions for children with fetal alcohol spectrum disorders. *Neuropsychology Review, 21*(2), 204–223.

Kodituwakku, P.W., & Kodituwakku, E.L. (2014). Cognitive and behavioral profiles of children with fetal alcohol spectrum disorders. *Current Developmental Disorder Reports, 1*, 149–160.

Kodituwakku, P.W., Segall, J.M., & Beatty, G.K. (2011). Cognitive and behavioral effects of prenatal alcohol exposure. *Future Neurology, 6*(2), 237–259.

Kooistra, L., Crawford, S., Gibbard, B., Ramage, B., & Kaplan, B.J. (2010). Differentiating attention deficits in children with fetal alcohol spectrum disorder or attention-deficit-hyperactivity disorder. *Developmental Medicine and Child Neurology, 52*(2), 205–211.

Koren, G., Chudley, A., Loock, C., MacLeod, S.M., Rosales, T., Rosenbaum, C., & Sarkar, M. (2014). Screening and referral to identify children at risk for FASD: Search for new methods 2006–2013. *Journal of Population Therapeutics and Clinical Pharmacology, 21*(2), e260–265.

Kuehn, D., Aros, S., Cassorla, F., Avaria, M., Unanue, N., Henriquez, C.,…Mills, J.L. (2012). A prospective cohort study of the prevalence of growth, facial, and central nervous system abnormalities in children with heavy

prenatal alcohol exposure. *Alcoholism: Clinical and Experimental Research, 36*(10), 1811–1819.

Kvigne, V.L., Leonardson, G.R., Borzelleca, J., Brock, E., Neff-Smith, M., & Welty, T.K. (2003). Characteristics of mothers who have children with fetal alcohol syndrome or some characteristics of fetal alcohol syndrome. *Journal of the American Board of Family Practice,16*(4), 296–303.

Lange, S., Shield, K., Rehm, J., & Popova, S. (2013). Prevalence of fetal alcohol spectrum disorders in child care settings: A meta-analysis. *Pediatrics, 132*(4), e980–995.

Loomes, C., Rasmussen, C., Pei, J., Manji, S., & Andrew, G. (2008). The effect of rehearsal training on working memory span of children with fetal alcohol spectrum disorder. *Research in Developmental Disabilities, 29*(2), 113–124.

Lupton, C., Burd, L., & Harwood, R. (2004). Cost of fetal alcohol spectrum disorders. *American Journal of Medical Genetics. Part C, Seminars in Medical Genetics, 127C*(1), 42–50.

Mattson, S.N., Roesch, S.C., Glass, E., Deweese, B.N., Coles, C.D., Kable, J.A.,…Riley, E.P. (2013). Further development of a neurobehavioral profile of fetal alcohol spectrum disorders. *Alcoholism: Clinical and Experimental Research, 37*(3), 517–528.

May, P.A., Baete, A., Russo, J., Eliott, A.J., Blankenship, J., Kalberg, W.O.,…Hoyme, H.E. (2014). Prevalence and characteristics of fetal alcohol spectrum disorders. *Pediatrics, 134*(5), 855–866.

May, P.A., Blankenship, J., Marais, A.S., Gossage, J.P., Kalberg, W.O., Barnard, R.,…Seedat, S. (2013). Approaching the prevalence of the full spectrum of fetal alcohol spectrum disorders in a South African population-based study. *Alcoholism: Clinical and Experimental Research, 37*(5), 818–830.

Moore, E.M., Migliorini, R., Alejandra Infante, M., & Riley, E.P. (2014). Fetal alcohol spectrum disorders: Recent neuroimaging findings. *Current Developmental Disorders Reports, 1*, 161–172.

National Institutes of Health, National Institute on Alcohol Abuse and Alcoholism. (n.d.). *Drinking levels defined*. Retrieved from http://www.niaaa.nih.gov /alcohol-health/overview-alcohol-consumption/moderate-binge-drinking

National Organisation for Foetal Alcohol Syndrome-UK. (n.). *Home page*. Retrieved from http://www.nofas-uk.org

O'Connor, M.J. (2014). Mental health outcomes associated with prenatal alcohol exposure: Genetic and environmental factors. *Current Developmental Disorders Reports, 1*, 181–188.

O'Connor, M.J., Frankel, F., Paley, B., Schonfeld, A.M., Carpenter, E., Laugeson, E.A., & Marquardt, R. (2006). A controlled social skills training for children with fetal alcohol spectrum disorders. *Journal of Consulting and Clinical Psychology,74*(4), 639–648.

O'Leary, C., Zubrick, S.R., Taylor, C.L., Dixon, G., & Bower, C. (2009). Prenatal alcohol exposure and language delay in 2-year-old children: The importance of dose and timing on risk. *Pediatrics, 123*(2), 547–554.

Olson, H.C., Oti, R., Gelo, J., & Beck, S. (2009). "Family matters": Fetal alcohol spectrum disorders and the family. *Developmental Disabilities Research Review, 15*(3), 235–249.

Paley, B., & O'Connor, M.J. (2011). Behavioral interventions for children and adolescents with fetal alcohol spectrum disorders. *Alcohol Research and Health, 34*(1), 64–75.

Rajaprakash, M., Chakravarty, M.M., Lerch, J.P., & Rovet, J. (2014). Cortical morphology in children with alcohol-related neurodevelopmental disorder. *Brain and Behavior, 4*(1), 41–50.

Rangmar, J., Hjern, A., Vinnerljung, B., Stromland, K., Aronson, M., & Fahlk, C. (2015). Psychosocial outcomes of fetal alcohol syndrome in adulthood. *Pediatrics, 135*(1), e52–58.

Spohr, H.R., Willms, J., & Steinhausen, H.C. (2007) Fetal alcohol spectrum disorder in young adulthood. *Journal of Pediatrics, 150*(2), 175–179.

Stevens, S.A., Nash, K., Fantus, E., Nulman, I., Rovet, J., & Koren, G. (2013). Towards identifying a characteristic neuropsychological profile for fetal alcohol spectrum disorders. 2. Specific caregiver- and teacher-rating. *Journal of Population Therapeutics and Clinical Pharmacology, 20*(1), e53–62.

Stratton, K., Howe, C., & Battaglia, F. (Eds.). (1996). *Fetal alcohol syndrome: Diagnosis, epidemiology, prevention, and treatment.* Washington, DC: National Academies Press.

Streissguth, A.P. (1994). A long term perspective of fetal alcohol syndrome. *Alcohol Health and Research World, 18*(1), 74–81.

Streissguth, A.P., Bookstein, F.L., Barr, H.M., Sampson, P.D., O'Malley, K., & Young, J.K. (2004). Risk factors for adverse life outcomes in fetal alcohol syndrome and fetal alcohol effects. *Journal of Developmental and Behavioral Pediatrics, 25*(4), 228–238.

Thomas, S.E., Kelly, S.J., Mattson, S.N., & Riley, E.P. (1998). Comparison of social abilities of children with fetal alcohol syndrome to those of children with similar IQ scores and normal controls. *Alcoholism: Clinical and Experimental Research, 22*(2), 528–533.

Wells, A.M., Chasnoff, I.J., Schmidt, C.A., Telford, E., & Schwartz, L.D. (2012). Neurocognitive habilitation therapy for children with fetal alcohol spectrum disorders: An adaptation of the Alert Program. *American Journal of Occupational Therapy, 66*(1), 24–34.

Werts, R.L., Van Calcar, S.C., Wargowski, D.S., & Smith, S.M. (2014). Inappropriate feeding behaviors and dietary intakes in children with fetal alcohol spectrum disorder or probable prenatal alcohol exposure. *Alcoholism: Clinical and Experimental Research, 38*(3), 871–878.

Whaley, S.E., O'Connor, M.J., & Gunderson, G. (2001). Comparison of the adaptive functioning of children prenatally exposed to alcohol to a nonexposed clinical sample. *Alcoholism: Clinical and Experimental Research, 25*(7), 1018–1024.

Wozniak, J.R., Fuglestad, A.J., Eckerle, J.K., Fink, B.A., Hoecker, H.L., Boys, C.J.,...Georgieff, M.K. (2013). Choline supplementation in children with fetal alcohol spectrum disorders: A randomized, double-blind, placebo-control trial. *American Journal of Clinical Nutrition, 102*(5), 1113–1125.

Zuccolo, L., Lewis, S.J., Smith, G.D., Sayal, K., Draper, E.S., Fraser, R.,...Gray, R. (2013). Prenatal alcohol exposure and offspring cognition and school performance. A "Mendelian randomization" natural experiment. *International Journal of Epidemiology, 42*(5), 1358–1370.

19

Fetal Alcohol Spectrum Disorder, Part II

Challenges in Adulthood

Valerie K. Temple, Leeping Tao, and Trudy Clifford

WHAT YOU WILL LEARN

- How fetal alcohol spectrum disorder is diagnosed in adults
- Intellectual abilities and impairments of people with fetal alcohol spectrum disorder
- Mental health challenges for adults with fetal alcohol spectrum disorder
- Treatment and support of adults with fetal alcohol spectrum disorder

Children with fetal alcohol spectrum disorder (FASD) eventually grow to become adults with FASD, and adults with FASD often have very different types of challenges from those of children. This chapter focuses on issues in adulthood for individuals with FASD, discussing diagnosis, treatment, and the support of adult individuals with this disorder.

DIAGNOSIS OF FETAL ALCOHOL SPECTRUM DISORDER IN ADULTS

FASD is a term that describes a group of disorders that may occur if an individual is exposed to alcohol prior to birth. Although a number of different guidelines for diagnosing FASD are used across North America and around the world (e.g., Astley, 2004; Chudley et al., 2005; Hoyme et al., 2005; May, 1995), most of these systems consider the following parameters when making a diagnosis. The presence

or absence and the severity of these parameters determines whether an individual is given a diagnosis and which one is given. The parameters are as follows:

1. Level of exposure to alcohol before birth, including how often, how much, and during what period of the pregnancy the mother drank

2. A constellation of specific facial features, including small eyes, a flat mid-face, a poorly developed philtrum (the two lines that run from the nose to the upper lip on the face), and a thin upper lip

3. Central nervous system (CNS) damage or brain dysfunction, including directly observable indicators such as seizures, microcephaly (small head circumference), or damage seen on brain imaging (e.g., computed tomography, magnetic resonance imaging), and/or dysfunction inferred through neurological, psychological, speech-language, or occupational therapy assessments

4. Physical growth deficits such as low birth weight or failure to gain weight and/or height after birth

Individuals with significant prenatal exposure to alcohol, all the facial features, central nervous system damage/dysfunction, and growth deficits generally

257

meet criteria for full fetal alcohol syndrome (FAS). Individuals with partial symptoms may receive other diagnoses on the spectrum, including alcohol-related neurodevelopmental disorder (ARND), neurobehavioral disorder, partial FAS, or FASD without sentinel facial features. The level of severity required for a positive finding on each parameter and the diagnosis given will vary depending on the diagnostic system used.

At the time of this writing in 2016, diagnostic guidelines for adults and children are the same, but a number of substantial challenges to diagnosing adults have been encountered (Chudley, Kilgour, Cranston, & Edwards, 2007). These include changes in, or the complete disappearance of, specific FAS facial features as an individual ages; "catch-up growth" or normalization in physical height and weight during adolescence and adulthood; and difficulties with obtaining information about alcohol exposure before birth because it is distant in time and memory for family members or because of estrangement from the family due to foster care or adoption. Spohr, Wilms, and Steinhausen (2007), in their follow-up study of 37 individuals with FASD 20 years after diagnosis, found that many of the physical features of FASD documented in childhood had disappeared. They noted significant gains in height, weight, and head circumference for the sample as a whole and reported that most individuals now fell within the average range for these measurements. In addition, facial features such as smaller than normal eyes had diminished across the group. This means that an individual who met criteria for full FAS in childhood, with the facial features and growth deficits, might not meet these criteria in adulthood. The authors noted, however, that brain dysfunction and intellectual impairments remained constant throughout the life span.

The issue of obtaining information regarding maternal alcohol consumption during pregnancy is difficult for individuals of all ages. However, it is especially problematic in adult diagnosis. For adults,

---

Case Study

At 19 years old, Melissa was referred for FASD assessment by child protective services (CPS) in her community. CPS could only support Melissa up until 20 years of age and requested services within the adult sector to assist in the future. Melissa was born full term and weighed 5 pounds, 2 ounces. Her mother drank heavily throughout the pregnancy and also smoked cigarettes. Melissa was a small, frail child who had difficulty gaining weight. When she was 6 years of age, CPS became involved with her family due to allegations by school personnel that she was being neglected and physically abused at home.

By 8 years of age, Melissa was removed from her mother's home and put into a series of foster home placements. Each placement began well but would break down after a short period, and Melissa would attempt to run away and go back to her mother. By 15 years old, Melissa was made a ward of the state and had been diagnosed with attention-deficit/hyperactivity disorder (ADHD), depression, oppositional defiant disorder, and attachment disorder. Teachers and caregivers believed Melissa was an intelligent but stubborn child who could do better if she would only try harder. At 16 years of age, Melissa was hospitalized for substance abuse problems and a suicide attempt. She became pregnant at 18 years of age, but the child was apprehended by CPS shortly after birth. Also around the same time, Melissa's mother died from complications related to liver disease and Melissa became profoundly depressed by these two serious losses in her life.

An assessment found that Melissa met criteria for ARND, a form of FASD. Her psychological testing found a scattered profile of skills, with some abilities in the mild range of intellectual disability, some in the borderline range, and some in the low average range. Following the assessment, Melissa received counseling services to address her bereavement issues, a supported housing placement, and financial assistance from the state disability support program. Her support workers learned that many of the problems they had previously attributed to stubbornness and oppositional behavior were actually due to her disability. This led them to view her in a different light and provide more support, which in turn led to less problem behavior.

it is at least 18 years since the pregnancy took place, and gaining information about alcohol consumption during a particular 9-month period that long ago is challenging at best. Mothers and other family members are often unavailable to report their activities or may even be deceased. At times, it is possible to obtain medical or other records documenting exposure, but the information is typically limited in terms of details. This makes it very difficult to establish whether there was alcohol exposure and exactly how much exposure occurred.

For individuals with the physical and facial features of FAS and substantial intellectual impairments early in life, a diagnosis in childhood is more likely. However, for those with less obvious symptoms, it could be late adolescence or adulthood before a diagnosis is reached. In some cases, FASD may be strongly suspected but a diagnosis cannot be assigned because the maternal drinking history is not available. As is the case for many disorders, early diagnosis and intervention generally leads to better outcomes. This means that individuals with FASD who are not recognized early in life and provided with appropriate supports may have greater challenges and develop more problems relative to those with an early diagnosis. Nevertheless, diagnosis at any point in the lifespan can lead to more positive future outcomes and improved support and well-being.

INTELLECTUAL AND FUNCTIONAL ABILITIES IN ADULTS WITH FETAL ALCOHOL SPECTRUM DISORDER

Adults with FASD can have a wide range of abilities and impairments. Some present with a global intellectual disability, whereas others function within the borderline or even average range of intelligence, with more limited areas of disability. Level of alcohol exposure, timing of the exposure, and preexisting genetic factors (e.g., intelligence levels of the parents) can all affect an individual's outcome (Kodituwakku, 2007; O'Leary et al., 2010). A person who is exposed to heavy alcohol consumption across the entire pregnancy, for example, may have a very different outcome than someone exposed to drinking only in the early stages of pregnancy.

The environment and experiences of an adult with FASD also work to shape his or her profile of intellectual strengths and weaknesses. As is true for everyone, life experiences influence ability and achievement. Both adverse and enriching life events can alter and affect brain development, as the vast literature on brain plasticity has documented (Doidge, 2007). Although environmental factors are also important for children with FASD, the effect is likely magnified in adults due to the greater period of time passed.

Because of the variable presentation of individuals with FASD, a set of impairments specific to FASD has been hard to identify. A common finding in the assessment of adults, however, is the existence of what is called a "scattered profile" (i.e., a set of scores on functional testing characterized by large peaks and valleys of ability). This is different from the smaller variability in scores seen in typically functioning individuals. Adults with FASD, for example, may have arithmetic skills at the primary school level along with reading skills at the high school level, or age-appropriate (average range) recognition memory but severe impairments (intellectual disability range) in recall memory (Kodituwakku, 2007).

Individuals with a scattered profile of abilities often present a special challenge to their families and care providers. This is because they may appear to be stubborn or oppositional if they do not perform at an age-appropriate level across different situations. For example, an individual with FASD may have average long-term memory skills but severe impairments in short-term memory. This would mean the person could recall what happened many weeks ago but not the day before. Therefore, care providers who do not know about the impairment may believe the individual chooses not to give complete or correct information about the previous day's events or that he or she is being evasive when in fact the person is simply unable to give it. This is just one possible example, but the general situation of mistaking inability for unwillingness is a common problem for this group.

Executive Functioning and Daily Living Skills

Despite the varying levels of ability and scattered profiles commonly seen in adults with FASD, there are at least two areas in which impairments almost always exist. These are executive functioning and daily living skills (Chudley et al., 2007; Rasmussen, McAuley, & Andrew, 2007; Streissguth et al.,

2004). Executive functioning is a group of abilities that involves managing, controlling, and organizing one's own actions and behavior. Executive functioning skills include planning and organizing, modulating emotional reactions, initiating activities, attention and focus, and impulse control. Considering all these skills together, it is easy to see how an individual with impairments in these areas would have challenges functioning as an adult. Because the activities of children are often controlled and managed by their parents or caregivers, executive functioning impairments may be less obvious or more easily managed in a child. An adult, however, is expected to self-direct most or all aspects of his or her own life, and individuals with executive functioning impairments are less able to do this.

Research in this area has suggested that executive functioning issues become more pronounced as an individual with FASD ages (Rasmussen et al., 2007). Studies of adults with FASD have shown that problems with anger management, impulse control, and social interaction are very common. This can lead to interactions with the criminal justice system, difficulties holding a job, and loss of residential placement (Streissguth et al., 1994). Diagnoses such as oppositional defiant disorder, conduct disorder, and antisocial personality disorder are also common in adults with FASD and are likely related to these difficulties with executive functioning skills.

Another important area of impairment for adults with FASD is daily living skills (Streissguth et al., 2004). *Daily living skills* refers to the ability to perform everyday tasks. This includes activities such as personal hygiene, domestic chores, traveling in the community, shopping for groceries, and using banking services. Adults with FASD frequently have very low skills in this area, regardless of their level of intellectual ability (Temple, Shewfelt, & Clifford, 2011), and even those with average or borderline intellect may have problems "applying" their intelligence on a daily basis. It is possible that this is because of their difficulties with planning and organizing, which in turn influence the ability to follow through on many types of tasks.

MENTAL HEALTH ISSUES ASSOCIATED WITH FETAL ALCOHOL SPECTRUM DISORDER

Adults with FASD are at very high risk for mental health problems. In the developmental literature, individuals with intellectual disability and a mental health problem are referred to as having a dual diagnosis. Whereas individuals with intellectual disability as a general group have a high rate of dual diagnosis, in the range of 14%–67% (Bradley & Summers, 2003), adults with FASD have been reported to have rates in the range of 85%–90% (Streissguth et al., 1994). Some common mental health challenges for adults with FASD include mood disorders such as depression, attention deficit disorders (e.g., ADHD), anxiety disorders, and personality disorders (Barr et al., 2006). Adults with FASD are also at high risk for problems such as abusing substances and suicide attempts (Chudley et al., 2007; Streissguth et al., 2004).

Environmental stressors and adverse life events are also very common for adults with FASD, and arguably these are important in the development of later mental health problems. In her longitudinal study completed in the state of Washington, Streissguth reported that 67% of individuals with FASD had been the victims of sexual or physical abuse or domestic violence. Also, 80% were not raised by their biological parents, suggesting a high level of disrupted family experiences. As adolescents or adults, 46% had drug or alcohol problems of their own, and by adulthood, 35% had spent time in jail (Streissguth et al., 2004). Of interest, in the longitudinal study of Spohr et al. (2007), conducted in Germany, there were far fewer negative events in childhood and adolescence reported. This suggests that cultural or social factors may also play a role in outcomes for this group.

Interventions and Supports

Adults with FASD can benefit from a variety of interventions and supports (see Tao, Temple, Casson, & Kirkpatrick [2013] for an overview). One critical area is assistance with organizing and structuring activities. Given their very poor daily living skills and executive functioning impairments, adults with FASD are generally in need of someone to organize and direct activities in their lives. For example, they may require someone to accompany them to appointments in the community, set schedules, plan events, or assist with managing their money. This may be done by a family member, a paid support worker, or residential staff. In the FASD literature, this role is sometimes referred to as being the "external brain" for the person with FASD.

Another important support issue is case management. There are very few community resources or interventions specifically for adults with FASD (Wheeler, Kenney, & Temple, 2013), and generic supports for individuals in the intellectual disability sector may not always be suitable for this group due to their unique challenges (e.g., high rate of substance abuse, mental health issues). In addition, many intellectual disability services require a formal diagnosis of intellectual disability (e.g., IQ below 70) and, given the broad range of scatter common in the intellectual scores of adults with FASD, they may not qualify for such services. Case managers can help by advocating for and finding structured and adapted work environments, residential supports, and appropriate leisure activities for adults with FASD.

Counseling services can also be helpful for this group. As adults with FASD have frequently experienced abuse, neglect, and/or trauma, counseling aimed at reducing symptoms of stress, increasing self-esteem, and teaching self-regulation strategies can be very useful. Counseling techniques aimed at reducing impulsivity and behavioral problems, however, are generally less effective. Because of difficulties with managing time and organizing, it is important to make accommodations in providing counseling services to people with FASD. Ideally, appointments should be set at the same time every week or biweekly. Also, it may be helpful, with the permission of the individual, to involve caregivers in counseling sessions to gain information about problems that the individual may have difficulty articulating and to help him or her to arrive at appointments on schedule.

Another intervention that has proved effective with this group is behavior therapy. Although traditional "learning theory" that may focus on the consequences of an individual's actions is less helpful for adults with FASD (Malbin, 2005), interventions aimed at modifying the environment to provide greater support and structure have been found useful. Role modeling, using visual cues, and using scheduling aids to improve organization are some examples of effective supports.

Although adults with FASD have high rates of mental health issues, at the time of this writing in 2016 there is very little information available regarding how well medications can help manage various mental health symptoms. Because of their unique etiology, the presentation of mental health problems in adults with FASD may be different from that in other individuals. At least one study, however, reported that pharmacological interventions can provide additional support for symptom management in the very common condition of ADHD (Doig, McLennan, & Gibbard, 2008).

SUMMARY

Adults with FASD present with a complex array of challenges. As a group, they often come from difficult family environments and many are adopted or placed in foster care. A large number have been physically or sexually assaulted at some time in their lives, and as adults they have very high rates of substance use and mental health problems. Diagnosing FASD in adulthood has many challenges, including the fact that individuals may "grow out" of some of the key indicators such as facial features and weight/height deficits. Functional assessment often finds these individuals have a scattered profile of intellectual abilities along with substantial impairments in executive functioning and daily living skills. These and other issues lead to the need for a high level of support around personal care, gaining employment, managing money, and living in the community. Case management, counseling, and behavior support services are some of the important interventions that can be helpful for adults with FASD. Although pharmacological interventions may help for some coexisting conditions (e.g., ADHD), research about the use of medications for adults with FASD is very limited at the time of this writing.

FOR FURTHER THOUGHT AND DISCUSSION

1. What additional challenges do you think you might encounter when working with adults with FASD as compared to working with children with FASD?

2. When individuals require a high degree of support and structure in their lives, ethical issues can arise for care providers (e.g., family members, professionals, case workers). What do you think could be some of the ethical issues encountered when managing someone else's life? Discuss with reference to the concepts of autonomy and dignity of risk.

REFERENCES

Astley, S.J. (2004). *Diagnostic guidelines for FASD: The 4-digit diagnostic code* (3rd ed.). Seattle: University of Washington.

Barr, H.M., Bookstein, F.L., O'Malley, K., Connor, P.D., Huggins, J.E., & Streissguth, A.P. (2006). Binge drinking during pregnancy as a predictor of psychiatric disorders on the structured clinical interview for DSM-IV in young adult offspring. *American Journal of Psychiatry, 163,* 1061–1065.

Bradley, E., & Summers, J. (2003). Developmental disability and behavioural, emotional, and psychiatric disturbances. In I. Brown & M. Percy (Eds.), *Developmental disabilities in Ontario* (2nd ed., pp. 751–771). Toronto, Canada: Ontario Association on Developmental Disabilities.

Chudley, A.E., Conry, J., Cook, J.L., Loock, C., Rosales, T., & LeBlanc, N. (2005). Fetal alcohol spectrum disorder: Canadian guidelines for diagnosis. *Canadian Medical Association Journal, 172,* S1–S21.

Chudley, A.E., Kilgour, A.R., Cranston, M., & Edwards, M. (2007). Challenges of diagnosis in fetal alcohol syndrome and fetal alcohol spectrum disorder in the adult. *American Journal of Medical Genetics, Part C, 145C,* 261–272.

Doidge, N. (2007). *The brain that changes itself.* New York, NY: Penguin.

Doig, J., McLennan, J.D., & Gibbard, W.B. (2008). Medication effects on symptoms of attention-deficit/hyperactivity disorder in children with fetal alcohol spectrum disorder. *Journal of Child and Adolescent Psychopharmacology, 18*(4), 365–371.

Hoyme, H.E., May, P.A., Kalberg, M.A., Kodituwakku, P., Gossage, P., Trujillo, P.,…Robinson, L. (2005). A practical clinical approach to diagnosis of fetal alcohol spectrum disorder: Clarification of the 1996 Institute of Medicine criteria. *Pediatrics, 115*(1), 39–47.

Kodituwakku, P.W. (2007). Defining the behavioral phenotype in children with fetal alcohol spectrum disorders: A review. *Neuroscience and Biobehavioral Reviews, 31,* 192–201.

Malbin, D. (2005, Summer). FASD and standard interventions: Poor fits? *British Columbia Teachers Federation-Alternative Education Association Newsletter.*

May, P.A. (1995). A multi-level comprehensive approach to the prevention of fetal alcohol syndrome (FAS) and other alcohol related birth defects (ARBD). *International Journal of Addiction, 30,* 549–602.

O'Leary, C.M., Nassar, N., Zubrick, S.R., Kurinczuk, J.J., Stanley, F., & Bower, C. (2010). Evidence of a complex association between dose, pattern and timing of prenatal alcohol exposure and child behaviour problems. *Addiction, 105*(1), 74–86.

Rasmussen, C., McAuley, R., & Andrew, G. (2007). Parental rating of children with fetal alcohol spectrum disorder on the Behavior Rating Inventory of Executive Functioning (BRIEF). *Journal of FAS International, 5*(e2), 1–8.

Spohr, H.L., Willms, J., & Steinhausen, H.C. (2007). Fetal alcohol spectrum disorders in young adulthood. *Journal of Pediatrics, 150,* 175–179.

Streissguth, A.P., Bookstein, F.L., Barr, H.M., Sampson, P.D., O'Malley, K., & Kogan Young, J. (2004). Risk factors for adverse life outcomes in fetal alcohol syndrome and fetal alcohol effects. *Developmental and Behavioral Pediatrics, 25*(4), 228–237.

Streissguth, A.P., Sampson, P.D., Carmichael Olson, H., Bookstein, F.L., Barr, H.M., Scott, M.,…Mirsky, A.F. (1994). Maternal drinking during pregnancy: Attention and short-term memory in 14-year-old offspring—A longitudinal study. *Alcoholism: Clinical and Experimental Research, 18*(1), 202–218.

Tao, L., Temple, V.K., Casson, I., & Kirkpatrick, S.M.L. (2013). *Healthwatch table: Fetal alcohol spectrum disorder.* Retrieved from http://vkc.mc.vanderbilt.edu/etoolkit/physical-health/health-watch-tables-2/fetal-alcohol-spectrum-disorder/

Temple, V.K., Shewfelt, L., & Clifford, T. (2011). Comparing daily living skills in adults with fetal alcohol spectrum disorder to an IQ matched clinical sample. *Journal of Population Therapeutics and Clinical Pharmacology, 18*(2), e397–e402.

Wheeler, J.A., Kenney, K.A., & Temple, V.K. (2013). Fetal alcohol spectrum disorder: An exploratory investigation of services and interventions for adults. *Journal on Developmental Disabilities, 19*(3), 64–77.

20

Cerebral Palsy

Darcy Fehlings and Carolyn Hunt

- What cerebral palsy is and what impact it has on a person's development and activities of daily living
- Different types of cerebral palsy
- Risk factors for cerebral palsy
- Medical complications associated with cerebral palsy
- Treatment approaches for people with cerebral palsy

Jessica is a 3½ year old girl who attends an inclusive child care center in the heart of the city. She has a twin sister, Kayla, who attends the same day care. Jessica loves to play at the sand station and with building blocks. She especially enjoys story time. Kayla's favorite activity is going out on the playground. She always helps Jessica get her walker out the door so that they can go outside and have fun! Jessica loves to play, and since she has learned to use her walker outside, nobody has been able to catch her! Jessica has spastic diplegia, a form of cerebral palsy, and uses a walker for mobility most of the time. She is having a little bit of difficulty learning her letters but is an enthusiastic participant in her care program and all of the children love her. Jessica and Kayla's mother, Cindy, is so proud of her twins. Who would have guessed they would have grown to be so big and strong, after being premature and weighing just 1.5 pounds each at birth?

WHAT IS CEREBRAL PALSY?

Cerebral palsy is a motor disorder caused by an injury to the developing brain. Rosenbaum et al. (2007) define cerebral palsy as follows:

> A group of permanent disorders of the development of movement and posture causing activity limitations that are attributed to non-progressive disturbances that occurred in the developing fetal or infant brain. The motor disorders are often accompanied by disturbances of sensation, perception, cognition, communication, and behavior, by epilepsy, or by secondary musculoskeletal problems. (p. 9)

The following are four main features of cerebral palsy:

1. Onset that is before, during, or after birth (usually before 2 years of age)

2. Motor difficulties that are secondary to brain injury or an abnormality of the developing brain

3. Decreased control of movements with poor motor coordination or balance, muscle stiffness, or abnormal movements (or a combination of these features)

4. A condition that is nonprogressive but permanent

A child is often suspected of having cerebral palsy in the first year of life if his or her motor milestones are delayed (i.e., late in sitting, crawling, and walking). Parents may also notice that their infant has an atypical way of moving, such as commando crawling (crawling by pulling the body forward with the arms and dragging the legs behind) or that their child always stands or walks on his or her toes. The child may have an early hand preference (before 2 years of age). There is a common misconception that all people with cerebral palsy also have an intellectual disability. Although this is sometimes the case, many children with cerebral palsy have typical intelligence.

Cerebral palsy is diagnosed by identifying abnormalities in a neurological exam including muscle tone (e.g., stiffness) and motor function. A diagnosis of cerebral palsy is usually made by a pediatrician. Pediatricians typically take a detailed history and review any potential risk factors for cerebral palsy. They also carry out a physical examination, concentrating on the neurological examination and careful observation the child's movement. They often order a special picture of the brain (e.g., magnetic resonance imaging scan). A formal diagnosis of cerebral palsy is usually made between 12 to 24 months of age; however, it is important to note that this should not delay a referral to early intervention services in the first year of life once a motor delay is identified (Noritz, Murphy, & Neuromotor Screening Expert Panel, 2013).

How Common Is Cerebral Palsy?

Cerebral palsy is the most common cause of childhood physical disability. In developed countries, the prevalence is estimated to be two out of every 1,000 children (Andersen et al., 2008). The prevalence of cerebral palsy has remained very stable despite improvements in obstetrical care.

What Causes Cerebral Palsy?

A great deal is understood about risk factors for developing cerebral palsy, and sometimes a specific cause can be identified. Often, a combination of risk factors leads to conditions that cause cerebral palsy. Prematurity is the greatest risk factor for cerebral palsy, but despite this, the majority of children with cerebral palsy were born at term; similarly, many children born preterm do not have cerebral palsy. It is likely that a combination of genetic vulnerability interacting with environmental stressors leads to the development of cerebral palsy. The presence of multiple risk factors markedly increases the risk. Possible risk factors are listed in Table 20.1. It is often assumed that most children who develop cerebral palsy have had a difficult birth. However, as outlined in Table 20.1,

there are many risk factors that do not relate to the intrapartum (i.e., during birth) period. Likely it is the intersection of preconception, prenatal, intrapartum, and neonatal risk factors that contribute to the development of cerebral palsy. Even when the risk factors are known, there are few strategies available for prevention (McIntyre et al., 2013; Nelson, 1996, 2008).

One condition that can be associated with the subsequent development of cerebral palsy is neonatal encephalopathy, when an infant experiences a low oxygen level during delivery (sometimes resulting in delayed crying and poor respiratory effort at birth). When this happens, the reduced oxygen to the brain causes cell death and, ultimately, damage to the very sensitive areas that control motor function. Neonatal encephalopathy is the strongest risk factor for cerebral palsy in term infants, present in up to 33% of children with cerebral palsy born at term (Kyriakipoulos, Oskoui, Degenais, & Shevell, 2013). Neonatal encephalopathy is significantly associated with Gross Motor Function Classification System (GMFCS) Level III–V cerebral palsy and is not a common risk factor in the milder forms of cerebral palsy. (See the Movement subsection later in this chapter for details about the GMFCS.) There are many risk factors leading to neonatal encephalopathy, such as chorioamnionitis (inflammation of the placenta), but the relationship between those risk factors and specific outcomes is still not well understood.

Types of Cerebral Palsy

There are three main types of cerebral palsy: spastic, dyskinetic, and ataxic (see Table 20.2). *Spasticity* refers to neurologic stiffness in the muscles associated with increased reflexes and can be further subdivided into *bilateral* (limbs on both sides of the body are involved) or *unilateral* (limbs on one side of the body are involved). Another term for unilateral spastic cerebral palsy is *hemiplegia*. When the spastic cerebral palsy is bilateral, it often involves both legs, and the term for this is *spastic diplegia;* if all four limbs are involved, this is *spastic quadriplegia*. Dyskinetic cerebral palsy is characterized by involuntary movements and consists of two subtypes: dystonic and choreoathetotic. The dystonic subtype consists of marked fluctuation in tone and getting "stuck" in abnormal postures. Choreoathetotic cerebral palsy is associated with hyperkinetic (increased activity) involuntary movements. Ataxic cerebral palsy is associated with poor balance and decreased muscle coordination. Mixed cerebral palsy occurs when there is a combination of subtypes.

Table 20.1. Risk factors for cerebral palsy

Preconception	Antenatal (before birth)	Intrapartum (during delivery)	Neonatal/postnatal
Maternal disease or disability (e.g., seizures, intellectual disability)	Prematurity	Abnormal length of labor	Neonatal encephalopathy
Maternal age > 40	Congenital malformations and antenatal infection, (e.g., cytomegalovirus)	Breech position and other abnormal fetal presentations	Respiratory distress syndrome
History of stillbirth or neonatal death	Low birth weight	Emergency delivery (either by cesarean section or with instrumentation)	Hypoglycemia
Low socioeconomic status	Chorioamnionitis (inflammation of the placenta)	Meconium aspiration	Neonatal infection
	Abnormal amount of amniotic fluid	Obstetric risk factors (e.g., shoulder dystocia, cord prolapse, true knot in cord)	Severe jaundice
	Maternal health in pregnancy (e.g., cardiac, respiratory, or cervical incompetence/insufficiency)		Neonatal stroke

Table 20.2. Types of cerebral palsy

Spastic

  Bilateral

    Spastic quadriplegia

    Spastic diplegia

  Unilateral

    Spastic hemiplegia

Dyskinetic

  Dystonic

  Choreoathetotic

Ataxia

Mixed

Source: Surveillance of Cerebral Palsy in Europe (2000).

Table 20.3. Gross Motor Function Classification System (GMFCS) for children ages 6–12 years

Level I	"Walks without restrictions; limitations in more advanced motor skills" such as speed of running
Level II	"Walks without assistive devices; limitations walking outdoors and in the community," such as difficulties with changes in terrain
Level III	"Walks with assistive mobility devices such as a walker or canes"
Level IV	"Self-mobility with limitations; children are transported or use power mobility outdoors and in the community"
Level V	"Self-mobility is extremely limited even with the use of assistive technology"

From Palisano, R., Rosenbaum, P., Bartlett, D., & Livingston, M. (2008). Content validity of the expanded and revised Gross Motor Function Classification System. *Developmental Medicine & Child Neurology, 50*(10), 744–750; adapted by permission.

IMPACT OF CEREBRAL PALSY ON DEVELOPMENT

Cerebral palsy can affect many aspects of an individual's life, including the ability to move, the ability to complete activities of daily living, cognitive and language abilities, and physical health.

Movement

One of the defining features of cerebral palsy is difficulty controlling and planning motor movements in the parts of the body that are affected. There is wide variability in function, with some individuals being completely independent and others using a manual or electric wheelchair for mobility. Most individuals with hemiplegic and spastic diplegic cerebral palsy are able to walk. A higher percentage of those individuals with spastic quadriplegia and/or dyskinetic cerebral palsy use a wheelchair for mobility. Researchers from McMaster University in Hamilton, Ontario, Canada, created a now well-established classification system, the GMFCS (Palisano et al., 1997), which classifies cerebral palsy according to gross motor function and divides cerebral palsy into five ability levels (see Table 20.3). This had a huge impact on how cerebral palsy is understood and gave researchers a critical measurement system to understand the impact of potential therapies and interventions. Jessica, from the anecdote at the beginning of this chapter, has GMFCS Level III cerebral palsy.

Hand Control and Activities of Daily Living

People with cerebral palsy vary from being completely independent in their activities of daily living (ADLs) to needing supports for the majority of their activities of daily living. The degree of independence often relates to the motor control a person with cerebral palsy has in his or her hands (e.g., those with hemiplegic cerebral palsy can become very good at doing tasks with one hand). Compared with the other types of cerebral palsy, there are higher needs for support in completing ADLs in individuals with spastic quadriplegia or dyskinetic cerebral palsy. The Manual Ability Classification System (MACS; Eliasson et al., 2006), similar to the GMFCS, describes the ability of the individual to do activities with their hands, from Level I (independent) to Level V (dependent).

Learning and Developmental Disabilities

People with cerebral palsy can have typical intelligence, but some people with cerebral palsy are at risk for developmental delays, intellectual disability, or learning disability. Reported rates of intellectual disability in people with cerebral palsy range from 30% to 60% (Evans, Evans, & Alberman, 1990). People with cerebral palsy can have both a physical disability and an intellectual disability, although this is not always the case.

Speech and Language

Many people with cerebral palsy are able to speak fluently and clearly. Some have difficulty with articulation, which can make speech difficult for a listener to understand. Others may be unable to speak because of motor problems and require alternate strategies to communicate, such as picture or symbol displays, or they may use a computer voice output system. Difficulty with articulation is common for people with dyskinetic cerebral palsy.

MEDICAL PROBLEMS ASSOCIATED WITH CEREBRAL PALSY

People with cerebral palsy are at risk for medical complications. The main medical complications are as follows:

- Seizures (seen in approximately 20%–30%)

- Visual impairment

- Strabismus (turning in or out of the eye)

- Hearing loss

- Dental cavities

- Drooling

- Swallowing difficulties

- Poor growth/nutrition

- Aspiration pneumonia

- Gastroesophageal reflux disease (GERD)

- Constipation

- Orthopedic complications

The medical complications associated with cerebral palsy require careful monitoring and active treatment. A developmental pediatrician is a physician who has specialized training in developmental problems, such as cerebral palsy and other areas, and coordinates the care of children who are medically complex and have a diagnosis of cerebral palsy.

Seizures occur when there is an episodic excess of electrical activity in the brain (often arising from an area that has been injured). This can lead to shaking of the arms and legs and a loss of consciousness. Seizures are usually treated with anticonvulsants that help to prevent or decrease their frequency and severity. Strabismus (more commonly known as lazy eye) is usually treated with eye surgery that helps to align both eyes. Hearing loss can often be addressed with a hearing aid. If there is persisting fluid in the middle ear, secondary to recurrent ear infections, the fluid can be drained with a small tube inserted into the eardrum. Drooling often improves with age and saliva management training. If it persists past 5 years of age, a small surgical procedure that moves the saliva ducts farther back in the mouth can be performed.

Eating difficulties—especially difficulties with swallowing—are commonly seen in people with spastic quadriplegia or dyskinetic cerebral palsy. It takes good muscle coordination to swallow food and beverages, particularly thin liquids such as juice. When the swallowing is poor, food can be taken into the lungs and can create aspiration pneumonia. It can also decrease the total amount of food and calories being taken in, which can cause poor nutrition and delayed growth. Thickening liquids and watching the physical position of individuals when they are eating can help (sitting up in a comfortable, supported seat is best). Sometimes a feeding tube (gastrostomy tube, or g-tube) placed in the stomach through the abdominal wall is required to provide nutrition. Although daunting at first, parents and caregivers are able to manage a g-tube in a home environment.

Orthopedic (bone) complications are frequently seen in cerebral palsy. Children with cerebral palsy may require surgical intervention by an orthopedic surgeon (i.e., bone doctor). The extra stiffness in the muscles decreases muscle growth. This can lead to joint contractures that can affect the individual's gait (i.e., walking pattern). An orthopedic surgeon can do an operation that lengthens the tendon of the muscle to help to increase flexibility. For instance, with a heel cord lengthening, a child can go from always standing on his or her toes to being able to bring the heel down to the floor. For children who are non-ambulatory and have more severe cerebral palsy (GMFCS Level IV and Level V), x-ray surveillance of their hips is important to assess their risk of future hip dislocation, which can occur because of the muscle tightness around their hip joint. The orthopedic surgeon can lengthen the muscles around the hip and reshape the bones of the hip to try to prevent a complete dislocation of the hip.

Life Expectancy

For children who are able to walk and do not have specific medical issues such as epilepsy, life expectancy is close to that of the general population, although still slightly reduced. A study reported the 5- and 18-year survival rates as 98% and 89%, respectively (Touyama, Touyama, Ochiai, Toyokawa, & Kobayashi, 2013). Level V cerebral palsy was the only significant risk factor for shortened life span in this study, with 85% of the mortality occurring in the children with Level V cerebral palsy (Touyama et al., 2013). Another group (Strauss, Brooks, Rosenbloom, & Shavelle, 2009) specifically noted that life expectancy is significantly reduced, particularly if the individual is not able to self-feed. Those with hard-to-control seizures, significant respiratory difficulties, and severe GERD associated with aspiration pneumonia are at risk of early death due to these complications. Life expectancy for these individuals would range from late 20s to early 50s (Strauss et al., 2009).

INTERVENTIONS FOR PEOPLE WITH CEREBRAL PALSY

The focus of interventions for people with cerebral palsy is to promote health, wellness, and participation. The aim is to help people with cerebral palsy achieve their developmental potential. Many health professionals can be involved: nurses, occupational therapists, orthopedic surgeons, orthotists (a professional who fabricates braces and splints), pediatricians, physical therapists (called physiotherapists in some countries), psychologists, recreation consultants, social workers, speech-language therapists, teachers, and others. Rehabilitation specialists use the World Health Organization's 2001 *International Classification of Functioning, Disability and Health (ICF)* framework when working with people with chronic health conditions such as cerebral palsy. This framework emphasizes interactions between body functions and structures (impairments affecting body structure and function), activities, participation, and contextual factors (e.g., personal and environmental factors) and can be used to conceptualize the impact of cerebral palsy on the individual. With so many people on the team, things can get confusing, although each person can play an important role. Families tell us that it is very important to coordinate services, to provide long-term continuity of care, and to focus on the whole individual and his or her family rather than just on problems or medical issues. In the disability field, this is called family-centered care (King, Teplicky, King, & Rosenbaum, 2004).

There are many different treatments available for people with cerebral palsy. It is increasingly recognized that treatment needs to be evidence based (showing through carefully constructed research projects that it does some good and that this outweighs any harmful side effects; Novak et al., 2013). Examples of commonly used treatments are listed in Table 20.4.

NEW DIRECTIONS IN MANAGEMENT AND PREVENTION

Treatments to assist individuals with cerebral palsy continue to evolve, with advances being made in pharmacologic management and rehabilitation interventions.

Advances in Management

The use of botulinum toxin type A to help manage spasticity (stiff muscles) has become a treatment option for individuals with cerebral palsy (Delgado et al., 2010; Fehlings et al., 2010; Love et al., 2010). Botulinum toxin type A is a neurotoxin that blocks the synaptic release of acetylcholine from cholinergic

Table 20.4.   Examples of therapies

Developmental area	Example of treatment	Health professional involved
Gross motor function	Physical therapy to teach stretching to maintain flexibility, improve muscle strength, and work on functional movements (e.g., walking, sitting, rolling)	Physical therapist
		Orthotist
	Use of special equipment such as walkers to help promote independence in walking	Physician
	Use of wheelchairs (manual and electric) to help promote mobility	
	Use of splints, braces (e.g., an ankle-foot orthosis that helps the individual put his or her heel on the floor)	
	Spasticity management, such as the use of botulinum toxin type A injections (Delgado et al., 2010)	
Fine motor function/ activities of daily living	Stretching and strengthening activities to promote hand control, splinting (e.g., a neoprene hand splint that helps to keep the thumb out of the palm to make grasping objects easier)	Occupational therapist
		Writing aid clinics (staffed by occupational therapists)
	Assessment for equipment to make activities of daily living easier (e.g., grab bars near toilets and baths, commode chairs, seating with trays to create a stable work or play area, lifting systems)	
	Home renovations to promote wheelchair accessibility	
	Computer-assisted writing aids	
	Training of the affected limb via constraint of the unaffected limb	
Speech and language	Parent training on encouraging young children's language development (e.g., the Hanen Program)	Speech-language pathologists
	Speech-language therapy to improve articulation and promote language development	Augmentative communication clinics (staffed by speech-language pathologists and occupational therapists)
	Augmentative and alternative communication systems used for individuals who are not able to speak effectively (e.g., a communication book with picture symbols that the individual looks at or points to, voice output computer systems)	
Learning/cognitive development	Infant stimulation programs for children younger than 2 years of age	Early childhood educators
	Preschool programs for children ages 2–4 years that include therapy consultation	School boards, teachers, psychologists
	Special education, including individualized education plans and accommodations for motor and learning difficulties	Teachers, occupational therapists, psychologists
	Psychoeducational assessment to evaluate learning strengths and weaknesses in order to assist with school and vocational planning	
	Vocational programs to provide training and support to individuals with special needs to enter the workplace	
Psychosocial development/ wellness	Support to family and siblings	Social worker
	Participation in recreational and extracurricular activities	Recreational therapist
	Promotion of peer interactions	

nerve terminals, mainly at the neuromuscular junction, resulting in irreversible loss of motor end plates. When botulinum toxin type A is injected into a stiff muscle, it causes partial temporary paralysis of this muscle. This decreases the muscle tone for about 3 months following the injection, which can allow the affected muscle to relax and move more easily. Botulinum toxin type A can also relieve painful muscle spasms (Lundy, Doherty, & Fairhurst, 2009). Injections can be paired with casting to increase the range of motion of the joint (Blackmore, Boettcher-Hunt, Jordan, & Chan, 2007)

For individuals with hemiplegic cerebral palsy, hand function can be improved with intensive motor therapy such as constraint therapy. Evidence suggests that if the nonhemiplegic hand is temporarily constrained via a splint/or cast and paired with intensive motor training of the hemiplegic hand, there will be improvements in use of the hemiplegic hand (Boyd et al., 2010; Hoare, Imms, Carey, & Wasiak, 2007).

Transitions

Making the transition from a supportive school environment to adult life in the community with employment and relationship opportunities requires careful planning (Logan, 1997). Planning for needed supports in adulthood should begin in the early teen years. Adults with cerebral palsy can be more isolated and have more difficulty with access to employment opportunities and establishing long-term relationships with a life partner. For example, in a large Swedish study, 55% of adults with cerebral palsy were not living with a partner, did not have biological children, and did not have competitive employment, compared with 4% of controls (Michelsen, Uldall, Hansen, & Madsen, 2006). There also are challenges associated with health care needs in the transition to adulthood. For example, adults with cerebral palsy who use wheeled mobility are at risk of developing cervical spinal stenosis (thickening of the bones around the spinal cord) because of a lifetime of looking upward to communicate with their ambulatory family and friends. Furthermore, it is not uncommon for people with cerebral palsy to experience a gradual decline in mobility as they move through adulthood (Young et al., 2006). However, more positive research is also starting to emerge. In a study of adults with cerebral palsy in Tel Aviv, Israel, 23% had their driver's license and were competitively employed (Mesterman et al., 2010). A study of adolescents with cerebral palsy without

intellectual disability studied over 5 years showed increasing levels of social participation, approaching the level of same-age peers by the end of adolescence (Tan et al., 2014). Other studies have demonstrated that both the presence of epilepsy and the degree of intellectual disability were the best predictors of long-term social participation (Michelsen et al.). Further research is needed to determine how treatment can be tailored to create the best transition to adulthood for all children with cerebral palsy.

Will Cerebral Palsy Ever Be Preventable?

A major focus of current research is aimed at increasing participation of individuals with disabilities in the community. However, strategies to minimize the amount of disability experienced by an individual should continue to be sought. Preterm birth is a significant risk factor for cerebral palsy. There is evidence that treating women who are in preterm labor (prior to 31 weeks) with magnesium sulfate substantially reduces the risk of cerebral palsy in infants (Doyle, Crowther, Middleton, Marret, & Rouse, 2009). A second strategy is the use of cooling (either head or total body cooling) for 72 hours for treatment in the immediate newborn period if an infant born at term has neonatal encephalopathy. Studies have shown that cooling may reduce both the frequency and severity of cerebral palsy (Schulzke, Rao, & Patole, 2007). Other promising treatments for the prevention of cerebral palsy are melatonin, with research being done to supplement pregnant mothers who are carrying a growth-restricted baby to reduce oxidative stress, and research studies evaluating stem cells or erythropoietin given to infants with or at risk for cerebral palsy.

SUMMARY

People with cerebral palsy have motor difficulties secondary to damage or an abnormality of the developing brain. It is a common condition, with prevalence rates of two for every 1,000 children. Having cerebral palsy can affect many areas of the individual's development and function. There is a high association with a coexisting intellectual disability (30%–60%) and medical complications. Rehabilitation often requires a team of many different social service and health professionals working together with individuals who have cerebral palsy and their families to maximize developmental potential and promote quality of life.

FOR FURTHER THOUGHT AND DISCUSSION

1. What are the best types of service delivery models for people with cerebral palsy?

2. Discuss the importance of providing treatments that are evidence based.

3. A new drug used for women who are pregnant is considered by some to have the potential to be associated with the infant developing cerebral palsy. How would you evaluate this drug as a potential risk factor?

4. What can you do personally to promote universal accessibility for people with disabilities?

REFERENCES

Andersen, G., Irgens, L., Haagaas, I., Skranes, J., Meberg, A., & Vik, T. (2008). Cerebral palsy in Norway: Prevalence, subtypes and severity. *European Journal of Paediatric Neurology, 12*(1), 4–13.

Blackmore, A.M., Boettcher-Hunt, E., Jordan, M., & Chan, M.D. (2007). A systematic review of the effects of casting on equinus in children with cerebral palsy: An evidence report of the AACPDM. *Developmental Medicine and Child Neurology, 49*(10), 781–790.

Boyd, R., Sakzewski, L., Ziviani, J., Abbott, D.F., Badawy, R., Gilmore, R.,...Jackson, G.D. (2010). INCITE: A randomised trial comparing constraint induced movement therapy and bimanual training in children with congenital hemiplegia. *BMC Neurology, 10*, 4.

Delgado, M., Hirtz, D., Aisen, M., Ashwal, S., Fehlings, D., McLaughlin, J.,...Vargus-Adams, J. (2010). Practice parameter: Pharmacologic treatment of spasticity in children and adolescents with cerebral palsy (an evidence-based review): Report of the quality standards subcommittee of the American Academy of Neurology and the practice committee of the Child Neurology Society. *Neurology, 74*(4), 336–343.

Doyle, L.W., Crowther, C.A., Middleton, P., Marret, S., & Rouse, D. (2009). Magnesium sulphate for women at risk of preterm birth for neuroprotection of the fetus. *Cochrane Database of Systematic Reviews*, Issue 1. doi:10.1002/14651858.CD004661.pub

Eliasson, A.C., Krumlinde-Sundholm, L., Rosblad, B., Beckung, E., Arner, M., Ohrvall, A.M., & Rosenbaum, P. (2006). The Manual Ability Classification System (MACS) for children with cerebral palsy: Scale development and evidence of validity and reliability. *Developmental Medicine and Child Neurology, 48*(7), 549–554.

Evans, P.M., Evans, S.J.W., & Alberman, E. (1990). Cerebral palsy: Why we must plan for survival. *Archives of Disease in Childhood, 65*, 1329–1333.

Fehlings, D., Novak, I., Berweck, S., Hoare, B., Stott, N., & Russo, R. (2010). Botulinum toxin assessment, intervention and follow-up for paediatric upper limb hypertonicity: International consensus statement. *European Journal of Neurology, 17*(2), 38–56.

Hoare, B., Imms, C., Carey, L., & Wasiak, J. (2007). Constraint-induced movement therapy in the treatment of the upper limb in children with hemiplegic cerebral palsy: A Cochrane systematic review. *Clinical Rehabilitation, 21*, 675–685.

King, S., Teplicky, R., King, G., & Rosenbaum, P. (2004). Family-centered service for children with cerebral palsy and their family: A review of the literature. *Seminars in Pediatric Neurology, 11*(1), 78–86.

Kyriakipoulos, P., Oskoui, M., Dagenais, L., & Shevell, M.I. (2013). Term neonatal encephalopathy antecedent cerebral palsy: A retrospective population-based study. *European Journal of Pediatric Neurology, 17*(3), 269–273.

Logan, S. (1997). In the UK the transition from youth to adulthood of people with cerebral palsy is poorly planned and co-ordinated. *Child: Care, Health and Development, 23*(6), 480–482.

Love, S.C., Noval, I., Kentish, M., Desloovere, K., Heinen, F., Molenaers, G.,...Graham, H.K. (2010). Botulinum toxin assessment, intervention and after-care for lower limb spasticity in children with cerebral palsy: International consensus statement. *European Journal of Neurology, 17*(2), 9–37.

Lundy, C., Doherty, G., & Fairhurst, C. (2009). Botulinum toxin type A injections can be an effective treatment for pain in children with hip spasms and cerebral palsy. *Developmental Medicine and Child Neurology, 51*, 705–710.

McIntyre, S., Taitz, D., Keogh, J., Goldsmith, S., & Badawi, N. (2013). A systematic review of risk factors for cerebral palsy in children born at term in developed countries. *Developmental Medicine and Child Neurology, 55*, 499–508.

Mesterman, R., Leitner, Y., Yifat, R., Gilutz, G., Levi-Hakeini, O., Bitchonsky, O.,...Harel, S. (2010). Cerebral palsy—long term medical, functional, educational and psychosocial outcomes. *Journal of Child Neurology, 25*(1), 36–42.

Michelsen, S.I., Uldall, P., Hansen, T., & Madsen, M. (2006). Social integration of adults with cerebral palsy. *Developmental Medicine and Child Neurology, 48*(8), 643–649.

Nelson, K.B. (1996). Epidemiology and etiology of cerebral palsy. In A.J. Capute & P.J. Accardo (Eds.), *Developmental disabilities in infancy and childhood: The spectrum of developmental disabilities* (2nd ed., Vol. 2, pp. 73–79). Baltimore, MD: York Press.

Nelson, K. (2008). Causative factors in cerebral palsy. *Clinical Obstetrics and Gynecology, 51*(4), 749–762.

Noritz, G., Murphy, N., & Neuromotor Screening Expert Panel. (2013). Motor delays: Early identification and evaluation. *Pediatrics, 131*, e2016. doi:10.1542/peds.2013-1056

Novak, I., McIntyre, S., Morgan, C., Campbell, L., Dark, L., Morton, N.,...Goldsmith, S. (2013). A systematic review of interventions for children with cerebral palsy: State of the evidence. *Developmental Medicine and Child Neurology, 55*, 885–910.

Palisano, R., Rosenbaum, P., Walter, S., Russell, D., Wood, E., & Galuppi, B. (1997). Development and reliability of a system to classify gross motor function in children with cerebral palsy. *Developmental Medicine and Child Neurology, 39*(4), 214–223.

Rosenbaum, P., Paneth, N., Leviton, A., Goldstein, M., Bax, M., Damiano, D., & Jacobsson, G. (2007). A report: The definition and classification of cerebral palsy April 2006. *Developmental Medicine and Child Neurology, 109*(Supplement), 8–14.

Schulzke, S.M., Rao, S., & Patole, S.K. (2007). A systematic review of cooling for neuroprotection in neonates with hypoxic ischemic encephalopathy—are we there yet? *BMC Pediatrics, 7,* 30. doi:10.1186/1471-2431-7-30

Strauss, D., Brooks, J., Rosenbloom, L., & Shavelle, R. (2009). Life expectancy in cerebral palsy: An update. *Developmental Medicine and Child Neurology, 50,* 487–493.

Surveillance of Cerebral Palsy in Europe. (2000). Surveillance of cerebral palsy in Europe: A collaboration of cerebral palsy surveys and registers. *Developmental Medicine and Child Neurology, 42,* 816–824.

Tan, S.W., Wiegerink, D.J., Vos, R.C., Smits, D.W., Voorman, J.M., Twisk, J.W.,...Roebroeck, M.E. (2014). Developmental trajectories of social participation in individuals with cerebral palsy. *Developmental Medicine and Child Neurology, 56*(4), 370–377.

Touyama, M., Touyama J., Ochiai, Y., Toyokawa S., & Kobayashi, Y. (2013). Long-term survival of children with cerebral palsy in Okinawa, Japan. *Developmental Medicine and Child Neurology, 55*(5), 459–463.

World Health Organization. (2001). *International Classification of Functioning, Disability and Health (ICF).* Geneva, Switzerland: Author.

Young, N., McCormick, A., Mills, W., Barden, W., Boydell, K., Law, M.,...Williams, J. (2006). The transition study: A look at youth and adults with cerebral palsy, spina bifida and acquired brain injury. *Physical and Occupational Therapy Pediatrics, 26*(4), 25–45.

21

Other Syndromes and Conditions Associated with Intellectual and Developmental Disabilities

Maire Percy, Miles D. Thompson, Ivan Brown, Wai Lun Alan Fung, and Others

WHAT YOU WILL LEARN

- Information about many syndromes and conditions associated with intellectual and developmental disabilities that are not presented in other chapters in this book
- Physical and behavioral characteristics; causes; incidence or prevalence; and interventions, supports, or services applicable to each condition
- Relevant resources that provide more information about the conditions described and promote independent learning

Due to the comprehensive nature of this chapter, references have been styled differently to streamline text and improve readability. The reference list at the end of the chapter has been divided into two sections. The first section lists references that have been cited within the chapter text. The second section lists current references pertaining to the individual syndromes and conditions. These have not been cited in the chapter text and have been arranged alphabetically according to the syndrome or condition name.

Individuals who were authors on the related chapter (Percy et al., 2007) are gratefully acknowledged. They include Tom Cheetham, Maria Gitta, Bev Morrison, Karolina Machalek, Sivan Bega, Alison Burgess, Christina de Rivera, Trish Domi, Youssef El Hayek, Everlyne Gomez, Amy Hayashi, Raquel Heskin Sweezie, Anthony Lau, Anya McLaren, Ewa Niechwiej-Szwedo, Oma D. D. Persaud, Nam Phan, Evan Jon Propst, Marcus Salvatori, Fiona Wong, Athena Ypsilanti, and Jennie Yum. Marika Korossy, Surrey Place Centre, provided some key references; Rivka Birkan-Bradley and Victoria Duda Milloy provided helpful comments.

This chapter presents more than 30 syndromes and conditions associated with intellectual and developmental disabilities that have not been featured in other chapters. The word *syndrome* refers to a complex of concurrent things—the signs and symptoms, including behaviors, that are characteristic of a particular condition. There are several reasons why awareness of syndromes or conditions associated with intellectual and developmental disabilities is important.

1. The main reason is that knowledge of specific syndromes or conditions enables the best interventions, supports, or services to be implemented at the earliest possible stages, as these often are specific for a given condition. For example, people who have Prader-Willi syndrome can eat compulsively; they also are at high risk of becoming overtly obese and developing diabetes and heart disease. Specific interventions, supports, and services can alleviate such complications; with an early diagnosis, it may be possible to prevent such complications from occurring.

2. Cognitive deterioration associated with certain syndromes or conditions can largely be prevented if appropriate intervention is initiated early enough. Two examples are congenital hypothyroidism and phenylketonuria.

3. Information in this chapter can facilitate a diagnosis. For example, certain syndromes or conditions have physical or behavioral features that are quite distinctive. Williams syndrome is one condition that has often been recognized by nonspecialists with a prepared mind who have recognized characteristic "cocktail party speech."

4. Finally, information in this chapter will be of interest to students, professionals, and support providers alike. Enriched learning will not only lead to better quality of life for affected individuals and their families but also will motivate and foster independent learning at all levels, a process that needs to be ongoing in this field.

The rest of this chapter is divided into three main sections. The first section (Etiological Overview of the Featured Syndromes and Conditions) provides a succinct overview of the syndromes and conditions that have been featured in this chapter according to their etiology—genetic or "other" (i.e., environmental or unknown)—and also by inheritance pattern (when relevant). (The word *etiology* refers to the primary cause, set of causes, or manner of causation of a disease or condition.) The second main section (Conditions with a Genetic Etiology: Group 1) presents information about individual conditions with a genetic etiology in greater depth and in parallel format so that readers can focus, for example, on the physical or behavioral features characteristic of each condition or on appropriate interventions. The third main section (Other Conditions: Group 2) presents analogous information about the conditions with other etiology in a similar format. For the second and third sections, information for each of the featured syndromes and conditions was compiled from the text and references in the related chapter by Percy et al. (2007) as well as from newer references listed at the end of this chapter. For more information about the featured conditions or others, search by subject in the following online resources: Inserm's (2016) Orphanet Encyclopedia, Jung (2010), National Institute of Neurological Diseases and Stroke's (n.d.) Disorder Index, Johns Hopkins University's (2016) Online Mendelian Inheritance in Man, the Online Metabolic and Molecular Bases of Inherited Diseases (Valle et al., n.d.), U.S. National Library of Medicine's (2015) MedlinePlus medical encyclopedia, University of Utah Learn.Genetics (2016), Whonamedit (2016), and National Center for Biotechnology Information's (n.d.) PubMed or American Psychological Association's (2016) PsycINFO. See also Accardo (2007a, 2007b); Accardo et al. (2011); Batshaw, Roizen, and Lotrecchiano (2013); Jones, Jones, and Del Campo (2013); Matson and Matson (2015); Rubin and Crocker (2006); Shapiro and Accardo (2010); and the Penn State Hershey web site Clinician Information Resources and Evidence-Based Practice (2016). Chapters 10 and 13 of this volume also contain information that complements that in the present chapter.

ETIOLOGICAL OVERVIEW OF THE FEATURED SYNDROMES AND CONDITIONS

The syndromes and conditions featured in this chapter are listed in Table 21.1. These are classified as having either a genetic or other etiology (Groups 1 and 2, respectively). Those with a genetic basis have been subdivided into six subgroups: chromosomal, single-gene disorders, imprinting disorders, genetically heterogeneous disorders, somatic mosaicism disorders, and those resulting from a combination of genetic and environmental factors. A number of conditions with other etiology are caused by environmental factors. Within each of the subsections in Groups 1 and 2, syndromes or conditions are in alphabetical order. Also shown in Table 21.1 are the inheritance patterns.

Chromosomal disorders include those resulting from abnormal numbers of chromosomes or abnormalities in DNA that involve large stretches of DNA. Single-gene disorders include those arising from relatively small abnormalities (including single nucleotide differences) in only one particular gene. For most genes, two working copies are inherited, one from the mother and one from the father. For some other genes, only one working copy is inherited—in this case, either the copy from the mother or from the father has been silenced. Imprinting disorders can occur for a variety of reasons that include problems with the silencing mechanism(s), chromosomal errors, and single-gene mutations. Genetically heterogeneous disorders listed in Table 21.1 actually are single-gene disorders, but in these cases mutations in any one of a number of different genes result in the same disorder. For example, in Mabry syndrome (also known

Table 21.1. Etiological overview of the featured syndromes and conditions[a]

Syndrome or disorder	Cause	Inheritance pattern
GROUP 1: CONDITIONS WITH A GENETIC ETIOLOGY		
Chromosomal disorders		
Cri-du-chat syndrome	Deletions of multiple genes on chromosome 5	Mostly sporadic
Klinefelter syndrome	Extra X chromosome	Sporadic
Smith-Magenis syndrome	Microdeletions on chromosome 17	Sporadic
Turner syndrome	Loss of one or part of one X chromosome, often the paternal X	Sporadic
Williams syndrome	Deletions of multiple genes on chromosome 7	Mostly sporadic; occasionally autosomal dominant
Single-gene disorders		
Hunter syndrome (mucopolysaccharidosis type II)	Mutations in the iduronate-2-sulfatase gene on the X chromosome	X-linked, recessive
Hurler syndrome (mucopolysaccharidosis type I)	Mutations in the alpha-L-iduronidase gene on chromosome 4	Autosomal recessive
Lesch-Nyhan syndrome	Mutations in the hypoxanthine-guanine phosphoribosyltransferase gene on chromosome X	X-linked recessive
Neurofibromatosis type 1	Mutations in the neurofibromatosis 1 gene on chromosome 17	Sporadic (about 50%) or autosomal dominant (about 50%)
Neurofibromatosis type 2	Mutations of the neurofibromatosis 2 gene on chromosome 22	Sporadic or autosomal dominant
Phenylketonuria	Most cases result from mutations in the phenylalanine hydroxylase gene on chromosome 12.	Autosomal recessive
Rett syndrome	Mutations of the methyl-CpG-binding protein 2 gene on chromosome X	X-linked dominant; usually affects females; lethal in males
Smith-Lemli-Opitz syndrome	Mutations in the 7-dehydrocholesterol reductase gene on chromosome 11	Autosomal recessive
Imprinting disorders		
Angelman and Prader-Willi syndromes	Prader-Willi syndrome and Angelman syndrome are markedly different, but they are caused by abnormalities in the same region of chromosome 15. This chromosome 15 region is imprinted; this means that some of the genes in this region are silenced in the egg, and at least one gene is silenced in the sperm. Depending upon whether a chromosome 15 defect came from the mother or father, different active genes will be missing. Individuals with Angelman syndrome are missing chromosome 15 gene activity that normally comes from the mother. Those with Prader-Willi syndrome are missing chromosome 15 gene activity that normally comes from the father. (University of Utah Learn.Genetics, 2016)	Usually sporadic, but Prader-Willi syndrome sometimes shows autosomal dominant inheritance
Genetically heterogeneous		
Congenital hypothyroidism (genetic forms; Szinnai, 2014)	As of 2014, genetic defects have been identified in at least 12 different genes	Sporadic, autosomal recessive, autosomal dominant
Cornelia de Lange syndrome	Defects in each of at least five different genes, leading to disruption of function of the cohesion complex	Autosomal dominant or X-linked dominant, depending on the genetic mutation
Mabry syndrome/ Hyperphosphatasia syndrome with mental retardation	Defects in each of at least five different genes, leading to dysfunction in the phosphatidylinositol glycan anchor biosynthesis pathway	Probably autosomal recessive

(continued)

Table 21.1.   *(continued)*

Syndrome or disorder	Cause	Inheritance pattern
Noonan syndrome	Defects in one of at least eight different genes	Sporadic or autosomal dominant
Progressive myoclonus epilepsies	Defects on various chromosomes	Most are autosomal recessive; one is mitochondrial
Sanfillipo syndrome/ mucopolysaccharidosis type III	Defects in genes causing four different enzyme deficiencies, resulting in four subtypes of the syndrome	Sporadic or autosomal recessive
Tuberous sclerosis complex/syndrome	Defects in the TC1 gene on chromosome 9 and the TC2 gene on chromosome 16	Sporadic or, in some cases, autosomal dominant
Somatic mosaicism		
Sturge-Weber syndrome	Mutations in the GNAQ gene on chromosome 9 that arise after zygote formation	Sporadic
Involvement of genetic and environmental factors		
Neuronal migration disorders (more than 25 have been described)	Defects in different genes are associated with different disorders, but roles of the defective genetic factors are not clear. Infections, poor nutritional status, and smoking during pregnancy may also be involved.	Often sporadic; different patterns of inheritance have been described for different syndromes
Tourette syndrome	Both genetic and environmental factors are thought to be involved; a few cases are associated with mutations in two different genes.	Inheritance pattern not clear

GROUP 2: OTHER CONDITIONS

Involvement of environmental factors		
Congenital hypothyroidism resulting from iodine deficiency	Deficiency of iodine	
Congenital rubella (German measles)	Consequences of rubella infection during the mother's pregnancy	
Hypoxic-ischemic encephalopathy/neonatal encephalopathy	Asphyxia (a condition associated with unconsciousness or death resulting from oxygen deprivation for any reason) from systemic hypoxemia and/or reduced cerebral blood flow	
Intraventricular hemorrhage in infants	Fragility of blood vessels as the result of premature birth	
Meningitis	Different types of bacterial infections; different types of viral infections such as herpes simplex	
Pediatric stroke	Hemorrhagic stroke occurs when a blood vessel bursts inside the brain. Ischemic stroke is caused by occlusion of a blood vessel supplying part of the brain.	
Shaken baby syndrome/ abusive head trauma	Abusive head trauma caused by direct blows to the head or dropping, throwing, or shaking a child	
Traumatic brain injury	Causes include falls, motor vehicle and pedestrian-related accidents; collision-related (being struck by or against) events; violent assaults; sports-related injuries; and explosive blasts/ military combat injuries.	
No known cause		
Developmental coordination disorder	May possibly be part of the spectrum of cerebral palsy and secondary to prenatal, perinatal, or neonatal insults	

ᵃThe most common syndromes and conditions associated with intellectual and developmental disabilities have been highlighted in other chapters of this book. These include Down syndrome (chromosomal disorder caused by an extra chromosome 21 or part of one; occurs mostly sporadically; Chapter 14), fragile X syndrome (single-gene disorder caused by expansion of the CGG trinucleotide repeat region on chromosome X; inheritance pattern is atypical X linked, with males being more severely affected than females; Chapter 15), autism spectrum disorder (a heterogeneous collection of conditions with different etiologies, known and unknown; Chapter 16), 22q11.2 deletion syndrome (a disorder resulting from small [micro-] deletions on the long [q] arm of chromosome 22; usually occurs sporadically, but the inheritance pattern is autosomal dominant; Chapter 17), fetal alcohol spectrum disorder (a spectrum of conditions resulting from excessive maternal consumption of alcohol during pregnancy; occurs sporadically; Chapters 17 and 18), and cerebral palsy (a group of permanent movement disorders associated with brain injury or malformation from a variety of causes while the brain is developing; Chapter 20—as noted by MacLennan, Thompson, & Gecz [2015], occurrence of cerebral palsy is mainly sporadic, but new-generation sequencing has identified single-gene mutations in approximately 14% of cases and relevant copy number variations in up to 31% of cases).

as hyperphosphatasia syndrome with mental retardation), mutations in each of several different genes that are involved in a common biosynthetic pathway result in very similar clinical outcomes. The term *somatic mosaicism* refers to the occurrence of a mutation after fertilization of an egg by a sperm (i.e., zygote formation); for this reason, abnormalities resulting from the genetic change are restricted to only the tissue or tissues that harbor the mutant gene. Finally, some conditions classified as genetic (e.g., Tourette syndrome) are thought to result from a variety of genetic and environmental factors, though mutations involving two different genes have been identified in a small number of people with Tourette.

As explained in more depth in Chapter 10, inheritance patterns include sporadic (i.e., those occurring de novo or without an obvious family history), recessive (i.e., the inheritance of two copies of a defective gene causes a given disorder), dominant (i.e., the inheritance of only one copy of a defective gene causes a given disorder), X-linked (i.e., a defective gene is on an X chromosome, one of the two sex chromosomes), and mitochondrial (i.e., the abnormal mitochondrial gene causing the given disorder is inherited only from the mother, since somatic cells do not contain mitochondria from the father). The word *autosomal* refers to gene localization on any of chromosomes 1 to 22 (the "autosomes"). Note from Table 21.1 that genetic conditions classified as chromosomal tend to occur sporadically (i.e., de novo)—that is, without an obvious history of the syndrome being inherited.

CONDITIONS WITH A GENETIC ETIOLOGY: GROUP 1

In this section, for ease of access, the syndromes and conditions included in each of the six subgroups of Group 1 in Table 21.1 have been pooled and arranged in alphabetical order. *Prevalence* is the proportion of a population found to have a disorder. In contrast, *incidence* is a measure of new cases arising in a population over a given period (e.g., at birth, within a month, within a year).

Angelman Syndrome

Harry Angelman, an English physician, first described this syndrome in three children who had a stiff and jerky gait, absent speech, excessive laughter, and seizures. It is sometimes called "happy puppet" syndrome because of the inappropriate laughter and puppet-like gait. It is caused by deletions of (or mutations in) the UBE3A gene on maternally inherited chromosome 15 at the 15q11.2-13 locus. The 15q11.2-13 locus also is involved in Prader-Willi syndrome, but in this case, abnormalities of the paternally inherited chromosome 15 are involved. Angelman syndrome usually occurs sporadically but sometimes is inherited in an autosomal dominant fashion.

Physical Characteristics

- Dysmorphic (malformed) facial features that develop by the age of 2 years include a wide and smiling mouth, pointed chin, prominent tongue, wide-spaced teeth, large jaw, and deep-set eyes.

- Approximately half of all affected individuals have fair-colored hair and skin, and most have blue eyes.

- Head circumference is usually below the 50th percentile; approximately one fourth of affected individuals have microcephaly (have a small head).

Incidence or Prevalence

- 1 in 10,000 to 1 in 20,000 live births; the condition is underdiagnosed

Genotype or Cause

- Mutations or deletions of the maternally inherited UBE3A gene at locus 15q11.2-13. UBE3A encodes an enzyme called ubiquitin ligase E3A, which puts ubiquitin residues on proteins to tag them for degradation. The paternal and maternal copies of UBE3A are expressed in most tissues, but only the maternal copy is expressed in certain brain regions. If the protein coded by UBE3A is not made, then certain proteins in the brain are not degraded.

- In a few cases, Angelman syndrome is caused when two paternal copies of the UBE3A gene are inherited, instead of one from each parent.

Functional and Behavioral Characteristics

- Severe to profound developmental delay is evident in 100% of cases by 6–12 months of age.

- Children laugh frequently and inappropriately; hand flapping may occur.

- Children walk with a wide-base gait and stiff legs, described as a puppet-like gait.

- Grabbing and hair pulling is frequently seen.

- Affected individuals tend to like water.

- Sleep disturbances are common.

- Affected individuals have a happy, sociable disposition.

- Profound speech impairment and delay occur in 98% of cases, and absent speech in 88%; the ability to comprehend is better than the ability to express.

- Affected individuals may exhibit alternating strabismus (squinting caused by inability of one eye to attain binocular vision with the other eye because of an imbalance of the muscles of the eyeball).

- Seizure disorder with a characteristic electro-encephalogram (EEG) occurs in approximately 80% of affected individuals.

- Maternally but not paternally derived defects, such as duplications, within the chromosome 15 critical region result in symptomatology similar to that of autism.

Interventions, Supports, and Services

- Genetic counseling is indicated.

- Seizure management is the main focus of the primary care physician; seizure control sometimes requires trials with more than one anticonvulsant.

- Pharmacotherapy (drug therapy) and behavior management may help with sleep disturbances.

- Sign language may be required for communication.

- Identification and treatment of behavior problems can improve adaptive functioning.

Congenital Hypothyroidism

The failure of normal infant growth and development associated with congenital hypothyroidism can result from a deficiency of iodine or, sometimes, of other micronutrients as well as from genetic or other causes. For information about congenital hypothyroidism from iodine deficiency, see this topic in the main section following and also Chapter 13. In the absence of iodine deficiency, congenital hypothyroidism is associated with thyroid gland agenesis (i.e., inadequate development or absence of development) or dysgenesis (i.e., faulty development) or with deficient production of thyroid hormones (T3 or T4) (thyroid hormone dysgenesis). In rare instances, a normal gland does not make enough thyroid hormone because of insufficient thyroid stimulating hormone (TSH) from the pituitary. Congenital hypothyroidism can be transient or permanent; 15%–20% of hypothyroid infants require only temporary treatment.

Physical Characteristics   Features may include the following:

- Arrested physical growth

- Puffy face; thick neck due to goiter (enlargement of thyroid gland)

- Dry, swollen skin

- Large abdomen

- Possible umbilical hernia

- Prolonged jaundice; feeding difficulties

- Respiratory difficulties aggravated by a large tongue

- Cold, mottled arms and legs

Incidence or Prevalence   In iodine replete areas of the world, congenital hypothyroidism affects approximately 1 in 3,000 to 1 in 4,000 newborns; more females are affected than males.

Genotype or Cause

- In the absence of iodine deficiency, 80%–85% of cases result from thyroid gland agenesis or dysgenesis and approximately 20% from thyroid hormone dysgenesis. As of 2014, approximately 20% of cases have been found to be associated with genetic mutations. Inheritance patterns can be sporadic, autosomal recessive, or autosomal dominant.

Functional and Behavioral Characteristics

- Lower intellectual functioning that develops progressively with age

- Sluggishness, sleepiness, poor cry

Interventions, Supports, and Services

- Genetic counseling is indicated.

- As early detection and treatment is vital to impede the progression, screen newborns for iodine deficiency or thyroid hormone deficiency.

- Treat for iodine deficiency if relevant.

- Treat for thyroid hormone deficiency if level of TSH is high and levels of thyroid hormones (T4 or T3, or both) are low.

Cornelia de Lange Syndrome

Cornelia de Lange syndrome is a congenital syndrome that was named after a Dutch pediatrician who described the syndrome in two children in 1933. This syndrome is also known as Brachmann-de Lange syndrome; German physician Winfried Brachmann wrote about a similar syndrome that he discovered in a child patient in 1916. Most of the physical and behavioral characteristics may be recognized at birth or shortly thereafter, but children with this disorder may not have all of them. Mutations in at least five different genes affecting function of the cohesin complex cause the syndrome. The syndrome usually arises sporadically. When inherited, the transmission pattern can be autosomal dominant or X-linked dominant.

Physical Characteristics

- Facies: Thin, down-turned lips, low-set ears, long eyelashes, bushy eyebrows that meet in the middle, ptosis (drooping of upper eyelid), hypertelorism (abnormal width between the eyes), and excessive body hair

- Brachycephaly (disproportionately short head); small hands and feet; and syndactylism (webbing or fusing) of the feet

- Infant swallowing difficulty; aspiration pneumonia risk; gastroesophageal reflux (i.e., reverse flow of stomach contents into the esophagus)

- Congenital heart defects; hearing deficits

- An unusual marbled (bluish, mottled) appearance of the skin on the arms and legs, particularly in the cold, in almost all cases

Incidence or Prevalence

- 1 in 10,000 to 1 in 30,000 live births; affects males and females equally

Genotype or Cause

- Mutations in at least five genes (NIPBL, SMC1A, HDAC8, RAD21, and SMC3) cause the syndrome by impairing the function of the cohesin complex; this disrupts gene regulation during critical stages of early development. Cohesin regulates sister chromatid cohesion during mitosis and meiosis. It also plays a critical role in the regulation of gene expression. Proteins in the cohesin pathway are involved in double strand DNA break repair, chromatin remodeling, and maintenance of genomic stability. When inherited, mutations in the NIPBL, RAD21, or SMC3 gene have an autosomal dominant pattern of inheritance; mutations in the HDAC8 or SMC1A gene have an X-linked dominant pattern of inheritance.

Functional and Behavioral Characteristics

- Delays in intellectual development and communication are characteristic.

- May be associated with features similar to those of autism, seizures, self-injury, hyperactivity, daily aggression, and sleep disturbances.

- Parents frequently report their children as happy and charming, loving to laugh and giggle and interact with others.

- Strengths include perceptual organization, visuospatial memory, and fine motor skills.

Interventions, Supports, and Services

- Genetic counseling

- May require speech therapy or sign language, or both

- Anticonvulsant therapy for seizures

- Pharmacotherapy and behavior management to help with sleep disturbances, hyperactivity, and aggression

- Management of gastroesophageal reflux through special diets, medications, and elevating a child after eating; a surgical procedure such as a gastrostomy (provision of a hole in the stomach for feeding through a G-tube) may be required

Cri-du-Chat Syndrome

Cri-du-chat syndrome was first described in 1964 by Dr. Jerome Lejeune, a French geneticist, who also codiscovered the chromosomal abnormality characteristic of Down syndrome. Cri-du-chat syndrome is also known as 5p-syndrome because of a defect on the short (p) arm of chromosome 5. The name of the syndrome comes from the infantile, high pitched, cat-like cry by which it is characterized. This syndrome generally occurs sporadically, but about 10% of people with this disorder inherit it from an unaffected parent who carries a balanced chromosomal rearrangement of chromosome 5.

Physical Characteristics

- Early hypotonia (i.e., loss of muscular tone)

- May include prominent epicanthic folds (i.e., skin fold from the root of the nose extending to the inner end of the eyebrow), microcephaly (i.e., small head), and low-set ears

Incidence or Prevalence

- 1 in 15,000 to 1 in 50,000 live births

Genotype or Cause

- Deletion of variable size on the short (p) arm of chromosome 5, called a 5p deletion

Functional and Behavioral Characteristics

- Affected individuals produce an infantile, high-pitched, cat-like cry.

- Severe motor, language, and developmental delay is exhibited.

- Stereotypic (repetitive) behavior has been observed, and hyperactivity is common.

- Occasionally, aggressive and self-injurious behaviors are seen, but more typically, individuals have a friendly and happy demeanor.

- More than 75% of affected individuals are easily distracted, restless, and excessively active.

Interventions, Supports, and Services

- Genetic counseling is indicated.

- Intensive early intervention should be undertaken to improve speech, motor, and self-help skills.

- Clinicians may consider medication to treat hyperactivity.

Hunter Syndrome/ Mucopolysaccharidosis Type II

Mucopolysaccharidosis (MPS) syndromes are characterized by excessive storage of complex carbohydrates, called mucopolysaccharides, in various tissues and organs. Hunter syndrome is a mucopolysaccharidosis type II (MPS II) lysosomal storage disorder. Hunter syndrome was first described in 1917 by Charles Hunter, a Scottish-Canadian physician. There are two forms of this disorder: a severe, early-onset form and a mild, late-onset form. The severe form of Hunter syndrome is typically diagnosed in children ages 18–36 months. The mild form causes later and less severe symptoms. This syndrome has an X-linked recessive mode of inheritance and, consequently, is usually seen only in males, but rare cases in females have been reported.

Physical Characteristics

- Affected individuals have a normal appearance at birth except for possible noisy breathing and umbilical or inguinal hernias, or both.

- Classic features begin to develop at around age 2, for the severe form, and later for the mild form, including coarse facial features, large head, frontal bossing (i.e., protuberance of frontal skull), and enlarged tongue.

- Other physical characteristics include the following:

  - Hydrocephaly (enlargement of ventricles of the brain due to an accumulation of cerebrospinal fluid in the brain, typically associated with an enlarged head)

  - Slowed growth rate

  - Stiffening of joints; wide spaces between erupting teeth

  - Hepatosplenomegaly (enlargement of liver and spleen); thickened heart valves

- Carpal tunnel syndrome; upper airway obstruction due to thickened airways

- Claw hands and skeletal changes referred to as dysostosis multiplex (e.g., wide medial clavicle [collar bone], flat ribs)

Incidence or Prevalence

- 1 in 16,000 to 1 in 30,000 live births for all MPS disorders

- 1 in 65,000 to 1 in 320,000 live births for MPS II; birth incidence is increased among Jewish population of Israel; usually affects only males

Genotype or Cause

- An X-linked disorder resulting from heterogeneous mutations in the iduronate-2-sulphatase gene, which results in lack of the enzyme iduronate sulfatase; in its absence, mucopolysaccharides collect in various body tissues, causing damage

Functional and Behavioral Characteristics

- The severe, early-onset form of the syndrome is characterized by mental deterioration, severe intellectual delay, aggressive behavior, and hyperactivity.

- The mild, late-onset form is characterized by mild to no intellectual deficiency.

- In the severe form, death occurs at approximately 10 to 15 years of age from cardiac or respiratory failure; in the mild form, individuals survive.

- Patients with MPS may have unusual sensitivity to anesthesia.

Interventions, Supports, and Services

- For MPS disorders in general, there is no consensus on effective treatments.

- Current treatment is primarily supportive: physical therapy and selected surgical procedures may be helpful in some patients. Hearing and need for a hearing aid should be assessed, as susceptibility to ear infections, colds, and meningitis can lead to deafness.

- Bone marrow transplantation lessens the effects of the MPS disorders, but the procedure is not generally recommended.

- Genetic counseling is indicated.

Hurler/Hurler-Scheie/Scheie Syndrome/Gargoylism

Hurler syndrome is one of the MPS syndromes and is known as mucopolysaccharidosis type I (MPS I), or gargoylism. This syndrome is named after the German pediatrician Gertrude Hurler, who described it in 1919. Hurler syndrome is also known as Hurler-Scheie or Scheie syndrome, after Harold Glendon Scheie, an American physician and ophthalmologist who, in 1962, described a less severe form of Hurler syndrome. Hurler-Scheie syndrome is less severe than Hurler syndrome but more severe than Scheie syndrome. All three syndromes are due to the same enzyme defect. Hurler syndrome has an autosomal recessive mode of inheritance.

Physical Characteristics

- Characteristic pattern of facial features known as gargoylism includes coarseness of facial features; thick, coarse hair; and bushy eyebrows.

- Skeletal abnormalities include dwarfism, kyphosis (an abnormal degree of forward curvature of part of the spine), a broad hand with short fingers, joint contractures, and radiological features of dysostosis multiplex (see Hunter syndrome).

- Other physical characteristics include the following:

  - Hepatosplenomegaly (i.e., enlargement of liver and spleen)

  - Structural abnormalities of the heart

  - Clouding of corneas

  - Umbilical and inguinal hernias (see Hunter syndrome subsection)

  - Conductive hearing loss in most individuals

Incidence or Prevalence

- 1 in 16,000 to 1 in 30,000 live births for all MPS disorders

- 1 in 76,000 to 1 in 150,000 live births for MPS I

Genotype or Cause

- Hurler syndrome results from mutations in the alpha-L-iduronidase gene located on chromosome 4 (4p16.3). Mutations in this gene are responsible for alpha-L-iduronidase enzyme deficiency, which leads to the accumulation of partially degraded mucopolysaccharides in the lysosomes of cells.

Functional and Behavioral Characteristics

- Intellectual development is usually normal in the first few years of childhood.

- Severe, progressive learning disorders are evident by later childhood.

- Death often occurs by the second decade of life due to heart failure and severe respiratory tract infections.

- Patients with MPS may have unusual sensitivity to anesthesia.

Interventions, Supports, and Services

- Genetic counseling is indicated.

- Complications should be supported and treated by means such as supplemental oxygen for breathing difficulties, continuous positive airway pressure machines for interrupted breathing during sleep (sleep apnea), tracheotomy (surgery for difficulties in breathing), physical therapy for joint stiffness, and heart valve replacement therapy for heart problems.

- Monitor or treat for severe respiratory illnesses.

- Severe MPS I is treated with palliative support, hematopoietic stem cell transplantation, and enzyme replacement therapy.

Klinefelter Syndrome

Klinefelter syndrome is also known as Klinefelter-Reifenstein-Albright syndrome, after the three men who described it. In 1942, Harry Klinefelter, an American physician, and his colleagues Edward Reifenstein and Fuller Albright, published a report on nine men who had enlarged breasts, sparse facial and body hair, small testes, and the inability to produce sperm. In 1959, Klinefelter syndrome was associated with an extra sex chromosome (genotype XXY) instead of the usual male sex complement (genotype XY). This syndrome usually occurs sporadically. However, there is a trend for chromosomal errors to be transmitted to the offspring.

Physical Characteristics

- Variable physical phenotype; affected individuals may have none, some, or all of the symptoms noted here

- Hypogonadism (i.e., small testes, small penis, inadequate testosterone)

- Gynecomastia (i.e., swelling of breast tissue in puberty) in about half of affected individuals

- Tall with slim stature, long legs, and a tendency for truncal obesity

- Female distribution of body fat in adults; sparse facial and body hair

- Hypotonia (i.e., low muscle tone); motor skill difficulties

- At increased risk for hypothyroidism, breast cancer, osteoporosis, leg ulcers, depression, dental problems, varicose veins, mitral valve prolapse

- At increased risk for autoimmune disorders, including type 2 diabetes and thyroiditis

- Most common cause of infertility in males

Incidence or Prevalence

- 1 in 500 to 1 in 1,000 live male births

- One fifth of males at infertility clinics have Klinefelter syndrome

Genotype or Cause

- Most commonly, males have three sex chromosomes (XXY) instead of two (XY).

- Some males are mosaic for this abnormality (i.e., have somatic mosaicism); some cells have the typical 46 chromosomes, while others have the extra X.

- In 50%–60% of cases, Klinefelter syndrome results from chromosomal nondisjunction that occurs during meiosis I in older mothers.

Functional and Behavioral Characteristics

- Most XXY males have average to superior intelligence, with only about 20% scoring below average on standardized intelligence tests.

- Intellectual disability is rare; when this occurs, IQ is lower by only 10 or 15 points.

- Affected individuals tend to have problems with expressive language.

- There is a risk of psychiatric disorders, poor social skills, anxiety, and low self-esteem.

Interventions, Supports, and Services

- Genetic counseling is indicated.

- Testosterone replacement corrects symptoms of androgen deficiency (e.g., loss of libido, decreased energy, increased abdominal fat) and may have positive effects on language or behavioral problems, but it has no positive effect on infertility; hormone treatment during adolescence may encourage a more normal puberty.

- Some individuals require help in school and some need special education programs; a substantial number go on to postsecondary education.

- Intracytoplasmic sperm injection (i.e., injection of a single sperm recovered from a testicular biopsy into the cytoplasm of a mature oocyte using a glass needle) offers an opportunity for procreation even when there are no spermatozoa in the ejaculate.

- Syndrome-specific health care should complement standard preventative health care recommendations.

Lesch-Nyhan Syndrome

Lesch-Nyhan syndrome is a genetic disorder that affects how the body builds and breaks down purines (compounds in RNA and DNA). Lesch-Nyhan syndrome was first discovered by Michael Lesch and William Nyhan (American cardiologist and American pediatrician, respectively) in 1964, when they described two affected brothers. The underlying enzyme defect was discovered in 1967, and the gene responsible was found in 1985. This syndrome is characterized by diffuse effects throughout the central nervous system and specific effects in the basal ganglia. (The term *basal ganglia* refers to several large clusters of nerve cells deep in the brain below the cerebral hemispheres; these are crucial in coordinating motor commands—e.g., movement, balance,

walking—and include the striatum and the substantia nigra.) Lesch-Nyhan syndrome has an X-linked recessive mode of inheritance, and the disease is seen mainly in males.

Physical Characteristics

- Prenatal and neonatal development is normal for the first 2 to 3 months.

- The first symptom is likely to be presence of urate crystals (orange-colored, crystal-like deposits, or orange sand) in the child's diaper or in the urine.

- Affected individuals have increased urate to creatinine ratio in blood or urine (ratio of more than 2 indicates dysfunction). (Urate is the breakdown product of dietary purines formed by action of the enzyme xanthine oxidase; creatinine is a by-product of muscular exertion.)

- Increased reflex sensitivity is found.

Incidence or Prevalence

- 1 in 380,000 live births; affects males almost exclusively

Genotype or Cause

- Mutations in the hypoxanthine-guanine phosphoribosyltransferase gene on chromosome X

Functional and Behavioral Characteristics

- Symptoms are first present by 3 to 6 months and include unusual irritability and nervous system impairment (e.g., inability to lift the head or to sit up).

- By the end of the first year, a typical motor development is evident, including writhing motions (athetosis) and spasmodic movements of the limbs and facial muscles (chorea).

- The majority of children affected never develop the ability to walk.

- Affected individuals are prone to compulsive self-injury that intensifies as the disease progresses, including biting of lips, tongue, and fingers, and head-banging.

- Kidney damage can occur due to kidney stones.

- Joints may be swollen and tender due to gout.

- Affected individuals have neurological dysfunction that resembles athetoid cerebral palsy (i.e., resulting from damage to the cerebellum or basal ganglia).

Interventions, Supports, and Services

- There are no known treatments for neurological defects.

- Behavioral extinction methods with positive reinforcement are most beneficial.

- Allopurinol (an inhibitor of the enzyme xanthine oxidase that slows down formation of urate) can lower blood uric-acid levels but does not reduce many of the symptoms.

- Lithotripsy (a nonsurgical procedure that breaks up stones in the kidneys and ureters by high-energy shock waves) reduces kidney stone formation.

- Parkinson's disease medication and tranquilizers are used to control involuntary movements.

- Patients often have teeth removed to prevent self-injury.

- Restraints are often used to reduce self-destructive behaviors.

- If properly managed, individuals can survive until their 20s or 30s.

Mabry Syndrome/ Hyperphosphatasia Syndrome

Mabry syndrome is a profound developmental disability syndrome with variable expression. It was first identified as hyperphosphatasia (i.e., increased blood levels of the alkaline phosphatase enzyme) with neurologic deficit by Charleton Mabry in 1970. Miles Thompson named the syndrome in 2010. In addition to hyperphosphatasia, typical Mabry syndrome is characterized by a trio of physical characteristics, detailed in the next subsection, in the first year of life. Hyperphosphatasia distinguishes Mabry syndrome from Cornelia de Lange syndrome. The condition results from mutations in at least five different genes that encode molecules of the glycosylphosphatidylinositol-anchor biosynthesis pathway. These mutations may be inherited in an autosomal recessive manner.

Physical Characteristics

- Facial seizures, facial dysmorphology (hypertelorism, a broad nasal bridge, and a rectangular face), and variable degrees of brachytelephalangy (i.e., shortened bones at the ends of the fingers)

Incidence or Prevalence

- Prevalence is currently unknown; although considered rare, this condition is underdiagnosed.

Genotype or Cause

- Mutations in at least five different genes (PIGV, PIGO, PGAP2, PGAP3, and PIGW) result in the syndrome. All of these affect the function of the glycosylphosphatidylinositol-anchor biosynthesis pathway. In some cases, the cause is still unknown.

Functional and Behavioral Characteristics

- Degrees of intellectual disability and physical abnormalities are variable. Those least severely affected have only intellectual disability and hyperphosphatasia.

Interventions, Services, and Supports

- Genetic counseling is indicated.

- In a few cases, seizure frequency may be reduced by vitamin B_6 therapy; it is not known whether B_6 deficiency in these cases is a characteristic of the syndrome or is a coincidence.

Neurofibromatosis Type 1 and Type 2

Neurofibromatosis was once known as "elephant man disease." This genetic syndrome was described in 1768 by Mark Akenside and, in 1882, by German pathologist Friedrich Daniel von Recklinghausen, who described autopsy findings in a female and male. There are two types of neurofibromatosis: neurofibromatosis type 1 (NF1), or von Recklinghausen disease, which is responsible for 85% of cases, and neurofibromatosis type 2 (NF2), which is responsible for 15% of cases. NF1 and NF2 can occur sporadically or be inherited in an autosomal dominant manner. Sturge-Weber syndrome and tuberous sclerosis complex/syndrome are related disorders.

Physical Characteristics

Neurofibromatosis Type 1   NF1 is diagnosed by the presence of two or more of the following:

- Six or more café-au-lait (coffee-with-cream/light brown) skin spots

- Two or more neurofibromas (i.e., tumors that grow on a nerve or nerve tissue, under the skin) or one plexiform neurofibroma (involving many nerves)

- Multiple freckles in axillary (arm pit) or inguinal (groin) region

- Osseous lesions (lesion on the bone); enlargement or deformation of certain bones other than the spine

- Optic glioma (tumor of the optic nerve)

- Two or more iris hamartomas (clumps of pigment in the pigmented part of the eye)

- Severe scoliosis (curvature of the spine)

- First-degree relative (parent, child, or sibling) with NF1

Neurofibromatosis Type 2   NF2 is diagnosed by the presence of one of the following:

- Bilateral acoustic neuromas, benign (noncancerous) tumors that originate in the cochlear vestibular nerves

- A first-degree relative (i.e., parent, child, or sibling) with NF2 plus one of the following: unilateral acoustic neuroma at less than 30 years of age; any two of meningioma (a benign tumor of the meninges), glioma (a tumor that arises from the glial cells), schwannoma (a usually benign tumor of the peripheral nerve fibers that is composed of Schwann cells), or juvenile cortical cataract (the cortex of the lens)

Incidence or Prevalence

- NF1: 1 in 3,000 to 1 in 4,000 live births

- NF2: 1 in 30,000 to 1 in 40,000 live births

Genotype or Cause

- NF1 is caused by mutation in the neurofibromin gene on chromosome 17; familial NF1 has

100% penetrance (i.e., the frequency, under given environmental conditions, with which a phenotype results from a specific genotype), and variable expressivity (i.e., the degree to which an expressed gene exerts an effect). One known function of neurofibromin is to inhibit another gene called Ras from sending signals to other genes and proteins. Mutations of the neurofibromin gene disrupt its ability to inhibit Ras.

- NF2 is caused by mutation in the merlin tumor suppressor gene on chromosome 22. Merlin-deficient cells cannot "sense" each other and continue to divide when there is no more room.

Functional and Behavioral Characteristics

Neurofibromatosis Type 1

- Depends on the system affected

- May include seizures, intellectual compromise, blindness, deafness, movement disorders, dislocations, endocrine abnormalities, autonomic involvement, bowel irregularities, hypertension, and symptoms of autism spectrum disorder

Neurofibromatosis Type 2

- Depends on the system affected

- Acoustic neuromas present with high-frequency sensorineural hearing loss, vertigo (dizziness), tinnitus (ringing of the ears), and facial paralysis

- Cataracts lead to blindness

- Spinal tumors cause pain and paraplegia or quadriplegia

Interventions, Supports, and Services

- Genetic counseling for familial cases of NF1 and NF2

- NF1: depends on organ being investigated

- NF2: surgical removal or radiotherapy for acoustic neuromas

Neuronal Migration Disorders

Neuronal migration disorders are a group of birth defects caused by the abnormal migration of neurons in the developing brain and nervous system during fetal development. More than 25 neuronal migration disorders have been described, including lissencephaly, which is highlighted in this section. *Lissencephaly* (LIS) literally means "smooth brain;" this is separated into two classes: classical (previously type I LIS) and cobblestone complex (previously type II LIS). Classical LIS is the more prevalent and presents itself clinically in two common ways: isolated lissencephaly sequence (ILS) and Miller-Dieker syndrome (MDS). MDS and ILS share a common genetic pathway and exhibit similar symptoms. MDS usually occurs sporadically and is the result of a chromosomal deletion. In rare cases, it can be associated with a familial reciprocal translocation (i.e., interchange of material between two chromosomes). ILS also occurs sporadically but in some cases is autosomal recessive. Both disorders primarily affect the cortex, and MDS also affects the cranium and facial tissues.

Physical Characteristics

- Magnetic resonance imaging demonstrates a very thick cortex (10 mm–20 mm), malformations of the gyri (i.e., ridges on the surface of the cerebellum) that are more severe in posterior than anterior brain regions, and a prominent cell-sparse zone in the cortex. These features are more severe in MDS than in ILS.

- MDS has characteristic craniofacial anomalies including a broad and often high forehead, a subtle indentation of the temples, a slightly upturned tip of the nose, a thin upper lip, and a small jaw.

Incidence or Prevalence

- The only published data on the prevalence of classical LIS comes from a 1991 Dutch study, which reported 11.7 in 1,000,000 live births; however, this statistic is probably an underestimation.

- MDS occurs in fewer than 1 in 100,000 people.

Genotype or Cause

- ILS can result from viral infections of the uterus or in the fetus during the first trimester, from insufficient blood supply to the fetal brain early in pregnancy, and from a number of genetic causes. These include mutations in at least three genes (PAFAH1B1, DCX, or TUBA1A). When

ILS is caused by mutations in the PAFAH1B1 or TUBA1A gene, it is inherited in an autosomal dominant pattern. When mutations in the DCX gene cause ILS, it is inherited in an X-linked pattern.

- Approximately 20% of cases of MDS are caused by a deletion on the small (p) arm of chromosome 17 that involves the loss of multiple genes.

- In 80% of the MDS cases, the cause is not known.

Functional and Behavioral Characteristics

- Patients exhibit severe intellectual and developmental delay, suffer from epilepsy, and usually die early in childhood. These symptoms are much more severe in MDS; furthermore, there is a gradient of severity in ILS that correlates with the mutation type.

- Feeding problems are common and include gagging while feeding, refusal of feeding, spitting up, and weight loss; these problems are usually the result of aspiration and reflux.

- Patients are at risk of recurrent pneumonia related to feeding problems.

Interventions, Supports, and Services

- Management is symptomatic. The use of a nasogastric tube (i.e., a feeding tube inserted through the nose to the stomach) and gastrostomy (i.e., an opening made through the abdominal wall into the stomach, usually for inserting a feeding tube) may alleviate complications that arise due to feeding problems; the use of medication is required to control seizures. These approaches have increased life expectancy to adolescence.

- Genetic counseling is important when there is risk of recurrence (e.g., in the case of a familial reciprocal translocation).

Noonan Syndrome

Noonan syndrome is a genetic disorder characterized by short stature, facial anomalies, and congenital heart defects. Noonan syndrome has characteristics resembling Turner syndrome, except that it has no chromosomal abnormality and occurs in both sexes. A male with webbing of the neck, incomplete folding of the ears, and a low posterior hair line was first reported in 1883 by Koblinsky, at the University of Dorpat in Estonia. Further characteristics of the syndrome were described by Jacqueline Noonan and Dorothy Ehmke (American cardiologist and pediatrician, respectively) in 1963. The syndrome can occur sporadically but also can be inherited in an autosomal dominant manner.

Physical Characteristics

- Affected individuals have short stature.

- Facial anomalies include hypertelorism (i.e., abnormal width between the eyes), ptosis (i.e., drooping) of eyelids, palpebral (eyelid) slant, epicanthal folds (i.e., skin fold from the root of the nose to the inner termination of eyebrow), micrognathia (i.e., small jaw), ear abnormalities (low-set, prominent, and abnormally rotated), and neck webbing.

- Skeletal abnormalities are present, such as cubitus valgus (i.e., increased carrying angle of the elbow) and hemivertebrae (i.e., an abnormality of the spine often apparent before the age of 6 months in which one or more of the vertebrae are half-formed, leading to lateral curvature of the spine [scoliosis]).

- In people with Noonan syndrome, congenital heart disease is common; of those affected, approximately 50% have pulmonary valvular stenosis—a condition in which a deformity on or near the pulmonary valve slows the blood flow from the heart to the lungs.

- Gonadal defects vary from severe deficiency to normal sexual development; defects include cryptorchidism (i.e., undescended testes) in males.

- Hepatosplenomegaly (i.e., enlargement of liver and spleen) and abnormal bleeding can occur.

Incidence or Prevalence

- 1 in 1,000 to 1 in 2,500 live births

Genotype or Cause

- Defects in at least six different genes (PTPN11, SOS1, RAF1, KRAS, NRAS, and BRAF) can cause the syndrome. These gene mutations are involved in the Ras/mitogen-activated protein kinase signal transduction pathway and currently explain ~61% of Noonan syndrome cases. In approximately 50% of cases, the condition is caused by a missense mutation in the PTPN11 gene on chromosome 12, resulting in a gain of function of the protein SHP-2—a protein tyrosine phosphatase produced by PTPN11.

- Individuals with Noonan syndrome who have mutations in PTPN11 are at risk of developing mild juvenile myelomonocytic leukemia.

Functional and Behavioral Characteristics

- There is no specific behavioral phenotype; affected individuals exhibit some features similar to those of autism.

- Most people with Noonan syndrome are intellectually normal as adults, but mild to moderate cognitive disability may affect up to 33%.

- Progressive high-frequency sensorineural hearing loss (a problem in the inner ear or auditory nerve) in Noonan syndrome may affect as many as 50%.

- Children with Noonan syndrome may exhibit stubbornness, clumsiness, mood problems, and communication problems, and/or be "fussy" eaters.

Interventions, Supports, and Services

- If no serious heart problem exists, life expectancy should be normal.

- Assessment is necessary to identify any delays and allow for intervention.

- Mildly affected individuals should respond well to traditional educational methods.

- Screening should be conducted for high-frequency sensorineural hearing loss, and this condition should be appropriately managed (e.g., with a hearing aid, reduction of background noise, or possibly with a cochlear implant if severe).

Phenylketonuria

Phenylketonuria (PKU) is a rare autosomal recessive disorder in which the amino acid phenylalanine is not properly metabolized. Phenylalanine is one of eight essential amino acids found in protein-containing foods. In PKU, phenylalanine cannot be normally metabolized because of a deficiency in an enzyme necessary for its breakdown. High levels of phenylalanine and its derivatives are toxic to the central nervous system and cause brain damage. This syndrome was first described by Norwegian physiologist Ivar Asbjørn Følling in 1934. It was characterized by paleness of skin, eyes, and hair; eczema; cognitive delay; and a characteristic odor of the urine due to high levels of the amino acid phenylalanine in the blood and excretion of the metabolite phenylketone in the urine. The name *phenylketonuria* was coined by Lionel Penrose, a British geneticist. By 1951, dietary treatment, involving restriction of phenylalanine from the diet, had begun. Most developed countries have been screening newborns for PKU since 1969. The accepted upper limit of phenylalanine in blood plasma for preschoolers is 360 μmol/L. This disorder has an autosomal recessive mode of inheritance. Women with untreated PKU are likely to have children with congenital and cognitive abnormalities; thus, it is important for affected women to stay on a low phenylalanine diet before conception through to delivery.

Physical Characteristics

- Affected individuals usually have the following:

    - Fair skin, blond hair, blue eyes

    - Eczema (skin rash)

    - Characteristic odor of the urine due to high levels of the amino acid phenylalanine in the blood and urinary excretion of the metabolite phenylketone

- If dietary intervention is not started soon after birth, a child with PKU will suffer from intellectual disability, stunted growth, seizures, tremors, and jerky hand and leg movements.

Incidence or Prevalence

- 1 in 15,000 live births in the United States; varies internationally: highest incidence in Turkey, with approximately 1 in 2,600 live births; high incidence also occurs in Yemenite Jews and in northern and eastern Europe, Italy, and China

Genotype or Cause

- The amino acid phenylalanine cannot be converted to tyrosine because the enzyme phenylalanine hydroxylase is absent or nonfunctional; the phenylalanine hydroxylase gene is on chromosome 12.

- A deficiency of tetrahydrobiopterin also causes some cases of the disorder.

Functional and Behavioral Characteristics

- If untreated, developmental delay is observable by mid-infancy.

- Severe behavioral disturbances may include hyperactivity, destructiveness, impulsiveness, uncontrolled rage attacks, and self-injury.

- Autism and schizophrenia-like symptoms are possible.

- Tonic-clonic seizures (i.e., epileptic seizures associated with loss of consciousness) are present in about 25% of affected children.

- Hyperreflexia (i.e., exaggerated reflexes) is present in about 50% of affected individuals.

- Spastic cerebral palsy may also appear.

- Athetosis (i.e., writhing motions), hand posturing, and behavioral stereotypies (i.e., frequent repetition of the same posture, movement, or form of speech) may be present.

Interventions, Supports, and Services

- No effects are apparent if low phenylalanine diet is started before 3 weeks of age; if started between 3 and 6 weeks, there are mild effects of disorder; after 6 months, there is little benefit.

- Treatment is associated with, on average, a normal life span and slightly lower intellectual functioning.

- Dietary restriction should be followed until an affected individual is at least 10 years of age. Women with PKU should consider dietary restriction of phenylalanine for life to prevent fetal abnormalities (see background section).

- Aspartame is a potent source of phenylalanine and should be avoided.

- People with PKU resulting from tetrahydrobiopterin deficiency may need supplementation with tyrosine as well as phenylalanine restriction.

Prader-Willi Syndrome/ Prader-Labhart-Willi Syndrome

This syndrome was first described in Switzerland in 1956 by Andrea Prader, Alexis Labhardt, and Heinrich Willi on the basis of nine children with the tetrad of small stature, mental retardation, obesity, and small hands and feet. Prader and Willi reviewed the condition in 1961, expanded the phenotype, and drew attention to the presence of hypotonia in infancy and the development of diabetes mellitus in later childhood. This syndrome involves the same region of chromosome 15 as Angelman syndrome, but the abnormalities of Prader-Willi syndrome occur on the paternally inherited chromosome 15. Most cases of this syndrome arise sporadically, but some have an autosomal dominant mode of inheritance.

Physical Characteristics

- Commonly, blond to light-brown hair, blue eyes, and sun-sensitive, fair skin

- Hypotonia in newborns, poor sucking response, weak cry, and feeding difficulties; overeating between 6 months and 2 years of age

- Obesity after infancy; some individuals suffer "Pickwickian syndrome" wherein severe obesity impairs breathing, leading to drowsiness, cyanosis (i.e., bluish discoloration due to decreased oxygen), and possibly heart failure; diabetes also possible

- Short stature

- Cryptorchidism (i.e., absence of one or both testes from the scrotum) and hypogonadism (i.e., small testes, small penis, inadequate testosterone production)

- Small hands and feet

- Dysmorphic facies (i.e., unusual facial features)

- Excessive daytime sleepiness

- Increased occurrence of scoliosis and other orthopedic problems

- Likely to have a hypothalamic growth hormone deficiency

Incidence or Prevalence

- 1 in 8,000 to 1 in 25,000 live births; same frequency in males and females

Genotype or Cause

- The syndrome is the first human disorder attributed to genomic imprinting, in which genes are expressed differentially based upon the parent of origin.

- An imprinting center has been identified on chromosome 15 within 15q11-13; expression may be regulated by DNA methylation at cytosine bases.

- The syndrome results from the loss of imprinted genomic material within the paternal 15q11.2-13 locus; the loss of maternal genomic material at the 15q11.2-13 locus results in Angelman syndrome.

- The loss of paternal genetic material in Prader-Willi syndrome may occur in three different ways: a deletion on the paternal chromosome 15, a mutation on the paternal chromosome 15, and maternal uniparental disomy (i.e., two copies of chromosome 15 from the mother and none from the father).

Functional and Behavioral Characteristics

- The majority of affected individuals exhibit mild to moderate developmental delay.

- Some cases are associated with autism.

- Typical behavioral patterns include irritability, anger, temper tantrums, stubbornness, low frustration tolerance, anxiety, compulsive eating (i.e., hyperphagia), and self-injurious behavior (skin picking is the most common).

- Serious personality problems in 70%; anger and hostility are common.

- Obsessive-compulsive disorder may be 20 to 40 times more common than in the general population, including nonfood-related behavior.

- Food-related behaviors include food seeking, overeating, and hoarding.

- Other maladaptive behavior includes argumentativeness and aggression.

- Affected individuals may have difficulty in sequential processing and short-term memory (visual and motor).

- Affected individuals may have relative strengths in expressive vocabulary, long-term memory, visual memory, and visual spatial integration (e.g., an unusual interest in jigsaw puzzles).

Interventions, Supports, and Services

- Genetic counseling is indicated.

- Life expectancy into the 50s is dependent upon weight management.

- Treatment involves a combination of dietary management, behavior management, family intervention and therapy, physiotherapy with passive exercises and frequent change in position to prevent disuse atrophy and joint contractures, as well as pharmacological interventions.

- Growth hormone is being tried on an experimental basis.

Progressive Myoclonus Epilepsy

Progressive myoclonus epilepsy (PME) refers to a group of rare catastrophic epilepsies, including Unverricht-Lundborg disease, Lafora disease, five forms of neuronal ceroid lipofuscinosis (e.g., Batten disease), myoclonic epilepsy with ragged red fibers and sialidosis (a disorder in which a lysosomal enzyme called neuraminidase is missing; this enzyme is involved in the first stage of breakdown of large carbohydrate groups, removing sialic acid residues). PME is associated with myoclonus (i.e., sudden, brief, jerky, shock-like, involuntary movements), tonic-clonic (formerly called "grand-mal") seizures (i.e., contraction of all skeletal muscles and loss of consciousness), and neurological decline. This group of disorders affects young children and adolescents. All types of PME are genetic. Most have an autosomal recessive mode of inheritance and one affects mitochondrial DNA.

Physical Characteristics

- Generalized or multifocal myoclonus that is stimulus sensitive

- Tonic-clonic seizures

- Cognitive deterioration

- EEG abnormalities

Incidence or Prevalence

- 1% of all epilepsy cases in childhood and adolescence

Genotype or Cause

(abbreviation/chromosomal region/mutation[s])

Unverricht-Lundborg Disease

- EPM1/21q22.3/cystatin B

Lafora Disease

- EPM2A/6q24/laforin

- EPM2B/6p22/malin

Neuronal Ceroid Lipofuscinosis—Infantile

- CLN1/1p32/palmitoyl-protein thioesterase 1

Neuronal Ceroid Lipofuscinosis—Late Infantile

- CLN2/11p15/tripeptidyl peptidase 1

Neuronal Ceroid Lipofuscinosis—Finnish Variant

- CLN5/13q22/novel membrane protein

Neuronal Ceroid Lipofuscinosis—Juvenile

- CLN3/16p12/novel membrane protein

Neuronal Ceroid Lipofuscinosis—Northern Epilepsy

- CLN8/8p23/novel membrane protein

Myoclonic Epilepsy with Ragged Red Fibers

- MTTK/mtDNA/tRNALys

Sialidosis

- NEU1/6p21/neuraminidase 1

Functional and Behavioral Characteristics

- Intellectual deterioration and dementia

- Cerebellar ataxia (i.e., impaired ability to coordinate voluntary movements)

- Sensorineural impairments (deafness, blindness)

- Optic atrophy (i.e., degeneration or destruction of the optic nerve) and macular "spots" (i.e., blind spots in the central part of the retina)

Interventions, Supports, and Services

- Antiepileptic medication is useful in controlling myoclonus and seizures.

- Therapeutic approaches for mitochondrial disease include vitamins (B, C, E), enzyme cofactors (coenzyme Q10), and antioxidants.

Rett Syndrome

Rett syndrome was originally described in 1966 by Andreas Rett, an Austrian pediatrician, but was not known worldwide until 2 decades later, following a report by Bengt Hagberg and colleagues describing 35 affected girls from Sweden, Portugal, and France. Most cases of Rett syndrome are sporadic. This disorder also has an X-linked dominant mode of inheritance, usually with lethality in males. Females have two X chromosomes, one of which provides enough normal protein for survival.

Physical Characteristics

- Typical development for the first 6 to 18 months
- Hypotonia—a first sign
- Slowing head growth beginning at approximately 2 to 6 months of age, with gray matter atrophy, leading to acquired microcephaly (i.e., small head)
- Shaky, unsteady, or stiff gait
- Scoliosis
- Poor circulation, leading to cold and bluish arms and legs and small feet
- Excessive saliva and drooling
- Four stages of disease development have been described: early onset stagnation, developmental regression, pseudostationary period, and late motor deterioration (Hagberg, 2002).

Incidence or Prevalence

- 1 in 23,000 live births in the United States; 1 in 10,000 to 1 in 45,000 live births internationally

Genotype or Cause

- Rett syndrome is caused by mutation of the gene encoding methyl-CpG-binding protein 2 (MeCP2) on the X chromosome; MeCP2 normally binds methylated DNA regulating gene expression and chromatin structure.
- Mutations have also been found in males and children with autism and mental delay.

Functional and Behavioral Characteristics

- Children with this disorder exhibit behaviors similar to those of autism—such as repetitive hand movements, toe walking, body walking, and sleep problems—though the brain pathology differs from that in autism. Other characteristics include the following:

  - Developmental regression (e.g., slowing of head growth)
  - Severely impaired language regression, loss of communication skills
  - Intellectual disabilities and learning difficulties
  - Apraxia (a neurogenic impairment involving planning, executing, and sequencing motor movements)
  - Seizures; loss of normal sleep patterns and sleep disturbances
  - Breathing abnormalities
  - Gastrointestinal complaints including ongoing, severe constipation and gastroesophageal reflux

Interventions, Supports, and Services

- Physical and occupational therapy to slow the progression
- Speech therapy; music therapy as an adjunct

Sanfilippo Syndrome/ Mucopolysaccharidosis Type III

Sanfilippo syndrome was recognized by American physician Sylvester Sanfilippo and colleagues in 1963. Sanfilippo syndrome is the most common form of the MPS disorders. It is a lysosomal storage disorder resulting from deficiency in one of the enzymes needed to break down heparan sulfate (a glycosaminoglycan found in the extracellular matrix and on cell surface glycoproteins). The MPSs are ubiquitous and, therefore, multiple organ systems can be involved. Like Hurler syndrome (MPS-I) and Hunter syndrome (MPS-II), Sanfilippo syndrome (MPS-III) can result in severe mental impairment. The mode of inheritance of Sanfilippo syndrome is autosomal recessive.

Physical Characteristics

- Children appear typical at birth and seem to develop typically for the first year or two; as more and more cells become damaged, symptoms appear.

- The syndrome is difficult to diagnose due to mild dysmorphic features and the lack of MPS in urine. Some features include the following:

  - Mild coarsening of facial features

  - Hairiness

  - Minimal dysostosis multiplex (incomplete/ defective bone formation)

  - Corneal clouding and hepatosplenomegaly (enlargement of liver and spleen) in rare cases

Incidence or Prevalence

- MPS disorders occur in 1 in 16,000 to 1 in 30,000 live births.

- MPS III accounts for approximately 50% of all cases of MPS diagnosed and has a combined prevalence of 1 in 53,000 to 1 in 280,000 live births.

- There are four different enzyme deficiencies that cause Sanfilippo, resulting in types A, B, C, and D.

- Prevalence of type A is 1 in 24,000 to 1 in 89,000 (the most severe and common).

- Type B is the second most common.

Genotype or Cause

- The syndrome results from a deficiency of one of four enzymes that are necessary to degrade heparan sulfate (a sulfated polysaccharide that consists of alternating hexuronate and glucosamine units):

  - Type A: deficiency of heparan sulfatase

  - Type B: deficiency of N-acetyl-alpha-D-glucosaminidase

  - Type C: deficiency of acetyl coA-alpha-glucose N-acetyl transferase

  - Type D: deficiency of N-acetylglucosamine-6-sulfate sulfatase

- In each case, a partially broken down sugar, or mucopolysaccharide, accumulates in the brain and the body's cells and tissues, causing progressive damage; the storage process affects children's appearances, bodily functions, and development.

Functional and Behavioral Characteristics

- Severe cognitive disability and joint stiffness are often difficult to manage.

- Symptoms can mimic those of autism.

- Severe behavioral disturbances can include hyperactivity, aggression, and sleep disturbances; some affected children chew objects.

- Affected individuals display loss of language and hearing, intellectual deterioration, and dementia.

Interventions, Supports, and Services

- Genetic counseling is indicated.

- Symptomatic treatment is needed for associated health and difficult behavioral problems.

- Enzyme replacement therapy and gene therapy are used; bone marrow transplants have been tried with disappointing results

- Those affected tend to have short life spans (10 to 20 years); pneumonia is common.

- Some people with a mild form of type B live well into adulthood.

- Patients with MPS may have unusual sensitivity to anesthesia.

Smith-Lemli-Opitz Syndrome

Smith-Lemli-Opitz syndrome (SLOS) was first described in three unrelated boys in 1964 by David Weyhe Smith, Luc Lemli, and John Marius Opitz. Smith-Lemli-Opitz syndrome is caused by a deficiency in the enzyme 7-dehydrocholesterol reductase (DHCR7), which acts in the sterol synthetic metabolic pathway to convert 7-dehydrocholesterol (7DHC) into cholesterol. The disease is thus characterized by a deficiency of plasma cholesterol as well as the presence of high levels of the precursor 7DHC, which is toxic at high concentrations. Severity of the disease generally correlates with plasma sterol concentration. Very severely affected individuals are subject to multiple congenital malformations and are often miscarried or die within the first few weeks of life, since cholesterol is required by practically all cells in the body. Morphogenic abnormalities are predominantly located in the following systems: craniofacial, limb or skeletal, urogenital, and internal organs such as the heart. SLOS is linked with a high rate of mortality due to multi-organ-system failure, congenital heart disease, and hepatic failure. The syndrome has an autosomal recessive mode of inheritance.

Physical Characteristics Severely affected individuals often present with the following characteristics:

- Intrauterine growth retardation, low weight, shortness of stature

- Dysmorphic facial features (cleft palate, anteverted nostrils); microcephaly

- Genital anomalies

- Syndactyly (i.e., joining or webbing of two or more fingers or toes) or polydactyly (i.e., having more than the normal number of fingers or toes)

- Cardiac malformation

Incidence or Prevalence

- Incidence is 1 in 20,000 to 1 in 60,000 live births; as many as 1 in 30 people carry one mutant gene, suggesting an incidence of 1 in 5,000 to 1 in 18,000. Incidence may be lower than expected due to fetal loss.

- The syndrome occurs most frequently in the Caucasian population of Eastern European descent and least frequently in Asian and African populations.

- SLOS is equally prevalent among males and females.

Genotype or Cause

- Caused by different mutations in the DHCR7 gene located on chromosome 11

Functional and Behavioral Characteristics

- Neuropsychiatric and neurodevelopmental abnormalities are frequent. Other characteristics include the following:

  - Antisocial, self-destructive, hyperactive, or aggressive behavior

  - Withdrawn personality, behaviors similar to those of autism, or both

- Borderline typical intelligence to profound mental delay

  - Language and hearing impairments

Interventions, Supports, and Services

- Interventions include surgery for congenital heart failure, repair of polydactyly, hearing aids for hearing impairments, and restriction of exposure to the sun.

- Current experimental therapy consists of dietary cholesterol supplementation, but effects are under evaluation.

- Preconceptual and prenatal therapy are under consideration.

Smith-Magenis Syndrome

This rare group of children was described in the 1980s by Ann Smith, a genetic counselor, and Ellen Magenis, a physician and chromosome expert. A variety of unusual physical and behavioral characteristics have been found in people with Smith-Magenis syndrome. This syndrome usually occurs sporadically.

Physical Characteristics

- Brachycephaly (i.e., a disproportionately short head); broad face; broad nasal bridge; flat midface; posteriorly rotated or low-set ears; short, broad hands; upper limb deformity; eye problems including strabismus (abnormal condition of one or both eyes that are not correctly aligned and pointing in different directions); and severe myopia (nearsightedness)

- Low muscle tone and feeding problems in infancy

- Short stature

- Prominent jaw in older children and adults

- Abnormalities of the palate, with or without cleft lip

- Downturned mouth

- Chronic ear infections and hearing impairments

- Short fingers and toes

- Heart defects and murmurs

- Urinary system problems

- Scoliosis (curvature of the spine); unusual gait (walking pattern)

Incidence or Prevalence

- 1 in 25,000 live births in the United States, but the condition is underrecognized and underdiagnosed

Genotype or Cause

- The syndrome is associated with deletion involving chromosome 17.

- Frameshift and missense mutations leading to protein truncation in the retinoic acid induced 1 gene have been observed in individuals exhibiting Smith-Magenis syndrome characteristics, but without a chromosome 17 deletion.

Functional and Behavioral Characteristics

- Affected individuals show moderate cognitive impairment (IQ in the 50 to 60 range) with speech and language delays.

- Some of those affected show maladaptive behaviors including hyperactivity, sleep problems (frequent awakenings), and features similar to those of autism.

- An abnormal movement described as "self-hugging" posture involving a spasmatic upper body squeeze is characteristic.

- Affected individuals show a tendency to repeat the same questions (e.g., "Where are you from?" "What's your name?").

- Aggression, self-injury, head banging, hand biting, pulling out fingernails and toenails, and polyembolokoilamania (i.e., insertion of foreign bodies or objects into bodily orifices) is observed in 70% of individuals; there may be a relative insensitivity to pain.

- Individuals are at risk of stereotypic (repetitive) movement disorders.

- Affected individuals are described as very appealing and affectionate, with untapped potential.

Interventions, Supports, and Services

- Strong need for behavioral intervention planning as part of family services

- Psychotropic drugs for modifying problem behaviors; therapeutic management of sleep disorders

- Speech and language therapy, occupational therapy, physical therapy, orthopedic intervention

- Support from families, schools, work, and residential service providers

- Important need for early intervention programs

Sturge-Weber Syndrome

During ancient times, visible birthmarks were thought to be caused by some adverse event experienced by the mother. The presence of neurological problems in individuals with visible birthmarks added to the lack of acceptance by society. The link between birthmarks and other features was made in 1860 by German ophthalmologist Rudolf Schirmer. In 1879, English physician William Allen Sturge clearly described the main clinical manifestations in a young girl and deduced that they resulted from a vascular lesion. In 1922, Frederick Parkes Weber described the radiographic features of the syndrome for the first time. Sturge-Weber syndrome occurs sporadically. Although it has a genetic basis, mutations causing the syndrome arise during development. It rarely occurs more than once in a family. Refer to the sections entitled Neurofibromatosis and Tuberous Sclerosis Complex/Syndrome for information on related disorders.

Physical Characteristics

- This neurodevelopmental disorder is characterized by an angiomatous facial malformation ("port-wine stain") caused by overgrowth of capillaries beneath the skin surface and excessive growth of blood vessels on the surface of the brain (posterior) on the same side as the birthmark; brain tissue beneath the growth may not receive adequate perfusion.

- Other physical symptoms may include the following:

  - Hemiparesis (i.e., a weakening or loss of the use of one side of the body) that develops on the side opposite to the port-wine stain

  - Buphthalmos (i.e., an enlarging of the eye that has been affected by the stain)

  - Glaucoma (i.e., increased pressure within the eyeball that can result in damage to the optic disk and gradual loss of vision)

Incidence or Prevalence

- The disease is sporadic; incidence or prevalence has not been estimated.

- Males and females are affected equally.

Genotype or Cause

- Occurs sporadically

- Caused by a somatic mutation in the guanine nucleotide binding protein (G protein), q polypeptide gene

- Persistence of the transitory primordial sinusoidal plexus stage of vessel development results from the somatic mutations

Functional and Behavioral Characteristics

- Seizures often occur, usually beginning between 2 and 7 months of age.

- Affected individuals display varying degrees of developmental delay in motor and cognitive skills.

- There is a high prevalence of attention-deficit/hyperactivity disorder in young people with this disorder.

- Autism spectrum disorder may be more frequent than in the general population.

- Older children and adolescents are at risk for depression.

Interventions, Supports, and Services

- Laser treatment is used to lighten or to remove port-wine stains in young children.

- Diagnosis of glaucoma and intracranial involvement, even in asymptomatic individuals, is fundamental.

- Early neuroimaging features are important to recognize.

- Management of associated neurologic and ocular abnormalities is required.

- Anticonvulsants are used to control seizures. Vagus nerve stimulator implants (i.e., electrical stimulation of the vagus nerve, leading to an antiepileptic effect) are used in children over 12 years of age, and brain surgery can be used for seizure management.

- Physical and occupational therapy are indicated.

- Special education services are required.

Tourette Syndrome

Tourette syndrome was recognized as early as 1825 by French physician Jean Marc Gaspard Itard. In 1885 French neurologist Georges Albert Édouard Brutus Gilles de la Tourette described a condition involving multiple tics, involuntary movements, echolalia (i.e., involuntary repetition of a word or sentence just spoken by another person), and coprolalia (i.e., involuntary utterance of vulgar or obscene words). Tourette syndrome, named after its discoverer, is a childhood-onset neurological disorder characterized by motor and vocal tics. In most cases, Tourette syndrome is thought to result from a variety of genetic and environmental factors, although in a small number of cases, causal genetic factors have been identified. Although symptoms are sometimes clustered in families, an inheritance pattern is not clear.

Physical Characteristics

- Not relevant

Incidence or Prevalence

- Not certain. One study indicated that between 3 and 6 of every 1,000 children in the United States are affected. The most severe form may affect 1 in 200,000 Americans. As many as 1 in 100 may have a mild form of the syndrome. The condition is three to four times more common in males than females.

Genotype or Cause

- Genetic and environmental factors are thought to be involved in most cases of this syndrome. Mutations causing histidine carboxylase deficiency have been identified in a small number of people with Tourette. Mutations in the SLITRK1 gene also are implicated in a small number of cases.

Functional and Behavioral Characteristics

- The condition is characterized by tics, sensorimotor gating deficiencies, and abnormalities of cortico-basal ganglia circuits.

- Symptoms begin between the ages of 2 and 15 years; most present by age 11.

- The syndrome is often not recognized in severe or profound intellectual or developmental disability.

- Affected individuals exhibit head and facial tics as well as vocalizations (e.g., throat clearing, barking, snorting, grunting, coughing, word accentuation).

- Other movement symptoms are frequently present and include touching, hitting, jumping, and smelling objects; involuntary and inappropriate obscene remarks; obsessive-compulsive behaviors; hyperactivity; attention-deficit disorder and learning disabilities; self-injury; inappropriate sexual activity; exhibitionism; and antisocial behavior.

- Sleep disorders are common.

Interventions, Supports, and Services

- It is critical to work with the family.

- Traditional neuroleptics (i.e., antipsychotic drugs) are standard; nonneuroleptic drugs, behavioral therapies, and surgical approaches may apply.

- Treatment begins with modification of the work and home environment.

- Treatment of tics may result in greater disability than the tics themselves.

- Although Tourette syndrome was once believed to be a lifelong condition, noticeable improvement or remissions may occur without the use of medication: 30%–40% of children have total remission; another 30% exhibit substantial improvement.

Tuberous Sclerosis Complex/Syndrome

Tuberous sclerosis (TS) complex/syndrome is one of the neurocutaneous syndromes, also referred to as phacomatoses (a group of congenital and hereditary diseases characterized by the development of hamartomas, benign tumor-like malformations, in various tissues). Neurocutaneous syndromes include neurofibromatosis, tuberous sclerosis, Sturge-Weber syndrome, and ataxia-telangiectasia. Tuberous sclerosis was probably first described by German pathologist Friedrich Daniel von Recklinghausen in 1862. French neurologist Désiré-Magloire Bourneville formally labeled the condition as tuberous sclerosis in 1880. The onset of TS occurs in the first decade of life. It is characterized by the classic triad of epilepsy, low cognitive functioning, and adenoma sebaceum (i.e., benign tumors of the sebaceous glands, the small glands associated with hair follicles that secrete oily substances or sebum to lubricate the skin and hair). TS occurs sporadically and may be inherited in an autosomal dominant fashion.

Physical Characteristics

- Benign tumors or growths on the brain, face, and organs (especially the kidneys, heart, liver, spleen, and lungs) can occur. (Facial growths typically appear as small, bright-red or brownish nodules occurring in a butterfly distribution on nose and cheeks; these facial growths become evident between 2 and 5 years of age.)

- Areas of hypopigmentation (i.e., decreased pigmentation) that can appear on the arms, trunk, and legs are often exhibited at birth.

- Tooth enamel defects are common.

- Periungual fibromas (i.e., tumors under the fingernails) occur in about half of affected individuals.

- Shagreen patches (i.e., irregularly thickened, slightly elevated soft plaques usually noted over the lumbosacral area) occur in about 70% of those affected.

- Cardiac rhabdomyoma (a benign tumor composed of striated muscle fibers), single or multiple, may be present.

Incidence or Prevalence

- 1 in 5,800 to 1 in 30,000 live births

Genotype or Cause

- Affected individuals have mutations to the TSC1 and TSC2 genes, encoding the proteins hamartin and tuberin, respectively.

- TSC1 maps to chromosome 9; TSC2 maps to chromosome 16.

- Tuberin, the protein gene product of TSC2, shows a small region of homologic identity to the Rap1 guanosine triphosphatase activity protein. Rap1 is involved in the regulation of cell proliferation and differentiation; loss of tuberin activity is thought to lead to activation of Rap1 in tumors.

- Hamartin, the TSC1 gene product, may function as a tumor suppressor.

Functional and Behavioral Characteristics

- Convulsions occur in approximately 80% of affected individuals.

- Mild to severe developmental disabilities are apparent in 70% of cases.

- TS is sometimes associated with behavior disturbances including autism, Asperger syndrome, and socially unacceptable behaviors (e.g., hyperactivity, screaming, destructiveness, temper tantrums, aggression, self-mutilation).

- Sleep disorders are common (e.g., night walking and early morning waking).

- Psychiatric comorbidities are common, especially behavioral disorders.

Interventions, Supports, and Services

- Interventions include the following:

  - Medication for seizures; pharmacological interventions

  - Surgery or plastic surgery for skin conditions

  - Psychoeducational and behavioral therapy

- Individuals with mild cases may live productive lives.

- Those with severe mental impairments and seizures require extensive medical and psychosocial treatment.

- Pharmacological treatment can be effective for psychiatric comorbidities.

Turner Syndrome

Turner syndrome was first described by American endocrinologist Henry Hubert Turner in 1938 as a condition consisting of sexual infantilism, short stature, webbed neck, and cubitus valgus (i.e., an increased carrying angle at the elbows). Also known as chromosome XO syndrome, Turner syndrome affects only females. Its most common characteristics include short stature and lack of ovarian development. A number of other physical features, such as webbed neck, arms that turn out slightly at the elbow, and a low hairline in the back of the head, are sometimes seen in Turner syndrome patients. Individuals with Turner syndrome are also prone to cardiovascular, kidney, and thyroid problems; skeletal disorders such as scoliosis (i.e., curvature of the spine) or dislocated hips; and hearing and ear disturbances. Turner syndrome occurs sporadically.

Physical Characteristics

- Early characteristics include low birth weight, edema (i.e., fluid retention) on dorsum (back) of hands and feet, and loose skin folds at nape of neck.

- Later-developing characteristics include short stature, webbing of the neck, low posterior hairline, small mandible, prominent ears, epicanthic folds, high-arched palate, broad chest and wide-spaced nipples, cubitus valgus, hyperconvex fingernails, ovarian dysgenesis (i.e., defective embryonic development) resulting in amenorrhea (i.e., absence of menstrual periods) and infertility, sensorineural hearing loss, and relative micrognathia (i.e., smallness of the jaw).

- Most affected individuals cannot become pregnant and may lack other secondary sex characteristics such as breast development.

- Affected individuals have a high rate of color blindness, short stature, chronic middle ear infections, kidney and urinary tract abnormalities, and coarctation of the aorta (i.e., malformation causing narrowing of the main outflow artery of the heart).

- Abnormalities of the earlobes are associated with progressive sensorineural hearing loss in the second decade of life.

Incidence or Prevalence

- 1 in 2,500 to 1 in 5,000 live female births; a common cause of miscarriages

Genotype or Cause

- Turner syndrome is a genetic condition specific to females caused by loss of one or part of one X chromosome. The missing or defective chromosome is often the paternal X.

Functional and Behavioral Characteristics

- Intelligence is typically in the normal to low range, with developmental disability occurring in fewer than 10% of those affected.

- Affected individuals may have attention-deficit/hyperactivity disorder, poor right-left directionality, impaired social cognition and low self-esteem, increased risk of depression and anorexia nervosa, dysgraphia (i.e., inability to write properly), dyscalculia (i.e., math inability), problems with visual-spatial organization (e.g., impaired shape copying), and psychomotor delays or disabilities.

Interventions, Supports, and Services

- Growth hormone, either alone or with a low dose of androgen, will increase growth velocity and probably also final adult height.

- Estrogen replacement therapy (ERT) will promote development of secondary sexual characteristics and help to maintain good tissue and bone integrity. ERT has been associated with a risk of breast cancer and blood clots, among other problems.

- Reproductive technologies may help women with Turner syndrome become pregnant (a donor egg can be used to create an embryo, which is carried by the woman with Turner syndrome).

- Hypertension in adulthood may need treatment.

- Psychiatric symptoms may be decreased by medical and psychological treatments for short stature and ovarian impairments.

- New information is ideally presented verbally to affected individuals.

- Affected individuals have a normal life expectancy

Williams Syndrome

Williams syndrome was first identified by New Zealand cardiologist J. C. P. Williams and colleagues in 1961 on the basis of a pattern of cardiovascular anomalies. In 1978, the syndrome was recognized to include specific heart defects (in about 80% of cases), developmental disabilities, and unusual facial features. Williams syndrome has a sporadic or autosomal dominant mode of inheritance.

Physical Characteristics

- Facial features: a broad forehead, medial eyebrow flare, depressed nasal bridge, star-like pattern in the iris, wide-spaced teeth, and full lips; face frequently described as "elfin-like"

- Low birth weight; growth delay; mild microcephaly (i.e., small head)

- Renal and cardiovascular irregularities

- Difficulties in feeding, digestion, constipation, and failure to thrive in infancy

- Hypertension (i.e., high blood pressure); supravalvular aortic stenosis (i.e., narrowing or stricture above the aortic heart valve); pulmonary stenosis (i.e., narrowing or stricture of the pulmonary heart valve); hypercalcemia (i.e., elevated calcium in the blood) with increased urination and water intake

- Possible urethral stenosis (i.e., narrowing of the ureter, the canal through which urine is carried out of the body from the bladder) and bladder diverticula (i.e., pouches in the bladder)

- Commonly, contractures (i.e., shortening of muscles or ligaments) in the legs

- High frequency of middle ear infections

Incidence or Prevalence

- 1 in 20,000 to 1 in 50,000 live births

Genotype or Cause

- Microdeletions on chromosome 7 that include about 20 genes are present.

- A submicroscopic deletion of variable size on chromosome band 7q11.23, that includes the elastin gene, is present in 95%–98% of affected individuals.

Functional and Behavioral Characteristics

- Developmental delays; severe cognitive impairment to average cognitive ability

- Auditory sensitivity

- Affected individuals have an increased risk of anxiety and attention-deficit/hyperactivity disorder.

- Despite lower overall mental age and visuospatial functioning, higher level language abilities are evident; those affected display "cocktail party speech."

- Emotional and behavioral difficulties can include irritability, poor concentration, temper tantrums, overactivity, eating difficulties, poor peer relationships, and sleep disturbances.

- Inappropriate attention-seeking behavior is displayed.

- Affected children show lack of social constraints (e.g., friendliness toward adults, including strangers).

Interventions, Supports, and Services

- Children respond better to verbal teaching methods.

- Early speech, language, and occupational therapy are indicated.

- Sociability needs to be appropriately directed (i.e., there is risk of exploitation due to affected individuals' friendly nature).

- Individuals and families may require help from mental health professionals.

- Most affected adults live and work in supervised settings.

- Life expectancy may be lessened if congenital heart disease is present.

OTHER CONDITIONS: GROUP 2

In this third main section, the conditions featured in Group 2 of Table 21.1 are listed alphabetically.

Congenital Hypothyroidism from Iodine Deficiency

The most common cause of preventable intellectual disability worldwide is iodine deficiency in pregnant women. This causes iodine deficiency in the fetus. Negative effects of severe iodine deficiency in pregnant women on their offspring have long been known, but there also are effects from moderate and mild iodine deficiency. Outcomes vary depending on when during pregnancy maternal hypothyroidism has occurred. Iodine deficiency is associated with lack of iodine in the soil in certain geographical regions of the world. Effects from iodine deficiency can be exacerbated by deficiencies

in certain other nutrients (e.g., iron, selenium, zinc, vitamin A). In quite a number of countries, effects of iodine deficiency are being counteracted by the addition of iodine to salt. See Chapter 13 for additional information

Characteristics

- From transient maternal hypothyroidism early in pregnancy: neurologic cretinism (intellectual disability, deaf-mutism, and gait disturbances but not hypothyroidism)

- From maternal hypothyroidism late in pregnancy: myxedematous cretinism (intellectual disability, short stature, and hypothyroidism)

- Growth failure

- Increased susceptibility of the thyroid gland to ionizing radiation

Incidence or Prevalence

- In 1990, 11.2 million people (28.9 % of the world population) were affected by overt cretinism and another 43 million people were affected by some degree of cognitive impairment (Eastman & Zimmermann, 2014).

- Iodine deficiency is particularly common in certain regions of Europe, the East Mediterranean, Africa, and Southeast Asia.

- Although salt is supplemented with iodine in North America, approximately one third of pregnant women in the United States are iodine deficient.

Causes

- Inadequate iodine in food

Functional and Behavioral Characteristics

- Intellectual disability

- Hearing impairment

- Low scores of verbal IQ, reading comprehension, and reading accuracy

- Various neurological problems

Interventions, Supports, and Services

- Test pregnant women, nursing mothers, neonates, and others for iodine deficiency.

- In cases of deficiency in mothers and infants, ensure that iodine nutrition is optimal.

- To prevent iodine deficiency, aim for intervention at the community level rather than at the personal level.

Congenital Rubella Syndrome

Rubella is a viral infection that affects the fetus but causes only a minor fever and rash in the mother. Early work on rubella was done by German and French scientists, and hence it is known as German measles and French measles. In 1941, Normann Gregg, an Australian ophthalmologist, observed that large numbers of cataracts and other birth defects in children occurred right after rubella outbreaks. Between 1964 and 1965, there was a worldwide epidemic of rubella. Pregnant women who contracted rubella in the first trimester of their pregnancy passed the rubella virus to their developing fetus, causing the child to be born with intellectual disability, developmental disability, or both, and other health problems. In the U.S. epidemic, approximately 20,000 children were born with two or more of the symptoms listed in the following subsection, which came to be known as congenital rubella syndrome (CRS).

Physical Characteristics

- Affected individuals display the following characteristics:

  - Central nervous system disorders, specifically microcephaly (i.e., small head) and developmental disabilities

  - Hearing impairment

  - Visual impairment, typically cataract (i.e., clouding of the eye lens), glaucoma (i.e., increased pressure within the eyeball), or chorioretinitis (i.e., inflammation of the choroid and the retina, two layers of the eye)

  - Congenital heart disease; patent ductus arteriosus (i.e., abnormal, persistent opening of a blood vessel between the outflow of the heart and the lungs after birth)

- Affected children can develop additional medical problems as they get older; glaucoma and diabetes (high blood sugar) are two of the most common late-onset manifestations.

Incidence or Prevalence

- A serious problem in some countries; rare in vaccinated areas; 100,000 cases per year worldwide

Genotype or Cause

- Immature blood–brain barrier and absence of antibodies to rubella may predispose an individual to rubella infection of the central nervous system.

- Ability to make antibodies to rubella is affected by the human leukocyte antigen type (i.e., a type of genetic marker on white blood cells).

Functional and Behavioral Characteristics

- Developmental disabilities are evident.

- In a pioneering study of 243 children with CRS, 15% had reactive bad behavior disorder and 7% had autism (Chess, 1971). Although vaccination has reduced the prevalence of CRS, vaccines are not given worldwide, and rubella may still cause autism (Hutton, 2016).

Interventions, Supports, and Services

- Primary preventive action is immunization between 9 and 15 months of age; women of childbearing age should be vaccinated and should avoid pregnancy for at least 28 days after immunization.

- A number of rubella vaccines are available, either as single antigen vaccines or combined with either measles vaccine (MR), mumps vaccine, or with measles and mumps vaccine (MMR); in most countries, the vaccine is given as MR or MMR.

Developmental Coordination Disorder

The term *developmental coordination disorder (DCD)* is used to describe children who exhibit difficulties in activities that require motor coordination, such as playing ball, writing, or tying shoelaces. DCD was introduced into the American Psychiatric Association's *Diagnostic and Statistical Manual of Mental Disorders, Third Edition, Revised (DSM-III-R)*, in 1987. Previous terminology was not consistent; DCD has also been referred to as developmental dyspraxia, sensorimotor dysfunction, perceptual-motor problem, minor neurological dysfunction, minimal brain dysfunction, and "clumsiness."

Physical Characteristics

- Characteristics of DCD include motor coordination during performance that is below that expected on the basis of age or measured intelligence, as well as motor coordination impairments that interfere with academic achievement and activities of daily living and that are not due to other neurological disorders such as cerebral palsy, hemiplegia, or muscular dystrophy.

Incidence or Prevalence

- 5%–6% in school-age children; more frequent in males than in females

Genotype or Cause

- The cause is unknown; hypotheses include atypical brain development, abnormal fatty acid metabolism, and the same risk factors that result in cerebral palsy.

Functional and Behavioral Characteristics

- There is variability of expression in perceptual and motor characteristics; children may have any or all of the following impairments:

  - Poor balance and control of distal movements during fine- and gross-motor tasks including writing, dressing, catching, or kicking a ball

  - Delayed motor development: sitting, crawling, walking

  - Increased reliance on visual information

  - Difficulties with motor imagery, visual memory, and learning new skills

  - Lower levels of academic skills (e.g., writing, reading, spelling, mathematics) compared with other children of the same age

  - Decreased social skills; lack of confidence

  - Attention-deficit disorder or attention-deficit /hyperactivity disorder in 41% of affected individuals

- Learning disability, such as dyslexia, in 38% of individuals

Interventions, Supports, and Services

- Affected individuals benefit from physical education, occupational therapy, and a life-course approach (i.e., physical and skills training along with classes that teach how to become an advocate for all individuals with disabilities).

- The intervention must be tailored individually to each child.

- Most interventions (e.g., sensory integration intervention, process-oriented treatment, perceptual motor training, and task-specific training) do not generalize to other tasks.

- Cognitive approaches have used a problem-solving framework, although this approach is still being validated.

Hypoxic-Ischemic Encephalopathy/ Neonatal Encephalopathy

Hypoxic-ischemic encephalopathy (HIE), also known as neonatal encephalopathy (NE), is an acquired clinical neurologic syndrome that involves acute brain injury due to asphyxia (i.e., insufficient oxygen availability). HIE is usually caused by hypoxia (i.e., subnormal oxygen concentration) of the brain as well as ischemia (i.e., inadequate blood supply) to the brain resulting from systemic hypoxia and reduced cerebral blood flow. HIE accounts for 25% of full-term neonatal mortality, and in cases of severe HIE, 50% of affected infants die. HIE is the most common cause of intellectual disability, learning disability, and the disability associated with chronic motor function in cerebral palsy; it is also a cause of epilepsy, behavior problems, and other intellectual impairments. The outcome of HIE is not always predictable from the severity of the injury. The damage associated with HIE includes neuronal death (necrosis) in the region (called the infarct) affected by shifting of metabolism from aerobic to anaerobic. The process of cellular destruction in infants is faster than in adults (1–2 hours vs. 1–2 days). Identification of HIE as soon as possible is paramount, especially in infants, as the therapeutic window is small. In cases in which people with severe HIE survive, 80% suffer serious complications and 10% will be normal.

Physical Characteristics

- The following must be present for diagnosis of HIE in a newborn:

    - Low pH (pH < 7) of umbilical artery blood

    - An Apgar score (i.e., a numbered rating of newborns, based on heart rate, skin color, breathing, response to stimulus, and muscle tone; a score of 10 means the infant is robust) of 0–3 for more than 5 minutes

    - Neurological symptoms such as seizures, coma, and hypotonia

    - Multiple organ involvement (e.g., kidney, lungs, liver, heart)

Incidence or Prevalence

- 1–4 in 1,000 live births in the United States

- Much higher prevalence in developing countries

- Affects males and females equally

Genotype or Cause

- Prolonged partial asphyxia due to disturbances in cerebral blood flow

- Brief intrapartum events leading to asphyxia such as placental abruption

Functional and Behavioral Characteristics

Mild HIE

- Muscle tone increases slightly and deep tendon reflexes are brisk.

- Transient behavioral abnormalities (e.g., poor feeding, irritability) are observed.

- By 3 to 4 days, central nervous system examination findings are normal.

Moderately Severe HIE

- Affected individuals display lethargia (drowsiness) with significant hypotonia and diminished deep tendon reflexes.

- Grasping, sucking, and Moro reflexes are sluggish or absent. (The Moro reflex is a normal reflex for infant when they are startled or feel like they are falling. An infant will have a "startled" look and the arms will fling out sideways with the palms up and the thumbs flexed.)

- Occasional periods of apnea (temporary breathing stoppage) occur.

- Seizures occur within first 24 hours of the hypoxic period.

- An initial period of well-being is followed by sudden deterioration or an increase in intensity of seizures.

Severe HIE

- Stupor or coma

- Irregular breathing; ventilatory support may be needed

- Generalized hypotonia and depressed deep tendon reflexes

- Neonatal reflexes absent; disturbances of eye motion—dilated, fixed, or poor reaction of pupils to light

- Increased frequency of seizures 2–3 days after their onset

- Irregular heartbeat and blood pressure

Interventions, Supports, and Services

- The 1–2 hour time frame after birth is critical for successful intervention.

- There is no uniform standard of care.

- Neurological assessment and treatment of seizures is essential; imaging is used, but there is concern that computed tomography scans may damage the brain.

- Ventilation, perfusion, and metabolic status are maintained.

- Hypoxia as well as hypercapnia (i.e., too much carbon dioxide in the blood) and hypocapnia (i.e., too little carbon dioxide in the blood) are prevented.

- Blood gases are maintained (by intubation and artificial ventilation) as well as acid–base status. In some cases, compensation by the lungs or kidneys is adequate to bring the pH imbalance under control.

- Mean blood pressure is maintained above 35 mm Hg with medications.

- Focal cooling of the brain by 3° to 6° C reduces the extent of tissue injury.

- Neurological functioning is evaluated.

Intraventricular Hemorrhage

The name of this syndrome describes the disease: *Intraventricular hemorrhage* (IVH) refers to bleeding from fragile blood vessels in the brain into the brain ventricles (i.e., the cavities in the brain through which the cerebrospinal fluid flows). Bleeding in the brain puts pressure on nerve cells and can damage them. Severe damage to nerve cells results in brain injury. IVH is most common in premature infants; the smaller and more premature the infant, the greater the risk of IVH. Most cases of IVH occur within the first 3 days of life, but cases in adults have been reported.

Physical Characteristics

- Apnea (i.e., temporary stoppage of breathing) and bradycardia (i.e., slow heart rate)

- Pale or blue coloring (cyanosis)

- Weak suck

- High-pitched cry

- Seizures

- Swelling or bulging of the fontanelles (the "soft spots" between the bones of the infant's head)

- Anemia (i.e., a low number of red blood cells in peripheral circulation)

- IVH is graded from 1 to 4 according to the severity of the bleeding; small amounts of bleeding (Grades 1–2) do not usually cause any long-term damage; Grades 3–4 cause long-term problems such as hydrocephalus (i.e., blockage of the circulation system for cerebrospinal fluid)

Incidence or Prevalence

- IVH accounts for 3%–10% of all intracerebral hemorrhages in the United States.

- IVH occurs in up to 50% of infants with very low birth weight (under 1,500 g) or less than 35 weeks of gestation in the United States.

- There is no evidence that prevalence is different in males and females.

Genotype or Cause

- No genetic link has been proved.

- IVH can result from head trauma; insertion or removal of a ventricular catheter (used to drain fluid from the ventricles); intraventricular vas-cular malformation; aneurysm (i.e., bulging in the wall of a blood vessel); tumor; hypertension; or conditions predisposing to bleeding.

- Other causes include rapid ventricle volume expansion, asynchrony between mechanically delivered and spontaneous breaths in infants on ventilators, hypertension or beat-to-beat blood pressure changes, blood clotting disorders, oxygen deficiency and/or poor blood flow to the brain, respiratory disturbances, acidosis (i.e., too much blood acid), infusions of hypertonic solution (e.g., sodium bicarbonate), anemia, vacuum-assisted delivery, frequent handling, and tracheal suctioning (to remove mucus from windpipe).

Functional and Behavioral Characteristics

- For Grade 1 and 2 hemorrhages, prognosis is good; neurodevelopment is slightly hindered compared with typical infants.

- For Grade 3 hemorrhage without white matter disease (i.e., disease characterized by demyelination), mortality is less than 10%; cognitive or motor disorder is 30%–40%.

- For Grade 4, mortality approaches 80%–90%; severe neurological sequelae include cognitive and motor disturbances.

Interventions, Supports, and Services

- For adults, treatment involves ventricular drainage and administration of recombinant tissue plasminogen activator to remove the blood clots.

- Treatment of infants involves supportive care for cardiovascular, respiratory, or neurological complications, including treatment of lung conditions and infections; blood transfusions; seizure treatment; and treatment for hydrocephalus by spinal taps (i.e., placement of a needle into the spinal canal to remove fluid) or surgical placement of tubes into the ventricles for draining of excess fluid, or in severe cases, permanent placement of a ventricular-peritoneal shunt to drain fluid from the ventricle to the abdominal cavity (where it is absorbed) or directly to the circulation.

- Giving a pregnant woman corticosteroids before a birth that is expected to be premature reduces the risk of IVH in the baby.

Meningitis
(Particularly Bacterial Meningitis)

Meningitis is an infection of the meninges (membranes surrounding the brain) and the fluid surrounding the brain and spinal cord. There are two types of this disease: viral meningitis and bacterial meningitis. In general, viral meningitis is less severe and can resolve without treatment, whereas bacterial meningitis can be quite serious and may result in brain damage, learning disability, and even death. More than 50 types of bacteria can cause meningitis, and the causative agent changes with age. The bacteria responsible for the majority of meningitis cases are *Neisseria meningitidis, Haemophilus influenzae* type b, and *Streptococcus pneumoniae*. The information presented in the following subsections pertains, for the most part, to bacterial meningitis.

Physical Characteristics

- Symptoms include high fever, headache, stiff neck, nausea, and vomiting; approximately one third of children have seizure activity; a red or purple rash caused by meningococcal bacteria is present in 75% of cases.

- Symptoms persist for hours to days and worsen with time.

Incidence or Prevalence

- In industrialized countries, as many as 13 in 100,000 people are affected yearly.

- In developing countries, meningitis outbreaks are more common.

Genotype or Cause

- There is no genetic predisposition to meningitis; however, certain conditions such as immunodeficiency and deafness are correlated with the disease.

- Meningitis often occurs secondary to a bacterial infection in another part of the body such as the respiratory tract, urinary tract, or the ear. The disease is contagious and can be spread by contact, particularly through body fluids from an infected person such as discharges from the nose and throat.

Functional and Behavioral Characteristics

- Infants show increasing distress when held and rocked.

- Patient appears disoriented and drowsy.

- If the disease is not treated directly, serious complications may result, including intellectual disability; epilepsy; visual, speech, and hearing disabilities; cognitive impairment; and death.

Interventions, Supports, and Services

- Many forms of meningitis can be prevented by vaccination.

- The utility of antibiotics is dependent on early diagnosis.

- The treatments for any ensuing complications are varied and specific to each case (e.g., anticonvulsants for seizure activity).

Pediatric Stroke

Pediatric patients (including neonates, infants, and adolescents) can suffer stroke—the sudden occlusion or rupture of cerebral arteries or veins resulting in focal cerebral damage and clinical neurological deficits. There are two types of stroke: hemorrhagic stroke and ischemic stroke. Hemorrhagic stroke occurs when a blood vessel bursts inside the brain; the brain is very sensitive to bleeding. Damage occurs very rapidly because of the blood itself or because of increased fluid pressure on the brain trapped against the skull. Ischemic stroke occurs when blood supply is reduced to a part of the brain due to occlusion of a blood vessel. In arterial ischemic stroke (AIS), occlusion in the artery is usually due to thromboembolism (i.e., a blood clot forms, breaks off, and travels through the bloodstream to another part of the body), which results in an infarct (i.e., a localized area of ischemic necrosis usually caused by vascular blockage). Neonates (infants younger than 28 days of age) make up 25% of pediatric AIS patients. Hemorrhagic stroke is less common but more frequently fatal than ischemic stroke. As a result, the majority of information presented in this section pertains to AIS. Pediatric stroke is largely an understudied condition.

Physical Characteristics
Neonates

- Presence of seizures, lethargy, or decreased consciousness

Older Infants and Children

- Acute focal neurological deficit—usually motor, speech, or visual—as well as one or more of the following:

- Weakness or inability to move a body part; numbness or loss of sensation

- Decreased or lost vision (may be partial)

- Speech difficulties

- Inability to recognize or identify familiar things

- Sudden headache; dizziness; loss of coordination

- Vertigo (sensation of one's surroundings spinning around)

- Swallowing difficulties

- Sleepy, stuporous, lethargic, comatose, or unconscious

Incidence or Prevalence

- From 2.3 cases per 100,000 per year (1.2 for ischemic stroke and 1.1 for hemorrhagic stroke) up to more than 8 cases per 100,000 per year

- More males are affected than females

Genotype or Cause

- Causes of hemorrhagic stroke in children include an artery malformation or disorder; a brain tumor; in rare cases, drug or alcohol abuse by the mother.

- Leading risk factors for ischemic stroke in children include heart disease (congenital and acquired); blood clotting disorders; illnesses and disorders that lead to blood clotting abnormalities including meningitis, sepsis, diarrhea, dehydration, and iron deficiency; and irregular arteries. Examples of congenital heart disease include ventricular or atrial septal defect (i.e., incomplete closure between walls of the heart), patent ductus arteriosus (i.e., failure of the ductus arteriosus to close), aortic or mitral stenosis (i.e., closure or narrowing of the valve openings). Examples of acquired heart disease include rheumatic heart disease, infection of a prosthetic heart valve, bacterial endocarditis (i.e., infection of a valve), arrhythmia, and other conditions.

- Some pediatric stroke cases have no known cause.

In about half the children with first-ever arterial ischemic strokes, the following genetic disorders predispose:

- Sickle cell disease, an autosomal recessive disorder of red blood cells that confers resistance to malaria

- Homocystinuria, an autosomal recessive amino acid disorder caused primarily by a deficiency in cystathionine

- Fabry disease, one of several disorders called lysosomal storage disorders

- Progeria, a rare disorder that accelerates the aging process about sevenfold

- Neurofibromatosis (see the section earlier in this chapter)

- Coagulation disorders: Factor V Leiden (the most common inherited blood abnormality that results in blood clots); activated protein C resistance (a condition that occurs in patients with the Factor V mutation)

Other risk factors for pediatric stroke include the following:

- Heart or brain surgery

- Systemic vascular disease: systemic hypertension, volume depletion or systemic hypotension, diabetes, and other conditions

- Vasculitis (i.e., inflammation of blood vessels—e.g., as the result of meningitis or systemic infection)

- Autoimmune disorders affecting the arteries (e.g., systemic lupus erythematosus, a chronic inflammatory disorder of connective tissue) and other conditions

- Vasculopathies (any disorder of blood vessels)

- Vasospastic disorders resulting from ergot (fungal parasite in the heads of grains) poisoning or nitric oxide poisoning

- Hematologic disorders and coagulopathies (e.g., leukemia, vitamin K deficiency, congenital coagulation defects)

- Structural abnormalities of the cerebrovascular system

- Trauma, especially to the brain or neck (e.g., child abuse, obstruction of a blood vessel by a blood clot, air bubble, fat deposit, other foreign substance, penetrating intracranial trauma)

Functional and Behavioral Characteristics

Poststroke, a wide range of behaviors and functional impairments have been reported, depending on the location of the infarct in the brain:

- Long-term neurological deficits after childhood AIS in 60%–85% of cases

- The most frequent neurological impairment is hemiparesis (one-sided weakness); other residual issues include speech, learning, and behavior problems.

Interventions, Supports, and Services

- No clinical trials have been completed in pediatric stroke; treatment is experimental.

- Initial strategies for AIS aim to reduce the size of the infarct.

- For older children, antithrombotic agents (e.g., antiplatelet drugs—such as aspirin—that prevent platelets from clumping) and anticoagulants (e.g., heparin, warfarin) prevent new blood clots from forming or existing clots from enlarging, and reduce the 20%–30% risk of recurrence of AIS.

- Rehabilitation; school reintegration

- Neuropsychology, occupational therapy, and physiotherapy

- Drug therapy: aspirin, anticoagulants

Shaken Baby Syndrome/ Abusive Head Trauma

Head injuries are the leading cause of traumatic death and the leading cause of child abuse fatalities. The term "whiplash shaken baby syndrome" was made popular in 1972 by a pediatric radiologist, John Caffey. Shaken baby syndrome (SBS) refers to a cluster of clinical findings in infants, including retinal hemorrhages, subdural and subarachnoid hemorrhages, and little or no evidence of external cranial trauma. The act of shaking leading to SBS is recognized as violent and likely to inflict serious injury or death. Of note is that although traumatic brain injuries can result from shaking events provoked by an infant's crying, these also can result from other causes (e.g., falls or mauling by a pet animal). In 2009, the American Academy of Pediatrics decided

that SBS should be called "abusive head trauma" to reflect the new understanding of the condition. Advances in neuroimaging, computed tomography scans, and magnetic resonance imaging have been helpful in detailing the extent of intracranial injury, directing neurosurgical intervention, and determining when injuries occurred.

Physical Characteristics

- A triad of symptoms—retinal hemorrhage, subdural hematoma (and/or subarachnoid hemorrhage), and acute encephalopathy are characteristic of SBS, but these do not prove that injury was caused by shaking.

- The symptoms usually occur in the absence of any external trauma to the head, face, and neck and with inadequate history or report by caregiver.

Incidence or Prevalence

- An estimated 50,000 cases occur each year in the United States.

- Victims range in age from a few days to 5 years (average 6–8 months)

- SBS is the leading cause of death in children less than 4 years in the United States.

Genotype or Cause

- Vigorous shaking of an infant by the arms, legs, chest, or shoulders such that the brain rotates more than the surrounding skull and dura.

- Angular deceleration forces exceed those found in routine play or falls.

- Males tend to predominate as the perpetrators in 65%–90% of cases.

Functional and Behavioral Characteristics

- Less severe cases include vomiting, poor feeding, lethargy or irritability, hypothermia, increased sleeping, difficulty arousing, failure to vocalize.

- More severe cases include seizures, apnea (transient cessation of respiration), bradycardia (relatively slow heart action), and complete cardiovascular collapse.

Interventions, Supports, and Services

- To treat a victim, interdisciplinary intervention by clinical teams and community programs is imperative and costly.

- Effective prevention strategies include increasing public awareness regarding the consequences of shaking a child and educating healthcare professionals to identify infants at high risk for abuse.

Traumatic Brain Injury

Traumatic brain injury (TBI) occurs as a result of either direct or indirect forces to the brain matter and is divided into two phases of injury. The primary phase includes damage to the brain and its structures as a direct result of the force of the injury. The secondary phase consists of a cascade of physiological, cellular, and molecular events that exacerbate the primary injury to neurons and worsen the neurological outcome of patients suffering from TBI. Structures that may be damaged during the primary phase of injury include the skull, the frontal and temporal lobes, nerve cells in the brain's connecting nerve fibers, and the cerebral vasculature. Tissues and cells that are affected by the secondary phase include all cells and tissue types in the brain.

Physical Characteristics

- Abnormalities in the brain anatomy following a TBI include edema (i.e., swelling of the brain), hematomas (i.e., bruising of the tissue), diffuse axonal injury lesions, various types of hemorrhages, as well as neuronal death in deep areas of the brain from lack of oxygen.

Incidence or Prevalence

- Each year, more than 1.6 million people in North America sustain TBIs resulting in 80,000 severe neurological disabilities and 52,000 deaths.

Genotype or Cause

- Falls; bicycle, sports, and motor vehicle accidents

- Direct or indirect forces that cause direct or indirect injury, respectively. Direct injury is immediate and results from the force of an object striking or penetrating the head. Indirect injury results from acceleration or deceleration generated by movements of areas of the brain against one another, and impact of the brain against the skull.

Functional and Behavioral Characteristics

- TBI patients can have psychiatric symptoms including amnesia; headaches; confusion; dizziness; blurred vision; fatigue or lethargy; a change in sleep patterns, behavior, and mood; and attention deficit.

- Moderate or severe TBI patients experience repeated vomiting or nausea, convulsions, slurred speech, weakness or numbness in the extremities, and loss of coordination.

- Permanent disabilities associated with TBI can include problems with cognition, communication, sensory processing, behavior, or mental health. Long-term complications associated with TBI include Alzheimer's and Parkinson's diseases, posttraumatic dementia or epilepsy, stroke, and dysfunction of the autonomic nervous system.

Interventions, Supports, and Services

- In addition to rehabilitation, successful intervention requires the support and patience of family members, society, and clinicians.

- For children, more extensive approaches include school-based behavioral treatments, teaching, and reinforcement of metacognitive thinking strategies.

SUMMARY

This chapter has served as a guide to basic information about more than 30 syndromes and conditions associated with intellectual and developmental disabilities not covered in other chapters. For each, the chapter presented background (historical) information; physical and behavioral characteristics; prevalence or incidence; causes; and applicable interventions, services, and supports.

GENERAL REFERENCES

Accardo, P.J. (Ed.). (2007a). *Capute and Accardo's neurodevelopmental disabilities in infancy and childhood: Vol. 1. Neurodevelopmental diagnosis and treatment.* (3rd ed.). Baltimore, MD: Paul H. Brookes Publishing Co.

Accardo, P.J. (Ed.). (2007b). *Capute and Accardo's neurodevelopmental disabilities in infancy and childhood: Vol. 2. The spectrum of neurodevelopmental disabilities.* (3rd ed.). Baltimore, MD: Paul H. Brookes Publishing Co.

Accardo, P.J., Whitman, B.Y., Accardo, J.A., Bodurtha, J.N., Farrell, A., Goelz, T.,...Smith, G.J. (2011). *Dictionary of developmental disabilities terminology* (3rd ed.). Baltimore, MD: Paul H. Brookes Publishing Co.

American Psychological Association. (2016). *PsycINFO.* Retrieved from http://www.apa.org/pubs/databases/psycinfo/

Batshaw, M.L., Roizen, N.J., & Lotrecchiano, G.R. (Eds.). (2013). *Children with disabilities* (7th ed.) Baltimore, MD: Paul H. Brookes Publishing Co.

Grasberger, H., & Refetoff, S. (2011). Genetic causes of congenital hypothyroidism due to dyshormonogenesis. *Current Opinion in Pediatrics, 23*(4), 421–428.

Inserm. (2016). *Orphanet encyclopedia.* Retrieved from http://www.orpha.net/consor/cgi-bin/Disease_Search.php?lng=EN

Johns Hopkins University. (2016, January 8). *Online Mendelian inheritance in man (OMIM).* Retrieved from http://www.omim.org/

Jones, K.L., Jones, M.C., & Del Campo, M. (2013). *Smith's recognizable patterns of human malformation* (7th ed.). Philadelphia, PA: Elsevier Saunders.

Jung, J.H. (2010). *Genetic syndromes in communication disorders* (2nd ed.). Austin, TX: Pro-Ed.

MacLennan, A.H., Thompson, S.C., & Gecz, J. (2015). Cerebral palsy: Causes, pathways, and the role of genetic variants. *American Journal of Obstetrics and Gynecology, 213*(6), 779–788.

Matson, J.L., & Matson, M.L. (Eds.). (2015). *Comorbid conditions in individuals with intellectual disabilities.* Basel, Switzerland: Springer International.

National Center for Biotechnology Information. (n.d.). *PubMed.* Retrieved from http://www.ncbi.nlm.nih.gov/pubmed

National Institute of Neurological Diseases and Stroke. (n.d.). *Disorder index.* Retrieved from http://www.ninds.nih.gov/disorders/disorder_index.htm

Penn State Hershey, George T. Harrell Health Sciences Library. (2016, January 4). *Clinical information resources and evidence-based practice.* Retrieved from http://harrell.library.psu.edu/c.php?g=344586&p=2321221

Percy, M., Cheetham, T., Gitta, M., Morrison, B., Machalek, B., Bega, S.,...Yum, J. (2007). Other syndromes and disorders associated with intellectual and developmental disabilities. In I. Brown & M. Percy (Eds.), *A comprehensive guide to intellectual and developmental disabilities* (pp. 229–267). Baltimore, MD: Paul H. Brookes Publishing Co.

Rubin, I.L., & Crocker, A.C. (Eds.). (2006). *Medical care for children and adults with developmental disabilities* (2nd ed.). Baltimore, MD: Paul H. Brookes Publishing Co.

Shapiro, B.K., & Accardo, P.J. (Eds.). (2010). *Neurogenetic syndromes: Behavioral issues and their treatment.* Baltimore, MD: Paul H. Brookes Publishing Co.

Szinnai, G. (2014). Clinical genetics of congenital hypothyroidism. *Endocrine Development, 26,* 60–78.

University of Utah Learn.Genetics. (2016). *Genetic disorders.* Retrieved from http://learn.genetics.utah.edu/content/disorders/

U.S. National Library of Medicine MedlinePlus. (2015, January 7). *Medical encyclopedia.* Retrieved from https://www.nlm.nih.gov/medlineplus/encyclopedia.html

Valle, D., Beaudet, A.L., Vogelstein, B., Kinzler, K.W., Antonarakis, S.E., Ballabio, A.,...Mitchell, G. (n.d.). *The online metabolic and molecular bases of inherited diseases (OMMBID).* Retrieved from http://www.ommbid.com/book.aspx?bookid=971

Whonamedit. (2016). *A dictionary of medical eponyms.* Retrieved from http://www.whonamedit.com/

REFERENCES FOR THE FEATURED SYNDROMES AND CONDITIONS

Angelman Syndrome

Margolis, S.S., Sell, G.L., Zbinden, M.A., & Bird, L.M. (2015). Angelman syndrome. *Neurotherapeutics, 12*(3), 641–650.

National Institute of Neurological Diseases and Stroke. (2011, October 7). *NINDS Angelman syndrome information page.* Retrieved from http://www.ninds.nih.gov/disorders/angelman/angelman.htm

Williams, C.A. (2010). The behavioral phenotype of the Angelman syndrome. *American Journal of Medical Genetics C. Seminars in Medical Genetics, 154C*(4), 432–437.

Congenital Hypothyroidism

Bongers-Schokking, J.J., Resing, W.C., de Rijke, Y.B., de Ridder, M.A., & de Muinck Keizer-Schrama, S.M. (2013). Cognitive development in congenital hypothyroidism: Is overtreatment a greater threat than undertreatment? *Journal of Clinical Endocrinology and Metabolism, 98*(11), 4499–4506.

Eastman, C.J., & Zimmerman, M. (2014, February 12). *The iodine deficiency disorders.* Retrieved from http://www.thyroidmanager.org/chapter/the-iodine-deficiency-disorders/

National Institutes of Health, Genetics Home Reference. (2016, July 12). *Congenital hypothyroidism.* Retrieved from https://ghr.nlm.nih.gov/condition/congenital-hypothyroidism

Szinnai, G. (2014). Clinical genetics of congenital hypothyroidism. *Endocrine Development, 26,* 60–78.

Vitti, P. (2016, May 4). *Iodine deficiency disorders.* Retrieved from http://www.uptodate.com/contents/iodine-deficiency-disorders

Wassner, A.J., & Brown, R.S. (2015). Congenital hypothyroidism: Recent advances. *Current Opinion in Endocrinology, Diabetes and Obesity, 22*(5), 407–412.

Congenital Rubella Syndrome

Chess, S. (1971). Autism in children with congenital rubella. *Journal of Autism and Childhood Schizophrenia, 1*(1), 33–47.

Duzak, R.S. (2009). Congenital rubella syndrome—major review. *Optometry, 80*(1), 36–43.

Hutton, J. (2016, February 1). Does rubella cause autism: A 2015 reappraisal? *Frontiers in Human Neuroscience, 10*, 25. doi: 10.3389/fnhum.2016.00025

Lambert, N., Strebel, P., Orenstein, W., Icenogle, J., & Poland, G.A. (2015). Rubella. *Lancet. 385*(9984), 2297–2307.

U.S. National Library of Medicine MedlinePlus. (2016, July 7). *Congenital rubella.* Retrieved from http://www.nlm.nih.gov/medlineplus/ency/article/001658.htm

Cornelia de Lange or de Lange Syndrome

Boyle, M.I., Jespersgaard, C., Brøndum-Nielsen, K., Bisgaard, A.M., & Tümer, Z. (2015). Cornelia de Lange syndrome. *Clinical Genetics, 88*(1), 1–12.

Cornelia de Lange Syndrome Foundation. (2016). *About CdLS.* Retrieved from http://www.cdlsusa.org/what-is-cdls/index.htm

Liu, J., & Krantz, I.D. (2009). Cornelia de Lange syndrome, cohesin, and beyond. *Clinical Genetics, 76*(4), 303–314.

Cri-du-Chat Syndrome

Cerruti Mainardi, P. (2006). Cri du chat syndrome. *Orphanet Journal of Rare Diseases, 1*, 33.

Inserm. (2016, July 21). *Orphanet Encyclopedia: Monosomy 5p.* Retrieved from http://www.orpha.net/consor/cgi-bin/OC_Exp.php?lng=EN&Expert=281

Rodríguez-Caballero, A., Torres-Lagares, D., Rodríguez-Pérez, A., Serrera-Figallo, M.A., Hernández-Guisado, J.M., & Machuca-Portillo, G. (2010). Cri du chat syndrome: A critical review. *Medicina Oral, Patología Oral y Cirugía Bucal, 15*(3), e473–478.

Developmental Coordination Disorder

American Psychiatric Association. (1987). *Diagnostic and Statistical Manual of Mental Disorders* (3rd ed., rev.). Washington, DC: Author.

CanChild, Centre for Childhood Disability Research (Canada). (2016). *Developmental coordination disorder.* Retrieved from http://dcd.canchild.ca/en/

Gomez, A., & Sirigu, A. (2015). Developmental coordination disorder: Core sensori-motor deficits, neurobiology and etiology. *Neuropsychologia, 9*(Pt. B), 272–287.

Vaivre-Douret, L., Lalanne, C., Ingster-Moati, I., Boddaert, N., Cabrol, D., Dufier, J.L., & Falissard, B. (2011). Subtypes of developmental coordination disorder: Research on their nature and etiology. *Developmental Neuropsychology, 36*(5), 614–643.

Hunter Syndrome/ Mucopolysaccharidosis Type II

Beck, M. (2011). Mucopolysaccharidosis Type II (Hunter syndrome): Clinical picture and treatment. *Current Pharmaceutical Biotechnology, 12*(6), 861–866. doi:1389-2010/11

Raluy-Callado, M., Chen, W.H., Whiteman, D.A., Fang, J., & Wiklund, I. (2013). The impact of Hunter syndrome (mucopolysaccharidosis type II) on health-related quality of life. *Orphanet Journal of Rare Diseases, 8*, 101. doi:10.1186/1750-1172-8-101

U.S. National Library of Medicine MedlinePlus. (2016, July 7). *Hunter syndrome.* Retrieved from http://www.nlm.nih.gov/medlineplus/ency/article/001203.htm

Hurler/Hurler-Scheie/Scheie Syndrome/ Gargoylism/Mucopolysaccharidosis Type I

Muenzer, J., Wraith, J.E., & Clarke, L.A. (2009). International consensus panel on management and treatment of mucopolysaccharidosis I. Mucopolysaccharidosis I: Management and treatment guidelines. *Pediatrics, 123*(1), 19–29.

U.S. National Library of Medicine MedlinePlus. (2016, July 7). *Hurler syndrome.* Retrieved from http://www.nlm.nih.gov/medlineplus/ency/article/001204.htm

Wraith, J.E., & Jones, S. (2014). Mucopolysaccharidosis type I. *Pediatric Endocrinology Reviews, 12*(Suppl. 1), 102–106.

Hypoxic-Ischemic Encephalopathy/Neonatal Encephalopathy

Newborn Services Clinical Guideline. (2016, July 22). *Neonatal encephalopathy (NE).* Retrieved from http://www.adhb.govt.nz/newborn/guidelines/neurology/NE.htm

Sadler, L.C., Farquhar, C.M., Masson, V.L., & Battin, M.R., Neonatal Encephalopathy Working Group. (2015). Contributory factors and potentially avoidable neonatal encephalopathy associated with perinatal asphyxia. *American Journal of Obstetrics and Gynecology.* Advance online publication. doi:10.1016/j.ajog.2015.12.037

Zanelli, F. (2016). *Medscape: Hypoxic-ischemic encephalopathy.* Retrieved from http://emedicine.medscape.com/article/973501-overview

Intraventricular Hemorrhage

Adcock, L.M. (2016). *Management and complications of intraventricular hemorrhage in the newborn.* Retrieved from http://www.uptodate.com/contents/management-and-complications-of-intraventricular-hemorrhage-in-the-newborn

Annibale, D.J. (2014, March 19). *Medscape: Periventricular hemorrhage-intraventricular hemorrhage.* Retrieved from http://emedicine.medscape.com/article/976654-overview

U.S. National Library of Medicine MedlinePlus. (2015, December 2). *Intraventricular hemorrhage of the newborn.* Retrieved from http://www.nlm.nih.gov/medlineplus/ency/article/007301.htm

Klinefelter Syndrome

American Association for Klinefelter Syndrome Information and Support. (n.d.). *About.* Retrieved from http://www.aaksis.org/about.cfm

Giltay, J.C., & Maiburg, M.C. (2010). Klinefelter syndrome: Clinical and molecular aspects. *Expert Reviews of Molecular Diagnostics, 10*(6), 765–776.

Groth, K.A., Skakkebæk, A., Høst, C., Gravholt, C.H., & Bojesen, A. (2013). Clinical review: Klinefelter syndrome—a clinical update. *Journal of Clinical Endocrinology and Metabolism, 98*(1), 20–30.

Lesch-Nyhan Syndrome

Jinna, H.A. (2015, December 14). *Medscape: Lesch-Nyhan disease.* Retrieved from http://emedicine.medscape.com/article/1181356-overview

National Institute of Neurological Disorders and Stroke. (2007, February 13). *NINDS Lesch-Nyhan syndrome information page.* Retrieved from http://www.ninds.nih.gov/disorders/lesch_nyhan/lesch_nyhan.htm

Nyhan, W.L., O'Neill, J.P., Jinnah, H.A., & Harris, J.C. (2014, May 15). Lesch-Nyhan syndrome. *GeneReviews.* Retrieved from http://www.ncbi.nlm.nih.gov/books/NBK1149/

Mabry Syndrome/ Hyperphosphatasia Syndrome

Horn, D., Wieczorek, D., Metcalfe, K., Barić, I., Paležac, L., Cuk, M.,…Krawitz, P. (2014). Delineation of PIGV mutation spectrum and associated phenotypes in hyperphosphatasia with mental retardation syndrome. *European Journal of Human Genetics, 22*(6), 762–767.

Krawitz, P.M., Schweiger, M.R., Rödelsperger, C., Marcelis, C., Kölsch, U., Meisel, C.,…Robinson, P.N. (2010). Identity-by-descent filtering of exome sequence data identifies PIGV mutations in hyperphosphatasia mental retardation syndrome. *Nature Genetics, 42*(10), 827–829.

Thompson, M.D., Nezarati, M.M., Gillessen-Kaesbach, G., Meinecke, P., Mendoza-Londono, R., Mornet, E.,…Cole, D.E. (2010). Hyperphosphatasia with seizures, neurologic deficit, and characteristic facial features: Five new patients with Mabry syndrome. *American Journal of Medical Genetics A, 152A*(7), 1661–1669.

Meningitis

Centers for Disease Control and Prevention. (2016, June 29). *Meningitis.* Retrieved from http://www.cdc.gov/meningitis/index.html

Mann, K., & Jackson, M.A. (2008). Meningitis. *Pediatrics in Review, 29*(12), 1–2. Retrieved from http://pedsinreview.aappublications.org/content/29/12/417

World Health Organization. (2016). *Health topics: Meningitis.* Retrieved from http://www.who.int/topics/meningitis/en/

Neurofibromatosis

Evans, D.G.R. (2009). Neurofibromatosis type 2 (NF2): A clinical and molecular review. *Orphanet Journal of Rare Diseases, 4,* 16. doi:10.1186/1750-1172-4-16

Friedman, J. (2002). Neurofibromatosis 1: Clinical manifestations and diagnostic criteria. *Journal of Childhood Neurology, 17,* 548–554.

Hirbe, A.C., & Gutmann, D.H. (2014). Neurofibromatosis type 1: A multidisciplinary approach to care. *Lancet Neurology, 13*(8), 834–843.

Neuronal Migration Disorders

Kato, M. (2015). Genotype-phenotype correlation in neuronal migration disorders and cortical dysplasias. *Frontiers in Neuroscience, 9,* 181. doi:10.3389/fnins.2015.00181

Liu, J.S. (2011). Molecular genetics of neuronal migration disorders. *Current Neurology and Neuroscience Reports, 11*(2), 171–178.

National Institute of Neurological Disorders and Stroke. (2015, June 30). *NINDS Neuronal migration disorders information page.* Retrieved from http://www.ninds.nih.gov/disorders/neuronal_migration/neuronal_migration.htm

Noonan Syndrome

Jongmans, M., Sistermans, E.A., Rikken, A., Nillesen, W.M., Tamminga, R., Patton, M.,…van der Burgt, I. (2005). Genotypic and phenotypic characterization of Noonan syndrome: New data and review of the literature. *American Journal of Medical Genetics A, 134,* 165–170.

National Organization for Rare Disorders. (2016). *Noonan syndrome.* Retrieved from http://rarediseases.org/rare-diseases/noonan-syndrome/

Roberts, A.E., Allanson, J.E., Tartaglia, M., & Gelb, B.D. (2013). Noonan syndrome. *Lancet, 381*(9863), 333–342.

Pediatric Stroke

Kirton, A., & deVeber, G. (2015). Paediatric stroke: Pressing issues and promising directions. *Lancet Neurology, 14*(1), 92–102.

National Stroke Association. (2016). *Pediatric stroke.* Retrieved from http://www.stroke.org/site/PageServer?pagename=PEDSTROKE

Tsze, D.S., & Valente, J.H. (2011). Pediatric stroke: A review. *Emergency Medicine International 2011,* 734506. http://doi.org/10.1155/2011/734506

Phenylketonuria

MedlinePlus. (2016, January 8). *Phenylketonuria.* Retrieved from https://www.nlm.nih.gov/medlineplus/phenylketonuria.html

Mitchell, J.J. (2013, January 31). Phenylalanine hydroxylase deficiency. *GeneReviews.* Retrieved from http://www.ncbi.nlm.nih.gov/books/NBK1504/

Van Spronsen, F.J. (2010). Phenylketonuria: A 21st century perspective. *Nature Reviews Endocrinology, 6*(9), 509–514.

Prader-Willi Syndrome

Angulo, M.A., Butler, M.G., & Cataletto, M.E. (2015). Prader-Willi syndrome: A review of clinical, genetic, and endocrine findings. *Journal of Endocrinological Investigation, 38*(12), 1249–1263.

Cassidy, S.B., Schwartz, S., Miller, J.L., & Driscoll, D.J. (2012). Prader-Willi syndrome. *Genetics in Medicine, 14,* 10–26.

Prader-Willi Syndrome Association (U.S.A.). (n.d.). *About Prader-Willi syndrome.* Retrieved from http://www.pwsausa.org/about-pws/

Progressive Myoclonus Epilepsies

de Siqueira, L.F. (2010). Progressive myoclonic epilepsies: Review of clinical, molecular and therapeutic aspects. *Journal of Neurology, 257*(10), 1612–1619.

Malek, N., Stewart, W., & Greene, J. (2015). The progressive myoclonic epilepsies. *Practical Neurology, 15*(3), 164–171.

MedLink Neurology. (2016). *Progressive myoclonus epilepsies.* Retrieved from http://www.medlink.com/article/progressive_myoclonus_epilepsies

Rett Syndrome

Hagberg, B. (2002). *Clinical manifestations and stages of Rett syndrome.* Retrieved from http://www.rettsearch.org/Dataforms/files/RTT_Clinical_Rev_MRDDRev_8_61_02.pdf

Samaco, R.C., & Neul, J.L. (2011). Complexities of Rett syndrome and MeCP2. *Journal of Neuroscience, 31*(22), 7951–7959.

Schultz, R.J., & Glaze, D.G. (2016). *Rett syndrome.* Retrieved from http://www.uptodate.com/contents/rett-syndrome

U.S. National Library of Medicine. (2016, July 7). *Medline Plus: Rett syndrome.* Retrieved from http://www.nlm.nih.gov/medlineplus/ency/article/001536.htm

Sanfilippo Syndrome/ Mucopolysaccharidosis Type III

Andrade, F., Aldámiz-Echevarría, L., Llarena, M., & Couce, M.L. (2015). Sanfilippo syndrome: Overall review. *Pediatrics International, 57*(3), 331–338.

de Ruijter, J., Valstar, M.J., & Wijburg, F. (2011). Mucopolysaccharidosis type III (Sanfilippo syndrome): Emerging treatment strategies. *Current Pharmaceutical Biotechnology, 2*(6), 923–930.

National MPS Society. (2011). *MPS III.* Retrieved from http://mpssociety.org/mps/mps-iii/

Shaken Baby Syndrome/Abusive Head Trauma

Hinds, T., Shalaby-Rana, E., Jackson, A.M., & Khademian, Z. (2015). Aspects of abuse: Abusive head trauma. *Current Problems in Pediatric and Adolescent Health Care, 45*(3), 71–79.

National Institute of Neurological Disorders and Stroke. (2015, September 11). *NINDS shaken baby syndrome information page.* Retrieved from http://www.ninds.nih.gov/disorders/shakenbaby/shakenbaby.htm

Szalavitz, M. (2012, January 17). The shaky science of shaken baby syndrome. *Time Magazine.* Retrieved from http://healthland.time.com/2012/01/17/the-shaky-science-of-shaken-baby-syndrome/

Smith-Lemli-Opitz Syndrome

Bianconi, S.E., Cross, J.L., Wassif, C.A., & Porter, F.D. (2015). Pathogenesis, epidemiology, diagnosis and clinical aspects of Smith-Lemli-Opitz syndrome. *Expert Opinion on Orphan Drugs, 3*(3), 267–280.

Nowaczyk, M.J.M. (2013, June 20). Smith-Lemli-Opitz syndrome. *GeneReviews.* Retrieved from http://www.ncbi.nlm.nih.gov/books/NBK1143/

Smith-Lemli-Opitz/RSH Foundation. (n.d.). *Smith-Lemli-Opitz/RSH syndrome overview.* Retrieved from http://www.smithlemliopitz.org/smith-lemli-opitz-rsh-syndrome-overview/

Smith-Magenis Syndrome

PRISMS: Parents and Researchers Interested in Smith-Magenis Syndrome: *In-depth review.* (2016). Retrieved from http://www.prisms.org/index.php/us/what-is-sms/in-depth-review

Shelley, B.P., & Robertson, M.M. (2005). The neuropsychiatry and multisystem features of the Smith-Magenis syndrome: A review. *Journal of Neuropsychiatry and Clinical Neurosciences, 17,* 91–97.

Smith, A.C.M., Boyd, K.E., Elsea, S.H., Finucane, B.M., Haas-Givler, B., Gropman, A.,…Potocki, L. (2012, June 28). Smith-Magenis syndrome. *GeneReviews.* Retrieved from http://www.ncbi.nlm.nih.gov/books/NBK1310/

Sturge-Weber Syndrome

Comi, A.M. (2011). Presentation, diagnosis, pathophysiology, and treatment of the neurological features of Sturge-Weber syndrome. *Neurologist, 17*(4), 179–184.

National Institute of Neurological Diseases and Stroke. (2015, June 30). *NINDS Sturge-Weber syndrome information page.* Retrieved from http://www.ninds.nih.gov/disorders/sturge_weber/sturge_weber.htm

Shirley, M.D., Tang, H., & Gallione, C. (2013). Sturge-Weber syndrome and port-wine stains caused by somatic mutation in GNAQ. *New England Journal of Medicine, 368*(21), 1971–1979.

Tourette Syndrome

Castellan Baldan, L., Williams, K.A., Gallezot, J.D., Pogorelov, V., Rapanelli, M., Crowley, M.,…Pittenger, C. (2014). Histidine decarboxylase deficiency causes Tourette syndrome: Parallel findings in humans and mice. *Neuron, 81*(1), 77–90.

Cavanna, A.E., & Seri, S. (2013). Tourette's syndrome. *British Medical Journal, 347,* f4964. doi:10.1136/bmj.f4964

Hallett, M. (2015). Tourette syndrome: Update. *Brain Development, 37*(7), 651–655.

Jancovic, J. (2016). *Tourette syndrome.* Retrieved from http://www.uptodate.com/contents/tourette-syndrome

Traumatic Brain Injury

Dinsmore, J. (2013). Traumatic brain injury: An evidence-based review of management. *Continuing Education in Anaesthesia, Critical Care and Pain, 13*(6), 189–195.

National Institute of Neurological Disorders and Stroke. (2016, February 11). *Traumatic brain injury: Hope through research.* Retrieved from http://www.ninds.nih.gov/disorders/tbi/detail_tbi.htm

Nature Reviews Neurology. (n.d.). *WebFocus: Traumatic Brain Injury.* Retrieved from http://www.nature.com/nrneurol/focus/tbi/index.html

Zatzick, D.F., Rivara, F.P., Jurkovich, G.J., Hoge, C.W., Wang, J., Fan, M.Y.,…Mackenzie, E.J. (2010). Multisite investigation of traumatic brain injuries, posttraumatic stress disorder, and self-reported health and cognitive impairments. *Archives of General Psychiatry, 67*(12), 1291–1300.

Tuberous Sclerosis Complex/Syndrome

Owens, J., & Bodensteiner, J.B. (2016). *Tuberous sclerosis complex: Genetics, clinical features, and diagnosis.* Retrieved from http://www.uptodate.com/contents/tuberous-sclerosis-complex-genetics-clinical-features-and-diagnosis

Tsai, V., & Crino, P.B. (2012). Tuberous sclerosis complex: Genetic basis and management strategies. *Advances in Genomics and Genetics, 2012*(2), 19–31.

Tuberous Sclerosis Alliance. (2016). *What is TSC?* Retrieved from http://www.tsalliance.org/pages.aspx?content=2

Turner Syndrome

Loscalzo, M.L. (2008). Turner syndrome. *Pediatrics in Review, 29*(7). Retrieved from http://pedsinreview.aappublications.org/content/29/7/219

Pinsker, J.E. (2012). Clinical review: Turner syndrome: Updating the paradigm of clinical care. *Journal of Clinical Endocrinology Metabolism, 97*(6), E994–1003.

Turner Syndrome Society of the United States. (2016). *About Turner syndrome.* Retrieved from http://www.turnersyndrome.org/#!about-turner-syndrome/c42u

Williams Syndrome

Morris, C.A. (2013, June 13). Williams syndrome. *GeneReviews.* Retrieved from http://www.ncbi.nlm.nih.gov/books/NBK1249/

Pober, B.R. (2010). Williams–Beuren syndrome. *New England Journal of Medicine, 362,* 239–252.

Williams Syndrome Association. (2014). *What is Williams syndrome?* Retrieved from https://williams-syndrome.org/what-is-williams-syndrome

22

Epilepsy

W. McIntyre Burnham

WHAT YOU WILL LEARN

- The nature of epilepsy and of intractable epilepsy
- Treatment options for epilepsy
- Intractable epilepsy as a disability
- The cognitive and psychiatric problems associated with intractable epilepsy in children
- The cognitive and psychiatric problems associated with intractable epilepsy in adults
- The resources available for people with epilepsy and intractable epilepsy

WHAT ARE THE EPILEPSIES?

The epilepsies are a group of neurological disorders characterized by the occurrence of seizures. The epilepsies are also called seizure disorders. After headache, epilepsy is the most common condition treated by neurologists. About 4% of the population will have epilepsy sometime during the course of their lives. About 1% of the population will have epilepsy at any particular time (Burnham, 2002; Guberman & Bruni, 1999).

Seizures are periods of neural hyperactivity caused by an imbalance between excitation and inhibition in the central nervous system. During a seizure, the neurons in the brain fire in massive and synchronized bursts. After some seconds or minutes, when the inhibitory mechanisms of the brain regain control, the seizure ends.

Author's note: The author would like to thank Dr. Paul Hwang, M.D., CMFRCPC; Irene Elliott, R.N., M.H.Sc.; Mr. Trevor Lee; and the staffs of Epilepsy Ontario and Epilepsy Toronto for their help in preparing this chapter.

The epileptic activity in the brain during seizures can be seen as a series of "spikes" or "spikes and waves" in electroencephalographic (EEG) recordings. The behavior of the patient during an epilepsy attack may involve convulsions; however, many seizures are nonconvulsive. If the behavioral seizure does involve convulsions, they may be tonic (rigid) or clonic (jerking) (Burnham, 2002). Seizures are also called attacks or fits. The term *fit* is acceptable in Britain but not in Canada or the United States.

Onset of Epilepsy

The onset of epilepsy may occur at any time during a person's life. In many individuals, seizure onset occurs before the age of 15. Seizure onset is less likely during young adulthood or in middle age. There is an increased incidence of seizure onsets again after the age of 60. Some of these late-onset epilepsies may be the result of small strokes.

Frequency of Seizures

The frequency of seizures varies with the patient. Some individuals experience only a few seizures during their whole lives, often in childhood. Other people experience many seizures every day.

Classes of Epileptic Seizures

There are many different types of epileptic seizures, some of which occur only in childhood. A description of all of the seizure types is beyond the scope of the present discussion, but some of the more common types are described in Table 22.1.

Table 22.1. Common seizure types (new names adopted by the International League Against Epilepsy in parentheses)

Seizure type	Description
Generalized seizure (involves both cerebral hemispheres)	
Absence seizure	This is a nonconvulsive seizure consisting only of a few seconds of unconsciousness, blank staring, and immobility. The eyelids may flutter. The electroencephalogram (EEG) shows three per second "spike and wave" activity all over the brain. The individual has no memory for the period of the attack. (The name is unchanged in the new classification. This was traditionally called a petit mal seizure.)
Tonic-clonic seizure	This is a dramatic seizure involving a loss of consciousness plus whole-body convulsions that consist first of stiffening (tonus) and then of jerking (clonus). The EEG shows constant "spiking" in both hemispheres. The individual has no memory for the period of the attack. (The name remains unchanged in the new classification. This was traditionally called a grand mal seizure.)
Partial seizure (involves only a part of the brain; new name: focal seizure)	
Simple partial seizure	This consists of a sensory or emotional experience or of contralateral jerking on one side of the body. Sensory experiences relate to the part of the brain involved and may be auditory, visual, or other. The EEG shows spiking limited to one part of the brain. The individual is conscious and will remember the period of the attack. (The new name is focal seizures without impairment of consciousness or responsiveness.)
Complex partial seizure	The individual is conscious but is out of touch with the surrounding world. There may be automatic movements, such as lip smacking and fumbling with the clothes. The EEG shows spiking in the temporal lobe. The individual has no memory for the period of the attack. (The new name is focal seizures with impairment of consciousness or responsiveness.)

Source: Burnham (2007).

The International League Against Epilepsy (ILAE) adopted new names for the seizures in 2010 (Berg et al., 2010). The older (1981) names are used in the table because they are still in more common use. The new names are indicated in parentheses.

Epileptic Syndromes

There has been a move to integrate epileptic seizures into larger entities known as epileptic syndromes. An epileptic syndrome consists not only of a seizure type (or types) but also of a prediction about the probable time of seizure onset, a possible cause, a prognosis and, in some cases, a prediction of the response to medication.

Two well-known—and very serious—epileptic syndromes are West syndrome and Lennox-Gastaut syndrome. West syndrome usually has its onset during the first year of life, whereas Lennox-Gastaut syndrome usually begins between ages 1 and 8. Both syndromes involve drug-resistant seizures, an abnormal EEG reading between seizures and, in most cases, mild to severe developmental delay (Burnham, Carlen, & Hwang, 2002;

Guberman & Bruni, 1999; Hrachovy, 2002; Niedermeyer, 2002). Syndromes of this sort are now called epileptic encephalopathies.

Causes of Epilepsy

In some individuals with seizures, there is a clear-cut metabolic or structural abnormality in the brain (e.g., a vitamin B_6 deficiency, a scar, a tumor). These patients are said to have symptomatic epilepsy, and their seizures are thought to be caused by the abnormality in their brains. (The new ILAE name for symptomatic is structural/metabolic.) In other individuals with seizures, the brain appears to be completely normal. These people are said to have idiopathic epilepsy. (The new ILAE name for idiopathic is genetic.) In patients with idiopathic epilepsy, the seizures are thought to be caused by an inherited biochemical or ionic imbalance.

In some rare types of idiopathic epilepsy, the genetic factor involves a single mutation, and inheritance follows simple Mendelian rules (see Chapter 10). In most cases of epilepsy, however, inheritance is multifactorial, meaning that two or more genes are

Table 22.2. Disabilities often associated with seizures (percentage of affected individuals likely to have seizures indicated in parentheses)

Genetic syndrome	Nongenetic syndrome
Tuberous sclerosis (> 80%)	Cerebral palsy (frequent, varies with type)
Sturge-Weber syndrome (70%–90%)	Acquired immunodeficiency syndrome (13%)
Fragile X syndrome (20%–40%)	Multiple sclerosis (5%–10%)
Rett syndrome (70%–80%)	Stroke (5%–10% embolic, 2.5%–25% hemorrhagic)
Down syndrome (2%–15%)	Alzheimer's disease (15%)
Huntington disease (5%–10%)	

Source: Guberman and Bruni (1999).

involved. In these cases, inheritance does not follow simple Mendelian rules (Burnham, 2002).

Epilepsy and Other Types of Central Nervous System Disability

A number of common disabilities, such as cerebral palsy, are caused by brain damage or dysfunction. People with these disabilities often experience seizures as well. Table 22.2 presents a list of common disabilities and indicates the percentage of affected individuals who also have epilepsy.

CAN EPILEPSY BE TREATED AND CONTROLLED?

There are a number of treatments that can be used to control epileptic seizures. The most common treatment is drug therapy. Surgery, diet, and vagal stimulation are utilized when drug therapy is ineffective.

Drug Therapy

In many cases of epilepsy, seizures can be controlled by medication. The medications are called antiepileptic drugs, anticonvulsant drugs, or antiseizure drugs. A wide variety of antiepileptic drugs is available. Among the most commonly prescribed classic medications are ethosuximide, which is used for absence seizures; phenytoin and carbamazepine, which are used for tonic-clonic and partial seizures; and valproic acid, which is a wide-spectrum anticonvulsant, effective against many types of seizures. Phenobarbital is an older drug that is still in use, most often in children.

A number of drugs have been introduced since 1990. These include gabapentin, lacosamide, lamotrigine, levetiracetam, oxcarbazepine, topiramate, and zonisamide. The newer drugs are thought to have fewer side effects than the older drugs. It is not clear, however, that they are better at stopping seizures—and they are often more expensive.

The anticonvulsant medications do not cure epilepsy. They simply suppress seizures on a temporary basis. People with seizures must continue to take their medications once, twice, or three times daily, sometimes for the rest of their lives (for discussion, see Burnham, 2007; Levy, Mattson, Meldrum, & Perucca, 2002). If the drugs are taken regularly, however, about two thirds of people with seizures will achieve seizure freedom. (For a full discussion of antiepileptic drugs, see Blaise et al., 2008.)

Nondrug Therapies

For about a third of people with epilepsy, the antiepileptic drugs are ineffective. These people are said to have intractable, or refractory, epilepsy. Intractable epilepsy affects about 1 in 300 people in the general population (Burnham, 2007; Guberman & Bruni, 1999).

When seizures prove intractable to drug therapy, several sorts of nondrug therapy are available. If the person experiences partial seizures—and if the seizures always arise from the same area in the brain (the "focus")—he or she may be a candidate for seizure surgery. In adults, the most common type of seizure surgery involves removal of the part of the brain that contains the focus—often, the anterior part of one of the temporal lobes. Surgery may stop the seizures or make them more controllable with medication (see Luders, 2001).

Another nondrug therapy is diet therapy. The diet most often used is the ketogenic diet. This is a high-fat diet that contains adequate protein and very little carbohydrate. Many patients find the diet unpalatable, and it is hard to maintain because all of the food must be weighed and measured. The ketogenic diet, however, stops seizures in about a third of people who have failed drug therapy and decreases seizures in another third. Traditionally, the diet has been used only in children, yet some reports suggest that it is effective in adults as well. Unfortunately, due to the nutritionally unbalanced nature of the diet, individuals usually stay on the diet for only 2–3 years (Vining, 1999). A few treatment centers have used a modified Atkins diet with some success; it is far easier to maintain than the traditional ketogenic diet and appears to be beneficial in some patients (Kossoff, Rowley, Sinha, & Vining, 2007).

A further treatment for drug-resistant seizures is vagus nerve stimulation. A device similar to a cardiac pacemaker is implanted into the chest muscle and a wire is connected to the vagus nerve—a nerve that originates in the brain. Intermittent stimulation of the vagus nerve is used to control seizures. Vagus nerve stimulation is not as effective as surgery or the ketogenic diet, but it can be considered when the other therapies fail; it is now the second most common type of nondrug therapy in the United States (see McLachlan, 1997).

Unfortunately, some people have seizures that cannot be controlled by any type of therapy. These individuals continue to experience intractable, uncontrolled seizures despite the best attempts at therapeutic intervention.

INTRACTABLE EPILEPSY AS A DISABILITY

Epilepsy is sometimes called the "invisible disability." *Disability* is probably too strong a word for people with drug-responsive seizures; such people can lead typical lives and reach their full potential for accomplishment. Intractable, drug-resistant epilepsy, on the other hand, is clearly a disability. People with intractable epilepsy face both social and economic discrimination and must surmount significant barriers in their struggles to live as others do. Some of these barriers relate to seizures per se, and others relate to the comorbidities of epilepsy: cognitive, psychosocial, and reproductive conditions that often coexist with seizures.

The Disabling Effect of Seizures

In part, the problems of intractable epilepsy relate to the seizures per se. Seizure-related problems include personal safety, driving, being able to hold a job, and economic and social discrimination.

First, there is the risk of injury during seizures. The falls that occur during some seizures can lead to head injury if they occur on pavement or near furniture with hard edges. Even more serious injuries occur when falls happen on stairs, on ladders, or at the edges of subway platforms. People with frequent, uncontrolled seizures are warned against swimming alone and may be told to take showers rather than baths. Thus, life is circumscribed not by physical incapacity but by fears related to personal safety.

In addition, people with seizures cannot legally drive. Drivers' licenses are typically suspended with the first seizure and are reissued only if the person is totally seizure free for a period of time—often 1 year. Thus, a person with even one seizure a year will never be able to drive or to participate in work or social activities that require driving.

Finally, there are social and economic problems related to society's response to seizures. People who seize in public often face stigma and discrimination, and people who seize at work are frequently fired. Thus, people with uncontrolled seizures are at risk of social isolation and, because they are

Table 22.3. Comorbidities of intractable epilepsy[a]

Cognitive
Lowered IQ
Severe developmental delay (West and Lennox-Gastaut syndromes)
Selective memory impairments (related to partial seizures)
Global memory problems
Memory problems due to the sedative side effects of anticonvulsant drugs
Psychosocial
Lowered self-esteem
Psychiatric disturbances (anxiety and/or depression found in at least 30% of patients)
Attention-deficit/hyperactivity disorder (found in 20%–30% of children)
Late-developing psychosis
Personality changes due to the sedative side effects of anticonvulsant drugs
Reproductive (adults)
Lowered fertility
Lessened desire and responsiveness

[a]Comorbidities vary from individual to individual. They are present in some people and absent in others.

often unemployed or underemployed, of financial stress and poverty (Wiebe, Bellhouse, Fallahay, & Eliasziw, 1999).

The Disabling Effect of Comorbidities

The comorbidities of epilepsy are often more serious than the seizures themselves. The common comorbidities are summarized in Table 22.3. They are discussed in the following sections first as they relate to children and then as they relate to adults.

THE COMORBIDITIES OF INTRACTABLE EPILEPSY IN CHILDREN

Children with intractable epilepsy often have problems with learning and memory, psychosocial problems, and problems at home and at school.

Cognitive Impairment in Children

Intractable epilepsy is often associated with some cognitive impairment, which seems to be a progressive process beginning after the onset of seizures (Resnick & Duchowny, 2008).

In addition, in some epileptic syndromes, there may be severe cognitive impairment. In West syndrome and Lennox-Gastaut syndrome, if the seizures cannot be stopped, children begin to regress mentally. Four out of five will eventually display developmental delay. Some of the children will later outgrow their seizures, but the developmental delay will remain. Fortunately, these syndromes are rare.

Even when IQs are in the typical range, children with uncontrolled seizures do less well in school than children without epilepsy. The following discussion outlines a number of factors that may contribute to this.

One cause of learning problems is frequent absence seizures. These mild, nonconvulsive attacks consist only of brief lapses of consciousness. Some children have hundreds every day, however, and clusters of dozens may occur within a few minutes. During these periods, the child cannot follow what is going on around him or her. Children with absence epilepsy, therefore, may give the appearance of being "slow learners." In fact, their intelligence is usually typical.

Severe seizures, such as tonic-clonic attacks, cause a major perturbation in the brain's signaling systems. The aftereffects of such seizures may last for hours or days. If a child has had one or more seizures

during the night, he or she may show excessive fatigue during the following day, may have trouble concentrating, and may appear to have forgotten things he or she knew perfectly well the day before.

Some children, and particularly those with complex partial epilepsy, have a series of brief, single epileptic "spikes" called interictal spikes between their seizures. These spikes produce no outward manifestation, but if they are frequent, they may slow down the child's ability to process and retrieve information, causing transient cognitive impairment.

Children with an epileptic focus in particular parts of the brain may show selective impairments related to that area. Children with a focus in the hemisphere dominant for language, for instance, often have trouble with finding or remembering words.

Memory issues form one of the most common complaints in children with intractable epilepsy. Children complain that they need their lessons to be repeated over and over again before they can remember them. They know that their classmates do not have this problem. The reasons for this memory impairment are not completely clear. In some cases, it may relate to changes in the brain. Individuals with long-standing intractable epilepsy arising in the temporal lobes begin to lose neurons in the hippocampus, a subcortical forebrain structure. This loss of neurons is called hippocampal sclerosis or mesial temporal sclerosis. The hippocampus is involved in memory formation and, if severe, hippocampal sclerosis is associated with memory problems. In other cases, memory impairment may relate to the side effects of anticonvulsant drugs, as discussed next.

In addition to the cognitive impairments associated with intractable seizures per se, impairments are associated with the sedative (sleep-inducing) side effects of anticonvulsant drugs. These side effects are most serious at the start of therapy and improve as tolerance develops, but they never entirely disappear. They are worse with the older drugs such as phenobarbital and primidone, but they may occur (in susceptible individuals) with almost any of the anticonvulsants. Table 22.4 presents some commonly used anticonvulsants and indicates whether they are more or less likely to significantly impair cognition.

Psychosocial Problems in Children

Emotional and behavioral difficulties are disproportionately high in children with uncontrolled

Table 22.4. Anticonvulsant drugs that are more and less likely to cause cognitive impairment (have sedative side effects)[a]

More likely
Phenytoin (high doses)
Phenobarbital
Primidone
Clonazepam
Topiramate

Less likely
Carbamazepine
Valproate
Clobazam
Vigabatrin
Gabapentin
Lamotrigine

Source: Guberman and Bruni (1999).
[a]Effects vary from individual to individual.

epilepsy. Psychologists working with children who have epilepsy report a greater level of disturbances in this population of children as compared with the other children they treat.

Estimates are that 20%–60% of children with epilepsy are at risk for psychopathology. In one epidemiological study, psychiatric disorders were identified in 37% of children with epilepsy, as compared with 9% in the general population and 11% in children with diabetes (Ekinci, Titus, Rodopman, Berkem, & Trevathan, 2009). Some of the more common problems associated with intractable epilepsy include anxiety, depression, irritability, aggression, and irrational periods of rage (Johannessen, Gram, Sillanpaa, & Tomson, 1995; Sahlholdt, 1995). These emotional problems are often responsive to therapy, including therapy with psychotropic medications but, unfortunately, these comorbidities are seldom diagnosed or treated. Therapy often focuses on seizure control, and the emotional problems are neglected.

In addition to emotional problems, children with uncontrolled seizures may have problems with hyperactivity. It is estimated that 20%–30% of children with epilepsy experience concurrent attention-deficit/hyperactivity disorder (ADHD). A still larger number of children with seizures show impairments in attention or in impulse control without showing the full ADHD syndrome.

The previously noted emotional and behavioral problems are often compounded by the effects of the anticonvulsant drugs. Children may show a change of personality after being started on the anticonvulsants; they may become impulsive, hyperactive, and irritable, and they may exhibit both verbal and physical aggression. These problems usually disappear when the drug is stopped. Behavioral side effects are most frequently associated with the benzodiazepines (i.e., clonazepam) and the barbiturates (i.e., phenobarbital).

Children with Epilepsy and the Family

Intractable seizures present significant strain and stress, not just for the affected child but also for the entire family. Psychologists working with the families of children with uncontrolled epilepsy report that these families show a greater level of disturbances than other families with whom they work. The unpredictable nature of epilepsy makes it particularly disturbing. Parents live in fear of the next attack, and parents go through the classic stages of denial, anger, and depression usually seen when a child dies. Some parents develop psychosomatic reactions, such as sleep disturbances, headaches, and loss of appetite.

Parents, and particularly mothers, also often blame themselves for their child's epilepsy. In some cases, shame is added to guilt as other family members blame the parents for their child's condition. Eventually, most parents come to terms with their child's epilepsy. Some, however, would benefit from short-term psychotherapy, although they seldom seek it or receive it.

Support groups consisting of other parents with similar problems are of considerable help to parents of children with epilepsy. These are usually organized by the regional epilepsy associations (see Supporting People with Epilepsy and Their Families). In the absence of therapy or support, there is unfortunately a very real possibility of divorce.

Siblings of children with epilepsy may also develop both emotional complaints (e.g., fear of becoming sick or dying, nightmares) and physical complaints (e.g., headache, vomiting). There may be sibling rivalry, as parents are often perceived as favoring the child with seizures. A large study found that about 25% of the siblings of children with chronic epilepsy were perceived as "disturbed" by their teachers (Johannessen et al., 1995). Siblings, as well as parents, may benefit from psychotherapy (Sahlholdt, 1995).

Children with Epilepsy and School

Children with intractable epilepsy often have major problems at school. These are partly due to the cognitive problems associated with seizures—problems with learning and memory. The majority of problems, however, seem to relate to behavior. As noted previously, children with epilepsy may show tendencies toward ADHD. Perhaps for this reason, children with epilepsy are frequently sent to the principal and are often suspended from school. The children may express anger toward their teachers, and their families often end up "at war" with the school system.

The school situation would be much improved if both schools and parents understood the gravity of the comorbidities associated with intractable epilepsy. What is needed is a partnership between health care providers, the parents, and the schools. The following are important areas of focus:

1. Parents and health care providers should inform the school about the child's seizures and about how they are to be managed.

2. The comorbidities of intractable epilepsy should be explained and dealt with.

3. An education plan to improve academic success should be documented.

4. Appropriate supports, such as providing an educational assistant, should be put in place.

5. The importance of the child's participation in recreational and class activities should be accepted.

6. Social interactions with peers should be encouraged.

THE COMORBIDITIES OF INTRACTABLE EPILEPSY IN ADULTS

As children grow, the comorbidities of intractable epilepsy grow with them. Like children with uncontrolled seizures, adults with uncontrolled seizures experience many hardships and difficulties. These relate not only to the seizures—which cause embarrassment, injury, and rejection—but also to comorbid cognitive, psychosocial, and reproductive problems. In combination, the seizures and the comorbidities lead to a very poor quality of life in adults with uncontrolled epilepsy.

Cognitive Impairment

Cognitive impairments, once acquired, are likely to remain, and the aftereffects of seizures continue to occur in adults, as do the sedative side effects of the anticonvulsant medications.

Psychosocial Impairment

Emotional disturbances, especially anxiety and depression, are also common in adults with intractable epilepsy. Often there is low self-confidence, social isolation, and withdrawal. Adults may continue to live with their parents (Jahnukainen, 1995). The suicide rate is five times higher than in the general adult population.

In addition to anxiety and depression, about 5%–10% of adults with intractable seizures may develop a schizophreniform psychosis. Usually the patient has complex partial seizures with a focus in one of the temporal lobes. Often, he or she has had uncontrolled epilepsy for at least 10 years. In a few patients, the psychosis will clear after a major seizure and then gradually reappear (Guberman & Bruni, 1999).

A study of adults with uncontrolled seizures has reported that about 30% had psychiatric disorders, including psychosis, antisocial personality disorders, anxiety, and depression (Blumer, 2002; Johannessen et al., 1995). Unfortunately, as with children, adult therapy for epilepsy tends to focus only on seizure control; the accompanying psychiatric problems are often neglected.

Reproductive Problems

Reproductive and hormonal disorders are common in both men and women with intractable epilepsy. This is particularly true if the epilepsy is of temporal lobe origin.

In women, menstrual disorders are seen, including irregular or missed menstrual cycles or cycles in which there is no ovulation. Fertility is reduced to 70%–80% of normal capacity. Possible hormonal disorders include hypogonadism, which occurs with too little estrogen, and polycystic ovaries, which occur with too much estrogen. Anticonvulsant drugs, in particular valproate, may contribute to these disorders.

In men with intractable epilepsy, there is an increased risk of erectile dysfunction. In addition, more than 90% of them have abnormal semen analyses, including decreased sperm count and impaired sperm mobility.

In both sexes, diminished sexual desire and responsiveness have been described.

Intractable Epilepsy, Work, and Driving

The majority of adults with uncontrolled seizures are unemployed or underemployed. They face problems related to driving, to getting and retaining jobs, and to disclosure.

The first problem relates to driving. As noted previously, in most countries, driver's licenses are revoked after the first seizure. They can be reinstated if the driver is seizure-free for a period of time—often a year. People with intractable epilepsy, however, are seldom seizure-free for as long as a year, and most of them will never legally drive again. They cannot take any job that requires driving or that can be reached only by car. A second problem relates to having seizures at work. People are often fired if they experience seizures at work. Even though the law in Canada forbids firing an employee because of epilepsy, employers often eliminate people with public seizures, usually using some other pretext. A third problem relates to disclosure. People with seizures fear that they will not be hired if they disclose their epilepsy to potential employers, but they also fear that they will be fired later if they do not disclose. There are no simple solutions to these problems. Work and a stable income are major concerns for adults with intractable epilepsy. (For a complete discussion of psychiatric and social issues, see Austin et al., 2008; for a comprehensive discussion of epilepsy, see Engel & Pedley, 2008.)

SUPPORTING PEOPLE WITH EPILEPSY AND THEIR FAMILIES

There are a number of resources available for people with intractable seizures and their families.

Medical Resources

Many of the larger cities in North America have hospitals with specialized programs for the treatment of epilepsy. Every person with uncontrolled seizures should be referred to such a program. Seizures should be considered "uncontrolled" when adequate trials of two appropriate anticonvulsant drugs have failed to produce seizure freedom.

Some of the larger urban hospitals also have programs for treating the cognitive and psychosocial problems related to epilepsy. These are called comprehensive programs, and they try to treat the whole person instead of just treating the seizure disorder.

Epilepsy Associations

Patient support and advocacy groups can also offer help and guidance. These nonprofit organizations offer brochures and information about epilepsy. In addition, they often offer support groups for people with seizures and their families. Some associations also offer job and personal counseling. Upon request, they may make presentations at schools and at workplaces.

FUTURE DIRECTIONS

Researchers are working to develop better ways to stop seizures and better treatments for the epileptic comorbidities. New antiepileptic drugs are being developed and better antiseizure diets are being tested. High-powered imaging is localizing epileptic lesions and foci to improve seizure surgery. Cognitive behavior therapy is being designed for people with comorbidities. Finally, genetic and epigenetic studies are investigating the gene-related causes of seizures in order to design genetic/epigenetic therapies to combat—or even prevent—epilepsy. There is now a hope that someday intractable epilepsy, the invisible disability, will be a thing of the past.

SUMMARY

In addition to experiencing seizures, children with intractable epilepsy may have a lowered IQ and/or encounter problems with learning and memory. They may also have significant psychosocial problems, some of which result from the use of antiepileptic drugs. People who work with these children must be patient and must develop new strategies to promote learning.

Adults with uncontrollable seizures also have cognitive and psychosocial problems. They cannot legally drive and they may develop reproductive disorders. They face discrimination in the workplace and are frequently either unemployed or underemployed. Work and a stable income are major concerns. Their emotional problems are frequently untreated, even though they are in considerable need of treatment. Intractable epilepsy is a true—if invisible—disability.

FOR FURTHER THOUGHT AND DISCUSSION

1. Much of the stigma associated with epilepsy arises from the fact that seizures can be frightening to watch. Should the public be made aware of what seizures look like? Should they become accustomed to seizures? Should they be taught first aid for seizures?

2. People with seizures who continue to drive have more accidents than those in the general population. However, they do not have more accidents than drivers who have diabetes or heart disease. People with diabetes or heart disease are allowed to drive. Neither people with seizures nor those with diabetes and heart disease have as many accidents as young adult males without disease or disorder diagnoses. Should people with seizures be allowed to drive?

3. What are the economic and social costs of intractable epilepsy? This disorder often starts in childhood, lasts through life, and is found in 1 in every 300 people.

4. Teachers receive little or no training related to the epilepsies they will encounter in the classroom. Should education in the epilepsies be a part of teacher training?

REFERENCES

Austin, J.K., Fraser, R.T., Kanner, A.M., Michael, R., Trimble, M.R., & Engel, J., Jr. (Section Eds.). (2008). Psychiatric and social issues. In J. Engel & T.A. Pedley, (Eds.), *Epilepsy: A comprehensive textbook* (Vol. 3, pp. 2075–2282). New York, NY: Lippincott, Williams and Wilkins.

Berg, A.T., Berkovic, S.F., Brodie, M.J., Buchhalter, J., Cross, J.H., van Emde Boas, W.,…Scheffer, I.E. (2010). Revised terminology and concepts for organization of seizures and epilepsies report of the ILAE Commission on Classification and Terminology, 2005–2009. *Epilepsia, 51*(4), 676–685.

Blaise F.D., Bourgeois, D.W., Chadwick, M.A., Dichter, J.A., French, R.L., Macdonald, B.S.,…Pedley, T.A. (Section Eds.). (2008). Antiepileptic drugs. In J. Engel & T.A. Pedley (Eds.), *Epilepsy: A comprehensive textbook* (Vol. 2, pp. 1431–1747). New York, NY: Lippincott, Williams and Wilkins.

Blumer, D. (2002). Psychiatric aspects of intractable epilepsy. In W. Burnham, P.L. Carlen, & P.A. Hwang (Eds.), *Intractable seizures: Diagnosis, treatment and prevention* (pp. 133–147). New York, NY: Plenum Press.

Burnham, W.M. (2002). Epilepsy. In L. Nadel (Ed.), *The encyclopedia of cognitive neuroscience* (Vol. 2, pp. 1–7). London, United Kingdom: Nature Publishing Group.

Burnham, W.M. (2007). Antiseizure drugs. In H. Kalant, D. Grant, & J. Mitchell (Eds.), *Principles of medical pharmacology* (pp. 223–235). Toronto, Canada: Elsevier Canada.

Burnham, W.M., Carlen, P.L., & Hwang, P.A. (Eds.). (2002). *Intractable seizures: Diagnosis, treatment and prevention.* New York, NY: Plenum Press.

Ekinci, O., Titus, J., Rodopman, A., Berkem, M., & Trevathan, E. (2009). Depression and anxiety in children and adolescents with epilepsy: Prevalence, risk factors, and treatment. *Epilepsy and Behavior, 14*, 8–18.

Engel, J., & Pedley, T.A. (Eds.). (2008). *Epilepsy: A comprehensive textbook.* New York, NY: Lippincott, Williams and Wilkins.

Guberman, A., & Bruni, J. (1999). *Essentials of clinical epilepsy.* Woburn, MA: Butterworth-Heinemann.

Hrachovy, R.A. (2002). West's syndrome: Clinical description and diagnosis. In W. Burnham, P.L. Carlen, & P.A. Hwang (Eds.), *Intractable seizures: Diagnosis, treatment and prevention* (pp. 33–50). New York, NY: Plenum Press.

International League Against Epilepsy. (n.d.). *Home page.* Retrieved from http://www.ilae.org

Jahnukainen, H. (1995). Psychosocial consequences of intractable epilepsy in adults. In S. Johannessen, L. Gram, M. Sillanpaa, & T. Tomson, (Eds.), *Intractable epilepsy* (pp. 165–169). Bristol, PA: Wrightson Biomedical.

Johannessen, S., Gram, L., Sillanpaa, M., & Tomson, T. (Eds.). (1995). *Intractable epilepsy.* Bristol, PA: Wrightson Biomedical.

Kossoff, E.H., Rowley, H., Sinha, S.R., & Vining, E.P.G. (2007). A prospective study of the modified Atkins Diet for intractable epilepsy in adults. *Epilepsia, 49*, 316–319.

Levy, R.H., Mattson, R.H., Meldrum, B.J., & Perucca, E. (Eds.). (2002). *Antiepileptic drugs.* Philadelphia, PA: Lippincott, Williams & Wilkins.

Luders, H.O. (Ed.). (2001). *Epilepsy surgery.* New York, NY: Raven Press.

McLachlan, R. (1997). Vagus nerve stimulation for intractable epilepsy: A review. *Journal of Clinical Neurophysiology, 14*, 358–368.

Niedermeyer, E. (2002). Lennox-Gastaut syndrome: Clinical description and diagnosis. In W. Burnham, P.L. Carlen, & P.A. Hwang, (Eds.), *Intractable seizures: Diagnosis, treatment and prevention* (pp. 61–75). New York, NY: Plenum Press.

Resnick, T., & Duchowny, M. (2008). Comorbidity and immunizations in children. In J. Engel & T.A. Pedley (Eds.), *Epilepsy: A comprehensive textbook* (Vol. 2, pp. 1431–1747). New York, NY: Lippincott, Williams and Wilkins.

Sahlholdt, L. (1995). Psychosocial consequences of intractable epilepsy in children. In S. Johannessen, L. Gram, M. Sillanpaa, & T. Tomson (Eds.), *Intractable epilepsy* (pp. 153–163). Bristol, PA: Wrightson Biomedical.

Vining, E.P.G. (1999). Clinical efficacy of the ketogenic diet. *Epilepsy Research, 37*, 181–290.

Wiebe, S., Bellhouse, D.R., Fallahay, C., & Eliasziw, M. (1999). Burden of epilepsy: The Ontario Health Survey. *Canadian Journal of Neurological Science, 26*, 263–270.

23

Introduction to Behavior and Mental Health

Maire Percy, Wai Lun Alan Fung, Ivan Brown, and Angela Hassiotis

WHAT YOU WILL LEARN

- Overview of normal and abnormal behaviors
- Relationship between abnormal behaviors, challenging behaviors, mental disorders, mental ill-health, and dual diagnosis
- Classification systems for mental health disorders
- Brain injury and other causes of abnormal behavior
- Issues of mental ill-health in people with intellectual and developmental disabilities
- Supports for people with behavioral and mental health issues

This chapter is an introduction to the topics of behavior and mental health and what constitutes "abnormality." These are complex issues that are addressed differently by different disciplines. The authors recognize that the terms *normal* and *abnormal* are understood a variety of ways and that use of these terms is not the norm in the field. For some, these terms are understood as social constructions that are unhelpful to people realizing their full potential. In this chapter, the authors use *normal behavior* to describe behavior that is accepted or tolerated in its sociocultural context and *abnormal behavior* to describe behavior that is troublesome or harmful to a person or others in its sociocultural context. The chapter begins with a description of what are considered in today's world to be normal and abnormal behaviors from a lay point of view. The relationship between abnormal behaviors and related terms (e.g., challenging behaviors, mental disorders, mental ill-health, dual diagnosis) used in the field of intellectual and developmental disabilities is then described. The reader is next introduced to systems currently used to classify different mental disorders associated with abnormal behavior in people with or without disability, with a focus on the American Psychiatric Association's *Diagnostic and Statistical Manual of Mental Disorders (DSM)* system. Some special topics in the abnormal behavior field—suicide, brain injury and other causes of abnormal behavior, as well as behavioral phenotypes and stereotypic and self-injurious behaviors—are also covered. The final sections deal with strategies for intervention and prevention and future directions in the field.

Although considerable detail is given, readers should focus on obtaining an overview. A better understanding of abnormal behavior should lead to more effective treatments and interventions and help to improve the quality of life for individuals affected by conditions that affect behavior and/or personality.

Authors' note: The authors acknowledge previous contributions of Dr. Sheldon Lewkis and Rivka Birkan in development of this text. The material in this chapter draws substantially upon that in Fung, Percy, and Brown (2011) and Percy, Brown, and Lewkis (2007).

WHAT IS BEHAVIOR?

According to the *Oxford Dictionaries* (Oxford University Press, 2016), the term *behavior* refers to "the way one acts or conducts oneself, especially toward others" and "in response to a particular situation or stimulus." A definition based on a meta-analysis of scientific literature states that "behavior is the internally coordinated responses (actions or inactions) of whole living organisms (individuals or groups) to internal and/or external stimuli" (Levitis, Lidicker, & Freund, 2009, p. 103). External stimuli are sometimes referred to as "environmental."

People do hundreds of things every day, from the moment they wake up to the time they go to sleep and even while sleeping. All these things people do constitute their behavior. Behavior is the way a person (or animal) acts or behaves—what other people see him or her doing; thus, it is a principal way others form their understanding of a person and their views on who the person is.

Behavior can take many forms and can be described in many ways. For example, it can be described as actions or reactions: conscious or unconscious, intentional or unintentional, or overt (obvious) or covert (secretive). For many years, there was a debate over whether behavior is the consequence of nature or nurture. It now is accepted that both factors are involved. Behaviors are also influenced by brain functioning, because one's behaviors, both normal and abnormal, are produced and controlled by the brain. Separate regions of the brain are responsible for different behaviors. One of the many reasons behavior differs so much is that the brain is affected not only by genetics but also by the endocrine and nervous systems, by the immune system, by nutrition, by exercise, by sleep, by many different environmental factors, and by learning experiences that occur throughout life. Such learning results from a person's unique life experiences, abilities and disabilities, and interactions with the numerous aspects of changing environments.

Behavior can also be a shortcut in communication. It can send a quick message to others about what a person is thinking, how he or she is reacting, or what he or she wished to do. As people move through life, they learn more and more ways in which behavior can be a valuable communication tool. Early in life, children learn to communicate through their behavior, especially before they are able to tell others what the problem is.

Behavior can occur spontaneously or be learned; it also can be initiated or influenced by learned social patterns or by personal motivation, internal processes, and feelings. Whatever the reason for its occurrence, behavior can change the relationship between a person or group of people and the environment (Dusenbery, 2009)—that is, what a person does or does not do can change the social and physical environments. Because behavior can be observed, measured, repeated, learned, and changed, characterization of behavior is especially important in the education field. For example, understanding behavior can help with the development of lesson plans and support strategies (Bicard, Bicard, & the IRIS Center, 2012). Characterization or observation of behavior can also help with the identification of certain medical conditions and disorders and suggest helpful treatments.

NORMAL AND ABNORMAL BEHAVIORS

This section deals with differences between normal and abnormal behaviors.

Normal Behavior

Behavior is expected to conform to certain patterns that are acceptable to most people. In the sociology field, acceptable patterns of behavior are called behavioral norms, although society in general usually thinks of these patterns as normal behaviors. Behavioral norms differ from one culture to another and from one time period to another, but they serve an important purpose. When almost everybody conforms to them, behavior is largely predictable. Predictable behavior exhibited by others alleviates stress and encourages trust.

At the same time, there is considerable variation in normal behavior at the personal level. Each person, while behaving generally in accordance with behavioral norms, also does things that are unique. In fact, people are often described in terms of the unique aspects of their behavior because that is what distinguishes them as individuals. One of the things most intriguing about other people is how their behavior is different from one's own, even if both people follow the same general behavioral norms.

Having some degree of unique behavior is also beneficial to humans as a species because it allows people to explore and experiment with new ideas independently. The human race would not have developed to where it is had each person held fast to the same behavioral norms. Still, the unique behaviors of individuals need to be acceptable to others and to fit into the broader rules set for behavioral norms. Thus, it is considered "normal" for humans to show a range of individual behaviors while conforming to a general set of behavior rules.

Abnormal Behavior

Abnormal behavior, in a literal sense, means "away from normal behavior." It is a behavior that seems too far from the behavioral norm, too odd, or too unusual to be acceptable. It usually means rare in the statistical sense. For example, a person walking down the street shouting angrily at unseen people is exhibiting a behavior that is usually considered to be abnormal because it seems too unusual, is not commonly seen, and is too far away from current behavioral norms.

Any person may exhibit some abnormal behaviors at certain times. A few less serious abnormal behaviors in any one person are typically acceptable, especially if they are counterbalanced by many more normal behaviors. If a person has a number of abnormal behaviors, however, these may outweigh the normal behaviors such that the behavior pattern as a whole deviates too far from acceptable norms.

Abnormal behavior is frequently troublesome—either to the people who exhibit the behavior or to others who experience it. Troublesome behavior is unpredictable and creates stress and uncertainty. It can lead to great personal distress and interfere with daily functioning. It can result in the breakdown of relationships with other people, and sometimes it even leads to the need for inpatient care. In a broader sense, troublesome abnormal behavior can threaten the well-being of family and community. The troublesome aspects of abnormal behavior can take many forms. It might, for example, be amoral, dangerous, compulsive, counterproductive to well-being, distressful, incomprehensible, irrational, maladaptive, painful or uncomfortable, unconventional, or unwanted. Because of the difficulties it creates, abnormal behavior is considered undesirable and, if possible, something to be improved through intervention.

In practice, abnormal behavior is usually referred to as either atypical behavior or challenging behavior. Abnormal behaviors are thought of as atypical if they are quite different from normal behaviors but are not particularly troublesome or unwanted, and as challenging if they are quite different from normal behaviors and are troublesome and unwanted.

What Is "Challenging" Behavior?

The term *challenging behavior* was first introduced in the 1980s to describe abnormal and problematic behaviors in people with intellectual and developmental disabilities that threatened their quality of life and/or the physical safety of an individual or others. Such behaviors are also known as behaviors that challenge services. Emerson (as cited in Emerson, 2001) defined challenging behavior as follows:

> Culturally abnormal behavior(s) of such intensity, frequency or duration that the physical safety of the person or others is placed in serious jeopardy, or behavior which is likely to seriously limit or deny access to the use of ordinary community facilities. (p. 3)

Some investigators have proposed that the term *challenging behavior* be replaced by *behavior of concern,* because the former term may result in labeling, stereotyping, and diagnostic overshadowing (i.e., the failure to see a problem because the symptoms are attributed to another disability) (Chan et al., 2012). Furthermore, challenging behavior can in some circumstances be adaptive. For the purposes of this chapter, though, we use the term *challenging behavior.*

Some common examples of challenging behavior include aggressive outbursts, self-injury (including ingesting or inhaling foreign bodies), destructive behavior (e.g., property destruction), stereotyped behaviors (e.g., repetitive rocking or echolalia), socially inappropriate behavior (e.g., inappropriate sexualized behavior such as public masturbation or groping and sexual assault), disruptive behaviors (e.g., throwing a tantrum), or noncompliant behaviors (e.g., refusing to put on one's shoes or to turn off a video game). Examples of more serious challenging behaviors, which are also illegal, include arson, assault, murder or attempted murder, rape, and theft, among others.

Challenging behaviors can be triggered by, or result from, several different types of factors (e.g., biological, social, environmental, psychological). They are particularly common in populations with psychiatric disorders but can occur in the absence of a psychiatric disorder, and not all people with mental illness exhibit challenging behaviors. Challenging

Table 23.1. Some factors that can trigger or result in challenging behaviors

General type of factor	Specific factors
Biological	Traumatic brain injury
	Physical conditions resulting in pain
	Side effects from medical drugs
	Lead and mercury toxicity
	Mental disorders, including various neurological disorders
	Genetic disorders associated with characteristic patterns of behaviors called behavioral phenotypes
	Symptoms of withdrawal when drug treatment is stopped too abruptly
	Genetic disorders associated with unusually high frequencies of mental disorders
Social	Boredom
	Need for social interaction
	Need to be in control
	Lack of knowledge of what is acceptable behavior in the community
	Insensitivity of others to an individual's wishes and needs
Environmental	Excessive noise, lighting
	Gaining access to preferred objects and activities
Psychological	Feeling excluded, lonely, devalued, labeled, or disempowered
	Living up to people's negative expectations
	Stress

Sources: Fung, Percy, and Brown (2011) and Percy, Brown, and Lewkis (2007); see also Chapters 28 and 47 in this volume for more information.

behaviors and emotional dysfunction are more common in people with severe intellectual and developmental disabilities than in the general population. Table 23.1 provides examples of some specific factors that can result in challenging behaviors.

Two Common Forms of Challenging Behavior

Two forms of abnormal, challenging behavior are singled out next because they are somewhat common, they can be quite serious, and they may or may not necessarily meet the full criteria of a mental disorder.

Stereotypic Behaviors Stereotypic behavior is a repetitive, invariant behavior pattern with no obvious goal or function (Garner, 2005). It sometimes is referred to as self-stimulatory, or stimming, behavior. This can involve any of the senses or a combina-

tion of them. Stereotypic behavior in humans—which can be considered abnormal if it is too unusual to be socially acceptable or causes undue distress—can be categorized in the following ways:

- *Visual:* staring at lights, blinking repetitively, moving one's fingers in front of one's eyes, flapping one's hands

- *Auditory:* tapping ears, snapping fingers, making vocal sounds

- *Tactile:* rubbing the skin with one's hands or with another object, scratching

- *Vestibular:* rocking front to back, rocking side to side

- *Taste:* placing body parts or objects in one's mouth, licking objects

- *Smell:* smelling objects, sniffing people

Self-Injurious Behaviors Self-injurious behaviors (SIBs) are among the most devastating behaviors exhibited by people with or without intellectual and developmental disabilities (Oliver & Richards, 2010). SIB often refers to any behavior by people to themselves that causes tissue damage such as bruises, redness, and open wounds, regardless of any underlying disorder. In people with intellectual and developmental disabilities, the most common forms of SIBs include head banging, hand biting, and excessive self-rubbing and scratching. SIBs occur with an unusually high frequency in a number of disorders, including autism spectrum disorder (Chapter 16) and fragile X (Chapter 15), Tourette, Lesch-Nyhan, Cornelia de Lange, Prader-Willi, and Smith-Magenis syndromes (Chapter 21); schizophrenia; borderline personality disorder; and stereotypic movement disorder (American Psychiatric Association [APA], 2013). They may also occur as the result of impulse-control disorders (e.g., intermittent explosive disorder), obsessive-compulsive spectrum disorders (e.g., trichotillomania, body dysmorphic disorder), misuse of certain substances (e.g., hallucinogens, cocaine), and eating disorders (e.g., purging, excessive exercising), as well as the result of abuse or incest. SIBs do not include suicidal behavior, but in people with schizophrenia, deliberate self-harm is a strong predictor of suicide. The causes and purposes of SIBs are not known, though physiological and social factors play a role, as do stereotypic and other challenging behaviors.

ABNORMAL BEHAVIOR, MENTAL HEALTH, AND MENTAL DISORDERS

Mental health (or well-being) is an ideal that is commonly sought by many people. It is a balance of mental, emotional, and spiritual health, all of which may be affected by physical health. Many positive aspects of life—such as caring relationships, a place to call home, a supportive community, satisfying work, and enjoyable leisure—all contribute to mental health. Because passage through life involves downs as well as ups, mental health also involves learning skills to cope with adversity.

The term *mental disorder* (also referred to as *mental illness* or *mental ill-health*) is frequently used in the psychiatric and psychological literature to mean something that is, in general, a psychological state that is the opposite of mental health. In the mental health field, the term *mental disorder* is used in reference to a number of conditions and concepts such as distress, dysfunction, dyscontrol, disadvantage, disability, inflexibility, irrationality, syndromal pattern, and etiological and statistical deviation. Each of these is a useful indicator for the broader concept of mental disorder.

The relationship between mental disorders and abnormal behavior is not a straightforward one. Although mental disorders are often characterized by abnormal behaviors, these vary considerably in nature and intensity. Furthermore, not all abnormal behaviors arise from mental disorders. For instance, someone walking naked in a public area, which would be considered as an abnormal behavior in most societies, may have done so for a reason other than mental ill-health. Thus, although abnormal behavior and mental disorders overlap considerably, abnormal behavior does not necessarily indicate a mental disorder, and a diagnosed mental disorder does not always result in abnormal behavior.

Abnormal or challenging behaviors may occur for many different reasons. They also may be present in people affected with a wide variety of mental disorders that are classified in manuals of mental disorders. Such disorders can occur in any person in the general population, regardless of any coexisting condition, including intellectual and developmental disabilities.

Two Classification Systems for Mental Ill-Health Disorders

Classification systems for mental ill-health disorders are intended to be guidelines for clinicians. Classification is the process by which the complexity of phenomena is reduced by arranging them into categories according to some established criteria for one or more purposes. A common misconception is that classification of disorders of mental ill-health

---

Psychiatric Disorders, Psychological Disorders, Mental Ill-Health and Other Terms

Other terms such as *psychiatric disorders* and *psychological disorders* are also used to describe mental disorders, but like the term *mental disorder*, the former terms also lack precise definitions. One may define mental disorders as those treated by psychiatrists and psychologists, although there is still no consensus on which disorders or behaviors would fall into each group. In addition, the treatment of psychiatric and psychological disorders often involves a multidisciplinary team consisting of mental health professionals other than psychiatrists and psychologists. Broadly speaking, the core elements of mental, psychiatric, and psychological disorders are cognitive, behavioral, and affective perturbations resulting in distress or disabilities. The term *mental ill-health* has been proposed as an all-encompassing term describing such behavioral, emotional, and psychiatric disturbances in people with or without intellectual and developmental disabilities. As such, this is the term of choice throughout this chapter though not necessarily in other chapters (e.g., 11, 16, 18, and 22). Of note, the term *dual diagnosis* is being used in the intellectual and developmental disabilities field to describe the co-occurrence of mental ill-health and intellectual and developmental disabilities in the same individual (Centre for Addiction and Mental Health [CAMH], 2012; NADD, 2016).

classifies people, when actually what are being classified are disorders that people have. Nevertheless, people who are diagnosed with having a mental disorder often experience stereotypes associated with having a label. The ultimate purpose of classification is to improve treatment and prevention efforts by clearly identifying such conditions in order to enhance knowledge about them. The two classification systems that are most widely used today are briefly described in the following subsections.

The *Diagnostic and Statistical Manual of Mental Disorders* The major classification system used by the majority of clinicians in North America to classify disorders associated with mental ill-health is the *DSM-5* (APA, 2013). In the *DSM-5*, a mental disorder reflects dysfunction in one or more processes that underlie mental functioning: psychological, biological, or developmental. Mental disorders tend to be accompanied by substantial distress or disability in social, work-related, or other activities that are very important in people's lives.

As explained by Grohol (2013), the *DSM-5* contains three major sections. The first explains how to use the *DSM*, the second provides information and categorical diagnoses, and the third provides self-assessment tools as well as categories that require more research. In Section II of *DSM-5*, the multiaxial system used in earlier versions of the *DSM* was eliminated in order to remove artificial distinctions between medical and mental disorders. Section II of *DSM-5* has approximately the same number of conditions as text revision of the fourth edition, known as the *DSM-IV-TR* (Grohol, 2013).

In *DSM-5*, a number of major changes were made in certain specific disorders (see Table 23.2). Of particular relevance to intellectual and developmental disabilities are changes to autism and related disorders, attention-deficit/hyperactivity disorder (ADHD), grief, and posttraumatic stress disorder (PTSD). Not known is how these changes might affect supports and services for people with dual diagnosis, a term used to describe people with a diagnosis of an intellectual or developmental disability as well as a mental health disorder.

The *International Statistical Classification of Diseases and Related Health Problems* A second system for classification of mental disorders is described in the *International Statistical Classification of Diseases and Related Health Problems, 10th Revision* (ICD-10; World Health Organization, 1992) in Chapter V: Mental and Behavioural Disorders. (See Tyrer [2014] for a discussion of differences between the *DSM-5* and ICD classification systems.) The ICD manual tends to be used in Europe and is undergoing revision as of this writing in 2016. The *International Classification of Diseases, Eleventh Revision* (ICD-11), to

Table 23.2. Major changes in selected disorders from the *Diagnostic and Statistical Manual of Mental Disorders, Fourth Edition, Text Revision (DSM-IV-TR)* to the *Diagnostic and Statistical Manual of Mental Disorders, Fifth Edition (DSM-5)*

DSM-IV-TR	DSM-5
Autistic Disorder (Autism), Asperger's Disorder, Childhood Disintegrative Disorder, Pervasive Developmental Disorder	These are now included in the umbrella term Autism Spectrum Disorder.
Child Bipolar Disorder	This is now called Disruptive Mood Regulation Disorder.
(There is a growing body of evidence—particularly among researchers—that bipolar disorder can exist in children, although this condition was not recognized in the *DSM-IV-TR* and there still is debate among professionals about the validity of this diagnosis [Grohol, 2015].)	
Attention-Deficit/Hyperactivity Disorder (symptoms must appear before age 7)	Symptoms must appear before age 12; this disorder can continue into adulthood and be diagnosed in adults.
Major Depressive Disorder (should not be diagnosed in individuals suffering grief from the loss of a loved one)	A diagnosis can now be made in individuals who are grieving.
Posttraumatic Stress Disorder	Diagnostic thresholds have been lowered for children and adolescents; separate criteria have been added for children age 6 years or younger.
Dementia and Amnestic Disorder	This is now included under Major Neurocognitive Disorder; another category called Mild Neurocognitive Disorders has been added.

Sources: American Psychiatric Association (2000, 2013), Grohol (2013, 2015), and Madra (2013).

Note: Binge Eating Disorder and Premenstrual Dysphoric Disorder are diagnoses in *DSM-5*. Hoarding Disorder is considered to be distinct from Obsessive-Compulsive Disorder (Grohol, 2013).

be released to the public in 2017, is a system of medical coding created by the WHO for documenting diseases, signs and symptoms, diagnoses, and social circumstances (Rouse, 2014). The ICD is being revised to better reflect progress in health sciences and medical practice. (See WHO [n.d.], section 4 for more detail about changes that are planned for the ICD.)

Some Forms of Abnormal Behavior Associated with Diagnosed Biomedical Conditions or Disorders

As mentioned previously, some forms of abnormal behavior are associated with particular biomedical conditions or disorders that have an etiological basis (i.e., have known causes or origins as determined by medical diagnosis). These include abnormal behaviors related to brain injury, neurological disorders, physical conditions causing pain, and reactions to certain drugs or their withdrawal. Although the causes of stereotypic and self-injurious behavior are still not fully understood, certain conditions are associated with increased risk of such behaviors under certain conditions. People with or without intellectual and developmental disabilities can be affected by the disorders described in the following subsections.

Brain Injury   Major causes of brain injury are physical impact (e.g., motor vehicle accidents, falls, bicycle accidents, sports injuries, assaults, bullet wounds), exposure to neurotoxic agents (e.g., lead and mercury poisoning, excessive alcohol use), disruption of cerebral blood supply (e.g., stroke), violent shaking of an infant's head, and hypoxia (lack of oxygen—e.g., from drowning or disruption

of breathing at birth). Such traumas may result in mild to severe brain injury and death. Brain injury also can result in a broad range of abnormal behaviors affecting neurocognitive and neurobehavioral functions. It is interesting to note that neonatal temporal lobe lesions (indications of brain damage in newborns) in monkeys result in behavioral changes strikingly similar to those characteristic of autism (Bachevalier, Málková, & Mishkin, 2001), suggesting that the basis of autism may be, at least in part, a problem of the central nervous system. Typically, emotional problems resulting from brain injury take the form of depression, anxiety, emotional blunting, and irritability. A number of rare disorders can result from brain injury. Some examples include loss of ability to recognize faces (prosopagnosia) or believing that one's family and friends are imposters who just look like friends and family (Capgras syndrome). For more details, see Percy et al. (2007).

Neurological Disorders   A neurological disorder is any disorder of the body's nervous systems. Structural, biochemical, or electrical abnormalities in the brain, spinal cord, or other nerves can result in a range of symptoms. Examples of symptoms involving behavioral changes include paralysis, muscle weakness, poor coordination, loss of sensation, seizures, confusion, pain, and altered levels of consciousness. See Table 23.3 for examples of some neurological disorders associated with characteristic behavior changes. Creutzfeldt-Jakob disease, Huntington disease, and seizure disorder (epilepsy) are some additional examples. See National Institute of Neurological Diseases and Stroke at http://www.ninds.nih.gov/disorders/disorder_index.htm for additional information.

Table 23.3.   Some neurological disorders associated with characteristic behavior changes

Neurological disorder	Underlying brain changes	Behavior changes
Alzheimer's disease	Progressive loss of connections between cells in the brain's cerebral cortex	Getting upset easily, pacing, being sad, cognitive impairment
Aphasia	Damage to regions of the brain involved with language, often from stroke	Difficulty remembering words; problems with speaking, reading, and writing
Cerebrovascular disease	Disorders (temporary or permanent) that result from bleeding into the brain or lack of blood flow to certain regions	Dizziness, balance problems, vision and speech disturbances, numbness and/or paralysis in certain parts of the body
Parkinson's disease	Loss of dopamine-generating cells in the substantia nigra, a region of the mid-brain	Physical behavior changes: tremor, rigidity, and postural imbalance Nonmotor behavior changes: depression, drug-induced psychosis and impulse control disorders, cognitive impairment, anxiety, and sleep disturbances

Note: See also the chapters on epilepsy (seizure disorders; Chapter 22) and dementia (Chapter 49) in this volume.

Pain Disorders In medicine, the term *pain* relates to a sensation that hurts. Hurt leads to feelings of discomfort, distress and, sometimes, agony. In people with intellectual and developmental disabilities, common indicators of pain include changes in motor activity, facial activity or expression, social-emotional indicators, and nonverbal vocal expression (e.g., crying, screaming) (de Knegt et al., 2013). Disorders associated with severe pain include migraines, sinus headaches, backaches, toothaches, sprains, strains, and central pain syndrome resulting from stroke, brain and spinal cord injury, multiple sclerosis, reaction to medications, cancer, and any condition that can cause damage to the nerves or brain. Although pain disorders often alter behavior, not all the responses would be considered abnormal.

Drug Side Effects and Drug Withdrawal Some people (with or without intellectual and developmental disabilities) experience serious side effects from drugs, whereas others do not. Furthermore, interaction between different medications can have serious consequences. All physicians treating patients need to be aware of all the medications their patients are taking (e.g., prescription drugs and over-the-counter medicines, including vitamins, minerals, and herbal supplements). People also need to discuss any alcohol or other drug use with their physicians. (See the National Institute of Mental Health web site at http://www.nimh.nih.gov/health/publications /mental-health-medications/complete-index.shtml for a list of side effects of antipsychotic medications.)

When a person stops using drugs or alcohol, there often is a rebound effect (i.e., the condition being treated becomes much worse). Side effects from withdrawal of some drugs can produce physical, emotional, or mental symptoms. For example, sudden withdrawal from the barbiturate clonazepam sometimes results in delirium (i.e., a serious disturbance in a person's mental abilities that results in a decreased awareness of one's environment and confused thinking; see http://www.addictionsandrecovery .org/withdrawal.htm and Chapter 30).

MENTAL ILL-HEALTH IN INTELLECTUAL AND DEVELOPMENTAL DISABILITIES

The diagnosis of mental disorders in people with intellectual and developmental disabilities using *DSM-5* or ICD-10 criteria is not straightforward. It is often difficult to distinguish between challenging behavior and emotional expression, distress, or consequences of a genetic syndrome. Also, many people with intellectual and developmental disabilities have medical conditions or sensory difficulties that complicate diagnosis. Furthermore, the rates of certain mental disorders in particular intellectual and developmental disabilities are unusually high. To aid with diagnosis of mental disorders in people with intellectual and developmental disabilities, readers should be aware of some special resources, including two manuals edited by Fletcher, Loschen, Stavrakaki, and First (2009a, 2009b) as well as other publications (e.g., Cooper, 2003; Cooper, Smiley, Morrison, Williamson, & Allan, 2006; Hassiotis, Barron, & Hall, 2009). The continuing medical education article by Perkins (2007) provides a comprehensive and succinct overview of this topic. See also Chapter 47 in this volume.

Prevalence of Mental Disorders and Abnormal Behaviors in Intellectual and Developmental Disabilities

Despite uncertainty associated with the diagnosis of mental disorders among people with intellectual and developmental disabilities, there is agreement that some mental disorders are as common as found in the general population and others (e.g., psychosis) are more common than found in the general population. A problem in prevalence estimates of mental disorders is whether to include challenging behaviors, which are common in people with intellectual and developmental disabilities (Buckles, Luckasson, & Keefe, 2013). One meta-analysis found the prevalence of mental disorders in children and adolescents with intellectual and developmental disabilities to be 30%–80%, versus 8%–18% in those without intellectual and developmental disabilities (Einfeld, Ellis, & Emerson, 2011). Another found the prevalence in adults with intellectual and developmental disabilities to be 14%–75% (Buckles et al., 2013).

Many people with intellectual and developmental disabilities have more than one mental health problem. The specific levels of impairment in intellectual and developmental disabilities appear to be differentially associated with the rates and types of mental health disorders that may be diagnosed. Psychopathology in individuals with intellectual and developmental disabilities with mild levels of impairment tends to be associated with psychiatric disorders, whereas behavioral issues are more pronounced in people with intellectual and developmental disabilities with profound levels of impairment. For individuals with intellectual disability with moderate and severe levels of impairment, behavioral and psychiatric disorders are demonstrated to exist at similar rates (Fletcher et al., 2009a, 2009b).

People who have both intellectual and developmental disabilities and a mental illness have more severe symptoms and are more likely to have co-occurring medical conditions and have fewer resources (e.g., access to education and social and economic supports). They are also more likely to require long-term hospitalization. The percentage of adults in tertiary-care psychiatric hospitals who have intellectual and developmental disabilities and a mental illness is as high as one in eight in some places (Lunsky, 2006). People with intellectual and developmental disabilities may be more susceptible to the effects of psychosocial stress than people in the general population, and this difference may contribute to their higher rates of mental ill-health (Buckles et al., 2013; CAMH, 2012).

Specific Disorders of Mental Ill-Health Common in People with Intellectual and Developmental Disabilities

In a two-stage epidemiological study of Dutch children, disruptive disorder, anxiety disorder, and mood disorder occurred with point prevalences of 25%, 22%, and 4% (Dekker & Koot, 2003). For information derived from a secondary analysis of British children and adolescents, see Emerson and Hatton (2007). Both studies found comorbid mental disorders to be common in people with intellectual and developmental disabilities. Information about some disorders of mental ill-health common in children and adults with intellectual and developmental disabilities is given in Table 23.4.

Syndromes with High Frequencies of Particular Mental Disorders

As mentioned previously, certain syndromes resulting in intellectual and developmental disabilities are associated with particular mental disorders that occur unusually frequently. These include the following:

- *Down syndrome (trisomy 21):* People with Down syndrome are at high risk of developing dementia resembling Alzheimer's disease 20–30 years earlier than people in the general population (see Chapter 49).

- *Chromosome 22q11 deletion syndrome (velocardiofacial syndrome):* Approximately 25% of affected individuals develop psychosis in adolescence, and schizoaffective and bipolar spectrum disorders are common (see Chapter 17).

- *Fetal alcohol spectrum disorder:* Conduct disorder and antisocial behavior can co-occur (see Chapters 18 and 19).

- *Prader-Willi syndrome:* Depression, anxiety, compulsive behavior, and psychosis can occur in affected individuals (see Chapter 21).

- *Fragile X syndrome:* Anxiety and avoidance and mood disorders can occur; also, males who carry a premutation are at risk of developing a Parkinson's-like disorder (see Chapter 15).

- *Autism spectrum disorder:* High rates of childhood-onset schizophrenia have been found to either be preceded by or comorbid with autism spectrum disorders (Rapoport, Chavez, Greenstein, Addington, & Gogtay, 2009; see Chapter 16).

Behavioral Phenotypes

The term *phenotype* refers to the observable characteristics or traits of an organism resulting from interaction of its genotype with the environment. The term *behavioral phenotype* does not have a precise definition. Cassidy and Morris (2002) described this as the characteristic cognitive, personality, behavioral, and psychiatric pattern that typifies a disorder. O'Brien's (2006) definition is broader and refers to behavioral phenotypes as "patterns of behavior that present in syndromes caused by chromosomal or genetic abnormalities. They have both physiological and behavioral manifestations with distinctive social, linguistic, cognitive and motor profiles" (p. 338). See also the review of behavioral phenotypes by Oliver et al. (2013).

A number of issues about behavioral phenotypes should be stressed. First and foremost, the underlying goal of defining behavioral phenotypes is to clarify how changes at the genetic level result in the distinctive physiological and/or behavioral features in order to pave the way for development of effective intervention and care. Second, the distinctive profiles characteristic of particular syndromes may include items of relative strength as well as others that are potentially problematic to others or harmful to the person with the genetic condition.

Table 23.4. Some disorders of mental ill-health common in children and adults with intellectual and developmental disabilities

Disorder	Abnormal behaviors
Adjustment disorder	Psychiatric disturbances that are related to identifiable life stressors and not severe enough to meet the criteria of a major mood or anxiety disorder
Anxiety disorders	Panic attacks, phobias, obsessions, and posttraumatic stress disorder, among others
Attention-deficit/hyperactivity disorder	Difficulty staying focused and paying attention, difficulty controlling behavior, and hyperactivity (overactivity)
Bipolar disorder	Ongoing cycles of feeling intensely happy and invincible, followed by depression
Borderline personality disorder	Behavior instability, creating chaos in one's own and other people's lives, severe difficulty with relationships, placing oneself in danger, making bad decisions (this disorder can be a consequence of a history of child abuse, abandonment, or neglect)
Conduct disorder	A serious behavioral and emotional disorder that can occur in children and teens; a child with this disorder may display a pattern of disruptive and violent behavior and have problems following rules
Depression	Intense feelings of sadness and worthlessness so severe that interest in life can be lost
Eating disorders	Anorexia (not eating), bulimia (eating too much and then vomiting), or binge eating disorder (eating too much and not purging, often leading to obesity)
Emotional disturbances	An umbrella term often used in the education field to include (but not limited to) anxiety disorders, bipolar disorder, conduct disorders, eating disorders, obsessive-compulsive disorder, and psychotic disorders (National Dissemination Center for Children with Disabilities, 2010)
Mood disorders	An umbrella term also known as affective disorders; the main types are depression, bipolar disorder, and anxiety disorder
Pica	Ingesting items of no nutritional value, such as dirt, paper, or paint
Posttraumatic stress disorder	A mental health condition triggered by a terrifying event, either from experiencing it or witnessing it; symptoms may include flashbacks, nightmares, and severe anxiety as well as uncontrollable thoughts about the event that persist for a very long time
Schizophrenia	Seeing, smelling, or hearing things that are not there (hallucinations) or holding firm beliefs that make no sense to anyone but the person affected (delusions); often called psychosis, a term that refers to loss of contact with reality
Sleep disorders	Include snoring (a sound generated during sleep by vibration of loose tissue in the upper airway), sleep apnea (involuntary cessation of breathing while a person is asleep), insomnia (difficulty falling and/or staying asleep), sleep deprivation, and restless legs syndrome (a neurological disorder characterized by unpleasant sensations in the legs and a strong urge to move them; symptoms occur mainly at night when a person is relaxing or resting and can increase in severity during the night); good sleep is necessary for optimal health, and lack of sleep can affect hormone levels, mood, and weight
Suicide	The act of taking one's life on purpose; suicide and suicidal behavior tends to occur more commonly in people affected by one or more of the following disorders: bipolar disorder, borderline personality disorder, depression, drug or alcohol use, posttraumatic stress disorder, schizophrenia, or stressful life issues such as serious financial or relationship problems
Substance abuse	Use of substances such as alcohol, street drugs, or pain killers to a point where they produce some form of intoxication that alters judgment, perception, attention, or physical control; abrupt cessation of use can result in withdrawal symptoms ranging from mild anxiety to seizures, hallucinations, or even death
Tic disorder	Short-lasting sudden movements (motor tics) or uttered sounds (vocal tics) that occur suddenly during what is otherwise normal behavior; tics are often repetitive, with numerous successive occurrences of the same action

Sources: Centre for Addiction and Mental Health (2012); Dekker, Koot, van der Ende, and Verhulst (2002); Fung, Percy, and Brown (2011); and Percy, Brown, and Lewkis (2007).

Third, although behavioral phenotypes may include examples of "abnormal" behavior, understanding their cause makes those people exhibiting them more "normal." Fourth, knowing the behavioral phenotype associated with a particular genetic condition can help others to understand how people interact with their environment and how to adapt the environment to suit their needs. Adapting the environment can include the implementation of effective educational strategies as well as medical interventions and be helpful to parents as well as people with the syndrome. Fifth, because they are

Table 23.5. Behavioral phenotypes associated with certain genetic syndromes and supports

Genetic disorder	Behavioral phenotype	Supports
Williams syndrome	• Strong conversational abilities • Lack of fear in social situations • Excessive empathy • Unusual affinity toward music • Unusual sensitivity to sound • Short attention span and distractibility	• Special education strategies • Attention to common health problems: cardiovascular, muscle and joints, kidney, colic, hypercalcemia
Prader-Willi syndrome	• Temper tantrums, obsessive-compulsive features, self-injurious behavior • Insatiable appetite predisposing to obesity and diabetes	• Dietary management • Weight control through meal planning • Drug treatment for anxiety and mood problems • Growth hormone to promote growth and decrease fat in developing children
Angelman syndrome	• General motor restlessness and overactivity • Short attention span • Ataxia (poor muscle coordination that may affect speech, eye movements, swallowing, walking, picking up objects) • Excessive and socially inappropriate laughter • Sleep disturbances • Depression in adulthood	• Recognition that unusual social behavior is not play-acting • Speech and language therapy • Management of sleep (e.g., with melatonin) • Attention to co-occurring depression, epilepsy • Behavioral analysis to identify triggers that provoke inappropriate laughter

Source: O'Brien (2006).

Note: For other examples of behavioral phenotypes, see Fung, Percy, and Brown (2011); Oliver et al. (2013); and Perkins (2007).

the consequences of known genetic alterations, behavioral phenotypes can provide important clues about genes that are important in cognition, determinants of personality, or certain psychiatric disorders. Finally, a behavioral phenotype can aid in making a diagnosis, just as a characteristic facial appearance aids with a diagnosis of Down syndrome. When a diagnosis is made of a particular genetic syndrome with a distinctive behavioral phenotype, the affected individual, their families, and caregivers should not have to completely reinvent the wheel with respect to current approaches to multidisciplinary management and supports.

Numerous genetic syndromes have been identified as having a distinctive and consistent behavior pattern (Cassidy & Morris, 2002; O'Brien, 2006; Oliver et al., 2013; Perkins, 2007). Three examples and a list of important supports are provided in Table 23.5.

SUPPORTS FOR ABNORMAL BEHAVIORS AND MENTAL HEALTH DISORDERS

At the broader, societal level, the focus on managing and treating abnormal behaviors should be on public

awareness, understanding the behaviors, and making accommodations that help to make the behavior less abnormal. People with schizophrenia were, in the not-so-distant past, feared and very often housed in psychiatric institutions only because their behavior was perceived as abnormal. Many people now understand that the behavior of someone with schizophrenia, though unusual at times, is rarely harmful to themselves or others and thus not something to be unduly feared. Moreover, community-based services for people with schizophrenia have allowed them to live in communities everywhere, which both contributes to their treatment and helps society provide for its citizens in natural ways. Similarly, people with intellectual and developmental disabilities; people who use wheelchairs, scooters, and other mobility aids; people with dementia; and people with many other physical and mental conditions are increasingly living more productive lives in their communities because the public is more aware of their needs, understands them better, and makes accommodations to include them in the way general society functions.

Easing Family Stress

Raising a child with intellectual and developmental disabilities who also has challenging behavior and/or mental health problems can be very stressful. Parents can experience stigma associated with these disorders and also become stressed from the rigors of navigating the social service and health care systems to get help. Although many different types of services exist, getting access to them can be difficult and waiting lists may be long. Relationships can suffer, siblings can feel neglected, and family income can be compromised if one parent has to leave work to provide child care.

Some strategies have been identified that can help families cope and alleviate such stresses. Going to school can be a source of distress for a child, but keeping a child home from school is not a good long-term solution. Stressful situations at school need to be addressed. Ideally, a child with challenging behavior needs a functional team that includes parents and a multidisciplinary group including the family doctor, teacher and principal, siblings, other family members, professionals with experience in mental health (including social workers, nurses, occupational therapists), and specialists such as a pediatrician and a psychiatrist. Parents should not be shy about asking for help from family, friends, and professionals to try to improve their quality of life and energy level. Remembering that each little step forward is progress in the right direction is important in maintaining a positive attitude (Szatmari, 2014).

Supports for Individuals with Intellectual and Developmental Disabilities

In addition, providing supports and services at the individual level can be very productive. The focus here should be on the recovery process for the associated mental health issue(s). The recovery process is not a cure, but it involves living life to the fullest despite challenges, and it needs a broader base of coping mechanisms other than diagnosis, medication, or therapy. The process of restoring and maintaining mental health should include the people who are affected as active participants along with their families and caregivers (CAMH, 2012).

Management of challenging behaviors needs to take into account the particular behavior and the setting in which it occurs, try to identify the possible cause or causes, and focus on reducing or eliminating the triggers in the individual who is affected (National Institute for Health and Care Excellence,

2015; U.S. Department of Health and Human Services, 2006). Multidisciplinary and multiagency involvement may be necessary. It is important to collect information about previous occurrences of abnormal behavior and the nature and outcome of previous interventions. Different treatment modalities (e.g., medical therapy, environmental changes, pharmacotherapy, psychological and social interventions) as well as applied behavior analysis (ABA) or positive behavior supports, alone or in combination, may be required.

Several different types of supports, either alone or in combination, have proved helpful for people with or without intellectual and developmental disabilities who exhibit challenging behaviors. In the intellectual and developmental disabilities field, these commonly include behavioral approaches, cognitive-behavioral therapy, and psychodynamic psychotherapy. However, the evidence base for these and their cost-effectiveness is limited (Bhaumik, Gangadharan, Hiremath, & Russell, 2011). It is recognized that people with intellectual and developmental disabilities can benefit from treatment that can range from general support to learn how to cope better with emotional distress to more specific treatments appropriate for common mental disorders (e.g., cognitive-behavioral therapy). Various supports that can be used to help people with abnormal behaviors are described in the following subsections.

Applied Behavior Analysis   ABA, previously known as behavior modification, is defined as the process of systematically applying interventions based upon the principles of learning theory to improve socially significant behaviors to a meaningful degree and to demonstrate that the interventions employed are responsible for the improvement of behavior (see Chapter 28 for more details).

Positive Behavioral Interventions and Supports   Positive behavioral interventions and supports (PBIS) has been derived from ABA. Although the two terms are sometimes used synonymously, PBIS differs from ABA in that it incorporates evaluative methods, assessment and intervention procedures, and conceptual perspectives associated with a number of additional disciplines (Dunlap, Carr, Horner, Zarcone, & Schwartz, 2008. It is a way to promote behavior expectations by teaching desired behaviors in order to prevent bad behaviors. (See https://www.pbis.org/.)

Table 23.6. Psychotherapeutic supports

Name of the support	Description
Cognitive-behavioral therapy	A short-term and focused therapy to help people change their behavior in relation to a particular situation or set of circumstances; during treatment, people learn how to identify and change destructive or disturbing thought patterns that have a negative influence on their behavior
Psychoanalysis	A method of studying the mind and treating mental and emotional disorders based on revealing and investigating the role of the unconscious mind
Gestalt therapy	Focuses on gaining an awareness of emotions and behaviors in the present rather than in the past; the therapist and patient work together to help the patient understand him- or herself
Interpersonal therapy	A time-limited treatment, typically lasting 12–16 weeks, that encourages the patient to regain control of mood and functioning
Eye movement desensitization and reprocessing	A physiologically based therapy that helps a person see disturbing material in a new and less distressing way; it has been used to treat people with mild intellectual disability and posttraumatic stress disorder

Sources: Flynn (2012) and Mevissen, Lievegoed, and de Jongh (2011).

Psychotherapeutic Supports Some psychotherapeutic supports that have been used in the intellectual and developmental disabilities field are described in Table 23.6. In addition, some supports have been developed or modified specifically for people with intellectual and developmental disabilities (see *Journal on Developmental Disabilities,* Volume 19, Number 1, 2013). Moreover, yoga is being used for anxiety and depression (Harvard Health Publications, 2016) and for children with autism (Betts & Betts, 2006), and mindfulness-based cognitive therapy is used to ward off recurrence of major depression (Piet & Hougaard, 2011).

Psychopharmaceutical Approaches The use of psychiatric medications is one form of biology-based treatment. Medications can be used to treat the symptoms of disorders such as schizophrenia, depression, bipolar disorder, anxiety disorders, and ADHD. Sometimes they are used in combination with other treatments such as psychotherapy (National Institutes of Health, 2008). For more information, see Chapter 30.

Other Biological Approaches A number of other biological approaches shown to have some benefit in alleviating severe mental disorders in the general population may possibly be considered for the treatment of people with intellectual and developmental disabilities. These include electroconvulsive therapy, psychosurgery including bilateral cingulotomy, and deep brain stimulation (Table 23.7). Note that those procedures rarely have been used in people with intellectual and developmental disabilities.

Supports for Stereotypic Behaviors Although stereotypic behaviors are seemingly purposeless, they may excite or arouse the nervous system and provide pleasure (Bascom, 2015).

Table 23.7. Some medical supports for severe mental health disorders

Name of the support	Description
Electroconvulsive therapy (ECT)	In this treatment, seizures are electrically induced in patients to provide relief from psychiatric illnesses. This approach is very specific to severe depression.
Psychosurgery	This involves severing or otherwise disabling areas of the brain to treat a personality disorder, behavior disorder, or other mental illness. Modern psychosurgical techniques target the pathways between the limbic system (the portion of the brain on the inner edge of the cerebral cortex), which is believed to regulate emotions, and the frontal cortex, where thought processes are seated. Use of psychosurgery is very controversial. It may be used for intractable mental disorders such as severe obsessive-compulsive disorder (OCD) not responsive to medication and for severe depression not responsive to medication and ECT.
Deep brain stimulation	This is a neurosurgical procedure involving the implantation of a medical device called a brain pacemaker, which sends electrical impulses through implanted electrodes to specific parts of the brain for the treatment of very severe movement and affective disorders (e.g., severe depression, anxiety, OCD, or tics).

Conversely, they may be calming (Higashida, 2013). They interfere with attention and learning but can be a positive reinforcer if a person is allowed to do them after finishing a task. It is possible to reduce the frequency of stereotypic behaviors by providing alternative, more socially appropriate forms of stimulation such as physical exercise. Drugs (e.g., risperidone) can be used to address such behaviors, but it is not known whether these reduce the behaviors directly or indirectly by slowing down overall motor movement. Intensive early behavioral intervention is reported to also reduce and/or eliminate stereotypical and other problem behaviors in youth with autism (Garner, 2005; Percy et al., 2007).

Supports for Self-Injurious Behaviors A variety of approaches are used in managing SIBs, including psychotropic medication (e.g., antidepressants, anxiolytics, risperidone, cognitive-behavioral therapy, behavioral intervention, massage and/or sensory integration therapy, group and family therapy). In the case of pica, treatment should first address any missing nutrients (e.g., iron, zinc) or other medical problems, such as lead poisoning if paint has been ingested. Then behavior modification, modification of the environment, and family education should be considered. With pica, for example, one form of treatment associates the pica behavior with negative consequences (mild aversion therapy). Then the person gets positive reinforcement for eating normal foods. Medications may help reduce the abnormal eating behavior in people with intellectual and developmental disabilities. Deep brain stimulation and psychosurgery have been used in severe, refractory cases of Tourette syndrome (Fung et al., 2011; Oliver & Richards, 2010; Percy et al., 2007). See Chapters 15, 16, 28, and 47 for more information about supports for self-injurious behaviors.

FUTURE DIRECTIONS

Research is exploding in the neurosciences. Researchers and clinicians in different fields are beginning to collaborate in order to provide new insight into the concepts of what it means to be human and what biological and molecular processes are involved in human behaviors. New advances in genetics are beginning to reveal how environmental effects act on the genome and alter gene expression via biochemical mechanisms that are distinct from the DNA coding sequence (Mehler, 2010).

Understanding of nervous system development and function, both normal and pathogenic, is expanding at an enormous rate. The profound importance of a healthy diet, exercise (Lachance & Ramsey, 2015; Logan & Jacka, 2015; Lopresti, Hood, & Drummond, 2013; Sarris et al., 2014) and good sleep (Richdale, Francis, Gavidia-Payne, & Cotton, 2000; Weiss, 2013) in the management of challenging behaviors and mental health disorders is finally being recognized.

New information about what causes abnormal behaviors is raising the prospect of more effective treatments and interventions for them. For example, it is known that excessive exposures to heavy metals such as lead and mercury can result in intellectual and developmental disabilities and unusual behavior, and excesses of other metals also may be problematic (Adal & Wiener, 2016; Kordas, 2010). There is increasing awareness that different types of microorganisms in the gut (i.e., the microbiome) can affect behavior in different ways and possibly have profound effects on mental health (Foster & McVey Neufeld, 2013; Khanna & Tosh, 2014).

Yet all of these advances are raising new social, ethical, and legal questions not previously anticipated. The mental health treatment system has an edgy relationship with the legal system. This is because under certain circumstances people can be forced into mental health treatment. Exploring new ground, illustrated by the previously presented examples, is adding tremendously to knowledge of challenging behaviors and mental health disorders for both those in the general population and people with intellectual and developmental disabilities.

SUMMARY

In this chapter, we approached the topic of abnormal behavior from psychosocial and biomedical perspectives. We introduced readers to the concepts of normal and abnormal (or challenging) behaviors, mental disorders, mental ill-health, dual diagnosis, and suicidal behavior and suicide, as well as to two classification systems commonly used in characterization of mental ill-health. Various causes for abnormal behavior were outlined, including stress and anxiety; attention problems; personality disorders; schizophrenia; depression; eating, psychosocial, and sleeping disorders; pain disorders; substance abuse; medication side effects and withdrawal effects; brain injury and various neurological disorders; and behavioral patterns associated with particular genetic syndromes and forms of intellectual and developmental disabilities. New research directions are elucidating the neurological processes that are involved in human behavior as well as the importance of a healthy diet, exercise, and good sleep. These efforts also are raising new social, ethical, and legal questions.

FOR FURTHER THOUGHT AND DISCUSSION

1. What are some types of behavior that you consider to be normal and abnormal? Explain why they seem normal or abnormal to you.

2. What types of behavior considered abnormal by some people in society might not really be abnormal? What can be done to change society's views and help behaviors that are considered to be abnormal to be seen as more normal?

3. In the field of intellectual and developmental disabilities, the term *dual diagnosis* refers to an individual who has been diagnosed with an intellectual or developmental disability as well as a mental health condition. It is also understood that some mental health problems and challenging behaviors are associated with some types of intellectual and developmental disabilities. Discuss whether (and, if so, how much or in what instances) intellectual and developmental disabilities and challenging behaviors or mental health problems overlap.

4. Researchers are continuing to unravel the understanding of the biological mechanisms underlying abnormal behavior. Do you think that such information may lead to new forms of stigmatization and to attempts to eliminate abnormal behaviors through genetic selection? Or might such information help to ameliorate different forms of mental ill-health and the consequences of this in society?

REFERENCES

Adal, A., & Wiener, S.W. (2016, June 30). *Heavy metal toxicity*. Retrieved from http://emedicine.medscape.com/article/814960-overview

American Psychiatric Association. (2000). *Diagnostic and statistical manual of mental disorders* (4th ed., text revision). Washington, DC: Author.

American Psychiatric Association. (2013). *Diagnostic and statistical manual of mental disorders* (5th ed.). Arlington, VA: American Psychiatric Publishing.

Bachevalier, J., Málková, L., & Mishkin, M. (2001). Effects of selective neonatal temporal lobe lesions on socioemotional behavior in infant rhesus monkeys (*Macaca mulatta*). *Behavioral Neuroscience, 115,* 545–559.

Bascom, J. (2015). *The obsessive joy of autism*. London, United Kingdom: Jessica Kingsley.

Betts, D.E., & Betts, S.W. (2006). *Yoga for children with autism spectrum disorders: A step-by-step guide for parents and caregivers*. London, United Kingdom: Jessica Kingsley.

Bhaumik, S., Gangadharan, S., Hiremath, A., & Russell, P.S. (2011). Psychological treatments in intellectual disability: The challenges of building a good evidence base. *British Journal of Psychiatry, 198,* 428–430.

Bicard, S.C., Bicard, D.F., & the IRIS Center. (2012). *Defining behavior*. Retrieved from http://iris.peabody.vanderbilt.edu/case_studies/ICS-015.pdf

Buckles, J., Luckasson, R., & Keefe, E. (2013). A systematic review of the prevalence of psychiatric disorders in adults with intellectual disability. 2003–2010. *Journal of Mental Health Research in Intellectual Disabilities, 6,* 181–207.

Cassidy, S.B., & Morris, C.A. (2002). Behavioral phenotypes in genetic syndromes: Genetic clues to human behavior. *Advances in Pediatrics, 49,* 59–86.

Centre for Addiction and Mental Health. (2012). *Mental illness and addictions: Facts and statistics*. Retrieved from http://www.camh.ca/en/hospital/about_camh/newsroom/for_reporters/Pages/addictionmentalhealthstatistics.aspx

Chan, J., Arnold, S., Webber, L., Riches, V., Parmenter, T., & Stancliffe, R. (2012). Is it time to drop the term "challenging behaviour"? *Learning Disability Practice, 15,* 36–38.

Cooper, S.A. (2003). *Classification and assessment of psychiatric disorders in adults with learning [intellectual] disabilities*. Retrieved from http://www.intellectualdisability.info/mental-health/classification-and-assessment-of-psychiatric-disorders-in-adults-with-learning-intellectual-disabilities/?searchterm=None

Cooper, S.A., Smiley, E., Morrison, J., Williamson, A., & Allan, L. (2006). Mental ill-health in adults with intellectual disabilities: Prevalence and associated factors. *British Journal of Psychiatry, 190,* 27–35.

Dekker, M.C., & Koot, H.M. (2003). DSM-IV disorders in children with borderline to moderate intellectual disability. I: Prevalence and impact. *Journal of the American Academy of Child and Adolescent Psychiatry, 42,* 915–922.

Dekker, M.C., Koot, H.M., van der Ende, J., & Verhulst, F.C. (2002). Emotional and behavioral problems in children and adolescents with and without intellectual disability. *Journal of Child Psychology and Psychiatry, 43,* 1097–1098.

de Knegt, N.C., Pieper, M.J., Lobbezoo, F., Schuengel, C., Evenhuis, H.M., Passchier, J., & Scherder, E.J. (2013). Behavioral pain indicators in people with intellectual disabilities: A systematic review. *Journal of Pain, 14,* 885–896.

Dunlap, G., Carr, E.G., Horner, R.H., Zarcone, J., & Schwartz, I. (2008). Positive behavior support and applied behavior analysis: A familial alliance. *Behavior Modification, 32,* 682–698.

Dusenbery, D.B. (2009). *Living at micro scale*. Cambridge, MA: Harvard University Press.

Einfeld, S.L. Ellis, L.A., & Emerson, E. (2011). Comorbidity of intellectual disability and mental disorder in children and adolescents: A systematic review. *Journal of Intellectual and Developmental Disability, 36,* 137–143.

Emerson, E. (2001). *Challenging behaviour: Analysis and intervention in people with severe learning disabilities* (2nd ed., p. 3). Cambridge, United Kingdom: Cambridge University Press.

Emerson, E., & Hatton, C. (2007). Mental health of children and adolescents with intellectual disabilities in Britain. *British Journal of Psychiatry, 191,* 493–499.

Fletcher, R.J., Loschen, E., Stavrakaki, C., & First, M. (Eds.). (2009a). *Diagnostic manual—intellectual disability (DM-ID): A clinical guide for diagnosis of mental disorders in persons with intellectual disability.* Kingston, NY: NADD Press.

Fletcher, R.J., Loschen, E., Stavrakaki, C., & First, M. (Eds.). (2009b). *Diagnostic manual—intellectual disability (DM-ID): A textbook of diagnosis of mental disorders in persons with intellectual disability.* Kingston, NY: NADD Press.

Flynn, A.G. (2012). Fact or faith? On the evidence for psychotherapy for adults with intellectual disability and mental health needs. *Current Opinion in Psychiatry, 25,* 342–347.

Foster, J.A., & McVey Neufeld, K.-A. (2013). Gut-brain axis: How the microbiome influences anxiety and depression. *Neurosciences, 36,* 305–312.

Fung, W.L.A., Percy, M., & Brown, I. (2011). Abnormal behaviour. In I. Brown & M. Percy (Eds.), *Developmental disabilities in Ontario* (3rd ed., pp. 610–640). Toronto, Canada: Ontario Association on Developmental Disabilities.

Garner, J.P. (2005). Stereotypies and other abnormal repetitive behaviors: Potential impact on validity, reliability, and replicability of scientific outcomes. *Institute for Laboratory Animal Research Journal, 46,* 106–117.

Grohol, J. (2013). *DSM-5 released: The big changes.* Retrieved from http://psychcentral.com/blog/archives/2013/05/18/dsm-5-released-the-big-changes/

Grohol, J.M. (2015, October 30). *Symptoms of childhood bipolar disorder.* Retrieved from http://psychcentral.com/lib/symptoms-of-childhood-bipolar-disorder/

Harvard Health Publications. (2016). *Yoga for anxiety and depression.* Retrieved from http://www.health.harvard.edu/mind-and-mood/yoga-for-anxiety-and-depression

Hassiotis, A., Barron, D.A., & Hall, I. (Eds.). (2009). *Intellectual disability psychiatry: A practical handbook.* Hoboken, NJ: Wiley.

Higashida, N. (2013). *The reason I jump: The inner voice of a thirteen-year-old boy with autism.* New York, NY: Penguin Random House.

Khanna, S., & Tosh, P.K. (2014). A clinician's primer on the role of the microbiome in human health and disease. *Mayo Clinic Proceedings, 89,* 107–114.

Kordas, K. (2010). Iron, lead, and children's behavior and cognition. *Annual Review of Nutrition, 30,* 123–148.

Lachance, L., & Ramsey, D. (2015). Food, mood, and brain health: Implications for the modern clinician. *Missouri Medicine, 112,* 111–115.

Levitis, D., Lidicker, W.Z., Jr., & Freund, G. (2009). Behavioural biologists do not agree on what constitutes behaviour. *Animal Behaviour, 78,* 103–110.

Logan, A.C., & Jacka, F.N. (2014). Nutritional psychiatry research: An emerging discipline and its intersection with global urbanization, environmental challenges and the evolutionary mismatch. *Journal of Physiological Anthropology, 33,* 22. doi:10.1186/1880-6805-33-22

Lopresti, A.L., Hood, S.D., & Drummond, P.D. (2013). A review of lifestyle factors that contribute to important pathways associated with major depression: Diet, sleep and exercise. *Journal of Affective Disorders, 148,* 12–27.

Lunsky, Y. (2006). The clinical profile and service needs of adults with mental retardation and a psychiatric diagnosis. *Psychiatric Services, 7,* 177–183.

Madra, N. (2013). *DSM-5 brief overview.* Retrieved from http://essentiallearning.com/courseresources/courses/REl-DSM5-BO-0/story_content/external_files/REL-DSM5-BO-0_DSM-5%20-%20Transcript.pdf

Mehler, M.F. (2010). Epigenetics and neuropsychiatric diseases: Introduction and meeting summary. *Annals of the New York Academy of Sciences, 1204*(Suppl.), E1–7.

Mevissen, L.A., Lievegoed, R., & de Jongh, A. (2011). EMDR treatment in people with mild ID and PTSD: 4 cases. *Psychiatric Quarterly, 82,* 43–57.

NADD. (2016). *Information on dual diagnosis.* Retrieved from http://thenadd.org/resources/information-on-dual-diagnosis-2/

National Dissemination Center for Children with Disabilities. (2010). *NICHCY Disability Fact Sheet #5: Emotional disturbance.* Retrieved from http://www.parentcenterhub.org/wp-content/uploads/repo_items/fs5.pdf

National Institute for Health and Care Excellence. (2015, May). *Challenging behaviour and learning disabilities: Prevention and interventions for people with learning disabilities whose behaviour challenges.* Retrieved from https://www.nice.org.uk/guidance/ng11/chapter/Personcentred-care

National Institutes of Health. (2008). *Mental health medications: Overview.* Retrieved from http://www.nimh.nih.gov/health/publications/mental-health-medications/index.shtml

O'Brien, G. (2006). Behavioural phenotypes: Causes and clinical implications. *Advances in Psychiatric Treatment, 12,* 338–348.

Oliver, C., Adams, D., Allen, D., Bull, L., Heald, M., Moss, J.,…Woodcock, K. (2013). Causal models of clinically significant behaviors in Angelman, Cornelia de Lange, Prader-Willi and Smith-Magenis syndromes. In R.P. Hastings & J. Rojahn (Eds.), *International review of research in developmental disabilities: Challenging behaviour* (Vol. 44, pp. 167–244). San Diego, CA: Elsevier Academic Press.

Oliver, C., & Richards, C. (2010). Self-injurious behaviour in people with intellectual disability. *Current Opinion in Psychiatry, 23*(5), 412–416.

Oxford University Press. (2016). *Behavior.* Retrieved from http://www.oxforddictionaries.com/definition/american_english/behavior

Percy, M., Brown, I., & Lewkis, S. (2007). Abnormal behavior. In I. Brown & M. Percy (Eds.), *A comprehensive guide to intellectual and developmental disabilities* (pp. 309–361). Baltimore, MD: Paul H. Brookes Publishing Co.

Perkins, C. (2007). Mental illness in people with intellectual disability. *New Zealand Family Physician, 34,* 358–362.

Piet, J., & Hougaard, E. (2011). The effect of mindfulness-based cognitive therapy for prevention of relapse in recurrent major depressive disorder: A systematic review and meta-analysis. *Clinical Psychology Review, 31,* 1032–1040.

Rapoport, J., Chavez, A., Greenstein, D., Addington, A., & Gogtay, N. (2009). Autism spectrum disorders and childhood-onset schizophrenia: Clinical and biological contributions to a relation revisited. *Journal of the American Academy of Child and Adolescent Psychiatry, 48,* 10–18.

Richdale, A., Francis, A., Gavidia-Payne, S., & Cotton, S. (2000). Stress, behaviour, and sleep problems in children with an intellectual disability. *Journal of Intellectual and Developmental Disability, 25,* 147–161.

Rouse, M. (2014). *IDC-11.* Retrieved from http://searchhealthit.techtarget.com/definition/ICD-11

Sarris, J., Logan A.C., Akbaraly, T.N., Amminger, G.P., Balanzá-Martínez, V., Freeman, M.P.,...Jacka, F.N. (2015). Nutritional medicine as mainstream in psychiatry. *Lancet Psychiatry, 2,* 271–274.

Szatmari, P. (2014, August 29). *Five ways to ease the family stress of a child with a mental health challenge.* Retrieved from http://www.theglobeandmail.com/life/health-and-fitness/health-advisor/five-ways-to-ease-the-family-stress-of-a-child-with-a-mental-health-challenge/article20077997/

Tyrer, P. (2014). A comparison of DSM and ICD classifications of mental disorder. *Advances in Psychiatric Treatment, 20,* 280–285.

U.S. Department of Health and Human Services. (2006). *Strategies for understanding and managing challenging behavior in young children: What is developmentally appropriate—and what is a concern?* Technical Assistance Paper No. 10. Retrieved from http://eclkc.ohs.acf.hhs.gov/hslc/hs/resources/ECLKC_Bookstore/PDFs/TA10%5B1%5D.pdf

Weiss, T.C. (2013, December 21). *Sleep issues and children with developmental disorders.* Retrieved from http://www.disabled-world.com/health/neurology/sleepdisorders/cdd.php

World Health Organization. (1992). *International Statistical Classification of Diseases and Related Health Problems, Tenth Revision (ICD-10).* Geneva, Switzerland: Author.

World Health Organization. (n.d.). *International Classification of Diseases (ICD) revision.* Retrieved from http://www.who.int/classifications/icd/revision/icd11faq/en/

IV

Support and Intervention

24

An Introduction to Assessment, Diagnosis, Interventions, and Services

Ivan Brown and Maire Percy

- Effectiveness of ongoing and continuous assessment
- Use of formal assessment to identify (but label) people with specific conditions
- Good intervention based on the results of assessment
- Pros and cons to giving a diagnosis, and best practices for doing so
- Following specific guidelines for effective interventions and using them for specific purposes

To introduce this book's Support and Intervention section, this chapter presents four topics that are very much interrelated in practice: assessment, diagnosis, intervention, and services. The term *assessment* refers to the process of investigating and documenting knowledge, skills, capabilities, attitudes, and beliefs. In the field of intellectual and developmental disabilities, assessment is used primarily to help determine the strengths and capabilities, as well as the support needs, of children or adults and to suggest the most appropriate types of interventions and services. Assessment is also sometimes used to determine whether a person has a developmental disability or other condition and, if so, to describe its nature or type on the basis of its signs, symptoms, and the results of various tests. The conclusion reached from this latter process is called a diagnosis. Making a diagnosis in the field

of intellectual and developmental disabilities can be complex and sometimes requires ongoing assessment over a number of months or years, as well as input from various types of professionals.

The word *intervention* refers, in a literal sense, to the act or an instance of interfering or intruding. In the field of intellectual and developmental disabilities, *intervention* means something slightly different. It refers to a group of methods for taking intentional action to help people improve their lives in a variety of positive ways. Intervention should be based on the results of sound assessment procedures that are ongoing in nature and should be amended continuously based on ongoing assessment.

The term *service* (often called *support*) refers to the resources and structures that are in place for the purpose of helping others, whether or not they are used and whether or not they are actually helpful. To complicate understanding, the term *service* is also commonly used to refer to the act of helping others or of doing work that provides assistance or benefits to someone. In this sense, it overlaps somewhat with the meaning of *intervention*, as the term *services* is used to refer to a group of interventions and to interventions in general. Service for people with intellectual or developmental disabilities is multidisciplinary, as it includes direct care, health, education, and support in a variety of areas of life. Some service is designed to be specifically for people with disabilities and other service is for broader populations but is also available to people with disabilities. Overall,

343

though, *service* means the presence of formal and informal resources and structures that are available to people with disabilities and that can directly help to improve their lives. Interventions, to be effective, very much depend on the availability of needed services. Services are referred to throughout this chapter but are not described in detail here. Instead, a summary of common service types and of services available in most developed countries is described in Chapter 25.

The present chapter provides an introduction to assessment, diagnosis, intervention, and services because it is critical to stress their importance to the overall support provided to children and adults with intellectual and developmental disabilities. These topics have been addressed through a vast number of books, articles, and practical materials. It is not possible to represent or summarize all of the information that is available in these resources; thus, this chapter serves as an introduction to a much larger area of study. Readers are encouraged to explore, through more specific reading and study, specific diagnostic criteria and guidelines, as well as the large number of specific methods of assessment and intervention strategies for a broad array of purposes that are available in the disability literature. For example, see the American Association on Intellectual and Developmental Disabilities (AAIDD) publication *Intellectual Disability: Definition, Classification, and Systems of Supports* (Schalock, Borthwick-Duffy, Buntinx, Coulter, & Craig, 2010). Also of note are two manuals that deal with the diagnosis of mental disorders in people with intellectual disability (Fletcher, Loschen, Stavrakaki, & First, 2009a, 2009b). Readers are encouraged to become fully familiar with services that are available in their local areas.

ASSESSMENT

The field of intellectual and developmental disabilities—like the fields of education, social work, psychotherapy, psychiatry, and medicine—has a well-developed literature on assessment for both individuals and populations (groups of individuals). This literature places a strong emphasis on individual assessment to identify and address the specific needs of individuals with disabilities and, to a lesser degree, on population assessment to identify and address the needs of groups of people with disabilities. This literature continues to evolve, yet its basic premise has remained stable over time—namely,

that assessment is crucial to providing information for identifying needs and difficulties that can be addressed through interventions or services, for the specific purpose of helping to maintain or improve people's lives.

Ongoing need for intervention and services is the most important reason for assessment, but it also has become important to deliver intervention and services in the most cost-effective and efficient manner that benefits individuals. In most developed countries, services and the funds to support them have expanded quite dramatically since the mid-20th century. Along with this expansion, there has been a shift toward attempting to ensure that these services are not wasted. This trend encourages use of the human and financial resources and structures available to carry out interventions in ways that both are efficient and have positive impacts on people's lives by directly addressing their needs and difficulties.

At the same time, broad concepts such as inclusion, quality of life, and self-determination have gained tremendous attention since about 1990, especially because they emphasize the importance of maximizing independence, abilities, and the quality within each person's life. Service has incorporated many of the core ideas and values related to these concepts into the daily work of frontline workers and has placed a stronger emphasis on person-centered approaches to service (see Chapter 25). The emphasis on these ideals has further increased the need for individual assessment that can accurately identify aspects of life that currently provide quality and thus need to be maintained and enhanced, as well as those aspects of life that are problematic and need to be improved or removed from the person's life (Brown & Brown, 2003).

Overall Approach to Assessment for Service and Intervention Needs

There is a large amount of literature on assessment for people with intellectual and developmental disabilities. Numerous texts, detailing assessment methods and strategies that are useful for many purposes and over the life span, are readily available in such places as university and professional libraries. Here, in keeping with the objectives of this chapter, an overall approach to assessment is outlined.

Individual and Population Assessment
Assessment involves gathering information about something and drawing conclusions based on that

information. In the field of intellectual and developmental disabilities, that "something" for an individual is most typically the person's health and social history; characteristics, skills, knowledge, or behavior; the environment in which the person lives; and the interaction between the person and that environment or the interaction between the person and other people. Assessment may occur for a variety of reasons, including understanding how best to teach a child or adult, to improve physical and mental health, to provide support in everyday activities, and to identify needed services and interventions. Whatever the reason for carrying out a specific individual assessment, its overall purpose is to identify an area of capability or incapability and to suggest strategies or interventions that help improve the way an individual does things, the support in an individual's life, or the environment in which an individual lives.

Assessment for populations, or a focus on a group of individuals, is also important in the field of intellectual and developmental disabilities. For example, by gathering data on a large number of individuals in a region, it may become apparent that a significant number of youth with disabilities do not have major daily activities immediately on leaving school and that this situation is problematic for both the youth and their families. Such information, once gathered, can lead to recommendations for establishing resources so that interventions that address these needs can be put in place.

Assessment for Specific Reasons and Ongoing Assessment Often, assessment is carried out for a very specific reason. Frontline support personnel, family members, or others may refer an individual for a formal assessment because they would like opinions or answers to questions that they have identified. For example, educators may want information on the learning strengths and preferred learning styles of an 8-year-old girl to help determine the most appropriate class setting and teaching strategies for her. In this case, they may refer her to a school psychologist for assessment. In another example, parents may want to understand why their 40-year-old son is showing symptoms of depression and is having mood swings. They may seek a referral to a psychologist or a psychiatrist for their son.

Not all individual assessment is carried out for a specific reason, at a specific time, or in such a formal way. At times, professionals or frontline workers may carry out an assessment themselves to address a specific question or problem that has arisen. In these types of cases, assessment may—and should—be conducted in an ongoing way by those who support people with disabilities. A simple example is a 5-year-old boy who is crying. His caregiver will probably wonder if he is hurt, frightened, hungry, or tired, or if there is another problem. She will, in all likelihood, try to find out why he is crying and attempt to do something about it. If she determines that he is crying because he is frightened, she will probably try to separate him from the source of his fear and offer him physical and emotional comfort. In doing these things, the caregiver has gathered information about a problem situation, made a decision about the cause of the problem, and taken steps to improve it. Using the same basic approach, effective caregivers, support personnel, and professionals notice numerous small and not-so-small things during the course of a day that they assess for the purpose of improving or maximizing their support or the environment. For example, if a caregiver notices that a child is having trouble tying his or her shoe, the caregiver may observe and perform a series of small tests to determine if the child does not have the manual dexterity to tie the shoe, if he or she needs step-by-step instruction for how to do it, if time and space needs to be allocated for the task, or if there is another reason. Once the reason has been determined, a plan of action can be generated for improving the situation. In this way, individual assessment is integrated into the ongoing daily care, education, and other support provided to individuals.

Five Basic Assessment Actions

Assessments are described and organized in many different ways. They differ quite markedly because the purposes of assessments are different. For example, one would use different methods to assess hearing, vision, speech and language ability, communication, motor skills, level of intelligence, daily

---

Assessment Tip

All effective disability professionals should be in the habit of carrying out ongoing and continuous assessment in a wide range of areas as they go about their daily work.

living skills, need for physical and occupational therapy, ability to be responsible for a pet, capacity for traveling independently on a bus, or friend-making skills. Regardless of the specific assessment methods, they share some basic, overall components. Five actions that describe such common components are as follows:

1. Attend to a situation or problem that has come to one's attention for a specific reason or simply because it is occurring in an individual's life.

2. Gather as much information as possible about the situation or problem.

3. Analyze which aspects of the situation are working well (strengths) and which aspects are not working well (needs).

4. Understand the factors that help improve the situation as well as factors that hinder its improvement.

5. Decide on plans to maintain or enhance factors that help improve the situation and to decrease or eliminate factors that hinder improvement; such plans, once put into action, are often referred to as intervention (Brown & Brown, 2003).

THEORETICAL FRAMEWORKS FOR ASSESSMENT

It is often helpful to conceptualize and conduct assessment within a set of procedures that reflect both a theoretical stance and sound professional-ethical practice. Many such sets of procedures are available in assessment texts. One example (see Table 24.1) was put forward by Brown and Brown (2003), who advocated from the theoretical perspective that effective quality of life is an inherent right for all people with disabilities.

Formal Assessment

Assessment can, and should, be carried out by all disability professionals on an ongoing basis. At times, however, it is advisable to have an assessment carried out in a more formal way by a qualified professional or group of professionals. Formal assessments are usually carried out when there is a need to explain an individual's achievement levels or behavior, when there is a need to understand more clearly what learning strategies or behavior

strategies might be best suited to the individual's abilities, when a health or life course problem arises and needs to be addressed, or when there is a need to ascertain if an individual is eligible for a specific service (e.g., special education, vocational support).

Table 24.2 summarizes common target areas of formal assessment in intellectual and developmental disabilities. Formal tests are very often included in an assessment battery (a group of tools that use a variety of methods—e.g., intelligence tests, tests of adaptive behavior, tests of motor skills, hearing and vision tests). Typically, formal tests are characterized as either objective or subjective, and both are often used in testing to provide balance. Objective tests include fixed and well-defined scoring procedures. Often, these tests are referred to as standardized tests. Being standardized means that the test has been applied to a group of individuals of defined age and sex; thus, test results of a person being tested for a disability are compared with the test results of others of similar age and sex. Subjective tests typically seek the perception or perspective of the person being assessed and those of other people, and they are often designed to be interpreted by the assessor (e.g., ink blot tests, tests of apperception—perception as modified and enhanced by one's own emotions, memories, and biases).

Should formal testing be required for eligibility to services? Due to fiscal restraints and a perceived need for greater accountability since the 1990s, it has become more common in many jurisdictions to require formal testing of individuals to confirm that they have an intellectual or developmental disability before some types of services are offered. There are a number of advantages to requiring formal testing to determine eligibility for services. The most important of these are ensuring that services are available to the individuals for whom they were intended, ensuring that people are not given inappropriate or unnecessary services, and being accountable to administrators (and indirectly to taxpayers) for monies spent on services (see also discussion in Chapter 1).

On the other hand, there is considerable literature available on the difficulties of obtaining reliable test results from some individuals. For example, difficulties with hearing, vision, mobility, speech and language, mood, anxiety, concentrating, distractibility, and hypersensitivity to bright light interfere with obtaining accurate results from formal testing. Another problem is that formal

Table 24.1. Steps for blending quality of life concepts into assessment and intervention

Look at the person and his or her environment.
Person's own life experiences
Personal domains common to most people (e.g., family, friends, accommodations, work, leisure)
Environmental, social, and historical conditions in which the person lives
Environmental domains common to most people (e.g., community resources, public safety)

Set priorities for action.
First: Basic necessities
Second: The important things in life that bring satisfaction
Third: Achieving high levels of fulfillment and meaning in life

Carry out the initial appraisal.
Determine individual strengths and needs.
Determine the individual's wishes.
Determine whether short term or long term and immediate or distant.

Determine how to assess.
Use objective indicators and standardized instruments.
Gather personal perceptions of the individual and others.
Take into account the importance and value to the person of the needs being assessed.
Shape information toward stated personal goals.

Consider two key aspects.
Holism/domains: Life is often thought of in parts but works as an integrated whole.
Life has a changing nature over time.

Focus on what to assess and apply.
What is valued, relevant, and important to the person?
What does the individual perceive as leading to satisfaction and happiness?
What offers opportunities for improvement?
What reflects personal choice?
What enhances self-image?
What contributes to personal empowerment?

Consider other practice factors.
Effect on family members and others close to the individual
Professional considerations
Ethical issues
Policy and management issues

Look to goals (end points) in five key areas of improvement.
Well-being
Enjoyment/satisfaction
Personal meaning
Positive self-image
Social inclusion

From Brown, I., & Brown, R. I. (2003). *Quality of life and disability: An approach for community practitioners* (pp. 117–118). London: Jessica Kingsley Publishers, Copyright © Ivan Brown and Roy I. Brown 2003, second impression 2004; reproduced with permission of JESSICA KINGLSEY PUBLISHERS via PLSclear.

assessment is not always widely available and it is expensive. Thus, not everybody who needs to be tested obtains access to this testing in a timely manner or, sometimes, at all. One of the problems with requiring a formal diagnosis of intellectual disability as part of eligibility is that many people who have IQ scores between 70 and 85 (approximately one seventh of the general population in North America) have social and emotional problems that are not well addressed by generic services. These individuals, however, are usually ineligible for developmental disability services because they do

Table 24.2. Common target areas of formal assessment in developmental disability

Formal assessment typically identifies needs and strengths in these areas:

Intellectual functioning (an essential component of most formal assessments)

Adaptive skills (an essential component of most formal assessments)

Learning abilities and learning styles

Neurosensory functions (i.e., hearing, vision, and motor skills)

Speech and language function

Health and medical conditions

Dental health

Nutrition

Neuropsychological issues

Life skills

Activities of daily living

Living environment

Available supports

not have a formal diagnosis or meet other eligibility criteria set by service providers (Tymchuk, Lakin, & Luckasson, 2001; Zetlin & Murtaugh, 1990).

Trend Toward Multifaceted Formal Assessment

Multifaceted (or multidisciplinary) assessment involves professionals with different areas of expertise (e.g., pediatrics, family medicine, neurology, psychiatry, clinical genetics, education, psychology, social work) and the compilation of information from these different sources. It often involves observing adaptive and maladaptive behaviors in more than one environment. This type of assessment is considered especially useful in developing individualized plans for supports and services. Multifaceted assessment is typically carried out in environments that reveal needs for early childhood services, educational services, and, in some cases, social services for adults or families that have children with disabilities.

The purposes of multifaceted assessment often differ according to the age-related needs of the individual. For example, a pediatric clinic conducts assessments of young children for diagnostic purposes or health care needs, an educational team assesses individuals to pinpoint educational strengths and weaknesses during the school years, and community agencies assess adult support needs for independent skill development and care management in relation to community living and/or special care.

DIAGNOSIS

A diagnosis of intellectual or developmental disability, or a specific type of such disabilities, is a formal statement of the presence of a condition affecting personal characteristics, intellect, development, and/or behavior. It is made as a conclusion of assessment, which is sometimes carried out over extended periods of time. A diagnosis need not be more specific than identifying a descriptive term such as intellectual disability, developmental disability, developmental delay, or learning disability. A diagnosis is almost always made in accordance with widely recognized criteria, typically provided by professional organizations or legislation (e.g., AAIDD and others as described in Chapter 1 of the publication by Schalock et al., 2010, or on the web site of the Royal College of Psychiatrists, 2015).

For many people, a more specific diagnosis can be made, sometimes in addition to the more general diagnosis of developmental disability. Again, this is made in accordance with widely recognized criteria such as those contained within the *Diagnostic and Statistical Manual of Mental Disorders, Fifth Edition* (American Psychiatric Association, 2013), and is also made based on known reasons for the disability. (See also Fletcher et al., 2009a, 2009b.) There are two main types of such diagnoses: 1) classification diagnosis (e.g., autism, Asperger syndrome, schizophrenia, dementia, behavior problem), which classifies disabilities according to characteristics or behaviors common to groups of people, and 2) primary diagnosis, also sometimes called etiological diagnosis (e.g., Down syndrome, fragile X syndrome, fetal alcohol syndrome), which addresses the cause(s) of the disability (see also Chapters 13 and 21).

An aspect of diagnosis that sometimes seems confusing is that the more specific diagnoses may be made for people who have a diagnosis of intellectual or developmental disability as well as for people who do not have such a diagnosis. For example, it may be helpful to understand in more detail the diagnosis of a person with intellectual disability by having a further diagnosis of cerebral palsy, but not all people with cerebral palsy have lower intellectual functioning, and thus these people would not have a diagnosis of intellectual disability. Similarly, some people with autism, Tourette syndrome, and many other syndromes or conditions (including Down syndrome or fetal alcohol spectrum disorder) may or may not have a diagnosis of intellectual or developmental disability.

Issues in Making a Diagnosis

A diagnosis of intellectual or developmental disability needs to be made after careful consideration by a qualified professional or group of professionals, in accordance with established diagnostic criteria, and with an understanding of the effects the diagnosis may have on the individual and his or her family.

Responsibility for Making a Diagnosis A diagnosis needs to be made and communicated in a serious and responsible manner. Often, such responsibility is set out in legal documents or formal policy by government bodies, service or educational organizations, or professional organizations (e.g., Reynolds, Zupanick, & Dombeck, 2015). In some jurisdictions, certain types of professionals, such as psychologists and medical doctors, are identified in laws or policies as the only professionals who can make an official diagnosis of intellectual or developmental disability.

Understanding the Reason for the Diagnosis A diagnosis is a formal designation that identifies a specific term describing a condition in a person. Thus, when an individual is diagnosed with intellectual disability or a developmental disability, he or she is formally identified as a person who has the characteristics of that disability.

A diagnosis that determines the reason(s) for the disability is often very helpful. It helps others understand the person's characteristics and behaviors, and it helps others identify services and interventions that will help the person develop and enjoy life. It can also be helpful because many of the support needs in diagnosed conditions are already known from studies of other people with the same condition. Practitioners, family members, and people with disabilities themselves can use this information to plan the most appropriate support resources and activities.

In spite of this beneficial intent, some individuals, family members, and service providers are somewhat cautious about seeking or making a diagnosis because of the possibility of stigma associated with being labeled, overidentification with specific characteristics, or assumptions that are made both by practitioners and others based on the diagnosis. Another reason for caution is that professionals at times provide a diagnosis without making provision for support services (e.g., counseling or information for parents), which distresses some families. Thus, professionals should make, or not make, a diagnosis

following careful thought and after consultation and discussion with families, and they should be certain that the benefits of making a diagnosis outweigh the drawbacks. Professionals should also bear in mind the possibility of dual diagnosis (intellectual or developmental disability as well as mental illness).

Typically, professionals exercise some flexibility in whether to make a diagnosis of intellectual or developmental disability, except where the cause is clearly genetic (e.g., as in Down syndrome or fragile X syndrome). For some parents, having a diagnosis is a relief because it explains behavior and delayed development. For others, it is a source of stress and worry, and it might be best to postpone a diagnosis. Access or lack of access to services is another reason for flexibility in diagnosing. For example, a child may be diagnosed if the diagnosis is required for a needed and helpful service, but he may not be diagnosed if those services are not required or are not available in the area where the person lives.

When a diagnosis is made, it is often permanent and becomes part of the way that individual is seen by others and how he or she sees him- or herself throughout life. For this reason, a diagnosis should be made with care. This is especially important because conditions and skills change over the life span. For example, in order to be eligible for early intensive behavioral intervention services in some jurisdictions, a child must be diagnosed as having "severe autism." Nonetheless, this program can be so successful in some instances that the child is able to participate successfully in the general education classroom and enjoy most aspects of family and community life without undue negative effects (Hayward, Eikeseth, Gale, & Morgan, 2009; Mudford, Martin, Eikeseth, & Bibby, 2001; Peters-Scheffer, Didden, Korzilius, & Matson, 2012). In these cases, the diagnosis is still relevant, but the support needs are considerably reduced. The stigma attached to the diagnosis may be more harmful than the benefits from it. Thus, it is essential to think of a diagnosis in terms of the present need of the person with a disability and the supports that are indicated.

It is sometimes important, as well, to exercise flexibility in interpreting the results of formal assessment instruments. Results for people with intellectual and developmental disabilities are not always accurate, may change over time, and may reflect a different set of values or needs (e.g., results may be low because mathematics or expressive language skills are low, but the person may not actually need mathematics skills in daily life or may have a useful alternative expressive language system). The main purpose of assessments, or indeed of making a diagnosis, must remain to clarify personal characteristics and needed supports that are helpful in improving skills and enjoyment of life.

The Challenge of Determining Whether People Have Disabilities   Determining whether a person has an intellectual or developmental disability can be a challenge at times because it is not an exact science (see Chapter 1), it is sometimes difficult to conduct an accurate assessment, meanings and definitions of disabilities vary somewhat over time and place, and policies or regulations that set out diagnostic requirements for services are not always consistent.

A diagnosis needs to be based on a set of criteria, as mentioned previously. Around the world, regions and services use a variety of available sets of criteria for determining whether a diagnosis should be made. For example, psychologists within a school system may use one set of criteria for diagnoses and those in an adult living services agency may use another. There are many similarities among the common sets of criteria, but there are also some significant differences (see Chapter 1). In addition, some services have their own sets of criteria, and if those services are to be used, the diagnosis has to be in accordance with them. Even when one set of criteria is used, it may be interpreted in different ways. Moreover, there are rigorous and less formal ways of assigning a diagnosis (e.g., as in autism; see Chapter 16).

Certain aspects of diagnostic criteria are sometimes stressed more than others for particular reasons. Different services—such as residential services, vocational services, mental health services, recreational programs, life-skills development, and schools—may require demonstration of need in a particular area, resulting in its being overstressed for the purpose of getting the needed support. Unfortunately, there are wait lists for many services, and to compete for eligibility for those services, family members and professionals sometimes present the needs (diagnosis) of the person with the disability in ways that minimize ability and maximize disability.

Perhaps the most important limitation to any one set of diagnostic criteria is that it is impossible to design a set of criteria that works well for every

individual in every circumstance. There are people who match diagnostic criteria well but do not need services and people who very much need services but do not quite match the diagnostic criteria. Moreover, matching criteria and individual needs change over time with developing skills, maturation, and different environmental demands. There has been considerable debate in the disability literature about how strictly criteria should be interpreted, and there have been many calls for allowing for a degree of flexibility, especially to reflect clinical opinion that people are in need of services.

INTERVENTION

The term *intervention* in disability support work refers to action intentionally taken by others to positively affect the life of a person with intellectual or developmental disabilities. It is essential for disability workers to understand clearly that the only intent of intervention is to maintain or improve the person's life in some way. In this section, numerous interventions are identified or briefly described. Those mentioned are not intended to represent all that are used. Rather, they are intended to illustrate the richness of interventions that are available in some areas and that might be developed in others.

Interventions are carried out by a wide variety of professional frontline workers and specialists of various kinds. It is what these professionals do in their working time when they are supporting, advising, or treating people with disabilities. Family members or other nonprofessionals may also carry out interventions at times, especially when working as part of a team with professionals.

General Guidelines for Effective Intervention

Numerous sets of guidelines for effective intervention are available from a wide variety of sources, and readers are encouraged to seek out some of these. General guidelines are highlighted here to provide an overall context to understanding and using such guidelines. Intervention should

- Address a specific assessed need

- Set clear and achievable objectives that are designed to improve the life of the person with disabilities

- Be based on a sound theoretical or practical rationale

- Use methods that 1) are the choice of the person with disabilities, 2) are agreeable to the person with disabilities, and/or 3) do not cause the person with disabilities harm

- Use ongoing evaluation to assess the degree to which progress is being made and, using this information, adjust the methods to move toward the objectives in a more effective way

- Ensure a smooth transition away from the intervention

- Provide for follow-up intervention, if required

Types of Interventions

Many types of intervention are described in other chapters of this book, and readers are encouraged to seek additional information by consulting the many comprehensive texts on intervention that are available in academic and professional libraries. Intervention can take a wide variety of forms and is practiced in numerous service areas (e.g., social services, education, health). Intervention may be carried out in specialized settings (e.g., school classrooms, psychotherapy, medical intervention, special behavioral intervention), in the home or workplace, or in other settings. The specific types of interventions used in intellectual and developmental disabilities are extremely varied because they need to respond—sometimes in creative ways—to the assessed needs of individuals and to promote benefits to individuals within their unique life circumstances. Among these, a variety of general types of interventions and therapies have been particularly important to people with intellectual and developmental disabilities. Some examples are:

- *Activity-focused therapies:* art therapy, aquatic therapy, music therapy and music participation, pet therapy, play therapy, recreation therapies, sand play therapy; for a discussion of complications associated with Internet use, see Katz (2001)

- *Age-related therapies:* intensive early childhood behavioral intervention, transition counseling, grief and loss counseling

- *Communication:* audiology, speech-language therapy

- *Education and training:* academic upgrading (e.g., completion of school or courses; improvement of specific skills such as reading, writing,

or working with numbers), special educational programs, vocational programs

- *Health and medicine:* alternative medicine, correction of hearing and vision problems, gene therapy, hormone replacement, nutritional therapy (general and for specific problems, e.g., phenylketonuria), physiotherapy, pharmacotherapy, surgery for heart and gastrointestinal defects, correction of physical deformities

- *Lifestyle and personal support:* personal support, assistance animals, assistive technology, helpful specialized techniques (e.g., special feeding methods, hygiene and toileting assistance, community involvement, training to travel independently, bathing assistance, medicine schedule monitoring, enhancement of social skills)

- *Personal and skills development:* assertiveness training, behavior therapy for issues in behavior problems and mental health, counseling, family therapy, individual therapy, group therapy, life skills training, money management training, occupational therapy, psychotherapy, promoting friendships for people with disability, sex education, social skills training, and travel training

It should be noted that in practice not all interventions are helpful, and some might even be harmful to a particular person. For example, the administration of psychotropic medications is common for behavior disorders because it helps many people, yet not all people with disabilities respond to these drugs as expected and, at the same time, they may experience serious side effects (see Chapters 30 and 47 for more details). Children and adolescents with intellectual disability or developmental disabilities may experience functional impairment and akathisia (involuntary changes in posture), tics (pointless rapid movements or repeated sounds), and other dyskinesias (movement disorders) when administered traditional neuroleptic medications (Brasić, Barnett, Kowalik, Tsaltas, & Ahmad, 2004). Another example is the response to phenytoin for treatment of epileptic seizures. Although this drug has beneficial effects for many people, it may have life-threatening adverse effects in people with Down syndrome who have developed late-onset seizures, especially in those who have dementia of the Alzheimer's type (Tsiouris, Patti, Tipu, & Raguthu, 2002; see also Chapters 14, 46, and 49).

Issues in Interventions for Behavior Problems and Mental Health

At least four issues should be considered regarding interventions for behavior problems and mental health:

1. It is crucial to distinguish clinical symptoms of problem behavior and/or psychiatric illness from symptoms that might be characteristic of an underlying disability. Although both may be treatable, they may require different intervention techniques.

2. Psychotropic drugs appear to still be considerably overused among people with developmental disabilities, especially those with challenging behavior (see Chapter 30 for a full discussion).

3. It is important to ask what standards professionals should use for making decisions about interventions for behavior problems and mental health. Some special consensus statements have been developed to guide professionals. For example, AAIDD (under its former name of the American Association on Mental Retardation; Rush & Frances, 2000) published a special volume of its journal *American Journal on Mental Retardation* (called the *American Journal on Intellectual and Developmental Disability* since 2010), and the American Academy of Child and Adolescent Psychiatry also published guidelines (1999).

4. Attempts have been made to educate and empower individuals with developmental disabilities regarding use of their medication. For example, the Ohio State University's Project MED group published a set of several booklets intended for individuals with such disabilities. These booklets explain the uses of psychotropic medications and their side effects in an easy-to-understand manner (Aman et al., 1999–2001, 2007).

New Interventions

New interventions, sometimes for particular intellectual or developmental disabilities, are continually being developed and evaluated (Picker & Walsh, 2013). Some of these may prove to be effective in the future, and others may not. For this reason, expert opinion should be sought, and care should be taken if interventions that have not been evaluated in clinical trials are undertaken.

There are three areas of investigation that hold particular promise in the treatment arena in the general population and in people with intellectual or developmental disabilities. The first involves investigation of the role of the gut microbiome (i.e., the spectrum of microorganisms in the gut) in human physical and mental health and indeed for the development of healthy infants and children (Bonham, 2015; MacFabe, 2015b). The second involves study of the therapeutic benefits of exercise and movement in different aspects of physical and mental health (Cotman, Berchtold, & Christie, 2007; Doidge, 2015; see also Chapter 23). The third involves utilization of the phenomenon that the brain is far more malleable than previously thought and exploring novel ways of stimulating the brain to improve its function and to overcome significant malfunction and damage (Doidge, 2015; see also Chapter 12). Some examples follow of new or emerging interventions related to these areas of investigation as well as others.

New Treatment Approaches that Have Shown Promise in Animal Models A new potential treatment approach for autism involves probiotics (beneficial microorganisms) or fecal transplants to alter the spectrum of microorganisms in the gut. The pioneering efforts of Dr. Derrick MacFabe and colleagues (MacFabe, 2015a; Suzuki, 2012) have been key in development of this approach to treatment. Treatment of autism-model mice with probiotics is promising (Hsiao et al., 2013). Clinical trials involving fecal transplants from healthy individuals are planned in the near future.

In a mouse model of Down syndrome, voluntary daily running sustained over several months improved cognition and motor functioning and altered the levels of several proteins important for brain function (Kida, Rabe, Walus, Albertini, & Golabek, 2013). This supports the idea that a properly designed physical exercise program could be a valuable adjuvant to physical and mental health in people with Down syndrome.

In a mouse model of Alzheimer's disease, voluntary running attenuated memory loss, decreased neuropathological brain changes, and induced neurogenesis (Tapia-Rojas, Aranguiz, Varela-Nallar, & Inestrosa, 2015). These results encourage optimism that a properly devised exercise program may similarly ward off the onset of Alzheimer's disease in people in the general population or who have intellectual or developmental disability.

New Treatments that Have Shown Promise in Intellectual and Developmental Disabilities

Deep brain stimulation is a widely accepted surgical procedure that has proved successful in the treatment of people with Parkinson's disease, dystonia, and depression in the general population. This procedure now is being used in the intellectual and developmental disabilities field to treat disorders that include fragile X-associated tremor/ataxia syndrome (Weiss et al., 2015), refractory epilepsy with intractable challenging behaviors (Benedetti-Isaac et al., 2015), extrapyramidal movements and speech impairment in the inherited metabolic disorder of Lesch-Nyhan syndrome (Piedimonte et al., 2015), and life-threatening injurious behavior as well as other core symptoms in severe autism (Sturm et al., 2013).

Treatment of Smith-Lemli-Opitz syndrome, an inborn error of cholesterol synthesis, with cholesterol or cholesterol plus an antioxidant is being evaluated. A clinical trial yielded promising results with the latter approach (Fliesler, 2013).

There presently is cautious optimism about treatment of chronic posttraumatic stress disorder in people with intellectual disability by means of adapted eye movement desensitization and reprocessing (EMDR) intervention (Gilderthorp, 2015; see also Chapter 23).

The prenatal repair of myelomeningocele (commonly known as spina bifida) results in a decreased need for ventriculoperitoneal shunting after birth and improved lower extremity motor function. However, this prenatal surgery is associated with fetal and maternal risks (Adzick et al., 2011; Keller & Farmer, 2015).

In utero blood transfusions for severe hemolytic disease of the newborn (e.g., from Rh disease) keeps developing fetuses alive until delivery, though this approach is not without risks. The long-term outcome of this procedure on child development is under evaluation (Sainio et al., 2015).

Hematopoietic stem cell transplantation for high-risk inherited inborn errors of metabolism has proved to be effective in adrenoleukodystrophy, metachromatic leukodystrophy, or globoid cell leukodystrophy (Krabbe disease). This protocol is also being evaluated in other inherited metabolic diseases such as GM1 gangliosidosis, Tay-Sachs disease, Sanfilippo syndrome or Sandhoff disease, and I-cell disease (mucolipidosis II) (ClinicalTrials.gov, 2015).

Finally, gene therapy has been investigated for the neurological mucopolysaccharidoses (Hunter, Hurler, and Sanfilippo syndromes) (Wolf, Banerjee, Hackett, Whitley, & McIvor, 2015).

SUMMARY

Assessment, diagnosis, intervention, and services are closely linked. They must go hand in hand if improvements are to be made to support people with intellectual and developmental disabilities, their families, and their care providers. Some people with disabilities receive formal assessment and diagnosis, but others do not. Assessment should identify needed supports, and diagnosis should identify causes or classification of an individual's disability with the goal of helping provide needed supports. Numerous types of interventions are applicable to improving the lives of people with intellectual and developmental disabilities. Although assessment and specific interventions are essential for support to people with disabilities, more general interventions in the form of services must also be available.

FOR FURTHER THOUGHT AND DISCUSSION

1. Think of a person you know who has intellectual disability or a developmental disability. What types of assessment would be best to ascertain what his or her support needs are? Who would be best suited to carrying out this assessment?

2. When a diagnosis is made, when should it be thought of as long term and when should it be thought of as short term? Illustrate your view by giving examples of people with disabilities. When, if ever, is it appropriate not to give a diagnosis? What diagnostic criteria are used in the main service in which you work (or plan to work)?

3. Working in a small group with others, identify the services that are available locally for a teenager with intellectual disability and for a 40-year-old woman with a developmental disability. What diagnosis, if any, is required for these services? What are the main interventions these services offer for each person?

4. Think of one person with intellectual disability who has a specific need or problem. Describe that need or problem, then set out a plan for how you would assess it in the short term and over a 1-year period.

REFERENCES

Adzick, N.S., Thom, E.A., Spong, C.Y., Brock, J.W., Burrows, P.K., Johnson, M.P.,...Farmer, D.L. (2011). A randomized trial of prenatal versus postnatal repair of myelomeningocele. *New England Journal of Medicine, 364*, 993–1004.

Aman, M.G., Benson, B.A., Campbell, K.M., & Haas, B.A. (1999–2001). *Project MED booklet series.* Columbus: Ohio State University.

Aman, M.G., Benson, B.A., Farmer, C.A., Hall, K.L., Malone, K.M., & Taylor. S.J. (2007). Project MED: Effects of a Medication EDucation booklet series for individuals with intellectual disabilities. *Intellectual and Developmental Disabilities, 45*(1), 33–45.

American Academy of Child and Adolescent Psychiatry. (1999). Practice parameters for the assessment and treatment of children, adolescents, and adults with mental retardation and co-morbid mental disorders. *Journal of Child and Adolescent Psychiatry, 38*(12, Suppl.), 5S–31S.

American Psychiatric Association. (2013). *Diagnostic and statistical manual of mental disorders* (5th ed.). Washington, DC: Author.

Benedetti-Isaac, J.C., Torres-Zambrano, M., Vargas-Toscano, A., Perea-Castro, E., Alcalá-Cerra, G., Furlanetti, L.L.,...Contreras Lopez, W.O. (2015). Seizure frequency reduction after posteromedial hypothalamus deep brain stimulation in drug-resistant epilepsy associated with intractable aggressive behavior. *Epilepsia, 56*(7), 1152–1161.

Bonham, K. (2015). *Growing a baby microbiome.* Retrieved from http://blogs.scientificamerican.com/food-matters/growing-a-baby-microbiome/

Brasić, J.R., Barnett, J.Y., Kowalik, S., Tsaltas, M.O., & Ahmad, R. (2004). Neurobehavioral assessment of children and adolescents attending a developmental disabilities clinic. *Psychological Reports, 95*(3, Pt. 2), 1079–1086.

Brown, I., & Brown, R.I. (2003). *Quality of life and disability: An approach for community practitioners.* London, United Kingdom: Jessica Kingsley.

ClinicalTrials.gov. (2015). *HSCT for high risk inherited inborn errors.* Retrieved from https://clinicaltrials.gov/ct2/show/NCT00383448?term=leukodystrophy&rank=17

Cotman, C.W., Berchtold, N.C., & Christie, L.A. (2007). Exercise builds brain health: Key roles of growth factor cascades and inflammation. *Trends in Neuroscience, 30*(9), 464–472.

Doidge, N. (2015). *The brain's way of healing. Remarkable discoveries and recoveries from the frontiers of neuroplasticity.* New York, NY: Viking Press.

Fletcher, R., Loschen, E., Stavrakaki, C., & First, M. (Eds.). (2009a). *Diagnostic manual–intellectual disability (DM-ID): A clinical guide for diagnosis of mental disorders in persons with intellectual disability.* Kingston, NY: NADD Press.

Fletcher, R., Loschen, E., Stavrakaki, C., & First, M. (Eds.) (2009b). *Diagnostic manual–intellectual disability (DM-ID): A textbook of diagnosis of mental disorders in persons with intellectual disability.* Kingston, NY: NADD Press.

Fliesler, S.J. (2013). Antioxidants: The missing key to improved therapeutic intervention in Smith-Lemli-Opitz Syndrome? *Hereditary Genetics, 2*(2), 119. Retrieved from http://www.omicsonline.org/antioxidants-the-missing-key-to-improved-therapeutic-intervention-in-smithlemliopitz-syndrome-2161-1041.1000119.pdf

Gilderthorp, R.C. (2015). Is EMDR an effective treatment for people diagnosed with both intellectual disability and post-traumatic stress disorder? *Journal of Intellectual Disability, 19*(1), 58–68.

Hayward, D., Eikeseth, S., Gale, C., & Morgan, S. (2009). Assessing progress during treatment for young children with autism receiving intensive behavioural interventions. *Autism, 13*(6), 613–633.

Hsiao, E.Y., McBride, S.W., Hsien, S., Sharon, G., Hyde, E.R., McCue, T.,...Mazmanian, S.K. (2013). Microbiota modulate behavioral and physiological abnormalities associated with neurodevelopmental disorders. *Cell, 155*, 1451–1463. doi:10.1016/j.cell.2013.11.024

Katz, G. (2001). Adolescents and young adults with developmental disabilities interface the Internet: Six case reports of dangerous liaisons. *Mental Health Aspects of Developmental Disabilities, 4*(2), 77–84.

Keller, B.A., & Farmer, D.L. (2015). Fetal surgery for myelomeningocele: History, research, clinical trials, and future directions. *Minerva Pediatrica, 67*(4), 341–356.

Kida, E., Rabe, A., Walus, M., Albertini, G., & Golabek, A.A. (2013). Long-term running alleviates some behavioral and molecular abnormalities in Down syndrome mouse model Ts65Dn. *Experimental Neurology, 240*, 178–189.

MacFabe, D.F. (2015a). Enteric short-chain fatty acids: Microbial messengers of metabolism, mitochondria, and mind: Implications in autism spectrum disorders. *Microbial Ecology in Health and Disease, 26*, 28177. doi:10.3402/mehd.v26.28177

MacFabe, D.F. (2015b, March 31). *How the digestive system affects autism.* Retrieved from http://www.huffingtonpost.ca/dr-derrick-macfabe/digestive-system_b_6924428.html

Mudford, O.C., Martin, N.T., Eikeseth, S., & Bibby, P. (2001). Parent-managed behavioral treatment for preschool children with autism: Some characteristics of UK programs. *Research in Developmental Disabilities, 22*, 173–182.

Peters-Scheffer, N., Didden, R., Korzilius, H., & Matson, J. (2012). Cost comparison of early intensive behavioral intervention and treatment as usual for children with autism spectrum disorder in the Netherlands. *Research in Developmental Disabilities, 33*(6), 1763–1772.

Picker, J.D., & Walsh, C.A. (2013). New innovations: Therapeutic opportunities for intellectual disabilities. *Annals of Neurology, 74*(3), 382–390.

Piedimonte, F., Andreani, J.C., Piedimonte, L., Micheli, F., Graff, P., & Bacaro, V. (2015). Remarkable clinical improvement with bilateral globus pallidus internus deep brain stimulation in a case of Lesch-Nyhan disease: Five-year follow-up. *Neuromodulation, 18*(2), 118–121; discussion 122.

Reynolds, T., Zupanick, C.E., & Dombeck, M. (2015). *Diagnosis of intellectual disabilities*. Retrieved from http://www.eastcentralmhc.org/208-intellectual-disabilities/article/10345-the-diagnosis-of-intellectual-disabilities

Royal College of Psychiatrists. (2015). *OP48. DC-LD: Diagnostic criteria for psychiatric disorders for use with adults with learning disabilities/mental retardation*. Retrieved from http://www.rcpsych.ac.uk/usefulresources/publications/collegereports/op/op48.aspx

Rush, A.J., & Frances, A. (Eds.). (2000). Expert consensus guideline series: Treatment of psychiatric and behavioural problems in mental retardation [Special issue]. *American Journal on Mental Retardation, 105*(3).

Sainio, S., Nupponen, I., Kuosmanen, M., Aitokallio-Tallberg, A., Ekholm, E., Halmesmäki, E.,...Stefanovic, V. (2015). Diagnosis and treatment of severe hemolytic disease of the fetus and newborn: A 10-year nationwide retrospective study. *Acta Obstetricia et Gynecologica Scandinavica, 94*(4), 383–390. doi:10.1111/aogs.12590

Schalock, R.L., Borthwick-Duffy, S.A., Buntinx, W.H.E., Coulter, D.L., & Craig, E.M. (2010). *Intellectual disability: Definition, classification, and systems of supports* (11th ed.). Washington, DC: American Association on Intellectual and Developmental Disabilities.

Sturm, V., Fricke, O., Bührle, C.P., Lenartz, D., Maarouf, M., Treuer, H.,...Lehmkuhl, G. (2013). DBS in the basolateral amygdala improves symptoms of autism and related self-injurious behavior: A case report and hypothesis on the pathogenesis of the disorder. *Frontiers in Human Neuroscience, 6,* 41. doi:10.3389/fnhum.2012.00341 Retrieved from Frontiers in Human Neuroscience http://journal.frontiersin.org/article/10.3389/fnhum.2012.00341/full

Suzuki, D. (Host). (2012, July 26, August 2). Autism enigma [Television series episode]. In CBC (Producer), *The nature of things*. Toronto, Canada: Canadian Broadcasting Corporation. Retrieved from http://www.cbc.ca/natureofthings/episodes/autism-enigma

Tapia-Rojas, C., Aranguiz, F., Varela-Nallar, L., & Inestrosa, N.C. (2015). Voluntary running attenuates memory loss, decreases neuropathological changes and induces neurogenesis in a mouse model of Alzheimer's disease. *Brain Pathology, 26*(1), 62–74. doi:10.1111/bpa.12255

Tsiouris, J.A., Patti, P.J., Tipu, O., & Raguthu, S. (2002). Adverse effects of phenytoin given for late-onset seizures in adults with Down syndrome. *Neurology, 59,* 779–780.

Tymchuk, A.J., Lakin, K.C., & Luckasson, R. (2001). *The forgotten generation: The status and challenges of adults with mild cognitive limitations*. Baltimore, MD: Paul H. Brookes Publishing Co.

Weiss, D., Mielke, C., Wächter, T., Bender, B., Liscic, R.M., Scholten, M.,...Krüger, R. (2015). Long-term outcome of deep brain stimulation in fragile X-associated tremor/ataxia syndrome. *Parkinsonism and Related Disorders, 21*(3), 310–313.

Wolf, D.A., Banerjee, S., Hackett, P.B., Whitley, C.B., & McIvor, R.S. (2015). Low WC Gene therapy for neurologic manifestations of mucopolysaccharidoses. *Expert Opinion on Drug Delivery, 12*(2), 283–296.

Zetlin, A., & Murtaugh, M. (1990). Whatever happened to those with borderline IQs? *American Journal on Mental Retardation, 94,* 463–469.

25

Introduction to Intellectual and Developmental Disability Service Systems and Service Approaches

Ivan Brown, Diane Galambos, Denise Poston Stahl, and Ann P. Turnbull

WHAT YOU WILL LEARN

- Existence of several service systems in every country, of which the intellectual and developmental service system is one
- Necessity of both informal and formal supports for the efficient functioning of the intellectual and developmental disability service system
- Change of service systems over time with changing conditions and values
- Centrality of person-directed and family-directed approaches to good planning
- Importance of monitoring the implementation of plans
- Professional and personal dilemmas for disability support personnel as a result of the person-centered and family-centered approach

Chapter 24 described the important relationship between assessment and intervention for individuals with intellectual and developmental disabilities. It also noted that groups of interventions, or specific interventions for groups of people, are referred to as services—increasingly called supports—and that the systems that are set up for the purpose of providing services or supports are called service systems. This chapter provides an overview of service systems and of person-centered and family-centered support; such support is currently considered to be best practice in providing supports and services to individuals with intellectual and developmental disabilities and their families.

WHAT IS A SERVICE SYSTEM?

Every country has a number of major service systems, and we use many of these over the course of our lives. Almost all of us attend one or more parts of the education system (e.g., preschools, elementary schools, secondary schools, colleges, universities) and use at least some part of the health care system (e.g., family doctors, hospitals, nursing homes/skilled nursing facilities, emergency care, dental care, a broad array of health specialists). Some of us use financial support systems, and a few are involved in the legal system. The social service system is another of the many major service systems that many of us use in various ways.

All major service systems have common features. Their functions and the scope of what they can and cannot do are set out in a law or, more typically, in a series of laws. They have a defined funding mechanism that is relatively stable over time. They have policies and rules that describe what services are offered and how they are offered. They have personnel—professionals and nonprofessionals—whose jobs are to provide the service to service users. They have standards of conduct to govern the way things are done. Finally, they have physical places where the services are provided (e.g., schools, hospitals, community centers) and standard, recognized sets of ways they are provided (e.g., in person, online, communication by letter).

For people with intellectual and developmental disabilities, the trend since the 1980s has been to use, where possible, the services that are available to the general population. This trend has resulted in large numbers of people with disabilities becoming involved in generic social services, health services, education services, income support, and many other services. In other words, they use, wherever possible, the same services that are available to all people. At times, though, some additional services are required to address the special needs of people with intellectual and developmental disabilities and their families. Together, these special services can be thought of as the intellectual and developmental disability service system.

The Importance of Informal and Formal Support within Service Systems

All people, both with and without disabilities, need support from others. For people with disabilities, the word *support* is used in another sense as well: to refer to the additional actions, routines, structures, and resources that others provide because of the disability to help make life better or easier. The intellectual and developmental disability service system, to function efficiently, relies on both informal and formal supports from a wide variety of people. Some of these people work within the service system, but a great many do not.

Informal supports are offered within the natural settings of home and community. They include the countless ways that family members, friends, neighbors, co-workers, community members, and others assist those needing help. People contribute to informal supports when they hold a door open for someone who uses a wheelchair or offer to look after a neighbor's child while the parents go shopping. Some give much more substantial informal support.

Many parents and other family members make very large commitments to children and adults with disabilities. Relatives, friends, and neighbors often give a great deal of their time and other resources. Volunteers contribute time, energy, and expertise in any number of areas of life. On the whole, the contribution of informal supports to people with intellectual and developmental disabilities is enormous, and without such supports a large number of people would be experiencing a very poor quality of life.

Formal supports are those that are set up purposely to address the needs of groups of people, although there is usually latitude for them to be tailored to individuals' needs. Because formal supports require planning, organization, legislation or policy, and resources, they have a structure and are usually called services. Services for children and adults with intellectual and developmental disabilities are most often funded by governments, but other services are funded and provided by private groups, not-for-profit organizations, charitable groups and organizations, local governing bodies, and others. Especially in the more affluent countries of the world, services have expanded considerably since the 1970s, and they have become increasingly diverse.

Why Service Systems Change Over Time

Service systems for people with intellectual and developmental disabilities evolve over time. They change to follow philosophical trends that occur within the general society and within the field of intellectual and developmental disabilities. At one time, the service system in the intellectual and developmental disability field almost entirely took the form of institutional care. In the mid-1900s, due to parent groups and other pressures, schools and day programs emerged that provided alternate opportunities for both children and adults. Increasingly, because of changing attitudes and values, community agencies funded primarily by governments have taken on these responsibilities, and the philosophy of inclusive community living has replaced that of institutional care (see Chapter 2, in particular, for more information). Such changes illustrate how the intellectual and developmental disability service system has evolved since the early 20th century.

There is almost always some push and pull of philosophies and ideas in a service system as it changes over time. For example, consider the tensions that have been experienced—and are still being experienced—between the following:

- Institutional care versus community living
- Independent living versus supported care
- Family responsibility versus public responsibility

Over time, such tensions tend to work themselves out but are usually replaced by other new ones.

The intellectual and developmental disability service system is still changing in keeping up with philosophical, social, and economic changes. The mission statements of numerous service organizations and agencies set the goals for change by speaking to the value placed on independence, community participation and inclusion, quality of life, and self-determination. Yet it is up to those who work within the service system to put such goals into practice in the best way they can within the context of its social and economic realities. This application typically results in a series of smaller, but ongoing, changes to the structure and function of the service system, although sometimes major shifts occur, such as when new laws or policy directions are introduced. The following are three important changes that have begun to occur:

1. The role of community agencies is being reframed to reflect the support needs of individuals and families rather than to generate programs for groups of people with intellectual and developmental disabilities.

2. Financial and other resources are being allocated in accordance with the assessed support needs of individuals and families.

3. Individuals with disabilities and their families are being provided more control over how funding and other resources are used.

DEALING WITH THE INTELLECTUAL AND DEVELOPMENTAL DISABILITY SERVICE SYSTEM

Families who have a child or adult with an intellectual or developmental disability can find it very frustrating to understand, obtain access to, and navigate the disability service system. Some strategies that can make it easier are detailed in this section.

When Are Services Needed?

Disability services are needed if a child or adult with a disability is experiencing problems that are difficult or troublesome and if dealing with those problems extends beyond the capabilities of usual family and community supports. Family members in particular should gather information from professionals (e.g., family doctors, pediatricians, teachers, social workers) about what services are available for their child, even if they think those services are not needed at the present time.

Are All Services Available?

Numerous services are available for children and adults with disabilities. Most have eligibility criteria, and these are not necessarily the same from one service to another. Family members and disability support workers need to inquire and be knowledgeable about eligibility criteria for specific services. For some services, a formal diagnosis is required. Many services cannot be made available immediately; rather, applicants must "wait their turn" on a waiting list. Applicants should follow the progress of waiting lists and remain open to alternatives that might provide similar service.

Applying For Services

Various procedures are used for applying for services. Families and support workers should become familiar with the procedures used in the area where they live. This is useful information to have on hand even if the services are not needed at the present time.

Hints for Staying Informed

Keeping up with what services are available, and how and when to apply for them, takes time and effort. For parents who are busy with their own lives and have a son or daughter with a disability, keeping on top of changing services may not be something they cherish doing. Still, most people find it helpful to be knowledgeable about services and to have some involvement in ongoing advocacy for better services. Family members and disability professionals find it useful to keep on top of service changes in the following ways:

- Keep up with new developments in services (e.g., through web sites, information from local community agencies).

- Know local service providers such as community agencies and people who work for government funders, and consult with them when needed.

- Visit web sites of reputable organizations or subscribe to one or more of the many excellent magazines about intellectual and developmental disability.

- Explore ways to keep abreast of new research findings and new ideas of disability scholars.

- Read books, blogs, and other accounts written by people with disabilities and family members.

- Join social media discussions and exchange views and new discoveries.

- Become involved in community leisure and recreational activities for children and adults with disabilities.

- Become involved in fund-raising for specific causes.

- Join parent and family advocacy groups.

- Become familiar with politicians who exercise influence over disability policy and funding.

PERSON-CENTERED AND FAMILY-CENTERED SUPPORT

The field of intellectual and developmental disabilities has moved away from using the phrase "providing services to people with disabilities" and toward "supporting people with disabilities" (Thompson & Viriyangkura, 2013). This may appear to be a small change in terminology, but the change in meaning is significant. *Supporting* implies action by others associated with helping to strengthen the fundamental abilities and conditions of life of a person with a disability. An important aspect of support, and one that is central to much of what services do today, is its person-centered and family-centered focus (Kim & Turnbull, 2004). The concept here is that support given emerges from, and is fully in keeping with, the wishes and choices of people with disabilities or their families (Brown & Brown, 2009).

Since the 1980s, there has been an increasing trend toward taking person-centered approaches to providing services and supports to people with intellectual and developmental disabilities across the life span (Dunst, Trivette, & Hamby, 2007; Feinberg, 2014;

Simpson, O'Brien, & Towell, 2013). Since the turn of the 21st century family-centered support has been increasingly adopted (Samuel, Rillotta, & Brown, 2012). For this reason, these concepts are explored in some detail here, especially as they relate to planning and providing supports.

Person-centered support for people with intellectual and developmental disabilities means focusing attention and resources on the wants and needs of the person with disabilities when planning, providing, or reviewing services and supports. Simply put, it means respecting the person's opinions and choices. Person-centered support is a way of providing services and supports that place the person—rather than the service, organization, or system—at the center. A number of useful resources have been developed to help professionals take person-centered approaches (e.g., Holburn, Gordon, & Vietze, 2007; Smull, 2000; Strock-Lynskey & Keller, 2007).

Family-centered support is very similar to person-centered support with the exception that the family of the person with a disability is the focus of supports and services. Family-centered support is particularly relevant to the service system in cases when the child or adult with a disability lives with his or her family (Zuna, Brown, & Brown, 2014). It is recognized that the family is the immediate environment for the person and that the functioning of the family unit in this environment very much affects the life of the person with a disability. In addition, family members (and parents in particular) have a responsibility for providing care and a positive living environment for their family member with a disability, and many family members require some support to do this effectively.

Family-centered support, which began to take on special importance in the 1980s in the early childhood and early intervention fields (Epley, Summers, & Turnbull, 2010), represents a shift away from "fixing" the child and his or her mother and toward providing supports to key people in the various environments of the child's life. It is also characterized by a shift away from parental involvement, whereby parents (mostly mothers) were expected to be involved in a service system that was the "center of the universe," with family members revolving around it. Family-centered approaches put the family at the center of the universe, with service systems revolving around the family (Turnbull & Summers, 1987).

Person-centered and family-centered supports encompass four of the most important aspects of good services and supports:

1. Respect each person with a disability and family member as an individual human being with unique and valued characteristics.

2. Consider the rights and privileges of individual people with disabilities and individual families over the rights and privileges of groups of people or service providers, except when there is harm to self or others.

3. Develop and provide services and supports that are tailored to the needs and wants of individual people with disabilities and individual families and that enhance the quality of their lives.

4. Determine the cost of services and supports, and the responsibility for administering funds, for each person or each family rather than for groups or programs.

Person-centered and family-centered supports often incorporate other trends. It is often assumed, for example, that for people with disabilities to have a high quality of life they should live in ways that are close to the way the general population lives. This involves living in communities and taking part in the resources and activities that communities have. A person-centered approach explores how these things might be best accomplished in ways that are suited to the person's capabilities and that reflect his or her wishes to enjoy life. Similarly, a family-centered approach seeks to provide support for other trends in the field in ways the family chooses and that suit the family's characteristics. Thus, the trend toward person-centered and family-centered support builds on other trends in the field of intellectual and developmental disabilities and on existing values held by most members of society. At the same time, it represents a shift in values toward respecting people with disabilities as individuals and their families by addressing their unique needs and working toward effective choice and self-determination (Brown & Brown, 2009; Wehmeyer & Little, 2013) and also by improving individual and family quality of life (Chiu et al., 2013; Schalock & Verdugo Alonso, 2013).

Person-Centered Planning

Planning is a normal, everyday activity in which all people engage—some with more or less skill and

success than others. Most planning is informal and does not have accompanying documentation. From time to time, however, people engage in more formal planning activities such as career planning, education planning, financial planning, or retirement planning.

One's everyday plans focus on how one wants things to be, what one would like to happen next, and how it should happen. Planning may take place at home, at work, at school, or during leisure activities. Although some plans may be quite comprehensive and might even be thought of as life plans, others are very specific—focusing on only one aspect of a person's life at a particular time. The nature and scope of planning, therefore, varies.

Over several years, a person usually develops many plans, each one being somewhat different and having unique features. When one considers the complexities related to planning for an individual in a range of settings, for singular or comprehensive purposes, and across the life span, the idea of individualizing becomes paramount. There is simply no one way to formulate a plan that will work with all people in every setting. Thus, planning guides should be used only as guides.

In support of this, person-centered planning values the unique characteristics of each person and emphasizes the importance of each person having control over his or her life, what Brown, Raphael, and Renwick (1998) called "being the boss of your life" (p. 16). No one has total control over the events of his or her life, but planning helps to give a compass on life's journey. When people's life circumstances, which may include disabilities, make them vulnerable to control by others, their journeys may be restricted. For them, a person-centered planning approach that implies involvement and control is critical to having a rich and meaningful life (see also Beadle-Brown, Hutchinson, & Whelton, 2012; Emerson & Stancliffe, 2004; Felce, 2004; Mansell & Beadle-Brown, 2004).

What Person-Centered Planning Involves

One service provider described the person-centered planning process in this way: "An individual, along with his or her support network, develops a tailor-made support plan that identifies specific goals, expected outcomes, and natural and/or specialized support services required to actualize community living, participation, and quality of life" (Galambos, 2003, p. 394). Another description of person-centered planning is that the person selects others to assist in a process of developing the plan that is the basis of support arrangements, whether the plan involves informal supports or more formal services.

Whatever description is used, person-centered planning is a shift away from planning by others and toward supporting people with disabilities in planning for themselves. Such planning is no longer based on what a service organization has to offer; rather, it is based on the person's wants and needs, as well as on his or her dreams and hopes for life—whatever those may be.

Quality of Life: The Goal of Person-Centered Planning

Quality of life as a concept and a goal has been described as "close to most of our hearts, both personally and professionally" (Landesman, 1986, p. 141). For the most part, it is something that individual human beings and human civilizations throughout history have sought—and still seek. Quality of life has become commonly accepted in services for people with intellectual and developmental disabilities as both an overall goal and an effective organizing principle (Brown & Brown, 2003; Brown, Hatton, & Emerson, 2013; Butterworth, Steere, & Whitney-Thomas, 1997; Schalock, 1997; Schalock & Verdugo Alonso, 2013; Schippers, Zuna, & Brown, 2015). As such, this term has been useful for asking two fundamental questions pertaining to the lives of people with intellectual and developmental disabilities:

1. To what degree is life good?

2. How can life be improved?

At an individual level, it is now accepted that many aspects of quality of life are common to all humans (e.g., personal control, safety, self-efficacy, health), whereas other aspects are unique to individuals (e.g., personal tastes, treasured possessions, meaningful experiences, valued activities) (Beadle-Brown et al., 2012; Brown & Brown, 2003; Brown, Hatton, & Emerson, 2013).

Quality of life, as an overall concept, is useful for helping to set person-centered planning goals (Schalock, 2004). The following are two basic questions that people with disabilities should ask themselves (Brown & Croce, 2015; Renwick, Brown, & Raphael, 1994):

1. What things currently add to the quality of my life, and how can they be maintained or enhanced?

2. What things detract from the quality of my life, and how can they be improved, abandoned, or otherwise addressed?

When using quality of life for the purpose of more specific individual goal-setting, it is often helpful to use one or more of the several conceptual frameworks available to ask these same two questions about the domains and subdomains. (see Table 25.1 and Schalock & Verdugo, 2002, for two examples). The framework in Table 25.1 is the basis of a 54-item quality of life questionnaire (Raphael, Brown, & Renwick, 1999; Raphael et al., 1996), and the individual questionnaire items can also be useful starting points for thinking about person-centered goals. The nine domains of this conceptual framework are organized around three main concepts: Being, Belonging, and Becoming.

A great deal has been written about quality of life (e.g., see Brown & Brown, 2003; Brown & Faragher, 2014; Schalock & Verdugo, 2002; Schalock & Verdugo, 2014), but the following are the most important ideas for person-centered approaches that affect quality of life:

1. Living and working in environments that promote contentment and belonging

2. Having a wide range of opportunities available from which to choose

Table 25.1. Use of quality of life conceptual frameworks for setting person-centered goals

Being: Who you are as a person
Physical being: Your body and your health
Psychological being: Your thoughts and feelings
Spiritual being: Your values and beliefs
Belonging: The people and places in your life
Physical belonging: Where you live
Social belonging: The people in your life
Community belonging: Your connection with the people, places, and things in your community
Becoming: What you do in life for fulfillment
Practical becoming: The practical work you do at home, school, or place of employment
Leisure becoming: What you do for fun and enjoyment
Growth becoming: What you do to learn, develop, and adjust

From Brown, I., Raphael, D., & Renwick, R. (1997). *Dream or reality? Quality of life for adults with developmental disabilities in Ontario.* Toronto, Canada: Centre for Health Promotion, Faculty of Medicine, University of Toronto; adapted by permission.

Also available at http://sites.utoronto.ca/qol; for a description of the framework, see Woodill, Renwick, Brown, and Raphael (1994).

3. Exercising personal choice

4. Being able to act on personal choices by having necessary supports available

5. Engaging in activities that reflect personal values and interests and that result in satisfaction

6. Engaging in life experiences that have personal meaning

These six quality of life ideas serve as one good set of principles for achieving desired outcomes from person-centered planning. There are many other useful sets of principles available in various countries. The example in Table 25.2 is provided by the first author and captures the core principles that guide person-centered planning.

Other Guidelines for Person-Centered Planning When engaging in person-centered planning, first remember who is in charge. The person at the center of planning should ideally "own" and direct his or her plan as well as the process for developing and implementing it. Optimal involvement in and control of planning may, at times, be best achieved with help from unpaid members of a support circle and/or an advocate.

All those involved have a responsibility to help ensure that plans developed are personal and individual. Focus on people, not on disabilities. Being acknowledged as people first has become a prominent personal (and political) goal for people with disabilities. At the personal level, this involves affirmation as a unique individual who happens to have a disability that may require some form of additional support. Consequently, the wants and needs of the person should govern what supports are required and how supports will be provided.

Table 25.2. Guiding principles for person-centered planning

People with disabilities identify their own support needs.

Family members and others close to people with disabilities identify their needs in relation to the support they provide to those with disabilities.

A blend of informal (family, friends, community, etc.) and formal (services) supports is used.

The role of informal supports is to respond to the identified needs of people with disabilities in ways that enhance their quality of life.

The role of formal supports is to respond as closely as possible to the identified needs of people with disabilities and those who support them.

Available community and interpersonal resources are used.

Second, connect people to natural supports, not just to programs. Connecting people who have disabilities with natural supports is especially important for some individuals, to whom this approach is particularly meaningful. These partnerships and access to community resources have the potential to add positively to quality of life in an ongoing way as well as to make existing services more effective.

Third, avoid mindlessness. In paid service provision, attempts to reduce the complexities of the workplace have at times resulted in planning processes and documents that are used like recipes. Interactions can become routine, hampering positive mindsets and creativity. Mindful staff members remain alert to new ideas, especially those that emerge from natural interaction, and they participate in planning in ways that are both innovative and focused on the individual.

Fourth, plan for today, not just tomorrow. A problem associated with traditional planning approaches has been the idea that planning must focus on the long-term future—on accomplishments that may be realized "someday." As a consequence, some people with disabilities have plans outlining a vision for a far-off tomorrow but none for today. It is important to remember that most people make plans for the next hour, day, and week. Plans are not always realized, and they may be interrupted, changed, or even eliminated by welcome or unwelcome events. Yet it is important to plan, because not to plan is to surrender control to other people and events. People without plans and visions of the future are more likely to be passive and depressed than active and joyful. The thrill of spontaneity comes largely from one's power to alter one's own plans and to decide to willingly embrace unexpected events and opportunities.

Finally, plan for individuals, but remember universal principles. Make plans that reflect the fact that all people share the same universal needs for security, belonging, recognition, achievement, and control over one's life. These needs touch on the following areas (see also Gardner & Carran, 2005; Schwartz, Jacobson, & Holburn, 2000):

- A home

- A safe environment

- Relationships and mutual respect

- A sense of belonging

- Opportunities to grow and develop

- Opportunities to build self-respect

- Opportunities to engage in meaningful life activities

- Opportunities to make decisions and choices

- Freedom to exercise personal rights and to take personal responsibility

- The right to make mistakes and take reasonable risks

- Opportunities to see oneself and to be seen by others as unique and valued

Participant The individual with disability should be involved as much as possible in developing the plan. The level of involvement may depend on his or her age, ability, and preferences. Anyone who knows and is committed to the person and/or the family might also be involved. Thus, other members of the support network or planning team may include the following:

- Parents/guardians

- Other family members (e.g., brothers, sisters, grandparents, aunts, uncles, cousins)

- Friends and neighbors

- People from school, work, place of worship, and so forth

- An individual who specializes in planning and who has been asked (or hired) to facilitate the planning process

- Service providers

- A government or funding representative

- Medical personnel

The general principle for involving others is that the person himself or herself has the last word in who helps to construct the plan.

Style and Content The plan can be written by the person, family members, a facilitator, a friend, an advocate, or an experienced consultant. Plans can be simple or elaborate, of varying lengths, and in formats other than that of a formal report. They can include stories, journals, portfolios, photos, drawings, and diagrams—any form of representation or communication favored by the person.

The written plan is a compilation of materials reflecting endeavors to understand who the person is and how his or her quality of life can be established, maintained, and enhanced. The plan usually includes the following information:

- An outline, or "map," of the person's support network

- Relevant information about the person's background and present circumstances

- A vision for the future

- A description of the person's likes and dislikes, wants and needs, and desires and hopes

- A statement of objectives to be attained

- A description of the support that is required to attain the objectives

- A list of specific ways the objectives will be attained

- A list of the people who will help to attain the objectives

- A description of how the planning team will know when the objectives have been attained

All of the preceding items are often put together and formalized into a document that contains personal and private information. It is always important to remember that not everyone needs to know everything about a person with a disability. Involvement in planning begins with people with disabilities being in control over who knows what about their lives and circumstances. People with disabilities and their written plans become the focal point of a planning process that involves understanding, deciding, doing, and reviewing.

Potential Applications of Person-Centered Planning Person-centered planning has been applied in a wide variety of situations involving both children and adults with intellectual and developmental disabilities. The examples provided here illustrate this broad scope of application:

- Career choice and employment outcome (e.g., Menchetti & Garcia, 2003; Wehman, 2013)

- Individualized funding (e.g., Fortune et al., 2005)

- Later-life planning (e.g., Heller et al., 2000; Middleton & O'Brien, 2009)

- Goals, especially for people with profound and multiple disabilities (e.g., Green, Middleton, & Reid, 2000; Reid, Everson, & Green, 1999; Wigham et al., 2008)

- Residential settings (e.g., Cocks, Thoresen, Williamson, & Boaden, 2014; Davis & Faw, 2002; Heller, 2002)

- Sexuality (e.g., Lumley & Scotti, 2001)

- Transition planning in schools (e.g., Miner & Bates, 1997; Wehman, 2013)

Family-Centered Planning

Family-centered support is a general approach and a service philosophy that sometimes is informal in nature and other times is more formal, with family-centered support plans drawn up. When there is a family-centered support plan, the family member with a disability may have a separate person-centered support plan, supports for the individual may be included in the family-centered plan, or there may be a person and family interdependent plan (Kim & Turnbull, 2004).

Family Quality of Life: The Goal of Family-Centered Planning Like person-centered planning, the goal of family-centered planning is enhanced family quality of life. This is an area of study that has emerged in a formal sense since the year 2000, although there is a vast amount of related literature in several disciplines that looks at family structure and functioning. The domains and the questionnaire items that have emerged in family quality of life studies can be very useful places to start considering what aspects of family life could be the focus of family-centered goal setting (Brown, Hong, Shearer, Wang, & Wang, 2010; Chiu et al., 2013).

Common Characteristics Although there are many definitions and descriptions of family-centered supports (Bailey, Raspa, Humphreys, & Sam, 2011; Epley, Summers, & Turnbull, 2010), three common characteristics across many definitions include family as the unit of support, family choice, and emphasis on family strengths.

Family as the Unit of Support The primary component of a family-centered support approach is the focus on the family as a functional social unit, which requires a family systems approach for

understanding and supporting all family members (Turnbull, Turnbull, Erwin, Soodak, & Shogren, 2015). Previously, the main focus of services was the person with a disability (and sometimes his or her mother). There has been a growing research and service focus on support for the family as a whole, as well as a corresponding focus on father, siblings, and extended family members (Arnold, Heller, & Kramer, 2012; Carroll, 2013; Kresak, Gallagher, & Kelley, 2014). Research points to the importance of the family's role on child development, caregiving, and support, but most policies and programs still view the person as the beneficiary of supports and services (Turnbull et al., 2007).

Family Choice Just as choice is central to person-centered support, it is a key component of family-centered support. The family-centered support model encourages families to voice their preferences and priorities, and encourages professionals to respond to those needs. Family choice may be expressed in different ways, but its essence is that the family is the final decision maker regarding issues related to child or family (Bailey et al., 2011). One way this can be accomplished is to change the power relationship between families and professionals from one of power *over*—in which professionals have authority over families in decision making—to power *with*—in which families make decisions in partnership with professionals (Turnbull et al., 2015), thereby leveling the playing field and focusing on the authenticity and authority of parents' experience and knowledge.

Emphasis on Family Strengths The family-centered approach abandons the pathological orientation that focuses on the impairments of individuals and families and instead focuses on their strengths. Every person and family has strengths, but often the environment around the family is such that their strengths cannot be easily identified or used effectively to address effective living. One role of support professionals is to facilitate relationships and environments in which strengths can be enhanced and put to effective use. Another is to focus on and build strengths and resources rather than to emphasize impairments or needs. Building family strengths requires that service systems enhance families' knowledge, skills, and resources.

Service Challenges for a Family-Centered Approach Any change in service approach brings with it some challenges. Three such challenges that professionals and families might encounter when implementing a family-centered approach are described next.

First, getting to know families well enough to provide effective family-centered supports is essential but requires time and other resources. Families may be reluctant to share details of their family life, or some family members may not be available due to temporary geographic separation, work hours, or other reasons. Service providers need to value their relationships with family members and must be prepared to be flexible yet thorough in getting to know families.

Second, policy and organizational missions and structures have not always changed in keeping with the trend toward a family-centered approach. For example, many organizations do not have a funding mandate to provide supports to anyone other than the person with a disability; thus, they have to be creative in the way that family-centered supports are structured and implemented. This may be most feasible for organizations providing services to young children, who almost always live with families upon whom they are highly dependent. As children get older and become adults, the tendency for many organizations has been, and still is, to focus more on the person than the family. This is problematic because a great many adults with intellectual and developmental disabilities—in both the more developed and less developed countries of the world—are encouraged by policy and practice trends (see Chapter 4) to continue to live with their families.

Third, individual family members may have distinct values, preferences, and needs. As a consequence, there may not be one right service that is appropriate for the family as a whole. Service providers may believe that family members may actually need their own person-centered plans, but this is not always feasible in view of high caseloads. Approaches need to be developed that help professionals support the needs of families as a whole, as well as the needs of individual family members, in ways that are time and cost efficient.

MOVING FROM PLANNING TO IMPLEMENTATION

Once a person-directed or family-directed plan has been developed, it is essential to put it into action and to monitor progress. In doing so, it is typically the case that those involved in the planning discuss and agree upon who will do what to make sure the plan comes to life. It is also an excellent idea to discuss and agree upon how, and at what points in time, progress will be monitored and how it will be recognized (i.e., How will it be determined if the expected results or outcomes have been achieved?). Finally, no plans work out fully as anticipated and there are always some changes along the way. This is not a bad thing, because there are usually very good reasons why some changes need to be made. For example, life circumstances can change, or members of the planning team may realize that another course of action would lead to better results. Because there are always some changes, it is important to document what these are, why they have occurred, and what the revised outcomes are expected to be. A record of the implementation process needs to be kept, and kept up to date. There are many ways to record such information, and each team should devise a way that best suits its needs; the chart shown in Figure 25.1 provides an example of one simple method.

One aspect of this chart is the inclusion of quality of life outcomes. It was noted previously that enhanced quality of life is the goal of person-centered planning and enhanced family quality of life is the goal of family-centered planning. When tracking and documenting how plans are carried out and changed over time, it is important to note the degree to which this process has achieved its goal (enhancing quality of life) and, more specifically, how this has occurred. Information in this column should, in turn, be used to help alter plans in the future or develop new ones (for a conceptual framework for this process, see Schippers, Zuna, & Brown, 2015).

PROFESSIONAL ISSUES REGARDING PERSON- AND FAMILY-CENTERED SUPPORT

Providing the person-centered or family-centered support that results from planning almost always requires flexibility and creative problem solving. This can lead to numerous interesting and exciting activities. Along the way, however, those who are helping to implement the support plan will invariably face issues requiring decisions that are sometimes difficult and sometimes contrary to the plan. Six of these issues are described next as examples, although readers may think of others and, indeed, are invited to do so. Furthermore, readers are encouraged to think of each of these six issues as

Planned activity	What will be done?	Who will do it?	What are the expected results?	How and when will we know it has been accomplished?	What changes have been made and why?	How has it enhanced quality of life?
1.						
2.						
3.						
4.						

Figure 25.1.   Sample recording chart for plan implementation process.

if they occurred in their own communities, then to discuss how to move to an ethical decision (i.e., how to decide on the best course of action to follow in this particular situation). Thus, for each issue that follows, the dilemma is set out but the solution is not provided, precisely because there is no solution that fits all situations. (For more on professional ethics and person-centered planning, see O'Brien, 2002.)

Personal Choice versus Professional Role

A central idea in providing person- or family-centered support is to listen to the voice, and the choice, of the person with disabilities or the family. At times, though, what the person or family needs or wants to do may conflict with the perceived role of a professional. In an example cited in Brown and Brown (2003), a man with disabilities was on probation and under court order not to be in any establishment that served liquor. When his support worker passed by a pub and saw the man sitting in the window drinking a beer and beckoning him to come in, the worker was faced with a dilemma: Should he follow what he saw as his professional role and report this man for not obeying the terms of his probation, or should he support the man in doing what it was he wanted to do—enjoy his beer?

Personal Choice versus Professional Personal Opinion

People with intellectual and developmental disabilities or their families sometimes make decisions that professional staff who support them find difficult to accept. Decisions may be difficult to accept because the professional has learned from experience that the consequences probably are not in the person's or the family's best interest, because the decision is contrary to basic tenets of the professional's experience, or because the professional personally does not condone the decision. For example, Laila (mother of 8-year-old Kiera, who has intellectual disability) wanted to quit her job, move away from the city where her family and friends lived, and move to another city to live with a man she had known only for a brief time. The family support worker considered this to be an unwise decision, as it removed Kiera from the supports that helped with her challenging behavior at home and at school and it was fraught with other risks. The support worker recognized that this was Laila's personal wish, one that she was certain she wanted to pursue, but the

support worker simply did not agree with it. The dilemma she faced was whether to put her personal feelings aside and support Laila in what she wanted to do or to set her value of supporting a family member's decision aside and counsel Laila to change her mind.

Personal Choice versus Family Members' Choice

A common issue that arises in person-centered support, especially for people who live with their families or who are closely associated with them, is that the person's choice may differ from the choice of family members. Marcus, for example, was quite happy living in the basement of his mother's home. He expressed a wish to continue living there "forever." His mother wanted Marcus to be more independent and to learn to live on his own in supported independent living. She thought he should learn to take greater responsibility for his own life, and she felt worn out after many years of helping him. She asked his support worker to convince Marcus to look for another place to live. The worker then faced the difficult choice of supporting Marcus and asking the mother to reconsider or supporting the mother and asking Marcus to reconsider.

Personal Choice versus Resource and Funding Limitations

A limitation to the success of person- or family-centered support is that the personal resources are not always available (there is no one available to help carry out the plan) or that the financial resources do not support the activity (there is not enough money available to carry out the plan). One possible solution to this is that the support worker might consider it as part of his or her role to advocate for or seek such resources. This is not always feasible, however, especially in situations when people with disabilities have little contact with family and friends or are in parts of the world where financial resources are limited. If a personal choice cannot be supported, the support worker must consider whether it is advisable to support another personal choice, such as a second or third choice, and whether it is a valuable lesson simply to help the person with a disability understand that the choice cannot be met.

The story of Anita, who was searching for a new place to live, serves as an example. Anita's family was financially well off and she had grown up in a large house that had many amenities. When it was time for Anita to look for a place of her own, she informed her support worker that she wanted to buy a house in an affluent area. Her parents could easily afford to buy her a small house, although they were not prepared to support her financially for this purpose. Moreover, Anita had developed no particular skills in maintaining a house, and her disability allowance was much too low to support upkeep of a house. It seemed to the support worker that Anita's personal choice was not going to be supported by her family or her available funds. The worker had to decide whether to try to think of a way to make Anita's choice work at least partially or to explain to her that her choice was not possible and that she would have to make another choice.

Personal Choice and Service Organization Standards

Person- and family-centered support necessarily features the needs and wishes of the person or family rather than the service provider organization. This leads to a number of very interesting dilemmas for professionals who work for the organization. Two are highlighted next as examples.

First, most organizations have mandates, or visions of what they consider they should be doing. Needs and wishes, as expressed by people with intellectual and developmental disabilities or their families, are not always in accordance with these mandates. In fact, many people with disabilities and their families do not even know what these mandates are. A challenge for such service organizations is to adopt a mandate that is flexible enough to respond to the expressed needs and wishes of people with disabilities and families. Janice asked her employment support worker to help her find a new place to live because she said she was being harassed by the superintendent in her apartment building. Residential support was not part of the support worker's job nor was it part of the mission of the agency she worked for.

Second, the personal choice of a person with a disability may be contrary to professional or ethical standards and policies that are adhered to by members of the service organization. In some situations and in some jurisdictions, these standards are actually required by law. In more serious cases, the decision may be obvious, but in less serious cases it may not be. Maria, for example, was a support worker

at a supported employment organization that had a strict policy: People with disabilities they supported would be taken off the job if they stole from their employers. When Maria learned that an employee she supported had taken several rolls of tape to pack some boxes at home, she had to decide whether to go by her organization's policy, to counsel the employee to return the rolls of tape, or to ignore the situation.

Personal Choice and the Need for Advocacy or Behind-the-Scenes Planning

Personal and family choice suggests that the person with a disability or family is, for the most part, in control of making the decision and deciding how it will be carried out. In many instances, this is indeed possible. In other cases, though, those who are supporting the person with a disability or the family may need to do some advocacy or behind-the-scenes planning for the plan or activity to work out well. As a simple example, Juan liked to plan weekend trips by train to visit family and friends who lived in nearby cities. However, he had difficulty understanding that it was important to make sure those meeting him at the train station knew what day and time he would be arriving. He gave explicit instructions to his worker not to telephone ahead; rather, he claimed he would just wait at the station until they arrived, as he had done many times before. It appeared that he did not actually mind waiting for long periods of time, and it also appeared that this arrangement gave Juan a sense of being in control of the situation. His support worker realized that those meeting him needed to know that he was arriving and had to decide if it was ethical to go against Juan's explicit wishes and instructions and telephone those in the other city to give the arrival date and time.

SUMMARY

There are several types of service systems that people with disabilities and people without disabilities use (e.g., education, health, financial, legal). The intellectual and developmental disabilities service system provides services that are needed specifically by people with disabilities and their families. Both informal and formal supports are essential to the effective functioning of this service system. A person-centered approach to support is central to how disability services are provided today. Here, the needs and wishes of the person who has a disability, rather than service organizations or funders, are at the center of planning and providing support. Similarly, a family-centered approach makes the family of the individual with a disability the focus of supports and services. These approaches have occurred along with the trends toward more people with disabilities living in community settings and toward consideration of people's strengths rather than their impairments as was primarily the case in the past. There are many ways to make and implement person-centered and family-centered plans, but they should adhere to valued service principles, enhance quality of life, and reflect the specific characteristics of the person with a disability or family. Inherent in these approaches are a number of new and interesting challenges for support workers and for service organizations. These often require creative solutions.

FOR FURTHER THOUGHT AND DISCUSSION

1. It is important to understand wants and needs rather than to judge what services are needed. What are some good ways of understanding what a person or family wants and needs? How can you listen to the person's or family's opinions rather than present your own?

2. Create a person-centered plan for your own life. It is worth mentioning that a difference between planning for yourself and for a person with a disability may be the amount of control that you have over all aspects of the plan. Give serious thought to these differences as you note them, and write down the specific lessons you have learned for helping a person with intellectual disability or developmental disabilities to develop a plan.

3. Using your own family as an example, reflect on how person-centered support would differ from family-centered support.

4. If you currently are affiliated with a service organization, what would have to happen in your organization to fully implement family-centered supports? What facilitators or barriers are present in your organization?

5. It is important to understand that you will have to make some tough choices. Select four examples from the six issues described in the Professional Issues Regarding Person- and Family-Centered Support section of this chapter. Gather opinions from three colleagues about what they would do in each case. Discuss their reasons for their opinions.

REFERENCES

Arnold, C.K., Heller, T., & Kramer, J. (2012). Support needs of siblings of people with developmental disabilities. *Intellectual and Developmental Disabilities, 50*(5), 373–382.

Bailey, D.B., Raspa, M., Humphreys, B.P., & Sam, A.M. (2011). Promoting family outcomes in early intervention. In J.M. Kauffman & D.P. Hallahan (Eds.), *Handbook of special education* (pp. 668–684). New York, NY: Routledge.

Beadle-Brown, J., Hutchinson, A., & Whelton, B. (2012). Person-centred active support—increasing choice, promoting independence, and reducing challenging behaviour. *Journal of Applied Research in Intellectual Disabilities, 25*(4), 291–307.

Brown, I., & Brown, R.I. (2003). *Quality of life and disability: An approach for community practitioners.* London, United Kingdom: Jessica Kingsley Publishers.

Brown, I., & Brown, R.I. (2009). Choice as an aspect of quality of life for people with intellectual disabilities. *Journal of Policy and Practice in Intellectual Disabilities, 6*(1), 11–18.

Brown, I., & Croce, L. (2015, May). *Enhancing quality of life for individuals and families with intellectual and developmental disabilities.* Paper and workshop presented at the 1st Americas Congress, International Association for the Scientific Study of Intellectual and Developmental Disabilities, Honolulu, HI.

Brown, I., Hatton, C., & Emerson, E. (2013). Quality of life indicators for individuals with intellectual disabilities: Extending current practice. *Intellectual and Developmental Disabilities, 51*(5), 316–332. doi:10.1352/1934-9556-51.5.316

Brown, I., Raphael, D., & Renwick, R. (1997). *Dream or reality? Quality of life for adults with developmental disabilities in Ontario.* Toronto, Canada: Centre for Health Promotion, Faculty of Medicine, University of Toronto.

Brown, I., Raphael, D., & Renwick, R. (1998). *Quality of life instrument package for adults with developmental disabilities, full version: Manual and instruments.* Toronto, Canada: Centre for Health Promotion, University of Toronto.

Brown, R.I., & Faragher, R.M. (2014). *Quality of life and intellectual disability: Knowledge application to other social and educational challenges.* New York, NY: Nova Science.

Brown, R.I., Hong, K., Shearer, J., Wang, M., & Wang, S. (2010). Family quality of life in several countries: Results and discussion of satisfaction in families where there is a child with a disability. In R. Kober (Ed.), *Enhancing the quality of life of people with intellectual disability: From theory to practice* (pp. 255–264). Dordrecht, The Netherlands: Springer.

Butterworth, J., Steere, D.E., & Whitney-Thomas, J. (1997). Using person-centered planning to address personal quality of life. In R.L. Schalock (Ed.), *Quality of life: Vol. II. Applications to persons with disabilities* (pp. 5–23). Washington, DC: American Association on Mental Retardation.

Carroll, D.W. (2013). *Families of children with developmental disabilities: Understanding stress and opportunities for growth.* Washington, DC: American Psychological Association.

Chiu, C., Kyzar, K., Zuna, N., Turnbull, A., Summers, J.A., & Gomez, V.A. (2013). Family quality of life. In M.L. Wehmeyer (Ed.), *The Oxford handbook of positive psychology and disability* (pp. 365–392). New York, NY: Oxford University Press.

Cocks, E., Thoresen, S., Williamson, M., & Boaden, R. (2014). The individual supported living (ISL) manual: A planning and review instrument for individual supported living arrangements for adults with intellectual and developmental disabilities. *Journal of Intellectual Disability Research,58*(7), 614–624.

Davis, P., & Faw, G. (2002). Residential preferences in person-centered planning: Empowerment through the self-identification of preferences and their availability. In S. Holburn & P.M. Vietze (Eds.), *Person-centered planning: Research, practice, and future directions* (pp. 203–221). Baltimore, MD: Paul H. Brookes Publishing Co.

Dunst, C.J., Trivette, C.M., & Hamby, D.W. (2007). Meta-analysis of family-centered help giving practices research. *Mental Retardation and Developmental Disabilities Research Reviews, 13*, 370–378.

Emerson, E., & Stancliffe, R.J. (2004). Planning and action: Comments on Mansell & Beadle-Brown. *Journal of Applied Research in Intellectual Disabilities, 17*, 23–26.

Epley, P., Summers, J.A., & Turnbull, A. (2010). Characteristics and trends in family-centered conceptualizations. *Journal of Family Social Work, 13*, 269–285.

Feinberg, L.F. (2014). Moving toward person- and family-centered care. *Public Policy and Aging Report, 24*, 97–101.

Felce, D. (2004). Can person-centred planning fulfill a strategic planning role? Comments on Mansell & Beadle-Brown. *Journal of Applied Research in Intellectual Disabilities, 17*, 27–30.

Fortune, J.R., Smith, G.A., Campbell, E.M., Clabby, R.T., II, Heinlein, K.B., Lynch, R.M., & Allen, J. (2005). Individual budgets according to individual needs: The Wyoming DOORS system. In R.J. Stancliffe & K.C. Lakin (Eds.), *Costs and outcomes of community services for people with intellectual disabilities* (pp. 241–262). Baltimore, MD: Paul H. Brookes Publishing Co.

Galambos, D. (2003). Individual approaches to support. In I. Brown & M. Percy (Eds.), *Developmental disabilities in Ontario* (2nd ed.), Toronto, Canada: Ontario Association on Developmental Disabilities.

Gardner, J.F., & Carran, D.T. (2005). Attainment of personal outcomes by people with developmental disabilities. *Mental Retardation, 43*(3), 157–174.

Green, C.W., Middleton, S.G., & Reid, D.H. (2000). Embedded evaluation of preferences samples from person-centered plans for people with profound multiple disabilities. *Journal of Applied Behavior Analysis, 33*, 639–642.

Heller, T. (2002). Residential settings and outcomes for individuals with intellectual disabilities. *Current Opinion in Psychiatry, 15*, 503–508.

Heller, T., Miller, A.B., Hsieh, K., & Sterns, H. (2000). Later-life planning: Promoting knowledge of options and choice-making. *Mental Retardation, 38*, 395–406.

Holburn, S., Gordon, A., & Vietze, P.M. (2007). *Person-centered planning made easy: The PICTURE method*. Baltimore, MD: Paul H. Brookes Publishing Co.

Kim, K., & Turnbull, A.P. (2004). Transition to adulthood for students with severe intellectual disabilities: Shifting toward person-family interdependent planning. *Research and Practice for Persons with Severe Disabilities, 29*(1), 53–57.

Kresak, K.E., Gallagher, P.A., & Kelley, S.J. (2014). Grandmothers raising grandchildren with disabilities: Sources of support and family quality of life. *Journal of Early Intervention, 36*(1), 3–17.

Landesman, S. (1986). Quality of life and personal satisfaction: Definition and measurement issues. *Mental Retardation, 24*(3), 141–143.

Lumley, V.A., & Scotti, J.R. (2001). Supporting the sexuality of adults with mental retardation: Current status and future directions. *Journal of Positive Behavior Interventions, 3*, 109–119.

Mansell, J., & Beadle-Brown, J. (2004). Person-centred planning or person-centred action? Policy and practice in intellectual disability services. *Journal of Applied Research in Intellectual Disabilities, 17*, 1–9.

Menchetti, B.M., & Garcia, L.A. (2003). Personal and employment outcomes of person-centered career planning. *Education and Training in Developmental Disabilities, 38*, 145–156.

Middleton, C., & O'Brien, G. (2009). Living with aging in developmental disability. In G. O'Brien & L. Rosenbloom (Eds.), *Developmental disability and ageing* (pp. 90–114). London, United Kingdom: Mac Keith Press.

Miner, C.A., & Bates, P.E. (1997). The effect of person centered planning activities on the IEP/transition planning process. *Education and Training in Mental Retardation and Developmental Disabilities, 32*, 105–112.

O'Brien, J. (2002). Numbers and faces: The ethics of person-centered planning. In S. Holburn & P.M. Vietze (Eds.), *Person-centered planning: Research, practice, and future directions* (pp. 399–414). Baltimore, MD: Paul H. Brookes Publishing Co.

Ontario Association for Community Living. (1995). *Evolving our service practices toward more person-centred approaches.* Toronto, Canada: Author.

Raphael, D., Brown, I., & Renwick, R. (1999). Psychometric properties of the full and short versions of the Quality of Life Instrument Package: Results from the Ontario province-wide study. *International Journal of Disability, Development and Education, 46*(2), 157–168.

Raphael, D., Brown, I., Renwick, R., & Rootman, I. (1996). Assessing the quality of life of persons with developmental disabilities: Description of a new model, measuring instruments, and initial findings. *International Journal of Disability, Development, and Education, 43*(l), 25–42.

Reid, D.H., Everson, J.M., & Green, C.W. (1999). A systematic evaluation of preferences identified through person-centered planning for people with profound multiple disabilities. *Journal of Applied Behavior Analysis, 32*, 467–477.

Renwick, R., Brown, I., & Raphael, D. (1994). Linking a conceptual approach to service provision. *Journal on Developmental Disabilities, 3*(2), 32–44.

Samuel, P.S., Rillotta, F., & Brown, I. (2012). Review: The development of family quality of life concepts and measures. *Journal of Intellectual Disability Research, 56*(1), 1–16.

Schalock, R.L. (1997). Preface. In R.L. Schalock (Ed.), *Quality of life: Vol. II. Applications to persons with disabilities* (pp. xi–xiv). Washington, DC: American Association on Mental Retardation.

Schalock, R.L. (2004). Quality of life from a motivational perspective. In H.N. Switzky (Ed.), *Personality and motivational systems in mental retardation* (Vol. 28, pp. 303–319). San Diego, CA: Elsevier Academic Press.

Schalock, R.L., & Verdugo, M.A. (2002). *Handbook on quality of life for human service practitioners.* Washington, DC: American Association on Mental Retardation.

Schalock, R.L., & Verdugo, M.A. (2014). Quality of life as a change agent. In R.I. Brown & R.M. Faragher (Eds.), *Quality of life and intellectual disability: Knowledge application to other social and educational challenges* (pp. 19–34). Hauppauge, NY: Nova Science Publishers.

Schalock, R.L., & Verdugo Alonso, M.A. (2013). The impact of the quality of life concept on the field of intellectual disability. In M.L. Wehmeyer (Ed.), *The Oxford handbook of positive psychology and disability* (pp. 37–47). New York, NY: Oxford.

Schippers, A., Zuna, N., & Brown, I. (2015). A proposed framework for an integrated process of improving quality of life. *Journal of Policy and Practice in Intellectual Disabilities, 12*(3), 151–161.

Schwartz, A.A., Jacobson, J.W., & Holburn, S.C. (2000). Defining person centeredness: Results of two consensus methods. *Education and Training in Mental Retardation and Developmental Disabilities, 35,* 235–249.

Simpson, J., O'Brien, J., & Towell, D. (2013). Person-centered planning in its strategic context: Towards a framework for reflection-in-action. *Interaction: The Australian Magazine on Intellectual Disability, 27*(2), 10–30.

Smull, M.W. (2000). *Listen, learn, act.* Annapolis, MD: Support Development Associates.

Strock-Lynskey, D., & Keller, D. (2007). Integrating a family-centered approach into social work practice with families of children and adolescents with disabilities. In F.K.O. Yuen, C.B. Cohen, & K. Tower (Eds.), *Disability and social work education: Practice and policy issues* (pp. 111–134). New York, NY: Routledge.

Thompson, J.R., & Viriyangkura, Y. (2013). Supports and support needs. In M.L. Wehmeyer (Ed.), *The Oxford handbook of positive psychology and disability* (pp. 317–337). New York, NY: Oxford.

Turnbull, A.P., & Summers, J.A. (1987). From parent involvement to family support: Evolution to revolution. In S.M. Pueschel, C. Tingey, J.W. Rynders, A.C. Crocker, & D.M. Crutcher (Eds.), *New perspectives on Down syndrome* (pp. 289–306). Baltimore, MD: Paul H. Brookes Publishing Co.

Turnbull, A.P., Summers, J.A., Turnbull, R., Brotherson, M.J., Winton, P., Roberts, R.,...Stroup-Rentier, V. (2007). Family supports and services in early intervention: A bold vision. *Journal of Early Intervention, 29*(3), 187–206.

Turnbull, A.P., Turnbull, H.R., Erwin, E., Soodak, L., & Shogren, K. (2015). *Families, professionals, and exceptionality: Positive outcomes through partnerships and trust* (7th ed.). Boston, MA: Merrill/Prentice Hall.

Wehman, P. (2013). *Life beyond the classroom: Transition strategies for young people with disabilities* (5th ed.). Baltimore, MD: Paul H. Brookes Publishing Co.

Wehmeyer, M.L., & Little, T.D. (2013). Self-determination. In M.L. Wehmeyer (Ed.), *The Oxford handbook of positive psychology and disability* (pp. 116–136). New York, NY: Oxford.

Wigham, S., Robertson, J., Emerson, E., Hatton, C., Elliott, J., McIntosh, B.,...Joyce, T. (2008). Reported goal setting and benefits of person centered planning for people with intellectual disabilities. *Journal of Intellectual Disabilities, 12*(2), 143–152.

Woodill, G., Renwick, R., Brown, I., & Raphael, D. (1994). Being, belonging, becoming: An approach to the quality of life of persons with developmental disabilities. In D. Goode (Ed.), *Quality of life for persons with disabilities: International perspectives and issues* (pp. 57–74). Cambridge, MA: Brookline Press.

Zuna, N., Brown, I., & Brown, R.I. (2014). Family quality of life in intellectual and developmental disabilities: A support- based framework. *International Journal of Public Health, 6*(2), 161–184.

26

The Roles, Skills, and Competencies of Direct Support Professionals

Amy S. Hewitt and Matthew Bogenschutz

WHAT YOU WILL LEARN

- The vital roles that people who provide direct support to people with disabilities play in the quality of life of people with intellectual and developmental disabilities
- Historic models that have driven how disability was understood and how those models determined how services and supports were provided
- Major legislation that has influenced the delivery of services and supports
- Competencies of direct support professionals and trends in training and education
- Self-directed and consumer-controlled services for people with intellectual and developmental disabilities and their families
- How trends in an aging society are affecting the delivery of services and supports

Authors' note: Development of this chapter was funded through Grant #133B130006 to the Research and Training Center on Community Living by the National Institute on Disabilities and Rehabilitation Research, U.S. Department of Education, and through cooperative agreements #90DN0291-01 and #90DN0297 from the Administration on Community Living, U.S. Department of Health and Human Services. Grantees undertaking projects under government sponsorship are encouraged to express freely their findings and conclusions. Points of view or opinions do not therefore necessarily represent official National Institute on Disabilities and Rehabilitation Research or Administration on Community Living policy.

People with intellectual and developmental disabilities, like all people, rely on others around them to provide supports in many areas of their life. Much of this support comes from informal sources such as family members, friends, neighbors, or classmates. More formal support comes from professional practitioners in medical, social service, or educational fields, such as physicians, social workers, or teachers. Many people with intellectual and developmental disabilities also receive support provided by direct support professionals (DSPs): workers with a specific focus on honoring the preferences and supporting the day-to-day needs of people with intellectual and developmental disabilities with the intent of facilitating positive outcomes in many areas of life, such as health, wellness, safety, employment, home living, relationship-building, and other areas of community participation.

This chapter focuses on the vital roles that DSPs have in supporting people with intellectual and developmental disabilities where they live, work, learn, and play. Discussion includes an overview of the types of places in which DSPs work, people with whom DSPs most often work, the values and skills that are essential for effective DSP practice, and emerging issues that will affect direct support work in the coming years. All of these topics, however, are shaped by the context of the service and support system for people with intellectual and developmental disabilities; thus, the chapter first provides a brief overview of how services for people with intellectual and developmental disabilities have evolved and how these changes have updated the roles and duties of DSPs.

THE CHANGING LANDSCAPE OF DISABILITY SUPPORTS

In the United States and most other developed countries, the model for providing supports to people with intellectual and developmental disabilities has changed drastically since the 1960s. Prior to the 1960s, people with intellectual and developmental disabilities who were not living with their family spent the majority of their lives in institutional settings. Institutions were large, segregated living centers that provided basic services to many people with intellectual and developmental disabilities in the same location. In 1965, before deinstitutionalization, about 223,590 people with intellectual and developmental disabilities lived in large, state-operated institutions in the United States (Larson, Salmi, Smith, Anderson, & Hewitt, 2013). DSPs working in institutional settings were often called attendants and supervised by medical, nursing, or psychological professionals, and they were responsible for assisting people with intellectual and developmental disabilities with completing daily personal care and meeting basic needs or participating in activities within the institution.

Although institutions with 16 or more residents still existed in the United States as of June of 2011 (Larson et al., 2013), the vast majority of people with intellectual and developmental disabilities who receive services live in community settings, whether on their own, with family, or in smaller group homes. Similar trends toward community living exist in Australia, the United Kingdom, Ireland, Canada, and Scandinavia. As community living has expanded, so have opportunities for community work and vocational training as well as opportunities for people with intellectual and developmental disabilities to participate in the community. As a result of the continuing shift to supporting people with intellectual and developmental disabilities in the community, the roles and responsibilities of DSPs have dramatically changed. DSPs working in community settings have much greater autonomy, have less supervision, and require a comprehensive and advanced skill set (which is described later in

this chapter). DSPs now not only help people with intellectual and developmental disabilities with their personal needs but are also responsible for supporting people with intellectual and developmental disabilities as they participate within their communities, gain skills for community living, work, develop friendships, participate in a spiritual life, lead active social lives, and contribute as responsible citizens, among many other roles.

Medical and Social Models of Disability

The movement to supports that focus on community inclusion and participation also represents a fundamental shift in how DSPs and other professionals are challenged to think about people with disabilities. Institutional supports were (and in some places still are) driven mostly from the medical model of providing supports for people with intellectual and developmental disabilities. In the medical model, much emphasis is placed on "fixing" a person's disability, because it is assumed that those impairments prevent a person from doing certain activities. Thus, before the shift, the support provided by DSPs was often focused on teaching a person things he or she could not do. The goal, in those times, was to change the things about the person that prevented her or him from doing typical activities like other people.

As more people with intellectual and developmental disabilities have become involved in their communities, the social model of disability has become more important and a greater focus. In the social model, disabilities are viewed as a part of each person's uniqueness, and abilities are emphasized over disabilities. Rather than attempting to make the person with intellectual and developmental disabilities conform to society's preferences, as in the medical model, the social model seeks to find ways in which society's barriers can be broken down to be more inclusive of people of differing abilities. The shift in thinking toward the social model of disability has had many outcomes, including more accessible transportation, job accommodations that help people at work, and technological advances that help people with intellectual and developmental disabilities live independently at home. DSPs who support people with intellectual and developmental disabilities in the community are expected to adopt the social model, and many of their duties are now aimed at helping people with intellectual and developmental disabilities find ways to fully participate

---

Direct Support Professionals in the Medical and Social Models

Medical Model Scenario

Amina works as a direct support professional (DSP) in an institution that provides services to 56 people with intellectual and developmental disabilities. Specifically, she is assigned to work with eight individuals, all of whom have lived at the institution for many years. Although Amina knows the people she supports very well, she is sometimes frustrated that they do not have very many opportunities to grow and explore their individual interests. All of the people eat together in a cafeteria-style dining room where everyone comes to eat at the same time, with little choice in what they have to eat each day. At mealtime, Amina is responsible for making sure that everyone she supports eats a full meal, and she is supposed to document it if someone has not been eating what is served. If a person on her caseload wants to go to a social event, Amina must make arrangements in advance and often needs to find other people living in the institution to go along so that other DSPs do not have to support more people than is possible. Opportunities to interact with people outside of the institution are limited. Every day, Amina is responsible for the evening medication administration, when people living in the institution come to the nursing office to receive their prescribed medications. Much of Amina's direct work with the people she supports is to implement their goals. Goals are developed by the interdisciplinary team for each of the people Amina supports. They focus on helping the individuals with intellectual and developmental disabilities gain life skills, but Amina is often frustrated because the goals do not seem to fit well with an individual's skills and interests. Still, she "runs the goals" and documents progress using a standardized form. Amina loves her job and always enjoys interacting with the people she supports, but she often wonders if there might be better ways to support people with intellectual and developmental disabilities so they can pursue their own interests.

Social Model Scenario

Alex works as a DSP with people who have their own apartments in the community. He drives from apartment to apartment to check in on each person several times throughout the week. The work he does with each person varies quite a bit. Although it can be hard to keep everything straight, Alex really likes the variety in this job and often feels challenged to grow professionally, as his work requires so many different skills. For instance, one person he supports, James, is working on learning to cook nutritious meals, so he helps James choose a recipe, get ingredients at the supermarket, and then follow the cooking directions. Alex also supports Shonda, who is hoping to find more social activities that she can do with friends. She loves gardening, so together they have searched the Internet for a local gardening club that collaboratively manages a community garden. With Alex's help, Shonda has come to know several other gardeners who live in her neighborhood, and she enjoys talking and gardening with them. Alex works with the people he supports on goals that are important to them and helps them live healthy lives and be a part of their community. He believes his work makes a real difference in improving lives.

---

in their communities. The examples provided in the box show how DSPs might approach situations differently based on whether they work in an organization that embraces a medical or social model.

Legislation and Litigation

It is important to understand that the evolution of a community-dominated service system of support has been prompted by a long series of legislation and litigation. Although policies differ from country to country, most developed countries currently have an antidiscrimination law that protects people with intellectual and developmental disabilities. Examples of antidiscrimination laws include the Americans with Disabilities Act of 1990 (PL 101-336), Australia's Disability Discrimination Act (1992), and the United Kingdom's Equality Act of 2010. Typically, these laws prohibit discrimination against people with intellectual and developmental disabilities and other disabilities in employment, housing, and access to buildings. On the international level, the United Nations *Convention on the Rights of Persons with Disabilities* (United Nations General Assembly, 2007) is designed to protect the basic human rights of people with disabilities throughout the world. Although most countries have signaled their support by ratifying the Convention, some countries, including the United States, the Netherlands, Ireland, and Finland, have not. Taken together, these laws have been an important building block for community living. In addition, each country has laws and public policy that authorize certain types of services to be available to support people with intellectual and developmental disabilities as they live in the community. For instance, in the United States, the Medicaid Home and Community-Based Services programs (often called Waiver programs), originally enabled by the Omnibus Budget Reconciliation Act of 1981 (PL 97-35), provide a powerful avenue by which people with intellectual and developmental disabilities can receive supports to help them live and work in the community.

Litigation is another method for improving availability of and access to community living options and supports for people with intellectual and developmental disabilities, particularly in the United States. For instance, the Olmstead decision by the U.S. Supreme Court (*Olmstead v. L.C.*, 1999) stipulated that Americans with disabilities should be afforded the opportunity to live and learn in the "most integrated setting" possible and reinforced the importance of prioritizing integration and community living over segregation and institutionalization. Despite this ruling, highly restrictive living situations are still present in many locations in the United States, prompting the federal government to bring lawsuits against states in some instances. For example, a settlement in the lawsuit by the United States against the Commonwealth of Virginia (*U.S. v. Commonwealth of Virginia*, 2012) is driving downsizing of that state's remaining institutions and the transformation to a more community-based service system. In other states, litigation is underway to ensure that people with intellectual and developmental disabilities have opportunities to have paid, inclusive employment instead of attending a sheltered workshop or day program for employment programming (*U.S. v. Rhode Island*, 2014).

All of this legislation and litigation has been instrumental in changing how DSPs perform their work. It has also influenced the profile of the people who work as a DSP and the demographics of the DSP work force, as outlined in the next section.

WHO ARE DIRECT SUPPORT PROFESSIONALS AND WHAT DO THEY DO?

DSPs work in a variety of settings with many different populations of people. In addition to people with intellectual and developmental disabilities, DSPs may work with older adults, people with mental illness, and people with physical disabilities. All DSPs, regardless of the population of people with whom they work, provide person-to-person assistance to support personal health and safety, community participation, household upkeep, and employment of the people they support. DSPs are often the people who work most closely with people with intellectual and developmental disabilities and often know them as well as anyone.

Across all sectors (including, e.g., disability supports, supports to older adults, supports for people with mental illness), there are roughly 3.38 million DSPs working in the United States today, and that number is expected to grow to 5 million by 2020, by which time direct support may become the largest single occupational category in the country (PHI, 2013). Although the demand for DSPs is growing rapidly in the United States and many other countries, the supply of workers who have traditionally found employment in direct support is shrinking. This means that people who hire DSPs will likely need to reach out to an increasingly diverse labor pool in the upcoming years (Scan Foundation, 2012). This is a very important change that is likely to affect how employers (including individuals and families who direct their own services) recruit and train new DSPs.

DSPs have many job titles including, but not limited to, residential support counselor, direct care staff, aide, personal care attendant, home health aide, nursing aide, employment specialist, job coach, and habilitation specialist. Job titles are those that an employer gives to workers to describe their role within the organization. Since the mid-1990s, this group of workers has commonly been referred to by the occupational title of direct support professional. An occupational title describes a group of workers who are employed across various organizations within a given industry. DSPs have varied job titles, but they have some similar—and some differing—job duties, depending on where and with whom they work.

DSPs working with people with intellectual and developmental disabilities may do so in a number of settings. DSPs may support people with intellectual and developmental disabilities where they live, which can include supporting them in their own homes, a family home, a semi-independent living setting, a shared living setting, a group home with 24-hour staffing, or an institutional setting. Vocationally, DSPs support people with intellectual and developmental disabilities in competitive community work, in customized employment situations, in self-contained work crews, or in day programs where DSPs focus on teaching basic work skills in a setting with limited community integration. Most of these residential and vocational support settings are organization-based, meaning the DSP is hired by a human service organization and assigned to work with particular individuals in a specific setting. Although people with intellectual and developmental disabilities may have some say in how their supports are provided, in organization-based services, supervision for DSPs is typically provided by a supervisor within the organization.

Another approach to supports for people with intellectual and developmental disabilities is self-directed supports. Also called consumer-directed or participant-directed services, self-directed services place the person with intellectual and developmental disabilities and her or his family in charge of hiring, training, and directly managing workers. The person with intellectual and developmental disabilities and his or her family can have substantial control over which DSPs to hire, how much to pay them, and what tasks they are asked to perform. In the self-directed model, DSPs are employed by people with intellectual and developmental disabilities directly. This emerging model, which is available in only some U.S. states, has potential to strengthen the person-centeredness of supports for people with intellectual and developmental disabilities and may change the nature of the relationship between people with intellectual and developmental disabilities and the DSPs who support them. Sometimes, DSPs working in self-directed supports will work in settings similar to those noted for organization-based services. However, because the person with intellectual and developmental disabilities may choose what types of supports are provided in self-direction, DSPs will often be asked to play a larger role in facilitating inclusion in social events and other activities that will help the person with intellectual and developmental disabilities enhance his or her community inclusion.

Typically, DSPs receive relatively low wages for performing complex work. Studies suggest that wages tend to be higher in state-operated services (i.e., those services that are funded and delivered by the state) than in private human service organizations (i.e., those services that are funded by the state but provided by private nongovernmental organizations) (American Network of Community Options and Resources, 2010; Braddock & Hemp, 2004) and higher in vocational services than in residential services (Bogenschutz, Hewitt, Nord, & Hepperlen, 2014; Larson, Hewitt, & Knoblauch, 2005). There is some evidence that DSPs working in self-directed supports for people with intellectual and developmental disabilities may receive higher wages than their colleagues in traditional organization-based services, though DSPs in self-directed supports may receive fewer fringe benefits such as health insurance, paid leave time, and retirement savings accounts (Bogenschutz, Hewitt, Hall-Lande, & LaLiberte, 2010).

Overall, the estimated typical wage for a DSP was $10.01 per hour as of 2012, which amounts to about $20,830 annually for full-time employment (PHI, 2013). This figure represents the average wage for DSPs regardless of what population they support (i.e., includes DSPs in intellectual and developmental disabilities as well as those supporting older adults, people with mental illness, and other populations). Specifically considering DSPs who support people with intellectual and developmental disabilities, surveys suggest that the pay rate ranges from $8.68 per hour (Lakin, Polister, & Prouty, 2003) to a high of $11.26 (Bogenschutz et al., 2014). In self-directed supports, a Minnesota-based study found that mean wages were $12.76 per hour (Bogenschutz et al., 2010).

THE SKILLS AND VALUES OF DIRECT SUPPORT PROFESSIONALS

Because DSPs play such an important role in the lives of people with intellectual and developmental disabilities, it is essential to understand the skills and values that guide direct support. Underlying the discussion in this section is the assumption that direct support workers are professionals. Although working as a DSP has not always had the occupational status it deserves, recognition has grown in recent years that direct support work requires a vast skill set and a commitment to a unique set of values. It is this combination of skills and values commitments that define direct support as a profession.

Direct Support Professional Competencies

As outlined previously, the movement away from institutionally based services to community supports and services has necessitated major changes in the ways in which DSPs work in the United States and many other countries. Rather than specializing in a relatively narrow scope of duties performed while working in institutions, DSPs now need to work with high autonomy to support people with intellectual and developmental disabilities in a multitude of ways.

Essential to understanding the way in which the duties of DSPs are defined is the idea of competency. Broadly speaking, a competency may be thought of as the knowledge, skill, and attitudes that must be mastered in order to perform a job. By defining the work performed by DSPs in terms of competencies, it is assumed that the profession is action and value oriented, not simply knowledge based. Although building knowledge is essential for building competency, it is not enough. In order to develop competency, knowledge must be put into action, practiced, and improved. It is the application of knowledge and the constant refinement of skills that leads to competency in a particular task.

In 1996, the Community Support Skill Standards (CSSS; Taylor, Bradley, & Warren, 1996) were developed to summarize and validate the competencies required of DSPs in community settings. The CSSS identified 144 distinct skills that DSPs need to perform well, organized into 12 main categories: 1) participant empowerment; 2) communication; 3) assessment; 4) community and service networking; 5) facilitation of services; 6) community living skills and supports; 7) education, training, and self-development; 8) advocacy; 9) vocational, educational, and career supports; 10) crisis intervention; 11) organizational participation; and 12) documentation. Community services for people with intellectual and developmental disabilities have continued to change since the CSSS were developed, and additional competency sets have been developed since that time.

Building on the work of Hewitt (1998), which revalidated and expanded the CSSS's conceptualization of DSP competencies specific for people with intellectual and developmental disabilities, the National Alliance for Direct Support Professionals (NADSP, 2011a) published a new schema of DSP competencies. The NADSP competency set follows the basic outline of the CSSS with broad competency areas being defined by more specific skill statements. In the NADSP competency set, the first 12 competencies from the original CSSS remained the same, with three new competency areas added to reflect the most up-to-date skills that most DSPs need in order to do their work. The three new competency areas in the NADSP competency set are 1) supporting the person to build and maintain friendships and relationships, 2) providing person-centered supports, and 3) supporting health and wellness. With the original 12 competencies and the three newly validated competencies, NADSP's set of 15 validated competencies provides the most comprehensive picture of the depth of skill that DSPs require in order to support people with intellectual and developmental disabilities.

In addition to the competency sets that have been developed specifically for DSPs working with individuals with intellectual and developmental disabilities, other competency schemas have been developed for DSPs regardless of the population with whom they work. For instance, the cross-sector conceptualization of DSP competency by the U.S. Department of Labor (2011) is meant to guide the development of apprenticeships in direct support across long-term care settings. Likewise, direct support competencies were developed across service sectors for DSPs working in Alaska (Hoge & McFaul, 2010). Although not focused specifically on the needs of DSPs supporting people with intellectual and developmental disabilities, this competency outline may be of particular use in rural communities, where DSPs are sometimes asked to work with people from multiple populations, because specializing in supporting only people with intellectual and developmental disabilities would be difficult due to small populations and large geographical areas. Most recently, the U.S. Centers for Medicare and Medicaid Services developed a set of core competencies for people working in long-term services and supports providing direct support to people with various disabilities across settings (Sedlezky et al., 2014). A summary of each of these competency sets may be found in Table 26.1.

Table 26.1. Direct support professional competency sets

Community Support Skill Standards	National Alliance for Direct Support Professionals	U.S. Department of Labor long-term services and supports	Centers for Medicare and Medicaid Services core competencies
1. Participant empowerment	1. Participant empowerment	1. Long-term care, supports, and services	1. Communication
2. Communication	2. Communication	2. Supporting daily living	2. Person-centered practices
3. Assessment	3. Assessment	3. Crisis prevention and conflict resolution	3. Evaluation and observation
4. Community and service networking	4. Community and service networking	4. Ethics	4. Crisis prevention and intervention
5. Facilitation of services	5. Facilitation of services	5. Documentation	5. Safety
6. Community living skills and supports	6. Community living skills and supports	6. Laws and regulations	6. Professionalism and ethics
7. Education training and self-development	7. Education training and self-development	7. Health and safety	7. Empowerment and advocacy
8. Advocacy	8. Advocacy		8. Health and wellness
9. Vocational, education, and career support	9. Vocational, education, and career support		9. Community living skills and supports
10. Crisis intervention	10. Crisis prevention and intervention		10. Community inclusion and networking
11. Organizational participation	11. Organizational participation		11. Cultural competency
12. Documentation	12. Documentation		12. Education, training, and self-development
	13. Building and maintaining friendships and relationships		
	14. Providing person-centered supports		
	15. Supporting health and wellness		

Sources: National Alliance for Direct Support Professionals (2011a); Sedlezky et al. (2014); Taylor, Bradley, and Warren (1996); and U.S. Department of Labor (2011).

Each set of DSP competencies is extensive, and it may seem overwhelming for many DSPs and supervisors to focus on gaining high levels of competence in each skill area. It is important to understand competencies in relation to the most important duties a DSP performs in her or his job. Depending on the needs and preferences of the people with intellectual and developmental disabilities whom a DSP supports, some competency areas may be more or less important at a particular time. Though it is likely that a DSP will want to have some degree of proficiency in all of the competency areas, concentrating on development of those of most importance may be a smart way to specialize in supporting the needs of a particular person with intellectual and developmental disabilities.

Code of Ethics

As with many professions, direct support is guided by a set of defining principles that shape the values and commitments that DSPs should bring to their work. For DSPs in the United States, NADSP has developed a code of ethics (NADSP, 2011c) to guide professional practice for DSPs who support individuals with intellectual and developmental disabilities. Emphasizing the importance of ethics in creating partnerships between DSPs and people with intellectual and developmental disabilities, the NADSP Code of Ethics focuses on nine principles that should guide the attitudes and actions of DSPs as they seek to support people with intellectual and developmental disabilities in leading healthy and happy lives. The ethical principles aim to promote freedom, justice, and equality and include 1) person-centered supports; 2) promoting physical and emotional well-being; 3) integrity and responsibility; 4) confidentiality; 5) justice, fairness, and equity; 6) respect; 7) relationships; 8) self-determination; and 9) advocacy.

Much of the NADSP Code of Ethics concentrates on the values that underlie work as a DSP. For instance, the values of self-determination and respect for the person with intellectual and developmental disabilities are meant to propel DSPs' desires to support the people they serve to have a voice, direct their own lives, and be regarded as full members of their communities. Furthermore, the value of integrity and responsibility is meant to hold DSPs accountable for building their own skills, taking accountability for their work and decisions, and being aware of their own personal values and how they influence professional choices. These values are meant to be a guide for how a DSP practices her or his profession, not a handbook for how the profession must be practiced.

Indeed, the values outlined in the Code of Ethics are not operationalized as competencies. Here, it is important to note that competency schemas such as the CSSS and the NADSP competencies are grounded in the Code of Ethics. Competency sets seek to guide DSPs and their supervisors in developing skills that reflect the intent of the Code of Ethics. In this way, the development of competencies may be seen as a method for bringing abstract ideas from ethics into a practicable form that a DSP may use in her or his everyday work with people with intellectual and developmental disabilities.

DIRECT SUPPORT PROFESSIONAL EDUCATION AND TRAINING

The amount of education and training needed to become a DSP varies widely from country to country. In the United States, DSPs typically need to have a high school diploma or the equivalent, though many DSPs have an associate's degree in human services or a bachelor's degree in a field such as psychology, social work, human development, or disability studies. In other countries, including the Netherlands, Chile, and Canada, DSPs are required to have a bachelor's degree.

Aside from the educational requirements to become eligible for work, there are a variety of other considerations regarding training for DSPs who will support people with intellectual and developmental disabilities. Service systems differ greatly depending on country; therefore, this chapter focuses primarily on the service system in the United States. Readers should be aware that education and training regulations and approaches may vary considerably in other locations throughout the world.

Required versus Enhanced Training

Most DSPs are required by state regulations to participate in certain types of training. In organization-based service settings, the organization's license to provide services to individuals with intellectual and developmental disabilities may be contingent upon DSPs having certain types of training (usually defined by topic and number of hours) before starting the job and annually thereafter. Typically, this statutory training includes a course in basic first aid, cardiopulmonary resuscitation (CPR), blood-borne pathogens and infection control, medication administration procedures, and training on the basic rights of people with intellectual and developmental disabilities. Most often, this type of training is provided during on-boarding, when a DSP initially begins working for an organization. In many organizations that provide supports to individuals with intellectual and developmental disabilities, DSP training does not go much beyond this required training, yet, as community services have become more person centered, the need to go above and beyond regulatory training has become more pronounced. In addition, as DSPs focus more on providing supports that are based in their code of ethics and competency standards, the need for training that will help them build specific competencies has become more important.

Although competency-based training and education is practiced in many professions, including medicine, social work, nursing, and other allied health professions, it is not common in direct support. However, it needs to be commonly practiced, and tools and resources exist to implement effective training practices that go beyond mandated requirements. As the name implies, competency-based training aims at building competencies among people who practice a particular profession. Competency-based training is typically structured around a profession's validated competency set; for DSPs, the NADSP competencies are useful for direct support. The goal of competency-based training is to equip a new DSP with the knowledge base necessary to practice the profession and then apply that knowledge to real work circumstances in order to develop competence. Competency-based training takes a large commitment from DSPs, employers, and people with intellectual and developmental disabilities alike, but the results are more sustainable and applicable to supporting people with intellectual and developmental disabilities than would be expected from typical regulatory training.

There are a myriad of ways of organizing and implementing competency-based training. In a typical model, the DSP may begin with knowledge building, whether in an employer or postsecondary classroom setting or through online training. The DSP may learn about various parts of his or her job, the ethical foundation of being a DSP, the theoretical foundation of support of people with disabilities, disability history, the rights of people with disabilities, policy and laws that protect rights, the characteristics and needs of people with certain types of disabilities, and approaching their work through a person-centered lens. This knowledge can set the stage for more applied learning. For instance, case studies or active learning activities may be added to the acquisition of knowledge so a new DSP can think about how she or he might apply new learning to a typical work scenario. The DSP may be asked to keep a journal about a learning topic and how it would apply to her or his work, or he or she may be asked to talk with a supervisor or a person with intellectual and developmental disabilities about a particular topic in order to deepen understanding. In most circumstances, the DSP is working while engaged in training and can apply the new knowledge and ethical foundation to real work situations.

In competency-based learning, however, the training does not end in the classroom or with the completion of online training. It is critical to bring that learning into the real world. On-the-job training in which a supervisor or a person with intellectual and developmental disabilities helps the DSP apply his or her learning to specific work situations is essential to competency-based learning. Just as a medical student must practice surgical procedures under the supervision of a more experienced doctor or a psychology student must practice various counseling techniques under the supervision of a licensed psychologist, the ultimate proving ground for a DSP who is learning a new skill is to practice the skill while receiving feedback from a more experienced peer, supervisor, or person with intellectual and developmental disabilities. By engaging in practice, feedback, and refinement of a new skill, a DSP can work toward greater levels of competence in which knowledge is transformed into action. See the example of how a DSP may engage in competency-based training. See the Competency-Based Training discussion that follows for an example of how a DSP may engage in this practice.

On-Boarding versus Ongoing Training

As discussed previously, in many human service organizations that provide supports for people with intellectual and developmental disabilities, training emphasis is placed on the time when a DSP is new to the job. This time is called on-boarding and focuses on gearing DSPs up to do the basic tasks required of their job. On-boarding is important, because early turnover within the first 6 months of employment is common among DSPs (Larson, Lakin, & Bruininks, 1998), especially if they are not adequately trained and supported as they join the organization.

In addition to regulatory required training, on-boarding often includes an orientation to an organization's mission, values, policies, and procedures; an overview of the specific needs and preferences of the people with intellectual and developmental disabilities whom the DSP will support; and practice in documentation. It also includes basic health and safety training such as medication administration, CPR, and emergency procedures. To the extent possible, it is helpful for on-boarding to involve, or even be directed by, the people with intellectual and developmental disabilities who will receive supports from the DSP. In the case of self-directed supports, the person with intellectual and developmental disabilities will need to lead the on-boarding in most cases, and the DSP will need to be open to learning directly from the person with intellectual and developmental disabilities in an employee–employer relationship.

Although on-boarding training is quite important, it is only designed to support DSPs during the early months of their employment and rarely seeks to build higher-level competency, and it almost never prepares a DSP to have the problem-solving and person-centered skills required to excel at this work. For this reason, ongoing training is also essential for building skills for DSPs who support people with intellectual and developmental disabilities. No matter how much experience a DSP has, ongoing training can always be beneficial. The field changes, and new values, interventions, and expectations emerge. Training can support upgrading skills and competence of all DSPs. For newer DSPs, ongoing training can help to develop essential competencies for performing basic job tasks. For more experienced DSPs, ongoing training can be used to refresh skills, learn new approaches, and reinforce the application of new theories or attitudes. In addition, for either new or experienced DSPs, ongoing training may be used to help the DSP gain specialized competencies for supporting people with certain support needs.

Competency-Based Training

Anna is a DSP at a supported living home on a tree-lined suburban street. Three women with intellectual and developmental disabilities and varied strengths and needs live together, and Anna is responsible for providing individualized supports to all of them. One of the women, Claudia, has recently been diagnosed with diabetes. As a result of the diagnosis, it has been recommended by her physician that Claudia monitor her blood sugar, adjust her diet, and get more exercise. This is the first time Anna has worked with someone with a diagnosis of diabetes, so she needs to get specialized training to prepare her to provide Claudia with the best supports possible.

Anna begins by taking an online class about supporting people with diabetes that she found from an accredited, competency-based training source. The class teaches her a lot of good basic facts about diabetes and gives pointers about how to best support the needs of people with intellectual and developmental disabilities who have diabetes. The thing she likes most about the online training is that it provides the real-life examples of DSPs supporting people with diabetes. There are even activities to do that help her to apply the facts she is learning to how she may provide support to Claudia.

When she is done with the online training, Anna applies her new knowledge when she goes to work at Claudia's home. Her supervisor and a nurse are especially helpful in providing on-the-job training that brings her online learning into the real world. Through modeling, demonstration, and feedback, they train her to use a blood glucose monitor, how to document the readings, and what to do if blood glucose readings are too low or too high. They support her as she practices taking blood glucose readings, first on herself and then with Claudia in a real-life situation, and assist her with developing a plan to teach Claudia how to monitor her blood sugar with the greatest autonomy and independence. In addition, they discuss Claudia's rights and practice how they might approach circumstances if Claudia refuses to monitor her blood levels.

Knowing that Claudia needs to be involved in the learning process as well, Anna then begins to apply what she learned about diet, exercise, and monitoring blood glucose levels. She works with Claudia, her supervisor, and the nurse to develop a weekly meal plan that Claudia can help cook. Anna and Claudia also work out an exercise schedule, which includes walks in a nearby park and trips to a local pool where Claudia can do light exercise in ways that she thinks are fun and that are motivating to her. Anna takes a very person-centered approach to designing an exercise plan, considering Claudia's preferences, needs, schedule, and capabilities.

Anna gains a combination of new knowledge and applied, on-the-job training and is on her way to competence in providing supports to Claudia—and perhaps to other individuals with diabetes. She develops a new skill set that will stay with her no matter whom she supports in the future.

DIRECT SUPPORT PROFESSIONALS IN THE CONTEXT OF OTHER PROFESSIONALS

Although the primary role of DSPs is to provide direct supports to people with intellectual and developmental disabilities where they live, work, socialize, and play, they also have a pivotal role in making sure the needs of people with intellectual and developmental disabilities are met by other professionals. In most community services for people with intellectual and developmental disabilities, multidisciplinary teams are composed of service providers from various professions who come together to support a person with intellectual and developmental disabilities. Each professional on the team brings his or her own expertise to the table to determine, with the person with intellectual and developmental disabilities, the best support plan and to ensure needed services are secured. Within such a multidisciplinary team, DSPs are often the professionals with the most detailed knowledge of how a person with intellectual and developmental disabilities lives day to day. Given their comprehensive knowledge of the strengths, preferences, needs, and future dreams of the people they support, DSPs are ideally suited to serve as a link between a person with intellectual and developmental disabilities and other members of the support team. However, despite his or her unique lens and knowledge about the person, in some organizations the DSP may not be invited to be a part of the multidisciplinary team.

It is important for DSPs to understand their role in representing the person with intellectual and developmental disabilities in a multidisciplinary setting. People with intellectual and developmental disabilities have the right to self-determination when interacting with the professionals who support them. This means that the person with intellectual and developmental disabilities should be able to represent her or his own desires and needs in meetings with service providers, to the degree that she or he wishes to do so. The DSP should help to create an environment in which the person with intellectual and developmental disabilities may advocate for her or his own needs and preferences. In instances in which the person with intellectual and developmental disabilities prefers the DSP to take a more active role in representing her or his needs and preferences, the DSP should remain careful about speaking *as a partner* in the person's support, rather than speaking *for* the person with intellectual and developmental disabilities. By doing so, DSPs can help to empower people with intellectual and developmental disabilities as members of multidisciplinary teams and may even model appropriate ways of interacting with individuals with intellectual and developmental disabilities to other professionals, who often do not have specific training in how to respectfully work with people with intellectual and developmental disabilities.

In addition to interacting with other professionals within the context of multidisciplinary teams, DSPs also engage with and interact with other professionals when they take people with intellectual and developmental disabilities to appointments. It is common for DSPs to interact with health professionals (e.g., medical doctors, dentists, psychologists,

Table 26.2. Direct service professionals in interprofessional practice

Professional	Role of professional	Role of direct service professional (DSP) in interprofessional practice
Physician	Physicians, as well as medical specialists, are responsible for monitoring physical health and intervening when health challenges are present.	DSPs may serve as a facilitator of communication and information-sharing between a person with intellectual and developmental disabilities and a physician. DSPs are also responsible for implementing physicians' orders in many cases.
Social worker or case manager	Social workers are often responsible for coordinating services (e.g., residential services and day support services). In many places, they monitor program eligibility and authorize participation in certain programs.	DSPs coordinate service plans with social workers by helping people with intellectual and developmental disabilities advocate for their needs and preferences. They may also be asked to provide updates on how certain services are working.
Nutritionist	Nutritionists are responsible for making sure that a person with intellectual and developmental disabilities receives nutritionally balanced food to support well-being.	DSPs may need to take a nutritionist's recommendations and help a person with intellectual and developmental disabilities design a meal plan that represents the nutritionist's findings. They also support people with intellectual and developmental disabilities in learning to cook nutritious foods.
Counselor	Mental health counselors such as clinical social workers or marriage and family therapists provide support for an individual's psychological and mental health.	With the permission of the person they support, DSPs may provide updates on mental health. Often, DSPs will not be invited to share in the specific contents of counseling.
Psychiatrist	Psychiatry is a medical specialty focusing on mental health. Psychiatrists are concerned with the relationship between a person's mental health and the use of psychotropic medications or other interventions.	Often, DSPs will be asked to monitor certain behaviors of people they support so a psychiatrist can gauge whether a medication is working as intended. Objective, systematic reporting is important for DSPs in such cases.
Physical therapist	Physical therapists work with people to improve their movement and the functional ability of major muscle groups.	DSPs may be responsible for helping a person do exercises that are prescribed by a physical therapist. It is important for the person to do exercises regularly and exactly as recommended by the therapist.
Occupational therapist	Occupational therapists (OTs) help people develop skills they need for everyday life. For example, an OT might help a person eat, use a pen, or use the restroom.	Similar to their role with physical therapists, DSPs may be asked to help a person with exercises that reinforce in the person's home setting what an occupational therapist does in the clinic.

psychiatrists, specialists, occupational therapists) as well as educators and other community professionals such as faith leaders and hair stylists. Because such a wide range of professionals support individuals with intellectual and developmental disabilities, DSPs must develop a wide variety of skills and knowledge in order to help facilitate quality services for the people they support. Table 26.2 displays a mere sampling of the types of professionals that a DSP may have contact with as well as potential roles of DSPs in those interactions.

In their interactions with other professionals, it is essential that DSPs remain aware of their actions and their professionalism. DSPs working in multidisciplinary settings represent not only themselves but also the people they support and the profession of direct support as a whole. Communicating clearly, maintaining respectful demeanor and language, and being prepared to factually represent the strengths, preferences, and needs of a person with intellectual and developmental disabilities help DSPs present themselves and the field of direct support with the professionalism that the work demands. It is also extremely important that DSPs always remember that a person with intellectual and developmental disabilities can and should direct interactions with professionals to the degree they wish to do so.

FUTURE DIRECTIONS

Just as the roles of DSPs have changed in the years since the start of the deinstitutionalization movement, their roles will continue to evolve in the years ahead. Innovations in how people with intellectual and developmental disabilities seek and receive support, new methods and foci of training, and shifting population demographics will all have an impact on people with intellectual and developmental disabilities and the DSPs who provide support to them.

Specialized Training

Earlier in this chapter, the importance of competency-based training was emphasized as a key to enhancing DSPs' skill sets to match the extensive demands of their work. As DSPs gain mastery of general competencies, many would be well served to pursue more specialized training. This is particularly true because many DSPs will work intensively with just a few people with intellectual and developmental disabilities, who may often share some common support needs. For instance, if a DSP is working

to support independent living for individuals with autism who have high behavioral support needs, she or he may wish to receive specialized training in positive behavioral supports, behavioral training techniques, or even simply about autism spectrum disorders. Seeking out opportunities to pursue specialized competency is common in other professions, and it can also help DSPs to become better equipped to support the specific needs of specific individuals with intellectual and developmental disabilities, as is often required in order to provide truly person-centered supports.

Aside from gaining skills to better support people with intellectual and developmental disabilities, increasing DSP competency in specialized areas may benefit organizations as well. For many DSPs who work for a human service organization, there is little chance for promotion without moving into a frontline supervisor role. Whereas such a career shift may be good for some DSPs, many others may not want to go into a management position or may not have a skill set that is well suited for being a frontline supervisor. Many DSPs would prefer to make a career in direct support, where they can be more intimately involved in the lives of the individuals they support. Specialization may add another way for some DSPs to seek increased responsibility and even promotions within direct support. Many organizations have initiated career ladder programs that recognize DSPs who specialize their skill set with pay raises, assignments in which their skills can be most useful, and leadership opportunities. This ability for career advancement without having to leave direct support can be a benefit for DSPs, people with intellectual and developmental disabilities, and human service organizations alike. Likewise, for DSPs who want to move into a supervisory role, taking specialized training in leadership may help them to prepare for the new roles and responsibilities such a move would require.

Specialized training is also supported by credentialing in the United States. NADSP offers credentialing for DSPs who exhibit basic competence and for those who wish to specialize in building their competence in inclusion, health supports, positive behavior support, mentoring and supervision, employment supports, or aging supports (NADSP, 2011b). The credential for specialized DSPs provides formal recognition of competence and certifies the DSP's commitment to excellence in providing supports to people with intellectual and developmental disabilities with specific support needs.

Self-Directed Supports

In many places in the United States, people with intellectual and developmental disabilities may exercise considerable autonomy in hiring and managing their own DSPs when they utilize self-directed supports. DSPs working in self-directed supports are typically employed directly by a person with intellectual and developmental disabilities, often with the help of a family member or other close support person. Being employed by a person with intellectual and developmental disabilities directly, DSPs will need to provide increasingly person-centered supports.

Like many community services for people with intellectual and developmental disabilities, self-directed supports aim largely to promote social inclusion. DSPs working for a person with intellectual and developmental disabilities may, for example, assist the person to participate in community activities, to develop capacity for independent living, or to build skills to seek or maintain community employment. In any case, the self-directed supports provided by a DSP are highly tailored to the needs and preferences of the person with intellectual and developmental disabilities who is the employer.

It is important to note that although a person with intellectual and developmental disabilities will have the authority to hire, train, set wages, determine worker responsibilities, provide bonuses, and terminate employment if necessary, another organization often serves as the official employer of record. The external organization, often a human service agency or a human resource management company, is typically responsible for processing payroll, collecting taxes, making sure that payroll is within the amount budgeted, and maintaining employment records. Despite the presence of the employer of record, DSPs working in self-directed supports should regard the person with intellectual and developmental disabilities as the employer.

Because people with intellectual and developmental disabilities can hire their own staff, they often choose to employ people who they already know and trust (Bogenschutz et al., 2010; Heller, Arnold, van Heumen, McBride, & Factor, 2012). Quite often, relatives, friends, or neighbors serve as DSPs for people with intellectual and developmental disabilities who use self-directed supports, whereas people who were previously unknown to the person with intellectual and developmental disabilities are hired less often. The hiring of DSPs who come to work with a deep knowledge of the person's needs and preferences can have many positives. However, one potential drawback of self-directed supports may be in the area of DSP training. People with intellectual and developmental disabilities may have some difficulty in training their DSPs using competency-based methods, and access to external training material may be expensive and hard to obtain for people who use self-directed supports. This may mean that it is particularly important to assess the competence of potential DSPs up front by carefully checking references, using behavioral interviewing techniques, recruiting using trusted sources, and giving potential DSPs a realistic preview of what working with the individual with intellectual and developmental disabilities will be like (Hewitt, Keiling, Sauer, McCulloh, & McBride, 2006).

Supports Across the Life Span

DSPs support people with intellectual and developmental disabilities throughout their lifetimes, with various forms of support being offered to young children, adolescents, adults, and older individuals with intellectual and developmental disabilities. This is not to say that a single DSP will necessarily provide supports to the same individual throughout his or her life, but it does mean that DSPs should understand the needs of people with intellectual and developmental disabilities at particular stages in their lives.

For many DSPs, understanding the needs of people with intellectual and developmental disabilities as they enter old age may be of particular importance. The populations of many countries are getting older. Although people with intellectual and developmental disabilities used to have shorter life expectancies than members of the general population, life expectancies for people with most types of intellectual and developmental disabilities are now similar to the population as a whole (Coppus, 2013). DSPs providing support to older adults with intellectual and developmental disabilities may need to be prepared to help in the management of complex medical needs, declining cognitive functioning, and limited mobility. In addition, and of importance, DSPs serving older adults are challenged to find ways to support the social integration preferences of the people they support. Because most older adults with intellectual and developmental disabilities no longer participate in work or vocational training programs, and because participation in typical social activities may become more difficult as a person ages, DSPs need to work closely with older adults with intellectual and developmental disabilities to determine what types of social activities they prefer, how participation in those activities may be complicated by each individual's support needs, and the specific accommodations that may be necessary in order to facilitate participation.

Just as the provision of supports to older adults with intellectual and developmental disabilities is of emerging importance for DSPs, so too is the opportunity to provide supports for young children with intellectual and developmental disabilities. Traditionally, support for young children with intellectual and developmental disabilities has been provided mainly by parents or other caregivers. Although this is still the case, emerging programs such as self-direction and stipends to help pay for family respite have been opening up more options for DSPs to work with young children, and this trend seems likely to continue.

SUMMARY

DSPs are an integral part of the support systems for many people with intellectual and developmental disabilities. Over the years, working as a DSP has changed, as the social model of disability has begun to replace the medical model and as community living has become the focus of disability supports. DSPs support people with intellectual and developmental disabilities in many different ways and in a multitude of settings but are always focused on promoting self-determination and community inclusion of people with intellectual and developmental disabilities. Working as a DSP is incredibly complex, with dozens of unique competencies necessary to do the work well. These competencies can be developed by engaging in competency-based training, which goes beyond knowledge building to apply new skills in real-life work. A competent and well-trained DSP will be prepared to engage with the people he or she supports in ways that honor each person with intellectual and developmental disabilities' right to person-centered supports and will be ready to engage with other professionals with respect, expertise, and professionalism.

FOR FURTHER THOUGHT AND DISCUSSION

1. Considering the ways in which the provision of services and supports to people with intellectual and developmental disabilities have changed since the 1960s, consider how the provision of such services and supports will change in the coming decade or quarter century.

2. DSPs are often the most important people in the delivery of high-quality services and supports, but it is often difficult to hire and retain qualified people to fill these roles. Why is that? How might that be changed?

3. What do you think are the best ways to ensure that DSPs have the skills and knowledge they need to be effective?

4. Self-directed or consumer-controlled services are a fast-growing part of the disability services sector. What are the benefits and disadvantages to such models?

5. As the Baby Boomer generation retires and ages, how might that affect the provision of supports to people with intellectual and developmental disabilities?

REFERENCES

American Network of Community Options and Resources. (2010). *2009 Direct support professionals wage study*. Alexandria, VA: Author.

Americans with Disabilities Act (ADA) of 1990, PL 101-336, 42 U.S.C. §§ 12101 *et seq.*

Bogenschutz, M., Hewitt, A., Hall-Lande, J., & LaLiberte, T. (2010). Status and trends in the direct support workforce in self-directed supports. *Intellectual and Developmental Disabilities, 48,* 345–360. doi:10.1352/1934-9556-48.5.345

Bogenschutz, M., Hewitt, A., Nord, D., & Hepperlen, R. (2014). The direct support and frontline supervision workforce supporting community living for individuals with IDD: Current wages, benefits, and stability. *Intellectual and Developmental Disabilities, 52,* 317–329. doi:10.1352/1934-9556-52.3.317

Braddock, D., & Hemp, R. (2004). *Developmental disabilities in North Dakota: A study of the structure, financing and quality of residential and community services*. Boulder: University of Colorado, Department of Psychiatry.

Coppus, A. (2013). People with intellectual disability: What do we know about adulthood and life expectancy? *Developmental Disabilities Research Reviews, 18,* 6–16.

Disability Discrimination Act 1992. Act No. 135 of 1992 as amended. (1992).

Equality Act of 2010. Great Britain Parliament. (2010).

Heller, T., Arnold, C., van Heumen, L., McBride, E., & Factor, A. (2012). Self-directed support: Impact of hiring practices on adults with intellectual and developmental disabilities and families. *American Journal on Intellectual and Developmental Disabilities, 117,* 464–477.

Hewitt, A. (1998). *Identification of competencies and effective training practices for direct support staff working in community residential services for people with developmental disabilities* (Doctoral dissertation, University of Minnesota).

Hewitt, A., Keiling, K., Sauer, J., McCulloh, N., & McBride, M. (2006). *Find, choose, and keep great DSPs: A toolkit for people with disabilities.* Minneapolis, MN: Institute on Community Integration.

Hoge, M.A., & McFaul, M. (2010). *Alaskan core competencies for direct support workers in health and human services.* Anchorage, AK: Alaska Mental Health Trust Authority.

Lakin, K.C., Polister, B., & Prouty, R.W. (2003). Wages of non-state direct-support professionals lag far behind those of public direct-support professionals and the general workforce. *Mental Retardation, 41,* 141–146.

Larson, S.A., Hewitt, A.S., & Knoblauch, B.A. (2005). Recruitment, retention, and training challenges in community human services: A review of the literature. In S.A. Larson & A.S. Hewitt, *Staff recruitment, retention, and training strategies for community human services organizations* (pp. 1–18). Baltimore, MD: Paul H. Brookes Publishing Co.

Larson, S., Lakin, K., & Bruininks, R. (1998). *Staff recruitment and retention: Study results and intervention strategies.* Washington, DC: American Association on Mental Retardation.

Larson, S.A., Salmi, P., Smith, D., Anderson, L., & Hewitt, A.S. (2013). *Residential services for persons with intellectual or developmental disabilities: Status and trends through 2011.* Minneapolis: University of Minnesota, Research and Training Center on Community Living, Institute on Community Integration.

National Alliance for Direct Support Professionals. (2011a). *15 NADSP competency areas.* Retrieved from https://nadsp.org/2011-09-22-14-00-06.html

National Alliance for Direct Support Professionals. (2011b). *List of accredited curricula.* Retrieved from https://nadsp.org/accreditation/list-of-accredited-organizations.html

National Alliance for Direct Support Professionals. (2011c). *The NADSP code of ethics.* Retrieved from https://nadsp.org/library/code-of-ethics.html

Olmstead v. L.C., 527 U.S. 581 (1999).

Omnibus Budget Reconciliation Act (OBRA) of 1981, PL 97-35, 95 Stat. 357.

PHI. (2013). *Occupational projections for direct-care workers 2010–2020.* New York, NY: Author. Retrieved from http://phinational.org/sites/phinational.org/files/phi_factsheet1update_singles_2.pdf

Scan Foundation. (2012). *Who provides long term care in the United States?* Long Beach, CA: Author.

Sedlezky, L., Taylor, M., Nord, D., Hoge, M., Robbins, R., Dilla, B., & Flin, B. (2014). *Phase III-B: Road map of core competencies for the direct service workforce project validation.* Baltimore, MD: Centers for Medicare and Medicaid Services.

Taylor, M., Bradley, V., & Warren, R. (1996). *The community support skill standards: Tools for managing change and achieving outcomes.* Cambridge, MA: Human Services Research Institute.

United Nations General Assembly. (2007). *Convention on the Rights of Persons with Disabilities.* General Assembly Res. A/RES/ 61/106, entered into force May 3, 2008.

U.S. Department of Labor. (2011). *Long-term care, supports, and services competency model.* Retrieved from http://www.careeronestop.org/CompetencyModel/pyramid.aspx?LTC=Y

U.S. v. Commonwealth of Virginia. 3:12-cv-00059-JAG. (E.D. Virginia 2012).

U.S. v. Rhode Island. 1:14-cv-00175. (D.R.I. 2014).

27

Responding to Cultural and Linguistic Differences Among People with Intellectual Disability

Tawara D. Goode, Wendy Alegra Jones, and Joan Christopher

WHAT YOU WILL LEARN

- To define culture and multiple cultural differences among people with intellectual and developmental disabilities
- The link between culture and language and its implication for individuals with intellectual and developmental disabilities
- Conceptual frameworks and definitions of cultural competence and linguistic competence
- How a new demographic reality is reflected in shifting racial, ethnic, and linguistic diversity among populations in the United States, its territories, and tribal nations
- How culturally and linguistically competent policies and practices can improve the quality and effectiveness of services and supports for people with intellectual and developmental disabilities
- The role of cultural and linguistic competence in addressing racial, ethnic, and linguistic disparities that affect people with intellectual and developmental disabilities

This chapter is designed to examine culture and the convergence of cultural contexts that affect people with intellectual disability, their families, and the communities in which they attend school, love, marry, parent, work, play, and live their lives. The chapter delineates rationales for and explores the role of cultural and linguistic competence in

supporting people with intellectual disability and their families across the life span. Finally, the chapter highlights values and areas of awareness, knowledge, and skills for the broad range of professionals who provide services and supports to people with intellectual disability and their families.

DEFINING CULTURE

To respond effectively to cultural and linguistic differences among people with intellectual disability, one must first have a shared understanding of what culture is and what culture is not. Culture influences every aspect of life and defines our identity as humans. Culture has multiple dimensions that intersect in time and space with common and distinct manifestations for individuals, groups, and societies (Goode & Jones, 2008). Culture is learned or transmitted beginning, as social scientists believe, at birth or at initiation, in the context of families and the social groups to which a person belongs or consciously seeks to belong. Culture is almost always defined within the context of a group—by providing the code of behavior and the identity of a group and its members. Culture is often described as a paradox—although many aspects remain constant from generation to generation, many other aspects of culture are dynamic and change over time. The Definition of Culture discussion that follows underpins how culture is conceptualized throughout the chapter.

Definition of Culture

"Culture is the learned and shared knowledge that specific groups use to generate their behavior and interpret their experience of the world. It comprises beliefs about reality, how people should interact with each other, what they 'know' about the world, and how they should respond to the social and material environments in which they find themselves." Culture is reflected in, but is not limited to, our values, morals, beliefs, practices, customs, rituals, languages, spirituality, religions, and even our technologies. (Gilbert, Goode, & Dunne, 2007, p. 15)

From Gilbert, J., Goode, T., & Dunne, C. (2007). Cultural Awareness-Curricula Enhancement Module Series. Washington, DC: National Center for Cultural Competence, Georgetown University Center for Child and Human Development. Copyright © 2007 Georgetown University. Retrieved from http://www.ncccurricula.info/awareness/C4.html; Included with permission of the Georgetown University National Center for Cultural Competence, Georgetown University Center for Child & Human Development, Georgetown University Medical Center.

Although the aforementioned definitions and conceptualizations present culture in terms of the group and group behavior, it is essential to note that aspects of culture are manifested differently in each person. A member of a cultural group may neither exhibit nor embrace all of the beliefs, values, practices, modes of communication, or behaviors attributed to a given group. This understanding of culture recognizes the individuality of human beings and the unique diversity among group members. It is important to note that accepting this understanding of culture minimizes the tendency to stereotype and serves as a reminder that one's cultural identity is influenced by a constellation of interrelated and distinct factors, including having an intellectual or other developmental disability.

Because of the social history of the United States, particularly, there is a tendency among many to associate the terms *cultural diversity* or *diverse populations* solely with race or ethnicity. Although race and ethnicity are important defining social constructs in the United States society, they are only two of many factors that influence cultural diversity among individuals and groups. Other factors—such as a person's age, gender, gender identity, sexual orientation, socioeconomic status, education, family constellation, language of origin, and the lived experience of disability and mental illness—are all culturally influenced. For example, culture defines the concept of *family* in ways that include, but are not limited to 1) the people who comprise the family (i.e., extended, nuclear, blended, and not related by blood), 2) the expected roles of its members (i.e., male, female, children, adults, and other relatives such as grandparents, uncles, aunts, cousins, godparents, and fictive kin—individuals who are not related by birth or marriage yet are bonded by strong emotional ties or relationships), and 3) how family members interact with those outside of the family (e.g., health, education, and human services professionals), including

the types of external relationships they choose to forge. Culture influences perceptions, beliefs, and practices about a child, adolescent, or adult family member with intellectual disability. The box that follows highlights a constellation of factors that are

---

Cultural Factors That Influence Diversity Among Individuals and Groups

Cultural/racial/ethnic identity

Tribal affiliation/clan

Nationality

Acculturation/assimilation

Socioeconomic status/class

Education

Language

Literacy

Family constellation

Social history

Perception of time

Health beliefs and practices

Health and mental health literacy

Beliefs about disability or mental health

Lived experience of disability or mental illness

Age and life cycle issues

Gender, gender identity, and expression

Sexual orientation

Religious and spiritual views

Spatial regional patterns

Political orientation/affiliation

From The National Center for Cultural Competence (NCCC) (2006) (PowerPoint Slide). A closer look at culture. Retrieved from http://nccc.georgetown.edu/documents/pptculture.pdf; Adapted with permission from James L. Mason, Ph.D., NCCC Senior Consultant.

---

useful in understanding the multiple dimensions of culture and their influence on diversity.

In addition to the previous discussion of family constellation, the authors of this chapter chose to emphasize the perception of time because of its relevance to the theme of the chapter. *Time* is typically defined as past, present, and future. Belief systems about time are deeply embedded in all cultures and influence the behaviors of its members. Cultures that are past oriented often value family roots from previous generations, traditions, and ancestral figures and practices. Cultures that are present oriented believe that life is lived in the here and now and that the future is not promised. Cultures that are future oriented plan in advance and routinely project life experiences, finances, and living conditions 5–25 years in the future. The cultural beliefs and practices of the United States are consistent with those of future oriented cultures. Understanding and responding to these culturally defined belief systems about time is an important, yet often overlooked, aspect of services and supports to people with intellectual disability and their families.

For example, a family has a preschool age child diagnosed with significant developmental delays. The family's belief system is solidly present oriented. An early intervention provider recommends a range of therapeutic interventions to support the child's development and minimize adverse outcomes in the future. These are two very different world views, two very different cultural perspectives that, if unaddressed, may lead to a less than desirable outcome for all in this situation.

THE LANGUAGE–CULTURE LINK

In many ways, language and culture are inextricably linked; in other words, culture is embedded or encoded in language. For the purposes of this chapter, *language* is defined as a shared system of communication in which group members receive and deliver concepts, thoughts, needs, and emotions. Language is one of the most symbolic aspects of any culture, as it transmits messages not only in words but through symbols and nonverbal expressions such as gestures, facial expressions, silence, space, and touch. Just like culture, language is learned, is socially constructed, and changes over time, with new words emerging based on new realities and shared group experiences. For example, rapid advances in technology have not only ushered in dramatic changes in how people communicate but also have introduced numerous new concepts and

words to the U.S. lexicon. When the term *app* is heard or used, there is almost a universal understanding across U.S. society that an app is a software application that helps people do things on computers and smartphone devices. This is a perfect example of the integral and dynamic relationship between language and culture; the term *app* was voted Word of the Year by the American Dialect Society in 2010. Language is the means by which communication takes place among and between cultures, including the cultures of the professionals, disciplines, and service systems that support people with intellectual disability and their families.

Applying the Definitions and Concepts of Culture and Language to Intellectual Disability

The beliefs about and responses to people with disabilities in general, and those with intellectual disability in particular, have evolved over time among global societies and within the sociocultural contexts of the United States (Priestly, 2001; Wehmeyer, 2013). The definition of culture cited previously provides a lens through which to examine the evolution of how U.S. society has treated people with intellectual disability (i.e., "culture is reflected in, but not limited to, our values, morals, beliefs, practices, customs, rituals, and language," "culture is learned," and "aspects of culture are dynamic and change over time"). The extant literature documents that people with intellectual disability were viewed historically as being childlike, vulnerable, and in need of protection from the harms of society, and the consensus was that their best interests were served by placing them in segregated institutional settings. During the eugenics movement (1880–1950), youth and adults with intellectual disability (and those deemed to have other socially undesirable traits) were viewed by proponents as deviants and a threat to "normal" society, and the proposed solution was that they required sterilization to preserve the integrity and sanctity of future generations of human beings (Pfeiffer, 1994). The pervasive attitude about individuals with intellectual and other disabilities was that they were a burden and were not capable of making a positive contribution to their own well-being or to society. Language to describe people with intellectual and other disabilities also reflected the belief systems of the times and included terms that would be considered derogatory and offensive today, such as *feebleminded, imbecile, idiot, moron, mentally defective, retarded, backward, slow, deformed, crippled,* and *afflicted with insanity* (Pfeiffer, 1994). These belief systems reflected the culture of U.S. society and were legitimized by both state and federal statutes that justified forced sterilization and other oppressive practices of the eugenics movement.

The Developmental Disabilities Assistance and Bill of Rights Act Amendments of 2000 (DD Act of 2000; PL 106-402) states that "disability is a natural part of the human experience." (Administration for Community Living, U.S. Department of Health and Human Services, 2016). The belief system expressed in that definition, and the realization of its truth, continue to evolve in the cultural contexts of U.S. society—marking a most dramatic shift (Priestly, 2001; Snow, 2013). This cultural shift has not come easily. It has been hard fought, and achievements have been made because of the sheer unrelenting determination and advocacy of people who experience a broad spectrum of disabilities, their families, and allies who demanded that the human rights, freedoms, and dignity of people with disabilities be acknowledged, respected, and protected. Changes are evidenced by enactment of major legislation that espouse these cultural values, such as the Rehabilitation Act of 1973 (PL 93-112), the Education for All Handicapped Children Act of 1975 (PL 94-142) and its successor the Individuals with Disabilities Education Act of 1990 (PL 101-476), the landmark Americans with Disabilities Act of 1990 (PL 101-336), and the Assistive Technology Act of 1998 (PL 105-394), to name a few.

Regrettably, the commitment to changes in the cultural belief systems and practices of the United States has not permeated all aspects of society. As of this writing in 2016, the *Convention on the Rights of Persons with Disabilities* (CRPD; United Nations [U.N.] General Assembly, 2007) has been signed by 160 countries worldwide. The CRPD espouses the same belief systems and goals of U.S. legislation designed to affirm, protect the rights, and ensure the full inclusion of all people with disabilities, in all aspects of community life (see box). Yet the sociopolitical contexts in the United States have prevented it from joining members of the global community in ratifying this convention.

Concurrently, these shifts have also resulted in changes in how to understand intellectual disability and the language used to communicate with and about those who experience intellectual disability (Schalock et al., 2007; Schalock, Borthwith-Duffy, Buntinx, Coulter, & Craig, 2010). Led by self-advocates and their families, and supported by many within the broad disability community, a successful campaign was launched to change the term *mental retardation*. Self-advocates argued, and rightfully so, that the term is demeaning, offensive, and does not demonstrate an understanding of intellectual disability. These efforts brought about a monumental cultural shift in thinking and language and ultimately served to terminate the use of the term among disability professionals, disciplines, and service systems. Beginning in 1992, national organizations and academic

---

Disability Language from Landmark American and International Legislation

Developmental Disabilities Assistance and Bill of Rights Act Amendments of 2000

"Disability is a natural part of the human experience that does not diminish the right of individuals with developmental disabilities to live independently, to exert control and choice over their own lives, and to fully participate in and contribute to their communities through full integration and inclusion in the economic, political, social, cultural, and educational mainstream of United States society." (Office of the Law Revision Counsel, U.S. House of Representatives, n.d.)

Convention on the Rights of Persons with Disabilities

Recognizing:
"That disability is an evolving concept and...results from the interaction between persons with impairments and attitudinal and environmental barriers that hinder their full and effective participation in society on an equal basis with others"

"The valued existing and potential contributions made by persons with disabilities to the overall well-being and diversity of their communities." (UN General Assembly, 2007; see http://www.un.org/disabilities/convention/conventionfull.shtml)

journals publically removed the term *mental retardation* and changed their names, such as The Arc of the United States, the American Association on Intellectual and Developmental Disabilities, the U.S. President's Committee for People with Intellectual Disabilities, and the *Journal of Intellectual Disability Research*.

This cultural shift was subsequently legitimized in federal statute. In 2010, the U.S. Congress passed and President Obama signed Public Law 111-256, known as Rosa's Law, which required 1) *mental retardation* to be referred to as *intellectual disability* in specific federal laws and 2) federal agencies administering these laws to revise their regulations to conform to this terminology. In the 2014 *Hall v. Florida* case, the U.S. Supreme Court ruled that it is no longer appropriate for that institution to use the term *mental retardation* and that *intellectual disability* should be used in all future references to this condition (see also http://www.supremecourt.gov /opinions/13pdf/12-10882_kkg1.pdf).

We would be remiss if we did not address another factor, rooted in the social fabric of the United States, that influences cultural views of intellectual disability. It is a topic that some within the disability professions are uncomfortable or reticent to discuss. There is a well-documented history of belief systems and practices in the United States that considered African Americans as intellectually inferior to non-Hispanic whites (Fish, 2002). Regrettably, this historical context, combined with contemporary experiences, continues to have far-reaching implications for African American children and families and manifests in a number of ways. The legacy and ongoing impact of these belief systems are most apparent in the over-representation of African American students diagnosed with intellectual disability (considered to be "slow learners" in the past) and the disproportionality of African American students in special education settings—specifically for intellectual disability, emotional-behavioral disorders, learning disabilities, and diagnoses of language delays and disorders based on their use of African American Vernacular English, sometimes referred to as Black English (Cartledge & Dukes, 2009; Goode, Jones, & Jackson, 2011; Harry & Klingner, 2014).

In addition to African Americans, research documents that Latino children who have limited English proficiency or are English language learners are also disproportionately assigned to special education (see, e.g., Artiles, Harry, Reschly, & Chinn, 2002, & Harry & Klingner, 2014). A complex array of dynamics

contributes to this pattern of disparate treatment, that includes but is not limited to stereotyping, conscious and unconscious biases among educators, culturally biased assessment instruments and practices, discrimination, institutional and structural racism, and the debilitating effects on students of living in marginalized and disadvantaged families and communities. It is essential that professionals have an understanding of these historical cultural factors and their impact on current realities facing people with intellectual disability from racially and ethnically diverse groups across the life span. In today's work force, a professional's capacity to respond to cultural and linguistic differences among people who experience intellectual and other disabilities is an essential area of knowledge and skill.

A CONVERGENCE OF CULTURAL CONTEXTS

Our discussion in the chapter, thus far, has centered on culture from the perspective of individuals and groups. People with intellectual disability and their families may require involvement in a number of systems throughout the life span. Figure 27.1 provides a graphic representation of the possible array of systems as cultural contexts converge. Each system has its own culture: norms, rules, language,

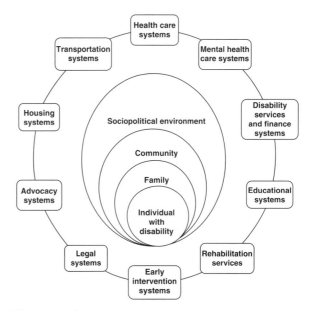

Figure 27.1. Convergence of cultural contexts: A focus on intellectual and developmental disabilities. (From Goode, T. [2016] Convergence of Cultural Contexts: A Focus on Intellectual and Developmental Disabilities. Figure Copyright © 2016 Tawara D. Goode; reprinted by permission.)

decision-making processes, approaches to communication, defined roles and responsibilities, ways of interacting with those seeking or receiving services, and so forth (Goode & Maloof, 2010). The culture of each of these systems is learned by employees and transmitted through policies, structures, and practices, both in formal and informal ways. Although slow to change, these systems are dynamic—and must respond to the sociocultural, economic, political, technological, and other environmental changes that take place internally and externally.

Imagine the magnitude and complexity of each system and the need for individuals with intellectual disability and their families or allies to navigate these systems in order to receive the services and supports that they prefer and need. Imagine a family that has little to no experience with any given system, perhaps other than education. Imagine that the family has limited English proficiency and requires interpretation and translation services in its first language to derive any benefit from the service system. Now imagine this family having to interact with four different service systems for their child, adolescent, or adult member with intellectual disability. Using the convergence of cultural contexts framework as a lens to examine the broad parameters of culture is humbling and, as such, can provide valuable insights to professionals to respond to cultural and linguistic differences among people who experience intellectual disability and their families.

To summarize our discussion on culture, as a disability professional, it is helpful to keep the following in mind:

- You are a cultural being and have multiple cultural identities, one of which may be your professional discipline or position in a school, university, clinic, community-based organization, or governmental entity.

- You view and interpret the world through your own cultural lens, which is comprised of both individual and group experiences over time.

- Your cultural frame of reference may or may not be shared by the individuals to whom you provide care, services, supports, or teaching.

- Your world view or cultural frame of reference influences your approach to delivering services, supports, or other responsibilities associated with your position or role. In addition, your world view is influenced by the "culture" of the organization, program, or agency in which you are employed.

- You, as well as all people, have biases that manifest at both conscious and unconscious levels. A bias is a preference for one thing, person, or group over another. Bias only becomes a concern when it becomes a prejudice against certain people or groups in ways that are unfair and lead to discrimination. Because one's cultural frame of reference contributes to biases, it is necessary to identify, acknowledge, and address such biases if they interfere with your capacity to perform day-to-day responsibilities in a competent and respectful manner.

- Your willingness and capacity to address cultural misunderstandings are essential to 1) supporting people with intellectual and other disabilities and their families and 2) the working relationships with colleagues and others involved in the array of systems that provide services and support to this diverse population.

CULTURAL COMPETENCE AND LINGUISTIC COMPETENCE

This section provides definitions from conceptual frameworks and explains the essential role of cultural and linguistic competence in disability services and supports.

Definitions and Conceptual Frameworks

There is no single definition of cultural competence. Definitions have evolved from diverse perspectives, interests, and needs and are incorporated in state legislation, federal statutes and programs, health and mental health organizations, and academic settings. The DD Act of 2000 defines culturally competent as

> Services, supports, or other assistance that is conducted or provided in a manner that is responsive to the beliefs, interpersonal styles, attitudes, language, and behaviors of individuals who are receiving the services, supports, or other assistance, and in a manner that has the greatest likelihood of ensuring their maximum participation in the program. (Administration for Community Living, U.S. Department of Health and Human Services, 2016)

For the purposes of this chapter, we use the definitions and conceptual frameworks presented in Table 27.1 that have been created or adapted by the National Center for Cultural Competence at Georgetown University.

Table 27.1. Definitions and conceptual frameworks

Cultural competence

"Cultural competence requires that organizations:

- have a defined set of values and principles, and demonstrate behaviors, attitudes, policies, and structures that enable them to work effectively cross-culturally.
- have the capacity to (1) value diversity, (2) conduct self-assessment, (3) manage the dynamics of difference, (4) acquire and institutionalize cultural knowledge and (5) adapt to diversity and the cultural contexts of the communities they serve.
- incorporate the above in all aspects of policy making, administration, practice, service delivery and involve systematically consumers, key stakeholders, and communities.

Cultural competence is a developmental process that evolves over an extended period. Both individuals and organizations are at various levels of awareness, knowledge, and skills along the cultural competence continuum. (adapted from Cross et al., 1989)"

Linguistic competence

Linguistic competence is "the capacity of an organization and its personnel to communicate effectively, and convey information in a manner that is easily understood by diverse groups, including persons of limited English proficiency, those who have low literacy skills or are not literate, individuals with disabilities, and those who are deaf or hard of hearing. Linguistic competency requires organizational and provider capacity to respond effectively to the health and mental health literacy needs of populations served. The organization must have policy, structures, practices, procedures, and dedicated resources to support this capacity."

From Goode, T., & Jones W. (modified 2009). Cultural Competence: Definition and Conceptual Framework; Linguistic Competence: Definition. Washington, DC: National Center for Cultural Competence, Georgetown University Center for Child & Human Development, Copyright © 2009 Georgetown University. Retrieved from http://nccc.georgetown.edu/foundations/frameworks.html; Included with permission of the Georgetown University National Center for Cultural Competence, Georgetown University Center for Child & Human Development, Georgetown University Medical Center.

The Essential Role of Cultural and Linguistic Competence in Disability Services and Supports

Cultural competence and linguistic competence are recognized across education, health, mental health, disability, and other human services as essential to quality, appropriateness, and effectiveness. Content that underpins the values and practices of cultural and linguistic competence is found nationally in curricula (K–12, postsecondary, graduate, and postgraduate education). Professional associations, accreditation bodies, and licensing authorities in many disciplines view cultural and linguistic competence as essential areas of knowledge and skills (e.g., American Psychological Association, American Speech-Language-Hearing Association, American Physical Therapy Association, American Occupational Therapy Association, National Education Association, American Academy of Pediatrics, American Psychiatric Association, National Association of Social Workers, National Association of Special Education Teachers, American Evaluation Association). The following subsections describe five salient reasons for cultural and linguistic competence in diverse disciplines, professions, and systems concerned with intellectual and developmental disabilities.

A New Demographic Reality There have been dramatic shifts in the demographics of the United States and its territories, and this trend is expected to continue. Data from the 2010 Census reveals that more than one third of those in the U.S. population are from racial and ethnic groups other than non-Hispanic white alone, representing an increase from 86.9 million to 111.9 million between 2000 and 2010 (U.S. Census Bureau, 2010). According to 2010 census data, the Hispanic population grew by 43%, from 35.3 million in 2000 to 50.5 million in 2010 and comprises 16% of the total population of 308.7 million people. Census data indicate the following percentages of self-identified members of single-race categories: 13% Blacks or African Americans, 5% Asians, 0.9% American Indians/Alaska Natives, and 0.5% Native Hawaiians/Other Pacific Islander (U.S. Census Bureau, 2010). More than 9 million people, 3% of the population, self-identified as having more than one race. For example, the American Indian and Alaska Native in combination population grew by 39%. Texas joined California, the District of Columbia, Hawaii, and New Mexico in what is coined as having a "majority-minority" population, where more than 50% of the population is from a group other than non-Hispanic white.

Diversity in World Views About Disability Definitions and beliefs about disability, including intellectual disability, vary widely, with more than 40 definitions in U.S. federal statutes alone, all of which are culturally influenced. Such beliefs range from viewing disability as a natural occurrence to viewing it as an accident of nature, a punishment from God, a blessing from God or another deity, a disruption in the body's equilibrium, or as something explained by medicine of science (Goode & Maloof, 2010). The prevailing view that, as defined by the National Institute on Disability Rehabilitation and Research, "disability is the result of an interaction between characteristics of the individual and those of the natural, built, communications (IT), cultural, and social environments" (U.S. Department of Education, n.d.) represents an emerging belief system embraced by self-advocates and many within academia, government, and the disability system of services and supports. However, this belief system is not shared by all. Cultural competence requires that disability professionals acquire or have knowledge of these belief systems in order to be responsive to the diverse populations with intellectual disability and their families.

Improve the Quality and Effectiveness of Services and Supports

There is a compelling body of research documenting that cultural and linguistic competence improves quality, effectiveness, and satisfaction in human services. The preponderance of this evidence is found in education, health and allied health disciplines, and mental health. Although both scholarly and practical work is emerging, overall the disability research community has been slower to contribute to this literature (Balcazar, Suarez-Balcazar, Taylor-Ritzler, & Keys, 2010; Blacher & McIntyre, 2006; Goode, Dunne, & Bronheim, 2006; Nehring, 2007). Because of the growing trend toward the use of evidence-based practices (EBPs) in education and human services, important cultural considerations for disability professionals include 1) the representation of diverse racial, ethnic, and socioeconomic groups in EBP validation processes; 2) whether the EBPs have proved equally effective for all racial, ethnic, or cultural groups; and 3) whether the EBPs have been culturally adapted for specific populations, including those with intellectual disability from culturally and linguistically diverse groups. Culturally competent organizations design and implement services that are tailored or matched to the unique needs of individuals, children, families, and the communities served.

Federal and State Legislation

There are numerous federal and state statutes that require cultural and linguistic competence in education, health, mental health, and social and other human services and are too numerous to cite here. Two areas of federal and state legislation are highly relevant to disability professionals. First is Title VI, Section 601 of the Civil Rights Act of 1964 (PL 88-352), which prohibits national origin discrimination against populations with limited English proficiency among any entity receiving federal funds. Although Title VI focuses on the responsibility of organizations, it is important that the professionals within these organizations understand the implications of this law for their respective positions and responsibilities, including those concerned with intellectual disability. The mandates of Title VI span almost all federal agencies (i.e., housing, education, health, social services). Second, numerous states have enacted legislation requiring cultural competence as a condition for licensure and for continuing education for specific disciplines (National Center for Cultural Competence, 2009). The education requirements mirror that of accreditation bodies and professional associations that view cultural competence as a key area of knowledge and skill. Systems and organizations must sanction, and in some cases mandate, the incorporation of cultural knowledge into policy making, infrastructure, and practice.

Address Racial, Ethnic, and Linguistic Disparities

There is consensus among educators; health, mental health, and social service providers; and many within the research community that cultural and linguistic competence is effective in addressing racial, ethnic, and linguistic disparities or disproportionality as commonly referred to in education and mental health. For a host of reasons, the disabilities field as a whole has, to a large degree, been a late adaptor of cultural and linguistic competence, even though the DD Act of 2000 defines cultural competence as essential to services and supports for people with the broad range of developmental disabilities. In 2014, the Association of University Centers on Disabilities identified increasing cultural and linguistic competence and diversity as a priority area of focus within its network of more than 100 programs concerned with intellectual and developmental disabilities in the United States and its territories. The role of cultural and linguistic competence in addressing racial, ethnic, and linguistic disparities for individuals with intellectual disability cannot be understated. Ensuring adoption and implementation across the network will require concerted effort on the part of many, including those who teach and provide therapies, direct services, or other supports to individuals with intellectual disability across the life span. Cultural competence embraces the principles of equal access and nondiscriminatory practices in service delivery.

Table 27.2 offers five elements of cultural competence at the individual level to provide guidance to disability professionals. Table 27.3 presents an example inventory for assessing selected examples of linguistically competent practices.

Table 27.2. Five elements of cultural competence at the individual level

Element of cultural competence	Application for professionals supporting individuals with intellectual disability and their families
Acknowledge cultural differences	• Be attuned to both similarities and differences between all cultural groups.
	• Recognize the within-group diversity among racial and ethnic populations (e.g., literacy, socioeconomic status, education, sexual orientation, gender identity, religiosity or spirituality, English language proficiency).
	• Recognize and accept differences in beliefs and practices about intellectual disability. Avoid judgment, and respect other disability beliefs systems or explanatory models even if they differ from your own.
	• Accept that some racial, ethnic, and other cultural groups have historical and present-day experiences of bias, stereotyping, discrimination, and disparate treatment in education and health and human services. These experiences affect their capacity for trust and confidence in service systems.
	• Identify and participate in professional development forums designed to increase knowledge and skills to address cultural differences in supports and other services.
Understand your own culture	• Reflect upon your own cultural belief systems, including the culture of the discipline or profession to which you belong.
	• List these values and beliefs systems.
	• Ask yourself this question: "Do I assume that these values are shared among the individuals and families that I support?"
	• Think "culture" when you notice that others are not behaving in ways that you expect. Consider what norms, beliefs, and values you bring to the situation.
	• Write a list of your beliefs systems that may lead to insensitive and biased thoughts and behaviors toward others.
	• Ask one or more colleagues, with whom you have a relationship of trust, to share their views about what they see as insensitive or biased beliefs or behaviors that you demonstrate, and with whom.
	• Reflect on whether and how your cultural belief systems negatively affect communication or relationships with
	— People to whom you provide services and supports or teach
	— Staff and colleagues with whom you work
	• Make a personal and professional commitment to address cultural belief systems and behaviors that compromise the services and supports you deliver.
	• Find out the professional code of ethics, guidelines, or standards for cultural and linguistic competence for your discipline or profession. Incorporate them in your day-to-day responsibilities.
Engage in self-assessment	• Identify and respond to assessment tools and checklists that probe the values and practices of cultural and linguistic competence. Engage in self-assessment as a routine component of your professional practice.
	• Maintain a query list designed to stimulate self-examination of your personal reactions, particularly when communications and interactions with others do not go well.
	• Ask colleagues, with whom you work closely, to complete an assessment of what they perceive as strengths and areas for growth relative to cultural and linguistic competence and compare it with your own assessment.
Acquire cultural knowledge and skills	• Learn strategies to see similarities rather than only differences in individuals from racial, ethnic, or cultural groups other than your own.
	• Identify and pursue both formal and informal opportunities for learning (i.e., about culture, cultural beliefs, and practices of the people you serve or support and their families, cultural and linguistic competence, and disparities and disproportionality affecting diverse populations).
	• Use self-assessment results to develop personal learning goals that enhance knowledge about cultural and linguistic competence.
	• Value the diversity within your organization or program setting and reach out to learn from colleagues and staff that have cultural experiences and perspectives other than your own.
View behavior within a cultural context	• Consider the following questions when reflecting on behaviors, both yours and those of individuals with intellectual disability and their families:
	• What does culture have to do with the behavior or attitude that I observe?

(continued)

Table 27.2.   *(continued)*

Element of cultural competence	Application for professionals supporting individuals with intellectual disability and their families
	• What is my cultural lens? Consider both professional and personal world views.
	• What is the other cultural lens (i.e., individual with intellectual disability, the family)?
	• Discover the strengths and resiliencies of individuals and families from racial and ethnic backgrounds that are typically described as disadvantaged, disempowered, marginalized, and not well educated. Use these strengths to inform your work.
	• Seek the experience and knowledge of cultural brokers or others who are familiar with the world view, belief systems, and practices of diverse families.
	• Widely accepted values and practices in disability services mean different things to different groups. It is helpful to view the concepts of self-determination, self-advocacy, and independence within a cultural context. Selected examples include the following:
	• *Self-determination:* In some cultures, decisions are made that do not rest solely with the individual but take the impact on the larger group (family or community) into consideration.
	• *Self-advocacy:* In some cultures, the notion and practice of advocacy is not well embraced. It is culturally unacceptable to challenge authority figures or the government, and in some instances such actions have resulted in punishment (e.g., jail, bodily harm).
	• *Independence versus interdependence:* In some cultures, interdependence is more highly valued and practiced than independence. The belief system that one person lives life totally independently—without the assistance of family, neighbors, or the faith community—is implausible in such cultures.

Goode T., Haywood S., Wells N., Rhee K. Family-centered, Culturally, and Linguistically Competent Care: Essential Components of the Medical Home. Pediatr Ann. 2009; 38(9): 505–512; Reprinted with permission from SLACK Incorporated.

Table 27.3.   Example inventory for assessing linguistically competent practices

Please select A, B, or C for each item listed below. Use the key to indicate your response to each item, remembering that there are no correct answers. If you frequently cite "C," however, you may not necessarily demonstrate areas of knowledge and the types of practices that are congruent with linguistic competence.

A = *Things I do frequently, or statement applies to me to a great degree*

B = *Things I do occasionally, or statement applies to me to a moderate degree*

C = *Things I do rarely or never, or statement applies to me to minimal degree or not at all*

1. For individuals who speak languages other than English, I attempt to learn and use key words in their language so that I am better able to communicate with them during assessment, treatment, or other interventions and supports.

2. I attempt to determine any familial colloquialisms used by individuals (children, adolescents, adults) and families that may affect assessment, treatment, teaching, or other interventions and supports.

3. I use bilingual staff or qualified interpreters when conducting assessments, providing treatment, and convening meetings and for other events for families who would require this level of assistance.

4. When interacting with parents or family members who have limited English proficiency, I always keep in mind the following:

   — Limitations in English proficiency are in no way a reflection of their level of intellectual functioning.

   — Their limited ability to speak the language of the dominant culture has no bearing on their ability to communicate effectively in their language of origin.

   — They may or may not be literate in their language of origin or English.

5. I ensure (and/or advocate) that all written documents and communiqués to individuals with limited English proficiency are written in their preferred language.

6. I understand the principles and practices of linguistic competence and

   — Apply them within my organization, program, agency, or educational setting

   — Advocate for them within my program or agency

7. I understand the implications of the following statutes, standards, or practices within the context of my roles and responsibilities:

   — Title VI, Section 601 of the Civil Rights Act of 1964 (PL 88-352)

   — The National Standards for Culturally and Linguistically Appropriate Services in Health and Health Care (National CLAS Standards; see U.S. Department of Health and Human Services, Office of Minority Health, n.d.)

   — Health literacy

From Goode, T. (2009). Promoting Cultural Diversity and Cultural Competency: Self-Assessment Checklist for Personnel Providing Services and Supports to Children with Disabilities & Special Health Needs and their Families. Washington, DC: National Center for Cultural Competence, University Center for Excellence in Developmental Disabilities, Copyright © 2009 Georgetown University. Retrieved from http://nccc.georgetown.edu/documents/ChecklistCSHN.pdf; Included with permission of the Georgetown University National Center for Cultural Competence, Georgetown University Center for Child & Human Development, Georgetown University Medical Center.

SUMMARY

This chapter sought to deepen the understanding of culture, its multiple dimensions, and the convergence of cultural contexts that affect people with intellectual disability, their families, and the communities in which they attend school, love, marry, parent, work, play, and live their lives. It explored the historical and contemporary factors that affect the experience of intellectual disability, including the impact of disparities and disproportionality for specific racial and ethnic groups. This chapter also introduced the definitions and conceptual frameworks of cultural competence and linguistic competence and their relevance to the provision of services and supports to individuals with intellectual and other disabilities across the life span.

The following thoughts about culture are offered as considerations for disability professionals.

• Understanding another culture is a continuous, not a discrete, process.

• It requires experience as well as study to understand the many subtleties of another culture.

• Stereotyping is inevitable in the absence of frequent contact with or study of other cultures.

• What seems to be logical, sensible, important, and reasonable in one culture may seem illogical, irrational, senseless, and unimportant to an outsider of that culture.

• Differences between cultures are often seen as threatening and are often described in negative terms.

• Language and culture are integrally linked. It is probably necessary to know the language of another culture to understand that culture in depth (Goode & Jones, 2008).

Remember, achieving cultural and linguistic competence is a journey that takes places over time. We encourage you to join the ranks of professionals who accept and understand the essential role of culture in disability services and supports.

FOR FURTHER THOUGHT AND DISCUSSION

1. Culture influences every aspect of life and defines identity as humans. In what ways does this affect people with intellectual and developmental disabilities?

2. How would you define *cultural competence*, and how does that affect how you act in supporting people with intellectual and developmental disabilities?

3. How will changing demographics affect services and supports for people with intellectual and developmental disabilities? Think about these changes in association with the aging population and its demands on the system.

4. How can the field ensure that professionals and direct support professionals supporting people with intellectual and developmental disabilities are adequately prepared to provide culturally and linguistically competent supports?

5. Discuss how the application of the five elements of cultural competence described in Table 27.2 could benefit people with intellectual and developmental disabilities and their families.

REFERENCES

Administration for Community Living, U.S. Department of Health and Human Services. (2016). *The Developmental Disabilities Assistance and Bill of Rights Act of 2000.* Retrieved from http://www.acl.gov/Programs/AIDD/DDA_BOR_ACT_2000/p2_tI_subtitleA.aspx

American Dialect Society. (2011). *"App" 2010 Word of the Year, as voted by American Dialect Society.* Retrieved from http://www.americandialect.org/American-Dialect-Society-2010-Word-of-the-Year-PRESS-RELEASE.pdf

Americans with Disabilities Act (ADA) of 1990, PL 101-336, 42 U.S.C. §§ 12101 *et seq.*

Artiles, A.J., Harry, B., Reschly, D.J., & Chinn, P.C. (2002). Over-identification of students of color in special education: A critical overview. *Multicultural Perspectives, 4*(1) 3-1.

Assistive Technology Act of 1998, PL 105-394, 29 U.S.C. §§ 3001 *et seq.*

Balcazar, F.E., Suarez-Balcazar, Y., Taylor-Ritzler, T., & Keys, C.B. (2010). *Race, culture, and disability: Rehabilitation science and practice.* Sudbury, MA: Jones and Bartlett.

Blacher, J., & McIntyre, L.L. (2006). Syndrome specificity and behavioural disorders in young adults with intellectual disability: Cultural differences in family impact. *Journal of Intellectual Disabilities Research, 50,* 184–198.

Cartledge, G., & Dukes, C. (2009). Disproportionality of African American children in special education: Definitions and dimensions. In L.C. Tillman (Ed.), *The Sage handbook of African American education* (pp. 383–398). Thousand Oaks, CA: Sage.

Civil Rights Act of 1964, PL 88-352, 20 U.S.C. §§ 241 *et seq.*

Developmental Disabilities Assistance and Bill of Rights Act Amendments of 2000, PL 106-402, 42 U.S.C. §§ 6000 *et seq.*

Education for All Handicapped Children Act of 1975, PL 94-142, 20 U.S.C. §§ 1400 *et seq.*

Fish, J.M. (Ed.). (2002). *Race and intelligence: Separating science from myth.* Mahwah, NJ: Lawrence Erlbaum.

Gilbert, J., Goode, T., & Dunne, C. (2007). *Cultural awareness curricula enhancement module series.* Washington, DC: National Center for Cultural Competence, Georgetown University Center for Child and Human Development. Retrieved from http://www.nccccurricula.info/

Goode, T. (2004). *Promoting cultural competence and cultural diversity in early intervention and early childhood settings.* Retrieved from http://nccc.georgetown.edu/documents/ChecklistCSHN.pdf

Goode, T., Dunne, C., & Bronheim, S. (2006). *The evidence base for cultural and linguistic competence in health care.* New York, NY: Commonwealth Fund.

Goode, T., & Jones, W. (2008). Cultural influences on child development: The middle years. In T.P. Gullotta & G.M. Blau (Eds.), *Family influences on childhood behavior and development: Evidence-based prevention and treatment approaches* (pp. 63–95). New York, NY: Routledge.

Goode, T.D., Jones, W., & Jackson, V. (2011). Families with African American roots. In E.W. Lynch & M.J. Hanson (Eds.), *Developing cross-cultural competence* (4th ed., pp. 142–189). Baltimore, MD: Paul H. Brookes Publishing Co.

Goode, T.D., & Maloof, P. (2010). End-of-life through a cultural lens. In S. Friedman & D. Helm (Eds.), *End-of-life care for children and adults with intellectual and developmental disabilities* (pp. 219–243). Washington, DC: American Association on Intellectual and Developmental Disabilities.

Hall v. Florida, 134 S. Ct. 1986, 1990 (2014).

Harry, B., & Klingner, J. (2014). *Why are so many minority students in special education: Understanding race and disability in school* (2nd ed.). New York, NY: Teachers College Press.

Individuals with Disabilities Education Act (IDEA) of 1990, PL 101-476, 20 U.S.C. §§ 1400 *et seq.*

National Center for Cultural Competence. (2009). *State-level strategies to address health and mental health disparities through cultural and linguistic competency training and licensure: An environmental scan of factors related to legislative and regulatory actions in states.* Princeton, NJ: Robert Wood Johnson Foundation. Retrieved from http://www.rwjf.org/pr/product.jsp?id=49249

National Center for Cultural Competence. (2014). *Foundations, conceptual frameworks/models and definitions.* Retrieved from http://nccc.georgetown.edu

Nehring, W. (2007). Cultural considerations for children with intellectual and developmental disabilities. *Journal of Pediatric Nursing, 22,* 93–102.

Office of the Law Revision Counsel, U.S. House of Representatives. (n.d.). *42 USC 15001: Findings, purposes, and policy.* Retrieved from http://uscode.house.gov/view.xhtml?req=granuleid:USC-prelim-title42-section15001&num=0&edition=prelim

Pfeiffer, D. (1994). Eugenics and disability discrimination. *Disability and Society, 9,* 481–499.

Priestly, M. (2001). *Disability and the life course: Global perspectives.* New York, NY: Cambridge University Press.

Rehabilitation Act of 1973, PL 93-112, 29 U.S.C. §§ 701 *et seq.*

Rosa's Law, PL 111-256, 20 U.S.C. 1400.

Schalock, R., Borthwith-Duffy, S., Buntinx, W., Coulter, D., & Craig, E. (2010). *Intellectual disability: Definition, classification, and systems of supports* (11th ed.). Washington, DC: American Association on Intellectual and Developmental Disabilities.

Schalock, R., Luckasson, R.A., Shogren, K.A., Borthwick-Duffy, S., Bradley, V., Buntinx, W.H....Yeager, M.H. et al. (2007). The renaming of *mental retardation*: Understanding the change to the term *intellectual disability. Intellectual and Developmental Disabilities, 45,* 116–124.

Snow, K. (2013). *Disability is natural* (3rd ed.). Woodland Park, CO: Braveheart Press.

United Nations General Assembly. (2007). *Convention on the Rights of Persons with Disabilities.* General Assembly Res. A/RES/ 61/106, entered into force May 3, 2008.

U.S. Census Bureau. (2010). *2010 census shows America's diversity.* Retrieved from http://www.census.gov/newsroom/releases/archives/2010_census/cb11-cn125.html

U.S. Census Bureau. (2012). *American FactFinder, 2012 American community survey—1 year estimates, table S1601.* Retrieved from http://factfinder2.census.gov/faces/tableservices/jsf/pages/productview.xhtml?src=bkmk

U.S. Census Bureau. (2013). *International migration is projected to become primary driver of U.S. population growth.* Retrieved from http://www.census.gov/newsroom/releases/archives/population/cb13-89.html

U.S. Department of Education. (n.d.). *National Institute on Disability Rehabilitation and Research. Definition of disability.* Retrieved from http://www2.ed.gov/about/offices/list/osers/nidrr/faq.html#question12

U.S. Department of Health and Human Services, Office of Minority Health. (n.d.) *The national standards for culturally and linguistically appropriate services in health and health care.* Retrieved from https://www.thinkculturalhealth.hhs.gov/content/clas.asp

Wehmeyer, M.L. (Ed.). (2013). *The story of intellectual disability: An evolution of meaning, understanding, and public perception.* Baltimore, MD: Paul H. Brookes Publishing Co.

28

Behavioral Intervention

Rosemary A. Condillac and Daniel Baker

WHAT YOU WILL LEARN

- Why many people with intellectual disability need behavioral intervention
- Behaviors that need intervention
- Types of behavioral intervention
- Why behavioral intervention is effective for people with intellectual disability
- Best practices regarding interventions for problem behavior

Behavioral intervention is the term used to describe a wide range of techniques that are based on learning theories. These theories focus on observable environmental events that prompt, increase, maintain, and decrease the occurrence of both appropriate and inappropriate behaviors. Another term used to describe this type of behavioral intervention is applied behavior analysis (ABA). ABA is the use of behavioral methods to solve practical problems, including those of a serious clinical nature (Baer, Wolf, & Risley, 1968).

Figure 28.1 shows the relationship among the four key tenets in ABA. Conditions that are known to prompt a particular behavior are called antecedents. Antecedents precede a behavior and set the stage for it to occur. For example, the smell of freshly baked bread might be an antecedent for entering a bakery.

Spilling water on a table might be an antecedent for getting a cloth to wipe it up. Being asked to do dishes might be an antecedent for doing dishes at first, but the hope would be that seeing dirty dishes in the sink would eventually be the antecedent (or cue) to wash them. Antecedents for problem behavior can include any events that set the stage for the behavior to occur, such as being asked to complete a difficult task or to end a preferred task or activity.

Conditions that increase, decrease, or maintain behaviors are called consequences. Consequences are the responses (or lack of responses) that immediately follow an individual's behavior. A consequence that results in a future increase in a particular behavior is called reinforcement. *Reinforcement* literally means "strengthening," as when a bridge is reinforced, it is made stronger. For example, a student who stays up all night to cram for a midterm exam might be reinforced for that behavior if he or she receives a good grade. Evidence of reinforcement would be the student cramming for the next exam. The effect on future behavior is the key to understanding reinforcement. Reinforcement is a process that results in an increased likelihood that the behavior will happen again in the future. Despite the best intentions, rewards are only considered as reinforcement if they are demonstrated to strengthen the behavior that they followed.

Figure 28.1. The four-term contingency.

Conversely, a consequence that decreases the likelihood that specific behavior will occur in the future is called punishment. The consequence only counts as a punisher if the behavior in question decreases. For example, if a person who regularly leaves a car in a no-parking zone returns to the car to find a sizeable parking ticket and consequently stops parking in such zones, an effective punishment has occurred. It is important to note that it is not one's intention, but rather the effect of the consequence upon the individual's behavior, that determines whether an event is reinforcing or punishing (see the case example about Zack). These basic tenets of ABA (antecedent, behavior, and consequence) are also called the three-term contingency and are essential to a clear understanding of behavioral intervention.

Behavior analysts have become interested in a fourth contingency term, *motivating operations*, which can influence the effectiveness of reinforcement or punishment and/or influence the rates of behavior that are associated with the established reinforcement or punishment. For example, some conditions, such as hunger, thirst, and fatigue can make access to food, drink, and rest more powerful reinforcers and may also increase the rates of behaviors that result after access to the corresponding reinforcer. In addition to paying attention to naturally occurring motivating operations when planning interventions (e.g., providing food reinforcers when a person is more likely to be hungry), behavior analysts can alter the environment to create motivating conditions (e.g., reserve a particular treat or activity to be earned only as a reward and not freely available).

WHY PEOPLE WITH INTELLECTUAL DISABILITY CAN BENEFIT FROM BEHAVIORAL INTERVENTION

Behavioral teaching methods have been demonstrated to be effective methods for increasing communication skills, social skills, activities of daily living, and academic skills in community settings (Repp, Favell, & Munk, 1996). There are several reasons why teaching new skills and increasing independence of emerging skills are important for people with intellectual disability. When people are not taught the skills to effectively participate in meaningful activities, the alternative can be inactivity or boredom, which can affect quality of life and can underlie some behavioral challenges. People with intellectual disability can also require more targeted and specific teaching to learn skills. This is particularly important given research by Emerson and Hatton (2007) that suggests that people with intellectual disability may be exposed to fewer models of skills to participate in meaningful activities. Behavioral methods for skill development can be used to teach skills to enhance the aforementioned situations and/or to meet objectives that are important to the person or

---

Is This an Example of Reinforcement or Punishment?

Zack is a 10-year-old with limited communication and motor skills. During art class, he is asked to cut out shapes and glue them together. After approximately 1 minute, Zack throws the glue on the floor. The teacher, wanting to punish him for this behavior, sends Zack out to the hallway for 5 minutes. When 5 minutes are up, Zack is returned to his table in the classroom and given his project back. He immediately throws the glue again and is sent back to the hallway for 5 minutes. This scenario is repeated three more times in the next 20 minutes.

Did the consequence of being removed from the task have a reinforcing or a punishing effect on Zack's behavior? Because Zack threw glue repeatedly, the consequence had a reinforcing effect. Zack's teacher intended the consequence of sending him into the hallway to be a punishment. However, it was not an effective punisher because the throwing did not decrease. Instead, Zack's throwing *increased* as a result of being sent out of the classroom. This is what is known as inadvertent reinforcement of problem behavior. In other words, being sent out of class for throwing glue actually strengthened Zack's throwing behavior, although this was certainly not the teacher's intention.

From Condillac, R. (2003). Behavioral intervention and developmental disabilities. In I. Brown & M. Percy (Eds.), *Developmental disabilities in Ontario* (2nd ed., p. 409). Toronto, Canada: Ontario Association on Developmental Disabilities; reprinted by permission.

family members and/or are identified by professionals (e.g., speech-language pathologists, occupational therapists, teachers, psychologists). Enhanced skills can lead to more meaningful day-to-day experiences, which can improve quality of life.

Behavioral intervention can also be useful when people with intellectual disability engage in problem behaviors. North American reports suggest that between one third and one half of people with intellectual disability exhibit some form of problematic behavior (e.g., Kats, Payne, Parlier, & Piven, 2013; Matson & Rivet, 2008) that can increase the risk of social isolation and decrease the quality of life they experience. People with intellectual disability may be more likely to exhibit problem behaviors when they do not have supports that address their communicative, cognitive, social, emotional, and adaptive needs (Feldman & Griffiths, 1997). For example, people whose communication support needs are not addressed with appropriate communication systems may exhibit challenging behavior to make their needs and wants known. Boredom, or a lack of enjoyable skills to occupy one's time, can also lead to problem behavior. Some people have learned over time that problem behavior can be an effective way to elicit change in an environment where they may otherwise lack power and freedom of choice. Thus, it is important that behavioral assessment and intervention practices take into account the person's support needs and the environmental events that might affect his or her challenging behavior.

In a review of multinational population-based prevalence studies published between 2000 and 2008, Rojahn & Meier (2009) found variable rates of problem behavior across the studies (0.1%–23%). Across the main categories of problem behavior, overall prevalence was highest for aggressive behavior (6%–32%). Relatively fewer individuals exhibited self-injurious behavior (4%–21%), with still fewer reported to engage in destructive behavior (2%–19%). The samples included rates for children and adults. There were more than 20 different measures used to determine prevalence, which, along with the ranges in age and functioning levels likely accounts for the variability. As mentioned previously, such behaviors can affect social relationships and quality of life and also lead to an increase in stress and sense of caregiving burden for the caregivers of individuals with intellectual disability who exhibit problem behaviors (Maes et al., 2003). This stress has been found to have a direct impact on the caregivers and on the people with disabilities (Baker et al., 2003).

Before attempting to change a behavior, it is important to determine why it is a problem (Cooper, Heron, & Heward, 2007). It is not ethical to target a behavior for change simply because it is "annoying." If this were acceptable, virtually everyone with or without intellectual disability would have at least one behavior program! However, some behaviors—such as hitting, spitting, or head banging—can be considered problem behaviors if they cause physical harm to the person or others and/or limit opportunities for learning and community inclusion. Other behaviors—such as screaming, having tantrums, or throwing items—can be problems if they disrupt routines or limit opportunities for social interaction. Another important reason for targeting a specific behavior for change is because the person him- or herself has expressed a desire to change. In other situations, support providers discuss possible reasons why a behavior needs to be changed. It is important to note that in addition to behavioral excesses (e.g., hitting, screaming), deficits in behavior can also require intervention. As mentioned previously, behavioral intervention can be used to teach new skills including communication skills, social skills, dressing skills, eating skills, and leisure skills.

TYPES OF BEHAVIORAL INTERVENTION

For decades, behavioral intervention has been used in the education of people with intellectual disability. One of the great debates in the treatment of problem behaviors for such individuals has been the use of intrusive versus nonintrusive procedures (Repp & Singh, 1990). Intrusive procedures can include contingent electric shock, time-out in seclusion, physical or mechanical restraint, and various other techniques that emphasize punishment. These intrusive punishment procedures can adversely affect the relationship between the person and the punisher, and they often bring about decreases in the problem behavior only in the presence of the punisher or in the environment where it was used (LaVigna & Donnellan, 1986). Furthermore, the use of such techniques in community settings (e.g., at a restaurant or shopping mall) may have a negative impact on community acceptance and/or inclusion of people with intellectual disability. There is also concern that more intrusive procedures have a negative impact on the dignity and personal freedoms of people with intellectual disability.

Since the mid-1980s, there has been extensive research into and development of positive behavior support (PBS; e.g., Carr et al., 2002; Koegel, Koegel, & Dunlap, 1996). PBS emphasizes redesigning environments to make problem behavior irrelevant and using antecedent interventions to teach skills and create systems of supports. Carr, Horner, and Turnbull (1999) completed a research synthesis of PBS in response to a request from the U.S. Department of Education. They did a comprehensive review of articles published between 1985 and 1996 that evaluated the use of PBS to treat individuals with intellectual disability and problem behavior. The major findings of this research included the following: PBS is widely applicable for individuals with intellectual disability living in community settings and can be implemented by direct support professionals and families. The major growth in the field is in the area of changing deficient environments and emphasizing antecedent strategies. PBS is effective for between one half and two thirds of reported cases of challenging behavior. There is an almost twofold improvement in outcome when intervention is based on the results of a functional analysis and implemented by care providers in natural environments.

Interventions involving PBS have been demonstrated to be effective in treating self-injurious, aggressive, and severely disruptive behavior exhibited by children and adults with intellectual disability in community settings (Feldman et al., 2002). An additional aspect of PBS is that it endeavors to affect behavior change in ways that avoid pain and loss of dignity (Jackson & Panyan, 2002). This is accomplished through environmental changes, increased positive reinforcement, skill building, and planned natural consequences. A major emphasis of PBS is the notion of addressing behavior in the context in which it naturally occurs, using natural caregivers as vital participants in the assessment and treatment process (Carr et al., 2002). Many of these approaches attempt to decrease problem behavior by changing antecedents. When successful, these techniques result in reduced rates of problem behavior through prevention, thus avoiding the need for more intrusive punitive consequences. The emphasis has shifted from cookbook-style applications of behavioral procedures (e.g., if the person is aggressive, use time-out) to the idea of focusing on the comprehensive assessment of medical and environmental patterns and determining the function of the problem behavior for the individual (Feldman & Griffiths,

1997). PBS focuses on natural consequences (e.g., if a person throws his music player and it breaks, he or she may have to be without the device until it can be repaired or he or she can afford to replace it) and teaching alternative behaviors that lead to the same outcome.

WHY BEHAVIORAL INTERVENTION IS EFFECTIVE FOR PEOPLE WITH INTELLECTUAL DISABILITY

A large North American study that examined treatment effectiveness found that behavioral intervention that was functionally related to the cause of problem behaviors had the most demonstrated effectiveness for people with intellectual disability (National Institutes of Health [NIH], 1991). In this study, experts developed a consensus report based on existing scientific evidence. They found that there was scientific evidence to support the use of behavioral intervention that included behavior enhancement strategies (aimed at increasing desirable behavior), behavior reduction strategies (aimed at decreasing undesirable behavior), educational strategies (aimed at teaching adaptive replacement skills), and ecobehavioral strategies (aimed at preventing problem behavior by changing the environment).

The researchers in this study also found that an alarming number of people with intellectual disability who engaged in serious problem behavior were treated only with psychotropic medication, despite the absence of scientific evidence for this approach (in isolation) as a treatment for behavior problems. Medication should be used, when appropriate, to treat medical and psychiatric issues that are diagnosed by a qualified practitioner and that can potentially underlie the person's problem behavior. In the absence of a psychiatric diagnosis, psychotropic medication should be used as a last resort or as a temporary crisis intervention measure only when other less intrusive methods have proved ineffective. In these situations, effects and side effects should be monitored closely by a physician in conjunction with a behavioral or mental health intervention program. The final recommendation of this panel was to endorse the use of multi-elemental behavioral intervention as the treatment of choice for people with intellectual disability who exhibit severe problem behaviors. The panel's findings serve as a reminder that regardless of the type of intervention used, valid, informed, legal, and voluntary consent must be obtained from the individual and/or the legal guardian (NIH, 1991).

Consistent with this panel's report, a federal law in the United States, the Individuals with Disabilities Education Improvement Act (IDEA) of 2004 (PL 108-446), includes a strong recommendation that PBS be used to support children and youth with disabilities who demonstrate problem behaviors in schools. Furthermore, if a child with a disability is suspended from school or is offered alternate placement due to problem behavior, IDEA requires that a functional behavioral assessment (FBA) be completed before (or within 10 days of) the suspension. IDEA 2004 requires the individualized education program team in the school to implement a behavior plan based on the FBA or to adjust the existing behavior plan accordingly. In other words, U.S. federal law mandates the use of positive behavior interventions to support students with disabilities who exhibit serious problem behavior. In reality, however, there is variable interpretation of these requirements and there is a need for a focus on implementation.

BEST PRACTICES REGARDING INTERVENTIONS FOR PROBLEM BEHAVIOR

Behavioral intervention should be based on two complementary parts: a comprehensive assessment and a written intervention plan. An intervention plan should be guided by the information gleaned from the assessment and should be developed using the least intrusive approaches that will be effective for the individual. The intervention plan should flow naturally from the results of the assessment and should include recommendations that stem from a working hypothesis. More intrusive approaches should be considered only for cases in which careful and systematic attempts at using less intrusive approaches have been unsuccessful (Feldman, 1990).

Comprehensive Behavioral Assessment

A comprehensive behavioral assessment should be undertaken by a trained professional, such as a Board Certified Behavior Analyst (BCBA) or a psychologist with specific training in ABA or PBS. The assessment must consider biomedical, environmental or interactional, and functional explanations for the problem behavior. Any combination of these factors may influence the emergence and maintenance of challenging behavior (NIH, 1991; Gardner, 2002).

Biomedical Assessment Biomedical issues can underlie problem behavior in people with intellectual disability (Feldman & Griffiths, 1997). This can be magnified if a person is unable to communicate his or her symptoms. Medical questions can arise if the person is taking medication with potentially adverse side effects. It is essential to uncover any potential biomedical or psychiatric explanations for problem behavior and to ensure that they are ruled out or treated before addressing the problem using a behavioral approach. In some situations, problem behavior can be the manifestation of mental health issues in people with intellectual disability. Rates of mental illness have been reported to be higher in samples of people with intellectual disability than

---

Case Example of Biomedical Assessment

Lisa, a 7-year-old with extensive communication support needs, was engaging in self-injurious behavior (banging her head) with increasing frequency over the course of a few weeks. Her behavior increased in the evening, and it was highest when she was lying down on her bed or in the living room.

Given the sudden onset of this behavior, a medical checkup would be recommended to confirm or rule out a possible medical condition. This was done, and Lisa was found to have otitis media, a painful ear infection. Self-injurious behavior, such as head banging, may have served to decrease or distract from the pain brought on by Lisa's medical condition. Once Lisa's ear infection was successfully treated by her physician, head banging decreased significantly.

From Condillac, R. (2003). Behavioral intervention and developmental disabilities. In I. Brown & M. Percy (Eds.), *Developmental disabilities in Ontario* (2nd ed., p. 412). Toronto, Canada: Ontario Association on Developmental Disabilities; reprinted by permission.

in the population in general (Rojahn & Meier, 2009). If the onset of the problem behavior is recent, or if there has been a sudden increase in problem behavior, there may be an underlying medical issue. It is unethical to provide behavioral intervention without ruling out an underlying medical cause.

Many people with intellectual disability who do not have communication supports in place may use problem behavior to communicate medical issues (Singh, Oswald, & Ellis, 1998), such as earaches, toothaches, headaches, and other forms of pain. It is important to note that even if physical or medical issues have been the initial cause of problem behavior, environmental factors may be maintaining the behavior even after these issues have been properly addressed. This is illustrated in the biomedical assessment case example involving Lisa.

Environmental or Interactional Assessment Routines and interactions in the person's natural environment may also influence problem behavior. Sometimes activities are too difficult; other times, activities are not adequately challenging. Some activities involve participation with a group and others require independence. Unfortunately, many people with intellectual disability are not given the choice of participating in preferred activities. Many are taught to comply with requests from direct support professionals or family members at the expense of personal preference. As a result, some activities may be associated with more problem behavior because they do not align with the person's interest and preference (Brown et al., 1984). Therefore, it is important to determine which activities and situations are associated with the highest rates of problem behavior and which situations are associated with the lowest rates or absence of the problem behavior (Touchette, MacDonald, & Langer, 1985).

With this information, routines can be altered to create a better match between the person and his or her environment. Wherever possible, it is essential to involve a person with intellectual disability in the creation of any intervention plan and to consider his or her personal preferences when suggesting alternate activities.

Some potential antecedent events that may prompt problem behavior can include 1) the end of a preferred activity, 2) task demands that are too difficult, 3) interaction (or lack thereof) with people in the environment, 4) denial of access to something that the person has requested, or 5) a lack of opportunities for meaningful activities. This information is used to develop environmental change procedures that can prevent or reduce problem behavior by reducing or eliminating the occurrence of antecedent events. For example, if a behavior occurs every time an individual is asked to wash the dishes, a prevention strategy might include not asking him to wash the dishes, asking him to wash only one dish or a few dishes, or asking him to choose one of three times when he will begin to wash the dishes.

Functional Behavioral Assessment All behavior serves a purpose. It may serve to increase attention or to end an unpleasant situation; Jerome's example illustrates things to think about when conducting an environmental assessment. In order to determine the purpose that problem behavior serves, an FBA should be completed, and informed consent should be obtained in writing (Behavior Analysis Certification Board [BACB], 2014).

Case Example of Environmental Assessment

Jerome is a 53-year-old who lives in a community group home. His direct-care staff are concerned about his aggressive behavior. After keeping track of his hitting for 2 weeks, it becomes evident that the majority of problems occur just before, or on the way to, evening outings with the other residents.

What possible antecedent change might you suggest? Simply offering Jerome more control over his environment by allowing him to choose between two desirable evening activities might prevent many incidents of aggression. Of course, it would be important to know other information as well. With whom does he sit in the van? Does he like the places they go? Is there something he would rather be doing at home? What does he do all day long? Is he too tired to go out in the evening? Would he do better with community recreation in the morning?

From Condillac, R. (2003). Behavioral intervention and developmental disabilities. In I. Brown & M. Percy (Eds.), *Developmental disabilities in Ontario* (2nd ed., p. 413). Toronto, Canada: Ontario Association on Developmental Disabilities; reprinted by permission.

An FBA is used to determine the antecedents and sources and types of reinforcement that an individual receives in response to his or her behavior. Multiple sources of information are needed to complete an FBA. Functional assessment techniques can be descriptive or experimental. Descriptive assessments include both indirect and direct measurement of behavior. Indirect assessments include interviews (e.g., Functional Assessment Interview [FAI]; O'Neill et al., 1990) and rating scales (e.g., Durand & Crimmins, 1988). Direct assessments include naturalistic observations (e.g., O'Neill et al.). Experimental approaches, often referred to as *experimental functional analyses,* are systematic experimental manipulations that attempt to reveal functional relationships between environmental events and problem behaviors (e.g., Iwata et al., 1982). Research regarding intervention effectiveness has demonstrated that the use of FBA predicts greater success when implementing behavioral intervention. That is, interventions that are guided by the results of functional analysis have proved more effective than those that do not use this method (Carr et al., 1999). Once the function(s) of the behavior is (are) determined, the person can be supported through environmental modifications and teaching strategies that promote the use of alternative behaviors that serve the same purpose(s) as the problem behavior (Carr & Durand, 1985). The case example about Kevin illustrates things that are considered during an FBA.

Behavioral assessment is typically based on the collection of relevant information from interview

Case Example of a Functional Assessment

Kevin is a 23-year-old with severe physical disabilities and intellectual disability. He has no scheduled activities inside or outside of his home with the exception of supports for activities of daily living and meals. His problem behavior consists of screaming for periods ranging from 10 to 30 minutes. His support staff try to calm him down by talking to him, but the only thing that appears to calm him down is when staff (as a last resort) make him a cup of tea and sit with him. In fact, he has been getting so much tea to calm him that his staff members have stopped making Kevin tea at other times.

Functional analysis focuses on the consequences of an individual's behavior; in this case, it was necessary for staff members to ask, "What happens when Kevin screams?" Their data show that after he screams, staff members talk to him for a while, then make him a cup of tea. The next question they ask is, "When else do staff give Kevin their undivided attention and a cup of tea?" Unfortunately, the answer is only when he screams. His screaming serves to gain him both increased attention (staff talk to him) and increased access to tangibles (tea). Furthermore, an examination of the antecedent conditions shows that Kevin often sits unoccupied for long periods of time.

First and foremost, Kevin needs to have more productive and meaningful activities built into his day. A person-centered life plan for Kevin should be developed with his input and that of his family, support staff, and others who know him well. An important aspect of the life plan should include increasing Kevin's time spent in meaningful activities, teaching him skills that would be applicable to job sites, and helping him to find suitable community employment that would be meaningful to him. Of course, there should also be natural opportunities to stop for tea and a visit with his support staff.

From a functional perspective, Kevin needs to learn a way to make his needs known without having to scream. One approach might be for staff to teach Kevin to raise his hand or activate a switch when he wants their attention. An augmentative communication device could be used to communicate once someone approaches him. Once learned, these new skills may serve the same purpose for Kevin as his screaming and thus make screaming unnecessary. It is important, however, not to wait until Kevin's screaming occurs at lower rates before exposing him to new opportunities and activities. It is possible that these antecedent changes will serve to decrease his screaming by virtue of adding interesting and meaningful activity to his life.

and observational methods. Several data collection techniques may be required to carry out a single comprehensive assessment. These can include interviewing the person and the support providers, keeping track of the specific problem behavior and the context (antecedents and consequences) in which it occurs, and monitoring the form, frequency, intensity, and duration of a problem behavior.

Content and Development of Behavior Support Plans

After the comprehensive behavioral assessment is complete, a behavior support plan specific to the person's needs should be developed. A behavior support plan needs to be developed in consultation with a trained professional, documented, and monitored (Feldman et al., 2004).

The behavior support plan should flow directly from the findings of the behavioral assessment and be based on the collected data. The goal of the plan is to prevent or decrease problem behavior by modifying the environment to make the behavior less effective and teaching the person alternative behaviors using the least intrusive procedures. The benefits of formal behavior support plans derived from assessment data are described in the case example about Kevin. All behavior support plans should be clearly and thoroughly reviewed by the person with intellectual disability and his or her parent or guardian. Informed, voluntary, and legal consent must be obtained before the plan can be implemented (BACB, 2014).

Behavior support plans should be individualized. Nonetheless, all such plans generally touch on these basic areas: prevention, skill promotion, intervention, and training and evaluation. These are discussed next.

Prevention Prevention strategies are developed from the findings of the environmental assessment. The goal of this phase of intervention is to prevent challenging behavior from occurring by making appropriate changes to the environment and the antecedents (e.g., routines, interactions) that prompt the individual's problem behavior. A key goal is to create the best match possible between the person with intellectual disability and his or her living and learning environments. In some cases, making changes to these systems-level antecedents (e.g., moving to one's own home with supports) can result in significant decreases in problem behavior

and increases in quality of life. Prevention strategies create an environment in which "problem" behaviors are not needed because the person's interests and preferences are respected and incorporated into the environment. A careful look at the antecedents might suggest, for example, that a person exhibits more challenging behavior when watching television alone and rarely acts out when out to dinner with friends. For this person, opportunities to interact with friends should be maximized (Touchette et al., 1985). Antecedent changes can result in rapid decreases in problem behavior.

Skill Promotion Once problem behaviors are successfully being prevented, the next stage is set to teach new adaptive behaviors. The goal of the second phase of intervention, skill promotion, is to teach skills that will serve the function that was originally served by the problem behavior. Naturally, this phase depends on the results of the FBA.

If, for example, the FBA suggests that the person is using the behavior to escape from difficult tasks, the person may need supports to learn how to request breaks from tasks. There are several ways to request a break, including use of the following:

- A verbal request, such as "Break, please"

- A signed request, such as manual signs for "break" or "finished"

- A picture communication symbol or card, such as touching a picture of a stop sign or handing over a "break" card

- A gesture, such as pointing to the chair that is used for taking a break

This approach is called functional communication training (see Carr et al., 1994, and Martin & Pear, 2014, for comprehensive coverage of this topic).

It is essential to consider the person's support needs and preferred communication modality level when selecting an appropriate replacement skill. If a person does not communicate verbally, then perhaps he or she could be taught to use a manual sign. If the person cannot gesture or identify pictures, then perhaps using actual objects would be a better way to start.

Once the replacement skill has been selected, a systematic teaching program should be implemented. The teaching program should include the methods for prompting and reinforcing the new desired behavior. Another aspect of the teaching program must include strategies for generalization. *Generalization* refers to a person's ability to apply or transfer skills across people, settings, materials, and responses (Martin & Pear, 2014). For example, a person who is learning to gain attention more appropriately also needs to know a variety of responses that achieve that outcome, such as raising a hand, calling a person's name, or tapping someone on the shoulder. This allows the individual to gain attention in many situations with many different people.

Intervention During the implementation of the behavior support program, the problem behavior is typically ignored (i.e., no eye contact or verbal response) and, if necessary, physically blocked (to prevent injury to others in the environment). The person is redirected to use the replacement behavior. This leads to the extinction (or gradual elimination) of the problem behavior following or during the acquisition of socially appropriate alternative skills (see the Skill Promotion subsection). If the behavior is of a serious nature and the person and/ or others are at increased risk, a crisis plan should be developed by a trained professional. This plan should detail the steps in handling problem behavior if it does occur.

Training and Evaluation It is important to note that unlike other treatment approaches, behavioral intervention typically relies on consistent implementation by support providers in the person's natural environment. Families, direct support professionals, and teachers often require hands-on training in behavioral techniques. Training can include topics such as data collection, environmental modifications, effective use of reinforcement, ways to teach skills, and crisis intervention techniques. Training improves the quality of the behavioral intervention and has been demonstrated as essential to the success of treatment. In addition to teaching concepts and reviewing plans, skills-based training using on-the-job feedback should be used to ensure the intervention is implemented accurately and consistently (Parsons, Rollyson, & Reid, 2012).

The final component should include clear guidelines for monitoring progress and fine-tuning the program (Martin & Pear, 2014). Data should be collected on both the behavior targeted for change and the skill(s) being taught to replace the problem behavior. Criteria for success should be identified (e.g., 80% increase in the replacement skill and 80%

decrease in the problem behavior). It is essential to monitor both the desired effects and the potential side effects of the behavioral intervention. Regularly scheduled reviews by a trained professional can offer opportunities for discussing progress, dealing with setbacks, and troubleshooting for potential difficulties.

SUMMARY

Behavioral intervention is important for people with intellectual disability because it can support the development of behaviors that promote success in community environments and the design of environments that enable the use of those behaviors to achieve valued outcomes. Assessment procedures should consider biomedical, environmental or interactional, and functional explanations for behavior. The assessment should lead to the development of a formal, documented behavior support plan that uses positive behavioral intervention. Once the environment has been redesigned, the person can be supported to develop new skills. Because behavioral intervention is typically implemented by support providers with minimal training in PBS, providing additional training in behavioral methods is often essential to the success of the intervention. Training of direct support professionals must convey an understanding of behavior principles and strategies and techniques for ongoing evaluation.

FOR FURTHER THOUGHT AND DISCUSSION

1. Why do you think problem behavior is so prevalent among people with intellectual disability?

2. Behavioral intervention can increase the control that a person with intellectual disability has on her or his environment. Why is this statement true?

3. Because behavioral intervention focuses on information that can be seen, heard, and counted, why is biomedical assessment so important?

4. Why would enhancing a person's life to include meaningful activities be a first course of treatment before focusing intervention on the elimination of problem behavior?

5. Research has found that FBA is critical to the effectiveness of behavioral intervention. Why do you think this is the case?

REFERENCES

Baer, D.M., Wolf, M.M., & Risley, T.R. (1968). Some current dimensions of applied behavior analysis. *Journal of Applied Behavior Analysis, 1,* 91–97.

Baker, B.L., McIntyre, J., Blacher, J., Crnic, K., Edelbrock, C., & Low, C. (2003). Pre-school children with and without developmental delay: Behavior problems and parenting stress over time. *Journal of Intellectual Disability Research, 47,* 217–230.

Behavior Analysis Certification Board. (2014). *Professional and ethical compliance code for behavior analysts.* Littleton, CO: Author.

Brown, L., Shirage, B., York, J., Zanella, K., & Rogan, P. (1984). *A life-space analysis strategy for students with severe handicaps.* Madison: University of Wisconsin and Madison Metropolitan School District.

Carr, E.G., Dunlap, G., Horner, R.H., Koegel, R.L., Turnbull, A.P., Sailor, W.,...& Fox, L. (2002). Positive behavior support: Evolution of an applied science. *Journal of Positive Behavior Intervention, 4,* 4–16.

Carr, E.G., & Durand, M.V. (1985). Reducing behavior problems through functional communication training. *Journal of Applied Behavioral Analysis, 18,* 111–126.

Carr, E.G., Horner, R.H., & Turnbull, A.P. (1999). *Positive behavior support for people with developmental disabilities: A research synthesis.* Washington, DC: American Association on Mental Retardation.

Carr, E.G., Levin, L., McConnachie, G., Carlson, J.I., Kemp, D.C., & Smith, C.E. (1994). *Communication-based intervention for problem behavior: A user's guide for producing positive change.* Baltimore, MD: Paul H. Brookes Publishing Co.

Condillac, R. (2003). Behavioral intervention and developmental disabilities. In I. Brown & M. Percy (Eds.), *Developmental disabilities in Ontario* (pp. 407–419). Toronto, Canada: Ontario Association on Developmental Disabilities.

Cooper, J.O., Heron, T.E., & Heward, W.L. (2007). *Applied behavior analysis* (2nd ed.). Upper Saddle River, NJ: Pearson.

Durand, V.M., & Crimmins, D.B. (1988). Identifying the variables maintaining self-injurious behavior. *Journal of Autism and Developmental Disorders, 18,* 99–117.

Emerson, E., & Hatton, C. (2007). *The mental health of children and adolescents with learning disabilities in Britain.* Lancaster, United Kingdom: Institute for Health Research, Lancaster University.

Feldman, M.A. (1990). Balancing freedom from harm and right to treatment for persons with developmental disabilities. In A.C. Repp & N.N. Singh (Eds.), *Perspectives on the use of nonaversive and aversive interventions for persons with developmental disabilities* (pp. 261–272). Sycamore, IL: Sycamore.

Feldman, M.A., Atkinson, L., Foti-Gervais, L., & Condillac, R.A. (2004). Formal versus informal interventions for challenging behavior in persons with intellectual disabilities. *Journal of Intellectual Disability Research, 48,* 60–68.

Feldman, M.A., Condillac, R.A., Tough, S.E., Hunt, S., & Griffiths, D. (2002). Effectiveness of community positive behavioral intervention for persons with developmental disabilities and severe behavioral challenges. *Behavior Therapy, 33,* 377–398.

Feldman, M.A., & Griffiths, D. (1997). Comprehensive assessment of severe behavior disorders. In N.N. Singh (Ed.), *Prevention and treatment of severe behavior problems: Models and methods in developmental disabilities* (pp. 23–48). Pacific Grove, CA: Brooks/Cole.

Gardner, W.I. (2002). *Aggression and other disruptive behavioral challenges: Biomedical and psychosocial assessment and treatment.* Kingston, NY: NADD Press.

Individuals with Disabilities Education Improvement Act (IDEA) of 2004, PL 108-446, 20 U.S.C. §§ 1400 *et seq.*

Iwata, B.A., Dorsey, M.F., Slifer, K.J., Bauman, K.E., & Richman, G.S. (1982). Toward a functional analysis of self-injury. *Analysis and Intervention in Developmental Disabilities, 2,* 1–20.

Jackson, L., & Panyan, M.V. (2002). *Positive behavioral support in the classroom: Principles and practices.* Baltimore, MD: Paul H. Brookes Publishing Co.

Kats, D., Payne, L., Parlier, M., & Piven, J. (2013). Prevalence of selected clinical problems in older adults with autism and intellectual disability. *Journal of Neurodevelopmental Disorders, 5*(1), 27. doi:10.1186/1866-1955-5-27

Koegel, L.K., Koegel, R.L., & Dunlap, G. (Eds.). (1996). *Positive behavioral support: Including people with difficult behavior in the community.* Baltimore, MD: Paul H. Brookes Publishing Co.

LaVigna, G.W., & Donnellan, A.M. (1986). *Alternatives to punishment: Solving behavior problems with non-aversive strategies.* New York, NY: Irvington.

Maes, B., Brokeman, T.G., Dosen, A. & Nauts, J. (2003). Caregiving burden of families looking after persons with intellectual disability and behavioral or psychiatric problems. *Journal of Intellectual Disability Research, 47,* 447–455.

Martin, G., & Pear, J. (2014). *Behavior modification: What it is and how to do it* (10th ed.). New York, NY: Pearson.

Matson J.L., & Rivet, T.T. (2008). Characteristics of challenging behaviours in adults with autistic disorder, PDD-NOS, and intellectual disability. *Journal of Intellectual and Development Disability, 33*(4), 323–329.

National Institutes of Health. (1991). *Treatment of destructive behaviors in persons with developmental disabilities: Consensus Development Conference, September 11–13, 1989.* Bethesda, MD: Author.

O'Neill, R.E., Horner, R.H., Albin, R.W., Storey, K., & Sprague, J.R. (1990). *Functional analysis of problem behavior: A practical assessment guide.* Pacific Grove, CA: Brooks/Cole.

Parsons, M., Rollyson, J., & Reid, D. (2012). Evidence-based staff training: A guide for practitioners. *Behavior Analysis in Practice, 5*(2), 2–11.

Repp, A.C., Favell, J., & Munk, D. (1996). Cognitive and vocational interventions for school-age children and adolescents with mental retardation. In J.W. Jacobson & J.A. Mulick (Eds.), *Manual of diagnosis and professional practice in mental retardation* (pp. 265–276). Washington, DC: American Psychological Association.

Repp, A.C., & Singh, N.N. (Eds.). (1990). *Perspectives on the use of nonaversive and aversive interventions for persons with developmental disabilities.* Sycamore, IL: Sycamore.

Rojahn, J., & Meier, L.J. (2009). Epidemiology of mental illness and maladaptive behavior in intellectual disabilities. *International Review of Research in Mental Retardation, 38,* 239–287.

Singh, N.N., Oswald, D.P., & Ellis, C.R. (1998). Mental retardation. In T.H. Ollendick & M. Hersen (Eds.), *Handbook of child psychopathology* (3rd ed., pp. 91–116). New York: Plenum.

Touchette, P.E., MacDonald, R.F., & Langer, S.N. (1985). A scatterplot for identifying stimulus control of problem behavior. *Journal of Applied Behavior Analysis, 18,* 343–351.

29

Challenging Families, Challenging Service Systems

A Positive Intervention Model

J. Dale Munro

WHAT YOU WILL LEARN

- Why professionals in the intellectual and developmental disabilities field find some families so challenging
- Behavior patterns of challenging families
- Barriers created by challenging service systems
- Four roles for social workers and other trained family therapists
- The Positive Intervention-Family Support Model

Families are the emotional shock absorbers of society that ideally help people cope with and face the struggles of life. This holds for families of people with intellectual and developmental disabilities, most of whom are supportive of their family members with a disability and the professionals and organizations working with them. Yet, in every community agency or school setting, there are a few families that might be described as "challenging." In this chapter, the term *challenging family* is used to describe a group of two or more blood or adopted relatives, at least one of whom has

Author's note: Additional references can be found in Munro, J.D. (2011). Challenging families: Mending broken spirits through support and therapy. In I. Brown and M. Percy (Eds.), *Developmental disabilities in Ontario* (3rd ed., pp. 459–473). Toronto, Canada: Ontario Association on Developmental Disabilities.

an intellectual or developmental disability, who repeatedly and chronically behave in a manner that seems extremely self-destructive, intimidating, unpredictable, aggressive, or resistant. As much as they might hate to admit it, some of the most challenging behavior that frontline professionals and managers ever face may not be from people with intellectual and developmental disabilities but from their families.

Challenging families pose one of the greatest dangers to the emotional well-being of the person with intellectual and developmental disabilities and are a constant source of frustration for frontline professionals and service managers in agencies, school systems, and service organizations. These families (approximately 5% to 10% of all the families with whom frontline professionals and managers work) tend to draw attention to themselves and their own needs, inadvertently obstructing service delivery to the person with a disability. Professionals need to become familiar with strategies for diffusing the frustrations, anger, and tension that challenging families are experiencing, not only to assist these families but also to promote mental wellness in the person with a disability.

This chapter—written to provide direction to frontline professionals, managers, and college students—examines probable causes of challenging family behavior and describes behavior patterns exhibited by these complex families. At the same time, discussion will also focus on ways that existing service systems frustrate families. A positive intervention model is presented, along with a discussion of how more highly trained therapists can help these needy and complicated families. It is worth noting that professionals and managers who develop more sophisticated skills in understanding, helping, and coping with challenging families will find it easier to deal with the majority of families who present less complex problems.

WHY DO FAMILIES SOMETIMES SEEM SO DIFFICULT?

Most parents suffer almost unbearable pain and trauma when they first learn (at birth or later) that their child has intellectual and developmental disabilities. The entire family is confronted with new demands that tax relationships both within and outside the family. Most parents and other family members go through a coping (grieving) process that is life changing. As illustrated in Figure 29.1, normally this grieving process is thought to comprise five phases, starting with initial shock and family crisis when first learning that the child has a permanent disability. The process proceeds slowly through several phases to eventual spiritual renewal and relative acceptance of the child and the disability. Years later, even healthy families may periodically experience short periods of cyclic or recurrent grief around transition or crisis times in the life of the child, teen, or adult with a disability (e.g., starting/graduating school, birthdays, staff changes, leaving home, major illness, anniversary date when the disability was identified). However, most parents and other family members gradually learn to accept the person and the disability—often becoming positively transformed and psychologically stronger (Munro, 2011, 2013).

In contrast, challenging families seem permanently stuck in the three earliest phases in this grieving and coping process. Their intense reaction and nonacceptance of the child and the disability is chronic and does not diminish with time, resulting in what has been called "chronic sorrow" (Olshansky, 1961). Siblings and grandparents of the family member with intellectual

and developmental disabilities also can become trapped in the parents' cycle of grief, denial, guilt, drama, and anger. The self-destructive, extremely aggressive, highly emotional, or resistant behavior exhibited by challenging families results from what has been referred to as complicated grief. Sanders (1999) suggested that complicated grief occurs when the typical family grieving process is confounded by extenuating factors. In the case of families of people with intellectual and developmental disabilities, five extenuating factors contribute to complicated grief and family–service system conflict. These factors include the following:

1. Personality variables or the basic thinking style of individual family members can impede the family coping process. For example, parents or siblings who typically blame someone or something else about life problems, or persist in blaming themselves, frequently will respond in a similar manner (toward service system representatives) when confronted with the reality of a family member with a permanent disability.

2. Other unresolved grief or situational factors may negatively influence personality factors. For instance, the family may experience a serious family crisis (e.g., loss of employment, unexpected financial burdens, critical illness or injury, marital discord, a recent death).

3. Some challenging family members may have intellectual or communication impairments or significant learning disabilities, making it more difficult to work cooperatively with them.

4. Family members may have sensory sensitivities (e.g., certain noises, perfume smells, brightness of light, textures of food) or allergies (e.g., gluten-and casein-based food, animal dander, mold in their home) that can contribute to irritable moods or behavioral or physical symptoms.

5. Untreated psychiatric difficulties, such as clinical depression, severe anxiety, obsessional thinking, alcohol or drug abuse, posttraumatic stress (e.g., from past abuse), psychosis, autism spectrum disorder, or personality disorders, can cause parents or family members to behave in a manner that makes them appear to be totally unreasonable.

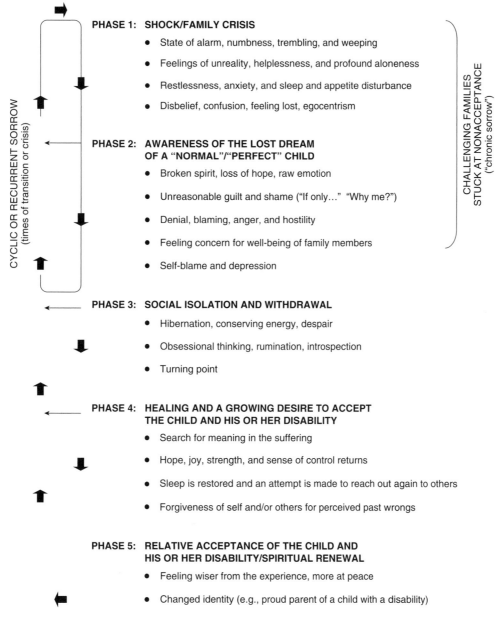

Figure 29.1. Family coping/grieving process. (Appreciation is expressed to Keith Anderson and Susan Hutton for their consultation.)

How "Challenging Service Systems" Affect Families

In the intellectual and developmental disabilities field, what professionals perceive as challenging families usually reflects families with complicated backgrounds and problems coming into conflict with rigid, overextended, and unresponsive human service systems. In fact, problems with communication and cooperation within formal service systems (i.e., health, education, corrections, and social services) can make family problems appear much more serious than they really are. Consider the following system-related concerns:

1. In today's diverse society, language, cultural, religious, sexual orientation, or socioeconomic differences, or differing definitions of what actually constitutes a family (e.g., nuclear, blended, same sex, single-parent, common law), can bring out latent prejudices in frontline professionals or managers and contribute to tension, misunderstanding, and conflict between families and service providers.

2. Power imbalances that disproportionately favor service system representatives or family members (e.g., sitting on agency boards) can create mean-spirited exchanges.

3. Frequently, overworked professionals experience burnout or behave in a defensive, insensitive, or unsophisticated manner when confronted by frustrated family members.

4. In the intellectual and developmental disabilities field, less than 10% of funding goes toward family support (Abbott, 2013). There is a startling lack of concern for the specific needs of family members (e.g., respite, alternative supported residential option who provide the majority of care and support).

5. The bureaucratic and somewhat impersonal nature of "the system" can frustrate otherwise reasonable family members. In fact, it is a misnomer to refer to it as a system at all. The service system is actually made up of a group of somewhat disconnected, scattered programs. The skill level of service representatives can vary greatly. Government attempts to amalgamate agencies and school boards frequently have divorced families from their local communities. Efforts ostensibly to be more fair and efficient in streamlining services have been perceived by many frustrated families as an attempt to curtail costs. These efforts have tended to bureaucratize application processes and create overly rigid eligibility criteria. Families complain that services are unavailable, and cutbacks have left many parents fearing for the future of their (young, teen, or adult) child with intellectual and developmental disabilities.

RECOGNIZING CHALLENGING FAMILY PATTERNS

Challenging families often seem overwhelmed with guilt, ambivalence, hostility, isolation, and loneliness. They may deny these feelings when confronted directly but show their emotional pain in a variety of overt or passive-aggressive ways. They sometimes try to present an image that everything is okay in their families, or they may mistakenly believe that most of their problems result from having a family member with a disability. In response to tremendous family tension, individuals with intellectual and developmental disabilities often begin to exhibit disturbed behavior, inadvertently making them a spokesperson for the underlying dysfunction in the entire family.

As professionals become involved to try to help the family with their "problem" relative, they sometimes encounter tremendous resistance. The homeostasis (balance) in the family may depend on maintaining the relative with intellectual and developmental disabilities in the scapegoat or problem role in order that tension is not refocused on the real source of conflict: the parental and family dysfunction. Challenging families frequently show one or more of the following behavior patterns—any one of which signifies that serious needs are being expressed that require a professional response (Munro, 2011).

1. Mental exhaustion and a "broken spirit" may be prevalent when family members have spent years trying to support a relative with significant intellectual, behavioral, psychiatric, and/or physical needs. Many of these family members have quit jobs, lost contact with friends, and unsuccessfully tried advocacy to obtain additional and needed support for their relative. They frequently show symptoms of clinical depression, bitterness, and disillusionment with the service system and express a sense of hopelessness that their home life will ever improve.

2. Loud, chronic complaining is a common pattern. These families literally scream and create crises out of minor concerns, even when special and repeated efforts have been made to meet their needs. They seem preoccupied with the way agencies, professionals, and school systems "should" and "must" provide quality and expanded services, with little appreciation for large caseloads or limited service resources. Some of these families complicate situations by turning to lawyers, agency or school

executives, or the mass or social media before first trying to resolve concerns with frontline professionals or managers.

3. Program (or person) sabotage is shown by some families who seem to insistently perceive professionals and service providers as adversaries. These families may block attempts to provide treatment interventions, such as psychotropic medication or behavioral approaches, that are needed to assist relatives exhibiting extreme self-injury or suicidal or aggressive behavior. They may insist on their family member being discharged against advice from specialized treatment settings just as the person is beginning to show progress. They may fail to show up for scheduled appointments or have unrealistically high or overly pessimistic expectations for their relative with intellectual and developmental disabilities that impede the person's potential for positive change and emotional growth.

4. Extreme overprotectiveness is demonstrated by some families who seem overwhelmed by guilt, anxiety, and obsessional thinking. These overinvolved families tend to infantilize their relative (e.g., providing child-like haircuts and clothing, bathing otherwise capable individuals) and sometimes want competent people protected in extreme ways (e.g., refusing to allow dating or independent use of public transportation). They may be unwilling to go away on vacations without their relative for fear that something awful might happen when they are gone or may tolerate seemingly intolerable behavior from the person with intellectual and developmental disabilities (e.g., repeated physical violence, property destruction). Parents may become family "martyrs" who, on one hand, seem totally devoted to their child but who secretly resent the lifelong cost (e.g., friends, a career) of constantly caring for the person.

5. False hope or jumping on treatment bandwagons is a pattern shown when long-term denial and unrealistically high expectations are a potent underlying dynamic in the family. Every new treatment "advance" is met with near-religious fervor. Shopping around from one specialist to another to find a miracle (and often expensive) cure for their relative's disability is not uncommon. Some families may unilaterally discontinue helpful anticonvulsant or psychotropic medication, falsely thinking it is no longer necessary. These families may even demand that physicians perform unnecessary surgery, use improperly tested drugs,

or change the person's treatment to some "medical breakthrough" described in sensationalized popular publications. Though rare, a few families may sincerely believe that their religion, prayer, or the right faith healer will cure the disability. Unfortunately, the ongoing zeal of these families to try the latest panacea often gets in the way of initiating more helpful, practical approaches.

6. Symbiotic (enmeshed) relationships are found in which there is a pathologically close relationship between the person with intellectual and developmental disabilities and at least one parent and an uncanny sensitivity for the other's pain. These relationships stifle independent thought and action on the part of the person with intellectual and developmental disabilities and trap the family member. Also, healthy parent–child emotional boundaries are continually violated. More troubled families may have shared delusions of grandeur in which the person with a disability is idolized beyond any realistic dimensions and may become the recipient of too much family attention and concern.

7. Open warfare and abuse is observed in some families, with overt hostility, "mind games," sarcastic exchanges, backbiting, and violent arguments among family members. Intense sibling rivalry may last into adulthood. Brothers and sisters vacillate between displacing enormous anger onto their sibling with a disability to competing to prove who loves the person more (e.g., overindulgent gift giving). Shared family secrets (e.g., incest, physical violence, alcohol and drug problems, criminal behavior, past mental illness) create ongoing tension. The individual with intellectual and developmental disabilities can be an easy target for the ever-present hostility, as can professionals or school or agency representatives who try to get involved.

8. Paranoia and pervasive evasiveness are manifested by some families who, because of social isolation or delusions of persecution, begin to believe that professionals, agencies, school systems, neighbors, family, or associates are conspiring against them. These families may leave cryptic or hostile messages on agency or school phone systems, refuse to meet or fail to show up for scheduled appointments, show hypervigilance to criticism or bear grudges, be preoccupied with unjustified doubts about the loyalty of others, fabricate stories or communicate in a confused manner, or physically threaten outsiders. Serious psychiatric disturbance and avoidance are the distinguishing characteristics of these

exceedingly suspicious families—and communication and support planning with them concerning their relative with intellectual and developmental disabilities can be particularly difficult.

9. Avoidance of the person is a pattern shown by families who completely terminate contact with the individual with intellectual and developmental disabilities. They may never visit, write to, or even acknowledge the existence of their relative. Such total rejection can destroy the person's self-worth, precipitate severe depression, and leave the individual fantasizing about the family that never comes. Other family members may maintain contact only until money from an inheritance runs out or may make promises that are never kept (e.g., visits, gifts); one parent may withdraw totally into work, volunteer, or leisure activities, leaving the other parent to deal almost single-handedly with the person.

10. Psychosocial deprivation characterizes families frequently found in isolated rural or urban slum areas. Neglect and harsh discipline may be common, and often little attention is paid to the special needs of the person with intellectual and developmental disabilities, because all family members face day-to-day struggles meeting basic needs. The disability may never even be diagnosed unless it is severe or a major crisis occurs. These families tend to distrust professionals, schools, and agencies because many are frustrated after long-term contact (sometimes involving more than one generation) with services and government programs.

POSITIVE INTERVENTION-FAMILY SUPPORT MODEL

Based on more than 4 decades of work in the intellectual and developmental disabilities field, I have developed a family support and intervention model that combines the best elements of traditional family assessment and counseling approaches with interventions that recognize the complexity of human service systems. The Positive Intervention-Family Support Model (PIFS Model) is particularly helpful in situations in which family and service system cooperation must be high. This is a highly effective and positive model that reduces family–system distress; improves communication and interpersonal relationships among key people; clarifies roles; and improves planning, case management, and advocacy for people with intellectual and developmental disabilities.

The Necessity of Being Positive: Mending Broken Spirits

There is a unique type of pain, grief, and trauma found in most families of people with intellectual and developmental disabilities that psychotherapists in the general counseling community, as well as frontline professionals, clinicians, and managers in the intellectual and developmental disabilities field, seldom understand. Professionals working from a traditional biopsychosocial model may not recognize that many of these families have broken spirits and that effective intervention must also focus on spiritual healing. Spiritual (not necessarily religious) approaches include showing compassion and kindness; helping families discover meaning in suffering; offering hope and developing faith that current painful circumstances can improve; and striving to find some degree of peace, joy, harmony, fellowship, and untapped sources of energy, even in seemingly "hopeless" situations (Munro, 2011, 2013). The PIFS Model suggests that frequently there are viable approaches that can be helpful if the professional is really motivated to assist such people. To a large extent, success depends on the professional's persistence, high energy, unflappable optimism (just short of being annoying), flexibility, knowledge of community resources, persuasiveness, charisma, patience, and ability to be satisfied with small gains.

The PIFS Model emphasizes that a positive or unconditionally constructive attitude on the part of frontline professionals and managers often leads to beneficial results when working with challenging families (Munro, 1997). In fact, professionals working in the intellectual and developmental disabilities field seldom meet people who could accurately be described as "bad" parents or family members. However, they do meet family members with broken spirits who are exhausted, disillusioned, burned out, and frightened about the future. Most families are trying too hard to do the right things for their relatives with a disability—almost to the point of making themselves sick. In this sort of emotional climate, negativity on the part of professionals can breed a self-perpetuating cycle of frustration, antiprofessional feelings, and hopelessness in family members.

The PIFS Model incorporates many elements of the strengths-based perspective of social work practice and positive psychology (Harris, Thorensen, & Lopez, 2007; Russo, 1999). This perspective—along

---

Broken Spirits in Service Providers: Managing Expectations, Stress, and Burnout

Professionals and managers often find working with challenging families emotionally demanding and, at times, discouraging. Self-destructive or intimidating family behavior can raise self-doubt and unconscious emotional reactions, causing professionals to question their own helping abilities. One senior manager reported that staff sometimes become so "rattled" by the behavior of some family members that their job performance suffers ("Staff [managers] operating out of fear make mistakes!"). This can result in professionals and managers themselves experiencing broken spirits (i.e., their original dream of helping others seems crushed) and exhibiting burnout symptoms.

Service providers and organizations must prepare themselves for family antagonism without being provoked into defensiveness, angry outbursts, or power struggles. In order to cope, survive, and thrive, the PIFS Model suggests that professionals and managers should do the following:

- Simplify thinking and abandon perfectionism and unrealistic "rescue fantasies" when dealing with highly complex families and emotionally charged situations. Keep expectations realistic and achievable.

- Remind families that their situation is very complex. Let them know that there are no quick fixes for the complicated family's difficulties. Slow and careful planning and collaboration usually results in the best long-term outcome for everyone involved ("This is a marathon, not a sprint!").

- Insist that discussion in family counseling sessions and meetings between the family and service providers focus on the "here and now" problems and solutions. This avoids the tendency of some families to dwell on past problems and perceived injustices against them.

- Use (appropriate and well-timed) humor, if possible, to reduce tension and defuse potentially hurtful interactions.

- Carefully document agency and school involvement as a safety precaution, just in case the family considers a lawsuit or creates bad publicity, which does occur on occasion.

- Hold regular professional or manager meetings to privately air frustrations and discuss positive approaches for helping and coping with disturbing family behavior.

- Practice good stress management every day (e.g., mindfulness meditation, time management, healthy diet, physical exercise) and encourage service organizations to hold wellness and self-care seminars for their personnel.

- Consider personal psychotherapy, family counseling, or psychiatric consultation if professionals or managers are not coping well with an "impossible" family or other work or personal distress.

---

with the strategies suggested for addressing broken spirits and managing stress that can help professionals deal with their own burnout, distress, and spiritual pain—provides a positive foundation for building effective working relationships with challenging families. The strengths-based approach is antithetical to the historical family pathology model on which many past generations of professionals relied. The professional's sense of humor, insight, and loyalty are often viewed as important ingredients for successful family work. Real problems are not ignored, but this perspective focuses on what is right, rather than wrong, with families. Family empowerment and resilience—and the possibility of positive transformation and rebound from personal trauma, abuse, oppression, sickness, and tragedy—are emphasized. This perspective liberates family members to pursue their own personal dreams and accepts that people are more motivated for positive change when they have genuine decision-making power and their strengths are respected (King, Baxter, Rosenbaum, Zwaigenbaum, & Bates, 2009).

Essential Family-Work Skills
for Frontline Professionals and Managers

Agency and school professionals often find themselves in situations in which they are confronted by
frustrated and angry challenging families (Munro,
2011). The PIFS Model insists that professionals
should ask themselves this question: "When a family is really struggling or upset with you or your
agency or school, what tools do you have in your
toolkit?" With this in mind, it is recommended that
all frontline professionals and service managers
should learn some essential family-work skills, such
as the following (Munro, 2009, 2013):

1. *Understanding history:* As a starting point, it
is vitally important to help professionals who may
be overly critical of families to gain some level of
historical perspective. They need to be informed
that almost every significant service advance for
people with intellectual and developmental disabilities has come about because of hard-fought
advocacy by dedicated family members. It is also
worth noting that there have been tragic times in
human service history when professionals reck-
lessly blamed parents for their children's disabilities (e.g., the outrageous belief that "refrigerator
mothers" cause autism; Bettelheim, 1967). Professionals must never allow themselves to return to
this sad historical tendency to blame parents and
must vigorously guard against viewing families as
the enemy.

2. *Recognizing healthy families:* Professionals are
often too quick to criticize the relatives of people
with intellectual and developmental disabilities
and may tend to pathologize family behavior that
is essentially normal (e.g., appropriate assertive expression of concerns). Professionals must recognize
that even healthy families can become negative
at times if they are exhausted or not comfortable
with how services are provided. They can have a
rough day or can be argumentative, on occasion,
if frustrated. Also, professionals can be taught that
healthy behavior is manifested by those families
who project a sense of pride, safety, mutual support, affection, and fun; who are protective of each
other; and who regularly involve the person with a
disability in family and community activities.

3. *Building positive relationships:* Professionals
sometimes need to be reminded that collaborative
relationships with families frequently begin in the
simplest of ways, by initially engaging in casual

small talk, using empathic listening, and sharing a
coffee. Rapport with families can be enhanced by
professionals who focus on here and now issues;
avoid jargon; celebrate (even small) successes with
the family; and strategically use well-timed (appropriate) humor, frankness, cheerleading, and brief in-
spirational and motivational speeches. When dealing
with people with intellectual and developmental
disabilities whose disturbances are severe, families
often are desperate for and appreciate staff suggestions about calming activities that allow visits with
the individual to go better (e.g., going for walks in
nearby parks, going for car rides, taking trips to
the beach, preparing favorite foods together). This
advice can contribute to a growing sense of family–
service system teamwork and cooperation. Also,
family–professional relationships can improve
through the use of regular planning or support circle meetings that may include the individual, family
members, friends, volunteers, and key professionals. These meetings help to reduce family isolation,
improve planning, and create strong family–service
system networks.

4. *Becoming aware of unspoken family questions:* To
ensure family–service system cooperation, agency,
school, or other service representatives need to
become more skilled at reassuring families. This
reassurance (requiring examples of positive experiences from the individual's typical week) must
address questions that are seldom stated openly.
Family members often continuously "test" professionals and organizations to reassuringly answer
four unspoken (but vitally important) questions: Do
you really care about my relative/me? Is my child
/relative really safe? Is my child/relative happy? Am
I a good parent/sibling/grandparent?

5. *Learning that "the name of the game is reframe":*
In my clinical experience (and from conducting
presentations across North America), it is not unusual for some professionals who work in agency
or school programs to talk in private about families in an extremely pejorative manner. Reframing
is a very positive and powerful strategy that professionals need to learn to help counteract this tendency. Reframing involves teaching professionals
to rethink, in a more constructive, less emotional,
and more rational manner, their negative descriptions, perceptions, or thoughts about a family
member or situation. To be effective, professionals
must learn to purge negative and degrading words
not only from their everyday speech but also from

their beliefs and thoughts. For example, a professional's angry statement such as "That mother is a control freak, a manipulator, and a real b****" might be much more accurately and sensitively reframed as "She is a concerned, courageous, and passionate advocate." When professionals begin to utilize reframing in their thoughts and verbal interactions, their relationships with families tend to immediately improve. When professionals teach family members to reframe their perceptions of professionals, agencies, and events around them, families ultimately become healthier, cope better, and become more cooperative (Minnes & Woodford, 2005).

6. *Clarifying roles:* One of the greatest sources of acrimony and confusion between service providers and families results from unclear roles and expectations. Families and professionals can improve their relationships and reduce distress by deciding who does what, how, and when. To illustrate, in order to enhance the possibility of treatment success in particularly complicated situations, a written service agreement is often useful in outlining the responsibilities of service organizations, professionals, families, and the individual. To minimize miscommunication and emotional upset, it is often wise to designate only one contact person (usually a supervisor or middle manager) through whom families can raise serious concerns with an agency, school, or organization. Likewise, staff should feel empowered to suggest positive ideas or raise concerns about the family's behavior with the designated contact person. Staff ideas or concerns can then be addressed with the family at regularly scheduled planning or support circle meetings.

7. *Learning to cope with "difficult" people:* Strategies have been developed that can help professionals maintain confidence and assertiveness and balance power when facing families who seem intimidating, explosive, or manipulative. These coping techniques often utilize role-play to help each staff member or manager practice strategies and focus on maintaining politeness and using mindfulness-based approaches to find one's center of calm. These approaches emphasize the need to "stand up without fighting" because families will never respect people whom they believe they can push around (Bramson, 1981). In addition, staff can be taught to respond effectively with angry or anxious family members by calmly speaking more quietly, slowly, succinctly, and firmly, while remaining positive and systematically ignoring most outrageously negative family comments and personal attacks.

8. *Setting proper boundaries:* Boundaries are the physical, psychological, and spiritual spaces that professionals create around themselves that define how they will relate to individuals and their families and how they are willing to let others treat them (Black & Enns, 1997). Frontline professionals and managers who learn to set appropriate work-related boundaries (e.g., reducing excessive overtime, politely ending acrimonious meetings, demonstrating team solidarity in not disclosing certain personal information with families, showing caution about receiving gifts or giving hugs, not giving out home phone numbers) tend to manage stress better—and families benefit from dealing with healthier, more positive professionals.

9. *Teaching families how to advocate:* Many families of people with disabilities seem hesitant or unsure about how to gain access to human service systems. However, professionals (with their vast knowledge of community services) can teach family members how to successfully navigate service systems. Families are empowered and strengthened by the knowledge that they have had the courage to stand up for their relative with a disability. The Step Approach Model for effective family advocacy is recommended (Munro, 1991, 2013).

Family Therapy Strategies

Obviously, most agencies, school professionals, or service providers cannot be expected to be sophisticated family therapists. In the intellectual and developmental disabilities field, clinical social workers tend to be the primary designated profession systematically trained in family therapy and support methods. As noted in the discussion What Role Can Family Therapists Play?, trained family therapists can play many useful roles in helping more complex families. Commonly, there is a need for private therapy sessions with families to help them deal with unresolved social, emotional, trauma, sexuality, and grief issues.

In many ways, challenging families seem caught in a bind. They desperately need clinical help but simultaneously push away potentially helpful outsiders with abusive or socially unacceptable behavior. Nevertheless, the PIFS Model emphasizes that therapists must persist—with the objective of

---

What Role Can Family Therapists Play?

Frontline professionals and managers in agencies and school systems need to know when and how to involve social workers or other clinicians with specialized family therapy skills. The PIFS Model suggests that there are four possible roles for family therapists in the intellectual and developmental disabilities field:

1. The family therapist may play a consultant role, offering advice regarding family support strategies to professionals and managers, with the therapist having little or no actual face-to-face involvement with the family.

2. The professional might act as an outside mediator who is brought in as an impartial third party to meet with key people and to help resolve complicated family–service system disputes (Munro, 1997).

3. The professional may feel a necessity to work directly with the challenging family—playing a role similar to that of a traditional family therapist. This might involve several private counseling sessions focusing on clearly agreed-upon clinical goals. If the professional does provide direct family therapy, a key feature of the PIFS Model is that a service system representative (e.g., from a local human service organization) who knows the individual with the disability well should act as a co-therapist. This provides an excellent learning opportunity for the co-therapist in effective family work. It also helps to monitor whether any real and positive change is occurring in terms of family functioning and family–system collaboration, and it helps to provide a reliable check-in as to how the individual with intellectual and developmental disabilities is coping.

4. On occasion, the family therapist may provide individual psychotherapy to the person with intellectual and developmental disabilities without getting directly involved with the family. This counseling can provide emotional support and develop assertive and coping skills in individuals who are being rejected, abused, or treated as a scapegoat by their family members. Again, it is sometimes advantageous to include a service system representative who knows the individual well to act as a co-therapist.

---

building a positive therapeutic alliance or relationship with the family. Counseling support usually is gradually accepted after the family has had time to test out the therapist's degree of commitment and concern. With this in mind, the following therapeutic family approaches can be particularly helpful.

1. Family therapy sessions usually should be held in the privacy of a counselor's office. Occasionally, it may be useful to meet at the family's home in order to obtain a greater understanding of the family's everyday living environment or in cases in which family members use wheelchairs or have mobility problems. However, it is better to meet in a professional office that is a more neutral site—especially in particularly tense situations. During interviews, professionals must ensure that people adhere to basic rules of etiquette (e.g., no interrupting the person speaking). Sometimes it is helpful to meet the entire family together. Other times, it is better to meet alone with parents, siblings (often an untapped resource), or the person with a disability in order to permit free expression of troubling feelings and concerns and discussion of possible solutions.

2. All promises or commitments that therapists and co-therapists make to the family must be faithfully kept, and any constructive ideas presented by family members should be supported and carried out in order to gradually encourage desired behavior and to gain trust.

3. Therapists must utilize (and teach frontline professionals and managers) listening approaches that promote assertiveness, rather than aggressiveness or passive resistance, in families. Professionals must be cautioned against treating the problems raised by chronically complaining families too lightly. Usually, even the most "dysfunctional" families have some legitimate concerns hidden behind what others may perceive as excessive griping.

Professionals are encouraged to use active or empathic listening, which involves putting oneself emotionally in the family's shoes, paraphrasing briefly the family member's words and message, and acknowledging how she or he is feeling. Being really listened to, as simple as it might seem, is a powerful therapeutic tool with even the most demanding family. Challenging families often have a history of being ignored, put off, or not taken seriously by others, which can lead them into treating others in a passive-aggressive manner. They may have to tell stories about the pain and grief in their lives over and over again until they feel truly understood. Only then do many families begin to let go of guilt and hostility, begin to exhibit assertiveness rather than "manipulation," and begin to accept the reality of their family member's disability and the need for outside help.

4. "Negative inquiry" is another positive and powerful technique that can be used in conjunction with active listening to encourage assertiveness in families. Therapists should actively utilize this approach in their practice and, as clinical consultants, teach it to frontline professionals and managers. Negative inquiry involves calmly and rather paradoxically prompting family members to criticize existing services even more than they might want to (e.g., "Are there any other concerns that you have?" "Are you sure there isn't anything else?"). This brings information to the surface that might be helpful or exhausts criticism if it is manipulative. This process guides both family members and professionals to become more assertive and less critical and to feel really understood. This process works even better if the professional takes written notes and carefully records family concerns, with the understanding that each concern will be taken seriously and addressed in turn (sometimes at a prearranged later date).

5. Therapists can "give permission" to family members to take part in activities that otherwise they would not do. For instance, parents may be encouraged to plan vacations or evenings or weekends away without their children; continue their education; return to work outside the family; join support groups; attend physical exercise programs, mindfulness meditation, and stress management seminars; use parent respite services; spend more time with their children who do not have disabilities; or (for divorced or widowed parents) consider dating again.

6. Many siblings believe they have benefited from having a brother or sister with intellectual and developmental disabilities (Findler & Vardi, 2009). However, clinical sessions with siblings can be a significant role for family therapists. Siblings may feel extreme rejection, guilt, depression, or even envy because of the excessive attention that is sometimes directed at the individual with special needs (Siegel & Silverstein, 1994). Some siblings may worry about genetic disorders and whether having children is even a viable option for them. Others may need trauma counseling related to feeling violated or being physically assaulted by a brother or sister with intellectual and developmental disabilities.

7. Psychoeducation can be an important part of family therapy. Often families need accurate information regarding their relative's specific syndrome (e.g., Prader-Willi), autism spectrum disorder, mental health diagnoses, and treatment; helpful web sites and books (e.g., Baskin & Fawcett, 2006); ways of adapting home and school environments to better meet the specific sensory sensitivities of individuals with intellectual and developmental disabilities (Bradley & Caldwell, 2013); and other methods for improving family wellness.

8. When appropriate, therapists can suggest to family members that they might benefit from a psychiatric assessment, psychotropic medication, or specialized counseling. Many family members who at first seem challenging are much less so after receiving proper professional help.

SUMMARY

Professionals and managers should view each family with whom they have contact—especially the more difficult families—as presenting a sophisticated college course (i.e., a wonderful opportunity) to further develop their family-work skills. Sometimes the dynamics, behavior, and circumstances of a particular family create great challenges. However, professionals, managers, and helping organizations always must remain aware that sometimes they may be the real problem based on their practice style or their organization's service philosophy or policy. It takes guts, creativity, training, and positive thinking for service providers to constructively contribute to viable solutions to serious family–service system problems. However, effectively and positively dealing with problems that arise can bring out the strengths in families; contribute to improvements in the overall functioning of agencies and schools; and promote mental wellness in the child, youth, or adult with intellectual and developmental disabilities.

FOR FURTHER THOUGHT AND DISCUSSION

1. What specific behaviors might be associated with each of the 10 behavior patterns of challenging families described in this chapter?

2. What problems in service systems can create great challenges for families?

3. What skills must professionals and managers learn in order to improve relations with families?

4. What strategies might trained family therapists use to help agencies, schools, and service systems work better with challenging families?

REFERENCES

Abbott, A. (2013). Love in the time of autism. *Psychology Today, 46*, 60–67.

Baskin, A., & Fawcett, H. (2006). *More than a mom: Living a full and balanced life.* Bethesda, MD: Woodbine House.

Bettelheim, B. (1967). *The empty fortress: Infantile autism and the birth of self.* New York, NY: Collier-Macmillan.

Black, J., & Enns, G. (1997). *Better boundaries: Owning and treasuring your life.* Oakland, CA: New Harbinger.

Bradley, E., & Caldwell, P. (2013). Mental health and autism: Promoting autism favourable environments. *Journal on Developmental Disabilities, 19,* 8–23.

Bramson, R.M. (1981). *Coping with difficult people.* New York, NY: Ballantine.

Findler, L., & Vardi, A. (2009). Psychological growth among siblings of children with and without intellectual disabilities. *Intellectual and Developmental Disabilities, 47,* 1–12.

Harris, A.H.S., Thorensen, C.E., & Lopez, S.J. (2007). Integrating positive psychology into counseling: Why and (when appropriate) how. *Journal of Counseling and Development, 85,* 3–13.

King, G., Baxter, D., Rosenbaum, P., Zwaigenbaum, L., & Bates, A. (2009). Belief systems of families of children with autism spectrum disorders or Down syndrome. *Focus on Autism and Developmental Disabilities, 24,* 50–64.

Minnes, P., & Woodford, L. (2005). Well-being in aging parents caring for an adult with a developmental disability. *Journal on Developmental Disabilities, 11,* 47–66.

Munro, J.D. (1991). Training families in the "Step Approach Model" for effective advocacy. *Canada's Mental Health, 39,* 1, 1–6.

Munro, J.D. (1997). Using unconditionally constructive mediation to resolve family–system disputes related to persons with disabilities. *Families in Society, 78*(6), 609–616.

Munro, J.D. (2009). Working with families: Essential skills every professional and manager should know! *The NADD Bulletin, 12*(3), 45–49.

Munro, J.D. (2011). Challenging families: Mending broken spirits through support and therapy . In I. Brown and M. Percy (Eds.), *Developmental disabilities in Ontario* (3rd ed., pp. 459–473). Toronto, Canada: Ontario Association on Developmental Disabilities.

Munro, J.D. (2013). Families of children and teens with dual diagnosis: Therapy and support strategies. In D.J. Baker and R. Blumberg (Eds.), *Mental health supports for youth with dual diagnosis* (pp. 185–208). Kingston, NY: NADD.

Olshansky, S. (1961). Chronic sorrow: A response to having a mentally defective child. *Social Casework, 43,* 190–193.

Russo, R.J. (1999). Applying a strengths-based practice approach in working with people with developmental disabilities and their families. *Families in Society, 80,* 25–33.

Sanders, C.M. (1999). *Grief: The mourning after: Dealing with adult bereavement.* New York, NY: Wiley.

Siegel, B., & Silverstein, S. (1994). *What about me? Growing up with a developmentally disabled sibling.* New York, NY: Insight Books.

30

Psychopharmacology in Intellectual and Developmental Disabilities

Jessica A. Hellings and Kenneth Boss

WHAT YOU WILL LEARN

- The history of psychoactive medication use
- Challenges with diagnosis and choosing medications
- Principles of treating people with intellectual and/or developmental disabilities with psychoactive medications
- Some common psychiatric medications and their mechanisms of action
- Evidence-based intervention and promising treatments warranting further study for targeting psychiatric diagnoses
- Balancing benefits and risks

This chapter is divided into five main sections. The first provides an introduction to the history of psychoactive medication use. The second highlights challenges that clinicians face in making diagnoses of mental disorders in people with intellectual and/or developmental disabilities and in choosing appropriate medications. The third discusses the principles of treating people with intellectual and developmental disabilities with psychoactive medications. The fourth introduces the different classes of psychoactive medications. The fifth discusses evidence for the effectiveness of psychoactive medications. The text ends with an overview of the field and a brief discussion of future directions. The chapter is based, in part, upon that by Boss (2011).

HISTORY OF PSYCHOACTIVE MEDICATION

Psychoactive drugs have been used by humans since prehistoric times. Various psychoactive mushrooms have been used as intoxicants in tribal rituals for millennia. Alcohol production and consumption by humans began in the Neolithic period. St. John's wort, a common medicinal herb used for mild to moderate depression, was recommended by ancient Greek physicians. The systematic use of chemical compounds for the treatment of psychiatric disorders, however, did not exist prior to the middle of the 20th century. The provided introduction to chlorpromazine describes the birth of the field of psychopharmacology.

The principal therapeutic tools available to psychiatrists prior to 1950 were convulsive therapies, which involved the induction of a seizure, as in electroconvulsive therapy (ECT); insulin coma therapy; and psychosurgery in which white matter connections within the brain were severed (i.e., lobotomy, which also is called prefrontal leucotomy). Whereas lobotomy and insulin coma therapy are no longer performed today, ECT remains a life-saving treatment for severe depression and treatment-resistant mania.

The Birth of Psychopharmacology

The birth of modern psychopharmacology coincides with the introduction of chlorpromazine (CPZ) in France in the early 1950s, although psychoactive compounds such as opiates and barbiturates were used for their calming properties prior to that time. CPZ was originally used to inhibit the physiological stress reaction of the central nervous system during surgery. The effects on anxiety and emotional stress were so marked that Henri Marie Laborit, who conducted the first clinical trials of CPZ in surgery in 1951, suggested its use in psychiatry. The following year, Pierre Deniker and Jean Delay, working at Sainte-Anne Hospital in Paris, conducted the first pivotal studies of CPZ treatment in psychiatric patients. They described a "neuroleptic syndrome," in which CPZ slowed motor activity and promoted affective indifference and emotional neutrality, and proposed the name *neuroleptic* to designate a class of medications that produced this syndrome (López-Muñoz et al., 2003). The eventual discovery that antipsychotic medications tended to share the feature of blocking dopamine type 2 receptors led to the dopamine hypothesis of schizophrenia. This posits that too much dopaminergic activity in certain areas of the brain causes the "positive symptoms" of hallucinations, delusions, and disorganized behavior and speech of the disorder.

As of this chapter's writing in 2016, medication is an important focus of psychiatric treatment. The burgeoning field of neuroscience has progressed greatly in the past decade, together with increased professional and public awareness of psychiatric disorders as medical illnesses, leading to a decrease in stigma and increased recognition and treatment. Recently, the U.S. pharmaceutical industry has been given limits regarding the provision of meals and payments to teaching physicians in order to minimize marketing influences on university teaching and practice. The U.S. 2010 Patient Protection and Affordable Care Act (PL 111-148) includes the National Physician Payment Transparency Program (Open Payments) section (commonly referred to as the Sunshine Act), which says that reimbursements to physicians by industry must be publicly available and posted on a web site (Carpenter & Joffe, 2011).

It is important that pharmacologic drug treatment be accompanied by other therapies—notably psychotherapy, behavioral supports and interventions, recreational and social activities, and appropriate housing settings. Furthermore, developmental progress in some people with intellectual and developmental disabilities or autism spectrum disorder (ASD) may be improved by appropriate pharmacotherapy. For example, people who have intellectual disability or ASD and co-occurring attention-deficit/hyperactivity disorder (ADHD), which predisposes to impulsive aggression, may benefit from pharmacotherapy.

CHALLENGES WITH DIAGNOSIS AND CHOOSING PSYCHOTROPIC MEDICATIONS

In 2003, Nottestad and Linaker found that between 20% and 45% of all people with intellectual and developmental disabilities were already taking psychotropic medications, making them the most medicated group in society. A decade later, a study of 33,565 children with autism found that 64% received at least one psychotropic medication, 35% received two or more, and 15% received three or more (Spencer et al., 2013). Thus, combination treatments have become common, but clinical trials of combination treatments are lacking. Whereas antipsychotics remain a commonly prescribed class of drug in this population, and the atypical antipsychotics risperidone and aripiprazole are FDA-approved for irritability in Autistic Disorder for ages 5 and older, many other classes of medications can be effective if used correctly.

Challenges in Making Comorbid Psychiatric Diagnoses in People with Intellectual and Developmental Disabilities

Contemporary psychiatry dictates that a medication be prescribed to target a specific diagnosis for which the medication has proved effective. However, in people with intellectual and developmental disabilities, especially people with moderate and severe levels of intellectual impairment, comorbid psychiatric diagnoses may be less likely to be identified, and presentation may be with self-injury, hyperactivity, or aggression. (The term *comorbid* refers to one or more disorders that co-occur with the primary one.) Problem or "challenging" behaviors occur in more than 20% of people with intellectual and developmental disabilities (Cooper, Smiley, Morrison, Williamson, & Allen, 2007). Psychiatric illness is three to four times more likely in people of all ages with intellectual and developmental disabilities. Seizures may also confound the clinical picture for these people. It is not uncommon that a physician must assess and treat a person with intellectual and developmental disabilities who is engaging in behaviors that are clearly harmful (i.e., those that endanger self or others), although their problem behaviors may not be easily categorized as any particular diagnosis in the *Diagnostic and Statistical Manual of Mental Disorders, Fifth Edition* (*DSM-5*; American Psychiatric Association, 2013) or *Diagnostic Manual—Intellectual Disability, Second Edition* (DM-ID2; Fletcher, Barnhill, & Cooper, in press). (The DM-ID2 is a companion manual to the *DSM-5* that aims to provide guidelines for adapting *DSM-5* criteria for people with intellectual and developmental disabilities and ASD.) In such cases, if warranted by severity, medications are prescribed based on a working diagnosis that is the most likely scenario of a number of differential (i.e., possible "working") diagnoses.

The Concept of Dual Diagnosis

The presence of comorbid psychiatric conditions together with intellectual and developmental disabilities may also be referred to as dual diagnosis. However, the latter term originally referred to the co-occurrence of substance abuse and psychiatric illness. More studies are needed to distinguish comorbid psychiatric disorders from seizure activity and other underlying causes, especially in people with minimal verbal skills. Seizures may be especially difficult to diagnose, because the routine electroencephalogram only records approximately 35% of brain waves, and sedation needed to perform an electroencephalogram in poorly compliant individuals may inhibit the seizure activity.

Some Common Psychiatric Disorders in People with Autism Spectrum Disorder and/or Intellectual and Developmental Disabilities

DSM-5 recognizes comorbid ADHD in people with autism, although the ADHD-associated affective dysregulation (i.e., emotional dysregulation) and impulsive aggression are still too often misdiagnosed and wrongly treated as anxiety or bipolar mood disorder. The misdiagnosis of bipolar mood disorder accounts partly for treatment resistance and repeated emergency room visits for aggression. Although ADHD is common, bipolar disorder is relatively rare. Likewise, ASD is still missed or incorrectly diagnosed as schizophrenia in many instances. (Refer to DM-ID2, Fletcher et al., in press, for more information about such complexities.) Anxiety disorders such as obsessive-compulsive disorder (OCD) co-occur commonly with ASD and/or intellectual and developmental disabilities, as does ADHD. Other co-occurring psychiatric diagnoses include Tourette syndrome, major depressive disorder, posttraumatic stress disorder, and generalized anxiety disorder.

When to Use Psychotropic Medications

In spite of risks associated with using psychotropic medications as interventions for people with intellectual and developmental disabilities, there are times when doing so is the best option. The two principal scenarios for using medications for people with intellectual and developmental disabilities or ASD are 1) the presence of interfering or challenging behaviors that impede developmental progress or community inclusion and have not responded to environmental or behavioral interventions or 2) the presence of one or more comorbid psychiatric diagnoses.

Many patients with intellectual and developmental disabilities or ASD presenting for psychiatric treatment have challenging behaviors, including aggression, self-injury, property destruction, or inappropriate sexual behaviors. Because *DSM-5* does not have these diagnostic categories, clinicians continue to try to target drug treatment toward a working diagnosis made with the aid of DM-ID2. Although nutritional and nonpharmacologic interventions (i.e., behavioral interventions) are preferred as treatment for challenging behaviors, some factors (e.g., when the patient will not or is not able to work with the therapist) limit the feasibility of behavioral interventions as the sole intervention.

Increasingly, the gut is recognized as an important contributor to behavioral problems in the general population as well as in people with ASD and/or intellectual and developmental disabilities. A prime example of gut influence on behavior is celiac disease (Percy & Propst, 2008), an allergic condition in which wheat ingestion produces antibodies to wheat gluten in the gut. The antibodies attack the lining of the small intestine, causing the junctions between small intestinal lining cells to become "leaky" and impairing absorption of nutrients. This process also allows antibodies to enter the bloodstream and target major organs and the central nervous system. (Other grains containing gluten also can have this effect.) Celiac disease predisposes to anemia and a host of medical complaints including an underactive thyroid gland (hypothyroidism); gastrointestinal symptoms such as irritable bowel syndrome, bloating, constipation or diarrhea; and liver disease. Associated psychiatric illness includes anxiety, depressive disorders, and psychotic disorders. The condition of gluten intolerance (in which such symptoms respond to a gluten-free diet but gluten antibody tests are negative) possibly also may contribute to behavior problems. Clinicians and others providing support to individuals with intellectual and developmental disabilities should be vigilant for associated symptoms of celiac disease or gluten intolerance, which also tend to be familial. In people with celiac disease or gluten intolerance, a gluten-free diet may allow improvement with or without the use of medications.

GENERAL PRINCIPLES FOR TREATING PEOPLE WITH INTELLECTUAL AND DEVELOPMENTAL DISABILITIES AND/OR AUTISM SPECTRUM DISORDER WITH PSYCHOACTIVE MEDICATIONS

There are a number of precautions to consider when psychotropic drugs are prescribed for people with intellectual and developmental disabilities and/or ASD.

1. Prescribing should be tailored to the individual patient after consideration of the beneficial and unwanted (side) effects of the medication proposed and, at the same time, avoiding daytime sedation. An example would be to avoid prescribing atypical antipsychotics that cause weight gain to an already obese individual.

2. An important principle is to "start low and go slow" with medications; in this case, any worsening then may be of a smaller degree than if large doses were used. This principle also allows for poorer medication tolerance in people with intellectual and developmental disabilities.

3. Medication tapering is usually done gradually and by very small amounts, especially in the case of antipsychotic reduction, unless serious allergic reactions occur and the medication must be stopped immediately according to physician orders.

4. Another principle is to "go up before giving up" in situations where the dose of a medication seems to be only partly effective. In this case, the person will have had an adequate trial of the drug if he or she is able to tolerate it.

5. Care must be taken when existing medications are being replaced. In general, for treatment-resistant individuals, the practice is to add in a low dose of new medication that is believed could be beneficial prior to tapering existing drugs very gradually.

6. Certain selective serotonin reuptake inhibitor (SSRI) antidepressants have the potential to cause drug–drug interactions by inhibiting liver enzymes called cytochrome P450 (CYP450) isoforms. In particular, paroxetine, fluoxetine, and sertraline are potent CYP2D6 inhibitors (Hemeryck & Belpaire, 2002). CYP2D6 normally is responsible for breakdown by oxidation of many psychotropic and nonpsychotropic medications. Thus, inhibition of breakdown of a drug can increase its potency and side effects. For example, in the case of atypical antipsychotics, CYP2D6 inhibition will result in weight gain, or in the case of benzodiazepines, will result in increased sedation and falling. CYP450 inhibition also can interfere with actions of nonpsychoactive medications. For example, fluoxetine and sertraline negatively interfere with the activity of tamoxifen, a drug used for breast cancer recurrence prevention (Harvard Health Publications,

2010). Potentially important drug–drug interactions require vigilance on the part of clinicians who prescribe medications and pharmacists who fill the prescriptions.

7. There may be a need to gradually taper existing medications that may be worsening behavior prior to starting anything new. Such medications include SSRIs that may appear to have helped initially but later worsen behaviors or remain only partially effective.

8. Some medications (e.g., the benzodiazepines) need to be tapered gradually. This is because abrupt cessation can result in withdrawal, especially after long-term use.

9. Medications that increase an electrocardiogram heart conduction indicator called the QTc interval should not be used together; one example is tricyclic antidepressants and lithium. When used together, these medications increase the risk for the potentially fatal cardiac arrhythmia called torsades de pointes.

10. Using several antiseizure medications in combination (e.g., phenytoin, phenobarbital, and mysoline) may worsen behavior and also increase liver metabolism of psychotropic and other medications.

11. Medications that are central nervous system depressants, such as benzodiazepines and lamotrigine, may impair balance and coordination and predispose to falling. Clumsiness and falls may also occur due to muscle stiffness (e.g., from antipsychotics).

12. Medications known to worsen cognitive performance and behavior, such as topiramate (used to control seizures), should be closely monitored.

13. Medications can cause unusual side effects that do not follow recognized patterns in people with intellectual and developmental disabilities, and the possibility that a new unusual behavior is due to a medication must always remain foremost in the minds of care providers.

See the Factors Affecting the Use of Psychoactive Drugs discussion for more information on using these types of medications for people with intellectual and developmental disabilities.

Neurotransmitters, Receptors, and Nutritional Precursors

A neurotransmitter binds to a receptor, akin to a key fitting into a lock, in order to produce electrical impulses for neurotransmission. Neurotransmitters are chemicals that, upon binding to a receptor, cause transmission of electronic impulses from one neuron to another. Receptors on the second neuron (nerve cell) are specifically configured to recognize neurotransmitters released from the end of the transmitting neuron into the space between the two neurons, called the synapse. Neurotransmitters released into the synapse go through a reuptake process back into the synapse through special reuptake channels, in a process that may be blocked by various types of psychiatric drugs in order to increase neurotransmitter action.

Since the latter part of the twentieth century, there has been a growing appreciation of diet and food allergies and the vital role of the gastrointestinal tract in absorption of nutrient precursors needed for manufacture of neurotransmitters. Examples are the amino acids tyramine and tryptophan, which are nutritional precursors of dopamine and serotonin respectively. Absorption of these neurotransmitter precursors is disturbed, for example, in celiac disease, which is caused by an allergy to the wheat protein gluten (see previous discussion).

Important Diagnostic Pitfalls Contributing to Treatment Resistance

As detailed in the following subsections, it is especially important to recognize and appropriately treat ADHD, which is often overlooked or misinterpreted as anxiety in people with intellectual and developmental disabilities and/or ASD. Failure to do so will result in what is sometimes called treatment resistance.

Diagnosing and Treating Attention-Deficit/Hyperactivity Disorder in the Presence or Absence of Obsessive-Compulsive Disorder

Although ADHD, inattentive subtype is the more common form of ADHD—both among people with intellectual and developmental disabilities and in the general population—many people with intellectual and developmental disabilities present for psychiatric treatment due to the related hyperactive,

---

Factors Affecting the Use of Psychoactive Drugs

Unusual and challenging behavior in people with intellectual and developmental disabilities can result from a number of different factors. These include difficulties with adaptation due to the intellectual disability (e.g., lack of developmental maturity, limited self-expression skills), mental illness (e.g., schizophrenia, bipolar disorder, generalized anxiety disorder), or learning history (e.g., banging one's head because of the attention received when one does so). Any of these factors can obscure the contribution of the others in certain settings.

Attributing all problem behaviors in people with intellectual and developmental disabilities to their disability is referred to as diagnostic overshadowing. In the original experiment designed to explore this phenomenon, a scenario describing an individual with a severe phobia was presented to a number of psychologists. In some cases, the individual was presented as having typical intelligence and in others as having intellectual and developmental disabilities. The psychologists were less likely to diagnose this phobia in the individual with an intellectual disability, suggesting that they regarded such symptoms as normal for someone with an intellectual disability (Reiss, Levitan, & Szyszko, 1982). Diagnostic overshadowing presents a barrier to the delivery of proper medical diagnosis and treatment and can hinder the identification not only of psychiatric diagnoses, but also of physical causes of challenging behaviors (e.g., dental pain, esophagitis, gallstones).

The opposite occurs when behaviors tend to be attributed to psychiatric illness without other causes being considered. This is especially problematic when the psychiatric diagnosis is made on the basis of behaviors, as is often the case. Once an individual receives a psychiatric diagnosis, mental health workers often come to regard various behaviors as indicative of mental illness. This tendency is referred to as diagnostic overemphasis. Someone who is demonstrating moodiness, for whatever reason, may be told that his or her "bipolar is acting up." An individual who is particular about details may be described as having OCD. Someone who engages in a lot of psychomotor activity may be described as anxious.

It also frequently occurs that behaviors are overattributed to the individual's learning history. For example, a certain behavior may be described as attention-seeking because of the presumption that previous emissions of that behavior led to attention, resulting in the individual learning to emit the behavior when attention is sought. This sort of overattribution is referred to as behavioral overshadowing.

---

disruptive, and/or aggressive behavior that is categorized as the ADHD combined hyperactive-impulsive subtype. For either subtype, certain ADHD medications are prescribed, notably stimulants and/or nonstimulant ADHD medications, or both medication types in combination.

If ASD is also present along with ADHD, accompanying repetitive behaviors resulting from OCD may often complicate pharmacotherapy, because stimulants may worsen anxiety, irritability, OCD, and repetitive behaviors. In such cases, a nonstimulant ADHD medication such as atomoxetine is preferable to stimulant trials, although a low dose of stimulant may be added later to improve focus. Bhatti and colleagues (2013) found that the tricyclic antidepressant (TCA) amitriptyline was useful in a

50-patient series of such cases, although randomized controlled studies are needed. In addition, Bhatti and co-workers reported that a low dose of antipsychotic such as risperidone was also often needed in such cases to reduce anxiety, self-injury, or irritability. Likewise, a presentation of repetitive behaviors and obsessive thoughts by a person with ASD may respond to nonstimulant ADHD medications, rather than OCD treatments, due to missed ADHD comorbidity.

ADHD together with intellectual and developmental disabilities continues into adulthood in many cases and often does not improve with age, as may occur in some typically developing individuals. The hyperactivity component may be reduced while the impulsivity continues together with irritability and explosive behavior, related to affect dysregulation that is characteristic in ADHD. The latter is often misreported and interpreted as bipolar mood disorder, which is rare in comparison to ADHD and results in treatment resistance as well as unnecessary exposure to multiple trials of antipsychotics and mood stabilizers. This is contributed to by the fact that psychiatrists treating adults often lack adequate training in ADHD manifestations in intellectual and developmental disabilities, the lack of a literature base of such studies, and failure to elicit a developmental history. Parents may not inform new providers involved after the transition to adult services at age 18 that the person received ADHD diagnoses and treatments during childhood and adolescence, and providers may not ask.

Diagnosing and Treating Bipolar Disorder

Bipolar disorder, although rare, may occur among people with intellectual and developmental disabilities; however, optimal treatment often warrants a combination of medications to achieve the best response, as also occurs in the general population (Hellings, 1999). Differences from ADHD include pressured speech or vocalization, hypersexual behavior, and grandiosity; an example of the latter in an individual with intellectual and developmental disabilities may simply be that he or she claims to drive and own a car when that is not the case. A commonly used combination for mood stabilization is a low dose of antipsychotic, divalproex, and lithium or gabapentin (Hellings, 2006). Gabapentin add-on to valproic acid appears safer and has fewer disabling side effects than lithium in this population; this likely is because problems related to monitoring and regulating fluid intake to prevent lithium toxicity are avoided. Tremor, thirst, and wetting are common lithium side effects.

CLASSES OF MEDICATIONS

Psychiatric medications are often grouped into five major classes: antipsychotics, antidepressants, mood stabilizers, sedative-hypnotics, and psychostimulants. These and others are described next (see also Table 30.1).

Antipsychotic Medications

The antipsychotics are probably the most studied and most prescribed class of medications for the management of mental health problems in people with intellectual and developmental disabilities. Their uses include schizophrenia, mania, psychotic depression, irritability, self-injury, and aggression. The antipsychotics are separated into two major groups: typical (classical) and atypical (novel) antipsychotics. The medium-potency typical antipsychotic loxapine in low dose has atypical characteristics and is thus unique (Stahl, 2002).

Typical Antipsychotics Typical antipsychotics are the older group and also are referred to as neuroleptics or major tranquilizers due to their ability to decrease agitation and anxiety and to cause muscle paralysis in laboratory animals. Their principal pharmacological mechanism of action is blockade of brain dopamine type 2 receptors. This prevents dopamine from exerting effects at this receptor type. Although is it not clear why this blockade results in antipsychotic action, it has led to the dopamine hypothesis of schizophrenia (see the prior discussion under The Birth of Psychopharmacology).

Dopamine blockade is also responsible for one of the major side effects caused by typical antipsychotics, namely neuroleptic-induced Parkinsonism. This refers to the tendency of typical antipsychotics, in dose-related fashion, to cause symptoms that resemble those seen in Parkinson's disease, including the triad of resting tremor, rigidity, and bradykinesia (or akinesia). The tremor has a typical appearance often referred to as "pill-rolling" because of its resemblance to the movement performed by pharmacists in the days when pills were prepared by hand. Rigidity refers to decreased flexibility at the joints that results from increased muscle tone. It can usually be detected when an examiner flexes the joints (e.g., holds the person's wrist and moves that hand slowly up and down while the person is at rest). This rigidity is often "cogwheel" in type, which refers to the tendency of superimposed rigidity and tremor to create a rhythmic, ratchet-like resistance when the joint is manipulated, particularly in rotation of the wrist. *Bradykinesia* and *akinesia* refer to a decrease in spontaneous movements, resulting in a lack of facial expression such as eye-blinking or "mask-like" lack of smiling or eye blinking, decreased use of hand gestures, reduced arm swing, and slowness in initiating speech and gait. Drooling often accompanies these, due to lack of swallowing. These symptoms are also referred to as extrapyramidal side effects. They are most common with high- and medium-potency typical antipsychotics such as haloperidol and fluphenazine but can occur even with atypical antipsychotics in a dose-related manner.

Table 30.1.   Selected psychiatric medications and typical adult dose ranges

Generic name	Trade name	Dose range (mg/day)[a]
Antipsychotics		
Typical		
Chlorpromazine	Largactil/Thorazine	50–1,000
Flupenthixol	Fluanxol	1–12
Haloperidol	Haldol	0.5–20
Loxapine	Loxapac/Loxitane	5–250[b]
Methotrimeprazine	Nozinan	25–500
Thioridazine	Mellaril	30–800
Trifluoperazine	Stelazine	2–40
Zuclopenthixol	Clopixol	10–100
Atypical		
Risperidone	Risperdal	0.5–6
Paliperidone	Invega	3–12
Olanzapine	Zyprexa	2.5–40
Clozapine	Clozaril	12.5–900
Aripiprazole	Abilify	2.5–30
Ziprasidone	Zeldox/Geodon	20–200
Quetiapine	Seroquel	50–800
Lurasidone	Latuda	40–60
Iloperidone	Fanapt	12–24
Asenapine	Saphris	2.5–20
Brexpiprazole	Rexulti	2–4
Cariprazine	Vraylar	1.5–6
Depot (long-acting injectable)		
Aripiprazole	Abilify Maintena	300–400 monthly
Risperidone	Risperdal Consta	25–50 every 2 weeks
Paliperidone	Invega Sustenna	39–234 monthly
Flupenthixol	Fluanxol depot	5–100 every 2–3 weeks
Fluphenazine	Modecate	2.5–100 every 2 weeks
Haloperidol	Haldol LA	50–300 every 4 weeks
Zuclopenthixol	Clopixol depot	100–400 every 2 weeks
Zuclopenthixol acetate	Clopixol accuphase	25–150 every 2–3 days
Antidepressants		
Selective serotonin reuptake inhibitors		
Citalopram	Celexa	10–60
Escitalopram	Cipralex/Lexapro	5–20
Fluvoxamine	Luvox	50–300
Fluoxetine	Prozac	10–80
Paroxetine	Paxil	10–60
Sertraline	Zoloft	25–200
Novel		
Bupropion	Welbutrin	150–300
Venlafaxine	Effexor	37.5–375
Mirtazapine	Remeron	15–60
Tricyclic antidepressants		
Desipramine	Norpramin	50–300
Nortriptyline	Aventyl	25–150
Amitriptyline	Elavil	10–300
Clomipramine	Anafranil	25–300

Table 30.1. *(continued)*

Generic name	Trade name	Dose range (mg/day)[a]
Tricyclic antidepressants		
Doxepin	Sinequan	25–300
Imipramine	Tofranil	25–300
Monoamine oxidase inhibitors		
Phenelzine	Nardil	15–90
Tranylcypromine	Parnate	20–40
Selegiline	Emsam	6–12
Mood Stabilizers		
Lithium	Carbolith, Duralith	Based on drug levels
Carbamazepine	Tegretol	200–1,600
Oxcarbazepine	Trileptal	300–2,400
Valproate	Epival	250–3,000
Topiramate	Topamax	25–800
Lamotrigine	Lamictal	25–250
Gabapentin (off label)	Neurontin	100–1,800[c]
Sedative-Hypnotics/Anxiolytics		
Benzodiazepines		
Alprazolam	Xanax	0.5[d]
Clonazepam	Rivotril	0.25[d]
Diazepam	Valium	5[d]
Lorazepam	Ativan	1[d]
Oxazepam	Serax	15[d]
Non-benzodiazepines		
Zopiclone	Imovane	7.5
Buspirone	BuSpar	5–60
Trazodone	Desyrel	25–500
Melatonin	—	0.3–12
Psychostimulants		
Methylphenidate	Ritalin	5–60
Methylphenidate SR	Ritalin SR	20–60
Methylphenidate ER	Concerta	18–54
Dextroamphetamine	Dexedrine	5–40
Mixed Amphetamine Salts	Adderall	5–60
Lisdexamphetamine	Vyvanse	30–70
Nonstimulant ADHD Medications		
Atomoxetine	Strattera	40–100
α_2-Adrenergic Receptor Agonists		
Clonidine	Catapres	0.1–0.6
Clonidine Extended-Release	Kapvay	0.1–0.4
Guanfacine	Tenex, Intuniv	1–3
Guanfacine Extended-Release		1–6
Opioid Receptor Antagonists		
Naltrexone	Revia	12.5–200

[a]Unless otherwise indicated

[b]Optimal loxapine dose of 5mg/day–15 mg/day in adolescents and adults with autism spectrum disorder, as described by Hellings and colleagues (2015)

[c]Hellings (2006)

[d]Typical starting doses; maximum dose depends on tolerance

Other movement disorders are frequently caused by typical neuroleptics. Akathisia is a common side effect consisting of subjective feelings of restlessness and/or an inability to remain still. This may occur also with atypical antipsychotics, especially aripiprazole, and may be confused with the underlying illness. Acute dystonia, which typically occurs in young males given a neuroleptic for the first time, consists of a severe contraction of small muscles that results in abnormal sustained postures such as oculogyric crisis. In this case, the eyes roll up intermittently, which may be very disabling and painful and also may be mistaken for hysteria, as the person's eyes may normalize when he or she is spoken to. Other dystonias include torticollis (i.e., a spasm affecting the neck), sustained tongue protrusion, an eye pulling to the side, or breathing difficulty due to laryngeal spasm. Acute dystonia may thus be a medical emergency; however, it responds very well to the administration of antiparkinsonian medications such as benztropine or diphenhydramine (Benadryl). Tardive dyskinesia usually occurs after long-term treatment with typical antipsychotics and involves involuntary writhing movements that are most commonly seen in the mouth and tongue as tongue protrusion, tongue in cheek, or grimacing and sucking movements, but that can occur in various parts of the body, particularly the upper body, and may be irreversible and very disabling. Neuroleptic malignant syndrome is a potentially fatal emergency in which muscle rigidity develops, along with altered consciousness and mental confusion, salivation, high fever, fluctuating blood pressure, and high serum levels of muscle creatine phosphokinase. Treatment often requires admission to an intensive care unit, immediate cessation of the antipsychotic drug, and administration of the muscle relaxant dantrolene.

Atypical Antipsychotics Typical antipsychotics have been largely supplanted by the advent of the atypical antipsychotics due to the latter being marketed as having a safer side effect profile. An unanticipated side effect of atypical antipsychotics was a marked reduction in satiation after eating, with marked appetite increase, weight gain, Type 2 diabetes, and related serious medical illness including steatohepatitis (fatty liver). Thus, although atypical antipsychotics were developed to be safer than typical antipsychotics, they may cause greater morbidity and mortality unless used

with caution. Also, careful monitoring of weight, fasting glucose and lipids, and blood pressure is important. Although atypical antipsychotics may have a lower risk of causing movement disorders in usual doses than do typical antipsychotics, they are much worse when it comes to metabolic side effects such as weight gain, elevations in serum lipid levels (e.g., low-density lipoprotein, or LDL, cholesterol), and increased fasting blood glucose levels (associated with an increased risk of diabetes). Atypical antipsychotics are also distinct from the typical antipsychotics in that they cause much less dopamine type 2 blockade (which may be partly responsible for the reduced incidence of movement disorders) and tend to block serotonin type 2A (5-HT2A) receptors. Thus, they are sometimes referred to as serotonin-dopamine antagonist medications.

The first serotonin-dopamine antagonist drug developed was clozapine, which remains a gold standard for antipsychotics due to its being the most effective drug for treating psychosis. Clozapine causes negligible movement disorder symptoms but has a host of other potential side effects, including seizures, cardiomyopathy, weight gain, and agranulocytosis. Agranulocytosis is a life-threatening disorder of bone marrow production of white blood cells, which are necessary to prevent and fight infections. This rare but potential side effect necessitates as much as weekly monitoring of the blood count when clozapine is used. The typical medium-potency antipsychotic loxapine is a designer drug from the 1980s based on clozapine but lacks the agranulocytosis risk. Although loxapine in usual doses may be used in schizophrenia, low doses of 5mg–15mg/day may be more like an atypical antipsychotic and effective in intellectual and developmental disabilities and ASD but with lesser weight gain; prospective studies are needed (Hellings et al., 2015; Stahl, 2002).

Of all antipsychotics, risperidone is the most likely to cause prolactin elevation resulting in breast development and lactation also in males, as well as movement disorders, although risk of weight gain is often marked, albeit less than with olanzapine and clozapine (Hellings, Zarcone, Crandall, Wallace, & Schroeder, 2001; Hellings et al., 2005). Quetiapine causes almost no early-onset movement disorders at all, but sedation and significant weight gain are often problematic. The newer atypical antipsychotic medications paliperidone, ziprasidone, aripiprazole, iloperidone, and lurasidone are marketed as causing less weight gain and fewer movement disorders than prior medications, but such side effects are nonetheless relatively common and are more so in younger individuals.

Depot Antipsychotics Depot antipsychotics are special preparations of antipsychotic medications that are given by intramuscular injection every 2 to 4 weeks, depending on the drug. As of this writing in 2016, the available depot antipsychotics are typical antipsychotics as well as the atypicals risperidone (Risperdal Consta), depot ziprasidone, and depot aripiprazole (e.g., Abilify Maintena). Depot antipsychotics have the same side effects as their oral counterparts, but it is believed that these side effects may be less severe due to a lower fluctuation in blood levels than is seen with oral administration. Depot antipsychotics are often used with people living independently in the community for whom compliance with medication regimens may be difficult or uncertain. The regular administration of a depot antipsychotic leaves no doubt as to whether a person is receiving his or her medication.

Antidepressant Medications

Antidepressants are also divided up into subclasses. The newest and by far the most commonly used are the SSRIs and the novel antidepressants bupropion, venlafaxine, desvenlafaxine, mirtazapine, and duloxetine. Antidepressants are used for a number of psychiatric illnesses, including major depressive disorder, bipolar depression, anxiety disorders, eating disorders, premenstrual dysphoric disorder, and some personality disorders, in addition to their somewhat equivocal use in challenging behaviors in intellectual and developmental disabilities. Generally, their pharmacological action is to prevent the reuptake of certain neurotransmitters from the synaptic cleft by presynaptic neurons.

Selective Serotonin Reuptake Inhibitors
Selective serotonin reuptake inhibitors, as their name implies, selectively block the reuptake of serotonin, which results in an increase in serotonin concentration in the synapse. How this translates into antidepressant activity is unknown, especially given the fact that antidepressants have a delayed onset of action of about 2–4 weeks. It is hypothesized that the antidepressant effect coincides with changes in receptors (downregulation) in the presynaptic neurons that occur secondary to the increased availability of serotonin, which would explain the delay.

Although SSRIs are widely used for depression, there is significant evidence that their actual effectiveness in treating depression is only partial. On the other hand, their ability to treat anxiety (particularly panic disorder) is greater. One particular type of anxiety disorder, OCD, is treated with SSRIs as well as with the most serotonin-specific of the older antidepressants, clomipramine. Overall, however, their efficacy is variable in autism (King et al., 2009), and in spite of a seeming initial improvement, they may later produce behavioral worsening and activation. The SSRI fluoxetine may be especially useful for self-picking and explosive outbursts in Prader-Willi syndrome (Hellings & Warnock, 1994).

Typical side effects of SSRIs are not life-threatening, especially when the SSRI is not prescribed together with the older antidepressants. Certain combinations of SSRIs with these older antidepressants can lead to a fairly severe condition called serotonin syndrome, a form of toxicity that produces symptoms of increased heart rate and blood pressure, fever with shivering and sweating, nausea and diarrhea, hypervigilance, agitation, and confusion. In severe cases, high fever can lead to life-threatening complications. Perhaps the most troubling side effect of SSRIs and other serotonergic medications (e.g., venlafaxine) is sexual dysfunction, which occurs to varying degrees in a significant number of people taking these medications. This can include lack of desire as well as difficulties with performance, including inability to achieve erections (in men) or orgasm (in both men and women). However, this side effect has also been used to advantage in the treatment of premature ejaculation.

Non-selective Serotonin Reuptake Inhibitor (Novel) Antidepressants Most of the non-SSRI antidepressants also cause varying degrees of serotonin reuptake inhibition, but they tend to block the reuptake of other neurotransmitters associated with depression, known as the catecholamines, as well. This chemical group includes norepinephrine (also known as noradrenaline), epinephrine (adrenaline), and dopamine. The catecholamines are much more highly associated with antidepressant effects (and less so with antianxiety effects) than is serotonin.

Dopamine, for example, is the neurotransmitter that is responsible for the effects of amphetamines (which cause dopamine release) and cocaine (which blocks dopamine reuptake). Both of these drugs are recognized for their tendency to enhance well-being and mood in the short term (although they are also known for causing paranoia and other psychotic symptoms, lending further support to the dopamine hypothesis of schizophrenia). Norepinephrine and epinephrine are associated with the increased energy, alertness, and "fight or flight" syndrome of the sympathetic nervous system.

Venlafaxine is a drug that blocks reuptake of serotonin, norepinephrine, and dopamine; the norepinephrine and dopamine effects are seen at higher dose ranges. Although venlafaxine is marketed for use as an antidepressant as well as an antianxiety agent, many people find that at higher doses (i.e., above 150 mg/day), or even at lower doses, it can cause unpleasant physical anxiety symptoms. In addition, at higher doses it is associated with occasional mild to moderate increases in blood pressure. Despite these potential side effects, venlafaxine may have a faster onset of action, greater effectiveness in severe depression, and a more "activating" effect than the SSRIs.

Bupropion has no effect on serotonin and, in fact, its mechanism is not clear, although inhibition of presynaptic norepinephrine and dopamine reuptake transporters is implicated in its mechanism of action. It is notable for not causing sexual dysfunction, a common rationale for its use. It is also regarded as an activating antidepressant in that it generally does not cause fatigue and often causes increases in energy. It has also been used as an antismoking drug under the trade name of Zyban.

Mirtazapine potentiates serotonin and norepinephrine transmission by blocking receptors (α_2-adrenergic type) that decrease their activity. Mirtazapine tends to be sedating and has negligible gastrointestinal side effects (e.g., nausea), properties that theoretically make it a possible choice for those with depressive symptoms associated with loss of appetite and insomnia. However, its relative effectiveness as an antidepressant is not clear, and weight gain and daytime sedation are associated problems.

Tricyclic Antidepressants and Monoamine Oxidase Inhibitors Prior to the advent of the SSRIs and the novel antidepressants, the two classes of antidepressants available were the TCAs and the monoamine oxidase inhibitors (MAOIs). Tricyclic antidepressants take their name from their molecular structure, which contains three rings of atoms, and their mechanism of action is to block the reuptake of the neurotransmitters serotonin and norepinephrine. First-generation TCAs include imipramine, amitriptyline, doxepin, and clomipramine. Second-generation TCAs were designed to cause less side effects of sedation, drop in blood pressure, blurred vision, and urinary retention, and include nortriptyline and desipramine. Preliminary evidence suggests that low-dose amitriptyline, in particular, appears effective in ASD, more so than the other TCAs (Bhatti et al., 2013). Amitriptyline improves problems associated with sleep, appetite, anxiety, impulse control, and hyperactivity; it also is less likely to cause gastrointestinal discomfort, although it may cause constipation. Bhatti et al. reported using it in combination with stimulants and low-dose antipsychotics such as risperidone and aripiprazole. More controlled studies are needed. It is interesting to note that amitriptyline is fairly commonly added to SSRIs in adults in the general population with treatment-resistant depression, bearing in mind possible drug interactions, as mentioned previously, and the need for TCA blood level and EKG monitoring.

MAOIs work by deactivating monoamine oxidase, the enzyme that degrades serotonin, norepinephrine, and dopamine, resulting in greater amounts of all three in the brain. Despite being superior in efficacy to the newer antidepressants, MAOIs can cause a hypertensive crisis if the user consumes foods containing tyramine; that in addition to other significant side effects means they are currently seldom used. Selegiline (Emsam) is available in patch form.

Ketamine, a glutamate N-methyl-D-aspartate receptor antagonist, has shown rapid antidepressant efficacy as well as resolution of suicidal ideation, but studies are still underway of this promising drug.

Mood Stabilizers

Mood stabilizers are generally used to treat and prevent serious mood alterations in bipolar disorder, particularly mania. One notable exception is lamotrigine, which is used largely for the treatment and prevention of bipolar depression. All except lithium are also anticonvulsants, meaning that they are used in the treatment of epilepsy to prevent seizures.

Mood stabilizers are particularly dangerous to the fetus, and their use should be avoided during pregnancy and in women trying to become pregnant. For example, the fetal valproate syndrome resembles fetal alcohol syndrome.

Lithium   Lithium is one of the oldest psychiatric medications, with great efficacy if used for the right indications. It is an element, which alone sets it apart from all other psychiatric medications. Like valproic acid, it remains a drug of first choice in the treatment of acute episodes of bipolar mania and depression; it is also used on an ongoing basis to prevent episodes of both types. It has consistently been shown to decrease suicidality and improve brain health, and it is used as an add-on treatment to antidepressants in treatment-resistant depression.

On the other hand, lithium is a drug with many risks. It has a low therapeutic index, which means that the difference between an effective and a toxic dose is fairly small, necessitating regular monitoring of blood levels. Lithium toxicity is characterized by a drunken appearance, including marked tremor, ataxia (i.e., severe lack of coordination, especially of gait), and confusion or, in more severe cases, stupor and coma. This is a life-threatening condition that can be brought on by dehydration, diarrhea, vomiting, interactions with other medications (including several diuretics, anti-inflammatory agents, and angiotensin-converting enzyme inhibitors), or impaired kidney function.

The side effects of lithium are many, including thirst, skin problems (acne and psoriasis), cognitive dysfunction (lack of spontaneity and memory problems), tremor, thyroid underactivity, and kidney impairments. Although actual kidney failure caused by lithium is quite rare, nephrogenic diabetes insipidus, an impairment of the ability of the kidneys to concentrate urine resulting in loss of body water due to a large output of dilute urine, is very common. The side effects of lithium can be particularly challenging for people with intellectual and developmental disabilities, who are particularly affected by increased urine output, tremor, diabetes insipidus, and cognitive impairments. Although increased urine output and memory problems may be annoying to a person without a disability, for a person with intellectual and developmental disabilities, these side effects can mean the difference between continence and incontinence and between relative independence and dependence. It is crucially important to remain aware of lithium's potential side effects with this population. Lithium toxicity may be unnoticed until advanced stages, partly due to caregiver shifts and weekend clinicians not knowing the risks in a particular patient.

Gabapentin   Gabapentin is an add-on anti-seizure medication that is often effective as a mood stabilizer in combination with valproic acid and can replace lithium for this purpose in many cases of adults with intellectual and developmental disabilities and bipolar-like illness (Hellings, 2006). Provided it is started slowly, gabapentin has far fewer side effects than lithium. It is not uncommon when treating bipolar disorder even in the general population that two mood stabilizers plus a low dose of antipsychotic are needed in order to achieve mood control.

Valproate and Carbamazepine   Valproate (valproic acid) and carbamazepine are anticonvulsant medications that both show evidence of effectiveness in bipolar disorder. Both are used to prevent mania and depression and in the treatment of mania. Carbamazepine is sometimes prescribed for aggressive behaviors in nonpsychotic individuals; however, its use for this purpose is not established, and behavioral activation may occur related to its tricyclic structure. Carbamazepine has somewhat more serious side effects than valproate, such as aplastic anemia (i.e., loss of new blood cell production) as well as an allergic type of hepatitis. Valproate has resulted in severe hepatitis in children younger than 10 and may rarely cause jaundice, liver failure, and death. The most common side effects related to its use are weight gain, hair loss, increase in blood levels of liver enzymes, and decrease in blood platelets predisposing to bruising and bleeding, nausea, and tremor. The hair loss may be counteracted by giving a multivitamin containing selenium.

Lamotrigine   Lamotrigine is an anticonvulsant used for treatment and prevention of depression in bipolar disorder. Bipolar depression has long been a difficult condition to treat because of the propensity of antidepressant medications to cause mania or "mixed states" in which depressive symptoms such as suicidal ideation co-occur with many symptoms such as racing thoughts and increased activity. Lamotrigine has been shown to have an antidepressant effect in individuals with bipolar disorder without causing a switch into mania or mixed states. Most side effects are mild, apart from possible clumsiness and injuries due to falling. In very rare cases, a life-threatening skin condition can develop known as Stevens-Johnson syndrome or toxic epidermal necrolysis. Any rash, especially in the first few weeks of treatment, should be closely monitored.

Sedative-Hypnotics

A sedative is a drug that tends to produce a calming, sedating effect, whereas a hypnotic is a drug that is used to promote sleep. Sedative-hypnotics are a very commonly used class of medications, given the fact that sleep complaints and anxiety are such common therapeutic targets. Some of these medications are primarily hypnotics (e.g., trazodone, melatonin) and others are principally anxiolytics (e.g., buspirone), whereas benzodiazepines are used for both purposes.

Benzodiazepines   The benzodiazepine class contains a number of medications that have in common their actions on γ-aminobutyric acid (GABA) type A (GABAA) receptors in the brain. GABA is an inhibitory neurotransmitter that causes a decrease in the activity of neurons through its activity on GABA receptors that are located throughout the brain. Benzodiazepines, which bind to the GABAA receptor at a site adjacent to the site where GABA binds, enhance the activity of the receptor, resulting in greater inhibition and, as a result, produce a calming and sedating effect. Nonetheless, disinhibition resulting in worsening of aggression is possible. Benzodiazepines are also very effective at stopping and preventing seizures.

The most commonly used benzodiazepines are probably lorazepam (Ativan) and clonazepam (Rivotril or Klonopin). Lorazepam is a short-acting benzodiazepine (half-life of about 15 hours) that is often used for occasional difficulty falling asleep or for "as needed" treatment of anxiety or agitation. Clonazepam, a long-acting benzodiazepine (half-life of 34 hours) may be given to prevent frequent anxiety states and agitation that occurs regularly; however, again, it is best avoided because it can cause behavioral disinhibition.

Long-term regular use of any benzodiazepine can result in tolerance and dependence. The implications of this are that individuals who use benzodiazepines regularly for longer than a few weeks may find that if they stop taking the medication very suddenly they will experience greater anxiety than they did before they started taking it (withdrawal) and will need to keep taking it (dependence). In addition, they may find that the effect begins to wear off and that they need higher doses to fall asleep or manage their anxiety than they did initially (tolerance). Finally, the sudden discontinuation of high-dose, long-term use of benzodiazepines can lead to withdrawal seizures. Because of these qualities, benzodiazepines are recommended only for short-term use. In addition, they should not be stopped "cold turkey" unless already at the lowest possible dose; rather, they should be slowly decreased until discontinuation. Even with slow tapering, when the lowest dose is discontinued, many individuals experience an emergence of anxiety and insomnia. Another potential side effect of benzodiazepines mentioned previously is the effect of paradoxical disinhibition. Although benzodiazepines may decrease anxiety and insomnia, some people become aggressive, impulsive, or silly after ingesting a benzodiazepine. Although this effect is reported as being rare, it may be more common among those with intellectual disability or brain injury, making it an important reason to avoid ongoing use in people with intellectual and developmental disabilities.

Non-benzodiazepines   So-called "non-benzodiazepine" drugs that act at the same site on the GABA receptor as benzodiazepines, such as zopiclone, were touted as lacking the dependency potential of benzodiazepines. Clinical experience has proved this untrue, however, and they also are now recommended for occasional use only.

Trazodone was originally developed as an antidepressant and has a structure similar to that of some of the older antidepressants. Although it is seldom used for depression, it is widely used off-label for chronic sleep disturbances. Trazodone is highly sedating, increases total sleep time, and decreases the amount of rapid eye movement sleep relative to the much more restorative Stage 4 sleep. It rarely may produce the serious side effect of priapism, a sustained erection in males that may become a medical emergency. Trazodone has no concerns related to issues of dependence and tolerance; however, drug interactions are possible when prescribed in combinations (e.g., with SSRIs).

Psychostimulants

Psychostimulants are used in the treatment of ADHD and as add-on treatments to antidepressants in treatment-resistant depression. The most well-known is methylphenidate, better known as Ritalin.

Methylphenidate and dextroamphetamine both block the reuptake of dopamine into presynaptic axon terminals. As noted, this is the same mechanism of action of cocaine, although the euphoria that one gets from cocaine does not occur with methylphenidate when it is taken orally (rather than injected or snorted) and at therapeutic doses. Dextroamphetamine is similar to Ritalin; however, it is twice as potent and its action lasts twice as long. Yet, the short half-life of these medications (rapid wear-off) and the need for lunch time doses at school led to the development of formulations that are not only longer acting but also more difficult to abuse, such as the stimulant precursor lisdexamfetamine (Vyvanse) that is only converted to the active drug once it enters the bloodstream.

Although it seems counterintuitive to give a stimulant for hyperactivity, the overall effect generally is an increased ability to focus on tasks and a decrease in impulsive behaviors. Common side effects of stimulants include loss of appetite, nervousness, and insomnia, and it is usually recommended that stimulants not be taken in the evening to avoid sleep disturbance.

Atomoxetine is a nonstimulant medication used in the treatment of ADHD. Marketed as Strattera, atomoxetine is a norepinephrine reuptake inhibitor that was originally developed as an antidepressant. Atomoxetine has important safety concerns, including the potential for worsening suicidal thoughts. These side effects have also been reported to occur in young people prescribed antidepressants and are likely related to starting treatment in a too-high dose or increasing the dose too rapidly.

Opioid Receptor Antagonists

Naltrexone, a drug that blocks opioid receptors, merits mention due to its (somewhat equivocal) use in treating self-injurious behavior (SIB). It is chemically very similar to naloxone (Narcan) nasal spray and injection, also an opioid receptor blocker, used as a treatment for opioid overdose. Opioids are addictive chemicals that decrease pain and include morphine and the endogenous (i.e., produced by the human body) opioids, which include the endorphins. Opioid receptor antagonists block opioid receptors and prevent these chemicals from exerting their effects. Their use in SIB is based on the hypothesis that individuals who engage in SIB do so to cause the release of endorphins, which occurs as a natural physiological response to pain stimuli. There are about equal numbers of positive and negative studies regarding naltrexone efficacy for reducing SIB in individuals with intellectual and developmental disabilities, and it is seldom used as of this writing.

α_2-Adrenergic Receptor Agonists

Originally produced as a medication for the treatment of high blood pressure, clonidine stimulates α_2-adrenergic receptors on presynaptic terminals, which results in a decrease in the amount of norepinephrine released into the synaptic cleft. This results in lower blood pressure, heart rate, and levels of arousal. Clonidine may be used in the treatment of ADHD to try to decrease hyperactivity and aggression. Although it may be effective, its short half-life requires dosing three to four times a day. This led to the development of the longer-acting formulation, Kapvay. Likewise, because the half-life of the alpha agonist guanfacine is short, a longer acting formulation, Intinuv, was developed and marketed. Rapid discontinuation of clonidine can cause an increase in blood pressure; thus, it must be tapered off gradually.

EVIDENCE BASE FOR PHARMACOLOGICAL INTERVENTIONS

This section begins with a background on evidence-based medicine. The following subsections then expand on the topic to discuss randomized controlled trials and their limitations, statistical versus clinical significance, the influence of the pharmaceutical industry, evidence for using psychotropic medications for challenging behaviors, and consensus guidelines and surveys.

Evidence-Based Medicine

Evidence-based medicine is a term that refers to the implementation of health research into medical practice (Haynes, Devereaux, & Guyatt, 2002) and could be said to represent an organized attempt to transform the "art" of medicine into the "science" of medicine. The primary goal of evidence-based medicine is to ensure that physicians are making decisions based on research that is of the highest scientific standard. Although there are many types of research study designs, the highest standard of scientific research with respect to the evaluation of the effectiveness of pharmacological interventions is the randomized controlled trial (RCT). In reality, however, many key treatments in the field of medicine are used off-label because they may not have received adequate study. This practice is common even in neonatal medicine.

Randomized Controlled Trials and Their Limitations

A pharmacological RCT is a study in which a drug and placebo or two or more drug treatments are compared. The subjects of the study, to whom the treatments will be administered, are randomized, meaning they are randomly assigned to different treatment groups rather than being assigned to a treatment group by nonrandom means. Non-random treatment allocation can lead to what is known as selection bias or sampling bias, in which the groups selected differ in ways that influence outcome. Ideally, the randomization procedure also includes matching, a process that ensures that important demographic factors, such as age, gender, and other factors, are equally represented in both groups. The trial is controlled by the presence of a placebo group to prevent factors other than the treatment itself causing the outcome being studied. A placebo is a treatment that contains no active ingredient but is identical in appearance to the active treatment. If, for example, scientists wish to study the ability of a certain vitamin to cure the common cold and no placebo group is studied, the vitamin will appear to cure the cold due to the fact that colds usually resolve on their own. If the group receiving the vitamin is compared to a group that does not receive anything—vitamin or placebo— that comparison group may recover more slowly

than the vitamin group because the psychological effect of receiving treatment in the vitamin group may lead to a quicker recovery. If, however, the control group is provided with a pill that looks exactly the same as the vitamin but contains only inert ingredients, then both groups should have equal expectations of benefit due to receiving treatment. The expectation of improvement due to receiving a treatment is called the "placebo effect" and is particularly important in psychiatry, as 1) it still is not understood exactly how psychiatric medications cause improvements in psychiatric disorders, 2) RCTs of psychiatric medications may show only small differences in improvements between placebo groups and active treatment groups (e.g., Kirsch & Sapirstein, 1998), and 3) brain activity studies have shown that similar brain changes may occur in placebo and active treatment groups (Mayberg et al., 2002), suggesting that the placebo effect has a psychological expectancy effect similar to that of active treatments.

Whether or not the groups being compared include a placebo group, a study should be blinded. "Blinding" refers to a state of ignorance in participants and evaluators with regard to which treatment group subjects belong to. If only the subjects are unaware of their treatment allocation, the trial is considered to be a single-blind trial, which is problematic because researchers, like study subjects, may believe that one of the treatments is superior and as a result be inclined to rate improvement as greater in that group. If both the subjects and the investigators responsible for evaluating response to treatment are unaware of who belongs to which group (preferable), the study is considered to be double-blind. However, there are limitations to blinding procedures. For example, in the case of a placebo-controlled trial in which the active treatment causes side effects (a common scenario), subjects may become "unblinded" by either experiencing or not experiencing side effects; as a result, the study becomes uncontrolled. Another criticism of RCTs is that subjects are often a select group meeting stringent criteria, whereas many individuals in the general population have more mixed, atypical, and comorbid conditions. A part of the art of medicine is matching the beneficial as well as adverse effects to the individual patient, and this should not be overshadowed by so-called evidence-based practices if off-label medications may be more beneficial.

Statistical versus Clinical Significance

Even in a properly conducted trial, it is possible to draw misleading conclusions. One of the most common of these relates to the difference between statistical significance and clinical significance. *Statistical significance* refers to the likelihood that a result did not occur due to chance. For example, if one wants to know which of two sports teams is better, one could ask them to play a game against each other. If the final score is 20–0, the conclusion might be that the team that won is the better team. If the final score is 3–2, one might be less convinced that the winning team is the better team but instead consider that the win may have been due to a "fluke" (i.e., to chance) and ask for a best four out of seven series. If the result of each of the games in this series is a score of 3–2, one might still not be convinced. If these two teams went on to play a thousand games, all with a close result, one might still not be convinced which team was better. Statistically, however, the greater the number of games played, the greater the chance of finding a statistical difference favoring one of the teams, even if the difference in the average scores is so small that one might not consider it significant.

In the same way, if a study comparing two treatments enrolls enough subjects, statistical analysis may reveal superiority of one treatment that statistically is not due to chance. However, if the difference is of a very small magnitude, it is likely clinically insignificant or of negligible real benefit. Alternatively, if too few subjects are enrolled, researchers may fail to find a statistically significant difference when in fact there is a clinically significant difference.

The general public, physicians, and researchers also need to be aware that statistics are not always correctly applied in the medical and other literature and that the conclusions of a study do not always reflect what the data indicate. Furthermore, reporting by journalists is not always accurate. These issues indicate that although the results of research that uses sound methodology need to be closely heeded when deciding whether to use specific medications, qualified medical practitioners also need to interpret how such results are best applied to individuals in their clinical practices. This process recalls the art of medicine, as mentioned previously. In addition, clinical improvement is often set at only 25% in RCTs, which in practice may be insufficient to improve severe challenging behaviors and the quality of life of the individual and his or her family.

The Influence of the Pharmaceutical Industry

Although since about 2000 the development of psychotropic medications by pharmaceutical companies has reduced significantly, the majority of data available regarding the efficacy and safety of psychiatric medications comes from research projects that were funded by the pharmaceutical companies themselves. Although it is in the financial interest of the pharmaceutical industry to portray their products in the most positive light possible, controls are now in place that prohibit certain interactions between academia and industry in terms of physician gifts, meals, and payments. In the United States, these interactions must be disclosed on a public web site under the Sunshine Act, and research presentations and publications are required to list investigator conflicts of interest. Negative trials (i.e., those in which the treatment in question demonstrates no apparent benefit over the placebo) are now also required to be published.

Evidence for Using Psychotropic Medications for Challenging Behaviors

Matson and Neal (2009) reviewed the evidence for the use of psychotropic medications for challenging behaviors exhibited by people with intellectual and developmental disabilities. In their review, the authors included only those studies that had, in their design, placebo control, randomization, double-blind subjects, standardized doses, standardized evaluations of symptoms, and appropriate statistical procedures. The authors identified 12 studies that met all of those criteria. Of these 12 studies, three studied typical antipsychotics, seven studied the atypical antipsychotic risperidone, one studied the antidepressant imipramine, and one studied both a typical (haloperidol) and an atypical (risperidone) antipsychotic. Of the 12 studies, eight found a significant benefit associated with medication use and four found no benefit. The eight that found a benefit included all of the seven that studied risperidone alone, whereas of the four that failed to demonstrate medication advantage, one examined imipramine, two focused on the typical antipsychotic thioridazine, and one studied both risperidone and the typical antipsychotic haloperidol. It is interesting to note that the four that found no benefit were the only ones that utilized both objective observation and standardized rating scales, whereas the eight that found a significant benefit relied only on the use of rating scales. The largest and highest quality study (Tyrer et al., 2008) was judged to be the one that found no advantage to risperidone or haloperidol compared with placebo.

In summary, the majority of studies that have employed a rigorous methodology have focused on risperidone. This makes it difficult to conclude that risperidone is superior to other medications for this purpose, as little evidence supporting or refuting the use of other medications has been obtained. Furthermore, despite the number of RCTs showing benefit from risperidone compared with placebo, the fact that a high-quality study using a more rigorous methodology failed to replicate this finding does cast some doubt on the relevance of these results.

Consensus Guidelines and Surveys

Despite the lack of adequate research data regarding all of their uses, it is still generally accepted that pharmacological interventions play an important role in the treatment of challenging behaviors in individuals with intellectual and developmental disabilities. As outlined previously, there are many situations in which the risk of harm due to agitated behavior is so great that the failure to administer psychiatric medications would be unethical. Most psychiatrists working with people with intellectual and developmental disabilities have many examples from their own practice of situations in which the initiation of psychiatric medications appeared to provide significant, and sometimes dramatic, benefits. It may be that the dearth of research evidence to support these benefits is due to inadequacies in study design, lack of study funding, or in the current capacity to predict which individuals will benefit from which particular medications. Although considered a low level of evidence in an evidence-based framework, the opinion of those with experience in the field is the best, and often only, guide in how to proceed.

When high-level evidence for interventions is lacking, or if evidence is conflicting, experts will often convene to create consensus guidelines. Expert consensus is considered a level of evidence, though not a very strong one, as it is based on clinical experience and opinion, which are vulnerable to various types of bias. A number of consensus guidelines have been created to help guide the use of psychotropic medications in those with intellectual and developmental disabilities (e.g., Reiss & Aman, 1997). However, the consensus guidelines published by Deb et al. (2009) concluded that there was insufficient evidence to make any recommendations regarding specific medication treatments for challenging behaviors and that nonpharmacological interventions should be tried first when no medical or psychiatric disorder is found to explain the behaviors. Another significant problem is lack of training, among general psychiatrists who treat adolescents and adults, in the presentation and treatment of ADHD. As is common in the general population, there is significant overdiagnosis of bipolar disorder, as discussed previously, when ADHD is the underlying cause of impulsive aggression and irritability.

In the absence of expert consensus, consensus surveys can be conducted to determine the practices of a broad sample of clinicians working in the field. Although this type of information is subject to major biases and nonscientific trends, it can at least provide a framework to make treatment decisions that would be considered reasonable by a majority of colleagues.

The overwhelming choice of antipsychotics, and risperidone in particular, likely reflects the greater evidence base supporting this medication to address aggressive behavior by people with intellectual and developmental disabilities. However, many psychiatrists try to avoid antipsychotics if at all possible when there is no evidence of psychosis, and for this reason, antianxiety drugs for many are the drug of first choice for aggression not due to psychosis. Finally, the relatively greater preference for antidepressants for SIB than for aggression likely reflects fears that aggression may be due to an underlying bipolar disorder that could be exacerbated by the administration of antidepressant medications (resulting in manic or mixed features), whereas SIB may be regarded as resulting from anxious or depressive symptoms. Among the antidepressants, SSRIs were the overwhelming choice for both the treatment of aggression and SIB, with 81.6% choosing an SSRI as their preferred antidepressant for SIB. Citalopram and fluoxetine were the top two first choices for both aggression and SIB.

Although no respondents chose mood stabilizers as their first choice for the treatment of aggression, it was the most popular second choice, selected by 40.7% for this ranking. This likely indicates that many psychiatrists would first choose an antipsychotic for the treatment of aggression and would then add a mood stabilizer if the antipsychotic was incompletely effective, or would switch to a mood stabilizer if the antipsychotic had to be stopped because of unacceptable side effects. The preferred mood stabilizers for both aggression and SIB were carbamazepine, chosen first among mood stabilizers by 44.4% for aggression and 40.7% for SIB, respectively, and valproate, ranked first by 37.0% for aggression and 31.5% for SIB. Carbamazepine and valproate were also the top-ranked second choices, indicating that most psychiatrists see these two medications as the mood stabilizers of choice. Lithium was relatively unpopular, chosen by only about 10% as the mood stabilizer of first choice for both aggression and SIB. It is interesting to note that naltrexone for the treatment of SIB was not mentioned in this study, nor were ADHD medications.

FUTURE DIRECTIONS

The following are areas of importance in the future pertaining to the field of psychopharmacology and people with intellectual and developmental disabilities:

- Increased awareness and active screening for intellectual and developmental disabilities, including ASD, will afford earlier detection and intervention (including with psychotropic medications if warranted). This will lead to improved developmental and behavioral outcomes for these individuals as adults.

- Research into nutrition, allergies to food proteins such as lactose and gluten, and bacteria in the gut (also called the microbiome) that may influence brain neurotransmitter synthesis should have high priority.

- Further studies are urgently needed of combination medications and of substitutes for antipsychotic medications such as loxapine and amitripyline when weight gain and metabolic illness complicate the treatment.

- The holy grail in psychopharmacology continues to be that treatment will reverse the disability by

acting on the specific molecular mechanism or pathway producing it in particular individuals. An example is the study of baclofen in fragile X syndrome that targeted a well-established molecular abnormality. Unfortunately, baclofen did not meet the goals set for it in clinical trials, though some patients may have been helped, and further development of the drug has been halted (Pollack, 2013).

SUMMARY

Although psychiatric disorders occur at a three to four times higher rate among people with intellectual and developmental disabilities than in the general population, the most common mental health problem that brings people with these disabilities to mental health and psychiatric services is a poorly defined group of disruptive and dangerous behaviors commonly referred to as "problem behaviors" or "challenging behaviors." The most commonly examined of these are hyperactivity, impulsive aggression toward others, SIBs, and property destruction. These behaviors are responsible for the majority of psychiatric medications prescribed to people with intellectual and developmental disabilities, who are the group of people in society that receive these medications at the highest rate. Although most physicians would agree that nonpharmacological interventions should be the first line of treatment, issues regarding the degree of risk posed by the behaviors and the unavailability of appropriate behavioral interventions, as well as other factors, frequently lead to medication administration. The latter can be very successful if used correctly, although more combination studies are needed. Old psychiatric medications warranting further study in this population include amitriptyline and loxapine.

Psychiatric medication is a huge industry, and much of the medical research that is available to support its use is produced and controlled by the pharmaceutical companies themselves. More high-quality studies of medication treatment of challenging behaviors in intellectual and developmental disabilities have been published recently, and many focus on the use of risperidone for aggression. Although these studies generally indicate that risperidone is superior to placebo, some data have cast some doubt on the generalizability of these results. Despite the lack of empirical data, psychiatrists employ a variety of psychiatric medications to treat behaviors that often are beyond current understanding. This is especially the case in situations in which the risk of doing nothing seems to significantly outweigh the risk of providing medications.

FOR FURTHER THOUGHT AND DISCUSSION

1. People with an intellectual disability generally have communication impairments, making it difficult for psychiatrists to evaluate the effects of medications using traditional interviewing methods. What can primary caregivers do to support psychiatrists in the evaluation of the effects of medications?

2. Debate with your classmates or colleagues: To what degree do frontline workers need to be knowledgeable about the effects (including side effects) of medications that they administer?

3. What would you do, as a frontline worker or supervisor, if you suspected that a prescribed medication was not having the intended effect?

4. Consider ways that research results that are sound, scientific, and, above all, unbiased can be obtained about medications.

5. Sometimes, psychiatric medications are given regularly (i.e., at the same time every day) for behavior problems, whereas sometimes they are given as needed. What are the potential advantages and disadvantages to each approach?

6. How can caregivers and families assist treating clinicians by providing observations and past school records to clarify a diagnosis, especially that of ADHD?

REFERENCES

American Psychiatric Association. (2013). *Diagnostic and statistical manual of mental disorders* (5th ed.). Washington, DC: Author.

Bhatti, I., Thome, A., Oxler-Smith, P., Cook-Wiens, G., Yeh, H.W., Gaffney, G.R., & Hellings, J.A. (2013). A retrospective study of amitriptyline in youth with autism spectrum disorders. *Journal of Autism and Developmental Disorders, 43*(5), 1017–1027.

Boss, K. (2011). Psychopharmacology of people with developmental disabilities. In I. Brown & M. Percy (Eds.), *Developmental disabilities in Ontario* (3rd ed., pp. 599–618). Toronto, Canada: Ontario Association on Developmental Disabilities.

Carpenter, D., & Joffe, S. (2011). A unique researcher identifier for the Physician Payments Sunshine Act. *Journal of the American Medical Association, 305*(19), 2007–2009.

Cooper, S., Smiley, E., Morrison, J., Williamson, A., & Allen, L. (2007). Mental ill-health in adults with intellectual disabilities: Prevalence and associated factors. *British Journal of Psychiatry, 190,* 27–35.

Deb, S., Kwok, H., Bertelli, M., Salvador-Carulla, L., Bradley, E., Torr, J., & Barnhill, J. (2009). International guide to prescribing psychotropic medication for management of problem behaviors in adults with intellectual disabilities. *World Psychiatry, 8,* 181–186.

Fletcher, R., Barnhill, J., & Cooper, S.-A. (Eds.). (in press). *Diagnostic manual—Intellectual disability 2: A textbook of diagnosis of mental disorders in persons with intellectual disability.* Kingston, NY: National Association for the Dually Diagnosed.

Harvard Health Publications. (2010). *Antidepressants and tamoxifen.* Retrieved from http://www.health.harvard.edu/newsletter_article/antidepressants-and-tamoxifen

Haynes, R.B., Devereaux, P.J., & Guyatt, G.H. (2002). Physicians' and patients' choices in evidence-based practice. *British Medical Journal, 324,* 1350.

Hellings, J.A. (1999). Psychopharmacology of mood disorders in persons with mental retardation and autism. *Mental Retardation and Developmental Disabilities Research Reviews, 5,* 270–278.

Hellings, J.A. (2006). Much improved outcome with gabapentin–divalproex combination in adults with bipolar disorders and developmental disabilities. *Journal of Clinical Psychopharmacology, 26*(3), 344–346.

Hellings, J.A., Reed, G., Cain, S.E., Zhou, X., Barth, F.X., Aman, M.G.,...Han, J.C. (2015). Loxapine add-on for adolescents and adults with autism spectrum disorders, aggression and irritability. *Journal of Child and Adolescent Psychopharmacology, 25*(2), 150–159.

Hellings, J.A., & Warnock, J.K. (1994). Self-injurious behavior and serotonin in Prader-Willi syndrome. *Psychopharmacology Bulletin, 30*(2), 245–250.

Hellings, J.A., Zarcone, J.R., Crandall, K., Wallace, D., & Schroeder, S.R. (2001). Weight gain in a controlled study of risperidone in children, adolescents and adults with mental retardation and autism. *Journal of Child and Adolescent Psychopharmacology, 11*(3), 229–238.

Hellings, J.A., Zarcone, J.R., Valdovinos, M.G., Reese, R.M., Ali, M., Gaughan, E., & Schroeder, S.R. (2005). Risperidone-induced prolactin elevation in a prospective study of children, adolescents and adults with mental retardation and pervasive developmental disorders. *Journal of Child and Adolescent Psychopharmacology, 15*(6), 885–892.

Hemeryck, A., & Belpaire, F.M. (2002). Selective serotonin reuptake inhibitors and cytochrome P-450 mediated drug–drug interactions: An update. *Current Drug Metabolism, 3*(1), 13–37.

King, B.H., Hollander, E., Sikich, L., McCracken, J.T., Scahill, L., Bregman, J.D.,...Ritz, L.; STAART Psychopharmacology Network. (2009). Lack of efficacy of citalopram in children with autism spectrum disorders and high levels of repetitive behaviors. *JAMA Psychiatry, 66*(6), 583–590.

Kirsch, I., & Sapirstein, G. (1998). Listening to Prozac but hearing placebo: A meta-analysis of antidepressant medication. *Prevention and Treatment, 1,* article 0002a.

López-Muñoz, F., Alamo, C., Rubio, G., García-García, P., Martín-Agueda, B., & Cuenca, E. (2003). Bibliometric analysis of biomedical publications on SSRI during 1980–2000. *Depression and Anxiety, 18*(2), 95–103.

Matson, J.L., & Neal, D. (2009). Psychotropic medication use for persons with intellectual disabilities: An overview. *Research in Developmental Disabilities, 30,* 572–586.

Mayberg, H.S., Silva, J.A., Brannan, S.K., Tekell, J.L., Mahurin, R.K., McGinnis, S., & Jerabek, P.A. (2002). The functional anatomy of the placebo effect. *American Journal of Psychiatry, 159,* 728–737.

Nottestad, J.A., & Linaker, O.M. (2003). Psychotropic drug use among people with intellectual disability before and after deinstitutionalization. *Journal of Intellectual Disability Research, 47,* 464–471.

Patient Protection and Affordable Care Act, 42 U.S.C. § 18001 *et seq.* (2010).

Percy, M., & Propst, E. (2008). Celiac disease: Its many faces and relevance to developmental disabilities. *Journal on Developmental Disabilities, 14*(2), 105–110.

Pollack, A. (2013, June 6). An experimental drug's bitter end. *The New York Times.* Retrieved from http://www .nytimes.com/2013/06/07/business/an-experimental-drugs-bitter-end.html?_r=0

Reiss, S., & Aman, M.G. (Eds.). (1997). *Psychotropic medications and developmental disabilities: The international consensus handbook.* Columbus: Ohio State University Nisonger Center.

Reiss, S., Levitan, G.W., & Szyszko, J. (1982). Emotional disturbance and mental retardation: Diagnostic overshadowing. *American Journal of Mental Deficiency, 86*(6), 567–574.

Spencer, D., Marshall, J., Post, B., Kulakodlu, M., Newschaffer, C., Dennen, T.,...Jain, A. (2013). Psychotropic medication use and polypharmacy in children with autism spectrum disorders. *Pediatrics, 132*(5), 833–840.

Stahl, S.M. (2002). *Essential psychopharmacology of antipsychotics and mood stabilizers.* New York, NY: Cambridge University Press.

Tyrer, S.P., Oliver-Africano, P.C., Ahmed, Z., Bouras, N., Cooray, S., Deb, S.,...Crawford, M. (2008). Risperidone, haloperidol and placebo in the treatment of aggressive, challenging behavior in patients with intellectual disability: A randomized, controlled trial. *Lancet, 371,* 57–63.

31

Speech, Language, and Communication Assessments and Interventions

Nancy Brady and Laura Hahn

- Communication forms and functions
- Preintentional communication: early communication before the communicative meaning is clear, including assessment and interventions for this stage of communication
- Intentional nonsymbolic communication: how communication becomes meaningful through the use of eye gaze, gestures, and vocalizations, including assessment and interventions for this stage of communication
- Symbolic communication: communicating through the use of speech, signs, and symbols, including assessment and interventions for this stage of communication
- Improving communication through an interdisciplinary team approach

Communication can be achieved in many ways. Most people think of speech as the primary way that individuals express themselves. Similarly, hearing is the typical way that communication is received for comprehension. However, communication can take on almost unlimited means. For example, all people communicate with gestures, body positions, vocal tone, facial expressions, laughing, and crying. These and other means of communication take on increasing importance for people with severe intellectual and developmental disabilities who may rely on nonspeech communication to convey important messages. Within this chapter, we briefly review communication forms and functions in people with intellectual disability, including people with limited vision and hearing. Our aim is to provide a knowledge base that serves as a platform to increase understanding of the value of all forms of communication, to inform assessment and intervention practices, and to improve interactions between all people, including those with severe intellectual and developmental disabilities.

Researchers and practitioners studying communication in people with severe intellectual and developmental disabilities have frequently employed a developmental perspective to describe communication in people with intellectual and developmental disabilities. Typically developing children attain well-recognized milestones by certain ages, and there also are well-recognized warning signs of developmental delay. The focus of a developmental approach is to describe a sequence of communication based on typically developing infants and young children. In our work, this approach has been useful for identifying communication behaviors that an individual currently uses to communicate as well as identifying communicative behaviors that may be appropriate goals for interventions. However, there are many exceptions to the typical developmental sequence of communication, particularly in the case of people with physical or sensory limitations. In the following sections, we present information about communication milestones within a developmental perspective, with the understanding that this perspective provides a basis for appreciating the many forms and functions of early communication. This approach is not meant to limit explorations of augmentative and alternative communication (AAC) forms (i.e., any form of communication other than speech—e.g., sign language, gesture use, use of graphic symbols with or without speech output). AAC may be appropriate for an individual at any stage of communication development (Beukelman & Miranda, 2013). Assessment and intervention strategies that have been developed and used within specified developmental stages are presented. The chapter concludes with a discussion of service delivery implications and future directions.

COMMUNICATION FORMS AND FUNCTIONS

Borrowing from the work on typical development, researchers have described the many ways that people can and do communicate with and without speech. In typical development, the focus of nonspeech communication has been on describing behaviors that occur within the first year, before an infant's first word. These communication behaviors include gestures, vocalizations, and facial expressions. Important transitions occur during this period leading up to word use. Notably, infants make a transition from perlocutionary (or preintentional) to illocutionary (or intentional) communication (Iverson & Thal, 1998). This transition, which occurs almost without notice in typical development, can be a major accomplishment for some people with severe intellectual and developmental disabilities. Another transition point is moving into more symbolic forms of communication such as speech, sign language, or graphic AAC communication. Further transitions in communication are typically marked by increased linguistic complexity such as multiword utterances. Figure 31.1 depicts the continuum of early communication development in typically developing children.

The following subsections describe major accomplishments at the stages bounded by these transitions, specifically the preintentional, intentional, and symbolic stages of communication. Examples from people with severe intellectual and developmental disabilities are included, along with assessment and intervention strategies within these stages.

Single orientation (person or object/event)

Person-directed eye gaze (or body orientation)

Person-directed eye gaze with vocalization

Person-directed eye gaze with gesture

Object-directed eye gaze

Object-directed eye gaze with vocalization

Object-directed eye gaze with gesture

Dual focus (person and object; triadic eye gaze)

Gesture with dual focus

Vocalization with dual focus

Triadic eye gaze

Independent production of single words

Independent production of multiword phrase

← Preintentional ──── ← Intentional nonsymbolic ─── ← Intentional symbolic

Figure 31.1. Continuum of early communication development.

Preintentional Communication

The hallmark of preintentional communication, the earliest stage of communication, is that the meaning or intent of the communicator must be inferred by communication partners—that is, the people with whom an individual is communicating. For example, when an infant cries, partners infer that the infant is hungry or uncomfortable. Similarly, when an individual with severe intellectual and developmental disabilities vocalizes loudly, partners may infer that he or she is uncomfortable or unhappy. Partners may have to guess the cause of the apparent discontent. For example, the individual may need to be repositioned or may be too hot or too cold. However, other than a specific history of experiences with the individual, there are no clear indications of the meaning of the individual's vocalizations. This type of communication can be extremely difficult for unfamiliar partners to interpret.

Assessments Assessing how an individual communicates in various contexts (i.e., in different communication contexts) can help educational teams to plan interventions and measure progress resulting from those interventions. Standardized assessments are of limited value because they do not accommodate the unique ways in which many people with severe intellectual and developmental disabilities communicate. Assessments for people who are communicating primarily with preintentional behaviors may be most useful when the assessment describes or catalogs the different ways in which the individual responds across various communicative contexts or situations (e.g., home, school; Crais, 2011; Wilcox & Woods, 2011). The Inventory of Potential Communicative Acts (IPCA; Sigafoos et al., 2000) is an instrument developed to guide interviews with knowledgeable partners about an individual's communication. The interview presents open-ended questions that ask, for example, how the individual indicates that he or she is glad, content, or enthusiastic about a particular activity or object. Responses to these questions are then transferred to a summary grid organized according to potentially communicative behaviors and communication functions. Through this process, behaviors such as tensing or extending body parts, lip smacking, or grimacing might be recognized as communicative. The communication functions referenced on the IPCA include requests for objects and actions, protests, comments, attention to self, and social conventions (e.g., greetings). Once behaviors are added to the grid, the assessment team can then inspect it to determine how the participant is using various behaviors to communicate different functions. For example, an individual may have a small set of behaviors that are used across many different functions, such as stiffening the body to indicate fear and also to indicate when he or she does not want to change positions. Alternatively, the individual may have many different forms that all correspond to the same communicative functions, such as smacking his or her lips, vocalizing loudly, or reaching toward food to indicate hunger.

Another valuable assessment tool is the Communication Matrix (Rowland & Fried-Oken, 2010). This assessment tool also relies on parent or caregiver report but utilizes a computerized interface. Parents (or other knowledgeable caregivers) indicate how the individual communicates for various functions (e.g., that he or she is hungry, tired, or uncomfortable). Based on the responses obtained, the computer program generates a profile that indicates the individual's current stage of communication.

For example, based on the answers given by a caregiver, it could be determined that an individual frequently communicates with preintentional means, such as smiling to express comfort, and sometimes will use gestures to communicate requests or protests. In this case, it could be said that the individual had mastered the level of preintentional behavior and was at an emerging level for intentional communication. This information can be very helpful in terms of educational programming, because the educational team can identify strengths and weaknesses in a person's communication profile. Goals that aim to increase the use of existing behaviors across multiple environments, as well as goals aimed at helping people learn new communication behaviors, can be based on the person's profile, derived from this assessment.

The IPCA and the Communication Matrix are two examples of methods that have been developed to help assess communication in people who communicate with nonconventional, idiosyncratic means. They serve as models of how to obtain information about the communicative intent of various behaviors that may not have been thought of as communicative. Hence, these and similar assessments are also a valuable part of the intervention process because they facilitate recognition and validation of these preintentional communicative behaviors. As described in the next subsection, this recognition is critical in helping people develop additional means to communicate and in helping people to be more effective with their current communication.

Interventions Interventions for people who are communicating primarily at the preintentional level have two broad areas of focus. First, an emphasis should be directed on increasing the number of communication partners who understand the individual's communication by teaching them what behaviors to look for and what functions those behaviors serve. Preintentional communication is often idiosyncratic. Once the functions of these behaviors have been identified using assessment instruments such as those discussed previously, interventionists should educate additional partners about specific behaviors. For example, if assessment results indicate that the participant cries and stands in front of the refrigerator when he or she is hungry, this information can be shared with other communication partners. When more communication partners are aware of the communication function of these behaviors, the individual will likely be a more successful communicator. Intervention teams may create "dictionaries" that describe the meanings of these behaviors. These dictionaries can accompany the individual across environments and may be particularly helpful for interactions with unfamiliar partners and during transitions to new communication environments.

A second focus should be on teaching new behaviors that may be intentional communication behaviors and may be more readily understood by others. These strategies will be described more in the upcoming subsection on interventions for intentional communicators. In addition to teaching new behaviors, the information derived from the assessment interviews can help identify optimal intervention contexts, such as specific activities at home or school, for intervention to take place.

Intentional Nonsymbolic Communication

Intentional communication marks a change from partners needing to infer the intent of communication to that intent being made clear to the communication partner. This clarity comes from the use of eye gaze, gestures, and vocalization, which are used to request or share interest with a communication partner. In our work, we have invoked the terminology put forth by Sigafoos and colleagues and refer to these as potentially communicative behaviors (PCBs; Sigafoos et al., 2000). For example, when a toddler looks from her father to her cup, vocalizes, and reaches toward her cup on a shelf, it is clear that she wants the cup. Or when a student with severe disabilities looks up when a teacher walks in, reaches his arm out toward the teacher, and smiles broadly, it is clear the student is greeting the teacher. However, what is it about this behavior that enables one to make these inferences?

First, there must be evidence that the child is attending to both a communication partner and an object or event of interest (Brady, McLean, McLean, & Johnston, 1995; Wetherby, Cain, Yonclas, & Walker, 1988). In the example in the previous paragraph, this was shown by shifting eye gaze between the communicative partner (the father) and the object of interest (the sippy cup). An eye gaze shift is one of the most common means used to show dual attention to a communicative partner and object or event of interest. However, it is not the

only means. Another way to show dual attention is to gesture toward a person and an object or event. For example, giving an object to someone clearly indicates dual orientation between the object being given and the person who is receiving the object. Similarly, placing someone's hand on an object or pushing an object toward someone indicates focus on both the object and person. Individuals with very limited vision and/or motor movements may demonstrate dual orientation through other means, such as shifting their body toward or away from their communication partner and an object of interest (Brady & Bashinski, 2008).

Second, there must be some indication that the individual intends to communicate something through this PCB that is directed toward a communicative partner. As was the case for preintentional communication, it is often easier for familiar communication partners to recognize the communicative intent, but there are clues that can help unfamiliar as well as familiar communicative partners to infer what someone is trying to communicate. The clues that led to inferring that the child in our example was requesting her sippy cup included the child reaching toward the cup and orienting to the communication partner and a history of frequently drinking out of the sippy cup. In addition, it is likely that she will persist in this behavior until she is given the sippy cup. Also, if she stops reaching once she receives the cup, it is another clue that this was indeed what she wanted. In our work, if we cannot make a reasonable assumption about the intended meaning using all the available clues, then we would not describe the behavior as intentional. For example, if a child gestured toward a favorite toy with the focus of attention directed solely toward that object, we would describe this act as preintentional. However, if the child combined his or her gesture with a look toward the communication partner and persisted in gesturing until he or she received an appropriate consequence, we would consider the act to be intentional.

Distinguishing intentional from nonintentional communication is important for several reasons. Communication partners are more likely to respond to intentional (as opposed to unintentional) communication behaviors (Warren & Yoder, 1998). Often, these responses serve to promote further communication developments by adding linguistic information. For example, following the gesture-plus-look example, a common response would be something like, "Oh, you want the toy," while giving the toy to the child. This verbal mapping is thought to be associated with improved vocabulary gains by children (Carey, 1978; Harris, Barrett, Jones, & Brookes, 1988). In addition, increased rates of prelinguistic communication are associated with the transition to symbolic communication. Typically developing children who are communicating intentionally at a rate of at least once per minute during motivating interactions begin to talk within a short period of time (Wetherby et al., 1988). Thus, it is important to assess the amount and types of intentional communication used and also encourage the use of intentional communication through intervention.

Assessments   Obtaining information from parents or caregivers, as discussed in the previous section on preintentional communication, is still an extremely helpful and valid method for identifying communication forms and functions used at this stage. An example of a caregiver assessment that was developed specifically for support workers who work with people with severe intellectual and developmental disabilities is the Triple C: Checklist of Communicative Competencies (Iacono, West, Bloomberg, & Johnson, 2009). It is intended to be used with people who are preintentional communicators or in the early stages of intentional communication. Based on the caregiver's report, a speech-language pathologist (SLP) or other communication specialist determines which of six communication stages best describes the individual's communication. Similarly, Cascella (2005) created a checklist with 14 different communication forms (e.g., reaching gestures, head nods or shakes) and 14 different communicative functions (e.g., communicates to draw attention to self). The checklist was used to describe the expressive communication behaviors of 14 adults with severe intellectual and developmental disabilities. Cascella (2004) also developed a similar checklist to assess receptive communication abilities. Items for this checklist were drawn from established measures of early receptive communication. Fourteen behaviors are on the checklist, including those related to physically turning toward sounds in the environment (e.g., television) and comprehending social greetings (e.g., "Hi"). The author points out that checklists such as these have high validity (i.e., they measure what was intended) because they ask about behaviors that are within familiar contexts.

In addition to these caregiver report measures, a number of direct assessments have been designed to determine how children will respond when provided with specific opportunities (or temptations). These assessments are designed to provide opportunities for children to communicate nonsymbolically (i.e., with gestures and vocalizations). Two common assessments are the Communication and Symbolic Behavior Scales Developmental Profile (CSBS DP™; Wetherby & Prizant, 2002) and the Early Social Communication Scales (ESCS; Seibert, Hogan, & Mundy, 1982). The protocols used in each of these assessments are scripted interactions with a predictable pattern. Activities designed as request opportunities provide motivation to communicate by use of sabotage (e.g., a wind-up toy is broken so that it will not work) or using a delay (e.g., the tester holds up an unblown balloon to her lips and waits). Activities designed as joint attention opportunities involve some element of surprise, such as presentation of a novel action toy in a bag of toys.

Modified assessment protocols have been developed that are aimed at minimizing the effect of sensory deficits and maximizing interest for different ages and abilities. For example, Brady and Bashinski (2008) modified their assessment protocol for use with deafblind children. Vestibular and movement activities, such as bouncing on a minitrampoline or feeling a slinky, replaced visual activities that required vision or eye–hand coordination. For example, children were bounced on a minitrampoline, and then the bouncing stopped and the assessor waited expectantly. Once a child indicated, through body movement, orientation, and/or vocalizations, that he or she wanted the bouncing to continue, the assessor would start bouncing again. In a different study, Brady and colleagues (1995) created versions of assessment protocols that were designed to be motivating and age-appropriate for adults with intellectual and developmental disabilities. For example, interesting flashlights were available for assembly but batteries were missing—creating a need to ask for the batteries. The aim of all of these assessment protocols is to provide motivating contexts for sampling how people can and do communicate, rather than focusing on communication limits.

There are many different ways to summarize the results of the observational assessments we discussed. The overall rate of communication can be a helpful measure, as are descriptions of the different types of communicative behaviors observed and the types of functions communicated during the assessment protocol. Functions are usually described as behavior regulation, which include requests (i.e., indicating a want or desire) and rejecting communication acts (e.g., pushing away to indicate one does not want something), or joint attention, which includes commenting on an interesting object, event, or person; sharing affect (e.g., smiling to indicate enjoyment or to please in an activity); and, sometimes, making social greetings (Didden et al., 2009; Reichle, Rogers, & Barrett, 1984; Wetherby, 1986). We developed a scoring system to describe the communication observed during scripted assessment protocols—like those described previously—using a 12-point scale called the Communication Complexity Scale (CCS; Brady et al., 2012). The scale is designed to reflect preintentional, intentional nonsymbolic, and beginning symbolic forms of communication. Level 1 on the scale refers to basic alerting responses, such as a change in posture or tone that might be observed in someone with physical and/or sensory impairments. The highest level (12) refers to combining two or more symbols or words into a communicative utterance. In the Brady and colleagues (2012) study, we derived a score by averaging the highest three scores observed across the different tasks in our communication assessment protocols. This procedure seemed to compensate for individual preferences and associated differences in the motivational values of different assessment activities. That is, we expect participants to respond to only some of the items, so averaging the top three scores allowed for differential responsiveness. These overall scores are interpretable according to the developmental continuum discussed previously, spanning preintentional nonsymbolic (Scores 1–5) to intentional nonsymbolic (Scores 6–10) and, finally, intentional symbolic (Scores 11–12).

An important goal for assessment is that it helps formulate effective interventions. Results of caregiver assessments and direct observational assessments can be combined in order to create a more complete picture of communication strengths and needs (Brady & Halle, 1997; Ogletree & Fischer, 1996). For example, results of an observational assessment may indicate that an individual rarely produced PCBs during scripted interactions, yet the caregiver report indicates that the individual frequently uses idiosyncratic behaviors to request objects in familiar contexts. A profile such as this would suggest that the individual requests when motivated to do so but uses forms that are not likely to be recognized by unfamiliar communication partners. Interventions

for this individual could focus on teaching him or her to request with more conventional gestures and/or symbols that are readily understood by others.

Interventions   Interventions have been developed to increase the use of intentional nonsymbolic communication. For example, Fey and colleagues (2006) found that children who participated in 6 months of an intervention package described as prelinguistic milieu teaching (PMT) showed significant increases in prelinguistic communication, including natural gestures and vocalizations, compared with a control group that did not experience this intervention. Much like the assessments described earlier, the goals of this intervention are to support and promote the use of communicative gestures and vocalizations during motivating routines (Warren et al., 2006). These routines can be as basic as rolling a ball back and forth or can be more complicated routines such as playing Peekaboo. Franco, Davis, and Davis (2013) demonstrated that PMT can also be successful with nonverbal school-age children with autism. Individualized routines in this study included requesting an adult to rub hands and feet with a therapy brush and requesting an adult to play "five little piggies." Brady and Bashinski (2008) developed routines that were motivating and accessible for children with deafblindness. For example, one child liked to spin on a Sit 'n Spin toy. During intervention, he learned to request more spinning by placing the communication partner's hand on the Sit 'n Spin when spinning paused.

Gesture communication has also been targeted in behavioral interventions such as functional communication training (Carr & Durand, 1985). Functional communication training is aimed at decreasing challenging behaviors (e.g., hitting, biting, and repetitive behaviors such as rocking) by increasing appropriate functional communicative skills to share basic needs and wants. These behaviors are ideal for teaching new functional communications, because the individual is already attempting to communicate and motivated to do so. Most of this work focuses on requesting and rejecting skills, including escape and avoidance behaviors (i.e., a form of rejecting behavior that focuses on getting away from or avoiding an undesired item or unwanted activity in an appropriate way). For example, instead of throwing a toy to show that it is unwanted, a child may learn to shake his or her head to reject the unwanted item. Similarly, instead of screaming to request a wanted toy, a child may learn to reach or point to the wanted item. Both of these examples highlight the use of replacement of a behavior that is socially inappropriate, socially stigmatizing, or hard to interpret with a behavior that is more socially appropriate (Brady & Halle, 2002; Reichle, Halle, & Drasgow, 1998). An important aim of this approach is reducing the inappropriate behaviors by replacement with behaviors that are socially acceptable and clearly communicative. Challenging behaviors may decrease because the individual can clearly indicate what he or she wants or does not want with socially acceptable means. An important consideration, however, is that new communication behavior needs to be as efficient and easy to use as the replaced behavior (Johnston, 2006). In other words, partners should respond as consistently to the new behaviors as they did to the behaviors they are trying to replace.

Other intervention approaches have focused on the use of objects to represent meaning. For example, use of tangible symbol systems is a communication approach that lies somewhere between nonsymbolic intentional and symbolic communication (Rowland & Schweigert, 2000). Tangible symbols include both three-dimensional and two-dimensional symbols that are created to suit the sensory and cognitive abilities as well as the experiences of individual users. Note that tangible symbols bear a physical resemblance to their referent (i.e., the object they represent) and hence are designed to be highly representative. For example, a miniature bowling ball could be used to represent bowling or a piece of Velcro could be used to represent Velcro shoes. The symbol has or acquires meaning for an individual user based on his or her unique experiences. Hence, tangible symbol systems do not come ready-made and must be developed for each individual. It has been suggested that tangible symbols may be particularly useful for people with severe intellectual and developmental disabilities, including those with visual and/or hearing impairments, because this system places low demands on the individual's memory and representational skills. Common communication skills taught through tangible symbol systems include requesting, naming, choice making, and directing the attention of others (for a review, see Roche et al., 2014).

Both receptive and expressive communication can be addressed through tangible symbol systems. On the receptive end, people may learn to respond to tangible symbols as cues for upcoming events. For example, an individual may learn that when the bowling ball symbol is presented, it is time to get ready to bowl. Another frequently employed receptive use of tangible symbols is within schedules or calendar boxes (i.e., a visual representation of the activities that are to happen during the school day; Janssen, Riksen-Walraven, & van Dijk, 2004). An individual could learn that the order of the symbols represents the order of activities to be followed in the classroom or at home. Once an activity is completed, the adjacent symbol indicates what is to follow, and so on. Expressive requesting can be achieved by selecting from an array of tangible symbols that represent highly motivating activities. These skills can be taught with familiar teaching approaches such as by prompting for a response (e.g., signing and/or saying "what do you want?") and then waiting for the individual to select a specific tangible symbol. For people with severe intellectual and developmental disabilities and visual impairments, the teacher or SLP will often help guide the individual's hand to the array of available tactile symbols for them to manually scan. Once a specific symbol is selected, the individual gets the opportunity to play with or use the item requested. Individuals can "select" a symbol by physically handing it to a partner or directly touching or pointing to the symbol, or through directed eye gaze. Individuals with multiple disabilities including deafblindness have learned to request preferred activities using tangible symbols (Rowland & Schweigert, 1989; Trief, 2007). Additional communicative functions such as commenting or sharing an experience could also be accomplished through tangible symbols, though more research on using tangible symbol systems beyond requesting is needed.

Symbolic Communication

Symbolic communication includes expressing oneself through the use of speech, signs, or graphic symbols with or without accompanying speech generation. The advantages to using any of these forms of communication, in comparison to nonsymbolic forms, are that the individual can communicate about something outside of his or her immediate context. For example, if someone is hungry and wants to request pita chips, he or she could request pita chips by signing or symbol selection even if there are no chips present. Nonsymbolic gestures would not be adequate in this scenario because chips are not present to point to or reach toward. In addition, symbolic communication can be used to communicate more complex, sentence-like utterances and thus is less limiting than nonsymbolic forms.

Although speech is the form of symbolic communication used by most people in face-to-face communication, it is not frequently targeted in interventions for older children or adults with severe intellectual and developmental disabilities. However, facilitating speech sound development may be an appropriate goal for many people, because improved speech can improve overall communication, even for people who communicate primarily with nonspeech modes. For example, communication partners may respond more to people who make speech sounds, even if they are not intelligible (Gros-Louis, West, Goldstein, & King, 2006). Increased partner responsiveness has been associated with better communication outcomes (Brady, Herynk, & Fleming, 2010; Hart, 1991). One of the best predictors of speech development is the ability to imitate speech (Rogers, Hepburn, Stackhouse, & Wehner, 2003); however, children with severe intellectual and developmental disabilities often do not imitate. DeThorne, Johnson, Walder, and Mahurin-Smith (2009) summarized alternative strategies that could be used to promote speech sound development in nonimitators, including use of AAC and partners' imitation of child sounds with or without exaggerated intonation. Beyond promoting speech sound use in general, behavioral approaches have demonstrated success in shaping the development of specific speech sounds in children with autism (e.g., Koegel, O'Dell, & Dunlap, 1988). In shaping, successive approximations of target sounds are reinforced in a massed-trial training paradigm. Shaping procedures require extensive, intensive interventions applied by skilled interventionists.

For the reasons presented previously, expressive communication interventions have increasingly targeted symbolic forms of AAC for people with severe intellectual and developmental disabilities (Snell, Lih-Yuan, & Hoover, 2006). The following subsections summarize the assessment concerns that are specific to symbolic communication and summarize some of the primary AAC interventions that have been applied with people with severe intellectual and developmental disabilities. As another chapter (Chapter 32) in this volume is devoted to AAC, only a brief summary of assessing and teaching AAC will be provided here.

Assessment   In addition to identifying how an individual currently communicates using the strategies previously discussed, it may be necessary to assess the sensory, motor, and discrimination requirements associated with the use of different AAC modes such as signing or selecting graphic symbols. For example, communicating through the exchange of small graphic symbols requires visual acuity sufficient to identify the symbol, motor ability to pick up and give the symbol, and the ability to discriminate this symbol from others and associate it with a referent.

A review of assessment of specific capabilities associated with various forms of AAC is presented in Beukelman and Mirenda (2013). Strategies to formally and informally assess motoric, sensory, cognitive, and language capabilities are discussed. Beukelman and Mirenda point out that the goal of capability assessment is to gather sufficient information to make current and future decisions regarding AAC. Because many different specialty areas are represented by these various capabilities, it is best to involve a team of specialists who represent expertise in each area of capability as part of the AAC team. More on using a team approach to assessment and intervention is presented in a following section.

Two important points should be remembered when planning and conducting AAC assessments for learners with severe intellectual and developmental disabilities. First, the goal is to find systems that will or could work with an individual (rather than identifying limits). The second is that the assessment process may be lengthy and it may be best to use an ongoing assessment model that incorporates assessment during intervention activities. For example, the intervention team may periodically conduct probes to determine what items are preferred by a particular individual. Similarly, the team may periodically probe different sizes of symbols to determine the visual acuity needed to use different symbols. Incorporating assessment during intervention will prevent a lengthy period of waiting for the assessment results before beginning intervention—an undesirable course (Beukelman & Mirenda, 2013).

In addition to assessing the capabilities required to communicate with various forms of AAC, assessing an individual's preference for one system over others may lead to more successful long-term outcomes and promote self-determination (Sigafoos, O'Reilly, Ganz, Lancioni, & Schlosser, 2005). Van der Meer, Sigafoos, O'Reilly, and Lancioni (2011) synthesized results from seven studies (with a total of eight different participants) that compared preferences for communicating with a speech-generating device (SGD; i.e., an electronic device that allows the user to select or type out a message that the device will then speak aloud), physical exchange, or manual signs (although only one study included manual signs). Participants in the reviewed studies were taught to use multiple AAC systems, such as a SGD and the Picture Exchange Communication System (PECS; a form of AAC in which the individual gives a picture to request an item), and then the participants were allowed to choose which form of AAC to use in requesting opportunities. The authors found that most of the participants showed a preference for one form of AAC over another. Although additional research is needed, preference for one form of AAC over another is likely to influence long-term use of a particular form of AAC. For example, if an individual preferred to communicate with a SGD, it seems likely that the individual would communicate more often and with less prompting using this preferred method.

Interventions Intervention strategies outlined for use in presymbolic interventions have also been applied to symbolic AAC interventions. The key difference is that instead of modeling and prompting the use of a gesture or vocalization to communicate, interventionists model and prompt the individual to say a word, make a sign, or select a symbol.

Sign language was initially a popular mode of communication targeted in intervention, but today it is less popular because communication partners must also learn sign language, and this limits its use across a variety of communication partners. Many research and intervention programs have demonstrated progress learning to communicate with graphic symbol systems (for review, see Mirenda, 1997; Sigafoos et al., 2008; Snell et al., 2006; Van der Meer & Rispoli, 2010). The type of symbol used may make a difference for some learners; therefore, assessments should determine whether an individual is better able to discriminate pictures, line drawings, or more abstract types of symbols (Schlosser & Sigafoos, 2002). In addition, symbols can be "selected" in a variety of ways. They can be directly pointed to or selected through eye gaze, selected via scanning methods, or exchanged. In exchange-based systems such as PECS (Bondy & Frost, 1994), the individual is taught to physically exchange a symbol with his

or her communication partner. The advantage of exchange-based systems such as PECS is that the communication partner is aware of communication attempts because the partner actively receives the symbol(s), thus assuring that the partner is attending to the learner's communication attempts.

The mode of symbol selection can vary in accordance with the capabilities of the individual communicator. For example, microswitches have been used to indicate preferences and make choices (for reviews, see Lancioni, O'Reilly, & Basili, 2001; Parker, Grimmett, & Summers, 2008). Switches can be activated by any voluntary movement such as eye movement, head movement, or limb movement. Individuals without voluntary movement have learned to use computers with brain–computer interfaces (Jirayucharoensak, Hemakom, Chonnaparamutt, & Israsena, 2011), but use of this technology for learners with severe intellectual and developmental disabilities, as well as physical impairments, is still under investigation.

Interventions have been adapted to meet the needs of people with sensory impairments. For example, Ali, MacFarland, and Umbreit (2011) demonstrated that children with multiple disabilities that included a visual impairment learned to request items using a modification of the PECS system. Instead of using two-dimensional graphic images that would not be discriminable by these participants, three-dimensional tangible symbols with Velcro on the bottom were used. The participants learned to select and exchange these tangible symbols to request preferred objects. Two-dimensional symbols can also be modified to enhance visibility (e.g., Heller, Allgood, Ware, Arnold, & Castelle, 1996). Sign language for people who are deafblind has been adapted by teaching communication partners to sign directly into the hands of the individual in order to allow him or her to feel the hand shapes (Knoors & Vervloed, 2003).

Summary of Communication Forms and Functions

The previous sections have summarized a developmental approach to assessing and treating communication in people with severe intellectual and developmental disabilities. It is our view that identifying an individual's current communication forms and functions and describing these communication acts within the developmental perspective provided in this chapter can facilitate goal setting and attainment. A number of different assessments and interventions were described for each stage of communication. Thus, it is clear that there are appropriate communication assessments and interventions for all people, no matter their cognitive or sensory abilities.

Many of the intervention approaches described in this chapter can be combined to optimize communication outcomes. For example, a modified object-exchange communication system could be addressed through a specific intervention program at school. As the individual is learning to use this system, additional interventions could target the use of nonsymbolic communication acts including gestures and vocalizations at specific times when it would be difficult to use the tangible symbols, such as during swim class or on the playground. This combined approach is aimed at promoting communication across contexts and with many different communication partners. A key component to achieving communication improvements is the instructional environment, including the communication partner. The following section describes intervention teaming.

IMPROVING COMMUNICATION THROUGH AN INTERDISCIPLINARY TEAM APPROACH

Throughout this chapter, we have emphasized the complex communication needs of people with severe intellectual and developmental disabilities. A team approach to assessment and intervention is ideal because it allows for people with unique and complementary skill sets to join forces in providing comprehensive individualized communication interventions. Clearly, the most important members of the team are the individual with severe intellectual and developmental disabilities and her or his communication partners. Ideally partners would include people who have close personal relationships as well as friends and people who are primarily service providers. Blackstone and Hunt-Berg, (2003) developed a comprehensive tool for assessing complex communication needs within a social networks framework. Goals that promote social interactions are identified by team members, including the various partners identified for a given individual.

Additional team members for school-age children typically include teachers and paraprofessionals and specialists such as occupational therapists, physical therapists, vision specialists, audiologists, social workers, and SLPs. School personnel such as teachers and paraprofessionals provide information about the communication needs associated with the student's curriculum and typical social communication within the school settings. The specialists are skilled in assessing people's sensory and motor needs related to communication. Social workers provide invaluable information about additional related services and often can help identify funding sources for communication equipment needs. Oftentimes, the SLP not only assesses communication strengths and needs of the student within contexts but also serves as the person who gathers information from the rest of the team and helps design interventions based on these assessments. The SLP, teachers, and other team members share responsibility for measuring progress and making changes as needed.

Team membership will vary according to the life stage of the individual with severe intellectual and developmental disabilities. At different transition points, people with knowledge about contexts that the individual is likely to move into are vital for effective planning. For example, communication needs in high school will be markedly different from those in elementary school, and it is important to plan for these differences as early as possible. Similarly, planning for the communication needs of future living environments is necessary.

Team members help educate each other about the best ways to interact with each other and with the person with severe intellectual and developmental disabilities to promote communication. For example, a vision specialist can help identify optimum lighting or visual field restraints for an individual and help ensure that these parameters are taken into consideration during instruction (and outside of instruction). Family members can alert team members about special events going on at home that might be potential communication topics. Communication between team members can be enhanced with social media so that all team members stay abreast of current developments.

FUTURE DIRECTIONS

People with severe intellectual and developmental disabilities are more visible and included in society than ever before. This means that it is incumbent upon the professionals who serve them to support the communication needs of these people and promote their functioning and participation in everyday life. This has led to improved research on communication assessments and interventions for people with severe intellectual and developmental disabilities, as we discussed in this chapter. In 2010, Snell et al. reported that more than 100 articles in the previous 20 years reported positive changes in some aspect of communication for people with severe intellectual and developmental disabilities as a result of communication interventions. Thus, evidence for varied approaches exists, and an important current and future direction is to increase awareness of this literature and thereby promote interventions for people with severe intellectual and developmental disabilities.

Also, changes in the way that the World Health Organization (WHO) classifies people with intellectual and developmental disabilities may lead to significant changes in the way communication disorders are assessed and treated. The WHO developed the *International Classification of Functioning, Disability and Health* (*ICF;* 2001, 2007) as a holistic framework that addresses the individual's functional abilities that may be related to a health condition. The goal of the ICF is to change how disability is thought about and to provide a set of descriptors that can be used, shared, and understood by practitioners in multiple fields (e.g., health, education, social services) to promote positive outcomes and life experiences. The ICF can be used at an individual level (e.g., assessment of functioning or treatment planning), at an institutional level (e.g., determining what services are needed and how effective those services are), and at a social level (e.g., determining eligibility criteria for state or government entitlements or developing policies to improve human functioning).

The five domains of the ICF are Body Functions, Body Structures, Activity, Participation, and Environmental and Personal Factors. All of these domains can be used by a member of the instructional team to help develop and implement treatment and intervention plans. For example, the Body Functions domain can be used by an SLP to classify issues related to voice and speech functions or global mental functions that affect an individual's ability to use and produce speech. An SLP or teacher can also use the Activity and Participation domains to explain that an individual's capacity for functioning in his or her environment can be improved with the support of AAC to help the

person communicate with others. Furthermore, the ICF, especially its focus on participation in everyday life, aligns with the assessment and intervention model most AAC specialists use (Beukelman & Mirenda, 2013).

There are several barriers to the utility of the ICF for people with severe intellectual and developmental disabilities and complex communication needs. The ICF does not use a developmental approach for describing functioning abilities, which has implications for proper identification of impairments or delays in speech and language development. In response, Ellingson and Simeonsson (2011) have refined some of the ICF codes from a developmental perspective to create developmental code sets for children of ages 0–2 years, 3–5 years, 6–12 years, and 13–17 years (visit http://www.icfcydevelopmentalcodesets.com for details). It has also been noted that within the communication items of the ICF, there is redundancy coupled with a need for more clarity or rewording (Rowland et al., 2012). The biggest challenge associated with the ICF, however, is how to implement the ICF as a universal qualifier (Simeonsson, Sauer-Lee, Granlund, & Bjorck-Akesson, 2010. In response to this challenge, the WHO and the American Psychological Association are working to develop a standardized manual for using the ICF (Threats, 2008).

In addition to improved research on communication assessments and interventions, recent and future technological advancements will be particularly important for promoting communication and supporting day-to-day functioning in people with severe intellectual and developmental disabilities. Many common consumer technologies can be used to support the communication needs of people with severe intellectual and developmental disabilities, such as tablet computers, which offer affordability, portability, and acceptability in today's society. In addition, numerous apps have been, and are being, developed that can be used to promote communication needs in people with severe intellectual and developmental disabilities. Innovative technologies are also creating new opportunities for communication, such as eye gaze and brain behavior interfaces. However, these technologies are more expensive, and access to them is more difficult. Nonetheless, in the coming years, technology, including innovative technologies, will become even more supportive of complex communication needs and more accessible for those who need it.

SUMMARY

Individuals with severe intellectual and developmental disabilities are more visible and included in today's society, which has led to improved understanding of the communication needs of these people. The use of a developmental approach for assessing and treating communication in people with severe intellectual and developmental disabilities is important for identifying an individual's current communication forms and functions and facilitates goal setting and attainment. In addition, this approach helps to identify effective assessments and interventions for the individual's level of communication. The use of a team approach to assessment and intervention is ideal for people with severe intellectual and developmental disabilities because it allows for people with unique and complementary skill sets to join forces in providing comprehensive individualized communication interventions. Recent and future technological advancements, as well as continued research on communication assessment and intervention, will be particularly important for promoting communication and supporting day-to-day functioning in people with severe intellectual and developmental disabilities.

FOR FURTHER THOUGHT AND DISCUSSION

1. A new student who has severe intellectual and developmental disabilities is assigned to your special education classroom. What would you do to figure out the student's stage of communication?

2. You have decided to take a team approach to help support the communication needs of a student in your class. Who would you want to include on your team, and why?

REFERENCES

Ali, E., MacFarland, S.Z., & Umbreit, J. (2011). Effectiveness of combining tangible symbols with the Picture Exchange Communication System to teach requesting skills to children with multiple disabilities including visual impairment. *Education and Training in Autism and Developmental Disabilities, 46*(3), 425–435.

Beukelman, D.R., & Mirenda, P. (2013). *Augmentative and alternative communication: Supporting children and adults with complex communication needs* (4th ed.). Baltimore, MD: Paul H. Brookes Publishing Co.

Blackstone, S., & Hunt-Berg, M. (2003). *Social networks: Augmentative communicators and their communication partners.* Verona, WI: Attainment.

Bondy, A.S., & Frost, L.A. (1994). The Picture Exchange Communication System. *Focus on Autistic Behavior, 9,* 1–19.

Brady, N., & Bashinski, S. (2008). Increasing communication in children with concurrent vision and hearing loss. *Research and Practice for Persons with Severe Disabilities, 33*(1–2), 59–71.

Brady, N.C., Fleming, K., Thiemann-Bourque, K., Olswang, L., Dowden, P., Saunders, M., & Marquis, J. (2012). Development of the Communication Complexity Scale. *American Journal of Speech-Language Pathology, 21,* 16–28.

Brady, N., & Halle, J. (1997). Functional analysis of communicative behaviors. *Focus on Autism and Other Developmental Disabilities, 12,* 95–104.

Brady, N.C., & Halle, J.W. (2002). Breakdowns and repairs in conversations between beginning AAC users and their partners. In D.R. Beukelman & R. Reichle (Series Eds.) & J. Reichle, D.R. Beukelman, & J.C. Light (Vol. Eds.), *Communication and Language Intervention Series. Exemplary practices for beginning communicators: Implications for AAC* (pp. 323–352). Baltimore, MD: Paul H. Brookes Publishing Co.

Brady, N., Herynk, J., & Fleming, K. (2010). Communication input matters: Lessons from prelinguistic children learning to use AAC in preschool environments. *Early Childhood Services, 4,* 141–154.

Brady, N., McLean, J., McLean, L., & Johnston, S. (1995). Initiation and repair of intentional communication acts by adults with severe to profound cognitive disabilities. *Journal of Speech and Hearing Research, 38,* 1334–1348.

Carey, S. (1978). The child as a word learner. In M. Halle, J. Bresnan, & G.A. Miller (Eds.), *Linguistic theory and psychological reality* (pp. 264–293). Cambridge, MA: MIT Press.

Carr, E., & Durand, V. (1985). Reducing behavior problems through functional communication training. *Journal of Applied Behavior Analysis, 2*(2), 111–126.

Cascella, P.W. (2004). Receptive communication abilities among adults with significant intellectual disability. *Journal of Intellectual and Developmental Disability, 29*(1), 70–78.

Cascella, P.W. (2005). Expressive communication strengths of adults with severe to profound intellectual disabilities as reported by group home staff. *Communication Disorders Quarterly, 26*(3), 156–163.

Crais, E.R. (2011). Testing and beyond: Strategies and tools for evaluating and assessing infants and toddlers. *Language, Speech, and Hearing Services in Schools, 42*(3), 341–364.

DeThorne, L.S., Johnson, C.J., Walder, L., & Mahurin-Smith, J. (2009). When "Simon Says" doesn't work: Alternatives to imitation for facilitating early speech development. *American Journal of Speech-Language Pathology, 18*(2), 133–145.

Didden, R., Sigafoos, J., Korzilius, H., Baas, A., Lancioni, G.E., O'Reilly, M.F., & Curfs, L.M.G. (2009). Form and function of communicative behaviours in people with

Angelman syndrome. *Journal of Applied Research in Intellectual Disabilities, 22*(6), 526–537.

Ellingson, K.M., & Simeonsson, R.J. (2011). *WHO ICF-CY developmental code sets.* Retrieved from http://www.icfcydevelopmentalcodesets.com

Fey, M., Warren, S.F., Brady, N., Finestack, L., Bredin-Oja, S., & Fairchild, M. (2006). Early effect of prelinguistic milieu teaching and responsivity education for children with developmental delays and their parents. *Journal of Speech, Language, and Hearing Research, 49*, 526–547.

Franco, J.H., Davis, B.L., & Davis, J.L. (2013). Increasing social interaction using prelinguistic milieu teaching with nonverbal school-age children with autism. *American Journal of Speech-Language Pathology, 22*(3), 489–502.

Gros-Louis, J., West, M.J., Goldstein, M.H., & King, A.P. (2006). Mothers provide differential feedback to infants' prelinguistic sounds. *International Journal of Behavioral Development, 30*(6), 509–516.

Harris, M., Barrett, M., Jones, D., & Brookes, S. (1988). Linguistic input and early word meaning. *Journal of Child Language, 15*(1), 77–94.

Hart, B. (1991). Input frequency and children's first words. *First Language, 11*, 289–300.

Heller, K.W., Allgood, M.H., Ware, S., Arnold, S.E., & Castelle, M.D. (1996). Initiating requests during community-based vocational training by students with mental retardation and sensory impairments. *Research in Developmental Disabilities, 17*(3), 173–184.

Iacono, T., West, D., Bloomberg, K., & Johnson, H. (2009). Reliability and validity of the revised Triple C: Checklist of Communicative Competencies for adults with severe and multiple disabilities. *Journal of Intellectual Disability Research, 53*(1), 44–53.

Iverson, J.M.., & Thal, D.J. (1998). Communicative transitions: There's more to the hand than meets the eye. In S.F. Warren & J. Reichle (Series Eds.) & A.M. Wetherby, S.F. Warren, & J. Reichle (Vol. Eds.), *Communication and Language Intervention Series: Vol. 7. Transitions in prelinguistic communication* (pp. 59–86). Baltimore, MD: Paul H. Brookes Publishing Co.

Janssen, M., Riksen-Walraven, J.M., & van Dijk, J. (2004). Enhancing the interactive competence of deafblind children: Do intervention effects endure? *Journal of Developmental and Physical Disabilities, 16*(1), 73–94.

Jirayucharoensak, S., Hemakom, A., Chonnaparamutt, W., & Israsena, P. (2011, July 21–23). *Design and evaluation of a picture-based P300 AAC system.* Paper presented at the Proceedings of the Fifth International Conference on Rehabilitation Engineering and Assistive Technology, Bangkok, Thailand.

Johnston, S. (2006). Considering response efficiency in the selection and use of AAC systems. *Journal of Speech-Language-Pathology and Applied Behavior Analysis, 1*, 193–206.

Knoors, H., & Vervloed, M.P. (2003). Educational programming for deaf children with multiple disabilities: Accommodating special needs. *Oxford handbook of deaf studies, language, and education* (pp. 82–94). Oxford, United Kingdom: Oxford Handbooks Online. Retrieved from http://www.oxfordhandbooks.com/view/10.1093 /oxfordhb/9780199750986.001.0001/oxfordhb-978019 9750986-e-006

Koegel, R.L., O'Dell, M.C., & Dunlap, G. (1988). Producing speech use in nonverbal autistic children by reinforcing attempts. *Journal of Autism and Developmental Disorders, 18*, 525–538.

Lancioni, G.E., O'Reilly, M.F., & Basili, G. (2001). Use of microswitches and speech output systems with people with severe/profound intellectual or multiple disabilities: A literature review. *Research in Developmental Disabilities, 22*(1), 21–40.

Mirenda, P. (1997). Supporting people with challenging behavior through functional communication training and AAC: Research review. *Augmentative and Alternative Communication, 13*, 207–224.

Ogletree, B.T., & Fischer, M.A. (1996). Assessment targets and protocols for nonsymbolic communicators with profound disabilities. *Focus on Autism and Other Developmental Disabilities, 11*, 53–59.

Parker, A.T., Grimmett, E.S., & Summers, S. (2008). Evidence-based communication practices for children with visual impairments and additional disabilities: An examination of single-subject design studies. *Journal of Visual Impairment and Blindness, 102*(9), 540–552.

Reichle, J., Halle, J.W., & Drasgow, E. (1998). Implementing augmentative communication systems. In S.F. Warren & J. Reichle (Series Eds.) & A.M. Wetherby, S.F. Warren, & J. Reichle (Vol. Eds.), *Communication and Language Intervention Series: Vol. 7. Transitions in prelinguistic communication* (pp. 417–436). Baltimore, MD: Paul H. Brookes Publishing Co.

Reichle, J., Rogers, N., & Barrett, C. (1984). Establishing pragmatic discriminations among the communicative functions of requesting, rejecting, and commenting in an adolescent. *Journal of the Association for Persons with Severe Handicaps, 9*, 31–36.

Roche, L., Sigafoos, J., Lancioni, G.E., O'Reilly, M.F., Green, V.A., Sutherland, D.,...Edrisinha, C.D. (2014). Tangible symbols as an AAC option for people with developmental disabilities: A systematic review of intervention studies. *Augmentative and Alternative Communication, 30*(1), 28–39.

Rogers, S., Hepburn, S., Stackhouse, T., & Wehner, E. (2003). Imitation performance in toddlers with autism and those with other developmental disorders. *Journal of Child Psychology and Psychiatry, 44*, 763–781.

Rowland, C., & Fried-Oken, M. (2010). Communication Matrix: A clinical and research assessment tool targeting children with severe communication disorders. *Journal of Pediatric Rehabilitation Medicine: An Interdisciplinary Approach, 3*, 319–329.

Rowland, C., Fried-Oken, M., Steiner, S.A.M., Lollar, D., Phelps, R., Simeonsson, R.J., & Granlund, M. (2012). Developing the ICF-CY for AAC profile and code set for children who rely on AAC. *Augmentative and Alternative Communication, 28*(1), 21–32.

Rowland, C., & Schweigert, P. (1989). Tangible symbols: Symbolic communication for people with multisensory impairments. *Augmentative and Alternative Communication, 5*, 226–234.

Rowland, C., & Schweigert, P. (2000). Tangible symbols, tangible outcomes. *Augmentative and Alternative Communication, 16*(2), 61–78.

Schlosser, R., & Sigafoos, J. (2002). Selecting graphic symbols for an initial request lexicon: Integrative review. *Augmentative and Alternative Communication, 18*(2), 102–123.

Seibert, J.M., Hogan, A.E., & Mundy, P.C. (1982). Assessing interactional competencies: The Early Social-Communication Scales. *Infant Mental Health Journal, 3*(4), 244–258.

Sigafoos, J., Didden, R., Schlosser, R., Green, V., O'Reilly, M., & Lancioni, G. (2008). A review of intervention studies on teaching AAC to people who are deaf and blind. *Journal of Developmental and Physical Disabilities, 20*(1), 71–99.

Sigafoos, J., O'Reilly, M., Ganz, J.B., Lancioni, G.E., & Schlosser, R.W. (2005). Supporting self-determination in AAC interventions by assessing preference for communication devices. *Technology and Disability, 17*(3), 143–153.

Sigafoos, J., Woodyatt, G., Keen, D., Tait, K., Tucker, M., & Roberts-Pennell, D. (2000). Identifying potential communicative acts in children with developmental and physical disabilities. *Communication Disorders Quarterly, 21*, 77–86.

Simeonsson, R., Sauer-Lee, A., Granlund, M., & Bjorck-Akesson, E. (2010). Developmental and health assessment in rehabilitation with the ICF for Children and Youth. In E. Mpofu & T. Oakland (Eds.), *Rehabilitation and health assessment: Applying ICF guidelines* (pp. 27–46). New York, NY: Springer.

Snell, M.E., Brady, N., McLean, L., Ogletree, B.T., Siegel, E., Sylvester, L.,...Sevcik, R. (2010). Twenty years of communication intervention research with people who have severe intellectual and developmental disabilities. *American Journal on Intellectual and Developmental Disabilities, 115*(5), 364–380.

Snell, M.E., Lih-Yuan, C., & Hoover, K. (2006). Teaching augmentative and alternative communication to students with severe disabilities: A review of intervention research 1997–2003. *Research and Practice for Persons with Severe Disabilities, 31*(3), 203–214.

Threats, T. (2008). Use of the ICF for clinical practice in speech-language pathology. *International Journal of Speech-Language Pathology, 10*, 50–60.

Trief, E. (2007). The use of tangible cues for children with multiple disabilities and visual impairment. *Journal of Visual Impairment and Blindness, 101*(10), 613–619.

Van der Meer, L., & Rispoli, M. (2010). Communication interventions involving speech-generating devices for children with autism: A review of the literature. *Developmental Neurorehabilitation, 13*(4), 294–306.

Van der Meer, L., Sigafoos, J., O'Reilly, M.F., & Lancioni, G.E. (2011). Assessing preferences for AAC options in communication interventions for people with developmental disabilities: A review of the literature. *Research in Developmental Disabilities, 32*(5), 1422–1431.

Warren, S.F., Bredin-Oja, S.L., Fairchild Escalante, M., Finestack, L.H., Fey, M.E., & Brady, N.C. (2006). Responsivity education/prelinguistic milieu teaching. In R.J. McCauley & M.E. Fey (Eds.), *Treatment of language disorders in children* (pp. 47–77). Baltimore, MD: Paul H. Brookes Publishing Co.

Warren, S.F., & Yoder, P.J. (1998). Facilitating the transition from preintentional to intentional communication. In S.F. Warren & J. Reichle (Series Eds.) & A.M. Wetherby, S.F. Warren, & J. Reichle (Vol. Eds.), *Communication and Language Intervention Series: Vol. 7. Transitions in prelinguistic communication* (pp. 365–384). Baltimore, MD: Paul H. Brookes Publishing Co.

Wetherby, A.M. (1986). Ontogeny of communicative functions in autism. *Journal of Autism and Developmental Disorders, 16*, 295–316.

Wetherby, A., Cain, D.H., Yonclas, D.G., & Walker, V.G. (1988). Analysis of intentional communication of normal children from the prelinguistic to the multiword stage. *Journal of Speech and Hearing Research, 31*, 240–252.

Wetherby, A., & Prizant, B. (2002). *Communication and Symbolic Behavior Scales Developmental Profile (CSBS DP™)*, first normed edition. Baltimore, MD: Paul H. Brookes Publishing Co.

Wilcox, M.J., & Woods, J. (2011). Participation as a basis for developing early intervention outcomes. *Language, Speech, and Hearing Services in Schools, 42*(3), 365–378.

World Health Organization. (2001). *International Classification of Functioning, Disability and Health: Children and youth version.* Geneva, Switzerland: Author.

World Health Organization. (2007). *International Classification of Functioning, Disability and Health: Children and youth version.* Geneva, Switzerland: Author.

32

Augmentative and Alternative Communication

Cathy Binger and Jennifer Kent-Walsh

People with intellectual disability and related developmental disabilities may communicate in a wide variety of ways, such as using speech, vocalizations, gestures, pointing, or sign language. This population is also at very high risk, however, for having a communication disorder of some sort; that is, people with intellectual and developmental disabilities may have difficulties understanding spoken language, have speech that is difficult to understand, speak in grammatically incorrect sentences, or have difficulties with reading and writing (Downing, Hanreddy, & Peckham-Hardin, 2015).

In these cases, it is often appropriate and necessary to provide someone with some form of augmentative and alternative communication (AAC),

which is the main focus of this chapter. As we subsequently discuss in greater detail, *AAC* refers to the use of tools and techniques, such as sign language or a communication device, to enable someone to communicate effectively. If, however, communication is to be truly improved, not only the person's means of expression but also other crucial elements of communication must be examined, such as the sender, the receiver, and the topic of communication (Schweigert, 2012). Therefore, before we delve into the area of AAC specifically, we first examine what communication is from a broader perspective; this will enable consideration of AAC from a more holistic viewpoint. We illustrate a variety of presented concepts and considerations through several case studies.

WHAT IS COMMUNICATION?

Since the 1980s, much has been learned about how to best support people with intellectual and developmental disabilities who have challenges with communicating. One way of looking at communication is to parcel it into four essential elements: sender, receiver, topic, and means of expression (Schweigert, 2012). When any one of these four elements is not working efficiently and effectively, the chances for successful communication decreases. In the following subsections, we examine each one of these areas in turn.

Sender

The sender element refers to a wide variety of characteristics of the person intending to communicate a message of some kind. Factors such as the ability to control one's own actions, having an awareness of other people, and having an awareness of the world are needed for successful communication to occur (Schweigert, 2012). Table 32.1 shows that Sabrina, a child with Down syndrome, has an awareness of her peers and wants to spend time with them. Similarly, Matteo, a young man with autism, often chooses to be in the same room as others, which demonstrates an awareness of other people and of his surroundings. Devan, an adult with intellectual disability, enjoys interacting with other people and seeks out those interactions. All three people in the case studies, then, demonstrate at least some characteristics of successful senders; they all have the ability to control themselves, at least to some extent, and they have an awareness of other people. In contrast, someone with intellectual disability with profound intellectual impairment who might, for example, spend a lot of time sitting in isolation engaging in repetitive, self-stimulating behaviors such as rocking and who demonstrates no change in behavior in the presence of others has significant challenges with the sender element of communication. For Sabrina and Devan, it is necessary to look to other areas to determine how they might improve their communication. For Matteo, issues in the sender category (e.g., standing nearby, instead of with, people) only partly encapsulate his communication challenges, so the other areas for him must be examined as well.

Table 32.1.   Case studies of individuals who could benefit from augmentative and alternative communication (AAC)

	Sabrina	Matteo	Devan
Broad context	School-age child with Down syndrome	Young adult with autism who recently moved into a home with two friends	Adult with intellectual and developmental disabilities who is moving into an independent living context (apartment) for the first time
Specific context	Participating in science centers with peers; the topic this month is ocean life	Participating with peers and staff in the evenings while playing board games and watching television	Interacting with people at the local coffee shop where he likes to spend time
What is working	• Enjoys being with peers • Is willing to go to each science center • Understands concrete directions	• Chooses to be in the same space as peers and staff in the evenings	• Can get to the coffee shop independently • Memorized the money he needs for his order (always the same)
Current challenges	• Has speech that is very hard for everyone to understand • Few teachers and peers understand manual signs • Communication breakdowns cause Sabrina to shut down and withdraw from interactions	• Sometimes stands in the doorway instead of sitting down • Engages in repetitive movements such as rubbing his fingers together • Says things that often seem irrelevant to those around him • Gets upset when not able to watch a preferred television show	• Becomes confused and frustrated if he does not have the exact bills and change to pay for his order • Coffee shop staff and customers do not understand his speech (mostly generalized vocalizations)
Communication-based solutions	• Create a communication book (or use a voice output device) with vocabulary relevant to the ocean life theme. • Include vocabulary options that mirror the vocabulary that peers use with Sabrina.	• Teach peers to ask Matteo to join in (using AAC as needed). • Provide Matteo with a communication book or device to participate in games (e.g., ask questions, take turns) and discuss television shows (e.g., state that he wants to watch something else, ask questions about other shows).	• Provide Devan with a laminated communication card he keeps with his money that says, "Can you help me count out the money I need to pay for my order?" to hand to the cashier when needed. • Provide Devan with a communication book, board, or device that allows him to use partner-focused phrases ("How are you?" "Nice to see you") and to answer questions posed by the coffee shop cashiers and other patrons.

Receiver

To be successful with the receiver element of communication, the person must understand that there is a need to engage other people for communication to take place and also to show an awareness of the relative availability of others (Schweigert, 2012). For example, a child who sits alone at a table and signs DRINK over and over again without first engaging the attention of another person is experiencing a communication breakdown with the receiver element of communication. Again, looking to the case studies shown in Table 32.1, Sabrina and Matteo both seek out other people when they want to say something, whereas Devan demonstrates a lack of awareness of the availability of others—that is, he often interrupts others (e.g., speaking with the cashier when she already is engaged with another customer)—and he also fails to read more subtle social cues as well (e.g., signs that someone sitting alone may prefer to read a book or work on a laptop rather than engage in conversation). Matteo, the young adult who recently moved into a home with two friends, has challenges with the receiver element as well. He tends to remain at more of a distance from others, often choosing to stand at the outskirts of events rather than joining in activities, and he sometimes says things that seem unrelated to the conversation. Also, he sometimes speaks without first engaging the attention of another person, so teaching Matteo to consistently engage the attention of others before conveying a message will be essential to his success.

Topic

The topic element of communication is what the conversation is about, and it often constitutes the reason for communicating. Topics of communication are driven by a person's motivations and preferences and also by his or her experiences with the world (Schweigert, 2012). When a person communicates with others, he or she needs to have something to say. At times, actual content of the topic is crucial (e.g., when giving someone directions to a specific location). At other times, such as when chatting with a close friend over a cup of coffee, the content of the interaction is less important; that is, communication may be more focused on maintaining social closeness than on the precise nature of the topic itself (Light, 1989). Some people with intellectual and developmental disabilities may have little motivation to communicate. At times, people with

intellectual disability with profound intellectual impairments may indicate few preferences, and intervention may need to focus on helping them to develop preferences (Tullis et al., 2011). It does not matter how seemingly appropriate or efficient a communication option is for someone in this situation if no motive for communication exists (e.g., having a switch that triggers the message "Can I have more, please?" is not meaningful if the person is not motivated to have more of anything). That is, what is the point in communicating if one is not interested in anything or anyone? Topics also may be challenging for people who are isolated, do not go very many places outside the home, or have few opportunities to interact with people. Most people enjoy sharing the events of their daily lives with others, but what if they went nowhere and did nothing? This sounds extreme, but some people with intellectual and developmental disabilities may find themselves in quite isolating conditions.

Again looking back at the case studies in Table 32.1, it may be noted that the main topic of conversation for Sabrina in her science center has been chosen for her: ocean life. However, it is important to attend to what else is commonly discussed in this situation among Sabrina's peers. For example, students may discuss places they have gone where they have seen ocean life, or they may talk about aquariums they have at home. Applying this kind of participation model (Beukelman & Mirenda, 2013) can enrich topics of conversation and help people with intellectual and developmental disabilities build genuine relationships with peers. The situation with Matteo is similar in that many of his topics of communication are somewhat predictable, although the content, of course, differs: discussing the rules of a board game, for example, or talking about who is winning. For Devan, one important topic is the need for him to calmly discuss money with the cashier. Also, he needs topics of communication to share with other customers he would like to engage in conversation. Thus, it is important to attend to the topics of conversation for Sabrina, Matteo, and Devan when seeking communication solutions.

Means of Expression

The final element of communication is the means of expression. Most people rely on spoken and written communication modes in everyday life, such as talking or texting with friends. To be successful, the means of expression must be doable, detectable, applicable, and efficient (Beukelman & Mirenda, 2013; Schweigert, 2012). This is a major area of challenge for many people with intellectual and developmental disabilities, which is why the remainder of this chapter will focus on this element. All three people in the case studies from Table 32.1 experience significant challenges in this area. Sabrina's speech is difficult to understand, and although she has learned a number of manual signs, most of the educators and peers at her school do not understand her signs. Matteo's speech may be comprehensible at times, but the language he uses often seems irrelevant to the situation. Devan's speech also is hard to understand, with customers in the coffee shop able to understand almost nothing of what he is trying to communicate. For Sabrina, Matteo, and Devan, then, appropriate means of expression to increase their communication successes must be found—while keeping in mind any accompanying challenges in the sender, receiver, and topic elements. Communication, then, involves a complex array of factors, all of which must be considered for successful communication to occur. For the remainder of this chapter, we primarily explore various means of expression that may be useful for people with intellectual and developmental disabilities, but it must always be kept in mind that finding an appropriate means of communication does not instantly lead to communication success; careful attention to the sender, receiver, and topic elements is also required, with consideration of changing needs over time.

WHAT IS AUGMENTATIVE AND ALTERNATIVE COMMUNICATION?

When people cannot fulfill their communication needs using speech alone, they may benefit from using AAC (Beukelman & Mirenda, 2013; Binger & Kent-Walsh, 2010). We have already discussed the term *communication* and what it refers to in some depth, so now we examine the other two words used in this term: *augmentative* means *supplemental*, and *alternative* means *replacement*—so essentially, AAC refers to using anything that either adds to or takes the place of typical forms of communication. For most people who use AAC, it is used to supplement or augment existing communication. For example, Sabrina, Matteo, and Devan are all using various means of expression, including speech, vocalizations, gestures, and manual signs, so any additional

means of expression would be augmenting their existing communication repertoires. In extreme cases in which someone has extremely limited movement (e.g., someone on the late stages of amyotrophic lateral sclerosis, also known as Lou Gehrig's disease), alternative communication modes, such as using switches sensitive to small movements of muscles near the eyes, may be employed to create messages through a computer (Beukelman, Fager, Ball, & Dietz, 2007).

Although the first thought, typically, is to focus on supplementing or replacing spoken messages, it is important to note that the formats of communication have expanded dramatically since the mid-1990s, and people with intellectual and developmental disabilities may require different means of expression when using different formats. Face-to-face communication is still a crucial part of daily life for most people, but people with intellectual and developmental disabilities likely will need to engage with others using the same broader range of formats used by support providers and peers—that is, not only phone calls, but also text messages, e-mail messages, video communications (e.g., FaceTime, Skype), and so forth. Written communication—even to oneself—is also important to remember. For example, Devan likely will need to construct shopping lists using a means of expression that will work for him (e.g., photos of needed items if he is not able to read).

Who Needs Augmentative and Alternative Communication?

The simple answer to the question of who needs AAC is this: anyone whose communication needs cannot be met by speech alone might benefit from using AAC. The use of AAC is not limited to people of a certain age or disability or background—anyone who needs help communicating might be able to benefit from AAC. Access to appropriate communication is the right of all people, and this includes access to appropriate forms of AAC (National Joint Committee for the Communication Needs of Persons With Severe Disabilities, 1992). People with intellectual and developmental disabilities who can benefit from AAC may have any of a range of disabilities, such as autism; cerebral palsy; childhood apraxia of speech; intellectual disability; Down syndrome; spina bifida; and a wide range of other syndromes such as Cornelia de Lange, Lejeune syndrome (cri-du-chat syndrome), and velocardiofacial syndrome

(DiGeorge syndrome). It also is important to note that many people benefiting from AAC have no specific diagnosis.

In addition, people can have a range of motor capabilities—that is, some people who benefit from AAC are able to walk independently and move around their environments without assistance, as with Sabrina, Matteo, and Devan. Other people, however, such as someone with cerebral palsy whose physical impairment limits mobility, may use a wheelchair to become mobile and also may need assistance with daily activities such as eating, toileting, bathing, or dressing. What matters, then, is not the person's diagnosis or physical status but that the person has unmet communication needs.

What Augmentative and Alternative Communication Options Exist?

There is a wide range of AAC options; the tricky part is finding the right option for the right person. In this subsection, we explore a range of AAC options that might help a person with intellectual and developmental disabilities and explain related AAC terminology.

Unaided versus Aided Augmentative and Alternative Communication

AAC can be divided into two major categories: unaided and aided communication. *Unaided communication* refers to using the body to communicate, without the use of any external aids. Unaided communication modes include the use of speech and vocalizations (i.e., sounds people make that are not really words), gaze, and gestures such as shrugging the shoulders or pointing, pantomime, and manual signs. In contrast, *aided communication* includes anything that is external to the body to help with communication. A wide array of options is available, ranging from extremely simple to highly complex. A simple form of aided AAC that Matteo or Devan might use, for example, would be to point to a photograph of an item on a menu to indicate what they would like to eat for dinner. On the other end of the spectrum are sophisticated computerized communication devices containing thousands of words and symbols that Sabrina, Matteo, or Devan might use to communicate.

No-, Low-, and High-Tech Aided Communication

Aided communication is further divided into no-tech, low-tech, and high-tech AAC solutions (Binger & Kent-Walsh, 2010). No-tech devices are nonelectronic aided AAC tools and include items such as communication books and wallets. Both low- and high-tech devices are electronic, although the low-tech options typically do not come with specialized rechargeable batteries (as would be found, e.g., on a laptop computer) and high-tech devices do. Low-tech devices also are typically simpler to program, and voice output is provided using recorded speech. In contrast, high-tech devices usually have rechargeable batteries and come with speech synthesizers (i.e., speech produced via computer algorithms) as well as the option to use recorded speech. Table 32.2 lists a range of no-tech, low-tech, and high-tech AAC options, along with examples of each.

Augmentative and Alternative Communication Symbols

Table 32.2 identifies several different types of symbols, such as line drawings, photographs, and remnants, that are often used for AAC purposes. When considering AAC options for someone with intellectual and developmental disabilities, it is important to consider what kinds of symbols that person might be able to use. First, it is important to understand what is meant by *symbol* in this context. A symbol, broadly speaking, is something that represents something else. Most communicative behaviors are symbolic in some way. For example, all spoken words, written words, and manual signs are symbols for something else: the spoken word *apple* is a symbol for a red, crunchy fruit; the written word *peace* is a symbol for an abstract concept that has to do with people getting along with each other (and the well-known peace symbol means the same thing), and the manual sign for *drink* represents an action referring to the consumption of liquids. Similarly, photographs or line drawings used to represent *apple, peace,* and *drink* are also symbolic. Some symbols may be easier to understand than others (e.g., a photograph of an apple is very transparent compared with the peace symbol), but nevertheless, they are still symbols. After all, eating an apple can be highly satisfactory, but eating a photograph of an apple is not.

Given this, all aided and unaided AAC solutions require that a person understands the symbolic nature of the provided AAC options. If a person is provided with a photograph of an apple and the person tries to eat the photo, he or she likely does not understand that the photo is a symbol for something else. Therefore, it becomes apparent that using

Table 32.2. Examples of aided augmentative and alternative communication (AAC) options with potential case study applications

Type of device	Description	Example
No-tech		
Single pictures: line drawings and photographs	• Line drawing symbol sets, such as Picture Communication Symbols (PCS; Johnson, 1994) that are part of Mayer-Johnson's Boardmaker family, are typically used. • Photos also can be used, from sources such as Google images, published photo sets, or personal photos. • The communicator shows or gives individual symbols to communication partners to deliver a message.	• Devan hands a line drawing or photo representing "help" to a cashier and gestures to his wallet to indicate he needs help in counting out the correct bills and coins.
Communication wallet	• A communication wallet contains a collection of single line drawings and photographs. • The communicator flips through the wallet to the appropriate line drawing or photograph and shows the symbol to the communication partner to deliver a message.	• Devan uses a communication wallet to say "good morning" to the cashier and "excuse me" to another patron in the coffee shop.
Communication album or book	• Multiple line drawings and photographs are arrayed on each page; pages are kept in a multipage book format. • The communicator flips through the book and points to appropriate line drawings and/or photographs to deliver a message.	• Matteo uses multiple communication boards to interact with peers about different television shows.
Remnant book	• A collection of memorabilia from outings—such as movie or theater tickets, menus, schedules, or receipts—is maintained in a book. • The communicator flips through the book and points to or shows appropriate remnants to deliver a message.	• Matteo shows the group-home staff a movie ticket from his outing with his brother to initiate an interaction about going to the movie.
Low-tech		
Single-message device	• An electronic communication device has one button to play one recorded message. • The communicator activates the recording in relevant contexts.	• Devan activates a single button he carries in his pocket to say "Please help me count out the proper change."
Multi-message device	• An electronic communication device has multiple buttons with different recorded messages. • The communicator activates the intended message in relevant contexts.	• Sabrina selects a range of messages pertaining to ocean life during science centers.
High-tech		
Dedicated communication device such as the DynaVox T10[a], Accent 800[b], or NOVA chat 8[c]	• High-tech computerized devices incorporate a dynamic display screen (similar to tablet/smartphone screens) and computer-generated speech; these devices are preprogrammed with thousands of words and messages. • The communicator activates individualized messages or spells out a message.	• Matteo uses a device that is programmed with extensive information about the television shows and movies that he likes and that are watched by his group home members.
iPad or tablet with communication app such as Proloquo2Go[d], TouchChat[c], or Sono Flex[e]	• Mass-market tablet is used with an AAC app; some apps are simple, containing relatively few symbols and preprogrammed vocabulary; others are more sophisticated and mirror software on dedicated communication devices. • The communicator activates individualized messages.	• Sabrina uses an iPad with programmed messages pertaining to ocean life during science centers.

[a]DynaVox, http://www.tobiidynavox.com/meet-t10/
[b]Accent 800, http://www.prentrom.com
[c]NOVA chat 8 and TouchChat, http://www.saltillo.com
[d]Proloquo2Go, http://www.assistiveware.com
[e]Sono Flex: http://www.tobiidynavox.com/sono-flex/

photographs as part of a communication system will not lead to successful communication until the person learns the symbolic relationship between the actual apple and the photograph of the apple. The following are examples of symbols (and symbol categories) that can be used to represent the concept or communicate the message "I'm thirsty" based on varying individual symbol comprehension skills: 1) a drawing of a cup (line drawing symbol), 2) a photo of a cup (photographic symbol), 3) an empty cup (real object symbol), 4) a portion of a straw (partial object symbol), 5) a miniature cup (miniature object symbol), 6) a Coca-Cola logo (logo symbol), or 7) the written word *thirsty* (traditional orthography symbol).

The main point is that different people with intellectual and developmental disabilities have different levels of symbolic competency, and this must be considered carefully on a case-by-case basis. For example, in the case studies described in the tables, Sabrina may have emerging literacy skills, and those who support her communication might want to incorporate use of written words (as well as line drawings and photographs) into her AAC solutions. Similarly, Matteo may have memorized virtually every logo and road sign he has ever seen, and those can be used as well. Devan, however, has no functional literacy skills, so those who support his communication need to make sure that this is accounted for in his communication solutions. For example, Devan may still be provided with a communication card to hand to the cashier that asks for help with counting money, as the cashier must understand what Devan needs, but Devan does not have to be able to read the card; therefore, an image of a cash register might be put on the card (because Devan understands line drawings and photographs of concrete objects) to remind him when and how to use the card. After considering these examples of how people can use various types of symbols when communicating, readers likely will reflect on people they have met or worked with in the past and others they will meet in the future and how AAC might apply to their communication.

Where Are People Who Need Augmentative and Alternative Communication?

As shown through the examples and contexts discussed so far, there are people who need AAC everywhere! Because people from across the life span can benefit from AAC, readers likely will find people who could benefit from AAC in any setting in which they work with people who have intellectual and developmental disabilities. The following subsections look at some examples.

Early Intervention/Birth-to-3 Programs
Families of young children who are identified early in life with a disability may receive services to learn how to maximize success with their children. Children identified in these early stages of development may have severe developmental delays or other types of disorders that put them at risk for difficulties with communication development. A few examples include children with various syndromes (e.g., Down syndrome, Prader-Willi syndrome), children with autism, children who experience a lack of oxygen at birth (also known as anoxia), and children who have undergone a trauma of some kind, such as abusive head trauma (also known as shaken baby syndrome; National Institute of Neurological Disorders and Stroke, 2014). Although it may be surprising that children this young can benefit from AAC, research indicates that very young children can and do experience success with AAC; providing AAC at very early stages of development can promote early success with communication and help build critical early language skills (Light & Drager, 2007). Although families or educators may express concerns that AAC might impede speech development, this is a myth; in fact, research shows that AAC can actually help with speech development (e.g., Kasari et al., 2014).

Preschools
Like the birth-to-3 population, preschool children require intervention to help meet their individual needs. All children discussed in the previous section on early intervention may continue services in preschool and beyond. In addition, children who have not previously received services may be identified in the preschool years as having communication needs, including children with intellectual and developmental disabilities. Many of these children receive no exact diagnosis and will qualify for services. Other children may be diagnosed during this time or somewhat later. Two relatively common specific disabilities diagnosed in the preschool years are autism spectrum disorders and cerebral palsy. As with children in early intervention, AAC should be provided as soon as there is a perceived need; there is no reason to wait to see

if speech develops. AAC can open up a whole world of successful experiences for preschoolers, allowing them to engage in early literacy activities, participate in classroom activities, and build relationships with peers—all of which provide a foundation for success during their school years.

Public and Private Schools Of course, the younger students discussed in the previous subsections are likely to continue to benefit from AAC throughout their school-age years. When provided with appropriate AAC access and instruction, many students with intellectual and developmental disabilities may be able to participate in typical instructional settings, given appropriate classroom supports (Chung, Carter, & Sisco, 2012). When devising an educational plan for a student with a disability, describing the specifics of the student's disabilities and needs is critical. Part of this process should include consideration of various assistive technologies, including AAC, that can assist students in meeting their educational and social potentials. Clearly defining and documenting AAC options and services are critical components of education plans that are tailored to students' individual needs. If one works in a school setting, he or she will have important information to contribute on the needs of the students with whom he or she works and frequently will be referred to the individualized education program (or IEP) for specifics on the supports that are required for individual students.

Residential, Community, and Support Programs Adults with intellectual and developmental disabilities may receive assistance through any number of types of programs. As is the case for anyone with communication challenges, AAC will be most successful when communication needs are carefully assessed in the context of the person's daily life activities. For example, adults with severe intellectual impairments typically need assistance with areas such as self-care, socializing, and coping with finances. Communication needs are not separate from these needs but, instead, are closely woven into each area. For example, part of successful self-care is a person learning how to tell support providers the ways in which he or she does and does not want assistance with getting dressed. AAC can help many adults with intellectual and developmental disabilities achieve a higher level of independence in all areas of self-care.

Long-Term Care Facilities Some people with intellectual and developmental disabilities may at some point in their lives need longer term supports. Like their peers without intellectual disability, for example, people with intellectual disability may experience dementia in their later years. Research indicates dementia rates for people with intellectual disability are comparable to or somewhat higher than the general population, with the exception of people with Down syndrome, in whom earlier dementia onset ages have been reported (Strydom et al., 2010). People both with and without intellectual disability who have dementia may benefit from AAC solutions such as memory books to support declining memory and to provide tangible contexts for communication (Bourgeois & Hickey, 2009).

As shown in the preceding discussion, people across the life span with intellectual and developmental disabilities can benefit from AAC, and the types of AAC they use must be fitted to their individual needs and circumstances. Note that regardless of the setting, successful AAC is not something that is added on as a special task but, instead, is integrated into daily life settings—such as the preschooler who is learning to build friendships, the adolescent who is learning how to talk to future employers, or the person with dementia who is sharing memories of the past. AAC, then, is all about adding to the richness of life. So then, how does one know when AAC might help? How can one recognize when someone has unmet communication needs?

Signs of Unmet Communication Needs

We mentioned toward the beginning of the chapter that if a person's communication needs are not met, then AAC should be considered. Recognizing someone who has unmet communication needs may not be as obvious as one might think; we have seen many individuals over the years, of all ages and in a wide range of settings, who have spent months, years, and even decades with insufficient access to appropriate communication solutions. This possibility raises questions about what signs to look for to make sure people with intellectual and developmental disabilities have the opportunity to reach their full communicative potential. We review a number of such signs in the following subsections.

Challenging Behaviors Some children and adults with intellectual and developmental disabilities exhibit challenging behaviors such as kicking, biting, hitting, yelling, and throwing objects. These behaviors can result in harm to the person him- or herself and to others. Much has been learned about people with intellectual and developmental disabilities who have challenging behaviors, with one of the major lessons being that these behaviors often can be traced back to challenges with communication (Ganz & Hong, 2014; Walker & Snell, 2013). For example, a child such as Sabrina might throw objects or bite herself during a craft activity, a young adult such as Matteo might bang his head against the wall when a nonpreferred program is on television, and an adult such as Devan might yell unintelligibly and wave his arms wildly in frustration in the coffee shop when he has trouble completing his order. At first glance, these may not appear to be communication issues, but providing functional communication-based solutions can potentially help eliminate all of these behaviors. Sabrina may be biting herself because she hates getting glue on her fingers, and providing a way for her to tell someone about this challenge might prevent this behavior. Matteo's frustration might be alleviated by telling a group-home worker that he wants to watch something different on television so they can negotiate a time to watch his preferred program. Devan's issue might be avoided by teaching him to use a card or a communication device containing a message asking for assistance with counting money. All this is to suggest that when working with people who have intellectual and developmental disabilities who are exhibiting challenging behaviors, it is necessary to ask oneself, "What is this person trying to tell me, and how can I help him or her do so in an equally efficient but more effective and socially appropriate manner?"

Learned Passivity People who experience learned passivity—also known as learned helplessness—essentially learn over time that their actions do not lead to the results they want, so they stop trying. At face value, learned passivity might seem to be the opposite of challenging behaviors, but in fact, these two responses can arise from the same kinds of situations. That is, just as challenging behaviors can result from unsuccessful communication, so can learned passivity (Light & Drager, 2007). For example, instead of Sabrina biting herself, Matteo banging his head, or Devan yelling, they may instead sit in silence, refusing to even attempt to communicate. People with severe motor impair-

ments, such as people with cerebral palsy, may simply hang their heads or shut their eyes as a form of escape. Furthermore, some people may fluctuate between these two responses—acting out in some situations and "shutting down" in others. Regardless, both types of behaviors can be an indication that a person's communication needs are unmet.

Low Expectations "Good enough" is not good enough. Our own personal experiences as clinicians and researchers over the years have taught us that expectations are often set too low for people with severe communication impairments. To put it simply, just because someone has difficulty speaking does not mean he or she does not have something to say! Similarly, just because someone has intellectual and developmental disabilities, that does not mean he or she cannot become a more sophisticated communicator. Often, it seems that as long as a person with severe intellectual and developmental disabilities can ask to go to the restroom and request preferred food items, his or her communication is deemed adequate (Light, Parsons, & Drager, 2002). However, one should ask, "What if those were the only things I could communicate? Would my quality of life be as high as it is right now?" When working with someone whose independence and opportunities for meaningful interaction seem to be significantly limited by natural speech, this may be a good indication of the need to explore AAC options. Many people with severe intellectual and developmental disabilities have the capacity to broaden their communication capabilities, and AAC may be able to help them move beyond communicating solely about their basic needs and wants and into other more rewarding communicative interactions.

Strong Comprehension Skills Something we hear repeatedly when working with people with communication disorders is that "they can understand far more than they can say." Virtually everyone's language comprehension skills are at least somewhat better than their expressive language skills; for example, most people would struggle to write the novels they can easily read and understand. However, this gap often is even larger for people with intellectual and developmental disabilities due to difficulty with verbal communication. Many of these people can make rapid progress with their ability to express themselves if they are provided with appropriate communication tools and appropriate instruction, so whenever a person with intellectual and developmental disabilities is said to have far better comprehension than expression, it is necessary to ask oneself how to assist the person in gaining access to relevant AAC services.

Finding Help with Augmentative and Alternative Communication Service Provision

At this point in the chapter, we have established a sense of what AAC is and how to identify people who might benefit from using AAC. We have provided examples of how AAC can improve the daily lives of people with intellectual and developmental disabilities, but it also is important to know who is primarily responsible for making AAC decisions. When thinking that someone has AAC support needs, the best thing to do is refer that person to a speech-language pathologist (SLP) who is an AAC specialist (Binger et al., 2012). Whether an AAC specialist is relatively easy to find depends on one's work setting and location. However, if one works in a place in which SLPs are employed, an SLP should be able to help locate—and take primary responsibility for finding—the right person to conduct an assessment and to provide suggested AAC solutions. In a broader sense, though, everyone involved with the person with intellectual and developmental disabilities contributes to communication successes. A direct service provider may spend far more time with the person with intellectual and developmental disabilities, for example, than the SLP or many other professionals, and therefore may have valuable—and even essential—information to contribute regarding the person's communication needs. The direct service provider is an important part of the team, and his or her insights and enthusiasm will have a direct impact on the communicative success of the people with whom he or she works.

SUMMARY

We hope that this chapter has provided some insights into communication and AAC for people with intellectual and developmental disabilities. We described the range of communication options that are available and explained how finding the right communication tools is a necessary but not sufficient part of communication success. That is, improving communication is not just about providing someone with a communication device; instead, a broad

perspective on the elements of communication (sender, receiver, topic, and means of expression) is required to identify the areas of need. We also have shown that people with intellectual and developmental disabilities who can benefit from AAC can be any age and may be found in a broad array of settings. Also, we presented some of the signs to look for to help identify when someone might benefit from AAC and who to refer that person to when the need arises. Finally, we hope we have left the reader with a sense of the power of AAC—that is, AAC has the ability to enrich quality of life for individuals with intellectual and developmental disabilities and can lead them into achieving goals that may not have been thought possible.

FOR FURTHER THOUGHT AND DISCUSSION

1. What role might AAC play in supporting better quality lives for people with intellectual and developmental disabilities?

2. What technology innovations are appearing now that might dramatically alter how AAC is provided?

3. What personal characteristics of people affect the types of AAC from which they might benefit?

4. Often, people think of high-tech devices when thinking about AAC, but what low-tech (or no-tech) and low-cost options might serve just as well?

5. Consider the reasons that people have unmet communication needs. How might barriers resulting in this situation be removed?

REFERENCES

Beukelman, D.R., Fager, S., Ball, L., & Dietz, A. (2007). AAC for adults with acquired neurological conditions: A review. *Augmentative and Alternative Communication, 23*(3), 230–242. doi:10.1080/07434610701553668

Beukelman, D.R., & Mirenda, P. (2013). *Augmentative and alternative communication: Supporting children and adults with complex communication needs* (4th ed.). Baltimore, MD: Paul H. Brookes Publishing Co.

Binger, C., Ball, L., Dietz, A., Kent-Walsh, J., Lasker, J., Lund, S.,...Quach, W. (2012). Personnel roles in the AAC assessment process. *Augmentative and Alternative Communication, 28*(4), 278–288. doi:10.3109/07434618.2012.716079

Binger, C., & Kent-Walsh, J. (2010). *What every speech-language pathologist/audiologist should know about augmentative and alternative communication*. Boston, MA: Allyn & Bacon.

Bourgeois, M.S., & Hickey, E. (2009). *Dementia: From diagnosis to management: A functional approach.* New York, NY: Taylor & Francis.

Chung, Y.-C., Carter, E.W., & Sisco, L.G. (2012). Social interactions of students with disabilities who use augmentative and alternative communication in inclusive classrooms. *American Journal on Intellectual and Developmental Disabilities, 117*(5), 349–367. doi:10.1352/1944-7558-117.5.349

Downing, J.E., Hanreddy, A., & Peckham-Hardin, K.D. (2015). *Teaching communication skills to students with severe disabilities* (3rd ed.). Baltimore, MD: Paul H. Brookes Publishing Co.

Ganz, J.B., & Hong, E.R. (2014). Functional communication training with aided AAC. In Ganz, J.B., *Aided augmentative communication for individuals with autism spectrum disorders* (pp. 95–111). New York, NY: Springer.

Johnson, R. (1994). *The Picture Communication Symbols.* Solana Beach, CA: Mayer-Johnson.

Kasari, C., Kaiser, A., Goods, K., Nietfeld, J., Mathy, P., Landa, R.,…Almirall, D. (2014). Communication interventions for minimally verbal children with autism: A sequential multiple assignment randomized trial. *Journal of the American Academy of Child and Adolescent Psychiatry, 53*(6), 635–646. Retrieved from http://linkinghub.elsevier.com/retrieve/pii/S08908567 14001634?showall=true

Light, J.C. (1989). Toward a definition of communicative competence for individuals using augmentative and alternative communication systems. *Augmentative and Alternative Communication, 5*(2), 137–144. doi:10.1080/074 34618912331275126

Light, J., & Drager, K. (2007). AAC technologies for young children with complex communication needs: State of the science and future research directions. *Augmentative and Alternative Communication, 23*(3), 204–216. doi:10.1080/07434610701553635

Light, J., Parsons, A., & Drager, K. (2002). "There's more to life than cookies": Developing interactions for social closeness with beginning communicators who use AAC. In D.R. Beukelman & J. Reichle (Series Eds.) & J. Reichle, D. Beukelman, & J. Light (Vol. Eds.), *Communication and Language Intervention Series: Exemplary practices for beginning communicators: Implications for AAC* (pp. 187–218). Baltimore, MD: Paul H. Brookes Publishing Co.

National Institute of Neurological Disorders and Stroke. (2014). *NINDS shaken baby syndrome information page.* Retrieved from http://www.ninds.nih.gov/disorders /shakenbaby/shakenbaby.htm

National Joint Committee for the Communication Needs of Persons With Severe Disabilities. (1992). Communication bill of rights. *ASHA, 34*(Suppl. 7), 2–3.

Schweigert, P. (2012). It takes two: Partners working with individuals who have sensory and multiple disabilities. In *Partner instruction in AAC: Building circles of support.* Paper presented at the online conference of the American Speech-Language-Hearing Association Special Interest Group on Augmentative and Alternative Communcation.

Strydom, A., Shooshtari, S., Lee, L., Raykar, V., Torr, J., Tsiouris, J.,…Maaskant, M. (2010). Dementia in older adults with intellectual disabilities—epidemiology, presentation, and diagnosis. *Journal of Policy and Practice in Intellectual Disabilities, 7*(2), 96–110. doi:10.1111/j.1741-1130.2010.00253.x

Tullis, C.A., Cannella-Malone, H.I., Basbigill, A.R., Yeager, A., Fleming, C.V., Payne, D., & Wu, P. (2011). Review of the choice and preference assessment literature for individuals with severe to profound disabilities. *Education and Training in Autism and Developmental Disabilities, 46*, 576–595.

Walker, V.L., & Snell, M.E. (2013). Effects of augmentative and alternative communication on challenging behavior: A meta-analysis. *Augmentative and Alternative Communication, 29*(2), 117–131. doi:10.3109/07434618 .2013.785020

V

Intellectual and Developmental Disabilities Through the Life Span

33

The First 1,000 Days of Fetal and Infant Development

Maire Percy, Karolina Machalek, Ivan Brown, Paula E. Pasquali, and Wai Lun Alan Fung

WHAT YOU WILL LEARN

- Why the first 1,000 days in the development of a fetus and infant (from conception to age 2 years) are critical for development and future health
- Milestones typical of the prenatal, neonatal, and early life periods
- Factors promoting optimal development in the first 1,000 days
- Screening for disabilities in the prenatal, newborn, and early childhood periods
- Dealing with a diagnosis, including diversity, cultural considerations, and religion or spirituality
- Future directions in the field

It is widely recognized that the first 1,000 days of fetal and infant development—from conception up until a child's second birthday—form the most crucial period of early childhood, with appropriate nutrition being of paramount importance (U.S.

Authors' note: The text of this chapter is based in part upon information in Machalek, Brown, Birkan, Fung, and Percy (2003); Machalek, Percy, and Brown (2007); and Machalek, Percy, Carter, and Brown (2011). Contributions by Karolina Machalek to these sources were made while based at the University of Toronto. Contributions to the present chapter were made on personal time and while on leave from employment with the Public Health Agency of Canada (PHAC). The authorship of Karolina Machalek on the present chapter and her present affiliation with PHAC should not be construed as PHAC approval of the chapter content. Recommendations featured in the chapter are based on U.S. guidelines and therefore may not align with recommendations and guidelines of the Public Health Agency of Canada and Health Canada. We thank Dr. John Percy for helpful discussion and advice.

Department of State, n.d.). Interaction between nature and nurture during this time period affects not only early development but also a person's physical, mental, and emotional health for the rest of his or her life (Harvard University Center on the Developing Child, 2010; Hoddinott et al., 2013; Mustard, 2009; Shonkoff et al., 2012). The chapter provides an introduction to "typical" development up to the age of 2 years and the key factors that promote attainment of an infant's optimal potential. Also discussed are how developmental disabilities can sometimes be identified in the first 1,000 days; some strategies and insights to consider when early diagnoses are made, including diversity and cultural considerations; and future directions in the field. For further information, quite a number of other chapters in the book contain material that is complementary to that in the present one—particularly Chapters 9, 10, 13, 27, 31, 34, 46, and 48.

TYPICAL MILESTONES ACHIEVED IN THE FIRST 1,000 DAYS

During the first 1,000 days of development, it is essential to provide appropriate nourishment, a healthy and secure environment, and the right sort of stimulation for brains and bodies to grow properly. At birth, an infant's brain has almost the same number of neurons that it will ever have. However, the brain continues to grow after birth. By 2 years of age, the brain is about 80% of the adult size. The increase in brain weight between birth and 2 years results largely from proliferation of glial (nonneuronal) cells, the formation of new connections between neurons, and the myelination of nerve fibers. (*Myelination* refers to the formation of myelin sheaths around nerves so that the nerve impulses move more quickly.) A typical infant's brain weighs approximately 350 grams at birth and increases to 1.1 kilograms (kg) by the age of 2 years and 1.4 kg by adulthood (Better Brains for Babies, 2015). In an appropriate environment, connections between neurons are formed and become strengthened, a phenomenon referred to as hardwiring. These hardwired connections, which form at an early age, are essential for cognitive and emotional functioning, including vision, hearing, language, movements, emotions, and subsequent development (Woods, 2014).

Table 33.1. Developmental milestone categories for children ages 0–2 years and sample resources

Milestone category	Examples of developmental milestones	Sample resources[a]
Gross motor skills	The child has the ability to perform tasks that utilize the gross or large muscles of the body (e.g., those in the arms, legs, and body core for crawling, running, and jumping).	World Health Organization: http://www.who.int /childgrowth/standards/motor_milestones/en/
Fine motor skills	The child has the ability to perform small movements of the hands, wrists, fingers, feet, toes, lips, and tongue.	Children's Hospital of Richmond at Virginia Commonwealth University: http://www .chrichmond.org/Resource-Library/Fine -Motor-Skills-Birth-to-2-years.htm
Hearing	Hearing develops early in fetal development and is fully functioning at birth. Hearing problems may be suspected in children who are not responding to sounds or who are not developing their language skills appropriately.	Hearing Speech and Deaf Center of Greater Cincinnati: http://hearingspeechdeaf.org/ Beaumont Health: http://www.beaumont.edu /childrens/health-and-safety/advice-for-parents /hearing-milestones/
Vision	The child develops ability in focusing, eye coordination and tracking, depth perception, seeing color, and object and face recognition.	American Optometric Association: http://www.aoa .org/patients-and-public/good-vision-throughout -life/childrens-vision/infant-vision-birth-to-24 -months-of-age?sso=y Top Five Milestones in Vision Development: http://vision.about.com/od/childrensvision/tp /vision_develop.htm
Speech and language[b]	The child develops the skills used to communicate with others. Milestones include babbling, saying "mama" or "dada," or putting two words together. Usually, a child needs to master one milestone before reaching the next.	National Institute on Deafness and Other Communication Disorders: http://www.nidcd.nih .gov/health/voice/pages/speechandlanguage .aspx#2 American Speech-Language-Hearing Association: http://www.asha.org/public/speech/development /chart/ Chapter 31 of this volume
Social and emotional development	The child initiates peer contact and participates in group play.	LD Online: http://www.ldonline.org/article/6050 Children's Therapy and Family Resource Centre: http://www.kamloopschildrenstherapy.org/social -emotional-infant-milestones
Adaptive/self-help skills	The child learns self-feeding, independent dressing and grooming, hygiene and toileting, and helping with daily chores such as putting away toys.	eXtension: Ways to Encourage Self-Help Skills in Children: http://www.extension.org/pages/26436 /ways-to-encourage-self-help-skills-in-children# .VecRvv_D9y0
Problem solving	The child exhibits reflex actions (rooting and sucking reflexes to feed), exploration of surroundings (putting hands and toys into the mouth), playing with toys that respond to his or her actions, observation and imitation, trial by error, and recalling solutions.	Life Stages Growth and Development: http://www .lifestagesinc.com/problem-solving-milestone -to-5/4558502494

[a]Numerous developmental milestone resources are readily available on the Internet. Parents and caregivers should check with professionals about the reliability of such resources.

[b]Speech is making the sounds that become words. Language is the system of using words to communicate and includes using words and gestures to say what is meant and understanding what others say.

Childhood development refers to physical, cognitive, emotional, social, and other growth that is indicated by the gradual acquisition of new characteristics and skills. Development can be monitored using developmental milestones—observable characteristics and skills that are reached by most children at various stages of their development. Such milestones reflect development in a number of areas, including physical growth, weight, gross motor, fine motor, vision, hearing, speech and language, social and emotional, adaptive or self-help skills, and problem solving. Typically developing children reach milestones in these areas at somewhat different ages, and this variability means that parents and professionals should not worry unduly if milestones are only somewhat early or somewhat delayed. However, if a child shows patterns of behavior that are unusual or reaches milestones markedly late, parents and professionals may consider the need for further assessment to determine whether a child might benefit from specialized early intervention (LeGeyt, 2012).

Charts describing developmental milestones that are achieved by typically developing children from birth to the age of 2 years are widely available. See Table 33.1 for examples of developmental milestones and some Internet sites that provide milestone charts. Table 33.2 lists some milestones that are achieved by most typically developing infants and toddlers by the given ages.

FACTORS IMPORTANT FOR DEVELOPMENT

This section provides an introduction to factors that might affect a child's development prior to conception, during pregnancy, during birth and the neonatal period (i.e., between birth and the first 28 days of life), and postnatally.

Importance of the Prenatal and Neonatal Periods

The importance of the prenatal and neonatal periods of development is frequently overlooked. According to the U.S. Department of Health and Human Services (n.d.),

> Every year nearly one million women in the United States deliver babies without receiving adequate medical attention. Babies born to mothers who received no prenatal care are three times more likely to be born at low birth weight, and five times more likely to die, than those whose mothers received prenatal care. A child's risk of dying is highest in the neonatal period, the first 28 days of life [after birth]. Safe childbirth and effective neonatal care are essential to prevent these deaths; 44% of deaths in children younger than 5 take place during the neonatal period.

Furthermore, according to the World Health Organization (WHO, 2015a),

Table 33.2. Ages by which some milestones are achieved by typically developing infants and toddlers

Age	Milestones
2 months	Responds to loud sounds; watches things that move; begins to smile at people; brings hands to mouth; holds head up when on stomach
4 months	Watches moving things; smiles at people; holds head steady; coos and makes sounds; brings things to mouth; pushes down with legs when feet are placed on a hard surface; moves both eyes in different directions
6 months	Tries to get things that are in reach; shows affection for caregivers; responds to sounds around him or her; gets things to mouth; makes vowel sounds ("ah," "eh," "oh"); rolls over in either direction; laughs and makes squealing sounds; is not stiff or floppy
9 months	Bears weight on legs with support; sits with help; babbles; plays games involving back-and-forth play; responds to own name; recognizes familiar people; looks where someone points; transfers toys from one hand to another
12 months	Crawls; stands when supported; searches for things he or she sees someone hide; says single words such as "mama" or "dada"; learns gestures such as waving or shaking the head; points to things
18 months	Points to show things to others; knows what familiar things are; copies others; has at least six words; gains new words; notices when a caregiver leaves or returns
2 years	Uses two-word phrases; knows what to do with common things such as a hair brush; copies actions and words; follows simple instructions; walks steadily; has a sense of empathy for others; has started to learn about self-control and rules; may become outraged at any form of discipline, whether for major or minor misbehaviors

Adapted from Centers for Disease Control and Prevention. (2015e, April 21). *Developmental milestones*. Retrieved from http://www.cdc.gov/ncbddd /actearly/milestones. See also charts from public health agencies of countries other than the United States, CDC (2015i), and sources listed in Table 33.1.

Preterm birth, intrapartum-related complications (birth asphyxia or lack of breathing at birth), and infections cause most neonatal deaths. From the end of the neonatal period and through the first five years of life, the main causes of death are pneumonia, diarrhea, and malaria. Malnutrition is the underlying contributing factor in about 45% of all child deaths, making children more vulnerable to severe diseases.

As of 2006, about half of pregnancies in the United States were not planned. Among women younger than 19 years of age, four of five pregnancies were unintended; among teens younger than 15, 98% of pregnancies were unintended (Finer & Zolna, 2011). This relatively high rate of unplanned pregnancies means that a substantial proportion of women and men are not able to take part in special programs that are available in many places to help prospective parents have a healthy infant.

Preconceptual Health for Women and Men

The term *preconception period* has been variously defined, but as Dean et al. (2013) noted, it can be thought of as "a minimum of one year prior to the initiation of any unprotected sexual intercourse among adolescents and women of reproductive age" (p. 1). The Centers for Disease Control and Prevention (CDC; 2014a) proposed sets of steps that are important for the health of potential parents—both women and men—during this preconceptual period, including seeing a doctor for prenatal care, learning the family history of health problems and considering genetic counseling if an infant might be at risk of having a developmental disorder, minimizing stress, keeping mentally healthy, and avoiding toxic substances and environmental contaminants.

Generally, good preconceptual health practices should continue through pregnancy for the healthy development of the fetus (Moore & Davies, 2005). Some specific aspects of good preconceptual health and health during pregnancy are explained more fully in the following subsections.

Healthy Nutrition   Healthy eating for men and women is an important component of preconceptual health. Good maternal nutrition (as well as other health factors) lessens the risk of a pregnant woman having a low birth weight infant or preterm birth, both of which are risk factors for intellectual and developmental disabilities. A pregnant woman needs about 300 calories more per day to support growth of her fetus and maintain her own body. Mother-and-child clinics should have access to a consultant dietitian (American College of Obstetricians and Gynecologists [ACOG], 2013).

Women need an adequate intake of folic acid and vitamin B_{12} to reduce the risk of neural tube defects (birth defects that happen in the first month of pregnancy involving the brain, spine, or spinal cord, such as spina bifida and anencephaly) in an infant (see Chapters 9 and 13, and the discussion later in this chapter for more information). The U.S. Public Health Service and CDC recommend that all women of childbearing age consume 0.4 mg (400 µg) of folic acid daily to prevent neural tube defects. In the United States, health care providers typically recommend that the dosage be increased by a factor of 10 a month before a woman is planning to get pregnant and prescribe one prenatal vitamin plus three 1 milligram (mg) tablets of folic acid a day to achieve a dosage of 4 mg of folic acid per day (4,000 µg) (CDC, 2015f). A Canadian panel recommends having adequate folic acid intake but not to exceed a daily dose of 1 mg, and also having an adequate intake of B_{12}. In addition, this panel recommends folic acid supplementation for male partners with a family history of neural tube defects (Wilson et al., 2015). Foods rich in folic acid include dark green vegetables like romaine lettuce, broccoli, and spinach, and dried legumes such as chickpeas, beans, and lentils. In North America, folic acid is added to all white flour, enriched pasta, and cornmeal products but, on average, such fortification increases the folic acid intake only by approximately 100 to 150 µg per day.

Regarding other nutritional factors, women who are considering pregnancy need to have adequate levels of iodine (for thyroid function), iron (to prevent anemia in mother and fetus), vitamin A (in the form of beta-carotene, not retinol, to prevent vision problems), and vitamin D (to reduce the risk of pregnancy and birth complications including gestational diabetes, preterm birth, and infection). Adequate vitamin B_6 (pyridoxine) may be important for development of an infant's brain (Boyles, 2015; Elmadfa & Meyer, 2012; Mayo Clinic, 2015; see Chapter 13). However, more clinical studies are needed to determine if supplementation with B_6 during pregnancy or labor is important for maternal or fetal outcomes (Salam, Zuberi, & Bhutta, 2015). In the United States, most people are thought to get enough B_6 from the foods they eat, though there are exceptions. It is important to note that too much B_6 is neurotoxic (National Institutes of Health, 2011). Some supplement pills have dosages of vitamin B_6 that exceed the recommended daily allowance (RDA).

People who take nutritional supplements should be cautioned about exceeding recommended dosages of vitamins, minerals, and other substances because too much as well as too little of many of these may be harmful. For information about RDAs of vitamins and minerals, see the guide by the U.S. Department of Agriculture (n.d.). For information about healthy eating, see Office of Disease Prevention and Health Promotion (2015).

Healthy Weight   It is important for potential parents to reach and maintain a healthy weight. Maternal obesity during pregnancy is also a problem (ACOG, 2013). According to University of California, Riverside (2015), it can "complicate pregnancy by increasing the mother's risk of having gestational diabetes, preeclampsia, preterm birth or a baby with birth defects. Maternal obesity is also linked to several adverse health outcomes for the infant that can persist into adulthood, such as type 2 diabetes, heart disease and mortality."

Behavioral Factors   When considering pregnancy, both women and men should stop smoking and not drink alcohol (see Chapters 18 and 19 on fetal alcohol spectrum disorder) or use recreational drugs. Taking part in activities that promote physical fitness is important for both men and women.

Vaccines and Similar Precautions   Vaccines help keep people healthy. Some contain live, though attenuated, viruses or bacteria. Examples of vaccines that contain live viruses include measles, mumps, rubella (MMR), chicken pox, and shingles vaccines. One that contains attenuated bacteria is the typhoid vaccine. Vaccines (including booster shots) containing live organisms should be given to women a month or more before pregnancy, whereas certain others can be given either before or during pregnancy (CDC, 2015a, 2015l). A flu vaccine that contains killed virus can be given before or during pregnancy or when breast feeding during the flu season (CDC, 2015l). The combined tetanus, diphtheria, and pertussis (Tdap) vaccine for adults who have never received this vaccine is another that can be given to pregnant women. Tdap contains inactivated forms of the toxins produced by the bacteria that cause each of these three

diseases. Men should also have their immunization status updated (CDC, 2014a, 2014b).

Metabolic and Endocrine Disorders   Maternal metabolic and endocrine disorders such as hypothyroidism and diabetes should be controlled because these are risk factors for intellectual and developmental disabilities (Canadian Diabetes Association Clinical Practice Guidelines Expert Committee, 2013; Mathur, 2015).

Treatment for Infections   It is also important to get treatment, prior to conception, for various infections (e.g., human immunodeficiency virus [HIV], vaginal infections) that might harm the fetus or infant after it is born (see later in this chapter and Chapter 13). For additional details about toxic environmental threats including HIV, see Chapters 9 and 13, Womenshealth.gov (2010), and AVERT (n.d.).

Other Environmental Factors   Some potentially harmful environmental factors to avoid before (and during) pregnancy include indoor air pollution, pesticides, and other toxic threats (e.g., fish that contain mercury, environmental sources of aluminum that can be avoided). See also Chapter 13.

Prenatal Care

Factors important for preconceptual health described previously are also important for a healthy pregnancy. A low level of caffeine intake is recommended. Physical exercise and movement are encouraged, though high-impact exercise should be undertaken with care (Melzer, Schutz, Boulvain, & Kayser, 2010). Some environmental factors that are particularly harmful to fetal development are x rays and hot tubs, which predispose to neural tube defects as well as to infections (Mayo Clinic, n.d.); certain drugs and vaccines (Gunatilake & Patil, 2013); and excessive exposures to heavy metals including cadmium, mercury, lead, and aluminum (Fanni et al., 2014; Karakis et al., 2014).

Prenatal care typically also includes the following: determining the mother's blood group; testing for anemia and anti-Rh antibodies (see next section); checking the growth of the uterus; listening to the fetal heart beat; checking the urine for protein (an indicator of kidney insufficiency) and sugar (an indicator of diabetes); monitoring blood pressure (to check for risk of eclampsia, a condition in which one or more convulsions occur in a pregnant woman experiencing high blood pressure, often followed by coma and posing a threat to the health of mother and infant); checking for other concerns such as blurred vision, leg cramps, abdominal cramps, and unusual headaches; optimizing oral health; and offering genetic screening if warranted (see later in this chapter).

Testing for infections such as hepatitis B virus (HBV), rubella (German measles), syphilis, and HIV is a standard aspect of prenatal care. HIV can be transmitted from the mother to the baby in utero, during the delivery process, and through breast feeding. There is strong evidence that use of antiviral medications during pregnancy can reduce maternal transmission of HIV. Thus, maternal testing for HIV is an extremely important aspect of prenatal health. If a father is HIV positive and a mother HIV negative, there is risk of fetal infection if the mother becomes HIV positive. (For more information about HIV, see CDC, 2015h).

Testing for vaginal streptococcus B infection is important. If a pregnant woman is positive, antibiotic treatment shortly before birth decreases an infant's risk of becoming infected. Correct dating of a pregnancy is important to prevent unnecessary induction of labor and to permit accurate treatment of preterm labor. Finally, testing for aneuploidy (e.g., an infant having an extra chromosome 21, 18, or 13) and neural tube defects (increasingly carried out by a series of biomarkers, or possible indicators shown through routine blood tests) should be offered to all pregnant women, with a discussion of the risks and benefits of such testing (CDC, 2015l; Zolotor & Carlough, 2014).

As of 2016, concern emerged from northeast Brazil that there may be a link between Zika virus infection during pregnancy and an increase in infants born with microcephaly (WHO, 2016). Although microcephaly can result from different causes, known and unknown, the CDC has declared that Zika virus is a teratogen that causes microcephaly and other serious brain anomalies (see Chapters 9 and 13). Zika is transmitted to people by the same type of mosquito that causes dengue, chikungunya, and yellow fever, and by possibly other types of mosquitos as well (CDC, 2016b). To avoid Zika virus infection, people should avoid being bitten by mosquitos. Those who live in areas where Zika virus outbreaks are rampant or who plan to travel to such areas (especially women who are pregnant or who are considering pregnancy) should consult health or travel authorities for advice. Unfortunately, Zika

may become an issue in more areas than originally thought. For example, although the Zika epidemic was first identified in Brazil, there is now evidence of Zika infection in Florida (CDC, 2016a). In addition, there is evidence that Zika can be transmitted sexually (CDC, 2016b). Other means of transmission such as by blood transfusion are under investigation (CDC, 2016b).

Since about 2010, there has been increasing recognition about potential negative effects of fetal exposure to "toxic" maternal stress, which can result from factors affecting the mother, her partner, and other members of the family (see Chapters 9 and 13). Although reactivity to stress is in part genetic, both animal and human studies have suggested that fetal exposure to maternal stress can influence later stress responsiveness. In animals, adverse effects of maternal stress have been demonstrated, not only in the offspring of the studied pregnancy, but also in subsequent generations (Shonkoff et al., 2012). Fortunately, the brain is plastic and can rewire. Negative effects of maternal stress can be improved after birth with reduction of stress, a secure parent–infant bond, and an enriched environment.

Midwifery care is an integrated part of some prenatal health care systems. This practice promotes a natural approach to birthing as well as additional support and flexibility for the mother and her family during the prenatal period, labor, and birth, as well as the postnatal period. For more information about midwifery care, see American Pregnancy Association (2015).

Birth and Neonatal Periods

According to the WHO, up to one half of newborn deaths occur within the first 24 hours after birth. Even in developing countries, the lives of many newborns and their mothers can be saved by interventions that require only simple technology (WHO, 2015b). This includes helping infants to breathe who do not breathe on their own, provision of eye care, supplementation with vitamin K, vaccinations (see later in this chapter), early access to breast feeding, and provision of special care for newborns who are sick, preterm, have been exposed to or infected by HIV, or have congenital syphilis. In the United States, guidelines specify the level of care that newborns and their mothers should receive, depending upon their health risks (American Academy of Pediatrics, 2012b).

The health benefits of breast feeding, in developed as well as developing countries, are well documented. Breast feeding confers nutritional benefits to the infant and nonnutritional benefits to the infant and the mother; as a result, breast feeding optimizes infant, child, and adult health as well as child growth and development (American Academy of Pediatrics, 2012a). As well as providing an ideal source of nutrition, breast feeding protects the infant against a host of illnesses and diseases (CDC, 2015j). Breast feeding provides many other benefits to both the mother and the infant, including lowered risk of allergies and asthma for the infant, lowered risk of breast and ovarian cancer for the mother, as well as psychological benefits by promoting the attachment and emotional bond between the mother and the infant, among other benefits (American Academy of Pediatrics, 2012a). Given its documented short- and long-term medical and neurodevelopmental benefits, breast feeding should be considered a public health issue and not only a lifestyle choice (American Academy of Pediatrics, 2012a). The American Academy of Pediatrics recommends exclusive breast feeding for the first 6 months of an infant's life, followed by continued breast feeding as complementary foods are introduced, with continuation of breast feeding for 1 year or longer as mutually desired by mother and infant (American Academy of Pediatrics, 2012a). Due to the overwhelming public health benefits of breast feeding, it should be encouraged, supported, and facilitated in hospitals and by health professionals (American Academy of Pediatrics, 2012a). Mothers who breast feed exclusively should consume an extra 500 calories per day and extra liquid. The American Academy of Pediatrics recommends that breast fed infants take a vitamin D supplement of 400 IU (international units) per day (American Academy of Pediatrics, 2012a). Contraindications for breast feeding are rare and include certain infections (e.g., tuberculosis, certain retroviruses) and when taking certain drugs (American Academy of Pediatrics, 2012a). Mothers who are breast feeding and need to take drugs should speak with a pharmacist about the safety and potential effects of the drugs on their babies. See the U.S. National Library of Medicine's LactMed web site for information about drug safety while breast feeding (https://toxnet.nlm.nih.gov/newtoxnet/lactmed.htm). Readers should be aware that being HIV positive is not necessarily a contraindication for breast feeding. For more information and guidance on specific cases, refer to new guidelines from the World Health Organization and the United Nations Children's Fund (2016) and seek advice from professionals. For mothers who cannot breast feed by necessity or choice, formula feeding can be a healthy and the next best alternative for infants (MedlinePlus, 2015a).

Postnatal Period

In order for children to realize their full potential and develop into productive and healthy adults, they need good nutrition, appropriate housing, protection from infectious diseases, access to primary health care, an adequate family income, and access to good education (Woods, 2014). Good nutrition is very important for mothers who breastfeed. Because infants are dependent on adults to regulate their stress levels, it is important that their environment be unstressful and be nurturing (see Chapter 13). An infant's environment also should be stimulating. In an appropriate environment, an infant will develop strong emotional attachments and learn to trust and love and to be socially competent (i.e., to get along with other people). For more information about social competence, see Illinois Early Learning Project (2015).

For postnatal care, a family needs to find a family doctor and, preferably, a pediatrician for the infant. At well-baby clinics, a nurse can answer questions and check the infant's growth. Well-baby examinations that involve a doctor should include height and weight measurements, a complete physical examination of the infant, and questions about the infant's motor skills and development. Vaccination is an important aspect of postnatal care. The HBV hepatitis B virus vaccine can be given at birth and again between 1 and 2 months. At 2 months, the full immunization schedule starts; this includes vaccinations against diphtheria, tetanus, pertussis, polio, meningitis, pneumococcal infections, and rotavirus. The CDC recommends that all children get two doses of the MMR vaccine, with the first dose at 12–15 months of age and the second dose at 4–6 years of age. Children can receive the second dose earlier as long as it is at least 28 days after the first dose. Flu shots are recommended for infants beginning at age 6 months (CDC, 2015a, 2015k).

Environments that are stimulating for infants and young children up to age 5 should provide safe objects to explore, allow freedom of movement, and offer a variety of experiences. A stimulating environment can be created in one room of a home, in a home child care setting, or in a center-based environment. For examples of how to create stimulating environments, see Kaplan-Sanoff (2002).

The importance of a nurturing environment cannot be overemphasized. It is recognized that in order to bond and develop trust, infants require a primary caregiver who responds appropriately to their needs and spends time cuddling and playing with them, smiling at them, and making plenty of eye contact (Hamilton, 2014). Infant attachment is a process that involves input from both the infant and the caregiver. The primary function of attachment is thought to be ensuring that the infant receives necessary care from the caregiver to promote survival. As important, the quality of the sensory stimuli associated with development of attachment serves to shape, organize, and affect pathways in the brain that are critical for the infant's cognitive and emotional functioning and development in the short and long terms (Sullivan, Perry, Sloan, Kleinhaus, & Burtchen, 2011).

Much of what is known about the importance of a nurturing environment during the first 6 months after birth has come from studies of children who lived in orphanages in Romania more than 25 years ago. For example, a study of Romanian orphans who were adopted before the age of 2 years by families in the United Kingdom revealed that those children adopted before the age of 6 months had better cognitive and physical status by age 4 years than those adopted after age 6 months. The development of Romanian children adopted within the United Kingdom before age 6 months was indistinguishable form a control group of U.K. orphans adopted within the United Kingdom before age 6 months (Rutter, 1998). Other studies of the Romanian orphans found that they had significantly more psychological disorders, including serious attachment issues, than children raised in homes from birth. These observations demonstrate that there is a window of time during which an appropriately nourishing, loving, and stimulating environment can overturn negative effects of a deprived environment to a considerable degree (Hamilton, 2014).

In addition to social factors, other factors such as diet, nurturing while feeding, and medical care are very important in a child's early life. Medical support includes all aspects of health care, including medications for the treatment and prevention of diseases and psychopharmacological interventions for mental disorders, surgical interventions, dental intervention, and intervention for any vision or hearing problems that might exist. Other forms of support include physiotherapy, speech and language therapy, interventions designated as assistive, infant stimulation programs, early childhood intervention programs, and other types of programs.

It has been said that some young children are "dandelions": They thrive no matter what the environmental circumstances. Others are likened to "orchids" and are exquisitely sensitive to their environment (Boyce & Ellis, 2005). There presently is much interest in identifying the genetic and biological bases for these differences and developing appropriate parenting strategies (Albert et al., 2015; Herbert, 2011).

DIAGNOSING DISABILITIES PRENATALLY AND POSTNATALLY

The focus of the preceding sections has been on factors that foster healthy development. This section addresses ways in which some forms of disability can be detected during the fetal period and the first 2 years of an infant's life. Before agreeing to prenatal or neonatal testing that might identify a serious problem with their unborn or newborn infant, women should consider what they would do if the results were positive (e.g., get support from the spouse, partner, family, and/or friends; seek help and guidance from a genetic counselor). Parents who know they are carriers of a genetic disorder may consider preimplantation genetic diagnosis to prevent the birth of children with genetic disorders by selecting unaffected embryos before pregnancy (Dahdouh, Balayla, & Audibert, 2015). However, as this option often involves the destruction of embryos not chosen for implantation, this option is not considered acceptable or ethical by everyone. They may also wish to consider adoption (USA.gov, n.d.). Should a problem be identified prenatally, elective termination of pregnancy might be considered (Trupin, 2015). The latter option is not considered acceptable or ethical by everyone. Furthermore, it is not always possible to predict how one will feel or react until one is faced with having to make a decision. Also, detecting a genetic mutation in one family member sometimes yields information about the risk status of family members who may or may not wish to be informed, resulting in a range of reactions and emotions. Families and professionals must always consider effects that genetic knowledge might provoke.

A recurring dilemma that has been discussed in other chapters (e.g., Chapter 1 and Chapter 24) is that diagnosis of a disability sometimes can lead to various forms of discrimination for families and relatives of a person with the disability as well as for the individual who is affected. It is important to note, however, that all intellectual and developmental disabilities benefit from interventions and supports and that development of intellectual and developmental disabilities can actually be prevented in some cases. Furthermore, the most appropriate support and services often are disorder specific and would not be available in the absence of a diagnosis (see Chapter 21). Finally, it is incontestable that the earlier interventions and supports start, the better off affected children and their families will be.

Prenatal Screening and Testing

Prenatal testing provides information about an infant's health before she or he is born. This can include the application of ultrasound, testing for Rhesus (Rh) disease, and blood tests to detect aneuploidy in the fetus (i.e., trisomy 21 [Down syndrome], trisomy 13, trisomy 18) as well as open neural tube defects (CDC, 20151). Tests denoted as screening tests detect risks for, or signs of, possible health problems in the mother or infant. Based on the results of screening tests, diagnostic tests may be conducted to confirm or rule out possible health problems. The following subsections provide an introduction to prenatal screening and testing. For more information, see MedlinePlus (2015b).

Ultrasound Ultrasound imaging is considered a safe and noninvasive procedure. It is used in early pregnancy to check fetal viability in the case of threatened miscarriage, determine gestational age (i.e., the time since conception) and assess fetus size, check the localization of the placenta, determine the number of fetuses, and check for signs of fetal malformation as well as other conditions. Many different structural abnormalities in the fetus, including neural tube defects and congenital cardiac abnormalities, can be recognized before 20 weeks of pregnancy. (For more information about the use of ultrasound, see Zolotor & Carlough, 2014.) Ultrasound is also used to assist in other diagnostic procedures requiring amniocentesis (i.e., sampling of the amniotic fluid that bathes the fetus), chorionic

villus sampling (CVS; sampling tissue in the uterus), and percutaneous umbilical cord sampling (PUBS; sampling the infant's blood in the umbilical cord). Amniocentesis, CVS, and PUBS are considered to be invasive tests because they increase the risk of miscarriage. See Chapter 9 for details about amniocentesis, CVS, and PUBS.

Testing for Rhesus (Rh) Disease Rh disease (hemolytic disease of the newborn) occurs during pregnancy when a mother who has Rh-negative blood makes antibodies to Rh factor and these antibodies cross the placenta to an infant who has Rh-positive blood. In this case, the antibodies will attack the infant's red blood cells and destroy them. Rh disease does not harm the mother, but it can cause the infant to become anemic and develop jaundice (i.e., yellowing of the skin and whites of the eyes caused by high blood bilirubin levels). If the fetal anemia is severe, the unborn infant may require blood transfusions while still in the uterus via the umbilical cord. Medication called Rhesus immune globulin is available to prevent the mother from making antibodies. This should be given to all Rh-negative women at 28 weeks of pregnancy and after the delivery of her first Rh-positive infant. If an infant with Rh disease is not treated, severe intellectual and developmental disabilities can result (March of Dimes, 2015; see Chapter 13).

Testing for Aneuploidy and Open Neural Tube Defects A class of tests that involves analysis of serum prepared from blood samples taken from a pregnant woman can detect certain types of abnormality in a fetus. For example, blood samples taken from a mother in the second trimester can be analyzed biochemically to see whether the concentrations of certain biomarkers in the blood indicate that she is at increased risk of having an infant with an aneuploidy (Down syndrome, trisomy 18, trisomy 13) or open neural tube defects. Because this form of testing is not perfect, some centers combine specialized first-trimester ultrasound with blood testing. Women with negative results on these blood tests or test combinations usually have no follow-up testing. Women with positive results may arrange to have a detailed ultrasound as well as invasive testing (i.e., amniocentesis, CVS, or PUBS) to rule out or confirm the results of the blood tests.

In some health centers, all women older than age 35 are offered invasive testing to detect aneuploidy without the need for preliminary testing.

This is because the risk of having a child with aneuploidy increases with increasing maternal age. For example, the risk of having a child with Down syndrome (trisomy 21) at maternal age 25 is 1 in 1,250; at age 35, the risk is 1 in 400; at age 45, the risk is 1 in 30 (ACOG, 2005). If parents know that they are at high risk of having a child with a particular inherited genetic disorder, diagnostic prenatal testing for this disorder involving amniocentesis, CVS, or PUBS can be specially arranged. An example of such a disorder is Tay-Sachs disease, an autosomal recessive disorder particularly common in Ashkenazi Jews (Kaback & Desnick, 2011).

Noninvasive Prenatal Genetic Testing   A newer type of blood test detects aneuploidies in the fetus by analyzing cell-free fetal DNA in the blood of a pregnant woman instead of levels of certain biochemicals. This is called noninvasive prenatal genetic testing (Skirton, Goldsmith, & Chitty, 2015). This test has a high sensitivity (true positive rate) and specificity (true negative rate), making it an attractive alternative to the serum screens and invasive tests currently in use (Allyse et al., 2015). In theory, this form of testing can detect almost any single gene disorder (i.e., involving an abnormality in one gene), though such applications are still being researched.

Newborn Screening Programs   Soon after birth, all infants born in the United States and other developed countries, as well as in some less-developed countries, are checked for certain medical conditions. Newborn screening is performed by analyzing a few drops of blood taken from an infant's heel. Two treatable conditions that can be detected at birth are phenylketonuria (PKU) and hypothyroidism (see Chapters 13 and 21). Brain damage from PKU can be prevented by putting an infant with the disorder on a special diet. Slowed growth and brain damage from hypothyroidism can be prevented by medication with thyroid hormone and/or iodine, depending upon the cause of the problem. Infants with sickle cell disease also are treatable; they are prone to infections and can be given a daily dose of antibiotic to help prevent these. In the United States, each state runs its own newborn screening program. Most states screen for a standard number of conditions, but some states may screen for more. Baby's First Test (n.d.) provides a list of conditions included in newborn screening in each state; see also CDC (2015d).

Genetic Testing in Infants and Young Children   Because of improvements in technology, the sequencing of genomic DNA has become not only feasible, but also increasingly more affordable. It is now possible to do genetic testing at any age. What has not kept pace is how to read the DNA sequences and interpret the findings (Knoppers, Zawati, & Sénécal, 2015). Genetic counseling and other forms of support should be arranged before genetic testing is initiated. (A genetic counselor is a professional who is specifically trained to help parents understand a diagnosis of a genetic condition.) Genetic testing is ethically more complex for infants and young children, who cannot make a choice for themselves. When testing is being considered for infants and children, the advantages and the disadvantages should be carefully considered by physicians and parents. For 2013 guidelines for physicians about such testing, see American Academy of Pediatrics (2013).

Hearing and Vision Screening   Problems with hearing and vision can delay the attainment of communication milestones and can affect the development of parent–child bonding. Infants begin to develop speech and language from the time they are born, especially during the first 6 months. The first 3 years are critical ones for acquisition of language. All infants should be screened for hearing loss no later than 1 month of age; it is best if they are screened before leaving the hospital after birth. If an infant does not pass a hearing screening, a full hearing test should be done as soon thereafter as possible, but no later than 3 months of age (CDC, 2015b).

Healthy eyes and equal input from both eyes are critical for proper development of the visual centers in the brain as well as for proper physical development and educational progress. If the developing brain does not receive a clear focused image from a child's eye, loss of vision may result and may be irreversible. A child with vision problems will benefit from early intervention services to help offset the effects of poor vision on development. The first vision screening should take place shortly after birth when the doctor or practitioner inspects the newborn's eye, pupil, and red reflex. From 1 month to 4 years of age, eye health should be assessed at each well-child visit (American Academy of Ophthalmology [ACO], 2013).

Screening for Critical Congenital Heart Defects   Infants with a critical congenital heart defect (CCHD) are at significant risk of disability or death if their condition is not diagnosed soon after birth. Infants with Down syndrome often have serious congenital heart defects (see Chapter 14). Newborn screening using pulse oximetry can identify some infants with a CCHD before they show signs of the condition. (Pulse oximetry is a noninvasive, painless procedure used to measure the oxygen level [or oxygen saturation] in the blood. The sensor is placed on a thin part of the patient's body such as a finger, an earlobe, or the nose. In an infant, it is placed across the foot.) After diagnosis, cardiologists can provide special care and treatment to prevent disability and death early in life. Many, but not all, hospitals routinely screen all newborns for CCHDs. For information, see CDC (2015g).

Postnatal Developmental Screening

As explained previously, hearing and vision play important roles in an infant's development. After birth, an infant's hearing and vision should continue to be checked (ACO, 2013; CDC, 2015b). Remediation should be provided if there is a problem. Middle ear infection is a common condition that can block hearing and lead to language difficulty in young children. Medical intervention and watchful waiting are preferred to the implantation of tubes to alleviate persistent inflammation of the inner ear (otitis media; Rettig & Tunkel, 2014).

There are many different causes of vision impairment in newborns and in infants younger than age 2. Corrective measures should be taken as soon as possible to ensure that children do not become blind as the result of potentially correctable causes such as cataracts and retinopathy of prematurity (ACO, 2013). See also the Urban Child Institute's article on the importance of vision development at http://www.urbanchildinstitute.org/articles/research-to-policy/overviews/seeing-the-importance-of-vision-development.

If an infant is at high risk for developmental problems (i.e., was born prematurely, had a low birthweight, or had a problem or potential problem indicated by a newborn screening test), or if there is concern about a child meeting typical milestones by particular ages (see Table 33.2) or about having autism spectrum disorder (ASD), parents should work with their infant's doctor to get any necessary follow-up tests as soon as possible (CDC, 2015c).

The CDC recommends that all children should have a short developmental screening test during well-child doctor visits at 9, 18, and 24 or 30 months to pick up delays in learning, speaking, behaviors, or moving. In addition, all children should be screened specifically for ASD during well-child visits at 18 and 24 months. If any signs of a problem are found, then a comprehensive diagnostic evaluation should be conducted. This evaluation may include looking at the child's behavior and development in more detail and interviewing the parents. It may also include hearing and vision screening, genetic testing, neurological testing, and other medical testing. In some cases, the primary care doctor might choose to refer the child and family to a specialist for further assessment and diagnosis. Such specialists include developmental pediatricians, child neurologists, and child psychologists or psychiatrists. For more information see CDC (2015e, 2015i), Rauh (2015), Sharma (2011), and WebMD (2015).

DEALING WITH AN EARLY DIAGNOSIS

This section deals with how parents react to the knowledge of having an infant or young child diagnosed with a disability. Some parents adjust quickly and well, whereas others have difficulty accepting the fact that their child is something other than what they had planned for. Lopez, Clifford, Minnes, and Ouellette-Kuntz (2008) pointed out that

> Increased levels of parental stress are often related to the severity of their child's behavior. However, the experience of stress is dependent on how individuals perceive their situation and whether coping strategies (i.e., problem-focused, emotion-focused, and appraisal- or perception-focused coping) are used to manage stress. (p. 99)

This is understandable, and effective support needs to be available to help such parents adjust. In the end, almost all parents make something positive out of disability, even if they initially saw it as negative (Brown, Anand, Fung, Isaacs, & Baum, 2003). As known to the editors and many of the chapter authors of this volume, a great many parents become advocates for disability and even work in the disability field.

Available on the Internet are many stories from parents of children who were diagnosed at an early age with a developmental disability. One moving testimony is called "Noah's Birth Story: How Down Syndrome Changed Our Lives...For the Better" (Smith, 2015). Another is entitled "I Didn't Know I Would Be Able to Love Her the Way I Do" (Reardon,

2015). For other positive stories about having children with disabilities, see the Canadian Down Syndrome Society (n.d.), the FORCE Society for Kids' Mental Health (n.d.), and web sites about other specific types of intellectual and developmental disabilities.

Complexities Associated with a Diagnosis

Diagnosis of a child's disability may result in shock or debilitating anxiety for parents. In retrospect, however, most parents agree that an early diagnosis enables action to help the child and the family. Parents' and other people's concerns about a child's development should always be taken seriously. Parenting a child with a disability can be very challenging in some cases and can include a grief reaction. However, it can also bring rewards and provide opportunities for parents and siblings to learn and experience many new things. It is essential for new parents of a child with a disability to understand the following:

- Their lives will be enriched in some ways.

- They will face many challenges that they would not face with a typically developing child.

- They are not alone—many other parents share their experiences.

- Support and practical help may come from a variety of sources, not just from medical or psychosocial specialists. For example, parent groups can be very helpful in emotional and pragmatic ways.

Breaking the News of an Unexpected Diagnosis

Breaking the news of an unexpected diagnosis to parents in prenatal or newborn settings is a common occurrence and often a difficult one for counselors and physicians (Dent & Carey, 2006). Sheets and colleagues (2011) formulated some helpful practice guidelines for communicating a prenatal or postnatal diagnosis of Down syndrome that could be adapted for other situations.

Finding Specialists

If parents suspect that their infant may have a disability, it is important to do the following:

- Check web sites of recognized organizations for people with disabilities for a list of common characteristics and symptoms.

- Visit a local library or search the Internet for additional reading material.

- Ask for a second professional opinion.

- Keep track of the child's progress and possible manifestations of disability, such as missed milestones.

Once parents are made aware of a delay or medical problem, they may be referred by a family doctor, pediatrician, or clinic to a specialist or a diagnostic group. Parents may also self-refer.

When parents suspect that their child may have a problem, finding the right specialist can be complicated, though a community health or social service organization can be helpful. Parents should remember that a multifaceted team can offer more information and can evaluate the child more comprehensively than a single specialist. This team may consist of a pediatrician, a children's education specialist, a physical therapist, an occupational therapist, a speech-language pathologist, an orthopedic surgeon, a psychologist, a psychiatrist, an ophthalmologist, and an audiologist, among others. Teams of specialists are often found at larger hospitals, especially at university teaching hospitals. In the United States, people seeking such information should check the Center for Parent Information and Resources (2015); that resource has an interactive map directing readers to resources available in different states.

Understanding a Diagnosis

Obtaining a diagnosis is one step forward for the child, and understanding the meaning and implications of the diagnosis—immediate and long term—is just as important for parents. Professionals should explain the diagnosis in terms that parents are able to fully comprehend. Parents need to learn as much as possible about their child's disability so that, in time, they will become familiar with special terms and other aspects of the disability.

There has been a dramatic increase and improvement in the quality of information available on the Internet. However, not all web sites provide credible and accurate information. Web sites linked with governments or universities tend to be more credible than those that are not. Other valuable sources of information come from articles available on such databases as PubMed, PsycINFO, and others. In order to have free access to such articles, having a library card from an organization that subscribes to these facilities is usually required. Some organizations for people with disabilities provide copies of relevant papers or links to them.

Parent–Professional Communication

The importance of communication between parents and professionals cannot be overemphasized. Often, because of their motivation to help their child, parents' knowledge about the disorder and available resources may exceed that of the professionals with whom they are interacting. Professionals should be receptive to learning from parents and be respectful of their knowledge, attitudes, and concerns. Occasionally, barriers to communication can lead to difficulties in relationships between professionals and families or caregivers.

Finding Programs to Assist with Child Care and Development

Parents to be and new parents should take advantage of prenatal education classes, well-baby clinics, and visits from public health nurses. A new birth can be very demanding for anyone. In many places, groups for new mothers provide opportunities for socializing, having adult conversations, and baby-sitting. Some new mothers have become inspired to form such groups themselves. Mothers of infants and young children, with or without disabilities, take part in such groups.

Learning Opportunities

Because the first 2–3 years are especially important ones for a child's development, the implementation of programs for a child with special needs should be considered as early as possible. These can help families gain access to community resources, help parents identify and achieve personal goals, provide up-to-date information on children's growth and development, help children gain access to developmental screening, and provide assistance with transportation to appointments.

Family support programs can provide support and information to individuals with intellectual and developmental disabilities and their families so that both personal and family crises can be assisted. These programs can also provide referrals, information about disabilities and genetic counseling, short-term care management, and crisis and stress

relief, including respite services to provide much-needed breaks on a short- or longer term basis. The programs' general health, safety, and technical advice ranges from information on feeding, playing, toilet training, hygiene, and taking medication to finding schools and advocacy groups and facilitating friendships. The support programs are also a source of information about entitlements, guardianship, and legal issues, as well as various types of counseling. Parent matching groups connect families who have children with the same or similar disorders. Such parent groups frequently provide a great deal of information and support. Parents can also seek advice from guides for parents with a child who has a disability. For example, see *One Miracle at a Time: Getting Help for a Child with a Disability* (Dickman & Gordon, 1993) and "Parenting a Child with a Disability" (Womenshealth.gov, 2009).

Effectively Parenting a Child with a Disability

Effective parenting of an infant or toddler with a disability includes learning as much as possible about the disability and keeping detailed records about the child. It is useful to have a binder or notebook (in hard copy or electronic form) with contacts and telephone numbers and additional information such as that shown in Table 33.3. Such information is often very helpful to professionals involved in the care of the child with a disability (e.g., physicians, therapists, teachers). It also provides families with evidence for progress and can be therapeutic on its own.

Managing Care for a Child with a Disability

The arrival of a child with a disability can create stresses in a family and can be very challenging. However, as documented by Dickman and Gordon (1993),

- A family with a child with a disability does not have to break down as the result of stress.

- It is not the child's disability that results in difficulties for families but the ways in which family members react to the disability and to one another.

It is crucial to find ways to deal with the added stresses, to minimize them, and to overcome them by discussing them. When a child with a disability becomes part of the family, tensions may begin to

Table 33.3. Information for a child history binder or notebook

Item	Details
Emergency phone numbers	First aid, ambulance, fire department, police, important health care suppliers and providers for the child
ID numbers of parents and child	Numbers pertaining to Social Security, health care, and private insurance
Child's medical history	If the child was born with a disability, to include prenatal information about the child and parents, genetic background, details about the birth and the period shortly after birth, copies of hospital and medical records
Child's medication records	Names of medicines and dates they were prescribed, why they were prescribed and if they worked, negative side effects
Copies of notes, record of names, and phone numbers of key individuals	From conferences, consults and conversations with professionals, agencies, and school officials (face to face, on the phone, or by web conference)
Correspondence	Letters or e-mails to and from government and voluntary agencies, health care suppliers, school officials
Educational history	Preschool programs and schools attended; infant stimulation and early intervention programs with dates, names of teachers, therapists, and resource personnel who worked with the child; copies of report cards, test results, comments, assessments, individual educational programs or other educational plans
Parents' observations	Child's behavior

Source: Machalek, Brown, Birkan, Fung, and Percy (2003); see also Dickman and Gordon (1993).

mount. However, some parents say that the experience of bringing up a child with a disability has brought them closer together. Essential to the well-being of the marriage or partnership and the child is communication between the parents and talking together about their child. This often means deliberately bringing other people, including the child's siblings, into the discussion. Each family needs to work out an effective communication pattern. Some families may sit around the kitchen table once a week, whereas others communicate more sporadically. Feelings should be shared, as this will foster an inclusive environment where all family members feel validated.

Involvement of Siblings Siblings are an important part of the support network, even when the child with a disability is an infant or a toddler. The child's brothers and sisters should be informed as much as possible about the nature of the disability. Joining a sibling group or a sibling–parent group can make it easier to realize why parents must spend extra time on the care of the child with a disability. Although siblings may understand this at an intellectual level, they may still feel jealous, neglected, or shortchanged (Moyson & Roeyers, 2012). In families that have one child with a disability, it is often not possible for parents to spend equal amounts of time with their other children. One way to manage this is to set aside "special time" for every child in

the family (Dickman & Gordon, 1993). The length of time is not as important as the fact that special attention and nurturing is given to the siblings, who can enhance family stability as well as development of the child with disability (Pit-Ten Cate & Loots, 2000). Respite care for the child with the disability can provide parents with time for their other children. Many parents also find it helpful to provide special rewards (e.g., praise or privileges) to sons and daughters for helping to care for and look out for their sibling with a disability. However, parents should ensure that children (especially girls) are not unduly burdened.

Siblings often form a special bond with a sister or brother who has a developmental disability (Cicirelli, 1982). However, types of sibling relationships can vary enormously. Factors that appear to help include setting a positive family atmosphere and interacting with others in positive ways (Greenberg, Seltzer, Orsmond, & Krauss, 1999; McPhail, 1996). However, parents should be aware that siblings of a child with a disability often feel an ongoing sense of loss and sometimes experience ridicule from other children (McPhail). When families cannot cope with managing a child with a disability or their sibling(s), they should seek professional counseling and help. A study found that siblings of children with intellectual and developmental disabilities either were not affected or were positively affected by their experiences (Carter, Cook,

Sutton-Boulton, Ward, & Clarke, 2016). These study authors described social pedagogy as a model to provide support for such siblings. A key principle of social pedagogy (a model that is gaining popularity in Europe) is that the child is in charge of his or her own life, and that the social pedagogue works alongside rather than dictating to him or her.

Helping Family and Friends New parents will probably need guidance and practical assistance to deal positively with family and friends. Two particular studies of parents of children with developmental disabilities found that most parents relied little on others (Brown et al., 2003; Renwick, Brown, & Raphael, 1999). Their reasons for doing so were as follows:

- People outside the family (others) do not understand a child with a disability.

- Others do not know how to handle or talk to a child with a disability.

- Parents feel embarrassed by their child's behavior.

- Parents do not want to burden others with their child's disability.

These results were replicated in numerous international studies that focused on family quality of life (Brown, 2010, 2015).

However, these parents did not identify acceptance by other people as being a particular problem for them. Relatives, friends, neighbors, and people in the general public were often more accepting of disability than many parents believed. Still, there are many ways that new parents can help others understand and accept disability in their child. First, they need to discuss the disability openly, explaining its nature and what can be expected in the future. Second, they can provide opportunities for others to interact with, and care for, their child with a disability—as they would for a child who does not have disabilities. Third, they can include the child with a disability in their social activities to the extent that is comfortable. Finally, they may need to make extra efforts to instruct others on what they should say, what they should do, and how they should react. It is important to realize that most people do not have experience with children who have disabilities and may not know what they should do. Typically, they welcome helpful pointers from the parents.

Finding Supports and Services for Parents
For both parents and siblings, it is important to take initiative in dealing with relatives, friends, and others in positive ways. Because parents and siblings usually do not have experience with this and may be dealing with considerable adjustment themselves, they very often need some help and guidance. Knowledgeable counselors or health, early childhood, or social services professionals can be very helpful in this regard. In North America and in many countries, there are also numerous parent and family support groups (known to local social service organizations) that provide valuable help to new parents of infants with developmental disabilities. Families should connect to these groups as soon as possible.

DIVERSITY AND CROSS-CULTURAL CONSIDERATIONS

Availability of many of the supports and services highlighted in this chapter varies markedly from one region to another. Furthermore, accessibility to these often is limited to those who are affluent and/or who have extensive medical insurance coverage. The importance of free well-baby clinics staffed by nurses cannot be overemphasized. Finally, because populations in North America are ethnically diverse and continually changing through arrivals of newcomers from other countries, cross-cultural considerations will affect attitudes of dealing with disability and relationships with professionals. Professionals in the field need always to be aware of and learning about diversity and cross-cultural issues while being cognizant of what are their own beliefs and attitudes. Culture, religion, and spirituality can be tremendous sources of strength to any person or family or, in some cases, the only support. For more information about diversity and cross-cultural issues, see Chapter 27, Nehring (2007), and the Canadian Paediatric Society web site at http://www.kidsnewtocanada.ca/screening/child-development.

FUTURE DIRECTIONS

At the global level, not enough is being done to provide every child the opportunity to have the best start in life by optimizing the first 1,000 days. In the United States, an organization called 1,000 Days is committed to improving nutrition for women and young children throughout the world. This organization was first established in 2010 and obtained independent public charitable status in 2015. For more information about 1,000 Days, its activities, and its partnerships (which include the U.S. Department of State), see 1,000 Days (2016a, 2016b).

In Canada, there is a movement to improve early childhood development by bringing together researchers from various disciplines, by generating new knowledge, and by breaking down academic silos that have tended to isolate professionals in biomedical fields from those in psychosocial disciplines. Efforts are being made to design health and education programs on the basis of the science of early childhood education. Also, researchers, policy makers, educators, families, and caregivers are being encouraged to create and share knowledge in an active and equal partnership (University of Toronto Fraser Mustard Institute of Human Development, 2016).

Finally, the next frontier of the genome revolution is sequencing DNA of fetuses that has been recovered from maternal peripheral blood samples. (DNA pieces in the mother's blood come from broken cells derived from the placenta.) Although fetal genomic sequencing likely will be technically and economically feasible within a few years from the time this chapter was written in 2016, what presently poses a roadblock is reading and understanding the sequence information. Furthermore, not presently clear is whether parents and professionals really want such comprehensive sequence information by the time the infant is born. Finally, there are other complex ethical issues arising from such technological advances. For example, although an adult can decide whether to undergo genomic sequencing, this is not the case for an unborn baby (Rigolato, 2013).

SUMMARY

The first 1,000 days of development (from conception to 2 years of age) are critical for optimal early development and for an infant's physical, mental, and emotional health throughout life. Good nutrition is crucial, as is a nurturing, stimulating, and supportive environment. Childhood development can be monitored using developmental milestones—particular skills achieved by typically developing children at certain ages. Such skills include gross and fine motor skills, hearing and vision, speech and language, social and emotional development, and problem solving. Factors that promote optimal early development begin in the parents

prior to conception and include important prenatal, neonatal, and postnatal issues, particularly good nutrition, good lifestyle habits, and good health care. Certain disorders can be identified prenatally, at birth, and afterward using biochemical, genetic, or developmental screening.

Although assignment of a diagnosis can lead to discrimination, it is important to bear in mind that virtually all disabilities benefit from supports and services at the earliest possible age and that some intellectual disabilities can actually be prevented. Parents react differently to the knowledge of having an infant or young child diagnosed with a disability. Effective and appropriate supports and services should be available to help parents and siblings of children who have a disability, regardless of issues of diversity and culture. Immediate future activities in the prenatal and early childhood development arenas include bringing together a wide array of partners dedicated to improving nutritional and health outcomes for mothers and children at levels ranging from local to global and addressing the ethical complexities that result from the technological ability to sequence an infant's DNA before it is born.

FOR FURTHER THOUGHT AND DISCUSSION

1. Kristen has just found out that her 18-month-old son has fragile X syndrome and that she is a carrier of the fragile X mutation. Kristen's parents decided to be tested for the fragile X mutation as well. Kristen found out that she inherited a fragile X mutation from her mother, who carried a premutation. Kristen and her parents know that Kristen's sister, Willa, wants very much to have a child but that Willa may have inherited a fragile X mutation from her mother. They do not know if they should tell Willa, as Willa once mentioned that she would never consider genetic counseling for an inherited disorder in the family. How would you handle the situation if you were Kristen or her parents? (For information about fragile X syndrome, see Chapter 15.)

2. Rose is a single mother of a 2-year-old girl with severe cerebral palsy. Rose has a job that enables her to manage financially. Until recently, she had a wonderful live-in caregiver for her daughter. Unfortunately, the caregiver became very ill and Rose had to arrange for nursing care for her daughter from an agency. Each week, a

different nurse comes to the house, and Rose has to spend an enormous amount of time training each new person about her daughter's needs. Rose's employer has become concerned about the amount of time Rose takes off from work. Also, professional nursing assistance is far more expensive than live-in care, and Rose knows that this cannot continue indefinitely. What course of action would you recommend?

3. Riva and Invid have a 2-year-old son just diagnosed with ASD who requires a great deal of their time. Their older son (age 6 years) is engaging in challenging behavior, though he does not have ASD. What can Riva and Invid do to help both of their children and improve their family life?

REFERENCES

Albert, D., Belsky, D.W., Crowley, D.M., Latendresse, S.J., Aliev, F., Riley, B.,...Dodge, K.A. (2015). Can genetics predict response to complex behavioral interventions? Evidence from a genetic analysis of the fast track randomized control trial. *Journal of Policy Analysis and Management, 34*(3), 497–518.

Allyse, M., Minear, M.A., Berson, E., Sridhar, S., Rote, M., Hung, A., & Chandrasekharan, S. (2015). Non-invasive prenatal testing: A review of international implementation and challenges. *International Journal of Women's Health, 7*, 113–126.

American Academy of Ophthalmology. (2013). *Vision screening for infants and children—2013.* Retrieved from http://www.aao.org/clinical-statement/vision-screening -infants-children-2013

American Academy of Pediatrics. (2012a). Breastfeeding and the use of human milk. *Pediatrics, 129*(3), e827–e841. Retrieved from http://pediatrics.aappublications.org /content/pediatrics/early/2012/02/22/peds.2011-3552 .full.pdf

American Academy of Pediatrics. (2012b). Levels of neonatal care. *Pediatrics, 130*(3), 587–597.

American Academy of Pediatrics. (2013). Ethical and policy issues in genetic testing and screening of children. *Pediatrics, 131*(3), 620–622.

American College of Obstetricians and Gynecologists. (2005). *Your pregnancy and birth* (4th ed.). Washington, DC: Author.

American College of Obstetricians and Gynecologists. (2013). *ACOG Committee opinion no. 549: Obesity in pregnancy. Committee opinion. Number 549. Obstetrics & Gynecology, 121*(1), 213–217.

American Pregnancy Association. (2015). *Prenatal testing.* Retrieved from http://americanpregnancy.org/prenatal -testing/

AVERT. (n.d.). *Global HIV and AIDS statistics.* Retrieved from http://www.avert.org/worldstats.htm

Baby's First Test. (n.d.). *Conditions screened by state.* Retrieved from http://www.babysfirsttest.org/newborn-screening /states

Better Brains for Babies. (2015). *Early and middle childhood.* Retrieved from http://www.bbbgeorgia.org/brain TimeEarlyChild.php

Boyce, W.T., & Ellis, B.J. (2005). Biological sensitivity to context, Vol. 1: An evolutionary-developmental theory of the origins and functions of stress reactivity. *Development and Psychopathology, 17*(2), 271–301.

Boyles, S. (2015). *High doses of vitamin D may cut pregnancy risks.* Retrieved from http://www.webmd.com/baby /news/20100504/high-doses-of-vitamin-d-may-cut- pregnancy-risk

Brown, I. (2010). Family quality of life: A comparison of trends in eight countries. In V.P. Prasher (Ed.), *Contemporary issues in intellectual disabilities* (pp. 255–264). New York, NY: Nova.

Brown, I. (2015). *Quality of life: Advances in individual and family quality of life for persons with neurodevelopmental disorders.* Keynote speech, Tenth International Congress, European Association for Mental Health in Intellectual Disability, Florence, Italy. Retrieved from https://www .researchgate.net/publication/285055792_Quality_of _Life_Advances_in_Individual_and_Family_Quality _of_Life_for_Persons_with_Neurodevelopmental _Disorders

Brown, I., Anand, S., Fung, W.L.A., Isaacs, B., & Baum, N. (2003). Family quality of life: Canadian results from an international study. *Journal of Developmental and Physical Disabilities, 15*(3), 207–230.

Canadian Diabetes Association Clinical Practice Guidelines Expert Committee. (2013). Canadian Diabetes Association 2013 clinical practice guidelines for the prevention and management of diabetes in Canada. *Canadian Journal of Disabilities, 37*(Suppl. 1), S1–S212.

Canadian Down Syndrome Society. (n.d.). *Personal stories.* Retrieved from http://www.cdss.ca/blog/information /personal-stories/

Canadian Paediatric Society, Caring for Kids New to Canada. (2015). *Developmental disability across cultures.* Retrieved from http://www.kidsnewtocanada.ca/mental -health/developmental-disability

Carter, S., Cook, J., Sutton-Boulton, G., Ward, V., & Clarke, S. (2016). Social pedagogy as a model to provide support for siblings of children with intellectual disabilities: A report of the views of the children and young people using a sibling support group. *Journal of Intellectual Disability Research, 20*(1), 65–81.

Center for Parent Information and Resources. (2015). *Find your parent center.* Retrieved from http://www .parentcenterhub.org/find-your-center/

Centers for Disease Control and Prevention. (2014a, August 29). *Preconception health and health care: Overview.* Retrieved from http://www.cdc.gov/preconception /overview.html

Centers for Disease Control and Prevention. (2014b, October 10). *Vaccines for pregnant women.* Retrieved from http://www.cdc.gov/vaccines/adults/rec-vac/pregnant .html

Centers for Disease Control and Prevention. (2015a, January 26). *Immunization schedules for infants and children.* Retrieved from http://www.cdc.gov/vaccines/schedules /easy-to-read/child.html

Centers for Disease Control and Prevention. (2015b, February 18). *Hearing loss in children: Screening and diagnosis*. Retrieved from http://www.cdc.gov/ncbddd /hearingloss/screening.html

Centers for Disease Control and Prevention. (2015c, February 26). *Autism spectrum disorder (ASD) screening and diagnosis*. Retrieved from http://www.cdc.gov/ncbddd /autism/screening.html

Centers for Disease Control and Prevention. (2015d, March 3). *Newborn screening*. Retrieved from http://www .cdc.gov/ncbddd/newbornscreening/

Centers for Disease Control and Prevention. (2015e, April 21). *Developmental milestones*. Retrieved from http://www .cdc.gov/ncbddd/actearly/milestones/

Centers for Disease Control and Prevention. (2015f, April 28). *Folic acid recommendations*. Retrieved from http://www .cdc.gov/ncbddd/folicacid/recommendations.html

Centers for Disease Control and Prevention. (2015g, May 26). *Screening for critical congenital heart defects*. Retrieved from http://www.cdc.gov/ncbddd/heartdefects /screening.html

Centers for Disease Control and Prevention. (2015h, June 23). *HIV among pregnant women, infants, and children*. Retrieved from http://www.cdc.gov/hiv/group/gender /pregnantwomen/index.html

Centers for Disease Control and Prevention. (2015i, August 24). *Child development: Developmental monitoring and screening*. Retrieved from http://www.cdc.gov/ncbddd /childdevelopment/screening.html

Centers for Disease Control and Prevention. (2015j, October 1). *Breastfeeding*. Retrieved from http://www .cdc.gov/breastfeeding/

Centers for Disease Control and Prevention. (2015k, October 16). *Flu vaccine safety and pregnancy*. Retrieved from http://www.cdc.gov/flu/protect/vaccine /qa_vacpregnant.htm

Centers for Disease Control and Prevention. (2015l, November 9). *Pregnancy*. Retrieved from http://www.cdc .gov/pregnancy/index.html

Centers for Disease Control and Prevention. (2016a). *Zika virus: Advice for people living in or traveling to Wynwood, a neighborhood in Miami, FL*. Retrieved from http://www .cdc.gov/zika/intheus/florida-update.html

Centers for Disease Control and Prevention. (2016b). *Zika virus: Transmission and risks*. Retrieved from http://www .cdc.gov/zika/transmission/index.html

Cicirelli, V.G. (1982). Sibling influence throughout the lifespan. In M.E. Lamb & B. Sutton-Smith (Eds.), *Sibling relationships*. Hillsdale, NJ: Lawrence Erlbaum.

Dahdouh, E.M., Balayla, J., & Audibert, F. (2015). Technical update: Pre-implantation genetic diagnosis and screening. *Journal of Obstetrics and Gynaecology Canada, 37*(5), 451–463.

Dean, S., Rudan, I., Althabe, F., Webb Girard, A., Howson, C., Langer, A.,...Bhutta, Z.A. (2013). Setting research priorities for preconception care in low- and middle-income countries: Aiming to reduce maternal and child mortality and morbidity. *PLoS Medicine, 10*, e1001508. doi:10.1371/journal.pmed.1001508

Dent, K.M., & Carey, J.C. (2006). Breaking difficult news in a newborn setting: Down syndrome as a paradigm.

American Journal of Medical Genetics: C. Seminars in Medical Genetics, 142C(3), 173–179.

Dickman, I.R., & Gordon, S. (1993). *One miracle at a time: Getting help for a child with a disability* (Rev. ed.). New York, NY: Simon and Schuster.

Elmadfa, I., & Meyer, A.L. (2012). Vitamins for the first 1,000 days: Preparing for life. *International Journal for Vitamin and Nutrition Research, 82*(5), 342–347.

Fanni, D., Ambu, R., Gerosa, C., Nemolato, S., Iacovidou, N., Van Eyken, P.,...Faa, G. (2014). Aluminum exposure and toxicity in neonates: A practical guide to halt aluminum overload in the prenatal and perinatal periods. *World Journal of Pediatrics, 10*(2), 101–107.

Finer, L.B., & Zolna, M.R. (2011). Unintended pregnancy in the United States: Incidence and disparities, 2006. *Contraception, 84*(5), 478–485.

The FORCE Society for Kids' Mental Health. (n.d.). Denise's story. Dual diagnosis from a parent's point of view. In *Dual diagnosis: A guide for families of a child with an intellectual/developmental disability and a mental disorder*. Retrieved from http://www.forcesociety.com/sites /default/files/Dual_Diagnosis_Guide.pdf

Greenberg, J.S., Seltzer, M.M., Orsmond, G.I., & Krauss, M.W. (1999). Siblings of adults with mental illness or mental retardation: Current involvement and expectation of future caregiving. *Psychiatric Services, 50*(9), 1214–1219.

Gunatilake, R., & Patil, A.S. (2013). *Drugs in pregnancy. Merck Manual*. Retrieved from http://www.merckmanuals .com/professional/gynecology-and-obstetrics/drugs-in -pregnancy/drugs-in-pregnancy

Hamilton, J. (2014). *Orphans' lonely beginnings reveal how parents shape a child's brain*. Retrieved from http://www.npr .org/blogs/health/2014/02/20/280237833/orphans-lonely -beginnings-reveal-how-parents-shape-a-childs-brain

Harvard University Center on the Developing Child. (2010). *The foundations of lifelong health are built in early childhood*. Retrieved from http://www.developingchild .harvard.edu

Herbert, W. (2011, November/December). On the trail of the orchid child. One genetic variant leads to the best and worst outcomes in kids. *Scientific American*. Retrieved from http://www.scientificamerican.com/article /on-the-trail-of-the-orchid-child/

Hoddinott, J., Behrman, J.R., Maluccio, J.A., Melgar, P., Quisumbing, A.R., Ramirez-Zea, M.,...Martorell, R. (2013). Adult consequences of growth failure in early childhood. *American Journal of Clinical Nutrition, 98*(5), 1170–1178.

Illinois Early Learning Project. (2015). *What do I need to know about young children's social competence?* Retrieved from http://illinoisearlylearning.org/faqs/socialcomp.htm

Kaback, M.M., & Desnick, R.J. (1999, March 11; updated 2011, August 11). Hexosaminidase A deficiency. In R.A. Pagon, M.P. Adam, H.H. Ardinger, S.E. Wallace, A. Amemiya, L.J.H. Bean, T.D. Bird, & K. Stephens (Eds.), *GeneReviews* [Internet]. Seattle: University of Washington, Seattle.

Kaplan-Sanoff, M. (2002). Stimulating environments. In N. Jellinek, B.P. Patel, & M.C. Froehle (Eds.), *Bright futures in practice: Mental Health: Volume II. Tool Kit.*

Arlington, VA: National Center for Education in Maternal and Child Health.

Karakis, I., Sarov, B., Landau, D., Manor, E., Yitshak-Sade, M., Rotenberg, M.,...Novack, L. (2014). Association between prenatal exposure to metals and neonatal morbidity. *Journal of Toxicology and Environmental Health, Part A, 77*(21), 1281–1284.

Knoppers, B.M., Zawati, M.H, & Sénécal, K. (2015). Return of genetic testing results in the era of whole-genome sequencing. *Nature Reviews Genetics, 16*(9), 553–559.

Le Geyt, J. (2012). Developmental screening for young children. *InnovAiT, 5*(10), 579–586.

Lopez, V., Clifford, T.P., Minnes, P., & Ouellette-Kuntz, H. (2008). Parental stress and coping in families of children with and without developmental delays. *Journal on Developmental Disabilities, 14*(2), 99–104.

Machalek, K., Brown, I., Birkan, R., Fung, M., & Percy, M. (2003). Prenatal and early life. In I. Brown & M. Percy (Eds.), *Developmental disabilities in Ontario* (2nd ed., pp. 511–530). Toronto, Canada: Ontario Association on Developmental Disabilities.

Machalek, K., Percy, M., & Brown, I. (2007). Prenatal and early life. In I. Brown & M. Percy (Eds.), *A comprehensive guide to intellectual and developmental disabilities* (pp. 433–450). Baltimore, MD: Paul H. Brookes Publishing Co.

Machalek, K., Percy, M., Carter, M., & Brown, I. (2011). Prenatal and early life. In I. Brown & M. Percy (Eds.), *Developmental disabilities in Ontario* (3rd ed., pp. 697–717). Toronto, Canada: Ontario Association on Developmental Disabilities.

March of Dimes. (2015). *Rh disease.* Retrieved from http://www.marchofdimes.org/baby/rh-disease.aspx

Mathur, R. (2015). *Hypothyroidism during pregnancy (thyroid deficiency during pregnancy).* Retrieved from http://www.medicinenet.com/hypothyroidism_during_pregnancy/article.htm

Mayo Clinic. (n.d.). *Pregnancy week by week: Is it safe to use a hot tub during pregnancy?* Retrieved from http://www.mayoclinic.org/healthy-lifestyle/pregnancy-week-by-week/expert-answers/pregnancy-and-hot-tubs/faq-2005

Mayo Clinic. (2015). *Vitamin B$_6$ (pyridoxine): Safety.* Retrieved from http://www.mayoclinic.org/drugs-supplements/vitamin-b6/safety/hrb-20058788

McPhail, E. (1996). A parent's perspective: Quality of life in families with a member with disabilities. In R. Renwick, I. Brown, & M. Nagler (Eds.), *Quality of life in health promotion and rehabilitation* (pp. 279–289). Thousand Oaks, CA: Sage.

MedlinePlus. (2015a, December 2). *Breastfeeding vs. formula feeding.* Retrieved from https://www.nlm.nih.gov/medlineplus/ency/patientinstructions/000803.htm

MedlinePlus. (2015b). *Prenatal testing.* Retrieved from https://www.nlm.nih.gov/medlineplus/prenataltesting.html

Melzer, K., Schutz, Y., Boulvain, M., & Kayser, B. (2010). Physical activity and pregnancy: Cardiovascular adaptations, recommendations and pregnancy outcomes. *Sports Medicine, 40*(6), 493–507.

Moore, V.M., & Davies, M.J. (2005). Diet during pregnancy, neonatal outcomes and later health. *Reproduction, Fertility, and Development, 17,* 341–348.

Moyson, T., & Roeyers, H. (2012). "The overall quality of my life as a sibling is all right, but of course, it could always be better": Quality of life of siblings of children with intellectual disability: The siblings' perspectives. *Journal of Intellectual Disability Research* [Special issue; Part Two: Family Quality of Life], *56*(1), 87–101.

Mustard, J.F. (2009). Canadian progress in early child development—putting science into action. *Paediatric and Child Health, 14*(10), 689–690.

National Institutes of Health, Office of Dietary Supplements. (2011). *Vitamin B$_6$ fact sheet for consumers.* Retrieved from https://ods.od.nih.gov/factsheets/VitaminB6-Consumer/

Nehring, W.M. (2007). Cultural considerations for children with intellectual and developmental disabilities. *Journal of Pediatric Nursing, 22*(2), 93–102.

Office of Disease Prevention and Health Promotion. (2015). *Dietary guidelines.* Retrieved from http://health.gov/dietaryguidelines/

1,000 Days. (2016a). *Home page.* Retrieved from http://thousanddays.org/

1,000 Days. (2016b). *Partners.* Retrieved from http://thousanddays.org/about/partners/

Pit-Ten Cate, I.M., & Loots, G.M. (2000). Experiences of siblings of children with physical disabilities: An empirical investigation. *Disability and Rehabilitation, 22*(9), 399–408.

Rauh, S. (2015). *Is your baby on track?* Retrieved from http://www.webmd.com/parenting/baby/features/is-your-baby-on-track

Reardon, M. (2015, March 20). *I didn't know I would be able to love her the way I do.* Retrieved from http://www.cbsnews.com/news/down-syndrome-mothers-story/

Renwick, R., Brown, I., & Raphael, D. (1999). *The family quality of life project: Final report. Report to the Ontario Ministry of Community and Social Services, Developmental Services Branch.* Toronto, Canada: Centre for Health Promotion, University of Toronto.

Rettig, E., & Tunkel, D.E. (2014). Contemporary concepts in management of acute otitis media in children. *Otolaryngologic Clinics of North America, 47*(5), 651–672.

Rigolato, A. (2013). *Prenatal DNA sequencing. MIT Technology Review.* Retrieved from http://www.technologyreview.com/featuredstory/513691/prenatal-dna-sequencing/

Rutter, M. (1998). Developmental catch-up, and deficit, following adoption after severe global early privation. English and Romanian Adoptees (ERA) Study Team. *Journal of Child Psychology and Psychiatry, 39*(4), 465–476.

Salam, R.A., Zuberi, N.F., & Bhutta, Z.A. (2015). Pyridoxine (vitamin B$_6$) supplementation during pregnancy or labour for maternal and neonatal outcomes. *Cochrane Database of Systematic Reviews, 2015*(6). doi:10.1002/14651858.CD000179.pub3

Sharma, A. (2011). Developmental examination: Birth to 5 years. *Archives of Diseases in Childhood Education and Practice Edition, 96,* 162–175.

Sheets, K.B., Crissman, B.G., Feist, C.D., Sell, S.L., Johnson, L.R., Donahue, K.C.,...Brasington, C.K. (2011). Practice guidelines for communicating a prenatal or postnatal diagnosis of Down syndrome: Recommendations of the

National Society of Genetic Counselors. *Journal of Genetic Counseling, 20*(5), 432–441.

Shonkoff, J.P., Garner, A.S.; Committee on Psychosocial Aspects of Child and Family Health; Committee on Early Childhood, Adoption, and Dependent Care; Section on Developmental and Behavioral Pediatrics. (2012). The lifelong effects of early childhood adversity and toxic stress. *Pediatrics, 129*(1), e232–e246. doi:10.1542/peds.2011-2663

Skirton, H., Goldsmith, L., & Chitty, L.S. (2015). An easy test but a hard decision: Ethical issues concerning non-invasive prenatal testing for autosomal recessive disorders. *European Journal of Human Genetics, 23*(8), 1004–1009.

Smith, R. (2015). *Noah's birth story: How Down syndrome changed our lives…For the better.* Retrieved from http://noahsdad.com/story/

Sullivan, R., Perry, R., Sloan, A., Kleinhaus, K., & Burtchen, N. (2011). Infant bonding and attachment to the caregiver: Insights from basic and clinical science. *Clinical Perinatology, 38*(4), 643–655.

Trupin, S.R. (2015). *Abortion overview and history.* Retrieved from http://www.emedicinehealth.com/abortion/article_em.htm

University of California, Riverside. (2015, May 18). *Maternal obesity compromises babies' immune system at time of birth.* Retrieved from http://www.sciencedaily.com/releases/2015/05/150518173501.htm

University of Toronto Fraser Mustard Institute of Human Development. (2016). *Research program.* Retrieved from http://fmihd.utoronto.ca/

USA.gov. (n.d.). *Family legal issues.* Retrieved from https://www.usa.gov/family-legal

U.S. Department of Agriculture. (n.d.). *Dietary reference intakes.* Retrieved from http://fnic.nal.usda.gov/dietary-guidance/dietary-reference-intakes

U.S. Department of Health and Human Services, Health Resources and Services Administration, Maternal and Child Health. (n.d.). *Prenatal services.* Retrieved from http://mchb.hrsa.gov/programs/womeninfants/prenatal.html

U.S. Department of State. (n.d.). *1,000 days. Change a life: Change the future.* Retrieved from http://www.state.gov/secretary/20092013clinton/rm/2010/09/147512.htm

U.S. National Library of Medicine. (2013). *LactMed: A new NLM database on drugs and lactation.* Retrieved from https://www.nlm.nih.gov/news/lactmed_announce_06.html

WebMD. (2015). *Recognizing developmental delays in children.* Retrieved from http://www.webmd.com/parenting/baby/recognizing-developmental-delays-birth-age-2

Wilson, R.D., Genetics Committee, & Special Contributors. (2015). Pre-conception folic acid and multivitamin supplementation for the primary and secondary prevention of neural tube defects and other folic acid-sensitive congenital anomalies. *Journal of Obstetricians and Gynaecologists of Canada, 37*(6), 534–552.

Womenshealth.gov. (2009). *Parenting a child with a disability.* Retrieved from http://womenshealth.gov/illnesses-disabilities/parenting/parenting-child-with-disability.html

Womenshealth.gov. (2010). *Pregnancy: Staying healthy and safe.* Retrieved from http://womenshealth.gov/pregnancy/you-are-pregnant/staying-healthy-safe.html

Woods, L. (2014). *Every child counts. Seven key reasons why the first 1,000 days are critical.* Retrieved from http://everychildcounts.org.nz/Seven+key+reasons+why+the+first+1000+days+are+critical

World Health Organization. (2015a). *Children: Reducing mortality.* Retrieved from http://www.who.int/mediacentre/factsheets/fs178/en/

World Health Organization. (2015b). *Newborn care at birth.* Retrieved from http://www.who.int/maternal_child_adolescent/topics/newborn/care_at_birth/en/

World Health Organization. (2016). *Zika virus.* Retrieved from http://www.who.int/mediacentre/factsheets/zika/en/

World Health Organization & United Nations Children's Fund. (2016). *Guideline: Updates on HIV and infant feeding: The duration of breastfeeding, and support from health services to improve feeding practices among mothers living with HIV.* Geneva, Switzerland: World Health Organization. Retrieved from http://apps.who.int/iris/bitstream/10665/246260/1/9789241549707-eng.pdf

Zolotor, A.J., & Carlough, M.C. (2014). Update on prenatal care. *American Family Physician, 89*(3), 199–208.

34

Early Intervention
for Young Children

Elaine B. Frankel, Kathryn Underwood, and Peggy Goldstein

WHAT YOU WILL LEARN

- How to define and understand early intervention and early intervention services
- The benefits accruing from high-quality early intervention services
- How to recognize and provide high-quality inclusive early education
- The role of assessment and evaluation in designing high-quality early intervention services
- How to plan for early intervention services
- Accommodations and classroom organization features that promote high-quality inclusive early intervention services
- The importance of involving families in early intervention

Creative Kids, a community-based early education and care program, and Creative Families, a family resource program, welcome Carlos, Jessica, and Matthew as they arrive, giggling at each other's hairstyles for "wacky hair day" at the center. They are followed by their parents, who bring them to the center each morning. They are 2- and 3-year-olds who live in the same neighborhood.

Carlos, age 2, has fragile medical conditions that have affected his development. After Carlos was

Authors' note: The authors acknowledge contributions from other versions of this chapter authored by Dr. Elaine B. Frankel and Dr. Kathryn Underwood (2011), Dr. Elaine B. Frankel and Dr. Susan Gold (2007), and Dr. Elaine B. Frankel, Susan Howson, and Ingrid Fish (2003). The authors thank Cherry Chan for her research assistance.

born, his developmental delays were identified during regular visits to his home by the public health nurse. His parents then met with an early intervention case manager, and an evaluation of him and an assessment of his family was conducted by a transdisciplinary team to develop an individualized family service plan (IFSP). He now receives occupational therapy in his home environment, and his parents attend family support groups at Creative Families with Carlos, where they discuss how to facilitate his development and are provided with referrals to financial and educational services. Carlos' parents emigrated from Peru and are learning to speak English.

Jessica, age 3, has a congenital hearing impairment that was diagnosed at birth at the local hospital. Her mothers have been teaching her sign language since she was an infant. As Jessica entered preschool at Creative Kids, a transdisciplinary team including her parents, itinerant early childhood special educator, preschool teacher, American Sign Language itinerant teacher, speech-language pathologist (SLP), and audiologist collaborated to formulate an individualized education program (IEP) for Jessica, with inclusion implementation recommendations to ensure a smooth program transition into the preschool classroom.

Matthew has fragile X syndrome and has recently been diagnosed with autism. He has been provided with early intervention services but will be turning 3 this year and making a transition to the services provided by the local education agency (LEA). His parents, early interventionist, child care teacher, occupational therapist (OT), and intensive behavioral therapist will attend a transition meeting that identifies Matthew's strengths, abilities, challenges, and goals. Because his family's first language is Korean, an interpreter will also be available at the meeting. If Matthew is eligible for special education services, goals will be written and services will be acquired based on his assessed abilities and needs, and these will be outlined in an IEP. Through this collaborative effort, the team will produce an IEP and inclusion plan that provides environmental adaptations and teaching strategies to best promote his development, learning, and success.

Carlos, Jessica, and Matthew are examples of the many children who are receiving services to address their individual needs in an inclusive early childhood intervention program. All children require environments and early experiences that support optimal outcomes for development. For infants, toddlers, and preschoolers, development is age sensitive. Therefore, it is essential that services and programs that promote healthy child development are available to them and their families early and when they are needed.

In general, children with disabilities have additional risks to their development, and appropriate early intervention can prevent further delays and additional impairments as well as minimize barriers to a child's learning and healthy development. Early intervention services also strive to provide families with support and resources to achieve positive patterns of parent–child interactions that enhance the child's development (Guralnick, 2011).

Early identification of vulnerable children and quality intervention services become critical to ensure that young children with disabilities are comprehensively and equitably served (World Health Organization, 2012). Early childhood services in the community assist in identifying young children who have an established condition (e.g., deafness), are experiencing delays in a particular aspect of their development (e.g., speech and language), or are at risk for developmental delays due to biological and/or environmental factors (e.g., a chronic health condition). Services and programs can then provide children and families with the appropriate interventions and support to facilitate development.

Internationally, *early intervention* does not have one definition, but it is generally conceptualized as a range of policies and services provided before school age to support children and families. It is predicated on the right of all children to equitable opportunities for growth and development in the early years. The rights of all children have been clearly articulated in international conventions and in the policies and laws of many countries.

The United Nations *Convention on the Rights of the Child* (1989) stipulated that all children with physical or mental disabilities "should enjoy a full and decent life, in conditions which ensure dignity, promote self-reliance, and facilitate the child's active participation in the community" (A. 23, s.1). The United Nations *Convention on the Rights of Persons with Disabilities* (2006) further stated that children with disabilities have a right to early intervention (A. 25 [health] s.b) and to education "on an equal basis with others in the communities in which they live" (A. 24 [education] s.2b.).

In some countries, this rights-based approach to early intervention is operationalized through national or state/provincial legislation. For example, in the United States, early intervention and special education services are provided for infants, toddlers, and preschoolers and their families by federal legislation, the Individuals with Disabilities Education Improvement Act (IDEA) of 2004 (PL 108-446). In this legislation, *early intervention* specifically refers to services for children from birth up to 3 years of age that must be provided by each state. Although not mandated in the law, states are permitted to continue to provide early intervention services (Part C) for children from age 3 until entry into kindergarten (Gargiulo & Kilgo, 2014). Free appropriate public education for young children 3–5 years old can also be provided under the Special Education Preschool Grants Part B of IDEA. There are regulatory differences between services under Part C and Part B (for further discussion, see U.S. Department of Education, 2013). These definitions differ from those used in many countries, such as Canada and Australia, where the provision of early intervention services for young children birth to 6 years of age is built into provincial/state or territorial government policies. Funding is available regionally by municipal, provincial/state, and territorial authorities in these countries where there is not a national mandate (Sukkar, 2013; Underwood & Frankel, 2012). In this chapter, we adopt the broad definition of *early intervention* to refer to services for families and children from birth to 6 years or school age.

This chapter describes principles of high-quality early intervention. High-quality early intervention services in the child's community are guided by the provision of inclusive programs, partnerships generated with families, and the formation of collaborative teams. Each of these is described more fully in the sections to follow.

HIGH-QUALITY EARLY INTERVENTION

Children and families requiring support and assistance are everywhere in communities. They attend infant development programs, child care centers, family resource centers, library events, and community health clinics. Health and educational research has made significant gains in illuminating the effects of nurturing environments on healthy development. In particular, there are believed to be critical periods in brain development that make the early years an important window for early intervention (Irwin, Siddiqi, & Hertzman, 2007). In the early years of a child's development, the brain's rapid growth and ability to self-correct offers a window of opportunity to reverse or minimize the effects of risk conditions such as brain injury, chromosomal anomalies, or environmental stress (McCain, Mustard, & McCuaig, 2011). Overall, better outcomes can be expected for children when they have exposure and access to quality early childhood and care programs.

The gains associated with high-quality early intervention are sustained and long-lasting. There is an increasing body of evidence that has demonstrated that high-quality early care and education promotes positive short-term outcomes for children's cognitive and social-emotional development (Barnett & Ackerman, 2006). Longitudinal findings from the Abecedarian project have shown that not only are educational and social benefits maintained, including lower crime rates and increased employment, but long-term health benefits also exist. Participants from low-income families, who as young children attended a high-quality child care program with an innovative early learning curriculum and health care on site, still display better intellectual, educational, and health outcomes 35 years later than their peers who did not attend (Campbell et al., 2014).

Beyond developmental, educational, and ethical rationales for high-quality intervention services, there is a strong economic rationale for providing quality care and early intervention. James Heckman's (2011) analysis of the economic return on investment in early childhood showed the highest returns were associated with children from disadvantaged families, when intervention happens very early, and when the programs are of high quality. His work suggested that when these conditions are present, the rate of return is as high as $7 for every dollar spent. Similarly, research in Canada citing returns in Canadian dollars showed that every $1 invested in child care returns $1.45 to the economy (Prentice & McCracken, 2004). Barnett and Ackerman (2006) cautioned that although the cost benefits can be substantial to society, these outcomes are only associated with high-quality programs.

The first step in a successful system of early intervention requires universal screening programs that identify children at risk for compromised healthy child development. Coordinated and integrated community services are necessary to ensure that early screening and detection efforts offer equitable and consistent access for all children (Macy, Marks, & Towle, 2014). Furthermore, effective detection requires screening tools that possess reliable psychometric characteristics and also requires knowledgeable professionals who appreciate and measure the abilities that children possess rather than assess only their weaknesses. These professionals must also be sensitive to the cultural context of development and the linguistic diversity of families.

The effects of merely identifying children and families are limited if resources are not available in the community for further assessments and interventions. Based on developmental–behavioral and family assessments, early intervention services can be truly individualized, ranging in intensity and degree depending on the child and family's strengths and priorities. Early interventionists who provide individualized services are trained professionals from a variety of disciplines who support children and families through home visits or consultations in their community child care center, preschool, or school.

INCLUSIVE EARLY EDUCATION

At the core of early intervention are high-quality inclusive services that provide access, full participation, and appropriate supports to enhance each child's learning and development (Division for Early Childhood [DEC] & National Association for the Education of Young Children [NAEYC], 2009). Within inclusive early childhood settings, children may have very different learning needs, learning styles, and rates of learning, yet each child's growth is appreciated and encouraged.

Four core principles of inclusion form the foundation for bridging the gap between a vision of full inclusion for all children and actual practice. First, as previously described, inclusive programs look to international conventions and mandates to provide the context for developing a vision of inclusion in each jurisdiction. Second, a philosophy that values the right of every child to be included must be embraced by all stakeholders in an organization, including parents. Third, there must be respect for the cultural and linguistic diversity of children and families and their preferences. Finally, instructional approaches and therapeutic interventions are required that are based on the child's strengths and embedded within the learning experiences and routines of the classroom (Frankel, Gold, & Ajodhia-Andrews, 2010).

Converging evidence suggests that the positive developmental outcomes associated with early intervention can be achieved in quality inclusive early childhood settings where children with a range of abilities play and learn together in a diverse group. In inclusive settings, children learn from modeling the play, language, and social interactions of their peers (Guralnick, 2011). When early childhood educators promote relationships, social competence, and close friendships between children with developmental disabilities and their peers in inclusive settings, it provides opportunities for all children to learn how to relate to each other as playmates and friends. The educators also help develop friendships that continue outside the early childhood program. In inclusive settings, children with disabilities have been shown to achieve significant gains in peer acceptance, friendships, and cognitive development (Odom, Buysse, & Soukakou, 2011). These empirical findings give support to inclusion as a strategy to achieve positive developmental and educational outcomes for children.

In an inclusive early childhood setting, all children benefit. They become more sensitive, tolerant, and accepting of people with disabilities. They learn to appreciate and embrace diversity. This is not to suggest, however, that a quality early childhood program that offers developmentally appropriate programming for its children is enough to ensure continued gains for children with developmental delays. In other words, mere proximity to peers does not guarantee developmental advances for the child with a disability. Research demonstrates that in order to promote successful developmental growth, individualized intervention plans must be provided that allow children with developmental delays to learn and apply functional behaviors and communication skills (Guralnick, 2004; Hollingsworth, Boone, & Crais, 2009).

Leadership

The provision of early intervention services in inclusive environments has been acknowledged as a recommended practice for preschoolers with disabilities (DEC, 2014). Yet inclusive early childhood education and care programs are not yet universally available for children (Odom et al., 2011). Transformational leaders can be instrumental in motivating administrators, teachers, and families to make fundamental changes to program philosophy, policies, and instructional practices that allow for inclusion.

Boards of directors, administrators, and teachers should review the program's philosophy and consider how it promotes inclusion. Supervisors need to be able to clearly articulate this philosophy of inclusion to staff and families. By having a written policy, position, or mission statement affirming inclusion, administrators demonstrate a commitment to ensuring children have access to both equity and quality in all aspects of their early childhood experience. Wait lists and admission practices should ensure equitable access. The number of children with developmental disabilities in an inclusive early childhood setting should reflect the prevalence of disability in each community. This allows all children in the community to come together in early childhood settings.

Although an inclusive philosophy and clear policies are the cornerstones of inclusion, there needs to be a planned process to ensure that the vision is carried out effectively. Administrators, families, early childhood educators, itinerant early childhood special education teachers, therapists, and resource consultants, as leaders in the field, must work together to plan, problem-solve, and decide on environmental adaptations and instructional strategies that include a child with developmental disabilities in all aspects of the program (DEC, 2014).

Assessment and Evaluation

Evaluation is critical to the continued improvement and expansion of inclusive early childhood programs (Guralnick, 2004). In addition to screening children for developmental disabilities and delays, ongoing assessments are used to plan instructional goals, monitor growth in children in all developmental domains, and evaluate the effectiveness of intentional interventions (DEC, 2014).

An assessment of the early childhood inclusive environment can provide guidance for embedding interventions for a child with a developmental delay in the routines and activities of the classroom (Hollingsworth et al., 2009) and can promote professional development of staff (Buysse & Hollingsworth, 2009). Ecobehavioral assessments of classroom environments and behavioral interactions between a child with disabilities and adults and peers have shown that positive social interactions of children with disabilities are established in inclusive settings (Tsao et al., 2008). By comparing assessments with quality indicators of inclusive early childhood education and care programs, families, educators, and specialized professionals can work together to improve the outcomes for children and programs. In addition, staff should be encouraged to regularly evaluate all aspects of their programs, including professional development and family satisfaction.

Instructional Environments

Children with developmental disabilities are included in a variety of early childhood programs, including specialized preschool classes, group child care centers, nursery schools, drop-in centers, family resource centers, and private home child care. The way that individualized goals and instructional approaches are implemented may be different from program to program. However, it is important to ensure that the goals and approaches in individual program planning take into account not only the abilities and needs of the child but also the environment in which the program will be implemented and the interactive skills of the caregiver who will implement them (Hollingsworth et al., 2009). In the United States, federal law ensures appropriate educational practice by mandating the

development and implementation of an IFSP for families with children from birth to age 3 or an IEP for any child identified with a disability age 3 or older. Globally, individualized program planning for children and families is viewed as best practice.

Individualized Family Service Plan The IFSP describes individualized supports for both the child and family as recipients of early intervention services and may include recommendations for health and human service organizations for the family. In the United States, the IFSP is developed after a child has been referred to the early Child Find system, identified, and evaluated by the early intervention team. This collaborative team determines whether the child meets the criteria for services based on the assessment results. If the child meets the criteria, the document includes a description of the strengths, concerns, and priorities of the family for themselves and their child, outlines the services to be provided, and sets procedures and timelines for evaluation. Direct and indirect services for the child are embedded in daily routines and natural environments.

Individualized Education Program The IEP is a statement of the child's specific educational program that includes, among other things, a description of the child's present level of performance, developmental goals, accommodations, and assessment. In the United States, IEPs are legislated to contain specific elements. An IEP is developed after a child has been referred to Child Find services for identification and the collaborative team, provided by the LEA, has completed an evaluation. If the evaluation information provides evidence that the child has a disability, an IEP is written by a collaborative team that includes the parents, teachers, evaluation specialists, and LEA representative. In other countries, the IEP might also include plans for implementing the child's program in the classroom (see Figure 34.1).

Program Accommodations and Adaptations Staff are responsible for developing activities that are interesting and promote the involvement of all children (Sandall, Schwartz, & Joseph, 2001). They are also responsible for implementing a child's IEP goals within the daily program. Universal instructional design should be used to benefit all children. This may require changes to the classroom environment, materials, and/or instructional methods.

Child: Jessica Reid

Date of birth: July 6, 2011

Chronological age: 3 years, 2 months

Grade: Preschool

Parent/guardian: Henni Reid and Tara Jackes

IEP date: September 12, 2014

Initiation date: September 12, 2014

Annual evaluation date: September 12, 2015

Eligibility: Hearing impairment

Evaluation Instruments

Batelle Developmental Inventory–Revised

Preschool Language Scale, Fifth Edition (PLS-5)

Peabody Picture Vocabulary Test, Fourth Edition (PPVT-4)

Language sample

Review of records

Informal play assessment

Audiological evaluation

Team Members Present

H. Reid (parent), T. Jackes (parent), E. Sloan (preschool teacher), C. Kwiatkowski (ECE), L. Davis (ASL teacher), J. Perry (SLP), T. Lang (audiologist), G. Park (LEA representative)

Area of Need: Language and Social-Emotional

Present Level of Performance

Jessica has a delay in receptive and expressive spoken English language skills. She communicates primarily in two- to three-word phrases. Occasionally, she uses ASL in order to convey a message. Receptively, Jessica is able to identify colors, group objects, and understand time concepts (night and day). There is a 6-month delay on receptive language tasks. Expressively, she combines two or three words spontaneously, uses plurals, and uses verb + -*ing*. She has difficulty answering *wh*- questions and yes/no questions, using possessives, and expressing the function of an object. Jessica relates to her peers through parallel play and attends to and engages in large-group activities. She enjoys expressive art activities, sensory experiences, and picture books.

Family Concerns, Implications of Formal and Informal Assessments

All formal assessments were conducted in spoken English without access to an assessor fluent in ASL. Her parents have expressed a preference to have her continue to learn ASL as well as spoken English, and they are making efforts to have her socialize with the Deaf community. All goals will be achieved in both ASL and spoken English. The child care center agrees to enhance its capability to communicate with Jessica in ASL.

Measurable Annual Goals and STOs or Benchmarks

Areas of development	Child's strengths	Child's needs	Short-term objectives	Long-term goal(s) (fundamental skills and concepts)
Language and communication: receptive and expressive	• Communicates primarily in two- to three-word phrases • Expressive signing well developed	Developing receptive and expressive language skills in ASL and spoken English Answering *wh*- questions and yes/no questions, using possessives	Jessica will • Identify vocabulary items and actions by pointing, 9 out of 10 times, when given multiple exposures to new vocabulary in ASL and spoken English • Name in ASL and spoken English common vocabulary items and actions, given multiple exposures to new vocabulary, 9 out of 10 times • Answer simple yes/no questions posed in ASL and spoken English with 90% accuracy after interactive play with peers	Jessica will • Increase receptive and expressive vocabulary development through high-interest activities in the preschool • Use sign language with verbal language to answer simple requests
Social/emotional: self-esteem	• Engages in parallel play with peers • Attends to and engages in large-group activities	Joining play with peers in small groups Maintaining associative play with peers in small groups	• When at a preferred play area (e.g., sand or water table, creative arts area), Jessica will join her peers in play with teacher support, 9 out of 10 times. • When at a small-group activity with peers, Jessica will initiate an action with her peers (e.g., sharing her doll) without teacher support, 9 out of 10 times. • When playing in a small-group activity, Jessica will maintain the play with her peers for 5 minutes, 75% of the time.	Jessica will • Engage in associative play with peers

Figure 34.1.   Individualized education program and implementation plan for Jessica. (*Sources for instruments cited:* Dunn & Dunn, 2007; Newborg, 2004; and Zimmerman, Steiner, Pond, Boland, & Marshall, 2011.) (*Key:* IEP, individualized education program; ECE, early childhood educator; ASL, American Sign Language; SLP, speech-language pathologist; LEA, local education agency; STOs, short-term objectives.)

Implementation plan (services to be provided)	1. Independent picture drawing	2. Library walks (once per week)	3. Dramatic play area	4. Visual, verbal, and behavioral teaching strategies
	• ECE and SLP will encourage and record children's verbal and ASL descriptions of creative art work. • ECE will verbalize in English and signed descriptions.	• ECE will pair children with a different partner each week. • Children will choose books to borrow. • Children will describe pictures in books.	• ECE will invite and record children's ideas for dramatic play area themes during circle time. • Dramatic area will change each week to reflect children's ideas. • Itinerant special education teacher will lead small-group art experiences that emphasize self-knowledge (i.e., body tracing).	• ECE will encourage emotional expression daily using verbal prompts. • ECE will encourage Jessica's entry into small-group sensory play using verbal prompts and physical proximity for support. • ECE will use positive verbal and behavioral reinforcement when Jessica is engaged in play with peers.

Related Services

Audiologist

Placement

Inclusion in community-based preschool with itinerant services from the SLP and ASL teacher and consultation services provided by the early childhood special education teacher.

Participants' Signatures

LEA representative _____

Parents _____

_____

Preschool teacher _____

SLP _____

ASL teacher _____

Audiologist _____

Early Childhood Special Educator _____

Figure 34.1. (continued)

Embedding learning within the natural and inclusive environment, and during daily routines and activities, is the most developmentally appropriate strategy for teaching. Many of the strategies presented herein can be applied universally but may be differentiated to accommodate the individual needs of specific children in the class. Some examples of accommodations and adaptations for an effective inclusive classroom include the following:

Classroom organization

• Physical space may need to be arranged to accommodate specialized equipment such as a wheelchair or medical devices.

• Routines may need to be adjusted. Some groups require physical activity, such as outside play, prior to sitting for circle time.

• Augmentative and alternative communication systems are used for choice making and socialization. Picture or symbol prompts should be provided to identify activities, procedures, and areas, in addition to a visual schedule.

Materials

• Limit the number of choices of toys or activities for children who may be easily distracted.

- Adjust expectations for each activity to allow children at a variety of developmental levels to participate in all domain areas. For example, encourage activities that facilitate development for a child with fine motor delays by having the child tear paper rather than use scissors.

- Adapt materials to support a child's participation. A child with a weak hand grasp may need the handles of paintbrushes and crayons to be made thicker with foam or Silly Putty or to be attached to his or her hand by a band of Velcro.

- Use adaptive designs to support a child's access to the learning environment (e.g., a weighted vest or fidget toy to help a child focus his or her attention, a specially designed and angled easel to allow a child to reach the paper while sitting in a wheelchair).

Instructional Methods

- Vary classroom groupings. It is important to encourage mixed skill groupings so peers can provide models for each other.

- Differentiated instruction should be embedded in routines and activities throughout the day. For example, during story time, the teacher might ask the child working on an objective to enhance vocabulary to name the pictures on the page but have the child with fine motor objectives turn the pages of the big book.

- Analyze tasks and teach the skill in smaller steps.

- Verbal and physical prompts such as praise or hand-over-hand assistance can be used to help children interact with materials and peers.

- Positive behavioral supports are highly recommended for children who have difficulty regulating their own behavior. For example, the child who has difficulty with the transition to clean up may need multiple prior verbal alerts that the activity will be changing.

The possible accommodations and adaptations are limitless. The teacher and staff must always consider the abilities, needs, and developmental goals for the child and then review the skills and knowledge needed for tasks and activities. Where the abilities of the child and the demands in the classroom do not match, the teacher may need to make adjustments and adaptations to the environment and to developmental expectations for the child.

Transitions   The transitions from early intervention to preschool education and from preschool education to kindergarten mark critical junctures for a child and family. In this process, the transition meeting has been found to be an essential conduit for sharing information, planning services, and developing an initial inclusion plan (Villeneuve et al., 2013). Transition planning includes parents (many who become the primary advocates for their children), early interventionists, resource consultants, educators, health care professionals, and program administrators.

CREATING PARTNERSHIPS WITH FAMILIES

Intervention programs that recognize the primary importance of the child's family, the social context in which the family operates, and the family's enduring relationship with the child are known as family-centered programs. However, families of children with developmental delays often experience stress related to the quality of supports available to them (Bailey, Golden, Roberts, & Ford, 2007; Tehee, Honan, & Hevey, 2009). For this reason, early intervention programs must not only effectively meet the needs of the individual child but must also recognize and support the whole family.

Guidelines for family-centered practice should be based on core principles that supports to the child 1) need to be embedded in a holistic understanding of the family members and their life context and 2) need to be based on parent–professional partnerships that maintain the family as primary caregiver and decision maker for the child. However, such guidelines should also stipulate that children with disabilities should be part of decisions that affect them and be informed in a manner appropriate to their ages and development. The United Nations *Convention on the Rights of the Child* (1989) stated that the views of the child should be given due weight in decisions that affect them (A. 12, s.1), or a representative should be heard on the child's behalf. This means that families should be included as children's representatives and, where appropriate, children should be kept informed. The child should, therefore, be central to family-centered practice.

The Developmental Systems Approach (DSA) can provide a structural framework for developing early intervention services to children and families (Guralnick, 2011). The DSA stresses that an important goal of early intervention is to strengthen family functioning to allow the family to effectively interact with their child to obtain positive child developmental outcomes (Guralnick, 2011). To serve the needs of families, parent involvement and family support have become central components of early intervention programs and services. Evidence suggests that family participation in early intervention services promotes positive parent attitudes and expectations for their child and strengthens family processes. Families who are able to create a stable and stimulating environment have positive long-term effects on child development outcomes (Guralnick, 2011).

Research supports that family-centered programs are guided by the following beliefs (Dempsey & Keen, 2008; Dunst & Dempsey, 2009; Dunst, Trivette, & Hamby, 2007):

- Strengthening and supporting the family in conjunction with the child will have a positive impact on all members of the family.

- Families and children should be empowered to become competent and capable rather than dependent on professional help-giving systems. This is accomplished by creating opportunities for families to acquire knowledge and skills to navigate the ongoing challenges that life presents.

- A proactive approach to families and children involves the acceptance of individual differences and the recognition of individual strengths, and encourages the acquisition of skills that will allow families and children increased control and decision-making power.

- The family and child, and not the professionals, should identify the needs and aspirations to target for intervention. It should be the role of the family to determine what is in the best interests of the family.

- All families and children have strengths, and these strengths should be recognized and built upon. Focusing on correcting weaknesses will prevent the development of a meaningful and

productive relationship between families and professionals and a positive self-concept for the child.

- Families often have informal social networks that can provide resources and support that they need. It should be the aim of intervention programs to strengthen and build social networks for families and children, not to replace them with professional services.

- The relationship among parents, children, and professionals should be considered a partnership in which the individual partners all have capabilities that become enhanced through the sharing of knowledge, skills, and resources.

- Inclusive practices should ensure that families have access to a broad range of early intervention services that are sensitive to and respectful of diverse cultural, religious, and social values and priorities.

Not only are families involved in assessing their own and their child's needs, but also they collaborate with the professionals to identify and prioritize goals and develop intervention plans and strategies as part of an IFSP. The IFSP, as discussed previously, is based on the expressed strengths and requirements of the family with a young child who is at risk for developmental delays and incorporates goals that enhance family functioning (see Figure 34.2). This process ensures that parental expectations and priority goals meaningful to the family are included (Xu, 2008).

FORMING COLLABORATIVE TEAMS

Early intervention services offer a variety of therapies (speech and language therapy, occupational therapy, physical therapy) and progress monitoring for the child, support to educators, and family services that include—but are not limited to—family support, resource referrals, and respite care. Many services for infants and toddlers are provided in the home and offer opportunities for the parents to learn appropriate activities to enhance their child's development. For preschoolers, itinerant consultative support is usually provided in the child's home, child care center, preschool, or school. Educators and parents provide valuable input into implementing programs to benefit the child. Multiple professionals and family members working together to support young children requires collaboration.

Child: Carlos Torres

Date of birth: July 21, 2012

Date of evaluation: October 1, 2014

Chronological age: 2 years, 2 months

Parent/guardian: Henri and Cassandra Torres

Present level of development

Carlos was diagnosed at birth with atrial septal defect, a congenital heart defect. Carlos' atrial septal defect is of moderate severity, but he continues to experience chronic fatigue, poor physical development, and frequent lung infections. This condition and frequent hospitalizations have affected his gross motor skills and cognitive abilities. He is walking upright and starting to run but tires quickly. He enjoys fine motor and sensory activities such as playdough and goop and is developing imitative skills and an understanding of cause and effect when he and his parents play with toys. His self-care skills are limited. His mother feeds him and he drinks from a bottle. He is using gestures and one-word utterances in Spanish and English to communicate his needs.

Family's resources, priorities, and concerns

His parents are concerned about his low muscle tone and weight. They have asked for more medical information about his condition. They want Carlos to be able to kick, throw, and catch a ball so that he can eventually play soccer with his father and cousins. His mother reports that Carlos has difficulty with daily transitions and with separating from her. She would like to start to work but requires full-time child care arrangements for Carlos and needs to improve her English language skills. His father was a bookkeeper in his country but needs to upgrade his skills. Both parents have asked for support from a settlement specialist to assist them in finding appropriate employment.

Major outcomes for child and family

Outcome 1: Parents will be provided with more information on atrial septal defect.

Times/criteria for progress: Goal will be met when parents have received information from medical sources regarding Carlos' health.

Strategies:
- The public health nurse will accompany the family to the child's doctor visits to help them ask questions and understand the medical recommendations.
- The public health nurse will make home visits and make recommendations as to how the family can help prevent the spread of colds and viruses.

Review date: 3 months

Outcome 2: Carlos will be able to kick, throw, and catch a ball.

Times/criteria for progress: Goal will be met when Carlos can kick, throw, and catch a ball by his fourth birthday.

Strategies:
- The family support practitioner will provide parents with reading material about the physical development of toddlers and preschoolers.
- The occupational therapist and family will encourage his participation in activities to improve muscle tone and ball-related activities.
- The early childhood resource consultant will assist the family resource center in adapting program equipment and activities to support Carlos' physical development.
- Parents will take Carlos to a local park to encourage the use of climbing equipment and balls.

Review date: 6 months

Outcome 3: Parents would like Carlos to attend a child care center.

Times/criteria for progress: Goal will be met when Carlos is enrolled in child care.

Strategies:
- The resource consultant will be a liaison between the child care subsidy office and the parents to ensure all materials and forms are complete.
- The family support practitioner will refer the parents to several child care centers and assist them with selecting an appropriate program.

Review date: 6 months

Service coordinator: Family support practitioner

Location of services: Home and family resource center

Figure 34.2. Individual family service plan for the Torres family.

Collaboration among parents, educators, and specialized professionals concerned with the child and family's educational and developmental progress has been shown to be a cornerstone of effective early intervention services and inclusion (Bailey et al., 2006). Together, families and professionals assess, plan, and evaluate the individual goals and objectives for the child. Collaborative teams are key to the successful changes children and families make as they move from one program to another, such as from child care to school-based kindergartens (Villeneuve et al., 2013). When individuals bring their discipline-specific professional perspective, knowledge, and experience with the child to the team, a shared understanding of the child evolves and the child's intervention plan can be formulated.

Collaboration involves effective communication, group decision making, team regeneration, interagency cooperation, and a team approach (see Figure 34.3).

Communication

Effective interpersonal communication skills assist all team members in listening and responding to the opinions and perspectives of others on the team. This requires participants to maintain an open mind, to show empathy to others, and to put aside the priorities of their own discipline to incorporate the views of others when appropriate. An environment of trust is most beneficial to the work of a collaborative team. When individuals feel supported and respected, they can, in turn, support and respect the views of others. Creative solutions can flow more freely in an atmosphere of trust and cooperation. Each participant feels freer to express ideas without fear of criticism (Keen, 2007). Differences of opinion should be viewed as opportunities to consider all perspectives, to be flexible, and to implement new intervention strategies.

Group Decision Making

The IFSP and IEP that result from the collaborative team's efforts are based on observations and assessments and guide the intervention. Group members exchange knowledge, share expertise, and make program recommendations. Decisions derived from group problem solving and decision making are superior to those that can be developed by any one individual alone. Ultimately, though, it is the family—as the consumer—that should hold the power to make final decisions related to the IFSP and IEP.

Regeneration

A collaborative team continually evaluates its efforts. Members leave the team as their expertise is no longer required, and new members may be added as the needs of the child and family change. The collaborative team is dynamic, with participants working together to plan strategies for including children with developmental disabilities in early childhood programs.

Child: Matthew

Chronological age: 2 years 11 months

Collaborative team: F. Hong (parent); M. Hong (parent); L. Davis (preschool teacher); C. Kole (early interventionist); E. Sloan (kindergarten teacher); L. Wan (developmental pediatrician); F. Frankfurt (occupational therapist); and G. Park (LEA representative)

The collaborative team met to begin the process of helping Matthew make the transition into a prekindergarten classroom next September. Mr. Hong expressed that he wanted Matthew to be a part of the class like the other children he had seen when visiting the school. He hoped that Matthew would have friends and participate in all areas of the program. He and Ms. Hong expressed concern that Matthew's physical and cognitive development may interfere with his ability to play and learn like the other children. Ms. Hong shared that Matthew enjoys looking at storybooks and listening to music. Both parents were concerned about his behaviors on a large school bus with many children that he did not know. Dr. Wan discussed the communicative intent of Matthew's idiosyncratic behaviors. Fabian, the occupational therapist, wanted to continue sensory integration experiences. Leah, the preschool teacher, provided examples of how the teachers in the child care center promote Matthew's social interactions with peers and engagement with sensory activities that reflect his interests. Fabian made some recommendations for environmental adaptations in the classroom that would assist Matthew's participation in the curriculum. Carol, the early interventionist, offered to observe Matthew's first few visits to the prekindergarten and to provide suggestions for activities that could be embedded in the curriculum and involve all children. Gloria, the LEA representative, expressed concern that Matthew's wandering through the room would be a distraction to the other children. She was invited to observe Matthew's routines in the child care center prior to the start of school in September. The team scheduled a time for the next team meeting.

Figure 34.3. Collaborative team transition meeting notes for Matthew. (*Key:* LEA, local education agency.)

Collaborative Team Approaches

Children with developmental disabilities and their families are often involved with service agencies and health providers other than early intervention (e.g., special services at home, respite care). This involves interagency cooperation. Although teams may function in a variety of ways, including multidisciplinary teams (i.e., professionals communicate with parents and other specialists but work separately within their discipline with the child) and interdisciplinary teams (i.e., parents, educators, and professionals communicate to share knowledge of the child and develop individual goals but work in discipline-specific fields), the use of a transdisciplinary team has been recognized as the ideal model for collaborating in inclusive early childhood settings (Gargiulo & Kilgo, 2014). A transdisciplinary team is characterized by interprofessional "role release" and "role acceptance" (Carpenter, 2005). Families, early childhood educators, itinerant special education teachers, and specialized health care providers (e.g., SLP, OT, physical therapist) share roles, cross traditional discipline-specific boundaries, and collaborate in order to jointly assess a child's learning, plan program goals and objectives for the child's success, determine environmental accommodations and teaching strategies, and evaluate the effectiveness of the program. A primary interventionist is determined by the team, whereas the transdisciplinary team ensures that the whole child is supported, resulting in more meaningful assessments, programming, and evaluation (Gargiulo & Kilgo, 2014).

SUMMARY

This chapter has described early intervention services for young children with disabilities and those at risk for developmental delays. Best practice in early intervention reflects the principles of inclusion, family-centered practice, and collaborative team approaches. Families, early childhood educators, and specialized consultants form the collaborative team. The team has responsibility to assess the abilities and requirements of the child and the family, to seek creative solutions for achieving goals, and to make mutual decisions about service. Based on the family's priorities, goals, and personal preferences, an IEP and/or IFSP is formulated to direct services for the family and the child. With the implementation of adapted instructional activities and family services in inclusive early intervention programs, all children like Jessica, Carlos, and Matthew—who are introduced in the chapter's opening and whose education and service plans are shown in the chapter's figures—will have an opportunity to reach their optimal developmental potential.

FOR FURTHER THOUGHT AND DISCUSSION

1. Discuss the benefits that children who receive early intervention receive, both in the short term and the long term.

2. What are some of the unique challenges in providing inclusive early intervention services? What are the benefits to children of providing inclusive early intervention services (compared with segregated early intervention services)?

3. How do the four core principles of inclusion that form the foundation for inclusive early education affect the education of young children with intellectual and developmental disabilities?

4. Discuss the differences between IFSPs and IEPs. What relative benefits exist in active family involvement in planning?

5. What strategies succeed in involving parents and family members in early intervention programs? What barriers exist that limit this outcome?

REFERENCES

Bailey, D., Bruder, M.B., Hebbeler, K., Carta, I., Defosset, M., Greenwood, C.,...Barton, I. (2006). Recommended outcomes for families of young children with disabilities. *Journal of Early Intervention, 28,* 227–251.

Bailey, D.B., Golden, R.N., Roberts, J., & Ford, A. (2007). Maternal depression and developmental disability: Research critique. *Mental Retardation and Developmental Disabilities Research Reviews, 13,* 321–329.

Barnett, W.S., & Ackerman, D.J. (2006). Costs, benefits, and long-term effects of early care and education programs: Recommendations and cautions for community developers. *Journal of the Community Development Society, 37*(2), 86–100.

Buysse, V., & Hollingsworth, H.L. (2009). Program quality and early childhood inclusion. *Topics in Early Childhood Special Education, 29*(2), 119–128.

Campbell, F., Conti, G., Heckman, J., Moon, S.H., Pinto, R., Pungello, E., & Pan, Y. (2014). Early childhood investments substantially boost adult health. *Science, 343,* 1478–1485.

Carpenter, B. (2005). Early childhood intervention: Possibilities and prospects for professionals, families, and children. *British Journal of Special Education, 32*(4), 176–183.

Dempsey, I., & Keen, D. (2008). A review of processes and outcomes in family-centered services for children with a disability. *Topics in Early Childhood Special Education, 28*(1), 42–52.

Division for Early Childhood. (2014). *DEC recommended practices in early intervention/early childhood special education 2014*. Retrieved from http://www.dec-sped.org/recommendedpractices

Division for Early Childhood & National Association for the Education of Young Children. (2009). *Early childhood inclusion: A joint position statement of the Division for Early Childhood (DEC) and the National Association for the Education of Young Children (NAEYC)*. Chapel Hill: University of North Carolina, FPG Child Development Institute.

Dunn, L.M., & Dunn, D.M. (2007). *Peabody Picture Vocabulary Test, Fourth Edition (PPVT-4)*. Minneapolis, MN: Pearson.

Dunst, C.J., & Dempsey, I. (2009). Family–professional partnerships and parenting competence, confidence and enjoyment. *International Journal of Disability, Development, and Education, 54*(3), 305–318.

Dunst, C.J., Trivette, C.M., & Hamby, D.W. (2007). Meta-analysis of family-centered helpgiving practices research. *Mental Retardation and Developmental Disabilities Research Reviews, 13*, 370–378.

Frankel, E.B., & Gold, S. (2007). Principles and practices of early intervention. In I. Brown & M. Percy (Eds.), *A comprehensive guide to intellectual and developmental disabilities* (pp. 451–466). Baltimore, MD: Paul H. Brookes Publishing Co.

Frankel, E.B., Gold, S., & Ajodhia-Andrews, A. (2010). Preschool inclusion: Bridging the gap between principles and practices. *Young Exceptional Children, 13*(5), 2–16.

Frankel, E.B., Howson, S., & Fish, I. (2003). Early intervention for young children with developmental delays. In I. Brown & M. Percy (Eds.), *Developmental disabilities in Ontario* (2nd ed.). Toronto, Canada: Ontario Association on Developmental Disabilities.

Frankel, E.B., & Underwood, K. (2011). Early intervention for young children. In I. Brown & M. Percy (Eds.), *Developmental disabilities in Ontario* (3rd ed.). Toronto, Canada: Ontario Association on Developmental Disabilities.

Gargiulo, R.M., & Kilgo, J.L. (2014). *An introduction to young children with special needs: Birth through age eight*. Belmont, CA: Wadsworth, Cengage Learning.

Guralnick, M.J. (2004). Effectiveness of early intervention for vulnerable children: A developmental perspective. In M.A. Feldman (Ed.), *Early intervention: The essentialist readings* (pp. 9–50). Oxford, United Kingdom: Blackwell.

Guralnick, M.J. (2011). Why early intervention works: A systems perspective. *Infants & Young Children, 24*, 6–28.

Heckman, J.J. (2011). The economics of inequality: The value of early childhood education. *American Educator, 35*(1), 31–35, 47.

Hollingsworth, H.L., Boone, H.A., & Crais, E.R. (2009). Individualized inclusion plans at work in early childhood classrooms. *Young Exceptional Children, 13*(1), 19–35.

Individuals with Disabilities Education Improvement Act (IDEA) of 2004, PL 108-446, 20 U.S.C. §§ 1400 *et seq.*

Irwin, L.G., Siddiqi, A., & Hertzman, C. (2007). *Early child development: A powerful equalizer*. Vancouver, Canada: Human Early Learning Partnership.

Keen, D. (2007). Parents, families and partnerships: Issues and considerations. *International Journal of Disability Development and Education, 54*(3), 339–349.

Macy, M., Marks, K., & Towle, A. (2014). Missed, misused, or mismanaged: Improving early detection systems to optimize child outcomes. *Topics in Early Childhood Special Education, 34*(2), 94–105.

McCain, M.N., Mustard, J.F., & McCuaig, K. (2011). *Early years study 3: Making decisions, taking action*. Toronto, Canada: Margaret and Wallace McCain Family Foundation.

Newborg, J. (2004). *Battelle Developmental Inventory, Second Edition (BDI-2)*. Itasca, IL: Riverside Publishing.

Odom, S.L., Buysse, V., & Soukakou, E. (2011). Inclusion for young children with disabilities: A quarter century of research perspectives. *Journal of Early Intervention, 33*(4), 344–356.

Prentice, S., & McCracken, M. (2004). *Time for action: An economic and social analysis of childcare in Winnipeg*. Winnipeg, Canada: Child Care Coalition of Manitoba.

Sandall, S., Schwartz, I., & Joseph, G. (2001). A building blocks model for effective instruction in inclusive early childhood settings. *Young Exceptional Children, 4*(3), 3–9.

Sukkar, H. (2013). Early childhood intervention: An Australian perspective. *Infants & Young Children, 26*, 94–110.

Tehee, E., Honan, R., & Hevey, D. (2009). Factors contributing to stress in parents of individuals with autistic spectrum disorders. *Journal of Applied Research in Intellectual Disabilities, 22*, 34–42.

Tsao, L., Odom, S.L., Buysse, V., Skinner, M., West, T., & Vitztum-Komanecki, J. (2008). Social participation of children with disabilities in inclusive preschool programs: Program typology and ecological features. *Exceptionality, 16*(3), 125–140.

Underwood, K., & Frankel, E.B. (2012). The Developmental Systems Approach to early intervention in Canada. *Infants & Young Children, 25*(4), 286–296.

United Nations. (1989). *Convention on the rights of the child*. Retrieved from http://www.ohchr.org/EN/Professional Interest/Pages/CRC.aspx

United Nations. (2006). *Convention on the rights of persons with disabilities*. Retrieved from http://www.un.org/disabilities/convention/conventionfull.shtml

U.S. Department of Education. (2013). *Building the Legacy: IDEA 2004*. Retrieved http://idea.ed.gov

Villeneuve, M., Minnes, P., Versnel, J., Hutchinson, N., Frankel, E.B., Chatenoud, C., & Dionne, C. (2013, November). *Collaborating for educational inclusion of young children with developmental delays and disability during entry to schools*. Paper presented at the 48th Australasian Society for Intellectual Disability Conference, Sydney, Australia.

World Health Organization. (2012). *Early childhood development and disability: Discussion paper*. Geneva, Switzerland: World Health Organization.

Xu, Y. (2008). Developing meaningful IFSP outcomes through a family-centered approach using the double ABCX Model. *Young Exceptional Children, 12*(1), 2–19.

Zimmerman, I., Steiner, V., Pond, R., Boland, J., & Marshall, E. (2011). *Preschool Language Scale–Fifth Edition (PLS-5)*. Bloomington, MN: Pearson/PsychCorp.

35

Maltreatment of Children with Developmental Disabilities

Ann Fudge Schormans and Dick Sobsey

WHAT YOU WILL LEARN

- An understanding of *child maltreatment* as a socially constructed term that refers mainly to physical, emotional, or sexual abuse, and to neglect
- An awareness that child maltreatment has always existed but that now children are entitled to protection by international rights legislation and by laws in their own countries
- Recognition that child maltreatment is a more common experience for children with developmental disability and that developmental disability can result from child maltreatment

The right to live free from fear and from want is a basic human right set out by the United Nations in the 1948 *International Declaration of Human Rights* (Centre for Human Rights, 1996). This was extended to expand protections to people with disabilities in 1971 *(Declaration on the Rights of Mentally Retarded Persons)*, in 1975 *(Declaration on the Rights of Disabled Persons)*, in 1982 *(World Program of Actions Concerning Disabled Persons)*, in 1994 *(Standard Rules on Equalization of Opportunities for Persons with Disabilities)* and, most recently, in 2006 *(Convention on the Rights of Persons with Disabilities* and its *Optional Protocol;* United Nations Enable, 2006).

The United Nations' (1989) *Convention on the Rights of the Child,* ratified by countries in both the Global North and Global South, guarantees every child the right to be free from abuse. Article 23 of the Convention specifically states that children with intellectual and physical disabilities share these rights and that states must make special efforts to meet their special needs. These declarations have prompted many developed and developing nations to begin to design policies, legislation, and practices to ensure these rights. The Canadian Charter of Rights and Freedoms, the Bill of Rights in the Constitution of South Africa, and the United States Constitution are among many national constitutional documents that also promise equal protection of the law for individuals with disabilities. In spite of these fundamental protections, however, child maltreatment remains a major problem for children worldwide and a more severe problem for children with disabilities.

WHAT IS MEANT BY THE TERM *CHILD MALTREATMENT?*

The term *child maltreatment* (or *child abuse*) is a socially constructed concept. This means that the ways that these terms are defined and understood are historically specific and differ across, and within, various nations. The definition of *child* similarly varies according to laws and customs that set out the ages at which individuals are considered adults. Child protection history, laws, and practices in the Anglo-American nations (e.g., Australia, Canada, United Kingdom, United States) typically share many major features (Waldfogel, 1998). These countries all have mandated institutions to deal with child protection. Most have laws that define child maltreatment in fairly similar ways—for example, as in Corso, Edwards, Fang, and Mercy's (2008) definition:

Any act or series of acts of commission or omission by a parent or other caregiver, in the context of a relationship of responsibility, trust, or power, that results in harm, potential for harm, or threat of harm to a child's health, survival, development, or dignity. (p. 1094)

This and similar definitions focus primarily on intrafamilial maltreatment and do not include extrafamilial abuse—acts committed by individuals who are not parents or caregivers (e.g., physical or sexual assault of a child by a stranger). Although not under the purview of mandated child protection services, such acts would nevertheless be considered child abuse under a broader definition.

HISTORICAL AND CURRENT CONTEXTS

Although child maltreatment almost certainly has existed as long as there have been children, the recognition of the right of children to protection from abuse is relatively recent. Prior to the late 1800s, children were granted few protections from abuse. The laissez-faire ideology of Western governments, combined with the liberal idea of the sanctity of the family (and concomitant view of children as the responsibility and property of their parents), minimized provision of social supports to children and deterred state intervention in situations involving disability and/or parental abuse of children (Macintyre, 1993). The child protection movement is commonly divided into two phases or "waves." The first wave began in the late 1800s, and the second started in the middle of the 1900s.

The first wave can be traced to 1874, when the Society for the Prevention of Cruelty to Animals met in New York City to discuss the possibility that children should also be protected. Responding to the exploitation of children wrought by industrialization and the deplorable conditions of foundling homes and orphanages—and informed by an emerging middle class, rising standards of health and welfare, and shifting understandings of childhood and child rearing—it formed the Society for the Prevention of Cruelty to Children (Bremner, 1971; Chadwick, 1999; Macintyre, 1993). Buttressed by women's suffrage, abolitionist, and labor movements, the child saving movement rapidly spread to Britain (1883), Canada (1891), Australia (1896), and many other countries (Waldfogel, 1998).

In many ways, the development of a systemic response to child abuse parallels the path of service provision to children with developmental disabilities in these countries, with the phenomena of child abuse and developmental disability being inextricably linked. Both were informed by eugenicist and social hygiene concerns to protect society from moral decay—that wrought by immoral, abusive parents and by those deemed genetically inferior (e.g., people with disabilities) (Carlson, 2001). Unfortunately, services for children with developmental disabilities and services for abused children were similar in that 1) both produced institutional care and 2) institutional care often produced more abuse.

Contemporary Context of Developmental Disabilities and Child Protection

The second wave in child protection began in the middle of the 20th century with a renewed interest in the areas of child maltreatment and child protection. Publication of x-ray studies showing children with multiple healed fractures and head injuries (Caffey, 1946) led to the identification of battered child syndrome (Kempe, Silverman, Steele, Droegemueller, & Silver, 1962), a key development in child protection. As a result, health care professionals joined the child protection movement, which had previously been primarily in the social reform domain. Growing feminist and human rights movements were also important drivers of emerging child protection initiatives. (Increasingly, child protection activism is adopting a strong orientation toward risk of maltreatment.)

Researchers were also beginning to explore the connection between child abuse and developmental disabilities during this period. For example, in 1967, Elmer and Gregg reported that 50% of abused children had intellectual disability and raised the question of whether the disabilities resulted from abuse or were risk factors for abuse. In addition, a growing movement of parents and advocates campaigned against abuse and other appalling conditions within institutions. Rescuing their children from institutional settings and returning them to their home communities became a strong advocacy focus, and gradually, deinstitutionalization policies and practices took hold (Malacrida, 2012; Panitch, 2008; Sobsey, 1994). It is important to note, however, that although some jurisdictions have adopted deinstitutionalization as a goal, others have not.

"Care" in large-scale institutions (and the risk of abuse engendered by such environments) remains a reality for many people with developmental disabilities. Nor has the move back to community meant the end of abuse: Children and adults with developmental disabilities living in family homes or service-based residential settings or living independently continue to experience and be at risk for abuse as defined in this chapter and for other forms of violence (Robinson, 2014).

THEORETICAL PERSPECTIVE FOR UNDERSTANDING MALTREATMENT

Child maltreatment, like all forms of violence, cannot be understood to result from any single determinant. The most accepted theoretical framework in much contemporary research is the integrative ecological model (Macdonald, 2001). From this perspective, child abuse and neglect are the result of the dynamic interplay of genetic, biological, psychological, environmental, and sociological factors that combine to create the conditions necessary for abuse or neglect to occur. Some of these factors act to increase the risk of maltreatment, others to protect the child from harm. Some factors are distal and have a long-lasting or cumulative effect (e.g., attachment disruptions). Current, or recent, factors are termed *proximal factors* (e.g., loss of housing). An understanding of abuse is best accomplished through an assessment of the interplay among the relevant factors over both space (i.e., the individuals involved and the environment) and time (past and present) and across four levels of analysis: the individual (child and caregiver), the family, the community, and society (Macdonald, 2001).

This theoretical orientation is extended by more recent critical theorizing in disability that attends to ableist beliefs, structures, practices, and processes that both define and privilege those deemed "able bodied" or "able minded" while simultaneously defining and "disabling" those understood to be "unable." Rejecting a limited focus on the individual (which serves often to pathologize, victimize, and blame people with disabilities), critical theorizing supports an analysis that makes plain the sources of oppression, discrimination, marginalization, and stigmatization experienced by people with disabilities (Fudge Schormans, 2010) and the ways these are involved in abuse and maltreatment.

CHILD MALTREATMENT AND DEVELOPMENTAL DISABILITY

There is no singular worldwide view of disability (see Chapters 1, 2, and 3). Across the vast array of world cultures can be found a similarly vast number of understandings of, and responses to, children and adults labeled with developmental disabilities (Ghai, 2001; Mallett & Runswick-Cole, 2014). A review of the international literature, however, reveals a strong connection between developmental disability and maltreatment. The available literature does not always distinguish between children and adults, and thus the following discussion makes reference to both.

Prevalence of Child Maltreatment

A variety of studies dating back at least to the 1960s (e.g., Elmer & Gregg, 1967) have reported an association between child maltreatment and intellectual and developmental disabilities. The strength of the association varied significantly, at least in part because of differences in sampling and procedures.

A meta-analysis of studies meeting strict methodological criteria (Jones et al., 2012), conducted under the auspices of the World Health Organization, provided a reliable estimate: children with intellectual disability or mental disabilities were 4.3 times more likely to experience some form of reported abuse than children without disabilities. They were 3.7 times more likely to experience physical abuse, 4.3 times more likely to experience emotional abuse, and 4.6 times more likely to experience sexual abuse. An odds ratio for neglect was not calculated in this meta-analysis for procedural reasons.

Sullivan and Knutson's (2000) study of a large cohort of more than 40,000 children in Omaha, Nebraska, only included school-age children but produced similar results. The cohort design allowed the same definitions of disability to be applied to children with and without histories of maltreatment. The study found that children identified by their schools as requiring special education services were 3.4 times more likely to be maltreated than children who had not been found to need such services. This meant that almost one quarter (22%) of children with a history of maltreatment were identified as needing special education, and almost one third (31%) of children receiving special education had a confirmed history of child maltreatment.

The strongest association between maltreatment and disability was for children with behavior disorders, who were 6.3 times more likely to have a confirmed history of maltreatment than children with no identified disability. Children with intellectual disability were 3.7 times more likely to have a confirmed history of neglect, 3.8 times more likely to have a confirmed history of physical abuse, 3.8 times more likely to have a confirmed history of emotional abuse, and 4.0 times more likely to have a history of sexual abuse than children with no identified disability. Among all maltreated children, 24.1% had intellectual disability.

Although these and other studies make it clear that maltreatment is a major problem for children with intellectual and developmental disabilities, it is impossible to determine the exact scope of this problem for three reasons: reporting issues, variability in research methodology, and lack of clarity in understanding the association. These topics are discussed in detail next.

Reporting Issues   Given its multiple causes and manifestations, complicated by variations in definition, developmental disability is believed to be underdiagnosed in the general population (Percy & Brown, 2003). It is often neither identified nor noted in child protective services records, particularly for infants and young children who experience high rates of abuse but may have as yet undiagnosed disabilities (Algood, Hong, Gourdine, & Williams, 2011). Two factors are important here. First, the normative understandings of *child* and *child abuse* used to guide many child protection policies are not designed with children who have disabilities in mind and thus may exclude them (Robinson, 2014). Second, child protection workers typically receive insufficient training to identify developmental disability at the time child abuse is being investigated (Shannon & Tappan, 2011).

Child maltreatment itself is underreported, most frequently because it is hidden by the abusers. It is estimated that 50%–75% of all cases of suspected child maltreatment are not reported (Fallon et al., 2010). Abused children have many reasons for not reporting: manipulation or threats by the abuser; the (false) belief that the abuse was their fault; fear of punishment, abandonment, rejection, or separation from family; negative consequences for family; and/or feelings of shame (Akbas et al., 2009; Department of Justice Canada, 2001). In addition,

many people are not familiar with the indicators of maltreatment. In places where reporting suspected child abuse is mandatory, people may be unaware of their legislated responsibility to do so or how and to whom to report their suspicions. Even when maltreatment and duty to report are recognized, there may be a reluctance to report. People may believe that reporting will have negative repercussions for themselves, the child, and/or the family; that it will cause more harm; or that nothing will be done (Department of Justice Canada, 2001).

Assuming equal proportions of abuse are reported and unreported for children with and without disabilities, the odds ratios identified in existing studies would remain the same (Sobsey, 1994). If the likelihood of reporting is different for these groups of children, however, the odds ratios of reported abuse may be misleading. Many children with intellectual and developmental disabilities may lack the communication skills to disclose abuse (Strickler, 2001), whereas others who do disclose may not be believed due to assumptions about (in)ability (Erikson, Isaacs, & Perlman, 2003; Robinson, 2014). A child's disability may mask signs of abuse (e.g., injuries may be attributed to seizures or frequent falls) (Manders & Stoneman, 2009), and emotional or behavioral signs of maltreatment may be overlooked or improperly labeled as a function of developmental or mental health disability (Ammerman et al., 1989). There may be a conscious and unconscious tendency for people to neither see nor report maltreatment of children with disabilities (Cooke & Standen, 2002). These factors may result in reduced rates of reporting among children with disabilities. A child's disability, however, may result in increased interactions and surveillance by health service providers, educators, and other professionals that could increase the chances of abuse being reported (Hibbard, Desch, Committee on Child Abuse and Neglect, & Council on Children with Disabilities, 2007). Consequently, the relative rates of reporting abuse of children with and without disabilities remain unknown.

Variability in Research Methodology   Variability in research methodology complicates determination of an accurate understanding of the rate of maltreatment in children with developmental disabilities (Stalker & McArthur, 2012). Research samples tend to be selective, targeting individuals with a particular diagnosis (e.g., Down syndrome), thus failing to represent the broad range of diagnoses and abilities captured under the label *developmental disability*. Many studies are concerned with only one type of abuse. In addition, incidence studies rarely control for age in comparing children with and without disabilities (Dufour & Chamberland, 2003). Finally, when data are collected from child protective service records, the lower socioeconomic classes and ethnic minorities—in particular, aboriginal populations—may be overrepresented in the results (Gorman-Smith & Matson, 1992; Trocmé et al., 2005).

Although children with intellectual and developmental disabilities reside in a wide variety of settings (i.e., family homes; foster, kinship, and adoptive homes; group homes; and institutions), samples tend to be drawn from very specific (usually clinical) settings (Perlman & Erikson, 1992). Estimates drawn from the records of child protective services typically include only cases of intrafamilial abuse, thereby excluding the situations of extrafamilial abuse investigated by the police authorities (Trocmé et al., 2005). For example, drawing on data taken from child protective services records alone, Sullivan and Knutson (2000) determined the incidence of maltreatment among children with developmental disabilities to be 1.7 times greater than for children without developmental disabilities. When they examined data derived by merging a number of sources (i.e., school, police, foster care, and child protective services records), children with developmental disabilities were found to be 3.4 times more likely to experience abuse.

An important concern is the Eurocentric bias to research. Although approximately 80% of people with disabilities live in the Global South, most available research originates from the Global North, specifically Western Europe and North America (Priestley, 2001). Differential definitions and understanding of the terms *developmental disability* and *abuse* further confound knowledge of prevalence worldwide (Govindshenoy & Spencer, 2006).

Lack of Clarity in Understanding the Association Another issue is that studies relating developmental disability to maltreatment do not typically clarify the nature of the association. They do not indicate whether children who already have disabilities are at increased risk, whether maltreatment results in the overrepresentation of cases of children with disabilities, or whether some other factors increase the risk for both disabilities and

maltreatment. Stalker and McArthur (2012) noted that "since impairment is as multi-faceted as abuse, it follows that the relationship between them is both complex and variable" (p. 30).

These factors suggest that any estimates to date are most likely an underreporting of the true extent of the problem. Despite this, it is still clear that children with intellectual and developmental disabilities are overrepresented in maltreatment.

DEVELOPMENTAL DISABILITY AS A RISK FOR, AND CONSEQUENCE OF, MALTREATMENT

Child maltreatment is implicated in a substantial number of developmental disabilities, and children with developmental disabilities are at an increased risk of experiencing maltreatment. Sobsey (1994) suggested that 3%–6% of all maltreated children have some degree of permanent developmental disability as a result of the abuse, and that child maltreatment is a factor in 10%–25% of all developmental disabilities. This is, however, not a simple cause-and-effect relationship, and it is neither universal nor inevitable. Yet it can, for some people, create a cycle of maltreatment and disability: childhood maltreatment leading to permanent developmental disability that precipitates lifelong risk and vulnerability to further maltreatment. These two concepts are discussed in detail next.

Child Maltreatment Increases the Risk of Developmental Disability

There are three primary mechanisms by which developmental disability becomes an outcome of child maltreatment: 1) physical trauma, 2) neglect, and 3) the emotional and psychological effects of maltreatment (Garbarino et al., 1987; Hughes & Rycus, 1998; Sobsey, 1994). As more is learned about how emotional and psychological effects produce physiological, and even anatomical, effects in developing children, the line between these categories begins to blur.

Physical Trauma Physical trauma leading to neurological damage may result in developmental disability. Permanent brain damage may be a sequela of physical abuse and may be implicated in developmental disability, cerebral palsy, epilepsy, neuromotor disabilities, speech and language impairments, and growth deficits. Shaken baby syndrome is a well-known example. Women face an increased risk of physical assault by their partner during pregnancy (Sobsey, 1994). Both the assaults and stress associated with spousal violence can result in traumatogenic developmental disabilities or low birth weights (also associated with developmental disability) (Teixeira, Fisk, & Glover, 1999). Maternal prenatal substance abuse (e.g., alcohol, street drugs, inhalants), which is associated with violence, also interferes with typical fetal development and may lead to serious, lifelong developmental problems (e.g., fetal alcohol spectrum disorder). The role of violence in pregnancy is relevant because 1) it is associated with maternal substance abuse, poor nutrition, and poor prenatal care and 2) prenatal family violence is a risk factor for postnatal child maltreatment (Algood et al., 2011). Although there is debate over whether assault to a developing fetus is definable as child maltreatment, the numbers of children born affected after assault warrants its inclusion in this discussion (see Covell & Howe, 2001).

Neglect   Neglect affects a child's development in several ways. Poor maternal nutrition and prenatal care negatively affects fetal development. Inadequate nutrition, especially in the first 2 years of life when the brain and central nervous system are growing rapidly, may stunt the child's development (Vig & Kaminer, 2002). Poverty—associated with increased vulnerability to conditions associated with disability—is a factor here: Intellectual disability is more prevalent in low-income countries and neighborhoods (Brown & Fudge Schormans, 2003; Maulik, Mascarenhas, Mathers, Dua, & Saxena, 2011), and many maltreated children live in poverty (Trocmé et al., 2005). In addition, inadequate supervision of children is implicated in child fatalities, serious injury, and exposure to toxic or poisonous substances. Furthermore, developmental disability may be a consequence of neglect of the child's needs for attention, stimulation, and learning opportunities (Hughes & Rycus, 1998).

Emotional and Psychological Effects of Maltreatment   Emotional and psychological effects of maltreatment frequently include delayed or arrested cognitive development. When a child's energies are directed toward surviving and/or trying to cope with extreme stress, learning and adaptive impairments may follow. Emotional and psychological trauma can result in changes to the child's developing brain (e.g., atypical brain wave patterns, higher than expected rates of seizure disorder), affecting cognition and learning and possibly increasing risk for future psychiatric disorders (Bremner & Vermetten, 2001; De Bellis & Thomas, 2003; Penza, Heim, & Nemeroff, 2003).

Developmental Disability Increases the Risk of Child Maltreatment

As noted, children born with developmental disabilities and those who acquire developmental disabilities from maltreatment in turn become more vulnerable to further maltreatment. How is this increased risk and vulnerability to maltreatment to be understood?

Children with disabilities are not substantially different from children without disabilities and therefore share risk factors that are common to all children (see Garbarino et al., 1987; Macdonald, 2001; and Sobsey, 1994, for common risk factors for maltreatment). Reflecting a critical disability perspective, people with developmental disabilities are, however, believed to be more vulnerable as a result of a number of factors specific to them as a group. Most of these factors do not apply to everyone with developmental disabilities, nor are they the result of immutable characteristics of people with disabilities. Instead, they reflect the typical life experiences of many people with disabilities in an ableist society that does not adequately understand, value, or protect them.

Developmental disability does not cause maltreatment. To assume a causal relationship serves only to engage in blaming the victim and to obscure the ideological, social, political, and economic variables that create the conditions for the abuse of people with developmental disabilities to occur. For example, a number of tenacious myths about the abuse of people with developmental disabilities continue to have serious consequences:

*   Children and adults with developmental disabilities are never abused.

*   The abuse of people with developmental disabilities is not a serious issue because they will neither understand what happened to them nor be affected as severely as would people without disabilities.

*   The abuse of people with developmental disabilities is acceptable because it is a natural

reaction to the burden of caring for someone with a disability.

- People with developmental disabilities are not sexually desirable—no one would want to sexually abuse them.

- People with developmental disabilities cannot provide a credible account of what happened; therefore, there is no point in dealing with the disclosure.

Acceptance of these myths serves as a rationale for denying the existence of maltreatment of people with developmental disabilities, minimizing the seriousness of the problem, failing to report suspected or disclosed abuse, failing to pursue conviction of the alleged perpetrator, and/or failing to provide appropriate support and interventions to the person who has been abused.

Some of the most frequently cited risk factors specific to this population are presented next (as reported in Gorman-Smith & Matson, 1992; Griffiths, 2003; Hibbard et al., 2007; Hughes & Rycus, 1998; Kvam, 2000; Malacrida, 2012; Manders & Stoneman, 2009; Mazzucchelli, 2001; Perlman & Erikson, 1992; Randall, Parilla, & Sobsey, 2000; Robinson, 2014; Strickler, 2001; Tharinger, Burrows Horton, & Millea, 1990; Westcott & Jones, 1999). It should be noted, however, that the following is not an exhaustive list.

1. *For some families living in an ableist society that devalues disability, their child's developmental disability may be more than they can manage.* Parents may mourn the loss of the "normal" child they had expected. The anger that often accompanies mourning may be directed at the child. Family members' perceptions of the child as "different" can impede their ability to form an attachment or appropriately care for the child. It may also precipitate sufficient emotional stress to create a family crisis, thus increasing the child's risk of and vulnerability to abuse. This is exacerbated for families without access to adequate economic, social, and professional supports. In many instances, parents are required to quit their jobs in order to meet the care and advocacy needs of their child with a disability. It would, however, be both erroneous and dangerous to assume all families interpret the birth of a child with a disability as a tragedy.

2. *Assumptions of (in)ability may mean reduced or no expectations for growth or development.* Failure to provide appropriate stimulation, educational, or other learning or training opportunities may accrue when one is deemed unable to learn.

3. *Dependence on others increases vulnerability to maltreatment.* Children and adults with developmental disabilities are frequently more dependent on caregivers (this may be a lifelong dependence) for their basic needs and the provision of intimate personal care. In addition, people with developmental disabilities may have multiple caregivers across a wide variety of situations (e.g., home, school, respite home, therapy center, day program), increasing the risk of maltreatment exponentially.

4. *Compliance training is a common experience for many people with developmental disabilities.* Compliance is often overemphasized at the expense of assertiveness or independence. An unintended consequence is an increased vulnerability, as it places the person in a situation of unusual trust while enhancing the possibility of coercion.

5. *The overuse and/or misuse of specialized interventions or treatments, such as aversive behavioral techniques and pharmacological interventions, creates risk.* Aversive behavioral techniques—especially when administered improperly, by insufficiently trained people, or in an aggressive or overly punitive manner—can create a situation of risk. Similarly, the misuse or overuse of pharmacological interventions (sometimes for purposes of compliance) can result in harm.

6. *Limited communication skills can play a role.* These limited skills may affect the ability to report abuse, to have disclosure understood or viewed as credible, to say "no," and/or to call for help. This may lead to some perpetrators identifying a person with developmental disabilities as an "easy mark."

7. *Additional physical, mobility, or sensory impairments pose a risk.* They may impede the ability to defend oneself, to anticipate or ward off an attack, or to run away.

8. *The need or desire to "fit in" and to feel accepted can work to create risk.* Low self-esteem, emotional and social insecurities, and an eagerness to please are often consequences of negative societal understandings of developmental disability. They can make one more vulnerable to coercion.

9. *Insufficient education and training regarding intimacy, sexuality, personal rights, self-protection, and abuse can be a risk factor.* People with developmental disabilities frequently have not been equipped to recognize or navigate dangerous situations, protect themselves, or report what has happened to them.

Some parents and service providers are reluctant to provide this information. They may believe that people with developmental disabilities are asexual, that sexual behavior is not appropriate for people with developmental disabilities, or that providing this information will lead to inappropriate behavior. Most often, such training is provided only after maltreatment has occurred.

10. *A lack of personal privacy also increases vulnerability.* This is most notably (but not exclusively) a concern for people with developmental disabilities living in congregate settings. As the number of residents and staff increases, so may risk.

11. *Segregation and out-of-home care arrangements are more likely for people with developmental disabilities, especially for those with more complex needs.* Segregated school, therapeutic, and leisure settings and/or residential placement in respite care, foster care, group homes, or institutional settings inflate the risk of maltreatment. This is due to increased exposure to potential offenders, fewer available protections, and more limited access to individuals who will act on disclosures. It should be noted, however, that most reported maltreatment occurs in the family home (Fudge Schormans & Fallon, 2009).

12. *Social powerlessness stems from power inequities in the settings designed to protect people with developmental disabilities (e.g., school, foster care, respite care, group homes, institutions).* In these settings, children and adults with developmental disabilities generally have little real control and limited influence on decision making.

13. *Social devaluation rooted in ableism is a particularly powerful risk factor.* Being regarded as abnormal or less than human decreases both internal inhibitions and social restraints against the abuse of people with developmental disabilities. That this devaluation matters is reflected in rates of abuse and violence, including hate crimes (Quarmby, 2011, as cited in Mallett & Runswick-Cole, 2014), that have not decreased (and seem instead to be increasing) over time. In addition, when societal devaluation is internalized by the person being devalued, it can facilitate an ongoing sense of powerlessness to resist or report abuse.

From ecological and critical disability perspectives, it is necessary to look beyond the personal characteristics of children and adults with developmental disabilities in an attempt to understand why they are maltreated more often than their peers without disabilities. Numerous factors are involved,

---

Case Study: Nina

Nina was born with a congenital syndrome that resulted in both physical and developmental disabilities. This syndrome was progressive in nature. It was anticipated at her birth that Nina would require increasing levels of care and that she would likely die before reaching adulthood. Nina's parents had no family support to assist with Nina's care. Nina's father was unwilling to accept respite or in-home support services. Feeling unable to cope with her daughter's care needs and impending death, Nina's mother abandoned Nina to her father's care when Nina was 9 years old. Her father began to sexually abuse her once she reached puberty. This continued for more than a year. A neighbor, who had known Nina for several years, suspected that Nina was being abused after observing changes in Nina's behavior with her father. Unable to speak, Nina would close her eyes and turn her head away whenever her father spoke to her or approached her. Previously a friendly child, her apparent sadness also prompted the neighbor's suspicions. When questioned by police and child protective services, Nina's father admitted to abusing his daughter but asserted his belief that he had acted within his rights as Nina's father.

From Fudge Schormans, A. (2003). Child maltreatment and developmental disabilities. In I. Brown & M. Percy (Eds.), *Developmental disabilities in Ontario* (2nd ed., pp. 551–582). Toronto, Canada: Ontario Association on Developmental Disabilities; reprinted by permission.

---

not the least of which are those related to the aforementioned devaluation and latent assumptions and prejudices about people with developmental disabilities in contemporary culture.

Characteristics of Maltreatment and Developmental Disability

Children with developmental disabilities are subject to the same maltreatment experiences as children without developmental disabilities, yet significant differences also exist. A few of the more significant similarities and differences are outlined next.

Most Common Type of Maltreatment For children with and without developmental disabilities, neglect is the type of maltreatment cited to occur most often (i.e., more frequently than sexual abuse, physical abuse, and emotional maltreatment). In addition, both groups of children are reported to frequently experience multiple forms of maltreatment simultaneously or at different times or ages. However, children with developmental disabilities appear to experience both neglect and multiple categories of maltreatment at a significantly higher rate (Fudge Schormans & Brown, 2002; Sullivan & Knutson, 2000). One hypothesis put forth to explain the high incidence of neglect is that the increased care demands of this group of children places them at greater risk (Ammerman et al., 1989), especially if the supports and services they and their families require are not readily available or accessible (Brown & Fudge Schormans, 2003; Fudge Schormans & Fallon, 2009).

Severity There is strong literature support for the view that the maltreatment of people with developmental disabilities is more severe than for people without developmental disabilities. People with developmental disabilities appear to experience more physical injuries and emotional harm as a result of physical abuse and emotional maltreatment (Ammerman et al., 1989; Fudge Schormans & Fallon, 2009; Tharinger et al., 1990). More severe maltreatment also occurs in sexual abuse, as having a developmental disability increases the likelihood of experiencing contact sexual abuse (e.g., inappropriate touching; oral, anal, or vaginal penetration; attempted penetration), as opposed to noncontact sexual abuse (e.g., indecent exposure, invitation to touch). Consequently, people with developmental disabilities also face greater risk of exposure to HIV/AIDS and other sexually transmitted diseases (Ammerman et al., 1989; Beail & Warden, 1995; Sobsey, 1994).

Chronic versus Acute Nature Abuse and neglect for people with developmental disabilities tends also to be chronic. They are much more likely than those in the general population to experience multiple episodes of maltreatment spanning a longer time period (Fudge Schormans & Brown, 2002; Jaudes & Mackey-Bilaver, 2008). While this may be partially explained by the higher rates of neglect (Fudge Schormans & Fallon, 2009), Sullivan and Knutson (2000) found that 71% of their sample of children identified as having a developmental disability reported repeated abuse, as opposed to 60.1% of their sample of children without an identified developmental disability. Regarding sexual abuse specifically, this may be even more pronounced for younger children and for children with more significant disabilities (Sobsey, 1994).

Degree of Impairment Degree of impairment is an important parameter. A common assumption is that people with more severe developmental disabilities are at greater risk of abuse and neglect, primarily as a result of several of the risk factors that were previously identified: increased dependence, multiple caregivers, less well-developed communication skills, additional impairments, and more involvement with out-of-home care and segregated services. A review of the literature, however, suggests that people with mild or moderate levels of developmental disability are at greater risk. One explanation is that children with more severe disabilities elicit more sympathy than anger, which serves to somehow protect them. A second explanation is that they are less able to engage in behaviors that may trigger an abusive incident (i.e., aggressive or self-stimulating behavior) (Ammerman et al., 1989). Strickler (2001) suggested they are less capable of interacting with others or reacting to a potential abuser in a way that precipitates abuse. Benedict et al. (1990) argued that because caregivers expect less from them, caregiver frustration (leading to abuse) is a less common response.

It must be remembered, however, that maltreatment is far less likely to be verbally disclosed by people with more severe impairments (largely as a result of more limited communication abilities). If abuse is disclosed behaviorally or emotionally, there is less chance it will be correctly identified by others, especially by people unfamiliar with indicators of maltreatment and/or the individual's nonverbal communication methods (Balogh et al., 2001; Kvam, 2000). Sobsey's (1994) finding that people with mild to moderate or severe to profound impairments are almost equally represented in reported cases of sexual abuse, and Herman's (2007) finding that for school-age children the risk of physical and sexual abuse increases in proportion to severity and multiplicity of disability, suggest the need to investigate this area further.

Age Two patterns emerge when age is examined. First, the maltreatment of children with developmental disabilities tends to begin at a younger age than for children without developmental disabilities. More preschool-age children with developmental disabilities are reported for all types of maltreatment than are their counterparts without developmental disabilities (Benedict et al., 1990; Howe, 2006; Sullivan & Knutson, 2000). Investigating children with multiple disabilities in psychiatric hospitals, Ammerman et al. (1989) found that before the age of 2 years, 46% of the children in this sample had been physically abused, 49% had been sexually abused, and 68% had experienced neglect. For both children with and without developmental disabilities, younger children are typically at greater risk for physical abuse and neglect, whereas the risk of sexual abuse increases in adolescence (Ammerman et al., 1989; Beail & Warden, 1995; Trocmé et al., 2005).

Second, an inverse relationship between age and maltreatment exists for children without developmental disabilities: As age increases, the rate of maltreatment decreases. As children grow, they typically develop better communication and self-protection skills and are physically better able to ward off an attack. Maturity frequently brings improved capacity to escape or avoid abusive situations (Randall et al., 2000). This is not always the case for children with developmental disabilities (especially those that are more severe), who develop such skills later or not at all. For this group, age is not necessarily a protective factor and vulnerability to maltreatment generally extends across the life span (Jaudes & Mackey-Bilaver, 2008; Randall, Sobsey, & Parilla, 2001).

Gender   The effect of gender is not equal for children with and without developmental disabilities. Among children without developmental disabilities, Sullivan and Knutson (2000) noted that girls are abused more often (56%) than boys (42%), whereas Trocmé et al. (2005) found an almost equal distribution (49.1% girls, 50.9% boys). Hershkowitz, Lamb, and Horowitz (2007) found boys to be abused more often than girls. An interesting finding is that boys with developmental disabilities are overrepresented in all categories of maltreatment: 63.8% of children with developmental disabilities reported for child maltreatment are boys and 36.2% are girls (Fudge Schormans & Fallon, 2009).

Does disability status actually increase the risk of abuse for boys? Children with developmental disability are more likely to have paid caregivers and, for boys, these are more likely to be male. As the characteristics "paid caregiver" and "male" are sometimes correlated with perpetrator status, this potentially contributes to this elevated risk of maltreatment for boys with developmental disabilities (Randall et al., 2000). Sullivan and Knutson (2000) argued instead that more boys than girls are identified as having developmental disabilities: the greater prevalence of maltreated boys reflects the increased prevalence of boys in the developmental disability population. Reporting issues may be a factor. Maltreated boys with developmental disabilities are more likely to act out to demonstrate behavioral concerns that bring them into contact with professionals, thus potentially increasing the probability of being reported for maltreatment. As a group, girls tend more toward withdrawal and other emotional and behavioral expressions that do not create the same type of problems for caregivers as the behaviors exhibited by boys. A consequence is that girls may be thus less likely to be diagnosed as being abused (Beail & Warden, 1995). To complicate matters, developmental disability, in addition to maltreatment, may be underreported more often for girls than for boys (Randall et al., 2000). Furthermore, although boys seem to be more reluctant to disclose abuse—especially sexual abuse—than do girls, girls are less likely to be believed. This not only affects understanding of the rates of maltreatment but also, more seriously, results in the threat of continued maltreatment for girls (Beail & Warden, 1995; Randall et al., 2000). In addition, as compared with their peers without a disability, disclosures by people with developmental disabilities are significantly less likely to be believed (Robinson, 2014). These factors skew understanding of the intersection between gender, disability, and maltreatment and point to the need for further investigation.

Alleged Perpetrator   For all children, irrespective of disability, the alleged perpetrator of maltreatment is usually someone the child knows. "Stranger abuse" is a rare event, accounting for less than 1% (Trocmé et al., 2005) to 6.6% (Sobsey, 1994) of child maltreatment. Worldwide, the alleged perpetrator of child maltreatment is most often a family member. For children with disabilities living in India, Ghai (2001) noted that, especially for families living in poverty, the family may be a "safe haven" or a "risk" from which they need protection. In Canada, the Canadian Incidence Study of Reported

Child Abuse and Neglect reported that only 6% of child maltreatment was committed by a nonfamily member (e.g., a teacher, professional, baby sitter, parental girlfriend or boyfriend, peer, stranger) (Trocmé et al., 2005). This figure is perhaps an underestimation, as instances of nonfamilial abuse are often investigated by the police rather than child protective services. For children without a developmental disability, and for many children with this label, immediate family members are believed to be responsible for the majority of neglect, physical, and emotional abuse. Extended family or nonfamily members are implicated in sexual abuse more often than in neglect, physical, or emotional abuse. Mothers and fathers are equally represented as perpetrators of physical abuse, with more mothers reported for neglect and emotional abuse and fathers for sexual abuse. It must be remembered, however, that globally, the responsibility for child care often still rests primarily with mothers. In addition, more single-parent families—a risk factor for child maltreatment—are headed by mothers than by fathers (Fudge Schormans & Brown, 2002; Sobsey, 1994; Trocmé et al., 2005).

Debate exists as to whether people with developmental disabilities are at greater risk of familial or nonfamilial maltreatment. Although, as noted, some studies report high levels of familial abuse, contradictory findings suggest that maltreatment at the hands of service providers is a greater threat. Sobsey (1994) reported that of those included in his sample, 56% of sexual abuse was perpetrated by service providers, compared with 28% by caregivers. The issue is muddied by the variety, multiplicity, and complexity of living arrangements for this group. Although deinstitutionalization policies have resulted in more people with developmental disabilities living in their family homes, the reality is that a significant number still reside in out-of-home placements. These placements may be permanent (i.e., foster care, group homes, or institutional settings) or temporary (i.e., respite care). Multiple moves are not uncommon (especially in the foster care system, where children sometimes bounce from one placement to the next) (Fudge Schormans, Coniega, & Renwick, 2006). One outcome of such discontinuity of care and involvement with the developmental disability service system is an increased vulnerability to maltreatment by nonfamily members. This is not restricted to alternative caregivers or staff members alone. A consequence of residential and

day program settings, in which several people with developmental disabilities are congregated together, is a higher risk of maltreatment by a peer who also has a developmental disability (Balogh et al., 2001).

Potential for Abuse in Institutions and Institutionalized Services Specific to children and adults with developmental disabilities is the notion that the institutionally sanctioned services and procedures may be abusive or neglectful. In some instances, administrative structures, philosophies, and institutional cultures—particularly those rooted in dehumanizing and pathologizing understandings of people labeled with intellectual and developmental disabilities—can permit, condone, or even encourage three forms of institutional maltreatment that are then enacted by employees: institutional child abuse, institutional child neglect, and wrongful abrogation of personal rights. Institutional child abuse involves the use of physical punishment, aversive behavior management techniques, excessive isolation, denial of freedom, physical or mechanical restraints, and/or the abuse or misuse of psychotropic drugs. Institutional child neglect refers to failure to provide needed services (including those for development) and negligent attitudes toward the use of punishment, restraints, and medication. Wrongful abrogation of personal rights includes such actions as improper segregation and restrictions on personal choice, decision making, communications, or socialization preferences (Garbarino et al., 1987; Malacrida, 2012; Robinson, 2014).

IMPACT OF MALTREATMENT ON CHILDREN AND ADULTS WITH DEVELOPMENTAL DISABILITIES

Childhood maltreatment has both short- and long-term effects on the physical, cognitive, psychological or emotional, behavioral, social, and material well-being of children with developmental disabilities— many of which are shared with children without developmental disabilities (see Garbarino et al., 1987; Macdonald, 2001; Sobsey, 1994; and Vig & Kaminer, 2002). Kvam (2000) cautioned that for each individual, the impact is affected by such factors as the seriousness of the abuse, age of onset, single or multiple episodes of maltreatment, characteristics of the individual, family response to disclosure, family situation, and the individual's relationship to the abuser. (Remember, the first five have already been identified as significant factors in the maltreatment of people with developmental disabilities.) It must be noted, however, that a much larger research literature exists regarding potential impacts for children and adults without disabilities.

The impact of maltreatment on children with developmental disabilities appears to be similar to, but more severe than, the impact on children without disabilities. Mansell, Sobsey, and Moskal (1998), for example, compared clinical findings among two samples of age- and gender-matched Canadian children served by the same treatment agency: children with developmental disabilities who had been sexually abused and children without disabilities who had been sexually abused. Clinical characteristics were similar, but the children with disabilities exhibited a higher number of clinically significant problems (e.g., increased vulnerability to sexual abuse, withdrawal into fantasy and self-abuse). This finding was supported by Fudge Schormans and Fallon (2009) in their analysis of Canadian Incidence Study of Reported Child Abuse and Neglect—2003 data: Maltreated children with developmental disabilities demonstrated more signs of emotional harm such as nightmares, bed wetting, and social withdrawal.

There are, however, effects of maltreatment that are unique to people with developmental disabilities. These include the following (as reported in Fudge Schormans et al., 2006; Gorman-Smith & Matson, 1992; Lightfoot, Hill, & LaLiberte, 2011; Manders & Stoneman, 2009; Perlman & Erikson, 1992; Robinson, 2014; Rosenberg & Robinson, 2004; Sobsey, 1994; Strickler, 2001; Tharinger et al., 1990):

1. The experience of maltreatment exacerbates feelings of social isolation and of "being different" that are common to people with developmental disabilities.

2. People with developmental disabilities are already stigmatized; further stigmatization may accrue as a result of maltreatment.

3. There is a tendency for individuals with developmental disabilities to believe they were abused because they have a developmental disability.

4. Notably higher rates of psychiatric disorder have been correlated with maltreatment of children and adults with developmental disabilities.

5. Because of frequent misdiagnosis of the emotional, social, and behavioral symptomatology of maltreatment, people with developmental disabilities are more likely to be mistreated and prescribed intrusive behavior management, inappropriate psychotropic medication, hospitalization, and/or unnecessary placement changes. For example, self-injurious behavior is a common clinical finding among children with and without developmental disabilities who have been abused. Punishment procedures used to eliminate this behavior without understanding why the behavior occurs will likely increase the trauma and do further harm.

6. The lack of education and training regarding developmental disabilities and discriminatory attitudes and biases of some professionals (e.g., child protective service workers) can result in the failure to recognize abuse or to believe disclosures. When disability is regarded as a burden and undue hardship for caregivers, abuse of people with developmental disabilities may be excused as understandable and blame may be attributed instead to the child or adult. In these instances, abuse is less likely to be investigated or substantiated and thus more likely to continue.

7. There is a mistaken belief that people with developmental disabilities are unable to benefit from therapeutic interventions for maltreatment. This is one reason why such services are rarely made available to them. Even if they are available, generic services are frequently unable to accommodate the unique needs of this group. Specialized therapeutic services are limited in number and are thus more difficult to obtain. Similarly, a lack of trained foster parents and specialized residential services creates problems, particularly as children and youth with developmental disabilities having substantiated maltreatment are more likely to be removed from the care of their families, to have multiple and longer stays in out-of-home care, and to be less likely to return to their families than their counterparts without disabilities. These factors increase the risk that the impact of maltreatment will be more severe and longer lasting and may precipitate emotional, behavioral, or psychological crises.

INVESTIGATING MALTREATMENT OF CHILDREN AND ADULTS WITH DEVELOPMENTAL DISABILITIES

Despite investigations, the abuse of people with developmental disabilities is punished less often than might be expected. Alleged perpetrators are rarely criminally charged, tried, and/or convicted; consequently, the abuser often continues to live with (or provide care for) the person with the developmental disability (Balogh et al., 2001; Beail & Warden, 1995; Trocmé et al., 2001).

In developed countries, criminal law provides children and adults some protection from physical and sexual abuse and/or from deprivation of the necessities of life. Such legislation is typically the legal basis for prosecution by criminal court systems, which are required to prove beyond a reasonable doubt the guilt of the alleged perpetrator. One consequence of this is that many cases of suspected child abuse are not pursued successfully through criminal law. Obtaining sufficient evidence to establish guilt beyond a reasonable doubt is often more difficult when dealing with child maltreatment and may also prove more challenging in cases of abuse against adults with developmental disabilities (for some of the reasons already addressed in this chapter).

The second means by which protection is afforded is through child welfare legislation that governs child protection agencies. Applying exclusively to children, this legislation is based on the less demanding civil law standard of proof of the preponderance of the evidence. The difference in these standards is the purpose of each process. Criminal proceedings are intended primarily to determine guilt and to punish criminal behavior. Child welfare proceedings are intended to determine if a child needs protection and to do what is best for the child.

Child protective services are primarily responsible for investigating reports of child maltreatment when the alleged perpetrator is someone acting in a caregiving capacity (e.g., family member, baby sitter, teacher, child care provider, foster parent, group-home staff member). There is typically a joint investigation between the child protective services and the police if the allegation involves sexual abuse, serious physical harm, criminal activity, and/or abandonment. The police are less likely to participate in situations involving neglect or emotional abuse (unless domestic violence is identified as a factor in the emotional abuse). The police maintain responsibility for investigating alleged child maltreatment if the alleged perpetrator is a stranger or nonfamily member. It is not uncommon, however, for the police to include child protective services in such investigations to take advantage of their expertise in interviewing children and linking maltreated children and their families to community supports and services. Adult protective services have been developed in many states and provinces in an attempt to provide a system of similar protection for adults who are vulnerable to maltreatment. These vary substantially from one jurisdiction to another.

The current issues and debates associated with the investigation of maltreatment, for people with and without developmental disabilities, are complex. Regarding people with developmental disabilities, the two case studies highlighted on the next pages reveal some of the myriad factors that complicate this process and have repercussions for the individual, family, and alleged perpetrator.

SUMMARY

Historically, societal attitudes about disability are reflected in legislated and professional practice responses to the maltreatment of people with intellectual and developmental disabilities. Differential treatment for this group—from social service, child protection, and criminal justice systems—is not uncommon and can serve to perpetuate, condone, or even authorize further maltreatment. Present structures are inadequate to effectively address this problem. Identification as being both part of the problem and of the solution necessitates stronger collaboration and information sharing among all the parties involved with this issue: child protective services, developmental disability services, police officers, lawyers, judges, school staff, child care providers, health care professionals, therapeutic services professionals, service planners and administrators, governmental administrators and policy makers, and advocates. People with intellectual and developmental disabilities and their families are a key element to the development of a more responsive system of protection, possessing invaluable insights into the factors contributing to maltreatment and what is required for prevention, protection, and healthy recoveries.

Case Study: Child Protection Investigation

A social worker received a call from a teacher. The teacher said that a 6-year-old boy reported that he and his 5-year-old sister had been sexually abused by their father. Both children had developmental disabilities. The girl was nonverbal, and her disability was more severe. The teacher conveyed the following: the mother forced the father to leave the home after witnessing the father in the act of abusing the children; the abuse was ongoing; the boy was anxious and frightened and was threatened by the father not to tell; the mother also had a developmental disability; and the school had ongoing concerns about the children's nutrition, clothing, and hygiene.

The worker completed a standardized tool for assessing risk and discussed the situation with her supervisor. They decided that eligibility criteria for services had been met. According to local government guidelines, the children had to be seen within 12 hours. This would be a joint investigation with police and would take place at the school. To account for the children's disabilities, minimize trauma, and maximize information obtained, the social worker tried to arrange for supports to assist the investigation (e.g., people familiar with and to the children and/or with experience in developmental disabilities, communication, behavior, and safety issues for children with disabilities). The only support people available that day were the children's classroom aides, so the social worker arranged for them to be present during the interview. Although the social worker and the police officer knew this had potential to contaminate evidence, they believed it would best facilitate information gathering.

In case the children were later unable to testify in court, the interview was videotaped. During the interview, the boy was anxious, distractible, and unable to give dates, but his aide kept him focused. Consistent details of sexual, physical, and emotional abuse of both children emerged from the boy's report. Despite being nonverbal, attempts were made to interview and gather nonspoken information from the sister, but she was unable to provide any information.

The mother was called and requested to accompany the children and the worker to the hospital's sexual assault unit, where she was interviewed and the children were examined. The boy complied with being examined. Although no physical evidence could be obtained, the physician noted that his behavior during the exam was consistent with abuse. The physician was unable to complete an exam of the girl, as she was distraught, even with her mother's support. Because the prosecuting attorney would need to prove guilt beyond a reasonable doubt, it became apparent that the lack of physical evidence might compromise prosecution of the father. The mother was interviewed and confirmed her son's account of the abuse. However, the mother reported that the father had returned home, and she believed herself unable to protect the children at that time. Because the children were clearly not safe, she agreed with the worker's plan to place the children in foster care until parenting supports could be arranged.

The police found the father at the family home. After questioning him, they decided to charge him despite his denial of wrongdoing and the lack of physical evidence. The boy's disclosure and behavioral indicators warranted this decision. Even if no conviction was obtained, it was hoped that this would be a deterrent in the future. The boy was referred to a victim witness program to be prepared for criminal court. His sister would not testify, as her communication was determined to be neither consistent nor reliable. Her brother was deemed competent as a witness because he knew right from wrong and the importance of telling the truth. He testified but, in part because of his cognitive, memory, and language difficulties, he was easily confused by the defense attorney and his credibility was damaged. Although behavioral evidence existed, the lack of physical evidence and the boy's difficulties in testifying due to his developmental disabilities meant that the father was found not guilty. The mother refused to testify. Later, it was learned that she had also been the victim of violence at the father's hands. During supervised-access visits with the children at the social services agency offices, however, the mother recanted this disclosure and stated her decision to remain with father. The children became wards of the state.

From Fudge Schormans, A. (2003). Child maltreatment and developmental disabilities. In I. Brown & M. Percy (Eds.), *Developmental disabilities in Ontario* (2nd ed., pp. 551–582). Toronto, Canada: Ontario Association on Developmental Disabilities; adapted by permission.

Case Study: Police Investigation

A 31-year-old woman with developmental disabilities was a frequent customer at a neighborhood variety store down the street from her home. Although she did not speak, she had some alternative communication abilities, and the shopkeeper came to know her well. During the day, the woman attended an adult day program funded by the local government.

Over time, the shopkeeper began to notice disturbing changes in the woman's behavior. She appeared overly interested in men in the store but also frightened of them. She openly masturbated in their presence and began to exhibit self-harming behaviors (e.g., head slapping). Concerned that she had been abused, the shopkeeper attempted to engage the woman in conversation and suggested that if she had been abused she should call the police and not let anyone hurt her. The woman was clearly distressed by this conversation. The shopkeeper decided to call the police, who advised her that if the woman could not or would not make a disclosure herself, then the shopkeeper could register a third-party complaint. This was done, and several days later the police met with the shopkeeper. The shopkeeper could provide little information about the woman's family. The police were reluctant to go to the woman's home, fearing that this might place her at greater risk. Deciding to meet with the woman at the store, the police were unsuccessful in their attempts to speak with her; however, they were convinced by observing her behavior that something had happened to her. As a result, the police decided to speak with the woman's family.

The woman lived with her mother. Appearing devastated by the suspicions of abuse, the mother agreed to facilitate a police interview with her daughter. The mother, able to communicate with her daughter using a system of yes/no responses to questions, elicited from her daughter that she had been sexually touched by staff at the day program. The daughter was then informed of her rights and her options, but it was not clear how much she understood. She refused to go to the hospital for an examination, and she did not agree to press charges. Because of her age, the woman was deemed responsible to make her own decisions. The police were unable to proceed without her consent. They reviewed with the mother the option of having her daughter legally declared incompetent so that they could go forward with the investigation. The mother refused, as she saw the risks this posed to her daughter's future ability to make decisions for herself. The police referred the woman and her mother to the local sexual assault center in an effort to assist them to receive information and support.

From Fudge Schormans, A. (2003). Child maltreatment and developmental disabilities. In I. Brown & M. Percy (Eds.), *Developmental disabilities in Ontario* (2nd ed., pp. 551–582). Toronto, Canada: Ontario Association on Developmental Disabilities; adapted by permission.

Maltreatment is a reality in the daily lives of many people with intellectual and developmental disabilities. People with intellectual and developmental disabilities face a much higher risk of and vulnerability to maltreatment that is both similar to and unique from that experienced by people without disabilities. However, maltreatment of these individuals is often unreported and/or undetected and, therefore, untreated. What is missing is recognition and acknowledgement of the magnitude and seriousness of this issue. Also, legislation, policies, and practices are needed that are preventive, as opposed to reactive. Society needs to value people with intellectual and developmental disabilities, demand active condemnation of the violence

perpetrated against them, and challenge the ableism and devaluation that lie at the root of such violence.

FOR FURTHER THOUGHT AND DISCUSSION

1. What might be the consequences of conceptualizing maltreatment of children with disabilities in the following ways: an individual pathology issue, a social welfare issue, a public health issue, a public safety issue, an economic issue, or a human or disability rights issue?

2. One thing that people with developmental disabilities share with other oppressed groups is a concern over the language used to describe

them. An example from the mental health field demonstrates this point. The current practice for many people labeled as having mental health concerns is to use the term *survivor* as opposed to *victim*. Explain the pros and cons of the use of each term in relation to children and adults with developmental disabilities who experience maltreatment.

3. Discuss the issues of prenatal practices (e.g., alcohol or drug use by pregnant women) and violence against women resulting in a child being born with developmental disabilities. Should either or both be defined as child abuse? Do these practices constitute a criminal offense? What are the salient factors at play in these instances? What role, if any, should child protective services play?

4. The child protection system lacks expertise in the area of developmental disability. The developmental disability service system lacks expertise in the area of child maltreatment. Which service system do you believe is most appropriate to deal with the issue of the maltreatment of children with developmental disabilities, and why? What alternatives might be possible? What other systems would you consider drawing into this mix?

5. Should people with developmental disabilities be treated as "special cases" within child welfare legislation and/or criminal law in light of their particular vulnerabilities and the systemic issues that have been identified?

REFERENCES

Akbas, S., Turia, A., Karabekirolgu, K., Pazvantoglu, O., Kekskin, T., & Boke, O. (2009). Characteristics of sexual abuse in a sample of Turkish children with and without mental retardation, referred for legal appraisal of the psychological repercussions. *Sexuality and Disability, 27,* 205–213.

Algood, C.L., Hong, J.S., Gourdine, R.M., & Williams, A.B. (2011). Maltreatment of children with disabilities: An ecological systems analysis. *Children and Youth Services Review, 33,* 1142–1148.

Ammerman, R.T., Van Hasselt, V.B., Hersen, M., McGonigle, J.J., & Lubetsky, M.J. (1989). Abuse and neglect in psychiatrically hospitalized multihandicapped children. *Child Abuse and Neglect, 13,* 335–343.

Balogh, R., Bretherton, K., Whibley, S., Berney, T., Graham, S., Richold, P.,...Firth, H. (2001). Sexual abuse in children and adolescents with intellectual disability. *Journal of Intellectual Disability Research, 45,* 194–201.

Beail, N., & Warden, S. (1995). Sexual abuse of adults with learning disabilities. *Journal of Intellectual Disability Research, 39,* 382–387.

Benedict, M.I., White, R.B., Wulff, L.M., & Hall, B.J. (1990). Reported maltreatment in children with multiple disabilities. *Child Abuse and Neglect, 14,* 207–217.

Bremner, J.D., & Vermetten, E. (2001). Stress and development: Behavioural and biological consequences. *Development and Psychopathology, 13,* 473–489.

Bremner, R.H. (1971). *Children and youth in America: A documentary history: Vol. II. 1866–1932.* Cambridge, MA: Harvard University Press.

Brown, I., & Fudge Schormans, A. (2003). Maltreatment and life stressors in single mothers who have children with developmental delay. *Journal on Developmental Disabilities, 10*(1), 61–66.

Caffey, J. (1946). Multiple fractures in the long-bones of infants suffering from chronic subdural hematoma. *American Journal of Roentgenology, 56,* 163–173.

Carlson, L. (2001). Cognitive ableism and disability studies: Feminist reflections on the history of mental retardation. *Hypatia, 16,* 124–146.

Centre for Human Rights. (1996). *The International Bill of Human Rights, Fact sheet No. 2.* Geneva, Switzerland: Centre for Human Rights, United Nations Office at Geneva.

Chadwick, D.L. (1999). The message. *Child Abuse and Neglect, 23,* 957–961.

Cooke, P., & Standen, P.J. (2002). Abuse and disabled children: Hidden needs...? *Child Abuse Review, 11,* 1–18.

Corso, P.S., Edwards, V.D., Fang, X., & Mercy, J. (2008). Health-related quality of life among adults who experienced maltreatment during childhood. *American Journal of Public Health, 98*(6), 1094–1100.

Covell, K., & Howe, R.B. (2001). *The challenge of children's rights for Canada.* Waterloo, Canada: Wilfred Laurier University Press.

De Bellis, M.D., & Thomas, L.A. (2003). Biologic findings of post-traumatic stress disorder and child maltreatment. *Current Psychiatry Reports, 5*(2), 108–117.

Department of Justice Canada. (2001). *Child abuse: a fact sheet from the Department of Justice Canada* Retrieved from http://publications.gc.ca/collections/Collection/J2-295-2002E.pdf

Dufour, S., & Chamberland, C. (2003). *The effectiveness of child welfare interventions: A systematic review.* Retrieved from http://cwrp.ca/publications/636

Elmer, E., & Gregg, G.S. (1967). Developmental characteristics of abused children. *Pediatrics, 40*(4), 596–602.

Erikson, C.,, Isaacs, B., & Perlman, N. (2003). Enhancing communication with persons with developmental disabilities: The special case of interviewing victim-witnesses of sexual abuse. In I. Brown & M. Percy (Eds.), *Developmental disabilities in Ontario* (2nd ed., pp. 465–476). Toronto, Canada: Ontario Association on Developmental Disabilities.

Fallon, B., Trocmé, N., Fluke, J., MacLaurin, B., Tonmyr, L., & Yuan, Y. (2010). Methodological challenges in measuring child maltreatment. *Child Abuse and Neglect, 34*(1), 70–79.

Fudge Schormans, A. (2003). Child maltreatment and developmental disabilities. In I. Brown & M. Percy (Eds.), *Developmental disabilities in Ontario* (2nd ed., pp. 551–582). Toronto, Canada: Ontario Association on Developmental Disabilities.

Fudge Schormans, A. (2010). Epilogues and prefaces: Research and social work and people with intellectual disabilities. *Australian Social Work, 63*(1), 51–66.

Fudge Schormans, A., & Brown, I. (2002). An investigation into the characteristics of the maltreatment of children with developmental delays and the alleged perpetrators of this maltreatment. *Journal of Developmental Disabilities, 9*(1), 1–19.

Fudge Schormans, A., Coniega, M., & Renwick, R. (2006). Placement stability: Enhancing quality of life for children with developmental disabilities. *Families in Society, 87*(4), 521–528.

Fudge Schormans, A., & Fallon, B. (2009, August). *Children with developmental disability and substantiation of child maltreatment.* Paper presented at 117th American Psychology Association Convention, Toronto, Canada.

Garbarino, J., Brookhouser, P.E., & Authier, K. (1987). *Special children, special risks: The maltreatment of children with disabilities.* New York, NY: Aldine De Gruyter.

Ghai, A. (2001). Marginalisation and disability: Experiences from the Third World. In M. Priestley (Ed.), *Disability and the life course: Global perspectives* (pp. 26–37). New York, NY: Cambridge University Press.

Gorman-Smith, D., & Matson, J.L. (1992). Sexual abuse and persons with mental retardation. In W. O'Donohue & J.H. Geer (Eds.), *The sexual abuse of children: Theory and research: Vol. 1* (pp. 285–306). Mahwah, NJ: Lawrence Erlbaum.

Govindshenoy, M., & Spencer, N. (2006). Abuse of the disabled child: A systematic review of population-based studies. *Child: Care, Health and Development, 33*(5), 552–558.

Griffiths, D. (2003). Sexuality and people with developmental disabilities: From myth to emerging practices. In I. Brown & M. Percy (Eds.), *Developmental disabilities in Ontario* (2nd ed., pp. 677–698). Toronto, Canada: Ontario Association on Developmental Disabilities.

Herman, B. (2007). CAPTA and early childhood intervention: Policy and the role of parents. *Children & Schools, 29*(1), 17–24.

Hershkowitz, I., Lamb, M.E., & Horowitz, D. (2007). Victimization of children with disabilities. *American Journal of Orthopsychiatry, 77,* 629–635.

Hibbard, R.A., & Desch, I.W., Committee on Child Abuse and Neglect, & Council on Children with Disabilities. (2007). Maltreatment of children with disabilities. *Pediatrics, 119*(5), 1018–1025.

Howe, D. (2006). Disabled children, maltreatment and attachment. *British Journal of Social Work, 36,* 743–760.

Hughes, R.C., & Rycus, J.S. (1998). *Developmental disabilities and child welfare.* Washington, DC: Child Welfare League of America Press.

Jaudes, P.K., & Mackey-Bilaver, L. (2008). Do chronic conditions increase young children's risk of being maltreated? *Child Abuse and Neglect, 32,* 671–681.

Jones, L., Bellis, M.A., Wood, S., Hughes, K., McCoy, E., Eckley, L.,…Officer, A. (2012). Prevalence and risk of violence against children with disabilities: A systematic review and meta-analysis of observational studies. *Lancet, 380,* 899–907.

Kempe, C.H., Silverman, F.N., Steele, B.F., Droegemueller, W., & Silver, H.K. (1962). The battered-child syndrome. *Journal of the American Medical Association, 181,* 17–24.

Kvam, M.H. (2000). Is sexual abuse of children with disabilities disclosed? A retrospective analysis of child disability and the likelihood of sexual abuse among those attending Norwegian hospitals. *Child Abuse and Neglect, 24,* 1073–1084.

Lightfoot, E., Hill, K., & LaLiberte, T. (2011). Prevalence of children with disabilities in the child welfare system and out of home placement: An examination of administrative records. *Youth Services Review, 33,* 2069–2075.

Macdonald, G. (2001). *Effective interventions for child abuse and neglect: An evidence-based approach to planning and evaluating interventions.* Hoboken, NJ: John Wiley & Sons.

Macintyre, E. (1993). The historical context of child welfare in Canada. In B. Wharf (Ed.), *Rethinking child welfare in Canada* (pp. 13–36). Toronto, Canada: McClelland & Stewart.

Malacrida, C. (2012). Bodily practices as vehicles for dehumanization in an institution for mental defectives. *Societies, 2,* 286–301.

Mallett, R., & Runswick-Cole, K. (2014). *Approaching disability: Critical issues and perspectives.* London, United Kingdom: Routledge.

Manders, J.E., & Stoneman, Z. (2009). Children with disabilities in the child protective services system: An analog study of investigation and case management. *Child Abuse and Neglect, 33*(4), 229–237.

Mansell, S., Sobsey, D., & Moskal, R. (1998). Clinical findings among sexually abused children with and without developmental disabilities. *Mental Retardation, 36*(1), 12–22.

Maulik, P.K., Mascarenhas, M.N., Mathers, C.D., Dua, T., & Saxena, S. (2011). Prevalence of intellectual disability: A meta-analysis of population-based studies. *Research in Developmental Disabilities, 32*(2), 419–436.

Mazzucchelli, T.G. (2001). Feel Safe: A pilot study of a protective behaviours programme for people with intellectual disability. *Journal of Intellectual and Developmental Disability, 26,* 115–126.

Panitch, M. (2008). *Disability, mothers, and organization: Accidental activists.* New York, NY: Routledge.

Penza, K.M., Heim, C., & Nemeroff, C.B. (2003). Neurobiological effects of childhood abuse: Implications for the pathophysiology of depression and anxiety. *Archives of Women's Mental Health, 6*(1), 15–22.

Percy, M., & Brown, I. (2003). Factors that cause or contribute to developmental disability. In I. Brown & M. Percy (Eds.), *Developmental disabilities in Ontario* (2nd ed., pp. 117–144). Toronto, Canada: Ontario Association on Developmental Disabilities.

Perlman, N., & Erikson, C. (1992). Issues related to sexual abuse of persons with developmental disabilities: An overview. *Journal on Developmental Disabilities, 1,* 19–23.

Priestley, M. (2001). Introduction: The global context of disability. In M. Priestley (Ed.), *Disability and the life course: Global perspectives* (pp. 3–14). Cambridge, United Kingdom: Cambridge University Press.

Randall, W., Parilla, R., & Sobsey, D. (2000). Gender, disability status and risk for sexual abuse in children. *Journal on Developmental Disability, 7*, 1–15.

Randall, W., Sobsey, D., & Parilla, R. (2001). Ethnicity, disability and risk for abuse. *Developmental Disabilities Bulletin, 29*, 60–80.

Robinson, R. (2014). Preventing abuse of children and young people with disability under the National Disability Insurance scheme: A brave new world? *Australian Social Work, 68*(4), 469–482. doi:10.1080/031240 7X.2014.950977

Rosenberg, S.A., & Robinson, C. (2004). Out-of-home placements for young children with developmental and medical conditions. *Children and Youth Services Review, 26*, 711–723.

Shannon, P., & Tappan, C. (2011). Identification and assessment of children with developmental disabilities in child welfare. *Social Work, 56*(4), 297–305.

Sobsey, D. (1994). *Violence and abuse in the lives of people with disabilities: The end of silent acceptance?* Baltimore, MD: Paul H. Brookes Publishing Co.

Stalker, K., & McArthur, K. (2012). Child abuse, child protection and disabled children: A review of recent research. *Child Abuse Review, 21*, 24–40.

Strickler, H. (2001). Interaction between family violence and mental retardation. *Mental Retardation, 39*, 461–471.

Sullivan, P., & Knutson, J.F. (2000). Maltreatment and disabilities: A population-based epidemiological study. *Child Abuse and Neglect, 24*, 1257–1273.

Teixeira, J.M., Fisk, N.M., & Glover, V. (1999). Association between maternal anxiety in pregnancy and increased uterine artery resistance index: Cohort based study. *British Medical Journal, 318*, 153–157.

Tharinger, D., Burrows Horton, C., & Millea, S. (1990). Sexual abuse and exploitation of children and adults with mental retardation and other handicaps. *Child Abuse and Neglect, 14*, 301–312.

Trocmé, N., MacLaurin, B., Fallon, B., Black, T., Tonmyr, L., Blackstock, C.,...Cloutier, R. (2005). *Canadian Incidence Study of Reported Child Abuse and Neglect (CIS-2003): Major findings*. Ottawa, Canada: Minister of Public Works and Government Services Canada.

Trocmé, N., MacLaurin, B., Fallon, B., Daciuk, J., Billingsley, D., Tourigny, M.,...McKenzie, B. (2001). *Canadian Incidence Study of Reported Child Abuse and Neglect: Final report*. Ottawa, Canada: Minister of Public Works and Government Services Canada.

United Nations. (1989). *Convention on the Rights of the Child*. Retrieved from http://www.unhcr.org/uk/4aa76b319 .pdf

United Nations Enable. (2006). *The United Nations focal point on persons with disabilities*. Retrieved from http://www.un.org/esa/socdev/enable/rights/convtexte .htm#convtext

Vig, S., & Kaminer, R. (2002). Maltreatment and developmental disabilities in children. *Journal of Developmental and Physical Disabilities, 14*(4), 371–386.

Waldfogel, J. (1998). *The future of child protection*. Cambridge, MA: Harvard University Press.

Westcott, H.L., & Jones, D.P.H. (1999). Annotation: The abuse of disabled children. *Journal of Child Psychology and Psychiatry, 40*(4), 497–506.

36

Education for Students with Intellectual and Developmental Disabilities

Michael L. Wehmeyer, Karrie A. Shogren, and Ivan Brown

WHAT YOU WILL LEARN

- The concept of special education as activities, supports, or services that are designed and provided for children or young adults who need extraordinary supports
- The concept of inclusive education as specially designed instruction and other accommodations needed for students with disabilities to be successfully educated in the same schools and the same classrooms as their peers without disabilities
- Enhanced benefits of inclusive settings for students with intellectual and developmental disabilities compared with the segregated settings that were provided historically
- The existence of a wide array of effective instructional methods, materials, and strategies for teaching learners with intellectual and developmental disabilities
- The critical importance of parental involvement in the education of students with intellectual and developmental disabilities

It is customary around the world for children to go to school. Most countries have laws requiring

Authors' note: Portions of this chapter are reprinted by permission from Brown, Percy, and Machalek (2007). The authors are grateful to Rhonda Faragher, Nick Gore, and Glynis Murphy for providing information on legislation and policy in Australia and the United Kingdom.

parents to ensure that their children attend school or receive accredited home schooling. These laws underscore the widely accepted view that education is an exceptionally useful tool not only for individual success but also for the betterment of society as a whole.

An internationally recognized standard for practice is that children with disabilities have a right to education. In 1994, the United Nations Educational, Scientific and Cultural Organization (UNESCO) issued the *Salamanca Statement and Framework for Action on Special Needs Education* (UNESCO, 1994), which stated, in part, that every child has a fundamental right to education and that children who have unique learning needs must have access to regular inclusive schools. Article 24 of the United Nations' *Convention on the Rights of Persons with Disabilities* (2006) confirmed this fundamental right, proclaiming the right of children with disabilities to a free public education with the accommodations and supports needed to ensure student participation in inclusive settings. These two international statements emphasize the rights of children with disabilities to free, inclusive public education (but see Chapter 5 and Chapter 6 for insight into limitations to the enforcement of international agreements).

This chapter focuses on issues pertaining to the education of children with intellectual and developmental disabilities. The special education field has attracted a great deal of research and related inquiry, and this has resulted in a very large amount of literature that cannot be adequately captured in one chapter. Thus, this chapter functions as an introduction to the education of students with intellectual and developmental disabilities, highlighting the main trends and issues and some of the important legislation that supports them.

DESCRIPTION OF SPECIAL EDUCATION SERVICES

The term *special education* has both legal and practical meanings. In the United States, special education is defined in the Individuals with Disabilities Education Improvement Act (IDEA) of 2004 (PL 108-446) as "specially designed instruction, at no cost to the parents, to meet the unique needs of a child with a disability" (Section 300.39). Similarly, in Australia (and other countries), *special needs education* is defined as teaching for students who have difficulties learning, including specialized exercises, subject matter, or techniques. In Canada, each province and territory sets its own educational policies, so *special education* or *special needs education* are defined in a variety of ways, but all of these are generally consistent with the aforementioned focus on the provision of individualized instruction for students who need additional or exceptional supports to be successful.

Thus, *special education* refers to activities, supports, or services that are designed and provided to ensure effective education for children (or, in some countries, young adults) who need extraordinary supports to learn. The settings in which children take part in such activities and receive such supports and services vary across the world, but the critical point is that *special education* refers to the *practices* pertaining to the instruction that is provided and not to the *place* where it occurs, as the term is often misunderstood to mean. For this reason, we use the term *special education services* to be clear that it means educational practices.

Although the settings in which children with disabilities receive these special education services vary from typical general education classrooms to specialized settings, in the United States and increasingly around the world, policy and best practice in the education of students with disabilities emphasizes a strong preference toward inclusive education. The term *inclusive education* means that students with disabilities are educated in the same schools and the same classrooms as their peers without disabilities, with the specially designed instruction and other accommodations they need to be successful provided for them.

This vision remains unrealized for many students with intellectual and developmental disabilities, unfortunately. For example, in the United States, federal law establishes a preference for educating students with disabilities in general education classrooms with their peers who do not have disabilities but leaves the decision for where a student is educated up to the individualized education program (IEP) planning team. According to IDEA 2004, a student with a disability should be removed from a general education classroom only when supplementary aids and services are not sufficient to ensure student success. If a student is not educated in a regular classroom, IDEA 2004 allows the IEP team to select the most "appropriate" setting from a continuum of available educational placement options ranging from home schooling to inclusive classroom settings.

Overall, during the 2010–2011 school year, 61% of students receiving special education services spent 80% or more of their day in the general education classroom (U.S. Department of Education, 2014). This percentage ranged, however, from only 13% of children with multiple disabilities spending 80% or more of their day in general education classrooms to 87% of children with speech and language difficulties. Only children with hearing impairments, orthopedic impairments, other health impairments, specific learning disabilities, speech and language impairments, and visual impairments spent 80% or more of their day in general education classes at greater than 50% rates. On the other end of the spectrum, more than 50% of children with deafblindness, intellectual disability, or multiple disabilities were in the general education classroom less than 40% of the day or were served in separate schools or in homebound instruction.

A BRIEF HISTORY OF SPECIAL EDUCATION

The compulsory education of students with intellectual and developmental disabilities is a relatively contemporary idea, although the seeds of this movement began prior to the 20th century (see Chapter 2 for more information about historical understandings of disability and intellectual and developmental disabilities). The box provides information about antecedents to and pioneers of special education practice leading up to the 20th century.

Special Education Before the 20th Century

Special education, as a formal and systematic service, began in the early 18th century, primarily as a result of the growth of egalitarian and humanitarian

---

Precursors to 20th Century Focus on Special Education

Pedro Ponce de Leon (1520–1584), a Spanish Benedictine monk, promoted the view that sensory disabilities do not prohibit learning. He demonstrated this belief by teaching boys who were deaf and mute to speak, read, and write. He wrote a book that described his methods, although it has been lost to history. However, another Spaniard who specialized in the same area, J. Pablo Bonet (1560–1620), published teaching methods in his 1620 *Reducción de las letras y arte para enseñar a hablar a los mudos,* the first known book on the topic (*Educación Especial,* 1991).

John Locke (1632–1704) had many innovative ideas in many fields, including education (Williams, 2006). He was the first to differentiate between intellectual disabilities and emotional difficulties, although this difference was not fully understood until the 20th century.

Jean-Marc-Gaspard Itard (1775–1838) was a French physician who specialized in diseases of the ear. He became known for his development of successful methods for educating children who were deaf. He is most famous for the 5 years he spent teaching a 12-year-old French boy named Victor who was deaf and found living in the wild. Itard described this partial success in his well-known book *The Wild Boy of Aveyron* (Itard, 1801, 1806/1962), and his teaching enabled Victor to live with some degree of dignity in society.

Laurent Clerc (1785–1869) was a deaf teacher whom Thomas Hopkins Gallaudet recruited from the Institution for Deaf-Mutes in Paris; together they founded the American School for the Deaf. Clerc taught for 50 years and was much celebrated as the man who brought deaf education to America. He also adapted the French system of manual signing for his American students, creating a somewhat separate American system of signing (Naranjo, 2008).

Thomas Hopkins Gallaudet (1787–1851), an American theologian, studied European methods of communicating with and educating people who are deaf. When he returned to the United States, he founded, in 1817, the first residential school for children who are deaf in Hartford, Connecticut. This school, later renamed the American School for the Deaf, was modeled after a well-regarded school for children who were deaf in Paris. Gallaudet's pioneering work and name are honored by Gallaudet University in Washington, D.C., the only U.S. institution of higher learning for students who are deaf (Hallahan & Kauffman, 2003).

Samuel Gridley Howe (1801–1876) was an American educator, physician, and social reformer for a variety of humanitarian causes, including abolition. In the disability field, he is remembered mostly for his pioneering work in the education of people who were blind and deaf. He helped found the New England Asylum for the Blind (now the Perkins School for the Blind) and was its head for 44 years. Over time, Howe developed methods that he and others used to help a great many people. Helen Keller was a student who later benefited from his pioneering work (TeacherLINK, 2006).

Edouard Séguin (1812–1880) was a student of Jean-Marc-Gaspard Itard in France. He emigrated to the United States in 1848 and became well known for his pioneering work with children who would now be considered to have developmental delays or intellectual disability (Kanner, 1960; Stainton, 1994; see Chapter 2 for historic usage of terms). His approach became known as the physiological method and involved motor and sensory physical training, intellectual training (including academic and speech techniques), and socialization (which was considered moral training at the time). He founded an organization that later evolved into the American Association on Mental Retardation (Winzer, 2007).

(continued)

Precursors to 20th Century Focus on Special Education *(continued)*

Johann Jakob Guggenbühl (1816–1863) was a well-known Swiss educator who opened a residential facility to educate people with intellectual disability in Abendberg, Switzerland, in 1816. Guggenbühl is usually considered to be the pioneer in institutional care for people with intellectual disabilities. His work in education, although later discredited, set the scene for many later advances (for details, see Kanner, 1959).

John Langdon Haydon Down (1828–1896) was an English physician who taught medicine and specialized in mental health. He was an early proponent of training for people now described as having intellectual disability. Down proposed an early classification system for such people (described in Chapter 2), but he is best known for his description of what was once called mongolism and is now known as Down syndrome. He made many other contributions to special education and the greater understanding of disability and mental health. During Down's life, he also became well known for his pioneering education and training methods in England, first at Earlswood Asylum for Idiots in Surrey and later at a home called Normansfield (Kanner, 1964).

---

ideas that swept France, the United States, and, other European countries and the countries in their empires. Numerous advances were made in a number of countries, beginning with France and Germany and later moving to England, the United States, and elsewhere. These improvements were led primarily by physicians who were appalled by the lack of care of children who were "idiots" and lived in orphanages, workhouses, asylums, schools for the poor, and other places of care (see Chapter 2 for a discussion of historical usage of terms). Despite efforts by religious and philanthropic organizations, conditions for these children often continued to be very poor, and the early pioneers in special education were interested in developing effective educational and training methods, primarily for the purpose of equipping children with skills that would enable them to take a better place in society.

Several events in the first half of the 19th century in Europe particularly shaped the history of special education and warrant highlighting here, but none more than the discovery of a young boy, found by hunters in the woods near Aveyron, a small village in south-central France, on January 8, 1800 (Lane, 1976). At the time it was thought that the boy, later named Victor, had grown up in the wild for most, if not all, of his 11 or 12 years, thus earning him the epithet "The Wild Boy of Aveyron." Victor was examined by the famous French physician, Phillipe Pinel, and declared an "incurable idiot." Eventually, though, Victor came under the care of Jean-Marc-Gaspard Itard (1775–1838), who was chief physician at the Institution

for Deaf-Mutes in Paris and who had been a student under Pinel. Itard did not, however, share Pinel's conviction of Victor's ineducability, and so he began a systematic program of intervention to teach Victor to speak, recognize words and letters, and care for himself. Itard's efforts contributed a number of firsts to the field, among them the first individualized education program and the first recognition of the importance of an enriched environment in mediating the impact of impairments. Ironically, Itard considered his work with Victor a failure due to his pupil's inability to acquire speech, but in reality Victor gained a number of social, academic, and independent living skills. Itard's pioneering work paved the way for the growth, throughout the 19th century, of efforts to educate people with intellectual and developmental disabilities (Lane, 1976).

In 1837, Edouard Seguin (1812–1880), a student of Itard, began work that would eventually change the view about the educability of people with intellectual disability and prove Itard correct. Itard was approached to take on another student like Victor, but due to failing health he declined and recommended Seguin. Seguin developed a pedagogy based on careful physiological training of all the senses, and by 1844, the French Academy of Sciences proclaimed that, with his method, Seguin "had definitely solved the problem of idiot education" (Blatt, 1987, p. 36). Even if the "problem" of special education had not been exactly "solved," Seguin's work launched the field of special education for people with developmental disabilities.

Special Education in the 20th Century

As discussed in Chapter 2, by the beginning of the 20th century, great numbers of asylums, hospitals, special schools, care homes, orphanages, workhouses, and other forms of residential and habilitation institutions and schools had sprung up across Europe, the United States, and countries that were strongly influenced by Europe (e.g., Australia, Canada, New Zealand). By then, however, the burgeoning populations and the focus on eugenics had resulted in the de-emphasis on habilitation and had turned to custodial care and efforts to protect society from the inmates of such institutions. This remained the case for most state-run institutions throughout the 20th century.

As the institution system grew, and as individual institutions themselves grew and changed missions, there emerged initial efforts in schools to educate students with disabilities. In the United States, the first public classes for "feebleminded" children opened in Boston, Massachusetts, in 1896 and in Providence, Rhode Island; in 1899, the Chicago public schools opened classes for "crippled" children. That same year, the U.S. National Education Association established a Department of Special Education, though the impetus for this pertained to education efforts for the deaf, spearheaded by Alexander Graham Bell and emphasizing lip reading and other accommodations to the hearing world rather than learning sign language.

Perhaps the first large-scale effort in the United States to educate students that included students who were then deemed to be "feebleminded" occurred in the New York City public schools under the direction of Elizabeth Farrell. Farrell, the daughter of immigrants from Ireland and Wales, began teaching in the New York system in 1899 and, in that same year, formed the first ungraded class in Public School #1 in Manhattan. Farrell's methods involved increased work in manual and physical training and, much like Seguin's work, emphasized motor training. The ungraded classes expanded through the New York system rapidly, with 10 in place by 1903, 14 by 1906, 61 by 1908, and 131 by 1912. The identification of children for these ungraded classes was, however, somewhat haphazard, and it was the introduction of intelligence testing that systematized identification and the delivery of special education services.

Intelligence Testing The mental testing movement began with the work of French psychologist Alfred Binet (1857–1911) and his doctoral student Théodore Simon. In 1904, the French government commissioned Binet to develop a reliable way to identify children who could benefit from instruction that was more specialized than that typically found in schoolrooms in France at the time. Binet and Simon developed the eponymous Binet-Simon Scale, which was revised in 1908 and again in 1911. This test was intended to provide information about a child within a broader assessment of functioning and learning ability.

In 1911, American psychologist Henry Herbert Goddard translated the Binet-Simon scale into English and began using it to measure the intelligence of inmates at the Vineland Training School, an institution for "feebleminded" children at which Goddard worked (Smith & Wehmeyer, 2012). In 1911, Goddard published a study of the use of the Binet-Simon Scale with 2,000 school children and, in 1914, published the results of a 2-year survey in the New York schools, recommending the increased use of intelligence testing to identify "defective children" and the creation of a segregated school system for them (Goddard, 1914). A few years earlier, in 1904, the Vineland Training School established a summer teacher training program. Goddard and his institution colleagues held very eugenic views of feeblemindedness, and this view was, in essence, codified by the growing use of intelligence testing and the establishment of a segregated school system over the course of the first half of the 20th century.

Last Half of the 20th Century After World War II, the dominant countries of the Western world started turning their attention toward social equality and human rights. The World Health Organization and the United Nations took leading roles in promoting international agreements that, at least on paper, spoke to the rights of individuals and the equality of all people. Parents of children with disabilities formed groups and began to advocate strongly for educational and social services for their children, especially as there was no legal entitlement to schooling for children with disabilities.

At first, such advocacy led to the growth of educational services primarily outside school systems. These services were not always ideal. Access was fairly arbitrary, the quality of instruction was uneven, and some sites were overcrowded and underfunded. As with the residential institutions, some children were left in these services simply because it appeared to be the only option available and not because their learning needs were being served. Similar problems plagued public school special education programs that some school boards offered but that were not required by law. These and other factors helped generate a number of important acts and laws across the world (see the next subsection) that set out educational rights for all children with disabilities and that have led to the current educational philosophy of inclusion and international conventions such as the *Convention on the Rights of Persons with Disabilities*.

Legislation Pertaining to Free Public Education for Students with Disabilities

As of this writing in 2016, many countries have passed legislation mandating a free appropriate public education, and this subsection is intended to highlight only a sampling of such legislative mandates. In the United States, numerous state and local laws and policies are in force that pertain to protecting the civil liberties of people with disabilities, but with respect to education, the primary legislation is the previously mentioned IDEA. Passed originally in 1975 as the Education for All Handicapped Children Act (PL 94-142), IDEA ensures a free appropriate public education for students with disabilities and regulates the actions school districts must take to meet this guarantee of equal access. IDEA requires such procedures as nondiscriminatory evaluation to determine a child's need for special education, requires the development of an IEP that addresses how students with disabilities will have access to the general education curriculum and have their other education needs met, identifies the types of related services and supplementary aids and services that should be delivered, and puts in place safeguards for parents and family members and a myriad of other protections, regulations, and recommendations.

In Canada, education is the constitutional responsibility of the provinces and territories, and all provinces and territories have enacted legislation that guarantees the right to free public education for all children, even if this right takes numerous forms both among and within provinces and territories (Winzer, 2007). Ontario, Canada's most populous province, serves as an example. Ontario amended its Education Act in 1980 (Ontario Ministry of Education, 1980) to require all school boards to ensure that all exceptional children are provided with free public education, that exceptional pupils are defined and categorized, and that exceptional pupils are identified and appropriately placed through an Identification, Placement, and Review Committee (Ontario Ministry of Education, 2015). Section 1 of the act describes an exceptional pupil as one "whose behavioural, communicational, intellectual, physical or multiple exceptionalities are such that he or she is considered to need placement in a special education program" (Ontario Human Rights Commission, 2002). The other main provisions of the amendment are that special education programs must 1) be based on, and modified by, ongoing assessment and evaluation, 2) provide an Individual Education Plan with specific learning objectives, and 3) specify educational supports that meet the needs of exceptional pupils. The act also established a Special Education Tribunal to "provide final and binding arbitration in disagreements between a parent and school board concerning the identification or placement of an exceptional pupil" (Ontario Ministry of Education, 2015). This legislation has been modified numerous times in the intervening years, but the basic principle remains the same: all children, including those with any disability, are entitled to a publicly funded education with appropriate supports provided.

The United Kingdom passed a series of laws to provide for the needs of children with learning difficulties and other special needs (see Mittler, 2002). The Education Acts (1993 and 1996) and the Disability Discrimination Act (1995) were updated for special education with the enactment of the Special Educational Needs and Disability Act 2001 (SENDA), applicable to England, Scotland, and Wales (see U.K. Centre for Legal Education, 2015; U.K. Office of Public Sector Information, 2015). This, in turn, has been updated and revised since its enactment (e.g., Special Educational Needs and Disability Code of Practice for England) (U.K. Department for Education and Department of Health, 2014). SENDA gave students with disabilities the right not to be discriminated against in education, training, and services pertaining to education (U.K. Centre for Legal Education). In general terms, this means that all students with disabilities, including students in higher education, were given the right not to be treated "less favorably" than students without disabilities, and that it is the responsibility of schools and educational institutions themselves to show that their treatment of individuals with disabilities is justified. The key features of SENDA include free access to public education, the right to inclusive education where possible, the right of students with disabilities not to be substantially disadvantaged, the right of families to be informed, and the right to appeal decisions (Brown, Percy, & Machalek, 2007). SENDA represents an important step forward for special education and for the rights of individuals with disabilities in the United Kingdom. It establishes legal rights for all students with disabilities, and it requires educational service providers to anticipate, plan for, and respond to the needs of exceptional students. Subsequently, other special education legislation and policy has been adopted. Although this varies among jurisdictions of the United Kingdom, "the right to local mainstream education for children with disabilities is enshrined in policy and guidance across England, Wales, Ireland, and Scotland (e.g., The Children [Scotland] Act, 1995; The Special Educational Needs and Disability [Northern Ireland] Order, 2005; Special Educational Needs Code of Practice for Wales, 2002; Children and Families Act, 2014)" (Gore et al., 2015, pp. 46–47).

In Australia, the Disability Discrimination Act 1992, and its supplement, the Disability Standards for Education 2005, ensure that students with a disability have access to and are able to participate in education free from discrimination and on the same basis as other children. The standards were reviewed in 2010 (Australian Government Department of Education, 2010), culminating in recommendations to improve awareness of the standards; to clarify key terms such as "on the same basis"; to acknowledge that *equitable* is different from *the same*" (p. 55, italics in the original); to affirm that the standards apply to child care and vocational training sectors; and to require the development of individual education plans for students in schools. These plans are to include advice on barriers to learning faced by the student and how these can be overcome. The fundamental principle remains: all learners in Australia are entitled to free, compulsory, secular education in their local school.

In South Korea, the Special Education Promotion Law similarly guarantees equal access to education, as do the Japanese Special Support Education system and the laws of many countries.

EFFECTIVE SPECIAL EDUCATION PRACTICES

We turn now to a discussion of what students with intellectual and developmental disabilities are often taught in the compulsory systems described earlier in this chapter. As was mentioned previously, despite legislation that establishes a vision for inclusive practices, the reality for most children with intellectual and developmental disabilities is that their education remains largely separate and segregated. Significant issues remain pertaining to labeling and the stigma associated with terms such as *mental retardation* and the consequent low expectations held for students with intellectual and developmental disabilities. However, there are trends in education that point toward a better future, and these are discussed herein.

Where Are Students with Intellectual and Developmental Disabilities Taught?

We previously described the historical trends that established a largely segregated system to educate students with intellectual and developmental disabilities. Though progress is slow, the clear trend for the future is toward educating students with intellectual and developmental disabilities in inclusive settings. The beginnings of a movement toward inclusive education date to the 1980s and efforts at mainstreaming (i.e., including students with disabilities in select, nonacademic courses). Turnbull, Turnbull, Wehmeyer, and Shogren (2013) suggested that the inclusion movement can best be described as three generations of related, though distinct, activities.

First-generation inclusive practices focused on the basics of including students with intellectual and developmental disabilities into the general education classroom, and efforts during this period were instrumental in changing prevailing educational settings for students with disabilities from primarily separate, self-contained settings to integration into the regular or mainstream education classroom. These basics of integration could be summarized in three "key components of first-generation inclusion":

- All students receive education in the school they would attend if they had no disability.

- School and general education placements are age- and grade-appropriate.

- Special education supports exist within the general education class. (Turnbull et al., 2013, p. 56)

The second generation of inclusive practices was more generative in nature in that instead of focusing on moving students from separate settings to regular classroom settings, efforts focused on improving practice in the general education classroom. Research and practice during this phase emphasized aspects of instructional practices that promoted inclusion, such as differentiated instruction and cooperative learning, several of which are described in subsequent sections.

The third generation of inclusive practices has emerged since 2000. School reform efforts have shifted the main focus of inclusion from where and how a student is educated to what the student is learning. Third-generation practices have shifted the focus from individual classrooms to schoolwide provision of high-quality instruction to all, with more intensive instruction as necessary for students who continue to struggle.

Schoolwide Interventions and Multi-Tiered Systems of Support One of the distinguishing features of third-generation inclusive practices is the focus on schoolwide interventions, which are, quite simply, interventions (including high-quality instruction) that are implemented throughout a school building and that are designed to maximally benefit all students. Recent models of schoolwide practices operate under models of multi-tiered systems of support (MTSS), which are designed to provide a tiered approach to academic, social, and behavioral instruction. These MTSS frameworks have emerged from the convergence of "tiered" interventions to address academic and behavioral issues, and the basis of such models is that 1) all students receive high-quality, evidence-based, and universally designed instruction, taking into consideration their linguistic and cultural backgrounds, disabilities, and other learning needs (primary or Tier 1 interventions); 2) some students who are not successful behaviorally or academically with only Tier 1 supports receive additional targeted instruction in addition to Tier 1 instruction (secondary or Tier 2 interventions); and 3) a few students who need the most intensive supports to succeed receive not only Tier 1 and 2 interventions but also more intensive, sometimes individualized, instruction and supports (tertiary or Tier 3 interventions). It is important to note that as students move to more intensive levels (tiers) of support, they do not need to be removed from general education classes (Sailor, 2009). Interventions can be embedded within general education instruction and activities, maintaining opportunities for the benefits of inclusion.

Classroom Ecological Modifications and Accommodations Teachers of children with disabilities must have an ongoing awareness of how the classroom environment (ecology) affects students with intellectual and developmental disabilities and then adapt it accordingly. Some students do not function well when they are in large-group instructional settings, whereas others do not do well in individualized seat work. For some students, being surrounded by colors, pictures, books, and so forth is positively stimulating, and other students find the presence of such things to be stressful and overwhelming. Equipment, routines, or presentation of material may need to be made to address these and other issues within the classroom environment that limit student learning.

What Are Students with Intellectual and Developmental Disabilities Taught?

There is, by now, a substantive body of evidence that students with intellectual and developmental disabilities can acquire new knowledge and skills across multiple domains (Wehmeyer et al., 2014). We have already indicated that there is a worldwide priority for educating students with disabilities—including students with intellectual and developmental disabilities—in inclusive settings. That said, historically, the educational programs of students with intellectual and developmental disabilities have been primarily, if not exclusively, focused on functional skills or life skills content, too often to the exclusion of instruction in core academic content (Jackson, Ryndak, & Wehmeyer, 2010). We use legislation in the United States to illustrate this shift, although similar movements have occurred worldwide (Wehmeyer et al., 2014). The 1997 amendments to IDEA (PL 105-17), in response to nationwide school reform efforts, contained requirements, referred to as the access to the general education mandates, to ensure that all students receiving special education services are involved with and progress in the general education curriculum. In this reauthorization, the educational programs of students with disabilities were required to include a statement of the special education and related services and supplementary aids and services to be provided to the student to advance appropriately toward attaining the annual goals, to be involved and progress in the general curriculum, and to be educated with children who do not have disabilities. *General education curriculum* was defined in the regulations as referring to the same curriculum as all children receive. The 2004 amendments to IDEA (PL 108-446) contained all of the original IDEA 1997 mandates and added several new requirements, including that schools ensure that the IEP team includes someone knowledgeable about the general education curriculum and that the team meet at least annually to address any lack of expected progress in the general education curriculum. Finally, the regulations in IDEA 2004 prohibited a student with a disability from being removed from the general education setting based solely upon needed modifications to the general education curriculum.

It is worth noting that research has established that students with intellectual disability who are educated in the general education classroom are disproportionally more likely to be working on academic tasks that are grade-level or near-grade-level than are their peers in self-contained classrooms (Matzen, Ryndak, & Nakao, 2010; Soukup, Wehmeyer, Bashinski, & Bavaird, 2007; Wehmeyer, Lattin, Lapp-Rincker, & Agran, 2003) and that, if provided instruction to do so, students with intellectual disability can make progress on core content instruction in the general education setting (Lee, Wehmeyer, Soukup, & Palmer, 2010; Roach & Elliott, 2006; Shogren, Palmer, Wehmeyer, Williams-Diehm, & Little, 2012; Wehmeyer, 2011).

So, the expectation for the education of students with intellectual and developmental disabilities is that they will be taught both functional skills as well as core academic content. Clearly, with regard to the latter, specialized instructional techniques are necessary to ensure success; how students with intellectual and developmental disabilities are taught is addressed next.

How Are Students with Intellectual and Developmental Disabilities Taught?

There are available in the literature far too many instructional strategies and techniques useful in the education of students with intellectual and developmental disabilities to describe in one chapter.

This subsection examines assessment, modifications to curricular materials, and instructional strategies pertinent to the education of students with intellectual and developmental disabilities.

Assessment of Learning and Instructional Needs Assessment in special education has two general purposes. First, assessment provides child-specific information that guides school personnel and parents in making decisions to provide individual students with the best learning environments, instructional methods, and supports. Such information may emerge from using some of the many available formal assessment tools, but it also may come from less formal assessment such as teacher and parent observations, checklists of child behaviors, classroom tests and other documentation of learning achievement, and notes on the effects of the environment (Friend & Bursuck, 2002; see Wodrich, 1997, for a good description of tests and assessment methods). Information that contributes to a special education assessment may be sought from school psychologists, speech-language specialists, physical therapists, medical professionals, social workers, and others.

Second, assessment identifies a child's specific skills and abilities, learning needs, most successful learning methods, and learning progress. In this sense, it is a basic and essential tool of good teaching. Formal assessment tools are sometimes helpful for identifying starting points, but effective teachers need to assess their students less formally in an ongoing way each day, adjusting for specific subject matter and specific skills as well as for what needs to be taught and the best ways to teach it. With experience, teachers learn to intuitively and continually evaluate children with special needs and to identify routes of learning that are best for a given child.

Universal Design for Learning and Curriculum Modifications Chapter 1 discussed models that conceptualize disability as a function of the gap between personal capacities and the demands of the environment or context. In education, the curriculum (in this case intended to mean the instructional materials that students receive, including textbooks and workbooks) forms an important part of the "context" of education. Like interventions derived from social-ecological models of disability in other areas (e.g., supported employment), modifications to the curriculum form an important part of specialized educational services. To that end, universal design for learning (UDL) constitutes a critical part of high-quality education. UDL refers to the design of instructional materials to be fully accessible for all students. Orkwis and McLane (1998) defined UDL as "the design of instructional materials and activities that allows learning goals to be achievable by individuals with wide differences in their abilities to see, hear, speak, move, read, write, understand English, attend, organize, engage, and remember" (p. 9). Meyer, Rose, and Gordon (2014) suggested three essential qualities of universally designed materials: that these materials 1) provide multiple representations of content, 2) provide multiple options for expression and control, and 3) provide multiple options for engagement and motivation.

The critical feature of UDL is that the curriculum is designed with a flexibility that enables learners with and without disabilities to have access to the content. Presentation of content in nonprint formats such as video, audio, graphic, or symbolic representation forms allows a wider range of students to gain access to the information. The use of e-books and digital texts rather than print texts, for example, allows for the representation of content in audio (text to speech), video (hyperlinked images or videos), and augmentative (electronic braille) format.

There are nontechnology forms of modifying the curriculum that can achieve similar purposes. The use, for example, of advance or graphic organizers to present the main ideas for a book chapter in a text enables learners with cognitive difficulties to pay attention to those themes or ideas when they appear in the reading. Learning-to-learn strategies (e.g., self-monitoring or self-evaluation skills) enable students to learn skills that improve their performance. Furthermore, there are other types of accommodations or task modifications that benefit students with intellectual and developmental disabilities, including modifications to the time available to complete tasks, alternative test items or lesson objectives, and the support of educational and assistive technology.

Research-Based Practices in Intervention

A number of instructional strategies or practices provide high-quality instruction when implemented schoolwide and have established efficacy with students with intellectual and developmental disabilities. These include direct instruction, modeling, match to sample, discrimination training,

discrete trial, prompting and fading, and generalization training. Many of these strategies have emerged from applied behavior analysis, including (in addition to discrete trial training and prompting and fading) task analysis, backward and forward chaining, stimulus shaping and facing, and errorless learning (Wehmeyer & Lee, 2007). Each of these strategies can be explored in detail elsewhere, but for now it is important to recognize that they constitute the types of more specialized interventions that might be useful with any learner who is having difficulty, including students with disabilities.

Peer-Mediated and Student-Mediated Instruction

The aforementioned instructional strategies are, by and large, teacher-mediated (i.e., are implemented by the teacher for the student). Another type of high-quality instructional strategy for use in schoolwide applications involves peer-mediated interventions. There are several approaches to peer-mediated strategies. One, peer tutoring, involves organizing students into pairs for brief periods of time to discuss their reactions or connections to content presented in class. In another version of paired tutoring, students work together to solve problems (Utley, Mortweet, & Greenwood, 1997), and with classwide peer tutoring (Delquadri, Greenwood, Whorton, Carta, & Hall, 1986), students are paired for frequent, brief periods of drill and practice of factual material, helping to focus the students' attention for intense practice periods.

Similarly, a number of student-directed learning strategies—in which the student mediates learning him- or herself—have been shown to be effective in enabling students with intellectual disability to self-regulate at least a portion of their own learning, including picture cues or antecedent cue regulation strategies (i.e., students use visual or auditory cues to complete a sequence of steps in a task), self-instruction (i.e., students provide their own verbal cues for learning), self-monitoring (i.e., students track their own completion of steps in a task), and self-evaluation (i.e., students evaluate whether they have completed a task or reached a goal) (Wehmeyer et al., 2014). A form of self-directed learning involves promoting self-determination, which involves instruction in areas such as goal setting, problem solving, decision making, self-advocacy, and self-regulation. Research has linked higher self-determination to positive adult outcomes, including employment and independent living, for youth with special educational needs (Shogren, Wehmeyer, Palmer, Rifenbark, & Little, 2015), as well as to a higher quality of life (Lachapelle et al., 2005; Nota, Ferrrari, Soresi, & Wehmeyer, 2007; Wehmeyer & Schwartz, 1998).

Meeting Other Educational Needs of Students with Intellectual Disability Although there is increased focus on teaching students with intellectual and developmental disabilities the content that is considered important for all children to acquire, it will remain the case that they need instruction in other educational areas if they are to be successful in life. Skills related to the transition from school to adult life or postsecondary education are covered in Chapter 37. Among the domains within other educational needs in which there is international consensus that students with intellectual and developmental disabilities need instruction are the areas related to life skills ranging from self-care and cooking skills to skills needed to live or work in one's community; skills and instruction to promote the transition from school to adulthood, including employment, independent living, and community inclusion; and skills leading to social inclusion and integration.

As students get older, such instruction in the general education curriculum is not typical. There are strategies that can be applied to continue to focus on such functional or life skills within the school setting while still being sensitive to the need for age-appropriate treatment. For example, from junior high or middle school onward, most students are involved in a physical education class, during which students typically change clothing. At such time, instruction to promote more independent dressing or self-care skills can be implemented without calling too much attention to the student's ongoing need for such supports. Furthermore, as students get older, it may be better to look at modifications to the object or task itself to enable a student to be more independent, as a social-ecological model would suggest. Velcro athletic shoes to replace shoestringed versions are an example of how modifications to the context can support independent functioning.

One of the learning characteristics of many students with intellectual disability is that they have a difficult time generalizing learning from one context to another (Wehmeyer, Sands, Knowlton, & Kozleski, 2002). As such, best practice has emphasized that instruction in many life skill areas—particularly as they pertain to independent living, community inclusion, and employment—should be provided in ecologically valid environments (i.e., the environment in which students will need to use the skill being taught). This community-based instruction approach requires that students leave the school campus to receive instruction in more appropriate environments for portions of the day or week.

Parent and Family Involvement

Schools have increasingly recognized the role of family members and others in their social network in influencing and supporting the overall development of children with intellectual and developmental disabilities (e.g., Hiatt-Michael, 2001; Leyser & Kirk, 2004). Ongoing communication and cooperation between teachers and parents is essential in maximizing the learning opportunities for children both inside and outside school and ensuring that the types of learning that occur in their various environments support one another.

This can be done in various ways. One good way is to establish a systematic method of communication. Many schools use some variation of a communications journal, which travels from home to school daily with the student and in which both teachers and family members make written comments that are helpful to the other. Other teachers use regularly scheduled telephone calls or meetings to ensure communication. Whatever the methods used, it is essential that teachers act as team members rather than as expert leaders, recognizing the value of ideas and suggestions made by family members and looking for ways the school can build on resources and customs in the family to enhance learning opportunities for the student. Another good way to enhance learning opportunities for students and improve the effectiveness of special education and general education teachers is for families to follow procedures at home similar to those used in the school (e.g., have similar behavior expectations, give praise in the same way for similar actions). Once more, ongoing communication between teachers and parents is necessary to make this work effectively, and some training may be necessary. It is important, here, that schools do not set their expectations for families too high. They need to recognize that families have lifestyles, skill sets, social and financial needs, and other personal circumstances that influence the support they are able to give their children at home. School personnel need to know and understand these factors when planning and carrying out IEPs.

SUMMARY

Special education or *special-needs education* refers to teaching and learning for children and adults who, because of their individual learning characteristics, require methods of instruction other than those provided in general education programs. The 19th and 20th centuries saw substantial growth in special education for children with intellectual and developmental disabilities, but it was not until the 1970s that laws began to be enacted requiring schools to provide education for all children with disabilities. The United States, in particular, enacted several laws that progressively ensured education rights. Other countries have followed closely. As a result, special education has undergone a dramatic change since the early 1970s, with the main thrusts being the development of publicly funded education for all students with disabilities, the ongoing refinement of individual assessment and learning plans, and the implementation of inclusive education practices within schools. However, a number of future challenges still need to be faced. Among these is the daunting challenge of providing special education worldwide, particularly for children who currently receive no education at all.

FOR FURTHER THOUGHT AND DISCUSSION

1. Educational rights for children with intellectual and developmental disabilities have improved dramatically since the early 1970s, especially with the passage of important laws. Select a child you know who has intellectual disability or a developmental disability. In what ways would this child's life differ if none of the education laws now in place in your country were enacted?

2. Think of the same child identified in the previous question. What rights and entitlements does this student need, in addition to the education laws that are in place in your country, to lead a successful life?

3. Ramos is a 7-year-old boy who has intellectual disability with mild cognitive impairments and cerebral palsy. His mobility is severely affected,

and he uses a wheelchair. Monica has just learned that Ramos will be a student in her class next year. What might Monica do to help prepare herself, her classroom environment, other students in the class, and Ramos' parents so that Ramos will have a successful learning experience?

4. What actions can a school initiate to be more inclusive?

5. What types of transition strategies can schools put in place? For example, what practical suggestions can a school give to employers to help students with intellectual or developmental disabilities succeed in the workplace? How can such suggestions be communicated to places of employment?

REFERENCES

Australian Government Department of Education. (2010). *Review of the Disability Standards for Education 2005.* Retrieved from http://education.gov.au/disability-standards-education

Blatt, B. (1987). *The conquest of mental retardation.* Austin, TX: PRO-ED.

Brown, I., Percy, M., & Machalek, K. (2007). Education for individuals with intellectual and developmental disabilities. In I. Brown & M. Percy (Eds.), *A comprehensive guide to intellectual and developmental disabilities* (pp. 489–510). Baltimore, MD: Paul H. Brookes Publishing Co.

Delquadri, J., Greenwood, C.R., Whorton, D., Carta, J.J., & Hall, R.V. (1986). Class wide peer tutoring. *Exceptional Children, 52,* 535–542.

Disability Discrimination Act. (1995). (c. 50), 1995, Chapter 50.

Educación especial. (1991). Retrieved from http://www.mercaba.org/Rialp/E/educacion_especial.htm

Education Act. (1993). (c. 35), 1993, Chapter 35.

Education Act. (1996). (c. 56), 1996, Chapter 56.

Education for All Handicapped Children Act of 1975, PL 94-142, 20 U.S.C. §§ 1400 *et seq.*

Esquirol, J.E. (1838/1845). *Mental maladies* (E. Hunt, Trans.). Philadelphia, PA: Lea and Blanchard.

Friend, M., & Bursuck, W.D. (2002). *Including students with special needs: A practical guide for classroom teachers* (3rd ed.). Boston, MA: Allyn & Bacon.

Goddard, H.H. (1914). *School training of defective children.* Yonkers-on-Hudson, NY: World Book.

Gore, N., Brady, S., Cormack, M., McGill, P., Shurlock, J., Jackson-Brown, F.,…Wedge, S. (2015). *Residential school placements for children and young people with intellectual disabilities: Their use and implications for adult social care.* London, United Kingdom: NIHR School for Social Care Research. Retrieved from http://www.sscr.nihr.ac.uk/PDF/ScopingReviews/SR10.pdf

Hallahan, D.P., & Kauffman, J.M. (2003). *Exceptional learners: Introduction to special education* (9th ed.). Boston, MA: Allyn & Bacon.

Hiatt-Michael, D. (2001). *Preparing teachers to work with parents* (Report No. EDO-SP-2001-2). Washington, DC: ERIC Clearinghouse on Teaching and Teacher Education.

Individuals with Disabilities Education Act Amendments (IDEA) of 1997, PL 105-17, 20 U.S.C. §§ 1400 *et seq.*

Individuals with Disabilities Education Improvement Act (IDEA) of 2004, PL 108-446, 20 U.S.C. §§ 1400 *et seq.*

Itard, J.M.G. (1801, 1806/1962). *The wild boy of Aveyron* (G. Humphrey & M. Humphrey, Trans.). New York, NY: Appleton-Century-Crofts.

Jackson, L., Ryndak, D., & Wehmeyer, M. (2010). The dynamic relationship between context, curriculum, and student learning: A case for inclusive education as a research-based practice. *Research and Practice in Severe Disabilities, 34*(1), 175–195.

Kanner, L. (1959). Johann Jakob Guggenbühl and the Abendberg. *Bulletin of the History of Medicine, 33,* 489–502.

Kanner, L. (1960). Itard, Seguin and Howe: Three pioneers in the education of retarded children. *American Journal of Mental Deficiency, 65,* 2–10.

Kanner, L. (1964). *A history of the care and study of the mentally retarded.* Springfield, IL: Charles C. Thomas.

Lachapelle, Y., Wehmeyer, M.L., Haelewyck, M.C., Courbois, Y., Keith, K.D., Schalock, R.,...Walsh, P.N. (2005). The relationship between quality of life and self-determination: An international study. *Journal of Intellectual Disability Research, 49,* 740–744.

Lane, H. (1976). *The wild boy of Aveyron.* Cambridge, MA: Harvard University Press.

Lee, S.H., Wehmeyer, M.L., Soukup, J.H., & Palmer, S.B. (2010). Impact of curriculum modifications on access to the general education curriculum for students with disabilities. *Exceptional Children, 76*(2), 213–233.

Leyser, Y., & Kirk, R. (2004). Evaluating inclusion: An examination of parent views and factors influencing their perspectives. *International Journal of Disability, Development and Education, 51,* 271–285.

Matzen, K., Ryndak, D., & Nakao, T. (2010). Middle school teams increasing access to general education for students with significant disabilities: Issues encountered and activities observed across contexts. *Remedial and Special Education, 31*(4), 287–304.

Meyer, A., Rose, D.H., & Gordon, D. (2014). *Universal design for learning: Theory & practice.* Wakefield, MA: CAST Professional Publishing.

Mittler, P. (2002). Educating pupils with intellectual disabilities in England: Thirty years on. *International Journal of Disability, Development and Education, 49,* 145–160.

Naranjo, D. (2008). *Laurent Clerc 1785–1869.* Retrieved from http://www.lifeprint.com/asl101/topics/clerc_laurent_7.htm

Nota, L., Ferrrari, L., Soresi, S., & Wehmeyer, M.L. (2007). Self-determination, social abilities, and the quality of life of people with intellectual disabilities. *Journal of Intellectual Disability Research, 51,* 850–865.

Ontario Human Rights Commission. (2002). *Report on education.* Retrieved from http://www.odacommittee.net/ohrc_education.html

Ontario Ministry of Education. (1980). *The Education Act.* Retrieved from http://www.edu.gov.on.ca/eng/general/elemsec/speced/edact.html

Ontario Ministry of Education. (2015). *The Education Act.* Retrieved from http://www.edu.gov.on.ca/eng/general/elemsec/speced/edact.html

Orkwis, R., & McLane, K. (1998). *A curriculum every student can use: Design principles for student access.* ERIC/OSEP Topical Brief, Fall 1998. Reston, VA: Council for Exceptional Children.

Roach, A.T., & Elliott, S.N. (2006). The influence of access to general education curriculum on alternate assessment performance of students with significant cognitive disabilities. *Educational Evaluation and Policy Analysis, 28*(2), 181–194.

Sailor, W. (2009). *Making RtI work: How smart schools are reforming education through schoolwide response-to-intervention models.* San Francisco, CA: Jossey-Bass.

Shogren, K., Palmer, S., Wehmeyer, M.L., Williams-Diehm, K., & Little, T. (2012). Effect of intervention with the Self-Determined Learning Model of Instruction on access and goal attainment. *Remedial and Special Education, 33*(5), 320–330.

Shogren, K.A., Wehmeyer, M.L., Palmer, S.B., Rifenbark, G., & Little, T. (2015). Relationships between self-determination and postschool outcomes for youth with disabilities. *Journal of Special Education, 48*(4), 256–267.

Smith, J.D., & Wehmeyer, M.L. (2012). Good blood, bad blood: Science, nature, and the myth of the Kallikaks. Washington, DC: American Association on Intellectual and Developmental Disabilities.

Soukup, J.H., Wehmeyer, M.L., Bashinski, S.M., & Bovaird, J. (2009). Classroom variables and access to the general education curriculum of students with intellectual and developmental disabilities. *Exceptional Children, 74,* 101–120.

Stainton, T. (1994). *Autonomy and social policy: Rights, mental handicap and social care.* London, United Kingdom: Avebury.

TeacherLINK. (2006). *Samuel Gridley Howe.* Retrieved from http://teacherlink.ed.usu.edu/tlresources/reference/champions/pdf/SamuelHowe.pdf

Turnbull, R., Turnbull, A., Wehmeyer, M., & Shogren, K. (2013). *Exceptional lives: Special education in today's schools* (7th ed.). Columbus, OH: Merrill Prentice-Hall.

U.K. Centre for Legal Education. (2015). *Welcome to UKCLE.* Retrieved from http://ials.sas.ac.uk/library/archives/ukcle/78.158.56.101/archive/law/index.html

U.K. Department for Education and Department of Health. (2014). *Special educational needs and disability code of practice for England.* Retrieved from https://www.gov.uk/government/uploads/system/uploads/attachment_data/file/273877/special_educational_needs_code_of_practice.pdf

U.K. Office of Public Sector Information. (2015). *Office of Public Sector Information.* Retrieved from http://www.opsi.gov.uk/psi/

United Nations. (2006). *Convention on the rights of persons with disabilities.* Retrieved from http://www.un.org/disabilities/convention/conventionfull.shtml

United Nations Educational, Scientific, and Cultural Organization. (1994). *The Salamanca statement and framework for action on special needs education.* Retrieved from http://www.unesco.org/education/pdf/SALAMA_E.PDF

U.S. Department of Education. (2014). *36th annual report to Congress on the implementation of the Individuals with Disabilities Education Act.* Washington, DC: Government Printing Office.

Utley, C.A., Mortweet, S.L., & Greenwood, C.R. (1997). Peer-mediated instruction and interventions. *Focus on Exceptional Children, 29,* 1–23.

Wehmeyer, M.L. (2011). Access to the general education curriculum for students with significant cognitive disabilities. In J.M. Kauffman & D.P. Hallahan (Eds.), *Handbook of special education* (pp. 544–556). New York, NY: Routledge.

Wehmeyer, M.L., Lattin, D., Lapp-Rincker, G., & Agran, M. (2003). Access to the general curriculum of middle-school students with mental retardation: An observational study. *Remedial and Special Education, 24,* 262–272.

Wehmeyer, M.L., & Lee, S.Y. (2007). Educating children with intellectual disability. In A. Carr, G. O'Reilly, P.N. Walsh, & J. McEvoy (Eds.), *The handbook of intellectual disability and clinical psychology practice* (pp. 559–605). London, United Kingdom: Routledge.

Wehmeyer, M.L., Sands, D.J., Knowlton, H.E., & Kozleski, E.B. (2002). *Teaching students with mental retardation: Providing access to the general curriculum.* Baltimore, MD: Paul H. Brookes Publishing Co.

Wehmeyer, M.L., & Schwartz, M. (1998). The relationship between self-determination and quality of life for adults with mental retardation. *Education and Training in Mental Retardation and Developmental Disabilities, 33,* 3–12.

Wehmeyer, M.L., Shogren, K., Verdugo, M.A., Nota, L., Soresi, S., Lee, S.H.,…Lachapelle, Y. (2014). Cognitive impairment and intellectual disability. In A.F. Rotatori, J.P. Bakken, S. Burkhardt, F. Obiakor, & U. Sharma (Eds.), *Advances in special education: Vol. 27. Special education international perspectives: Biopsychosocial, cultural, and disability aspects* (pp. 55–89). London, United Kingdom: Emerald Group.

Williams, A.N. (2006). Physician, philosopher, and paediatrician: John Locke's practice of child health care. *Archives of Disease in Childhood, 91,* 85–89.

Winzer, M.A. (2007). *Children with exceptionalities in Canadian classrooms* (8th ed.). Toronto, Canada: Prentice Hall.

Wodrich, D.L. (1997). *Children's psychological testing: A guide for nonpsychologists* (3rd ed.). Baltimore, MD: Paul H. Brookes Publishing Co.

37

The Transition
from School to Adult Life

Ivan Brown, Michael L. Wehmeyer, Kristine Weist Webb, and Janice Seabrooks-Blackmore

WHAT YOU WILL LEARN

- Key transition support questions
- The eclectic and pragmatic nature of theoretical foundations for transition
- The roles that families, schools, employers, and community services play in the transition to adult life of youth with disabilities
- The need for special support for individuals with severe disabilities and their families

All people experience many changes over the span of their lifetimes. Almost all of these changes are small and can be adjusted to with relative ease. There are times in most people's lives, however, when the changes are on a much larger scale, requiring people to follow patterns of behavior that are quite different from those with which they have become familiar. People with and without disabilities experience major changes, and most people require support at such times. People with intellectual and developmental disabilities, though, may require more, or somewhat specialized, support from professionals, family members, and others at times of change. The term *transition* is used in the field to describe times of major change and also to refer to the expanding body of literature and knowledge about such times of major change.

There are a number of key transitions that affect the lives of people with intellectual and developmental disabilities. Transitions arise from health and biology (e.g., growing up, losing parents, entering a later-life care facility), from social norms (e.g., cohabiting, marrying), from the way society is organized (e.g., entering or leaving school, entering or retiring from employment), and from current demographic trends (e.g., moving, becoming separated or divorced) (Wehmeyer & Webb, 2012a). Thus, transitions differ in nature from one country to another, due to social, cultural, and economic differences. They also differ in nature and importance from one person to another. For example, one person may retire after working for 30 years and experience the transition in a positive way, whereas another person may find this transition to be very problematic.

One transition that affects almost every person with intellectual or developmental disabilities (as well as young people without disabilities) in a fairly major way is the transition from school to adult life. As a consequence, this is the transition that has attracted the most attention and the most research to date in the disabilities field. There are a number of major changes in the lives of most people as they move from school to adult life, particularly those that affect people's places of residence and employment and their social interactions. Wehman (2013) identified seven common changes for youth with disabilities: employment, living arrangements, getting around the community, financial independence, making friends, sexuality and self-esteem, and having fun.

KEY TRANSITION SUPPORT QUESTIONS

As noted, the transition from school to adult life is a period when a number of changes can be expected in the lives of young people and when young people with intellectual or developmental disabilities may require more intensive support. What, then, are the key questions or issues that need to be addressed when preparing for and providing this support?

- *Theoretical foundations for support:* From what theoretical foundations is work in the transition area drawn?

- *Support to individuals and families:* Capie, Contardi, and Doehring (2006) set out three helpful support questions: How can families be supported to allow the young person to have increased autonomy? How many risks can be taken? How can young people be best helped to become full participants in society?

- *Exceptional support to individuals with severe disabilities and their families:* Most youth with severe disabilities need additional support. Florian et al. (2000) suggested that the following questions should be asked: What kinds of opportunities for further education are there? Are there other forms of provision? What are they? What options are currently available for young people with profound and complex learning difficulties after the age of 16?

The sections of this chapter do not address these questions fully; rather, they outline much of the progress that has been made to date.

Theoretical Foundations for Transition

Analyses of the transition from school to adult life draw on theory from a number of sources. In a review of the literature, Eisenman (2003) pointed out that the transition literature does not have a strong theoretical foundation. Instead, theory from a number of perspectives informs transition from school to adult roles. Some examples she provided to illustrate this point included the following:

Vocational psychology

- Person–environment fit theories suggest that positive work outcomes result from a good match between worker skills and abilities and the requirements of the job and work environment.

- Career development theories refer to people's awareness of, planning for, and response to work opportunities.

Developmental psychology

- The transition to adulthood is part of the overall process of individuation, or the movement from being largely dependent upon others for one's support to being largely dependent upon oneself for such support. Certain areas of focus in transition, particularly issues pertaining to self-determination, are derived heavily from research in developmental and personality psychology (Wehmeyer, Field, & Thoma, 2012).

Learning and cognitive psychology

- Learning and sociocognitive theories propose that such things as individuals' cognitive skills, motivation, perceptions, goals, attitudes, and expected rewards are key to successful adjustment.

Quality of life

- Quality of life theory proposes that addressing core quality of life concepts—such as allowing independence; including what is important to the individual; satisfying personal needs and wishes; and providing opportunities, choice, and social connectedness—is key to positive life adjustment outcomes (see Brown & Brown, 2003).

Sociology

- Status attainment theories look to social status and cognitive abilities as being most relevant to availability of opportunities and attainment of life and career options.

- Structuralist theories examine the relationship between major social institutions (e.g., schools, labor markets, health and social services, social policy) and an individual's characteristics.

- Identity theories (gender- and race-based theories; critical disability theory) focus on social stigma and roles, and the marginalization that accompanies them, as sources of inequality that require redress.

- Workplace culture theories emphasize the social patterns and behavioral norms that occur within workplaces.

These examples illustrate the eclectic nature of the theory that informs work in the area of transitions. Drawing from a variety of theoretical sources may add to the richness of this relatively new field of study, which involves virtually all aspects of a person's life, because some aspects of life are more important to individuals than others in times of change. Thus, one theoretical perspective may be more important than others when considering transition for individuals.

Approaches to Transition Arising from Theory

Reflecting the eclectic nature of its theoretical foundations, the practical work associated with successful transition from school to adult life appears to be multifaceted and, consequently, to reflect more than one theoretical approach. Eisenman (2003) summarized the approach most commonly used for work in the area of transition from school to adult life as being not strictly theory based but, rather, as being

> Pragmatically focused on solving culturally and socially determined problems (e.g., employment, graduation) that span multiple environments (educational, vocation, residential, and community) and involve multiple actors, including both individuals (e.g., children, young adults, family members, teachers, employers, social service workers) and corporations (e.g., school systems, community services, businesses, families), whose intrinsic and socially defined characteristics interact across time. (pp. 95–96)

Transition is, in fact, a practice-based field (Wehmeyer & Webb, 2012b).

In spite of this multifaceted approach, there are a number of specific ways to look at the transition from school to adult life. Each has its own emphasis on what is considered most important for youth undergoing transition, although they all overlap and all pursue the same ultimate goal—successful adjustment to adult life. Some of the ways to look at transition that are currently in use are as follows:

1. *Developmental life span:* Emphasizes opportunity-seeking skills, involving support groups, and making choices that are suited to the individual's

competencies and that will benefit the individual in the long term (e.g., Wehmeyer, Field, et al., 2012)

2. *Quality of life:* Emphasizes addressing basic needs, then enhancing the quality of a person's life experiences to promote enjoyment of life and reduce life problems (Moore & McNaught, 2014)

3. *Family:* Emphasizes the involvement of the family in transition planning and activities and the effects of transition on both individual family members and the family as a whole (Wandry & Pleet, 2012; Wehman, 2013)

4. *Social and psychological adjustment:* Emphasizes the stressful nature of the social and psychological changes that face young people as they move from school to adult life (Hepper & Garralda, 2001)

5. *Supports needed:* Emphasizes policy, service, work force, and family supports needed for successful transition to adult life (Wehman, Brooke, Lau, & Targett, 2012)

Conceptualizations of Transition Emerging from Theory

A number of conceptual frameworks for transition have been developed since the mid-1990s that are useful for transition planning and putting transition plans into practice. Four such conceptual frameworks are outlined in the following subsections to exemplify three different approaches. Readers are invited to explore the cited sources for full details of these frameworks.

Taxonomy for Transition Programs
The Taxomony for Transition Programs (Kohler, 1996) sets out concepts, subconcepts, and action objectives that are useful for carrying out transition plans and evaluating transition systems. The model comprises five key concepts:

1. Student-focused planning

2. Student development

3. Interagency collaboration

4. Program structure

5. Family involvement

Each of these five concepts has subconcepts that are accompanied by specific action objectives. For example, in the first concept, student-focused planning, one of the subconcepts is student participation. The following action objectives are set out for student participation:

- The planning team includes student, family members, and school and participating agency personnel.

- Assessment information is used as basis for planning.

- Transition-focused planning begins no later than age 14.

- Meeting time is adequate to conduct planning.

- Preparation time is adequate to conduct planning.

- Meeting time and place are conducive to student and family participation.

- Accommodations are made for communication needs (e.g., interpreters).

- Referral to adult service provider(s) occurs prior to the student's exit from school.

- A planning team leader identified.

Quality Indicators of Exemplary Transition Programs

Morningstar, Lee, Lattin, and Murray (2015) introduced a framework identifying quality indicators of adolescent transition programs. This model includes 47 quality indicators categorized into seven domains: 1) transition planning, 2) transition assessment, 3) family involvement, 4) student involvement, 5) transition-focused curriculum and instruction, 6) interagency collaboration, and 7) systems-level infrastructure. Morningstar and colleagues have developed a needs assessment using these indicators for use by students, educators, school districts, and others to evaluate transition program quality and areas of needed improvement.

Transition from a Family Perspective

Blacher (2001) offered a useful conceptual model that "considers transition from a family perspective, with family well-being as the primary outcome of interest" (p. 173). In Blacher's conceptual model, three interacting types of factors influence transition success:

1. Individual factors (cognitive level, adaptive behavior, psychiatric status)

2. Environment and culture (social supports, socioeconomic status, service supports, religious connectedness, cohesion/families, acculturation)

3. Involvement/detachment (behavioral, cognitive, emotional)

Transition success, in turn, is seen as a major influence on family well-being during the transition period. It is recognized, however, that the three interacting types of factors influence family well-being independently as well. Family well-being is described as both positive and negative indicators of adjustment (individual, dyadic or two-person interactions, and family) considered all together.

Outcomes Measures Synthesis

An outcomes measures synthesis was developed by Hughes et al. (1997). This is a helpful method of conceptualizing and categorizing the wide variety of outcome measures that have been used throughout the transition literature to indicate success for youth who make the transition from school to adult life. The authors conducted a thorough search of available literature in constructing their 11 major categories and numerous subcategories. In descending order of number of supporting references, these major categories were

> Employment (44), social interaction (39), community adjustment, competence, and independent living (35), psychological well-being and personal satisfaction (31), personal development and fulfillment (25), recreation and leisure (23), social acceptance, social status, and ecological-fit (19), self-determination, autonomy, and personal choice (17), physical and material well-being (17), individual and social demographic indicators (13), and civic responsibility and activity (6). (Hughes et al., 1997, p. 86)

PREPARING FOR TRANSITION

In many countries, but particularly in more developed countries, the point at which young people graduate from school has come to be seen as the true beginning of adult life. It is a significant milestone that is marked in a number of social ways, such as graduation ceremonies, physical moves, and the beginning of paid work. It is a rite of passage, and, as Ferguson, Ferguson, and Jones (1988) pointed out, it can be a stressful time because of the changes it entails. However, it is also a time of heightened expectations and hope for the future (Wehmeyer & Webb, 2012b). It is a time to begin new activities, make new friends, live in new places, and learn new skills. Both stress and heightened expectations can create interesting challenges for those who work with individuals and families to support successful transitions. Many of these are related to the overall dilemma inherent in letting go of young adults with intellectual or developmental disabilities and encouraging them to take greater charge of developing their own lives and their own futures in ways that are helpful and safe.

The Dilemmas Inherent in Letting Go

The transition from school to adult life is a period when most parents (of children without disabilities) naturally relinquish most of the control they had over the lives of their sons and daughters. This transition also marks a time when most young people (without disabilities) assume control and independence. They begin setting up their independent lives in the areas of their own accommodation, employment, and finances; making the final decisions about almost everything that affects their lives; and, sometimes, starting families of their own.

For families that include a transition-age youth who has intellectual or developmental disability, however, the shift is usually not nearly as straightforward. The difficulty these families face is that, at the very time when it would be natural for their sons and daughters to be assuming independence and for families (especially parents) to be letting go, the demands on families (especially parents) increase. A number of reasons for this—reasons that vary from family to family, and from country to country—have emerged in the literature and have remained remarkably consistent over time (Capie et al., 2006; Thorin, Yovanoff, & Irvin, 1996; Wehmeyer & Webb, 2012b):

- Some youth with disabilities do not want to leave school because they have become accustomed to a way of life they enjoy.

- Youth with disabilities do not have the life skills to assume control and independence.

- Parents and other family members do not know how to help the person with disabilities plan for or adjust to adult living.

- Parents and other family members feel worn out from many years of providing care and support,

and they lack hope and energy to address the future.

- Parents' friends (with children who do not have disabilities) are beginning lives free from child-rearing responsibilities.

- Established routines (e.g., preparing for school, traveling to and from school, and taking part in the daily school schedules) are no longer available, and this can be experienced as loss; in addition, there can be a feeling of void if lost routines are not replaced by other routines.

- There are few local options available for youth with disabilities.

- Formal supports (services) are underfunded, with insufficient staff and program alternatives.

- Moving to independent or shared living has a great many challenges that parents recognize, but youth with intellectual disabilities may perceive this as a positive event that lowers stress.

- People with disabilities face unemployment, underemployment, long-term dependency, inappropriate living conditions, inadequate financial resources, restricted opportunities for education and training, limited opportunities for leisure activities, and (in some countries) inadequate health care—all in larger measure than their peers without disabilities.

As a consequence, parents are faced with a number of dilemmas. On the one hand, they want their children with disabilities to become more independent and begin leading their own lives. On the other hand, they want to ensure that their children have both opportunities and support for their lives ahead. Thorin et al. (1996) identified six such dilemmas, and found them to be important to the 103 families they studied, for reasons and to degrees that differ among families:

Dilemma 1: Wanting to create opportunities for independence for the young adult and wanting to assure that health and safety needs are met.

Dilemma 2: Wanting a life separate from the young adult and wanting to do whatever is necessary to assure a good life for him or her.

Dilemma 3: Wanting to provide stability and predictability in the family life and wanting to meet the changing needs of the young adult and family.

Dilemma 4: Wanting to create a separate social life for the young adult and wanting to have less involvement in his or her life.

Dilemma 5: Wanting to avoid burn-out and wanting to do everything possible for the young adult.

Dilemma 6: Wanting to maximize the young adult's growth and potential and wanting to accept the young adult as he or she is. (pp. 118–119)

Two other factors, in particular, complicate what parents want for their sons and daughters with disabilities who are facing young adulthood. First, raising a child with a disability can be stressful, but there are also many positive emotional and practical advantages (Chiu et al., 2013). For example, many parents enjoy ongoing caregiving, a family member who has disabilities sometimes becomes a valued and central figure in a family, some people with disabilities are helpful in carrying out household chores, and some families rely on disability pensions to support their household income. Many parents are reluctant to give these up. Second, by the time youth reach transition age, most parents have invested a tremendous amount of time and energy in understanding the youth's personal skills, abilities, and personal characteristics, as well as in trying to develop strategies that make the youth's life as successful as possible (Wandry & Pleet, 2012). Quite understandably, many parents see themselves as the experts on their son's or daughter's life. Even though they may wish to have a break from caregiving, they are rather wary of handing the main responsibility for support to paid support workers who are less experienced. There are several legitimate reasons for this. The most important include the following: some transition-age youth choose to turn to those who are closest to them (usually parents or other family members) for additional emotional support in times of change; adult services are not always available; and, if services are available, frontline paid support workers often do not know the youth well, are often relatively inexperienced, and typically have limited time to spend with the youth.

Thus, the challenge of "letting go" is not as easy as most family members might wish it to be. The fault, if there is one, lies not in one place, but in many. The framework set out by Ferguson et al. (1988)—which identified bureaucracy, family life, and adult status as areas in which transition problems emerge—unfortunately still seems fully relevant.

Legal Independence

One factor that complicates the issues of letting go and accepting responsibility in the transition years is that they occur at about the age when people with disabilities who do not demonstrate incompetence become legally independent of their parents or guardians and, in many countries, are not legally subject to the direction of others at all (e.g., see Millar, 2003). Such legal independence means not only that young people with intellectual or developmental disabilities are entitled to make their own decisions, but also that they are responsible for both making decisions and being accountable for the outcomes of those decisions.

On one hand, legal independence is an assertion of equal rights for people with disabilities and encourages them to function among others adults in their societies in responsible ways. On the other hand, it sometimes creates stress for family members who feel unsure that their youth with disabilities can make sound decisions and who fear that youth may be held legally accountable for adverse consequences of unsound decisions.

A worldwide movement to address some of these issues involves the use of supported decision making (SDM) as a means to fully involve adults with intellectual disability in decisions that affect the quality of their lives (Bach & Kerzner, 2010; Jameson et al., 2015). In supported decision-making situations, as Blanck and Martinis (2015) noted, people with intellectual and developmental disabilities use "trusted friends, family members, and professionals to help them understand the situations and choices they face, so they may make their own decisions" (pp. 24–25). Shogren and Wehmeyer (2015) proposed a three-pronged framework for considering supports to promote SDM, with a focus on enhancing decision-making abilities, examining environmental demands for decision making, and identifying supports needed for decision making.

Importance of Planning

A dominant theme of the transition literature is the importance of planning. Generally accepted principles in transition planning include the following:

- *Self-determination:* Above all, transition planning must reflect the perspective of the youth with a disability and include his or her wishes, dreams, goals for the future, perceptions of him- or herself as an adult, and preferred ways of doing things. This includes actively involving students in their own planning process (Martin, Zhang, & Test, 2012).

- *Multisector participation:* Transition planning should include representatives—who are in a position to effect change—of the person's family, friends, other support group(s), school, adult services, and so forth.

- *Person–planning fit:* Transition planning should be carried out in a way that the person with the disability can understand. For those who express themselves verbally, this may require modifying or adjusting both the process and the content of the plan. For those who do not express themselves verbally, this may require direct experience, such as visiting places and introducing new people and carefully noting nonverbal expressions of likes and dislikes.

Generally accepted methods for enabling youth with disabilities and those who support them to plan successfully include these approaches:

- Provide the needed human and environmental support to a person with a disability throughout the planning process to allow full participation.

- Prepare the person for his or her roles in future planning.

- Provide the person with opportunities from which to choose.

- Have accurate information about the opportunities that are available.

- Ensure the person has the skills and feels free to express his or her choices independently.

- Expose the person to a variety of experiences to enable him or her to make life-enhancing choices.

- Allow adequate time for planning and for revisiting plans.

- Allow the person to make poor choices and to act on opportunities to learn from those experiences.

FAMILY ROLES IN TRANSITION

The most important thing that families can do is to ensure that a transition plan is in place and

that someone has taken responsibility for putting it into action. That responsibility may be taken by school or community agency staff, by a family member, or by another person such as a paid consultant. Most transitions work better, however, if parents participate in the process and have an active voice in how it is carried out (Wehman, 2013). This view has been supported by Mizutani, Hiruma, and Yanagimoto (2002), who recommended that parents keep involved in the transition planning through the school years and when the youth becomes involved in services from community agencies.

One aspect of entering adult life that is often viewed as a family concern, and thus that families can have a strong part in supporting, is addressing sexuality in transition youth, including both procreation and the role of sexuality in social relationships (Sinclair, Unruh, Lindstrom, & Scanlon, 2015). Although these topics may well have been covered in the school curriculum, families can help by providing additional sex education, offering practical help and advice, and, above all, being open to ongoing discussions about emerging issues related to sexuality. Some aspects of sexuality continue to be considered from a moral perspective (i.e., specific sexual acts are considered to be right or wrong) within some families and some cultures, and families can be helpful in explaining socially acceptable methods of satisfying adult sexual needs, dealing with the possibility of pregnancy, being a partner in a sexual relationship, and addressing concerns that arise from engaging in sexual activity.

SCHOOL-BASED PRACTICES IN TRANSITION

The National Secondary Transition Technical Assistance Center, funded by the U.S. Department of Education, identified a host of evidence-based practices that can be implemented in schools to promote more positive transition outcomes (Test, Fowler et al., 2009; Test, Mazzotti et al., 2009). Although it is not feasible to cover all of these practices, some of the primary school-based practices are described here.

Community-Based and Life Skills Instruction

The area of life skills instruction captures a broad array of skills needed to function in one's community and ranges from independent living skills to community inclusion skills and more. The domains in which life skills and community-based instruction are needed vary, as is always the case, by the student's unique strengths and areas of instructional need. Test, Fowler et al. (2009) identified a number of major critical life skills domains in which students with disabilities might require instruction such as purchasing and banking skills; grocery shopping, food preparation, and cooking skills; functional math and reading skills; leisure and recreation skills; home maintenance skills; computer skills; and daily living skills.

Promoting Self-Determination

We have touched on the importance of promoting self-determination, but it is worth emphasizing this as an important focus for schools. Wehmeyer, Palmer, Shogren, Williams-Diehm, and Soukup (2012) conducted a randomized trial, placebo control group study of the impact of interventions to promote the self-determination of high school students with learning disabilities or intellectual disability. They showed that students in the intervention condition (who received multiple instructional components to promote self-determination) had significantly greater growth in self-determination when compared with students in the control group. Wehmeyer, Shogren, et al. (2012) conducted a randomized trial study of the efficacy of the Self-Determined Learning Model of Instruction (SDLMI) to promote self-determination. Data on self-determination using multiple measures were collected with 312 high school students with learning disabilities and intellectual disability in both a control and treatment group. Findings showed that students who received the SDLMI significantly enhanced self-determination.

These two studies provide evidence of the causal impact of promoting self-determination on student self-determination. Shogren, Palmer, Wehmeyer, Williams-Diehm, and Little (2012) conducted a study examining the impact of the SDLMI on student academic and transition goal attainment and access to the general education curriculum for high school students with learning disabilities or intellectual disability. Findings supported the efficacy of the intervention for both goal attainment and access to the general education curriculum.

Finally, Shogren, Wehmeyer, Palmer, Rifenbark, and Little (2015) conducted a follow-up study of the students involved in the Wehmeyer, Palmer et al. (2012) randomized trial, placebo control group study of the impact of interventions to promote the self-determination of high school students with learning disabilities or intellectual disability. Upon completion of the intervention, students were surveyed, using items from follow-up surveys previously reported in the literature, 1 and 2 years after they left school. Self-determination status predicted more positive employment outcomes 1 year after school (and employment status 1 year after school predicted employment status 2 years after school) and community access at years 1 and 2.

In other words, there is clear evidence that students with intellectual and developmental disabilities can become more self-determined if provided instruction to promote this outcome and that such instruction leads to more positive school and post-graduation outcomes.

Career Development and Job and Employment Skills Instruction

Not unrelated to community-based and life skills instruction is instruction in job- and employment-related skills and a focus on career development. This often begins in elementary school with career-awareness-related activities in which students begin to learn about types of careers, career roles, and options. It is followed, typically in the middle school or junior high years, by a focus on career exploration in which students compare tasks in various jobs, try out specific tasks, and begin to narrow down areas of interest. Strategies including job shadowing, work samples, and service learning are explored (Repetto & Andrews, 2012). That is followed, in high school, by career preparation activities. Among the most important aspect of such activities is that students engage in paid work during high school. Research shows that students who have such experiences achieve more positive post-graduation employment outcomes (Benz, Lindstrom, & Yovanoff, 2000; Luecking & Fabian, 2009; Rabren, Dunn, & Chambers, 2002; Test, Mazzotti et al., 2009). A number of strategies have efficacy in promoting job- and employment-related outcomes, including internships, apprenticeships, and service learning (Lindstrom, Doren, Flannery, & Benz, 2012).

Social Skills, Supports, and Social Capital

Social relationships are critical to post-graduation success across all domains and will necessarily be the focus of instruction during the transition years. Whether such instruction focuses on interacting with co-workers or one's boss, relating to fellow students or teachers in postsecondary education, or having meaningful, loving relationships, promoting social inclusion is an important area for school practices. Practices to promote social inclusion for high school students with disabilities include linking students with disabilities to same-age peers without disabilities through peer buddy programs; supporting student engagement in extracurricular activities associated with the school; teaching basic social and friendship skills; role playing; modeling; assertiveness training; and teaching self-advocacy and leadership skills (Eisenman & Celestin, 2012).

Transition to Postsecondary Education

A college education is often noted as a predictor of stronger employment outcomes (Caruth, 2014; Helyer & Lee, 2014), a longer life, happiness, and strong community involvement (McMahon, 2009). In line with these findings, when people with disabilities complete postsecondary education, they increase their likelihood of finding employment and receiving higher wages than do their peers with disabilities who do not receive postsecondary degrees or certifications (Stodden, 2005; Summers, White, Zhang, & Gordon, 2014). With knowledge of these predictors, it is not surprising that students with intellectual and developmental disabilities and their families have begun to express similar expectations for college attendance (Grigal & Hart, 2013; Grigal, Hart, & Migliore, 2011).

There is a growing movement to provide postsecondary education programs for students with intellectual and developmental disabilities in 2- and 4-year colleges and universities (Ryan, 2014). For example, in 2015, more than 200 such programs for people with intellectual and developmental disabilities were available across the United States, most of which were created during the previous decade (Plotner & Marshall, 2015). The course offerings vary by institution and may be academically specialized courses, uniquely designed courses for only those participating in certain programs, and/or academically inclusive courses, which are courses that include both students with and without disabilities

(Grigal et al., 2014). The program locations differ, with individuals with intellectual and developmental disabilities attending 2-year colleges, technical schools, and 4-year colleges or universities. Approximately a third of these programs (in the United States) have a dual enrollment option in which students ages 18–21 remain in high school while attending college (Grigal, Hart, & Weir, 2012; Plotner & Marshall, 2015). Hart, Grigal, Sax, Martinez, and Will (2006) identified three types of postsecondary program models: the mixed model or hybrid, the substantially separate model, and the inclusive individual support model. The mixed/hybrid model incorporates primarily inclusive academic work and social activities; however, separate academic or life skill support is also provided. In the substantially separate model, courses and social activities are located on campus, but courses are offered separate from the rest of the student body and instruction focuses on life skills. In the inclusive individual support model, all activities and coursework take place in inclusive settings with individualized support for each student (Plotner & Marshall, 2015).

Leaders in this movement have developed standards, along with accompanying quality indicators and benchmarks for postsecondary education institutions to use when they design, implement, and revise programs for students with intellectual and developmental disabilities (Grigal, Hart, & Weir, 2011). These standards include inclusive academic access, career development, campus membership, self-determination, alignment with college systems and practices, coordination and collaboration, sustainability, and ongoing evaluation. Papay and Griffin (2015) urged program personnel to collaborate with a wide variety of stakeholders, gain knowledge from model programs, create a shared vision, present proposals to key players, and spend time considering factors such as admissions, marketing, interviewing, recruiting mentors, and creating guidelines and policies.

Student outcome data from inclusive postsecondary programs are promising. Not only do college students with intellectual and developmental disabilities have preparation for employment, but also they expand their minds and social networks (Eisenman, Farley-Ripple, Culnane, & Freedman, 2013; Grigal & Hart, 2013). Furthermore, the same-age peers who work and live alongside these students in inclusive programs have experienced a shift about the value of diversity and inclusion of underrepresented groups on campus (May, 2012) and have opportunities to reinforce their own career goals and professional practice (Izzo & Shuman, 2013).

Smith and Benito (2013) identified barriers for postsecondary education programs and the students who attend them, including 1) a lack of awareness of postsecondary education options, 2) a lack of research on effective postsecondary education programs for students with intellectual disabilities, 3) a lack of engagement of administrators at postsecondary education institutions, 4) limited nondegree options such as certificate programs, and 5) a lack of funding for necessary supports. Although one might believe that individuals with intellectual and developmental disabilities may encounter barriers that their peers without intellectual and developmental disabilities may not experience in a postsecondary education setting, Corby, Cousins, and Slevin (2012) noted that a review of the literature revealed that individuals with intellectual and developmental disabilities experienced issues similar to those identified for nontraditional students as they made the transition to higher education. The students required additional supports both prior to and during enrollment in postsecondary education programs. Other revealing results from Corby and her colleagues identified that difficulty with language and maintaining institutional rules and expectations could be barriers for students with intellectual and developmental disabilities. If students with intellectual and developmental disabilities do not understand that they must reveal their disabilities to the institution, they will not receive the needed and/or appropriate accommodations to be successful at this level. Therefore, students must learn to self-disclose; misinterpretation of that major responsibility could bring an individual's postsecondary education career to an unintended halt. Other barriers that students may face could include attitudinal barriers, safety and liability issues, and lack of appropriate training for university personnel in adequately addressing the needs of these young adults.

Nevertheless, the overwhelmingly positive outcomes of postsecondary education outweigh any obstacle and, in that vein, steps must be taken to ensure that students and their stakeholders are aware of various options and stated program outcomes. Some progress has already been made. As Rogan, Updike, Chesterfield, and Savage (2014)

noted, "seeing former students thrive in the campus environment motivated many teachers to teach differently in high school and have higher expectations for their students' adult outcomes" (p. 115). If the hope is to increase the number of students who attend inclusive postsecondary education institutions, students with intellectual and developmental disabilities and their stakeholders must insist on transition goals that reflect the best choice among achievable outcomes (Grigal, Hart, & Migliore, 2011).

ROLE OF THE COMMUNITY IN TRANSITION

One of the major problems in transition from school to adult living is that community service organizations very often do not plan for or make themselves available to students who will be graduating from school. This trend has been changing gradually so that schools and community service organizations in many areas of some countries have now developed joint programs to address transition in a systematic way. Many such programs are funded by governments that have identified transition from school to adult living as an important aspect of service to people with disabilities (e.g., see Wehman, 2013). Change has been slow, however, primarily because education and adult social services are typically administered and funded by separate government departments or ministries. In addition, the relatively low level of funding of community services for adults results in waiting lists for services that are sometimes many years long. Where this is the case, it is somewhat understandable that organizations that focus on adult services do not reach out to graduating students who might also need their services.

For those community service organizations that are in a position to take some action, the most important aspects of their role are as follows:

- Take action to coordinate the services that youth with disabilities get while they are in school and the services they will need when they leave school, especially health and social services (Noonan & Morningstar, 2012).

- Provide comprehensive case management for transition-age youth with disabilities (Wehman, 2013).

- Increase the number of options that are available to youth to engage in meaningful life activity (Wehmeyer, Shogren et al., 2012).

- Put in place personnel who have training, skill, and experience in helping young adults move from school to adult life (Morningstar & Benitez, 2013).

- Train youth in self-development and self-advocacy skills to promote themselves in workplace and other community settings (Wehmeyer, Palmer et al., 2012; Shogren et al., 2015).

- Invest time and energy in developing relationships with current and potential employers (Luecking, Fabian, & Tilson, 2004).

- Seriously consider self-employment as one option (Yamamoto & Alverson, 2015).

EMPLOYER ROLES IN TRANSITION

In spite of sustained efforts to involve people with intellectual disability in paid, community-based employment, large numbers of youth with intellectual and developmental disabilities continue to be unemployed (Lysaght, Siska, & Koenig, 2015). The U.S. Department of Education–funded National Longitudinal Transition Survey indicated that only 38.8% of young adults with intellectual disability were employed at the time of the interview (Newman et al., 2011). Certainly, schools and families play an important role in improving these outcomes, but employers, too, must be willing to play their part if youth are to be successfully included in the work force. They need to be open to providing a variety of job possibilities within their workplaces for which youth might be trained, moving beyond thinking only of the types of work that are repetitive and not mentally challenging (Braithwaite, 2003; Ramcharan &Whittell, 2003). In addition, they need to be open to providing training for staff without disabilities to be effective in their support for the employees who have disabilities.

POLICY ISSUES IN TRANSITION

Making the transition from school to adult living is a relatively new focus for policy in the field of intellectual and developmental disabilities. Legislation enhancing supported employment has existed in the United States (see Wehman, 2013, for a description of U.S. legislation) and many other countries since the mid-1980s, but a broader policy focus on transition to adult living has not yet emerged. Still, as Eisenman (2003) noted in her review, there

have been some helpful policy discussions about how to integrate transition into special education curricula, especially in relation to how this might more positively affect employment and other measures of successful living for youth after they leave school. Some helpful ideas have begun to emerge, and these will no doubt be expanded over the next few years. Policy makers can do the following:

- Address the issue of fair wages for people with disabilities by setting clear rules and guidelines (Lysaght, Siska, & Koenig, 2015).

- Develop helpful databases for the purposes of evaluating the effectiveness of transition activities such as making transition plans; putting plans into effect; gaining employment or other meaningful daily activity; acquiring independent accommodation; becoming interconnected with community services, people, and activities; and providing for financial independence (Kirby, 1997).

- Enhance the mandates of government-funded agencies to address transition issues (Johnson, 2012).

- Promote greater independence in early adult life by taking measures to ensure personal safety, financial security, and access to public transportation (Ramcharan & Whittell, 2003).

- Promote within industry the value of employing workers with disabilities, providing incentives if necessary.

- Put into place programs that link transition planning in the schools to assistance to youth after they leave school.

- Set out policy for training managers and workers in industry who do not have disabilities (Kirby, 1997).

SUPPORTING ADOLESCENTS WITH SEVERE DISABILITIES AND THEIR FAMILIES DURING TRANSITION

Successful transition to adult life is most challenging for people with severe intellectual, developmental, or behavioral disabilities, yet it is so essential to positive life outcomes (Bouck, 2012; Carter, Brock, & Trainor, 2014). It might be assumed that lower levels of cognition or other skills might be problematic to putting transition plans into effect. Cooney (2002) noted, however, that students were remarkably articulate about postschool plans; problems appeared to stem primarily from lack of available opportunities. This view was supported by a large study of 3,084 students 14 years of age and older with severe intellectual disability in England and Wales, where students were found to have few opportunities to participate in the community life of adults (Florian et al., 2000).

Central to the support needed by individuals with severe disabilities is the inescapable realization that dependency will continue into adulthood. This realization may contribute to families, schools, and community service organizations considering fewer options for people with severe disabilities. For example, youth, especially men, with challenging behavior problems are likely in the early transition years to enter residential care (Alborz, 2003). Regarding occupational activity, Kraemer and Blacher (2001) noted that more than half of youth with severe disabilities in their U.S.-based study worked in segregated environments. Family involvement may be especially important in broadening opportunities for youth with severe disabilities.

Overall, individuals with severe disabilities typically need to have some specialized support to help them successfully negotiate transition to adult life. For most people with severe disabilities, continued success needs to include ongoing personal and professional support. The specific methods for providing such supports are numerous and need to be person-specific. However, some general actions that have been described or suggested in the literature and that are helpful to almost all people are as follows:

- Begin with, and integrate throughout the transition process, a full assessment for all youth with severe disabilities (Carter et al., 2014).

- Facilitate social interaction in community settings in an ongoing way to help community integration (Eisenman et al., 2013).

- Involve families, individuals with disabilities, schools, community agencies, and other support people in the ongoing planning and implementation of transition activities.

- Provide a wide variety of community-based experience.

- Provide employment support in the form of employment specialists and trained co-workers (Wehman, 2013).

SUMMARY

A smooth transition from school to adult life is one of the major keys to the successful inclusion of young adults into community life. However, it is important to recognize that no one person, no one family, and no one service organization can provide the full range of services needed by an individual or that individual's family. If the best ways to bring about smooth transitions for youth to adult life are to be found, governments, community services, employers, and families will have to find a way to share and blend their responsibility for doing so.

FOR FURTHER THOUGHT AND DISCUSSION

1. What could be done to better connect the school system for students and the community supports for adults?

2. Consider the case of one youth with disabilities. What factors are most helpful to him or her in adjusting to adult life in the community? How many of these factors pertain to most youth with intellectual disability or developmental disabilities? How many are unique to the person you have selected to describe?

3. Think of a family that has a teenager with intellectual disability or a developmental disability. Now imagine that the parents are not satisfied that a transition plan is being developed in the school. What courses of action might the parents take? Discuss the advantages and disadvantages of each course of action.

4. Many employers are interested in helping people with disabilities, even if they are not required to do so. What can interested employers do to promote opportunities within their workplaces?

5. Not all families connect with community services when their children leave the school system. These families are sometimes described as "falling between the cracks" because their children need services but are not obtaining them. What can policy makers do to ensure that families do not fall between the cracks? What can community service organizations do? What can schools do?

REFERENCES

Alborz, A. (2003). Transitions: Placing a son or daughter with intellectual disability and challenging behaviour in alternative residential provision. *Journal of Applied Research in Intellectual Disabilities, 16,* 75–88.

Bach, M., & Kerzner, L. (2010). *A new paradigm for protecting autonomy and the right to legal capacity.* Toronto, Canada: Law Commission of Ontario.

Benz, M., Lindstrom, L., & Yovanoff, P. (2000). Improving graduation and employment outcomes of students with disabilities: Predictive factors and student perspectives. *Exceptional Children, 66*(4), 509–529.

Blacher, J. (2001). Transition to adulthood: Mental retardation, families, and culture. *American Journal on Mental Retardation, 106,* 173–188.

Blanck, P., & Martinis, J.G. (2015). "The right to make choices": The National Resource Center for Supported Decision-Making. *Inclusion, 3*(1), 24–33.

Bouck, E.C. (2012). Secondary students with moderate/severe intellectual disability: Considerations of curriculum and post-school outcomes from the National Longitudinal Transition Study-2. *Journal of Intellectual Disability Research, 56*(12), 1175–1186.

Braithwaite, M. (2003). Transition and changes in the lives of people with intellectual disabilities. *International Journal of Disability, Development and Education, 50,* 225–226.

Brown, I., & Brown, R.I. (2003). *Quality of life and disability: An approach for community practitioners.* London, United Kingdom: Jessica Kingsley.

Capie, A.C., Contardi, A., & Doehring, D. (2006). *Transition to employment.* Southsea, United Kingdom: Down Syndrome Educational Trust.

Carter, E.W., Brock, M.E., & Trainor, A.A. (2014). Transition assessment and planning for youth with severe intellectual and developmental disabilities. *Journal of Special Education, 47*(4), 245–255.

Caruth, G.D. (2014). Meeting the needs of older students in higher education. *Participatory Educational Research, 1*(2), 21–35.

Chiu, C., Kyzar, K., Zuna, N., Turnbull, A., Summers, J.A., & Gomez, V.A. (2013). Family quality of life. In M.L. Wehmeyer (Ed.), *Oxford handbook of positive psychology and disability* (pp. 365–392). Oxford, United Kingdom: Oxford University Press.

Cooney, B.F. (2002). Exploring perspectives on transition of youth with disabilities: Voices of young adults, parents, and professionals. *Mental Retardation, 40,* 425–435.

Corby, D., Cousins, W., & Slevin, E. (2012). Inclusion of adults with intellectual disabilities in post-secondary and higher education: A review of the literature. In P. Jones, J. Storan, A. Hudson, & J. Braham (Eds.), *Lifelong learning community development* (pp. 69–86). Stevenage, United Kingdom: Berforts Information Press. Retrieved from http://www.academia.edu/1786214/Inclusion_of_adults_with_intellectual_disabilities_in_post-secondary_and_higher_education_A_review_of_the_literature

Eisenman, L.T. (2003). Theories in practice: School-to-work transitions for youth with mild disabilities. *Exceptionality, 11,* 89–102.

Eisenman, L.T., & Celestin, S.A. (2012). Social skills, supports, and networks in adolescent transition. In M.L. Wehmeyer & K.W. Webb (Eds.), *Handbook of adolescent transition for youth with disabilities* (pp. 223–232). New York, NY: Routledge.

Eisenman, L.T., Farley-Ripple, E., Culnane, M., & Freedman, B. (2013). Rethinking social network assessment for students with intellectual disabilities (ID) in postsecondary education. *Journal of Postsecondary Education and Disability, 26*(4), 367–384.

Ferguson, P.M., Ferguson, D.L., & Jones, D. (1988). Generations of hope: Parental perspectives on the transitions of their children with severe retardation from school to adult life. *Journal of the Association for Persons with Severe Handicaps, 13,* 177–187.

Florian, L., Dee, L., Byers, R., & Maudslay, L. (2000). What happens after the age of 14? Mapping transitions for pupils with profound and complex learning difficulties. *British Journal of Special Education, 27*(3), 124–128.

Grigal, M., & Hart, D. (2013). *Transition and postsecondary education programs for students with intellectual disability: A pathway to employment.* Think College Fast Facts, Issue No. 4. Boston: University of Massachusetts Boston, Institute for Community Inclusion.

Grigal, M., Hart, D., & Migliore, A. (2011). Comparing the transition planning, postsecondary education, and employment outcomes of students with intellectual and other disabilities. *Career Development for Exceptional Individuals, 34*(1), 4–17.

Grigal, M., Hart, D., & Paiewonsky, M. (2010). Postsecondary education: The next frontier for individuals with intellectual disabilities. In M. Grigal & D. Hart, *Think college! Postsecondary education options for students with intellectual disabilities* (pp. 1–28). Baltimore, MD: Paul H. Brookes Publishing Co.

Grigal, M., Hart, D., Smith, F.A., Domin, D., Sulewski, J., & Weir, C. (2014). *Think College National Coordinating Center: Annual report on the transition and postsecondary programs for students with intellectual disabilities (2012–2013): Executive summary.* Boston: University of Massachusetts Boston, Institute for Community Inclusion.

Grigal, M., Hart, D., & Weir, C. (2011). *Think College standards, quality indicators, and benchmarks for inclusive higher education.* Boston: University of Massachusetts Boston, Institute for Community Inclusion.

Grigal, M., Hart, D., & Weir, C. (2012). A survey of postsecondary education programs for students with intellectual disabilities in the United States. *Journal of Policy and Practice in Intellectual Disabilities, 9*(4), 223–233.

Hart, D., Grigal, M., Sax, C., Martinez, D., & Will, M. (2006). *Postsecondary options for students with intellectual disabilities. Research brief #46.* Boston: University of Massachusetts, Institute for Community Inclusion.

Helyer, R., & Lee, D. (2014). The role of work experiences in the future employability of higher education graduates. *Higher Education Quarterly, 68*(3), 348–372.

Hepper, F., & Garralda, M.E. (2001). Psychiatric adjustment to leaving school in adolescents with intellectual disability: A pilot study. *Journal of Intellectual Disability Research, 45,* 521–525.

Hughes, C., Eisenman, L.T., Hwang, B., Kim, J.H., Killian, D.J., & Scott, S.V. (1997). Transition from secondary special education to adult life: A review and analysis of empirical measures. *Education and Training in Mental Retardation and Developmental Disabilities, 32*, 85–104.

Izzo, M.V., & Shuman, A. (2013). Impact of inclusive college programs serving students with intellectual disabilities on disability studies interns and typically enrolled students. *Journal of Postsecondary Education and Disability, 26*(4), 321–335.

Jameson, J.M., Riesen, T., Polychronis, S., Trader, B., Mizner, J., Martinis, J., & Hoyle, D. (2015). Guardianship and the potential of supported decision making with individuals with disabilities. *Research and Practice for Persons with Severe Disabilities.* Advance online publication. doi:10.1177/1540796915586189

Johnson, D.R. (2012). Policy and adolescent transition education. In M.L. Wehmeyer & K.W. Webb (Eds.), *Handbook of adolescent transition for youth with disabilities* (pp. 11–32). New York, NY: Routledge.

Kirby, N. (1997). Employment and mental retardation. In N.W. Bray (Ed.), *International review of research in mental retardation* (Vol. 20, pp. 191–249). San Diego, CA: Academic Press.

Kohler, P.D. (1996). *Taxonomy for transition programming: A model for planning, organizing, and evaluating transition education, services, and programs.* Champaign: University of Illinois. Retrieved from http://homepages.wmich.edu/~kohlerp/pdf/Taxonomy.pdf

Kraemer, B.R., & Blacher, J. (2001). Transition for young adults with severe mental retardation: School, preparation, parent expectations, and family involvement. *Mental Retardation, 39*, 423–435.

Lindstrom, L., Doren, B., Flannery, K.B., & Benz, M.R. (2012). Structured work experiences. In M.L. Wehmeyer & K.W. Webb (Eds.), *Handbook of adolescent transition for youth with disabilities* (pp. 191–207). New York, NY: Routledge.

Luecking, R., & Fabian, E. (2009). Paid internships and employment success for youth in transition. *Career Development for Exceptional Individuals, 23*(2), 205–221.

Luecking, R.G., Fabian, E.S., & Tilson, G.P. (2004). *Working relationships: Creating career opportunities for job seekers with disabilities through employer partnerships.* Baltimore, MD: Paul H. Brookes Publishing Co.

Lysaght, R., Siska, J., & Koenig, O. (2015). International employment statistics for people with intellectual disability: The case for common metrics. *Journal of Policy and Practice in Intellectual Disabilities, 12*(2), 112–119.

Martin, J.E., Zhang, D., & Test, D.W. (2012). Student involvement in the transition process. In M.L. Wehmeyer & K.W. Webb (Eds.), *Handbook of adolescent transition for youth with disabilities* (pp. 56–72). New York, NY: Routledge.

May, C. (2012). An investigation of attitude change in inclusive college classes including young adults with an intellectual disability. *Journal of Policy and Practice in Intellectual Disability, 9*(4), 240–246.

McMahon, W. (2009). *Higher learning, greater good: The private and social benefits of higher education.* Baltimore, MD: Johns Hopkins University Press.

Millar, D.S. (2003). Age of majority, transfer of rights and guardianship: Considerations for families and educators. *Education and Training in Developmental Disabilities, 38*, 378–397.

Mizutani, Y., Hiruma, T,, & Yanagimoto, Y. (2002). A nationwide investigation of individualized plans in Japanese special high schools: Implications for the collaborative practices of individualized transition support plans. *The Japanese Journal of Special Education, 39*(6), 41–58.

Moore, M., & McNaught, J. (2014). Virginia's self-determination project: Assisting students with disabilities to become college and career ready. *Journal of Vocational Rehabilitation, 40*, 247–254.

Morningstar, M.E., & Benitez, D.T. (2013). Teacher training matters: The results of a multistate survey of secondary special educators regarding transition from school to adulthood. *Teacher Education and Special Education, 36*(1), 51–64.

Morningstar, M.E., Lee, H., Lattin, D., & Murray, A.K. (2015). An evaluation of the technical adequacy of a revised measure of quality indicators of transition. *Career Development and Transition for Exceptional Individuals.* doi:10.1177/2165143415589925

Newman, L., Wagner, M., Knokey, A.-M., Marder, C., Nagle, K., Shaver, D.,...Schwarting, M. (2011). *The post-high school outcomes of young adults with disabilities up to 8 years after high school. A report from the National Longitudinal Transition Study-2 (NLTS2)* (NCSER 2011-3005). Menlo Park, CA: SRI International.

Noonan, P.M., & Morningstar, M.E. (2012). Effective strategies for interagency collaboration. In M.L. Wehmeyer & K.W. Webb (Eds.), *Handbook of adolescent transition for youth with disabilities* (pp. 312–328). New York, NY: Routledge.

Papay, C., & Griffin, M. (2015). Developing inclusive college opportunities for students with intellectual and developmental disabilities. *Research and Practice for Persons with Severe Disabilities, 38*(2), 110–116.

Plotner, A., & Marshall, K. (2015). Postsecondary education programs for students with an intellectual disability: Facilitators and barriers to implementation. *Intellectual and Developmental Disabilities, 53*(1), 58–69.

Rabren, K., Dunn, C., & Chambers, D. (2002). Predictors of post high school employment among young adults with disabilities. *Career Development for Exceptional Individuals, 25*, 25–40.

Ramcharan, P., & Whittell, B. (2003). Carers and employment. In K. Stalker (Ed.), *Reconceptualising work with carers: New directions for policy and practice* (pp. 137–159). London, United Kingdom: Jessica Kingsley Publishers.

Repetto, J., & Andrews, D. (2012). Career development and vocational instruction. In M.L. Wehmeyer & K.W. Webb (Eds.), *Handbook of adolescent transition for youth with disabilities* (pp. 156–170). New York, NY: Routledge.

Rogan, P., Updike, J., Chesterfield, G., & Savage, S. (2014). The SITE program at IUPUI: A post-secondary program for individuals with intellectual disabilities. *Journal of Vocational Rehabilitation, 40*, 109–166.

Ryan, S.M. (2014). An inclusive rural postsecondary education program for students with intellectual disabilities. *Rural Special Education Quarterly, 33*(2), 18–28.

Shogren, K.A., Palmer, S., Wehmeyer, M.L., Williams-Diehm, K., & Little, T. (2012). Effect of intervention with the Self-Determined Learning Model of Instruction on access and goal attainment. *Remedial and Special Education, 33*(5), 320–330.

Shogren, K.A., & Wehmeyer, M.L. (2015). A framework for research and intervention design in supported decision-making. *Inclusion, 3*(1), 17–23.

Shogren, K.A., Wehmeyer, M.L., Palmer, S.B., Rifenbark, G., & Little, T. (2015). Relationships between self-determination and postschool outcomes for youth with disabilities. *Journal of Special Education, 48*(4), 256–267.

Sinclair, J., Unruh, D., Lindstrom, L., & Scanlon, D. (2015). Barriers to sexuality for individuals with intellectual and developmental disabilities: A literature review. *Education and Training in Autism and Developmental Disabilities, 50*(1), 3–16.

Smith, T., & Benito, N. (2013). Florida college collaborative: Facilitating inclusive postsecondary education opportunities for youth with intellectual disabilities. *Journal of Postsecondary Education and Disability, 26,* 395–402.

Stodden, R.A. (2005). The use of voice recognition software as a compensatory strategy for postsecondary education students receiving services under the category of learning disabled. *Journal of Vocational Rehabilitation, 22*(4), 49–64.

Summers, J.A., White, G.W., Zhang, E., & Gordon, J.M. (2014). Providing support to postsecondary students with disabilities to request accommodations: A framework for intervention. *Journal of Postsecondary Education and Disability, 27*(3), 245–260.

Test, D.W., Fowler, C.H., Richter, S.M., White, J., Mazzotti, V., Walker, A.R.,…Kortering, L. (2009). Evidence-based practices in secondary transition. *Career Development and Transition for Exceptional Individuals, 32*(2), 115–128.

Test, D.W., Mazzotti, V.L., Mustian, A.L., Fowler, C.H., Kortering, L., & Kohler, P. (2009). Evidence-based secondary transition predictors for improving postschool outcomes for students with disabilities. *Career Development and Transition for Exceptional Individuals, 32*(3), 160–181.

Thorin, E., Yovanoff, P., & Irvin, L. (1996). Dilemmas faced by families during their young adults' transitions to adulthood: A brief report. *Mental Retardation, 34,* 117–120.

Wandry, D., & Pleet, A. (2012). Family involvement in transition planning. In M.L. Wehmeyer & K.W. Webb (Eds.), *Handbook of adolescent transition for youth with disabilities* (pp. 102–118). New York, NY: Routledge.

Wehman, P. (2013). *Life beyond the classroom: Transition strategies for young people with disabilities* (5th ed.). Baltimore, MD: Paul H. Brookes Publishing Co.

Wehman, P., Brooke, V., Lau, S., & Targett, P. (2012). Supported employment. In M.L. Wehmeyer (Ed.), *Oxford handbook of positive psychology and disability* (pp. 338–365). Oxford, United Kingdom: Oxford University Press.

Wehmeyer, M.L., Field, S., & Thoma, C. (2012). Self-determination in adolescent transition education. In M.L. Wehmeyer & K.W. Webb (Eds.), *Handbook of adolescent transition for youth with disabilities* (pp. 171–190). New York, NY: Routledge.

Wehmeyer, M.L., Palmer, S., Shogren, K.A., Williams-Diehm, K., & Soukup, J. (2012). Establishing a causal relationship between interventions to promote self-determination and enhanced student self-determination. *Journal of Special Education, 46*(4), 195–210.

Wehmeyer, M.L., Shogren, K.A., Palmer, S., Williams-Diehm, K., Little, T., & Boulton, A. (2012). The impact of the Self-Determined Learning Model of Instruction on student self-determination. *Exceptional Children, 78*(2), 135–153.

Wehmeyer, M.L., & Webb, K.W. (2012a). An introduction to adolescent transition education. In M.L. Wehmeyer & K.W. Webb (Eds.), *Handbook of adolescent transition for youth with disabilities* (pp. 3–10). New York, NY: Routledge.

Wehmeyer, M.L., & Webb, K.W. (Eds.). (2012b). *Handbook of adolescent transition and disability.* New York, NY: Taylor & Francis.

Yamamoto, S.H., & Alverson, C.Y. (2015). Factors of successful self-employment through vocational rehabilitation for individuals with disabilities. *Journal of Career Assessment, 23*(2), 318–335.

38

Work and Employment for People with Intellectual and Developmental Disabilities

Richard G. Luecking and Amy Dwyre D'Agati

WHAT YOU WILL LEARN

- Evolving expectations since the mid-1960s, from presuming that people with intellectual and developmental disabilities cannot work to presuming everyone is able to work
- Continuation of sheltered workshops and alternative to this model in providing ongoing employment for many people
- Evolution of customized employment, seamless transition from school, and employer-led initiatives as viable employment models
- Continuing underemployment of people with intellectual and developmental disabilities and legislative and policy changes that may help to redress this issue

Work is universally regarded as a defining component of adult life. One's worth and one's level of satisfaction are often measured by whether one is employed and, if so, in what capacity (Sandys, 2007). In turn, it is logical that programs and services for people with intellectual and developmental disabilities include some element of work activity. However, the types of work-related programs, and indeed the opportunities to work at all, have often been limited. Furthermore, when they have been available, work programs—or what are often called "vocational services"—have historically operated from the notion that for people with intellectual disability, the work is limited to routine and repetitive tasks in protected or sheltered environments where all the other workers also have a similar disability. Historically, then, low employment expectations have often framed the type of vocational services or employment available to individuals with intellectual and developmental disabilities.

Since the 1980s, however, there have been several key developments that support the notion that all people with disabilities, regardless of the nature or severity of the disability, can achieve employment given the opportunity and the necessary support in the job search and on the job. As the field of disability employment has evolved, there is more and more evidence that it can be realistic to presume that all people are employable, including those individuals previously thought to be unemployable or employable only under special conditions that segregate them from the mainstream workplace. Although higher expectations for employment have not always been common for individuals with intellectual and developmental disabilities, many legislative, policy, and practice developments are changing this. This chapter provides a brief history of employment opportunity for individuals with intellectual and developmental disabilities, discusses the current context for employment and employment services, and illustrates emerging strategies that promote employment.

HISTORICAL VIEWS OF EMPLOYMENT FOR PEOPLE WITH INTELLECTUAL AND DEVELOPMENTAL DISABILITIES

To understand the current context of employment for individuals with intellectual and developmental disabilities, it is helpful to review how employment opportunity for these individuals has evolved. In many respects, the notions of employment and employability have reflected overall perceptions of what individuals with intellectual and developmental disabilities could or should experience in all aspects of their lives. For example, in the 19th century in the United States, Canada, and the United Kingdom, large institutions proliferated for people with intellectual and developmental disabilities that segregated them from the rest of the community (Noll & Trent, 2004). This was partly for what were considered humane reasons; that is, there were few other options for their care. Unfortunately, conditions in many of these institutions were later revealed to be far from humane (Blatt & Kaplan, 1966).

Other reasons for institutionalization included societal attitudes about the worthiness or capacity of people with intellectual and developmental disabilities to live among the rest of the community. That is, they were seen as deviant and/or incapable of meaningful social engagement or productive activity. If residents of these institutions worked at all, it was to perform menial maintenance tasks within the institutions (e.g., cleaning, laundry, farm assistance). Institutions remained in operation well into the mid-1970s, when movements to develop community living alternatives to institutionalization began to emerge on a larger scale than had previously been the case. Fewer people moved into institutions, and there was a concerted effort to move people from institutions into community-based homes and residences. This simultaneously created the need for expanding options for how people with intellectual and developmental disabilities spent their days and how work-related opportunities could be incorporated in their daily activities.

EXPANDING OPTIONS FOR EMPLOYMENT

New vocational service models emerged along with deinstitutionalization programs. Views of the employment potential of individuals with intellectual and developmental disabilities influenced, and later corresponded to, the development of these new models.

Sheltered Workshops

Even prior to the large-scale depopulation of institutions, families of individuals with intellectual disabilities began forming organizations to advocate for and serve their family members with disabilities outside of institutions. One type of service, called sheltered employment, spread within this movement. Proliferating in the 1960s in America, Canada, Australia, and other countries, sheltered workshops, as they were called, became the predominant method of providing employment opportunity to individuals with intellectual and developmental disabilities (Migliore, 2010). Sheltered workshops were widely seen as a place where alternative vocational services could be available for those deemed as either unemployable in regular community jobs or as needing training to prepare them for eventual community employment. In their early days, sheltered workshops were regarded as the only likely option for employment of any kind for people with significant disabilities, whether they already resided in the community or were moving out of institutions.

Since the 1960s, sheltered workshops have continued to operate as facility-based vocational service programs attended by adults with disabilities thought to be unable to compete for jobs in the regular labor market. Sheltered workshops typically offer opportunities for simple work activities such as assembling, packaging, and light manufacturing for which individuals are paid a wage meant to be commensurate with productivity, as measured by comparison to performance of a person without disabilities performing the same task, or they are paid a wage that will not disqualify them from disabilities pensions and their accompanying benefits. Whatever the reason, the wage for most sheltered workers is substantially below minimum wage, and this is allowable, for example, as an exception to sheltered workshops in the United States under the Fair Labor Standards Act of 1938 (PL 75-718).

Although work is the ostensible focus of sheltered workshops, the activities available to individuals reflect a range-of-services focus. Other services available in sheltered workshops can include occupational readiness activities, such as work sampling tasks or simulated work tasks; educational activities, such as basic reading or even basic self-care skills; and a range of leisure and recreational activities. Thus, sheltered workshops offer what many see as safe and comfortable environments where there is consistent structure and operating hours, typically during an established 5-day work week. They are also places where individuals with disabilities can go during virtually their entire adult "working age" life. The threat of job loss is not a concern because the demands for work skills, performance, and even social skills are set at a level presumed to be commensurate with each individual's characteristics and circumstances. As opposed to an open labor market job, sheltered workshops provide a place to go even during economic downturns because, when there is no work, individuals can engage in unpaid or leisure activities.

Even when sheltered workshops concentrate their operation on work, they operate differently from a typical business in that there is a distinct emphasis on service provision over productivity. Individuals usually have individual service plans, which include goals and personal objectives that may not relate to progress toward employment or work productivity. In any case, even with at least some emphasis on work skills and employability, sheltered workshop programs are largely unsuccessful at helping individuals move into mainstream jobs. For example, in the United States, less than 4% of individuals who have worked in sheltered workshops move into jobs in the regular labor market (Rogan & Rinne, 2011). Consequently, sheltered workshops are often criticized as places that, at best, merely promote a state of "perpetual readiness" for work but rarely lead to actual employment in workplaces outside of the workshop (Murphy & Rogan, 1995; Wehman, Inge, Revell, & Brooke, 2006). This has caused advocates and governments in North America and the United Kingdom to reexamine the methods for achieving employment goals for individuals with intellectual and developmental disabilities (Beyer, Brown, Akandi, & Rapley, 2010; Martinez, 2013; Sandys, 2007).

Employment Potential of People with Significant Disabilities

The pioneering work of Marc Gold in the 1970s with his "try another way" approach demonstrated the capabilities of people with the most significant intellectual disabilities to perform a variety of complex tasks (Gold, 1980). Soon, Lou Brown and colleagues in the 1980s and many others presented ways in which these tasks could be taught in authentic workplaces (Brown et al., 1984). In schools, for example, community-referenced instruction gained acceptance as a method to teach students with significant disabilities by providing instruction in actual community settings. These developments enabled school teachers and professionals in vocational rehabilitation (VR) to begin to look seriously at supporting individuals with intellectual and developmental disabilities in the regular work force outside of sheltered workshops.

These early demonstrations were logical steps forward as the principle of normalization gained international recognition and acceptance (Wolfensberger, 1972). This principle calls for maximum integration and involvement between individuals with and without disabilities in daily activities, including employment. Thus, as people with intellectual and developmental disabilities began to gain access to a wide variety of community environments and activities, it was only reasonable that they also have access to integrated work settings where they could both increase income and benefit from interacting with peers who do not have disabilities.

These developments provided alternatives to the traditional "train and place" model of VR, which was useful for a large segment of those using VR services but did not yield employment for people with significant disabilities. Increasingly, providing training and support in authentic work environments (i.e., "place, and then train") enabled people to obtain and retain employment without first having to meet the artificial barrier of being "work ready" before job placement. From this concept emerged supported employment as both a VR strategy and a formal mechanism to fund the activities and services that lead to successful community employment of people with the most significant disabilities, including individuals with significant intellectual disabilities (Wehman & Kregel, 1985; Sandys, 2007).

Supported Employment as Evolving Methodology and as a Service Category

As field practice and advancing methodology further illustrated that integrated employment can be an achievable goal for individuals considered to have the most significant support needs, efforts were initiated to formalize these approaches. *Supported employment* became the accepted terminology for referring to the overall approach to effect employment for individuals who could not benefit from traditional VR approaches or gain entry into the workplace in the typical manner. *Supported employment* often refers to both the development of employment opportunities and the ongoing support for those individuals to maintain employment. Supported employment provides assistance that includes targeted job development, job coaching, and job retention support.

Early supported employment practice incorporated several models that included individual placement, enclaves (i.e., small groups of individuals with disabilities, trained and supervised, working among employees who do not have disabilities at the host company's work site), and mobile work crews (i.e., distinct units that operate as a self-contained business and generate employment for their crew members by selling a service—e.g., janitorial work or grounds maintenance). These models still exist in common practice but the individual placement model is increasingly preferred as a true reflection of sound integrated employment practice and consistent with the original concept of normalization discussed previously (Wehman et al., 2006). Regardless of the model, supported employment has been characterized by these common features:

- Employment in integrated work settings

- Support from professionals to seek, obtain, and retain employment

- Availability of other supportive services, such as job coaching, transportation, assistive devices, and other services necessary to sustain employment

- Ongoing support well beyond the initial hiring and training period as needed by individuals to sustain employment, perhaps in the form of continuous or intermittent job coaching or provided by VR professionals or through supports naturally existing in the workplace, such as co-workers and supervisors

The promise of this approach was reflected in legislative and policy activity. For example, in the United States, the 1984 amendments to the Developmental Disabilities Act (PL 98-527) and the 1986 reauthorization of the Rehabilitation Act (PL 99-506) both included definitions of supported employment. The latter defined supported employment as a service for individuals

> (i)(I) for whom competitive employment has not traditionally occurred; or
>
> (II) for whom competitive employment has been interrupted or intermittent as a result of a significant disability; and
>
> (ii) who, because of the nature and severity of their disability, need intensive supported employment services for the period, and any extension,...in order to perform such work. (Title 29. Labor; Chapter 16. Vocational Rehabilitation and Other Rehabilitation Services; General Provisions)

In addition to such legislative activity, policy initiatives put in place at the same time have served to increase the availability of supported employment and to improve its practice. Key among these were the supported employment systems change grants in the United States during the early 1990s that provided a major impetus for state VR, developmental disabilities, and mental health agencies to adopt policies and regulations to promote employment of people requiring additional support to find and retain integrated employment. Thus, the job search and job coaching supports associated with supported employment have become widely implemented strategies for facilitating employment for people with disabilities who previously had been unable to gain access to employment in traditional ways. Over time, supported employment has become a widely implemented strategy for facilitating employment for people needing more intensive assistance to find and keep integrated, community-based jobs. Data from 2014 indicate, for example, that there were more than 110,000 individuals with intellectual and developmental disabilities receiving ongoing supported employment services annually across the United States (Butterworth et al., 2014). Since the 1990s, there have also been simultaneous activities to adopt supported employment practice in Canada, the United Kingdom and other European countries, and Australia (Beyer & Kilsby, 1997; Sandys, 2007; Symonds & Luecking, 2013; Wehman et al., 2005). More recent attempts have also been made to initiate and expand supported employment in several South American countries (Luecking, 2013).

Supported Employment

Katie is 24 years old. She has cerebral palsy that slightly affects her gait and she has an intellectual disability. Katie had a variety of work experiences during high school and always enjoyed working with people and being in a job setting. She has difficulty reading and writing but is very sociable and friendly. She can be difficult to understand, often has trouble reading social cues, and always had direct support on job sites to prompt her to complete tasks. It would be difficult for her to complete the traditional application and interview process on her own to gain employment and then complete all the tasks required of a standard position.

Katie started working on an enclave (or small work crew) that worked at the local airport. This group of four individuals with disabilities traveled between three airport cafés and kept them stocked, cleaned, and prepped. After a period of time, Katie's job coach noticed that walking between cafés was hard on Katie due to her cerebral palsy. The job coach suggested that Katie be assigned to one café with less direct support while the rest of the enclave could cover the other two cafés. When the manager was approached, he agreed to the arrangement.

Katie's job was to keep all merchandise stocked. She also had to clear off and clean tables and keep the general areas clean. When not busy, she helped prepare food in the back—filling the deli stand, wrapping premade sandwiches, and performing other tasks. The job coach and the manager worked together to identify accommodations for areas where Katie had difficulty; a few examples include allowing her to use a push cart to get inventory boxes from the back room to the floor, placing smiley face stickers in containers to signal to her to refill items, practicing appropriate phrases to use with customers, and using a picture book of tasks in order to help her complete all parts of her job. The job coach remains in regular contact with both Katie and the manager.

EVOLVING EMPLOYMENT STRATEGIES

Since the early 2000s, the methodology associated with employment for individuals with the most significant disabilities has continued to undergo refinement. Variations of, and refinements to, supported employment have resulted in more effective ways for individuals with intellectual and developmental disabilities to achieve employment. Customized employment, service integration that allows youth to make a seamless transition from secondary school to adult life, and growing employer-led employment initiatives expand the possibilities that supported employment created.

Customized Employment

Customized employment represents an important enhancement of strategies that expand the promise for employment for more individuals previously thought unemployable. It represents a further refinement of supported employment, including ways in which the employment potential of individuals with significant disabilities can be identified, or "discovered," and ways in which jobs and conditions of employment are negotiated with prospective employers.

Customized employment is both a process and an outcome. The customized process is used for only one individual at a time. According to the Office of Disability Employment Policy (ODEP) of the U.S. Department of Labor, the following constitutes the typical steps in, or components of, the customized employment process (ODEP, 2005):

1. *Discovery:* identifying the individual's skills, interests, preferences, and support/accommodation needs through interactive, experiential methods

2. *Job search plan:* using the information gathered through discovery to identify potential job tasks for the job seeker and potential employers where these tasks can be performed and where they might be needed

3. *Employer contact and negotiation:* meeting with potential employers and negotiating a match between employer operational needs and tasks that can be performed by the job seeker, as well as other conditions of employment (e.g., schedule, supports, pay)

4. *Postplacement support:* job coaching and other supports as needed to insure satisfactory performance in a customized job

A customized employment outcome can then be defined as a job with negotiated tasks (i.e., those identified from an existing job description or created to meet a specific operational need). It also includes negotiated working conditions such as work schedules, productivity expectations, and the wage paid by the employer. Thus, the individual has a "customized" job description that did not exist prior to the negotiation process, along with other negotiated conditions of work. Self-employment delivering customized products or services, along with individualized supports to operate the business, is also considered to be a customized employment outcome.

The promise of this methodology, with its distinct process and with virtually unlimited numbers and types of customized job outcomes, is that individuals with unusual or intensive support and accommodation requirements—previously thought too "disabled" to work—can pursue integrated employment where they earn at least the legal minimum wage and where the wages are paid directly by their employer rather than by an employment service agency providing services to the individual.

Models of Seamless Transition

Research increasingly shows that employment is more likely to be a postschool expectation for youth with intellectual disability when they have experiences in authentic work places early and often during their secondary education years. This is especially so when paid employment is on a youth's resume by the time they graduate. In fact, those youth who are employed in one or more paid jobs while still enrolled in secondary education are far more likely to work as adults (Carter, Austin, & Trainor, 2011). In other words, work can be both an integral part of the educational experience for youth with intellectual disability as well as the expected outcome.

Collaborations between schools and partnering adult employment services have been shown to result in students seamlessly making the transition into postschool life with employment secured before they leave school (Certo et al., 2009; Luecking & Luecking, 2015). Seamless transition occurs when the first day after leaving school looks the same for

---

Customized Employment

Richard is a young man with Down syndrome. Although his speech is difficult to understand, he is very good at making friends and working in a team. Richard spent 5 years at a college-based transition program for students with intellectual disability after high school, taking courses, participating in recreational activities on campus, and trying out a variety of jobs on and off campus. He always had a direct support person with him on the job, and he would have difficulty going through an application/interview process for a traditional job position. As the end of his education program neared, an employment specialist with a local employment agency began to focus strongly on discovery and assessment of Richard's talents. Because he had been on campus for 5 years, he and his teachers had thorough knowledge of his strengths, interests, and support needs. Richard's preference was to work at the college—as an employee, not a student.

The employment specialist began to meet with each department on campus, conducting individual interviews with key people in each department to learn about what they did, what help they might need, and whether Richard might be able to offer value to their departments. After these meetings, the employment specialist and Richard negotiated a job description that matched Richard's interests and skills and included tasks that department managers expressed they needed completed. As a result, a full-time job, on the college pay scale for administrative support workers, was created for Richard that involved very specific tasks from a variety of departments on a specific schedule (mail sorting at the campus copy center, posting class cancellations for the registrar's office, setting up for campus activities, taking photos for events, and filing for Student Affairs). His job is customized to his skills and preferences and to the specific needs of this employer. Richard recently found an apartment near campus so he can walk to and from work.

Seamless Transition to Employment

During the 3 years prior to finishing his high school special education program, Tyree had several work experiences, including volunteering at a library and sampling tasks at a retail store and restaurant. These experiences helped him develop work skills, identify the best type of work environment for him, and identify the specific ways job coaching could help him learn and succeed in the workplace. In his second-to-last year in school, he was referred to the state VR agency for employment-related services. In his last year, he began working two paid jobs at local retail chain stores. He was supported in learning and retaining these jobs by both his teacher and an employment service provider funded by the state VR agency, which had an agreement with the school system to begin supporting Tyree in employment prior to school exit as well as to continue to do so after he exited school.

The result? The first day after he exited school looked the same as the day before. At "graduation," Tyree had the same jobs and the same adult agency supporting him to succeed in them. He seamlessly made the transition from being a student to being an employed adult. He hopes to continue in these jobs long after his departure from school.

youth as their last day of school. That is, they exit school already in an integrated job, with supports in place to keep this job. As more demonstrations of this approach are implemented, and as more policies are developed that support it, the prospects of postschool employment for youth with intellectual and developmental disabilities are likely to trend upward.

Employer-Led Employment Initiatives

Employers certainly have a stake in the preparation of their current and future work force. Developing effective ways to bring in new workers, including those with disabilities, is often in the employers' best interest. Walgreens, for example, is a business in the United States that has made concerted efforts to bring large numbers of people with disabilities into their distribution centers. The company has not only made recruitment of people with disabilities a priority but also has implemented procedures and physical adaptations in the work environment so that workers with disabilities can do their work more effectively. In these distribution centers, up to 30% of the total work force includes people with disabilities, many of whom have intellectual disability (Nicholas, Kauder, Krepcio, & Baker, 2011).

Another employer-led initiative that prominently includes individuals with intellectual and developmental disabilities is called Project SEARCH. Originating in Cincinnati Children's Hospital in the mid-1990s to offer work experiences to youth in transition, Project SEARCH has expanded to offer these experiences in hospitals, banks, and other large employers throughout the United States, Canada, the United Kingdom, and other countries of the world. Through partnerships with school systems, VR agencies, and developmental disabilities agencies, Project SEARCH offers a number of avenues for work experience and jobs for individuals with intellectual and developmental disabilities, often customized to accommodate individuals with ongoing support needs. Through these experiences, individuals learn job skills in actual workplace environments of participating companies, with the goal of later employment in the company or with other employers. The employment rate of individuals with intellectual and developmental disabilities and other significant disabilities participating in Project SEARCH is considered to be well above the norm (Rutkowski, Daston, Van Kuiken, & Riehle, 2006).

Although examples of businesses that have taken the initiative to offer work experience and jobs are expanding, they are of a scale sufficient to address the employment pursuits of only a tiny percentage of the job seekers with intellectual and developmental disabilities. However, they represent opportunities to learn from employers the most effective ways to engage them so that more employers are receptive to applicants with intellectual and developmental disabilities. These will counteract lingering stereotypical assumptions about inferior performance or skill sets. In fact, many in the field of disability employment have noted that effective employment programs, and professionals who support job seekers with intellectual and developmental disabilities, approach and negotiate with employers with the intent to meet specific employer needs, rather than simply promoting employer awareness of disability (Luecking, 2011).

THE CURRENT EMPLOYMENT CONTEXT

Despite the evolution of more sophisticated and effective methods of employment support, employment participation of individuals with intellectual and developmental disabilities has not yet matched the promise of these developments. In the United Kingdom, for example, a 2009 Department of Health report indicated a 10% employment rate of individuals with intellectual and developmental disabilities. Australia is reexamining how to maximize its employment services resource, which may affect the availability of "open employment," as supported employment is called in Australia, to address low community-based employment rates for individuals with intellectual and developmental disabilities (Symonds & Luecking, 2013). Illustrative of the challenges of work participation of individuals with intellectual and developmental disabilities, the most recent comprehensive report on employment services and outcomes in the United States indicated that only about 18% of individuals served through programs funded by state intellectual and developmental disabilities service systems were participating in nonsheltered, integrated employment (Butterworth et al., 2014). According to this report, the employment participation rate was relatively unchanged since 2002, as sheltered employment and nonwork activity remain the predominant service option for individuals with intellectual and developmental disabilities. In fact, in recent years, the rate of entry into sheltered work exceeds that of integrated employment (Butterworth et al., 2014). Furthermore, more often than not, those who are employed work limited hours and earn low wages (Human Services Research Institute, 2012). State VR systems in the United States have similarly achieved variable results for individuals with intellectual and developmental disabilities served by those programs. Although individuals with intellectual and developmental disabilities achieve a rehabilitation rate (i.e., the percentage of applicants for services who achieve employment as a result of the services) that is comparable to people with other disabilities, they work fewer hours and earn lower wages (Butterworth et al., 2014). Furthermore, this rate varies greatly from state to state, suggesting a less than uniform approach to facilitating employment for this group.

Finally, examination of employment outcomes of youth with intellectual and developmental disabilities exiting secondary special education programs in the United States illustrates the ongoing challenges such youth face in the pursuit of employment. For example, Wagner, Newman, Cameto, Garza, and Levine (2005) found that youth with intellectual disability as a group had among the lowest rates of postschool employment of any disability group. A study analyzing the National Longitudinal Transition Study 2 database found that only 26% of youth and young adults with intellectual and multiple disabilities were reported to be employed 2 years after high school (Carter, Austin, & Trainor, 2011). This study did not distinguish between community-based work and sub-minimum-wage employment in sheltered workshops, indicating the difficulty these youth have in experiencing work of any kind as a logical result of the education services they received.

These circumstances have caused groups of self-advocates, families, and professionals to openly advocate for continued policy and practice refinement as well as for legal and legislative actions to promote integrated employment options for individuals with intellectual and developmental disabilities. Some of the most prominent of these recent developments are summarized in the following subsections.

Employment First

The presumption of employability is the foundation of the recent growth of "Employment First" initiatives in the United States. Employment First is a concept intended to facilitate the full inclusion of people with the most significant disabilities in the workplace and community. As opposed to public funds applied to services for individuals with significant disabilities in sheltered employment in work or nonwork settings, the basis of the Employment First approach is that employment in the general work force should be the first and preferred outcome of services for all working-age citizens with disabilities, regardless of level of disability. Many states now have an official Employment First policy, based on legislation, policy directive, or official proclamation (Kiernan, Hoff, Freeze, & Mank, 2011). In some cases, these policies focus exclusively on individuals with intellectual and developmental disabilities. In others, they are cross-disability. What they all have in common is an overt recognition that integrated employment is a worthwhile, if not achievable, goal for individuals considered to have significant disability.

American federal policy is promoting more universal adoption of Employment First but not yet requiring it. For example, ODEP, an office of the U.S. Department of Labor, has taken several actions to promote Employment First, including creating the Employment First State Leadership Mentoring Program (Martinez, 2013). This program helps states align policies, regulations, and funding priorities to encourage integrated employment as the primary outcome for individuals with significant disabilities. Through the initiative, ODEP has provided support and informational resources for selected states that desire systems change reflecting the Employment First approach but have struggled to fully implement it as the primary service delivery system for people with disabilities. It is significant to note that ODEP's definition of integrated employment has been the one adopted by the larger Employment First movement:

> Integrated employment refers to jobs held by people with the most significant disabilities in typical workplace settings where the majority of persons employed are not persons with disabilities. In these jobs, the individuals with disabilities earn wages consistent with wages paid workers without disabilities in the community performing the same or similar work; the individuals earn at least minimum wage, and they are paid directly by the employer. (ODEP, n.d.).

Despite increasing state-level Employment First proclamations and federal endorsement of the concept, for the most part there are few clear directives to change employment policy. States do not have consistent policies about promoting integrated employment, and there is no universal legislative mandate to require it over segregated employment or nonemployment activities. In fact, only a handful of states prioritize their funding for integrated employment (Kiernan et al., 2011). Employment First does not impose any mandate about integrated employment, nor does it require any specific action to eliminate sheltered employment. States and employment service providers can adopt its tenets, or not, at their choosing. However, at its core, this movement represents an emerging catalyst for further promoting the notion of presumed employability and complementing the push for ever stronger legislative and policy support of integrated employment.

Legislative Developments

American federal legislation since the late 1990s has addressed the issue of integrated employment for individuals with significant disabilities in two ways. First, the Workforce Investment Act of 1998 (PL 105-220), which includes the reauthorization of the original Rehabilitation Act that funds the U.S. VR system, made it difficult to refuse service to individuals based on the severity of disability. In other words, the system ostensibly assumes people are employable, even though the actual outcomes for people with significant disabilities using the system so far do not show a high rate of employment success, as indicated in the VR outcomes cited previously.

Second, and significantly, newer American legislation, the Workforce Innovation and Opportunity Act of 2014 (PL 113-128), which replaces the Workforce Investment Act, includes provisions to make subminimum wage jobs—that is, those in sheltered workshops—less likely to be an option for individuals with significant disabilities. It also requires agreements between the VR, developmental disabilities, and other government-based systems so that they work together to fund integrated employment for youth in transition from special education programs to adult life. In addition, the act updates the definition of supported employment so that it includes "customized employment," a strategy, as described earlier, that enables individuals who cannot apply for "off-the-shelf" jobs due to significant disability achieve integrated employment with tasks that are individualized to their abilities and that meet an operational need of employers.

Employment and Disability Rights

Many countries have adopted specific laws and policies establishing that society must employ its resources in such a way that every individual has an equal opportunity to participate in community life, including employment. These initiatives range from banning discrimination in hiring practices for otherwise qualified individuals, as in the Americans with Disabilities Act (ADA) of 1990 (PL 101-336) in the United States, to laws that specify affirmative employment quotas in European countries (Vaughn-Jones, 2013) and in Brazil (Brazilian Ministry of Labor, 1991). The ADA is a representative example of how rights to employment are not the same as assurances that employment will be available. The ADA does not force employers to hire people with disabilities who are not qualified to perform the essential functions of the job, but employers must not discriminate against those who are otherwise qualified. Many job seekers with intellectual and developmental disabilities are not, by definition of the law's stipulations about qualifications, qualified to perform essential job functions in many available jobs. This, of course, does not preclude employment through strategies previously described.

However, one of the most significant ramifications of the ADA as it pertains to individuals with intellectual and developmental disabilities is a Supreme Court ruling in 1999 that requires states to eliminate unnecessary segregation of people with disabilities from regular community life and to ensure that people with disabilities receive services in the most integrated setting appropriate to their needs. Called *Olmstead v. L.C.* (1999) after the original litigants in a case involving segregation in a nursing home, this ruling has been interpreted as an important benchmark in deciding how individuals with intellectual and developmental disabilities are served in employment programs.

The U.S. Department of Justice Civil Rights Division has used the *Olmstead* decision as the basis for action to hold states accountable for unnecessarily segregating individuals with intellectual and developmental disabilities in sheltered workshops or similar programs. As a result, the State of Rhode Island and the Department of Justice reached a settlement in 2014 that mandates that in 10 years, all state residents with intellectual and developmental disabilities will receive help in obtaining typical jobs in the community by redirecting public funds previously used for sheltered employment services. Other American states are likely to make similar adjustments in employment services as a result of this ruling. This ruling, along with continued advances of the Employment First movement, supporting legislation, and vocational service delivery refinements, will strongly influence the ability of individuals with intellectual and developmental disabilities to achieve integrated employment as defined by ODEP.

SUMMARY

The history of work and employment for individuals with intellectual and developmental disabilities reflects steady changes in the way society regards them and their potential. There have been significant advances from the days of widespread institutionalization, when the prevailing notion was that these individuals should not live—much less work—among the rest of society. Sheltered workshops subsequently became a means of providing work and work activity when families, professionals, and advocates sought alternatives in situations in which open-market employment was not seen as a viable option. Then, advances in work strategies created new thinking about what was possible. Supported employment, and more recently customized employment, illustrated both the possibilities and the methods for achieving more integrated employment outcomes.

Legislation, policy, the Employment First movement, and even legal interpretations of such laws as the ADA are further advancing the idea of presumed employability—that is, that there is a job for everyone who wants to work, regardless of disability and need for support to find and keep a job. Work, including community-based employment, is becoming a stronger focus in designated government funding for services to individuals with intellectual and developmental disabilities. This is the case in the United States, other English-speaking countries, and in many other parts of the world (Luecking, 2013).

As of this writing in 2016, employment outcomes are relatively stagnant for individuals with intellectual and developmental disabilities. In addition, the relative merits of sheltered versus integrated employment continue to be debated and even litigated. In the meantime, sheltered employment remains far more prevalent than integrated employment options. However, through continued refinements in employment service strategies, and with evolving legislation and policy, it is likely that the future will see many more advancements in employment for individuals with intellectual and developmental disabilities.

FOR FURTHER THOUGHT AND DISCUSSION

1. In a small group, discuss this proposition: It is entirely realistic to expect all people with intellectual and developmental disabilities who want to work, no matter what their disabilities may be, to be employed and earn at least minimum wage.

2. A young woman with cerebral palsy who uses a wheelchair has an opportunity to be employed in a store that sells cans of paints and paint-related goods. How can the customized employment approach help her to be successful in her job?

3. What further legislation and policy would help more people with intellectual and developmental disabilities to be employed?

4. In two teams, debate the following:

   a. Under conditions of a plentiful labor supply, such as when unemployment is high, as an employer I would avoid hiring people with intellectual disabilities because there would be many available people who are more qualified.

   b. Even though I know I can have more job candidates to choose from during high unemployment, it is to my advantage to hire people with intellectual disabilities in my own community.

REFERENCES

Americans with Disabilities Act (ADA) of 1990, PL 101-336, 42 U.S.C. §§ 12101 *et seq.*

Beyer, S., Brown, T., Akandi, R., & Rapley, M. (2010). A comparison of quality of life outcomes for people with intellectual disabilities in supported employment, day services and employment enterprises. *Journal of Applied Research in Intellectual Disabilities, 23*(3), 290–295.

Beyer, S., & Kilsby, M. (1997). Supported employment in Britain. *Tizard Learning Disability Review, 2*(2), 6–14.

Blatt, B., & Kaplan, F. (1966). *Christmas in purgatory: A photographic essay on mental retardation.* Syracuse, NY: Human Policy Press.

Brazilian Ministry of Labor. (1991). Regulations related to people with disabilities at work. *Brasilia: Law, 8,* 213.

Brown, L., Shiraga, B., York, J., Kessler, K., Strohm, B., Rogan, P.,...Loomis, R. (1984). Integrated work opportunities for adults with severe handicaps: The extended training option. *Journal of the Association for Persons with Severe Handicaps, 9*(4), 262–269.

Butterworth, J., Smith, F.A., Hall, A.C., Migliore, A., Winsor, J., & Domin, D. (2014). *StateData: The national report on employment services and outcomes.* Boston: University of Massachusetts Boston, Institute for Community Inclusion.

Carter, E.W., Austin, D., & Trainor, A.A. (2011). Factors associated with the early work experiences of adolescents with severe disabilities. *Intellectual and Developmental Disabilities, 49,* 233–247.

Carter, E.W., Austin, D., & Trainor, A.A. (2012). Predictors of postschool employment outcomes for young adults with severe disabilities. *Journal of Disability Policy Studies, 3,* 1–14.

Certo, N., Luecking, R., Murphy, S., Brown, L., Courey, S., & Belanger, D. (2009). Seamless transition and long term support for individuals with severe intellectual disabilities. *Research and Practice for Persons with Severe Disabilities, 33,* 85–95.

Department of Health. (2009). *Valuing people now: A new three year strategy for people with learning disabilities.* London, United Kingdom: Stationary Office.

Developmental Disabilities Act of 1984, PL 97-527, 42 U.S.C. §§ 6000 *et seq.*

Fair Labor Standards Act of 1938, PL 75-718, 29 U.S.C. §§ 201 *et seq.*

Gold, M. (1980). *"Did I say that?" Articles and commentary on the Try Another Way system.* Champaign, IL: Research Press.

Human Services Research Institute. (2012*). Working in the community: The status and outcomes of people with intellectual and developmental disabilities in integrated employment.* NCI Data Brief, October 2012. Cambridge, MA: Human Services Research Institute.

Kiernan, W., Hoff, D., Freeze, S., & Mank, D. (2011). Employment First: A beginning, not an end. *Intellectual and Developmental Disabilities, 49,* 300–304.

Luecking, R. (2011). Connecting employers with people who have intellectual disability. *Intellectual and Developmental Disabilities, 49,* 261–273.

Luecking, R. (2013). International perspectives on integrated employment. *Journal of Vocational Rehabilitation, 38,* 163–164.

Luecking, D., & Luecking, R. (2015). Translating research into a seamless transition model. *Career Development and Transition for Exceptional Individuals, 38,* 4–13.

Martinez, K. (2013). Integrated employment, Employment First, and U.S. federal policy. *Journal of Vocational Rehabilitation, 38,* 165–168.

Migliore, A. (2010). Sheltered workshops. In J.H. Stone & M. Blouin (Eds.), *International Encyclopedia of Rehabilitation.* Retrieved from http://cirrie.buffalo.edu/encyclopedia/en/article/136/

Murphy, S.T., & Rogan, P.M. (1995). *Closing the shop: Conversion from sheltered to integrated work.* Baltimore, MD: Paul H. Brookes Publishing Co.

Nicholas, R., Kauder, R., Krepcio, K., & Baker, D. (2011). *Ready and able: Addressing labor market needs and building productive careers for people with disabilities through collaborative approaches.* New Brunswick, NJ: National Technical Assistance and Research Center, Rutgers University.

Noll, S., & Trent, J.W. (Eds.). (2004). *Mental retardation in America: A historical reader.* New York, NY: New York University Press.

Office of Disability Employment Policy. (n.d.). *Integrated employment.* Retrieved from https://www.dol.gov/odep/topics/IntegratedEmployment.htm

Office of Disability Employment Policy. (2005). *Customized employment: Practical solutions for employment success* (Vol. 1). Washington, DC: United States Department of Labor. Retrieved from http://www.dol.gov/odep/categories/workforce/CustomizedEmployment/practical/index.htm

Olmstead v. L.C., 527 U.S. 581 (1999).

Rehabilitation Act Amendments of 1986, PL 99-506, 29 U.S.C. §§ 701 *et seq.*

Rogan, P., & Rinne, S. (2011). National call for organizational change from sheltered to integrated employment. *Intellectual and Developmental Disabilities, 49,* 248–264.

Rutkowski, S., Daston, M., Van Kuiken, D., & Riehle, E. (2006). Project SEARCH: A demand-side model of high school transition. *Journal of Vocational Rehabilitation, 25*(2), 85–96.

Sandys, J. (2007). Work and employment for people with intellectual and developmental disabilities. In Brown, I., & Percy, M. (Eds.). *A comprehensive guide to intellectual and developmental disabilities* (pp. 527–543). Baltimore, MD: Paul H. Brookes Publishing Co.

Symonds, P., & Luecking, R. (2013). Open employment in Australia. *Journal of Vocational Rehabilitation, 38,* 215–222.

Vaughn-Jones, J. (2013). *The world and disability: Quotas or no quotas.* Retrieved from http://www.igloballaw.com/the-world-and-disability-quotas-or-no-quotas/

Wagner, M., Newman, L., Cameto, R., Garza, N., & Levine, P. (2005). *After high school: A first look at the post-school experiences of youth with disabilities. A Report from the National Longitudinal Transition Study-2 (NLTS2).* Menlo Park, CA: SRI International.

Wehman, P., Inge, K.J., Revell, W.G., & Brooke, V.A. (2006). *Real work for real pay: Inclusive employment for people with disabilities.* Baltimore, MD: Paul H. Brookes Publishing Co.

Wehman, P., & Kregel, J. (1985). A supported work approach to competitive employment of individuals with moderate and severe handicaps. *Journal of the Association for Persons with Severe Handicaps, 10*(3), 132–136.

Wolfensberger, W. (1972). *The principle of normalization.* Toronto, Canada: National Institute on Mental Retardation.

Workforce Innovation and Opportunity Act of 2014, PL 113-128, 29 U.S.C. 3101 §§ *et seq.*

Workforce Investment Act of 1998, PL 105-220, 29 U.S.C. §§ 2801 *et seq.*

39

Lifestyles of Adults with Intellectual and Developmental Disabilities

Pat Rogan

- Movement of policies and services from supporting segregated to more integrated lifestyles
- Preparation for successful typical lifestyles, beginning with inclusive early learning and school experiences and continuing with a smooth transition to adulthood and postsecondary education for some
- Values that serve as goals for successful adult lifestyles, including integrated, community-based employment; community living; positive social relationships; use of leisure time; and community engagement

What defines happiness and quality of life? Imagine people who experience dis/abilities defining and creating the lifestyle they desire with the supports they need. Most human beings desire a place to call home and meaningful and valued roles such as friend, partner, employee, neighbor, citizen, volunteer, and community member. Also valued, albeit differently by individuals throughout the world, are high-quality education, satisfying employment and income security, affordable and accessible housing, health, safety, social relationships and leisure time, and civil or human rights. Historically, youth and adults with substantial dis/abilities and high support needs have experienced lifestyles that reflect few, if any, of these quality of life indicators. Furthermore, there is a direct link between dis/ability, poverty, and social exclusion throughout the world (Degener & Quinn, 2002). Fortunately, this linkage is slowly changing and examples abound of adults with significant dis/abilities leading typical lifestyles.

The purpose of this chapter is to examine lifestyles of adults who are considered to have high support needs due to their intellectual and developmental disabilities. The word *dis/abilities* is intentionally used here to signify that all humans have abilities, strengths, interests, and desires, and that disabling conditions are often due to socially constructed conditions located outside of individuals, including attitudinal and environmental barriers, that impede rather than enhance one's access, rights, and, ultimately, one's equal opportunities as a citizen. The chapter begins with a brief historical perspective about the evolution of policies and services for those considered to have intellectual and developmental disabilities and issues that still exist. Subsequent sections provide an overview of current exemplary practices in inclusive education, school to adult life transition, postsecondary education, supported/customized employment, supported living, and social/leisure/community engagement. The chapter concludes with recommendations for significantly improving lifestyles and quality of life outcomes for adults who experience intellectual and developmental disabilities.

HISTORICAL EVOLUTION
OF POLICIES AND SERVICES

It is important to know the history of services for people considered to have significant dis/abilities in order to better understand how much progress has been made and how much remains to be accomplished. Throughout the world, youth and adults with dis/abilities have been excluded from their communities for centuries—either kept largely invisible at home or congregated and segregated in institutions and other group residential settings, segregated schools, sheltered workshops, and other "special" settings at the margins of their communities. Historically, societies have viewed these individuals as deficient and defective and needing to be fixed. If services were provided, they often followed a "medical model," with a focus on treatment and rehabilitation in hospital-like settings removed from one's family and community, or they followed a welfare or charity model. The eugenics movement, the dominant disability philosophy from about 1880 to 1945 in the United Kingdom, the United States, Germany, France, Canada, Australia, and many other countries, attempted to improve human genetic traits by promoting reproduction among those with positive traits and reducing reproduction by those with undesirable traits. To accomplish this, eugenics advocates successfully put into place public education about the evils of sexual activity, segregation by gender, and sterilization without consent for adults with disabilities.

Exposures of abuse and neglect in institutions and other settings served to bring public attention and outcry about the dehumanizing conditions of people who lived in them (Blatt & Kaplan, 1966; Brown & Radford, 2007), followed by efforts to reform and close or downsize institutions. For example, in the United States, the population of individuals in state-funded institutions has decreased over the past 40 years, with a growing number of states with no state-operated institutions (Braddock et al., 2011).

Concurrently, an increasing number of parents became strong advocates for more inclusive and community-based services for their children. This parent movement resulted in the development of advocacy organizations throughout the world that continue to push for integrated services and supports for youth and adults who experience dis/abilities.

The era from the mid-1970s to the present represents a significant shift, although slow and uneven, toward a human rights approach that recognizes the inherent dignity of each human being. This perspective has been endorsed by the United Nations (UN) for several decades (Quinn & Degener, 2002). The United States, Canada, and many other countries adopted antidiscrimination laws beginning in the 1970s. For example, the Education for All Handicapped Children Act of 1975 (PL 94-142) in the United States—now the Individuals with Disabilities Education Improvement Act (IDEA) of 2004 (PL 108-446)—mandated a free appropriate public education for youth with disabilities. Previously, children with dis/abilities had been largely excluded from public schools. Efforts to support students identified as having dis/abilities in inclusive schools and classrooms continue today, as discussed later in this chapter.

The self-advocacy movement represents a desire among individuals who experience dis/ability for self-determination in their lives, embracing the motto "nothing about me without me." Self-advocacy groups have been forming since the mid-1970s (e.g., People First and Self Advocates Becoming Empowered [SABE] in the United States). Among members of such groups and their allies, disability is viewed as a natural part of the human existence, with the barriers to full citizenship stemming from societal attitudes and systemic issues (e.g., restrictive policies, practices, and funding) rather than from within individuals themselves. Self-advocates continue to focus on removing barriers that impede full access to typical lifestyles in the community as well as choice and control of one's life.

As youth considered to have dis/abilities were gaining access to regular public schools and moving into adulthood, attention was also given to adult services. The United States passed the Rehabilitation Act of 1973 (PL 93-112), which provided funding to states for vocational rehabilitation (VR), with special emphasis on services for those with the most significant dis/abilities. The Rehabilitation Act prohibited discrimination on the basis of disability and authorizes funding for independent living centers and supported employment. Section 504 of the Rehabilitation Act stated that "no qualified individual with a disability in the United States shall be excluded from, denied the benefits of, or be subjected to discrimination under" any program or activity that receives federal financial assistance.

Nondiscrimination was emphasized in the 1982 UN *World Programme of Action Concerning Disabled Persons*. Equalization of opportunity was defined as

> The process through which the system of society, such as the physical and cultural environment, housing and transportation, social and health services, education and work opportunities, cultural and social life, including sports and recreational facilities, are made accessible to all. (Resolution 37/52, paragraph 12)

The Americans with Disabilities Act (ADA) of 1990 (PL 101-336), considered the "emancipation proclamation" for people with dis/abilities, is a significant piece of antidiscrimination legislation in the United States. The ADA prohibits discrimination on the basis of disability in employment, state and local government, public accommodations, commercial facilities, public transportation, and telecommunications. This legislation led to adoption of reasonable accommodation mandates around the world. It also requires schools to provide educational opportunities to youth identified with dis/abilities that are equal to their peers who have not been labeled as such. One of the federal regulations created to enforce the ADA, known as the integration mandate, required "services, programs and activities in the most integrated setting" (28 C.F.R. § 35.130[d] [the "integration mandate"]), which led to the U.S. Supreme Court's *Olmstead v. L.C.* decision (1999), discussed later in this section. The proposed European Accessibility Act (Ahtonen & Pardo, 2013) parallels the major elements of the ADA. Now, more than 25 years since the ADA's enactment, the United States and many countries around the world have made great strides in terms of access and nondiscrimination by people with disabilities, but this integration mandate has yet to be fully implemented.

The 1990s was a "banner" decade, with more than 40 nations enacting new equality and antidisability and antidiscrimination laws at the national, supranational, and international level (Degener & Quinn, 2002). The 1993 UN *Standard Rules on the Equalization of Opportunities for People with Disabilities* provided policy guidelines on promoting the same opportunities to people with disabilities that others enjoy, serving as model legislation and a moral imperative for change for other countries. However, the Standard Rules are not a legally binding instrument, and disability advocates note that there are no enforceable obligations without a convention,

thus laying the groundwork for the subsequent UN *Convention on the Rights of Persons with Disabilities* (2006), discussed later in this section.

The landmark U.S. Supreme Court decision known as *Olmstead v. L.C.* (1999) ruled that unjustified segregation of people with disabilities constitutes discrimination in violation of the ADA and affirmed the right of people with dis/abilities to live in the most integrated setting. This is considered by many to be the most important civil rights decision on behalf of people with dis/abilities in the United States. The decision upheld the right of people with dis/abilities to receive state-funded services and supports in the community instead of in congregate, segregated institutional settings (for further information, see http://www.olmsteadrights.org).

In 2006, an international treaty, the *Convention on the Rights of Persons with Disabilities* (UN, 2006), was adopted by the UN General Assembly. As of October 2015, it had 160 signatories and 159 parties, including 158 states (countries) and the European Union. Unfortunately, as of the same time, the United States had yet to ratify the treaty. The treaty was intended to promote, protect, and ensure full and equal rights of people with dis/abilities. The document addresses accessibility, personal mobility, health, education, employment, habilitation and rehabilitation, participation in political life, and equality and nondiscrimination. The Convention has been a major catalyst in the global movement away from viewing people with dis/abilities as objects of charity, medical treatment, and social protection and toward viewing them as full and equal members of society with all human rights. The Convention is monitored by the Committee on the Rights of Persons with Disabilities (Rioux, Pinto, & Parekh, 2015).

In sum, the evolution of services for people who are considered to have intellectual and developmental disabilities includes a movement away from a medical model of services, institutionalization, and mass segregation to socially valued roles such as citizen, employee, friend, neighbor, and homeowner in typical, inclusive settings. Thousands of positive examples are available of how to provide totally community-based supports for employment, community living, leisure, and other typical lifestyles (Rioux et al., 2015).

Preparation for typical lifestyles begins at birth and continues through youth and schooling into adulthood. The following sections describe a "cradle to career" focus for supporting individuals considered to have intellectual and developmental dis/abilities using a backward planning approach. In other words, planning is begun with the end in mind and inclusive experiences and supports are aligned throughout one's life to ensure positive outcomes as adults.

EARLY INTERVENTION AND INCLUSIVE EDUCATION

Both IDEA (PL 108-446; U.S. Department of Education, n.d.), initially passed in 1975 in the United States, and the 2006 UN *Convention on the Rights of Persons with Disabilities* put in place the right to free, compulsory, and inclusive (least restrictive) education at the primary and secondary levels, without discrimination and on the basis of equal opportunity. IDEA has been, and continues to be, a powerful force regarding the provision of special education services in the United States. Prior to 1975, children with dis/abilities, and especially those with more significant dis/abilities, were mostly excluded from attending school with their siblings, friends, and neighbors. IDEA requires the development of individualized education programs (IEPs), including specific special education and related services, to address the unique needs of each student and mandates that IEPs be developed by a knowledgeable team, including the child's teacher, parents, the student, and others as deemed appropriate, and be reviewed at least annually. Due process procedures allow families who disagree with their child's IEP to pursue a hearing and review.

IDEA Part C includes an early intervention program for infants and toddlers with disabilities to support the development of children from birth to age 3 and to assist their families at home. An individualized family service plan (IFSP), like an IEP, is developed with family and team members to specify the interventions to be provided to facilitate the child's development in those critical early years. Young children, ages 3–6, are served under Part B of IDEA in preschool programs prior to entering primary and secondary schools.

The mandate to provide services in the least restrictive environment has driven efforts to educate students in inclusive environments to the maximum extent possible. Special education is a set of services, not a place. The age-appropriate general education classroom in neighborhood schools is the first placement of choice for all students. This philosophy regarding educational placement is central to inclusive education, as are interdisciplinary team planning and the attitude that all children belong. In practice, however, children continue to receive a disability label and are then placed in self-contained classrooms according to their label (e.g., "severe disabilities," "emotional disabilities"), thus enacting practices that reinforce the notion that special education is a place.

More than 2 decades of research has consistently documented the benefits of educating students with and without disabilities together (Causton-Theoharis & Kasa, 2012; Causton-Theoharis & Theoharis, 2008; Fisher, Sax, & Pumpian, 1999; Hughes, Cosgriff, Agran, & Washington, 2013; Kasa-Hendrickson & Ashby, 2009), as all students benefit from teachers' efforts to meet the needs of diverse learners through a universal design for learning framework (see http://www.cast.org), differentiated instruction and curriculum modifications and adaptations, the use of technology, cooperative learning, peer-mediated instruction and supports, authentic assessment, and more (Bui, Quirk, Almazan, & Valenti, 2010; Carter, Cushing, & Kennedy, 2008; Hunt, Soto, Maier, & Doering, 2003; Lee et al., 2006; Sailor, 2002; Soukup, Wehmeyer, Bashinski, & Bovaird, 2007). According to Walker and colleagues (2011), inclusion in school provides greater opportunities to develop self-determination skills (i.e., choice making and decision making, goal setting) when compared with more restrictive settings and experiences, as well as increased social, language/communication, and positive behavior skills due to the age-appropriate role models in general education classrooms.

Historically, curriculum and instruction for students considered to have significant dis/abilities have focused on "functional life skills" that were taught in self-contained classrooms, often in isolated contexts (e.g., using a mock grocery store and fake money), and through community-based instruction—all outside of the general education curriculum (Soukup et al., 2007). In the early stages of promoting school integration, students with dis/abilities were "mainstreamed" based on a readiness approach. That is, students participated in general education classrooms only when they demonstrated the academic skills and behaviors to do grade-level work with little support. However, lack of such readiness need not be a barrier to inclusion in general education; as noted by Kluth, Villa, and Thousand (2001),

To be truly inclusive, [students with disabilities] do not need to engage in the curriculum in the same way that students without disabilities do; and they do not need to practice the same skills that students without disabilities practice. Learners need not fulfill any prerequisites to participate in inclusive education. (p. 4)

The inclusion of students considered to have significant intellectual and developmental dis/abilities requires school systems to shift their model of service delivery in order to allow access to the general education curriculum and programs (Kozleski, Artiles, & Waitoller, 2011; Loreman, Deppeler, & Harvey, 2010; Slee, 2011). Key elements of building an inclusive educational setting are the vision and leadership of the building administrator and developing the capacity of educators at each school to serve all children (All Inclusive, 2001), including the provision of supplemental aids and services in the general education classroom. Salend (2011) posited the following principles to guide inclusive education practices:

- Provide all students with challenging, engaging, and flexible general education curricula.

- Embrace diversity and responsiveness to individual strengths and challenges.

- Use reflective practices and differentiated instruction.

- Establish a school community based on collaboration among all team members, including students, teachers, family members, and other involved professionals.

Inclusive education does not mean that students must receive instruction in general education classrooms for the full school day. Decisions must be made for each individual student—regardless of whether the individual has a special education label or not—to determine the best location for instruction, which may involve one-to-one or small-group learning within or outside the school building (e.g., test-taking in the school Learning Center, work experiences in the community for high school students), and, to the maximum extent possible, with so-called typical peers.

The degree to which students considered to have significant intellectual and developmental dis/abilities are included in schools varies greatly. In many schools, there is a separate system of special education that operates parallel to general education programs and environments. As noted previously, students with labels of significant dis/abilities continue to be served in self-contained classrooms. Some continue to be served in "special" (segregated) schools or centers.

Transitions occur across the lifespan for all students as they move from preschool through high school and into adulthood. Unfortunately, far too many students with dis/abilities drop out of secondary school, do not attend postsecondary education, and face an adult life of unemployment or underemployment. For example, more than 86,000 students with disabilities in the United States dropped out of high school in 2010 (U.S. Department of Education, 2015), and the percentage of youth with disabilities employed full time (35 or more hours per week) dropped significantly from 71% in 1990 to 55% in 2005 (Wagner, Newman, Cameto, Garza, & Levine, 2005). These troubling outcomes point to the need for schools to improve outcomes and assist all students, including those with high support needs, in making a successful transition to postsecondary education, employment, and adult life.

SCHOOL TO ADULT LIFE TRANSITION

The 2006 UN *Convention on the Rights of Persons with Disabilities* states that adults with disabilities should have access to vocational training, adult education, and lifelong learning. The Convention goes further to state that people with dis/abilities should receive the necessary support, within the general education system, to facilitate their effective education. Within the United States, IDEA of 2004 (PL 108-446) also mandates preparation for adulthood via the provision of transition services. As stated in IDEA, transition services are a coordinated set of activities for students with a disability that

a) are designed to be results-oriented by focusing on the child's movement from school to post-school activities;

b) include postsecondary education, vocational education, integrated employment (including supported employment), continuing and adult education, adult services, independent living, or community participation;

c) are based on the students' individual needs, strengths, preferences, and interests; and

d) include instruction, related services, community experiences, the development of employment and other post-school adult living objectives, and, if appropriate, acquisition of daily living skills and functional vocational evaluation. [34 CFR 300.43 (a); 20 U.S.C. 1401(34)]

According to IDEA, individualized transition plans, including postsecondary goals and transition services needed to achieve the goals, must be developed by age 16, or younger if deemed appropriate by the IEP team, and updated annually thereafter. In addition, the student with a dis/ability label must be invited to attend any IEP meetings that address postsecondary goals, along with a representative from an agency responsible for paying for transition services, such as a VR agency.

As noted previously, it is important to take a lifespan approach to the transition from school to adult life. Preparation for adult roles encompasses employment, postsecondary education, community living, leisure time, lifelong learning, transportation, and community engagement. Essential components of effective practices that prepare youth considered to have significant dis/abilities and their families for transition to meaningful adult lives are as follows.

Facilitate the development of self-determination skills. People develop self-determination skills over the course of their lives, beginning at a young age. These skills include making choices and decisions that affect their lives, being responsible for their actions, gaining knowledge of their strengths and interests, advocating for their needs, and seeking assistance as needed. Students with a significant impact of dis/abilities on their daily lives have been denied opportunities to develop these skills due to low expectations, overprotection, and restricted opportunities, yet decades of research indicates that such individuals have demonstrated self-determination skills when provided appropriate instruction and experiences (Nota, Ferrari, Soresi, & Wehmeyer, 2007; Shogren, Wehmeyer, Palmer, Rifenbark, & Little, 2015). Such skills are critical as part of the transition planning process.

Use person-centered planning approaches. Individualized or person-centered planning forms the backbone of transition planning. Planning tools such as Planning Alternative Tomorrows with Hope (PATH; Pearpoint, O'Brien, & Forest, 1993), Personal Futures Planning (Mount, 2000), and Making Action Plans (MAPS; O'Brien, Pearpoint, & Kahn, 2010) help guide team members to get to know the student and her or his vision of a desirable adult lifestyle, as well as his or her interests, strengths, and support needs, which inform the development of short- and long-term goals. Plans are often depicted visually using colorful graphics and are used to guide team member roles, responsibilities, and timelines.

Involve students in transition planning. Students identified with dis/abilities have historically received little instruction regarding how to participate as an active member of their transition team and, as a result, have been excluded or had minimal involvement in planning meetings (Hughes et al., 2013; Thoma, Rogan, & Baker, 2001). Student-directed assessment and planning should be used to maximize student engagement in the transition process (Martin, Van Dycke, D'Ottavio, & Nickerson, 2007). Assistive technology, including alternative and augmentative communication devices, and presentation tools such as PowerPoint, videos, and graphics have been used successfully by students to promote communication and actively participate in their meetings (Held, Thoma, & Thomas, 2004).

Involve and empower parents or guardians in culturally responsive and respectful ways. Given the complexity of the adult service system and its funding, as well as the "silo" nature of services for each domain of one's life, transition planning must involve parents or guardians early and often, with special attention to each family's culture, preferences, and needs. Information and resources should be provided for families in easy-to-use formats (e.g., web sites, videos, or podcasts in the family's first or preferred language) in order for them to be coequal members of transition teams, and school personnel must exhibit the utmost respect for the strengths and assets that each family brings with regard to their child.

Provide multiple career exploration and job training experiences. Youth with and without dis/abilities benefit from career exploration and community-based work experiences during secondary school as they explore jobs and careers of interest. It has been well documented that having one or more paid jobs during secondary school is a strong predictor of postschool employment success for young adults with dis/abilities (Test et al., 2009). Furthermore, inclusive participation in school clubs, internships, vocational or technical classes, and volunteer opportunities can also serve to build the student's repertoire of skills and experiences that inform postsecondary choices.

Build "typical day" and postsecondary services for youth ages 18–21. As young adults with dis/abilities prepare to exit secondary school, school personnel (senders) and adult service personnel and funding organizations (receivers) must collaborate to gradually hand over responsibilities for supports. Ideally, instruction and supports should be put in place to assist young adults with intellectual and developmental dis/abilities to assume postschool daily routines in age-appropriate community settings. As described later in the chapter, young adults with intellectual and developmental dis/abilities can attend an inclusive postsecondary education program (e.g., see Think College in the United States) and/or go directly to work via supported or customized employment. Other daily routines should be taught and practiced during these transition years, including such things as moving into supported living arrangements, learning daily transportation routes using public or other forms of transportation, and connecting with friends and desired leisure or recreation establishments.

Engage in interagency collaboration and track student outcome data. Given that adult service funding may be limited and complex, with various eligibility criteria and application processes, and that service providers are typically siloed (e.g., some provide only day programs and others provide only residential services), interagency collaboration is essential to ensure smooth and seamless transitions. IDEA 2004 mandated the collection and reporting of transition data and postschool student outcome data. Tracking such outcome data is critical in order to assess progress and address issues that impede positive outcomes. One desirable outcome, postsecondary education, is described next.

POSTSECONDARY EDUCATION

For most individuals with dis/abilities, especially those identified with intellectual disability, formal education ended after high school. Higher education was rarely, if ever, considered as a viable option or appropriate opportunity until recently. The Higher Education Opportunity Act (HEOA) of 2008 (PL 110-315) in the United States defined the term *intellectual disability* and created the Comprehensive Transition and Postsecondary Program (CTP) that supports access for students with intellectual dis/abilities to academic, career and technical, and independent living instruction at institutions

for higher education in order to secure integrated employment (Grigal, Hart, & Weir, 2013), with a requirement that at least half of each student's program take place with peers who do not have dis/abilities. In addition, HEOA provides students with access to federal aid, including federal Pell grants and work-study funds (Boyle, 2012), and authorizes support for model demonstration projects at institutions of higher education (IHE). Consequently, in 2010 the U.S. Department of Education's, Office of Postsecondary Education awarded more than $10 million to 27 2-year and 4-year colleges and universities across the country as part of the Model Comprehensive Transition and Postsecondary Programs for Students with Intellectual Disabilities (TPSID; see http://www2.ed.gov/programs/tpsid/index.html). These grants have enabled the creation of inclusive transition and postsecondary programs for students with intellectual and developmental dis/abilities throughout the United States (Grigal & Hart, 2012). Think College (see http://www.thinkcollege.net/) serves as the national coordinating center for these grants and provides ongoing training and technical assistance to ensure high-quality inclusive programs are implemented and evaluated.

Young adults considered to have significant dis/abilities are typically engaged on college campuses in activities and routines that are similar to their peers without dis/abilities (Kleiner, Jones, Sheppard-Jones, Harp, & Harrison, 2012). They attend classes (both for credit and noncredit), use campus facilities and resources, hold e-mail accounts, receive tutoring and mentoring, socialize, work, develop self-advocacy and self-determination skills, learn to use public transportation, and engage in relevant community and independent or supported living activities (Rogan, Updike, Chesterfield, & Savage, 2014). According to Grigal et al. (2013), students with intellectual dis/abilities are increasingly receiving postsecondary education experiences in a dual enrollment program (high school students taking college classes) as part of their IEP transition services plan. Once again, collaboration between school personnel, students and family members, and IHE administrators and faculty is critical to the success of dual enrollment programs.

The key to campus-based transition programs is to ensure that young adults with intellectual and developmental dis/abilities exit with jobs and other typical lifestyle components in place. Thus, efforts to develop credentials are gaining attention in order to document critical skills acquired in higher education programs serving individuals with intellectual and developmental dis/abilities (Shanley, Weir, & Grigal, 2014), with the goal of informing employers and others.

Ultimately, the goal of primary, secondary, and postsecondary education is to secure paid employment that is fulfilling and supports one's interests, skills, and desired lifestyle. The next section describes supported employment practices for people considered to have significant dis/abilities.

INTEGRATED, SUPPORTED EMPLOYMENT

In most societies, employment is highly valued and serves as the anchor of a meaningful day and life. A job and paycheck help support other areas of one's life. Historically, people with significant dis/abilities have been totally excluded from the regular work force or relegated to congregated, segregated day activity programs and sheltered workshops, making no wage or subminimum wages. By the 1980s, the practice of supported employment emerged, buoyed in the United States by the Rehabilitation Act of 1973 (PL 93-112), as a viable opportunity to assist people with high support needs to get and keep employment in integrated settings and be provided intensive, ongoing supports from a trained job coach or employment specialist. Demonstrations of successful supported and customized employment are widespread, and the positive impact on the lives of supported employees has been well documented (Callahan & Garner, 1997; Griffin, Hammis, & Geary, 2007; Hagner & DiLeo, 1993; Rogan & Mank, 2011; Wehman, 2001).

The 2006 UN *Convention on the Rights of Persons with Disabilities* further advanced integrated employment throughout the world by requiring that States Parties recognize the right of people with dis/abilities to work on an equal basis with others, including work in environments that are open, inclusive, and accessible to them. The Convention prohibits discrimination on the basis of dis/ability with regard to all matters concerning all forms of employment, continuance of employment, career advancement, and safe and healthy working conditions. Furthermore, in alignment with United States law, the Convention ensures reasonable accommodations in the workplace and promotes opportunities for self-employment and entrepreneurship.

Federal legislation in the United States and recent legal decisions have served to nudge the service delivery system toward integrated employment. For example, the Workforce Innovation and Opportunity Act (PL 113-128), which amends the Rehabilitation Act of 1973, was signed into law in 2014. The act increases transition services to youth with dis/abilities, modifies eligibility for VR to promote access by people with the most significant dis/abilities, and emphasizes competitive, integrated employment, especially for VR and supported employment programs. Specific language addresses individuals with the most significant dis/abilities obtaining integrated work through customized employment, supported employment, and other individualized services.

The U.S Supreme Court's *Olmstead* decision, described previously, requires states to eliminate unnecessary segregation of people with disabilities and to serve them in the most integrated setting appropriate to their needs. The U.S. Department of Justice is enforcing *Olmstead*'s mandate. For example, in April 2014, the U.S. Department of Justice entered into the first statewide settlement agreement in the country that will address violations in Rhode Island (*U.S. v. Rhode Island* [2014]). The agreement focuses on the rights of people with dis/abilities to receive state-funded employment and daytime services in the community instead of segregated programs. This lawsuit mandates the closure of sheltered facilities and should lead to organizational change efforts nationwide to convert from segregated to integrated services.

Unfortunately, people with significant dis/abilities continue to be served primarily in segregated programs (Braddock et al., 2013). In 2012, a mere 27% of working-age adults with intellectual and developmental dis/abilities in the United States participated in some form of integrated employment, as reported by community rehabilitation providers (Butterworth et al., 2014).

The process of supported and customized employment begins with the job seeker, rather than job openings. That is, person-centered planning or a "discovery" process is used to get to know the job seeker's strengths, interests, preferences, individual complexities, support needs, preferred environments, and so on. Information is secured from the job seeker, family members, friends, professionals, and via observations and interactions with the job seeker in typical life activities rather than through testing and other comparative evaluation processes (Callahan & Condon, 2007). This information is compiled in a vocational profile and used to match the job seeker with job tasks and workplace environments and conditions. In some cases, employment specialists work with employers to develop "carved" jobs, comprised of tasks from existing jobs that can be performed by the job seeker. As noted by Griffin et al. (2007), "making each job seeker's personal genius visible to an employer, as well as to various funders and family members, is the task of the modern job developer" (p. 49).

Once a job is secured, the employment specialist collaborates with workplace personnel to facilitate natural supports among co-workers and supervisors, to the extent possible, in order to ensure that the supported employee is successful and integrated into the fabric of the workplace culture (Rogan, Banks, & Howard Herbein, 2003). It is critical that a "one person, one job" process is used in order to avoid grouping people with dis/abilities in any one workplace and to ensure individualized job matches.

More recently, individuals considered to have significant dis/abilities have been supported to develop self-employment opportunities that align directly with their interests and skills. Self-employment allows individuals to customize their work activities, location, and hours to meet their personal interests and needs (Griffin & Hammis, 2014) and to provide the possibility for more flexibility than traditional employment.

An Employment First movement is underway in the United States to make integrated employment the first priority and preferred outcome for people with dis/abilities (Association of People Supporting Employment First, 2010). With the growing alignment of binding and nonbinding international human rights instruments adopted by the General Assembly of the UN, as well as equal rights legislation, policies, and legal decisions in countries throughout the world, there is hope that the mass exclusion and segregation of individuals with dis/abilities in congregate sheltered and day services will cease to occur in the not-too-distant future.

COMMUNITY LIVING

As of 2015, no binding UN convention existed that guaranteed the right of people with dis/abilities to receive services in the community as opposed to in an institution (Kanter, 2015). In the United States, more than three out of every four people considered to have intellectual and developmental dis/abilities live with a family member (Braddock et al., 2015). Of those not living with a family member, most currently live in a home with five or fewer individuals with disabilities. One of the lessons learned as a result of deinstitutionalization is that people considered to have intellectual and developmental dis/abilities do not need to "get ready" to live in the community by moving through the continuum of services from most restrictive (e.g., an institutional setting) to least restrictive (e.g., an apartment or house with a roommate of choice, living alone) (Taylor, 1988).

Too often, social protection systems have entrapped people with dis/abilities. Self-advocacy groups such as SABE have stated their preference for small, community-based, person-centered residential settings. Similarly, the National Council on Disability (2015), composed primarily of individuals with dis/abilities, issued a report titled *Home and Community-Based Services: Creating Systems for Success at Home, at Work and in the Community*. The report called for smaller, individualized, and community-based services and supports, noting that individuals in these settings had more positive life outcomes, including greater personal choice, satisfaction, housing stability, community participation, and adaptive behavior (Bradley, Giordano, Bershadsky, Hiersteiner, & Bonardi, 2015; Nord et al., 2014).

With the drastic decline in institutionalization, aging family caregivers, the increasing longevity of people with intellectual and developmental dis/abilities, and litigation requiring services in the most inclusive setting, the demand for high-quality community-based residential service providers has grown. For example, Lakin, Larson, Salmi, and Webster (2010) estimated that 122,870 people identified as having intellectual and developmental dis/abilities were on formal state waiting lists for residential services in the United States. There is a critical need for more funding directed to community living; for well-qualified direct support professionals; and for person-centered, flexible, and culturally responsive services and supports in order for people with intellectual and developmental dis/abilities to have homes of their own.

SOCIAL RELATIONSHIPS, LEISURE TIME, AND COMMUNITY ENGAGEMENT

Having fun with loved ones and friends and participating actively in one's community are highly valued aspects of a quality life. The 2006 UN *Convention on the Rights of People with Disabilities* includes the right to full participation and inclusion in society and community life.

Individuals with significant dis/abilities often experience social isolation and loneliness, relying primarily on family members and paid professionals as their caregivers and social network. Options for recreation and leisure, like other life domains described thus far, have historically been limited to segregated activities. If recreation and leisure activities take place in the community, they are often agency directed and occur in a group with others with dis/abilities. Such group outings promote negative stereotypes and a "them and us" attitude among community members. Group approaches not only reduce personal choice but also minimize independence and opportunities for social interactions with community members. Although people with significant dis/abilities may be physically present in their communities, they are still not *of* their communities (Novak Amado, Stancliffe, McCarron, & McCallion, 2013).

Once again, supporting social relationships, recreation and leisure pursuits, and community engagement begins with getting to know the person with a dis/ability and his or her personal choices as well as the community resources and opportunities in the individual's neighborhood and locality. Activities associated with one's age group, gender, racial or ethnic group, language, and/or religious affiliation may lead to a stronger affiliation or sense of membership. Areas to explore include sports and fitness activities, theater and the arts, clubs, classes, involvement in social causes, and volunteer opportunities (Walker, 2007).

Active participation in the community most often requires a variety of supports that need to be coordinated between the person's caregivers and friends, service provider agencies, and the community entity. Such supports may include the need for accessible and affordable transportation, assistive technology (including alternative or augmentative communication devices), adaptations and accommodations, and personal care assistance. As a result of frequenting an establishment on a routine basis,

individuals with dis/abilities are more likely to be viewed as "regulars" who feel a sense of belonging and membership. In addition, individuals gain independence through familiarity with the routines and skills within each environment and have a greater chance of engaging in social interactions, developing personal relationships, and receiving natural supports from others. However, there may still be a need to facilitate interactions and actively model and teach social skills if individuals exhibit difficulty in this area.

CONCLUSION

Despite representing approximately 10% of the world's population, the 650 million individuals considered to have dis/abilities (of which two out of three live in developing countries) have lived in the shadows of global society. Until relatively recently, people with dis/abilities were largely ignored in international human rights law. Now, the basic values of human rights, including equality, autonomy, and dignity, are in place in laws and policies throughout the world. Translating these mandates into universal practice at the state and local levels is the challenge. Disability rights reform can be accelerated around the world if the UN human rights treaties are leveraged in order to provide guidance and place obligations on states to reform (Quinn & Degener, 2002). To coincide with the 25th anniversary signing of the Americans with Disabilities Act, a paper titled "Community Living and Participation of People with Intellectual and Developmental Disabilities" was released (Association of University Centers on Disability & American Association on Intellectual and Developmental Disabilities, 2015). Based on more than 50 years of research, the paper describes how the next 25 years should result in access, opportunity, and support for people with dis/abilities. Specifically, the authors recommend that scarce resources be used to accomplish the following:

- Ensure that children, youth, and adults with intellectual dis/abilities (IDD) have equal access to long-term services and supports in their home and communities;
- Ensure that children, youth, and adults with IDD and their families have the support they need to be independent, earn a living, and interact with others with and without dis/abilities;
- Provide access to specialized services that support individuals with IDD with an emphasis

on communication, social interaction, and positive behavior support;

- Ensure the availability of trained, committed, and caring professionals who have the knowledge, skills, and ability to deliver needed supports and services to people with IDD;
- Implement interventions designed to promote a stable and competent direct service workforce; and
- Ensure access to typical community living services and individualized supports for people with IDD who need them. (pp. 7–8)

Nations around the world are at a critical crossroads regarding progress toward full citizenship for individuals with dis/abilities. This chapter has provided an overview of the incredible progress that has been made toward typical lifestyles in inclusive communities for all members of society while highlighting the huge gaps and barriers that still exist. Hope and excitement lie in the fact that, for the first time in history, key laws and legislation, policies, legal mandates, and practices are aligned to mandate and enforce inclusive community-based services and supports for citizens with diverse abilities and dis/abilities. True systems change appears within reach. Ways to support people with high support needs in inclusive settings are known, and the money to do so is available if funding is redirected from segregated to integrated services. Ultimately, whether integrated outcomes are achieved depends on the will of governments, professionals, and citizens to work closely and collaboratively with people with dis/abilities and their families to design customized, flexible, and sufficient supports in order to achieve inclusive and meaningful lives for all.

SUMMARY

This chapter has examined the lifestyles of adults who are considered to have high support needs due to their intellectual and developmental dis/abilities. A brief historical perspective provided an overview of the evolution of policies and services for those considered to have intellectual and developmental dis/abilities and issues that still exist. Subsequent sections provided an overview of current exemplary practices in inclusive education, school to adult life transition, postsecondary education, supported employment, supported living, and social/leisure/community engagement. The chapter concluded with recommendations for significantly

improving lifestyles and quality of life outcomes for adults who experience intellectual and developmental disabilities.

FOR FURTHER THOUGHT AND DISCUSSION

1. What do you believe are the primary reasons that inclusive school and adult services have lagged behind legislation and legal mandates? What are the major barriers and how should they be overcome?

2. Consider ways that you can serve as an advocate for one or more individuals with dis/abilities in order to promote choice, inclusion, and a typical lifestyle.

3. Investigate outcome data in your state or country in the areas of inclusive education, postsecondary education, employment, and/or community living for individuals identified with dis/abilities.

REFERENCES

Ahtonen, A., & Pardo, R. (2013, March). *The Accessibility Act—using the single market to promote fundamental rights.* Brussels, Belgium: European Policy Centre.

All Inclusive. (2001, June). *Special education is a service—not a place.* Hanover, MD: Maryland Coalition for Inclusive Education.

Americans with Disabilities Act (ADA) of 1990, PL 101-336, 42 U.S.C. §§ 12101 *et seq.*

Association of People Supporting Employment First. (2010). *APSE statement on Employment First.* Retrieved from http://apse.org/employment-first/statement/

Association of University Centers on Disability & American Association on Intellectual and Developmental Disabilities. (2015, July 24). *Community living and participation for people with intellectual and developmental disabilities: What the research tells us.* Retrieved from http://aaidd.org/docs/default-source/policy/community-living-and-participation-for-people-with-intellectual-and-developmental-disabilities-nbsp-what-the-research-tells-us.pdf

Blatt, B., & Kaplan, F. (1966). *Christmas in purgatory: A photographic essay on mental retardation.* Syracuse, NY: Human Policy Press.

Boyle, M. (2012). *Federal financial aid for students with intellectual disabilities.* Think College Insight Brief 16. Boston: University of Massachusetts Institute for Community Inclusion.

Braddock, D., Hemp, R., Rizzolo, M., Haffer, L., Shea Tanis, E., & Wu, J. (2011). *The state of the states in developmental disabilities.* Boulder: Department of Psychiatry & Coleman Institute for Cognitive Disabilities, University of Colorado.

Braddock, D., Hemp, R., Rizzolo, M.C., Tanis, E.S., Haffer, L., Lulinski, A., & Wu, J. (2013). *The state of the states in developmental disabilities 2013: The great recession and its aftermath.* Washington, DC: American Association on Intellectual and Developmental Disabilities.

Braddock, D., Hemp, R., Rizzolo, M.C., Tanis, E.S., Haffer, L., & Wu, J. (2015). *The state of the states in intellectual and developmental disabilities* (10th ed.). Washington, DC: American Association on Intellectual and Developmental Disabilities.

Bradley, V., Giordano, S., Bershadsky, J., Hiersteiner, D., & Bonardi, A. (2015, November). *Housing for people with intellectual disabilities: How do we ensure a home of their own?* Presentation at the National Association of State Directors of Developmental Disabilities Services Annual Meeting, Alexandria, VA.

Brown, I., & Radford, J.P. (2007). Historical overview of intellectual and developmental disabilities. In I. Brown & M. Percy (Eds.), *A comprehensive guide to intellectual and developmental disabilities* (pp. 17–33). Baltimore, MD: Paul H. Brookes Publishing Co.

Bui, X., Quirk, C., Almazan, S., & Valenti, M. (2010). *Inclusive education research and practice.* Hanover, MD: Maryland Coalition for Inclusive Education. Retrieved from http://www.mcie.org/usermedia/application/6/inclusion_works_final.pdf

Butterworth, J., Winsor, J., Smith, F., Migliore, A., Domin, D., Ciulla Timmons, J., & Cohen Hall, A. (2014). *State-Date: The national report on employment services and outcomes.* Boston: ICI, University of Massachusetts, Boston.

Callahan, M., & Condon, E. (2007). Discovery: The foundation of job development. In C. Griffin, D. Hammis, & T. Geary, *The job developer's handbook: Practical tactics for customized employment* (pp. 23–33). Baltimore, MD: Paul H. Brookes Publishing Co.

Callahan, M.J., & Garner, J.B. (1997). *Keys to the workplace: Skills and supports for people with disabilities.* Baltimore, MD: Paul H. Brookes Publishing Co.

Carter, E.W., Cushing, L.S., & Kennedy, C.H. (2008). Promoting rigor, relevance, and relationships through peer support interventions. *TASH Connections, 34*(2), 20–23.

Causton-Theoharis, J., & Kasa, C. (2012). *Achieving inclusion: What every parent should know when advocating for their child.* Pittsburgh, PA: The PEAL Center.

Causton-Theoharis, J., & Theoharis, G. (2008, September). Creating inclusive schools for ALL students. *The School Administrator,* 24–30.

Degener, T., & Quinn, G. (2002). A survey of international, comparative and regional disability law reform. In M. Breslin & S. Yee (Eds.), *Disability rights law and policy: International and national perspectives* (pp. 3–124). Ardsley, NY: Transnational.

Education for All Handicapped Children Act of 1975, PL 94-142, 20 U.S.C. §§ 1400 *et seq.*

Fisher, D., Sax, C., & Pumpian, I. (Eds.). (1999). *Inclusive high schools: Learning from contemporary classrooms.* Baltimore, MD: Paul H. Brookes Publishing Co.

Griffin, C., & Hammis, D. (2014). *Making self-employment work for people with disabilities* (2nd ed.). Baltimore, MD: Paul H. Brookes Publishing Co.

Griffin, C., Hammis, D., & Geary, T. (2007). Person-centered job development strategy: Finding the jobs behind the jobs. In C. Griffin, D. Hammis, & T. Geary, *The job developer's handbook: Practical tactics for customized employment* (pp. 49–72). Baltimore, MD: Paul H. Brookes Publishing Co.

Grigal, M., & Hart, D. (2012). The power of expectations. *Journal of Policy and Practice in Intellectual Disabilities, 9,* 221–222.

Grigal, M., Hart, D., & Weir, C. (2013). Postsecondary education for people with intellectual disability: Current issues and critical challenges. *Inclusion, 1*(1), 50–63.

Hagner, D., & DiLeo, D. (1993). *Working together: Workplace culture, supported employment, and persons with disabilities.* Cambridge, MA: Brookline Books.

Held, C., Thoma, C., & Thomas, K. (2004). "The John Jones Show": How one teacher facilitated self-determined transition planning for a young man with autism. *Focus on Autism and Other Developmental Disabilities, 19*(3), 177–188.

Higher Education Opportunity Act (HEOA) of 2008, PL 110-315, 20 U.S.C. §§ 1001, *et seq.*

Hughes, C., Cosgriff, J., Agran, M., & Washington, B. (2013). Student self-determination: A preliminary investigation of the role of participation in inclusive settings. *Education and Training in Autism and Developmental Disabilities, 48,* 3–17.

Hunt, P., Soto, G., Maier, J., & Doering, K. (2003). Collaborative teaming to support students at risk and students with severe disabilities in general education classrooms. *Exceptional Children, 69*(3), 315–332.

Individuals with Disabilities Education Improvement Act (IDEA) of 2004, PL 108-446, 20 U.S.C. §§ 1400 *et seq.*

Kanter, A. (2015). *The development of disability rights under international law: From charity to human rights.* New York, NY: Routledge.

Kasa-Hendrickson, C., & Ashby, C. (2009). *Strength based classroom: How the presence of students with disabilities enhances the general education classroom.* Paper presented at the Ninth Second City Conference on Disability Studies in Education, Syracuse, NY.

Kleiner, H., Jones, M., Sheppard-Jones, K., Harp, B., & Harrison, E. (2012). Students with intellectual disabilities going to college? Absolutely! *Teaching Exceptional Children, 44,* 26–35.

Kluth, P., Villa, R., & Thousand, J. (2001, December/January). "Our school doesn't offer inclusion" and other legal blunders. *Educational Leadership, 59,* 24–27.

Kozleski, E., Artiles, A., & Waitoller, F. (2011). Introduction: Equity in inclusive education. In A. Artiles, E. Kozleski, & F. Waitoller (Eds.), *Inclusive education on five continents: Unraveling equity issues* (pp. 1–14). Cambridge, MA: Harvard Educational Press.

Lakin, K.C., Larson, S., Salmi, P., & Webster, A. (2010). *Residential services for persons with developmental disabilities: Status and trends through 2009.* Minneapolis: University of Minnesota, Institute on Community Integration, Research and Training Center on Community Living.

Lee, S.H., Amos, B.A., Gragoudas, S., Lee, Y., Shogren, K.A., & Theoharis, R., (2006). Curriculum augmentation and adaptation strategies to promote access to the general curriculum for students with intellectual and developmental disabilities. *Education and Training in Developmental Disabilities, 41,* 199–212.

Loreman, T., Deppeler, J., & Harvey, D. (2010). *Inclusive education: Supporting diversity in the classroom* (2nd ed.). Sydney, Australia: Allen & Unwin.

Martin, J., Van Dycke, J., D'Ottavio, M., & Nickerson, K. (2007). The student-directed summary of performance: Increasing student and family involvement in the transition planning process. *Career Development for Exceptional Individuals, 30*(1), 13–26.

Mount, B. (2000). *Person-centered planning: Finding directions for change using person-centered planning. A sourcebook of values, ideals, and methods to encourage person-centered development.* Amenia, NY: Capacity Works!

National Council on Disability. (2015). *Home and community-based services: Creating systems for success at home, at work and in the community.* Retrieved from https://www.ncd.gov/publications/2015/02242015

Nord, D., Kang, Y., Ticha, R., Hamre, K., Fay, M., & Mosley, C. (2014). *Residential size and individual outcomes: An assessment of existing National Core Indicators research.* Policy Research Brief 25(3). Minneapolis: Research and Training Center on Community Living, University of Minnesota.

Nota, L., Ferrari, L., Soresi, S., & Wehmeyer, M.L. (2007). Self-determination, social abilities, and the quality of life of people with intellectual disabilities. *Journal of Intellectual Disability Research, 51,* 850–865.

Novak Amado, A., Stancliffe, R., McCarron, M., & McCallion, P. (2013). Social inclusion and community participation of individuals with intellectual and developmental disabilities. *Intellectual and Developmental Disabilities, 51*(5), 360–375.

O'Brien, J., Pearpoint, J., & Kahn, L. (2010). *The PATH and MAPS handbook.* Toronto, Canada: Inclusion Press.

Olmstead v. L.C., 527 U.S. 581 (1999).

Pearpoint, J., O'Brien, J., & Forest, M. (1993). *PATH: A workbook for planning possible positive futures: Planning alternative tomorrows with hope for schools, organizations, businesses, and families.* Toronto, Canada: Inclusion Press.

Quinn, G., & Degener, T. (2002). *Human rights and disability: The current use and future potential of the United Nations human rights instruments in the context of disability.* Retrieved from http://www.ohchr.org/Documents/Publications/HRDisabilityen.pdf

Rehabilitation Act of 1973, PL 93-112, 29 U.S.C. §§ 701 *et seq.*

Rioux, M.H., Pinto, P.C., & Parekh, G. (2015). *Disability, rights monitoring, and social change: Building power out of evidence.* Toronto, Canada: Canadian Scholars' Press.

Rogan, P., Banks, B., & Howard Herbein, M. (2003). Supported employment and workplace supports: A qualitative study. *Journal of Vocational Rehabilitation, 19*(1), 5–18.

Rogan, P., & Mank, D. (2011). Looking back, moving ahead: A commentary on supported employment. *Journal of Vocational Rehabilitation, 35*(3), 185–188.

Rogan, P., Updike, J., Chesterfield, G., & Savage, S. (2014). The SITE program at IUPUI: A post-secondary program for individuals with intellectual disabilities. *Journal of Vocational Rehabilitation, 40*(2), 109–116.

Sailor, W. (2002, April 18). *Testimony submitted to President's Commission on Excellence in Special Education: Research Agenda Task Force.* Retrieved from http://www.beachcenter.org/books/fullpublications/pdf/presidentreport.pdf

Salend, S. (2011). *Creating inclusive classrooms: Effective and reflective practices* (7th ed.). New York, NY: Pearson.

Shanley, J., Weir, C., & Grigal, M. (2014). *Credential development in inclusive higher education programs serving students with intellectual disabilities.* Think College Insight Brief 25. Retrieved from http://www.thinkcollege.net/component/resdb/item/t-110/1948

Shogren, K.A., Wehmeyer, M., Palmer, S., Rifenbark, G., & Little, T. (2015). Relationships between self-determination and postschool outcomes for youth with disabilities. *Journal of Special Education, 48*(4), 256–267.

Slee, R. (2011). *The irregular school: Exclusion, schooling, and inclusive education.* Abingdon, United Kingdom: Routledge.

Soukup, J.H., Wehmeyer, M.L., Bashinski, S.M., & Bovaird, J. (2007). Classroom variables and access to the general education curriculum for students with disabilities. *Exceptional Children, 74,* 101–120.

Taylor, S. (1988). Caught in the continuum: A critical analysis of the principle of the least restrictive environment. *Journal of the Association for Persons with Severe Handicaps, 13*(1), 41–53.

Test, D.W., Mazzotti, V.L., Mustian, A.L., Fowler, C.H., Kortering, L., & Kohler, P. (2009). Evidence-based secondary transition predictors for improving postschool outcomes for students with disabilities. *Career Development for Exceptional Individuals, 32,* 160–181.

Thoma, C.A., Rogan, P., & Baker, S.R. (2001). Student involvement in transition planning: Unheard voices. *Education and Training in Mental Retardation and Developmental Disabilities, 36,* 16–29.

United Nations. (1982). *World Programme of Action Concerning Disabled Persons.* Retrieved from http://www.un.org/documents/ga/res/37/a37r052.htm

United Nations. (1993). *Standard Rules on the Equalization of Opportunities for People with Disabilities.* Retrieved from http://www.un.org/disabilities/documents/gadocs/standardrules.doc

United Nations. (2006). *Convention on the Rights of Persons with Disabilities.* Retrieved from http://www.un.org/disabilities/convention/conventionfull.shtml

U.S. v. Rhode Island – 1:14-cv00175-(D.R.I.2014).

U.S. Department of Education. (n.d.). *Building the legacy: IDEA 2004.* Retrieved from http://idea.ed.gov/

U.S. Department of Education. (2015, September). *OSERS Transition Data Fact Sheet.* Retrieved from https://www2.ed.gov/about/offices/list/osers/products/transition/osers-transition-activities-2015.pdf

Wagner, M., Newman, L., Cameto, R., Garza, N., & Levine, P. (2005, April). *After high school: A first look at the postschool experiences of youth with disabilities: A report from the National Longitudinal Transition Study-2.* Prepared for the Office of Special Education Programs, U.S. Department of Education. Menlo Park, CA: SRI International.

Walker, P.M. (2007). Promoting meaningful leisure and social connections: More than just work. In P.M. Walker

& P.M. Rogan, *Make the day matter! Promoting typical lifestyles for adults with significant disabilities.* Baltimore, MD: Paul H. Brookes Publishing Co.

Walker, H., Calkins, C., Wehmeyer, M., Walker, L., Bacon, A., Palmer, S., & Johnson, D. (2011). A social-ecological approach to promote self-determination. *Exceptionality, 19,* 6–18.

Wehman, P. (Ed.). (2001). *Supported employment in business: Expanding the capacity of workers with disabilities.* St. Augustine, FL: Training Resource Network.

Workforce Innovation and Opportunity Act of 2014, PL 113-128, 29 U.S.C. 3101 §§ *et seq.*

40

Providing Support that Enhances a Family's Quality of Life

Heather M. Aldersey, Ann P. Turnbull, and Patricia Minnes

WHAT YOU WILL LEARN

- Understand the four components of family systems theory and apply this theory to the families with whom you work
- Identify and work to address needs throughout all family subsystems—marital, sibling, parental, and extended family—and across the family life cycle
- Describe the eight types of family functions and identify how individuals with a disability can affect family functions
- Recognize the multiple roles that many family members take on, over and beyond parenting or caregiving
- Understand family–professional partnerships as helpful in attending to each domain of family quality of life

Chapter coauthor Heather Aldersey illustrates concepts throughout this chapter with text from a family that she interviewed in Kinshasa, Democratic Republic of the Congo. Salome Kavira is a mother of six who was married for 27 years at the time of the interview. Her youngest son, Jeremy, was 17 years old at the time of the interview and has significant intellectual and developmental disabilities resulting from brain damage at birth. Salome is a nurse by training, and she spends much of her free time helping other families in her role as secretary of a parent self-help group, known by its French acronym ANAPEHMCO. In addition to the Kaviras' own six children, at the time that Salome was interviewed,

her elderly mother and four nieces were also living in the family home.

The Kavira family has many strengths. It also faces some challenges, including finding appropriate services for Jeremy and securing transportation to get to the locations where the services are offered. Jeremy used to have regular physical therapy appointments, but because of cost and difficulty of transportation, Salome just does what she can for Jeremy on her own in the family home. Salome notes that the family gets by all right and is grateful that both she and her husband have steady jobs. Salome believes that she must constantly be an advocate for her son and for other families in Kinshasa. She is hopeful for both her family's future and Jeremy's future.

A fundamental role of families who have a member with a disability is to provide caregiving for that member (Singer, Biegel, & Conway, 2012). Without question, families are the primary source of caregiving worldwide for individuals with intellectual disabilities across the life span. In working to provide services and supports that will be beneficial to families, the most important tenet to remember is that each family is unique. Just as it is important to recognize, value, and take into account the individual differences of people with disabilities, it is important to take this same individualized perspective with families. This chapter's Perspectives from the Kavira Family sections also highlight potential commonalities of experiences of families worldwide.

FAMILIES AS DYNAMIC SYSTEMS

The caregiving roles of families can best be understood through a family systems perspective. Systems
theory, in general, addresses the interrelated parts of
an entity in order to understand it as a whole (Turnbull, Turnbull, Erwin, Soodak, & Shogren, 2015).
Family systems theory suggests that it is impossible
to understand the caregiving of a child with a disability within the family without an understanding
of how the family functions as a whole. A family
systems perspective is attuned to the well-being of
every family member and not just the individual
with the disability. Figure 40.1 visually illustrates a
family systems framework. This section highlights
each of the four components of the family systems
framework—characteristics, interaction, functions,
life cycle—by briefly highlighting its definition, noting illustrative related research, presenting a perspective from the Kavira family, and providing tips
for family–professional partnerships in providing
services and supports.

Family Characteristics

Definition Family characteristics include the
unique elements of each family. These elements can
be delineated as follows:

1. *Characteristics of the family as a whole:* family size
   and form, cultural background, socioeconomic
   status, and geographic location

2. *Each family member's personal characteristics:* health,
   the particular nature of impairment of the individual with a disability, and coping strategies

3. *Special challenges not specifically related to a family
   member's intellectual disability:* poverty, abuse,
   illness, disability considerations of other family members, or crises such as hurricanes or
   floods

   A systems perspective suggests that each family has a set of characteristics that provide the input
into the way that the family interacts and the way
the family members carry out their functions.

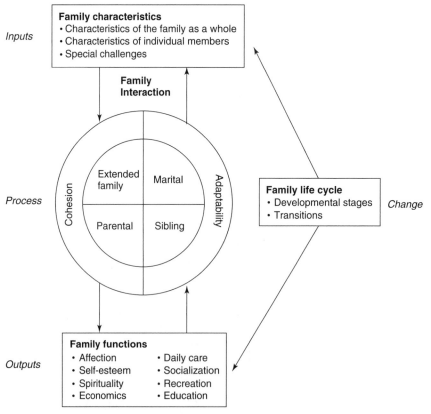

Figure 40.1. Family systems framework. (From Turnbull, A.P., Summers, J.A., & Brotherson, M.J.
[1984]. *Working with families with disabled members: A family systems approach* [p. 60]. Lawrence:
University of Kansas, Kansas Affiliated Facility; adapted by permission.)

Illustrative Research Highlights To illustrate family characteristics, this section focuses primarily on the second and third of the previously described elements—each family member's personal characteristics, specifically the particular nature of impairment of the individual with a disability, and special challenges, specifically poverty. Raising a child with a disability can be stressful for families (Carroll, 2013). Research has shown that the severity of a disability is significantly associated with both mothers' and fathers' satisfaction with family quality of life (Wang et al., 2004b) and that a child with medically complex needs often requires a family to make adaptations in daily routines, such as providing ongoing assistance, purchasing special equipment, and interacting frequently with medical personnel (Kuo, Cohen, Agrawal, Berry, & Casey, 2011).

Specific disabilities also have their own unique challenges. Families of young children with autism experience challenges with access to services following diagnosis, thus increasing parental stress (Braddock & Twyman, 2014). A child with a later onset of disability can cause major family readjustments (Cavallo & Kay, 2011). In addition, children with disabilities who exhibit problem behavior can be particularly stressful for families. A review of the literature on family outcomes showed that behavior problems of children with intellectual and developmental disabilities predict lower family well-being, adaptation, and family functioning (Turnbull, Summers, Lee, & Kyzar, 2007).

Until the late 1990s, research has tended to focus on negative outcomes and stress in family research (Blacher, Begum, Marcoulides, & Baker, 2013; Kayfitz, Gragg, & Orr, 2010). Research has begun to demonstrate that families can have positive as well as negative outcomes. Parents frequently report considerable stress, but they also report positive outcomes such as greater valuing of the family and increased family closeness, appreciation of new opportunities such as advocacy, and becoming more aware of others' strengths (King, Zwaigenbaum, Bates, Baxter, & Rosenbaum, 2012).

This chapter's example family is from the Democratic Republic of the Congo, a country that is characterized by high levels of poverty. It is also important to understand poverty as a special challenge that can affect family characteristics. Poverty challenges many families, especially those whose children have disabilities (Hughes & Fanion, 2014). Regardless of their home country, families who live in poverty are more likely to have lower educational attainment; be in poor health; have less access to health care services and higher medical expenses; and have infants who are born with a low birth weight, which is linked to later disability (Eide & Ingstad, 2013; Mitra, Posarac, & Vick, 2013). Even in countries with well-developed service delivery systems (e.g., the United States), poverty can be a factor in families having difficulty gaining access to community resources, and it can affect their interactions with service providers (Parish, Thomas, Rose, Kilany, & Shattuck, 2012). Although the Kaviras are fortunate in that both parents are presently employed, they are still living in a context in which finances are limited and it is difficult to gain access to social services and community resources.

Perspectives from the Kavira Family "Jeremy's arrival in the family changed things for us in terms of finances, but the family climate…really, the family love has always existed. I take primary caregiving responsibility for Jeremy, from washing him in the morning, to changing his diapers, to feeding him. This takes a lot of time and he is getting quite heavy! People around us may talk about Jeremy in a superstitious way or they may wonder why we take such good care of Jeremy, but we don't pay them any mind. Jeremy is an important part of our family."

Implications of Family Characteristics for Providing Supports and Services to Families

- In conversations with families, pay attention to the information that they share related to the characteristics of their family as a unit, the individual characteristics of each member, and any long-term or episodic special challenges that they are facing.

- If families are interested, connect them with other families who have similar characteristics.

- Recognize the unique strengths that each family has and find ways to positively affirm these strengths in your conversations and interactions. As you affirm these strengths, families can gain insight into their own strengths and potentially use them in the future when facing challenges.

Family Interaction

Definition As depicted in Figure 40.1, family interaction is the process hub of the family system and represents different subsystems that constitute family life. These subsystems include parental, extended family, marital, and sibling. Often, when caregiving is considered, it is thought about primarily in terms of the parental subsystem (often just the mother–child relationship). It is clear, however, that caregiving is influenced by the dynamics of each subsystem and the dynamics of the system as a whole. This perspective is expressed by a well-known family therapist as follows:

> In a mobile, all the pieces, no matter what size or shape, can be grouped together and balanced by shortening or lengthening the strings attached, or rearranging the distance between the pieces. So it is with the family. None of the family members is identical to any others; they are all different and at different levels of growth. As in a mobile, you can't arrange one without thinking of the other. (Satir, 1972, pp. 119–120)

In considering family interaction, it is important that families be able to identify and address needs throughout all of their subsystems—marital, sibling, parental, and extended family (Kriegsman & Palmer, 2013).

Illustrative Research Highlights
This section focuses on the sibling subsystem in terms of illustrating issues associated with balancing time and attention among all children in the family. Some studies have found that brothers and sisters of siblings with disabilities have a higher incidence of emotional problems, lower self-esteem, and greater responsibility for household chores (Mazaheri et al., 2013; Neely-Barnes & Graff, 2011). Professionals also express concerns about missed social experiences, stigma, and constant worry for parent and sibling in addition to jealousy regarding uneven parenting for the siblings without disabilities or chronic illnesses (Packman et al., 2008). A review of literature on outcomes of typically developing siblings of children with disabilities found that 61.1% of the studies reviewed reflected negative sibling outcomes, ranging from emotional concerns (e.g., anger, resentment, depression, and anxiety) to negative behavioral measures, including school problems (Dauz Williams et al., 2010). However, some researchers have argued that reports of negative sibling outcomes should be treated with caution because in studies where siblings have lower than expected levels of well-being, effect sizes and significance of these studies are generally small, and when environmental adversities (e.g., poor socioeconomic conditions of the family) are taken into account, low well-being of siblings is no longer significant (Emerson & Giallo, 2014).

Research has also shown that there are many positive benefits to having a sibling with a disability, such as increased empathy, kindness, involvement, and acceptance of differences (Dykens, 2005; Heller & Arnold, 2010; Stoneman, 2005). Some siblings benefit in terms of increased self-esteem, maturity, and tolerance and understanding (Mulroy, Robertson, Aiberti, Leonard, & Bower, 2008). Often, siblings serve in the role of socialization agent and tutor for their sibling with a disability (Rivers & Stoneman, 2008). Moreover, research has found that a positive relationship between a sibling with a disability and sibling without a disability may help negate the effects of (parental) caregiver burden and is more predictive of typically developing child outcomes (Platt, Roper, Mandleco, & Freeborn, 2014). Many parents struggle to meet the needs of other children in the family (Koch & Mayes, 2012), a struggle that Salome Kavira also highlights in the next subsection.

Perspectives from the Kavira Family
"We try to plan so that everyone in the family gets what he or she needs so that there is no animosity between siblings. For example, I tell my children that the most important thing for them is to go to school. So, I pay for all of their school fees, and I tell them 'to each according to his needs.' And little by little we try to meet the needs of all of our children, so that they don't think that we give everything to Jeremy. I make a conscious effort to give enough to all of my children to ensure that there isn't any jealousy in our household."

Implications of Family Interactions for Providing Supports and Services to Families

- Learn from families how they carry out their roles in terms of providing care to all members.

- Find out families' priorities of what they would consider the most useful support that could be provided to them in order to address the needs of all family members.

- Provide support to the individual with a disability that is focused on enabling that individual to make positive contributions to other family members and to other subsystems within the family.

- Encourage families to consider inviting siblings, grandparents, and other family members to the individualized planning meetings to encourage other family members to gain information and provide their perspectives.

Family Functions

Definition   As illustrated in Figure 40.1, family functions are the outputs of the interaction system. Thus, based on the unique characteristics of each family (input) and the way that the family members interact with each other (process), functions are the outputs or the way that families address their needs related to affection, self-esteem, spirituality, economics, daily care, socialization, recreation, and education needs. Clearly, one of the purposes of families is to meet the individual and collective needs of members. Individuals with a disability can affect each of the eight types of family functions in positive, neutral, or negative ways (Turnbull et al., 2015).

Illustrative Research Highlights

Related to the economics function, all families must have income and a way to spend the money earned to meet food, clothing, shelter, and other needs. The presence of a son or daughter with a severe disability can create excess expenses (Parish, Rose, & Swaine, 2010). Some of the devices and services for a child with a severe disability may include adaptive feeding utensils, special clothing, speech therapy, psychological assessments, ongoing medications required for seizures and other physiological or psychological needs, and adaptive mobility devices such as walkers and crutches (Zuna, Kyzar, Turnbull, & Turnbull, 2015). In addition, the presence of a family member with an intellectual or developmental disability may prevent parents from obtaining employment because of the level of care and supervision required. This situation may add to parental challenges, as data indicate that mothers of children with disabilities who are employed outside of the home experience better mental health than mothers of children with disabilities who are not employed (Morris, 2014).

A consideration to keep in mind is that most families are incredibly busy trying to balance needs across all eight family functions. As families give more time and attention to one function, such as meeting economic needs, time and attention has to be withdrawn from other functions. Many parents

are especially appreciative of respite care services that enable them to devote their time and attention to other important aspects of their lives.

Perspectives from the Kavira Family   "We have a nanny who helps us with Jeremy because I need to go to work. And because the nanny comes from her house every morning (she's not a live-in nanny), I need to make sure that she is here before I can leave the house. If, for whatever reason, she can't come, I am paralyzed, and I can't go to work. This has caused problems for me at work because I really need to be there. I have to make sure that I make arrangements so that the nanny is always here. If I am in between nannies, I try to arrange with Jeremy's older sisters or with our nieces that they will be here in the morning and stay for the day with Jeremy."

Implications of Family Functions for Providing Supports and Services to Families

- Make sure to provide up-to-date and evidence-based support so that parents will not have to spend their valuable time advocating for service improvements.

- Support the individual to learn skills that can contribute positively to the family meeting all of its functions (e.g., doing chores around the house to address needs related to the function of daily care).

- Encourage teachers and other professionals to assist the individual with a disability to make friends and to participate in community and school extracurricular activities that will also serve to give the family a break from caregiving responsibilities.

Family Life Cycle

Definition   The family life cycle can be thought of in terms of life cycle stages and life cycle transitions. Life cycle stages include the developmental periods of time in which family functions are relatively stable (Carter & McGoldrick, 2005). Researchers and theorists disagree concerning the number of life-cycle stages that exist. Some have identified as many as 24 stages, although others have identified as few as six (Turnbull et al., 2015). The number is not as important as the tasks that families are responsible for accomplishing at each stage. The six stages identified by Turnbull et al. (2015) are 1) birth and early childhood, 2) elementary school years, 3) adolescence, 4) early adulthood, 5) middle adulthood, and 6) aging. In each of these life stages, families often vary in how they interact with each other and how they meet their needs related to family functions. For example, parents may express affection differently toward their child when she is an infant than they will when he or she is a teenager.

Family life cycle transitions represent the dynamic changes that occur within the family system as the family encounters change. Developmental changes include changes expected due to the growth of family members (e.g., moving from elementary school to middle school, leaving school to begin working), and nondevelopmental changes represent changes that are not tied to the evolution of time (e.g., changing jobs, moving from one town to another).

Illustrative Research Highlights Research clearly documents that the times that are often the most stressful in families' lives are times of transition when significant changes are occurring (Turnbull et al., 2015). Transitions represent the periods of change as families move from one developmental stage to another. One way to think about life-cycle stages and transitions is that stages are similar to plateaus and that transitions resemble peaks and valleys that divide those plateaus. Because these times of transition often represent changes in expectations and service systems, typically they are the times that families identify as the most challenging (Rous, Hallam, Harbin, McCormick, & Jung, 2007; Winn & Hay, 2009; Ytterhus, Wendelborg, & Lundeby, 2008).

One of the most stressful periods of family life is when individuals with disabilities graduate from high school and face the choices available for how to lead their adult lives, such as where to work, where to live, and the nature of social relationships and recreation. Families vary greatly in their priorities for their son or daughter during adulthood, and these variations are influenced by family characteristics, interaction, and functions. Many individuals with intellectual disability and their families would like to pursue supported employment, which has the goal of developing independent work skills and the ability to earn competitive wages in an inclusive job market (Wehman, 2012). For example, in one

study of supported versus sheltered employment, the average monthly wage earned in supported employment ($390.96) was more than twice the average wage in sheltered employment ($164.79) (Cimera, 2011). Families need support in knowing how to assist their son or daughter in supported employment initially and in being successfully employed over the long term. One way to do this might be through family involvement in Family Employment Awareness Training (FEAT). FEAT is a project, created through partnership between university researchers and Parent Training and Information Center leaders, which provides trainings to families, including members with the disability, and professionals. The training provides attendees with real-life examples of successful competitive employment, information on employment services and supports, and opportunities to network with each other and with guest speakers (e.g., competitively employed individuals with disabilities, employers, local agency representatives) (Francis, Gross, Turnbull, & Turnbull, 2013). Research has shown that FEAT is a promising approach for improving competitive employment outcomes for individuals (Francis, Gross, Turnbull, & Parent-Johnson, 2013; Francis, Gross, Turnbull, & Turnbull, 2013).

For families of people with intellectual and developmental disabilities who require intensive and ongoing support, planning for their future adult life transitions can be particularly stressful. Parents often need support in planning for a time when they will no longer be alive or capable to provide the necessary caregiving for their children with disabilities (Ryan, Taggart, Truesdale-Kennedy, & Slevin, 2014). In terms of transitions, the Kaviras are most concerned about an ongoing key developmental transition: Jeremy has grown too big to be lifted easily by one individual. Salome is also concerned about the transition that will take place when she is no longer able to hold primary caregiving responsibility for Jeremy. She would prefer that Jeremy move to a residential facility when she dies so that he is not a "burden" on his siblings; however, such a facility does not exist in Kinshasa at this time.

Perspectives from the Kavira Family "I am very aware of the impact that life cycle has on Jeremy and our family. My greatest dream is that all of my children can do well in life, that each of Jeremy's siblings get a job and that Jeremy isn't a burden for them. I also hope that in the future, there will be a structure in place for Jeremy to live a good life as well. There will be a time when I am no longer here to take care of Jeremy, and I would like for there to be a place where Jeremy could live and his siblings could come and visit. I don't want Jeremy to be a problem for them. If a structure like that existed, Jeremy could go there; they could visit him and take him home with them on the weekends. But I can't go and drop Jeremy somewhere to live while I am still alive. But when we are no longer here, we need him in a sort of structure where he won't be a burden for his siblings."

Implications of Life Cycle Issues for Providing Supports and Services to Families

- Support families by identifying the cognitive and behavioral expectations of the next environment and helping to teach skills in advance.

- Develop partnerships with local employers so that students with disabilities can have successful job experiences before graduating from high school.

- Support individuals and families to gain information on resources that they may want to consider in the future and how they might go about arranging visits to adult programs and/ or services.

- When individuals with disabilities and their families are in the midst of making major life cycle transitions, talk with them about what kinds of additional supports you might provide that would be helpful to them.

MULTIPLE FAMILY ROLES

Families of individuals with disabilities often take on roles over and above caregiving. This section briefly highlights three of these roles—families as teachers, parents as educators of others, and parents as advocates—and points out advantages and disadvantages to families assuming these responsibilities. For more information on the roles of siblings, see Burke (2010) or Burbidge and Minnes (2014). An overview, perspectives from the Kavira family, and implications are provided for each role.

Families as Teachers

Overview of Role The role of families as teachers involves mothers, fathers, siblings, and

often other family members implementing a treatment or intervention. The professional meets with the family several times at the beginning of the intervention to do an assessment, formulate a plan, and teach the family to carry out the intervention in their home. The professional then collects and analyzes the data from the family and provides ongoing feedback. This approach allows more families to be served by a small number of trained professionals and enables professionals to work with many families simultaneously (Briesmeister & Schaefer, 2007; Feldman & Werner, 2002).

Involving families' expertise and firsthand experience can be indispensable in the assessment and implementation of the intervention. This collaboration between professionals and family members can be a catalyst for empowering families to take action to address their needs.

Alternatively, many parents whose sons and daughters need interventions do not have the time, energy, or personal resources to carry out the role of teacher (Turnbull et al., 2015). The expectation that the family will be able to carry out explicit intervention programs may be setting them up for frustration and even failure. Another problem is that in the teacher model, parents must be highly motivated, consistent, and capable of the dual role of teacher and parent. This dual role can create stressful interactions between parents and children. It can also result in individuals with disabilities perceiving themselves as recipients of perpetual instruction. Salome Kavira did not carry out the role of teacher for Jeremy, although, as noted later in this chapter, she often carried out the roles of educator of others and advocate. It is important to understand that families will choose the roles that work for them.

Implications of Teacher Role for Providing Supports and Services to Families

- Brainstorm with families about what role is comfortable and possible for them related to serving as teacher for the family member with a disability.

- Be sensitive to the fact that having a parent serving as a teacher can strain relationships with the individual with the disability.

- Look for additional community resources to provide teaching opportunities so that family members will not need to assume this role.

Parents as Educators of Others

Overview of Role   Professionals and parents often acknowledge the need for more information about intellectual and developmental disabilities for the general public and for professionals. In particular, many parents spend a significant amount of time informing themselves and then, in turn, sharing that knowledge with others. One of the reasons they adopt this role is that they are better equipped to deal with professionals if they are well informed. One parent quoted in a journal article on mothers' experiences of support services believed that obtaining health care for her child was made more difficult because some medical professionals have little knowledge on the specific disability of her child and, as a result, she thought that she must educate them:

> They won't admit to you they don't know much about Cri du Chat. [...] And they are asking me questions about Cri du Chat, and I'm saying "Are you not supposed to be telling me? You're the professionals, I'm just a Mum." (Griffith et al., 2011, p. 170)

Educating others about their child's disability helps many parents increase the knowledge and comfort of others. Another mother noted that going out in public with her child often required her to educate people who did not understand that her child had a disability:

> Because she looks like she does they don't really realize she is like how she is. They think she is being rude [...] Quite often they will have a go at her and I'm thinking "God" and I say "Do you mind?" Sometimes I just don't know what to say, and I say "Julia that is quite inappropriate and I'm very sorry for what she has said." And they say "Well she is old enough to know better." (Griffith et al., 2011, p. 170)

Serving as an educator of others can be an empowering experience for some parents. Researchers have found that empowering parents and engaging them in planning and decision making can improve family functioning (Nachshen & Minnes, 2005). Although parents who educate may feel empowered by helping to educate others, it is also an added responsibility.

Alternatively, other parents do not want the role of educator. Parents who have this perspective may perceive it as burdensome to be the "explainer" and "informer" when it comes to their child's condition. They may choose a much more normalized experience in which they are not serving as a disability expert.

Perspectives from the Kavira Family   "People here [in the Democratic Republic of the Congo] are often not trained to support children with intellectual and developmental disabilities. Cerebral palsy seems new in our society. If Jeremy falls ill with malaria or the flu or something unrelated to his disability, health professionals often can't see beyond his disability. We can go into an institution, and instead of giving us a consultation about whatever illness Jeremy has, they look at his disability and say, 'Has he always been like that? How do you do it? We can't treat him here.' It is too bad because parents are often discouraged by health professionals. Even when they give you a diagnosis of a disability they do it insensitively. For a parent who is not prepared, it can be really discouraging. I do my best to educate parents and health professionals about people with disabilities."

Implications of the Educator Role for Providing Supports and Services to Families

- Have conversations with families about their preferred role related to providing knowledge to others related to disability issues.

- Find out from families how to be helpful in providing resources to them so that they will have the information that they need.

- Ask parents what has worked well for them in the past and build on their successes rather than assuming that they lack sufficient knowledge and skills for a new challenge.

- As a team of professionals and families, consider how community education related to disability can be carried out so that all of the responsibility for this role will not fall on families.

Parents as Advocates for Services and Supports

Overview of Role   Parents of individuals with disabilities often experience gaps in the system of supports and services. These gaps may be related to education, health care, recreation, employment, residential options, or other issues. Historically, and still today, parents often assume the role of advocates. Advocacy consists of presenting, supporting, or defending a position in order to obtain a particular result. The role of parents as advocates involves acting on knowledge related to social, economic, and political environments in order to improve the life situation of their families. Research has shown that parent advocacy can be an important coping behavior (Ewles, Clifford, & Minnes, 2014).

All parents advocate for their children in various ways, but parents who have children with intellectual and developmental disabilities typically have a considerably greater need for advocacy. In responding to this need, they may advocate in numerous different situations and use a wide range of approaches. They may write letters, make telephone calls, and enlist the help of the media to address specific needs of their children or of all children with disabilities. Parents may act as advocates individually or as part of a group at the community, national, and/or international level.

A qualitative study examined advocacy behavior of diverse parents during special education home–school interactions (Trainor, 2010). The author found that patterns of parents' approaches to advocacy across groups could align under the following classifications:

1. *The intuitive approach:* Advocates emphasized the importance of "knowing my child" and of being in the best position to understand or accurately assess their children's needs.

2. *The disability expert:* Advocates incorporated knowledge about disabilities as they advocated for their children. These advocates developed such expertise from sources such as doctors, disability-specific organizations, and commercially available texts and web sites.

3. *The strategist:* Advocates combined their understanding and sense of disability, and knowledge of their children's unique strengths and needs, with their knowledge about special education. Parents who strategized often used knowledge about the U.S. special education law known as the Individuals with Disabilities Education Improvement Act (IDEA) of 2004 (PL 108-446). Strategists understood the role they could potentially play in making decisions about referrals and evaluations, services and accommodations, and inclusion.

4. *The change agent:* Advocates discussed concerns about the level of complex knowledge and social networking required to advocate for their individual children, motivating them to advocate for systemic change. Parents who were interested in activating systems change had to understand educational systems' functions as well as having special-education-specific knowledge. In addition, this type of advocacy required investments of time to establish relationships among parents, teachers, and administrators.

Parent advocates can often find that their advocacy opens many doors for them and their children or that a reputation of determination and persistence helps them be heard by social service providers (Griffith et al., 2011). As one mother explains,

> Am I listened to by services? Yes I am now, I am now, but that is only because half my life is spent... and they know that we are helping them. It's not because they love me. But I would say the only reason I am listened to is because they know that if they are not listening to me, somebody else will be. (as cited in Griffith et al., 2011, p. 173)

Advocacy can have negative outcomes as well as positive ones. For example, in another qualitative study, the authors found that the continual battle for meaningful inclusion can have negative consequences for parents (Resch et al., 2010). Several parents shared that they were personally labeled as "trouble parents" for their efforts to advocate on behalf of their children. Advocacy can result in parents being involved in adversarial struggles and can cause stress (Griffith et al., 2011) along with feelings of isolation or being separated and disconnected from their community and social groups. One parent notes,

> I've watched parents who I think would like to see the same kind of outcomes that our children are having as a result of what I believe are inclusive education experiences, but are not willing to put themselves in the political spot that they saw us get in. [They're] very fearful of the community backlash and so they don't. (Resch et al., 2010, p. 144)

Perspectives from the Kavira Family   "We need more things like media sensitization campaigns and educational brochures that explain disability and its causes. We need to combat stigma and misinformed or superstitious ideas about disability in our society. We also need more national programs so that families can find early and effective support for their child with a disability. I see myself as an ambassador for other families who have children with disabilities and I often advocate for improved information about disabilities and support for families, on both city and national levels."

Implications of Advocacy Role for Providing Supports and Services to Families

- Ensure that services are offered at such a quality level that it is not necessary for parents to advocate because of service deficiencies.

- Work collaboratively among professionals, families, and community citizens to start new programs for individuals with disabilities and ensure that this responsibility does not fall solely to parents.

- Provide advocacy training or support to parents so that they can optimally and efficiently advocate for their needs and priorities.

FAMILY QUALITY OF LIFE

A new way of addressing family support and family outcomes is through an emphasis on family quality of life. Various aspects of this concept are described next.

Definition

Family quality of life as a concept is a relatively new area of study. Most family research has focused on family systems, family roles, family stress and coping, and family dysfunction, as previously described. Family quality of life is the embodiment of a paradigm shift in disability services and family support (Poston et al., 2003). It moves the focus from "fixing" to support, from deficit to strengths, and from the child as the focus of intervention and support to the family as the target of supports.

Two parallel lines of research on family quality of life have emerged since 2000: one at the University of Kansas Beach Center on Disability and another among an international group of researchers from Canada, Australia, and Israel. Both lines of research have similar definitions of family quality of life. The Beach Center defines *family quality of life* as the conditions in which the family's needs are met, they enjoy spending time together, and members have opportunities to do things that they believe are important (Poston et al., 2003). Zuna, Summers, Turnbull, Hu, & Xu (2010) added that it is "a dynamic sense of well-being collectively and subjectively defined and informed by its members in which individual and family-level needs interact" (p. 262). Similarly, the international team describes family quality of life as both the place where the individual

quality of life of each family member mingles as well as the place where other factors affect the family as a whole (Brown & Brown, 2003). Both of these definitions share the concept that family quality of life concerns individual family members as well as the whole family.

Perspectives from the Kavira Family   "Life with Jeremy can be tough in terms of caregiving and finances, but first, I must say, Jeremy has truly brought an academic benefit to our family. When I completed my nursing degree, I needed a subject for my final project. I found that I had to write about disabilities. Also, in school, right away, the subject I understood the best and specialized in was home-based support. So, [the subject for my final project was] teaching families how to support their child with a disability in the home. My niece also took psychology in school, and she chose to specialize in disability and its impact on the family. So, having Jeremy in our lives has really opened our eyes and showed us that we need to protect people living with disabilities. Disability isn't always negative, as you can see with its impact on our family. Also, Jeremy really brought brotherly love into our home. No one can leave the house for the day without first going and saying hello to Jeremy. Even when someone is traveling away from home, they will call home and the first thing they ask is, 'How is Jeremy doing?'...So he really brought love into our home, and he taught us the sense of togetherness and sharing. The sense of sharing is also apparent because I cannot see another family that has a child with a disability without being interested in them. And when others have a problem related to their child with a disability, they just need to call. The little that I have, I will give them that....So Jeremy really brought us the ability to share support and experience as well."

Implications for Providing Supports and Services to Families

- Ask family members who they consider to be part of their family.

- Consider how the aspects of the family member's disability may both positively and negatively affect both individual family members and the family as a whole.

- Consider how the concept of family quality of life could change the way you provide supports to individuals with disabilities.

Domains of Family Quality of Life

Family quality of life is a holistic, multidimensional concept, intended to represent the totality of family life (Poston et al., 2003; Schalock & Verdugo Alonso, 2002). Its multidimensional nature is often represented by its component parts, typically referred to as domains. Considering the domains of family quality of life separately makes it a more practical concept, whereas thinking of these domains as being interrelated retains its holistic nature.

The domains of family quality of life differ somewhat, depending on the line of research. The international team offers the following domains: health, financial well-being, family relationships, support from other people, support from services, careers and preparing for careers, influence of values, leisure, and community interaction (Brown et al., 2006). A survey developed based on these domains enables families to respond in terms of their opportunities for participation, their initiative in taking advantage of opportunities, their attainment in getting or accomplishing things important to them, and their satisfaction with their overall family life (Brown, Anand, Fung, Isaacs, & Baum, 2003).

The Beach Center framework offers five similar domains: family interaction, parenting, emotional well-being, physical/material well-being, and disability-related support (Wang, Mannan, Poston, Turnbull, & Summers, 2004a). Each of these domains is described in more detail next.

1. *Family interaction:* The family interaction domain refers to the relationships among family members. It includes indicators such as communicating, problem solving, spending time together, and showing love and support.

2. *Parenting:* The parenting domain relates to the activities that adults in the family do to help their children grow and develop. The indicators include helping children learn to make good decisions, helping them learn to be independent, helping with schoolwork, knowing who the children's friends are, and having time for the needs of all the children in the family.

3. *Emotional well-being:* This domain concerns the emotional aspects of family life. Its indicators include having support to relieve stress, having

friends to provide support, having time to pursue interests, and having help from outside the family to care for family members.

4. *Physical/material well-being:* The physical/material well-being domain includes the basic physical needs of family members. Some representative indicators include getting medical and dental care, having transportation, taking care of expenses, and feeling safe.

5. *Disability-related supports:* The disability-related supports domain refers to the supports needed in the home and community for the family member with a disability. Indicators include having support to make progress at school, work, and home; having support to make friends; and having a good relationship with service providers.

The Beach Center Family Quality of Life scale measures family satisfaction in these five domains of family quality of life. This scale has proven psychometric properties and can be used as an outcome measure for family support (Hoffman, Marquis, Poston, Summers, & Turnbull, 2006). A review of the literature on family support found that across studies, family support was significantly related to improved family outcomes (Kyzar, Turnbull, Summers, & Gomez, 2012).

Perspectives from the Kavira Family "Even with our challenges, we have a good life. We have jobs and we are able to stretch our money to meet our needs. Our greatest need is on the day-to-day level—providing basic caregiving support to Jeremy. But when the nanny is not here, everyone works together to help Jeremy, even his brothers. For example, when his one brother wakes up, if he sees Jeremy is wet, he will change him. And my friends too, particularly colleagues. They are always interested in Jeremy, and they ask about his well-being and do what they can to help me. So Jeremy's issues are everyone's issues. But, often, we find that we have to organize our own lives around Jeremy's daily needs."

Although the Kavira family seems satisfied with the support they receive from other people, this is not always the case. For many families around the world, support from other people is often rated lowest of all nine domains in both attainment and satisfaction (Brown, 2012).

Implications for Providing Supports and Services to Families

- Use family quality of life domains to facilitate conversations with family members about what is happening within their family.

- Consider the impact of one or more of the family quality of life domains on the supports and services you provide.

- Recognize that families may need their basic needs met (i.e., housing, transportation, or family relationships) before a disability-related intervention can be effective.

- Provide the support that families ask for and particularly need.

- Develop strategies to encourage physical and emotional support from relatives, friends, and neighbors.

SUMMARY

A family systems perspective is helpful in identifying and understanding family priorities. This perspective includes recognizing the characteristics of families, the way that they interact through subsystems, and the priority that they give to different family functions. Furthermore, family systems change through the life cycle, especially at times of transition.

Family members assume many roles related to serving as a teacher of their child, an educator of others, and an advocate. Professionals can support families to be successful in these roles by understanding their family system and providing services and supports that are tailored to each family's circumstances. The most contemporary way of supporting families is to recognize that their quality of life as a family is critically important and that family–professional partnerships can be helpful in attending to each domain of family quality of life. A permeating theme throughout the chapter is the critical importance of individualization and a positive, strengths-based approach in forming and carrying out partnerships that support families to meet their needs, helping them enjoy spending time together and enabling them to have opportunities to do the things that are important to them.

FOR FURTHER THOUGHT AND DISCUSSION

1. What are your assumptions about the impact of having a person with a disability in the family?

2. How can professionals, paid caregivers, or volunteers be more supportive of families?

3. Ask yourself the following questions about working with families of children with intellectual and developmental disabilities, and illustrate with examples to help explain your point of view.

   a. Are we as service providers asking too much of families or too little, given their experience, capacity to overcome challenges, levels of stress, and resources?

   b. Are we giving too much or too little?

   c. Are our suggestions consistent with the family's priorities?

   d. Are our priorities consistent with the family's stage in the life cycle?

4. How can we partner with other professionals to address all of a family's priorities for support in a way that is consistent with a family quality of life perspective?

REFERENCES

Blacher, J., Begum, G.F., Marcoulides, G.A., & Baker, B.L. (2013). Longitudinal perspectives of child positive impact on families: Relationship to disability and culture. *American Journal on Intellectual and Developmental Disabilities, 118*(2), 141–155.

Braddock, B., & Twyman, K. (2014). Access to treatment for toddlers with autism spectrum disorders. *Clinical Pediatrics, 53*(3), 225–229. doi:10.1177/0009922814521284

Briesmeister, J.M., & Schaefer, C.E. (2007). *Handbook of parent training: Helping parents prevent and solve problem behavior* (3rd ed.). Hoboken, NJ: John Wiley & Sons.

Brown, I. (July, 2012). *Family quality of life: Comparison among 16 countries.* Paper presented at the IASSIDD World Congress, Halifax, Canada.

Brown, I., Anand, S., Fung, W.L.A., Isaacs, B., & Baum, N. (2003). Family quality of life: Canadian results from an international study. *Journal of Developmental and Physical Disabilities, 15,* 207–230.

Brown, I., & Brown, R.I. (2003). *Quality of life and disability: An approach for community practitioners.* London, United Kingdom: Jessica Kingsley.

Brown, I., Brown, R.I., Baum, N.T., Isaacs, B.J., Myerscough, T., Neikrug, S.,...Wang, M. (2006). *Family quality of life—2006: Main caregivers of people with intellectual disabilities.* Toronto, Canada: Surrey Place Centre.

Burbidge, J., & Minnes, P. (2014). Relationship quality in adult siblings with and without developmental disabilities. *Family Relations, 63,* 148–162.

Burke, P. (2010). Brothers and sisters of disabled children: The experience of disability by association. *British Journal of Social Work, 40*(6), 1681–1699.

Carroll, D.W. (2013). *Families of children with developmental disabilities: Understanding stress and opportunities for growth.* Washington, DC: American Psychological Association.

Carter, E.A., & McGoldrick, M. (2005). *The expanded family life cycle: Individual, family, and social perspectives* (3rd ed.). Boston, MA: Pearson/Allyn & Bacon.

Cavallo, M.M., & Kay, T. (2011). The family system. In J.M. Silver, T.W. McAllister, & S.C. Yudofsky (Eds.), *Textbook of traumatic brain injury* (2nd ed., pp. 483–504). Arlington, VA: American Psychiatric.

Cimera, R.E. (2011). Supported versus sheltered employment: Cumulative costs, hours worked, and wages earned. *Journal of Vocational Rehabilitation, 35,* 85–92.

Dauz Williams, P., Piamjariyakul, U., Graff, J.C., Stanton, A., Guthrie, A.C., Hafeman C., & Williams, A.R. (2010). Developmental disabilities: Effects on well siblings. *Issues in Comprehensive Pediatric Nursing, 33,* 39–55. doi:10.3109/01460860903486515

Dykens, E.M. (2005). Happiness, well-being, and character strengths: Outcomes for families and siblings of persons with mental retardation. *Mental Retardation, 43*(5), 360–364.

Eide, A.H., & Ingstad, B. (2013). Disability and poverty: Reflections on research experiences in Africa and beyond. *African Journal of Disability, 2,* 1–7.

Emerson, E., & Giallo, R. (2014). The well-being of siblings of children with disabilities. *Research in Developmental Disabilities, 35*(9), 2085–2092.

Ewles, G., Clifford, T., & Minnes, P. (2014). Predictors of advocacy in parents of children with autism spectrum disorders. *Journal on Developmental Disabilities, 20*(1), 74–83.

Feldman, M.A., & Werner, S.E. (2002). Collateral effects of behavioral parent training on families of children with developmental disabilities and behavior disorders. *Behavioral Interventions, 17,* 75–83.

Francis, G.L., Gross, J.M.S., Turnbull, H.R., & Parent-Johnson, W. (2013). Evaluating the effectiveness of the family employment awareness training in Kansas: A pilot study. *Research and Practice for Persons with Severe Disabilities, 38*(1), 44–57.

Francis, G.L., Gross, J.M.S., Turnbull, A.P., & Turnbull, H.R. (2013). The Family Employment Awareness Training (FEAT): A mixed-method follow-up. *Journal of Vocational Rehabilitation, 39,* 167–181.

Griffith, G.M., Hastings, R.P., Nash, S., Petalas, M., Oliver, C., Howlin, P.,...Tunnicliffe, P. (2011). "You have to sit and explain it all, and explain yourself." Mothers' experiences of support services for their offspring with a rare genetic intellectual disability syndrome. *Journal of Genetic Counseling, 20,* 165–177.

Heller, T., & Arnold, C.K. (2010). Siblings of adults with developmental disabilities: Psychosocial outcomes, relationships, and future planning. *Policy and Practice in Intellectual Disabilities, 7*(1), 16–25.

Hoffman, L., Marquis, J.G., Poston, D.J., Summers, J.A., & Turnbull, A. (2006). Assessing family outcomes: Psychometric evaluation of the family quality of life scale. *Journal of Marriage and Family, 68,* 1069–1083.

Hughes, C., & Fanion, L.L. (2014). Poverty and disability: Addressing the ties that bind. In M. Agran, F. Brown, C. Hughes, C. Quirk, & D.L. Ryndak (Eds.), *Equity and full participation for individuals with severe disabilities: A vision for the future* (pp. 25–40). Baltimore, MD: Paul H. Brookes Publishing Co.

Individuals with Disabilities Education Improvement Act (IDEA) of 2004, PL 108-446, 20 U.S.C. §§ 1400 *et seq.*

Kayfitz, A.D., Gragg, M.N., & Orr, R.R. (2010). Positive experiences of mothers and fathers of children with autism. *Journal of Applied Research in Intellectual Disabilities, 23,* 337–343.

King, G., Zwaigenbaum, L., Bates, A., Baxter, D., & Rosenbaum, P. (2012). Parent views of the positive contributions of elementary and high-school-aged children with autism spectrum disorders and Down syndrome. *Child: Care, Health and Development, 38*(6), 817–828.

Koch, C., & Mayes, R. (2012). The balancing act: Meeting the needs of all children including an adolescent with disabilities. *Journal of Applied Research in Intellectual Disabilities, 25,* 464–475.

Kriegsman, K.H., & Palmer, S. (2013). *Just one of the kids: Raising a resilient family when one of your children has a physical disability.* Baltimore, MD: Johns Hopkins University Press.

Kuo, D.Z., Cohen, E., Agrawal, R., Berry, J.G., & Casey, P.H. (2011). A national profile of caregiver challenges among more medically complex children with special health care needs. *Archives of Pediatric and Adolescent Medicine, 165*(11), 1020–1026.

Kyzar, K.B., Turnbull, A.P., Summers, J.A., & Gomez, V.A. (2012). The relationship of family support to family outcomes: A synthesis of key findings from research on severe disability. *Research and Practice for Persons with Severe Disabilities, 37*(1), 31–44.

Mazaheri, M.M., Rae-Seebach, R., Preston, H.E., Schmidt, M., Kountz-Edwards, S., Field, N.,...Packman, W. (2013). The impact of Prader-Willi syndrome on the family's quality of life and caregiving, and the unaffected siblings' psychosocial adjustment. *Journal of Intellectual Disability Research, 57*(9), 861–873.

Mitra, S., Posarac, A., & Vick, B. (2013). Disability and poverty in developing countries: A multidimensional study. *World Development, 41,* 1–18.

Morris, L.A. (2014). The impact of work on the mental health of parents of children with disabilities. *Family Relations, 63*(1), 101–121.

Mulroy, S., Robertson, L., Aiberti, K., Leonard, H., & Bower, C. (2008). The impact of having a sibling with an intellectual disability: Parental perspectives in two disorders. *Journal of Intellectual Disability Research, 52,* 216–229.

Nachshen, J.S., & Minnes, P. (2005). Empowerment in parents of school-aged children with and without developmental disabilities. *Journal of Intellectual Disability Research, 42*(12), 889–904.

Neely-Barnes, S.L., & Graff, J.C. (2011). Are there adverse consequences to being a sibling of a person with a disability? A propensity score analysis. *Family Relations, 60*(3), 331–341.

Packman, W., Mazaheri, M., Sporri, L., Long, J.K., Chesterman, B., Fine, J., & Amylon, M.D. (2008). Projective drawings as measures of psychological functioning in siblings of pediatric cancer patients from the Camp Okizu study. *Journal of Pediatric Oncology Nursing, 25,* 44–55.

Parish, S.L., Rose, R.A., & Swaine, J.G. (2010). Financial well-being of US parents caring for co-resident children and adults with developmental disabilities: An age cohort analysis. *Journal of Intellectual and Developmental Disability, 35*(4), 235–243.

Parish, S.L., Thomas, K.C., Rose, R., Kilany, M., & Shattuck, P.T. (2012). State Medicaid spending and financial burden of families raising children with autism. *Intellectual and Developmental Disabilities, 50*(6), 441–451.

Platt, C., Roper, S.O., Mandleco, B., & Freeborn, D. (2014). Sibling cooperative and externalizing behaviors in families raising children with disabilities. *Nursing Research, 63*(4), 235–244.

Poston, D., Turnbull, A., Park, J., Mannan, H., Marquis, J., & Wang, M. (2003). Family quality of life: A qualitative inquiry. *Mental Retardation, 41*(5), 313–328.

Resch, J.A., Mireles, G., Benz, M.R., Grenwelge, C., Peterson, R., & Zhang, D. (2010). Giving parents a voice: A qualitative study of the challenges experienced by parents of children with disabilities. *Rehabilitation Psychology, 55*(2), 139–150.

Rivers, J.W., & Stoneman, Z. (2008). Child temperaments, differential parenting, and the sibling relationships of children with autism spectrum disorder. *Journal of Autism and Developmental Disorders, 38,* 1740–1750.

Rous, B., Hallam, R., Harbin, G., McCormick, K., & Jung, L.A. (2007). The transition process for young children with disabilities: A conceptual framework. *Infants and Young Children, 20*(2), 135–148.

Ryan, A., Taggart, L., Truesdale-Kennedy, M., & Slevin, E. (2014). Issues in caregiving for older people with intellectual disabilities and their ageing family careers: A review and commentary. *International Journal of Older People Nursing, 9*(3), 217–226.

Satir, V. (1972). *Peoplemaking.* Palo Alto, CA: Science and Behavior Books.

Schalock, R.L., & Verdugo Alonso, M.A. (2002). *Handbook on quality of life for human service practitioners.* Washington, DC: American Association on Mental Retardation.

Singer, G.H.S., Biegel, D.E., & Conway, P. (2012). *Family support and family caregiving across disabilities.* New York, NY: Routledge.

Stoneman, Z. (2005). Siblings of children with disabilities: Research themes. *Mental Retardation, 43*(5), 339–350.

Trainor, A.A. (2010). Diverse approaches to parent advocacy during special education home-school interactions. *Remedial and Special Education, 31*(1), 34–47.

Turnbull, A.P., Summers, J.A., & Brotherson, M.J. (1984). *Working with families with disabled members: A family systems approach.* Lawrence: University of Kansas, Kansas Affiliated Facility.

Turnbull, A.P., Summers, J.A., Lee, S.H., & Kyzar, K. (2007). Conceptualization and measurement of family outcomes associated with families of individuals with intellectual disabilities. *Mental Retardation and Developmental Disabilities Research Reviews, 13,* 346–356.

Turnbull, A.P., Turnbull, H.R., Erwin, E.J., Soodak, L.C., & Shogren, K.A. (2015). *Families, professionals, and exceptionality: Positive outcomes through partnerships and trust* (6th ed.). Upper Saddle River, NJ: Merrill/ Pearson Education.

Wang, M., Mannan, H., Poston, D., Turnbull, A.P., & Summers, J.A. (2004a). Parents' perceptions of advocacy activities and their impact on family quality of life. *Research and Practice for Persons with Severe Disabilities, 29*(2), 144–155.

Wang, M., Turnbull, A.P., Summers, J.A., Little, T.D., Poston, D.J., Mannan, H., & Turnbull, H.R. (2004b). Severity of disability and income as predictors of parents' satisfaction with their family quality of life during early childhood years. *Research and Practice for Persons with Severe Disabilities, 29*(2), 82–94.

Wehman, P. (2012). Supported employment: What is it? *Journal of Vocational Rehabilitation, 37*(3), 139–142.

Winn, S., & Hay, I. (2009). Transition from school for youths with a disability: Issues and challenges. *Disability and Society, 24*(1), 103–115.

Ytterhus, B., Wendelborg, C., & Lundeby, H. (2008). Managing turning points and transitions in childhood and parenthood—insights from families with disabled children in Norway. *Disability and Society, 23*(6), 625–636.

Zuna, N., Kyzar, K., Turnbull, A.P., & Turnbull, R. (2015). Fostering family–professional partnerships. In F. Brown, J. McDonnell, & M. Snell (Eds.), *Instruction of students with severe disabilities* (8th ed.). Upper Saddle River, NJ: Pearson Education.

Zuna, N., Summers, J.A., Turnbull, A.P., Hu, X., & Xu, S. (2010). Theorizing about family quality of life. In R. Kober (Ed.), *Enhancing quality of life for people with intellectual disabilities: From theory to practice* (pp. 241–278). Dordrecht, The Netherlands: Springer.

41

Sexuality and People Who Have Intellectual and Developmental Disabilities

From Myth to Emerging Practices

Dorothy Griffiths, Stephanie Ioannou, and Jordan Hoath

WHAT YOU WILL LEARN

- Myths and facts pertaining to the sexuality of people with intellectual and developmental disabilities
- Policy suggestions for creating a positive atmosphere for teaching appropriate and responsible socio-sexual behavior
- The history of socio-sexual education and its importance to people with intellectual and developmental disabilities
- Forms of treatment and counseling for people with intellectual and developmental disabilities
- Teachable moments for people with intellectual and developmental disabilities to learn socio-sexuality skills
- The application of issues pertaining to sexual diversity to people with intellectual and developmental disabilities

Sexuality is often overlooked in relation to people who have intellectual and developmental disabilities. This chapter explores the subject in terms of myths and facts, matters related to changing sexual policy, socio-sexual education, birth control, sexual diversity, sexual victimization, and treatment and counseling.

MYTHS AND FACTS

The topic of the sexuality of people with intellectual and developmental disabilities conjures up many myths. It is surprising that myths that were commonly believed at the beginning of the last century still exist in the 21st century. Seven of the most common are listed in Table 41.1. After reading them, it may appear that some of the myths contradict others. However, all of them have the same effect; they give the impression that the sexuality of people who have an intellectual or developmental disability is outside of the "normal" range. Such myths allow society to continue to deny this aspect of life to people with intellectual and developmental disabilities.

DISPELLING THE MYTHS

The myth that people with intellectual and developmental disabilities are eternal children is based on a misunderstanding that mental age is a construct that has any validity and is a predictor of all aspects of the person's life. People with intellectual and developmental disabilities typically show an interest in closeness, affection, and contact with others, as do people without disabilities. However, from the moment of birth, others often treat people with

597

Table 41.1. Dispelling seven common myths about the sexuality of people with intellectual and developmental disabilities

Myth	Information that dispels the myth
1. People with intellectual and developmental disabilities are eternal children and are asexual.	Most people with intellectual and developmental disabilities develop secondary sexual characteristics at about the same rate as people without disabilities. Individuals may vary in their rate of development, however, especially individuals with certain genetic or endocrine dysfunctions. Generally, people with intellectual and developmental disabilities have sexual feelings and responses to the same kinds of things as do people without such disabilities.
2. People with intellectual and developmental disabilities need to live in environments that restrict and inhibit their sexuality to protect themselves and others.	People who have intellectual and developmental disabilities require environments that provide the types of learning about sexuality that are generally taught in their cultures. Like others in the general population, people with intellectual and developmental disabilities benefit from an environment that models and teaches personal, moral, social, and legal responsibility regarding sexuality.
3. People with intellectual and developmental disabilities should not be provided with sex education, as it will only encourage inappropriate behavior.	Socio-sexual education helps individuals to understand their changing bodies and feelings and provides the knowledge and guidance necessary to learn responsibility about one's sexuality. There appears to be a correlation between socio-sexual education and a reduced frequency of abuse (Hard, 1986, as cited in Roeher Institute, 1988). Socio-sexual education provides, for people who may be demonstrating inappropriate sexual behavior, knowledge and skills to replace their current inappropriate sexual behavior.
4. People with intellectual and developmental disabilities should be sterilized because they will give birth to children who also have disabilities.	Eighty-five percent of adult disability is caused after the age of 13, and more than 90% of infant disability is due to social, not genetic, causes (Rioux, 1996). Thus, the disabilities of most people with intellectual and developmental disabilities are not attributable to a known genetic abnormality. There is no physical reason to think people with intellectual and developmental disabilities will be more likely to give birth to children with disabilities unless there is a genetic cause for their particular disabilities. It should also be noted that the characteristics of some people's intellectual and developmental disabilities, especially those disabilities with genetic causes, are such that these individuals can never procreate (Griffiths, Richards, Federoff, & Watson, 2002).
5. People with intellectual and developmental disabilities are more likely to develop diverse, unusual, or deviant sexual behavior.	The sexual development of people with intellectual and developmental disabilities can be affected by many factors: lack of sexual education, deprivation of peer group interactions, family restrictions on activities, lack of social exposure, and even lack of motor coordination. People with intellectual and developmental disabilities do not develop any more sexually inappropriate behavior than is found in the general population if they have typical opportunities to learn about their sexuality.
6. People with intellectual and developmental disabilities are oversexed, promiscuous, sexually indiscriminate, and dangerous; children should not be left unattended with them.	Although it appears that people with intellectual and developmental disabilities may be somewhat overrepresented in the population of people who are convicted of sexual offenses, these data may reflect that they are more likely to get caught, confess, and waive their rights rather than indicating an increased rate of offense. Often the type of sexually inappropriate behaviors committed by people with intellectual disability represent less serious offenses than those committed by people without disabilities. An example might be masturbating in public. Some clinicians have suggested that sexual deviance may be less common in this population than among people without disabilities (Day, 1994). People with intellectual and developmental disabilities are more likely to be the victims of sexual offenses than the victimizers.
7. People with intellectual and developmental disabilities cannot benefit from sexual counseling or treatment.	A growing body of literature has demonstrated that people who have intellectual and developmental disabilities can benefit from treatment or intervention directed at 1) sexual abuse counseling or 2) teaching appropriate socio-sexual behavior to replace sexually inappropriate behavior.

Sources: Griffiths (1991, 2003).

intellectual and developmental disabilities as asexual and as children. In the 20th century, because of the fear of procreation by people with intellectual and developmental disabilities, they were isolated in institutions (see Chapter 2). As discussed later in this chapter, attitudes about the sexuality of people with intellectual and developmental disabilities have begun to evolve.

The remainder of this chapter explores some key issues revolving around sexuality and the field of intellectual and developmental disabilities: sexuality policy, socio-sexual education, birth control, sexual diversity, victimization, and treatment and counseling. For expanded discussions of these and other topics, the reader is referred to *Ethical Dilemmas: Sexuality and Developmental Disabilities*, edited by Griffiths, Richards, Federoff, and Watson (2002).

CHANGING SEXUALITY POLICY

People with intellectual and developmental disabilities have the right to be treated in the same way as anyone else, and this includes the realm of sexuality. In both Canada and the United States, this right is implied in various laws. The Canadian Charter of Rights (1982) guarantees protections against discrimination based on disability. The American Bill of Rights and the Rehabilitation Act of 1973 (PL 93-112) protect rights of privacy, choice of marital status, and freedom to procreate and raise a family. Globally, the United Nations *Declaration on the Rights of Mentally Retarded Persons* (1971) proclaimed that people with intellectual and developmental disabilities have the right to cohabitate and marry. In recent years, United Nations *Convention on the Rights of Persons with Disabilities* (CRPD; United Nations, 2006) has provided a more directive doctrine on rights. The CRPD moves signatory nations beyond the rhetoric of recognition of the rights of people with disabilities to bearing responsibility for creating a positive climate that respects and supports people's opportunities to understand and express their sexuality to the same degree that other citizens do. The CRPD further states that nations must provide support to individuals to ensure them opportunities to assert these rights, including education, counseling, and abuse prevention. It states that people who have a disability must not be denied their rights with regard to their sexuality and parenting.

As a consequence of such doctrines, there has been a growing awareness of the need for community agencies and other organizations to develop socio-sexual policies to ensure that the rights of people with intellectual and developmental disabilities are respected. Policies are vital in ensuring that there is a consistent and responsible atmosphere in which to learn about culturally appropriate socio-sexual interactions. Unless there are clear guidelines for staff in a school or community agency to provide direction on socio-sexual issues, each staff member might come up with his or her own individual approach. This would lead to great inconsistencies in what is being taught; certain behaviors might at times be accepted and at other times punished, depending on which staff member is present. This type of inconsistent treatment creates an environment in which it is very difficult for people to learn to take responsibility for their own behavior.

To create a positive atmosphere in which to teach appropriate and responsible socio-sexual behavior, it is recommended that a school or community agency provide the following:

- A statement that recognizes the sexuality of people with intellectual and developmental disabilities and recognizes related rights

- An educational program to ensure that staff members respond to socio-sexual issues, whether appropriate or inappropriate, in a consistent manner across staff and over time

- Opportunities for people with intellectual and developmental disabilities to learn appropriate socio-sexual education and behavior and to have input into the topics they would like to learn in an education program

- Access for people with intellectual and developmental disabilities to medical and counseling intervention, as needed, for sexual issues, including abuse counseling and treatment for inappropriate sexual behavior

- Clear policies and procedures to prevent abuse and procedures to follow should there be a suspicion of abuse

Parents of people with intellectual and developmental disabilities are becoming increasingly more verbal and less conservative about sexuality issues regarding their children. Numerous articles suggest that sexual education may reduce vulnerability to abuse in people with intellectual and developmental disabilities (Finkelhor, 2009; Swango-Wilson, 2011). As a result, families have come to recognize the importance of sex education for their children because of the growing awareness that without it, their children could be at greater risk of abuse (Johnson & Davies, 1989).

Staff attitudes have also become generally more accepting toward sexual behavior between consenting adults in private settings (Evans, McGuire,

Healy, & Carley, 2009), although there still remain inconsistent attitudes regarding abortion, sterilization, and same-sex attraction (Johnson & Davies, 1989; Löfgren-Mårtenson, 2009) that can be counteracted through education and training on issues related to the sexuality of people with intellectual and developmental disabilities. The rigid disapproval that existed in earlier years is giving way to indecision. Policy and training and education are the only means by which agencies can ensure that the sexuality of people with intellectual and developmental disabilities will be responsibly, consistently, and proactively addressed.

SOCIO-SEXUAL EDUCATION

Prior to the 1970s, sex education programs focused on behavioral control of inappropriate sexual activities rather than teaching about appropriate sexuality. It was not until the 1980s that sex education became focused on the socio-sexual learning needs of people with intellectual and developmental disabilities. In addition to education about anatomy, birth control, sexual intercourse, hygiene, and venereal disease, educators began to incorporate topics such as relationships, social behavior, self-esteem, decision making, sexual lifestyles, and abuse into their curricula.

Griffiths and Lunsky (2000) explored the increased emphasis on socio-sexual education in recent decades and a shift in the priorities of education. They noted four reasons for this shift: awareness of abuse, attention to inappropriate sexual expression, identification of HIV/AIDS, and enhanced interest in preventive health care. Each of these is discussed in the following subsections.

Sexual Abuse

People with intellectual and developmental disabilities are far more vulnerable to abuse than people without disabilities; abuse is most likely perpetrated by someone known to the victim, and the perpetrator is often a caregiver who gains access and opportunity to abuse through the disability system (Cambridge, Beadle-Brown, Milne, Mansell, & Whelton, 2011). It has been suggested that people with intellectual and developmental disabilities are vulnerable to abuse for a myriad of reasons related to the cultural circumstances of having a disability; also, because of a lack of sexual knowledge, they may not identify abusive situations and understand

their rights to refuse such advances. This was demonstrated in a study by Hard (as cited in Roeher Institute, 1988), who presented correlational data that showed that among people who had been provided with sex education, abuse rates were considerably lower than for those who had not. Sex education, therefore, became identified as a key factor in the reduction of abuse.

Inappropriate Sexual Expression

It has been recognized that a lack of sexuality education not only leaves people with intellectual and developmental disabilities vulnerable to abuse but may also play a role in some socially inappropriate expressions of their own sexuality (Griffiths, Quinsey, & Hingsburger, 1989). However, even in cases in which the person may be exhibiting more severe socio-sexual behaviors of an offensive nature, for some individuals, sexual education may also, but not necessarily, be a component of treatment (Griffiths, Hingsburger, Hoath, & Ioannou, 2013). This topic is further discussed later in this chapter.

HIV and AIDS Awareness

The discovery of HIV and AIDS changed society's perspective on sex education. People with intellectual and developmental disabilities are typically presented with little information about HIV and/or AIDS or with methods to minimize their risk of contracting it (Groce et al., 2013). As previously noted, this may have been a result of the widespread belief that individuals with intellectual and developmental disabilities cannot and should not engage in sexual activity. Though this belief almost certainly played a role in the reluctance to provide education in the past, in some jurisdictions, agencies are becoming legally mandated to provide sexual education and opportunities in some areas (e.g., Ontario Ministry of Community and Social Services, 2011). Despite this advancement, many individuals with intellectual and developmental disabilities are engaging in sexual activity, a large number of whom may have received no education or safety skills regarding sexually transmitted infections.

Servais (2006) noted that emergence of AIDS among people with intellectual and developmental disabilities has heightened the need for preventive action in sexual health. Agencies are beginning to recognize the critical importance of evaluating and documenting the effectiveness of their educational programs and the need for accountability regarding the quality of sexuality education, and research shows that education can increase a person's ability to assume responsibility in making sexuality-related decisions (Dukes & McGuire, 2009). It is important to determine whether the individuals being supported have sufficient knowledge and appropriate attitudes regarding safer sex practices. Assessments such as the Socio-Sexual Knowledge and Attitudes Assessment Tool (Griffiths & Lunsky, 2003) can be helpful in evaluating the knowledge the person has regarding these practices and whether the steps for safe sex (i.e., putting on a condom) can be appropriately followed. All comprehensive socio-sexual education programs will address issues of education for individuals with developmental disabilities within the context of teaching generalized socio-sexual knowledge. In addition, programs such as that prepared by the Young Adult Institute (Jacobs, Samowitz, Levy, Levy, & Cabrera, 1992) provide comprehensive AIDS staff training.

Preventive Health Care

Preventive health care has become an emerging concern in general society. Recent initiatives on preventive health extend beyond simple education regarding hygiene to include routine health checks that previously were not commonly provided for people with intellectual and developmental disabilities, such as Pap smears or prostate-specific antigen tests (Robertson, Roberts, Emerson, Turner, & Greig, 2011). (For a comprehensive description of preventive health care for people with intellectual and developmental disabilities, see Servais, 2006.)

In socio-sexual education, *how* it is taught is as important as *what* is taught. Learning about one's sexuality does not take place in six 1-hour sessions, nor is it restricted to a single period in a person's life. It is a lifelong process. This means that people with intellectual and developmental disabilities, just like people without disabilities, will learn about sexuality throughout their lives. People need access to accurate information when it is age-appropriate and contextually relevant for them to know it. Parents and staff can capitalize on these moments to teach about different parts of sexuality. Examples of natural "teachable moments" for sexuality education are when children begin to ask questions about

their bodies, when they want to know where babies come from, or when they experience body changes during puberty.

In addition to these teachable moments, people who have intellectual and developmental disabilities benefit from formal socio-sexual education programs. Although most professionals agree that sex education should be provided for people with intellectual and developmental disabilities, there are several major challenges with the way in which socio-sexual education is provided. It is generally

- Provided sporadically or only in response to a problem

- Based upon educational programs that have very little, if any, empirical evidence of effectiveness

- Incomplete and fails to address the full range of topics to allow for a comprehensive understanding of sexuality (including narrow teaching such as abstinence being the only method for safe sex)

- Not evaluated for effectiveness, generalization, or transfer of skill to the person's life

Consequently, although there is significant consensus about the value of socio-sexual education, the practice of it often does not follow.

One of the questions often asked is, "Where do I find a good sex education training package?" Some excellent programs are available commercially. One of the most widely used is the Life Horizons I and II program by Winifred Kempton, which was first developed in 1988 and has been revised over the years. This program is very comprehensive and includes hundreds of slides to aid instruction. Winifred Kempton, one of the most important founding educators in this field, suggests that a good socio-sexual education program should include male and female anatomy, human reproduction, birth control, and sexual health (including safer sex practices). However, she also recommends that training should include the moral, social, and legal aspects of sexuality; male and female socio-sexual behavior; dating, parenting, and marriage; prevention of and coping with abuse; building self-esteem; and establishing relationships. A fundamental part of socio-sexual education is teaching that there are responsibilities that come with sexual expression, not the least of which is the topic of consent.

BIRTH CONTROL

Dating back to the early part of the 20th century, the topic of the sexuality of people with intellectual and developmental disabilities was dominated by a concern about procreation, so much so that during World War II, about 300,000 people with intellectual and developmental disabilities in Nazi-occupied countries underwent forced sterilization because of a fear of procreation (see Scheerenberger, 1987). Primarily for the same reason, forced sterilization occurred throughout other parts of the world, including in North America until the 1970s. Sterilization of people with intellectual and developmental disabilities was based on beliefs that arose from the eugenics movement—popular both in North America and in Europe—that "feeble-mindedness" was largely inherited. Since institutionalization was expensive, people with intellectual and developmental disabilities were often sterilized so that they could then be put to work in the community.

These eugenics-oriented beliefs have long been discredited. It has been known for some time that many disabilities are not linked to genetic factors. Nongenetic causes such as child maltreatment, infections, accident, injury, and fetal alcohol spectrum disorder and related conditions account for a considerable percentage of etiologies leading to intellectual and developmental disabilities. Even if a person with intellectual or developmental disabilities has a genetic condition, the gene may not be passed on to the next generation (e.g., recessive genes need to be paired with similar recessive genes), or, if a dominant gene created the disability, the chance of passing the disability to a child is still only 50% (see Chapter 10).

The right to procreate and parent has stirred heated debate in the field of intellectual and developmental disabilities. In Canada, during the 1970s, the case of Eve (Rioux & Yarmol, 1987) provided very clear consent guidelines for nontherapeutic sterilization. As of this writing in 2016, in Canada and in many states in the United States, parents do not have the right to consent to nontherapeutic sterilization for their child, whether an adult or a minor. For a person who has a developmental disability to give consent to nontherapeutic sterilization, the nature and consequences of consenting to the procedure must be established.

The right to procreate and raise children does not end with the topic of sterilization. Concern is often expressed about whether people with intellectual and developmental disabilities can be adequate parents. It is common for a parent who has intellectual or developmental disabilities to be subject to considerable scrutiny regarding his or her ability to raise a child. The decision to have a child carries with it great responsibility, and society upholds the belief that the rights of the child must supersede the rights of parents. Counseling and support is very often vital to help people with intellectual and developmental disabilities make the right decision for themselves and their future child (see Chapter 42).

SEXUAL DIVERSITY

People with intellectual and developmental disabilities exhibit the same range of sexual expression that occurs in the population of people without disabilities, including heterosexual, same-sex, and bisexual relationships; dating; petting; masturbation; premarital coitus; and marriage. Some people with intellectual and developmental disabilities may be limited in their sexual expression because of physical challenges, interest, or opportunity. However, many people with intellectual and developmental disabilities are also limited in their sexual expression by the environments in which they live and by the attitudes of caregivers and of society. A great number of people with intellectual and developmental disabilities live in sex-segregated environments where it is almost impossible to develop a heterosexual relationship. In some environments, there are severe restrictions on the sexual behavior of people with intellectual and developmental disabilities, and the rights of association or privacy that would be afforded to people without disabilities are denied. In addition, people with intellectual and developmental disabilities have been punished or even abused for expressing their sexuality. There have been instances of people with intellectual and developmental disabilities being beaten, drugged, or emotionally berated for engaging in sexual behavior. Inappropriate sexual behavior can develop as a result, as a means of adapting to an aberrant environment.

As with all people, people with intellectual and developmental disabilities may choose to express or not to express their sexuality in various ways, depending on their learning experiences, family values, or religious background. However, some people with intellectual and developmental disabilities have experienced very different learning histories with regard to their sexuality. They may have been sheltered from sexual knowledge and typical experiences that would assist them in developing a healthy understanding of their sexuality.

Inappropriate sexual behavior can sometimes develop as a result of a lack of sexual knowledge and understanding and a lack of opportunity to engage in appropriate sexual expression. People with intellectual and developmental disabilities do not inherently have more unusual or inappropriate sexual behavior than people without disabilities, but it is common for them to encounter very different learning experiences about their sexuality. For this reason, they have sometimes learned unusual or inappropriate sexual behaviors through atypical life and learning experiences such as abuse and institutional living.

The importance of determining the reasons for the expression of an inappropriate sexual behavior—be it inappropriate learning experiences, a lack of education, a paraphilia (i.e., sexual diagnosis of deviance), or other factor (Griffiths et al., 2013)—must be recognized. Such a differential diagnosis of the reason for or function of the behavior serves as a basis for determining treatment. This consideration has important clinical implications related to the sexual diversity of people with intellectual and developmental disabilities.

SEXUAL VICTIMIZATION

Research has provided convincing evidence that the sexual abuse of people with intellectual and developmental disabilities is widespread and more common than for people without disabilities (Horner-Johnson & Drum, 2006; McEachern, 2012). It has been suggested that people with intellectual and developmental disabilities are two and a half times more likely to be sexually abused than people without disabilities (Lin, Yen, Kuo, Wu, & Lin, 2009). In a study of sexual abuse victims with intellectual and developmental disabilities, Cambridge et al. (2011) reported that 31% of victims were male and 68.8% were female; he also noted that perpetrators tended to be male (91.4%) and, most often, another person with intellectual and developmental disabilities (51.6%) or a family member or staff person (41.3%). These offenses frequently occurred in the residential environment of the person with intellectual and developmental disabilities.

The increased vulnerability to abuse of people with intellectual and developmental disabilities is not related directly to the nature of the person's disability. Rather, abuse is more likely to occur because of the way society treats and views people with intellectual and developmental disabilities and their sexuality and because of the systems in which people with intellectual and developmental disabilities live. In these systems, people with intellectual and developmental disabilities have little or no power, choice, or control over many aspects of their lives. Theorists believe that there is a need for a multidimensional approach to the reduction of abuse of people with intellectual and developmental disabilities (McEachern, 2012) that includes changing systems in terms of policy, screening staff, individual empowerment, addressing attitudes that dehumanize people with disabilities, and providing education about healthy boundaries and assertiveness skills for staff and for individuals who have intellectual and developmental disabilities.

TREATMENT AND COUNSELING

Until the 1980s, it was widely assumed that people with intellectual and developmental disabilities would not benefit from insight-oriented counseling or treatment for sexual issues. Since then, however, these therapies have been adapted in keeping with the cognitive abilities of people with intellectual and developmental disabilities and, as such, have gained utility in the field. The two primary areas of counseling and treatment of sexually related issues are victim (survivor) counseling and treatment of inappropriate sexual behavior.

Victim (Survivor) Counseling

Although people with intellectual and developmental disabilities have been sexually abused at higher rates than people without disabilities, until the 1980s, their access to appropriate supports and counseling services has been largely absent. A body of literature has been developed to help clinicians who work with sexual abuse survivors who have adapted their counseling procedures to support people who have intellectual or developmental disabilities. One of the foundational contributions to the field was the book *Counseling People with Developmental Disabilities Who Have Been Sexually Abused* and a training video, *Alone in a Crowd,* created by two of the leaders in this field (Mansell & Sobsey, 2001a, 2001b).

Treatment of Sexually Inappropriate Behavior

People with intellectual and developmental disabilities do not demonstrate any more sexually inappropriate behavior than people without disabilities if they are provided with a normative learning experience. However, the sexual learning experience of many people with intellectual and developmental disabilities has often been anything but normative. The nature of the offenses committed by people with intellectual and developmental disabilities includes the same range seen in the general population. Although more serious offenses do occur with some individuals, many of the offenses tend to be more inappropriate behaviors such as public masturbation rather than serious sexual violations.

The more serious offenses are categorized in the *Diagnostic and Statistical Manual of Mental Disorders, Fifth Edition* (*DSM-5;* American Psychiatric Association, 2013), as paraphilia, which is "any intense and persistent sexual interest other than sexual interest in genital stimulation or preparatory fondling with phenotypically normal, physically mature, consenting human partners" (p. 685). The group of disorders under paraphilia includes atypical activity preferences, which are subdivided into courtship disorders and sexual pleasure that involves inflicting pain and suffering. The second group of disorders involves unusual target preferences and can include sexual interest in children or objects (American Psychiatric Association, 2013). However, when assessing paraphilia in people with intellectual and developmental disabilities, it is vital to explore both the environmental and learning contexts and the experiential and medical factors in order to rule out that the person has engaged in the behavior because of "counterfeit deviance" (Fletcher, Loschen, Stavrakaki, & First, 2007; Griffiths et al., 2013). Individuals with intellectual and developmental disabilities can possess and display deviant sexual interests. These offenders can have inappropriate sexual interests based on age, coercion, or sadism. Their offenses can be contact based and even violent in nature. However, given

the unique history and circumstances of many in this population, counterfeit deviance should first be explored and can help to explain some nondeviant contributors to sexual offending.

Since the end of the 20th century, an increasingly rich body of clinical literature on intervention has emerged (see Griffiths, 2002). Based on a growing body of clinical experience, specialized treatment providers have reported that sexual problems of people with intellectual and developmental disabilities, particularly people with mild and moderate levels of disability, have been surprisingly responsive to treatment (Lambrick & Glaser, 2004). Treatment focus often involves teaching and reinforcing alternative replacement, altering the conditions sustaining the behavior, and the judicious use of medication or hormonal therapy, if appropriate (Griffiths, Richards, Federoff et al., 2002), self-regulation training (Langdon, Maxted, Murphy, & Group, 2007), and a combination of targeted therapies (Lindsay, Hasting, Griffiths, & Hayes, 2007). However, determining the components of treatment first requires a thorough assessment. Understanding the precipitating factors and "vulnerabilities" (Nezu, Greenberg, & Nezu, 2005) that are associated with the challenging sexual behavior and the potential risk for a reoffense is necessary in order for the treatment team to determine not only the approach to treatment but also the nature of the environment and the level of restrictions and supervision needed (Camilleri & Quinsey, 2011).

The self-regulation model of sex offender treatment (Ward & Hudson, 1998; Ward & Stewart, 2003) arose from the previous widespread use of relapse prevention. It has gained momentum and is intuitively more practical and more adaptable than relapse prevention. The self-regulation model suggests that offenders follow specific pathways to their offenses; these pathways are based on a combination of the offender's goals (approach or avoidant) and the strategies used to obtain that goal (passive or active). It would be natural to assume that offenders with intellectual and developmental disabilities do not plan their offenses but rather that they are the product of mistakes or impulsivity. These pathways would presumably be avoidant based or, if approach based, passive in nature. A 2006 study by Keeling, Rose, and Beech determined that 94% of participants in their study demonstrated approach-based offenses; in fact, 31% of offenders were approach-explicit, indicating a degree of planning and premeditation. The remainder of the participants represented approach-automatic offenders; they had goals to reoffend, were impulsive, and only utilized basic strategies or enacted behavioral schemas. Though research is preliminary, there is a great deal of promise in adapting this model for people with intellectual and developmental disabilities who offend (Keeling et al., 2006; Langdon et al., 2007).

In a study examining types of community settings that support people with intellectual and developmental disabilities who had offended, Ioannou, Griffiths, Owen, Condillac, and Wilson (2014) noted that there was great diversity in the community support homes. Some homes focused more on ensuring that risks were minimized; other homes, operating as more typical group homes, were concerned with how to provide support for an offender without violation of the person's rights. The critical issue that must be addressed in providing community support is to ensure that the risks and rights are balanced by the agency to ensure that there is responsible support to meet the level of needs of the individual. Where risk is greater, the responsibility of the agency must lean more toward protecting others; where risk is less, the responsibility of the agency can lean more toward ensuring that maximum rights are preserved (Ioannou et al., 2014). Assessment of the nature and function of the offense, and the individual's response to treatment, is the only way to be able to address where the needs of the individual and the responsibility of the agency fall.

Specialized treatment for people with dual diagnoses (i.e., mental health needs and intellectual disability) is, however, not available in all geographical areas and often requires coordination with generic mental health and correctional resources that may be reluctant or ill-informed to adapt resources for this population (see Griffiths, Stavrakaki, & Summers, 2002). In addition, special expertise in working with people with intellectual and developmental disabilities who have sexuality issues is even rarer. In many cases, it is necessary to work in an interdisciplinary manner using both experts in sexual challenges and experts in dual diagnosis. Where not readily available, creative options to gain appropriate assessments are vital if service providers are to understand the nature of the offending behavior and provide appropriate community supports that match the needs of the person with intellectual and developmental disabilities

who has sexually offended and to be responsible to the community.

SUMMARY

It is important to dispel the seven myths about the sexuality of people with intellectual and developmental disabilities described in Table 41.1, as these myths continue to influence how some people in society treat people with intellectual and developmental disabilities with respect to their sexuality. Available research and clinical evidence contradicts the myths, demonstrating that people with intellectual and developmental disabilities are sexual people and, like people without disabilities, need knowledge and a normal learning environment to understand and learn to act responsibly on their natural feelings.

FOR FURTHER THOUGHT AND DISCUSSION

1. Consider the discussion of the policy commitments that schools should make to create a positive atmosphere in which to teach appropriate and responsible socio-sexual behaviors. What barriers exist to establishing such practices? How might these barriers be overcome?

2. People with intellectual and developmental disabilities are at greater risk than other people for abuse, including sexual abuse. What could be done to reduce that risk? Consider both what the person with intellectual or developmental disability might do as well as what others need to do.

3. Discuss the overlap between health care and sexuality. How might strategies such as preventive health care affect sexuality education?

4. Issues pertaining to human sexuality, including sexual diversity, are often controversial, and yet people across sexual orientations are gaining greater equal rights and protections. To what degree are people with intellectual disability allowed to express their sexuality in various ways? What barriers exist to this? How can such barriers be removed?

REFERENCES

American Psychiatric Association. (2013). *Diagnostic and statistical manual of mental disorders*, (5th ed.). Washington, DC: Author.

Cambridge, P., Beadle-Brown, J., Milne, A., Mansell, J., & Whelton, B. (2011). Patterns of risk in adult protection referrals for sexual abuse and people with intellectual disability. *Journal of Applied Research in Intellectual Disabilities, 24*(2), 118–132.

Camilleri, J.A., & Quinsey, V.L. (2011). Appraising the risk of sexual and violent recidivism among intellectually disabled offenders. *Psychology, Crime and Law, 17*(1), 59–74.

Canadian Charter of Rights and Freedoms, Constitution Act (1982[1]) Schedule B, Part 1.

Day, K. (1994). Male, mentally-handicapped sex offenders. *British Journal of Psychiatry, 165,* 630–639.

Dukes, E., & McGuire, B.E. (2009). Enhancing capacity to make sexuality-related decisions in people with an intellectual disability. *Journal of Intellectual Disability Research, 53*(8), 727–734.

Evans, D.S., McGuire, B.E., Healy, E., & Carley, S.N. (2009). Sexuality and personal relationships for people with an intellectual disability. Part II: Staff and family carer perspectives. *Journal of Intellectual Disability Research, 53*(11), 913–921.

Finkelhor, D. (2009). The prevention of childhood sexual abuse. *The Future of Children, 19*(2), 169–194.

Fletcher, R., Loschen, E., Stavrakaki, C., & First, M. (2007). *Diagnostic manual—intellectual disability.* Kingston, NY: NADD.

Griffiths, D. (1991, May). *Myths and mythconceptions. Panel on sexuality and mental retardation—a glance at the present and a view to the future.* Panel discussion at the Annual Meeting of the American Association on Mental Retardation, Washington, DC.

Griffiths, D. (2002). Sexual aggression. In W.I. Gardner (Ed.), *Aggression and persons with developmental disabilities* (pp. 325–386). Kingston, NY: NADD.

Griffiths, D. (2003). Sexuality and people who have developmental disabilities: From myths to emerging practices. In I. Brown & M. Percy (Eds.), *Developmental disabilities in Ontario* (2nd ed., pp. 677–689). Toronto, Canada: Ontario Association on Developmental Disabilities.

Griffiths, D., Hingsburger, D., Hoath, J., & Ioannou, S. (2013). Counterfeit deviance revisited [Special issue: Pathways, assessment and treatment of offenders with intellectual disability]. *Journal of Applied Research in Intellectual Disabilities, 26*(5), 471–480. doi:10.1111/jar.12034

Griffiths, D., & Lunsky, Y. (2000). Changing attitudes towards the nature of socio-sexual assessment and education for persons with developmental disabilities: A twenty-year comparison. *Journal of Developmental Disabilities, 7,* 16–33.

Griffiths, D., & Lunsky, Y. (2003). *Socio-Sexual Knowledge and Attitudes Assessment Tool–Revised (SSKAAT-R).* Wood Dale, IL: Stoelting.

Griffiths, D., Quinsey, V.L., & Hingsburger, D. (1989). *Changing inappropriate sexual behavior: A community-based approach for persons with developmental disorders.* Baltimore, MD: Paul H. Brookes Publishing Co.

Griffiths, D.M., Richards, D., Federoff, P., & Watson, S.L. (Eds.). (2002). *Ethical dilemmas: Sexuality and developmental disabilities.* Kingston, NY: NADD.

Griffiths, D.M., Stavrakaki, C., & Summers, J. (Eds.). (2002). *Dual diagnosis—An introduction to the mental health needs of persons with developmental disabilities.* Sudbury, Canada: Habilitative Mental Health Resource Network.

Groce, N.E., Rohleder, P., Eide, A.H., MacLachlan, M., Mall, S., & Swartz, L. (2013). HIV issues and people with disabilities: A review and agenda for research. *Social Science and Medicine, 77,* 31–40.

Horner-Johnson, W., & Drum, C.E. (2006).Prevalence of maltreatment of people with intellectual disabilities: A review of recently published research. *Mental Retardation and Developmental Disabilities Research Reviews, 12,* 57–69.

Ioannou, S., Griffiths, D., Owen, F., Condillac, R., & Wilson, R.J. (2014). Managing risk in a culture of rights: Providing support and treatment in community-based settings for persons with intellectual disabilities who sexually offend. *ATSA Forum, 26*(1). Retrieved from http://newsmanager.commpartners.com/atsa/issues/2014-02-11/4.html

Jacobs, R., Samowitz, P., Levy, P.H., Levy, J.M., & Cabrera, G.A. (1992). Young Adult Institute's comprehensive AIDS staff training program. In A.C. Crocker, H.J. Cohen, & T.A. Kastner (Eds.), *HIV infection and developmental disabilities: A resource for service providers* (pp. 161–169). Baltimore, MD: Paul H. Brookes Publishing Co.

Johnson, P.R., & Davies, R. (1989). Sexual attitudes of members of staff. *British Journal of Mental Subnormality, 35,* 17–21.

Keeling, J.A., Rose, J.L., & Beech, A.R. (2006). A comparison of the application of the self-regulation model of the relapse process for mainstream and special needs sexual offenders. *Sexual Abuse: A Journal of Research and Treatment, 18*(4), 373–382.

Kempton, W. (1988). *Life Horizons I and II.* Santa Barbara, CA: James Stanfield Publishing.

Lambrick, F., & Glaser, W. (2004). Sex offenders with an intellectual disability. *Sexual Abuse: A Journal of Research and Treatment, 16*(4), 381–392.

Langdon, P.E., Maxted, H., Murphy, G.H., & Group, S.I. (2007). An exploratory evaluation of the Ward and Hudson Offending Pathways model with offenders who have intellectual disability. *Journal of Intellectual and Developmental Disability, 32*(2), 94–105.

Lin, L.P., Yen, C.F., Kuo, F.Y., Wu, J.L., & Lin, J.D. (2009). Sexual assault of people with disabilities: Results of a 2002–2007 national report in Taiwan. *Research in Developmental Disabilities, 30*(5), 969–975.

Lindsay, W.R., Hasting, R.P., Griffiths, D.M., & Hayes, S.C. (2007). Trends and challenges in forensic research on offenders with intellectual disability. *Journal of Intellectual and Developmental Disability, 32*(2), 55–61.

Löfgren-Mårtenson, L. (2009). The invisibility of young homosexual women and men with intellectual disabilities. *Sexuality and Disability, 27*(1), 21–26.

Mansell, S., & Sobsey, D. (2001a). *Alone in a crowd* [Video]. Kingston, NY: NADD.

Mansell, S., & Sobsey, D. (2001b). *Counselling people with developmental disabilities who have been sexually abused.* Kingston, NY: NADD.

McEachern, A.G. (2012). Sexual abuse of individuals with disabilities: Prevention strategies for clinical practice. *Journal of Child Sexual Abuse, 21,* 386–398.

Nezu, C., Greenberg, J., & Nezu, A.M. (2005). Project STOP: Cognitive behavioral assessment and treatment for sex offenders with intellectual disability. *International Journal of Behavioral Consultation and Therapy, 1*(3), 191–203.

Ontario Ministry of Community and Social Services (2011). *A guide to the regulation of Quality Assurance Measures.* Retrieved from http://www.mcss.gov.on.ca/en/mcss/publications/developmentalServices/guide_regulation_qualityassurance.aspx

Rehabilitation Act of 1973, PL 93-112, 29 U.S.C. §§ 701 *et seq.*

Rioux, M. (1996, Summer). Reproductive technology: A rights issue. *Entourage,* 5–7.

Rioux, M., & Yarmol, K. (1987, Winter). The right to control one's own body: A look at the "Eve" decision. *Entourage,* 28–30.

Robertson, J., Roberts, H., Emerson, E., Turner, S., & Greig, R. (2011). The impact of health checks for people with intellectual disabilities: A systemic review of evidence. *Journal of Intellectual Disability Research, 55*(11), 1009–1019.

Roeher Institute (1988). *Vulnerable.* Toronto, Canada: Author.

Scheerenberger, R.C. (1987). *A history of mental retardation: A quarter century of promise.* Baltimore, MD: Paul H. Brookes Publishing Co.

Servais, L. (2006). Sexual health care in persons with intellectual disabilities. *Mental Retardation and Developmental Disabilities Research Reviews, 12*(1), 48–56. doi:10.1002/mrdd.20093

Swango-Wilson, A. (2011). Meaningful sex education programs for individuals with intellectual/developmental disabilities. *Sexuality and Disability, 29,* 113–118.

United Nations. (1971). *Declaration on the rights of mentally retarded persons.* New York, NY: Author.

United Nations. (2006). *Convention on the rights of persons with disabilities.* Retrieved from http://www.un.org/disabilities/convention/conventionfull.shtml

Ward, T., & Hudson, S.M. (1998). A model of the relapse process in sexual offenders. *Journal of Interpersonal Violence, 13*(6), 700–725.

Ward, T., & Stewart, C.A. (2003). The treatment of sex offenders: Risk management and good lives. *Professional Psychology: Research and Practice, 34*(4), 353.

42

Parenting by People with Intellectual Disability

Marjorie Aunos, Maurice Feldman, Ella Callow, Traci LaLiberte, and Elizabeth Lightfoot

WHAT YOU WILL LEARN

- Challenges that people with intellectual disability face as parents
- Factors that influence parenting by people with intellectual disability
- Key elements of best practices in supports and services for families headed by people with intellectual disability

Ms. Smith is a 35-year-old single mother of four children ages 6 to 11 years. She has mild intellectual disability and attended special education classes when she was in school. Three of her children live in foster care because there were concerns about possible neglect. Ms. Smith's father (the children's grandfather) has custody of the fourth child. Ms. Smith is seen as having difficulties implementing discipline strategies with her preteen children. Furthermore, Ms. Smith has been described by a parenting capacity assessment as not having the capacity to parent her children due to her cognitive limitations. The assumption of parenting inadequacy is based primarily on her lower intellectual functioning label. Her case record in the child welfare system does not report any direct evidence of child maltreatment, a situation that is quite common concerning parents with intellectual disability.

Since the 1970s, researchers have studied parents like Ms. Smith, looking at their capacity and ability to parent and at assessment, support needs, interventions, and at other variables influencing their parenting abilities and child and family

outcomes (McConnell, 2008). Subsequent disability laws, statutes, and conventions (e.g., Pan-American Health Organization and World Health Organization, 2004; United Nations, 1989, 2006) have begun to recognize the parenting rights of people with disabilities and the need to provide services to preserve their families. Despite the equal rights movement and the wealth of research-based knowledge regarding effective services and supports, the child welfare system in many jurisdictions still routinely removes the children of parents with intellectual disability (McConnell, Feldman, Aunos, & Prasad, 2010). This chapter presents characteristics of families headed by parents with intellectual disability, highlights the overall challenges these parents face, presents a model for understanding factors that influence parenting by people with intellectual disability, and discusses key elements of best practices in supports and services for families headed by people with intellectual disability.

PARENTS WITH INTELLECTUAL DISABILITY

Researchers and clinicians have thoroughly looked at people with intellectual disabilities since the 1970s. Due to those studies, we are now able to trace a portrait of who most parents with intellectual disability are and what incredible odds they have to face.

Prevalence

As social attitudes and practices toward people with disabilities evolved during the 20th century, from institutionalization and compulsory sterilization toward a more community-based approach, the number of people with intellectual or developmental disabilities becoming parents increased (Llewellyn, 1990; Swain & Cameron, 2003). Unfortunately, despite these growing numbers, there is still somewhat limited knowledge on the prevalence of parents with disabilities for a variety of reasons, such as the lack of a common definition of disability used by agencies and the lack of administrative data on parents with disabilities (Llewellyn; McConnell & Llewellyn, 2002).

The most comprehensive data on prevalence of parents with intellectual and/or developmental disabilities come from the somewhat dated National Health Interview Survey-Disability Survey conducted by four federal agencies in the United States during 1994–1995. According to these data, in 1994–1995 an estimated 174,310 mothers with intellectual and/or developmental disabilities in the United States were living with children younger than 18 years (Anderson, Byun, Larson, & Lakin, 2005). Of these women, about 43,953 had intellectual disability, 49,719 had developmental disabilities, and 80,638 had both intellectual and developmental disabilities. Some newer population-based data analysis in the United States has estimated that less than 1% of all deliveries in 2010 were from women with intellectual disability (Parish, Mitra, Son, Bonardi, & Swoboda, 2014). A secondary analysis of the Canadian National Longitudinal Survey of Children and Youth identified 5% of parents as having a disability, not specific to intellectual disability (Hyun, Hahn, & McConnell, 2014). As researchers are better able to tap into those longitudinal population databases, it can be assumed that there will be a more accurate prevalence rate of children born to parents with intellectual disability.

As more people with intellectual disability have become parents, there has been a growing interest in their involvement with the child welfare system. It is clear that many countries still have policies and practices that might unfairly affect parents with disabilities (Lightfoot, Hill, & LaLiberte, 2010), but only since about 2006 has there been any comprehensive prevalence data that demonstrates how parents with disabilities are disproportionally represented in the child welfare system. The most comprehensive and recent data examining the prevalence of parents with disabilities in the child welfare system comes from Canada. Analysis

of data from the Canadian Incidence Study of Reported Child Abuse and Neglect (McConnell, Feldman et al., 2011) found that although parents with intellectual disability represent less than 3% of the general Canadian population, they comprise more than 10% of child maltreatment investigation reports. National-level data are not available in the United States, but risk ratios for parents with disability being involved in child welfare have been calculated using state administrative data from Minnesota. These risk ratios show that parents with a disability in the state of Minnesota were two times more likely than their peers without a disability label to experience child welfare involvement (LaLiberte, Lightfoot, Singh, Piescher, & Hong, 2012). It was further determined in that study that parents with disabilities were more than three times likely to experience a termination of their parental rights once involved with the child welfare system.

Characteristics

People with intellectual disability have, by definition, some cognitive limitations. International research over many years has also demonstrated that parents with intellectual disability often have incomes below the poverty line, seldom work, display a higher proportion of mental health issues (e.g., depression), experience high levels of stress related to their parenting role, and have poorer health in general (Feldman, Léger, & Walton-Allen, 1997; Hindmarsh, Llewellyn & Emerson, 2015). Most research conducted on mothers with intellectual disability finds that they are socially isolated with limited "informal" support (Feldman, Varghese, Ramsay, & Rajska, 2002). Too often, these mothers have been abused at a young age and continue to be exploited. A more recent study shows that mothers with intellectual disability are younger, less likely to be married, and more likely to smoke than mothers without intellectual disability (Hindmarsh et al., 2015.)

Research on pregnancy and postnatal outcomes show that women with intellectual disability are more likely to receive inadequate prenatal care; have early labor, preterm birth, or health issues such as preeclampsia; and deliver their children via cesarean section and consequently have longer hospital stays. More of their children are of low birth weight and are at higher risk of developing long-term health problems and developmental delays due to these pre- and postnatal issues (Hoglund, Lindgren, & Larsson, 2012; Mayes, Llewellyn, & McConnell, 2006; Mitra, Parish, Cui, & Diop, 2014; Parish et al., 2014).

The risk factors associated with these families are well known, with poverty and living conditions explaining only 50% of the prevalence of poorer mental health in the mothers and a higher risk for developmental or speech delays in the children (Emerson & Brigham, 2013, 2014).

CHALLENGES AND BARRIERS

All parents need support in their parenting at one time or another. Parents with intellectual disability may require additional or specialized training and support in order to parent effectively. Many barriers can make it difficult for them to receive the supports they need, however. Without appropriate supports, these parents may face severe consequences, which may include losing custody of their children.

Child Custody Litigation and Parents with Intellectual Disability

Parents with intellectual disability face significant challenges with serious consequences when they become involved in child custody litigation. Although exact structures vary by nation, there are commonalities in custody litigation systems in many Western nations, especially between Canada and the United States. It is important that professionals working with these families understand the basics of these systems (see the Basic Structure for Child Custody Litigation discussion) and the barriers they contain for parents with intellectual disability. In either type of litigation discussed in the box, parents with intellectual disability face barriers to retaining custody of their children.

Attitudinal Bias Defined loosely as a general belief in the pathology of people with disabilities, attitudinal bias remains prevalent (Kirshbaum, Taube, & Lasian Baer, 2003). Attitudinal bias leads to speculation by neighbors, family members, social service workers, educators, and health practitioners that a parent with intellectual disability cannot provide adequate and safe child care. Attitudinal bias is often caused by general misconceptions that people with intellectual disability 1) are incapable of providing adequate child care, 2) cannot benefit from parent training, and 3) will have children who also have disabilities (Aunos & Feldman, 2002; Espe-Sherwindt & Kerlin, 1990).

Those attitudinal biases can be the trigger for the state or another parent or family member to begin a child custody case. Once a case begins, professionals involved in custody cases (e.g., social

---

Basic Structure for Child Custody Litigation

There are primarily two types of court action that can result in a loss of child custody: 1) child welfare cases (called children in need cases in Canada and dependency cases in the United States) occurring in child welfare courts and 2) family court cases occurring in family courts.

Child welfare court cases involve the state seeking to remove, take jurisdiction over, and/or terminate parental rights to a child. These cases can be brought to court because states are in charge of protecting children and at times need to use the court process to do so. Because parenting is a fundamental civil and human right, the general rule is that the state must show the parent is unfit to care for the child and provide a procedure by which a parent can challenge the loss of his or her child (Canadian Children and Family Services Act, 1990; Watkins, 1995).

Family or divorce court cases involve two parents, or a parent and a family member, who are contesting the custody of a child. These cases can be brought by parents and family members because the state has authority to resolve disputes when a parent or family member requests such resolution via the filing of formal papers with the court. Because the state is not a party seeking jurisdiction or custody of the child, the standard is different from that in child welfare cases. Typically, courts consider which adult can best support the health, education, and welfare of the child and will determine that placement with this adult is in the best interest of the child.

Sources: Kohm (2008) and Northwest Territories Justice (2014).

workers, officers of the court, and legal and mental health professionals) are expected to participate in its fair adjudication. However, they often carry the same attitudinal bias as the society in general and may alter the outcome of the case through expressions of attitudinal bias within the process (Callow, Buckland, & Jones, 2011).

Following child custody litigations, the parenting rights of people with intellectual disability are too often terminated because of concerns about their capacity to raise children, often in the absence of factual evidence of abuse or neglect (Feldman & Aunos, 2010; McConnell, Feldman et al., 2010; McConnell, Llewellyn, & Ferronato, 2003). The unjustifiable severance of family ties raises ethical and legal concerns regarding the rights of individuals. In many cases, there is a negative impact on the children's development (Aunos & Feldman, 2008), especially if children grow up in state care where a stable family home is not provided. The unimaginable grief caused for the parents and the impact of family separation may have a profound effect on parents' and children's mental health (Booth & Booth, 2005; Mayes & Llewellyn, 2009). Although these consequences are known, only limited services are available to support many parents with intellectual disability and, in situations where family separation does occur, only limited counseling is available to parents following the loss of their child (Janeslätt, Springer, & Adolfsson, 2014; Tarleton, Ward, & Howarth, 2006).

Lack of Meaningful Participation Parents with intellectual disability particularly struggle with the high-level, formal language used in court case proceedings, the rapid pace of court and other formal hearings or meetings, and the requirement for quick processing of verbal or written information and decision making (National Council on Disability, 2012). While involved in a child welfare case, parents typically have access to an attorney for some portion of the case; however, in family law cases they often proceed in propria persona (i.e., they are self-represented). This particularly is a disadvantage to those with intellectual disability (National Council on Disability, 2012).

Meaningful participation also refers to the type of services parents received. Services that are not adapted to their cognitive strengths or pace of learning will not support parents and may have a negative impact on their self-esteem and self-confidence.

Parents with intellectual disability do not usually like to admit when they do not understand and thus, more often than not, try to hide their disability (Feldman & Aunos, 2010). This strategy can backfire when, in obvious need of support, the parents claim that they will do fine on their own.

Lack of Awareness or Knowledge Regarding Proper Services Adapted services for parents with intellectual disability can be used by professionals to determine the individual's true capacity to parent. As seen later in this chapter, such adapted services have unique elements. However, most social service and legal professionals are not educated or trained regarding these critical services (Callow, 2013a; Lightfoot & LaLiberte, 2006); even disability studies programs fail to provide coursework on this important issue (Callow & Miller, 2013). Attorneys infrequently request these services or challenge the court's reliance on unadapted and inappropriate evaluations, services, and/or interventions (Aunos & Feldman, 2007; Callow, Buckland et al., 2011).

Lack of Awareness or Knowledge Regarding Disabilities and Appropriate Adaptations Too often, disability, child welfare, and other family support professionals—and the systems within which they work—hold such misconceptions due to their little experience supporting families in which the parents have intellectual disability. They might have limited knowledge about disabilities in general, and their education and training might not have included any information about providing accommodations or supports to people with disabilities or introduced them to disability resources within their region (Lightfoot & LaLiberte, 2006).

Other professionals involved in the litigation process may also have limited understanding of how to use mediation services or represent parents with intellectual disability in court. They might fail to make use of informal supports and other resources, or they may simply work within a system that does not include needed services for parents with intellectual disability (McConnell, Feldman et al., 2011). They also may be located in a region with few service providers within driving distance (Lightfoot & LaLiberte, 2006). As a consequence, many parents with intellectual disability are not provided with the supports and resources they require, and some are not even given an opportunity to parent.

There are additional policies and practices that make parents with intellectual disability at a heightened risk to face termination of parental rights. Parents with disabilities often receive services and supports from a variety of providers who are mandated reporters of suspected child abuse or neglect. This increased scrutiny, particularly by people who might not have much experience with parents with intellectual disability, could lead to increased reports of maltreatment. It also creates a climate of mistrust between the worker and the parent.

Complex Legal Framework   Child custody litigation is seen as being squarely within the jurisdiction of the state, province, or territory in which the child resides (e.g., Uniform Child Custody Jurisdiction and Enforcement Act of 1997 [Blumberg, 2014], Divorce Act [Canada], 1985). However, when a parent has a disability, there are also the same or higher level laws relating to disability rights that either intersect, supersede, or inform these provincial, territorial, or state laws (i.e., Americans with Disabilities Act [ADA] of 1990 [PL 101-336]; Canadian Charter of Rights and Freedoms/Constitution Act, 1982). The result is a complex legal matrix.

For example, in the United States, each state makes its own laws regarding child custody. However, at the federal level, the ADA applies to all states and requires that child welfare agencies and courts refrain from discriminating against people with disabilities, provide accommodations in services, and ensure the opportunity for participation (Margolin, 2007). Courts have reached different conclusions as to what this means substantively and procedurally in cases involving parental disability and, as a result, cases with the same facts can be decided differently depending on the state in which the family lives.

Although there have been calls to change these state laws (National Council on Disability, 2012), many parents with intellectual disability can face a child welfare and court system that views parental disability in itself as a risk for child maltreatment.

Parents with Intellectual Disability in Indigenous Communities

Due to the history of colonization and oppression of indigenous peoples in Canada, the United States, Australia, and New Zealand, loss of child custody due to parental disability has a disparate and alarming effect on those communities to this day.

Indigenous people have the highest rates of disability in each of these nations by a significant margin (United Nations, 2014). They also share a history of state programs designed explicitly to remove indigenous children from their families and communities for political or philosophical reasons (Brown, Limb, Chance, & Munoz, 2002; Sinha & Kozlowski, 2013).

Although some nations, including Canada and the United States, have passed remedial legislation to attempt to address this dark history, indigenous children remain vastly overrepresented in the child welfare systems of both nations (Child Welfare Information Gateway, 2011; Sinha & Kozlowski, 2013). Review of 17 U.S. states reporting to the National Child Abuse and Neglect Data System revealed a 26.5% rate of disability among indigenous caregivers from whom the child welfare system removed children (Callow, 2013b; Callow, Gemmill, Jacob, & Riley, 2011).

More research is needed examining the intersection of parental disability and involvement in child welfare cases in indigenous communities where both disability and child welfare involvement rates are elevated. In the meantime, professionals working within these communities should keep in mind the history of child custody loss and strive to ensure that disability in a parent is not used as an "end run" around the remedial legislation and policy designed to protect indigenous communities.

FACTORS INFLUENCING PARENTING

Parenting is difficult to define, as it encompasses many different skills and sets of abilities. Parenting is also affected by different variables that rise from parents themselves—by their pasts, by their interactions with others who are involved in the parenting of a child, and by characteristics of the environment. Many studies in this field have tried to look at what variables influence (or do not influence) parenting by people with intellectual disabilities.

Intelligence Quotient and Parenting

In the first half of the 20th century, eugenicist policies struck preemptively at parenting by people with intellectual and other disabilities in the form of sterilization and institutionalization (Silver, 2004). These policies were viewed as being in the best interest of society (Lombardo, 1996), an effective way to "deny parenthood to the manifestly unfit" (Humphrey, 1920, p. 231). IQ testing was viewed and used as a scientific means to determine candidacy for involuntarily sterilization (Leslie-Miller, 1997). This era resulted in the involuntary sterilization of tens of thousands of people and, due to racism, had a disparate impact in communities of color (Gallagher, 1994).

However, since the 1970s, reliance on IQ in legal proceedings involving significant rights has largely fallen from favor. The Canadian Supreme Court banned the sterilization of people with intellectual disability in *E. (Mrs.) v. Eve* (1986), and the practice was largely eradicated throughout the United States during the 1970–1980s (Smith, 1988). In 2014, IQ testing was found to be unreliable as used to determine intellectual capacity in death penalty cases in the United States (*Hall v. Florida,* 2014).

In contrast, and in clear corollary to the history we reviewed previously, the one legal venue in which eugenics theory continues to thrive is child custody litigation involving parents with intellectual disability. In a pilot study examining 50 appellate-court-level or higher cases in Canada and the United States, researchers found that IQ was treated as a significant evidentiary element in a vast majority of cases when parents had intellectual disability and were appealing the termination of their parental rights by a lower court (Callow, Feldman, & Tahir, 2014). Within the sample, 78% of courts referenced the evidence of parental IQ and 66% took time to discuss a specific IQ score; 96% of the time, the appellate court upheld the termination of the parenting rights of the person with intellectual disability despite the fact that 69% of the parents had IQ scores that were borderline or mild (between 55 and 84) (Callow et al., 2014). While there are yet no similar data for family courts, there is little reason to believe that the family courts approach IQ testing differently.

Parenting Models

The belief in and reliance on IQ as a scientific predictor of parenting capacity seems to be still well in use in custody and child welfare cases, despite the fact that international research has largely debunked this theory. This method for prediction of parenting capacity can then be properly termed pseudo-scientific (Faigman, Monahan, & Slobogin, 2014), as research continues to demonstrate that other variables have a stronger effect on parenting than IQ per se (Feldman & Aunos, 2010; McGaw, Scully, & Pritchard, 2010; Spencer, 2001). This simplistic, univariate model has been replaced by more sophisticated multivariate, contextual parenting models that examine the interaction of internal and external variables that could affect parenting abilities and child outcomes.

Feldman (2002) proposed an interactional model that extended to parents with intellectual disability the complex, empirically supported, ecological parenting models from the general parenting literature (Belsky, 1984; Bronfenbrenner, 1979; Sameroff & Chandler, 1975). Figure 42.1 presents a modified version of Feldman's (2002) original interactional model that illustrates the complex interrelationships of a host of factors that need to be considered when trying to understand and assess parenting and child issues (Feldman & Aunos, 2010). When Feldman first proposed this parenting model, many of the relationships depicted were supported in the general parenting literature but not in research specifically with parents who have intellectual disability. Since then, several studies have been published that provide empirical evidence for several of the relationships in the model (see the arrows in Figure 42.1), with the most recent studies involving large sample sizes and sophisticated statistical analyses.

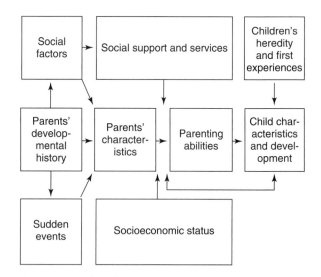

Figure 42.1. Feldman's parenting interactional model. (From Feldman, M.A. [2002]. Parents with intellectual disabilities and their children: Impediments and supports. In D. Griffiths & P. Federoff [Eds.], *Ethical dilemmas: Sexuality and developmental disability* [pp. 255–292]. Kingston, NY: NADD Press; adapted by permission).

Although not demonstrated with parents with intellectual disability, the negative impact of social stigma and discrimination on the lives of people with intellectual disability has been well established (Jahoda, Wilson, Stalker, & Cairney, 2010). Furthermore, several other studies illustrate the impact of social factors such as systemic discrimination and negative attitudes on families with parents who have intellectual disability. Booth, Booth, and McConnell (2005) reviewed court records in the United Kingdom and showed that parents with intellectual disability were vastly overrepresented (given their population prevalence) in child welfare proceedings. There was also evidence of systemic discrimination in the records, such as failure to provide any services to remediate identified parenting skill deficits. Booth, McConnell, and Booth (2006) showed how legislated time limits on adjudicating child welfare cases systematically discriminated against parents with intellectual disability. Using a Canadian child welfare sample of approximately 1,200 cases involving parents with cognitive limitations, McConnell, Feldman, Aunos, and Prasad (2011) found that workers' perceptions of noncooperation in parents with intellectual disability was the strongest predictor of court application to permanently remove the child, and that few parents with intellectual disability had access to mediation and services to improve socioeconomic advantage. Furthermore, less experienced child protection workers were more likely to keep cases open than experienced workers. Overall, these studies illustrated how social factors (e.g., negative bias due to parents being seen as cognitively impaired; arbitrary time limits) may impede service access and likelihood of permanency in families headed by parents with intellectual disability.

Other studies have examined the relationships among parental history and well-being, social support, parenting practices, and child outcomes. Feldman et al. (2002) interviewed 30 mothers with intellectual disability in Ontario, Canada, and found a positive relationship between self-reported support need and parenting stress and a negative relationship between social support satisfaction and parenting stress (size of the social support network was not significantly correlated with stress). They also found a positive relationship between social support satisfaction and positive parent–child interactions. Aunos, Feldman, and Goupil (2008) studied 32 mothers with intellectual disability in

Quebec, Canada, and reported a significant positive correlation between support network size and the provision of a stimulating home environment and positive parent–child interactions. Parenting stress was negatively correlated with positive parenting and positively correlated with inconsistent and hostile parenting; both inconsistent and hostile parenting, in turn, were positively correlated with total scores on the Child Behavior Checklist (Achenbach, 1991). McGaw et al. (2010) studied predictors of child protection registration in 101 parents with intellectual disability referred to a specialized parenting program in the United Kingdom. McGaw et al. showed that parental IQ, per se, was not associated with child protection involvement (including having children removed). Rather, child protection involvement was associated with the parent's history of childhood trauma (especially emotional abuse and physical neglect), parental physical disability, antisocial and criminal histories of male partners, and caring for a child with special needs (the later finding supports the reciprocal relationship between child functioning and parenting seen in the Feldman model).

Using structural equation modeling with 120 Australian families headed by a parent with intellectual disability, Wade, Llewellyn, and Matthews (2008) demonstrated that parenting practices and social support had direct effects on child well-being; parenting practices mediated the relationship between social support and child well-being. Using the same Canadian child welfare database as McConnell, Feldman, et al. (2011), Feldman, McConnell, and Aunos (2011) used logistic regression analysis and "found evidence consistent with a causal chain running from low parental social support, through parental mental health issues and (in turn) alleged emotional maltreatment, to child emotional/behavioral issues" (p. 82). Emerson and Brigham (2013) identified about 600 families with one or two parents with intellectual disability from a needs analysis survey of three United Kingdom primary care trusts (total number of households surveyed was 46,023). They found that poorer health outcomes in parents with intellectual disability were not due to the parents' intellectual disability per se, but rather were explained more by the parents' increased exposure to adversities related to socioeconomic disadvantage (e.g., social isolation, parental history of abuse and trauma, family characteristics, life crises) that led to poor health outcomes in the general population. Granqvist, Forslund, Fransson, Springer, and Lindberg (2014) compared 23 mothers with intellectual disability to 25 mothers without intellectual disability in Sweden and found that the parent's history of abuse and trauma, as opposed to their IQ, predicted insecure and disorganized attachment status in their children. Although the researchers did not measure parenting, they noted the considerable research showing the strong relationship between maternal sensitivity and responsivity and secure attachment in children (e.g., de Wolff & van Ijzendoorn, 1997). Indeed, Feldman, Sparks, and Case (1993/2004) in a randomized placebo-control trial taught mothers with intellectual disability to be more sensitive and responsive to their infants and found corresponding improvements in child language and social development that was considerably above maturation effects in the control group.

Thus, evidence is accumulating that although superficially, parental cognitive impairment may be a risk factor for parenting problems and child protection involvement, more in-depth analyses reveal an intricate web of connections between a host of external and internal variables that must be taken into consideration in predicting and assessing parenting practices, child outcomes, and placement decisions (Feldman & Aunos, 2010). The discussion on Feldman's Parenting Interactional Model provides the key indicators of these variables.

Early Life Challenges

Children of parents with intellectual disability are at risk for developmental delay (especially in the area of language), difficulties in school, and emotional and behavior problems (Collings, Llewellyn, & Grace, 2014; Feldman, Case, Towns, & Betel, 1985; Feldman & Walton-Allen, 1997/2002; Gillberg & Geijer-Karlsson, 1983; Hindmarsh et al., 2015). Developmental delay is seen in children as young as 6 months old, and cognitive development is typically more affected than physical and social development (Feldman et al., 1985; McConnell, Llewellyn, Mayes, Russo, & Honey, 2003). Such developmental problems are also typical of children growing up in poverty, but, for children of parents with intellectual disability, poverty is not the only reason, as school-age children from similar socioeconomic backgrounds who are raised by parents without intellectual disability have higher

IQ scores and fewer school and behavior problems (Feldman & Walton-Allen, 1997/2002). There is some evidence that developmental problems for children of parents with intellectual disability continue into adolescence and adulthood. For example, in a study of 30 adult offspring of parents with intellectual disability, 50% had learning problems and 23% had emotional or psychiatric problems (Booth & Booth, 1995).

Evidence highlights the potential relationship of these negative outcomes in children with high levels of stress during pregnancy (McConnell, Mayes, & Llewellyn, 2008a) and a high level of parenting stress (Aunos et al., 2008), particularly for parents raising school-age children (Feldman et al., 1997) and for women with a paucity of accessible prenatal care (McConnell, Mayes, & Llewellyn, 2008b; Mitra et al., 2014). Furthermore, in addition to a genetic predisposition for low intelligence in children of parents with intellectual disability (Reed & Reed, 1965), developmental delays may also be related in part to an impoverished environment (Emerson & Brigham, 2013, 2014). With adapted support, however, the home environment of parents with intellectual disability can become adequate (Feldman et al., 1993/2004; Llewellyn, McConnell, Honey, Mayes, & Russo, 2003; McConnell et al., 2003).

Returning now to the story of Ms. Smith, her four children were placed in foster care by child protective services following allegations of neglect and results from a private parenting capacity assessment. She was also referred to a specialized organization that works with parents with intellectual disability. A team of professionals (psychologist, social worker, and parent educator) worked with her. These professionals conducted an alternative parenting capacity assessment (see the section Best Practices in Service) following validated research methods and identified specific areas of needs. As per Feldman's interactional mode of examining supports and impediments, Ms. Smith's cognitive and adaptive functioning did not in themselves negatively affect her parenting skills. Rather, other issues seemed to impede her parenting. She was socially isolated, had poor parenting role models as a child, and had various recent stressful events (i.e., separation from her partner, loss of revenue, debts). Further elements of risk included high levels of anxiety related to her parenting role and symptoms related to depression (i.e., extreme fatigue, loss of energy, changes in eating patterns, irritability).

Key Indicators of Variables in Feldman's Parenting Interactional Model

Social factors

- Stigmatization (as a person with intellectual disability)
- Discrimination

Parent's developmental history

- Cognitive limitations and deficits in adaptive behaviors
- Past abuse
- Institutionalization
- Parental role models
- Past experiences in raising and taking care of children
- Age at the birth of the first child

Sudden events

- Currently experiencing abuse and violence
- Illnesses
- Loss of revenue
- Loss of a partner or an important person through separation or death
- Eviction and homelessness

Parent's characteristics

- Mental health issues such as depression, anxiety disorder, or substance abuse
- Physical health issues such as asthma, diabetes, and lupus
- High stress levels
- Adaptive behavior such as capacity to go about everyday life activities and vulnerability to exploitation

Parenting abilities

- Basic care needs of children
- Safe and healthy home environment
- Sensitive, responsive, and positive parent–child interactions
- Sound judgments (e.g., discipline, limit-setting, supervision)
- Positive child behavioral support
- Effective problem solving

Social support and services

- Supportive partner and family
- Satisfaction with social network

(continued)

Key Indicators of Variables in Feldman's Parenting Interactional Model *(continued)*

- Type of support and services, and proportion of formal (services) to informal (e.g., family members, neighbors, volunteers, friends)

- Involvement of child protection agency

- Supports and services needed versus received

Socioeconomic status

- Family income

- Employment status

- Quality of the neighborhood (e.g., safety; availability of services, transportation, and community activities)

Children's heredity and first experiences

- Family history of low IQ, genetic syndromes, mental illnesses

- Prenatal, perinatal, postnatal experiences and conditions that could affect development (e.g., prenatal maternal ingestion of alcohol or drugs, maternal hepatitis C or HIV/AIDS, birth complications, prematurity, low birth weight, early infections)

Children's characteristics and development

- Temperament and behavior (e.g., irritable, behavior problems)

- Developmental level (e.g., delay)

- School status (e.g., special education)

- Physical and mental health

- Number of children living at home

- Age and gender of child or children

In addition, her mother's interference seemed to be inhibiting her capacity to resolve problems related to disciplining her children. These impediments may have contributed to Ms. Smith's punitive and inconsistent styles of parenting that increased conflicts with her children and led to their subsequent apprehension. The report concluded that although Ms. Smith had the cognitive capacity to parent effectively, various factors were impeding her ability to do so. Many of these challenges were remediable with appropriate supports and services.

The Role of Social Support Networks

Parents with intellectual disability can learn to parent and sustain their learning over time (Aunos, 2000; Feldman, 1994, 1997, 1998; Feldman, Case, & Sparks, 1992; Feldman et al., 1993/2004). Furthermore, parents with intellectual disability have been found to seek appropriate and competence-promoting support—even during their pregnancies—from family, friends, and relatives and from services (Mayes, McConnell, & Llewellyn, 2008). A positive support network will foster increased understanding of how best to work with a family headed by a parent with an intellectual disability (de Kimpe, Kef, & Schuengel, 2014). Collaboration and a belief from all service providers that parents with intellectual disability can parent are also important in establishing a successful supportive partnership (Aunos & Pacheco, 2013).

Although most parents use a variety of formal or informal supports to assist in parenting their children, the child welfare system typically assesses whether a person can independently parent his or her children without parental supports. Support can be informal or formal. Typical formal supports include child care, after-school programs, self-help books and web sites, and parent training classes. Typical informal supports include carpools, relative caregiving, babysitting, loans, and parenting advice from family and friends. Parents with intellectual disability need similar types of supports as do parents without disabilities. These types of supports for parents with disabilities are called parental supports (Lightfoot & LaLiberte, 2011).

Lightfoot and LaLiberte (2011) noted that parental supports for parents with disabilities are simply "technologies or personal supports that enhance family functioning in families headed by a parent or guardian with a disability" (p. 390). The idea of parental supports builds on the general notion of supports in the field of intellectual and developmental disabilities (Schalock et al., 2010). However, although the provision of supports usually focuses on individual supports (e.g., assistance with activities of daily living, transportation, or employment), parental supports can be technologies such as a smartphone with an infant feeding schedule or personal supports such as a personal assistant.

Support that strengthens social ties may have a positive impact on the parents' well-being (e.g., lower stress levels, fewer depressive symptoms) and on their capacity to advocate for themselves (McConnell, Dalziel, Llewellyn, Laidlaw, & Hindmarsh, 2008; Traustadóttir & Björg Sigurjónsdóttir, 2008). The quality of the supports offered and the parent's satisfaction with it may be more important than the number of people and services involved (Feldman et al., 2002). In fact, too large a support network may evoke greater dependency (St.-Amand, Goupil, & Aunos, 2010). Thus, not all forms of social support are perceived as beneficial, and supports can either impair or empower parents (Espe-Sherwindt & Kerlin, 1990; Tucker & Johnson, 1989). The parents' attitude toward supports affects their willingness to accept them. Inversely, staff mindset toward parents' willingness to work has an impact on the satisfaction level of this working relationship (Meppelder, Hodes, Kef, & Schuengel, 2014).

Although most parents with intellectual disability recognize that they have learning difficulties, some reject the intellectual disability label. Some parents disguise their disability and deny that they need help (Feldman, 2002). They are leery of offers of support and especially distrust child welfare professionals. Parents with intellectual disability are in a double bind: the parents fear that an admission of need for assistance may result in their children being taken away by child protection authorities. Conversely, by rejecting offers of support, parents may be perceived as lacking judgment and not understanding how difficult it is to parent (Feldman, 2002). Rapport and trust are essential parts of effective supports. Rapport is well established when child welfare professionals recognize the central role of the parents in their child's life and development (Mayes et al., 2008).

BEST PRACTICES IN SERVICE: AIMING AT SUCCESSFUL PARENTING

A wealth of knowledge has been acquired to inform service providers on how best to support parents with intellectual disabilities. This knowledge base has also informed providers regarding gaps of services, training, and programs.

Support to Child Welfare Professionals

Despite calls since the mid-1990s for increased training on working with parents with intellectual disability (National Council on Disability, 2012), child welfare professionals have not typically received training and/or education related to working with this population. Psychologists, social workers, and other practitioners are not customarily exposed to relevant policies, practices, or research pertaining to people with intellectual disability, yet they are often the ones conducting assessments and providing services to this group of parents (LaLiberte, 2013). Even when child welfare workers perceived themselves to be adequately competent in their work with these parents, they reported high levels of need for training in both knowledge and skills related to working with parents with disabilities (LaLiberte). Child welfare agencies may want to refer to the Institute for Human Services (2003), as it created a specific subset of competencies for working with parents with disabilities in their development of a set of child welfare competencies.

Assessing Parenting Skills

Assessing parenting skills has been challenging because of the lack of a universally accepted operational definition of adequate or "good enough" parenting (Aunos & Feldman, 2002, 2007). In general, it is expected that parents can provide basic child care, home safety, nutrition, and surveillance to keep their children healthy and safe. Parents are also expected to provide a loving, warm, and stimulating environment to foster child development and secure attachment. These parenting skills are further supported by parallel skills such as problem solving, decision making, ability to succeed at community living, and social and communication skills. Of course, as noted previously, systemic risk and resilience factors also need to be taken into consideration, as poor mental health or lack of adequate resources could have a negative impact on the application of, or ability to learn, these parenting or parallel skills.

Essential components of a comprehensive, competence-based parenting capacity assessment for parents with intellectual disability are 1) an examination of impediments and supports in line with Feldman's interaction model (described previously; see Figure 42.1) and 2) direct observation of parenting skills, preferably using validated checklists (Aunos & Feldman, 2002; Feldman & Aunos, 2010). Another key element of such assessment is that it be conducted by an open-minded professional who has expertise in working with people with intellectual disability (Feldman & Aunos). Many parents with intellectual disability have been known to be defensive or fearful of any type of assessments, as they have lost custody of a previous child (Feldman et al., 1993/2004) and are therefore aware of the potential repercussions of such an assessment.

Parent Education Programs

Several specialized supportive parenting programs have been established for parents with intellectual disability (Aunos, 2000; Feldman, 1998, 2004, 2010; Hur, 1997; Tymchuk, 2006). Evaluation studies and reviews have shown that these programs increase selected parenting skills to levels seen in parents without intellectual disability and that they are of benefit to the children (Feldman, 1994; Feldman et al., 1992; Feldman et al., 1993/2004; Llewellyn et al., 2003; Wade et al., 2008).

Unfortunately, because few specialized services exist, many of these families are referred to early intervention, family support, public health, and child protective services that often do not have expertise to assist them. In fact, sometimes these services may have negative biases against parents with intellectual disability. Services often are fragmented and uncoordinated—as many as six different child welfare professionals may routinely visit the home! Most community agencies are geared to parents with higher cognitive skills. Important information is often presented in lecture-style "parenting classes," in a short time span, and in a limited number of sessions. The material may be too complex and presented in writing. These approaches are not very effective for most parents with intellectual disability (Feldman, 1994; Tymchuk, 1998). As described later in this chapter, parents with intellectual disability do better with concrete instruction of specific skills broken down into small steps, with training carried out in the home or a home-like setting over several sessions (Feldman, 1994, 1998, 2010).

As an increasing number of these families are appearing on agency caseloads, a more concerted effort is being made to provide relevant, adapted, and long-term supports. In turn, more specialized services and programs for parents with intellectual disability and their children have been developed and validated by research (MacLean & Aunos, 2010; Meppelder, Hodes, Kef, & Schuengel, 2014; Starke, Wade, Feldman, & Mildon, 2013; Wade et al., 2008). Efforts have begun for broader dissemination of information and training over the Internet (e.g.., Healthy Start in Australia [http://healthystart.net.au]; McConnell, Matthews, Llewellyn, Mildon, & Hindmarsh, 2008) and the Association for Successful Parenting (http://achancetoparent.net). Nonetheless, there is still a tremendous need to establish new services and to adapt existing services (see the Recommendations on How to Adapt Services sidebar) to meet the needs of these families so that their children may remain at home in a safe, healthy, and nurturing environment.

The Psychoeducational and Psychosocial Components for Assessment and Learning list presents the skills that should be assessed prior to intervention and that could be covered in a parenting program, depending on the age of the child and the family's needs (Aunos & Feldman, 2002, 2008; MacLean & Aunos, 2010). Each parent and family situation is different, so it may not be necessary to address all of these areas every time. Topics that will immediately improve the child's safety, health, and development should be covered first. Naturally,

Recommendations on How to Adapt Services

Services need to be adapted in view of the specific needs, capacities, and limitations of parents with intellectual disability. Here are some suggestions:

- Have a team (or at least one worker) who has expertise in working with these families.

- Establish trust and rapport with the family.

- Plan for an assessment of the family's needs and the needs of each family member, including the needs of the parents as individuals.

- Identify areas of need; use a systemic, interactional, and observational approach (Feldman & Aunos, 2010).

- Provide evidence-based interventions and other supports in areas identified as needing improvement (e.g., parental and child health, child development, social support, parenting and related skills).

- Involve the parents in designing the intervention plan as much as possible.

- Establish partnerships and coordinate between various agencies (particularly child protective services, if involved).

- Objectively monitor progress of the parents in learning new skills and the child's health and development.

- Have the parents identify and enlist others (i.e., informal supports) who could help support the intervention plan.

as children grow and a family's needs adapt and evolve, these elements could be targeted at different times. If the agency providing services lacks expertise in certain areas, this agency could and should refer to other agencies that do have such expertise.

This point highlights the importance of partnerships among public agencies and the need for a concerted effort to collaborate among organizations.

Training Strategies

Effective programs use concrete behavioral strategies that have been shown to rapidly increase complex skills in people with intellectual disability (Feldman, 1994). The general procedure involves task analysis and performance-based teaching methods (e.g., audiovisual materials, modeling, role playing, practice, reinforcement, and error correction). The Behavioral Training Components sidebar presents the specific strategies used to teach child care skills to parents with intellectual disability. More details regarding these strategies can be found in Feldman (1998, 2010).

The training can be carried out individually in the home or in a small group (preferably in a home-like setting). Home visits usually occur weekly and last 1–2 hours (of which only a portion focuses on training). The home visit starts with an exchange of pleasantries and updates on events since the last visit. Then the parent educator observes previously learned skills (to check for maintenance), skills to be trained soon (baseline), and/or skills currently being trained. Training time can vary depending on how long it takes to model and have the parent perform the task; most single-task training sessions last about 10 minutes. Following training, the parent and educator often will have tea or coffee and discuss other issues in the family's life (e.g., difficulties with neighbors, trying to find a job or child care). The parent educator may offer advice and assistance or recommend other services. If group instruction is used, it is important to conduct home visits and observations to check that the parent has generalized the skills learned in the group to the home (i.e., that he or she remembers them and uses them in home life).

Service Frameworks

Additional frameworks for child welfare practice exist that may provide more strengths-based, individualized case plans that better meet the needs of parents with intellectual disability and their children. One such practice framework is Signs of Safety (SOS; http://www.signsofsafety.net /signs-of-safety/#). This practice model, originating

Psychoeducational and Psychosocial Components for Assessment and Learning

Psychoeducational Components

Parenting Skills

- *Basic child care skills:* understanding how the child develops and what skills are acquired at different ages, newborn care, diapering, bathing, supervision, toilet training
- *Child positive behavior support:* establishing clear rules and instructions, enforcing limit-setting strategies, reinforcing appropriate behavior and correcting inappropriate behavior, noncorporal discipline
- *Safety:* recognizing home dangers and ensuring safety (environments: crib, sleep, home, street, playground, park, pool, beach, skating rink, public transportation, shopping center)
- *Parent–child interactions:* developing positive engagement and reciprocity and demonstrating responsiveness toward the child's needs; looking at attention, listening, supervising, choices, warmth, sensitivity, empathy, play skills
- *Health:* recognizing and intervening appropriately when health ailments occur—including treatment of diaper rash, cradle cap, colds, fever, infections, vomiting, teething; taking temperature; using medication, sunscreen, and protective clothing
- *Emergencies and first aid:* intervening during health crisis situations (e.g., cuts, burns, falls, head injury, poisoning, choking, insect bite, sunburn, heat stroke, frostbite)
- *Child development and secure attachment:* adapting interventions based on the child's age and being consistent in offering a stimulating home environment and interactions; looking at affection, sensitivity, contingent recognition, consistency, reading to the child, conversation, asking questions, telling stories, outings
- *Nutritional skills:* incorporating nutritional principles into meal time—including feeding, burping, preparing formula, serving wholesome foods, planning for nutritious and balanced meals, grocery shopping

Parallel Skills

- *Problem solving:* identifying problems and implementing strategies to resolve them—setting priorities, understanding the cause of the problem, identifying possible solutions, implementing the best solution, evaluating the outcome, generalization
- *Social skills training and communication skills:* recognizing and communicating one's own needs in an assertive way; using empathy, conversation skills, asking for help, listening, giving a compliment, responding to criticism, negotiating, apologizing, dealing with persuasion, group pressure, embarrassment
- *Stress or anger management:* identifying one's own emotions and anger triggers, relaxation, removal, self-control, incompatible responses, handling failure, handling stressors, time management

Psychosocial Components

Parental Characteristics and Parallel Skills

- *Empowerment training:* understanding how to navigate and deal with the "system," child welfare professionals, other professionals, and bureaucrats; assertiveness; self-advocacy; support groups
- *Dealing with one's own disability or a child's disability:* defining disability, identity, emotions, personal experiences, stages of grief, and experiences of loss; recognizing strengths, limitations, and rights of children with disabilities; locating resources
- *Dealing with death, adoption, and loss through custody:* recognizing when grief occurs and strategies to deal with it—sharing experiences of having a child placed, grief and loss, coping strategies, benefits of sharing experiences, death, reactions to loss, coping strategies

Factors of the Environment

- *Gaining access to community resources:* understanding how to gain access to community resources such as child care or preschool, library, community drop-ins, parent–tot programs, parenting courses, vocational and academic upgrading, counseling services, transit training

Sources: Aunos and Feldman (2002, 2008) and MacLean and Aunos (2010).

**Behavioral
Training Components
of Effective Parenting Programs**

- Through direct observation, assess how well the parent performs the set child care skills needed given the child's age.

- Use validated child care checklists that break down skills into smaller steps (e.g., Feldman & Case, 1997; McGaw, 2002).

- Teach skills one at a time.

- Teach skills in several locations in which the parent will need to learn the skill to promote generalization.

- Provide simple, concrete verbal explanations and instructions.

- Provide a picture book illustrating each step of the skill, along with simple text and an audio recording describing each picture (Feldman, 2004). Try these manuals first on their own as self-learning tools before adding more intensive training.

- Model the skill step by step, focusing on the steps that the parent missed in the assessment.

- Have the parent practice the skill in real or role-played situations. Roleplays also can be conducted in a game format.

- Use verbal, gestural, modeling, and physical prompts to guide correct performance as necessary.

- Provide immediate praise and feedback for correct performance.

- Give corrective feedback. Try to provide four times as much positive feedback as corrective feedback.

- Provide tangible rewards contingent on attendance and progress (e.g., parenting coupons exchangeable for small gift items contingent on improvements). Fade the tangible rewards after the parent shows generalization and maintenance of the skill (e.g., over a 3-month period).

in Western Australia, is organized in a context of safety and strengths, building partnerships and collaborations with the family, extended family, friends, and other formal and informal resources to prioritize safety planning. In this approach to child welfare practice, the parent is seen as the expert and positions the worker to help the parent identify the threats to their child's safety as well as the resources and strengths they have that lend themselves to protecting the child and providing appropriate care. The worker supports the parent to develop safety plans when necessary (Edwards & Turnell, 1997). For parents with intellectual limitations, SOS is an approach that engages them rather than one that places them in a defensive position. It allows them to use their strengths while identifying the areas in which they need help in order to parent their child safely—just like all other parents. It is an empowering approach to child welfare work that positions the parent with a disability in an expert role of parent rather than leading with the assumption of incompetence (Lightfoot, LaLiberte, & Semanchin-Jones, 2010).

Another approach to child welfare practice, Alternative Response (sometimes referred to as Differential Response) (Waldfogel, 1998), requires structure change in child welfare systems. It has been used in a variety of jurisdictions since about 2000 and has been received favorably by many child welfare professionals. Similar to SOS, this approach to child welfare practice is rooted in the belief that parents need to be partners in this work and that they are both capable of and desire to provide safe and appropriate parenting for their children. It is a strengths-based approach to engaging families who are facing significant challenges and supporting them in gaining access to and utilizing services that create real change for their families (Brown, Merkel-Holguin, & Rohm, 2012; Kaplan & Merkel-Holguin, 2008). The focus is not on investigating allegations and making a legal determination of maltreatment; rather, it is on partnering with a family to identify what problems exist and offering family members support and services to address their problems (Kaplan & Merkel-Holguin, 2008). Just as with SOS, parents with intellectual disability may find that this type of child welfare service approach allows them to tailor services to meet their unique set of needs in the context of parenting. It has a structure to recognize the parent's strengths and appreciates the interconnectivity of the support system in a person's life. In other words, parents do not have to be able to independently demonstrate the ability to do all parenting tasks but rather are allowed to co-construct a plan that works for them and uses their formal and informal supports to keep their children safe (Lightfoot, LaLiberte, & Semanchin-Jones, 2010).

Other child welfare practice approaches that could be effective in working with parents with intellectual disability include family group decision making, family-centered assessment, and comprehensive family assessment. Each of these has a strong foundation of strengths-based practices. Adequate training in working with people with disabilities (including but not limited to understanding modifications, use of accommodations, and the normative need for parental supports) coupled with any one of the aforementioned child welfare practice approaches could positively position parents with intellectual disability for day-to-day parenting activities.

Returning once again to Ms. Smith's story, goals and objectives were set with her following the results from a parenting capacity assessment. Ms. Smith's family physician prescribed antidepressants to target her symptoms of anxiety and depression. The psychologist from the parenting team worked with her on developing and implementing coping strategies and stress management skills. When Ms. Smith thought she had more energy, she agreed to develop new ties in her community. With the support of the social worker from the parenting team, Ms. Smith identified community support groups and chose to participate to meet other mothers like herself. She distanced herself from her mother, as she saw that her mother was denigrating her in unhelpful ways. An educator with expertise in working with parents with intellectual disability was referred to assist Ms. Smith. The objectives were to learn about child development and parenting strategies around discipline, limit-setting, and the development of positive parent–child interactions. As things got better in Ms. Smith's life, child protective services allowed an increased number of visitations with her children.

SUMMARY

Many factors, instead of or in addition to parental cognitive limitations, may influence parenting by parents with intellectual disability. There is an overrepresentation of parents with intellectual disability in court proceedings and child protective services. The informal support network and competency-enhancing services are very important in developing and empowering parenting abilities for this population. Programs that aim to enable young adults in their parenting roles are associated with increased positive birth outcomes.

Despite progressive changes in the recognition of rights of people with intellectual disability, the applicability of these rights to parenting lags behind. The erroneous perception that such individuals' low intellectual functioning precludes competent parenting still influences child custody decisions; indeed, it has been known for more than 2 decades that many factors apart from their cognitive disability may impede their ability to parent adequately and respond to interventions. Ironically, one of these obstacles is the continuing stigmatization and discrimination of parents with intellectual disability that may lead to a lack of referral to beneficial services that might allow the child to remain in or be returned to the home. Many of their children are prematurely removed from their biological parents and spend their childhoods in the foster-care system. The deleterious effects of living in foster care, which often lasts many years and involves living in several homes, often is not considered in these cases.

As is the case with parents without a disability, some parents with intellectual disability learn and apply new skills with supports and advice easily and some do not. For some parents with intellectual disability to be successful, a specialized teaching style and intermittent but ongoing supports may be needed. It has been shown that with appropriate, personalized services and supports, these parents can learn to be effective parents and raise their children in a safe, nurturing, and loving home.

To continue to move forward, evidence-based decision making and practices should be systematized and integrated into formal support services and child protection. More efforts need to be made to ensure that parents with intellectual disability have access to antenatal and prenatal care to increase the chances for positive birth and early developmental outcomes. The interaction model described in this chapter should serve as a template for parenting capacity assessments that aim to identify the impact on parenting abilities of such things as the parent's past and current experiences, health issues, social supports, and poverty. Families should have access to needed services and supports before the child is permanently removed. Finally, disability services should work closely with child protective services to ensure the ongoing protection of the children as the parents improve their skills.

FOR FURTHER THOUGHT AND DISCUSSION

1. What are the ethical ramifications of allowing or denying the right to parent in people with intellectual disability? How can parenting rights be balanced with what is in the best interests of the child?

2. Many studies have documented the need for and importance of adequate support in helping parents with intellectual disability. This need for support is also described as being, at times, intensive and long standing. On the other hand, many children are removed from the custody of their parents who have intellectual disability. Which solution is the most appropriate: offering extensive support or placing children into foster care? Which one would be most humane? Which one the most affordable?

3. Parents with intellectual disability face many challenges. What are these challenges, and how could parents be offered support in overcoming them?

4. Countries, and even individual states and provinces, have somewhat different approaches to providing services to people with intellectual disability. How could services be adapted to better meet the needs of parents with intellectual disability and their children? How do current child welfare laws and practices affect services and decisions regarding families headed by parents with intellectual disability?

5. In Ms. Smith's case, how would the analysis of her strengths or the way of assessing her parenting skills be different if she was a new immigrant?

REFERENCES

Achenbach, T.M. (1991). *Manual for the Child Behavior Checklist/4-18 and 1991 profile*. Burlington: University of Vermont.

Americans with Disabilities Act (ADA) of 1990, PL 101-336, 42 U.S.C. §§ 12101 *et seq.*

Anderson, L., Byun, S., Larson, S., & Lakin, C. (2005). *Mothers with disabilities—characteristics and outcomes: An analysis from the 1994/1995 NHIS-D. MR/DD Data Brief*

7(3). Minneapolis: University of Minnesota, Institute on Community Integration, Research and Training Center on Community Living.

Aunos, M. (2000). Les programmes de formation aux habiletés parentales pour des adultes présentant une déficience intellectuelle. *La revue internationale de l'éducation familiale, 4*(2), 59–75.

Aunos, M., & Feldman, M.A. (2002). Attitudes toward sexuality, sterilisation, and parenting rights of persons with intellectual disabilities. *Journal of Applied Research in Intellectual Disability, 15*, 285–296.

Aunos, M., & Feldman, M. (2007). Assessing parenting capacity in parents with intellectual disabilities. In C. Chamberland, S. Léveillé, & N. Trocmé (Eds.), *Des enfants à protéger, des adultes à aider: Deux univers à rapprocher* (pp. 223–240). Sainte-Foy, Canada: Presses de l'université du Québec.

Aunos, M., & Feldman, M. (2008). There's no place like home: The child's right to family. In T. O'Neill & D. Zinga (Eds.), *Children's rights: Multidisciplinary approaches to participation and protection* (pp. 137–162). Toronto, Canada: University of Toronto Press.

Aunos, M., Feldman, M., & Goupil, G. (2008). Mothering with intellectual disabilities: Relationship between social support, health and well-being, parenting and child behaviour outcomes. *Journal of Applied Research in Intellectual Disabilities, 21*, 320–330.

Aunos, M., & Pacheco, L. (2013). Changing perspectives via collaborative framework: Parents with intellectual disabilities and their families. *Journal of Public Child Welfare, 7*, 658–674.

Belsky, J. (1984). The determinants of parenting: A process model. *Child Development, 55*, 83–96.

Blumberg, D.A. (2014). *Understanding custody jurisdiction and the UCCJEA*. Retrieved from http://www.uccjea.net/FAQs/Understanding-Custody-Jurisdiction-And-The-UCCJEA.shtml

Booth, T., & Booth, W. (1995). Unto us a child is born: The trials and rewards of parenthood for people with learning disabilities. *Australia and New Zealand Journal of Developmental Disabilities, 20*, 25–39.

Booth, T., & Booth, W. (2005). Parents with learning difficulties in the child protection system: Experiences and perspectives. *Journal of Intellectual Disabilities, 9*, 109–129.

Booth, T., Booth, W., & McConnell, D. (2005). Care proceedings and parents with learning difficulties: Comparative prevalence and outcomes in an English and Australian court sample. *Child and Family Social Work, 10*(4), 353–360.

Booth, T., McConnell, D., & Booth, W. (2006). Temporal discrimination and parents with learning difficulties in the child protection system. *British Journal of Social Work, 36*(6), 997–1015.

Bronfenbrenner, U. (1979). Contexts of child rearing: Problems and prospects. *American Psychologist, 34*, 844–850.

Brown, B., Merkel-Holguin, L., & Rohm, A. (2012). *Differential response: Cross-site findings report*. Denver, CO: National Quality Improvement Center on Differential Response in Child Protective Services.

Brown, E.F., Limb, G.E., Chance, T., & Munoz, R. (2002). *The Indian Child Welfare Act: An examination of state compliance in Arizona.* Seattle, WA: Casey Family Programs.

Callow, E. (2013a). Common (higher) ground: What social workers and parents' attorneys can do to maximize justice for parents with disabilities and their children. *Child Welfare, 360,* 27, 36.

Callow, E. (2013b). The Indian Child Welfare Act: Intersections with disability and the Americans with Disabilities Act. *Clearinghouse Review Journal of Poverty Law and Policy, 46*(11–12), 501–508.

Callow, E., Buckland, K., & Jones, S. (2011). Parents with disabilities in the United States: Prevalence, perspectives and a proposal for legislative change to protect the right to family in the disability community. *Texas Journal on Civil Liberties and Civil Rights, 17*(1), 9–41.

Callow, E., Feldman, M., & Tahir, M. (2014). [Pseudoscientific measures and practice in American and Canadian appellate level and higher child welfare cases involving parents with intellectual disabilities.] Unpublished data. The National Center for Parents with Disabilities and Their Families.

Callow, E., Gemmill, A., Jacob, J., & Riley, S. (2011). *Summary of the 2008 National Child Abuse and Neglect Data System (NCANDS) child file: Victims of maltreatment and their caregivers' disabilities.* Unpublished report to National Institute on Disability and Rehabilitation Research. The National Center for Parents with Disabilities at Through the Looking Glass.

Callow, E., & Miller, C. (2013). [Review of disability studies programs regarding inclusion of parenting as a topic.] Unpublished data. The National Center for Parents with Disabilities at Through the Looking Glass.

Canadian Charter of Rights and Freedoms, s 2, Part I of the Constitution Act, 1982, being Schedule B to the Canada Act 1982 (UK), 1982, c 11.

Canadian Children and Family Services Act, R.S.O., 1990, Chapter C.11.

Case, L., & Gang, B. (2003). People with developmental disabilities as parents. In I. Brown & M. Percy (Eds.), *Developmental disabilities in Ontario* (2nd ed., pp. 709–724). Toronto, Canada: Ontario Association on Developmental Disabilities.

Child Welfare Information Gateway. (2011, January). *Addressing racial disproportionality in child welfare.* Retrieved from http://1.usa.gov/T16y04

Collings, S., Llewellyn, G., & Grace, R. (2014). Exploring the social worlds of children of mothers with intellectual disability. *Journal of Applied Research in Intellectual Disabilities, 27,* 356.

de Kimpe, J., Kef, S., & Schuengel, C. (2014). The cooperation between social network members and professionals for parents with intellectual disabilities: Insights in protective possibilities. *Journal of Applied Research in Intellectual Disabilities, 27,* 340–341.

de Wolff, M.S., & van Ijzendoorn, M.H. (1997). Sensitivity and attachment: A meta-analysis on parental antecedents of infant attachment. *Child Development, 68*(4), 571–591.

Divorce Act (Canada), R.S.C., 1985, c. 3 (2nd Supp.).

E. (Mrs.) v. Eve, (1986) 2 SCR 388.

Edwards, S., & Turnell, A. (1997). *Signs of Safety: A solution and safety oriented approach to child protection casework.* New York, NY: W.W. Norton.

Emerson, E., & Brigham, P. (2013). Health behaviours and mental health status of parents with intellectual disabilities: Cross sectional study. *Public Health, 127*(12), 1111–1116.

Emerson, E., & Brigham, P. (2014). Exposure of children with developmental delay to social determinants of poor health: Cross-sectional study. *Journal of Applied Research in Intellectual Disabilities, 27,* 305.

Espe-Sherwindt, M., & Kerlin, S. (1990). Early intervention with parents with mental retardation: Do we empower or impair? *Infants and Young Children, 2,* 21–28.

Faigman, D., Monahan, J., & Slobogin, C. (2014). Group to individual (G2I) inference in scientific expert testimony. *University of Chicago Law Review, 81,* 417, 448.

Feldman, M.A. (1994). Parenting education for parents with intellectual disabilities: A review of outcome studies. *Research in Developmental Disabilities, 15,* 299–332.

Feldman, M.A. (1997). The effectiveness of early intervention for children of parents with mental retardation. In M.J. Guralnick (Ed.), *The effectiveness of early intervention* (pp. 171–191). Baltimore, MD: Paul H. Brookes Publishing Co.

Feldman, M.A. (1998). Preventing child neglect: Child-care training for parents with intellectual disabilities. *Infants and Young Children, 11,* 1–11.

Feldman, M.A. (2002). Parents with intellectual disabilities and their children: Impediments and supports. In D. Griffiths & P. Federoff (Eds.), *Ethical dilemmas: Sexuality and developmental disability* (pp. 255–292). Kingston, NY: NADD Press.

Feldman, M.A. (2004). Self-directed learning of child-care skills by parents with intellectual disabilities. *Infants and Young Children, 17,* 17–31.

Feldman, M.A. (2010). Parenting education programs. In G. Llewellyn, R. Traustadóttir, D. McConnell, & H. Björg Sigurjónsdóttir (Eds.), *Parents with intellectual disabilities: Past, present and futures* (pp. 121–136). Chichester, United Kingdom: Wiley-Blackwell.

Feldman, M.A., & Aunos, M. (2010). *Comprehensive Competence-Based Parenting Assessment for parents with learning difficulties and their children.* Kingston, NY: NADD Press.

Feldman, M.A., & Case, L. (1997). *Step by step child care: Teaching aids for parents, child-care workers, and babysitters.* Unpublished Manuscript, Centre for Applied Disability, Brock University, St. Catharines, Ontario, Canada.

Feldman, M.A., Case, L., & Sparks, B. (1992). Effectiveness of a child-care training program for parents at-risk for child neglect. *Canadian Journal of Behavioural Science, 24,* 14–28.

Feldman, M.A., Case, L., Towns, F., & Betel, J. (1985). Parent education project I: The development and nurturance of children of mentally handicapped mothers. *American Journal of Mental Deficiency, 90,* 253–258.

Feldman, M.A., Léger, M., & Walton-Allen, N. (1997). Stress in mothers with intellectual disabilities. *Journal of Child and Family Studies, 6,* 471–485.

Feldman, M., McConnell, D., & Aunos, M. (2011). Parental cognitive impairment, mental health and child outcomes in child protection population. *Journal of Mental Health Research in Intellectual Disability, 5*(1), 66–90.

Feldman, M.A., Sparks, B., & Case, L. (2004). Effectiveness of home-based early intervention on the language development of children of parents with mental retardation. In M.A. Feldman (Ed.), *Early intervention: The essential readings* (pp. 134–150). Oxford, United Kingdom: Blackwell. (Reprinted from *Research in Developmental Disabilities, 14,* 387–408, 1993)

Feldman, M.A., Varghese, J., Ramsay, J., & Rajska, D. (2002). Relationship between social support, stress and mother–child interactions in mothers with intellectual disabilities. *Journal of Applied Research in Intellectual Disability, 15,* 314–323.

Feldman, M.A., & Walton-Allen, N. (2002). Effects of maternal mental retardation and poverty on intellectual, academic, and behavioral status of school-age children. In J. Blacher & B. Baker (Eds.), *The best of AAMR: Families and mental retardation: A collection of notable AAMR journal articles across the 20th century* (pp. 235–246). Washington, DC: American Association on Mental Retardation. (Reprinted from *American Journal on Mental Retardation, 101,* 352–364, 1997)

Gallagher, N. (1994). *Breeding better Vermonters: The Eugenics Project in the Green Mountain State.* Lebanon, NH: University Press of New England.

Gillberg, C., & Geijer-Karlsson, M. (1983). Children born to mentally retarded women: A 1–21 year follow-up study of 41 cases. *Psychological Medicine, 13,* 891–894.

Granqvist, P., Forslund, T., Fransson, L., Springer, L., & Lindberg, L. (2014). Mothers with intellectual disability, their experiences of maltreatment, and their children's attachment representations: A small-group matched comparison study. *Attachment and Human Development, 16,* 417–436. doi:10.1080/14616734.2014.926946

Hall v. Florida, 572 U.S. (2014).

Hindmarsh, G., Llewellyn, G., & Emerson, E. (2015). Mothers with intellectual impairment and their 9-month-old infants. *Journal of Intellectual Disability Research, 59*(6), 541–550.

Hoglund, B., Lindgren, P., & Larsson, M. (2012). Newborns of mothers with intellectual disability have a higher risk of perinatal death and being small for gestational age. *Acta Obstetricia et Gynecologica Scandinavica, 91,* 1409–1414.

Humphrey, S. (1920). The menace of the half-man. *Journal of Heredity, 11,* 228–231.

Hur, J. (1997). Review of research on parent training for parents with intellectual disability: Methodological issues. *International Journal of Disability, Development and Education, 44*(2), 147–162.

Hyun, E., Hahn, L. & McConnell, D. (2014). Experiences of people with learning disabilities in the criminal justice system. *British Journal of Learning Disabilities, 42,* 308–314.

Institute for Human Services. (2003). *The OCWTP universe of competencies.* Retrieved from http://www.ocwtp.net/universe%20of%20competencies.htm

Jahoda, A., Wilson, A., Stalker, K., & Cairney, A. (2010). Living with stigma and the self-perceptions of people with mild intellectual disabilities. *Journal of Social Issues, 66*(3), 521–534.

Janeslätt, G., Springer, L., & Adolfsson, P. (2014). Parents on the outside—A pilot study of a support group for parents with cognitive limitations who have lost the care of their children. *Journal of Applied Research in Intellectual Disabilities, 27*(4), 356.

Kaplan, C., & Merkel-Holguin, L. (2008). Another look at the national study on differential response in child welfare. *Exploring Differential, 23,* 4–21.

Kirshbaum, M., Taube, D., & Lasian Baer, R. (2003). Parents with disabilities: Problems in family court practice. *Journal of the Center for Families, Children and the Courts, 4,* 27–48.

Kohm, L.M. (2008). Tracing the foundations of the best interest of the child standard in American jurisprudence. *Journal of Law and Family Studies, 10,* 337–376.

LaLiberte, T. (2013). Child welfare workers' perceived competency in working with parents with intellectual and developmental disabilities. *Journal of Public Child Welfare, 7*(5), 633–657.

LaLiberte, T., Lightfoot, E., Singh, S., Piescher, K.N., & Hong, S. (2012). *Parental disability and termination of parental rights in child welfare. Minn-LInK Brief No. 12.* Retrieved from http://cascw.umn.edu/portfolio-items/parental-disability-and-termination-of-parental-rights-in-child-protection-ml-12revised/

Leslie-Miller, J. (1997). From Bell to Bell: Responsible reproduction in the twentieth century. *Maryland Journal of Contemporary Legal Issues, 8,* 123-150.

Lightfoot, E., Hill, K., & LaLiberte, T. (2010a). Disability in the termination of parental rights and other child custody statutes. *Child Abuse and Neglect, 34,* 927–934. doi:10.1016/j.chiabu.2010.07.001

Lightfoot, E., & LaLiberte, T. (2006). Approaches to child protection case management for cases involving people with disabilities. *Child Abuse and Neglect, 30*(4), 381–391.

Lightfoot, E., & LaLiberte, T. (2011). Parental supports for parents with intellectual and developmental disabilities. *Intellectual and Developmental Disabilities, 49*(5), 388–391. doi:10.1352/1934-9556-49.5.388

Lightfoot, E., LaLiberte, T., & Semanchin-Jones, A. (2010, September). *A new approach to partnering: Engaging child welfare to work with parents with disabilities.* Paper presented at the Association for Successful Parenting International Conference, Enhancing the Lives of Families When Parents Have Learning Difficulties, Denver, CO.

Llewellyn, G. (1990). People with intellectual disability as parents: Perspectives from the professional literature. *Australia and New Zealand Journal of Developmental Disabilities, 16*(4), 369–380.

Llewellyn, G., McConnell, D., Honey, A., Mayes, R., & Russo, D. (2003). Promoting health and home safety for children of parents with intellectual disability: A randomized controlled trial. *Research in Developmental Disabilities, 24*(6), 405–431.

Lombardo, P.A. (1996). Medicine, eugenics and the Supreme Court: From coercive sterilization to reproductive freedom. *Contemporary Health and Policy, 13,* 1–25.

MacLean, K., & Aunos, M. (2010). Addressing the needs of parents with intellectual disabilities: Exploring a parenting pilot project. *Journal on Developmental Disabilities* [Special issue: Falling Through the Cracks], *16*(1), 18–33.

Margolin, D. (2007). No chance to prove themselves: The rights of mentally disabled parents under the Americans with Disabilities Act and state law. *Virginia Journal of Social Policy and the Law, 15,* 112–117.

Mayes, R., & Llewellyn, G. (2009). What happens to parents with intellectual disability following removal of their child in child protection proceedings? *Journal of Intellectual and Developmental Disability, 34,* 92–95.

Mayes, R., Llewellyn, G., & McConnell, D. (2006). Misconception: The experience of pregnancy for women with intellectual disabilities. *Scandinavian Journal of Disability Research, 8,* 120–131.

Mayes, R., McConnell, D., & Llewellyn, G. (2008). Active negotiation: Mothers with intellectual disabilities creating their social support network. *Journal of Applied Research in Intellectual Disabilities, 21,* 341–350.

McConnell, D. (2008). Parents labeled with intellectual disabilities: Position of the IASSID SIRG on parents and parenting with intellectual disabilities. *Journal of Applied Research in Intellectual Disabilities, 21,* 296–307.

McConnell, D., Aunos, M., Feldman, M., & Prasad, N. (2011). Child maltreatment investigation outcomes for children of caregivers with cognitive impairments: Logistic regression analysis of the CIS-2003. *Child Maltreatment, 16*(1), 21–32.

McConnell, D., Dalziel, A., Llewellyn, G., Laidlaw, K., & Hindmarsh, G. (2008). Strengthening the social relationship of mothers with learning difficulties. *British Journal of Learning Disabilities, 37,* 66–75.

McConnell, D., Feldman, M., Aunos, M., & Prasad, N. (2010). *Child welfare process and outcome, caregiver cognitive impairment: Secondary analysis of the Canadian Incidence Study of Reported Child Abuse and Neglect (CIS-2003).* Edmonton, Canada: Family and Disability Studies, University of Alberta.

McConnell, D., Feldman, M., Aunos, M., & Prasad, N. (2011). Parental cognitive impairment and child maltreatment in Canada. *Child Abuse and Neglect, 35,* 621–632.

McConnell, D., & Llewellyn, G. (2002). Stereotypes, parents with intellectual disability and child protection. *Journal of Social Welfare and Family Law, 24*(3), 297–317.

McConnell, D., Llewellyn, G., & Ferronato, L. (2003). Prevalence and outcomes for parents with disabilities and their children in an Australian court sample. *Child Abuse and Neglect, 27,* 235–251.

McConnell, D., Llewellyn, G., Mayes, R., Russo, D., & Honey, A. (2003). Developmental profiles of children born to mothers with intellectual disability. *Journal of Intellectual and Developmental Disability, 28*(2), 122–134.

McConnell, D., Matthews, J., Llewellyn, G., Mildon, R., & Hindmarsh, G. (2008). "Healthy Start": A national strategy for parents with intellectual disabilities and their children. *Journal of Policy and Practice in Intellectual Disabilities, 5,* 194–202.

McConnell, D., Mayes, R., & Llewellyn, G. (2008a). Prepartum distress in women with intellectual disabilities. *Journal of Intellectual and Developmental Disability, 33,* 177–183.

McConnell, D., Mayes, R., & Llewellyn, G. (2008b). Women with intellectual disability at risk of adverse pregnancy and birth outcomes. *Journal of Intellectual Disability Research, 52,* 529–535.

McGaw, S. (2002). Should parenting be taught? *The Psychologist, 15,* 510–513.

McGaw, S., Scully, T., & Pritchard, C. (2010). Predicting the unpredictable? Identifying high-risk versus low-risk parents with intellectual disabilities. *Child Abuse and Neglect, 34,* 699–710.

Meppelder, M., Hodes, M., Kef, S., & Schuengel, C. (2014). Parents with intellectual disabilities seeking professional parenting support: The role of working alliance, stress and informal support. *Child Abuse and Neglect, 38*(9), 1478–1486.

Mitra, M., Parish, S.L., Cui, X., & Diop, H. (2014). Using longitudinal data to examine pregnancy outcomes among women with and without intellectual and developmental disabilities. *Journal of Applied Research in Intellectual Disabilities, 27,* 322–323.

National Council on Disability. (2012). *Rocking the cradle: Ensuring the rights of parents with disabilities and their children.* Retrieved from https://www.ncd.gov/publications/2012/Sep272012

Northwest Territories Justice, Canadian Department of Justice. (2014, August). *Family Law, Federal Divorce Act.* Retrieved from https://www.justice.gov.nt.ca/en/legislation/

Pan-American Health Organization and World Health Organization. (2004). *The Montreal declaration on intellectual disabilities.* Retrieved from http://www.opadd.on.ca/News/documents/montrealdeclarationMTL.pdf

Parish, S.L., Mitra, M., Son, E., Bonardi, A., & Swoboda, P. (2014). A national profile of deliveries by women with intellectual disabilities in the US: Maternal characteristics and pregnancy outcomes. *Journal of Applied Research in Intellectual Disabilities, 27,* 323–323.

Reed, E.W., & Reed, S.C. (1965). *Mental retardation: A family study.* Philadelphia, PA: W. B. Saunders.

Richardson, T. (1989). *The century of the child: The mental hygiene movement and social policy in the United States and Canada.* Albany, NY: State University of New York Press.

Sameroff, A.J., & Chandler, M. (1975). Reproductive risk and the continuum of caretaking causality. In F. Horowitz (Ed.), *Review of child development research* (Vol. 4, pp. 157–243). Chicago, IL: University of Chicago Press.

Schalock, R.L., Borthwick-Duffy, S.A., Bradley, V.J., Buntinx, W.H.E., Coulter, D.L., Craig, E.M., & Gomez, S.C. (2010). *Intellectual disability: Definition, classification, and systems of supports* (11th ed.). Washington, DC: American Association on Intellectual and Developmental Disabilities.

Silver, M.G. (2004). Eugenics and compulsory sterilization laws: Providing redress for the victims of a shameful era in United States history. *George Washington Law Review, 72*, 862–890.

Sinha, V., & Kozlowski, A. (2013). The structure of aboriginal child welfare in Canada. *The International Indigenous Policy Journal*, 4(2). Retrieved from http://ir.lib.uwo.ca/iipj/vol4/iss2/2

Smith, G. (1988). Limitations on reproductive autonomy for the mentally handicapped. *Journal of Contemporary Health Law and Policy, 4*. Retrieved from http://scholarship.law.edu/jchlp/vol4/iss1/8

Spencer, M. (2001, Winter). Proceed with caution: The limitations of current parenting capacity assessments. *Developing Practice*, 16–24.

St.-Amand, K., Goupil, G., & Aunos, M. (2010). Mères présentant une déficience intellectuelle: Perceptions de leur qualité de vie. *Journal on Developmental Disabilities, 16*(3), 18–27.

Starke, M., Wade, C., Feldman, M.A., & Mildon, R. (2013). Parenting with disabilities: Experiences from implementing a parenting support programme in Sweden. *Journal of Intellectual Disabilities, 17*, 145–156.

Swain, P., & Cameron, N. (2003). Good enough parenting: Parental disability and child protection. *Disability and Society, 18*(2), 165–177.

Tarleton, B., Ward, L., & Howarth, J. (2006). *Finding the right support: A review of issues and positive practice to support parents with learning difficulties and their children.* London, United Kingdom: Baring Foundation.

Traustadóttir, R., & Björg Sigurjónsdóttir, H. (2008). The "mother" behind the mother: Three generations of mothers with intellectual disabilities and their family support networks. *Journal of Applied Research in Intellectual Disabilities, 21*, 331–340.

Tucker, M.B., & Johnson, O. (1989). Competence promoting versus competence inhibiting social support for mentally retarded mothers. *Human Organization, 48*, 95–107.

Tymchuk, A.J. (1998). The importance of matching educational interventions to parent needs in child maltreatment: Issues, methods, and recommendations. In J. Lutzker (Ed.), *Handbook of child abuse research and treatment* (pp. 421–448). New York, NY: Plenum Press.

Tymchuk, A.J. (2006). *The health and wellness program: A parenting curriculum for families at risk.* Baltimore, MD: Paul H. Brookes Publishing Co.

United Nations. (1989). *Convention on the rights of the child.* Retrieved from http://www.ohchr.org/en/professionalinterest/pages/crc.aspx

United Nations. (2006). *Convention on the rights of persons with disabilities.* Retrieved from http://www.un.org/esa/socdev/enable/rights/convtexte.htm#convtext

United Nations Inter-Agency Support Group on Indigenous People's Issues. (2014). *Rights of indigenous peoples/persons with disabilities.* Retrieved from http://www.ohchr.org/EN/Issues/IPeoples/Pages/Declaration.aspx

Wade, C., Llewellyn, G., & Matthews, J. (2008). Review of parent training interventions for parents with intellectual disability. *Journal of Applied Research in Intellectual Disability, 21*, 351–366.

Waldfogel, J. (1998). Rethinking the paradigm for child protection. *The Future of Children, 8*(1), 104–119.

Watkins, C. (1995). Beyond status: The Americans with Disabilities Act and the parental rights of people labeled developmentally disabled or mentally retarded. *California Law Review, 83*, 1415–1475.

43

Gender Issues in Developmental Disabilities

Kruti Acharya, Abigail Schindler, and Tamar Heller

WHAT YOU WILL LEARN

- Issues in the history of gender and intellectual and developmental disabilities
- Gender studies and feminism and their application to the field of intellectual and developmental disabilities
- Issues pertaining to the intersection of disability and masculinity
- Gender issues in employment
- The impact of gender and disability on relationships and friendships
- Health care disparities and people with intellectual and developmental disabilities

Gender is an important part of each individual's identity, and this is no less true for people with intellectual and developmental disabilities. As in many other fields of inquiry, scholarship within the field of intellectual and developmental disabilities

Authors' note: This document was produced under Grant No. H133B130007 awarded by the U.S. Administration for Community Living's National Institute on Disability and Rehabilitation Research to the Rehabilitation Research and Training Center on Developmental Disabilities and Health at the University of Illinois at Chicago and Grant No. T73MC11047 (Leadership Education in Neurodevelopmental and Other Related Disabilities Program) awarded by the U.S. Department of Health and Human Services Health Resources and Services Administration (HRSA). The contents of this article do not necessarily represent the policy of the U.S. Administration for Community Living or HRSA and should not be assumed to be endorsed by the U.S. federal government.

often conflates the concepts of gender and sex. Although sex is an important and essential component of gender, *sex* refers to a biological characteristic and *gender* refers to socially constructed roles that are considered to be appropriate for men and women. What it means to be a man or a woman varies greatly based on the society in which an individual lives. Gender roles within cultures shape and dictate what is considered socially accepted behavior. As may be surmised by the fact that cultures shape gender roles, the differences between men and women are not only biologically determined but also socially constructed.

Due to many factors discussed further within this chapter, people with intellectual and developmental disabilities may have a complicated relationship with gender. Historically, sexuality has been restricted within this population and adherence to traditional gender roles has been impeded in various ways. It is important to acknowledge the intersectionality of various parts of an individual's identity, including race, gender, and disability status. For many, identity as a person with intellectual and developmental disabilities tends to supersede an identity as a man or a woman, so people with intellectual and developmental disabilities are seen as both asexual and agendered. However, in their view of themselves, people with intellectual and developmental disabilities often view their gender as an important part of their identity, though the opportunity to assume some gender roles (e.g., parenting) is often denied to them.

HISTORY OF GENDER AND INTELLECTUAL AND DEVELOPMENTAL DISABILITIES

Historically, residential institutions for people with intellectual and developmental disabilities included a variety of people classified as "deviants." This included both those who would now be described as having intellectual and developmental disabilities as well as others who did not conform to prevailing gender roles (e.g., a mother who did not nurture her children) or displayed some sort of sexual deviance (e.g., an unwed mother) (Starogiannis & Hill, 2008). These residential institutions were often segregated by sex in an attempt to regulate both gender and sexuality. People living within institutions were often assigned highly gendered tasks, with women working in laundry rooms and kitchens and men working in industrial shops within the institution (Starogiannis & Hill).

During the early to mid-20th century, the involuntary sterilization of women with intellectual and developmental disabilities was legal and common in Western societies. This may be due in large part to the eugenics movement, which aimed to improve society by preventing procreation in those who were determined to be inferior (including the "feebleminded") while encouraging the procreation of those who were considered to be of good stock (Trent, 1995). However, the practice of sterilization continued long past the time when eugenic views were discredited, with the reasoning reframed as giving women "unfit" for parenthood the freedom to live outside of institutions without the risk of pregnancy (Tilley, Walmsley, Earle, & Atkinson, 2012). Involuntary sterilization is now subject to increasing safeguards designed to protect the best interests of people with intellectual and developmental disabilities, such as requiring guardians to seek court oversight before enacting sterilization procedures. However, it may be argued that the legacy of sterilization continues through other forms of reproductive control such as long-term contraception with Depo-Provera, which can essentially become a form of chemical sterilization with limited understanding by the individual with intellectual and developmental disabilities (Tilley et al., 2012). For reasons that remain unclear, the sterilization of people with intellectual and developmental disabilities has focused almost exclusively on women.

GENDER STUDIES

Burns (1993) describes intellectual and developmental disabilities as a "master status," meaning other identity statuses (including gender) are often ignored within both research and service delivery. The concept of intersectionality, or "intersecting statuses," within the field of gender studies examines the way various parts of an individual's identity (e.g., race and gender) play a role in determining her or his overall identity. For people with intellectual and developmental disabilities, this means that they may simultaneously inhabit several identity statuses, and the extent to which each characteristic affects overall identity is unclear (Barnartt, 2013). Individuals with intellectual and developmental disabilities of both genders may be subject to double disadvantage wherein the stigma of intellectual and developmental disabilities combines with gender stereotypes, creating cumulative effects (Barnartt; Mehrota & Vaidya, 2008). For instance, being a woman with intellectual and developmental disabilities may challenge notions of femininity, and being a man with intellectual and developmental disabilities may similarly challenge the ability to prove masculinity within cultural norms (Mehrota & Vaidya).

INTELLECTUAL AND DEVELOPMENTAL DISABILITIES AND FEMINISM

Early feminist theory within Western contexts focused on proving that women are equal to men because they have the same physical, intellectual, and moral capabilities. Although this argument has been a key part of the women's movement, modern theorists, especially people within disability studies, have noted that this perspective can marginalize people with disabilities (Minister, 2013). Classic feminist works that depict disability as an icon of human vulnerability and deviation from cultural norms are challenged by disability politics, which tend to depict disability as a natural part of human variability (Herndl, 2013).

Women with disabilities have recognized that their needs, concerns, and experiences have not been addressed by either feminist or disability theories (Flintoff, Fitzgerald, & Scraton, 2008). Although the feminist movement has championed women to be in control of their own bodies, especially with regard to reproductive rights, it may be argued that women with intellectual and developmental disabilities have been largely ignored within this literature (Tilley et al., 2012). Women with intellectual and developmental disabilities who become pregnant often face predominantly negative reactions by family members, strangers, and professional staff. Despite this, qualitative studies have revealed that pregnant women with intellectual and developmental disabilities see pregnancy and motherhood as affirming their femininity in ways they believe were previously denied to them (Walsh-Gallagher, Sinclair, & McConkey, 2012).

The United Nations *Convention on the Rights of Persons with Disabilities* (2006) promotes policies and practices wherein reproduction is viewed as a human right. Parenting rights and responsibilities, however, are influenced by culture and societal traditions, which sometimes limit societies' behavior toward parents with intellectual and developmental disabilities (Llewellyn, 2013). Mothers who have intellectual and developmental disabilities are more likely to have their children removed from their custody, though researchers have noted that with supports in place, parents with moderate intellectual and developmental disabilities may be able to thrive as parents (Llewellyn; Wilson, McKenzie, Quayle, & Murray, 2014). Parents with intellectual and developmental disabilities are overrepresented in child welfare systems, constituting between 9% and 22% of child protection cases (Proctor & Azar, 2013). The involvement of child protection services in the lives of families can lead to shame, grief, distrust toward social services, and poor mental health (Mayes & Llewellyn, 2009). In a study investigating the attitudes and emotions of child support workers toward parents with intellectual and developmental disabilities, workers read vignettes describing parents who were either labeled as having intellectual and developmental disabilities or not. Child support workers had significantly higher rates of pity for parents with intellectual and developmental disabilities as well as lower rates of anger and disgust. However, when assessing risk in neglect situations, parents with intellectual and developmental disabilities were perceived as placing their child at greater risk, although the vignettes were the same for the two groups (Proctor & Azar, 2013).

Although the literature on parenting with intellectual and developmental disabilities often uses the genderless term *parents*, most data focus on mothers with intellectual and developmental disabilities rather than fathers (Mayes & Björg Sigurjónsdóttir, 2010), which is especially problematic given the dramatically gendered cultural experiences of parenting. To adequately provide support services to parents with intellectual and developmental disabilities, a gender-sensitive approach is paramount, with the needs of both mothers and fathers taken into account (Mayes & Björg Sigurjónsdóttir). (For further details about issues related to parenting, see Chapter 42 of this book.)

MASCULINITY

The majority of theory and research on the intersection of disability and masculinity has focused on men with physical disabilities, especially acquired physical impairments (Shuttleworth, Wedgwood, & Wilson, 2012). Among studies involving people with intellectual and developmental disabilities, it has been observed that men with intellectual and developmental disabilities have often been characterized as "eternal children," which denies them an adult masculine identity (Wilson, Parmenter, Stancliffe, & Shuttleworth, 2011). Masculinity may be seen as antithetical to intellectual and developmental disabilities, because masculinity is characterized by independence and strength, whereas having intellectual and developmental disabilities is more often perceived as a state of dependence characterized by limitations in adaptive functioning (Shuttleworth et al., 2012).

Another factor at play in the feminization of men with disabilities may be a lifetime of interacting with primarily female caregivers using highly gendered social scripts (Wilson, Shuttleworth, Stancliffe, & Parmenter, 2012). The predominance of female caregivers may help to explain the abundance of research on behavior challenges in men with intellectual and developmental disabilities involving physical aggression. An approach that values male physical aggression within this population may actually reduce the incidence of physical aggression while still maintaining individuals' masculinity (Wilson et al., 2012).

SEXUALITY

Although people with intellectual and developmental disabilities typically have the same sexual desires as people without intellectual and developmental disabilities, their right to sexuality has historically been denied (Richards, Watson, & Monger, 2012; Winges-Yanez, 2014). In particular, gay and lesbian people with intellectual and developmental disabilities are likely to have restrictions on how they express their sexuality (Abbott, 2013). The opportunity for people with intellectual and developmental disabilities to engage in sexual activities is complicated by questions about sexual knowledge, lack of privacy in many formal disability service settings, fear of sexual abuse, and concerns about individuals' capacity to consent to sex (Saxe & Flanagan, 2014).

Beginning in adolescence, people with intellectual and developmental disabilities generally have lower levels of sexual knowledge than their counterparts without disabilities (Jahoda & Pownall, 2014), and this knowledge gap may continue into adulthood (Eastgate, van Driel, Lennox, & Scheermeyer, 2011). This lowered understanding of sexuality is likely due both to not being included in formal sexual education in school (Tice & Harnek Hall, 2008) and to having more restricted social networks compared with their peers (Jahoda & Pownall, 2014). Without this sexual knowledge, people with intellectual and developmental disabilities may be less aware of how to use contraceptives, participate in sexual health screenings such as Pap smears, or prevent sexually transmitted infections.

In adulthood, one primary barrier to the expression of sexuality for people with intellectual and developmental disabilities is that of privacy. Whereas privacy is often taken for granted in the general public, in a system in which people are served in institutions or group homes, the right to privacy becomes murky, making sexual or romantic relationships difficult (Richards et al., 2012). Policies for sexual expression within these systems vary widely and often err on the side of paternalism (Winges-Yanez, 2014). Caregivers for people with intellectual and developmental disabilities report that fear and uncertainty, inadequate training on sexual issues, and balancing their role of protecting people from sexual abuse and simultaneously facilitating their sexuality all make it difficult to support sexual needs (Rushbrooke, Murray, & Townsend, 2014).

Both children and adults with intellectual and developmental disabilities are more likely to experience sexual abuse than people without disabilities (Hughes et al., 2012; Jones et al., 2012). Fear of sexual abuse within this population has, in many cases, led to a culture of paternalism and protectionism

for adults with intellectual and developmental disabilities with regard to their personal sexuality (Winges-Yanez, 2014). Women with intellectual and developmental disabilities, in particular, are often portrayed as "sexual innocents" or sexual victims, despite having a much more complex relationship to sex (Bernert & Ogletree, 2013; Lesseliers, van Hove, & van Hoey, 2010).

In contrast to the image of women with intellectual and developmental disabilities as sexual innocents or sexual victims, men with intellectual and developmental disabilities are frequently depicted as sexual aggressors or predators (Winges-Yanez, 2014). Some of the sexual deviance seen among men with intellectual and developmental disabilities may be due to "counterfeit deviance," meaning that although their sexual behavior is atypical or inappropriate, this behavior should be understood within the context of their lives. Because men with intellectual and developmental disabilities often live in situations in which appropriate sexual behaviors are not allowed or supported, any sexual behavior can be seen as problematic or deviant (Griffiths, Hingsburger, Hoath, & Ioannou, 2013). A strengths-based approach to supporting the sexuality of men with intellectual and developmental disabilities could target key problem areas in sexuality for this population: distinguishing between sexual behaviors that are acceptable in private but not in public, eliminating sexual behavior directed at others without their consent, managing sexual risks, and providing access to male-specific health screening (Wilson & Plummer, 2014). (For further details about issues related to sexuality, see Chapter 41 of this book.)

DOMAINS OF ADULT LIFE

Responsibilities of adult roles raise distinct issues for many adults with intellectual and developmental disabilities.

Work

Finding work remains a challenge for many adults with intellectual and developmental disabilities, with high rates of unemployment and limited job opportunities characterized by low wages and a lack of meaningful work experiences. Women with intellectual and developmental disabilities are at a particular disadvantage in finding employment. Much like their counterparts without disabilities, women with intellectual and developmental disabilities are more likely to earn less money and work fewer hours in low wage jobs than men of similar abilities (Boeltzig, Timmons, & Butterworth, 2009). In addition, there are significant gender differences in the types of jobs men and women with intellectual and developmental disabilities work, with more women working in food services and clerical fields and more men working in farming, gardening, janitorial work, assembly, manufacturing, packaging, and mail distribution (Boeltzig et al.; Umb-Carlsson & Sonnander, 2006). These gender differences in job types roughly mirror the same types of gender-based job distribution in the general public. (For further details about issues related to employment, see Chapter 38 of this book.)

Relationships

It has been well established that the social networks of people with intellectual and developmental disabilities are restricted compared with their peers without disabilities. These restricted social networks not only reduce quality of life but may also affect health, mental health, and security. People in congregate living situations have an especially difficult time sustaining relationships and friendships, relying instead on their staff and family members for friendship (Lippold & Burns, 2009). Although the companionship offered by paid staff has some value, it does not constitute the true "friendship" most of these adults desire. Engaging in same-sex or opposite-sex friendships remains elusive for many adults with intellectual and developmental disabilities, and support staff have difficulty facilitating these relationships for people with whom they work.

In addition to friendships, people with intellectual and developmental disabilities are often restricted in sustaining meaningful romantic relationships, especially because policies within the disability support system create environments in which they must engage in these relationships privately and often without the approval of staff members (Lafferty, McConkey, & Taggart, 2013). The legacy of the eugenics movement, which deliberately separated men and women for fear they would procreate, may live on in policies that restrict the relationships of adults with intellectual and developmental disabilities. Although the desire to engage in relationships and marry is similar to that of

people without disabilities, opportunities to engage in such relationships are rare among this population (Lafferty et al., 2013). Further complicating the opportunities for adults with intellectual and developmental disabilities to become involved in romantic relationships is the high risk of abuse for both women and men.

WOMEN'S HEALTH

Individuals with intellectual and developmental disabilities often face health service–related disparities across the spectrum of health care services. Women with intellectual and developmental disabilities face additional disparities in receiving women's health care such as mammograms, gynecological care, and reproductive care. Focus groups with women with intellectual and developmental disabilities revealed a number of barriers to receiving women's health care, including anxiety and fear, communication struggles, and inadequate education about women's health (Brown & Gill, 2009). It is startling to note that many women within these focus groups stated that they were refusing all gynecological pelvic exams and mammograms because they associated them with pain and anxiety (Brown & Gill, 2009). Similarly, studies have shown that women with intellectual and developmental disabilities are less likely to receive screening for cervical and breast cancer than women without disabilities, due both to not knowing the exam is needed as well as to discomfort during the exam (Swaine, Dababnah, Parish, & Luken, 2013). These findings emphasize the importance of support staff and health providers being sensitive to the anxiety of women with intellectual and developmental disabilities in these health care settings and providing more extensive education and support for women's health with these women.

Comorbid disorders and conditions related to intellectual disability may predispose women with intellectual and developmental disabilities to certain health problems. For instance, women with Down syndrome are more likely to have earlier onset of menstruation as well as concerns with menstrual conditions such as debilitating cramps (Pikora et al., 2014). The use of antiepileptic medication among people with intellectual and developmental disabilities may also contribute to vitamin D deficiencies, which are associated with osteoporosis and rickets (Teagarden, Meador, & Loring, 2014). Women with intellectual and developmental disabilities are also generally more likely to struggle with obesity than women in the general population (Rimmer & Yamaki, 2006).

MEN'S HEALTH

Much like women with intellectual and developmental disabilities, men with intellectual and developmental disabilities likely have reduced access to male-specific health screenings. Although it is known that hypogonadism and testicular cancer are more common in males with intellectual and developmental disabilities than in the general population, more research on these topics is necessary (McElduff, Center, & Beange, 2003; Sasco et al., 2008; Wilson & Plummer, 2014). It is unclear the extent to which screenings for testicular and prostate cancer are performed among men with intellectual and developmental disabilities. The lack of guidance and training within the intellectual and developmental disabilities service system on male-specific screenings as well as the penile health needs of men is an area that should receive further consideration in health care delivery (Wilson & Plummer, 2014).

GENDER AND CAREGIVING FOR PEOPLE WITH INTELLECTUAL AND DEVELOPMENTAL DISABILITIES

Within the United States, the majority of people with intellectual and developmental disabilities continue to live with family caregivers well into adulthood (Braddock et al., 2013). As the life expectancy for people with intellectual and developmental disabilities increases, families are likely to provide lifelong care (Factor, Heller, & Janicki, 2012). Caregiving for family members with intellectual and developmental disabilities most frequently falls on women, especially mothers. This gender disparity for caregiving begins in childhood but continues into the person with intellectual and developmental disabilities' adult life. Many studies have revealed detrimental effects of caregiving on mothers of children with disabilities as compared with parents of typically developing children, as well as on mothers caring for adult children with intellectual and developmental disabilities. These detrimental effects include poorer health and mental health; more restricted social networks; higher prevalence of high blood pressure, arthritis, and obesity; limitations in life activities; and decreased job prospects due to the

higher parenting demands at home (Seltzer, Floyd, Song, Greenberg, & Hong, 2011). However, a minority of studies on family caregiving for people with intellectual and developmental disabilities have used the social model of disability as a lens through which to focus on the positive aspects of this caregiving (Green, Darling, & Wilbers, 2013).

SUMMARY

Gender plays an important role in the lives of people with intellectual and developmental disabilities, despite the tendency for this aspect of their identity to be overlooked within research and in society at large. A view of people with intellectual and developmental disabilities as asexual and agendered does not take into account these individuals' self-identification as men and women and denies them gender roles that are an important part of how they think, act, and live. The legacy of eugenics and historical attempts to control and deny the gender and sexuality of people with intellectual and developmental disabilities can be seen in modern policies that continue to ignore and deny the importance of gender in these individuals' lives. This chapter has explored some of the ways in which gender affects the lives of people with intellectual and developmental disabilities, including their masculinity or femininity, sexuality, life domains such as work and relationships, and gender-specific health concerns. Professional organizations for people with intellectual and developmental disabilities and health care professionals, as well as family caregivers, would do well to take gender into consideration when forming policies and supporting individuals in living full and meaningful lives.

FOR FURTHER THOUGHT AND DISCUSSION

1. In the early 20th century, women with intellectual and developmental disabilities were often more prone to discrimination and segregation. Why was this? What factors contributed to this outcome? Might some of these issues persist?

2. What stereotypes and biases might affect men with intellectual and developmental disabilities?

3. Women with intellectual and developmental disabilities achieve less positive employment and community inclusion outcomes than do men with intellectual and developmental disabilities. Why

might this be the case? How does this affect the lives of women with intellectual and developmental disabilities?

4. Friends and romantic partners are important to all humans. How are people with intellectual and developmental disabilities denied opportunities to form meaningful relationships and build friendships? How does gender affect this? What actions might address these discrepancies?

5. There is a well-documented gap in access to health care for people with intellectual and developmental disabilities. Discuss how this affects women's health and men's health outcomes. What can be done to reduce the gap?

REFERENCES

Abbott, D. (2013). Nudge, nudge, wink, wink: Love, sex and gay men with intellectual disabilities—a helping hand or a human right? *Journal of Intellectual Disability Research, 57*(11), 1079–1087.

Barnartt, S. (2013). Introduction. In S. Barnartt (Ed.), *Disability and intersecting statuses.* Bingley, United Kingdom: Emerald Press.

Bernert, D.J., & Ogletree, R.J. (2013). Women with intellectual disabilities talk about their perceptions of sex. *Journal of Intellectual Disability Research, 57*(3), 240–249.

Boeltzig, H., Timmons, J.C., & Butterworth, J. (2009). Gender differences in employment outcomes of individuals with developmental disabilities. *Journal of Vocational Rehabilitation, 31*(1), 29–38.

Braddock, D., Hemp, R., Rizzolo, M.C., Tanis, E.S., Haffer, L., Lulinski, A., & Wu, J. (2013). *State of the states in developmental disabilities, 2013: The great recession and its aftermath.* Washington, DC: American Association on Intellectual and Developmental Disabilities.

Brown, A.A., & Gill, C.J. (2009). New voices in women's health: Perceptions of women with intellectual and developmental disabilities. *Intellectual and Developmental Disabilities, 47*(5), 337–347.

Burns, J. (1993). Invisible women—women who have intellectual disabilities. *The Psychologist: Bulletin of the British Psychological Society, 6,* 102–105.

Eastgate, G., van Driel, M.L., Lennox, N., & Scheermeyer, E. (2011). Women with intellectual disabilities: A study of sexuality, sexual abuse and protection skills. *Australian Family Physician, 40*(4), 226–230.

Factor, A., Heller, T., & Janicki, M. (2012). *Bridging the aging and developmental disabilities service networks: Challenges and best practices.* Retrieved from http://www.rrtcadd .org/resources/Resources/Publications/Policy/Service /Briefs-&-Reports/Bridging-Report.pdf

Flintoff, A., Fitzgerald, H., & Scraton, S. (2008). The challenges of intersectionality: Researching difference in physical education. *International Studies in Sociology of Education, 18*(2), 73–85.

Green, S.E., Darling, R.B., & Wilbers, L. (2013). Has the parent experience changed over time? A meta-analysis of qualitative studies of parents of children with disabilities from 1960 to 2012. *Research in Social Science and Disability, 7,* 97–168.

Griffiths, D., Hingsburger, D., Hoath, J., & Ioannou, S. (2013). "Counterfeit deviance" revisited. *Journal of Applied Research in Intellectual Disabilities, 26*(5), 471–480.

Herndl, D.P. (2013). Politics and sympathy: Recognition and action in feminist literary disability studies. *Legacy, 30*(1), 187–200.

Hughes, K., Bellis, M.A., Jones, L., Wood, S., Bates, G., Eckley, L.,…Officer, A. (2012). Prevalence and risk of violence against adults with disabilities: A systematic review and meta-analysis of observational studies. *The Lancet, 379*(9826), 1621–1629.

Jahoda, A., & Pownall, J. (2014). Sexual understanding, sources of information and social networks: The reports of young people with intellectual disabilities and their non-disabled peers. *Journal of Intellectual Disability Research, 58*(5), 430–441.

Jones, L., Bellis, M.A., Wood, S., Hughes, K., McCoy, E., Eckley, L.,…Officer, A. (2012). Prevalence and risk of violence against children with disabilities: A systematic review and meta-analysis of observational studies. *The Lancet, 380*(9845), 899–907.

Lafferty, A., McConkey, R., & Taggart, L. (2013). Beyond friendship: The nature and meaning of close personal relationships as perceived by people with learning disabilities. *Disability and Society, 28*(8), 1074–1088.

Lesseliers, J., van Hove, G., & van Hoey, T. (2010). Supporting relationships: Lessons from what people with learning disabilities have to say. In M. McCarthy & D. Thompson (Eds.), *Sexuality and learning disability: A handbook* (pp. 97–108). Brighton, United Kingdom: Pavilion.

Lippold, T., & Burns, J. (2009). Social support and intellectual disabilities: A comparison between social networks of adults with intellectual disability and those with physical disability. *Journal of Intellectual Disability Research, 53*(5), 463–473.

Llewellyn, G. (2013). Parents with intellectual disability and their children: Advances in policy and practice. *Journal of Policy and Practice in Intellectual Disabilities, 10*(2), 82–85.

Mayes, R., & Björg Sigurjónsdóttir, H. (2010). Becoming a mother—becoming a father. In G. Lewellyn, R. Traustadóttir, D. McConnell, & H. Björg Sigurjónsdóttir (Eds.), *Parents with intellectual disabilities: Past, present and futures* (pp.15–31). Hoboken, NJ: John Wiley & Sons.

Mayes, R., & Llewellyn, G. (2009). What happens to parents with intellectual disability following removal of their child in child protection proceedings? *Journal of Intellectual and Developmental Disability, 34*(1), 92–95.

McElduff, A., Center, J., & Beange, H. (2003). Hypogonadism in men with intellectual disabilities: A population study. *Journal of Intellectual and Developmental Disability, 28*(2), 163–170.

Mehrota, N., & Vaidya, S. (2008). Exploring constructs of disability and personhood in Haryana and Delhi. *Indian Journal of Gender Studies, 15*(2), 317–340.

Minister, M. (2013). Religion and (dis)ability in early feminism. *Journal of Feminist Studies in Religion, 29*(2), 5–24.

Pikora, T.J., Bourke, J., Bathgate, K., Foley, K., Lennox, N., & Leonard, H. (2014). Health conditions and their impact among adolescents and young adults with Down syndrome. *PLOS ONE, 9*(5).

Proctor, S.N., & Azar, S.T. (2013). The effect of parental intellectual disability status on child protection service worker decision making. *Journal of Intellectual Disability Research, 57*(12), 1104–1116.

Richards, D.A., Watson, S.L., & Monger, S. (2012). The right to sexuality and relationships. In D. Griffiths, F. Owen, & S.L. Watson (Eds.), *The human rights agenda for persons with intellectual disabilities* (pp. 103–128). Kingston, NY: NADD.

Rimmer, J.H., & Yamaki, K. (2006). Obesity and intellectual disability. *Mental Retardation and Developmental Disabilities Research Reviews, 12*(1), 22–27.

Rushbrooke, E., Murray, C.D., & Townsend, S. (2014). What difficulties are experienced by caregivers in relation to the sexuality of people with intellectual disabilities? A qualitative meta-synthesis. *Research in Developmental Disabilities, 35*(4), 871–886.

Sasco, A.J., Ah-Song, R., Nishi, M., Culine, S., Réthoré, M., & Satgé, D. (2008). Testicular cancer and intellectual disability. *International Journal on Disability and Human Development, 7*(4), 397–403.

Saxe, A. & Flanagan, T. (2014). Factors that impact support workers' perceptions of the sexuality of adults with developmental disabilities: A quantitative analysis. *Sexuality and Disability, 32*, 45–63.

Seltzer, M.M., Floyd, F., Song, J., Greenberg, J., & Hong, J. (2011). Midlife and aging parents of adults with intellectual and developmental disabilities: Impacts of lifelong parenting. *American Journal on Intellectual and Developmental Disabilities, 116*(6), 479–499.

Shuttleworth, R., Wedgwood, N., & Wilson, N.J. (2012). The dilemma of disabled masculinity. *Men and Masculinities, 15*(2), 174–194.

Starogiannis, H., & Hill, D.B. (2008). Sex and gender in an American State School (1951–1987): The Willowbrook class. *Sexuality and Disability, 26*, 83–103.

Swaine, J.G., Dababnah, S., Parish, S.L., & Luken, K. (2013). Family caregivers' perspectives on barriers and facilitators of cervical and breast cancer screening for women with intellectual disability. *Intellectual and Developmental Disabilities, 51*(1), 62–73.

Teagarden, D.L., Meador, K.J., & Loring, D.W. (2014). Low vitamin D levels are common in patients with epilepsy. *Epilepsy Research, 108*(8), 1352–1356.

Tice, C.J., & Harnek Hall, D.M. (2008). Sexuality education and adolescents with developmental disabilities: Assessment, policy, and advocacy. *Journal of Social Work in Disability and Rehabilitation, 7*(1), 47–62.

Tilley, E., Walmsley, J., Earle, S., & Atkinson, D. (2012). "The silence is roaring": Sterilization, reproductive rights and women with intellectual disabilities. *Disability and Society, 27*(3), 413–426.

Trent, J.W. (1995). *Inventing the feeble mind: A history of mental retardation in the United States.* Oakland, CA: University of California Press.

Umb-Carlsson, O., & Sonnander, K. (2006) Living conditions of adults with intellectual disabilities from a gender perspective. *Journal of Intellectual Disability Research, 50*(5), 326–334.

United Nations. (2006). *Convention on the rights of persons with disabilities.* Retrieved from http://www.un.org/disabilities/convention/conventionfull.shtml

Walsh-Gallagher, D., Sinclair, M., & McConkey, R. (2012). The ambiguity of disabled women's experiences of pregnancy, childbirth and motherhood: A phenomenological understanding. *Midwifery, 28*(2), 156–162.

Wilson, S., McKenzie, K., Quayle, E., & Murray, G. (2014). A systematic review of interventions to promote social support and parenting skills in parents with an intellectual disability. *Child: Care, Health and Development, 40*(1), 7–19.

Wilson, N.J., Parmenter, T.R., Stancliffe, R.J., & Shuttleworth, R.P. (2011). Conditionally sexual: Men and teenage boys with moderate to profound intellectual disability. *Sexuality and Disability, 29*(3), 275–289.

Wilson, N.J., & Plummer, D. (2014). Towards supporting a healthy masculine sexuality: Utilising mainstream male health policy and masculinity theory. *Journal of Intellectual and Developmental Disability, 39*(2), 132–136.

Wilson, N.J., Shuttleworth, R., Stancliffe, R., & Parmenter, T. (2012). Masculinity theory in applied research with men and boys with intellectual disability. *Intellectual and Developmental Disabilities, 50*(3), 261–272.

Winges-Yanez, N. (2014). Why all the talk about sex? An authoethnography identifying the troubling discourse of sexuality and intellectual disability. *Sexuality and Disability, 32*(1), 107–116.

44

Aging

Philip McCallion, Nancy Jokinen, and Matthew P. Janicki

WHAT YOU WILL LEARN

- The dramatic increase in life expectancy for people with intellectual disability since the 1960s and the growing need for services and supports for older-age people with intellectual disability
- The continued residence of many older-age people with intellectual disability with their aging parents and the need for support systems that address both families and older-age people with intellectual disability
- The importance of maintaining high quality of life, social connectedness, and physical and mental well-being as components of supports for older-age people with intellectual disability
- The need for a comprehensive reorientation of services and training to effectively deliver services to aging people with intellectual disability and their family caregivers

Life expectancy for people with intellectual disability in the United States has increased from an average 18.5 years in 1930 to 59.1 years in the 1970s to an estimated 66.2 years in 1993 (Braddock, 1999). There are reports of similar growth in the United Kingdom, other European countries, and Australia (Bigby, McCallion, & McCarron, 2014). However, data and discussions in *The Lancet* (Heslop et al., 2014; McCallion & McCarron, 2014) and symposia at the 2014 International Association for the Scientific Study of Intellectual and Developmental Disabilities European Congress have highlighted that continued growth in longevity may not have increased further since about 2005 (McCallion, Hastings, & McCarron, 2014; McCarron, Carroll, Kelly, & McCallion, 2014). Findings that there are higher

rates of avoidable deaths from manageable health conditions point to the need for more targeted and skillful health care delivery for people with intellectual disability as they age (Heslop et al., 2014). However, even with slowing increases in longevity, there is evidence from national databases that the numbers of individuals older than 35 and older than 60 has steadily risen (Kelly & Kelly, 2014; McCallion & McCarron, 2015), also meaning that there are increased needs for both family caregivers and formal services—a demand that services providers and staff groups are ill prepared to address (McCallion, 2006; McCallion & McCarron, 2015).

When people with intellectual disability were not expected to live into old age, there was a reasonable expectation that parents would outlive their offspring and offer a lifetime of care, and with most of that care provided in the home, few services for old age were developed or provided (McCallion & McCarron, 2015). Now with sizeable groups of people with intellectual disability aging, the demand for formal services is heightened to a level greater than that for the general population, which is also seeing increased longevity (Jackson, Howe, & Nakashima, 2011). This reflects the fact that people with intellectual disability have lower rates of employment than the general population, which means they have personal incomes close to or below poverty lines, resulting in a heavy reliance on government income supports. They also are less likely to have married or to have children or robust networks of close friends (McCarron et al., 2011) and are likely to have greater dependence either upon staffed living and programming situations and/or on the small number of family members who provide most of their care (Bigby et al., 2014;

Duggan & Linehan, 2013; McCallion & McCarron, 2015). Equally, there is little respite from such caregiving for the caregiver (Lightfoot & McCallion, in press), further straining the available informal resources. Needs for services and supports are considerable and varied, yet providing services for aging people with intellectual disability and supporting their families are areas in which many professionals have received little training (Bigby et al., 2014).

Increased aging must also be seen in the context of increasing life transitions. Living plans for people with intellectual disability assume that the individual will live in the community, control to the extent possible his or her life, have a vital and supportive network of friends and relationships, and experience more independence this year as compared to last (McCallion & McCarron, 2007). Aging challenges some of these assumptions, as it may be a time, as it is for many other aging people, when work experiences end and decrements rather than expansions in ability and independence occur. Caregiving transitions are also increased by the changing family structures due to increases in single-parent families, lowered birth rates that further reduce the size of caregiving networks, greater participation by women in the work force and increased conflict between work and caregiving responsibilities (Jackson et al., 2011), and delayed childbearing by siblings and increased age of parents together increasing multiple co-incident caregiving demands on siblings (Lightfoot & McCallion, in press). For people with intellectual disability, uncertainty about the integrity and sustainability of their family caregiving situations also means an increased need to consider staffed interventions to support existing caregiving, facilitate within-family transitions, and manage planned-for rather than abrupt transfers to new care arrangements (McCallion & Kolomer, 2003a).

Adulthood and old age may also be a time for further losses (e.g., loss of parents and valued friends and neighbors) and many transitions in key staff in day, residential, and community group home programs (from transfer and promotion of staff more than from death) (Lightfoot & McCallion, in press). In addition, such losses may also signal movement from the family home to an out-of-home placement and related separation from well-established and valued social networks and neighborhoods (Bigby et al., 2014).

As people with intellectual disability increasingly live community-based lives, they also face exposure to the potential for financial, physical, and sexual exploitation, yet efforts to avoid or manage such risks may have the unintended consequence of restrictions being imposed on the lives of people with intellectual disability (Aldridge, 2007). Instead, a focus is needed upon increasing self-advocacy and independence and on harm reduction strategies and the development of skills among staff to effectively interview those who may have been abused and to apply supportive interventions to address the toll of abuse (McCallion et al., 2008).

In his consideration of fundamental principles underpinning successful aging, Kahn (2002) argued for the importance of an absence of illness and of illness-related disability. However, he acknowledged that successful aging may also require acceptance of age-determined health-related decrements to independence and that responding to such decrements would also require compensating for the declines with external resources. The maintenance of good health and the application of additional external resources when ill health does occur are likely to be of particular concern for people with intellectual disability.

Given the life transitions and potential for aging-related health concerns experienced, the needs of both families and of people with intellectual disability are likely to change. Most services available continue to be based upon, and assume, fixed needs for people with intellectual disability, at levels established in their younger years. However, needs change with age and, therefore, so too must the services and the staff that support them (McCallion & McCarron, 2004a; McCallion, Swinburne, Burke, McGlinchey, & McCarron, 2013). New services needed include retirement planning, aging-focused day programming, support of chronic condition health needs, and adaptations of homes and program sites to maintain personal independence, given new or increased impairments associated with aging (Lightfoot & McCallion, in press).

OLDER-AGE ADULTS WITH INTELLECTUAL DISABILITY: A UNIQUE COHORT

Older-age adults with and without intellectual disability are a diverse group of people with differing values, personalities, interests, and living situations as well as a range of skills and abilities. The needs of all older adults are similar: housing that accommodates changing abilities with age, adequate nutrition, access to timely and appropriate health care, and opportunities for positive social engagement. However, due to their lifelong disability, older adults with intellectual disability also have unique life experiences and perceptions compared with age peers in the general population that must also be considered (Kåhlin, Kjellberg, Nord, & Hagberg, 2013).

As a cohort, older adults with intellectual disability were born and raised during a time that encouraged institutionalization and, in some cases, promoted their sterilization. As youth, educational opportunities were nominal and, as young adults, employment prospects limited. They were often denied the right to marry. Older-age adults with intellectual disability in receipt of services have seen a convoy of staff coming and going and witnessed significant changes in beliefs that framed their services and supports, including the embracing of community living and inclusion.

At the beginning of the 21st century, older-age adults with intellectual disability live in an array of situations: alone or with family members, a spouse, or other unrelated adults with and without disabilities, sometimes in formal settings such as group homes. In some locales, they may also live in institutions specifically designed for people with intellectual disability or for older people requiring extended care (e.g., a long-term care facility) (see, e.g., Braddock, 2013). In developed countries, there are longstanding concerns about the futures of adults with intellectual disability who continue to reside with aging family caregivers (Ryan, Taggart, Truesdale-Kennedy, & Slevin, 2014). Many older-age parents provide significant support to their sons or daughters who have intellectual disability—social, emotional, financial, and practical assistance—whether co-resident or not (Hines, Balandin, & Togher, 2014). The negative impact of this prolonged caregiving on parental health has been of concern, yet older-age parents living with their offspring also report their caregiving experience as rewarding and some of these relationships as reciprocal in nature (Cairns, Brown, Tolson, & Darbyshire, 2014; Lightfoot & McCallion, in press). The importance and benefits of reciprocity in familial relationships has had too scant attention (Perkins & Haley, 2013).

Working with Families Caring at Home

The greatest focus for service providers had traditionally been upon children and young adults with intellectual disability. In school and in residential care, there have been mandates, legal or implied, for a basic level of services, for example for special education services (McCallion, 1993). For adults with intellectual disability, mandates are less defined and attention is paid most to those in out-of-home placements. Those adults living at home may also receive some additional services. However, such adults are less likely to receive and may not receive professional services while they are in their young and middle adult years (Lightfoot & McCallion, in press; McCallion & Kolomer, 2003b). It is often a surprise to staff and administrators to realize how many people with intellectual disability and their families have minimal or no contact with services and that sustained contacts may only be in the older years.

The majority of people with intellectual disability are cared for at home, for all the attention paid to out-of-home care. There is every expectation that the large number of people with intellectual disability living at home in the second decade of the 21st century and being cared for by individuals in their 40s and 50s will, by 2030, still be cared for by these individuals, who will then be in their 60s and 70s. Greater and rapidly growing demands will be placed on limited out-of-home services when caregivers are having increased difficulties or are no longer able or available to provide care (Lightfoot & McCallion, in press). Better current and future planning for these families and thoughtful provision of respite and other supportive services will be needed (if not needed already), as will earlier encouragement of health promotion recommendations for both caregiver and care recipient and the designation of staff as specialists in such support.

Responsibility for the care of a person with intellectual disability is rarely shared equally by all family members. It is primarily, but not exclusively, a female responsibility (usually the mother), and generally there is one primary caregiver. The identification of a primary caregiver has led many service providers to focus attention solely on this family member. However, attention is also needed to the additional support provided by fathers (McCallion & Kolomer, 2003b), siblings (including sons), and adolescent grandchildren (Lightfoot & McCallion, in press), as illness or later absence of these individuals will change the caregiving situation. Transitions in caregiving are also an important concern; when a mother or father is no longer able or available to provide care, people with intellectual disability generally do not have spouses or children to assume that care, as do many other aging people, so the responsibility falls to siblings or to out-of-home placements (McCallion, 2006).

For staff assisting in the planning for future care of people with intellectual disability, out-of-home care may seem the easier and, in the case of community group home placement, even the preferable approach. However, this assumes that "a bed" is available and that this transition is the desire of the person with intellectual disability and the family. Future care planning should instead begin with an assessment of the desires of the individual with intellectual disability and the family, an understanding of the available social network and past patterns of care, consideration of improvement or supports to informal care, and where the strategic addition of formal services would be helpful. Families may need to be "helped" (not told) to include the person with intellectual disability in the planning process. Even if the chosen future plan is out-of-home placement, in the short term, enhanced support to families may be needed to allow them to continue to care for the older family member with intellectual disability until the placement becomes available (Bigby et al., 2014; McCarron & McCallion, 2007).

Families of a person with intellectual disability complain of being "referred around" or "falling through the cracks" and receiving few of the services they believe they need; they experience staff in their discipline roles as "partializing" the person with intellectual disability or the family and not spending enough time to understand the entire caregiving situation. These experiences contribute to a belief that service systems and professionals make families feel just as labeled and stigmatized as their child or adult family member. However, active participation of families and people with intellectual disability themselves in the planning and delivery of needed services will result in more appropriate services and greater functional achievement by the family member with intellectual disability (McCallion & Kolomer, 2003a). The challenge to service providers and staff is to create an environment of respect and inclusion and one where the strengths of the family and the aging person with intellectual disability are clearly included and appreciated.

Permanency Planning

Reviews of studies of the self-identified needs of families of people with intellectual disability report that addressing fears about future care was the highest rated need (Bigby et al., 2014; Lightfoot & McCallion, in press). Traditionally, permanency planning has focused on maintaining children with intellectual disability in their own homes (McCallion & Toseland, 1993). However, increased longevity has raised the issue of permanency, futures, or long-term planning for people with intellectual disability who outlive parents and siblings. The planning role with engaged families in future planning is to ensure that adequate and up-to-date information is available. Staff will be best prepared to offer families of people with intellectual disability assistance with planning if they understand the course and history of care they have provided, review all records available, and interview family members. In the absence of such planning, the illness or death of a caregiver requires a crisis response (McCallion, 2006). This often precludes choosing the best living options for the person with intellectual disability and exacerbates the sense of loss the individual with intellectual disability will feel (McCallion & Kolomer, 2003a). Families who successfully utilize respite and other services have been found to be more likely to consider residential placement (Caldwell & Heller, 2003). Therefore, as both the person with intellectual disability and the family age, a role for staff may be to encourage and facilitate such related service use. Key services to be familiar with include in-home respite, out-of-home respite or vacation programs, home-help services, transportation assistance, and day and recreation or leisure programs.

SOCIAL CONNECTEDNESS AND QUALITY OF LIFE

There have been long-standing beliefs that movement from institutions to the community and to group home and independent living from family care leads to greater community involvement, and older adults with intellectual disability who made such transitions earlier in life would be expected to benefit most from these strategies. As reviewed by Amado, Stancliffe, McCarron, and McCallion (2013), there is evidence of increases in the size of social networks and of greater participation in community-based activities, but concerns are also raised that success is much more about presence in the community than genuine involvement and engagement. Questions are also raised about the value (or lack of value) placed in such studies on relationships with family members, other people with intellectual disability, and staff members. To the extent that aging is time for reductions in social networks for all, the impact that living arrangements have on quality of life is of interest. It has been argued, for example, that preferred housing options are those that enable the individual to maintain peer relationships forged through involvement in previous supported employment or other day activities (Shaw, Cartwright, & Craig, 2011). There is little evidence that this arrangement is supported; it is more likely that changing needs will result in movement to settings that address health and other needs associated with aging (Janicki, Dalton, McCallion, Baxley, & Zendell, 2005).

Promoting and maintaining quality of life as people age are significant concerns. Many organizations seek various ways to enhance and assess quality of life for service users (Reinders & Schalock, 2014), and some intellectual disability funders utilize a quality of life framework and associated indicators to evaluate service outcomes (see, e.g., Alberta Human Services, 2014). Government initiatives also seek to promote quality of life across the ages (see, e.g., Healthy People 2020, National Center for Health Statistics, 2012). Research on the general population suggests that quality of life trajectories decline with older ages given relocations, death of family and friends, and other transitions. Improving the psychosocial context for older-age people as well as providing support for age-associated changes that affect daily living may help maintain quality of life (Zaninotto, Falaschetti, & Sacker, 2009). Research from the field of aging also suggests that perceptions of quality of life and priorities change with age (Plagnol & Scott, 2011). Studies of quality of life, whether from the field of intellectual disabilities or of general aging, agree on the importance of choice, autonomy, and social relations as cornerstones to maintaining quality of life (Jokinen, 2014) and that individuals' perceptions play a vital role in the measurement and experience of quality of life (Brown & Faragher, 2014).

More needs to be done in the field of intellectual disability to advance the cornerstones of quality of life and to understand its subjective experience.

Ageism

Ageist stereotypes have been reported as impinging on opportunities for older people to live fuller lives (World Health Organization, 2012) and, thereby, negatively affect quality of life. Among people with intellectual disability themselves, their perceptions of aging include references to physical body changes and other perceived negative declines (Burke, McCarron, Carroll, McGlinchey, & McCallion, 2014; Kåhlin et al., 2013). There were also findings of respondents feeling positive about their futures and believing that they could still do most things (Burke et al.), and Kåhlin et al. reported that some people with intellectual disability experienced later life as a time when they become the same as everyone else, when everyone needed support. However, in one study, staff acknowledged that reduced social networks, reliance on staff support, and the service environment were all barriers to promoting active aging (Buys, Aird, & Miller, 2012). Training and education are needed to counterbalance any tendencies toward ageism that might build upon the ableism barriers that people with intellectual disability have previously faced.

CHRONIC CONDITIONS THAT COMPROMISE THE AGING YEARS

The aging of people with intellectual disability is a credit to the sustained efforts of families, providers, communities, and professionals to improve their lives, but aging also presents its own challenges. Holland speculated that people with intellectual disability who survived into old age were probably healthier and hardier than those who did not (Holland, Hon, Huppert, & Stevens, 2000). However, he also expressed concern about the potential of additional age-related disabilities and the lack of preparedness of service networks. As of this writing in 2016, there are still concerns about system-level and professional readiness (Bigby et al., 2014).

The experience of chronic illness among people with intellectual disability and the similarities and dissimilarities with experiences of the general population have been the subjects of a number of investigations pointing to a high prevalence of disorders that go unrecognized and untreated

(Emerson, 2011; Emerson et al., 2011; McCarron et al., 2011; van Schrojenstein Lantman-De Valk, Metsemakers, Haveman, & Crebolder, 2008). There is a greater prevalence among people with intellectual disability of gastrointestinal disorders, respiratory disorders such as pneumonia, sensory impairments, epilepsy, dental disease, osteoporosis, dementia, mental illness, and behavioral challenges (Cooper et al., 2007; Emerson; McCarron et al., 2011; McCarron et al., 2014). People with intellectual disability, as they age, are therefore frequent users of primary health care services—both general population caregivers and intellectual disability specialists—and as aging people with intellectual disability make greater use of community-based health care resources, there are concerns that the staff and facilities involved are unprepared (McCarron & Lawlor, 2003). Different patterns and combinations of morbidities, less focus on preventive interventions, and inattention to population health among people with intellectual disability are symptomatic of a lack of preparedness for aging people with intellectual disability in general population health delivery (McCarron, Swinburne, et al., 2013).

Frailty

Another relevant concept that is increasingly influencing health care for older adults in the general population is frailty. Evenhuis, Hermans, Hilgenkamp, Bastiaanse, and Echteld (2012), taking a standard definition of *frailty* as high vulnerability to adverse health conditions, measured frailty in people with intellectual disability using five criteria: weight loss, poor grip strength, slow walking speed, low physical activity, and poor endurance or exhaustion. They found that people with intellectual disability at ages 50–64 had a prevalence of frailty (11%) that was similar to that of the general population at ages 65 and older (7%–9%). Although age, Down syndrome, dementia, motor disability, and severe intellectual impairment were associated with frailty, statistically they only explained 25% of the variance. Using an alternative Frailty Index, the researchers found that people with intellectual disability older than age 50 had frailty scores similar to most elderly people older than 75 (Schoufour et al., 2012). The index comprised 50 health-related deficits, including physical, social, and medical problems, and established that rather than irreversible

premature aging, high levels of frailty among people with intellectual disability were associated with potentially preventable and reversible factors including very low levels of physical activity, social relationships, and community participation (Hilgenkamp, Reis, Wijck, & Evenhuis, 2012). Such ideas are poorly understood in both intellectual disability–specific and in general population health services, and there is a need for leadership in incorporating such concepts in the services offered to people with intellectual disability.

Health Management and Health Promotion as People Age

Access and support are critical to health management and health promotion, including access to appropriate foods and health screening, participation in physical activity and follow-up preventive care, and provision of financial and personal support from social networks (McCallion, Swinburne, et al., 2013; Taggart, Coates, & Truesdale-Kennedy, 2013). People with intellectual disability embark on life from a particularly disadvantaged position (Emerson & Baines, 2011). They are more likely to have lived in poverty; have poorer physical and mental health; have higher levels of obesity (Lennox, Bain, & Rey-Conde, 2007); are more likely to lead sedentary lifestyles (McGuire, Daly, & Smyth, 2007); tend to have nutritionally poor diets with limited access to fruits and vegetables and excessive access to fats, candy or sweets, desserts, and junk food (Ewing, McDermott, Thomas-Koger, Whitner, & Pierce, 2004; Humphries, Traci, & Seekins, 2009); participate less than the general population in physical activity (Temple & Walkley, 2003); and are less likely to have benefitted from preventive health screening and health promotion (Bigby et al., 2014; Emerson et al., 2011; McCarron et al., 2011). The higher rates of obesity and cholesterol and lower rates of physical activity potentially increase risk of diabetes, hypertension, heart disease, and arthritis late in life (Bigby et al., 2014; Evenhuis, Theunissen, Denkers, Verschuure, & Kemme, 2001; McCallion, Burke, et al., 2013). There is a particular concern about screenings. Samele et al. (2006), for example, estimated that in the United Kingdom, uptake of cervical cancer screening was 84%–89% overall but only 13%–47% in the population of people with intellectual disability. There are similar findings for vision and hearing impairment and for dental care

(MacGiolla-Phadraig et al., 2014; Emerson & Baines, 2011). Yet Robertson et al. (2011) concluded that based upon systematic review evidence, screening for people with intellectual disability is so beneficial that specifically designed health checks should become a routine part of primary care.

Physical Health

Compared with older adults in the general population, aging people with intellectual disability have the following:

- Higher rates of chronic conditions such as dementia (Jokinen, Janicki, Keller, McCallion, & Force, 2013)

- Different patterns of co-occurring conditions with greater levels of co-occurring mental health concerns (McCarron et al., 2013)

- Higher rates of unhealthy lifestyles (Haveman et al., 2010; McCarron et al., 2013)

- Higher levels of medication use (Raghavan & Patel, 2010)

These physical health challenges increase demands on caregivers, particularly when they may be dealing with their own increasing health concerns. Also, many health professionals are unfamiliar with and have received little training in the typical health and functioning issues in older adults with intellectual disability (Haveman et al., 2010), meaning they may miss health problems (McCarron et al., 2013). There are also reports that communication barriers (Scheepers et al., 2005), higher and different comorbidity, poorer management of health conditions, and minimal emphasis on prevention mean poorer care and mean that significant physical health-related burdens fall upon caregivers (Bigby et al., 2014; Lightfoot & McCallion, in press; McCarron et al., 2013).

Mental Health

Health concerns include psychosocial or mental health. A summation of available studies of mental health and behavioral concern prevalence suggested total rates ranging from 20% to 40% of assessed older people with intellectual disability and that psychiatric disorders, including dementia, increase as people with intellectual disability age (for a review, see Tyrrell & Dodd, 2003). Other

reviews argue that the picture is more complex, with most mental health concerns appearing to decline with age, except for dementia, which increases (Jacobson, 2003). Regardless, mental health issues are of concern, and aging people with intellectual disability are particularly at risk because of their life experiences; behavioral phenotypes (particularly for dementia); side effects of medications that they may metabolize differently from others; higher rates of sensory impairments that increase communication difficulties; aging-specific disorders such as Alzheimer's disease, which may predispose to depression and anxiety; and life events such as bereavements and abuse (Tyrrell & Dodd, 2003). Findings from the Intellectual Disability Supplement to the Irish Longitudinal Study on Ageing confirm such findings, with epilepsy, mental health concerns, unaddressed pain, comorbidity, and the consequences of polypharmacy appearing of most concern (McCallion et al., 2014; McCarron, O'Dwyer, Burke, McGlinchey, & McCallion, 2014; McCallion, Swinburne, et al., 2013).

Dementia

Dementia in people with Down syndrome exceeds that of the general population; one study reported a prevalence of 2% in people ages 30–39 years, 9.4% in people ages 40–49 years, 36.1% in people ages 50–59 years, and 54.5% in people ages 60–69 years (Prasher, 1995), as compared with general population rates of between 4.3% to 10% in people ages 65 years and older. Reports of the prevalence of dementia for other people with intellectual disability (who do not have Down syndrome) are more equivocal, with findings of rates similar to the general population (Janicki & Dalton, 2000) and also of higher rates (Cooper, 1997). People with Down syndrome and dementia experience an early and precipitous but then extended decline; pose care concerns given wandering, sleep disturbance, and incontinence; and in some cases experience auditory and visual hallucinations (McCarron, McCallion, Reilly, & Mulryan, 2014). In addition, depression and other mental health symptoms may be mistaken for dementia or may co-occur with dementia, further impairing functioning and compromising behavior (McCarron & Griffiths, 2003). A longitudinal follow-up of a group of women with Down syndrome confirmed increased incidence of other health conditions when dementia symptoms were present, including hearing, vision, and mobility impairments as well as depression, epilepsy, and lung disease (McCarron, O'Dwyer, et al., 2014).

Assessing and Managing Age-Related Chronic Conditions

A useful framework drawn from work by McCallion and McCarron (2007) identifies three principles— 1) absence of pain, 2) maintenance of health, and 3) psychosocial well-being—and offers an important basis for multidisciplinary work to assess and manage health concerns as people with intellectual disability age.

Absence of Pain   Diseases of old age, in people with and without intellectual disability, tend to be chronic rather than acute and may be accompanied by pain, yet people with intellectual disability are often unable or unaware of the need to complain about that pain in order for it to be treated (McCallion, 2003; McCallion & McCarron, 2007). Identifying pain in people with intellectual disability, particularly people with multiple and profound impairments, is complex (Bromley et al., 1998; McCallion, McCarron, Fahey-McCarthy, & Connaire, 2012). Health professionals, in their investigations of the causes of behavior problems and other symptoms, should be sensitive to identifying pain issues, and when such issues are identified, to providing appropriate responses. Medications may be appropriate, but given metabolism issues, multidisciplinary input should be encouraged to identify other strategies including positioning, complementary therapies, and proactive addressing of comfort needs.

Maintaining Health   Staff, families, and people with intellectual disability themselves should question what preventive and supportive health strategies are part of service delivery and not accept beliefs that decline is just something to be "expected" (McCarron & McCallion, 2007). In particular, they should advocate for receipt of recommended aging- and intellectual-disability-related routine health screenings. Modification of diet and exercise patterns have been shown to be effective for improved health for people with intellectual disability, similar to effects in the general population, but are not yet part of routine programming (Rimmer et al., 2010). This is another area in which multidisciplinary advocacy and support is needed. When referrals are received for assessment of behavioral

concerns, potential physical causes or explanations must be assessed and ruled out. Finally, as changes to programming are considered as people age, the manner in which health issues and concerns for the individual will be supported must also be addressed (McCarron & McCallion).

Assessing and Managing Grief and Bereavement and Preparing for End of Life   Some authors argue that families have been in a perpetual state of bereavement since the birth of an individual with intellectual disability (Todd, 2004). For aging people with intellectual disability, the loss of the primary caregiver or another significant family member is also a late point at which to address issues of death and bereavement (McCallion, McCarron, et al., 2012). There is a need to be prepared to support people with intellectual disability, their family caregivers, and their peers when end of life approaches. A study of collaboration and training needs among intellectual disability services and a specialist palliative care provider highlighted a number of critical steps in successful delivery of palliative care for people with intellectual disability (Fahey-McCarthy, McCarron, Connaire, & McCallion, 2009):

- Raising awareness, among staff in both systems, of the philosophies underpinning care and the expertise inherent in both intellectual disability and specialist palliative care services

- Recognizing staff in intellectual disability services as highly dedicated and committed to providing optimal care but sometimes lacking knowledge and skills in managing pain, constipation, dyspnea, and fevers as well as lacking care experience in siting subcutaneous lines and managing nutrition and hydration

- Recognizing that staff in specialist palliative care offer skills in symptom management and also offer an external source of support that may be vital to navigating final days

- Developing procedures and protocols within intellectual disability services to address understanding the wishes of the individual for their last days, the suitability of extraordinary measures, and the management of last days and death, including the postdeath grieving period

- Recognizing the need for advance planning, education, palliative care intervention guidelines, and supportive policies to support needed care in the last days.

Psychosocial Well-Being For psychosocial concerns, including dementia symptoms, successful identification requires capturing over time what may be subtle changes from previous functioning using instruments appropriate for people with intellectual disability, routine and repeated assessment, and completion of documentation in ways that permit comparison with previous reports of functioning. For example, it has been suggested that annual assessments of physical and psychosocial functioning with a recommended battery of instruments be initiated for people with Down syndrome older than 35 and other people with intellectual disability older than 50 (see Burt & Aylward, 2000; Jokinen et al., 2013). The same should be considered for depression and anxiety to enable the early identification of symptoms and their causes. In addition, the development of proactive, appropriate, and sensitive programs and services, and their effective delivery, will all contribute to psychosocial well-being.

Retraining the Work Force

The effective delivery of services to aging people with intellectual disability and their family caregivers requires a comprehensive reorientation of services and a multidisciplinary approach to best address long-term planning, differential diagnosis, treatment of dementia and other aging-related health concerns, and responses to bereavement. Specific strategies include the following (McCarron & McCallion, 2007; McCallion, McCarron, et al., 2012):

1. Training for staff on the general aging processes and related assessments for people with intellectual disability and their family caregivers

2. Systematic and sensitive approaches to helping families engage in long-term planning

3. Supports for self-advocacy and decision making for people with intellectual disability

4. Documentation, screening, and routine assessment processes to monitor change in functioning of people with intellectual disability and to offer critical information to inform differential diagnosis

5. Holistic approaches to presenting problem behaviors that facilitate understanding of the causes of those behaviors; how they may be avoided; and the delivery of appropriate, effective responses

6. Interdisciplinary and inter-sector (i.e., intellectual disability specialist and general health delivery) approaches to chronic disease management and end-of-life care

SUMMARY

People with intellectual disability who have reached old age have often lived through changing service systems, changing philosophies, and changing views of what is possible in the lives they will lead and where it is best they should live. Their families, in particular, should be forgiven for being suspicious of service systems that may have told them that their children with intellectual disability would not live to old age and would be best served in institutions. Later, many of those families were told that the best settings were large group homes, then small group homes, then independent living (including leaving the family home), and then—most recently—that family caregivers need to rely more upon their informal supports. Absent from the discussion was that intellectual disability would not be their only challenge to successful aging; there was little discussion of the onset of chronic conditions. Clearly, the conversation about aging with people with intellectual disability themselves and with families needs to change. Service providers also must recognize that they are becoming old-age service providers, and general population service providers—including hospitals and physician practices—need to reorient to include this growing aging population and build supportive professional relationships with intellectual disability specialist providers. There must also be a rethinking of what integration in the community truly means when, with age, social networks become more limited and chronic health conditions increase. Too little of this reorientation has already occurred, and this will be a critical challenge in the years ahead.

FOR FURTHER THOUGHT AND DISCUSSION

1. In what ways might the current work force need to change in order to support people with intellectual and developmental disabilities and their families as they age?

2. What role might technology play in supporting older-age people with intellectual disability? What barriers might exist to the integration of such technology?

3. Supports for mental health will become even more important as people with intellectual and developmental disabilities age. Is the system prepared to deal with this? What might need to change to ensure that it is?

4. Social connectedness is important throughout the life span. In what way might people with intellectual and developmental disabilities who are aging remain connected? With family? With friends? With other networks?

REFERENCES

Alberta Human Services. (2014). *My Life Survey: The Personal Outcomes Index.* Retrieved from http://www.humanservices.alberta.ca/disability-services/pdd-poi.html

Aldridge, J. (2007). Risk assessment, risk management and safety planning. In M. Jukes & J. Aldridge (2007), *Person-centred practices—a holistic and integrated approach.* London, United Kingdom: Quay Books.

Amado, A.N., Stancliffe, R.J., McCarron, M., & McCallion, P. (2013). Social inclusion and community participation of individuals with intellectual/developmental disabilities. *Intellectual and Developmental Disabilities, 51*(5), 360–375. doi:10.1352/1934-9556-51.5.360

Bigby, C., McCallion, P., & McCarron, M. (2014). Serving an elderly population. In M. Agran, F. Brown, C. Hughes, C. Quirk, & D.L. Ryndak (Eds.), *Equality and full participation for individuals with severe disabilities: A vision for the future* (pp. 319–348). Baltimore, MD: Paul H. Brookes Publishing Co.

Braddock, D. (1999). Aging and developmental disabilities: Demographic and policy issues affecting American families. *Mental Retardation, 37*(2), 155–161.

Braddock, D. (2013). *Summary of national trends: 2013. The state of the states in developmental disabilities.* Retrieved from http://www.stateofthestates.org/images/documents/PowerPointBraddock-LongTermCareCommission.pdf

Bromley, J., Emerson, E., & Caine, A. (1998). The development of a self-report measure to assess the location and intensity of pain in people with learning disabilities. *Journal of Intellectual Disability Research, 42,* 72–80.

Brown, R.I., & Faragher, R. (Eds.). (2014). *Quality of life and intellectual disabilities: Knowledge application to other social and educational challenges.* New York, NY: Nova Science.

Burke, E., McCarron, M., Carroll, R., McGlinchey, E., & McCallion, P. (2014). What it's like to grow older: The aging perceptions of people with an intellectual disability in Ireland. *Intellectual and Developmental Disabilities, 52*(3), 205–219. doi:10.1352/1934-9556-52.3.205

Burt, D.B., & Aylward, E.H. (2000). Test battery for the diagnosis of dementia in individuals with intellectual disability. Working Group for the Establishment of Criteria for the Diagnosis of Dementia in Individuals with Intellectual Disability. *Journal of Intellectual Disability Research, 44,* 175–180.

Buys, L., Aird, R., & Miller, E. (2012). Service providers' perceptions of active ageing among older adults with lifelong intellectual disabilities. *Journal of Intellectual Disability Research, 56*(12), 1133–1147. doi:10.1111/j.1365-2788.2011.01500.x

Cairns, D., Brown, J., Tolson, D., & Darbyshire, C. (2014). Caring for a child with learning disabilities over a prolonged period of time: An exploratory survey on the experiences and health of older parent carers living in Scotland. *Journal of Applied Research in Intellectual Disabilities, 27*(5), 471–480. doi:10.1111/jar.12071

Caldwell, J., & Heller, T. (2003). Management of respite and personal assistance services in a consumer-directed family support programme. *Journal of Intellectual Disability Research, 47*(4–5), 352–367.

Cooper, S.A. (1997). High prevalence of dementia among people with learning disabilities not attributable to Down's syndrome. *Psychological Medicine, 27,* 609–616.

Cooper, S.A., Smiley, E., Morrison, J., Williamson, A., & Allan, L. (2007) Mental ill-health in adults with intellectual disabilities: Prevalence and associated factors. *British Journal of Psychiatry, 90,* 27–35.

Duggan, C., & Linehan, C. (2013). The role of natural supports in promoting independent living for people with disabilities: A review of existing literature. *British Journal of Learning Disabilities, 41,* 199–207.

Emerson, E. (2011). Health status and health risks of the "hidden majority" of adults with intellectual disability. *Journal of Intellectual and Developmental Disabilities, 49*(3), 155–165.

Emerson. E., & Baines, S. (2011). *Health inequalities and people with learning disabilities in the UK: 2010.* Lancaster, United Kingdom: Improving Health and Lives Learning Disabilities Observatory.

Emerson, E., Madden, R., Graham, H., Llewellyn, G., Hatton, C., & Robertson, J. (2011). The health of disabled people and the social determinants of health. *Public Health, 125*(3), 145–147.

Evenhuis, H., Hermans, H., Hilgenkamp, M., Bastiaanse, L., & Echteld, M. (2012). Frailty and disability in older adults with intellectual disabilities: Results from the healthy ageing and intellectual disability study. *Journal of American Geriatric Society, 60,* 934–938.

Evenhuis, H.M., Theunissen, M., Denkers, I., Verschuure, H., & Kemme, H. (2001). Prevalence of visual and hearing impairment in a Dutch institutionalized population with intellectual disability. *Journal of Intellectual Disability Research, 45*(5), 457–464.

Ewing, G., McDermott, S., Thomas-Koger, M., Whitner, W., & Pierce, K. (2004). Evaluation of a cardiovascular health program for participants with mental retardation and normal learners. *Health Education and Behaviours, 31,* 77–87.

Fahey-McCarthy, E., McCarron, M., Connaire, K., & McCallion, P. (2009). Developing an education intervention for staff supporting persons with intellectual disability and advanced dementia. *Journal of Policy and Practice in Intellectual Disabilities, 6*(4), 267–275.

Haveman, M., Heller, T., Lee, L., Maaskant, M., Shoosharti, S., & Strydom, A. (2010). Major health risks in aging persons with intellectual disabilities: An overview of recent studies. *Journal of Policy and Practice in Intellectual Disabilities, 7*, 59–69.

Haveman, M., Perry, J., Salvador-Carulla, L., Walsh, P.N., Kerr, M., Van Schrojenstein Lantman-de Valk, H.,... Weber, G. (2011). Ageing and health status in adults with intellectual disabilities: Results of the European POMONA II study. *Journal of Intellectual and Developmental Disability, 36*(1), 49–60.

Heslop, P., Blair, P.S., Fleming, P.J., Hoghton, M.A., Marriott, A.M., & Russ, L.S. (2014). The confidential inquiry into premature deaths of people with intellectual disabilities in the UK: A population-based study. *The Lancet, 383*(9920), 889–895.

Hilgenkamp, M., Reis, D., Wijck,R., & Evenhuis, H. (2012). Physical activity levels in older adults with intellectual disabilities are extremely low. *Research in Developmental Disabilities, 33*, 477–483.

Hines, M., Balandin, S., & Togher, L. (2014). The stories of older parents of adult sons and daughters with autism: A balancing act. *Journal of Applied Research in Intellectual Disabilities, 27*(2), 163–173. doi:10.1111/jar.12063

Holland, A.J., Hon, J., Huppert, F.A., & Stevens, F. (2000). Incidence and course of dementia in people with Down's syndrome: Findings from a population-based study. *Journal of Intellectual Disability Research, 44*(2), 138–146.

Humphries, K., Traci, M.A., & Seekins, T. (2009). Nutrition and adults with intellectual or developmental disabilities: Systematic literature review results. *Intellectual and Developmental Disabilities, 47*(3), 163–185.

Jackson, R., Howe, N., & Nakashima, K. (2011). *Global aging preparedness index.* Washington, DC: Center for Strategic and International Studies.

Jacobson, J. (2003). Prevalence of mental and behavioural disorders. In P.W. Davidson, V.P. Prasher, & M.P. Janicki (Eds.), *Mental health, intellectual disabilities and the aging process* (pp. 9–21). Oxford, United Kingdom: Blackwell Publishing.

Janicki, M.P., & Dalton, A.J. (2000). Prevalence of dementia and impact on intellectual disability services. *Mental Retardation, 38*, 277–289.

Janicki, M., Dalton, A., McCallion, P., Baxley, D., & Zendell, A. (2005). Group home care for adults with intellectual disabilities and Alzheimer's disease. *Dementia, 4*, 361–385.

Jokinen, N.S. (2014). Quality of life and older-aged adults. In R.I. Brown & R. Faragher (Eds.), *Quality of life and intellectual disabilities: Knowledge application to other social and educational challenges* (pp. 247–264). New York, NY: Nova Science.

Jokinen, N., Janicki, M.P., Keller, S., McCallion, P., & Force, L.T. (2013). Guidelines for structuring community care and supports for people with intellectual disabilities affected by dementia. *Journal of Policy and Practice in Intellectual Disabilities, 10*(1), 1–24.

Kåhlin, I., Kjellberg, A., Nord, C., & Hagberg, J.-E. (2013). Lived experiences of ageing and later life in older people with intellectual disabilities. *Ageing and Society, FirstView, 35*(3), 602–628. doi:10.1017/S0144686X13000949

Kahn, R.L. (2002). Guest editorial on "Successful aging and well-being." *The Gerontologist, 42*, 725–726.

Kelly, F., & Kelly, C. (2013). *Annual report of the National Intellectual Disability Database Committee.* Dublin, Ireland: Health Research Board.

Lennox, N., Bain, C., & Rey-Conde, T. (2007). Effects of a comprehensive health assessment programme for Australian adults with intellectual disability: A cluster randomized trial. *International Journal of Epidemiology, 36*, 139–146.

Lightfoot, E., & McCallion, P. (in press). Older adults and developmental disabilities. In B. Berkman & D. Kaplan (Eds.), *Handbook of social work in health and aging* (2nd ed.). New York, NY: Oxford University Press.

MacGiolla Phadraig, C., el-Helaali, R., Burke, E., McCallion, P., McGlinchey, E., McCarron, M., & Nunn, J.H. (2014). National levels of reported difficulty in tooth and denture cleaning among an ageing population with intellectual disabilities. *Journal of Dentistry and Oral Health, 15*(3), 48–53.

McCallion, P. (1993). *Social worker orientation to permanency planning* (Unpublished doctoral dissertation). University at Albany, NY.

McCallion, P. (2006). Older adults as caregivers to persons with developmental disabilities. In B. Berkman & E. D'Ambruoso (Eds.), *Handbook of social work in health and aging* (pp. 363–370). New York, NY: Oxford University Press.

McCallion, P., Burke, E., Swinburne, J., McGlinchey, E., Carroll, R., & McCarron, M. (2013). Influence of environment, predisposing, enabling and need variables on personal health choices of adults with intellectual disability. *Health, 5*(4), 749–756.

McCallion, P., Hastings, J., & McCarron, M. (2014). Understanding increasing longevity for people with intellectual disability: Findings from New York State administrative data. *Journal of Applied Research in Intellectual Disabilities, 27*(4), 310.

McCallion, P., & Kolomer, S.R. (2003a). Aging persons with developmental disabilities and their aging caregivers. In B. Berkman & L. Harootyan (Eds.), *Social work and health care in an aging world* (pp. 201–225). New York, NY: Springer.

McCallion, P., & Kolomer, S.R. (2003b). Understanding and addressing psychosocial concerns among aging family caregivers of persons with intellectual disabilities. In P. Davidson, V. Prasher, & M.P. Janicki (Eds.), *Mental health, intellectual disabilities and the aging process* (pp. 179–196). London, United Kingdom: Blackwell.

McCallion, P., & McCarron, M. (2004a). Aging and intellectual disabilities: A review of recent literature. *Current Opinion in Psychiatry, 17*(5), 349–352.

McCallion, P., & McCarron, M. (2004b). Intellectual disabilities and dementia. In K. Doka (Ed.), *Living with grief: Alzheimer's disease* (pp. 67–84). Washington, DC: Hospice Foundation of America.

McCallion, P., & McCarron, M. (2007). A perspective on quality of life in dementia care. *Intellectual and Developmental Disabilities, 45*(1), 56–59.

McCallion, P., & McCarron, M. (2014). Death of people with intellectual disabilities in the UK. *The Lancet, 383*(9920), 853–855. doi:10.1016/S0140-6736(13)62026-7

McCallion, P., & McCarron, M. (2015). People with disabilities entering the third age. In R. McConkey, R. Gilligan, & E.G. Iriarte (Eds.), *Disability in a global age: A human rights based approach* (pp. 217–230). London, United Kingdom: Palgrave McMillan.

McCallion, P., McCarron, M., Fahey-McCarthy, E., & Connaire, K. (2012). Meeting the end of life needs of older adults with intellectual disabilities. In E. Chang & A. Johnson (Eds.), *Contemporary and innovative practice in palliative care* (pp. 255–267). Rijeka, Croatia: Intech.

McCallion, P., Swinburne, J., Burke, E., McGlinchey, E., & McCarron, M. (2013). Understanding the similarities and differences in aging with an intellectual disability: Linking Irish general population and intellectual disability datasets. In R. Urbano (Ed.), *Using secondary datasets to understand persons with developmental disabilities and their families (IRRDD-45)*. New York, NY: Academic Press.

McCallion, P., & Toseland, R.W. (1995). Supportive group interventions with caregivers of frail older adults. *Social Work with Groups, 18*(1), 11–25.

McCallion, P., Zendell, A., Ferretti, L.A., & Aldrich, D. (2008). *Facing the challenges: Addressing needs for persons with intellectual disabilities* [CD-ROM]. Albany, NY: New York State Office of Children and Family Services.

McCarron, M., Carroll, R., Kelly, C., & McCallion, P. (2014, July). *To understand differing patterns of age of death by gender and level of ID, for people with ID in Ireland.* Presentation at IASSIDD Europe Regional Congress, Vienna, Austria.

McCarron, M., & Griffiths, C. (2003). Nurses' roles in supporting aging persons with intellectual disability and mental health problems: Challenges and opportunities for care. In P. Davidson, V. Prasher, & M.P. Janicki (Eds.), *Mental health, intellectual disabilities and the aging process,* (pp. 223–237). London, United Kingdom: Blackwell.

McCarron, M., & Lawlor, B.A. (2003). Responding to the challenges of ageing and dementia in intellectual disability in Ireland. *Ageing and Mental Health, 7,* 413–417.

McCarron, M., & McCallion, P. (2007). End of life care challenges for persons with intellectual disability and dementia: Making decisions about tube feeding. *Intellectual and Developmental Disabilities, 45*(2), 128–131.

McCarron, M., McCallion, P., Reilly, E., & Mulryan, N. (2014). A prospective 14 year longitudinal follow-up of dementia in persons with Down syndrome. *Journal of Intellectual Disability Research, 58*(1), 61–70.

McCarron, M., O'Dwyer, M., Burke, E., McGlinchey, E., & McCallion, P. (2014). Epidemiology of epilepsy in older adults with an intellectual disability in Ireland: Associations and service implications. *American Journal on Intellectual and Developmental Disabilities, 119*(3), 253–260.

McCarron, M., Swinburne, J., Burke, E., McGlinchey, E., Carroll, R., & McCallion, P. (2013). Patterns of multimorbidity in an older population of persons with an intellectual disability: Results from the Intellectual Disability Supplement to the Irish Longitudinal Study on Ageing (IDS-TILDA). *Research in Developmental Disabilities, 34,* 521–527.

McCarron, M., Swinburne, J., Burke, E., McGlinchey, E., Mulryan, N., Andrews, V.,...McCallion, P. (2011). *Growing older with an intellectual disability in Ireland in 2011: First results from the Intellectual Disability Supplement of the Irish Longitudinal Study on Ageing.* Dublin, Ireland: Trinity College Dublin.

McGuire, B.E., Daly, P., & Smyth, F. (2007). Lifestyle and health behaviours of adults with an intellectual disability. *Journal of Intellectual Disability Research, 51,* 497–510.

National Center for Health Statistics. (2012). *Healthy People 2020 final review.* Hyattsville, MD: Author.

Perkins, E.A., & Haley, W.E. (2013). Emotional and tangible reciprocity in middle- and older-aged carers of adults with intellectual disabilities. *Journal of Policy and Practice in Intellectual Disabilities, 10*(4), 334–344. doi:10.1111/jppi.12061

Plagnol, A.C., & Scott, J. (2011). What matters for well-being: Individual perceptions of quality of life before and after important life events. *Applied Research in Quality of Life, 6,* 115–137. doi:10.1007/s11482-010-9119-1

Prasher, V.P. (1995). End-stage dementia in adults with Down syndrome. *International Journal of Geriatric Psychiatry, 10,* 1067–1069.

Raghavan, R., & Patel, P. (2010). Ethical issues of psychotropic medication for people with intellectual disabilities. *Advances in Mental Health and Intellectual Disabilities, 4*(3), 34–38.

Reinders, H.S., & Schalock, R.L. (2014). How organizations can enhance the quality of life of their clients and assess their results: The concept of QOL enhancement. *American Journal on Intellectual and Developmental Disabilities, 119*(4), 291–302. doi:10.1352/1944-7558-119.4.291

Rimmer, J.H., Chen, M.D., McCubbin, J.A., Drum, C., & Peterson, J. (2010) Exercise intervention research on persons with disabilities: What we know and where we need to go. *American Journal of Physical and Medical Rehabilitation, 89*(3), 249–263.

Robertson, J., Roberts, H., Emerson, E., Turner, S., & Grieg, R. (2011). The impact of health checks for people with intellectual disabilities: A systematic review of evidence. *Journal of Intellectual Disabilities Research, 55*(11), 1009–1019.

Ryan, A., Taggart, L., Truesdale-Kennedy, M., & Slevin, E. (2014). Issues in caregiving for older people with intellectual disabilities and their ageing family carers: A review and commentary. *International Journal of Older People Nursing, 9*(3), 217–226.

Samele, C., Seymour, L., Morris, B., Central England People First, Cohen, A., & Emerson, E. (2006). *A formal investigation into health inequalities experienced by people with learning difficulties and people with mental health problems.* London, United Kingdom: Sainsbury Centre for Mental Health.

Scheepers, M., Kerr, M., O'Hara, D., Bainbridge, D., Cooper, S.A., Davis, R.,...Wehmeyer, M. (2005). Reducing health disparity in people with intellectual disabilities: A report from Health Issues Special Interest Research Group of IASSID. *Journal of Policy and Practice in Intellectual Disabilities, 2,* 249–255.

Schoufour, J., Echteld, M., & Evenhuis, H. (2012). Frailty in elderly with intellectual disabilities. *Journal of Intellectual Disabilty Research, 56,* 661.

Shaw, K., Cartwright, C., & Craig, J. (2011). The housing and support needs of people with an intellectual disability into older age. *Journal of Intellectual Disability Research, 55*(9), 895–903. doi:10.1111/j.1365-2788.2011.01449.x

Taggart, L., Coates, V., & Truesdale-Kennedy, M. (2013). Management and quality indicators of diabetes mellitus in people with intellectual disability. *Journal of Intellectual Disability Research, 57*(12), 1152–1163.

Temple, V.A. & Walkley, J.W. (2003). Physical activity of adults with intellectual disability. *Journal of Intellectual and Developmental Disability, 28,* 323–334.

Todd, S. (2004). Death counts: The challenge of death and dying in learning disability services. *Learning Disability Practice, 7,* 12–15.

Tyrrell, J., & Dodd, P. (2003). Psychopathology in older age. In P.W. Davidson, V.P. Prasher, & M.P. Janicki (Eds.), *Mental health, intellectual disabilities and the aging process* (pp. 22–37). Oxford, United Kingdom: Blackwell Publishing.

van Schrojenstein Lantman-De Valk, H.M., Metsemakers, J.F., Haveman, M.J., & Crebolder, H.F. (2000). Health problems in people with intellectual disability in general practice: A comparative study. *Family Practice, 17*(5), 405–407.

World Health Organization. (2012). *Good health adds life to years: Global brief for World Health Day 2012.* Geneva, Switzerland: Author.

Zaninotto, P., Falaschetti, E., & Sacker, A. (2009). Age trajectories of quality of life among older adults: Results from the English Longitudinal Study of Ageing. *Quality of Life Research, 18*(10), 1301–1309. doi:10.1007/s11136-009-9543-6

VI

Health

45

Ethics of Decision Making and Consent in People with Intellectual and Developmental Disabilities

John Heng and William F. Sullivan

WHAT YOU WILL LEARN

- The importance and meaning of respect for moral agency
- Components of decision making, including ethical deliberation
- The notion of supported decision making
- The deliberative model of the health care professional–patient relationship
- The substitute interests model of substitute decision making
- Advance care planning

This chapter uses the term *health care professionals* for physicians, nurses, psychologists, and others who provide health care services. It refers to people with intellectual and developmental disabilities. These are lifelong challenges to cognitive, adaptive, and social skills that result from differences in neuropsychological development before adulthood. These challenges vary in type and severity from individual to individual, affecting capacity for decision making and consent. The term *intellectual and developmental disabilities* in this chapter overlaps in meaning with other terms that might be encountered elsewhere, such as *intellectual disability, developmental disabilities, learning disability, developmental delay, mental handicap,* and *mental retardation*.

This chapter discusses various clinical and ethical issues regarding health care decision making and consent in people with intellectual and developmental disabilities. Although the focus of this chapter is on health care, many similar issues arise in other aspects of the lives of people with intellectual and developmental disabilities, such as decisions about living arrangements (Robertson et al., 2001; Struhkamp, 2005), employment, relationships (Murphy & O'Callaghan, 2004), and participation in research (Dye, Hare, & Hendy, 2007).

THE IMPORTANCE OF SUPPORTING MORAL AGENCY IN HEALTH CARE

For people in need of health care or their substitute decision makers, giving consent to health care interventions entails having engaged in ethical deliberation. Health care providers are obligated not only to obtain voluntary and informed consent from patients before providing some health care intervention but also to support their moral agency (i.e., ability to make moral judgments based on some notion of right and wrong and to be held accountable for these actions) and authentic decision making. These obligations follow from respecting the intrinsic dignity of the person to whom they provide care.

Dignity and Moral Standing

Some thinkers believe that dignity is an attribute that can be withheld or withdrawn by others when certain qualities and capacities of a human being (e.g., rationality, moral agency) are impaired. According to this view, people with intellectual and developmental disabilities who do not have such capacities have lower moral standing relative to those who do (Singer, 1993; McMahan, 1996). Other thinkers hold that every human being has intrinsic dignity (Sulmasy, 2013) and equal moral worth to others in the human community (Kittay, 2008). According to such thinkers, people with intellectual and developmental disabilities have moral standing that does not vary according to their capabilities. The authors of this chapter affirm this second view.

A health care professional's positive obligation to do good and negative obligation to avoid harming his or her patient might sometimes appear to conflict with the professional's obligation also to respect the patient's moral agency. In the chapter authors' opinion, such dilemmas can often be resolved ethically through a correct understanding of what moral agency entails and how the person's community can support it.

Not respecting or supporting a person's moral agency always harms that person, even if the health care provider thinks that there are desirable consequences of a proposed health care intervention. Health care professionals, however, should be aware of certain vulnerabilities in a person's attempts to exercise his or her moral agency, such as by engaging in ethical deliberations. They also should recognize the importance to the person of family, loved ones, and others who provide care and support. Some people with intellectual and developmental disabilities require support from others to discern or communicate their authentic values and wishes and how these might relate to specific health care decisions. Others have very limited capacity to engage in ethical deliberation and require the assistance of a substitute decision maker. Substitute decision makers themselves might need help to discern and apply the authentic values and wishes of the person with an intellectual and developmental disability for whose benefit they are making the decision.

Models of the Health Care Professional and Patient Relationship

There are at least four models of the health care professional and patient relationship (Emanuel & Emanuel, 1992). In the paternalistic model, the health care professional decides on behalf of the patient or substitute decision maker. In the informative model, the health care professional simply provides factual information regarding interventions and answers questions, but refrains from discussing values. In the interpretive model, the health care professional both provides information and helps the patient or substitute decision maker to apply the patient's values to a health care decision. In the deliberative model, the health care professional not only gives information and helps to apply the patient's values but also supports the patient's or substitute decision maker's discernment of what these values ought to be for promoting the patient's overall health and wellness. It is the fourth type of health care professional–patient relationship, the deliberative model, that best fosters supporting moral agency in health care.

Distinguishing Legal and Ethical Approaches to Consent

Most legal jurisdictions in the world have laws on consent regarding health care interventions. Health care professionals should be aware of and understand the legal requirements in their jurisdiction. They should, however, also be aware of and understand the difference between legal and ethical approaches to consent to health care interventions. Although there are areas of overlap between these approaches, there are also noteworthy differences.

First, the law sets down general standards and rules with which every member of society is expected to comply. By contrast, ethical inquiry is concerned with the basis of decisions to act or to refrain from acting in particular circumstances. Sometimes, applying a general legal standard or rule to a specific circumstance without taking into account relevant exceptional factors could result in harm being done. Health care professionals should be aware that laws on consent in health care might not take into account the capacities or vulnerabilities of individuals with intellectual and developmental disabilities in relation to their moral agency.

Second, laws regarding consent to health care interventions typically consider a patient's decision-making capacity to be an all-or-none attribute. That is, either a person meets some standard threshold of capacity for such decisions or that person does not. If the person does not meet such a standard, then a substitute decision maker is authorized to provide consent to a health care intervention on behalf of that person. The philosophical basis of this approach in the law is a narrow understanding of moral agency as only the capacity for independent choice. Health care providers might mistakenly identify ethical deliberation simply with the act of choosing among alternatives, which is its outcome. Furthermore, health care providers might mistakenly regard moral agency as simply freedom from interference or help from others. To the extent that health care providers reduce ethical deliberation to acts of choosing and moral agency to freedom from the input or interference of others, they will tend to overlook and not support sufficiently the capacities required for different aspects of ethical deliberation that some people with intellectual and developmental disabilities might need from others.

Third, there can be a tendency for health care providers to focus more on assessing that a patient meets the legal requirements for capacity to consent to some health care intervention and on documenting such consent than on developing the clinical and ethical skills they need to promote authentic decision making by patients with intellectual and developmental disabilities and their substitute decision makers. As a result, carefully observing, listening to, and communicating with their patient and family can be neglected. Health care providers should also be aware that giving consent to a health care intervention is the outcome of a process of ethical deliberation. This process depends, to a large extent, on the quality of the relationship between the health care provider and the patient with intellectual and developmental disabilities and his or her substitute decision maker and on discussions among all relevant stakeholders who should contribute to such deliberations.

Elements of Consent

Most ethicists agree that there are at least four essential elements of informed consent. The client must have sufficient, although not necessarily technically detailed, information on which to base a decision; understand this information; be able to appreciate the consequences of giving or withholding consent; and be free to give or withhold consent (Evans, 1997). Some ethicists have proposed a fifth element, being able to weigh the benefits and burdens of various options in light of a person's values or what that person judges to be good in life (Grisso, 1986; Sulmasy, 1997). The addition of this fifth

element raises the contentious question of whether there is a distinction between being capable of understanding information and being capable of making an ethical judgment. It is the chapter authors' opinion that a person's ability to consider various options in light of his or her values is an integral part of giving consent. Giving consent expresses a person's evaluation that an intervention is, on the balance, good in that it contributes to what that person holds to be ultimately worthwhile and is consistent with that person's desire for overall and lasting well-being and flourishing in life, even if this intervention could be disagreeable in the short term. In other words, such judgments are about values.

COMPONENTS OF DECISION MAKING

Properly understood, giving or withholding consent is the outcome of a process of ethical decision making (American Association on Mental Retardation, 2000). Suto, Clare, Holland, and Watson (2005) identified what they regard as an emerging consensus among health care providers on the distinct but related capacities required in the various aspects of this decision-making process. These capacities include the following:

1. Realizing that a decision needs to be made

2. Understanding sufficient information that is relevant to the decision

3. Reasoning with that information to come to a decision

4. Appreciating who is affected by the decision

5. Communicating a choice

Abilities 3 and 4 involve discerning values and weighing the benefits and burdens for oneself of various medical options in light of those values. Ability 5 corresponds to what the law typically means by giving or withholding consent and comes at the end of this decision-making process.

Assessing Decision-Making Capacities

Because consent is the outcome of a decision-making process with different aspects, from a clinical perspective, it is more accurate to speak about assessing decision-making capacities rather than the capacity to give consent. There are no universally accepted criteria for such assessments by health care providers. Nevertheless, the five abilities described by Suto et al. (2005) and listed previously seem to be a reasonable guide for assessments of decision-making capacity. Some have found the MacArthur Competence Assessment Tool for Treatment (MacCAT-T), which has been validated for use with people with dementia, depression, and schizophrenia, to be helpful for assessments (Keywood & Flynn, 2009). A tool developed by the Developmental Disabilities Primary Care Initiative (2011) in Ontario, Canada, specifically for people with intellectual and developmental disabilities is another resource that could be used in such assessments.

Particular Issues in Assessing Decision-Making Capacity

It follows that assessing decision-making capacities of a person with intellectual and developmental disabilities should involve more than simply testing his or her ability to understand and to recall information, for this is only a part of ethical deliberation. There should also be some assessment of the other capacities involved. For a person with intellectual and developmental disabilities, this might entail the use of hypothetical vignettes, described in pictures or stories or a mixture of both, to determine the match between an individual's decision-making abilities and the level of complexity of the actual decision to be made (Morris, Niederbuhl, & Mahr, 1993). It is important to offer vignettes that are relevant to the health care decision.

The decision-making capacity of people with intellectual and developmental disabilities is usually compared with that of people in the general population faced with similar decisions. There is, however, a range of decision-making capacities in individuals in the general population as well as in those with intellectual and developmental disabilities. Although, as a group, the latter's decision making is more likely to be impaired when compared with what some researchers call the "very able" decision makers in the general population, this is not always the case. For instance, there are often similarities in the decision-making abilities of people with mild developmental disabilities and the very able in the general population (Gunn, Wong, Clare, & Holland, 2000). People with moderate developmental disabilities might not have all the skills necessary to make complex health care decisions. Here, the support of family and other significant caregivers might enable them to participate in the decision-making process. It is unlikely that a person whose intellectual and functional abilities are in the severe to profound range of intellectual and developmental disabilities (i.e., a person with an IQ score below 40 who needs significant supports in the areas of self-care, health, and safety) is capable of providing consent for most health care interventions (Dinerstein, Herr, & O'Sullivan, 1999). Nevertheless, the health care provider should always conduct a thorough assessment of the person's decision-making capacities. This is important not only for people with moderate intellectual and developmental disabilities, in which such capacities are uncertain, but also for those with mild and borderline intellectual and developmental disabilities, in whom such capacities might routinely (but sometimes mistakenly) be assumed (Sullivan & Heng, 2014).

People with intellectual and developmental disabilities, whatever their level of function, are usually better able to make decisions about health care if they have had some prior experience with making any decisions. Some people with intellectual and developmental disabilities have had a limited range of life experiences and opportunities to make decisions, as many live or have lived in a protective family environment or a highly structured institution; this might often account for their underdeveloped decision-making capacities (Cea & Fisher, 2003). Learned helplessness, acquiescence, and suggestibility can predispose a person with intellectual and developmental disabilities to be overly compliant with requests from health care professionals, thereby diminishing the voluntary nature of their decisions. In addition, having experienced or witnessed something distressing or harmful in the past can influence a person's judgment and willingness to consent to health care that he or she associates with that negative experience. These difficulties point to the importance of taking extra time for discussion and making the effort to involve others who know the person well in ethical deliberation. When considering health care that lasts over time, health care professionals should periodically ask for feedback from the person or the person's substitute decision maker.

A further consideration in assessments is that a person's decision-making abilities might change over time. This is particularly important for individuals who have disabilities that result in progressive functional deteriorations, such as dementia in some adults with Down syndrome. Also there might be factors affecting a person's capacity for decision making in some circumstances but not in others. The stresses and distresses caused by an illness, or the presence of depression even if it does not meet the criteria for a psychiatric diagnosis, are examples of such factors. Health care professionals should not simply assume that the results of a prior assessment of an individual's capacity to make decisions and to give consent are still valid in the present circumstances.

In addition, it is important to know that some people with intellectual and developmental disabilities might have limited verbal communication skills. Some might use body language, sign language, or other means of communication with which their health care professionals are unfamiliar. In these situations, the health care professional assessing a person's decision-making abilities must be a keen observer and attentive listener and should use an appropriate level of language or means of communication. Often the involvement of interpreters who know the person well is very helpful (Morris et al., 1993).

Finally, health care professionals should be aware that a significant number of people with intellectual and developmental disabilities also have some form of affective disorder or psychiatric illness (i.e., a dual diagnosis). Health care professionals should obtain an adequate psychosocial history to recognize various mental health factors that might affect decision making and the freedom to give or to withhold consent, and should involve others with psychological or psychiatric expertise, particularly those familiar with mental health issues in people with intellectual and developmental disabilities, in assessments as needed.

Discerning People's Values

A question might be raised about whether people with intellectual and developmental disabilities are capable of apprehending and holding values for ethical deliberation. Values are apprehended by means of morally attuned feelings. Having some notion of what is ultimately worthwhile and what contributes to one's overall well-being and flourishing in life is an ability that is distinct from, and does not necessarily depend on, one's intellectual abilities (Sullivan & Heng, 2007). Health care professionals should not dismiss the possibility that

people with intellectual and developmental disabilities can apprehend and hold values, but they should be attentive to individuals' various strengths and weaknesses in this area, such as discerning, expressing, evaluating, and applying them. Individuals with disabilities that primarily affect intellectual performance generally can develop morally attuned feelings that enable them to apprehend values. In comparison, some individuals with an autism spectrum disorder can have highly developed intellectual capacities in areas such as mathematics but could have significant affective and social challenges that affect their ability to apprehend some values.

Although many people with intellectual and developmental disabilities might be capable of apprehending values, they might still need assistance in discerning, expressing, evaluating, and connecting those values to a concrete decision regarding health care. Giving or withholding consent for a particular intervention sets into motion a series of events that might have an effect contrary to what a person ultimately values and judges to be good in life. For example, a person with an intellectual and developmental disability who requires physiotherapy might not truly want to be immobilized but might refuse consent to the procedures that are necessary to recover some motor function. Health care professionals should not consider a person's expression of consent or refusal without taking the time and making the effort to probe the value basis for this choice. Health care professionals ought to discern, as much as possible, through appropriate means of communication and by consulting those who know the individual well, whether a given choice reflects what that person ultimately judges or would judge to be worthwhile.

Many people with intellectual and developmental disabilities are unable to understand what is meant by *value* or to relate their apprehension, through feelings, of what is ultimately worthwhile in their life with this term. What often is needed to discern a person's values is attentive communication with that person as well as a history of that person's pattern of preferences and choices in health care and in other areas of life (Wong, Clare, Gunn, & Holland, 1999). According to a deliberative model of the health care professional–patient relationship, such interactions can be conducted in a manner that does not give undue weight to a health care professional's own values but raises questions that might help a person or his or her substitute decision maker to consider what health-related values for the person might have been overlooked and should be considered.

Uncertainty About a Person's Decision-Making Capacities

When there is uncertainty regarding the decision-making capacities of a person with intellectual and developmental disabilities, assessment by a health care professional who is familiar with people with intellectual and developmental disabilities should be sought. The decision to seek expert assessment should not be based only on disagreement with the person's consent or refusal; there must be reasonable grounds to hold that the person might be having difficulty participating in one or more of the aspects of decision making.

Different Types of Decision Making

Decisions can be made in various ways: through supported decision making, substitute decision making, or advance care planning. These are discussed next, as are issues to consider for decision making during emergencies.

Supported Decision Making   The authors of this chapter have argued for a notion of partial decision-making capacity and thus urge that the goal of capacity assessments should not simply be to conclude that a person is or is not capable of giving or refusing consent. The primary goal ought to be to identify strengths and weaknesses in particular aspects of the decision-making process in order to determine what supports are needed to enable a person with intellectual and developmental disabilities to be involved as much as possible in making decisions affecting his or her life, health, and participation in the community. Examples of such support include adapting the format for disclosing information relevant to the decision (Cea & Fisher, 2003), using alternative means or drawing on the help of interpreters to communicate, providing reassurance and counseling to address emotional and psychological challenges, helping a person to identify his or her values and to relate them to the medical options at hand, and involving a member of the person's family or some other caregiver whom the person trusts to give advice. In assessing capacity and supporting decision making in health care, health care professionals should continually address the person being assessed and not merely his or her accompanying caregiver.

Substitute Decision Making   Sometimes, even with supports, a person with developmental disabilities might not be capable of participating very much or at all in the process of decision making, either in a particular situation or in general. In these cases, it is necessary to find a substitute decision maker. *Surrogate, representative,* or *proxy consent giver* are other terms for a substitute decision maker. This is someone who has the legal authority to give or to refuse consent on behalf of the person with intellectual and developmental disabilities when that person is incapable of doing so. Most laws concerning consent for health care specify which individuals are authorized to be substitute decision makers and in what order of priority. Usually, priority is given to the legal guardian, whether a family member or publicly appointed figure, or to someone whom the person has designated in an advance directive. This might not be the person accompanying the person with intellectual and developmental disabilities to obtain health care. Health care professionals and accompanying caregivers should not routinely assume that it is their role to take over decision making for the person with intellectual and developmental disabilities.

Substitute decision makers should be educated to decide for the best interests of the person with intellectual and developmental disabilities who has very limited decision-making capacities by applying a prudential weighing of each medical option's benefits and burdens for the person. This judgment should be informed by known or presumed values of the patient. Substitute decision makers, therefore, should ideally know the person well over time, even if they do not know the person's precise wishes regarding the health care decision to be made. Hence, a substitute interests model of decision making (in which the values of the person are taken into account and applied by the substitute decision maker) rather than simply substitute judgment (which relies on explicit prior instructions) should be used (Sulmasy & Snyder, 2010).

Care must be taken to ensure that those who are incapable of participating very much or at all in health care decision making are not undertreated or inappropriately overtreated. Vigilance is important for health care decisions in life-threatening or end-of-life circumstances, where negative attitudes regarding the value of the life of the person with intellectual and developmental disabilities or the burden of care on the person's community can sometimes have an undue influence on substitute decision makers and health care professionals. It is important to be vigilant even in regard to routine health care, including health care prevention and promotion, to ensure that the substitute decision makers of people with intellectual and developmental disabilities who cannot request the care that they need should be informed of the availability of these interventions. Likewise, substitute decision makers should be informed of and take into account both the risk of harm and burdens of interventions on the patient with intellectual and developmental disabilities as well as the benefits for this person. Substitute decision makers should always be able to provide and justify reasons to others for their decisions on behalf of people with intellectual and developmental disabilities. Health care professionals cannot routinely assume that substitute decision makers are aware of their role or their ethical responsibilities (Redley et al., 2013). Education and discussion with substitute decision makers is often required.

Advance Directives and Advance Care Planning

An advance directive is a written document or verbal instruction made at a time when a person is capable of making decisions about health care in anticipation of some future possible medical circumstance in which the person may no longer be capable of making such decisions (Friedman, 1998). Advance directives can outline particular procedures or treatments that a person would accept or refuse in various medical situations. Because these situations are not always possible to predict, however, it is usually more prudent for the advance directive to take the form of a statement of values held by the person and to designate a substitute decision maker, ideally someone who has known the person well for a long time and whose judgment and goodwill the person trusts. Moreover, the focus for people with intellectual and developmental disabilities should be on advance care planning as an ongoing process in providing health care rather than on any single document such as an advance directive. Health care professionals should inform people with intellectual and developmental disabilities and their family and other significant caregivers about the importance of advance care planning and should have periodic discussions with them regarding who and what values and goals should guide health care decisions when a patient cannot participate fully in decision making.

Emergencies

In emergency situations, the consequences of delaying decision making could be life threatening. When the patient is assessed to have very limited decision-making capacities, even with supports, and an authorized substitute decision maker cannot be located despite reasonable efforts to do so, it is ethically acceptable for the health care professional to proceed with treatment based on a prudential judgment of its benefits and burdens for that person. In these situations, health care professionals must be careful to act out of a concern for the individual's best interest and overall well-being.

End-of-Life Decisions

People with intellectual and developmental disabilities can be supported to participate as much as possible in ethical deliberations regarding end-of-life care. Current best health care practices demand that providers of curative and life-sustaining treatments always attend to palliative concerns. Health care professionals should discuss the availability of palliative care with people with intellectual and developmental disabilities and their designated substitute decision maker as part of ongoing advance care planning. If palliative care runs concurrently with other forms of health care, shared support for end-of-life decisions and communication of those decisions among all involved health care professionals will foster patients' trust and the continuity and integration of their care.

Where physician-assisted suicide and voluntary euthanasia are legal practices, care must be taken to protect people who have intellectual and other developmental challenges that impair their decision making. Mental health issues, loneliness, low self-esteem, sensitivity to the negative evaluations of others, and other psychosocial factors that might be behind a request for assistance in suicide or euthanasia should be addressed with alternative therapeutic interventions and supports. Negative attitudes toward people with intellectual and developmental disabilities in society and in health care can place such people at risk of harm if physician-assisted suicide and euthanasia become normalized practices.

Jack's Story

Many of the ethical and clinical issues discussed in this chapter are illustrated in Jack's story. Jack, age 28, had mild-to-moderate intellectual and developmental disabilities. He attended school, found work, and had recently moved from his parents' house into a group home. Jack's transition to increased independence and responsibility in adulthood was complicated by two limitations: his frequent tendency to become constipated and his long-standing fear of health care procedures based on adverse past experiences.

Although Jack was typically in excellent health, his first major encounter with the health care system occurred when he was 21 and developed severe abdominal pain and persistent diarrhea. His family physician referred him to a nearby hospital to be assessed. The hospital's emergency physician determined that Jack's diarrhea was due to severe constipation. Through attentive communication with Jack, at the level of his functioning, and drawing on the help of the family member who had accompanied Jack to the hospital, the physician became aware that Jack's desire to avoid the proposed health care investigations and treatments for his constipation was due to his past adverse experiences. Jack nevertheless also expressed that he wanted to get better soon in order to return to work and his friends at the group home. After discussion with Jack and his family member, who was his legal substitute decision maker, a shared decision was made to pursue the interventions. Following these interventions, Jack's constipation improved and he was released from the hospital.

Approximately 2 years later, Jack again developed symptoms of severe constipation. As before, Jack's family physician referred him to the hospital, but this time, Jack went on his own. Jack again refused the investigation and treatment proposed by the emergency physician, who was a different physician than the one before. This physician was unfamiliar with people with intellectual and developmental disabilities. He assessed Jack and thought that Jack understood the information he was given and was communicating his choice without coercion. He decided not to refer Jack for a

more thorough assessment of his decision-making capacities or to contact Jack's family. He prescribed some medications for Jack and allowed him to return home.

Over the next 5 days, no one at the group home was monitoring Jack's condition or was aware of the medication he had been prescribed until it became apparent that his abdomen had become greatly distended and Jack expressed great distress. Jack was brought back to the hospital emergency service by one of the group home workers but, by then, his condition and distress had worsened significantly. Presumably, Jack had developed a bowel obstruction from being constipated. Jack had been prescribed liquid medication to help relieve his constipation. A person with a bowel obstruction, however, should not take anything by mouth, because food and fluids will accumulate in the patient's stomach, causing vomiting. Jack's aspiration of liquid into his lungs resulted in respiratory distress and precipitated a cardiac arrest at the hospital. He was unable to be revived and died.

Discussion of the Case

The ethical starting point for the health care professionals in this case should be respecting Jack's intrinsic human dignity. This entails an obligation to provide Jack with adequate and appropriate health care in accordance with his desire to enjoy the goods he values, such as his work and his relationships with his family and people at his group home.

This case is an illustration of the classic dilemma in ethics of conflicting duties for health care professionals both to respect their patients' moral agency and to avoid harming them. The first emergency physician understood correctly that moral agency in patients means more than understanding information and communicating an independent choice. In assessing Jack's decision-making capacities, the physician took the time and made the effort to discuss with Jack what was behind his choice, using language and means that were appropriate for his level of functioning and involving his family. Jack, his family, and the physician came to a shared decision based on what Jack ultimately valued rather than the immediate but transient distress Jack wished to avoid. The physician applied a model of supported decision making that took into account both Jack's capabilities and vulnerabilities in various aspects of decision making and enabled him to be involved as much as possible in the decision. The physician respected Jack's moral agency by engaging him and his family in ethical deliberation regarding Jack's values as an integral part of promoting authentic decision making.

The second emergency physician was unfamiliar with people with intellectual and developmental disabilities. To his credit, the physician realized that just because Jack had consented to similar interventions at the hospital 2 years ago, his refusal on this occasion should not be disregarded. An assessment of a person's decision-making capacities must be undertaken every time health care is proposed. The physician, however, was unfamiliar with people with intellectual and developmental disabilities and how to assess their decision-making capacities and vulnerabilities. If he was uncertain of Jack's decision-making capacities, he should have sought a health care professional with the necessary expertise and experience to conduct a more thorough assessment of Jack. Moreover, the physician's understanding of moral agency was unduly narrow. He made no effort to adapt his communication to Jack's level of functioning, did not try to locate and involve Jack's family, did not engage in ethical deliberation with Jack, and did not follow up with Jack's caregivers in the group home. In the end, in the view of the authors of this chapter, the physician in this case neither truly respected Jack's moral agency nor avoided harm to him.

Communication and discussions about the ethical application of health care interventions for people with intellectual and developmental disabilities are better undertaken in advance of emergency situations. The reality that Jack had recurrent problems with constipation suggests both that Jack's family physician should have involved Jack in discussing possible preventive interventions, and that they, together with Jack's designated substitute decision maker, should have engaged in advance care planning for acute crises.

SUMMARY

Weighing an intervention's benefits and burdens for a particular patient is an essential component of the decision-making process in health care. Doing this is a matter not only of understanding and applying factual information but also of ethical deliberation—apprehending values and relating them

to the decision. Many people with intellectual and developmental disabilities can apprehend and hold values, although they might require assistance from health care professionals, family, and others whom they trust to discern, evaluate, express, and apply such values. Providing such support is not the same as imposing values or taking over decision making. When a person with intellectual and developmental disabilities does not have the capacity to weigh the benefits and burdens of various health care options for himself or herself, even with appropriate supports, a substitute decision maker may do this in the person's stead, informed by that person's known or presumed values.

Harmful under- or overtreating of a person with intellectual and developmental disabilities can be avoided if respect for moral agency is understood to entail enabling the person with intellectual and developmental disabilities to participate in various aspects of decision making according to his or her capacities while addressing aspects for which the person needs support from others. Advance care planning should be incorporated into the provision of health care to people with intellectual and developmental disabilities. Promoting ethical deliberation and authentic decision making in health care ultimately depends on good relationships among the person with intellectual and developmental disabilities, the health care professional, the family, and others from whom the person receives care and support. Those relationships should be based on familiarity over time, trust, and respect for the intrinsic human dignity of people with intellectual and developmental disabilities.

FOR FURTHER THOUGHT AND DISCUSSION

1. How is an ethical approach to obtaining informed consent similar to and different from a legal approach?

2. In your opinion, is the ability of an individual to understand medical information, including the health benefits and risks of a treatment, sufficient evidence of his or her capacity to give or to refuse consent? Ought the individual also need to show that he or she can judge the broader personal implications of such a decision?

3. Is capacity to consent to a proposed therapeutic intervention or treatment only present or absent in an individual? Can an individual have a partial

capacity to consent to a treatment such that he or she requires the support of a family member or other regular caregiver for some aspects of the decision-making process?

4. Should the same ethical standard of respecting an individual's informed consent apply to a diagnostic procedure as to a medical treatment? What about a low-risk intervention to which most people would consent?

5. Should a substitute decision maker go along with the expressed wish of a person who is incapable wholly of giving informed consent to a treatment or try to judge what would be in the overall best interest of that person? Is it ethical for a substitute decision maker to refuse treatment on behalf of a person who is incapable fully of giving informed consent to a treatment for the reason that prolonging life with an intellectual and developmental disability is too burdensome?

REFERENCES

American Association on Mental Retardation. (2000). Expert consensus guideline series: Treatment of psychiatric and behavioral problems in mental retardation. Guideline 2: Informed consent. *American Journal on Mental Retardation, 105,* 159–226.

Cea, C.D., & Fisher, C.B. (2003). Health care decision-making by adults with mental retardation. *Mental Retardation, 41,* 78–87.

Developmental Disabilities Primary Care Initiative. (2011). *Informed consent in adults with developmental disabilities.* Retrieved from http://www.surreyplace.on.ca /documents/Primary%20Care/Informed%20Consent %20in%20Adults%20with%20Developmental%20 Disabilities%20(DD).pdf

Dinerstein, R.D., Herr, S.S., & O'Sullivan, J.L. (1999). *A guide to consent.* Washington, DC: American Association on Mental Retardation.

Dye, L., Hare, D.J., & Hendy, S. (2007). Capacity of people with intellectual disabilities to consent to take part in a research study. *Intellectual Disabilities, 20,* 168–174.

Emanuel, E.J., & Emanuel, L.L. (1992). Four models of the physician–patient relationship. *Journal of the American Medical Association, 267,* 2221–2226.

Evans, D.R. (1997). *The law, standards of practice, and ethics in the practice of psychology.* Toronto, Canada: Edmond Montgomery.

Friedman, R.I. (1998). Use of advance directives: Facilitating health care decisions by adults with mental retardation and their families. *Mental Retardation, 36,* 444–456.

Grisso, T. (1986). *Evaluating competencies: Forensic assessments and instruments.* New York, NY: Kluwer Academic /Plenum.

Gunn, M.J., Wong, J.G., Clare, I.C., & Holland A.J. (2000). Medical research and incompetent adults. *Journal of Mental Health Law, 2,* 60–72.

Keywood, K., & Flynn, M. (2009). Healthcare decision-making by adults with learning disabilities: Ongoing agendas, future challenges. *Psychiatry, 8,* 429–432.

Kittay, E.F. (2008). At the margins of moral personhood. *Bioethical Inquiry, 5,* 137–156.

McMahan, J. (1996). Cognitive disability, misfortune and justice. *Philosophy and Public Affairs, 25,* 3–34.

Morris, C.D., Niederbuhl, J.M., & Mahr, J.M. (1993). Determining the capability of individuals with mental retardation to give informed consent. *American Journal on Mental Retardation, 98,* 263–272.

Murphy, G.H., & O'Callaghan, A. (2004). Capacity of adults with intellectual disabilities to consent to sexual relationships. *Psychological Medicine, 34,* 1347–1357.

Redley, M., Prince, E., Bateman, N., Pennington, M., Wood, N., Croudace, T., & Ring, H. (2013). The involvement of parents in healthcare decisions where adult children are at risk of lacking decision-making capacity: A qualitative study of treatment decisions in epilepsy. *Intellectual Disability Research, 57,* 531–538.

Robertson, J., Emerson, E., Hatton, C., Kessissoglou, S., Hallam, A., & Walsh, P.N. (2001). Environmental opportunities and supports for exercising self-determination in community-based residential settings. *Research in Developmental Disabilities, 22,* 487–502.

Singer, P. (1993). *Practical ethics.* New York, NY: Cambridge University Press.

Struhkamp, R.M. (2005). Patient autonomy: A view from the kitchen. *Medicine, Health Care and Philosophy, 8,* 105–114.

Sullivan, W.F., & Heng, J. (2007). Moral education for health care professionals. In J.J. Liptay & D.S. Liptay (Eds.), *The importance of insight* (pp. 172–182). Toronto, Canada: University of Toronto Press.

Sullivan, W.F., & Heng, J. (2014). Ethics. In L. Taggart & W. Cousin (Eds.), *Health promotion for people with intellectual and developmental disabilities* (pp. 204–210). New York, NY: Open University Press & McGraw-Hill Education.

Sulmasy, D. (1997). Futility and the varieties of medical judgment. *Theoretical Medicine, 18,* 63–78.

Sulmasy, D. (2013). The varieties of human dignity: A logical and conceptual analysis. *Medicine, Health Care, and Philosophy, 16,* 937–944.

Sulmasy, D., & Snyder, L. (2010). Substitute interests and best judgments: An integrated model of surrogate decision making. *Journal of the American Medical Association, 304,* 1946–1947.

Suto, W.M., Clare, I.C., Holland, A.J., & Watson, P.C. (2005). Capacity to make financial decisions among people with mild intellectual disabilities. *Journal of Intellectual Disability Research, 49,* 199–209.

Wong, J.G., Clare, I.H., Gunn, M.J., & Holland, A.J. (1999). Capacity to make health care decisions: Its importance in clinical practice. *Psychological Medicine, 29,* 437–446.

46

Physical Health

Tom Cheetham and Shirley McMillan

WHAT YOU WILL LEARN

- Key primary care differences
- Challenges to providing quality care
- Critical role of caregivers
- Special problems and easily overlooked issues
- Screening and prevention—proactive care
- Tools for successful health care

This chapter focuses on primary care, the point of first contact with the health care system that provides continuity of care that is comprehensive and coordinated. The perspective is predominantly that of adults because there is a separate system for children and adolescents; no adult specialty comparable to either developmental-behavioral pediatrics or child and adolescent psychiatry exists, except in intellectual disability medicine in two European countries and in nursing and psychiatry in the United Kingdom (where intellectual disability is termed *learning disability*). Thus, health care for people with intellectual and developmental disabilities is unrecognized as distinct in North America. Regarding physical health for people with intellectual and developmental disabilities, it is important to know 1) that there are differences from the general (here also referred to as neurotypical) population, 2) what the differences are, and 3) what factors influence physical health for people with intellectual and developmental disabilities. The chapter addresses these questions. Optimal health underpins a good quality of life, as determined by the person, but easily can be taken for granted until ill health arises. Here the reader only need think of how a simple, self-limiting upper respiratory infection

has affected his or her functioning for a few days. Physical health is significant to everything else in a person's life; it is foundational, a cornerstone. In addition, the way physical health issues present is closely intertwined with behavioral and mental health issues, which are presented in Chapter 47.

Beange, McElduff, and Baker's (1995) landmark study in the mid-1990s drew attention to the high prevalence of physical health problems among people with intellectual and developmental disabilities (a mean of 5.4 health conditions per person), many of which went undetected and, even when diagnosed, were inadequately managed. These researchers also noted poor screening and prevention activities, frequent use of medication, and an increased mortality rate. Since the publication of the first edition of *A Comprehensive Guide to Intellectual and Developmental Disabilities*, health research has increased dramatically, and although knowledge is improved, sadly, many of the health issues identified by Beange and colleagues remain. For example, a population-based database linkage study on health issues and use of primary care services in more than 66,000 adults with intellectual disability confirmed unmet health needs, lack of screening and prevention, and high use of medications, particularly antipsychotic drugs (Lunsky, Klein-Getlink, & Yares, 2013).

People with intellectual and developmental disabilities have about twice the health issues compared with the neurotypical population (van Schrojenstein Lantman-de Valk & Walsh, 2008), but discussion here necessarily is general because people with intellectual and developmental disabilities encompass a very heterogeneous group. With some people, the underlying cause (i.e., etiology) of the intellectual disability is known; with others, it is not. For a specific syndrome (e.g., Down syndrome, Angelman syndrome, Prader-Willi syndrome, fetal alcohol syndrome), associated health issues may be defined, thus helping the clinician in making diagnoses. Often, the prevalence and severity of health problems in a person with a mild intellectual disability is different from those of someone with severe or profound impairments, and even in the case of a defined genetic syndrome, significant variability can exist. Consider epilepsy as an example: the prevalence is about 1% in the general population but approximately 25% in people with mild intellectual impairment, and it rises to about 40% in people with profound intellectual impairment. Moreover, epilepsy has a different prevalence in different syndromes; for example, it is infrequent in Down syndrome (where it may herald dementia) but very common in Sturge-Weber syndrome.

Many positive developments in the field of intellectual and developmental disabilities that affect health care have occurred in the interval since 1995. Early principles of patient-centered primary care have had wide influence in health care, and person-centered approaches now dominate social services. This has resulted in giving voice to the person with intellectual disability (e.g., Kripke, 2014). Empowerment and self-determination were identified some time ago as critical to meeting needs of people with intellectual and developmental disabilities, including health needs, but similar to the evolution of patient-centered medicine (McWhinney & Freeman, 2009) and person-centered supports and services, the views of self-advocates only recently have informed action. People with intellectual and developmental disabilities can develop skills following training in health self-advocacy. Another influence on health care is the United Nations *Convention on the Rights of Persons with Disabilities* (2006), which has advanced the human rights of people with disabilities, including the right to the highest possible standard of health (Article 25).

Discussion of the social determinants of health is beyond the scope of this chapter; nevertheless, issues such as poverty, residential segregation, stigma and discrimination, and education level affect physical health. People with intellectual and developmental disabilities increasingly live at home with parents. Parents, like their sons and daughters with intellectual and developmental disabilities, are aging and may experience health issues similar to those of their children. For example, dementia occurs at an earlier age in people with Down syndrome than in those without Down syndrome, and the parent of such an individual may himself or herself have dementia. Perkins and Haley (2010) have termed this "compound caregiving." Investigators have examined the needs of caregivers and future caregiving implications to the person's siblings. Another trend influencing physical health is the move away from segregated, sheltered work to integrated supported employment in the community (Rogan & Rinne, 2011) and therefore, at some point, retirement. Research on adverse childhood experiences in neurotypical children found that early life events set the stage both for health problems in adulthood and for shortened life expectancy. This is particularly relevant knowing the alarming rate of abuse experienced by people with intellectual and developmental disabilities (Sobsey, 1994) and has given rise to a greater emphasis on trauma-informed therapeutic approaches (e.g., Keesler, 2014; Wigham, Hatton, & Taylor, 2011).

Additional challenges to high-quality health care should be mentioned. *Diagnostic overshadowing,* a term coined by Reiss (1994), has evolved to mean that any behavior erroneously can be attributed to the person's intellectual and developmental disabilities. For example, it might be assumed that a person is remaining in his or her room or avoiding others due to the intellectual and developmental disabilities; however, such a conclusion may preclude identification of a treatable condition such as depression. One tip that can be helpful: If it is reported that "he is always like that" or "that's just her," beware of diagnostic overshadowing. Also, reimbursement to health care providers is viewed by some as a challenge because it is disproportionate to the work involved. Although it seems reasonable that care requires more time, given communication difficulties, to obtain the history and engage with the person to understand what is required for the examination, obtain informed consent, and other needed elements of care, nevertheless, data to support the clinical observation of longer appointment times being required are lacking.

People with intellectual and developmental disabilities have been excluded from research and, of serious concern given the high rate of medication use, face barriers to inclusion in medication trials. Therefore, decisions may be made based on extrapolation from research on neurotypical people, yet the epilepsy example presented previously suggests that neurotypical people and people with intellectual and developmental disabilities are not equivalent in terms of underlying brain function. Fortunately, this exclusion is changing with a growing body of research that includes people with disabilities in, for example, determining what to research (Northway et al., 2014). Consent to participate in research has been a barrier, but with training, people with intellectual and developmental disabilities may be able to give consent. With such changes in research, over time the knowledge base on which health care decisions for people with intellectual and developmental disabilities are based should improve.

With this overview of some broad influences on health, we next focus more specifically on the process (health appointment) and content (knowledge base) of the health encounter. Starting with the process, we consider who is involved and what happens at the appointment.

THE PROCESS—WHO IS INVOLVED

Health problems can be complex, even overwhelming, to providers (Wilkinson, Dreyfus, Cerreto, & Bokhour, 2012) who may have minimal or no training or supervised experience with people with intellectual and developmental disabilities. Many of the issues presented in this chapter apply equally to medical specialists and subspecialists (i.e., secondary and tertiary care, respectively) as well as other health care professionals who need to collaborate for optimal care to be provided. A number of disciplines may be required and include medical specialists, nurse practitioners, registered nurses, licensed practical nurses (termed licensed vocational nurses in California and Texas and registered practical nurses in Ontario, Canada), physician assistants, dentists, dental hygienists, psychiatrists, occupational therapists, speech-language pathologists or therapists, audiologists, optometrists, psychologists, behavior analysts (sometimes called behavior therapists), physical therapists (physiotherapists), social workers, dietitians, pharmacists, podiatrists (chiropodists), kinesiologists, recreation therapists, social workers, and others. Considerable research has examined attitudes of medical students (see Ryan & Scior, 2014, for a review), nurses, and psychiatrists and other professionals toward people with intellectual and developmental disabilities. Specialist care is beyond the scope here; however, a study reported

that adult neurologists had lower confidence in diagnosing and treating epilepsy associated with childhood-onset and intellectual disability (Borlot et al., 2014), highlighting that the issue applies beyond primary care providers. An encouraging finding from this literature is that early and frequent contact with people with disabilities improves comfort level (Karl, McGuigan, Witham-Leitch, Akl, & Symons, 2013) and specific training increases knowledge, skills, and attitudes (Minihan et al., 2011). Similarly, with dentists, training improves these attributes (Fisher, 2012), as it does by training caregivers on providing dental care (Fickert & Ross, 2012).

CRUCIAL ROLE OF CAREGIVERS

People with perhaps the most crucial role in ensuring high-quality health care for individuals often are not recognized as key professionals. They are support staff, direct support professionals, and family members, here referred to as caregivers. These individuals are knowledgeable, caring, and involved, and they have an important advantage possessed by no other professional. Caregivers who are with the person with disabilities day in and day out, often know that person best for most of their lives. A caregiver is ideally positioned to detect a change from the person's usual functioning and interpret idiosyncratic forms of communication, wants and needs, behavior indicating pain, and other vital information for accurate assessment and diagnosis. A change in some aspect of the person's appearance or behavior may be subtle—and the only clue to a health problem that might be serious, even life-threatening. Atypical presentation of such health problems could be general irritability, inactivity, disturbed appetite or sleep, or self-injurious behavior. If a person experienced abuse in a health care setting, "inexplicable" behavior might indicate a trigger to the past trauma. This contrasts with how medical problems present in the general population; it underscores the complexity and challenge of making an accurate assessment. Not surprisingly, these challenges increase as a person is closer to the profound end of a continuum from mild, moderate, severe, to a profound level of intellectual impairment. An additional factor complicates physical health: the extent to which challenging behavior and psychiatric ill-health overlap with physical health issues (see de Winter, Jansen, & Evenhuis, 2011, for a systematic review).

Physical, mental, and behavioral health issues may be far more intertwined in people with intellectual and developmental disabilities who have a limited repertoire of ways to interact with their environment compared with the neurotypical population. Therefore, medical problems, emotional problems, or problems with supports provided all can present as challenging behavior—a final common pathway.

In addition to identifying health issues requiring attention because of a change in functioning of a person who may not recognize the need to see a health care provider or be able to express discomfort or pain, caregiver activities include providing information for diagnosis, assisting with the medical encounter, and carrying out and monitoring subsequent treatment. Furthermore, the caregiver can advocate for health screening and prevention strategies to maintain health. These roles demand detailed health knowledge; therefore, tools to assist are presented later in the chapter. One paid caregiver stated it best when, describing her frustration with having her observations ignored by the clinician as she tried to have a client's problem with constipation addressed, said, "We are in the business of observation." She understood that constipation was potentially a life-threatening problem for her client, something the provider failed to appreciate based on training and experience with patients who did not have intellectual and developmental disabilities. (Various terms are used to refer to a person with intellectual and developmental disabilities: In a medical context *patient* may be the term, although it may be frowned upon based on a rejection of the historical medicalization of disability; in social services *person served* or *client* may be heard; increasingly, *person* is the appropriate term. Managed care organizations refer to the "member" of their health plan.) On the other hand, caregiver observations sometimes require clarification or an additional source to confirm the information. For example, sometimes vision and hearing problems were underreported. An experienced nurse teaching direct support professionals put it succinctly, "As front line staff, you are the eyes, ears, and voice for those you support."

With increased awareness of the caregiver's central role has come research exploring relevant caregiver issues. Important roles include recognition of health problems (e.g., determining a decline in everyday functioning heralding dementia), carrying out treatment plans (e.g., implementing

treatment of visual impairment), and supporting health promotion (e.g., support for women through menopause). A systematic review of caregiver-led interventions to monitor and improve health of adults with intellectual disability called for involvement of people with intellectual disability and caregivers in the planning and development to improve adherence with interventions that will have a positive impact (Hithersay, Strydom, Moulster, & Buszewicz, 2014). An interesting example is the HealthMatters Program: Train the Trainer model, which provides 8 hours of training to direct support professionals, who then start a 12-week health promotion activity together with the people with intellectual and developmental disabilities they support (Marks, Sisirak, & Chang, 2013).

However, the need for additional staff education to improve the quality of care has been recognized. In addition, research has explored caregiver job stress and burnout. Of concern, given the importance of knowing the person, is the low wages and lack of benefits, which contribute to an annual turnover rate of about 26% per year (Bogenschutz, Hewitt, Nord, & Hepperlen, 2014). More positively, emerging research has focused on positive aspects of the work of direct support professionals (Lunsky, Hastings, Hensel, Arenovich, & Dewa, 2014).

One discipline deserves special mention. Besides medicine, nursing is the one clinical discipline that can bridge physical, behavioral, and mental health issues and support a multidisciplinary or interdisciplinary team in understanding the multimorbidity and complexity and integrate the perspectives of various other disciplines. Primary care providers do not have sufficient time to assume this role. Another important nursing role is health teaching for adults with intellectual and developmental disabilities. Some jurisdictions outside North America have specialist nurses to support better health outcomes for people with intellectual and developmental disabilities. However, in North America, the Developmental Disabilities Nurses Association has advanced recognition of this unique branch of nursing.

Even this chapter's authors, each having 35 years' experience with people with intellectual and developmental disabilities within health care settings, continue to be surprised at how apparently trivial and nonspecific observations can herald significant health problems. In many instances, it has been the caregiver's concern that has led to discovery of important medical problems. High-quality medical care for people with intellectual and developmental disabilities is a collaborative effort between the person with disabilities, the caregiver(s), and the health care providers. Having considered the people involved in providing care, we next consider the primary care encounter using the health record as a structure to organize health information.

THE HEALTH RECORD

The health record, which may also be called the medical record, increasingly an electronic health record, is the summary of all the health information—past and current—about a patient that forms the basis for health care diagnosis, treatment planning, and progress.

Content-Knowledge Base: Guidelines and Tools

In Ontario, Canada, the Developmental Disabilities Primary Care Initiative developed evidence-based primary care guidelines (Sullivan et al., 2011) and tools to operationalize implementation of the guidelines (all available at http://www.surreyplace .on.ca/primary-care). A Special Hope Foundation grant allowed Tennessee to develop electronic versions of several of the tools that were compatible with U.S. legislation such as the Americans with Disabilities Act (ADA) of 1990 (PL 101-336). The tools are organized into three broad sections: General Issues, such as Today's Visit and Office Organizational Tips; Physical Health Issues, including Health Watch Tables; and Behavioral and Mental Health Issues. The Health Watch Tables are checklists for several specific syndromes and provide content (i.e., the knowledge base, for providers but also for people with intellectual and developmental disabilities and caregivers). Health issues for each syndrome are listed by body system, together with recommendations that address screening and prevention activities. The tool kit is available at www .iddtoolkit.org. Usual health screenings done for the general population apply—for example, recommendations of the U.S. Preventive Services Task Force (http://www.uspreventiveservicestaskforce.org) or the Canadian Task Force on Preventive Health Care (http://canadiantaskforce.ca); the Health Watch Tables highlight those additional evidence-based interventions for a particular syndrome.

Screening and Prevention—Health Checks

Considerable evidence shows that people with intellectual and developmental disabilities are not included in health screening and prevention activities. For example, almost twice as many women with intellectual and developmental disabilities are not screened for cancer of the cervix and one and a half times as many do not have mammography. A breast health promotion program may fall to nurses and residential staff. Preventive care guidelines for adults with Down syndrome are followed inconsistently. Obesity is prevalent and higher in women with intellectual and developmental disabilities than in men. A number of health promotion activities may be less frequently offered for people living in family homes or independent living situations. Even with Special Olympics athletes, presumably healthier than people with intellectual and developmental disabilities who do not participate, 25% are overweight and 32% are obese. It is not surprising that activity levels in older adults are very low; however, there is good evidence of positive effects of physical activity on balance, muscle strength, and quality of life. Health promotion works and must be broadened (Marks, Sisirack, Heller, & Wagner, 2010).

In contrast to the general population, in which periodic health checks have been found to be ineffective and possibly harmful, structured health checks have been proved effective in randomized controlled clinical trials for people with intellectual disability. A systematic review found improved detection of unmet health needs and specific actions to address these issues and an updated review 3 years later confirmed the effectiveness of this approach, with even life-threatening conditions being detected (Robertson, Hatton, Emerson, & Baines, 2014).

Autism Spectrum Disorder

Adults with autism spectrum disorder (ASD) experience increased obesity, hyperlipidemia, hypertension, epilepsy, and higher mortality compared with the neurotypical population. For a comprehensive review of primary care for adults on the autism spectrum, see Nicolaidis, Kripke, & Raymaker (2014). A brief tool that organizes health conditions and suggested monitoring is the Autism Health Watch Table, available at www.iddtoolkit.org. Other useful tools may be obtained there without charge. A more detailed Autism Spectrum Disorder Health Watch Table tool is available at http://www.surreyplace .on.ca/primary-care.

Aging and Dementia

People with intellectual and developmental disabilities are living longer and, therefore, are at risk for age-related health problems against a background of lifelong disabilities plus the long-term effects of medications taken to treat the comorbidities. One study of people with intellectual disability older than 50 found that 80% had multimorbidity, defined as two or more chronic conditions, associated with increased age and severity of intellectual disability, and almost 50% had four or more chronic health conditions (Hermans, & Evenhuis, 2014). Aging in people who have ASD requires health surveillance and screening for preventable health conditions. Risks include lifestyle issues such as lack of exercise and poor nutrition, obesity, and the high occurrence of gastroesophageal reflux disease (GERD), constipation, and infection with *Helicobacter pylori*, a bacteria that can cause stomach inflammation, ulcers, and cancer (Haveman et al., 2010). These digestive system conditions are common and not confined to older individuals with intellectual and developmental disabilities.

With aging can come dementia, particularly in, but not limited to, people with Down syndrome, where onset is earlier—at a mean age of 55.4 years in one report—and this may be associated with epilepsy and impairment of vision and hearing. The National Task Group on Intellectual Disabilities and Dementia Practices has accomplished a great deal, including advocacy, identification of screening instruments, development of guidelines for care of people with dementia and intellectual disability, and national trainings (Jokinen, Janicki, Keller, McCallion, & Force, 2013).

End of Life and Palliative Care

Although people with intellectual and developmental disabilities require similar end-of-life services such as palliative and hospice care, as with other services, they face many barriers, including their wishes not being considered.

Mortality

Despite people with intellectual and developmental disabilities living longer, death rates continue to be higher than in the neurotypical population and the causes of death differ. A large multiyear investigation into premature deaths in people with intellectual disability found the median age of death was 64 years; men with intellectual disability died, on average, 13 years sooner, and women died, on average, 20 years sooner than the general population (Heslop et al., 2014). In addition, 22% of people who died were younger than 50 years of age, compared with 9% of people without intellectual disability. The authors concluded that 37% of the deaths were avoidable by good-quality health care. People with ASD die at a rate more than five times higher than expected. Lauer and McCallion (2015) found that average age at death of people receiving services in state intellectual and developmental disabilities service systems averaged 50.4–58.7 years.

As noted previously, epilepsy is more prevalent in adults with intellectual disability. One study reviewed 898 deaths of adults with intellectual disability older than 18 years. Two hundred and forty-four of the deaths (27%) occurred in people with intellectual disability who had epilepsy; 26 of the 244 had probable sudden unexpected death in epilepsy (SUDEP). The standardized mortality ratio (i.e., the ratio of observed deaths compared with expected deaths in the general population) for SUDEP was 38 for men and 52 for women; this means that men with intellectual disability died at 38 times the rate at which men without intellectual disability died and women died at 52 times the rate compared with women without intellectual disability. Moreover, not only do people with intellectual and developmental disabilities have a shorter life expectancy, the causes of death are different. For adults in the general population, the top causes of death are circulatory disease (29%), respiratory disease (26%), and cancer (22%), whereas for people with intellectual and developmental disabilities they are respiratory disease (52%), circulatory disease (12%), and infections and parasites (6%) (Glover & Ayub, 2010). These researchers noted that aspiration and epilepsy stood out as possible preventable causes. In addition, suicide may be underrecognized.

Drug Side Effects

Medications, especially psychotropics, are overused; they are discussed in Chapter 30. The topic is included here only as a reminder that drug side effects may be common, present as physical health problems, and easily missed if the person is not able to report feeling different or unwell. Long-term psychotropic medication use can cause neurological conditions such as tardive dyskinesia, an involuntary, repetitive, often irreversible movement disorder; effects on bone metabolism and metabolic effects, including overweight and obesity; and metabolic syndrome. Metabolic syndrome includes glucose intolerance, lipid abnormalities, and increased waist circumference; prevalence was 25% and much higher than the general population (de Winter, Magilsen, van Alfen, Willemsen, & Evenhuis, 2011). Neuroleptic malignant syndrome and serotonin syndrome are rare idiosyncratic side effects that can appear initially as a flu-like illness but can be life threatening. Once again, the important thing here for the direct support professional or other caregiver is to notice a change or some difference and report it to the health care provider.

Other medications used more frequently in people with intellectual and developmental disabilities can have serious side effects. For example, proton pump inhibitors, used to treat GERD, may cause nutritional deficiencies, infections and bone fractures, and possibly pneumonia. Selective serotonin reuptake inhibitors used to treat depression and anxiety, as well as sleeping medications, can contribute to bone fractures, to give but two examples. Medications require careful monitoring by someone who can recognize subtle differences in the person with intellectual and developmental disabilities.

Infections

An investigation of people with Down syndrome suggests a much higher risk from influenza. A database study of the 2009 H1N1 influenza pandemic revealed that patients with Down syndrome, compared with patients without Down syndrome, had an increased risk of hospitalization (61.7% compared to 9.2%), endotracheal intubation (18.2% versus 2.6%), and death (23.3% versus 0.1%) (Pérez-Padilla et al., 2010). The study emphasized the importance of preventive measures such as seasonal influenza immunization.

Often, studies suffer from methodological issues and intellectual disabilities are not distinguished from other disabilities. Nevertheless, people with intellectual disability may have an increased risk of human immunodeficiency (HIV) infection.

Surgery

Research on surgical intervention is scarce. It has long been recognized that presentation can be late in the course of an illness and, with minimal signs and symptoms of intestinal obstruction, surgical risk is an important issue. One study found a higher surgical mortality rate but a similar rate of nonfatal complications; in addition, 85% of the diagnostic delays resulted in death (Bernstein & Offenbartl, 1991). A subsequent population study of inpatient major surgery between 2004 and 2007 reported increased kidney failure, pneumonia, postoperative bleeding, and septicemia (Lin, Liao, Chang, Chang, & Chen, 2011). Retrospective study of placement of a percutaneous endoscopic gastrostomy tube found that complications were common (in 74%), and more than 10% of those treated had ongoing vomiting (Ayres, Black, Scheepers, & Shaw, 2014). A more extensive procedure for reflux in children, Nissen fundoplication and gastrostomy, reported pneumonia recurrence was unchanged, reflux recurrence was 30%, and mortality rate was 20% (Cheung, Tse, Tse, & Chan, 2006).

Dental

Oral health affects the person's systemic health (Sheiham, 2005). Dental care for people with intellectual and developmental disabilities mirrors other physical health issues with considerable unmet needs, even for Special Olympics athletes. Barriers to dental care include both patient and financial issues. A national review of Medicaid Home and Community-Based Waivers found that a minority offered any type of dental services. Not surprisingly, there is a greater likelihood of visiting an emergency department for nontraumatic dental conditions. Even in people who do receive routine dental care, oral health problems persist.

SPECIFIC PHYSICAL HEALTH ISSUES

Two gastrointestinal problems that have received little recent attention in the research literature should be mentioned here because of their high prevalence: constipation and GERD. Both are easily overlooked because of their early nonspecific presentation and both can have serious consequences and even result in death. What follows are some reflections of the authors, from long clinical experience with people with intellectual and developmental disabilities, on a variety of other common physical health issues that may not be readily distinguished based on the neurotypical population. The authors have chosen epilepsy, obesity, diabetes, osteoporosis, cardiovascular disease, cancer, sensory impairment, substance misuse, sexuality, and sleep.

Epilepsy

As previously discussed in the chapter, epilepsy is more prevalent in individuals with intellectual disability and increases with the severity of the intellectual disability. However, between 25% and 38% of cases of epilepsy may be misdiagnosed. Given the high proportion of people with intellectual disability living at home, it is concerning that adherence to antiepileptic medications is less in family homes or semi-independent living. Kerr and colleagues (2009) set forth epilepsy management guidelines. Sudden unexpected death in epilepsy was discussed earlier in the Mortality subsection.

Obesity

Obesity (defined as a body mass index ≥ 30 kg/m^2) is an even larger problem for adults with intellectual disability compared with the neurotypical population, including morbid obesity (body mass index ≥ 40 kg/m^2)—more so in women with intellectual disability. Special Olympics athletes might be presumed to be healthier than nonathletes; however, they also have very high levels of obesity and overweight. Programs that address both the person with intellectual and developmental disabilities and his or her caregivers, such as the HealthMatters Program, may result in better outcomes (Marks et al., 2013). Clearly, this health issue requires urgent action with a significant focus on including younger people with intellectual and developmental disabilities.

Diabetes

Diabetes is a significant health problem in the general population, yet there is a paucity of research that focuses on the prevalence, incidence, and impact of diabetes among individuals with intellectual and developmental disabilities. This research is needed in order to raise awareness among individuals, caregivers, and health care providers, especially if the individual is unable to communicate symptoms, thus making diagnosis and management difficult. There is a link between obesity and

developing other chronic diseases such as diabetes. The individual may also experience limited opportunities to engage in physical activity and healthy diets. Another concern is the increased use of atypical antipsychotic drugs that predispose to metabolic syndrome. One study of people enrolled in a state Medicaid plan found people with developmental disability had lower quality indicators of diabetes care compared to people without developmental disability (Shireman, Reichard, Nazir, Backes, & Greiner, 2010). Health care providers need to be aware of the challenges facing the individual with intellectual and developmental disabilities and how best to offer the appropriate supports to the person and his or her caregivers. Research has found that caregivers require more education in order to better support people with diabetes.

Osteoporosis

Osteoporosis is a disease characterized by low bone mineral density and leading to an increased risk of fractures and also increased risk of pain, deformity, loss of mobility, and independence. Osteoporosis is highly prevalent in the intellectual and developmental disabilities population. A review of screening noted that fractures occur between almost two to three and a half times more often. Individuals with Down syndrome may have an increased risk of osteoporosis relative to other people with other intellectual disability. Factors that may be associated with low bone mineral density include small body size, hypogonadism, and Down syndrome in both males and females; in addition, high phosphate levels in females and low vitamin D levels have long been recognized. The use of medications such as anticonvulsant medications also increases the risk of osteoporosis. Another reason for the increased risk of osteoporosis may be related to the lack of physical activity, especially weight-bearing activities, which was discussed in the Obesity subsection. Individuals with intellectual and developmental disabilities who are at risk for low bone quality should periodically be screened for osteoporosis and be given advice related to nutritional supplements and lifestyle changes related to weight-bearing activities.

Cardiovascular Disease

Individuals with intellectual and developmental disabilities are living longer and have been shown to have similar, if not increased, risk for cardiovascular disease compared with the general population. Jansen, Rozeboom, Penning, and Evenhuis (2012) identified that underdiagnosis and selection bias may be leading to an underestimation of age-related cardiovascular death in individuals with intellectual and developmental disabilities. As with other health issues, usual approaches to physical examination may require modification or occasionally may not be possible; one study of hypertension reported that in 28% of people with severe or profound intellectual disability, no accurate blood pressure measurement was possible.

From the studies, the one modifiable risk factor for cardiovascular disease is the implementation of regular physical activity starting at a young age. Moss (2009) found that a 12-week physical activity intervention resulted in a significant increase in cardiorespiratory fitness and decrease in body fat in both males and females. Inactivity in the community setting for individuals with intellectual and developmental disabilities is a major risk factor for cardiovascular disease, and implementing a regular physical activity program reduces the risk and also decreases body fat. Also encouraging is research showing that people can be supported to have an active role in self-management of cardiovascular disease.

Cancer

As individuals with intellectual and developmental disabilities live longer, their chances of developing cancer also increases. The frequency of all cancers has been estimated to be similar to the general population, although the pattern of cancer types may differ (Sullivan, Hussain, Threlfall, & Bittles, 2004). For example, breast cancer rates appear to be similar in both women with and without intellectual and developmental disabilities, but there is evidence to suggest diagnosis in women with disabilities may be delayed (Satgé et al., 2014). As with other health conditions, early detection of signs and symptoms of cancer is not easily identified by the individual or caregivers, thus making screening important. However, women with intellectual and developmental disabilities have limited knowledge and are less likely to receive cervical and breast cancer screenings, which is similar to findings in family caregivers; therefore, interventions should focus on people with intellectual disability and their families together (Greenwood, Dreyfus, & Wilkinson, 2014).

Health promotion and cancer prevention programs are a challenge, though individuals with intellectual and developmental disabilities have an equal right to these important services. Raising the awareness of caregivers as well as the individual to the early signs and symptoms of cancer and the importance of a healthy lifestyle as a protective factor may lead to informed healthier choices and may lower the risk of cancer and death. There is a need for accessible information for individuals with intellectual and developmental disabilities in an easy-to-read format as it relates to preventive screening and signs and symptoms for early detection of cancer. Tyler, Zyzanski, Panaite, and Council (2010) argued that nurses engage with adults with intellectual and developmental disabilities through educational, workplace, residential, and recreational as well as health care settings and offer a unique perspective as to what factors promote and impede cancer screening with this population. The nurses in this study noted that the reasons for cancer screening procedures not being successful were related to not tailoring the recommendations to the individual, overcoming the barrier of the need for sedation, and the failure of the health care provider to order the necessary cancer screening tests—in other words, to not being person-centered. A study of colonoscopy screening for colorectal cancer reported a high failure rate of preparation and thus the examination could not be performed.

Sensory Impairment

The prevalence of hearing and vision impairment is greater in adults with intellectual and developmental disabilities compared with the general population and increases with age (Kiani & Miller, 2010). This may be the result of not having access to generic health care and the communication and language deficits that may be experienced. According to Kiani and Miller (2010), diagnostic overshadowing may be occurring, with the intellectual disability or mental health issues contributing to a change in behavior. Often these problems are missed and, therefore, regular screening is required. Other researchers have confirmed undetected prevalent hearing loss in individuals with intellectual and developmental disabilities. A hearing impairment leads to the individual missing out on important information in conversations, social events, and entertainment, which can contribute to isolation. A review of Special Olympics athletes reported that 22% of participants failed hearing screening and 60% received recommendations for follow-up. A detailed study of vision in adults with Down syndrome illustrates the complexity of visual processing beyond simple visual acuity (Krinsky-McHale et al., 2013).

Substance Misuse

People with intellectual and developmental disabilities experience substance misuse, but there is a lack of empirical evidence to inform prevention and treatment efforts for them. Little is known about the demographics of the individuals with intellectual and developmental disabilities engaging in substance misuse. The identified consequences of substance misuse include social isolation, experience of stigma, reduced social functioning, and the development of serious health conditions (Steinberg, Heimlich, & Williams, 2009). Alcohol use among those with intellectual and developmental disabilities may be on the increase, which may in part be a result of the individuals being more involved in community activities. Alcohol use appears to be a hidden problem coexisting with multiple physical and mental health needs. There is a lack of large-scale population-based surveys on the use of tobacco among individuals with intellectual and developmental disabilities. The limited data that do exist show that men are more likely to smoke, and those individuals in the mild to moderate range of disability tend to use tobacco. As with so many health problems, little evidence is available to guide practice for health promotion interventions for tobacco and alcohol use among people with intellectual and developmental disabilities (Kerr, Lawrence, Darbyshire, Middleton, & Fitzsimmons, 2013).

Sexuality

There continue to be social and cultural barriers to the individual with intellectual and developmental disabilities in having sexual autonomy. Providing the individual with appropriate sex education training and promotion of positive attitudes is critical in the realization of sexual autonomy for the individual with intellectual and developmental disabilities (Healy, McGuire, Evans, & Carley, 2009a, 2009b). Service providers and caregivers struggle with the rights of the individual with intellectual and developmental disabilities to have sexual autonomy (Rushbrooke, Murray, & Townsend, 2014). As has been evident in other sections of this chapter, providing the individual and caregivers with accurate information in a format that is easily understood (e.g., Easy Read—a format with an accessible, easy-to-understand presentation; Social Stories) is critical. Offering a safe environment in which sexuality can be openly discussed and dispelling any myths will also assist the individual in making informed choices and keeping safe. (See Chapter 41 for a more complete discussion of issues related to sexuality.)

Sleep Difficulties

Sleep problems are common in people with intellectual and developmental disabilities, in part because sleep difficulties increase with age and life expectancy in people with intellectual and developmental disabilities has been rising. A systematic review reported significant sleep problems in almost 10% of people with intellectual and developmental disabilities (van de Wouw, Evenhuis, & Echteld, 2012). These were associated with challenging behaviors, psychiatric conditions, and a number of medications, including psychotropics, antiepileptics, and antidepressants. As van de Wouw et al. (2012) pointed out, it is not possible to determine whether the sleep disorders are a result of the medication or the underlying condition. Further research is required to make recommendations for clinical practice, but it is a significant health issue that can result in irritability and challenging behaviors, daytime drowsiness and sedentary behaviors, and overweight and obesity. Staff training can help improve sleep in the people they support.

Braam and colleagues (2010) reported that some people treated with melatonin for sleep problems responded well initially but that the response was lost after a few weeks of treatment. Investigation found that these individuals metabolized melatonin slowly and required a much reduced dose. This again highlights the fact that medications require close monitoring.

SUMMARY

This chapter presented some of the challenges in reaching quality health care for adults with intellectual and developmental disabilities and highlighted the essential role of the caregiver. Some relevant health issues were reviewed. Equipped with this information, individuals with intellectual and developmental disabilities, their families, and other caregivers will be positioned to support the individuals, advocate, and achieve optimal health care.

FOR FURTHER THOUGHT AND DISCUSSION

1. How might health care needs for people with intellectual and developmental disabilities differ from those in the general population?

2. Consider the role of empowerment and self-determination in enabling people with intellectual and developmental disabilities to maintain a healthy lifestyle. What other strengths-based approaches to health care support exist?

3. How do environmental and other social factors (e.g., socioeconomic status) affect access to and quality of health care for people with intellectual and developmental disabilities?

4. In what ways are caregivers important to supporting more positive health-related outcomes for people with intellectual and developmental disabilities?

5. Consider how some of the specific physical health issues discussed in the chapter can be addressed in ways that empower people with intellectual and developmental disabilities.

REFERENCES

Americans with Disabilities Act (ADA) of 1990, PL 101-336, 42 U.S.C. §§ 12101 *et seq.*

Ayres, L., Black, C., Scheepers, M., & Shaw, I. (2014). An audit to evaluate the safety and efficacy of percutaneous endoscopic gastrostomy placement in patients with learning disabilities. *British Journal of Learning Disabilities, 43*(3), 201–207.

Beange, H., McElduff, A., & Baker, W. (1995). Medical disorders of adults with mental retardation: A population study. *American Journal on Mental Retardation, 99*(6), 595–604.

Bernstein, G., & Offenbartl, S. (1991). Adverse surgical outcomes among patients with cognitive impairments. *American Surgeon, 57*(1), 682–690.

Bogenschutz, M., Hewitt, A., Nord, D., & Hepperlen, R. (2014). Direct support workforce supporting individuals with IDD: Current wages, benefits, and stability. *Intellectual and Developmental Disabilities, 52*(5), 317–329.

Borlot, F., Tellez-Zenteno, J., Allen, A., Ali, A., Carter Snead, O., & Andrade, D. (2014). Epilepsy transition: Challenges of caring for adults with childhood-onset seizures. *Epilepsia, 55*(10), 1659–1666.

Braam, W., Van Geijlswijk, I., Keijzer, H., Smits, M., Didden, R., & Curfs, L. (2010). Loss of response to melatonin treatment is associated with slow melatonin metabolism. *Journal of Intellectual Disability Research, 54*(6), 547–555. doi:10.1111/j.1365-2788.2010.01283

Cheung, K., Tse, H., Tse, P., & Chan, K. (2006). Nissen fundoplication and gastrostomy in severely neurologically impaired children with gastroesophageal reflux. *Hong Kong Medical Journal, 12*(4), 282–288.

de Winter, C., Jansen, A., & Evenhuis, H. (2011). Physical conditions and challenging behaviour in people with intellectual disability: A systematic review. *Journal of Intellectual Disability Research, 55*(7), 675–698. doi:10.1111/j.1365-2788.2011.01390.x

de Winter, C., Magilsen, K., van Alfen, J., Willemsen, S., & Evenhuis, H. (2011). Metabolic syndrome in 25% of older people with intellectual disability. *Family Practice, 28*, 141–144. doi:10.1093/fampra/cmq079

Fickert, N., & Ross, D. (2012). Effectiveness of a caregiver education program on providing oral care to individuals with intellectual and developmental disabilities. *Intellectual and Developmental Disabilities, 50*(3), 219–232. doi:10.1352/1934-9556-50.3.219

Fisher, K. (2012). Is there anything to smile about? A review of oral care for individuals with intellectual and developmental disabilities. *Nursing Research and Practice, 2012*, Article ID 860692, 6 pages. doi:10.1155/2012/860692

Glover, G., & Ayub, M. (2010). *How people with learning disabilities die.* Durham, United Kingdom: Improving Health and Lives Learning Disabilities Observatory.

Greenwood, N., Dreyfus, D., & Wilkinson, J. (2014). More than just a mammogram: Breast cancer screening perspectives of relatives of women with intellectual disability. *Intellectual and Developmental Disabilities, 52*(6), 444–455. doi:10.1352/1934-9556-52.6.444

Haveman, M., Heller, T., Lee, L., Maaskant, M., Shooshtari, S., & Strydom, A. (2010). Major health risks in aging persons with intellectual disabilities: An overview of recent studies. *Journal of Policy and Practice in Intellectual Disabilities, 7*(1), 59–69. doi:10.1111/j.1741-1130.2010.00248.x

Healy, E., McGuire, B., Evans, D., & Carley, S. (2009a). Sexuality and personal relationships for people with an intellectual disability. Part I: Service-user perspectives. *Journal of Intellectual Disability Research, 53*(11), 905–912. doi:10.1111/j.1365-2788.2009.01203.x

Healy, E., McGuire, B., Evans, D., & Carley, S. (2009b). Sexuality and personal relationships for people with an intellectual disability. Part II: Staff and family carer perspectives. *Journal of Intellectual Disability Research, 53*(11), 913–921. doi:10.1111/j.1365-2788.2009.01202.x

Hermans, H., & Evenhuis, H. (2014). Multimorbidity in older adults with intellectual disabilities. *Research in Developmental Disabilities, 35*, 776–783.

Heslop, P., Blair, P., Fleming, P., Hoghton, M., Marriott, A., & Russ, L. (2014). The confidential inquiry into premature deaths of people with intellectual disabilities in the UK: A population-based study. *The Lancet, 383*(9920), 889–895. doi:10.1016/s0140-6736(13)62026-7

Hithersay, R., Strydom, A., Moulster, G., & Buszewicz, M. (2014). Carer-led health interventions to monitor, promote and improve the health of adults with intellectual disabilities in the community: A systematic review. *Research in Developmental Disabilities, 35*(4), 887–907. doi:10.1016/j.ridd.2014.01.010

Jansen, J., Rozeboom, W., Penning, C., & Evenhuis, H. (2012). Prevalence and incidence of myocardial infarction and cerebrovascular accident in ageing persons with intellectual disability. *Journal of Intellectual Disability Research, 57*(7), 681–685. doi:10.1111/j.1365-2788.2012.01567.x

Jokinen, N., Janicki, M., Keller, S., McCallion, P., & Force, L. (2013). Guidelines for structuring community care and supports for people with intellectual disabilities affected by dementia. *Journal of Policy and Practice in Intellectual Disabilities, 10*(1), 1–24. doi:10.1111/jppi.12016

Karl, R., McGuigan, D., Withiam-Leitch, M., Akl, E., & Symons, A. (2013). Reflective impressions of a precepted clinical experience caring for people with disabilities. *Intellectual and Developmental Disabilities, 51*(4), 237–245. doi:10.1352/1934-9556-51.4.237

Keesler, J. (2014). A call for the integration of trauma-informed care among intellectual and developmental disability organizations. *Journal of Policy and Practice in Intellectual Disabilities, 11*(1), 34–42. doi:10.1111/jppi.12071

Kerr, S., Lawrence, M., Darbyshire, C., Middleton, A., & Fitzsimmons, L. (2013). Tobacco and alcohol-related interventions for people with mild/moderate intellectual disabilities: A systematic review of the literature. *Journal of Intellectual Disability Research, 57*(5), 393–408. doi:10.1111/j.1365-2788.2012.01543x

Kerr, M., Scheepers, M., Arvio, M., Beavis, J., Brandt, C., Brown, S.,...Wallace, R. (2009). Consensus guidelines into the management of epilepsy in adults with an intellectual disability. *Journal of Intellectual Disability Research, 53*(8), 687–694. doi:10.1111/j.1365-2788.2009.01182.x

Kiani, R., & Miller, H. (2010). Sensory impairment and intellectual disability. *Advances in Psychiatric Treatment, 16*, 228–235.

Krinsky-McHale, S., Silverman, W., Gordon, J., Devenny, D., Oley, N., & Abramov, I. (2013). Vision deficits in adults with Down syndrome. *Journal of Applied Research in Intellectual Disabilities, 27*(3), 247–263. doi:10.1111/jar.12062

Kripke, C. (2014). Primary care for adolescents with developmental disabilities. *Primary Care: Clinics in Office Practice, 41*(3), 507–518. doi:10.1016/j.pop.2014.05.005

Lauer, E., & McCallion, P. (2015). Mortality of people with intellectual and developmental disabilities from select US state disability service systems and medical claims data. *Journal of Applied Research on Intellectual Disabilities, 28*(5), 394–405. doi:10.1111/jar.12191

Lin, J-A., Liao, C-C., Chang, C-C., Chang, H., & Chen, T-L. (2011). Postoperative adverse outcomes in intellectually disabled surgical patients: A nationwide population-based study. *PLoS ONE, 6*(10), e26977. doi:10.1371/journal.pone.0026977

Lunsky, Y., Hastings, R., Hensel, J., Arenovich, T., & Dewa, C. (2014). Perceptions of positive contributions and burnout in community developmental disability

workers. *Intellectual and Developmental Disabilities, 52*(4), 249–257. doi:10.1352/1934-9556-52.4.249

Lunsky, Y., Klein-Getlink, J.E., & Yares, E.A. (Eds.). (2013). *Atlas on the primary care of adults with developmental disabilities in Ontario.* Toronto, Canada: Institute for Clinical Evaluative Sciences and Centre for Addiction and Mental Health.

Marks, B., Sisirak, J., & Chang, Y. (2013). Efficacy of the HealthMatters Program Train-the-Trainer model. *Journal of Applied Research in Intellectual Disabilities, 26*(4), 319–334. doi:10.1111/jar.12045

Marks, B., Sisirak, J., Heller, T., & Wagner, M. (2010). Evaluation of community-based health promotion programs for Special Olympics athletes. *Journal of Policy and Practice in Intellectual Disabilities, 7*(2), 119–129. doi:10.1111/j.1741-1130.2010.00258.x

McWhinney, I., & Freeman, T. (2009). Clinical method. In I. McWhinney & T. Freeman (Eds.), *Textbook of family medicine* (3rd ed., pp. 140–192). New York, NY: Oxford University Press.

Minihan, P., Robey, K., Long-Bellil, L., Graham, C., Hahn, J., Woodard, L., & Eddey, G. (2011). Desired educational outcomes of disability-related training for the generalist physician: Knowledge, attitudes, and skills. *Academic Medicine, 86*(9), 1171–1178. doi:10.1097/acm.0b013e3182264a25

Moss, S. (2009). Changes in coronary heart disease risk profile of adults with intellectual disabilities following a physical activity intervention. *Journal of Intellectual Disability Research, 53*(8), 735–744. doi:10.1111/j.1365-2788.2009.01187.x

Nicolaidis, C., Kripke, C., & Raymaker, D. (2014). Primary care for adults on the autism spectrum. *Medical Clinics of North America, 98*(5), 1169–1191. doi:10.1016/j.mcna.2014.06.011

Northway, R., Hurley, K., O'Connor, C., Thomas, H., Howarth, J., Langley, E., & Bale, S. (2014). Deciding what to research: An overview of a participatory workshop. *British Journal of Learning Disabilities, 42*(4), 323–327. doi:10.1111/bld.12080

Pérez-Padilla, R., Fernández, R., Garcia-Sancho, C., Franco-Marina, F., Aburto, O., López-Gatell, H., & Bojórquez, I. (2010). Pandemic (H1N1) 2009 virus and down syndrome patients. *Emerging Infectious Diseases, 16*(8), 1312–1314. doi:10.3201/eid1608.091931

Perkins, E., & Haley, W. (2010). Compound caregiving: When lifelong caregivers undertake additional caregiving roles. *Rehabilitation Psychology, 55*(4), 409–417. doi:10.1037/a0021521

Reiss, S. (1994). Psychopathology in mental retardation. In N. Bouras (Ed.), *Mental health in mental retardation: Recent advances and practices* (pp. 67–78). Cambridge, United Kingdom: Cambridge University Press.

Robertson, J., Hatton, C., Emerson, E., & Baines, S. (2014). The impact of health checks for people with intellectual disabilities: An updated systematic review of evidence. *Research in Developmental Disabilities, 35*(10), 2450–2462. doi:10.1016/j.ridd.2014.06.007

Rogan, P., & Rinne, S. (2011). National call for organizational change from sheltered to integrated employment.

Intellectual and Developmental Disabilities, 49(4), 248–260. doi:10.1352/1934-9556-49.4.248

Rushbrooke, E., Murray, C., & Townsend, S. (2014). What difficulties are experienced by caregivers in relation to the sexuality of people with intellectual disabilities? A qualitative meta-synthesis. *Research in Developmental Disabilities, 35*(4), 871–886. doi:10.1016/j.ridd.2014.01.012

Ryan, T., & Scior, K. (2014). Medical students' attitudes towards people with intellectual disabilities: A literature review. *Research in Developmental Disabilities, 35*(10), 2316–2328. doi:10.1016/j.ridd.2014.05.019

Satgé, D., Sauleau, E-A., Jacot, W., Raffi, F., Azéma, B., Bouyat, J-C., & Assaf, N. (2014). Age and stage at diagnosis: A hospital series of 11 women with intellectual disability and breast carcinoma. *BMC Cancer, 14,* 150. doi:10.1186/1471-2407-14-150

Sheiham, A. (2005). Oral health, general health and quality of life. *Bulletin of the World Health Organization, 83*(9), 644–645. Retrieved from www.who.int/bulletin/volumes/83/9/editorial30905html/en

Shireman, T.I., Reichard, A., Nazir, N., Backes, J.M., & Greiner, K.A. (2010). Quality of diabetes care for adults with developmental disabilities. *Disability and Health Journal, 3*(3) 179–185.

Sobsey, D. (1994). *Violence and abuse in the lives of people with disabilities: The end of silent acceptance?* Baltimore, MD: Paul H. Brookes Publishing Co.

Steinberg, M., Heimlich, L., & Williams, J. (2009). Tobacco use among individuals with intellectual or developmental disabilities: A brief review. *Intellectual and Developmental Disabilities,47*(3), 197–207.

Sullivan, W.F., Berg, J.M., Bradley, E., Cheetham, T., Denton, R., Heng, J.,...McMillan, S. (2011). Primary care of adults with developmental disabilities: Canadian consensus guidelines. *Canadian Family Physician, 57*(5), 541–568.

Sullivan, S., Hussain, R., Threlfall, T., & Bittles, A. (2004). The incidence of cancer in people with intellectual disabilities. *Cancer Causes and Control, 15*(10), 1021–1025. doi:10.1007/s10552-004-1256-0

Tyler, C., Zyzanski, S., Panaite, V., & Council, L. (2010). Nursing perspectives on cancer screening in adults with intellectual and other developmental disabilities. *Intellectual and Developmental Disabilities, 48*(4), 271–277. doi:10.1352/1934-9556-48.4.271

United Nations. (2006). *Convention on the rights of persons with disabilities.* Retrieved from http://www.un.org/disabilities/convention/conventionfull.shtml

van de Wouw, E., Evenhuis, H., & Echteld, M. (2012). Prevalence, associated factors and treatment of sleep problems in adults with intellectual disability: A systematic review. *Research in Developmental Disabilities, 33*(4), 1310–1332. doi:10.1016/j.ridd.2012.03.003

van Schrojenstein Lantman-de Valk, H., & Walsh, P. (2008). Managing health problems in people with intellectual disabilities. *British Medical Journal, 337,* a2507. doi:10.1136/bmj.a2507

Wigham, S., Hatton, C., & Taylor, J. (2011). The effects of traumatizing life events on people with intellectual disabilities: A systematic review. *Journal of Mental Health Research in Intellectual Disabilities, 4*(1), 19–39. doi:10.1080/19315864.2010.534576

Wilkinson, J., Dreyfus, D., Cerreto, M., & Bokhour, B. (2012). "Sometimes I feel overwhelmed": Educational needs of family physicians caring for people with intellectual disability. *Intellectual and Developmental Disabilities, 50*(3), 243–250. doi:10.1352/1934-9556-50.3.243

People with Intellectual and Developmental Disabilities and Mental Health Needs

Jane Summers, Robert Fletcher, and Elspeth Bradley

- Ways to understand, prevent, assess, and treat mental and emotional distress, psychiatric disorders, and problem behaviors in people with intellectual and developmental disabilities
- Mental health service systems in the United States and Canada for those with intellectual and developmental disabilities
- Equipping care providers to overcome challenges when working with this population

In this chapter, we outline approaches to assist with understanding, assessing, and treating mental health concerns in people with intellectual and developmental disabilities. We talk about how best to support people with intellectual and developmental disabilities so as to prevent, wherever possible, mental health problems from occurring. We have created an infographic (Figure 47.1) to convey key facts about mental health issues in individuals with intellectual and developmental disabilities. We also introduce the analogy of using "mental health detectives" who work as a team to gather information

Authors' note: The authors would like to acknowledge Rita Khamis and Terameet Kaur for their assistance in creating Figures 47.1 and 47.2.

about individuals who present with problem behaviors and/or mental distress.

Throughout this chapter, we use the broad term *mental health problems* to refer collectively to psychiatric disorders, mental and emotional distress, and problem behaviors. See the Terms Used in This Chapter discussion for a more complete understanding of these and related concepts.

OVERVIEW OF THE LIVES OF PEOPLE WITH INTELLECTUAL AND DEVELOPMENTAL DISABILITIES

People with intellectual and developmental disabilities show increased vulnerability to physical and mental health problems. Their health needs may be unrecognized and unmet. Bradley, Sinclair, and Greenbaum (2012) summarized some of the factors involved in mental health issues in people with intellectual and developmental disabilities:

- Seizures and complex seizure patterns are more common, which add to unusual and unique bodily experiences not easily understood by care providers or articulated by clients.
- They experience more social disadvantage, neglect, abuse (i.e., sexual and/or physical abuse)

Terms Used in This Chapter

- *Intellectual and developmental disability* (intellectual and developmental disabilities): significant limitations in intellectual and adaptive behavior that originate before the age of 18 years; current approaches to the evaluation and classification of intellectual and developmental disabilities (*Diagnostic and Statistical Manual of Mental Disorders, Fifth Edition* [*DSM-5*], American Psychiatric Association, 2013; *Intellectual Disability: Definition, Classification, and Systems of Support, Eleventh Edition,* Schalock et al., 2010) place an emphasis on assessing the impact of intellectual impairments on an individual's adaptive behavior (in relation to social, practical, and conceptual skills); assessment of adaptive functioning is of primary importance, as it determines the level of supports that are required to enhance an individual's personal and social competence

- *Mental health:* "a state of well-being in which every individual realizes his or her own potential, can cope with the normal stresses of life, can work productively and fruitfully, and is able to make a contribution to her or his community" (World Health Organization, 2016)

- *Mental distress:* a self-reported experience of worry, preoccupation, frustration, confusion, anguish, or emotional pain or a behavior observed by others, suggesting that the individual is worried, preoccupied, frustrated, confused, in anguish, or in emotional pain (e.g., facial and bodily expressions, nonverbal vocalizations)

- *Emotional distress:* mental distress specifically associated with emotional experience (e.g., happy, sad, disappointed) and/or emotional dysregulation as observed by others

- *Psychiatric disorders:* patterns of symptoms and behaviors, described in *DSM-5,* that are underpinned by changes in the neurobiology of the brain and nervous system; specific disorders are specific patterns meeting specific criteria

- *Mental (psychiatric) illness:* overlaps with *psychiatric disorders*; may be used to refer specifically to active episodes of a psychiatric disorder or to severe mental ill-health

- *Problem behaviors:* behaviors engaged in by an individual that are of concern to care providers, the individual, or both and that can result from a variety of underlying etiologies (discussed later in this chapter); sometimes referred to as "challenging" behaviors; may develop when an individual's unique needs (e.g., communication) or health conditions (e.g., pain) are unrecognized or unmet or not adequately accommodated

- *Dual diagnosis:* mental or emotional distress, psychiatric illness or disorder, or problem behaviors co-existing with intellectual and developmental disabilities

---

and negative life events than people without such disabilities.

- Many experience stigma and exclusion. Being teased is a common experience; this and similar negative responses from others may be experienced as posttraumatic stress disorder.

- Effects of trauma may present as deterioration in skills and behavior; the nature of this trauma may remain unrecognized and, instead, individuals may be considered to have "problem behaviors" or "challenging behaviors."

- Life events are associated with psychological problems and may play a causal role; trauma may play an even more important role in risk for psychopathology.

- Emotional and behavioral disturbances are responsive to a range of psychological therapies and other interventions that focus on the interpersonal environment.

- A focus on each individual's unique pattern of developmental issues and provision of "capable environments" (Banks et al., 2007; Banks &

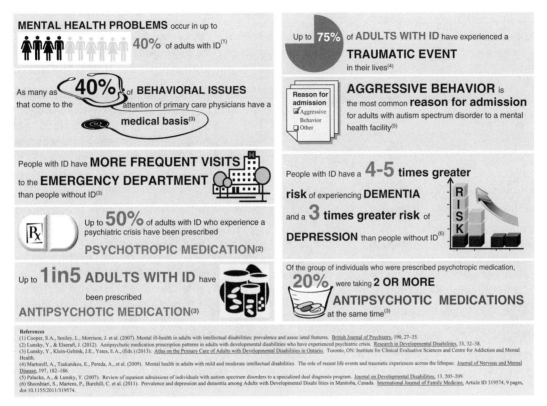

Figure 47.1. Infographic showing intellectual and developmental disabilities and mental health by the numbers. (Figure copyright © Summers & Bradley, 2016.) (*Key*: ID, intellectual disability.)

Bush, 2016) that are sensitive to and supportive of the developmental and emotional needs of people with intellectual and developmental disabilities rather than on "challenging behaviors" may prevent many of these emotional disturbances and problem behaviors.

MENTAL HEALTH PROBLEMS IN PEOPLE WITH INTELLECTUAL AND DEVELOPMENTAL DISABILITIES

People with intellectual and developmental disabilities experience the kinds of mental health problems experienced among the general population, but these problems occur more frequently (Cooper, Smiley, Morrison, Williamson, & Allan, 2007). Figure 47.1 illustrates the prevalence of various factors in the lives of individuals with IDD and the resulting clinical implications. Organic, psychosocial, and environmental factors may individually and in combination play a major role in the development of these mental health problems. Organic factors including genetic influences, brain injury, trauma,

disease, or infection may underlie both the intellectual disability and mental health problem (Leonard & Wen, 2002). Etiological differences include genetic syndromes (e.g., Down and fragile X) and behavioral syndromes (e.g., autism spectrum disorder [ASD]) and are differently associated with certain mental health vulnerabilities and psychiatric conditions. For example, up to 30% of individuals with intellectual and developmental disabilities may have coexisting ASD and, as such, show increased prevalence of anxiety and mood disorders, inattentive behaviors, hyperactive behaviors, compulsive behaviors, and stereotypies (Bradley, Ames, & Bolton, 2011; Bradley & Bolton, 2006; Bradley & Isaacs, 2006) compared to those with intellectual and developmental disabilities alone; Down syndrome is associated with earlier onset of age-related dementia and fragile X is associated with increased prevalence of anxiety disorders (O'Brien, 2016). In terms of environmental and psychosocial influences on mental health problems, many people with intellectual and developmental disabilities live in impoverished environments, lack strong support systems, do not have access to meaningful activities, and lack control over many aspects of their lives (Emerson, 2007). They may also have poor or inadequate social and coping skills. When these conditions occur on top of cognitive and communication impairments, feelings of frustration, a sense of failure, and an awareness of being "different" can be heightened, contributing further to mental health vulnerability.

Some of the more common psychiatric conditions found in people with intellectual and developmental disabilities include mood and anxiety disorders and adjustment problems. (Figure 47.1) These overlap considerably with behavioral disturbances, which include verbal and physical aggression, self-injury, attentional problems, and oppositional behavior. Many individuals with intellectual and developmental disabilities have multiple psychiatric diagnoses.

CLINICAL CHALLENGES IN DIAGNOSING MENTAL HEALTH PROBLEMS

A number of clinical challenges may arise when trying to correctly diagnose mental health problems in people with intellectual and developmental disabilities. Some of these challenges are highlighted in the following sections.

Communication Difficulties

Clinical challenges may arise, in part, because fully understanding mental distress and making a diagnosis of a psychiatric disorder require feedback from the individual about his or her inner experience (i.e., thoughts and feelings). Accurate diagnosis of mental health disorders becomes more difficult with increasing severity of communication impairments. Most individuals with intellectual and developmental disabilities have mild disabilities and often have good use of speech. As a result, it is easy to overestimate their comprehension and is important to check for shared comprehension. Some individuals who do not have well-developed verbal skills are able to respond to pictures, textual information, and other forms of visual input. However, with increasing severity of intellectual and developmental disabilities, people are generally unable to understand or use symbolic forms of communication and rely on those around them to anticipate their needs and interpret their vocalizations and body language (Boardman,

---

> **Trying to Imagine What It Is Like to Have Difficulties Communicating Your Needs to Others**
>
> *Scenario:* Your plane lands unexpectedly in a country you do not know, where the language and local customs are totally unfamiliar to you. How would you let someone know that you need to use the washroom?

Bernal, & Hollins, 2014). Often, practitioners are left to make interpretations, even after a comprehensive assessment of all possible contributors, as to what circumstance is underpinning changes in behavior (e.g., whereas one individual when in pain or when depressed might start to withdraw, another might start to self-injure). Many people with intellectual and developmental disabilities are "unique communicators." To truly engage in meaningful relationships with them (whether this is in friendship, therapy, or treatment) one needs to learn their unique ways of communicating so as to provide optimal supports, prevent mental distress, and prevent mental health problems or—when these arise—to ensure accurate diagnosis and appropriate treatment. We present an exercise (Trying to Imagine What It Is Like to Have Difficulties Communicating Your Needs to Others) to help the reader understand what it feels like when it is difficult to communicate one's most pressing needs.

Recognition of Pain

With increasing communication difficulties, recognition of pain often becomes problematic. It is likely that mental distress caused by pain and discomfort is greatly underrecognized in people with intellectual and developmental disabilities, even though this may underlie many problem (challenging) behaviors (Waite et al., 2014). It is essential for care providers to routinely identify how the individuals they are working with usually communicate their pain, whether this is with words, gestures, or problem behaviors or a combination of ways. For example, how do they speak and behave when they hurt themselves or have a toothache or headache? Knowing these usual patterns of behavior in response to injury, discomfort, and pain is helpful when trying to understand the causes of unusual behaviors that may arise.

Diagnostic Overshadowing

An additional concern is that a psychiatric disorder (and also medical conditions) may be masked because of the individual's intellectual and developmental disabilities. For example, absence of initiative may be attributed by a clinician who does not know the individual well, to the individual's intellectual and developmental disabilities rather than to onset of depression. This is referred to as diagnostic overshadowing—the tendency of professionals to underestimate signs of psychiatric or emotional disturbance in people with intellectual and developmental disabilities (Jopp & Keys, 2001). In determining whether someone with intellectual and developmental disabilities does indeed have a psychiatric disorder, it is most important that care providers who know the individual well provide information about his or her usual baseline functioning prior to the onset of concerns. A comparison of the individual's usual everyday functioning and behavior (baseline) against documented changes is crucial in determining whether there has been onset of a psychiatric disorder.

Acquiescence

Interviewing someone who has an intellectual disability and obtaining accurate information about the individual's symptoms can be confounded by an increased tendency for the person to agree quickly. The person may tell the clinician or care provider what he or she thinks the interviewer wants to hear or agree to things in order to avoid the risk of disapproval. The person may be more likely to report "yes" or "no" to all questions rather than provide the true response.

Medication Masking

The sedative effects of certain medications (e.g., atypical antipsychotic medications) can suppress, or mask, the presence of significant mental health symptoms. For example, a person may be experiencing agitation related to depression but, due to limited communication skills, may be unable to describe symptoms of his or her depression. If the person is prescribed an atypical antipsychotic medication, the agitation may stop. However, the medication has not effectively treated the person's illness, and he or she may continue to suffer with symptoms of depression.

ASSESSMENT OF PROBLEM BEHAVIORS AND MENTAL DISTRESS

This section outlines the steps that are involved in assessing someone with intellectual and developmental disabilities who presents with problem behaviors and/or mental distress. We have used a detective theme to organize the information in this section (see Figure 47.2). Our "mental health detectives" work as a team to systematically carry out an investigation that focuses on the following areas: 1) physical health and medical conditions, 2) environment and support needs, 3) life experiences and emotional needs, and 4) psychiatric problems (Bradley & Korossy, 2015). While conducting their investigation, the mental health detectives collect, examine, and analyze evidence and then use this evidence to "solve" (diagnose) the problem(s).

The starting point for this process is the recognition that an individual with intellectual and developmental disabilities is experiencing emotional or mental distress. For individuals who have difficulty telling others directly about their distress, this is often expressed in the form of changes in coping or functioning or in the emergence of behavior concerns. People who know the individual well (e.g., family members, support staff who work with the individual on a regular basis) are often among the first to recognize these behavioral changes or expressions of distress. Once recognized, these issues

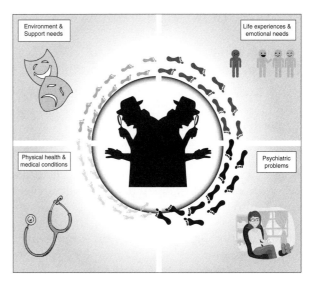

Figure 47.2. Mental health investigation involves four keys areas. (Figure copyright © Bradley & Summers, 2016. Detective art by Terameet Kaur. Clip art copyright © clipart.com and istockphoto.)

need to be brought to the attention of someone (e.g., supervisor, case manager, general practitioner) who can help to organize a comprehensive investigation. Initially, it may be necessary to attend to the individual's immediate safety and support needs. Our team of mental health detectives is called into action to conduct a careful and systematic search for evidence that can be used to diagnose the problem. The team can be made up of many people, including caregivers who know the individual best, along with specialists from medicine (e.g., developmental pediatrics, genetics, psychiatry, neurology, family medicine, audiology, ophthalmology), nursing, psychology, social work, speech-language pathology, behavior therapy, occupational therapy, and/or physiotherapy.

The first major form of evidence comes from investigating physical health and medical conditions as a possible source of the individual's problem behaviors or mental distress. This is followed by an exploration of the individual's environment and support system, along with a consideration of his or her emotional experiences and emotional needs. Once all of these factors have been investigated, the evidence can be integrated and analyzed to determine whether the individual meets the diagnostic criteria for a psychiatric disorder. It may be tempting to jump ahead and try to diagnose a psychiatric disorder without first conducting a thorough investigation. However, this means that important evidence may be missed. If so, the problem could be misdiagnosed and inadequate or even harmful treatment prescribed.

When Is the Problem Related to Physical Health and Medical Conditions?

There is strong evidence that physical and mental health are closely linked. This statement has particular relevance for people with intellectual and developmental disabilities, who experience higher rates of physical health problems and medical conditions and may be at higher risk for pain-related conditions than the general population. Unfortunately, their health problems may go undetected and subsequently undertreated, contributing to changes in mood, functioning, and behavior that can resemble psychiatric disorders (see Common Medical Conditions Contributing to Changes in Well-Being, Functioning, or Behavior). As an example, pain caused by constipation, reflux, dental problems, or

headache can result in sleep disturbance, increased irritability, and aggressive outbursts, which themselves become the focus of intervention rather than treating the underlying health problem. Identification of medical issues may be relatively straightforward for individuals with better verbal skills who can talk about the source of their discomfort but is more challenging when individuals are less able to communicate about their inner experiences. In these latter situations, caregiver reports are often an important source of information. Some individuals with intellectual and developmental disabilities may have a high pain tolerance or may not show outward signs of distress or discomfort that care providers recognize as pain behaviors until their situation is more serious (often labeled as a "behavioral crisis"). Others may have difficulties with access to and navigation of the health care system or avoid seeking treatment when feeling unwell due to negative or traumatic experiences they encountered in the past when trying to obtain help.

When investigating medical conditions and physical health issues, the team of mental health detectives should gather information from a variety of sources. They should speak directly with the individual with intellectual and developmental disabilities to obtain information first hand. If

---

Common Medical Conditions Contributing to Changes in Well-Being, Functioning, or Behavior

- Constipation
- Reflux
- Respiratory problems
- Cardiovascular-related problems
- Headache, earache
- Vision and hearing problems
- Dental problems
- Allergies
- Side effects from medication
- Seizures
- Problems related to cerebral palsy (e.g., spasticity, orthopedic or urinary issues)

**Clues a Person May
Feel Unwell or Be in Pain**

- Sudden changes in habits or behavior

- Behavior occurs at specific times, such as after a meal

- Shows signs of distress—crying, grimacing, moaning

- Refuses to eat or drink

- Has difficulty calming or settling

- Touches or protects certain part of his or her body

Environmental Issues to Consider

Physical environment

- Level of lighting

- Noise levels

- Activity and stimulation levels

- Temperature

- Odors and scents

- Presence of visual and auditory distractions

- Physical layout

- Adaptations to support those with visual, hearing, or ambulatory disabilities

Note: Autism Speaks (https://www.autismspeaks.org) offers autism video simulations to help others understand the experience of sensory overload.

Social environment

- All staff familiar with strategies and aids to support communication and unique communicators (Boardman et al., 2014)

- Person-centered plans to promote inclusion, participation, and friendships

---

the individual has difficulty communicating about symptoms of pain or illness, visually based tools such as body maps to indicate pain location and colored scales to indicate pain intensity (Temple et al., 2012) may be helpful. People who know the individual best (e.g., parents, teachers, support workers) should also be interviewed to obtain their perspectives. The individual's health history needs to be compiled and carefully reviewed. Sometimes this information is kept by different care providers, so the team needs to work out how to track this down. Finally, the team may need to observe the individual's behavior in a variety of situations to uncover additional evidence of physical and medical problems (see Clues a Person May Feel Unwell or Be in Pain). Resources are available to assist with recognition of pain and discomfort (e.g., Chronic Pain Scale for Nonverbal Adults with Intellectual Disabilities, Burkitt Breau, Salsman, Sarsfield-Turner, & Mullan, 2009; Disability Distress Assessment Tool, Pain Resource Center, n.d.).

When Is the Problem Related to the Environment, Supports, and Expectations?

Behavioral and mental health problems can also arise when there is a mismatch between the needs of individuals with intellectual and developmental disabilities and the characteristics and demands of their environment. For instance, individuals who are highly sensitive to noise and crowds may be better suited to an environment that has fewer people who engage in a limited number of activities (see Environmental Issues to Consider). However, this type of environment may not appeal to individuals

who prefer a variety of fast-paced activities. Individuals who are sensitive to noise and crowds may become overwhelmed and show signs of distress in a busy or chaotic environment. In contrast, individuals who prefer a more stimulating environment may show signs of anxiety and restlessness when placed in a quieter setting.

It is also important to consider the supports that are needed to optimize the personal competence and well-being of individuals with intellectual and developmental disabilities. Some individuals need frequent and intensive support to perform a wide variety of tasks successfully, such as taking care of their personal needs, helping out around the home, participating in activities in the community, and interacting with others. Other individuals only need occasional or less intensive assistance in relation to specific tasks, such as managing their finances or learning job-related skills. Planning for supports

---

Support Issues to Consider

• What do caregivers understand about the individual's disability?

• Are caregivers' expectations in line with the individual's abilities, goals, and preferences?

• What supports are available at home, at school, at work, and in recreational or leisure settings?

• What supports are available for caregivers (e.g., training, mentoring, reporting)?

Examples of Significant Life Events and Potentially Traumatic Events

Life events

• Moving to a different home

• Transitions (e.g., school, work)

• Becoming seriously ill

• Coping with the death, serious illness, or loss of a close friend, relative, or paid care provider

Traumatic events

• Exposure to physical, sexual, and verbal or emotional abuse

• Witnessing violence

• Teasing, bullying, or harassment

• Abandonment

• Experience of discrimination

• Puberty, for some

---

should be individualized and person-centered, taking into account individuals' preferences and goals in addition to the intensity and range of supports that are needed to improve their personal outcomes (Thompson et al., 2009). Providing the appropriate level of support requires an understanding of individuals' profile of strengths and needs across different areas, including their cognitive, adaptive, language, and academic skills. Some strengths may hide or mask weaknesses and give rise to unreasonable expectations by caregivers and/or underestimates for support needs, which in turn can lead to behavioral and mental health problems (see Support Issues to Consider).

When investigating environmental and support issues, the team of mental health detectives needs to gather information from different sources, including interviews with the individual and his or her caregivers (current and past), review of reports and other documentation, direct observation, and assessment. The detectives will look for evidence of behavioral and mental health problems in relationship to specific features or demands of the environment.

When Is the Problem Related to Life Experiences and Emotional Factors?

Individuals with intellectual and developmental disabilities may grow up in disadvantaged and less than optimal circumstances. They may be excluded from learning and social opportunities that are available to their peers without intellectual and developmental disabilities. They may be exposed to situations that have resulted in physical and psychological harm. They may not have a say in what happens to them based on the assumption that they are incapable of making informed decisions. Many (if not most) individuals with intellectual and developmental disabilities have experienced a significant life event or trauma at some point in their lives (see Examples of Significant Life Events and Potentially Traumatic Events). They may be particularly affected by losses in their lives (e.g., early separations, frequent changes in care providers, and death of peers due to greater mortality at younger ages). As a result, they may develop feelings of sadness, loneliness, inadequacy, fear, anger, or powerlessness but lack the skills or access to supports that would enable them to stop what is happening and cope more effectively with their unpleasant or distressing emotions. Their emotional pain may be expressed outwardly in different ways, such as through aggressive, self-injurious, noncompliant, or avoidant behavior.

The mental health detectives need to look for clues that life experiences and emotional factors may underlie the individual's problem behaviors. Once again, information will be gathered through interviews with caregivers as well as the individual with intellectual and developmental disabilities to obtain his or her own personal account, along with assessments, review of past records, and observations in different settings and circumstances. The team should become familiar with common types of trauma and abuse and look for clues that this may be happening, including evidence of physical injury and changes in mood and behavior patterns.

When Is the Problem Due to a Psychiatric Illness?

Once the mental health detectives have systematically investigated medical conditions and physical health issues, environment and support needs, and life experiences and emotional factors, the final step in the process is to determine whether the individual's symptoms of mental distress and changes in behavior meet standard diagnostic criteria for psychiatric disorders. The *DSM-5* (American Psychiatric Association, 2013) and the *International Classification of Diseases, 10th Edition (ICD-10) Classification of Mental and Behavioural Disorders* (World Health Organization [WHO], 1993) are standard diagnostic and classification tools for mental disorders. Adaptations to these standard manuals have been developed for use with people with intellectual and developmental disabilities. The *DSM* adaptation is called the *Diagnostic Manual–Intellectual Disability* (Fletcher, Loschen, Stavrakaki, & First, 2007) and the ICD-10 adaptation is called the *Diagnostic Criteria for Psychiatric Disorders for Use with Adults with Learning Disabilities/Mental Retardation* (Royal College of Psychiatrists, 2001). These adapted manuals include helpful descriptions of symptoms and behaviors representing the range of psychiatric disorders that occur and the "atypical" presentations that may arise in people with intellectual and developmental disabilities. Mental health professionals should be familiar with these standard and adapted diagnostic systems.

The goals of the psychiatric assessment are 1) to determine whether behaviors of concern are underpinned by a psychiatric disorder and, 2) if so, to accurately diagnose this disorder and initiate appropriate treatment, ideally without adding to the intellectual disability or the physical problem (e.g., memory problems or motor dysfunction from side effects of medication). A further goal is to identify stressors and other circumstances that trigger

or contribute to the psychiatric or behavioral disturbance so that future crises and relapses can be prevented or minimized. Because of the challenge in diagnosing psychiatric disorders in individuals with intellectual and developmental disabilities, the precise diagnosis may not be clear. When this situation occurs, the steps to follow are to 1) generate the best diagnostic hypothesis using information currently available, 2) collect data to confirm or disprove this hypothesis, 3) review these data along with the information that has been collected by the team of mental health detectives, and 4) review psychiatric formulation and adjust this and interventions as required. By following this approach, it should be possible to minimize the potential for inappropriate treatment, particularly with psychotropic medication. The discussion Common Psychiatric Disorders in People with Intellectual and Developmental Disabilities provides a starting point for considering whether someone with intellectual and developmental disabilities may have a psychiatric disorder.

A comprehensive psychiatric assessment typically takes longer when the individual has intellectual and developmental disabilities. It requires a coordinated approach across all of the settings and involves care providers where the individual with intellectual and developmental disabilities lives, works, and spends leisure time. An effective mental health team will have developed a systematic approach to assessment and treatment of psychiatric disorders based on the most up-to-date evidence and will be using valid and reliable instruments and

---

Common Psychiatric Disorders in People with Intellectual and Developmental Disabilities

- Problem behaviors (not a *DSM-5* diagnosis but a most prevalent mental health concern)

- Depression or mood-related disorder

- Anxiety, including posttraumatic stress disorder

- Adjustment disorder

- Psychotic disorder

Source: Cooper and van der Speck (2009).

procedures. Team members will be able to adapt their usual clinical approaches so they can be applied to individuals across the developmental spectrum. The team should be able to coordinate the assessment findings in a meaningful manner and provide a formulation upon which treatment recommendations should be based. Fragmented or incomplete assessments and those conducted by professionals who are unfamiliar with the emotional responses of people with intellectual and developmental disabilities may, unfortunately, contribute to misdiagnoses and result in inappropriate and sometimes harmful treatment. For example, some psychiatric conditions (e.g., psychotic disorder) may be overdiagnosed in people with intellectual and developmental disabilities, resulting in high rates of antipsychotic medication usage (Lunsky, Klein-Geltink, & Yates, 2013). On the other hand, anxiety and adjustment disorders may be overlooked, resulting in underutilization of some psychological therapies. Differentiating new-onset psychiatric disorders (e.g., mood disorder episodes) from those that may be of longer standing (e.g., attention-deficit/hyperactivity disorder) will assist in determining more targeted interventions according to best practices for the particular psychiatric disorder and better treatment outcomes (Bradley & Hollins, 2010).

NEXT STEPS

Once an accurate diagnosis is made, care providers should consider the relative roles of different possible interventions (e.g., psychological and pharmacological therapies, environmental accommodations) for individuals with intellectual and developmental disabilities and mental health needs. In doing so, coordination is important so that care providers can ensure that those they serve derive optimum benefit from services.

Intervention

Intervention may be focused initially on the management of the behavioral disturbance so as to ensure everyone's safety (i.e., the individual with intellectual and developmental disabilities, people he or she lives with, and other care providers) until a clearer understanding of its cause is available. A comprehensive assessment will identify the presence (or absence) of a psychiatric disorder and utilize information about medical, environmental, and emotional factors that may have a bearing on

the individual's problem behaviors and mental distress. While the assessment is underway, it may be necessary to develop a proactive crisis intervention plan to manage serious or dangerous behaviors. Depending on the seriousness of the concerning behaviors, this crisis plan may need to identify the potential roles of increased staff support, specific use of psychotropic medication and behavioral interventions, involvement of the police, or emergency room and inpatient admission. The individual's response to these crisis interventions should be documented carefully, as it can provide additional insight into the underlying cause of the disturbance and be relevant to future treatment recommendations. As a clearer understanding of the underlying disorder emerges, treatment becomes more focused and individualized (see Table 47.1).

Intervention is based on information that is gathered during the assessment. After a diagnosis, medication is required only to the extent that it is recommended for the optimal treatment of a clearly defined psychiatric disorder (Alexander, Branford, & Devapriam, 2016; Bhaumik, Branford, Barrett, & Gangadharan, 2015; Deb et al., 2009). Effective treatment involves educating the patient and caregivers about the individual's psychiatric disorder, options that are available for treatment, and strategies to minimize relapses and promote mental well-being. It is important to map out a proactive response in the event of a crisis or relapse, with a clear outline of the involvement of community, emergency, and inpatient services (see tools for primary care providers and caregivers at http://www.surreyplace.on.ca/primary-care). This will stabilize the system supporting the individual and consolidate the treatment plan, minimize anxiety and the escalation of distress in both the person with intellectual and developmental disabilities and his or her caregivers, and most important, ensure continuity of care and specialized treatment.

With supportive strategies such as counseling or psychotherapy, individuals can be helped to develop alternative coping strategies and learn to regulate their emotional responses and manage frustration and stress more effectively. Caregivers have a key role to play in managing the amount of stress in the individual's environment and in helping him or her gain access to lifestyles that promote physical and emotional well-being. Individuals with intellectual and developmental disabilities and psychiatric disorders require regular follow-up and

Table 47.1. Treatment principles and approaches

Treatment principles and approaches	Comments and examples
Treat underlying physical and medical conditions that contribute to behavior and mental health problems.	• Treat medical conditions that may cause pain and discomfort. • Treat vision and hearing problems and neurological conditions that may impair functioning.
Treat psychiatric disorders using medication and nonmedication approaches according to evidence-based practice for specific disorder.	• When medication is used, avoid using multiple medications when possible and monitor closely for side effects. • Adapt psychological treatment approaches to align with cognitive and communication abilities. • Develop strategies to minimize relapses and promote mental well-being.
Modify the environment and provide needed supports to meet daily life and emotional needs.	• Reduce levels of lighting and noise. • Decrease crowding. • Increase or decrease opportunities for activity and stimulation. • Increase access to preferred items, people, and activities. • Offer choices. • Enhance opportunities for inclusion and meaningful relationships and participation.
Decrease stress.	• Protect from physical, emotional, financial, and sexual harm. • Realign expectations to match abilities. • Provide appropriate levels of support.
Increase coping and skills.	• Increase or improve communication, social, self-help, play, and leisure skills. • Provide opportunities to develop coping skills. • Enhance autonomy and self-esteem. • Teach stress management strategies.
Develop a coordinated system of supports.	• Ensure coordinated care (e.g., when moving from child to adult system or inpatient to outpatient care). • Identify primary and specialist supports (e.g., family physician, medical specialists, case manager, behavioral specialist) and how and when to obtain these. • Develop proactive crisis management protocols.
Use medication for crisis intervention versus treatment of behavior problems.	• Not infrequently, individuals are on medications originally started to treat behavior problems—in this situation, the behaviors are being "managed." This is not good practice and can be harmful. The underlying cause of the behavior problems needs to be determined (e.g., As outlined previously, is the cause medical, related to the environment, an emotional issue, or psychiatric illness?) and this cause treated. Psychotropic medications should only be used to treat psychiatric disorders according to evidence-based practice for that disorder.

careful monitoring of their medication. Shared care involving a psychiatrist, nurse, and family doctor, with access to specialist services (e.g., psychology, behavior therapy, speech-language pathology, occupational therapy), can work well. The roles of the different team members are determined by the needs of the individual, the service context within which each of these professionals work, and the comfort level of each in working with people with intellectual and developmental disabilities.

Psychotherapy

As the provision of psychotherapy for people who have intellectual and developmental disabilities is increasingly accepted, the issue is no longer whether they are entitled to psychotherapy or will benefit from it but, rather, how psychotherapy techniques can be adapted to meet the needs of individuals who may have limitations in expressive and receptive language skills (Beail, 2016).

It has taken a number of years to reach a level of understanding of the extent of mental health problems among people with intellectual and developmental disabilities and the efficacy and effectiveness of psychotherapy—when appropriately modified—for these individuals. Historically, there have been several reasons why psychotherapy has not been used broadly for this group of people. First, maladaptive behaviors were often perceived as part of the condition of intellectual disability. Second, psychotherapy was not viewed by the professional community as being effective in this population. Third, there has been a bias on the part of mental health clinicians that echoes the thought that providing therapy for people with intellectual disabilities is not challenging or interesting. Fourth, there has been a near absence of academic training for professionals in providing psychotherapy treatment for this group of people. Furthermore, there has been a lack of professional literature on this subject. Traditionally, the concept of addressing people's feelings and emotions in this population has neither been fully addressed nor sufficiently acknowledged (Fletcher, 2011b).

Fortunately, there has been sufficient work done in the field to disprove myths, disbeliefs, and misunderstanding regarding the lack of efficacy of mental health treatment, including psychotherapy for people who have these co-occurring disorders. Informed clinicians now recognize that psychotherapy is a best practice in working with this population.

Effective psychotherapy with people who have intellectual and developmental disabilities and mental health concerns requires the clinician to modify therapy approaches, although the principles of therapy remain the same. The needed modifications are in accordance with the expressive and receptive language skills of the individual client. Modifications may entail shorter time of sessions, keeping language simple, avoiding abstractions, and being reflective (to ensure understanding of the conversation). Focusing on pictures rather than words is often helpful (e.g., Books Beyond Words series; Hollins, 2003). For those with little or no language, specific psychotherapeutic approaches using body language to engage emotionally with the individual are now available (e.g., Intensive Interaction [Caldwell, 2013] and Integrative Therapy for Attachment and Behaviour [Sterkenburg, 2008]). Individual, group, or family therapy modalities can be used in psychotherapy with individuals who have intellectual and developmental disabilities co-occurring with mental illness. Fletcher (2011a) edited a book entitled *Psychotherapy for Individuals with Intellectual Disability* in which there are chapters on adaptations of theoretical models such as dialectical behavioral therapy, mindfulness-based psychotherapy, positive psychotherapy, and cognitive-behavioral therapy, among other approaches.

Service Coordination

Various service systems in North America exist to meet the mental health needs of individuals with intellectual and developmental disabilities. These needs span the traditional administrative boundaries of health, social services, criminal justice, and education and their age-related mandates (see Figure 47.3). Addressing these needs requires teamwork and a coordinated approach to assessment and intervention (see Summers et al., 2002, for an example of an interdisciplinary mental health team).

The need for better integration and coordination of these services and systems of care is routinely acknowledged but is difficult to achieve and sustain. The Ohio Model (see related discussion) is an example of a statewide initiative to create a coordinated infrastructure that is designed to address the mental needs of individuals with intellectual and developmental disabilities. In Canada, the lead ministry for intellectual and developmental disabilities in most provinces is the social services ministry. Canadians with intellectual and developmental disabilities experience barriers and inequities in gaining access to health care. A significant development to addressing these issues has been the creation of national guidelines for the primary care of adults with intellectual and developmental disabilities (see http://www.surreyplace.on.ca/primary-care). Tools to support these guidelines

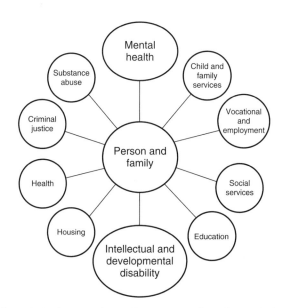

Figure 47.3. Example of a coordinated system of care for individuals with intellectual and developmental disabilities and mental health needs.

The Ohio Model

Ohio is the only state in America that has developed an infrastructure for addressing issues concerning individuals with intellectual and developmental disabilities and mental illness. The mission of Ohio's Mental Illness Developmental Disabilities Coordinating Center of Excellence (MIDD CCOE, n.d.) is to make life better for people with both mental illness and developmental disabilities. The MIDD CCOE is funded by the Ohio Department of Developmental Disabilities, Ohio Department of Mental Health and Addictions Services, and the Ohio Developmental Disabilities Council. The MIDD CCOE has four major functions:

1. To fund expert psychiatric diagnostic assessments; complex cases can be referred for diagnostic assessments and consultation services

2. To sponsor and support statewide and local or county trainings and conferences; the National Association on Dual Diagnosis (NADD), along with the three funders, sponsors an annual conference, and local or county training funds are available

3. To encourage county mental health and intellectual and developmental disabilities systems to talk to each other and train their staff to improve their work together; each county is expected to have intellectual and developmental disabilities and mental illness teams

4. To help colleges, universities, and professional schools include dual diagnosis in their programs; several universities are involved in the MIDD CCOE with regard to interdisciplinary training in the field of intellectual and developmental disabilities and mental illness

Guiding principles for MIDD CCOE collaboration:

- Shared responsibility for clients

- Administrative buy-in and support at the upper levels

- Strong relationships among system leaders and among direct service staff

- Willingness to create new things

- Good training for staff

- Close communication, especially during crises when expert help is needed

- Multidisciplinary and multisystem team membership (e.g., enforcement and/or court system and educational system as well as intellectual and developmental disabilities and mental health systems)

(e.g., *A Guide to Understanding Behavioural Problems and Emotional Concerns in Adults with Developmental Disabilities, Auditing Psychotropic Medication Therapy*) are also available online as well as periodic workshops, online training, and participation in clinical networks of care.

In both the United States and Canada, there is a lack of training with regard to mental illness in people who have intellectual and developmental disabilities. In Canada, specialist training in psychiatry now requires some training in intellectual and developmental disabilities (i.e., Royal College of Physicians and Surgeons, Canada, training requirements), but the extent of this inclusion usually depends on local champions. In the United States, there are few academic institutions that provide courses in psychopathology of intellectual and developmental disabilities. The National Association on Dual Diagnosis (NADD) trains approximately 2,000 people per year through conferences, consultation services, webinars, and other methods. All of this is important, but it is not enough. There is a need for more systematic training. The development of NADD's accreditation and certification programs, together with trainings intended to help agencies and individuals prepare for accreditation or certification, is intended to raise the bar and develop greater agency competency and greater personnel competency.

Ensuring Optimal Benefit from Services

As shown in the previous subsections, individuals with intellectual and developmental disabilities and mental health needs can benefit from various services. The following are recommendations for preparing care providers to overcome challenges when working with these individuals.

- Recognize that the person with intellectual and developmental disabilities is experiencing emotional or mental distress.

- Bring concerns forward to someone who can help organize a comprehensive investigation.

- Work in a team.

- Take advantage of ongoing opportunities to improve knowledge and skills.

- Develop positive attitudes toward people with intellectual and developmental disabilities.

- Attend to one's own self-care needs to reduce stress and burnout.

- Involve people with intellectual and developmental disabilities and their families to the greatest extent possible. For example, remember "Nothing about us without us," a key principle in United Kingdom policy for people with intellectual and developmental disabilities (Department of Health, 2009).

SUMMARY

In this chapter, we presented key issues in understanding, assessing, treating, and preventing mental distress and problem behaviors in people with intellectual and developmental disabilities. People with intellectual and developmental disabilities experience mental distress and psychiatric disorders similar to those of their peers without such disabilities but are relatively more prone to these conditions. In addition, both physical and mental distress as well as emotional concerns and psychiatric disorders may present as problem behaviors. We discussed how problem behaviors and mental distress have many different causes that need to be identified in order to provide the correct treatment.

Left untreated, mental distress may become chronic and crippling, contributing further to the disability. Furthermore, many emotional disturbances can be prevented, and both emotional and psychiatric disorders are significantly diminished with appropriate intervention and treatment. As we have shown in this chapter, service systems affect optimal assessment, treatment, and mental health support.

FOR FURTHER THOUGHT AND DISCUSSION

1. A new family recently has moved into your neighborhood. The parents are worried about their teenage daughter, Sophie, who has an intellectual disability. Sophie used to be happy and looked forward to going to school. Since moving, she has become more withdrawn and is unhappy most of the time. What might be going on, and what assistance may be required?

2. Consider the origins of negative attitudes toward individuals with intellectual disabilities. How can these attitudes affect their access to proper mental health services?

REFERENCES

Alexander, R.T., Branford, D., & Devapriam, J. (Eds.). (2016, April). *Psychotropic drug prescribing for people with intellectual disability, mental health problems and/or behaviours that challenge: Practice guidelines* (Report No.: FR/ID/09). Retrieved from London, United Kingdom: The Royal College of Psychiatrists. Retrieved from http://www.rcpsych.ac.uk/pdf/FR_ID_09_for_website.pdf

American Psychiatric Association. (2013). *Diagnostic and statistical manual of mental disorders* (5th ed.). Washington, DC: Author.

Banks, R., & Bush, A. (2016, April). *Challenging behaviour: A unified approach—update: Clinical and service guidelines for supporting children, young people and adults with intellectual disabilities who are at risk of receiving abusive or restrictive practices* (Report No.: FR/ID/08). London, United Kingdom: The Royal College of Psychiatrists. Retrieved from http://www.rcpsych.ac.uk/pdf/FR_ID_08.pdf

Banks, R., Bush, A., Baker, P., Bradshaw, J., Carpenter, P., Deb, S.,...Xenitidis, K. (2007). *Challenging behaviour: A unified approach* (College Report CR 144). Retrieved from http://www.rcpsych.ac.uk/files/pdfversion/cr144.pdf

Beail, N. (Ed.). (2016). *Psychological therapies and people who have intellectual disabilities*. Leicester, United Kingdom: The British Psychological Society, Division of Clinical Psychology. Retrieved from http://www.bps.org.uk/system/files/Public%20files/Policy/psychological_therapies_and_people_who_have_id_pdf_for_review.pdf

Bhaumik, S., Branford, D., Barrett, M., & Gangadharan, S.K. (Eds.) (2015). *The Frith prescribing guidelines for people with intellectual disability* (3rd ed.). Hoboken, NJ: John Wiley & Sons Inc.

Boardman, L., Bernal, J., & Hollins, S. (2014). Communicating with people with intellectual disabilities: A guide for general psychiatrists. *Advances in Psychiatric Treatment, 20,* 27–36.

Bradley, E., Ames, C., & Bolton, P. (2011). Psychiatric conditions and behavioural problems in adolescents with intellectual disabilities: Correlates with autism. *Canadian Journal of Psychiatry, 56*(2), 102–109.

Bradley, E., & Bolton, P. (2006). Episodic psychiatric disorders in teenagers with learning disabilities with and without autism. *British Journal of Psychiatry, 189,* 361–366.

Bradley, E.A., & Hollins, S. (2010). Assessment of patients with intellectual disabilities. In D. Goldbloom (Ed.), *Psychiatric clinical skills* (Rev. ed., pp. 235–253). Toronto, Canada: Centre for Addiction and Mental Health.

Bradley, E.A. & Isaacs, B.J. (2006). Inattention, hyperactivity, and impulsivity in teenagers with intellectual disabilities, with and without autism. *Canadian Journal of Psychiatry, 51*(9), 598–606.

Bradley, E., & Korossy, M. (2015). Behaviour problems. In M. Woodbury-Smith (Ed.), *Clinical topics in the psychiatry of intellectual developmental disorders.* London, United Kingdom: Gaskell Press.

Bradley, E., Sinclair, L., & Greenbaum, R. (2012). Trauma and adolescents with intellectual disabilities: Interprofessional clinical and service perspectives. *Journal of Child and Adolescent Trauma, 5,* 33–46.

Burkitt, C., Breau, L.M., Salsman, S., Sarsfield-Turner, T., & Mullan, R.(2009). Pilot study of the feasibility of the Non-Communicating Children's Pain Checklist—Revised for pain assessment in adults with intellectual disabilities. *Journal of Pain Management, 2*(1), 37–49.

Caldwell, P. (2013). Intensive interaction: Using body language to communicate. *Journal on Developmental Disabilities, 19*(1), 33–39.

Cooper, S.A., Smiley, L., Morrison, J., Williamson, A., & Allan, L. (2007). Mental ill-health in adults with intellectual disabilities: Prevalence and associated features. *British Journal of Psychiatry, 190,* 27–35.

Cooper, S.A., & van der Speck, R. (2009). Epidemiology of mental ill-health in adults with intellectual disabilities. *Current Opinion in Psychiatry, 22,* 431–436.

Deb, S., Kwok, H., Bertelli, M., Salvador-Carulla, L., Bradley, E., Torr, J., & Barnhill, J. (2009). International guide to prescribing psychotropic medication for the management of problem behaviours in adults with intellectual disabilities. *World Psychiatry; 8*(3), 181–186.

Department of Health. (2009). *Valuing People Now: A new three-year strategy for people with learning disabilities.* Retrieved from http://webarchive.nationalarchives.gov .uk/20130107105354/http:/www.dh.gov.uk/prod _consum_dh/groups/dh_digitalassets/documents /digitalasset/dh_093375.pdf

Emerson, E. (2007). Poverty and people with intellectual disabilities. *Mental Retardation and Developmental Disabilities Research Reviews, 13,* 107–113.

Fletcher, R.J. (Ed.). (2011a). *Psychotherapy for individuals with intellectual disability.* Kingston, NY: NADD Press.

Fletcher, R.J. (2011b). Psychotherapy: The North American experience. *Advances in Mental Health and Intellectual Disabilities, 5*(5), 3–5.

Fletcher, R., Loschen, E., Stavrakaki, C., & First, M. (Eds.). (2007). *Diagnostic manual–intellectual disability (DM-ID): A textbook of diagnosis of mental disorders in persons with intellectual disability.* Kingston NY: NADD Press.

Hollins, S. (2003). *Books beyond words: Empowering people through pictures.* Retrieved from http://booksbeyondwords .co.uk/

Jopp, D.A., & Keys, C.B. (2001). Diagnostic overshadowing reviewed and reconsidered. *American Journal on Mental Retardation, 106*(5), 416–433.

Leonard, H., & Wen, X. (2002). The epidemiology of mental retardation: Challenges and opportunities in the new millennium. *Mental Retardation and Developmental Disabilities Research Reviews, 8,* 117–134.

Lunsky, Y., & Elserafi, J. (2012). Antipsychotic medication prescription patterns in adults with developmental disabilities who have experienced psychiatric crisis. *Research in Developmental Disabilities, 33,* 32–38.

Lunsky, Y., Klein-Geltink, J.E., & Yates, E.A. (Eds.). (2013). *Atlas on the primary care of adults with developmental disabilities in Ontario.* Toronto, Canada: Institute for Clinical Evaluative Sciences and Centre for Addiction and Mental Health.

Martorell, A., Tsakanikos, E., Pereda, A., Gutiérrez-Recacha, P., Bouras, N., & Ayuso-Mateos, J.L. (2009). The role of recent life events and traumatic experiences across the life span. *Journal of Nervous and Mental Disease, 197,* 182–186.

Mental Illness Developmental Disabilities Coordinating Center of Excellence. (n.d.). *Welcome to MIDD CCOE.* Retrieved from http://dodd.ohio.gov/Initiatives-and-Partnerships/Pages/CCOE.aspx

O'Brien, G. (2016). *Behavioural phenotypes in adulthood.* Retrieved from http://www.intellectualdisability.info /mental-health/articles/behavioural-phenotypes-in -adulthood

Pain Resource Center. (n.d.). *Disability Distress Assessment Tool (DisDAT).* Retrieved from http://prc.coh.org/pain _assessment.asp

Palucka, A., & Lunsky, Y. (2007). Review of inpatient admissions of individuals with autism spectrum disorders to a specialized dual diagnosis program. *Journal on Developmental Disabilities, 13,* 205–209.

Royal College of Psychiatrists. (2001). *DC-LD: Diagnostic criteria for psychiatric disorders for use with adults with learning disabilities/mental retardation.* London, United Kingdom: Gaskell.

Schalock, R.L., Borthwick-Duffy, S., Bradley, V., Buntinx, W., Coulter, D., & Craig, E. (2010). *Intellectual disability: Definition, classification, and systems of support* (11th ed.). Washington, DC: American Association on Intellectual and Developmental Disabilities.

Shooshtari, S., Martens, P., Burchill, C. Dik, N., & Naghipur, S. (2011). Prevalence of depression and dementia among Adults with Developmental Disabilities in Manitoba, Canada. *International Journal of Family Medicine* (Article ID 319574, 9 pages). doi:10.1155/2011/319574

Sterkenburg, P.S. (2008). *Intervening in stress, attachment and challenging behaviour: Effects in children with multiple disabilities.* Retrieved from http://dare.ubvu.vu.nl/bitstream /handle/1871/15813/8494.pdf?sequence=5

Summers, J., Boyd, K., Reid, J., Adamson, J., Habjan, B., Gignac, V., & Meister, C. (2002). The interdisciplinary mental health team. In D. Griffiths, C. Stavrakaki, & J. Summers (Eds.), *Dual diagnosis: An introduction to the mental health needs of persons with developmental disabilities* (pp. 325–357). Sudbury, Canada: Habilitative Mental Health Resource Network.

Temple, B., Dube, C., McMillan, D., Secco, L., Kepron, E., Dittberner, K.,...Vipond, G. (2012). Pain in people with developmental disabilities: A scoping review. *Journal on Developmental Disabilities, 18*(1), 74–86.

Thompson, J.R., Bradley, V.J., Buntinx, W.H.E., Schalock, R.L., Shogren, K.A., Snell, M.E.,...Yeager, M.H. (2009). Conceptualizing supports and the support needs of people with intellectual disability. *Intellectual and Developmental Disabilities, 47*(2), 135–146.

Waite, J., Heald, M., Wilde, L., Woodcock, K., Welham, A., Adams, D.,...Oliver, C. (2014). The importance of understanding the behavioural phenotypes of genetic syndromes associated with intellectual disability. *Paediatrics and Child Health, 24*(10), 468–472.

World Health Organization. (1993). *The ICD-10 classification of mental and behavioural disorders: Diagnostic criteria for research.* Geneva, Switzerland: World Health Organization.

World Health Organization. (2016). *Mental health: A state of well-being.* Retrieved from http://www.who.int/features /factfiles/mental_health/en/

48

Nutritional Considerations for Children with Intellectual and Developmental Disabilities

Diana R. Mager

- Nutrition concerns in children with intellectual and developmental disabilities
- Common causes of malnutrition and obesity in children with intellectual and developmental disabilities
- How nutritional and feeding problems are identified and managed

The most common nutritional concern in children with intellectual and developmental disabilities is growth failure caused by feeding difficulties. Thirty to thirty-five percent of children with neurodevelopmental disabilities have feeding problems that result in slow growth, inadequate weight gain, developmental delay, psychosocial problems, anemia, and vitamin and/or mineral deficiencies (Marchand, Motil, & North American Society for Pediatric Gastroenterology, Hepatology and Nutrition Committee on Nutrition, 2006; Stevenson et al., 2006). Overnutrition leading to obesity is also common in this population. This usually results from dietary intake in excess of energy requirements and diminished physical activity or mobility. Proper nutrition is an important issue for children with intellectual and developmental disabilities. A comprehensive approach to nutrition support in this population can result in improved rates of growth, improvement in development, and enhanced quality of life.

Assessment of feeding difficulties should include an interdisciplinary approach involving at least a physician, nurse, and registered dietitian. The team also could include a speech-language pathologist, occupational therapist, physiotherapist, radiologist or interventional radiologist, dentist and dental hygienist, psychiatrist, social worker, teacher, and pharmacist. Some countries have laws mandating that infants and children at risk for intellectual and developmental disability are entitled to nutritional assessment and treatment within the context of a family-centered approach (Marchand et al., 2006).

The Nutritional Considerations at a Glance feature provides an overview of some key nutritional considerations in children with developmental disabilities with regard to feeding issues, nutrition screening, and laboratory investigations.

COMMON CAUSES OF MALNUTRITION

Malnutrition in children with developmental disabilities may be caused by several factors, including the presence of significant swallowing and gastrointestinal dysfunction, medication, development, and behavioral issues. Swallowing problems, or dysphagia, are very common in children with developmental delay (Marchand et al., 2006). The most common causes of dysphagia in this population include neurological impairment and structural abnormalities (e.g., cleft palate) of the oral and

Nutritional Considerations at a Glance

Feeding Issues

Factors That Affect Food Intake

- Acute and chronic illness (e.g., gastrointestinal dysfunction, neurological impairment)
- Psychosocial variables (e.g., depression, poverty, drug abuse)
- Drug therapy side effects (e.g., anorexia, nausea, vomiting, diarrhea)
- Functional capacity
- Dysphagia (i.e., inability to swallow or dysfunctional swallow)

There is a need to differentiate between a normal and abnormal swallow (dysphagia) and to define issues regarding functional capacity. Impairment of fine and gross motor skills and the presence of dysphagia can affect functional capacity or the ability to self-feed.

Signs of Oral/Pharyngeal Dysphagia

- Drooling
- Slow eating (i.e., low feeding efficiency or time to finish one meal)
- Altered posturing of head and neck during swallow
- Large food residual in mouth following a swallow
- Coughing during and after the swallow
- Choking with significant shortness of breath
- Voice quality changes
- Expectoration of food and/or saliva

Signs of Impairment of Fine and Gross Motor Skills

Causes may be neurological or structural:

- Ataxia (i.e., failure of muscle coordination resulting in poorly judged movements)
- Dysarthria (i.e., imperfect articulation of speech due to disturbances in muscle control)
- Abnormal reflexes (e.g., tongue thrusting in the infant)
- Apraxia (i.e., inability to plan and execute a skilled movement in the absence of sensory and motor deficits)

Compensatory Feeding Strategies

- Changes in food bolus consistency (e.g., puree textures vs. soft, thin vs. thickened liquids)
- Postural change (e.g., head should be in upright position vs. over on one side)
- Verbal cues (e.g., gentle reminders or cues to redirect attention to eating)
- Controlled intake (e.g., pacing of intake, portion size, limits on outside distracters—e.g., noise)
- Adaptive equipment (e.g., adaptive utensils, wrist or hand splints)
- Other therapies (e.g., effortful swallow, supraglottic swallow vs. super-supraglottic swallow)

Nutritional Considerations at a Glance

Food Intake Assessment Techniques

- Food frequency

- Intake records or diary

- 24-hour recall

- Food preferences (likes vs. dislikes)

- Direct observation

- Diet history, including a review of current and past food intake and food preferences, and also usually including a review of issues related to food intake (e.g., dental health, psychosocial factors such as depression, socioeconomic status, occupation, physical health, age, allergies, medication) and functional capacity (e.g., ability to self-feed, prepare food, have access to food)

Food Frequency Assessment Techniques

- Determination of food portion size

- Determination of food type or food group

- Determination of food frequency and number of servings per day, per week, and per month

- Single food type versus multiple food types (e.g., cheese slice vs. cheese casserole in terms of estimating portion size and/or nutrient composition)

Strategies to Aid with Food Identification and Estimation of Food Portion Size

- Pictures of foods, food labels

- Food models (especially plastic food models)

- Commercial product containers and labels to identify food types, food products, and food ingredients (especially important in cases of food allergy and/or intolerance)

- Food utensils (e.g., commercial product containers, measuring cups, cups, bowls, plates, cutlery) to approximately measure food portion size

- Hand-measures or rulers to identify thickness or dimensions of foods

- Kitchen scales to precisely measure food portions

Factors Affecting Accuracy of Food Intake Assessment

- Recollection or memory of the interviewee about issues regarding duration or length of time of particular food intake (i.e., Is this the usual intake, the most recent intake, seasonal intake, holiday or special occasion intake?)

- Seasonal variations in food intake

- Food preparation techniques (e.g., baking vs. frying to estimate fat content)

- Methods used to estimate portion sizes

- Method or type of interview

- Order of presentation of food groups (bias may be introduced)

- Socioeconomic factors

(continued)

Nutritional Considerations at a Glance   *(continued)*

Screening Issues

Purpose of Nutrition Screening

- Identification of individuals with inadequate nutritional status

- Identification of risk factors for malnutrition

- Prevention of inadequate or suboptimal nutritional status

Nutritional Risk Factors

- Inadequate oral intake

- Significant or recent weight loss (i.e., ideal body weight, percentage of recent weight change)

- Psychosocial variables (e.g., depression, poverty, drug abuse)

- Chronic or acute illness

- Drug therapy side effects (e.g., drug–nutrient interactions, anorexia, nausea)

- Altered functional capacity (due to changes in mobility, muscle strength)

Anthropometrics

- Body mass index (BMI)

- Percentage of ideal body weight, percentage of usual body weight

- Percentage of recent weight change, calculated using the following formula: usual weight – current weight × 100)/usual weight

- Significant weight loss:

    >1%–2% over 1 week

    >5% over 1 month

    >7.5% over 3 months

    >10% over 6 months

Biochemical Measurements of Blood Samples

- Hemoglobin—to detect iron deficiency anemia

- Triglyceride/cholesterol—to detect hyperlipidemia

- Albumin—to estimate visceral protein status when hepatic, renal, gastrointestinal functions, and hydration status are normal

Diet History

- Suboptimal intake for more than 3 days

- Abnormal eating pattern

- Nutrition-related problems present (e.g., teeth, gums, and surrounding soft tissue; gastrointestinal upset [acute and chronic]; dysphagia; food intolerance; anorexia)

Screening Tools

- Canada's Guide to Healthy Eating

- Computer nutrient data base (e.g., Canadian Nutrient File; https://food-nutrition.canada.ca/cnf-fce/index-eng.jsp)

Nutritional Considerations at a Glance

- Food frequency questionnaires

- Nutrition screening checklists (include information about past medical history, food consumption patterns, socioeconomic status, multiple medications, weight history, mobility, and other data)

Labs at Admission

This section explains the various tests that are usually ordered at admission to a hospital for nutritional assessment.

- Albumin (serum): normal, 33–58 g/L; 31 g/L is indicative of decreased visceral protein stores or inflammation in gut

- Erythrocyte sedimentation rate (ESR): normal, 1–10; elevated in collagen vascular disease, inflammatory states, acute phase reactions

- Electrolytes (serum): measures of ions such as sodium, potassium, calcium, and magnesium

- Platelets: normal, 150–450; 617 or above is a nonspecific gut inflammatory marker (e.g., of Crohn's disease)

- Hemoglobin: normal, 120–160; 76 or below is indicative of blood loss, microcytic anemia

- Mean corpuscular (red cell) volume (MCV): normal, 80–94; 63 or below is indicative of microcytic, hypochromic anemia

- Mean corpuscular (red cell) hemoglobin (MCH): normal, 24–31; 20 or below is indicative of microcytic anemia

- Serum iron: normal, 9–27 millimole (mmol)/L; 8 or below is abnormal

- Ferritin (serum): normal, 18–300 ng/mL

- Transferrin (serum): normal, 24–48 mmol/L; 14.6 or below is abnormal

- Transferrin saturation (_serum iron_/2 × _serum transferrin_): normal, 20%; 6% or below is abnormal

- Transferrin saturation is a marker of iron supply to the tissues. Low values are indicative that iron stores are inadequate for erythropoiesis.

- Glucose (serum): normal 4–6 mmol/L (random/fasting); indicative of normal glycemic control

---

pharyngeal cavities (Marchand et al.). Dysphagia can lead to poor food intake, impaired feeding efficiency (i.e., length of time to finish a meal), choking, regurgitation, and aspiration of food contents into the lung. Severity and duration of swallowing impairment has also been linked to a lag in the developmental progress in children with neurological impairment (Marchand et al.; Samson-Fang & Bell, 2013). Significant improvement in nutritional status in children with developmental disabilities can occur following assessment of nutritional requirements, dietary intake, type and severity of swallowing dysfunction, and functional capacity to self-feed (Marchand et al.; Samson-Fang & Bell).

Common causes of gastrointestinal dysfunction in children with developmental disabilities may include delayed gastric emptying, impaired intestinal motility (i.e., movement through the intestine),

and gastroesophageal reflux disease (GERD). Severe and persistent GERD can cause esophagitis (i.e., inflamed mucosa of the esophagus), vomiting, failure to thrive, or lung disease from aspiration (Marchand et al., 2006; Vernon-Roberts & Sullivan, 2013). GERD and delayed gastric and/or intestinal motility are usually treated with medications that promote motility and block acid production in the gut. Treatment of GERD and delayed gastric emptying with these medications can promote increased dietary intake and improved weight gain (Marchand et al.; Vernon-Roberts & Sullivan). Impaired intestinal motility can also cause constipation, leading to vomiting, decreased food intake, and weight loss. Improvement in the frequency of bowel movements can lead to significant improvement in dietary intake (Marchand et al.). Treatment of constipation in children includes the use of motility agents, stool-softening agents, suppository or fleet enemas, and assessment of fluid and fiber intake to ensure that adequate amounts are present in the diet.

Patients with persistent GERD and delayed gastric emptying may develop feeding aversions (Marchand et al., 2006). Feeding aversions may include partial or total food refusal and selectivity of food choices (picky eating) and food texture (e.g., a child may refuse to eat solids or liquids) (Rodas-Arts & Benoit, 1998). Behaviors such as tantrums associated with eating or changes in food texture and delay in self-feeding may also result in impairment of feeding efficiency. These problems can be exacerbated by swallowing problems. Treatment and management of behavioral problems associated with feeding is complex (Rodas-Arts & Benoit). Assessment of behavioral feeding problems should include a review of functional (e.g., posture) and physiological (e.g., swallowing function, gastrointestinal function) aspects of feeding.

The use of medications in children with developmental disabilities may have a significant impact on nutritional status, including potential drug–nutrient interactions or such side effects as nausea, vomiting, diarrhea, or poor appetite. For example, anticonvulsant medications (e.g., phenytoin) used in children with seizure disorders may interfere with the absorption and utilization of vitamin D and calcium, leading to increased risk for bone fracture (Henderson, Kairalia, Barrington, Abbas, & Stevenson, 2005). Use of antibiotics may produce gastrointestinal symptoms (e.g., diarrhea), and use of psychotropics may cause depressed appetite (Roe, 1982). In addition, many children with developmental disabilities take multiple medications (prescribed and nonprescribed) that potentially may interact and cause adverse reactions (Roe, 1982).

NUTRITION ASSESSMENT OF CHILDREN

Nutrition assessment of children includes the assessment of growth, body composition, dietary intake (past and present), and current health status. Assessment of growth includes examining weight and height growth to determine the adequacy of nutritional status. Deficits in growth and reductions in fat and lean body mass are the most common indicators of malnutrition (Marchand et al., 2006; Samson-Fang & Bell, 2013; Stevenson et al., 2006). Assessment of body composition is also necessary to establish severity of obesity in overnutrition. Assessment of dietary intake (past and present) is important for identifying causative factors in over- and undernutrition. This assessment includes a review of current and past intake; preferences; food frequency; use of caloric, vitamin, and mineral supplementation; food availability; and a review of feeding patterns (Marchand et al.; Samson-Fang & Bell). The review of feeding patterns can include timing of meals, behavioral patterns associated with feeding, and difficulties with feeding. A review of current health status may include a review of medical history (acute and chronic) and current medications (drug–nutrient interactions) in order to identify potential factors affecting current nutritional status. The history includes a review of body systems with emphasis on the child's ability to chew, swallow, and digest food in order to identify potential causes for under- or overnutrition (e.g., nausea, vomiting, malabsorption, reflux, diarrhea) (Marchand et al.; Samson-Fang & Bell).

Blood tests are also done in a nutritional assessment to screen for vitamin and mineral deficiency. These blood values should be assessed along with the medical, growth, and nutritional history to ensure completeness of assessment. The most common blood parameters used in nutrition assessment are measurements of serum albumin and a complete blood count (CBC). Serum albumin is a good indicator of adequacy of visceral protein status over the previous month in the absence of kidney and liver disease (half-life is 18–20 days) (Jensen, Hsiao, & Wheeler, 2012). Other markers of visceral protein status include transferrin, thyroxine-binding prealbumin (transthyretin), and retinol-binding protein. Evaluation of the CBC (hemoglobin, hematocrit, and red cell indices) is a useful screening tool for the detection of nutrition-related anemias (Jensen et al., 2012). A more complete analysis of iron status includes assessment of ferritin (iron stores), serum iron, transferrin, and iron-binding capacity (Marchand et al., 2006; Samson-Fang & Bell, 2013).

ASSESSMENT OF GROWTH IN CHILDREN

Assessment of growth in children is an important part of nutritional assessment. A complete assessment includes measurement of height (lying or standing), weight, and skinfolds (Marchand et al., 2006; Samson-Fang & Bell, 2013). Height and weight of a child should be plotted using standard growth curves (Goldbloom, 1997). Children grow at different rates over time. The highest rates of growth occur in utero, during early infancy, and around puberty. Differences in growth may occur annually, with faster rates during the spring and summer and slower rates in the fall and winter months in some countries (Goldbloom, 1997). Growth measurements should be recorded at regular intervals to account for these changes in growth patterns. Assessment of growth can be done by comparing height and weight percentiles, channel differences (one channel is representative of the distance between two percentile curves), or velocity curves. Children usually maintain their heights and weights in the same channels during the preschool and early childhood years (Goldbloom, 1997). However, growth in any particular channel may not be defined until after 2 years of age (Goldbloom, 1997). Genetic inheritance also plays a large role in growth in infancy and early childhood. Adjustment of stature of length measurements using mid-parental stature charts is a technique that may be used to correct for differences in genetic potential for linear growth (Himes, Roche, Thissen, & Moore, 1985).

For children with neurological impairment, growth may be impeded by dysphagia, chronic illness, and the presence of skeletal disorders. Weight loss or lack of weight gain, in particular, may place these children at significant risk for malnutrition. Obesity can also be a problem in these children. This can hamper their mobility and can result in additional complications, including increased risk for cardiovascular disease.

Assessment of Specific Indicators of Growth

Specific indicators of growth include height, height velocity, and weight. Each is discussed in the next subsections.

Height Measurement of height is an important tool in the assessment of a child's nutritional status. Linear growth is an excellent marker of a child's nutritional history and helps in distinguishing between short- and long-term nutritional problems (i.e., height reflects longer term nutritional issues). Recumbent lengths (lying down) are used for infants and children younger than 2 years of age or for children older than 3 years of age who are unable to stand. Recumbent length is not identical to standing height and must be measured using a device called a length board (Goldbloom, 1997; Roche & Davila, 1974). Plotting of height on reference growth curves should be done at sequential intervals for assessment of growth (Dietitians of Canada, 2004; Himes et al., 1985).

The U.S. Centers for Disease Control and Prevention (CDC, 2009) growth charts can be used for comparative purposes (http://www.cdc.gov/growth charts/clinical_charts.htm#Set1). The CDC charts consist of charts for infants from birth to age 3 for weight, recumbent length, head circumference, and weight-for-recumbent length, and a set for children and adolescents from ages 2 to 20 for weight, height, and body mass index. The charts are available in two forms: individual charts and clinical charts. The clinical charts were designed for use by health care providers (Dietitians of Canada, 2004). The World Health Organization (WHO), in collaboration with the United Nations Children's Fund, has developed newer growth standards for children that are more representative of an ethnically diverse population (available at http://www.who.int/childgrowth/standards /en/; WHO, 2011; see also de Onis et al., 2007).

More recently, the Canadian Pediatric Endocrine Group made modifications to the WHO curves to extend the weight-for-age curves beyond 10 years of age (http://cpeg-gcep.net) and to harmonize the choice of BMI percentiles with adult definitions of overweight and obesity (Lawrence et al., 2013). Use of these curves to evaluate growth in children with developmental disabilities needs to be evaluated.

Measurement of recumbent or standing height may be inappropriate for children with spinal curvature or contractures because proper positioning for these measurements may not be possible (Goldbloom, 1997). The use of arm span, or upper, lower, and segmental arm length measures may be more appropriate. Comparison to reference standard tables should be used to compare growth when using these measures (Schenker & Ward, 1999; Spender, Cronk, Charney, & Stallings, 1989). Sometimes, severe physical disabilities make even these measurements difficult. For example, the presence of severe contracture or spinal curvature may make it difficult to measure arm span or upper and lower arm lengths accurately. Assessment of height using arm span lengths is also not appropriate in children with bony skeletal disorders (e.g., achrondroplasia), as lower bone growth may be significantly different from upper bone growth, leading to overestimates of stature (Goldbloom, 1997). The use of upper and lower arm lengths for assessment of linear stature is the most appropriate method to use when recumbent and standing lengths are not possible (Schenker & Ward). Repeated measures on the same side of the body with the least involvement and comparison of both upper and lower measure should be done to minimize error and to ensure accuracy of height estimates (Goldbloom).

Height Velocity   Assessment of height velocity (how height changes over time) should be used to assess rates of linear growth. Calculation of height velocity over time should be done at 1-year intervals to account for seasonal variations in growth. Comparison to reference curves may be done to assess rates of linear growth (Roche & Himes, 1980). The use of these curves for the assessment of linear growth in children with skeletal impairment may be of limited value because growth patterns may be significantly different due to impairment of bone growth.

Weight   Infants and children should be weighed wearing little or no outer clothing on the same scale to ensure accuracy in measurements. Weight should be measured to the nearest 0.1 kg for older children and to the nearest 0.01 kg in infants (Goldbloom, 1997; Zemel & Stallings, 1997). The scale should be zeroed between measurements to ensure precision of the weight measurement. Factors that affect accuracy of weight measurements in children include the presence of edema, organomegaly (i.e., an enlarged organ), and measurement technique. It is important to distinguish between these variables when assessing weight in terms of a child's nutritional status. Plotting of weight on reference growth curves should be done at sequential intervals for assessment of growth (Roche & Himes, 1980).

Head Circumference   Below-normal head circumference in children and infants is often associated with developmental delay (Goldbloom, 1997). Hence, head circumference is not a useful marker of nutritional status in children with central nervous system impairment. Another cause of poor cranial growth includes premature fusion of cranial sutures, known as premature synostosis. Premature synostosis can lead to increased intracranial pressure and abnormal cranial skeletal development (Goldbloom, 1997). Head circumference that is larger than normal is usually familial (known as familial megalencephaly). Head circumference should be serially monitored on clinical charts as an integral part of assessment of neurological development in children (see CDC and WHO growth charts mentioned earlier).

Nutritional Status Using Weight as a Percentage of Ideal Body Weight   Evaluation of the nutritional status of children includes assessment of growth parameters. Plotting the height and weight of a child on standard growth curves over time is critical when assessing height and weight growth failure. Growth failure may include lack of height or weight growth or both. Lack of weight gain or loss of weight over several months may be indicative of the presence of severe undernutrition, disease, or psychosocial disturbance (Goldbloom, 1997). Excessive weight gain may be indicative of excessive energy intake, edema, or organomegaly. Disturbances of linear growth may also be due to the presence of chronic under- or overnutrition, chronic disease, and/or endocrine abnormalities (Goldbloom, 1997).

Assessment of weight as a percentage of ideal body weight assists the clinician in identifying the risk and severity of either under- or overnutrition (see Table 48.1) (McLaren & Read, 1972). Calculation of ideal body weight should be done using the 50th percentile weight for chronological age or by determining the child's height percentile and finding the corresponding weight for that percentile. Calculation of the ratio between the child's actual weight and ideal body weight is used to identify the risk for protein-energy malnutrition. The way in which such ratios are used to classify the risk for protein-energy malnutrition is given in Table 48.1.

Plotting growth (height and weight) patterns of children on standard growth curves (e.g., CDC clinical curves, WHO growth curves) may not be appropriate in children with quadriplegia, as linear growth retardation is common in this population (Samson-Fang & Bell, 2013; Stevenson et al., 2006). Growth studies in children with cerebral palsy indicate that growth is severely depressed (Stevenson et al., 2006). Growth retardation has been attributed to nutritional and nonnutritional factors in this

Table 48.1.   Classification of the risk for protein-energy malnutrition

Ratio of actual weight to ideal body weight	Risk of protein-energy malnutrition (PEM)
90%–110%	Normal
85%–90%	Mild PEM
75%–85%	Moderate PEM
< 75%	Severe PEM

Reprinted from The Lancet, Vol. 300, McLaren, D.S, & Read, W.C., Classification of nutritional status in early childhood, Pages 146–148, Copyright (1972), with permission from Elsevier.

population. One reason for this is a lack of weight bearing, which plays a direct role in the growth of long bones (Stevenson et al., 2006). Depressed weight gain is likely due to the prevalence of oral-motor dysfunction, decreased feeding efficiency, dysphagia, and/or gastroesophageal reflux.

Skinfold Measures   Skinfold measures may be used to assess subcutaneous fat and lean body mass stores in the body. Triceps and subscapular skinfold measures are good indicators of whole body fat stores (Goldbloom, 1997). Calculation of mid-arm muscle circumference (MAMC) using mid-arm circumference (MAC) and triceps skinfold measures may be used to assess lean body stores. Decreased MAMC measures reflect skeletal muscle wasting due to denervation and/or malnutrition, and decreased triceps skinfold measures reflect wasting secondary to malnutrition only (Marchand et al., 2006). Comparison of MAMC and triceps skinfold measures with reference standards may be done to assess the adequacy of lean body mass and fat stores (Cronk & Roche, 1982). Assessment of body composition using these measures is most useful with sequential measurements.

There are limitations to the use of these measures (Spender, Hediger, Cronk, & Stallings, 1988). Use of single-site skinfold measurements may lead to inaccurate assessments of body composition because fat deposition in the body may be site-dependent. Measurement technique may also affect the accuracy and precision of information derived from use of this technique. Individuals responsible for measurement of skinfolds should be trained in this method, and measurements should be done in triplicate to minimize errors due to technique. A repeat measure by the same individual over time also ensures that the values obtained from these measurements are consistent over time. Measurement of skinfolds should also be done using the same calipers to reduce the potential for instrument error. Hence, standardizing the method of measurement of skinfolds and MAC is important to reduce the potential for error in assessment of body composition.

ASSESSMENT OF ENERGY REQUIREMENTS

Assessment of energy requirements is an essential component of nutrition assessment. Under- and overnutrition in children with developmental disabilities may be caused by deficits or surpluses of dietary intake over current energy requirements. Total energy requirements (i.e., total amount of energy expenditure in 24 hours) may be divided into the following components: basal requirements (i.e., energy expended at rest, shortly after awakening, after a 12–14 hour fast), energy requirements secondary to activity, thermic effect of food (i.e., energy required to digest and store food eaten), and disease-related losses (e.g., from fever or burns) (Walker, Bell, Boyd, & Davies, 2012). Resting energy expenditure (REE) refers to the amount of energy expended under conditions of rest, 2 hours after feeding.

There are several methods that may be used to determine energy requirements in children with intellectual and developmental disabilities. These include measurement of resting energy requirements using such techniques as indirect calorimetry, doubly labeled water techniques, reference equations, or recommended nutrient intake data (Spender et al., 1988). The use of recommended nutrient data is not appropriate in this population, as it does not reflect the differences in activity, body composition, and body size that are characteristic of people with intellectual and developmental disabilities (Marchand, Motil, & NASPGHAN, 2006). The use of the doubly labeled water technique is most appropriate in research settings due to its high costs and demands for technical support. Use of indirect calorimetry is appropriate for assessment of resting energy requirements in this population but requires the availability of a skilled technician for use in a clinical setting (Walker et al., 2012).

The most convenient tool to assess energy requirements of children with intellectual and developmental disabilities in the clinical setting are the WHO formulas (WHO, 1985). These formulas allow individualized assessment of resting energy requirements based upon the age and weight of the child. Assessment of total energy requirements may be accomplished by adjustment for activity and disease factors. For healthy children, this translates into total energy requirements. Total energy requirements is equal to REE (based on WHO standards) multiplied by a factor of 1.5–1.7. However, for children with spastic quadriplegic cerebral palsy, estimates of total energy requirements should be based on REE (based on WHO standards) multiplied by a factor of 1.1 (Azcue, Zello, Levy, & Pencharz, 1996). Adjustment of REE (based on

WHO standards) should be done to account for estimations of total energy requirements that also consider current neuromuscular function. For example, children with cerebral palsy with significant athetosis (i.e., continuous, involuntary motion) or who are ambulatory have increased energy needs that may also require adjustment of the REE values (Johnson, Goran, Ferrara, & Poehlman, 1995). Hence, adjustments to estimates of resting energy requirements based on the WHO standards should consider neuromuscular status in children with spastic quadriplegic cerebral palsy to ensure that accurate assessments of total energy requirements are made (Azcue et al., 1996). The case study about Mary demonstrates how a nutritional assessment resulted in improved growth and quality of life for an 8-year-old girl with spastic quadriplegia.

NUTRITIONAL MANAGEMENT

Feeding difficulties that result from dysphagia can be managed as follows (Marchand et al., 2006; Samson-Fang & Bell, 2013):

- Altering food textures to ensure safety of swallowing

- Increasing the energy density of the diet

- Proper positioning during feeding

- Selecting appropriate feeding utensils

- Assessing the route of feeding

Alteration in food texture to minimize the risk of aspiration of food contents into the lungs is the most common compensatory strategy for children with dysphagia. Food texture alterations may

---

Mary

Clinical History

Mary was admitted to the hospital because of frequent recent admissions to the hospital with pneumonia. It was thought that this was related to the aspiration of food in her lungs. This child had a gastrostomy tube inserted at the age of 3 years because she was malnourished. Her current feeds through the gastrostomy tube were overnight feeds that provided 500 kcal per day, including 15 g of protein.

Height and Weight

- Current height (estimated): 110 cm (3rd percentile)

- Current weight: 15 kg (3rd percentile)

Current Issues

- Failure to thrive

- Intolerance to overnight gastrostomy feeds; Mary was experiencing vomiting with these feeds, thought to be due to gastroesophageal reflux

- Diet history indicated an energy intake of 200–300 kcal per day and a difficulty with chewing meats and raw vegetables. There was no history of choking on liquids. Mary was now vomiting after each meal. Mealtimes were associated with a lot of stress associated with feeding. Her caregivers were very anxious about her food intake.

- Diagnostic tests such as a gastric emptying study and a pH probe indicated delayed gastric emptying and gastroesophageal reflux. A feeding study indicated feeding difficulty with solids. Soft foods were tolerated.

Assessment

- Ideal body weight: 19.5 kg

- Current percentage of ideal body weight: 77%; this indicated a moderate protein-energy malnutrition or that Mary needed more nutrition

Mary

- Total energy requirements (based on the World Health Organization formula: resting energy expenditure × 1.1): 950 kcal per day; Mary's total energy intake (by gastrostomy tube and oral intake) was not sufficient to meet these needs; her current intake was providing only 75% of total energy requirements

Recommended Interventions

- Provide increased energy diet with soft textures that are more easily tolerated.

- Document intake with the goal of meeting total energy intake via oral intake and gastrostomy feeds. Gastrostomy tube feeds should be kept at present level with the goal to adjust the regimen in accordance with her tolerance and rate of weight gain. The goal should be to promote oral intake and supplement with feeds via the gastrostomy tube. Weight is to be monitored monthly in an outpatient setting.

- Focus on normalizing the feeding environment by promoting self-feeding. Initiate occupational therapy referral regarding positioning and feeding utensils to facilitate self-feeding. Mealtimes are to be limited to 20–30 minutes.

- Start on gastric motility agents and/or proton pump inhibitors for treatment of delayed gastric emptying and gastroesophageal reflux.

Outcome

Mary started to gain weight. She gained 1 kg (2.2 pounds) over the next 8 weeks. Her oral food intake started to increase. Her mother believed that this was due to the medications, as her vomiting had stopped. Mary still did not want to feed herself but was more willing to take food from her mother.

---

include the use of minced, pureed, or thickened textures. Choice of food texture(s) is based on feeding efficiency and on the ability to swallow a food texture safely. Limitations in food texture choices and selections may result in decreased food intake and weight loss. Energy intake may be enhanced by the addition to foods of protein, carbohydrate, and/or fat modules or by the addition to the diet of high-energy and/or high-protein oral supplements.

Persistent undernutrition can lead to the necessity of enteral (intestinal) support to meet nutritional and hydration requirements (Marchand et al., 2006). Enteral support involves the insertion of enterostomy devices such as nasogastric (short-term) or gastrostomy (long-term) feeding tubes (Marchand et al., 2006). These tubes are used to deliver nutrition and hydration to children unable to meet their requirements orally. Feeding with these devices is usually supplemental. However, when the risk of aspiration from oral feeding is significant or when oral intake is severely limited, the insertion of enterostomy devices may be necessary to meet total nutritional and hydration needs of the child. Careful monitoring of tolerance to tube feeding regimens, oral intake, and enterostomy devices

can make this mode of nutrition support successful. Transition from tube to oral feeding should be a primary goal in supplemental tube feeding. The weaning process should be directed toward supporting optimal nutrition, growth, and development during transition to oral feeding, with feeding interventions directed toward the developmental stage of the child (Marchand et al., 2006). Assessment of nutritional status, swallowing function, and feeding behaviors (i.e., willingness to eat) should be done throughout this process to ensure a successful transition to oral feeding. Tube feeding should be discontinued when more than 75% of total energy needs can be met through oral intake (Marchand et al.; Schauster & Dwyer, 1996). Removal of gastrostomy devices should occur after 8–12 weeks of discontinuing nutrition support through these devices and when oral intake and rate of weight gain has become consistent (Marchand et al., 2006; Schauster & Dwyer, 1996).

FUNCTIONAL CAPACITY

Assessment of the functional capacity to self-feed is also very important in children with neurological impairment (Samson-Fang & Bell, 2013). Significant impairment in gross and fine motor skills may lead to a loss of independence to self-feed by limitations of food access, inability to participate in food preparation, and loss of fine motor skills that are required to self-feed. Adaptive feeding devices and assistance with positioning may be useful in increasing independence and safety in feeding. Functional impairments may include ataxia (i.e., failure of muscle coordination resulting in poorly judged movements), apraxia (i.e., inability to plan and execute a skilled movement in the absence of sensory and motor defects), and skeletal-muscular limitations (e.g., upper limb contracture). When possible, patients should be comfortably positioned in an upright position during a meal to facilitate ease and safety of feeding. Assistance with feeding by caregivers should promote independence with feeding. Pace of feeding, volume of the food bolus (i.e., how much food is being chewed at one time), and alterations in food textures can promote a self-feeding environment for the child with neurological impairment. Length of meal times should be limited to approximately 30 minutes to ensure optimal feeding efficiency.

Intervention by a behavioral feeding specialist can also assist in identifying and treating feeding problems in children with intellectual and developmental disabilities. Focus is placed on the child–feeder interaction in addition to oral-motor skills and functional capacity to assist in normalizing the feeding environment (Rodas-Arts & Benoit, 1998). This usually includes mealtime observation for assessment of caregiver responses to adaptive and maladaptive feeding behaviors and intervention to promote appropriate eating behaviors (Rodas-Arts & Benoit, 1998).

NUTRITION-RELATED MEDICAL PROBLEMS

Numerous medical problems can arise from improper nutrition. Two of these, obesity and celiac disease, are described here because they are commonly encountered.

Obesity

The most common causes of obesity in children with developmental delay include dietary intake in excess of energy requirements and lack of mobility.

A few children with spastic quadriplegic cerebral palsy have been shown to have decreased resting energy expenditure (Azcue et al., 1996; Walker et al., 2012). Caregiver overestimation of energy requirements can lead to overfeeding and excessive weight gain in this population. Obesity is also common in children and adults with Prader-Willi syndrome, where a much smaller than average number of calories is required to maintain normal body weight, and in children and adults with Down syndrome. Special growth charts are available for use in Down syndrome (Cronk et al., 1988).

Assessment of obesity in children with developmental disabilities may be difficult due to limitations in the ability to measure height, weight, and skinfolds, which limits the use of BMI to quantify or serial track the onset and severity of obesity in this population. Waist circumference measurement has been used to provide information regarding the severity of obesity in children and is a simple and easy tool that can be used in this population.

Dietary treatment of obesity in children with intellectual and developmental disabilities involves modification of energy intake. Dietary intake should include all food groups to prevent macro- and micronutrient deficiency with energy restriction. Pediatric enteral formulas should be used in children fed via enterostomy devices. These formulas contain higher nutrient to energy ratios, which decrease the risk of micronutrient deficiency with energy restriction (Azcue et al., 1996; Marchand et al., 2006). Dietary counseling of caregivers by a registered dietitian regarding food portion size and food selection is an essential component to the successful dietary treatment of obesity in this population (Marchand et al., 2006). A weight management program that has been used with considerable success by many people with Prader-Willi syndrome is called the Red, Yellow, Green Weight Control Program. This is based on the traffic light color system. Green means "go!" Yellow means "caution—be careful, go slow," and red means "stop!" (Balko, 2006). The program requires support from a dietitian skilled in its application.

Celiac Disease

Celiac disease (CD) is an autoimmune disease that is commonly found in individuals in the more affluent countries of the world. Children and adults with this disorder have an autoimmune intolerance to gluten or gliadin, a common protein found in wheat, rye, and barley. Evidence suggests that the prevalence is approximately 1 in 100 (Mager, Qiao, & Turner, 2012; Rajani, Huynh, & Turner, 2010). Individuals with CD may have a variety of symptoms at time of presentation that include gastrointestinal symptomology (e.g., nausea, anorexia, constipation, irritability), iron deficiency anemia, fatigue, and poor growth and bone health. However, it is not uncommon for children and adults to be diagnosed with CD without any apparent gastrointestinal symptomology at all; in fact, many children present with only fatigue and poor bone health as the major symptomology. Poor bone health can be of considerable concern, particularly in adolescence, due to the increased risk for osteoporosis later in life (Mager et al., 2012).

Although serological markers to screen for CD have been developed (anti-tissue transglutaminase and endomysial IgA antibodies), the only way to definitively diagnose CD is through jejunal (i.e., the middle portion of the small intestine) biopsy. The hallmark feature of intestinal biopsy is the presence of a flattened jejunal mucosa, which is associated with macronutrient and micronutrient malabsorption (i.e., absorbing too few or too many nutrients). The potential for micronutrient deficiency is particularly high for iron, zinc, magnesium, and the fat-soluble vitamins (A, D, E, and K) if CD is left untreated. Vitamins D and K, in particular, are important for healthy bone development and growth, and hence children and adolescents with chronic undiagnosed CD are at increased risk for poor bone health (Mager et al., 2012).

For children with intellectual and developmental disabilities, poor bone health can be further exacerbated by issues related to immobility. Treatment for children and adolescents requires lifelong restriction of dietary gluten or gliadin. Complete exclusion of gluten or gliadin from the diet can bring about full gastrointestinal recovery for individuals with CD and can quickly contribute to improved overall well-being. Although controversial, exclusion of dietary avenin, a common protein found in oats, is still recommended.

Vitamin supplementation may be required in the period following diagnosis of CD, but it should not be routinely needed if compliance to the gluten-free diet is achieved. For the child with developmental disabilities and CD, following the gluten-free diet carefully can result in significant overall improvements in quality of life. Education regarding the diet by a registered dietitian is imperative to ensure that the child or adult with CD is following a gluten-free diet (Mager et al., 2012). For information regarding the gluten-free diet, consult http://www.celiac.ca/.

SUMMARY

Under- and overnutrition are common concerns in children with developmental delay. Under- and overnutrition are the deficit or surplus of dietary intake over total nutritional needs. The common causes of malnutrition in children with developmental delay include poor dietary intake and diminished feeding efficiency that result from swallowing and gastrointestinal dysfunction. Feeding problems and functional impairments to self-feeding may compound this issue. Assessment of nutritional status should include assessment of growth parameters, body composition, diet and medical history, and energy requirements to identify risk for under- and overnutrition. Management of nutritional disorders in children with intellectual and developmental disabilities is complex and should include a multidisciplinary approach.

FOR FURTHER THOUGHT AND DISCUSSION

1. Consider both the children and adults with intellectual and developmental disabilities who you have known. How common do you think malnutrition might be in this population?

2. Think of a child you know who might benefit from a nutrition assessment. What steps would you take to ensure that a full multidisciplinary assessment occurs?

3. In a group with three others, identify four children with intellectual and developmental disabilities who have feeding difficulties of various kinds. What are some practical ways in which each could be helped that promote their independence?

REFERENCES

Azcue, M.P., Zello, G.A., Levy, L.D., & Pencharz, P.B. (1996). Energy expenditure and body composition in children with spastic quadriplegic cerebral palsy. *Journal of Pediatrics, 129,* 870–876.

Balko, K.A. (2006). *The ABCs of nutrition. Implementation of the Red, Yellow, Green system (RYG) of weight management.*

Retrieved from http://www.pwsnetwork.ca/pws/docs/abcs_nutrition_2.pdf

Centers for Disease Control and Prevention, National Center for Health Statistics. (2009). *CDC growth charts: United States*. Retrieved from http://www.cdc.gov/growthcharts/

Cronk, C., Crocker, A.C., Pueschel, S.M., Shea, A.M., Zackai, E., Pickens, G., & Reed, R.B. (1988). Growth charts for children with Down syndrome: 1 month to 18 years of age. *Pediatrics, 81,* 102–110.

Cronk, C.E., & Roche, A.E. (1982). Race- and sex-specific reference data for triceps and subscapular skinfolds and weight/stature. *American Journal of Clinical Nutrition, 35*(2), 347–354.

de Onis, M., Onyango, A.W., Borghi, E., Siyam, A., Nishida, C., & Siekmann, J. (2007). Development of a WHO growth reference for school-aged children and adolescents. *Bulletin of the World Health Organization, 85,* 660–667.

Dietitians of Canada. (2004). A health professional's guide to using growth charts. *Paediatrics and Child Health, 9*(3), 174–176. Retrieved from http://www.ncbi.nlm.nih.gov/pmc/articles/PMC2720489/

Goldbloom, R.B. (1997). Assessment of physical growth and nutrition. In R.B. Goldbloom, *Pediatric clinical skills* (2nd ed.; pp. 23–48). New York, NY: Churchill Livingston.

Henderson, R.C., Kairalia, C., Barrington, J.W., Abbas, A., & Stevenson, R.D. (2005). Longitudinal changes in bone density in children with moderate to severe cerebral palsy. *Journal of Pediatrics, 146*(6), 769–775.

Himes, J.G., Roche, A.F., Thissen, D., & Moore, W.M. (1985). Parent-specific adjustments for evaluation of recumbent length and stature of children. *Pediatrics, 75,* 304–313.

Jensen, G.L., Hsiao, P.Y., & Wheeler, D. (2012). Adult nutrition assessment tutorial. *Journal of Parenteral and Enteral Nutrition, 36*(3), 267–274.

Johnson, R.K., Goran, M.I., Ferrara, M.S., & Poehlman, E.T. (1995). Athetosis increases resting metabolic rate in adults with cerebral palsy. *Journal of the American Dietetic Association, 95,* 145–148.

Lawrence, S., Cummings, E., Chanoine, J.P., Metzer, D.L., Palmert, M., Sharma, A., & Rodd, C. (2013). Canadian Pediatric Endocrine Group extension to WHO growth charts: Why bother? *Paediatrics and Child Health, 18,* 296–297.

Mager, D.R., Qiao, J., & Turner, J.T. (2012). Vitamin D and K status influences bone mineral density and bone accrual in children and adolescents with celiac disease. *European Journal of Clinical Nutrition, 66,* 488–495.

Marchand, V., Motil, K.J., & North American Society for Pediatric Gastroenterology, Hepatology and Nutrition Committee on Nutrition. (2006). Nutrition support for neurologically impaired children: A clinical report of the North American Society for Pediatric Gastroenterology, Hepatology and Nutrition. *Journal of Pediatric Gastroenterology and Nutrition, 43,* 123–135.

McLaren, D.S., & Read, W.C. (1972). Classification of nutritional status in early childhood. *The Lancet, 2,* 146–148.

Rajani, S., Huynh, H.Q., & Turner, J. (2010). The changing frequency of celiac disease diagnosed at the Stollery Children's Hospital. *Canadian Journal of Gastroenterology, 24*(2), 109–112.

Roche, A.F., & Davila, G.H. (1974). Differences between recumbent length and stature within individuals. *Growth, 38,* 313–320.

Roche, A.F., & Himes, J.H. (1980). Incremental growth charts. *American Journal of Clinical Nutrition, 33*(9), 2041–2052.

Rodas-Arts, D., & Benoit, D. (1998). Feeding problems in infancy and early childhood: Identification and management. *Paediatrics and Child Health, 3,* 21–27.

Roe, A. (1982). *Handbook: Interactions of selected drugs and nutrients in patients* (3rd ed.). Chicago, IL: American Dietetic Association.

Samson-Fang, L., & Bell, K. (2013). Assessment of growth and nutrition in children with cerebral palsy. *European Journal of Clinical Nutrition, 67,* 55–58.

Schauster, H., & Dwyer, J. (1996). Transition from tube feedings to feedings by mouth in children: Preventing eating dysfunction. *Journal of the American Dietetic Association, 96,* 277–281.

Schenker, J., & Ward, R. (1999). Development and application of a pediatric anthropometric evaluation system. *Canadian Journal of Dietetic Practice and Research, 60,* 20–26.

Spender, Q.W., Cronk, C.E., Charney, E.B., & Stallings, V.A. (1989). Assessment of linear growth of children with cerebral palsy: Use of alternative measures to height or length. *Developmental Medicine and Child Neurology, 31,* 206–214.

Spender, Q.W., Hediger, M.L., Cronk, C.E., & Stallings, V.A. (1988). Fat distribution in children with cerebral palsy. *Annals of Human Biology, 15,* 191–196.

Stevenson, R.D., Conaway, M., Chumlea, W.C., Rosenbaum, P., Fund, E.B., Henderson, R.C.,…Stallings, V.A. (2006). Growth and health in children with moderate-to-severe cerebral palsy (North American Growth in Cerebral Palsy Study). *Pediatrics, 118,* 1010–1018.

Vernon-Roberts, A., & Sullivan, P.B. (2013). Fundoplication versus postoperative medication for gastro-oesophageal reflux in children with neurological impairment undergoing gastrostomy. *Cochrane Database of Systematic Reviews, 8,* CD006151. doi: 10.1002/14651858.CD006151.pub3

Walker, J.L., Bell, K.L., Boyd, R.N., & Davies, P.S. (2012), Energy requirements in preschool-age children with cerebral palsy. *American Journal of Clinical Nutrition, 96*(6), 1309–1315.

World Health Organization. (1985). *Energy and protein requirements. Technical report series #724*. Geneva, Switzerland: Author.

World Health Organization. (2011). *The WHO child growth standards*. Retrieved from http://www.who.int/childgrowth/standards/en/

Zemel, B.S., Riley, E.M., & Stallings, V.A. (1997). Evaluation of methodology for nutritional assessment in children: Anthropometry, body composition, and energy expenditure. *Annual Review Nutrition, 17,* 211–235.

49

Alzheimer's Disease and Dementia

Implications for People with Down Syndrome and Other Intellectual or Developmental Disabilities

Vee P. Prasher, Matthew P. Janicki, Emoke Jozsvai, Joseph M. Berg,
John S. Lovering, Ambreen Rashid, Wai Lun Alan Fung, and Maire Percy

WHAT YOU WILL LEARN

- Alzheimer's disease in the general population
- Normal aging and other dementias
- Dementia of the Alzheimer's type in people with Down syndrome
- Dementia and Alzheimer's disease in people with other intellectual or developmental disabilities
- Multidisciplinary approach to the management of dementia

Alzheimer's disease can affect any adult as age advances. Understanding of this disorder in people with intellectual or developmental disability has lagged behind knowledge of the disease in the general population, with many clinical and biological issues still unresolved. In view of overall improvements in life expectancy—often dramatic in Down syndrome and in other types of intellectual and developmental disabilities—aging issues (including Alzheimer's disease in people with intellectual and developmental disabilities) are receiving increased attention, leading to prospects of better care for adults with intellectual and developmental disorders. The first three sections of this chapter

provide an introduction to Alzheimer's disease and dementia and how these disorders affect people with Down syndrome and other types of intellectual and developmental disabilities. The final section deals with the multidisciplinary management of dementia.

It is not our intent to lead with the impression that dementia attributed to Alzheimer's disease is the sole type of dementia that affects adults with intellectual and developmental disabilities. With the exception of Down syndrome, in which dementia of the Alzheimer's type occurs 2–3 decades earlier than in the general population, adults with intellectual and developmental disabilities are thought to be affected by the same range of related dementias (e.g., frontotemporal, vascular, Lewy body) as are same-age peers in the general population, with Alzheimer's disease being the most common. We recognize that in some instances, an adult may exhibit dementia with multiple causal features. As most of the primary research with adults with intellectual and developmental disabilities focuses on Alzheimer's disease, this is the main focus of this chapter; when other dementias have relevance to an issue discussed, they are cited accordingly.

ALZHEIMER'S DISEASE IN THE GENERAL POPULATION

In 1907, Alois Alzheimer, a German neuropathologist, reported clinical and postmortem neuropathological findings in a 56-year-old woman who had developed progressive severe loss of memory, disorientation, disturbance of language, and paranoid ideas over the last 5 years of her life (Alzheimer, 1907). At autopsy, her brain tissue was treated with a newly developed silver stain and examined microscopically. It was found to be riddled with numerous diffuse deposits and intensely staining fibrils that now are called amyloid plaques and neurofibrillary tangles, respectively. This disease process was first named Alzheimer's disease by Emil Kraepelin in 1910, a tribute that has since become the general designation for the condition. In addition, although others noted cognitive deterioration (Fraser & Mitchell, 1876) or senile plaques (Struwe, 1929) in adults with Down syndrome, George Jervis, a researcher in the United States, published the first article directly linking Alzheimer's-disease-type neuropathology to clinical dementia in adults with Down syndrome (Jervis, 1948).

Abnormal Brain Features

Deposition of amyloid-β peptides in plaques and intracellular neurofibrillary tangles are the two main characteristic pathological features of Alzheimer's disease (National Institute on Aging, n.d. b). Amyloid plaques (also called senile or neuritic plaques) are areas of degeneration associated with a central core containing a protein often referred to as amyloid-β, itself formed from another larger protein called amyloid precursor protein (APP), the gene for which is located on chromosome 21. In the healthy brain, amyloid-β fragments either are not formed or are broken down and eliminated. In Alzheimer's disease, the fragments accumulate to form hard, insoluble plaques.

Neurofibrillary tangles are found within the nerve cells (neurons) and consist of insoluble twisted fibers in the form of paired helical filaments. They primarily consist of a protein called tau, which forms part of a structure called a microtubule. The microtubules help transport nutrients and other important substances from one part of the neuron to another. In Alzheimer's disease, the tau is abnormal (it carries too many phosphate groups) and the microtubule structures collapse.

Plaques and tangles are not specific to Alzheimer's disease. They are found in other brain diseases such as Parkinson's disease (although in that disease, the brain regions involved differ from those affected in Alzheimer's). They are also found in the brains of up to about 30% of older adults who do not have intellectual impairments. However, in adults who have been diagnosed with Alzheimer's disease on the basis of their clinical symptoms, the numbers of plaques and tangles in particular regions of the brain are markedly increased above the "normal limits" expected in people of the same age without dementia. Also of significance is that the plaques are surrounded by activated nonneuronal cells (astrocytes, microglia and, possibly, macrophages), and it is thought that this activity contributes to the pathology. To reach a diagnosis of Alzheimer's disease after death on the basis of a brain autopsy, attention is necessary not just to the presence of plaques and tangles but also to how many there are and in which brain regions they are located (Khachaturian, 1985; Robinson et al., 2011; Wilcock & Esiri, 1982).

The two characteristic features of the Alzheimer's disease brain are shown in Figure 49.1. Along with plaques and tangles, which are microscopic abnormalities only seen with special staining techniques or with high-powered microscopes, other brain changes associated with Alzheimer's disease also occur, as listed in Table 49.1.

Some 40 years after Alzheimer's initial account, an association between Alzheimer's disease and Down syndrome was established (Jervis, 1948). It was recognized that the brains of virtually all people with Down syndrome older than about 40 years had features resembling those characteristic of Alzheimer's disease. However, not all aging people with Down syndrome develop clinical manifestations of Alzheimer's disease (Mann, Royston, & Ravindra, 1990;). During the latter part of the 20th century and into the 21st, there have been numerous reports concerning clinical, pathological, and genetic links between Alzheimer's disease and Down syndrome, although investigations of Alzheimer's disease in relation to intellectual and developmental disabilities other than Down syndrome have been much more limited.

There are widespread changes in the brains of people with Alzheimer's disease (see Table 49.1). Also, chemicals called neurotransmitters (e.g., acetylcholine, noradrenalin, serotonin), which

(a)

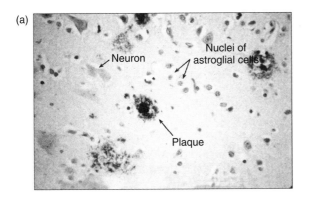

(b)

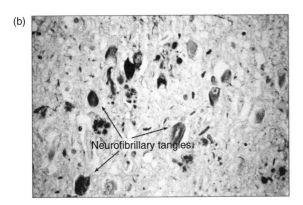

Figure 49.1. a) Characteristic amyloid plaques of Alzheimer's disease. The brain of all individuals with Alzheimer's disease is riddled with amyloid plaques. Brain tissue from the cortex of an individual with Alzheimer's disease was stained with antibody (Dako M872) that recognized amyloid-β, a breakdown product of APP. The large, dense, roundish deposits in this section are amyloid plaques that have been stained with this antibody. b) Characteristic neurofibrillary tangles of Alzheimer's disease. The brain of all individuals with Alzheimer's disease is also riddled with neurofibrillary tangles. Brain tissue from the cortex of an individual with Alzheimer's disease was stained with antibody (Sigma T5530) that recognizes tau protein in neurofibrillary tangles. The densely staining deposits that are present inside some of the neurons (triangular cells with a large, oval nucleus) are neurofibrillary tangles that have been stained with this antibody. (Copyright © 2006 Peter Barber. The authors thank Peter Barber, Senior Lecturer in Pathology, University of Birmingham, United Kingdom, for prints of the amyloid plaques and neurofibrillary tangles.)

maintain communication between nerve cells and normal brain function, are progressively reduced as pathological brain changes increase. All of these brain changes are believed to contribute to the characteristic clinical picture of Alzheimer's disease (see section on clinical manifestations).

Prevalence and Risk Factors

The reported prevalence of Alzheimer's disease (i.e., the number of affected people in a population at a given time) in the general population varies in different studies and among different ethnic groups,

Table 49.1. Quantitative brain changes in Alzheimer's disease

Type of change	Reduction compared with normal brain (%)
Brain weight	7.5–18
Weight of cerebral cortex	20–58
Thickness of cortex	10–15
Hemispheral volume	13–18
Number of nerve cells	22–60

but the striking age dependence of Alzheimer's disease is always evident. In North America, Alzheimer's disease prevalence doubles every 5 years beyond age 65. By 2050, approximately 11 million Americans are expected to have Alzheimer's disease (Thies & Bleiler, 2012). Alzheimer's disease and death from Alzheimer's disease affects more women than men (Maki, 2013). Studies of the brains of older adults suggest that Alzheimer's disease begins some 15–20 years prior to clinical manifestation (Norton, Matthews, Barnes, Yaffe, & Brayne, 2014).

There is no single known cause of Alzheimer's disease and no known cure. It is generally accepted that Alzheimer's disease is the "end product" of a number of different pathways that all lead to the formation of plaques and tangles and result in clinical dementia. Alzheimer's disease likely results from a combination of genetic predisposing, environmental, and lifestyle risk factors (Armstrong, 2013). Some factors that cause or contribute to Alzheimer's disease are listed in Table 49.2. Advancing age of adults is the most obvious predisposing factor in all populations. In about 95% of people with Alzheimer's disease, the condition occurs sporadically (i.e., without any affected relative being apparent). Down syndrome is considered to be a strong risk factor for an early-onset form of Alzheimer's disease. A gene called apolipoprotein E (APOE) is involved in sporadic Alzheimer's disease. APOE protein occurs in three major forms: E2, E3, and E4. Every person inherits one APOE gene from each parent. The E4 form of the protein leads to earlier development of Alzheimer's disease in Caucasians. People with two copies of E4 tend to develop Alzheimer's disease several years earlier than those with one E4. However, not everyone with one or two E4s develops Alzheimer's disease (Prasher, Percy, Jozsvai, Lovering, & Berg, 2007). A variant in the TREM2 gene (which encodes

Table 49.2.   Factors that predispose to Alzheimer's disease

Causal	Confirmed	Possible
Mutations in genes (amyloid precursor protein gene; presenilin 1 and presenilin 2 genes)[a]	Advancing age	Inflammatory conditions
	Family history of Alzheimer's	Clinical depression
	Apolipoprotein E4 gene	Stress
	Female sex	Inadequate physical exercise, socializing, and brain stimulation
	Down syndrome	Herpes simplex virus 1 in the brain
	Low levels of formal education	Excessive metal ions in the brain (e.g., iron, copper, aluminum, zinc, mercury)
	Mild cognitive impairment	Vascular risk factors (e.g., cardiovascular disease and carotid artery atherosclerosis)
	TREM2 gene variant	Type 2 diabetes
		Vitamin D deficiency

Sources: Alzheimer Society of Canada (2015), Daulatzai (2013), Littlejohns et al. (2014), and Prasher et al. (2007).
[a]More than 20 genetic factors are associated with Alzheimer's disease (see chapter text).

a receptor found on microglial cells) is associated with sporadic Alzheimer's disease as strongly as APOE E4 (Hampel & Lista, 2013). Genome-wide association studies and whole-exome and whole-genome sequencing have revealed more than 20 loci associated with Alzheimer's disease (Barber, 2012; Bird, 2015; Karch, Cruchaga, & Goate, 2014).

In a small number of families, Alzheimer's disease can recur in an inherited form, known as familial autosomal dominant, that can be passed on from one generation to the next, accounting for about 5%–10% of all cases of the disease. It usually occurs before the age of 65 years, even as early as in the person's 40s. Rare mutations in one of three genes—APP and presenilins 1 and 2 (PS1 and PS2)—are considered to cause Alzheimer's disease in such families, because people who carry one of these mutations almost always develop Alzheimer's disease in their lifetime (Prasher et al., 2007).

"NORMAL" AGING, DEMENTIA OTHER THAN ALZHEIMER'S, AND MILD COGNITIVE IMPAIRMENT

With normal aging into late life, mental and physical decline of varying extent is a general phenomenon among all people. Most people, including many with intellectual and developmental disabilities, maintain their cognitive abilities and adaptive behavior skills fairly well throughout their adult lives. However, normal aging is associated with declines in some areas of cognitive functioning.

Different cognitive abilities decline at different rates with advancing age. Abstract reasoning and verbal skills (expressive and receptive language ability) tend to remain relatively intact, whereas perceptual and motor skills decrease more substantially and earlier. As people age, they generally show some reduction in their capacity to learn and recall new information, their reaction time increases, and their motor movements become slower. There are many causes of age-related changes in cognitive functioning. Some that affect cognitive functioning in old age include sensory deficits (particularly reduced hearing and vision), general health status, and diminished motivation (Prasher et al., 2007).

Beyond normal aging and extending into the realm of disease, *dementia* is a term used to designate the development, generally in adults, of serious cognitive and associated disorders with an often detectable pathological basis that affect the ability to cope on a day-to-day basis. More precisely, in a diagnostic sense, Wherrett (1999) described the term as being applied to "persons in whom cognitive decline sufficient to impair personal, social, or occupational adaptation is the main presenting symptom, is persisting and progressive, and is associated with a chronic diffuse or multifocal brain disorder" (p. 91). There are many actual or potential causes of dementia (see Table 49.3) with various designations to indicate particular specific types with distinctive characteristics (e.g., vascular dementia, multi-infarct dementia, dementia pugilistica [a neurodegenerative disease with features of

Table 49.3. Some causes of dementia other than Alzheimer's disease

Vascular dementia

Multi-infarct dementia

Frontotemporal lobe dementia

Depression[a]

Head trauma

Alcohol abuse

HIV infection

Bacterial, fungal, and protozoan infections[a]

Huntington disease

Aluminum overload in chronic kidney disease[a]; acute aluminum toxicity[a]

Parkinson's disease

Dementia pugilistica

Lewy body disease

Pick disease

Hypothyroidism[a]

Drug-induced dementias (e.g., from benzodiazepines such as clonazepam)

Vitamin deficiencies (e.g., B_{12}[a])

Normal pressure hydrocephalus[a]

Multiple sclerosis

Brain tumor

[a]Potentially reversible.

dementia that may affect amateur or professional boxers and wrestlers as well as athletes], frontotemporal lobe dementia). Some other forms are potentially reversible if treated early enough (e.g., severe deficiency of B_{12}, severe hypothyroidism, normal pressure hydrocephalus, acute aluminum toxicity, dialysis dementia from aluminum overload in patients with chronic kidney disease). The state of delirium should be distinguished from that of dementia. *Delirium* refers to an abrupt change in the brain that causes mental and emotional confusion, particularly among older adults during hospitalization or following surgery (Fong, Davis, Growdon, Albuquerque, & Inouye, 2015).

A disorder called mild cognitive impairment (MCI) is now recognized as a predisposing factor for Alzheimer's disease. There is debate about the definition of MCI. Not everyone develops MCI, and not all cases of MCI progress to dementia, with some cases of MCI regressing. It has been proposed that dementia prevention strategies should target not only individuals with MCI but even asymptomatic individuals identified as being at risk of developing MCI or Alzheimer's disease (Geda, 2012).

Clinical Manifestations of Alzheimer's Disease

Symptoms of Alzheimer's disease range from early mild ones, which may go unnoticed and have little detrimental effect, to severe ones at the end stages of the disease process that can cause considerable stress to caregivers and lead to the individual requiring nursing care. The disorder can be artificially divided into three clinical stages (see Table 49.4).

Onset of Alzheimer's disease is slow and gradual, with the precise age of clinical onset often difficult to determine, as the clinical symptoms of the disorder tend to develop gradually over a number of years. Onset of behavioral changes is more

Table 49.4. Main stages of Alzheimer's disease

Stage I: Early (duration 1–3 years)	Stage II: Middle (duration 2–5 years)	Stage III: Late (duration 4–8 years)
Memory loss (particularly short-term memory)	Very forgetful	Marked intellectual deterioration
Changes in personality	Loss of self-care skills	Inability to recognize family, friends, caregivers
Difficulties with language	Greater dependence on others	Dependence on others for dressing, washing, eating, toileting
Disoriented in time	Increased speech difficulties	Immobility
Lost in familiar places	Wandering	Bladder and bowel incontinence
Loss of motivation	Seizures	More severe seizures
Signs of depression and aggression	Reduced mobility	Limb rigidity and flexed postures
Loss of interest	Behavior problems	Marked physical deterioration
	Hallucinations	

readily detected than some others. Those close to affected individuals frequently do not recognize that there is deterioration until it has become quite pronounced. As the disease progresses, it becomes increasingly apparent that there is progressive and significant decline in memory and other mental functions, sometimes associated with severe depression. There is a gradual loss of self-care skills and growing additional problems with day-to-day living. Late-onset seizures may be the first indication for medical attention. The later stage of Alzheimer's disease is marked by intellectual and physical deterioration. Total dependency and inactivity with increased need for nursing care becomes evident. Pneumonia or urinary tract infection is often the immediate cause of death.

The manifestations of Alzheimer's disease vary among individuals. Some adults may have a rapid, short illness, whereas others may experience a longer, more gradual decline in function. Affected people are unlikely to experience all symptoms and signs listed in Table 49.4 or to decline precisely as outlined in the table, which should be used only as a guide.

Diagnosis of Alzheimer's Disease

For a confident diagnosis of Alzheimer's disease, the declines of memory and other cognitive functions should be present for at least 1 year, show a progressive nature, and be irreversible. In Alzheimer's disease, deterioration of cognitive functioning is typically accompanied by personality, mood, and behavioral changes. For the general population, there are reliable clinical diagnostic tests for Alzheimer's disease based on signs and symptoms, although diagnosis can be certain only on direct brain examination. In 1984, McKhann and colleagues published criteria for the diagnosis of possible, probable, and definite Alzheimer's disease. Particularly in settings that specialize in Alzheimer's disease and related disorders, these exacting diagnostic criteria enable an accurate clinical diagnosis to be made in 70% to 80% of patients. As of July 2010, the National Institute on Aging (n.d. a) and the Alzheimer's Association (2015) in the United States have been leading efforts to update diagnostic criteria for Alzheimer's disease. See the web sites of these organizations for current information.

There are several important reasons for a diagnosis of Alzheimer's disease to be made. Such diagnosis enables

- Families and caregivers to understand what is happening to the person concerned

- Families and caregivers to plan for the future

- Provision to be made, with support if necessary, for appropriate care

- Exclusion of other, often treatable, causes of intellectual decline

- Consideration of appropriate medication

A clinical diagnosis of Alzheimer's disease is principally based on initially identifying the presence of behaviors associated with dementia and then excluding other possible treatable causes of the behavioral change. Over time, the characteristic deterioration of function associated with Alzheimer's disease often becomes evident. Diagnosis is generally made as shown in Figure 49.2. There are indications that the diagnosis of Alzheimer's disease may be aided by sensitive brain imaging techniques (e.g., computed or positron emission tomography, magnetic resonance imaging) or by measuring the amounts of particular substances (biomarkers) in other bodily fluids and tissues such as peripheral blood and cerebrospinal fluid (e.g., amyloid-β, tau). Biomarkers can also include particular genetic variants known to be predisposing risk factors for Alzheimer's disease.

Active Research Initiatives

A notable area of active research is whether Alzheimer's disease can be prevented through lifestyle changes. However, various other research initiatives are underway as well. These are discussed in the following subsections.

Prevention of Alzheimer's Disease Through Lifestyle Changes The potential prevention of Alzheimer's disease in the general population through lifestyle changes (e.g., physical activity, socializing, healthy diet) is an active research area (Table 49.5). It also is a topic that can be addressed by individuals and families, though best in consultation with health professionals.

The role of regular physical activity is of particular interest because preliminary biological research, epidemiological studies, and randomized

| Interview of family members/caregivers for evidence of mental deterioration and possible differential diagnosis |

⇩

| Formal assessment of mental condition including detailed psychological assessment of memory and other intellectual functions[a] |

⇩

| Comprehensive physical examination—including sensory testing, blood tests, and urinalysis—to exclude treatable conditions |

⇩

| Electroencephalography, brain scan (computed tomography, magnetic resonance imaging, single photon emission computed tomography) |

⇩

| Review of information and provisional diagnosis |

⇩

| Follow-up, including further regular assessments to confirm diagnosis |

Figure 49.2. Diagnosing Alzheimer's disease. (*Key:* [a]Dependent on availability of resources.)

controlled trials suggest that this may not only contribute to prevention of cognitive decline in older adults but also slow down the course of Alzheimer's disease and delay the onset of dementia (Blondell, Hammersley-Mather, & Veerman, 2014). More high-quality studies involving older adults with MCI and dementia are needed (Öhman, Savikko, Strandberg, & Pitkälä, 2014).

Other factors associated with a good lifestyle also might help to prevent cognitive decline and dementia. In addition to those shown in Table 49.5, lifestyle strategies to consider include reducing emotional stress, obesity, high blood pressure, and high cholesterol; avoiding polluted air; and drinking safe water (Prasher et al., 2007).

Other Research Initiatives Some other important questions under investigation include the following:

- Are plaques and tangles inherently harmful or protective? (Mondragón-Rodríguez et al., 2010)

- Does amyloid-β protect against infection in the central nervous system? (Soscia et al., 2010)

Table 49.5. Factors that might help to protect against Alzheimer's disease

Factors	Examples
Antioxidants	Vitamin E, vitamin C, selegiline (deprenyl)
Nonsteroidal anti-inflammatory drugs	Ibuprofen
Conditions resulting in increased blood flow to the brain	Physical exercise, intellectual stimulation, socializing
Healthy diet	Following a Mediterranean-style diet, having a low to moderate alcohol intake, eating fish at least once a week, ensuring an adequate intake of vitamins that regulate folate and homocysteine metabolism (folate, B_6, B_{12}), ensuring an adequate intake of vitamin D, avoiding foods associated with heart disease or diabetes

Sources: Alzheimer Society of Canada (2015), Arab and Sabbagh (2010), Daviglus et al. (2011), and Prasher et al. (2007).

- Is herpes simplex virus 1 a risk factor for Alzheimer's disease? (Itzhaki, 2014)

- Does excessive aluminum intake contribute to Alzheimer's disease? (Bhattacharjee, Zhao, Hill, Percy, & Lukiw, 2014; Percy, Kruck, Pogue, & Lukiw, 2011; Walton & Wang, 2009)

- Is mismetabolism of zinc, copper, and iron involved in Alzheimer's disease? (Ayton, Lei, & Bush, 2015)

- Does mercury contribute to Alzheimer's disease? (Mutter, Curth, Naumann, Deth, & Walach, 2010)

- Does prenatal infection in utero contribute to accelerated aging and development of Alzheimer's disease? (Madhusudan et al., 2011)

- Do microorganisms in the gut (i.e., part of the microbiome) contribute to circulating amyloid and amyloid in the brain? (Hill & Lukiw, 2015)

Still controversial is whether cognitive training (i.e., brain training) might be useful in Alzheimer's disease or help to ward off dementia or cognitive decline associated with aging (Mowszowski, Batchelor, & Naismith, 2010; Reichman, Fiocco, & Rose, 2010).

Unfortunately, aside from use of approved drugs that have minimal beneficial effects, no "magic bullet" has been found to cure or ward off Alzheimer's disease. Hence, much activity in Alzheimer's disease research is devoted to the development of novel therapeutic strategies and testing these in clinical trials (ClinicalTrials.gov, n.d.). Because brain glucose regulation has been found to be abnormal in Alzheimer's disease, the role of brain insulin resistance and deficiency has been highlighted as one of the ways toward novel therapeutic strategies (de la Monte, 2012; de la Monte & Wands, 2008). Because cholesterol and lipid-related metabolic processes are disturbed in Alzheimer's disease, these also are under investigation as prime targets for Alzheimer's disease therapeutics (Jones, Holmans, & International Genomics of Alzheimer's Project, 2013). Identifying biomarkers to aid with the early diagnosis of Alzheimer's disease also is topical (see the preceding section). Last but not least, there is recognition that understanding why dementia resembling Alzheimer's disease occurs 20–30 years earlier in people with Down syndrome will help to solve the mystery of what causes

Alzheimer's disease in the general population (Wiseman et al., 2015).

DEMENTIA OF THE ALZHEIMER'S TYPE IN PEOPLE WITH DOWN SYNDROME

This section provides an introduction to the early-onset dementia that is so common in people with Down syndrome.

Prevalence

Interest in Alzheimer's disease in people with intellectual and developmental disabilities has focused primarily on the association between Down syndrome and dementia resembling Alzheimer's disease. As already noted, virtually all adults with Down syndrome older than age 40 have a considerable amount of amyloid-β in their brains. Furthermore, people with Down syndrome are at risk of developing clinical dementia 20–30 years earlier than is usually the case in the general population. In this chapter, we refer to dementia that develops in older people with Down syndrome as dementia of the Alzheimer's type (DAT). The high frequency of DAT in Down syndrome has become increasingly apparent as people with Down syndrome live longer, largely due to improved health care, nutrition, and housing conditions. In the 1920s, the life expectancy for Caucasians with Down syndrome was about 9 years, but by the 1980s it had reached about 35 years (Thase, 1982). In addition, there is a greater expectation of longevity once adults are middle age. Studies have shown that the average age at death for those older than 40 is in the mid-50s (Janicki, Dalton, Henderson, & Davidson, 1999). In North America, the expected life span of a 1-year old Caucasian child with Down syndrome and mild-to-moderate intellectual impairment is 55 years; about a decade less in those with profound cognitive impairment (Strauss & Eyman, 1996); and about a decade less as well when compared with other adults with intellectual and developmental disabilities (Janicki et al., 1999).

Most studies have found that life expectancy among women with Down syndrome is lower than that for men (Day, Strauss, Shavelle, & Reynolds, 2005; Esbensen, 2010; Strauss & Eyman, 1996)—with speculation that earlier menopause may be a risk factor for DAT (Schupf et al., 1997). The opposite finding is prevalent among adults with other types of intellectual and developmental disabilities, with women generally outliving men—similar to findings in the general population (Glasson et al., 2003). Furthermore, the life expectancy of non-Caucasians with Down syndrome has often been considerably less than for Caucasians with the syndrome. This may in part be due to such factors as access to, use of, or quality of health care (Day et al., 2005; Yang, Rasmussen, & Friedman, 2002).

The frequency of DAT in Down syndrome increases from about 8% to 25% in those between 35 and 40 years, to approximately 60% to 75% in those older than 60 years. In individuals with Down syndrome who have a mild-to-moderate level of disability, the average age of onset of dementia is approximately 52–55 years, but early signs of dementia may appear before the age of 50 in some (Janicki & Dalton, 2000; Prasher et al., 2007). Individuals with Down syndrome who have higher intellectual functioning tend to remain free of symptoms longer than those with lower intellectual functioning (Temple, Jozsvai, Konstantareas, & Hewitt, 2001). Caregivers must be alerted to this possibility and be knowledgeable about how to cope with it.

Factors Predisposing to Dementia of the Alzheimer's Type

Although DAT research is not as extensive as for Alzheimer's disease in the general population, studies of Down syndrome are helping not only to clarify what causes DAT but also to clarify the controversy about what causes Alzheimer's disease in the general population. Because people with Down syndrome carry an extra chromosome 21, and the gene for APP (which becomes degraded into amyloid-β) is located on the long arm of that chromosome, overproduction of APP is thought to be primarily responsible for DAT. Jiang et al. (2010) have shown that a small derivative of APP protein, and not the amyloid-β breakdown product of APP, is essential for induction of an abnormality found early in DAT and Alzheimer's disease called endosome dysfunction. (An endosome is a membrane-bound compartment inside the cell that aids transport of large molecules from the plasma membrane of the cell to the lysosome, i.e., garbage disposal unit, or vice versa.) A review of literature exploring the link between oxidative stress and neurodegeneration (Perluigi, Di Domenico, & Butterfield, 2014) hypothesized that trisomy 21 affects gene or protein expression, causing increased oxidative stress conditions

and impaired mitochondrial function. Percy and colleagues (1990) previously implicated excessive oxidative stress in DAT and noted that Alzheimer's disease manifestations in older people with Down syndrome were associated with changes in the red cell oxygen scavenging processes.

As in the general population, in Down syndrome, the APOE E2 allele is associated with longevity and the preservation of cognitive functioning (Tyrrell et al., 1998). However, in Down syndrome, the APOE E4 allele not only is associated with lower age of dementia in males, but it also has an independent and strong relation to early mortality even in people with Down syndrome who do not have dementia (Prasher et al., 2008). The link between oxidative stress and neurodegeneration is an area of ongoing research, and there is support for the presence of oxidative damage in the brains of individuals with Down syndrome. There is evidence that herpes simplex virus 1 infection may play a role in the development of DAT in Down syndrome, as may be the case in the general population (Cheon, Bajo, Gulesserian, Cairns, & Lubec, 2001). Finally, among females with Down syndrome, a correlation has been noted between early age of menopause and frequency of dementia and between the age of menopause and age of onset of dementia (Cosgrave, Tyrrell, McCarron, Gill, & Lawlor, 1999; Zigman & Lott, 2007). As in the general population, genetic variation also may contribute to DAT. For example, recent studies suggest that a number of variants of genes previously associated with Alzheimer's disease in the general population are also associated with DAT in Down syndrome. These genes include APOE, SORL1, RUNX1, BACE1, and ALDH18A1 (Patel et al., 2011, 2014). An association has been found with certain gene variants and age of onset of DAT in Down syndrome (Mok et al., 2014).

Diagnosis of Dementia of the Alzheimer's Type in Down Syndrome

The clinical diagnosis of DAT remains problematic in people with Down syndrome and other etiologies of intellectual and developmental disabilities. Clinicians still have difficulty in distinguishing symptoms of dementia from cognitive deficits resulting from the intellectual impairment. Because there is a wide variation in the degree of cognitive impairment among people with Down syndrome, some tests that are used in dementia screening are too easy for some or too difficult for others. Also, there are a number of medical conditions that can mask as DAT (see later discussion). Longitudinal neurological assessment is the best approach for diagnosing DAT in Down syndrome (also see later discussion).

When onset of dementia is suspected in a person with Down syndrome (as for people in the general population), it is vital to determine as early as possible if there is a treatable cause. Such causes in people with Down syndrome that can be effectively treated include early vitamin B_6, B_{12}, or folate deficiency; early hypothyroidism; and severe depression and anxiety states (see the Conditions That Can Mimic Dementia of the Alzheimer's Type subsection).

Early Signs of Dementia of the Alzheimer's Type

Early signs of possible DAT in people with Down syndrome who have relatively higher levels of functional ability may include changes in personality (e.g., uncharacteristic irritability, mood swings) and reduced verbal communication (Ball et al., 2006). Initial symptoms often involve memory loss, problems in learning new things, and changes in behavior. As the disease progresses, activities of daily living are further impaired. For example, performance at work may gradually deteriorate, capacity to follow an instruction may decline, ability to use a telephone or to write may dissipate, and loss of language skills (especially word-finding abilities) may occur. At a more advanced stage, seizures frequently develop. The seizures, including myoclonic ones (i.e., frequent small jerks of the body), often appear after 2 years of evidence of dementia but usually occur somewhat later in higher functioning individuals with Down syndrome. Mobility typically becomes limited, and there may be bowel and bladder incontinence. Hallucinations and delusions may also develop. In addition, weight loss is common in people with Down syndrome and DAT (Prasher et al., 2007).

For people with Down syndrome who have higher functioning abilities, early indicators of memory loss may be forgetting the location of commonly used objects such as a key, eye glasses, bus tickets, or a lunch bag. With lower functioning abilities and Down syndrome, the first indicators of possible DAT may be diminished social interaction, loss of interest in hobbies and previously enjoyed

activities, or loss of self-care skills. As the disease progresses, memory deficits become more prominent and signs of spatial disorientation appear. The affected person may get lost in familiar surroundings and become unable to travel independently on previously familiar routes. Supervisors in work situations may begin noticing poorer work performance than previously, with the need for increased supervision. Biological (diurnal) rhythms are sometimes disturbed, with frequent confusion between day and night. Motor functions slow down and gait disturbances (i.e., problems with walking) may appear. The ability to perform the sequence of previously mastered complex tasks, such as toileting, dressing, or setting the table, diminishes. Bladder or bowel incontinence may begin to develop. Individuals without a previous history of epilepsy may commence having seizures. A strong association between seizures and cognitive decline has been noted in this group of patients (Lott et al., 2012; Menéndez, 2005).

As the disease progresses further, affected individuals are unable to recall the names of, or even recognize, close relatives and friends. Ability to communicate awareness of recent life experiences diminishes. Symptoms differ in sequence and degree from one person to another, but some include loss of purposeful activity, quiet resignation, delusional behavior, visual and auditory hallucinations, and myoclonus. At the late stages of their dementia, all verbal abilities and the ability to walk are typically lost, although not in a predictable sequence. Assistance with washing, toileting, and eating is required. Death is frequently caused by infectious disease such as aspiration pneumonia, urinary tract infection, and infected bedsores; sometimes, it simply results from a loss of basic life functions such as the ability to swallow solid food and even liquids.

Conditions That Can Mimic Dementia of the Alzheimer's Type

There are various physical conditions that can diminish cognitive function in older people with Down syndrome, as is the case in the general population, and thus be mistaken for early evidence of Alzheimer's disease. Hypothyroidism, which affects about 40% of people with Down syndrome, may precipitate decline by causing weight gain, apathy, mental slowing, and diminished levels of energy. Depression related to grief from loss of friends or relatives, or changes in residence and support workers, may lead to withdrawal or loss of daily living skills and may be associated with the onset of incontinence, irritability, and insomnia.

Mental functions may deteriorate as a result of hearing loss and visual impairment. A large proportion of adults with Down syndrome (about half to three quarters) experience hearing loss, and approximately half develop cataracts. Impaired hearing and vision may lead to withdrawal, apathy, and reduced interest in one's environment, mimicking early symptoms of DAT. Degenerative changes in the upper part of the cervical spine and joint problems in the hip and knee may cause pain and impair functioning in daily living. Vitamin B_{12} or folate deficiency and infectious diseases (e.g., pneumonia) may cause weight loss, tiredness, and consequent decrease in activity levels. Excessive daytime sleepiness, chronic fatigue, and irritability can also result from sleep apnea, a disorder characterized by frequent, brief pauses in respiration while asleep. Prescribed drugs (e.g., seizure medication, tranquilizers) can interfere with cognitive functioning. Cardiac disease and diabetes may produce functional decline in the general population and may have similar effects in people with Down syndrome. It is important to identify all medical conditions that co-occur with deterioration of cognitive function in older people with Down syndrome (see Chapter 14), because with medical attention and treatment, cognitive functioning and skills of daily living often return to previous levels (Prasher et al., 2007).

Early Detection and Screening

A precursor to diagnosis is early detection and screening, usually by acting upon suspicions that some changes in function are becoming evident. Family members and provider personnel may employ formal screening devices to help capture key information about health and function, and that may help track diminishing capabilities over time. Most extant instruments in use for assessment can be used for capturing this information, although they are generally more practical for use with early diagnosis and often are restricted for use by clinicians as part of an assessment process.

One early detection and screening instrument in use in the United States and other countries was specifically developed to capture and record observable changes by people without specific clinical training. The National Task Group Early Detection Screen for Dementia (National Task Group on Intellectual Disabilities and Dementia Practices, 2013b) was developed to be used by nonprofessionals and permits the recording of a range of behavioral, functional, and health data that can be used for serial tracking and for engaging a clinician in a discussion that may result in a more detailed examination. Such screening can often obviate the need for more detailed examinations if the changes noted can be linked to environmental or other nondisease factors.

Differential Diagnosis of Dementia of the Alzheimer's Type

If referral for full assessment or diagnostic examination is warranted, then more precise methods are warranted. In the general population, dementia is diagnosed by comparing performance on cognitive tests to established standards (norms) for the person's age group. In Down syndrome, however, dementia is generally superimposed on already reduced cognitive functioning. Furthermore, there are significant individual differences in the abilities of people with Down syndrome who do not have dementia. Some have strengths in the verbal domain but weaknesses in visuospatial or motor abilities, and the opposite pattern occurs in other people.

As noted previously, other disorders can mask as dementia. Hence, people with Down syndrome suspected of developing DAT should undergo a multidisciplinary and longitudinal evaluation. (In longitudinal evaluation, each person serves as his or her own control.) Ideally, this should include a thorough physical examination that includes assessment of hearing and vision; screening for thyroid dysfunction and infectious diseases; blood work to identify vitamin B_{12} and folate deficiencies; psychiatric evaluation for depression or anxiety; and neuropsychological assessment to evaluate memory function, language functions, visuospatial abilities, and adaptive behavior skills. Interviews with various caregivers (e.g., relatives, supervisors at the workplace, support workers in group homes) are an essential part of a neuropsychological assessment, as such people are usually the first to notice signs of cognitive decline and to initiate referrals. Imaging or electroencephalography also may be considered in order to rule out disorders such as stroke or brain tumor (Prasher et al., 2007).

Neurological Tests to Aid with Detection of Dementia

Until the early 1980s, a limited number of neurological tests were available as aids for the diagnosis of dementia in people with developmental disabilities. Since about 1990, however, several neurological measures have been developed (see Prasher, 2008). For example, for nonverbal individuals who cannot be assessed with formal test instruments, the Adaptive Behaviour Dementia Questionnaire (Prasher, Farooq, & Holder, 2004) and/or the Gedye Dementia Scale for Down Syndrome developed by Gedye (1995) may be administered to caregivers to elicit information about changes in functioning. See the National Task Group on Intellectual Disabilities and Dementia Practices (2013a, p. 10) for a table of prevalent test instruments used for diagnosing dementia in people with intellectual and developmental disabilities in the United States, along with their strengths and weaknesses. In a large, international multisite trial of vitamin E in older people with Down syndrome, a brief praxis test was used as the primary outcome measure to monitor cognitive functions expressed as performances of simple, short sequences of voluntary movements every 6 months over a 35-month period (Sano, Aisen, Dalton, Andrews, & Tsai, 2005). This simple praxis test can be administered by almost any trained individual, including the primary care provider. Though the Mini Mental State Examination (MMSE) is in general use in conducting screening for people with dementia, it is generally too complex for individuals with Down syndrome to undertake. For example, although a study of cognitive assessment in individuals with Down syndrome using the MMSE found it was successfully completed for 43 out of 49 subjects with an average score of 18.4 (± 5.1) (Meiner et al., 2011), the MMSE is generally not appropriate for people with intellectual and developmental disabilities due to their variability of information retention and cognitive skills.

Longitudinal Evaluation

Because DAT occurs so early in people with Down syndrome, it is recommended that all adults be evaluated at least once in early adulthood (by age 25 years) to establish a record of baseline cognitive functioning. When DAT is suspected, such earlier baseline data are useful for comparison with current test data to ascertain the nature and magnitude of changes in various areas of functioning.

Such testing may be available in hospital clinics that specialize in Alzheimer's disease and related disorders as well as in some settings serving adults with Down syndrome and other intellectual or developmental disabilities. Alternatively, less formal methods can be employed, such as digitally recording select activities (e.g., movement and gait, speech and conversation, fine and gross motor activities, and informational awareness); these recordings can be repeated at intervals depending upon any indications of change. The recordings can then later be presented to a clinician so as to demonstrate the person's "personal best" functioning.

The case report of K.D. illustrates clinical manifestations and progression of DAT often observed in people with Down syndrome. Readers are also referred to the paper by Devenny et al. (2005) that follows the course of decline of a woman with Down syndrome and DAT over an 11-year period until her death at age 57. As stated by Devenny et al.,

> This case illustrates features of premature aging that are typically associated with Down syndrome, and the progressive changes in memory and cognition that are usually associated with DAT. Although the subject's cardiovascular condition and thyroid disorder were treated, they may have contributed to the decline of her memory. This case shows the difficulty in diagnosing dementia in an individual with mental retardation who suffered comorbid episodes of depression and psychosis. (p. 1)

Histopathological findings revealed upon brain autopsy are included in Devenny and colleagues' report. The study shows the invaluable contribution that detailed studies of only one individual can make to the field and the key role that caregivers can make by collaborating with researchers and by facilitating the donation of brain tissue from their loved ones to "brain banks."

DEMENTIA AND ALZHEIMER'S DISEASE IN PEOPLE WITH INTELLECTUAL AND DEVELOPMENTAL DISABILITIES OTHER THAN DOWN SYNDROME

People with intellectual and developmental disabilities other than Down syndrome also are living into middle age and beyond, and the development of psychiatric symptomatology and dementia in this adult population also is receiving increasing attention. In some respects, elucidation of these issues is more complex than is the case with Down

Case Report of K.D.

K.D. is a 59-year-old man with Down syndrome. He was referred for an assessment of cognitive functioning following a baseline evaluation 2 years prior. The referral was made by a group home staff member who had concerns about deterioration in K.D.'s behavior. K.D. was reported to have episodes of confusion, and staff questioned his ability to distinguish fantasy from reality. K.D. was originally seen for one neuropsychological assessment and then for another 6 months later. At that time, test results showed mild-to-moderate decline in verbal learning and memory for verbal material as well as deterioration in fine motor control in his hands. Cognitive deterioration was coupled with the onset of seizures, at which time he was prescribed seizure medication by a neurologist. Staff from the group home where K.D. lived made referrals to screen for thyroid functions as well as visual and hearing impairment. Blood tests were requested by his physician to test for possible vitamin B_{12} and folate deficiency. A psychiatric examination showed no overt signs of depression.

On examination, K.D. presented as a frail "elderly" man. He walked slowly with assistance. He was unable to follow test instructions. Consequently, formal testing could not be implemented. Instead, information was gathered from staff regarding K.D.'s current difficulties. Interviews with staff at K.D.'s residence revealed significant deterioration in his cognitive functioning and skills of adaptive behavior over the past 2 years. According to reports from residential support workers, K.D. frequently misplaced objects, forgot the names of people he knew, and partly lost track of familiar routines. Over the past 2 years, his speech had slowed and had become difficult to understand. K.D. got lost several times while alone in the community and, more recently, had experienced difficulty finding his own bedroom. He was no longer able to dress or bathe himself and required assistance eating. He was regularly incontinent of feces and urine if he was not prompted to use the toilet. There were incidents suggesting that he experienced hallucinations and paranoid ideas. At times, K.D. complained of imaginary people wanting to beat him up, putting him into a closet, or attacking him. Sometimes he got angry for no apparent reason, banging his head into, or kicking, the walls.

Staff expressed concerns about their capability to continue to provide supports due to the deterioration of K.D.'s functioning and began making arrangements to have him transferred to another setting more able to provide dementia-related care. In the meantime, supervision of K.D. at the group home was intensified and he was given assistance with bathing, eating, and walking. The safety of his current environment was assessed by an occupational therapist and modifications were made to prevent injury. K.D. was issued a MedicAlert identification bracelet and was registered at the Alzheimer's Society.

Sources: Prasher et al. (2007) and Jozsvai (2003).

syndrome because, unlike Down syndrome, other types of intellectual and developmental disabilities constitute a wide-ranging "mixed bag" of entities with diverse etiology and symptomatology. However, while bearing such considerations in mind, some notable findings (although not always consistent) with significant implications have been documented, aspects of which are referred to in the following subsections.

Prevalence

There have been discrepancies in the limited studies of the frequency with which dementia occurs in older adults with intellectual and developmental disabilities other than Down syndrome. In the Netherlands, Evenhuis (1997) noted that the age-related frequency (and natural history) of dementia in this group was comparable to that in the general population. In the United States, Janicki and Dalton (2000) and Zigman and Lott (2007) reported the rate of dementia in adults with intellectual and developmental disabilities older than 64 years to be equivalent to or lower than the rate that would be expected compared with general population rates. In the United Kingdom, Strydom, Livingston, King, and Hassiotis (2007) concluded that dementia in adults with intellectual and developmental disabilities was two to three times more common than in the general population. A subsequent study found the prevalence to be five times more common (Strydom, Chan, King, Hassiotis, & Livingston, 2013). Cooper and van der Speck (2009) reported that the prevalence of dementia in people with intellectual and developmental disabilities was fourfold higher in people older than age 64 as compared with the general population. Discrepant findings in these regards are not surprising in view of such factors as relatively small sample sizes from different sources, with variable etiologies (most unknown), intellectual levels, age distributions, disability definition inclusion factors, and dementia diagnostic criteria—all this in circumstances in which preceding cognitive, behavioral, and chronic physical health problems (e.g., sensory and motor impairments) can seriously hamper accurate diagnosis of dementia.

Assessment of Dementia in People with Intellectual and Developmental Disabilities

A variety of different tools are used for the assessment of dementia in intellectual and developmental disabilities (see the relevant earlier section in the chapter). Nevertheless, a universally agreed-upon approach or instrument is missing (Zeilinger, Stiehl, & Weber, 2013). Some of the instruments are better for early detection and screening and some are more functional with respect to assessment and diagnosis. In the studies referred to previously, there was some mention of a diagnosis of Alzheimer's disease in a number of people in the groups investigated, but the information available was not sufficiently extensive for firm generalizations. As outlined in Prasher et al. (2007), there have been reports (albeit scanty in number) of postmortem brain examinations focused on Alzheimer's disease neuropathology in groups of non-Down–syndrome adults with intellectual and developmental disabilities. In these studies, the range was in keeping with that in a number of comparably aged population groups of those who are intellectually typical and do not have dementia. However, from the retrospective clinical data available in each of the studies referred to, it was uncertain to what extent the neuropathology noted was associated with dementia. It can be anticipated that further exploration and clarification of these issues will lead to improved therapeutic, quality of life, and even preventive prospects for those actually or potentially affected. These considerations become increasingly important as people live longer.

Early Detection

Early identification and follow-up form the basis for dementia-related long-term care planning in the intellectual and developmental disabilities field, as for people with Down syndrome and in the general population. Even in the absence or suspicion of MCI or dementia, it is generally accepted practice to collect midlife baseline function data and then conduct periodic reassessments for surveillance purposes of at-risk adults. Assessments can also be beneficial to identifying and tracking comorbid medical conditions and in identifying residents at high risk of hospitalization or institutionalization. The leading reason for identifying people with Alzheimer's disease is because they are often hospitalized for falls from syncope (i.e., temporary loss of consciousness resulting from low blood pressure), ischemic heart disease, gastrointestinal disease, pneumonia, and delirium (Rudolph et al., 2010). Tracking complex medical issues is important in reducing nursing home referrals among adults with intellectual and developmental disabilities, as many adults in the latter stages of dementia also experience physical debilitation and coincident medical conditions (Janicki, 2011). Such periodic reassessments can help determine the degree of degradation of function and progressive decline and to identify existing strengths and targets for rehabilitation and service provision in their later years.

Virtually no published information exists about risk factors that predispose to or protect from dementia in people with intellectual and developmental disabilities who do not have Down syndrome. It is assumed that the risk factors are the same as those generally attributed to the general population. Approaches for the diagnosis of dementia in this group are the same as for those who have Down syndrome (see the earlier section).

MULTIDISCIPLINARY MANAGEMENT OF DEMENTIA

There is no cure for Alzheimer's disease. However, appropriate management of the disease in people with or without intellectual and developmental disabilities improves the quality of life of those affected and their caregivers. Such management involves a multidisciplinary approach combining medication, psychological therapies, environmental changes, and support for caregivers. Treatment may involve trying to minimize the disease process as such, dealing with specific symptoms, and assisting caregivers to cope in the best way possible. Clinical trials in the general population of proposed medication for Alzheimer's disease are common. Until recently, such trials usually excluded people with intellectual and developmental disabilities. However, such people are now more often the focus of attention in this regard. The final section in this chapter provides an overview of multidisciplinary approaches to management for people with dementia.

Pharmacological Approaches

A number of developments have taken place in the role of pharmacological agents to treat dementia. Development of preventive drugs is very much in its infancy.

Drugs for Treating Alzheimer's Disease

There is no drug that can cure or stop Alzheimer's disease. As of this writing in 2016, most approved drugs are intended to increase availability of neurotransmitters (especially acetylcholine) and have effects that are minor and only temporary. As of 2015, four medications have been approved by the U.S. Food and Drug Administration to treat Alzheimer's disease. Donepezil (Aricept), rivastigmine (Exelon), or galantamine (Razadyne) are used to treat mild to moderate Alzheimer's disease (donepezil can be used for severe Alzheimer's disease as well). Memantine (Namenda) is used to treat moderate to severe Alzheimer's disease. These drugs regulate neurotransmitters; the first three inhibit the breakdown of acetylcholine by cholinesterase, and the fourth inhibits the action of glutamate (see http://www.nia.nih.gov/alzheimers/topics/treatment). Unfortunately, these drugs do not change the underlying disease process; they help some people, but not others, for a limited time. These drugs also are being used to treat Alzheimer's disease in people with Down syndrome and other intellectual and developmental disabilities. However, Hanney and colleagues (2011) concluded that there is a striking absence of evidence about pharmacological treatment of cognitive impairment and dementia in people older than 40 years with Down syndrome. Potential new drugs continue to be tested. Despite disappointing results from two recent medication trials on memantine and antioxidants for dementia in Down syndrome, it is clear that randomized controlled trials are feasible in older people with intellectual and developmental disabilities—a group often excluded from trials (Sinai, Bohnen, & Strydom, 2012). For a list of clinical trials that are underway, refer to ClinicalTrials.gov (n.d.), a service provided by the U.S. National Institutes of Health.

Medications for Alleviating Distressing Symptoms That Occur in Alzheimer's Disease

Medications to alleviate specific distressing symptoms that can occur in Alzheimer's disease should be used cautiously, with regular review, and usually only on a temporary basis (Prasher et al., 2007). Such medications include the following:

- Hypnotics for night sedation

- Low-dose neuroleptics for aggression, restlessness, and paranoid behavior

- Antidepressants for low mood

- Anticonvulsants for seizures

- Antibiotics for infections

Nonpharmacological Approaches

Most nonpharmacological approaches use a combination of specialized housing and care practices that are deemed "dementia capable." (*Dementia capable* refers to services and supports that are tailored to the unique needs of people with dementia and their caregivers and in which workers who interact with people with dementia and their caregivers have appropriate training in identifying a possible dementia in people they serve, the symptoms of Alzheimer's disease and other dementias, the likely illness trajectory, and services needed.) Given the nature of dementia and its progression and complexities, caregivers and provider organizations may face a range of challenges in accommodating the needs of affected adults. In most instances, organizations will need to radically change their approaches to services in order to best address the onset and evolution of dementia symptoms for people with intellectual and developmental disabilities in a supportive and respectful manner. A proactive (as opposed to reactive) response to dementia care requires preparation, strategic planning, redesign, and integration of services. This also includes supports provided to families and other direct caregivers (Jokinen et al., 2013).

Community Living Recommendations for dementia-related care universally promote the notion that supports of adults with Down syndrome (and other intellectual and developmental disabilities) affected by dementia take place as much as possible in community settings. As noted by Jokinen et al. (2013), continued community living is viable and warranted both from human rights and best practices perspectives. With appropriate supports and supervision, most, if not all, adults with Down syndrome can continue to reside in some type of community living setting and enjoy an enhanced quality of life. In such circumstances, threats to an individual's continued stay within his or her current living situation need to be identified and planning for remediation initiated. Similarly, medical follow-up for treatment of dementia and surveillance and management of comorbid conditions should also be planned for and should occur in tandem with gradual increases in supports as dementia progresses. Given these considerations, care plans should be revised to emphasize 1) skill maintenance rather than skill acquisition; 2) continuation in community participation, including day programs; 3) provision of spiritual support and engagement; 4) standardization of routines so the person is able to manage his or her own day and living situation to the greatest extent possible (e.g., meal, activity, exercise, bathing, bed and wake times) and to aid overcoming resistance to care in later stages; 5) modification of demand situations in the home or program to ease aggravation of dementia symptoms and the experience of declining independence; 6) modifications in the home or day program and/or its routine so that the individual's community participation and quality of life is maintained; 7) proactive management of any related physical or mental health issues, including pain management, likely to affect or be affected by dementia symptoms; and 8) sensitivity to and identified resources for staff and family caregivers who may experience compassion fatigue, stress, and caregiver burden and grief.

Specialized Housing Movement (change of housing) may be indicated when staging is a consideration (i.e., when progression of dementia causes significant deficits in function and different approaches to care and potentially different staffing is called for). In such cases, an appraisal needs to be undertaken to demonstrate that 1) the current physical environment is not suitable, 2) the current housing resources provided (including staff or availability of family members) are not meeting needs, 3) others in the household are being adversely affected, and/or 4) the demands placed on the caregiver are beyond his or her capacities. Planning for a change in residence should consider challenges in each of these four areas and determine whether some additional environmental modification should be made. Further considerations include what additional resources may be necessary (and for how long), how changes in managing the individual could improve the lives of others, and whether alternative ways of coping or new supports for the caregivers may increase their ability to manage (Jokinen et al., 2013).

Reality Orientation and Reminiscence Activities Reality orientation and reminiscence activities are forms of nonpharmacological interventions for adults with dementia that may help delay intellectual impairment and maximize remaining abilities. Reality orientation tries to keep the affected person oriented in time and place as much as possible by having caregivers provide appropriate clues (e.g., "It's noon—time for the toilet," "It's 1 o'clock—time for your lunch"). The environment may be modified by the use of signs and colors (e.g., blue doors for toilets). Reminiscence therapy uses prompts (e.g., objects, photographs) to help people with dementia relive past memories and thereby enable them to remain stimulated and to adjust to recent changes, as well as to maximize the effectiveness of recalling memories to maintain cognitive faculties.

Behavior Modification Behavior modification can enhance maintenance of preexisting skills such as dressing, washing, eating, and communication. The technique can also reduce difficult behaviors, including restlessness, agitation, and aggression. Suitable behaviors are targeted and encouraged with positive consequences. Conversely, undesirable behaviors are discouraged by avoiding the situations that lead to these and excluding confrontation about them. It is important to establish and maintain routines, avoid confrontation, keep tasks simple, speak clearly in short sentences, and try to maintain the person's existing abilities. Support that emphasizes action (behavior) often works better than that based on verbal exchange (conversation and reasoning) for people with Alzheimer's disease, especially after the understanding of words deteriorates.

Environmental Changes for Safe Living

The home must be made safe to prevent serious accidents and adapted for progressive limitations in mobility.

Making the Home Safe Often, universal design features that can accommodate the needs of the home's residents can be put in place—for example, removing mobility barriers for walkers and wheelchairs, installing grab bars in bathing and toileting areas, widening of door openings, replacing doorknobs with handle-type levers, and installing chair lifts for stairs. Safety assessments are valuable in enabling measures to be put in place for preventing accidents in the kitchen, bathroom, stairs, and other areas. Such assessments should include looking for loose rugs that may promote slipping or tripping, furniture placements that are inconvenient or pose risk for falling or being hurt when bumped into, doors that open in awkward manners and may cause injuries or that may be missing at the top of stairs, and controls on water temperature setting to prevent scalding. Some simple, low-cost physical accommodations can be made that enhance safety in family homes or in group homes or supervised apartments. These modifications can include leveling walkways and eliminating clutter on steps, installing easily grasped and sturdy railings, providing for adequate lighting, locking cabinets holding cleaning and other nonfood materials, and minimizing clutter. Controlling wandering may be a challenge, depending upon the physical design of the home and its outdoor spaces. Wandering itself can be beneficial if it provides an outlet for exercise and movement—as long as the home is designed with indoor wandering paths and the outdoor areas are fenced or otherwise protective. Individuals who wander with the intent to go outside of the home may pose challenges for the caregivers. Most often, wandering can be controlled with the use of enclosed areas, door alarms, and safety gates. Also beneficial, in the event that the adult does wander off, are "wandering registries," MedicAlert identification bracelets, and other technologies that should be in place to locate adults who may be wanderers. Incontinence is a major contributor to burnout in caregivers, so advice should be readily available regarding incontinence management and the use of a waterproof mattress, commode, bedpan, or bed bottle (Alzheimer's Disease International, 2006).

Different Types of Housing Most intellectual disability advocacy organizations are committed to enabling aging associated problems to be addressed within the context of continued community living, including wanting to see dementia-capable care be the keystone of a package of supports provided in a noninstitutional setting (National Task Group on Intellectual Disabilities and Dementia Practices, 2012). Studies of family preferences for alternative care seem to support this notion, as most parents opt for some type of community care, mostly in small group homes (Janicki, Zendell, & DeHaven, 2010). Organizations have evolved two primary models for community-based housing, one following an "aging-in-place" model, wherein the affected adult gradually ages and receives daily stage-appropriate supports for dementia. This model requires a commitment from the housing provider to continue providing supports and aid, with end-of-life care when indicated. The other model, "in-place progression," generally follows a housing provider setting up a specialty home for "dementia-capable" care, with all residents affected by dementia. In some cases, further specialization occurs, with the housing provider providing specialty homes based on stage-associated care and supports (see Figure 49.3). Based on a number of factors (e.g., reimbursement rates, staff capabilities, home designs, funder regulatory restrictions), administrators of such small group homes are often supportive about allowing residents with dementia or Alzheimer's disease to remain living in the homes for as long as possible.

Health Promotion

Meaningful activity that promotes health, and that uses and strengthens remaining daily living skills and abilities or that prevents these qualities from deteriorating, should be encouraged. Such activities can provide a sense of accomplishment, improve mood, and increase overall physical conditioning. Exercise can be beneficial by serving as a means for other social, memory, and language stimulation activities. Local day programs specifically for people with dementia provide opportunities for such activities and reduce continuous pressure on caregivers. The involvement of volunteers in the life of people with all forms of dementia cannot be underestimated.

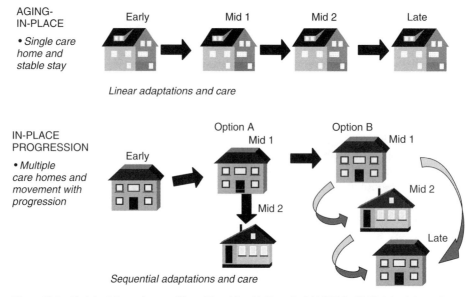

Figure 49.3.   Models of dementia care. (*Key:* mid = midlevel.) (From Janicki, M.P. [n.d.]. Models of dementia care; Reprinted by permission.) (Clip art copyright © istockphoto/A7880S.)

Support of Caregivers

In the United States, the National Task Group on Intellectual Disabilities and Dementia Practices (2012) has recognized the essential role of family caregivers in maintaining a place at home for adults with intellectual and developmental disabilities who are affected by dementia. Family caregivers of such adults have specialized needs and are challenged to continue to provide dementia care at home. There may also be multiple members of the family involved in various aspects of care or willing to assist even when they live at a distance. Oftentimes, families may be unaware of what resources are available and are confused by the requirements related to gaining access to services. Active outreach by and to families undertaking dementia care is critical to preparing them for what is to come and preventing social isolation. Talking with other families facing similar challenges in the decline of their relative is comforting and provides a sense of not "going it alone."

Support of caregivers of individuals with dementia, particularly long-standing caregivers who are family members, is essential. Such support includes emotional backing, information, advice, practical aids, and help with future planning. The many aspects of care, which vary as the disease progresses, require maintenance of the affected person's dignity, retaining a sense of humor and understanding, and making sure that the home is

safe. This includes encouraging those with the disease to themselves attend to such needs as dressing, washing, and eating. For example, if clothes are laid out in the order in which they are usually put on, and are easy to put on, distress can be minimized.

Caregivers and family members need guidance over time in coping with new negative emotions that can result from their experience with someone who has dementia. These emotions can involve feelings of loss, guilt, frustration, unrealistic hope, bitterness, sadness, and depression. It is important for others to recognize the challenges that caregivers and family members are going through, particularly as the behavior of people with dementia distressingly changes from previously familiar patterns.

Typically, support for primary caregivers is essential, in some cases including financial support. Generally, there is a need for caregivers and family members to learn more about the nature of Alzheimer's disease, its manifestations, and necessary practical changes to facilitate effective coping. Many national groups have assembled guides for caregivers that can be found on the Internet and used for a variety of situations (e.g., Alzheimer Society of Canada, 2015; Alzheimer's Association, 2015; Alzheimer's Disease International, 2006; National Institute on Aging, n.d. a, n.d. b; National Task Group on Intellectual Disabilities and Dementia Practices, 2012, 2012, 2013a). Caregiving help is almost always required, including practical in-house support from home-care workers and emotional backing from relatives, friends, and various professionals. An important beneficial source of guidance is presence of local support groups organized by disability agencies or Alzheimer's organizations. Joining such a group makes it possible to meet others who are facing similar issues with Alzheimer's disease or another form of dementia and enables sharing of information, feelings, and practical suggestions for coping and for helping a person with the disease to enjoy life as fully as possible. Such support groups for caregivers can be a useful vehicle for sharing information on dealing with stress, managing difficult situations or behaviors, and helping with strategizing for solutions to problems.

Services and Resources Needed by People with Dementia and Their Caregivers

Early detection of Alzheimer's disease and other dementias facilitates prompt attention by family and other caregivers to learn about the nature of the condition, to establish a support network, and to plan for the possibility of future alternative living arrangements. Services and other resources that are needed for people with dementia, whether with or without preceding intellectual and developmental disabilities, are listed in Table 49.6. The availability of such attention varies substantially, even among communities in the same country.

Some social services systems have implemented person-centered long-term planning to provide individualized services. This involves comprehensive examination of such issues as residential, financial, and legal planning requiring individual resolution. Planning for guardianship and residential changes benefits from an interdisciplinary approach, with the affected person's needs and desires taken into account. If still capable, the adult should be an active participant in such efforts. Personal care is an aspect of dementia care that is essential for a reasonable quality of life because people with dementia have complex medical and other needs. Supporting such people in small group-home settings or in their family residences as long as possible tends to respectfully enhance their dignity, even in difficult times (Kerr, 1997). Also, an effective support system is needed to assist those concerned with the emotionally draining process of dealing with terminal illness and death (e.g., Harvard Health Publications, 2014). Many provider organizations are responding to the growing number of clientele affected by

Table 49.6.   Needs of people with dementia and of their caregivers

Service	Education	Research
Differential diagnosis of dementia (to distinguish reversible and treatable forms from Alzheimer disease)	Brochures, guides, manuals, videos	Proposed therapeutic interventions
Counseling	Internet articles	Longitudinal studies of the development of dementia
Advocacy	Conferences, workshops, forums, and symposia	Donation of brain tissue for research
Case management and coordination	Courses and study programs	
Adult day care programs	Help lines	
Home care	Legal and financial assistance	
Home chores		
Home safety assessment by occupational therapists		
Delivered meals		
Respite care for temporary relief of caregivers		
Nursing assistance		
Long-term care facilities		
Wandering registries		
Support groups		

neuropathologies or frailty and are developing and maintaining small in-community group homes that are dementia-capable. Such homes are often structured along two primary models of care: aging in place or in-place progression (Janicki, 2011; Jokinen et al., 2013).

The aging-in-place approach considers the group home as the adult's home for the long term and, as such, commits to supporting the adult as the effects of dementia progress, much like long-term caring for any other chronic illness. Staff are oriented to understanding the nature of dementia and to the particulars of the specific dementia present (whether the dementia is attributable to Alzheimer's disease, vascular accident, or other brain neuropathologies—e.g., frontotemporal dementia or Lewy body dementia). In these disorders, the changes expected are stage dependent and the special surveillance and supports needed are dementia-specific. In most instances, such commitment includes end-of-life care and the introduction of palliative care and hospice.

The in-place progression approach is similar, with the exception that it usually applies to specialty homes for dementia care, wherein all residents have been diagnosed with or are suspected of having dementia. Such homes accommodate a small number of residents (usually from three to ten) and have staff who have been specifically trained in caring for people with dementia. In some situations, the providers operating such a home have moved to stage-dependent specialization, considering decline trajectories, to maintain homogeneity of residents and to maintain the best match between staff skills and care demands. This may involve some homes that primarily serve mid-stage dementia ambulatory residents and some homes that primarily serve late-stage dementia nonambulatory residents. Each model would have somewhat different physical features and designs and staff who are trained in providing different levels, intensities, and foci of care.

Gaining Access to Support Services and Community Resources

Even in the early stages of dementia, increased supervision of the affected person in his or her home is necessary, with consideration of various compensatory cognitive and environmental strategies to reduce the impact of the disease. Residential support staff are usually very cooperative in applying such strategies, but nursing home placement may be necessary if care requirements become too onerous.

Information about available services, community resources, and intervention strategies can be elicited from multiple sources, including Alzheimer's societies and family support groups, social service agencies that provide dementia screening, Alzheimer's disease and related disorder clinics, religious organizations, the Internet, and home care and safety agencies. Please also refer to this book's chapter on aging (Chapter 44).

Advocacy and Dementia

Among all of the older-age-associated conditions, dementia is the most insidious, as it affects and diminishes quality of life and robs affected individuals of their minds, capability to be independent, and often their dignity. The World Health Organization (WHO) and Alzheimer's Disease International, in their report, *Dementia: A Public Health Priority* (2012), noted that prevalence and incidence projections indicate that the number of people with dementia will continue to grow, particularly among the oldest adults. WHO has called for countries to adopt national plans that would address such diverse issues as encouraging research into the causes and eventual prevention of dementia, promoting the support of treatment strategies and managing supports for caregivers, setting up public education programs, and enhancing the capabilities of workers to care for and support adults affected by dementia. In most countries, such dementia plans are directed toward the general population and often omit mention of specific needs groups, such as people with lifelong disability who may be at higher risk of dementia. In the WHO and Alzheimer's Disease International report, special mention was made of the situation of people with intellectual and developmental disabilities, in particular those adults with Down syndrome who manifest high risk for Alzheimer's disease. In the United States, the national plan includes a focus on specific populations, including people with intellectual and developmental disabilities. A U.S. task group cited in the WHO and Alzheimer's Disease International report coalesced into a collective of interested people and organizations that are working toward ensuring that the needs and interests of adults with intellectual and developmental disabilities who are affected by Alzheimer's disease and related dementias—as well as their families and friends—are taken into account as part of the National Plan to Address Alzheimer's Disease (National Institute on Aging, 2012–2013). The National Task Group on Intellectual Disabilities and Dementia Practices is a voluntary-membership organization composed of families, association and organization representatives, clinicians, practitioners, academics, and others who contribute time and effort to its activities. Members represent a range of disciplines and educational backgrounds and serve on the task group as volunteers. Such a national effort can bring needed attention to the needs of adults with Down syndrome and ensure their inclusion in national efforts designed to aid people affected by Alzheimer's disease and related dementias (Janicki & Keller, 2015).

On a person-centered level, to help caregivers recognize and communicate symptoms of dementia in people with intellectual and developmental disabilities as well as find appropriate health care practitioners, the National Task Group prepared three sets of guidelines to help frame services: one focusing on community supports (Jokinen et al., 2013), one on advocacy for proper care related to their health needs (Bishop et al., 2015), and one for medical personnel when undertaking assessments (Moran, Rafii, Keller, Singh, & Janicki, 2013). For further details, see http://aadmd.org/ntg.

SUMMARY

Alzheimer's disease is the most common form of dementia. This disease is characterized by the presence of large quantities of amyloid plaques and neurofibrillary tangles in particular areas of the brain. The first clinical evidence of Alzheimer's disease tends to be memory loss, but other areas of intellectual functioning are progressively affected, leading to loss of self-care and social skills and to marked deterioration of physical health. The prevalence of Alzheimer's disease increases with increasing age in the general population and in people with intellectual and developmental disabilities. When older people begin to show signs of developing dementia, it is important that a differential diagnosis be undertaken promptly because there are various reversible causes of dementia.

DAT is more common (though not inevitable) in middle-age and older adults with Down syndrome than in similarly aged adults in the general population or in those with intellectual and developmental disabilities not due to Down syndrome. The association of DAT with Down syndrome is thought to be principally due to the trisomy 21 in Down syndrome, resulting in three copies of the APP gene instead of the normal two. People with Down syndrome are at risk of developing DAT at a much earlier age than is the case in the general population. Because these individuals are now living longer, more will be affected by this disorder than heretofore. The diagnosis of DAT in people with Down syndrome and other forms of intellectual and developmental disabilities is more difficult than in the general population because dementia must be distinguished from the previously existing cognitive impairment. Diagnosis should include a multidisciplinary assessment. A baseline assessment at about 25 years of age is an advantageous reference in identifying later changes in function. Suspicious manifestations should be thoroughly evaluated because there are many treatable medical conditions that can mask as Alzheimer's disease.

Dementia other than that in Down syndrome has not been as extensively studied in people with intellectual and developmental disabilities, although it may be at least as prevalent as in the general population. New drugs are now available to slow down the Alzheimer's disease process, but they are not curative. Despite absence of a cure for Alzheimer's disease, diagnosing and managing it effectively improves the quality of life of those who are affected and of their caregivers. Family and caregiver support is an essential part of care management. People with dementia and their caregivers play a key role in better understanding dementia by collaborating with researchers and donating brain tissue to brain banks.

FOR FURTHER THOUGHT AND DISCUSSION

1. To what degree do people with intellectual and developmental disabilities experience cognitive and behavioral skill losses as they get older?

2. If you were a caregiver of a person who has Down syndrome and is in his or her early 40s, what would you need to know about Alzheimer's disease and related dementias?

3. If you notice evidence of early signs of cognitive decline in a person under your care, what steps should you take to gather more information and pursue the matter further?

4. What might be the key things you should discuss with a professional who may be examining a

person with Down syndrome suspected of having dementia?

5. Discuss the implications of professionals and family members lacking an understanding of the possible causes and characteristics of Alzheimer's disease and other causes of dementia.

6. Should drug therapies targeting dementia in the general population be used for people with intellectual and developmental disabilities? Why or why not?

7. How can caregiving skills be modified with respect to attending to relatives with Alzheimer's disease, including changes in daily routines, in communication, and in attitude?

8. How might you introduce a dementia-related early detection and screening effort in your community?

9. What services are available in your area to help support people with Alzheimer's disease and related dementias and their families?

10. What might be some ways that you might advocate for more public awareness of the needs of families providing primary care at home for adults with intellectual or developmental disability and dementia?

REFERENCES

Alzheimer, A. (1907). Über eine eigenartige Erkrankung der Hirnrinde. *Allgemeine Zeitschrift für Psychiatrie und Psychisch-Gerichtliche Medizin, Berlin, 64*,146–148.

Alzheimer Society of Canada. (2015). *Home page.* Retrieved from http://www.alzheimer.ca/en

Alzheimer's Association. (2015). *New diagnostic criteria and guidelines for Alzheimer's disease for the first time in 27 years.* Retrieved from http://www.alz.org/documents _custom/Alz_Assoc_diag_criteria_guidelines_press _release_041911.pdf

Alzheimer's Disease International. (2006). *Help for caregivers.* Retrieved from https://www.alz.co.uk/adi/pdf /helpforcaregivers.pdf

Arab, L., & Sabbagh, M.N. (2010). Are certain lifestyle habits associated with lower Alzheimer's disease risk? *Journal of Alzheimer's Disease, 20*(3), 785–794.

Armstrong, R.A. (2013). What causes Alzheimer's disease? *Folia Neuropathologica, 51*(30), 169–188.

Ayton, S., Lei, P., & Bush, A.I. (2015). Biometals and their therapeutic implications in Alzheimer's disease. *Neurotherapeutics, 12*(1), 109–120.

Ball, S.L., Holland, A.J., Hon, J., Huppert, F.A., Treppner, P., & Watson, P.C. (2006). Personality and behaviour changes mark the early stages of Alzheimer's disease in adults with Down's syndrome: Findings from a prospective population-based study. *International Journal of Geriatric Psychiatry, 21*(7), 661–673.

Barber, R.C. (2012). The genetics of Alzheimer's disease. *Scientifica, 2012,* Article ID 246210, 14 pages. Retrieved from http://dx.doi.org/10.6064/2012/246210

Bhattacharjee, S., Zhao, Y., Hill, J.M., Percy, M.E., & Lukiw, W.J. (2014). Aluminum and its potential contribution to Alzheimer's disease (AD). *Frontiers in Aging Neuroscience, 6,* 62. doi:10.3389/fnagi.2014.00062

Bird, T. (2015, September 24). Alzheimer disease overview. In R.A. Pagon, M.P. Adam, H.H. Ardinger, et al. (Eds.), *GeneReviews* [Internet]. Seattle: University of Washington, Seattle. Retrieved from http://www.ncbi .nlm.nih.gov/books/NBK1161/

Bishop, K.M., Hogan, M., Janicki, M.P., Keller, S.M., Lucchino, R., Mughal, D.T.,…Health Planning Work Group of the National Task Group on Intellectual Disabilities and Dementia Practices. (2015). Guidelines for dementia-related health advocacy for adults with intellectual disability and dementia: National Task Group on Intellectual Disabilities and Dementia Practices. *Intellectual and Developmental Disabilities, 53*(1), 2–29.

Blondell, S.J., Hammersley-Mather, R., & Veerman, J.L. (2014). Does physical activity prevent cognitive decline and dementia? A systematic review and meta-analysis of longitudinal studies. *BioMedCentral Public Health, 27*(14), 510. doi:10.1186/1471-2458-14-510

Cheon, M.S., Bajo, M., Gulesserian, T., Cairns, N., & Lubec, G. (2001). Evidence for the relation of herpes simplex virus type 1 to Down syndrome and Alzheimer's disease. *Electrophoresis, 22,* 445–448.

ClinicalTrials.gov. (n.d.). *Guidelines for registering with ClinicalTrials.gov.* Retrieved from https://clinicaltrials .gov/

Cooper, S.A., & van der Speck, R. (2009). Epidemiology of mental ill health in adults with intellectual disabilities. *Current Opinion in Psychiatry, 22*(5), 431–436.

Cosgrave, M.P., Tyrrell, J., McCarron, M., Gill, M., & Lawlor, B.A. (1999). Age at onset of dementia and age of menopause in women with Down's syndrome. *Journal of Intellectual Disabilities Research, 43*(Pt. 6), 461–465.

Daulatzai, M.A. (2013). Neurotoxic saboteurs: Straws that break the hippo's (hippocampus) back drive cognitive impairment and Alzheimer's disease. *Neurotoxicity Research, 24*(3), 407–459.

Daviglus, M.L., Plassman, B.L., Pirzada, A., Bell, C.C., Bowen, P.E., Burke, J.R.,…Williams, J.W., Jr. (2011). Risk factors and preventive interventions for Alzheimer disease: State of the science. *Archives of Neurology, 68*(9), 1185–1190.

Day, S.M., Strauss, D.J., Shavelle, R.M., & Reynolds, R.J. (2005). Mortality and causes of death in persons with Down syndrome in California. *Developmental Medicine and Child Neurology, 47*(3), 171–176.

de la Monte, S.M. (2012). Contributions of brain insulin resistance and deficiency in amyloid-related neurodegeneration in Alzheimer's disease. *Drugs, 72*(1), 49–66.

de la Monte, S.M., & Wands, J.R. (2008). Alzheimer's disease is type 3 diabetes—evidence reviewed. *Journal of Diabetes Science and Technology, 2*(6), 1101–1113.

Devenny, D.A., Wegiel, J., Schupf, N., Jenkins, E., Zigman, W., Krinsky-McHale, S.J., & Silverman, W.P. (2005, April 6). Dementia of the Alzheimer's type and accelerated aging in Down syndrome [online publication]. *Science of Aging Knowledge Environment, 14,* dn1. doi:10.1126/sageke.2005.14.dn1

Esbensen, A.J. (2010). Health conditions associated with aging and end of life of adults with Down syndrome. *International Review of Research in Mental Retardation, 39*(C), 107–126.

Evenhuis, H.M. (1997). The natural history of dementia in ageing people with intellectual disability. *Journal of Intellectual Disability Research, 41,* 92–96.

Fong, T.G., Davis, D., Growdon, M.E., Albuquerque, A., & Inouye, S.K. (2015). The interface between delirium and dementia in elderly adults. *Lancet Neurology, 14*(8), 823–832.

Fraser, J., & Mitchell, A. (1876). Kalmuc idiocy: Report of a case with autopsy with notes on 62 cases. *Journal of Mental Science, 22,* 161–162, 169–179.

Geda, Y.E. (2012). Mild cognitive impairment in older adults. *Current Psychiatry Reports, 14*(4), 320–327.

Gedye, A. (1995). *Gedye Dementia Scale for Down Syndrome.* Vancouver, Canada: Gedye Research & Consulting. Retrieved from http://www.gedye.ca/

Glasson, E.J., Sullivan, S.G., Hussain, R., Petterson, B.A., Montgomery, P.D., & Bittles, A.H. (2003). Comparative survival advantage of males with Down syndrome. *American Journal of Human Biology, 15,* 192–195.

Hampel, H., & Lista, S. (2013). Have we learnt all we need to know from genetic studies: Is genetics over in Alzheimer's disease? *Alzheimer's Research and Therapy, 5*(2), 11. doi:10.1186/alzrt165

Hanney, M., Prasher, V., Williams, N., Jones, E.L., Aarsland, D., Corbett, A.,...Ballard, C. (2011). Memantine for dementia in adults older than 40 years with Down's syndrome (MEADOWS): A randomised, double-blind, placebo-controlled trial. *The Lancet, 379*(9815), 528–536.

Harvard Health Publications, Harvard Medical School. (2014). *Coping with grief and loss.* Boston, MA: Author.

Hill, J.M., & Lukiw, W.J. (2015). Microbial-generated amyloids and Alzheimer's disease (AD). *Frontiers in Aging Neuroscience, 7,* 9. doi:10.3389/fnagi.2015.00009

Itzhaki, R.F. (2014). Herpes simplex virus type 1 and Alzheimer's disease: Increasing evidence for a major role of the virus. *Frontiers in Aging Neuroscience, 6,* 202. doi:10.3389/fnagi.2014.00202

Janicki, M.P. (2011). Quality outcomes in group home dementia care for adults with intellectual disabilities. *Journal of Intellectual Disability Research, 53*(8), 763–766.

Janicki, M.P., & Dalton, A.J. (2000). Prevalence of dementia and impact on intellectual disability services. *Mental Retardation, 38,* 277–289.

Janicki, M.P., Dalton, A.J., Henderson, C.M., & Davidson, P.W. (1999). Mortality and morbidity among older adults with intellectual disability: Health services considerations. *Disability and Rehabilitation, 21,* 284–294.

Janicki, M.P., & Keller, S.M. (2015). Why do we need national guidelines for adults with intellectual disability and dementia? *Alzheimer's and Dementia: Diagnosis, Assessment and Disease Monitoring, 1*(3), 325–327. Retrieved from http://www.journals.elsevier.com/alzheimers-and-dementia-diagnosis-assessment-and-disease-monitoring/recent-articles/

Janicki, M.P., Zendell, A., & DeHaven, K. (2010). Coping with dementia and older families of adults with Down syndrome. *Dementia, 9*(3), 391–407.

Jervis, G.A. (1948). Early senile dementia mongoloid idiocy. *American Journal of Psychiatry, 105,* 102–106.

Jiang, Y., Mullaney, K.A., Peterhoff, C.M., Che, S., Schmidt, S.D., Boyer-Boiteau, A.,...Nixon, R.A. (2010). Alzheimer's-related endosome dysfunction in Down syndrome is Abeta-independent but requires APP and is reversed by BACE-1 inhibition. *Proceedings of the National Academy of Sciences U.S.A., 107*(4), 1630–1635.

Jokinen, J., Janicki, M.P., Keller, S.M., McCallion, P., Force, L.T., & National Task Group on Intellectual Disabilities and Dementia Practices. (2013). Guidelines for structuring community care and supports for people with intellectual disabilities affected by dementia. *Journal of Policy and Practice in Intellectual Disabilities, 10*(1), 1–28.

Jones, L., Holmans, P., & International Genomics of Alzheimer's Project. (2013). The genetics of lipid metabolism in Alzheimer's disease susceptibility. *Alzheimer's and Dementia, 9*(4 Suppl.), 121. doi:http://dx.doi.org/10.1016/j.jalz.2013.04.033

Karch, C.M., Cruchaga, C., & Goate, A.M. (2014). Alzheimer's disease genetics: From the bench to the clinic. *Neuron, 83*(1), 11–26.

Kerr, D. (1997) *Down's syndrome and dementia: Practitioner's guide.* Birmingham, United Kingdom: Venture Press.

Khachaturian, Z.S. (1985). Diagnosis of Alzheimer's disease. *Archives of Neurology, 42,* 1097–1104.

Littlejohns, T.J., Henley, W.E., Lang, I.A., Annweiler, C., Beauchet, O., Chaves, P.H.,...Llewellyn, D.J. (2014). Vitamin D and the risk of dementia and Alzheimer disease. *Neurology, 83*(10), 920–928.

Lott, I.T., Doran, E., Nguyen, V.Q., Tournay, A., Movsesyan, N., & Gillen D.L. (2012). Down syndrome and dementia: Seizures and cognitive decline. *Journal of Alzheimer's Disease, 29*(1), 177–185.

Madhusudan, A., Doehner, J., Breu, K., Riether, C., Schedlowski, M., & Knuesel, I. (2011). A prenatal immune challenge provides a key impetus for wild-type mice to undergo accelerated aging and develop AD-like neuropathology. *Neurodegenerative Diseases, 8,* 1660–2854.

Maki, P.M. (2013). Sex differences in Alzheimer's disease. *Menopause, 20*(12), 1313–1314.

Mann, D.M., Royston, M.C., & Ravindra, C.R. (1990). Some morphometric observations on the brains of patients with Down's syndrome: Their relationship to age and dementia. *Journal of the Neurological Sciences, 99*(2–3), 153–164.

McKhann, G., Drachman, D., Folstein, M., Katzman, R., Price, D., & Stadlan, E.M. (1984). Clinical diagnosis of Alzheimer's disease: Report of the NINCDS-ADRDA Work Group under the auspices of Department of Health and Human Services Task Force on Alzheimer's disease. *Neurology, 34,* 939–944.

Meiner, Z., Raban, O., Schickler, E.S., Kerem, E., Tenenbaum, A., & Newman, J.P. (2011). Cognitive assessment of adults with Down syndrome. *Neurodegenerative Diseases, 8*(Suppl. 1), AD/PD Abstracts. Retrieved from http://www.karger.com/ProdukteDB/miscArchiv/NDD_2011_008_s_1/AbstractCD/pdf/563.pdf

Menéndez, M. (2005). Down syndrome, Alzheimer's disease and seizures. *Brain Development, 27*(4), 246–252.

Mok, K.Y., Jones, E.L., Hanney, M., Harold, D., Sims, R., Williams, J.,...Hardy, J. (2014). Polymorphisms in BACE2 may affect the age of onset Alzheimer's dementia in Down syndrome. *Neurobiology of Aging, 35*(6), 1513 (e1–e5). doi:10.1016/j.neurobiolaging.2013.12.022

Mondragón-Rodríguez, S., Basurto-Islas, G., Lee, H.G., Perry, G., Zhu, X., Castellani, R.J., & Smith, M.A. (2010). Causes versus effects: The increasing complexities of Alzheimer's disease pathogenesis. *Expert Review of Neurotherapeutics, 10*(5), 683–691.

Moran, J.A., Rafii, M.S., Keller, S.M., Singh, B.K., & Janicki, M.P. (2013). The National Task Group on Intellectual Disabilities and Dementia Practices consensus recommendations for the evaluation and management of dementia in adults with intellectual disabilities. *Mayo Clinic Proceedings, 88*(8), 831–840.

Mowszowski, L., Batchelor, J., & Naismith, S.L. (2010). Early intervention for cognitive decline: Can cognitive training be used as a selective prevention technique? *International Psychogeriatrics, 22*(4), 537–548.

Mutter, J., Curth, A., Naumann, J., Deth, R., & Walach, H. (2010). Does inorganic mercury play a role in Alzheimer's disease? A systematic review and an integrated molecular mechanism. *Journal of Alzheimer's Disease, 22*(2), 357–374.

National Institute on Aging. (n.d. a). *Alzheimer's diagnostic guidelines.* Retrieved from http://www.nia.nih.gov/research/dn/alzheimers-diagnostic-guidelines

National Institute on Aging. (n.d. b). *Alzheimer's disease: Unraveling the mystery.* Retrieved from https://www.nia.nih.gov/alzheimers/publication/part-2-what-happens-brain-ad/hallmarks-ad

National Institute on Aging. (2012–2013). *The national plan to address Alzheimer's disease.* Retrieved from https://www.nia.nih.gov/alzheimers/publication/2012-2013-alzheimers-disease-progress-report/national-plan-address-alzheimers

National Task Group on Intellectual Disabilities and Dementia Practices. (2012). *"My thinker's not working": A national strategy for enabling adults with intellectual disabilities affected by dementia to remain in their community and receive quality supports.* Retrieved from www.aadmd.org/ntg/thinker

National Task Group on Intellectual Disabilities and Dementia Practices. (2013a). *Guidelines for structuring community care and supports for people with intellectual disabilities affected by dementia.* Retrieved from http://aadmd.org/sites/default/files/NTG-communitycareguidelines-Final.pdf

National Task Group on Intellectual Disabilities and Dementia Practices. (2013b). *National Task Group Early Detection Screen for Dementia (NTG-EDSD).* Retrieved from http://aadmd.org/sites/default/files/NTG-EDSD-Final.pdf

Norton, S., Matthews, F.E., Barnes, D.E., Yaffe, K., & Brayne, C. (2014). Potential for primary prevention of Alzheimer's disease: An analysis of population-based data. *Lancet Neurology, 13*(8), 788–794.

Öhman, H., Savikko, N., Strandberg, T.E., & Pitkälä, K.H. (2014). Effect of physical exercise on cognitive performance in older adults with mild cognitive impairment or dementia: A systematic review. *Dementia and Geriatric Cognitive Disorders, 38*(5–6), 347–365.

Patel, A., Rees, S.D., Kelly, M.A., Bain, S.C., Barnett, A.H., Prasher, A.,...Prasher, V.P. (2014). Genetic variants conferring susceptibility to Alzheimer's disease in the general population: Do they also predispose to dementia in Down's syndrome? *BMC Research Notes, 7,* 42. doi:10.1186/1756-0500-7-42

Patel, A., Rees, S.D., Kelly, M.A., Bain, S.C., Barnett, A.H., Thalitaya, D., & Prasher, V.P. (2011). Association of variants within APOE, SORL1, RUNX1, BACE1 and ALDH18A1 with dementia in Alzheimer's disease in subjects with Down syndrome. *Neuroscience Letters, 487*(2), 144–148.

Percy, M.E., Dalton, A.J., Markovic, V.D., McLachlan, D.R., Hummel, J.T., Rusk, A.C., & Andrews, D.F. (1990). Red cell superoxide dismutase, glutathione peroxidase and catalase in Down syndrome patients with and without manifestations of Alzheimer disease. *American Journal of Medical Genetics, 35*(4), 459–467.

Percy, M.E., Kruck, T.P., Pogue, A.I., & Lukiw, W.J. (2011). Towards the prevention of potential aluminum toxic effects and an effective treatment for Alzheimer's disease. *Journal of Inorganic Biochemistry, 105*(11), 1505–1512.

Perluigi, M., Di Domenico, F., & Butterfield, D.A. (2014). Unraveling the complexity of neurodegeneration in brains of subjects with Down syndrome: Insights from proteomics. *Proteomics—Clinical Applications, 8*(1–2), 73–85.

Prasher, V.P. (Ed.). (2008). *Neuropsychological assessments of dementia in Down syndrome and intellectual disabilities.* New York, NY: Springer.

Prasher, V., Farooq, A., & Holder, R. (2004). The Adaptive Behaviour Dementia Questionnaire (ABDQ): Screening questionnaire for dementia in Alzheimer's disease in adults with Down syndrome. *Research in Developmental Disabilities, 25*(4), 385–397.

Prasher, V., Percy, M., Jozsvai, E., Lovering, J.S., & Berg, J.M. (2007). Implications of Alzheimer's disease for people with Down syndrome and other intellectual disabilities. In I. Brown & M. Percy (Eds.), *A comprehensive guide to intellectual and developmental disabilities* (pp. 681–700). Baltimore, MD: Paul H. Brookes Publishing Co.

Prasher, V.P., Sajith, S.G., Rees, S.D., Patel, A., Tewari, S., Schupf, N., & Zigman, W.B. (2008). Significant effect of APOE epsilon 4 genotype on the risk of dementia in Alzheimer's disease and mortality in persons with Down syndrome. *International Journal of Geriatric Psychiatry, 23*(11), 1134–1140.

Reichman, W.E., Fiocco, A.J., & Rose, N.S. (2010). Exercising the brain to avoid cognitive decline. Examining the evidence. *Aging Health, 6*(5), 565–584.

Robinson, J.L., Geser, F., Corrada, M.M., Berlau, D.J., Arnold, S.E., Lee, V.M.-Y.,...Trojanowski, J.Q. (2011). Neocortical and hippocampal amyloid-beta and tau measures associate with dementia in the oldest-old. *Brain, 134*(Pt. 12), 3705–3712.

Rudolph, J.L., Zanin, N.M., Jones, R.N., Marcantonio, E.R., Fong, T.G., Yang, F.M.,...Inouye, S.K. (2010). Hospitalization in community-dwelling persons with

Alzheimer's disease: Frequency and causes. *Journal of the American Geriatric Society, 58*(8), 1542–1548.

Sano, M., Aisen, P., Dalton, A.J., Andrews, H.F., & Tsai, W.-Y. (2005). Assessment of aging individuals with Down syndrome in clinical trials: Results of baseline measures. *Journal of Policy and Practice in Intellectual Disabilities, 2*(2), 126–138.

Schupf, N., Zigman, W., Kapell, D., Lee, J.H., Kline, J., & Levin, D. (1997). Early menopause in women with Down's syndrome. *Journal of Intellectual Disability Research, 41*(3), 201–283.

Sinai, A., Bohnen, I., & Strydom, A. (2012). Older adults with intellectual disability. *Current Opinion in Psychiatry, 25*(5), 359–364.

Soscia, S.J., Kirby, J.E., Washicosky, K.J., Tucker, S.M., Ingelsson, M., Hyman, B.,...Moir, R.D. (2010). The Alzheimer's disease-associated amyloid beta-protein is an antimicrobial peptide. *PLOS One, 5*(3), e9505. doi:10.1371/journal.pone.0009505

Strauss, D., & Eyman, R.K. (1996). Mortality of people with mental retardation in California with and without Down syndrome, 1986–1991. *American Journal on Mental Retardation, 100*(6), 643–653.

Struwe, F. (1929). Histopathologische Untersuchungen über Entstehung und Wesen der senilen Plaques [Histopathological studies on the origin and nature of senile plaques]. *Zeitschrift für die gesamte Neurologie und Psychiatrie, 122,* 291–307.

Strydom, A., Chan, T., King, M., Hassiotis, A., & Livingston, G. (2013). Incidence of dementia in older adults with intellectual disabilities. *Research in Developmental Disabilities, 34*(6), 1881–1885.

Strydom, A., Livingston, G., King, M., & Hassiotis, A. (2007). Prevalence of dementia in intellectual disability using different diagnostic criteria. *British Journal of Psychiatry, 191,* 150–157.

Temple, V., Jozsvai, E., Konstantareas, M.M., & Hewitt, T.A. (2001). Alzheimer dementia in Down syndrome: The relevance of cognitive ability. *Journal of Intellectual Disability Research, 45,* 47–55.

Thase, M.E. (1982). Longevity and mortality in Down's syndrome. *Journal of Mental Deficiency Research, 16,* 177–192.

Thies, W., & Bleiler, L. (2012). 2012 Alzheimer's disease facts and figures. *Alzheimer's and Dementia, 8*(2), 131–168.

Tyrrell, J., Cosgrave, M., Hawi, Z., McPherson, J., O'Brien, C., McCalvert, J.,...Gill, M. (1998). A protective effect of apolipoprotein E e2 allele on dementia in Down's syndrome. *Biological Psychiatry, 43,* 397–400.

Walton, J.R., & Wang, M.X. (2009). APP expression, distribution and accumulation are altered by aluminum in a rodent model for Alzheimer's disease. *Journal of Inorganic Biochemistry, 103*(11), 1548–1554.

Wherrett, J.R. (1999). Neurological aspects. In M.P. Janicki & A.J. Dalton (Eds.), *Dementia, aging and intellectual disabilities: A handbook* (pp. 90–102). Philadelphia, PA: Taylor & Francis.

Wilcock, G.K., & Esiri, M.M. (1982). Plaques, tangles and dementia: A quantitative study. *Journal of the Neurological Sciences, 56,* 343–356.

Wiseman, F.K., Al-Janabi, T., Hardy, J., Karmiloff-Smith, A., Nizetic, D., Tybulewicz, V.L.,...Strydom, A. (2015). A genetic cause of Alzheimer disease: Mechanistic insights from Down syndrome. *Nature Reviews Neuroscience, 16,* 564–574. doi:10.1038/nrn3983

World Health Organization & Alzheimer's Disease International. (2012). *Dementia: A public health priority.* Retrieved from http://www.who.int/mental_health/publications/dementia_report_2012/en/

Yang, Q., Rasmussen, S.A., & Friedman, J.M. (2002). Mortality associated with Down's syndrome in the USA from 1983 to 1997: A population-based study. *The Lancet, 359,* 1019–1025.

Zeilinger, E.L., Stiehl, K.A.M., & Weber, G. (2013). A systematic review on assessment instruments for dementia in persons with intellectual disabilities. *Research in Developmental Disabilities, 34*(11), 3962–3977.

Zigman, W.B., & Lott, I.T. (2007). Alzheimer's disease in Down syndrome: Neurobiology and risk. *Mental Retardation and Developmental Disabilities Research Reviews, 13*(3), 237–246.

VII

The Future

50

Future Trends and Advances in Intellectual and Developmental Disabilities

Michael L. Wehmeyer and Karrie A. Shogren

WHAT YOU WILL LEARN

- The importance of strengths-based approaches to disability to improve the lives of people with intellectual and developmental disabilities
- The rising prominence of the supports model to improve the lives of people with intellectual and developmental disabilities
- The importance of the community in the lives of people with disabilities and their families
- The importance of technology to support people in their communities

This book has covered a lot of territory, from an exploration of the history and meaning of intellectual and developmental disabilities through legal, medical, intervention and supports, and life span issues affecting the lives of people with intellectual and developmental disabilities. Many of the book's chapters have discussed both current and future trends in their respective areas. In closing this text, it seems appropriate to turn the lens toward those trends and advances in the field that, in the authors' estimation, have the most likelihood to influence the field of intellectual and developmental disabilities, as well as the lives of people with intellectual and developmental disabilities, as the 21st century continues.

THE DECLINING IMPORTANCE OF PATHOLOGY

Chapter 1 discussed the various meanings of *intellectual disability*; personal, public, critical, and definitional. We mentioned that intellectual disability is a social construct, and we want to begin the current chapter discussion by reminding readers of that fact. This is not a new idea, as is evident from noted Yale psychologist Seymour Sarason's comment from 1985: "[Mental retardation] is never a thing or a characteristic of an individual, but rather a social invention stemming from time-bound societal values and ideology that makes diagnosis and management seem both necessary and socially desirable" (p. 233).

Here we parse some of the meanings of that quote: Intellectual disability, as the state of functioning is now termed, is not a thing or a characteristic of a person but a social invention that makes diagnosis and management seem both necessary and socially desirable. First, intellectual disability is not a thing. In the 9th edition of *Mental Retardation: Definition, Classification, and Systems of Supports*, the American Association on Intellectual and Developmental Disabilities (AAIDD; then named the American Association on Mental Retardation) stated this same fact most clearly:

[Mental retardation] is not something you have, like blue eyes or a bad heart. Nor is it something you are, like being short or thin. It is not a medical disorder, although it may be coded in a medical classification of diseases....Nor is it a mental disorder, although it may be coded in a classification of psychiatric disorders....Mental retardation refers to a particular state of functioning.... (Luckasson et al., 1992, p. 9)

Intellectual disability is not a thing. It is not something one has or is. It is a state of functioning. Just what is meant by *functioning*? As we discussed in Chapter 1, the *International Classification of Functioning, Disability and Health (ICF)* (World Health Organization, 2001) defines *functioning* as an umbrella term for all life activities of an individual that encompasses the areas of body structures (i.e., anatomical parts of the body) and functions (i.e., physiological and psychological functions of body systems), personal activities (i.e., the execution of tasks or actions), and participation (i.e., involvement in a life situation).

So, human functioning involves all life activities of a person, including body system and functions, personal activities, and participation in life situations. Problems or limitations in functioning are labeled a disability. Disability can result from any problem in one or more of the three dimensions of human functioning: Problems in body structures and functions are referred to as impairments; problems in personal activities are referred to as activity limitations; and problems in participation are referred to as participation restrictions. The ICF situates these impairments, activity limitations, and participation restrictions within the interactions among health conditions, environmental factors, and personal factors.

So, does this shift from conceptualizing disability as a disease or disorder to a state of functioning matter? It does, in several ways. First, the ICF (and subsequent definitional frameworks, such as the AAIDD model; Schalock et al., 2010) positions intellectual disability within the context of typical human functioning, not separate or apart from it. Under historic disease or disorder models, the "problem" was viewed as being the person him- or herself, and people (perhaps unavoidably) came to be seen as different and, inevitably, were treated differently (and inequitably; reread Chapter 2 to see how). Second, these understandings of disability as a state of functioning shift focus onto the types and intensities of supports a person needs to function

successfully in typical contexts. We talk more about supports later in the chapter.

A new era is beginning in which what a person cannot do will become less important and what supports that person has will become more important. Much of this will be technology-mediated (again, we discuss this later in the chapter). For example, for someone who has problems with directions, the ubiquity of GPS-enabled devices makes that irrelevant. However, along with successful functioning (with supports) come raised expectations. Some of the changes will come about because people will quit presuming that people with intellectual and developmental disabilities are incompetent and incapable because of their pathology and instead will begin to think about what kinds of supports— education to enhance personal capacity, modifications to the environment or context, or supports that mitigate the effects of activity limitations and participation restrictions—a person needs to be successful.

Intellectual disability is a state of functioning that is manifested not because of a predestined disease symptom but because problems in body structures and functions result in activity limitations and participation restrictions. That state of functioning is not permanent and unchanging. With adequate supports, the life circumstances of people with intellectual and developmental disabilities can improve, and people with intellectual and developmental disabilities can and do function successfully in typical life areas. (Do not mistake this discussion to imply that there are not etiological reasons for a person's activity limitations and participation restrictions. Chromosomal anomalies do result in medical conditions such as Down syndrome or fragile X syndrome, and environmental toxins can result in central nervous system impairments. Intellectual disability is always associated with central nervous system impairments, but those impairments manifest as intellectual disability only as a function of the interaction between the person and his or her environment and contexts.)

Before turning to this issue of supports, we return to Sarason's (1985) quote and consider the last sentence, indicating that what is now referred to as intellectual disability is "a social invention ... that makes diagnosis and management seem both necessary and socially desirable." Consider what that means for a minute. People with certain central nervous system impairments have, over the history of time, had difficulty participating fully in life situations. However, those participation restrictions are as much a function of the context as the impairment. Think about how advancing technology has, unfortunately, made some older adults who functioned fine their entire life actually less able to function in some life situations. Sarason is saying that this state of functioning called intellectual disability is a social invention; when people are having difficulty with life activities and participation, members of society feel compelled to do something, and that something has been diagnosis and treatment. Society, in essence, invents or constructs intellectual disability in order to fit people into societally constructed norms of ableness. If one cannot walk, one is identified as having a mobility disability. If the environment is adequately engineered, however, there are few (if any) life functions a person using a wheelchair cannot perform. To what degree, then, is "disability" a function of the person or the environment? In what manner, then, does society determine that diagnosis and management of the "problem" of disability is both necessary and important? Could, in fact, systems continue to operate in historic ways (i.e., segregated, emphasizing pathology) because of *their* interests and not the interests of the people they are supposed to support?

THE INCREASING IMPORTANCE OF SUPPORTS

Historically, the most important indicator that a person "has" intellectual disability has been an IQ score generated by intelligence testing. There is, however, an increased dissatisfaction with this indicator. For one thing, a score on an intelligence test is an imperfect indicator of what people need to be successful. People with exactly the same IQ score almost always have very different support needs, based upon the context in which they are functioning, the presence of exceptional medical or behavioral issues that affect functioning, and so forth. Perhaps what best characterizes people who are identified as manifesting intellectual and developmental disabilities is that they need more support than most people do to function successfully in life situations. Note that everyone needs supports to function successfully in life situations, so needing supports is not a unique experience—it is just that people with intellectual

and developmental disabilities need more, and more extensive, supports. Which begs the question, what are supports?

The ICF and AAIDD models of disability are conceptualized as social-ecological models or person–environment fit models, because disability resides not within the person but in the gap between the person's capacities and the demand of the environment or context. Schalock et al. (2010) noted that supports are "resources and strategies that aim to promote the development, education, interests, and personal well-being of a person and that enhance individual functioning" (p. 18). A related construct, support needs, is also important to understand. Schalock et al. wrote that *support needs* "refers to the pattern and intensity of supports necessary for a person to participate in activities linked to normative human functioning" (p. 109). People with intellectual disability have higher support needs than most people. As noted in the 11th edition of the AAIDD manual,

> A person's intensity of support needs reflects an enduring characteristic of the person rather than simply a point-in-time description of the need for a particular type of support. People with [intellectual disability] require the provision of ongoing, extraordinary (when compared with their peers with no intellectual disability) pattern and intensity of supports. (Schalock et al., 2010, p. 113)

Supports themselves can range widely in nature, scope, and form. *Supports* can refer to technology that enables enhanced functioning, to people in the person's life (either paid or unpaid) who enable that person to be more successful, to resources such as money or products, to education to promote capacity, and so on. Supports are, really, anything that promote the development, education, interests, and personal well-being of a person and that enhance individual functioning.

One important aspect of a supports model (and of the social-ecological or person–environment fit conceptualizations of disability) is that these are strengths-based models; they presume a person can be successful and place the onus on identifying and putting in place the supports needed to be successful. Furthermore, unlike responses to pathology-based understandings of disability, which emphasized programs and treatments, supports are individualized and highly personalized. A subsequent section emphasizes the important role of personalized technology supports, so at this point, it is worth simply emphasizing that as service systems implement supports-based (and strengths-based) systems, they will be driven by the design and provision of individualized, personalized supports.

THE INCREASING IMPORTANCE OF COMMUNITY

The place in which one engages in typical life activities is, of course, one's community—from one's home to the neighborhood, to the villages, towns, or cities in which one lives. One's personalized supports are inextricably linked to the community in which one lives, learns, works, and plays. Although this may seem all too obvious, the fact is that throughout history, people with intellectual and developmental disabilities have been denied the opportunity to participate in, and be a part of, their communities. The systems that were created emphasized pathology, segregation, and homogenous grouping.

This began to change in the 1970s. An early statement pertaining to the importance of the community to the field of intellectual and developmental disabilities was illustrated by *The Community Imperative* (most recently published in 2000), a declaration supporting the rights of all people with disabilities to community living. The original version of *The Community Imperative* was issued in 1979 by the Center on Human Policy at Syracuse University. The purpose of *The Community Imperative* was to serve as a vehicle for people in the field to communicate their belief that all people, regardless of the nature or severity of their disability, have the right to community inclusion. The document was drafted by the Center on Human Policy under the leadership of Dr. Burton Blatt (author of *Christmas in Purgatory*, the 1966 exposé on institutions that prompted the Kennedy administration to significant action in the field of intellectual and developmental disabilities) and was endorsed by more than 300 parents, people with disabilities, researchers, and professionals. *The Community Imperative* made the following brief but powerful statement:

In the domain of Human Rights:

- All people have fundamental moral and constitutional rights.
- These rights must not be abrogated merely because a person has a mental or physical disability.
- Among these fundamental rights is the right to community living.

In the domain of Educational Programming and Human Services:

- All people, as human beings, are inherently valuable.
- All people can grow and develop.
- All people are entitled to conditions which foster their development.
- Such conditions are optimally provided in community settings.

Therefore:

In the fulfillment of fundamental human rights and in securing optimum development opportunities, all people, regardless of the severity of their disabilities, are entitled to community living. (Center on Human Policy, 2000)

It would seem that the time to debate the place of people with intellectual disability in the society and the community has long since passed. However, far too many people with intellectual and developmental disabilities have no options other than to live in congregate settings, to attend school in classes that are segregated and not in their neighborhood, or to work in segregated, sheltered workshops.

Why should the situation change in the future if not much has changed since *The Community Imperative* was originally issued? For one reason, things are better, and though incremental, progress has been made. In the United States, for example, the institutional census (e.g., population) of people with intellectual and developmental disabilities living in large, state-run institutions peaked at around 250,000 people in the late 1970s. As of this writing in 2016, around 25,000 people live in such settings—still too many, but markedly down from earlier eras. Too many people have moved from these large institutions to what are, in essence, mini-institutions in the community, so much yet needs to be done, but there is progress. Similarly, as discussed in Chapter 38, although far too many people with intellectual and developmental disabilities are unemployed or "work" in congregate sheltered settings, there are well-established methods to support people with intellectual and developmental disabilities in meaningful, integrated, competitive employment settings and, in both the United States and Canada, these issues (e.g., ongoing segregated settings as the only work opportunities) are being seen in the context of violations of human rights and existing laws addressing unequal access and discrimination.

There has been progress, but there remains much to be done. One of the implied dimensions of the definition of *supports* is that the word refers to resources and strategies in typical environments and contexts; supports promote the development, education, interests, and personal well-being of a person and enhance individual functioning in typical contexts and environments. As such, as the field moves away from pathology-based models and creates systems of supports, this will be in the context of the community in which a person lives, learns, works, and plays.

THE CRITICAL IMPORTANCE OF TECHNOLOGY

Among the most important types of supports that will have the most impact on the lives of people with intellectual and developmental disabilities in the future is the use of technology. Wehmeyer and Shogren (2013) proposed a new "field of study" referred to as applied cognitive technologies and identified initial waves of research and development associated with this field as including a number of promising issues and technologies that could provide important supports for people with intellectual and developmental disabilities in the future. The first wave of this field emphasized research and development involving the following:

- Prompting and cuing technologies to assist in memory and organization functions

- Literacy supports and universal design for learning

- Sociobehavioral, adaptive behavior, and independent living supports

- Communication technologies (primarily e-mail)

- Monitoring technologies

The second wave of emphasis in the field built on first-wave research and development activities to extend efforts toward the following:

- Wayfinding and navigational supports

- Smart homes and smart technology, including remote monitoring devices

- Voice communication technologies (mobile phones, then smartphones)

- Use of multimedia and Internet accessibility

A third wave of research and development, still emerging, focuses on some of the following (Wehmeyer & Shogren, 2013, p. 92):

- Cloud- and app-based technologies

- Social media and social networks

- Self-determination and personal autonomy supports (e.g., PhotoVoice, survey and life planning tools, remote monitoring that is not invasive, technology that is participation based)

- Mobile digital image communication applications

- Health-related technologies

- Context-aware and location-based learning

Think about the rapid growth in technology supports (for the general population) from 2000 to 2015. e-Commerce did not exist until roughly the year 2000; smartphones were introduced a few years later, as were social media sites. In March of 2010, nobody had an iPad—they were introduced the following month. As of 2015, more than 200 million iPads had been sold. The growth of cloud-based technologies emerged in 2008 and will soon make the specific device one uses irrelevant, as all personalization features will reside in the cloud and will be accessible from anywhere, with any type of device. Early years of the 2010 decade saw the emergence of predictive analytics that used big data to help people identify products and activities that best fit their interests and abilities. 3-D printing will, in the coming years, change the face of manufacturing. Futurists predict that in 50–75 years, bioprinted organs will be produced. Instead of buying mass-produced products that do not fit the need of every person, 3-D printing will allow people experiencing disability to manufacture exactly what they need to be supported to live, learn, work, and play in their communities.

Finally, the "Internet of Things" or the Internet of Everything will create a vast network of supports and accommodations. This is the idea that someday—and that day will be sooner rather than later—everyday objects, people, processes, and data will be networked and connected such that what someone cannot do will be irrelevant; what will matter will be the supports available for that person to succeed. As of 2015, about 10 billion objects were connected to the Internet; by 2020, that figure is estimated to be 50 billion objects. If a person cannot drive, it will not matter; cars will drive themselves and when one's car pulls into one's driveway, the garage door opener will recognize the vehicle (and the car's occupant) and open automatically. Difficulty with meal preparation? Microwave ovens that scan universal product codes to obtain heating information will mean that all one has to do is put the package in the microwave and shut the door. Wearable computing is only now emerging as commonplace (e.g., Fitbit), but the applications of such technology are significant for sensory information and providing supports to gain cognitive access to the world (e.g., think about the role of wearable devices and face-recognition technology to support someone with name- or face-memory difficulties).

Furthermore, such technology will be highly personalizable. Personal support technologies already exist, to some extent, in the form of the smartphone or tablet. One adds the apps one wants, configures what one uses the most, and locates it appropriately. Even considering the capacity of today's smartphones, there are endless opportunities to provide supports. Smart transportation systems can enable people with intellectual disability to use mass transit by incorporating wireless network and smartphone technologies such that devices can "recognize" the right bus and bus drivers can be alerted to the fact that someone who needs supports is waiting at a bus stop—and, if something does go wrong, the person using the technology can contact transportation authorities for support through audio or video communication, with data transmitted to support people via GPS, video, or voice information (Braddock, Rizzolo, Thompson, & Bell, 2004).

In every area of life, technology will provide supports that enable more and more people, including people with intellectual and developmental disabilities, to succeed. Smart homes will incorporate computers, tracking technology, and environmental control technologies that will enable people who need supports to live more independently (Stock, Davies, & Gillespie, 2013). Educational materials that utilize Internet technologies will make written materials usable by all learners through text-to-speech supports, graphic and video representations, and other alternate means of representation. From workplaces to home to the movie theater, technology is changing how everyone lives and is creating opportunities to support people with intellectual and developmental disabilities to live rich, full lives in their communities.

SUMMARY

The field of intellectual and developmental disabilities is at a tipping point for achieving a future of full participation for people with intellectual and developmental disabilities. Malcolm Gladwell, in his book *The Tipping Point: How Little Things Can Make a Big Difference* (2000), described a tipping point as that moment of critical mass at which a phenomenon goes from obscurity to popularity—the threshold right before some idea or practice becomes widely adopted. All of the ingredients to achieve a future of equity and full participation already exist. The recognition and adoption of the idea that disability is not a problem within a person but the gap between personal capacity and the demands of the context that can be closed with adequate supports is, we believe, the final and critical element to achieving the goal of full participation and inclusion for people with intellectual and developmental disabilities and their families.

FOR FURTHER THOUGHT AND DISCUSSION

1. Consider how changing understandings of disability can alter the opportunities people with intellectual and developmental disabilities have to live, learn, work, and play in their communities.

2. How is disability, and thus intellectual and developmental disability, socially constructed, and what implications does that have for the future of the field of intellectual and developmental disabilities?

3. Think about what kinds of supports enable people to function in typical contexts and the barriers that exist to the provision of those supports.

4. It seems logical that people with disabilities, like all other people, want to live, learn, work, and play in their communities. As such, why does segregation remain such a dominant force in the lives of people with intellectual and developmental disabilities?

5. How will technology enable people with intellectual and developmental disabilities to lead fuller lives in their communities?

REFERENCES

Blatt, B., & Kaplan, F.M. (1966). *Christmas in purgatory: A photographic essay on mental retardation.* Boston, MA: Allyn and Bacon.

Braddock, D., Rizzolo, M.C., Thompson, M., & Bell, R. (2004). Emerging technologies and cognitive disability. *Journal of Special Education Technology, 19*(4), 49–56.

Center on Human Policy. (2000). *The community imperative.* Syracuse, NY: Author.

Gladwell, M. (2000). *The tipping point: How little things can make a big difference.* New York, NY: Little Brown.

Luckasson, R., Coulter, D.L., Polloway, E.A., Reiss, S., Schalock, R.L., Snell, M.E.,…Stark, J.A. (1992). *Mental retardation: Definition, classification, and systems of supports* (9th ed.). Washington, DC: American Association on Mental Retardation.

Sarason, S. (1985). *Psychology and mental retardation: Perspectives in change.* Austin, TX: PRO-ED.

Schalock, R.L., Borthwick-Duffy, S.A., Bradley, V.J., Buntinx, W.H.E., Coulter, D.L., Craig, E.M.,…Yeager, M.H. (2010). *Intellectual disability: Definition, classification, and systems of supports* (11th ed.). Washington, DC: American Association on Intellectual and Developmental Disabilities.

Stock, S.E., Davies, D.K., & Gillespie, T. (2013). The state of the field in applied cognitive technologies. *Inclusion, 1*(2), 103–120.

Wehmeyer, M.L., & Shogren, K.A. (2013). Establishing the field of applied cognitive technology. *Inclusion, 1*(2), 91–94.

World Health Organization. (2001). *International Classification of Functioning, Disability and Health (ICF).* Geneva, Switzerland: Author.

World Health Organization. (2002). *Towards a common language for functioning, disability, and health: ICF—The International Classification of Functioning, Disability and Health.* Retrieved from http://www.who.int/classifications/icf/icfbeginnersguide.pdf

Index

Page numbers followed by *f* and *t* indicate figures and tables, respectively.

745